CONTRACTS:
LAW IN ACTION

(2016–Pub.3025)

CONTRACTS: LAW IN ACTION

Volume I
The Introductory Course

Fourth Edition

Stewart Macaulay
Professor of Law Emeritus
University of Wisconsin Law School

William Whitford
Professor of Law Emeritus
University of Wisconsin Law School

Kathryn Hendley
William Voss-Bascom Professor of Law and Political Science
University of Wisconsin Law School

Jonathan Lipson
Harold E. Kohn Chair and Professor of Law
Temple University Beasley School of Law

CAROLINA ACADEMIC PRESS
Durham, North Carolina

ISBN: 978-1-5221-0404-9

Library of Congress Control Number: 2016939504

Carolina Academic Press, LLC
700 Kent Street
Durham, NC 27701
Telephone (919) 489-7486
Fax (919) 493-5668
www.caplaw.com

Printed in the United States of America
2018 Printing

(2016–Pub.3025)

Preface to the Fourth Edition

New editions of *Contracts: Law in Action* allow us to offer new cases and statutes to keep our materials up to date. In this edition, we continue the philosophy and the coverage of the first three editions; once again, we are republishing the preface to the second edition, in which that philosophy is described.

As in previous editions, the cases have been edited to make them easier to read. We have used ellipses whenever substantive text has been omitted from the body of an opinion, but some case citations and many footnotes have been omitted without indication. The footnote numbers in our text do not match the footnote numbers in the cases, since we number our footnotes sequentially by chapter. When we reproduce footnotes from cases, we have indicated the original footnote number by putting it in brackets: [ ]. When we have added our own footnote to a case, it is indicated by an "Eds. note," also in brackets.

The list of authors has changed; we have added Kathryn Hendley and Jonathan Lipson to our group. Each of them brings something new to the enterprise. Professor Hendley is one of the foremost scholars of law in the transition from socialism to capitalism in Russia. Professor Lipson has long experience as a corporate lawyer and transaction planner. Each has used earlier editions of *Contracts: Law in Action* for a number of years.

Sadly, two of the authors of our third edition have died since it was published. John Kidwell's participation in the creation and development of the book dates back to its earliest days. First and foremost, John was a great and award-winning teacher, and he insisted that the materials had to work in class. We knew that if John had a problem teaching something in the book, it had to be fixed.

John also wrote bar exam questions, and he insisted that our course had to play a real part in transforming beginners into skilled lawyers. John was sympathetic to the goal of fashioning a modern contracts course that emphasized law in action, but he worried about losing something important if and when we abandoned what had long been in the traditional course.

He was a wonderful colleague, always prepared to go above and beyond any possible call of duty to get the manuscript to the publisher in a timely manner, to get a jointly composed exam completed, or to help newly minted law school professors cope with their first classes. John wrote the following about himself for his law school profile: "He enjoys reading, listening to music,[1] idle conversation, and the game of poker. His favorite composer is J.S. Bach, and his favorite writer is John McPhee. He subscribes to too many magazines."

Jean Braucher first used a photocopied version of *Contracts: Law in Action* in 1992 at the University of Cincinnati Law School, and she continued teaching from it when she

---

[1] John often opened class by playing a song that fit one or more of the cases for that day. For example, when he taught *Vokes v. Arthur Murray*, he treated students raised on rock and roll to an ancient Jimmy Dorsey big band recording of "Arthur Murray Taught Me Dancing in a Hurry."

Jonathan Lipson carries on John's tradition, albeit with a lower brow. He opens the class on *Hadley v. Baxendale* with the "Theme from Shaft," for example.

moved to the University of Arizona in 1998. We appreciated her kind words about the book when it was first published:[2]

> [*Contracts: Law in Action*] weaves the history, philosophy, sociology, and doctrine of contract into a vibrant if troubling picture, confronting students with the conflicts, complexities, and above all, the limits of the subject. [The authors] challenge students to become "skeptical idealists" in the practice of law. Their approach is both theoretically sophisticated and thoroughly practical.

Jean had done empirical research on the practices of lawyers in consumer bankruptcy,[3] and she worked on law reform in many places, including the American Law Institute and the Uniform Law Commission (formerly known as the National Conference of Commissioners on Uniform State Laws).

In November 2007, Jean accepted our offer to become an author and editor for the third, and all subsequent, editions of *Contracts: Law in Action*. The publisher had insisted that the new edition of the book not be any longer than the previous one: if we added anything, we had to take something out. Jean enforced this rule, pushed us to bring the book up to date, and was always on the lookout for ways in which new statutes, new standard contracts clauses — and especially recent advances in technology — presented new settings for the classic problems dealt with in traditional contracts courses.

Jean used these materials for 22 years and edited them for seven. She concluded from this and other experiences: "The law does not march forward so much as stumble on . . . Law is about social struggle, and we never get neat, perfect conclusions."[4]

We have missed, and will continue to miss, John and Jean. Both contributed so much to this project. In the preparation of both this edition and the third edition, we also had the extraordinary assistance of Ellen Vinz (J.D., University of Wisconsin Law School, 2011), a professional copyeditor as well as a former lawyer. We were also assisted by Erica Maier at Temple University Beasley School of Law and the following student research assistants: Andrew Brehm (J.D., University of Wisconsin Law School, 2015); Miranda Bullard (J.D., Temple University Beasley School of Law, 2017); and Nicholas Zuiker (J.D., University of Wisconsin Law School, 2015).

Stewart Macaulay
William Whitford
Kathryn Hendley
Jonathan Lipson

September 15, 2015

---

[2] Jean Braucher, *The Afterlife of Contract*, 90 Nw. U.L. Rev. 49, 52–53 (1995).

[3] *See* Jean Braucher, *Lawyers and Consumer Bankruptcy: One Code, Many Cultures*, 67 Am. Bankr. L.J. 501 (1993).

[4] *See* William Whitford, *Jean Braucher's Contracts World View*, 58 Ariz. L. Rev. 13, 31 (2016).

Preface to the Second Edition

We revised our book for a number of reasons. Most importantly, our original book and this revision reject the idea that contract law is no more than a small collection of timeless principles. Contracts problems change as the society changes. Corporate lawyers also have been busy, seeking ways to use the form of contract to ward off liability to employees and consumers. Fashions in scholarly work reflect changes in the academy as we move through cycles of classical contract; realist judging in the grand style; dedication to the consumer movement; reductionist pursuits of efficiency, default rules, and formalism; and, perhaps, the coming new realism that reflects a law and society perspective. We have reviewed the entire book to see where we should reflect these changes and new developments, but the major effort has been devoted to bringing up to date our materials on such matters as unconscionability, form contracts printed in fine print or hidden in other ways (particularly in the area of computer programs), and the growing uses of arbitration to repeal the reform statutes of earlier decades. These are the interesting and important matters coming before the courts when this revision was prepared, and we expect these topics to have a fairly long shelf life.

At the same time, those who have used *Contracts: Law in Action* in the past will find much of the book unchanged or only slightly modified. After teaching *Contracts: Law in Action* and earlier photocopied versions for about 20 years, the authors think that the book works. Moreover, it has worked for instructors who emphasize very different approaches in their teaching. The original book and the revision both take the "Law in Action" part of the title seriously. Putting contract problems in context makes the course both more theoretical and more practical at the same time. Whatever a person's theoretical outlook, there is a high price to be paid if he or she forgets such things as that law is not free; most disputes end in settlement; crafting nice-sounding legal standards is one thing but finding evidence to establish a cause of action is another; and that all institutions, including the market, are flawed. American contract law is messy and often contradictory. Even when the form of the rules stay more or less the same, their application varies from court to court over time. Yet the flaws in our contract law have not blocked great economic progress or caused recessions. We quote Wittgenstein near the beginning of the course: "Is it even always an advantage to replace an indistinct picture by a sharp one? Isn't the indistinct one often exactly what we need?" At the very least, the answer to this question cannot just be assumed away. We also have been pleased to discover that many of our former students find that our course prepares them to hit the ground running when they begin practice. We have tried to focus on live contracts problems that our students will face when they become lawyers.

We are heavily in debt to contracts teachers at schools other than Wisconsin who have used *CLA*. We have had an e-mail list for those interested in the book. Our friends at other schools have contributed ideas and suggestions, and they have asked us to explain why we did certain things. Sometimes we have been able to explain choices we made long ago, and when we could not we rethought what we had done. We have learned a great deal from these friends. While we risk leaving out people who deserve mention, we wish to thank particularly Tom Russell, Tom Stipanowich, Bill Woodward, Sandy Meiklejohn, Alan Hunt, Jean Braucher, Peter Linzer, and Carolyn Brown. In addition, we staged a conference in the fall of 2001. We gathered many who had used the book and

Preface to the Second Edition

other friends whose contributions we wanted to hear. The papers were later published in 2001 *Wisconsin Law Review* 525–1006. The papers, discussions, and final articles helped us in the revision process.

The authors are not the only people at Wisconsin who have taught from the book. We have a small-group program in which each first-year student gets one class of around 20 students, and Contracts 1 often has been that class. This means that we have many contracts teachers at Wisconsin. Those teaching the course have met for lunch once a week during the semester. The authors have been challenged by the experiences and questions of their colleagues. In addition to Joe Thome, who was thanked in our original preface and who continued to teach from the materials until recently, we should acknowledge the many contributions of Kathryn Hendley, Lawrence Bugge, Gordon Smith, and Lori Ringhand (now at the University of Kentucky Law School). Lori was a beginning law teacher when she joined us, and she helped us rewrite the employment-at-will material and paid particular attention to the teaching notes that we have made available to those who use the book. She has revised them, pulling together the one set created by John Kidwell and the other by Stewart Macaulay. Our colleague Marc Galanter decided not to participate in the second edition of *Contracts: Law in Action*. He has not taught contracts for some time. However, he did present a paper at our 2001 contracts conference, and the revision still reflects his many contributions to the original version of the book. Also, Nicole Denow (J.D., Wisconsin, 2001) was a talented and hard-working research assistant in the revision of the materials dealing with policing contracts, and Nora Kersten (J.D., Wisconsin, 2002) did many memos that were helpful in expanding some of the notes, or in verifying that no changes were required.

We also owe a debt to the thousands of law students who have worked their way through *Contracts: Law in Action* and its photocopied predecessors. For example, Donovan Bezer, then a student at Rutgers Law School, sent us his reactions, which we found provocative. Other students have known one or more of the parties who appear in the cases in the book, or they have known much about the kinds of transactions involved. We have been reassured that the book has prompted students to see the hard choices lurking behind what seem to be the simple rules of contract law.

Americans, of course, always want to have their cake and eat it too. One student, who identified herself as a liberal, sent us an e-mail saying, "This class has put me in touch with my inner Republican, and I am not sure that I like *him*." Students have also reminded us that most of them are twenty-something, and what we see as things "everyone knows" are but ancient history to them. Students stay about the same age while authors age. Thus, we have tried to change examples so that they will not date too fast and explain a little about such "commonplace things" as the Vietnam conflict, OPEC, the consumer movement, and other manifestations of pre-Reagan politics — as well as what were ice houses, dial telephones, and typewriters. While we find it hard to believe, many of our students have never heard of Shirley MacLaine, Lee Marvin, or Bette Davis. We, on the other hand, are not great followers of River Phoenix. All of these stars, of course, play the parts of litigants in contracts cases.

During the past decade or so, the National Conference of Commissioners on Uniform State Law and the American Law Institute have attempted to revise Article 2 of the Uniform Commercial Code. We debated what to do with the proposed revisions. Then our friend Richard Speidel found the process intolerable and felt that he had to resign as the Reporter after twelve years of work. At the time this is being written, it seems unlikely that there will be ambitious changes to Article 2, with the possible exception of the addition of a highly controversial separate statute dealing with computer-related transactions. There is a risk that states may end up moving in the direction of creating "Un-Uniform Commercial Codes." As a result, we decided not to include material on the proposed revisions. Instructors, of course, may want to offer their classes particular proposals as a way to raise policy questions about the current law. However, we think that it is hard enough finding your way around Article 2 without having to navigate two or more versions.

Table of Contents

Table of Contents

Table of Contents

Table of Contents

Table of Contents

Table of Contents

Table of Contents

Table of Contents

Chapter 1

INTRODUCTION

A. OVERVIEW OF LAW IN ACTION

This book takes a law in action approach to the study of contract law. This approach questions overemphasis on legal rules. Of course law students must learn legal doctrine, but they need to learn much more. Legal reasoning has a tendency to overclaim for the impact of law on human relations. Furthermore, most lawyers are not litigators but rather play an advisory role in the planning and adjusting of relationships. In law practice, contract doctrine is a tool, but it is often less important to a lawyer's work than the ability to understand the business or other context, assess the goals and positions of parties, and find common interests and compromises.

The law in action approach stresses that very few disputes become lawsuits, let alone progress to an appeal that produces the appellate opinions typically studied in law schools. In most situations, legal rights serve as but a vague bargaining entitlement in a negotiation process. People settle differences in the shadow of the law. For example, the victim and an insurance adjuster who is not a lawyer settle most auto accident claims in a fairly routine way. Even in the small percentage of disputes where the victim hires a lawyer, that lawyer is likely to negotiate a settlement without bringing a lawsuit. In the tiny fraction of cases where a complaint is filed in court, lawyers usually settle before a trial begins. Of course, legal rules play a part in the outcome, but often a minor one. As a result, the liability rules discussed in law school classes often will not have the impact on behavior assumed in approaches such as legal realism or law and economics, discussed further below.

Moreover, we may err if we assume that appellate decisions are final resolutions of matters. The loser may battle on through administrative agencies or state and national legislatures to change the rules. And sometimes people win victories in these other law-making institutions so slighted in the first year of legal education. Furthermore, even where a plaintiff wins an appellate decision affirming a judgment for a large sum of damages, one must execute the judgment and turn it into money. However, the defendant may have no assets subject to execution in the jurisdiction. The defendant may file for bankruptcy or delay matters through a state creditor-debtor proceeding. One of the lessons of a law in action approach is that while rules and upper-level decisions are important, one has to look at the real options open to the parties. This approach insists that we look at the legal system from the bottom up as well as from the top down. Criminal law, for example, is both a matter of the statutory definitions of crimes as interpreted by appellate courts, and behavior as seen from the front seat of a police squad car.

The law in action approach reminds us of practical issues lawyers face, particularly in contract law. The approach emphasizes the gaps between stated policies of legal rules and their impact and the ways in which business norms and imperatives are often more powerful "law" than formal law on the books.

Use of "law stories," investigations of the background of cases, can help to bring out law in action insights. Your professor may choose to use another book with such material to provide detailed background about cases in this book.[1] Furthermore, the notes in this book often contain background such as excerpts from trial transcripts and briefs and information from interviews of lawyers and parties about their motivations and what happened after the reported decision. While cases often announce elegant abstract principles, implementation is usually partial and messy. Lawsuits do not necessarily reveal truth or produce justice.

B. STUDYING LAW: WHAT AM I HERE FOR?

1. Classical Legal Education

Beginning law students often have difficulty understanding what they are supposed to learn. Students may bring expectations with them to law school that cause part of the problem. Some assume that being a law student is a larger version of learning the rules of the road in order to get a motor vehicle driver's license. Law is rules, and the best student is the one who knows the most rules. Some expect to be offered a cookbook approach to such things as how to write and probate a will, how to draft a contract, and how to transfer real estate. Others expect basic training in how to try a lawsuit, including how to trip up a lying witness by vigorous cross-examination. These students' model is learning golf or tennis from a pro — law is a game, and they want to know how to win. Most law schools — certainly those with the highest prestige — will disappoint all of these expectations. Legal education directs primary attention elsewhere. Memorizing rules alone will not get a student very far. Moreover, while students may get some exposure in law school to skills such as legal drafting and cross-examination techniques and questions of tactics and strategy, their skills will be greatly refined in practice once formal legal education is over.

The traditional style of law school teaching causes many law students to misunderstand the game they are called upon to play. In the old-fashioned style, a professor assigns a collection of legal raw materials — appellate opinions and occasionally statutes — for preparation before class. Then the professor questions students about them, pointing out flaws in their answers. If a student takes the plaintiff's side in discussing a case, the professor attacks with challenges supporting the defendant. But if another student offers support for the defendant's arguments, the professor neatly leaps to the other side and attacks the defendant's case. At the very least, students in such a class are supposed to learn to impose

---

[1] *See* RICHARD DANZIG & GEOFFREY WATSON, THE CAPABILITY PROBLEM IN CONTRACT LAW (Foundation Press 2004); CONTRACTS STORIES (Douglas Baird, ed., Foundation Press 2007). For discussion of the advantages of law stories, see Stewart Macaulay, *Contracts, New Legal Realism, and Improving the Navigation of the Yellow Submarine*, 80 TUL. L. REV. 1161, 1175–77 (2006).

structure on what seems to be a jumble of cases, questions, fellow students' attempts at answers, jokes, and perhaps professorial war stories. They are supposed to recognize that plausible arguments can be made by a lawyer for just about any proposition but that some arguments are easier to sell than others. Judicial opinions offer examples of formal legal argument and conventional assumptions of legal culture. Needless to say, students are misguided if they assume that studying involves only memorizing what a professor or textbook author states. Students who have firm, simple ideas of right and wrong may be disturbed by the apparent chaos and relativism of many law school classes.

Law professors often speak of class discussion, but this phrase suggests more equality between professor and student than usually exists. Students cannot remain passive note takers. They can be forced to participate and fear making fools of themselves.[2] Moreover, the professor controls the agenda, grants and withholds permission to speak, and is armed with rhetorical ploys that few in the class will have mastered. Students learn to make cautious statements and recognize that the other side often has a good argument. Beginning law students can find themselves at the end of a limb arguing that a particular result is "just" or "fair." After having the limb sawed off a few times, students learn to say something qualified.

Today, professors often want law students to learn both the classic approach to doctrine and several other ways of looking at cases and legal problems. In classic legal education, one learns the application of legal doctrine to various situations. For example, suppose the tort of X allows a plaintiff to recover damages from a defendant if the plaintiff can prove (1) defendant hit plaintiff, (2) defendant intended to hit plaintiff, and (3) plaintiff did not consent to being hit. A professor expects students to discover "the elements" (that is, factors (1), (2), and (3)) of the tort of X from reading one or more cases. These elements are legal doctrine, but knowing them is only the start of the game.

A classic law professor would push students to unearth many difficult problems of definition lurking within this seemingly simple example. At the outset, what does "hit" mean? Suppose Defendant (hereafter D) tried to hit Plaintiff (hereafter P) but missed. However, as D's fist swung past P's chin, the sleeve of D's jacket brushed the sleeve of P's shirt. Did D "hit" P? And what does "intend" mean? Suppose D tried to hit Mr. A, but hit P instead when P jumped in the way trying to defend Mr. A. Suppose, alternatively, D intended to swing his fist at P but only to scare P, not to hit him. However, P moved into the path of D's punch and took it on the chin. Suppose, to change the case again, D swung his fist at P but was

---

2 *See* Elizabeth Mertz, The Language of Law School: Learning to "Think Like a Lawyer" 51 (Oxford University Press 2007) (noting that forcing students to participate in classroom dialogue is in one sense authoritarian but in another empowering, because students "are pushed to remain in and master the dialogue. The law school professor is thus at once giving students no choice and telling them that they are capable of performing this genre."). Mertz's study of legal education in the first-year contracts course is a work of anthropological linguistics. She concludes, at 219, that legal education inculcates "methodological arrogance," in which the main focus is examination of legal textual authority with great rigor, but "when it is time to discuss the assumptions about society and people that underlie the judicial decisions students read, law professors routinely invite speculation and anecdote." The law in action approach attempts to bring more rigor to questions about the impact of legal rules on human relations and reduce reliance on supposition.

indifferent whether he hit P or came close enough to scare him. Suppose, finally, D testifies at trial that he actually intended only to make a broad gesture while arguing with P, but D's fist came in contact with P's chin by accident. X, Y, and Z, three reasonable people who watched the encounter, testify that D seemed to them to have intended to hit P. Does the definition of "intend" in the tort refer to some subjective inner state? Must actors in the legal system judge it objectively by outward appearances?

The next step would be to ask: what does "consent" mean?[3] Few people who are not masochists would want others to hit them. Nevertheless, many do put themselves into situations where it is likely they will be hit. Does this constitute "consent" and thus a defense to the tort of X? Suppose that both P and D are professional football players for rival teams. In the course of a game, D hits P to block him so that a runner can advance the ball. Does P "consent" to D's hitting him just by participating in the game of football? Or does consent require a formal act such as signing a written contract whereby P gives up his protection from being hit by D in exchange for the privilege of playing the game? Suppose that D's block was illegal under the rules of football.[4] Would P's consent to being blocked in the game extend to being blocked illegally under the league rule? Would it matter if the rule were frequently broken or almost never broken? Suppose during a time-out, P took off his helmet, and D then punched P in the face. Does P's consent to being hit during the course of a game extend to this kind of behavior that is not part of the contest?

Suppose, to shift the situation again, P and D are baseball players. P, a pitcher, threw a ball at D, a batter, that just missed him. D ran to the mound and hit P in the face. P knew that while this is not an everyday occurrence, it is not unheard-of. Did P consent to D's retaliatory blow just by playing the game? Suppose that P is a spectator at a baseball game and a foul ball off D's bat went into the stands, hitting P. Did P consent to being hit in this way just by attending the game? Suppose P is French, and this is the first time he has ever seen a baseball game. On the back of P's ticket of admission to the game a number of sentences appear printed in tiny type. They say that anyone attending the game shall be deemed to have consented to being hit by foul balls coming into the stands. Is P bound by a contract whereby he gave up his rights as a result of accepting such a ticket and entering the stadium?

---

[3] The meaning of consent has become the focus of political controversy in the crime of rape. A man has not raped a woman who consented to sexual intercourse. Whatever the formal definition of consent, what is the folk definition of the term as imposed by juries? One study suggests American jurors often rule that if the woman knew the man, if sexual intercourse took place in a social situation, and if no weapon was used, the woman will be deemed to have consented. Many feminists see the social definition of rape as a reflection of the sexism in the society. Apart from the merits of their argument, the example suggests that consent is not a simple concept, and its definition often involves controversial normative choices.

[4] Notice the interesting use of the term *illegal.* Can we say that the National Football League has its own "law"? If so, should lawyers, and law students, concern themselves with this kind of "private government"? Is this footnote an example of a digression from the main theme of the discussion? If so, is it unimportant? Can you just ignore these questions without fear of sanction?

It is possible to dream up hypothetical situations endlessly that test what seems to be a straightforward rule of law. This illustrates something about the nature of the words so often used to state legal rules such as "hit," "intend," and "consent." Constructing hypotheticals is itself an important lawyer's skill, often useful in argument. Could we avoid all of these problems of classification by drafting rules of law more carefully and using more precise terms? Drafters of legal rules pay a price when they try to anticipate most situations. Think of the Internal Revenue Code and the regulations drafted under it. They are exceedingly complex, and complexity creates work for accountants and tax lawyers.

How do we answer these endless questions? The classic law professor, by questions and body language, would push students toward several possible sources of answers. First, we could search for *authority* — cases, statutes, administrative regulations, and other sources of law dealing with some aspect of the problems we have posed. Suppose we add to one of our hypothetical cases that P played football for the Chicago Bears, and D played for the Green Bay Packers. D hit P in a game played in Green Bay. Thus, we can assume that the case is governed by the law of Wisconsin. Suppose, further, that the Supreme Court of Wisconsin decided in 1960 that professional football players consent, within the meaning of that term in the tort of X, to the common and ordinary hitting involved in the game by their participation in the sport. If we assume that the Wisconsin court would not overrule its 1960 decision (and this might be a large assumption), then we could answer some of the questions about the meaning of consent with a degree of assurance.

We could consider the implications of this decision by using the techniques of common law case analysis. This is the art of generating both broad holdings for cases, so that they may be applied beyond their intuitive scope, and narrow holdings, so that they will not apply where it seems they should. Most narrowly, a court could limit the 1960 decision to professional football and the particular facts of the case. More broadly, a court could read the decision as establishing that a player takes the risk of common and ordinary physical contact in *any* sport. Of course, we still would have to determine whether the particular hitting involved in our case would be deemed common and ordinary within the sport. We might expect that some hitting would clearly be part of football while other hitting clearly would be outside the ordinary risks assumed by anyone who played the game. Even so, we might expect to find a large range of cases in the middle where reasonable people might differ about how common and ordinary the type of hitting involved was. These would be the close and difficult cases where both P and D would have good arguments — the type of case likely to be posed on a law school examination. Even skilled and experienced lawyers would not be able to be certain of the outcome of these cases; at best, they could make informed judgments about the probabilities that P or D would win.

Law students must learn to "spot the issues" — that is, to identify ambiguities in rules, conflicts among rules, and gaps where particular situations fail to fit rules. Clearly, this 1960 decision does not answer all the questions we raised. For example, does it apply to baseball players as well as football players? The classic law professor would push his or her students to reason by *analogy*. One could say, for example, that the key idea in the 1960 decision was that professional athletes —

whatever the sport — can be assumed to understand the ordinary risks of the game. As a result, they can be deemed to choose to take those risks when they choose to play. In this sense, baseball is like (analogous to) football, although the precise risks assumed by baseball and football players would differ as the two sports differ. Of course, this judgment based on an analogy would be strengthened if we were to discover that the highest courts in 10 other states had decided just this way on these very grounds. Then we could combine an argument by analogy with an appeal to authority. While the decisions of the courts in other states would not bind the Wisconsin Supreme Court in interpreting its 1960 decision, it is likely that its members would find these other cases *persuasive* since, absent good reason to the contrary, uniformity among the states itself is an important value.

Classic legal thought refers to the ordinary meaning of language as a second major source of answers to the questions we raised earlier. This approach might ask whether most people (which unfortunately might mean most educated people, or most members of the same socioeconomic class as the legal elite) understand "hit," "intend," or "consent" to include or exclude the cases presented. On occasion, judges, lawyers, and law professors look to dictionary definitions, raising the vexing questions whether words have fixed meanings apart from context and whether dictionaries capture meanings accurately. Resort is sometimes made to "common sense," but different people may have different views of easily accepted common norms.

2. Criticism of Classical Legal Thought: Other Perspectives

Legal realism: Beginning just before the First World War, a group of American law professors attacked the kinds of approaches we have just described. Their movement, traceable to the pragmatism of Oliver Wendell Holmes Jr.,[5] was called "legal realism," and its leading figure was Karl Llewellyn, later the chief architect of the Uniform Commercial Code. It is far easier to describe what the legal realists were against than what they were for. One idea common to the group was that judges do not "find" the law in the clouds or by manipulating techniques of distinguishing cases. Rather, judges "make" the law by normative choices. And if this is true, the realists told us that we would get better decisions and more predictable law if judges openly recognized their role and candidly explained how they arrived at their choices. Many realists relied on the teachings that came to be known as general semantics to attack definitional approaches. Words such as "hit," "intend," and "consent" have many meanings in ordinary speech, and definitions serve better to rule out extreme cases than to decide close ones. Since past decisions almost never involve the identical situation now brought before the court, cases almost always can be distinguished if a judge wants to do so. Thus, appeals to authority may affect judgment but they do not compel one result rather than another.

---

[5] Oliver Wendell Holmes Jr., The Common Law 1 (1881) ("The life of the law has not been logic; it has been experience. The felt necessities of the time, the prevalent moral and political theories, intuitions of public policy, avowed or unconscious, even the prejudices which judges share with their fellow-men, have had a good deal more to do than the syllogism in determining the rules by which men should be governed.").

Analogies, too, are suspect. For example, baseball and football are both professional sports, and those who play them are likely to be aware of certain risks of being hit by another player that are just part of the game. But football is supposed to be a contact sport while baseball is not. We could say that a football player has less need of the deterrent of the law of torts than a baseball player because of the nature of his athletic equipment and the opportunity to retaliate. Or one could argue that football needs the support of tort law more than baseball because it is necessary to control the violence inherent in the sport. Whatever the merit of these arguments, they illustrate that the very nature of an analogy is that the things being viewed are both *like* one another in some respects and *not like* one another in others. The problem is to decide if the common factors are more important than the uncommon ones. However, this is a judgment that rests on values, facts, and predictions about the consequences of decisions each way. Analogy may be a step in the process of decision, but it does not end the discussion.

A law professor who embraced realism would ask a student to argue in terms of the goals to be served by one decision or another. For example, a student might argue for a consent rule in professional sports that turned on the likely reaction of fans viewing the event. A player should be deemed to consent to the normal risks of the game, even including blows that violate its rules, but those blows that would likely incite fans to violence should be deterred by all means available, including tort liability. This, the student might argue, would aid in crowd control — a worldwide problem at sporting events — and, in the long run, in the continuation of professional sports. Another student might disagree, arguing that the private government of professional sports has enough internal sanctions to control the behavior of competitors so that we need not incur the costs of trying lawsuits between athletes. She might remind us that players in any sport, from golf to boxing, who hit others outside the rules of the game can be suspended or thrown out of the game for good. Those who violate the working norms of competitors are subject to a variety of sanctions ranging from attacks on their reputations in the form of gossip to ostracism and even physical retaliation. We should have evidence that more is needed before we waste the time of over-crowded judicial machinery on such cases.

Whatever the merit of these arguments, they accept that the term "consent" could be interpreted to include or exclude the behavior in question, and they attempt to influence the choice of a meaning in a particular situation on the basis of some impact on behavior that the advocate thinks good or bad. Definitions and analogies only offer a number of possibilities. Choices must be made on the basis of normative evaluation of statements of the rule or predictions about its consequences. This being the case, one must argue policy just as if one were trying to convince a legislator to vote for passage or defeat of a statute.

Realism, of course, relies on wise judges to make policy choices. How, then, does law differ from politics? Republican governors appoint one group of judges while Democratic governors appoint another. These political backgrounds might play important roles in forming attitudes and coming to decisions. In its extreme form, realism might see each judge as having a roving commission to do good as he or she sees fit. Many find this unsatisfactory and in fact an abandonment of the rule of law.

"Neutral principles," or "legal process": By the 1950s, most law professors accepted many of the teachings of realism. Predictably, there was a reaction, sometimes known as the "legal process" or "neutral principles" school of thought. This view holds that judges should leave major policy decisions to legislatures because the courts lack the capacity to make such decisions well or to implement them. This approach, which advocates legal craft and procedure to restrain judicial innovation to an incremental, step-by-step approach, is subject to the criticism that it favors the status quo and thus is inherently conservative rather than apolitical. Furthermore, particularly when it comes to common law such as contracts and torts, made by judges without the necessity of legislative intervention, it is the traditional role of the courts to review and adapt the law to current needs and norms.

Law and Economics: An influential school of thought derived from legal realism is the law and economics approach, which has become popular in many American law schools and among some judges. The founding fathers of the movement are identified with the University of Chicago and its tradition in economics. Realism tells judges and other decision-makers to make normative choices openly, but offers little advice about how to choose among possible normative positions. Legal process thinking imposes a requirement of due process on almost every important decision but accepts whatever substantive choices emerge from formally fair procedures. Law and economics, in contrast, generally favors efficient allocation of resources; if one wants to seek some other goal, at least one should be aware of the costs.

For example, we must pay a price if we insist that all decisions be taken only after procedures that comply with due process. Sometimes the cost will be outweighed by the benefits, but sometimes not. The position teaches a powerful lesson overlooked in much of legal realism or legal proceduralism — sometimes the lesson is summarized as "there is no such thing as a free lunch." In the 1960s and 1970s, Congress decided to regulate the safety of automobile design, environmental pollution caused by automotive exhaust, and the fuel consumption of cars. The law and economics approach emphasizes that such regulation is not free, and the cost of these changes in the design of vehicles raises prices for cars. This, in turn, is likely to have many consequences, some of which may be hard to see at first. On the one hand, the regulation reduces externalities — costs imposed on third parties in the form of impact on habitats and on human health from pollution and safety risks. On the other hand, less transportation may be available to the poor if higher prices cause middle-class owners to drive their cars longer so there is less usable life left when they trade in their cars. The total market for automobiles may contract as prices increase, and this limits the number of available jobs connected with automobile manufacturing, servicing, tourism and so on. People may be willing to accept these costs of regulation as the price for what they see as real benefits. Nonetheless, we cannot pretend that there is no cost or that costs just come out of the pocket of wealthy corporations in some magical fashion. This approach reminds us that law is not free.

The law and economics approach also suggests that, absent transaction costs, it makes no difference where legislatures and courts place liability for accidental injuries and deaths.[6] Suppose we have a rule that says car buyers must pay for repairs to their vehicles whatever the cause of damage. A court or legislature changes the rule to place the burden of certain repairs on car sellers. We then can expect sellers to raise prices or to make contracts shifting the burden of repairs back to buyers. In either event, buyers will still pay for repairs.

Many who advocate the law and economics approach see it as value-neutral. If we care about efficiency, we should try to predict the economic consequences of proposed changes in legal rules. Moreover, we can explain much of what courts have done since the Industrial Revolution in terms of seeking efficiency. Many proponents of law and economics tell us that it does not deal with the justice or fairness of the present distribution of wealth, status, privilege, or power in the society. Law and economics, however, has much to say about the costs of measures designed to change such distributions.

Critics of the approach see it as a highly successful effort to legitimate the position of the well-off in society. Law and economics just ignores law's role in symbolizing values and morals.[7] Often the message of the approach is that reform is impossible or unwise, and if only government would go away, all would be as good as it can be. Some law and economics scholars hold as an article of faith that competition and free markets solve all problems, and they deny that there can be any private power unchecked by the market apart from advantages granted by government.

Critics also point out that the law and economics approach is highly abstract and based on logical deduction from doubtful assumptions. A great deal of law and economics assumes a world without transaction costs, but that is not the world in which we live. Too little attention is given to implementation of rules — writers sometimes treat people as if they were puppets tied by strings to legal rules that control their behavior. That the formal statement of a legal rule can be rationalized in efficiency terms does not necessarily indicate that the rule promotes efficiency in practice. Of course one could take a law and economics approach to the law in action, looking at whether social relations are efficient. It just has not been done often.

In recent decades, behavioral economics has complicated the earlier assumptions of law and economics. Neoclassical economics assumed, with elegant parsimony but some sacrifice in accuracy, that humans act rationally in their own self-interest. Behavioral economics complicates this assumption and emphasizes that humans have bounded rationality and bounded willpower. People sometimes systematically fail to predict accurately their future behavior because they do not fully understand their own desires and risks. People may think they will always

---

[6] *See* Ronald H. Coase, *The Problem of Social Cost*, 3 J.L. & Econ. 1 (1960). It is sometimes lost on those who cite the "Coase theorem" (which refers to the idea that allocation of resources is independent of default legal rules if transaction costs are zero) that Coase was not arguing that transaction costs typically *are* zero. Rather, transaction costs of changing a background rule of law, for example by entering into a contract, are often high, so it very much does matter what the background rule is. *See* Coase, *The Problem of Social Cost: The Citations*, 71 Chi.-Kent L. Rev. 809 (1996) (noting many more citations for the "Coase Theorem" than for the reciprocal point).

[7] *See* Lawrence Friedman, *Two Faces of Law*, 1984 Wis. L. Rev. 13.

pay credit card bills on time and avoid interest charges and thus not pay attention to interest rates. They may underestimate the bad things that could happen to them, such as getting sick or losing their jobs, events that would make it hard or even impossible to pay on time. They may engage in impulse purchases and regret them later. This behavior is more problematic for big purchases than small ones, where people can learn over time to make better decisions without suffering large losses.

In addition, buyers typically act under limited information, not the perfect information of simple economic models. It is time-consuming to shop for the best deal, and some deals are very complicated, so that looking into competitors' terms on many points is virtually impossible. Cellphone contracts are a good example of consumer contracts with very complex terms. In theory a small number of shoppers might introduce competition in such terms, but the terms of competitors often look the same. Furthermore, sellers may be able to segment the small number of shoppers into better deals, while giving poorer deals to those who do not shop. In other words, markets do not work perfectly for a multitude of reasons. Onerous terms may be suggestive of market failure. Behavioral economics and attention to market failures can lead to very different conclusions about how to design legal rules than a more simple law and economics approach.

Critical Legal Studies and its variants: In the 1970s, legal realism developed a more radical branch known as "critical legal studies." From this perspective, the existing distribution of wealth, status, privilege, and power is central, and legal doctrine is mystification, legitimating the status quo. For example, in the 19th century lawyers and judges came to see the business corporation as a legal person with all the rights of real individuals. More generally, there is great inequality in wealth and power between a large business such as Microsoft and an individual. In theory, if Microsoft breaches a contract, an individual consumer could sue and recover damages as compensation. But all of this is ideology that ignores the advantages Microsoft has over any individual who attempts to assert legal rights against it.[8] Lawyers are both necessary and expensive. Wealth has an impact on the outcome of litigation. People and organizations with wealth can better afford the long delays that so characterize our legal system. Moreover, organizations that engage in repeated standardized transactions can plan these relationships to their advantage. Individuals who deal with them sign standard form contracts that serve to ward off most unwanted liability from the large organization. Most individuals are not aware of what they are giving away when they sign. Even if they were aware, one could say they have little *real* choice but to sign away their rights.

Scholars associated with the Conference on Critical Legal Studies (CLS) examined the assumptions hidden within legal doctrine concerning what is necessary, tolerable, and just. What do those who make and work with our law take as "common sense"? Which groups in society benefit from these tacit assumptions in our law and which are disadvantaged by them? Critical scholars see American legal consciousness as favoring wealth and privilege. Some of these scholars find American law characterized by contradictory principles. They hope that by

---

[8] *See* Marc Galanter, *Why the "Haves" Come Out Ahead: Speculations on the Limits of Legal Change*, 9 Law & Soc'y Rev. 95 (1974).

showing underdeveloped but long established counterthemes in our law, they can open the way to a new conception of rights more consistent with a less competitive and more cooperative society.

Critical feminists and critical race theorists have challenged the white male law professors who made up most of CLS. They have charged them with insensitivity to the benefits of a rule of law. While rights may be flawed weapons, women and people of color can use them both as symbols and as instruments to better their position. Moreover, when we look at any body of law, including contracts, from the perspective of gender or race, we recognize easily overlooked and debatable assumptions. For example, the alleged neutrality of contract ideas served well the institution of slavery in the United States until the Civil War — humans bought and sold other people under a law that claims to be one of the foundations of liberty.[9] People of color are almost entirely absent from contracts casebooks, suggesting that this body of law deals with power as much as it deals with questions of free choice. A leading critical feminist wrote an analysis of how a popular contracts casebook treated women either as sex objects or as the subject of paternal care.[10]

Radical lawyers sometimes see all varieties of critical legal thinkers as trying to bring about a revolution from within the academy rather than taking risks and fighting the battle on the front lines. Critical scholars respond that it is better to change ideas about what could be, than to win court victories seeking rights: lawyers championing the "have-nots" can implement rights only marginally in legal institutions controlled by the powerful. When workers, people of color, women, or other less powerful groups threaten to win significant victories through the assertion of rights, the system tends to adjust to support the status quo. Statutes are construed narrowly, procedural rules are put in place to minimize the chances of success, the costs of asserting rights are raised to limit their use, jurors reject valid claims as something they do not wish to believe, and businesses use standard form terms mandating arbitration to prevent their customers from going to court, restricting them to a private forum chosen by the contract drafter.

We could debate most of these assertions. Nonetheless, all varieties of critical legal thought invite students to consider how the legal system works in practice and what kinds of people benefit. Seemingly neutral legal rules may privilege certain positions.[11] Whatever the statement of legal ideals, law on the books may differ from law in action, and the differences may not be random or neutral.

Law in action: The law in action approach, also known as the law and society approach, can be seen as another branch of legal realism, along with law and economics and critical approaches. Its particular concern is with how human relationships actually play out in the shadow of the law. This approach is not

---

[9] Patricia Williams, The Alchemy of Race and Rights 17–21, 216, 224 (1991).

[10] Mary Jo Frug, *Re-reading Contracts: A Feminist Analysis of a Contracts Casebook*, 34 Am. U. L. Rev. 1065 (1985).

[11] Anatole France once wryly noted that "[t]he law in its majestic egalitarianism, forbids the rich as well as the poor to sleep under bridges, to beg in the streets, and to steal bread." Le lys rouge, Ch. 7 (1894).

opposed to pursuing policy goals through law, but it is highly skeptical of claims that particular policies will be easily implemented by adopting legal rules. Read again the opening pages of this introduction for an overview of law in action. As for criticism of this approach, its dependence on empirical examination of the impact of law may make it focus on things that are easy to study empirically rather than on bigger justice concerns. Furthermore, law and society research is not always up to the most rigorous standards of the social sciences, although sophisticated empirical study of the impact of law has been gaining favor in the legal academy in recent decades.

3. Law School Examinations

Part of the "what am I here for" topic concerns law school exams and how the skills tested on exams relate to preparing for the practice of law. Once a student masters the blend of approaches demanded by his or her professor, the student still must pass an exam. Typically, a student will be confronted with a story (often called a fact pattern) and asked to play the role of judge or that of a lawyer for plaintiff or defendant. To take a very simple example, suppose the question set out the story of P and D, two professional baseball players employed by rival teams. P, a pitcher, threw a ball that just missed hitting D, who was batting. D ran to the mound and threw a punch at P. However, D hit U, the first base umpire. U had come to the mound to try to prevent a fight. You are U's lawyer. Make the best case you can to justify recovery of a judgment against D.

In an exam, the student's job is often to identify the relevant legal doctrines and the elements of those doctrines that are debatable (debatable elements raise "legal issues," which must be "spotted" and then discussed) and then bring policy considerations to bear to develop opposing arguments. Arguments about legal issues are typically more important than "answers."

Your first task would be to try to fit the facts into some legal category. You recognize that it is worth considering the tort of X. There is no question that D hit U, and so the first element of the tort seems to be present, a point you should mention. However, unless you can persuade a judge and jury to interpret the word "intent" very broadly, you face trouble establishing the second element of the tort. Moreover, you should at least recognize the possibility that D's lawyer is going to argue that just by being an umpire U "consented" to the risks of getting hit in a fight between players. (The process of fitting facts into legal categories is "spotting the issues," the first step in legal analysis. Most of those who get low grades do so because they fail to see that they should discuss the tort of X or that there would be difficulty in establishing that D "intended" to hit U or that U did not consent.)

How would you argue that it was enough that D intended to hit someone and that the tort of X does not, or should not, require that he have intended to hit his actual victim, your client U? You could turn to whatever authority had been discussed in your course. You probably would not have a case directly deciding the question. You would have to draw analogies to those decisions that adopted a broader definition of "intent" in other contexts. You would do what you could with the ordinary understanding of the word "intent." Perhaps you could argue that in common speech we assume that one "intends" the ordinary consequences of one's actions, and one consequence of throwing a punch is missing the intended target and hitting something else. You would make policy arguments that would justify an expanded definition of the term so that the rule would include third parties such as U. You would deal with D's likely arguments that changes in liability rules are properly the task of a legislature and that such broader liability is economically inefficient. You might consider whether all a new rule would do is prompt disclaimer clauses in umpires' contracts. You might consider a distributional argument concerning highly paid players striking lesser paid employees of organized baseball such as umpires.

Then after all of this analysis concerning "intent," you would turn to the consent issue. Do umpires assume the risk of injury in fights between players just by being umpires? Again, you would make all the types of arguments we've catalogued. You would anticipate those arguments your opponent is likely to make and respond to them as best as you could.

Once you had dealt with the tort of X, you would then consider whether D's conduct came within the tort of Y. It applies to unintentional but "negligent" hitting of others. Why not start with tort Y and avoid all the difficult problems with the idea of "intent" in tort X? Because, as you should state in your answer, U might be able to get punitive damages in addition to compensation for his actual injuries if the hitting were deemed intentional. He could recover only actual compensatory damages for negligence. Indeed, this possibility might affect arguments about how a court should define intent for purposes of tort — in essence, you would assert that D's conduct warranted strong punishment so both he and others would be deterred in the future and therefore the word "intent" should be defined broadly to achieve this goal. D's lawyer, of course, would argue that D's conduct did not warrant such punishment. This may seem to be arguing backwards. Logically, one might expect a determination of whether D has committed tort X and then the remedies would just follow if he had. Here, we begin by asking what remedy makes sense in light of D's conduct. You will find that many of your courses reflect this concern with the bottom line. This is another example of the realists' point that deciding cases involves policy choices and not just definitions and deductions.

Yet, you might ask, what am I here for? What does all this have to do with becoming a lawyer? You did not come to law school to become an expert in taking examinations. Examinations are supposed to be a means to the end of becoming a lawyer. The theory is that those who can write good exam answers will be able to evaluate and make persuasive arguments to legal decision-makers. Lawyers who are good at evaluating arguments will know what cases to accept from potential clients and what to do with those they do take. When a lawyer has a strong legal argument — assuming all other things are equal — he or she can demand far more as the price of a settlement than when he or she has a weaker legal position. Furthermore, lawyers who can anticipate legal arguments can also write contracts to address them directly and perhaps create greater predictability for their clients. They will be better planners.

Notice that here we arrive at an explanation for legal education's emphasis on arguments rather than answers. A lawyer who can fashion a plausible argument, even one involving creative new theories, usually is in a better bargaining position in settlement negotiations or when drafting a contract than a lawyer who can do little more than blunder through a cookbook approach to practice. A lawyer who can anticipate arguments can rearrange the relationship at the outset to minimize the risk that those arguments will be successful. All lawyers are equal only in the yellow pages of the telephone directory; savvy, well-prepared, creative lawyers do better than foolish, ill-prepared ones who proceed by rote. Of course, creative theories must fall within the range of arguments acceptable within legal culture. Whatever the merit of Marxist theories about American law, one would be a fool to offer them so labeled to most American judges. There are fashions in ideas acceptable to the courts. Certain views are "in the air" at one time but not another. A wise lawyer would not make the same arguments before the present Supreme Court of the United States as she made when Earl Warren was Chief Justice. Consumer protection was far more popular in the early 1970s than in the early 1980s. Also, some judges delight in technical lawyering while others are annoyed by nice distinctions among cases and clever readings of statutes.

Indeed, the law of nearly every state as applied in its cities, towns, and villages will reflect the state's diversity and is likely to differ substantially around a common core found in the state's statutes, administrative regulations, and appellate cases. Knowing what is likely to sell before the judges who would decide a case is also part of a lawyer's skill. Of course, a sociologist of law would remind us that bargaining power flows from far more than legal arguments and so settlements may turn on other factors. One party may need money now while the other is able to await a final decision after several appeals, and this fact is likely to affect how they settle a case. This, too, is part of our subject matter.

In a sense, good lawyers never cease being law students. The practice of law is far more than knowing a body of formal statements of rules. Of course, learning certain rules and a vocabulary is an essential step in the process of becoming a lawyer. However, it is but one step. Moreover, many of the rules one must learn to practice are not what one normally thinks of as laws. Lawyers who represent those injured in auto accidents and lawyers who represent insurance companies know the going rate for various kinds of accidents. They know how much it will take to settle a rear end collision where the police gave neither driver a traffic ticket and where the plaintiff has suffered damage to his car and personal injuries. While all this is true, a great deal of law practice also involves judgments about probabilities in light of specialized knowledge. Lawyers must cope with the knowledge that they cannot be certain: a court or legislature may change the rule, there are good arguments for alternative interpretations of the rule as applied in the present situation, and what one knows and what one can prove in court are very different things. Legal education aims to provide part of the basis for making such informed judgments in the practice of law.

While legal education could always do a better job in preparing students for practice, it is impossible to mint finished lawyers in only three years at a university. "Lawyer" is a label applied to many distinct professions, and faculty and students cannot predict whether certain students will go to Wall Street or Main Street, work in governmental agencies, or enter politics. Formal legal education is just the beginning of a career-long process of learning. This is why law, like medicine, is known as a "learned profession."

C. CONTRACTS COURSES

1. The Goals of the Law-in-Action Approach to the Contracts Course

Almost all law students in what was once the British Empire begin their study with a course called "contracts." Students naturally assume that the course deals with an important part of law practice. However, in recent years many law professors and others have questioned this conventional view. They point out that there are large gaps between the law school law of contract, what happens in courts, and what practicing lawyers do. *Contracts: Law in Action* reflects our doubts about the traditional course.

Professors and students long assumed that contract rules were fundamental to the practice of law. While this may or may not be the case, contract doctrine clearly is only part of what lawyers need to understand to serve their clients. Lawyers are involved in the planning and structuring of business relationships. Producing a successful contract involves, first, an assessment of the goals and positions of the parties. What a lawyer proposes must be acceptable so that the parties can make a deal. Second, success involves planning a relationship so that both sides will be satisfied with the performance of the contract. Thus, the lawyer must understand business and social relationships, the techniques of planning and writing, and many bodies of law so that the arrangement will have desired legal consequences. Clearly, a good deal more is involved than a knowledge of contract doctrine.

Lawyers also perform an important advisory role in managing ongoing contractual relationships. For example, the parties may disagree about their obligations under a contract. One party may come close to performing but not quite make it. Is a miss as good as a mile or must a client accept substantial but not complete performance? Or the seller may fall far short of full performance, but the buyer may need the defective performance so badly that she takes it. Once the need has passed, can the buyer assert the original obligation or has she modified the contract by accepting the defective performance? Or the seller's failure to live up to the letter of the contract may have been caused by an unexpected event such as a fire, a strike, or a flood. To what extent, if at all, do such contingencies constitute excuses from contractual duties? Finally, once relationships are wrecked, lawyers may face questions of salvage. Can one turn to the legal system to force the other party to assume some or all of the losses caused by the breach of the contract? Again, contract doctrine speaks to all these questions, but lawyers and clients often must make difficult business judgments that are more important than legal arguments.

Lawyers do play a part in planning contracts, carrying them out, and clearing away the wreckage of those that fail, but business people are often able to handle these problems themselves without legal advice, and real estate brokers, land developers, investment bankers, sales people, engineers, and accountants all compete with lawyers to offer this kind of advice. Nevertheless, complicated contracts problems do arise in many contexts — not just in business — and their solution may require the services of someone who understands the law of contract. However, lawyers are more likely to face some questions than others. All lawyers must recognize the important contracts issues, but exposing every law student to all the classic contracts puzzles is an inefficient use of law school time and resources.

Contract ideas are indirectly relevant to most lawyers' practices. Contract ideas form part of the ideology[12] of capitalism, and this ideology affects many branches of the law and many lawyers' tasks. The ideology is familiar to us all. Many writers see contract as the solution to the conflict between individualism and community. In a society based on command, rulers order people to perform tasks. In a free society, individuals make choices about what they will and will not do. There are, however, ends that cannot be achieved without social interaction that is only possible by coordinating individual choices. By exchanging some measure of our freedom or property for what we value, our choices serve to allocate resources to desired uses. Contract thus enables people to unlock the value of their labor and the tangible and intangible things they control. I want your money more than I want my Chevrolet. You want a car more than you want your money. By making an exchange we are both better off. Neither of us can take advantage of the other in a perfect market (which involves a lot of assumptions, including perfect information). Others will offer you cars and others will offer me money for my car. These alternative potential contracts serve to limit our bargain so that we exchange the automobile at a price within the range of many similar choices by willing sellers and buyers. Self-interest, in this way, is channeled into a tool for cooperation in collective action.

Many theorists see contract law in capitalist societies as providing needed security of transactions. Any bargain where people exchange goods and money at the same time is almost self-policing. This is not true, however, when the exchange involves complex performances that take place over time. Suppose I am to paint your house and you are to pay me when I finish. Until I complete the job, you risk losing opportunities to hire someone else who might do the job more quickly and better. I risk your willingness and ability to pay me when I finish. Of course, many nonlegal sanctions give both of us incentives to perform. For example, we both may want to be known as people who carry out commitments. We may want to deal again, and I must worry that what I do under this contract will affect your willingness to enter new ones in the future. Members of my family may work for members of yours and depend on their good will for their economic success. You might badmouth me to other potential customers if I do not perform. Nonetheless, those who write about law see a need for official sanctions to reinforce nonlegal ones that support the making and performance of contracts.

Contract law tells those who would plan and take risks how to make legally binding commitments. One who follows the accepted formula can know that she has made a contract. Contract law provides standardized interpretations of forms of language — it is a kind of authoritative dictionary. Contract law fills in gaps in agreements so that it is unnecessary to plan everything in each contract. Economists call legal rules that can be changed by contract "default rules." Most gap-filling terms are default rules, but there are some mandatory rules that cannot

---

[12] We use the term *ideology* rather than *political philosophy* because ideology connotes a system accepted and assumed, rather than a thought-out view.

be changed. Contract law also offers remedies for breach, and these are mostly default rules. While these remedies may provide some salvage of wrecked bargains, perhaps their most important function is to deter breach in the first place. One who would default must consider the threat that contract law will cause trouble. It costs money to defend oneself, even if one is successful. Moreover, contract law symbolizes the importance of commitments. Society spends resources supporting performance of bargains, and this itself is a statement of what is right.

There is a vast literature debating the assumptions we have sketched. If one truly believes in freedom, why say that a person loses it by making a promise? To reject the freedom to change one's mind, one must look to policies other than choice. Suppose, for example, College makes a five-year contract with Coach to guide its football team. Two years later, State University offers Coach twice the salary to coach its team. Why should he not be free to change his mind and take the offer? Suppose Manufacturer Corporation orders parts from Supplier Corporation but then finds that the sales of the product in which it used these parts are very disappointing. Why should it not be free to cancel the order? If we look at customs in the football and manufacturing industries, we find that coaches and industrial buyers do feel free to cancel their commitments, whatever contract law says. Both universities and suppliers often accept cancellations without too much objection. And we should note that the law of contracts seldom, if ever, would tell judges to order either Coach or Manufacturer Corporation to perform or send them to jail for breach. Both could buy their way out by paying damages if either College or Supplier Corporation did not release them. Thus, the law itself suggests there may be reasons to allow people to break promises at not too great a price. Capitalist law does not seem to find absolute security of transactions an overriding value.

Some writers argue that free choice never really exists anyway, except in theorists' ivory towers. Suppose a robber with a gun sticks it in the back of a man walking past and says, "Your money or your life!" The victim cannot say "None of the above"; he is being given a choice between unpleasant alternatives. In the example about buying a car, your real preference might have been a better car for a lower price, but people are always constrained by their circumstances. The line between a choice we deem free and one we call coerced usually is difficult to draw. It is a normative evaluation rather than a description. The distribution of advantages in society affects freedom of choice in important ways. Perhaps seeing all but a few choices as free and not the product of coercion is a useful working assumption, but it cannot be confused with an empirical description.

Furthermore, the theorists' model is that of a negotiated deal, in which the parties give and take and are aware of the terms or accept the risks of incomplete knowledge. While this may describe some transactions involving expert buyers and sellers, it is a poor representation of many bargains. It is hard for most consumers to appraise products before they buy them. Few consumers understand that the form contracts they sign drastically limit their ability to do anything about unsatisfactory purchases. Of course, other-than-legal sanctions operate in this area, and many consumers' complaints will prompt real efforts by sellers to produce a remedy. However, the power of these sanctions is not equally distributed across society. Mercedes-Benz buyers are likely to have more attention paid to their complaints than Chevrolet buyers, and buyers of new Chevrolets will do better than buyers of used ones.

When you examine contract law closely, you will discover that it reflects competing tendencies. Scholars have fashioned an abstract system of rules that appear relatively clear and suitable for use for almost any purpose by anyone. Courts have used some parts of this system at various times and places. Nonetheless, if we look carefully in area after area within the body of contract doctrine, we find counterrules and approaches that seek substantive justice at the expense of predictable abstraction. While skilled lawyers can predict the results of cases with some degree of accuracy, they must draw on information outside the rules of law to do this.

It is a mistake, then, to assume that your professors are going to hand you a beautifully worked out, consistent, and coherent system called "contract law." We doubt that such a system could exist without great changes in American society. Instead, we hope to show you the contradictions within contract law and how to use this imperfect language to accomplish your clients' goals. This is what the good contracts lawyer must take from a law school class, rather than details of doctrinal refinements.[13] First, you should understand the rhetoric of contract with all of its ambiguities and inconsistencies. Whatever the doctrinal area, you will find that certain basic but inconsistent themes appear again and again. Lawyers have to learn to speak contract rhetoric because it will be the accepted vocabulary in negotiation as well as before trial and appellate courts.

Second, you must understand that contract law is a tool that you can use to try to solve your client's problems, rather than a set of answers to all your questions. Instead of offering certainty and predictability, it often offers good arguments for all concerned. Lawyers are people who know how things work and how to get things done. They spend a good deal of their time coping with uncertainty and risk. They may turn to drafting contract provisions that define what the law has left unclear. They may use uncertainty about the meaning of rules or about proving facts as bargaining tools and not as legal arguments before decision makers — for example, a client's uncertain chance of winning at trial is something you can sell to the other side for a price; that's called a settlement.

Lawyers often turn out to be policy makers. The actual jobs of lawyers often surprise law students. Rather than spending all their time in trial or appellate courtrooms, many lawyers act politically, both directly and indirectly. They are in the business of making deals with both public officials and representatives of private organizations. Contract often provides a vocabulary for negotiations in all kinds of settings. Furthermore, lawyers are elected to legislatures at all levels of government and even more often serve on legislative staffs. Much legislation of the past century has involved withdrawing areas from the domain of contract and

---

[13] Details of doctrinal refinements might prove important sometime in your practice. However, there is not time to teach everything in three years of law school. Furthermore, contracts doctrine, as all law, has a short shelf life; details learned today may be out of date tomorrow. Fortunately, there is an impressive literature in contract law to help you exhaust the refinements of any nice point of doctrine. This course certainly should acquaint you with enough of the conventional wisdom in the field so that you will recognize a problem and understand what you read in treatises and journal articles.

creating specialized bodies of law. However, when we shift to these new areas, we do not leave contract assumptions behind. They continue to color thought, particularly in labor law, real estate transactions, business organizations, commercial law, family law, trusts and estates, and regulation of specific areas. For example, since the 1960s, consumer advocates have made effective use of phrases such as "inequality of bargaining power" and "unconscionability" that have long been a countertheme in contract. In the 1980s, ideas about consumers' needs for protection began to change. Once again there was talk of self-reliance, efficiency, and the power of the market to impose all the discipline needed. In the 1970s through the 1990s, the debate was about where we should draw the boundaries of free contract and social control, and much of it was carried on in contract rhetoric. In the wake of the worldwide financial crisis that began in 2007, reregulation became an important theme. Of course, we must be sensitive to the possibility that the terms of debate can get in the way of seeing what really is at stake, but that, too, is on our agenda.

2.   The Law-in-Action Course in Historical Perspective

The classic course from about 1900 until World War II followed a life history of contract. Materials were considered in what seemed a simple, logical order: (1) the parties formed a contract by indicating agreement or by doing certain things that courts deemed to constitute concluding a bargain; (2) the contract was interpreted so that the obligations of each party could be established; (3) the performances of the parties were appraised, both as to whether one had fallen short of what had been promised and the importance of the degree of nonperformance involved; and (4) appropriate remedies for breach would be given. In short, a lawyer did not think about performance or remedies until she established that the parties had made a contract in the first place.

The course followed a blend of several scholarly positions. Samuel Williston, Harvard's great authority on the subject, developed in the first decades of the last century a system of contract based on relatively few principles.[14] Professor Williston saw contract law as largely formal and abstract. One system of concepts, with but few exceptions, should govern formation, performance, and remedies for insurance, employment, sales of goods, building construction, and all other kinds of contracts. The law was the same even if one party was rich and the other poor, or skilled lawyers advised one while the other was uneducated and lacked legal advice, or one party had behaved according to usual expectations but had failed to comply with all the rules. Contract law was objective. It depended on outward

---

[14] Samuel Williston, a famous professor at Harvard Law School, lived from 1861 to 1963. He taught contracts to several generations of American law teachers, influential lawyers, and judges, and wrote the classic American treatises on contracts (published in 1920 and in 1936) and sales of goods. He edited leading casebooks in contracts, sales, and bankruptcy and drafted several uniform commercial statutes passed by many states. Justice Felix Frankfurter of the Supreme Court of the United States, a former student of Williston's, said, "While Williston enchanted by his charm and wit, he elevated and stimulated by these moral qualities which were ingrained in the man. . . . And upon each of us he left not only the happy memory of having seen the greatest artist in teaching, but the indelible impress of having had aroused in us the ambition to approach and reflect his moral qualities." Felix Frankfurter, *Samuel Williston: An Inadequate Tribute to a Beloved Teacher*, 76 HARV. L. REV. 1321, 1323 (1963).

appearances rather than subjective intentions and hopes. One applied the rules and accepted the result. One did not ask whether the outcome was fair as judged by some standard apart from contract law.

Professor Lon Fuller, in a 1939 essay criticizing Williston, comments:[15]

> Turning to Professor Williston's legal method, if we ask at what point he gives up the attempt to shape the law by direct reference to social interests, I think the answer will have to be, at the very outset. What may be called the bases of contract liability, notions like consideration, the necessity for offer and acceptance, and the like, are nowhere in his work critically examined in the light of the social interests they serve. These things are accepted on faith. This neglect to refer to underlying social desiderata cannot properly be called "logic." It is simply an acceptance of what is conceived to be received legal tradition. . . .

> It seems reasonably clear that our American law has been going through a positivistic phase during the last seventy-five years, and that it is this positivistic philosophy which has been the predominant influence in shaping Professor Williston's legal method. He believes that there exists in the cases "a law of contract," and that it must be sufficiently simple and consistent with itself to be capable of intelligible statement. Believing this, he fears the intrusion of vague ethical and philosophical considerations, even in the interpretation of existing law, because their corruptive and dissolving influence threatens to make impossible the very task which the positivist sets for himself, that of stating what "the law" is.

Arthur Corbin, who lived from 1874 to 1967, was Yale's great contracts scholar. He published an influential casebook in 1921, and revised it in 1933 and 1947. His eight-volume treatise on the subject appeared in 1950. While later writers often use the two men as symbols of opposing approaches to the subject, Williston and Corbin were good friends. Corbin wrote that he viewed Williston as "an older brother." He said that Williston was his chief teacher in contracts. "As a beginning instructor in that subject at Yale, sixty years ago, it was to his articles and his edition of Pollock that I had to go for instruction."[16]

However, Williston's and Corbin's approaches to the subject differed. Corbin edited an edition of *Anson on Contracts* in 1919. In the preface he said that students

> . . . should be warned that the law does not consist of a series of unchangeable rules or principles. . . . Every system of justice and of right is of human development, and the necessary corollary is that no known system is eternal. In the long history of the law can be observed the birth and death of legal principles. . . . The law is merely a part of our changing civilization. The history of law is the history of man and society. Legal principles represent the prevailing *mores* of the time, and with the *mores* they must necessarily be born, survive for the appointed season, and perish.

---

[15] Lon L. Fuller, *Williston on Contracts*, 18 N.C. L. Rev. 1 (1939).

[16] Arthur Corbin, *Samuel Williston*, 76 Harv. L. Rev. 1321 (1963).

Corbin called his great treatise "a Comprehensive Treatise on the Working Rules of Contract Law." He explained that *"all* rules of law and human society are no more than tentative working rules, based on human experience, necessarily changing in form and substance as human experience varies in the evolutionary process of life." Compared to Williston, Corbin makes a more direct use of the purposes and policies behind specific legal rules in order to analyze how they are likely to be applied to specific instances.

American legal realists saw Professor Williston's work as a symbol of what was wrong with traditional legal thought.[17] Arthur Corbin was an inspiration to the realists. Karl Llewellyn and Harold Havighurst developed a very different view of contract in the 1920s and 1930s. They argued that no one simple set of rules could govern transactions as distinct as dealings among family members, sales of goods in business, real estate transfers, and employment relations. Moreover, they pointed out that Professor Williston's system failed to take into account large bodies of both American and British contract law inconsistent with Williston's assumptions. They called for a contract law that sought substantive rather than formal justice. Everything was to depend upon the particulars of each case. Rules were to be based on general standards such as "good faith," "reasonableness," and "risk assumption" that called for judges to make choices. The realists dealt in a new way with what Williston had seen as the important problems in the field. However, they did not challenge his view about what the important problems were. Moreover, with a few exceptions, they accepted the traditional assumption that appellate cases were the only appropriate subject for analysis.

In the decade following World War II, two contracts casebooks appeared that changed the very definition of the field. The first, Professor Lon Fuller's *Basic Contract Law*, was published in 1947. The most obvious innovation was that the course began with contract remedies. Students considered most of the other topics in light of Fuller's concern with remedial theory. By now, this part of Fuller's revolution is a recognized way to begin a course.

There are several justifications for beginning a contracts course with remedies. Fuller argued that decisions in the chain of reasoning about formation and performance of contracts were affected by their remedial consequences. One cannot understand judicial decisions about contract formation or performance without understanding what difference they make. Fuller insisted that courts did not decide abstract questions of whether there had been an offer and an acceptance so that a legally enforceable contract had been formed. He suggested that the real problem was whether the parties' conduct justified awarding a remedy to one of them or whether the court should just leave both parties where they were after their transaction had failed.

There are other good reasons to start with remedies. The subject is a good introduction to the conflicting goals of this body of law. There is a large gap between announced policy and the likely impact of the rules. Moreover, the material is

---

[17] For a famous critical treatment of Williston's treatise on contracts, see Walter Wheeler Cook, *Williston on Contracts*, 33 ILL. L. REV. 497 (1939). Williston replied to both Fuller and Cook, although he did not mention them by name. *See* Samuel Williston, *Fashions in Law With Illustrations From the Law of Contracts*, 21 TEX. L. REV. 119 (1942).

difficult to learn on your own. If we put it at the end of the course, we will teach it hurriedly if at all. Indeed, if we begin at the beginning of a relationship — asking whether a contract has been formed — we are likely to spend most of our time on problems of least practical and theoretical importance.

Fuller also included excerpts from classics in political philosophy and jurisprudence relevant to issues of individualism and altruism, freedom and regulation, and the nature of the process of judging. He offered materials that compared American and British approaches to those found in continental legal systems. He also introduced a few selections dealing with the way American businesses used contract. For example, he included provisions of the Worth Street Rules. These are the practical law of the cotton grey goods industry, a form of private government that codified norms and resolved disputes by arbitration apart from the public legal system.

In spite of Fuller's then-radical innovations, his work was recognizable as a contracts casebook and enjoyed great success from the start. The classic Willistonian problems were all there plus many of the familiar cases. Also, during the preceding decade Fuller had written two great articles. They enabled law teachers to see what he was trying to get across by the arrangement of materials in his book. One of those articles — *The Reliance Interest in Contracts Damages*[18] — is by now part of the conventional wisdom of any contracts course — though it has recently come under attack.[19]

The second post–World War II book that broke out of the classic mold was by Friedrich Kessler and Malcolm Sharp. The influence of their innovative contract materials was more subtle and indirect. Relatively few teachers used this book because it looked too hard and too different. The book's message spread more widely when Grant Gilmore became Kessler's co-author for the second edition after Sharp declined to participate further.[20] Kessler and Sharp, and later Kessler and Gilmore, saw contracts as an expression of the political philosophy and ideological struggles of this nation. On one hand, there was an ideal of free contract and a minimal limited state. This was rationalized in the name of freedom and unleashing creative energies. On the other hand, there was always a countertheme calling for regulation in various forms seeking substantive justice. Kessler and Sharp saw American contract law as expressing theme and countertheme, overgeneralizations and overcorrections. In short, they saw it as contradictory. Contract doctrine reflected deeper, more basic, but inconsistent themes in the national consciousness. Furthermore, these themes could be traced back to classic views about law, government, markets, and justice.[21]

---

[18] Lon L. Fuller & William R. Perdue, *The Reliance Interest in Contracts Damages* (pts. 1 & 2), 46 YALE L.J. 52, 373 (1936–1937). Professor Fuller became one of the great figures in American legal scholarship. He taught contracts, jurisprudence, and sociology of law at Harvard Law School.

[19] Richard Craswell, *Against Fuller and Perdue*, 67 U. CHI. L. REV. 99 (2000); *see also* Symposium: *W(h)ither the Reliance Interest?*, 38 SAN DIEGO L. REV. 1–230 (2001).

[20] A third edition was revised by Professors Kessler and Anthony Kronman of Yale Law School.

[21] Karl Klare, after praising the book's innovations, offers the following criticism of Kessler and Sharp:

The book does not suggest a theory to explain *why* an advanced capitalist society must

Although Kessler and Sharp devoted most of their attention to the traditional problems of law school contracts, the first cases in their book were an overview of the underlying policy themes running throughout the course. Then a last section looked at modern commercial problems expressing the tension between free contract and regulation. For example, they described the struggle between automobile manufacturers and dealers over the balance of power in their relationship. Kessler and Sharp saw contract law as but one of many tools for coping with these larger social problems. In this section, their focus was on important problems, rather than the logic of doctrine. They saw law in the mid-20th century as involving statutes and administrative regulations rather than common law cases. Although it was not emphasized in their book, both Kessler and Sharp were interested in the relationship of business practice to contract law, and such issues were raised easily at many places in their course.

In the late 1960s, Ian Macneil published his contracts materials. He began with contract remedies, and he also saw contracts as expressing fundamental philosophical conflicts. His distinct contribution was a relational approach. Macneil argued that underlying contract law was the assumption of a single discrete transaction between strangers. However, Macneil pointed out that the reality of most modern business is the long-term continuing relationship.[22] Sometimes lawyers formally structure business relationships in a requirements contract (in which the buyer commits to buy all its requirements from a particular seller) or a blanket order system (in which any order is subject to agreed terms). Often, however, X Corporation just views Y Corporation as a valued long-term customer. While no formal contract may exist, officials of both organizations feel there are rights against and duties to one another, although they may be imprecisely defined. Obviously, such relationships have their own norms and sanctions. Do contract law

---

continually reproduce the conflict between private autonomy and state regulation. The resulting impression, perhaps contrary to Kessler and Sharp's intentions, is that the dichotomy of individualism and social control is a necessary and unresolvable conflict in all modes of social organization. Autonomy and community ultimately become reified "first principles" or "fundamental values" to be, as though by some inevitable process, "balanced." The possibility that personal autonomy and communal need are not, in principle, in conflict and that, indeed, autonomy and community might support and enhance each other in a different, noncapitalist mode of social organization is not explored. One of the central ideological missions of law in advanced capitalism is to legitimate state regulation of private economic activity while upholding private enterprise as the proper system of ownership and control. Kessler and Sharp, perhaps unwittingly, contribute to this ideological mission. No matter how vital Kessler and Sharp's historical, antiformalist emphasis, in the end key categories such as individual autonomy and social control become for them abstractions cut off from their historical roots. Kessler and Sharp thereby not only revitalize conceptualism, but, ironically, by suggesting that freedom of contract and state regulation of private behavior can be comfortably balanced within our institutional framework, they obscure the fundamental contradictions of our mode of social organization which they must have intended to illuminate.

Klare, *Contracts Jurisprudence and the First-Year Casebook*, 54 N.Y.U. L. REV. 876, 886–87 (1979).

Consider the degree to which Klare's criticism of Kessler and Sharp applies to these contracts materials. Insofar as it does, in what "different, noncapitalist mode of social organization" would "autonomy and community support and enhance each other"? In terms of the schools of thought discussed above, Klare's criticism is an example of what approach to legal scholarship?

[22] *See* Robert Gordon, *Macaulay, Macneil, and the Discovery of Solidarity and Power in Contract Law*, 1985 WIS. L. REV. 565.

and the legal system offer anything to the management of these relationships? Or is the law necessarily limited to performing a salvage function at the time of a divorce?

Macneil's large body of writing on the subject and his casebook seek to develop the implications of a relational contract law. Some of these issues relate to contract law's call for careful and specific definition of obligations. This call conflicts with custom in many business relationships. People leave things to be worked out as a long-term transaction progresses. They want flexibility to deal with changed circumstances. Some issues relate to whether the parties have overriding duties requiring them to attempt to keep the relationship alive and beneficial to both in the long run. He emphasizes that parties in relational contracts frequently temper wealth maximization goals with other objectives:

> Macneil believes the legal system needs to take radically different approaches to relational contracts than it traditionally has. In dealing with disputes, he favors greater reliance on procedures oriented towards mediation and less emphasis on adversary processes looking towards adjudication. In regulating contracts, he counsels greater reliance on proactive administrative agencies that can take account of the many third-party interests at stake and less reliance on courts able to apply regulatory rules only when a disadvantaged party initiates a court procedure.[23]

Professor Jay Feinman describes Macneil's approach to deciding contracts cases. First, a court must decide whether a transaction involves a discrete or a relational contract. Discrete transactions call for enforcing the agreement struck by the parties when they entered the deal. However, in a relational contract,

> the court would consider how . . . [norms of flexibility and contractual solidarity] are manifest in the parties' action, the community's actions and understanding, the broader society's values, and the legal system's principles. That inquiry suggests the choices to be made: not what would the parties have done, but what kind of relationship is most desirable in this setting. What the parties would have done is but one element that goes into that assessment. Finally, the effect of legal intervention in support of these norms must be considered. . . . [T]he resort to law may upset the operation of several of the most important values of the relation; imposing a norm of flexibility may cause parties to be more precise in specifying the terms of their contracts and therefore less flexible.[24]

So much for a brief history of American contracts scholarship as it has been translated into teaching materials. When you read works by legal scholars, opinions by judges, and statutes passed by legislatures you must recall that they were written by people who were influenced by the kinds of people they were and the times in which they lived. To make matters more complicated, legal writers of a later generation often construct their own picture of a scholar who wrote at an earlier

---

[23] William C. Whitford, *Ian Macneil's Contribution to Contracts Scholarship*, 1985 WIS. L. REV. 545, 551.

[24] Jay Feinman, *The Significance of Contract Theory*, 58 U. CIN. L. REV. 1283 (1990).

time, the meaning of an earlier case, or the purposes of a statute passed in response to a particular now-forgotten crisis. Often these later understandings are little better than caricature or parody. For examples, the names Williston and Corbin today have each come to stand for ideas and assumptions that seem oversimplified in light of what they actually wrote.[25]

3.   Law in Action — Building on this History

These materials, *Contracts: Law in Action*, offer a blend of all these approaches plus their own features. Following Fuller, we begin with remedies. Following Kessler and Sharp, we look at issues of freedom and regulation, and we highlight the contradictions and inconsistencies found in contract doctrine. Following Macneil, we emphasize long-term continuing relationships. We adopt a law and society perspective. We examine the gap between the law on the books and the law in action. We emphasize both the virtues and vices of symbolic law that declares ideals but hides a reality that is less pleasing. We stress the functions of contract law as delivered to its ultimate consumers. We see contract doctrine as but one of many tools with which lawyers and others attempt to cope with individual and larger social problems.

We try to put contract law into its full context. We stress such things as the costs of using courts and bringing appeals. We see lawyers playing active roles reflecting both their clients' and their own interests. We see litigation and appeals as only part of a much larger social process. The chance that one might sue plays an important part in negotiation. Processes such as mediation and arbitration are supported by tacit threats of what might happen if one party declines to participate. Lawyers themselves often judge the merits of both sides' claims and attempt to work out problems in acceptable ways. We also try to keep students well aware that modern law involves legislation and administrative regulation. We see our course as helping beginning law students learn to be lawyers rather than just masters of the fine points of legal doctrine. At the same time, legal craft demands that lawyers recognize the conflicting goals of the field. Good lawyers understand the ways things work whether or not they work as they should.

Students have mixed reactions to the course. Some find to their surprise that our contracts course is not as dull as they feared the subject would be. It is, after all, about very real problems. Other students, however, sometimes find it hard to

---

[25] Williston had a formalist streak (note, for example, his use of the phrase "correct results" in the quote below), but he was also a progressive, as indicated in this excerpt from his treatise:

> When it is now said that courts "will neither make nor modify contracts, nor dispense with their performance," if it is meant that such power will not be exercised except in accordance with legal principles, the statement is sound; but if the meaning is that parties to contracts are always liable in accordance with their terms, it is far too narrow a limitation of the functions of the common law, and a court which insists upon such a statement obliges itself in various situations to use the confusing language of fiction in order to achieve correct results. Under the name of implied contracts (quasi-contracts) courts have wisely imposed obligations on parties to contracts which they never agreed to assume; and because of fraud, mistake, duress, impossibility, and illegality, have modified contracts or dispensed with their performance, simply because justice required it.

SAMUEL WILLISTON, 3 THE LAW OF CONTRACTS 3281–82 (1920) (footnotes omitted).

understand what we are driving at and may think we are "hiding the ball." Doctrinal structure can be comforting, as Elizabeth Mensch notes:[26]

> Viewed in retrospect, Williston's majestic doctrinal structure may have been silly, but . . . appeals to reasonableness and justice appear sloppy and formless by comparison. Williston's structure was, at least, a real structure, however misguided. Perhaps much Willistonian dogma survives simply because it provides a challenging intellectual game to learn and teach in law school — more fun than the close attention to commercial detail required by thorough-going realism.

This demand for structure reminds us of a statement printed on a bookbag carried by one of our former students. It said, "I have given up the search for truth. Now all I want is a good fantasy." We understand our students' desire for simple answers and structure. Students, particularly beginners, assume there are clear rules and seek to master them. Commercial publishers play to that demand and offer outlines and books aimed at students. They may assist some students in their struggle with the basic issues of a topic. However, professors hope to encourage students to go beyond the comforting half-truths of doctrinal knowledge.

In addition, the approach taken in these materials questions many things some students want to hold dear. Macaulay suggests:[27]

> The classical model of contract . . . appeals to many legal professionals [and law students] because it seems to offer those without political or economic power the possibility of overturning the structures of the powerful in the society. Judges are supposed to respond to reasoned argument, and if their decisions importantly affect behavior, then a single skilled advocate or author of a law review article, armed only with reason, could right wrongs by persuading judges. Not only would the powerless win, but the legal professional who championed their cause would need to do only honorable and enjoyable things in order to help them. The champion works through appeals to reason and intelligence, and talks of economic and social norms, the "findings of science," efficiency, or some other highly valued body of thought. Problems of politics, interest, power, and dominance need not be faced because they do not appear to be relevant in the world of doctrine, where it is assumed that right ideas will be crystallized into rules that are self-enforcing. . . . But many of those who examine the legal process in operation today find it difficult to retain their faith that the key to the good society resides in appellate judges, administrative agencies exercising discretion, pluralism, the morality of adjudication, or economic theory. Instead of justice, the empiricists describe a system of bargaining where "the haves come out ahead."[28]

One major theme of the course is that things are not as they seem. But debunking can be upsetting. It can lead to a resigned cynicism that undercuts any effort toward

---

[26] Elizabeth Mensch, *Freedom of Contract as Ideology*, 33 Stan. L. Rev. 753, 769 (1981).

[27] Stewart Macaulay, *Elegant Models, Empirical Pictures, and the Complexities of Contract*, 11 Law & Soc'y Rev. 507, 521–22 (1977).

[28] *See* Galanter, *supra* note 8.

bettering the world. It is true that naive idealism may seriously mislead those whose goal is to effect change. However, legal rules do often matter. Lawyers for various causes have won remarkable victories, and reform efforts have affected life in the United States over the past half-century or more. We think good lawyers are skeptical idealists, aware of how the system works but unwilling to retreat into an easy cynicism.

The authors of these materials organized them to emphasize what they see as important problems. In many places this calls for something other than a doctrinal arrangement. Indeed, often a doctrinal arrangement would distort our thinking. For example, Professor David Trubek argues that the behavioral system related to processing particular types of disputes — including the relevant doctrine — "not only transforms the various individual conflicts: in so doing it 'transforms,' so to speak, a raw conflict of interest into a social process with limited possibilities. The disputes that do emerge are those in which basic economic relationships are not challenged: all other possibilities are filtered out."[29] We want to avoid these limitations on what we can see. Nonetheless, we make a major effort to explain the ins and outs of the doctrines and traditional approaches. We accept the point that as silly as some may be, they influence the vocabulary and expectations of lawyers. We have struggled to explain the logical structure of, say, the consideration doctrine without allowing it to set boundaries around our thought.

In sum, these materials are challenging, but they only reflect the difficulty in both the claims of contract law and its actual role in social life in this country. Those who find the materials disorganized are looking for something other than the organization that is there. We have signaled where we are going and why.

These materials, divided into two volumes, were designed for two courses: Contracts I, a required course that meets four hours a week for the first semester, and Contracts II, an elective that meets three hours a week in the second semester. Contracts I deals with a background we think useful to everyone. Contracts II is a course designed for those with particular interest in the field. Contracts I introduces ideas that Contracts II develops in much greater detail. However, the more basic notions found in Contracts I also find expression in many other law school courses and areas of practice.

We divide Contracts I into three parts. First, we consider contracts remedies, looking at many of the difficulties involved in announced goals and means to implement them. Then, in the second part, we turn to the long-term continuing relationship. Here we look at problems in applying the contracts remedies system to these common and important situations. We also look at alternatives to the formal legal system, considering both their merits and flaws when applied to various kinds of relationships. In the course of this second part, we also address the rudiments of the law of contract formation. Finally, in the third part, we look at attempts to regulate the bargaining process in various ways. On the one hand, this material raises all of the tensions between freedom and regulation and the conflicting

---

[29] David Trubek, *The Construction and Deconstruction of a Disputes-Focused Approach*, 15 Law & Soc'y Rev. 727, 743 (1980–81).

principles found in American contract law. On the other hand, it stresses the limits of various kinds of legal action.

This structure emphasizes what we see as important problems. Examination of the materials reveals we do cover most of the important contract doctrines associated with traditional courses. Offer, acceptance, consideration, the parol evidence rule, and conditions all appear on stage as do the expectation, reliance, and restitution interests. Wise students will master the rules as they would have if they attended law school in 1935. However, this knowledge is necessary but not sufficient. We show these doctrines playing their parts in dealing with real problems. Abstract rules of contract could govern any kind of relationship, but each of these rules is likely to come into play only in particular situations. We see doctrine as a means and not as an end. We seek not only to understand the internal logic and political or philosophical positions the statement of these rules reflect but also their likely impact on different kinds of people.

Contracts II is a more technical course building on Contracts I. Here we try to select some of the issues of offer, acceptance, mistake, and interpretation that are very much alive in modern business transactions. We give major emphasis, however, to issues of performance and excuse both at common law and under the Uniform Commercial Code, issues that seem to matter most to modern business. Moreover, we do what we can to put those cases into context so that students can understand the real disputes that brought the parties into the legal process rather than turning to some other means of resolution. Just as in Contracts I, there is great emphasis on cost barriers to use of the legal process and on the roles played by lawyers.

These materials accept that messy reality provokes messy answers to difficult questions. The discussion in class flowing from the materials may push you to the boundaries of your Republican, Democratic, independent, reactionary, or radical beliefs. You should expect this, for most of the fights about the good, the true, and the beautiful lurk just beneath the surface of the law of contracts. Contract law mirrors the conflicting visions that many of us accept as just common sense. Whether you find satisfying answers will depend in large part on your vision of the society in which you live and your definition of social justice. In good liberal fashion, we have not written the materials to indoctrinate students with any political point of view. During the late 1960s and early 1970s, those teaching from the earliest versions questioned students from somewhat to the right of the accepted wisdom of the vocal members of the class. In the 1990s, many students had moved toward the right, and our challenges seemed to come from the left. It may be that another shift in student perspective has occurred too recently to accurately identify it. Whatever your perspective, we strive to test ideas and assumptions and see this as a valuable experience for those learning to be lawyers.

After many years of exploring the area, those who have contributed to these materials still find the subject fascinating and find something new each trip through them. The process of learning anything worth learning probably must involve a degree of frustration. Everything is related to everything else, and it seems impossible to understand anything without understanding everything. Moreover, many Americans, including entering law students, expect law to be clear and consistent with simple ideas of right and wrong. Whatever the merit of that idea, students learn that the law embraces complexity and reflects a view that concepts of right and wrong are anything but simple. We hope that you will share our interest in contracts as a way of learning about life in this country and considering possibilities for stability and change.

Chapter 2

REMEDIES FOR BREACH OF CONTRACT

We begin with contract remedies, the "so what?" of the subject. Suppose Williston makes a contract to supply goods to Corbin at an agreed price. Williston fails to deliver the goods and has no excuse that the law recognizes. What can Corbin do? He is likely to talk with Williston to try to persuade him to perform. If that fails, Corbin can buy from someone else and resolve never to deal with Williston again. Corbin can gossip at a trade show, telling atrocity stories about Williston that will make it harder for Williston to make contracts with other potential customers. Corbin might decide to consult a lawyer to see whether it makes sense to seek legal relief against Williston.

What would the lawyer tell Corbin? He would state facts and opinions about what the law might offer, what it might cost to get a remedy, and the chances of winning. Law school courses too seldom stress the costs and risks involved in delivering law to its consumers, but lawyers and clients must confront these factors. We will continually remind you that law is not free. Keeping this in mind, what has the legal system to offer someone when another party has breached his or her contract? In a famous article, Professor Lon Fuller and William Perdue tell us that the law could protect the *expectation interest, the reliance interest,* or the *restitution interest,* or some combination of them.[1] While there are problems with Fuller and Perdue's classification system since the categories overlap, one must master it because these terms have become part of the vocabulary of the contracts field.[2] This chapter of *Contracts: Law in Action* will take up the expectation, the reliance, and the restitution interests and then turn to some difficult problems drawing on aspects of all of them.

A. PROTECTING THE EXPECTATION INTEREST

From the middle of the 19th century to today, judges and legal writers have told us that the primary goal of contract remedies is to protect what Fuller and Perdue call the "expectation interest." The Uniform Commercial Code announces in § 1-305(a):[3]

---

[1] Lon Fuller & William Perdue, *The Reliance Interest in Contracts Damages* (pts. 1–2), 46 Yale L.J. 52, 373 (1936 & 1937).

[2] *But see* Richard Craswell, *Against Fuller and Perdue,* 67 U. Chi. L. Rev. 99 (2000); *see also* Symposium: *W(h)ither the Reliance Interest?,* 38 San Diego L. Rev. 1–230 (2001).

[3] In this book, unless otherwise indicated, we cite to Revised Article 1. Revised Article 1 has been generally adopted, as will be explained later in the text.

The remedies provided by [the Uniform Commercial Code] must be liberally administered to the end that the aggrieved party may be put in as good a position as if the other party had fully performed but . . . penal damages may [not] be had except as specifically provided in [the Uniform Commercial Code] or by other rule of law.

While the Code does not apply to all contracts cases, it shares this statement of goals with all the other bodies of contract law. Thus, the law says that it will attempt to put aggrieved parties where they expected to be as the result of performance. The ordinary objective is to approximate a hypothetical state — where the aggrieved party would have been had the contract been performed — and not to punish breach or put the aggrieved party in a better position than would have resulted from performance.

The goal is easy enough to state, but it ought to provoke questions. Why seek this objective? What function does it serve? And what about the means to the end? We have no contract police to watch those who enter into contracts. One who threatens breach or does not perform is not arrested. Such an approach might encourage performance, but few of us would be willing to pay to have contract police to ensure performance. We have balanced the ends and costs of alternative ways to respond to breach and collectively chosen to protect the "expectation interest" — hoping this will achieve an optimal level of performance at an acceptable cost.

But what do we mean by the phrase "the expectation interest"? What are the likely actual consequences of the compromises embodied in our contracts damages norms when they are filtered through the legal system in operation? How far is the law of contract remedies actually an instrument designed to produce changes in behavior, and how far is it an exercise in political and cultural symbolism and ideology? This is the agenda for our first body of material.

1. A Long, But Necessary, Digression: Of Two Codes, Reading Statutes, and the Application of Article 2 of the Uniform Commercial Code

We want to begin with some simple examples of how the Uniform Commercial Code (UCC) attempts to put aggrieved buyers and sellers of goods in as good a position as they would have been had the contract been performed, and why the law dealing with sales of goods adopts this as a goal. We will also examine the assumptions and compromises involved in the techniques that the UCC uses to protect the expectation interest. Then we can turn to examples of the expectation interest in areas not covered by the Code.

However, before beginning students can embark on this enterprise, they have to learn a little about what the Uniform Commercial Code is, techniques of reading statutes, and, since Article 2 of the Code does not apply to all contracts, when they can use its provisions. We will also (very briefly) mention another important codification of commercial law — the United Nations Convention on Contracts for the International Sale of Goods (CISG). We will refer to its provisions from time to time in these materials.

The Uniform Commercial Code: A great deal of this course will involve learning about the Uniform Commercial Code. It is a lengthy statute that has been the law in all but one state since the late 1960s. However, it is not all of commercial law. It does not cover taxation, bankruptcy, government contracts, patents and copyrights, consumer protection, environmental protection, cooperatives, antitrust and the protection of competitive markets, the regulation of banks and securities markets, and a lot more.

What does the Code deal with? It has nine articles or major sections: Article 1 covers the purposes of the Code, definitions, and a few provisions that apply to all the other articles. Article 2 deals with transactions in goods — roughly, buying and selling cars, chairs, cows, crowbars, and other movable things. Article 3 covers the law of commercial paper — checks and promissory notes, for example. Article 4 concerns bank deposits and collections. Article 5 governs letters of credit. Article 6 regulates bulk transfers. Article 7 covers warehouse receipts, bills of lading, and other documents of title. Article 8 deals with some aspects of investment securities, and Article 9 has provisions relating to secured transactions (buying a car "on time," for example), sales of accounts and chattel paper. We will be concerned in Contracts almost entirely with Articles 1 and 2. The rest of the Code is the turf of upper-level courses in commercial law.

Uniform laws attempt to deal with some of the costs of federalism. The United States has 50 states, as well as districts and territories, all with power to make laws affecting transactions within their borders. However, the economy of this country does not respect national or state lines. It would be difficult for General Motors to sell cars under 50 different state laws, and it would be even harder for smaller companies that could not afford to hire a staff of lawyers to keep things straight. The Congress of the United States could pass national legislation, but commercial law has traditionally been and remains the states' responsibility.

The UCC is the product of a collaboration between the Uniform Law Commission (ULC) and the American Law Institute (ALI). Both are examples of the odd mixture of public and private functions so often found in this country. ULC, formerly the National Conference of Commissioners on Uniform State Laws (NCCUSL), promotes uniform laws. It is largely funded by state governments, which appoint its members, but it has no official powers. It supervises experts who draft proposed uniform laws to submit to the state legislatures. Sometimes legislatures pass these model laws as written; sometimes they tinker with them; sometimes they ignore them. Between 1896 and 1933, the Commissioners proposed seven different uniform laws dealing with negotiable instruments, sales, warehouse receipts, stock transfers, bills of lading, conditional sales, and trust receipts. They had mixed success. The UCC was more successful; every state has enacted most of it. Forty-nine states (all but Louisiana) have enacted Article 2.

The American Law Institute (ULC's collaborator in creating the UCC) is a private group performing what we might see as public functions. It has attempted to distill, organize, and state precisely the judge-made common law developed by state appellate courts. In a sense, the ALI's "restatements of the law" are proposals to judges, who may or may not choose to follow the version of a common law rule put forward. However, these restatements are influential for many reasons. They are the product of drafting by experts and careful review by committees of elite judges, lawyers, and law professors.

The Uniform Commercial Code did not appear by magic on the pages of statute books. People with thought-out positions, biases, and human failings drafted proposed versions, which committees reviewed and interest groups tried to change. These committees and groups insisted on and got revisions. Then the final product had to be sold to 50 legislatures. While the proponents of the Code tried to claim that it was the work of neutral experts and expressed a consensus of those who understood the area, opposition developed. In the late 1950s, many thought the whole project was dead and would never become law. The Code you will study reflects the process of drafting, editing, fighting, and compromising that produced it.

In the late 1930s, many commercial lawyers thought that the Uniform Sales Act was out of date. Professor Karl Llewellyn, who then taught at the Columbia Law School, sought radical reform of commercial law. Llewellyn was a member of NCCUSL. He maneuvered to take the leading role in a reform effort. Zipporah Wiseman tells us:[4]

> In "five weeks' work by the clock, and uninterrupted," Llewellyn wrote an 88-page draft of a "Uniform Sales Act 1940." . . .
>
> Llewellyn's vision of sales law, reflected in that 1940 draft and in his earlier writings and subsequent revisions of the draft, was no mere update of [the Uniform Sales Act] . . . Obsolescence in general was an important starting point, but modernization was not Llewellyn's only end. Llewellyn's objective was to reformulate sales law in light of his normative vision of both merchant practice and judicial decision making.

Of course, as Wiseman chronicles, Llewellyn and his allies had to battle for a long time before the UCC ultimately assumed its final form. As a result, it is filled with compromises.

Professor (and later Justice) Robert Braucher was an insider who took part in this long process that led to the adoption of the Code. He taught contracts and sales at the Harvard Law School, and participated in many activities of both the National Conference of Commissioners on Uniform State Laws and the American Law Institute. He also served as a justice of the Supreme Judicial Court of Massachusetts. The following excerpt from his article speaks to the history of the statute.

---

[4] Zipporah Wiseman, *The Limits of Vision: Karl Llewellyn and the Merchant Rules*, 100 HARV. L. REV. 465, 490–93 (1987).

Robert Braucher, *Legislative History of the Uniform Commercial Code*
58 COLUM. L. REV. 798 (1958)[5]

The Code itself began with the address of President William A. Schnader to the fiftieth annual meeting of the [National] Conference [of Commissioners on Uniform State Laws]. . . . In 1942 the American Law Institute agreed to participate, and the Uniform Revised Sales Act was approved by the Conference in 1943 and by the Institute in 1944. Professor Llewellyn was the reporter and . . . Soia Mentschikoff was the assistant reporter in this first part of the project; they later became chief reporter and associate chief reporter for the Code as a whole.[6]

The comprehensive joint project officially got under way on January 1, 1945. Supervision of the Code was the responsibility of a five-man editorial board, under the chairmanship of Judge Herbert F. Goodrich. The method of operation, described in the initial comment to the Code, followed in outline the Institute's procedure in work on the various Restatements. A draft prepared by one of the reporters was reviewed by a small group of "advisers," then by the Council of the Institute and the Conference, often at a joint meeting. By May 1949 the Code had reached the stage of an integrated draft of nine articles with notes and comments. . . .

As the Code neared completion, published references to it increased in volume. A judicial opinion stated that provisions of the Code "which do not conflict with statute or settled case law are entitled to as much respect and weight as courts have been inclined to give to the various Restatements. It, like the Restatements, has the stamp of approval of a large body of American scholarship." People who had participated in the drafting wrote explanatory articles in legal periodicals. . . . Later the American Law Institute published a series of monographs on the Code, and new casebooks in fields covered by the Code were spattered with Code references.

The result was that groups that had not previously taken part in the project came to examine it critically. In addition to a great volume of favorable discussion, there appeared some highly critical academic comment on particular provisions of the Code. Professor Frederick Beutel of the University of Nebraska announced his all-out hostility, branding the Code as "the Lawyers and Bankers Relief Act," involving "a deliberate sell-out of the American Law Institute and the Commission-

---

[5] Copyright © 1958 by the Directors of the Columbia Law Review Association, Inc. All Rights Reserved. Reprinted by permission.

[6] [Eds. note: Llewellyn married Soia Mentschikoff during the early stages of drafting the Uniform Commercial Code (she lived from 1915 to 1984). She was one of the first women to become a partner in a Wall Street law firm and then became a visiting professor at Harvard Law School. In the 1940s and 1950s, most universities prohibited married couples from serving on the faculties of the same department. The University of Chicago had the same rule, but its Law School appointed Llewellyn as a professor of law and Mentschikoff as a "professorial lecturer with tenure." This seemed to satisfy the University, Karl, and Soia. Mentschikoff contributed a great deal to the drafting and lobbying for the enactment of the Uniform Commercial Code. She had a distinguished career apart from her professional and personal relationship with Llewellyn. She was Dean of the University of Miami Law School from 1974 to 1984.]

ers of Uniform Laws to the bank lobby." The other principal opponent, Emmett F. Smith, house counsel to the Chase National Bank of New York, was in strange contrast. Late in 1952 he began a one-man campaign to defeat the Code, circulating far and wide over the nation two mimeographed memoranda of forty-odd pages each. Far more effective than the Beutel attacks, the Smith memoranda provoked a printed reply from the Conference. Opposition by other groups seems to be traceable at least in part to the Smith memoranda, and it seems a fair guess that Smith was largely responsible for the fact that no state except Pennsylvania enacted the Code before 1957.

[Beginning in 1953 the Code was the subject of review by Massachusetts, New York, and Pennsylvania — with the New York study being watched with particular care.] . . . Finally, after three years of work and the expenditure of some $300,000, the [New York Law Revision Commission] early in 1956 rendered its report. The report's major conclusions may be summarized as follows:

    (1) The "preponderance" of the arguments for or against codification "is in favor of careful and foresighted codification of all or major parts of commercial law."

    (2) Such a commercial code "would be of greater value to the public and the legal profession than the enactment, even with revisions, of separate uniform laws."

    (3) Such a code "is attainable with a reasonable amount of effort and within a reasonable amount of time."

    (4) The Uniform Commercial Code "is not satisfactory in its present form."

    (5) The Uniform Commercial Code "cannot be made satisfactory without comprehensive re-examination and revision in light of all critical comment obtainable."

Following publication of the New York report, the subcommittees of the editorial board reviewed their previously formulated tentative recommendations and made final reports to the editorial board. The sponsoring organizations authorized the publication of a revised edition of the Code, and by November 1956 the board had completed action on a revised statutory text. . . . The subcommittees also prepared revised official comments during the spring of 1957, but publication was withheld to await developments in the 1957 legislative sessions in Massachusetts and Pennsylvania. A complete revised text and comments edition was finally published early in 1958.

––––––––––

At the time Braucher wrote, only Pennsylvania, Massachusetts, and Kentucky had passed the Uniform Commercial Code. The judgment of the Law Revision Commission in New York was a blow to the hopes of the proponents, and the editorial board made revisions to meet some of its objections. Many academics who taught commercial law participated in a lobbying movement, reassuring legislators that the Code was a progressive reform.

It is unlikely that many state legislators read and understood the Code. In most states, scholars prepared lengthy section-by-section commentaries discussing the impact of the Code's provisions on the law of the state. A few legislators may have looked at these efforts, but their length and complexity suggest that most legislators had to take the Code on faith or rely on the opinions of those they trusted. By 1962, fourteen states had passed the UCC, including important commercial states such as Illinois and New Jersey. By 1967 it was the law in 49 states, the District of Columbia, and the Virgin Islands. Louisiana, with its French Civil Code tradition, was the lone exception. Finally, in 1974, Louisiana passed all of the Code's articles but 2 and 6. Guam also adopted the entire UCC in 1977. Many of the states passed the statute with their own amendments here and there so that the result is not complete uniformity.

The Uniform Commercial Code has a style that many lawyers dislike. Professor Karl Llewellyn, its Chief Reporter, was a famous jurisprudential scholar.[7] He thought that the common law tradition was one of the important inventions of English-speaking people. Llewellyn argued that American courts had engaged in three styles of reasoning since 1800. The "Grand Style" typified 1800 to 1850. This was a creative and flexible approach. Judges looked back to precedent but also forward to prospective consequences and prospective future problems. "[P]recedent is carefully regarded, but if it does not make sense it is ordinarily re-explored; 'policy' is explicitly inquired into; alleged 'principle' must make for wisdom as well as for order if it is to qualify as such. . . ."[8] He contrasted this Grand Style with a "Formal Style" that predominated from 1850 to 1920. This approach was formal and logical, but remote from life. Formal style opinions ignored or concealed change and growth in the law. Llewellyn said that since the mid-1920s, courts had attempted to recapture the Grand Style of an earlier time. Judges, he wrote, had a sense of the situation that helped them find sensible results in particular cases, whatever the quality of the reasoning in opinions explaining what they had done. Rather than attempting to spell out precise rules in detail, lawmakers should attempt to help judges by giving guidance as to factors to consider. Thus, the Code often speaks qualitatively, using terms such as "good faith," "unconscionable," "commercial reasonableness," and the like. The Code does not purport to offer a solution for all possible problems.

Article 2 of the UCC is not pure Llewellyn. While he wrote the first draft in 1940, by 1958 many cooks had had a hand in making the broth. Zipporah Wiseman has studied Llewellyn's original papers, and she details how much of Llewellyn's original vision was lost in the process of building coalitions and making compromises.[9] Llewellyn, himself, said:[10]

---

[7] *See, e.g.,* WILLIAM TWINING, KARL LLEWELLYN AND THE REALIST MOVEMENT (1973); Kenneth Casebeer, *Escape from Liberalism: Fact and Value in Karl Llewellyn,* 1977 DUKE L.J. 671; Note, *How Appellate Opinions Should Justify Decisions Made Under the UCC,* 29 STAN. L. REV. 1245 (1977).

[8] Karl Llewellyn, *On the Current Recapture of the Grand Tradition,* 9 U. CHI. L. REV. 6 (1960).

[9] Zipporah Wiseman, *The Limits of Vision: Karl Llewellyn and the Merchant Rules,* 100 HARV. L. REV. 465 (1987).

[10] Karl Llewellyn, *Why a Commercial Code?* 22 TENN. L. REV. 779, 784 (1953).

I am ashamed of [the UCC] in some ways; there are so many pieces that I could make a little better; there are so many beautiful ideas I tried to get in that would have been good for the law, but I was voted down. A wide body of opinion has worked the law into some sort of compromise after debate and after exhaustive work. However, when you compare it with anything that there is, it is an infinite improvement.

Whatever Llewellyn's views about grand-style judging, the UCC still is a statute with its own logic and vocabulary. You must master them if you are to do a technically adequate job. Seldom, for example, can one read a phrase or a section in isolation and understand the Code's meaning. One must understand the structure, or architecture, of the Code before one can understand any particular provision.

While all states have passed a major part of the Code, there is a real gap between its text and the living law. The Code is not easy to understand. At the most elementary level, it lacks an index compiled by its authors, and the cross-references in the Official Comments often are incomplete. Some lawyers fight its underlying philosophy; they would be happier with a statute that provided more answers. Whatever your ultimate judgment about the UCC, it is the law. Command of its logic and vocabulary is an important skill for lawyers who encounter the subjects it deals with in their practice.

Revising Articles 1 and 2 and drafting UCITA: By the late 1980s, serious questions had arisen about some of the Code's provisions, and many were concerned about its ability to deal with new technologies. An ambitious (but controversial) revision process was initiated. Revisions of some articles, such as Article 1 on definitions and general provisions and Article 9 on secured transactions, were very successful. Almost all states have enacted Revised Article 1, and all have adopted Revised Article 9. The Article 2 revision process, however, broke down and was abandoned in 1999. This effort was replaced by a substantially more modest effort to amend Article 2, as well as an ambitious proposal for a freestanding Uniform Computer Information Transactions Act (UCITA) — not part of the UCC because the ALI refused to endorse it — to deal with contracts involving software, databases, and other computer-related transactions. Ultimately, no state enacted the Article 2 amendments, which have now been "withdrawn" by their sponsors, the ULC and the ALI. UCITA has only been enacted in two states, Maryland and Virginia, and it seems very unlikely it will be enacted by others. The courts have for the most part adapted by applying the existing Article 2 to software transactions even if they are labeled "licenses." In *Micro Data Base Systems, Inc. v. Dharma Systems, Inc.*, 148 F.3d 649, 651–54 (7th Cir. 1998), the court applied Article 2 to a transaction in customized software under an agreement involving a "license fee." The opinion by Judge Richard Posner notes that this approach represents "the weight of authority" and reaches "the right result — for we can think of no reason why the UCC is not suitable to govern disputes arising from the sale of custom software."). But as Professor Jean Braucher explains in the following excerpt, this was not the result favored by the software industry.

Jean Braucher, *New Basics: 12 Principles for Fair Commerce in Mass-Market Software and Other Digital Products*, *in* CONSUMER PROTECTION IN THE AGE OF THE "INFORMATION ECONOMY" 177 (Jane K. Winn ed., 2006)[11]

Overall, the [Article 2] study group's report did not identify any major reason for the revision project; instead, it surveyed a series of minor issues that might be addressed. With twenty-twenty hindsight, one can see that the project was doomed from the start because the study committee did not envision any significant efficiency gain that could justify the transition costs to businesses of many changes in statutory language. Despite the lack of a compelling reason to pursue the project, the Revised Article 2 drafting project began after the study committee report was published.

The issue of whether to cover software remained in limbo in the early years of the Revised Article 2 project. In 1995, the Article 2 drafting committee experimented with a draft covering both sales of goods and licenses of software (a development that might have supplied the missing rationale for the project), but later that year NCCUSL [now renamed the ULC] decided to go forward with a separate UCC article, Article 2B, on licenses of "computer information." The two projects then proceeded in tandem, with separate drafting committees, although there were periodic efforts to harmonize sections dealing with the same issues in the two projects.

The politics of the two committees were quite different. The majority of the Article 2B drafting committee consistently voted for positions favored by software producers, while the Revised Article 2 drafting committee was more balanced in its treatment of sellers and buyers. The Article 2 revision project ultimately faltered when NCCUSL sided with strong seller interests and pulled the project from final consideration in 1999. The original Article 2 reporters resigned and a new, more seller-oriented drafting committee was appointed. The project was scaled back somewhat, from a revision to a set of amendments. The ALI membership narrowly approved proposed Amended Article 2 in May 2003, following final approval by NCCUSL in August 2002. . . . [Eds. note: Amended Article 2 has now been withdrawn, having failed to be adopted by any state.]

In an unsuccessful effort to minimize controversy, proposed Amended Article 2 punted on the issue of the coverage of software and other digital products. . . . [The article then explains detailed provisions that had the effect of leaving various issues to judicial discretion, without statutory guidance.] Overall, as applied to software transactions, the amendments would be a step backwards, further confusing rather than clarifying the law.

The bias of the Article 2B project in favor of the software industry ultimately doomed it. In 1999, the ALI pulled out of the Article 2B project, ending its status as a UCC Article. The major reasons included amorphous scope, complex and unclear drafting, overreaching into issues best left to intellectual property law, and

---

a failure to require pre-transaction presentation of terms even in Internet transactions.

NCCUSL then decided to proceed alone with the Article 2B project, turning it into a freestanding uniform law and renaming it the Uniform Computer Information Transactions Act, or UCITA. NCCUSL first approved UCITA in 2000. After two quick enactments in Maryland and Virginia, the opposition effectively organized. Since then . . . opponents of UCITA have succeeded in defeating it in every jurisdiction where it has been promoted.

––––––––––

ALI's Principles of the Law of Software Contracts: ALI went forward with its own independent project concerning the law of software, called Principles of the Law of Software Contracts, which was approved by the membership in May 2009 and published in 2010. This is a more modest project in that it is not a proposed statute, but rather an attempt to influence common law decisions. It is called a "principles" project, rather than a restatement, to reflect the less settled nature of the law in this area.

United Nations Convention on Contracts for the International Sale of Goods, and the UNIDROIT Principles: The development of trade across state boundaries led to the need for a code of commercial law which was more or less uniform from one state to another — hence the UCC. Similarly, growth of international trade led to a perceived need for a code which would govern international sales of goods — hence the Convention on Contracts for the International Sale of Goods (CISG). The Convention was approved by a Diplomatic Conference in Vienna in 1980, and the process of adoption by individual countries began immediately. As of 2014, 83 nations, including the United States, Australia, Canada, China, France, Germany, Israel, Italy, Japan, Mexico, the Russian Federation, and Sweden had subscribed to the Convention. Contracts for the international sale of goods that are entered into by parties in at least two different countries, both of which have ratified the convention, are subject to CISG unless the contract for sale explicitly designates another law (such as the UCC) as the governing law. Many of the rules of the Convention are the same as those of the U.S. common law, or the UCC, but there are important differences. We will, on occasion, call your attention to the Convention when we think it would be useful or interesting to do so; we do not intend, however, to provide an exhaustive summary of the Convention's rules. It is important that you know that the Convention provides the presumptive standards for international sales of goods involving parties from participating nations, and that the rules may be different from those you might otherwise expect to apply.

Another body of norms of increasing significance can be found in the "UNIDROIT Principles." UNIDROIT is the commonly used name for the International Institute for the Unification of Private Law, an organization that was formed to prepare uniform international rules of contract law. Delegates from 58 countries, including the United States, make up the organization's membership. In 1994 UNIDROIT produced the UNIDROIT Principles, which constitute a set of general rules for international commercial contracts. These Principles were revised and updated in 2004 and 2010. They are applied primarily when parties agree to make them the governing rules, but they can also serve to supplement other international uniform law instruments, as well as providing a resource for general legal principles. The Principles address issues of formation, validity, interpretation, content, performance, and non-performance (including remedies). The Principles generally embody rules similar to those found in the Restatement (Second) of Contracts and the Uniform Commercial Code, though there are important differences. The Principles specifically address contract problems that are especially important in international transactions, such as contracts written in multiple languages and currency-related problems. The Principles also contain rules addressing requirements of good faith and fair dealing, gross disparity in bargaining power, and hardship as a ground for relief from a contract, or as a ground for re-negotiation, which may be different in important ways from the Restatement or the UCC.[12]

Reading statutes: While in many ways the Uniform Commercial Code is an unusual statute, still it is a statute. Lawyers have techniques for reading and applying words passed by legislatures. Law students, professors, judges, and lawyers often forget an obvious and simple one: *you must read the statute.* When Section 10 refers to Section 7, and both use terms defined in Section 1, you must read all three sections and put them together in some plausible way. English may be a terribly imprecise language, far better suited to poetry than lawmaking, but this does not justify neglect of what precision it does have.

We cannot forget that the reader of anything written must create its meaning. Judges often write of seeking the "plain meaning" of legislation. Many legal scholars, borrowing the teaching of those who study language, have attacked the idea that documents can have a plain meaning. Words take on meaning *for me* as I interpret them in light of context and my experiences. However, the meaning I create by this active process may not be the one you create because we are different people. Undoubtedly, the scholars' attack on the conceit that interpretation is a mechanical translation of a code available to everyone was a valuable corrective to the "plain meaning" position.

However, lawyers have a professional interest in asserting that there is some possibility of communication among people. Someone who decides to interpret "yes" to mean "no," "stop" to mean "go," "up" to mean "down," "right" to mean "left," and "I promise" to mean "I will if I feel like it" is likely to experience a good deal of difficulty in interaction with others. Most lawyers share a culture, and they have some success in predicting how others might react if they translate words one way or another. The more you understand that culture, the better you will be able to predict how lawyers are likely to interpret language. To restate the first rule of statutory construction: read the statute, but read it intelligently.

Judges also say that when the language of a statute is "ambiguous," then they may use various extrinsic aids to give it meaning. Ambiguity is a matter of degree. When the words in a statute seem to draw on the meanings common to lawyers, probably it is not worth wasting a judge's time by asking him or her to consider other plausible meanings. It is a good idea to hold legislators to using words with

---

[12] For the principles themselves, go to www.unidroit.org/instruments/commercial-contracts/unidroit-principles-2010.

something like the meaning expected in legal culture. But at some point, even words taken in context may leave most lawyers uncertain. Then materials other than the text of a statute should be consulted.

Often judges say that the goal of statutory construction is the "intention" of the legislature. At first glance, you might find this a strange idea. A legislature, after all, is not a person but a collective body. Representative A votes for the Good Works Act because the director of a political action committee that contributes to A's reelection campaign tells him to do so. Representative B has studied the matter and reached a reasoned conclusion that the Good Works Act best balances the competing interests of all the affected public. Representative C relies on Representative B's judgments on such matters while she specializes in other legislative issues. And so on. Furthermore, a great deal of the work of modern legislatures is done by members of the legislative staff who, in turn, may draw on suggestions from lobbyists, the governor's staff, people in administrative agencies, and professors. Given the workload and the complexity of the issues coming before a legislature, there must be a great division of labor, and representatives must often rely on others. Intention, then, often means no more than that members of the legislature had a *chance* to read the committee reports explaining the bill, though few did.

Returning to the Uniform Commercial Code, the problem of determining the legislature's intention in the face of textual ambiguity is even more difficult. The Code is technically state legislation, but it was not drafted in any particular state. Any meaningful effort to ascertain the intention of a section has to take into account the intentions of the experts who drafted the Code, as described in the excerpt from Professor Robert Braucher's article, *supra*. But these experts (professors and elite lawyers) are not legislators in any state, and it is not clear why their views should be considered authoritative. Could it be argued that the members of the state legislatures that enacted the Code had studied and embraced the views of these experts?

In practice, when faced with ambiguity in the provisions of the Code, especially Article 2, courts often refer to the Official Comments to each section. However, you should be aware that the text of the Code was enacted as law by legislatures; in most states, the Comments were not. The Comments were drafted by the same committees that drafted the text to the Code, as Professor Robert Braucher described, *supra*. It is unlikely that the Comments (which may themselves be ambiguous) were considered as carefully as the text (if at all) by the enacting legislatures. Courts sometimes feel free to ignore the import of a Comment in interpreting a Code provision.

 Applicability of Article 2 of the UCC: Article 2 of the Uniform Commercial Code governs many but not all contracts. It is important that you use Article 2 when it is clearly applicable. Before you turn to particular sections in Article 2, you always must give some thought to whether you have an Article 2 transaction. Obviously, in many situations it will not matter whether a case fits into Article 2 because its rules and those of general contract law are the same. The problem comes when Article 2 has provisions that favor your client but which are not found in other bodies of law. We will explore some of these differences in due course. Appellate courts have had to wrestle with the scope of Article 2 in a surprising number of cases.

At this point you should read §§ 2-102, 2-105(1), and 2-107(1) and (2) of the Uniform Commercial Code and the related Comments. Then consider the following questions (some of these are quite difficult and complicated):

(1) Owner buys a wooded hillside lot located at 123 N. Main Street for $20,000 from the Subdivision Development Corporation. Would Article 2 of the UCC apply to this transaction? *See* §§ 2-102, 2-105(1), 2-107. If not, does this mean that their contract is not legally enforceable? *See* § 1-103(b).

(2) Owner hires Woodsman to cut the trees and remove the stumps from the wooded hillside lot. Under the contract, Woodsman is to trim the felled trees to create marketable logs, stack the logs neatly, and transport the stumps and non-marketable small branches to the municipal dump. Is this transaction between Owner and Woodsman within Article 2 of the UCC? *See* § 2-105(1). If Owner later sells the stacked logs to Lumber Mill for an agreed price, is this transaction within Article 2?

(3) Businessperson leases an automobile for one day from Rent-A-Car. Is this transaction within Article 2 of the Code? *See* §§ 2-102, 2-106(1).[13]

(4) Owner buys components for a music system from StereoLand. Consider two variations:

(a) Owner receives cartons containing components at the store, and she assembles the system at her house. Is this transaction within Article 2 of the UCC?

(b) The contract calls for a StereoLand employee to go to Owner's house and set up the system. Does it matter whether the dispute is about the quality of the goods before installation, whether the installation was done right, or whether there is a writing to make the transaction enforceable under § 2-201?

(5) Owner makes a contract with Engineer to produce a specially designed automobile. Engineer is to supply the design, labor, and parts and deliver a completed automobile to Owner. Is this transaction within Article 2 of the UCC? *See* § 2-105(1); *cf.* § 2-704(2). What about a case in which Client consults Lawyer, and Lawyer prepares a will reflecting Client's wishes for the disposition of his property after his death? Lawyer produces a 10-page typewritten document on expensive paper with a fancy cover. This is handed to Client, who pays Lawyer's fee. Does this transaction fall within the boundaries of Article 2? If you have any question about the application of Article 2 here, how does the transaction differ from the production of a specially designed automobile?

In *Bonebrake v. Cox*,[14] the court said,

---

[13] This is a bit of a trick question. Article 2A, Leases, was proposed for adoption in 1987 to resolve the special issues involved in leasing goods. All states except Louisiana have now adopted it. The Article applies to short-term rentals of automobiles or do-it-yourself equipment by consumers, on the one hand, and to commercial leases of such items as aircraft and industrial machinery, on the other. Under Article 2A, you do not have to worry about the question we asked in the text.

[14] 499 F.2d 951, 960 (8th Cir. 1974).

The test for inclusion or exclusion [in Article 2 of the UCC] is not whether they [goods and services] are mixed, but, granting that they are mixed, whether their predominant factor, their thrust, their purpose, reasonably stated, is the rendition of service, with goods incidentally involved (*e.g.*, contract with artist for painting) or is a transaction of sale, with labor incidentally involved (installation of a water heater in a bathroom).

Do you find that this test helps you solve these problems? Another approach sometimes used by the courts is to look at the "gravamen of the action," that is, the aspect of the transaction in dispute. If the dispute in a mixed transaction is about the goods aspect of the transaction, Article 2 will apply, but if it is about the services element, it will not.

(6) Owner makes a contract with General Contractor to build a house on Owner's lot. General Contractor is to supply labor and materials. Is this transaction within Article 2 of the UCC? *See* §§ 2-106, 2-107, and 2-501(1)(a) and (b).

(7) After the house is built, Owner sells it to Buyer. Is this transaction within Article 2 of the UCC? Does it matter whether Owner sells only the house or sells the house and the lot on which it is built? *See* § 2-107(2).

(8) Local Fast Food enters a dealer franchise agreement with National Chain. Under this agreement, Local leases from National the land and building constituting the local restaurant; agrees to provide various services such as keeping the restaurant open during certain hours, keeping records in certain forms, and running the restaurant; and agrees to buy various food products and cleaning supplies from National. The franchise agreement provides that National can cancel the arrangement upon giving 60 days' notice, and National exercises this right. Local's lawyer wants to argue that National's action violated the obligation of "good faith" imposed by the Code under §§ 1-304 and 2-103(1)(b). National's lawyer argues that the UCC is not applicable to this transaction, and that the general contract law of the particular jurisdiction imposes no such obligation. The courts have had a great deal of trouble with this problem. Do you see why?[15]

(9) Lawyer buys a software package for her law office for billing, tracking documents, and so forth. A dispute arises with the seller with respect to whether the software has performed as promised. Should the UCC apply? In Maryland and Virginia, where UCITA has been enacted, that statute would govern. In other states, most courts have applied Article 2 to software transactions, even involving custom software.

Article 2 of the UCC applies to "transactions in goods." These problems have shown that application of this rather simple phrase yields considerable uncertainty in a variety of situations. You may find this troubling. If you do, you might find solace in suggestions by Ludwig Wittgenstein (1889–1951) in his *Philosophical Investigations*, an enigmatic landmark in 20th-century philosophy. Wittgenstein

---

[15] As we will see later, Local may have rights under federal and state franchise protection statutes passed in the 1960s and 1970s, but those statutes do not cover all situations involving franchisees. Furthermore, the general contract law of many jurisdictions will impose a duty of good faith and fair dealing, making the applicability of the Code of little importance in this circumstance. *See* Restatement (Second) of Contracts § 205 (1981).

suggests a radical defect in a long tradition in philosophy that says one knows what a thing is (for example, a "game" or a "transaction in goods") only if one knows some property or set of properties that *all* things, and *only* things, of that type have.

LUDWIG WITTGENSTEIN, PHILOSOPHICAL INVESTIGATIONS
(G.E.M. Anscombe, trans., Macmillan 3d ed. 1972)[16]

66. Consider for example the proceedings that we call "games." I mean board-games, card-games, ball-games, Olympic games, and so on. What is common to them all? — Don't say: "There *must* be something in common, or they would not be called 'games' " — but *look and see* whether there is anything common to all. — For if you look at them you will not see something that is common to *all*, but similarities, relationships, and a whole series of them at that. To repeat: don't think, but look! — Look for example at board-games, with their multifarious relationships. Now pass to card-games; here you find many correspondences with the first group, but many common features drop out, and others appear. When we pass next to ball-games, much that is common is retained, but much is lost. — Are they all 'amusing'? Compare chess with noughts and crosses. Or is there always winning and losing, or competition between players? Think of patience. In ball games there is winning and losing; but when a child throws his ball at the wall and catches it again, this feature has disappeared. Look at the parts played by skill and luck; and at the difference between skill in chess and skill in tennis. Think now of games like ring-a-ring-a-roses; here is the element of amusement, but how many other characteristic features have disappeared! And we can go through the many, many other groups of games in the same way; can see how similarities crop up and disappear.

And the result of this examination is: we see a complicated network of similarities overlapping and criss-crossing: sometimes overall similarities, sometimes similarities of detail.

67. I can think of no better expression to characterize these similarities than "family resemblances"; for the various resemblances between members of a family: build, features, colour of eyes, gait, temperament, etc., etc. overlap and criss-cross in the same way. — And I shall say: 'games' form a family. . . .

69. How shall we explain to someone what a game is? I imagine that we should describe *games* to him, and we might add: "This *and similar things* are called 'games.' " And do we know any more about it ourselves? Is it only other people whom we cannot tell exactly what a game is? — But this is not ignorance. We do not know the boundaries because none have been drawn. To repeat, we can draw a boundary — for a special purpose. Does it take that to make the concept usable? Not at all! (Except for that special purpose.) No more than it took the definition: one pace = 75 centimeters, to make the measure of length 'one pace' usable. And if you want to say "But still, before that it wasn't an exact measure," then I reply: very well, it was an inexact one. — Though you still owe me a definition of *exactness*.

---

70. "But if the concept 'game' is uncircumscribed like that, you don't really know what you mean by a 'game.' " — When I give the description: "The ground was quite covered with plants" — do you want to say I don't know what I am talking about until I can give a definition of a plant? . . .

71. One might say that the concept 'game' is a concept with blurred edges. — "But is a blurred concept a concept at all?" — Is an indistinct photograph a picture of a person at all? Is it even always an advantage to replace an indistinct picture by a sharp one? Isn't the indistinct one often exactly what we need?

———————

Wittgenstein's notion of "family resemblances" may be an incomplete solution to the problem he raises, but it does provide a provocative backdrop against which to think about the problem under discussion. For our purposes, it is especially useful to reflect upon the questions raised in § 71 of Wittgenstein's text. Why would it be an advantage for the UCC to employ an indistinct or blurred concept of "transaction in goods?" What disadvantages can you see?

Our long march through this digression ends at last. Now you are ready to begin by reading some Uniform Commercial Code sections and applying them to problems dealing with the expectation interest.

2. The Expectation Interest: The Substitute Contract as the Preferred Means to the End

Contract remedies generally are based on encouraging the aggrieved party to enter a substitute contract and then awarding damages to make up any loss remaining. Suppose Seller promises to sell 100 shares of Hot Property Software Corporation stock to Buyer for $10 a share. Seller breaches the contract. Buyer then immediately purchases 100 shares of this stock from someone else for $12 a share. Had the Seller/Buyer contract been performed, Buyer would have paid $1000 for 100 shares of stock. Because of the breach, Buyer had to pay $1200. A court would award Buyer damages of $200. Assuming no transaction costs, Buyer then will have paid $1000 ($1200 − 200 = $1000) for the 100 shares — that is, Buyer will be where he or she would have been had the contract been performed. The expectation interest is protected.

We will illustrate this principle in more detail by a series of examples of how the Uniform Commercial Code has codified this simple approach. As so often is the case, complexity lurks at the margins of a seemingly simple idea. In each instance, ask yourself not only what is the proper answer under the applicable statutes, but whether it is a sensible answer. First, read §§ 2-703, 2-706, and 2-708 of the Uniform Commercial Code as well as the relevant Official Comments. Then answer the following questions:[17]

———————

[17] The dollar amounts in these problems keep the math simple, but probably make a lawsuit impractical because of the cost of litigation. In such circumstances it is unclear to what extent legal analysis will affect any dispute resolution by the parties. However, if the contract were for 100,000 crates of apples, a threat of litigation could be credible, and in that case, predicting how a court would resolve any litigation would likely have an impact on any settlement discussions between the parties.

(1) On June 1st, Seller contracted to sell 100 crates of apples to Natural Foods at $8/crate. The crates of apples were to be delivered to Natural Foods on July 1st. On July 1st, Seller arrived at Natural Foods with 100 crates of apples that met the quality the contract required. However, Natural Foods Produce Manager breached the contract by refusing to accept or pay for the apples. Seller returned to his farm and kept the apples. The market price for this quality and type of apples on July 1st was $7.10/crate. How much, if anything, should Seller recover under the UCC?

(2) Suppose we learned that the market value of apples of this type and quality on both June 1st and July 1st was $7.10/crate. Would this change the result? Why or why not?

(3) Suppose the facts are as stated in question (1), except that Seller had resold the apples on July 1st at $7/crate to a supermarket located near Natural Foods' place of business. The owner of the supermarket was Seller's neighbor and close personal friend. How much, if anything, would Seller recover from Buyer?

(4) Suppose the facts are as stated in question (1), except that Seller upon leaving Natural Foods' place of business parked his truck by the side of the road and resold all the apples at $7.50/crate to people who stopped. How much, if anything, would Seller recover from Buyer?

Problem (4) is much more difficult than it looks. The UCC does not provide a clear answer, and scholars have debated the issue. You can find a summary of the contending positions in a leading authority on the interpretation of the UCC: WHITE & SUMMERS, THE UNIFORM COMMERCIAL CODE, at pp. 362–66 (6th ed., 2010). However, at this point in the course your task is simply to articulate what might be contending interpretations of the UCC relevant to the solution of problem (4).

B.   THE EXPECTATION INTEREST: OF INFERIOR SUBSTITUTES, OTHER ENDS, AND OTHER MEANS

The contract-price/market-price approach offers a simple solution to many cases. However, it won't always work. For example, go back once again to our apple case. Suppose the Produce Manager at Natural Foods refuses to take the apples because there is a glut, and apples are so plentiful that one can buy them at every roadside for a penny an apple. Commercial buyers are not purchasing apples from anyone, and one cannot sell them to consumers at roadsides at prices adequate to pay for the gasoline burned to drive the truck there. Section 2-709 makes it clear that "if the seller is unable after reasonable effort to resell [the goods] at a reasonable price or the circumstances reasonably indicate that such effort will be unavailing," then the seller may recover the contract price from the buyer. The seller must hold the goods for the buyer unless resale becomes possible.

The next three cases illustrate some of the difficulties in the application of the expectation principle.

PARKER v. TWENTIETH CENTURY-FOX FILM CORP.
California Supreme Court
3 Cal. 3d 176, 474 P.2d 689 (1970)

BURKE, J.

Defendant Twentieth Century-Fox Film Corporation appeals from a summary judgment granting to plaintiff the recovery of agreed compensation under a written contract for her services as an actress in a motion picture. As will appear, we have concluded that the trial court correctly ruled in plaintiff's favor and that the judgment should be affirmed.

Plaintiff [Shirley MacLaine Parker] is well known as an actress, and in the contract between plaintiff and defendant is sometimes referred to as the "Artist." Under the contract, dated August 6, 1965, plaintiff was to play the female lead in defendant's contemplated production of a motion picture entitled "Bloomer Girl." The contract provided that defendant would pay plaintiff a minimum "guaranteed compensation" of $53,571.42 per week for 14 weeks commencing May 23, 1966, for a total of $750,000. Prior to May 1966 defendant decided not to produce the picture and by a letter dated April 4, 1966, it notified plaintiff of that decision and that it would not "comply with our obligations to you under" the written contract. By the same letter and with the professed purpose "to avoid any damage to you," defendant instead offered to employ plaintiff as the leading actress in another film tentatively entitled "Big Country, Big Man" (hereinafter, "Big Country"). The compensation offer was identical, as were 31 of the 34 numbered provisions or articles of the original contract. Unlike "Bloomer Girl," however, which was to have been a musical production, "Big Country" was a dramatic "Western-type" movie. "Bloomer Girl" was to have been filmed in California; "Big Country" was to be produced in Australia. Also, certain terms in the proferred contract varied from those of the original.[18]

---

[18] [2] Article 29 of the original contract specified that plaintiff approved the director already chosen for "Bloomer Girl" and that in case he failed to act as director plaintiff was to have approval rights of any substitute director. Article 31 provided that plaintiff was to have the right of approval of the "Bloomer Girl" dance director, and Article 32 gave her the right to approval of the screenplay.

Defendant's letter of April 4 to plaintiff, which contained both defendant's notice of breach of the "Bloomer Girl" contract and offer of the lead in "Big Country," eliminated or impaired each of those rights. It read in part as follows: "The terms and conditions of our offer of employment are identical to those set forth in the 'Bloomer Girl' Agreement, Articles 1 through 34 and Exhibit A to the Agreement, except as follows:

"1. Article 31 of said Agreement will not be included in any contract of employment regarding 'Big Country, Big Man' as it is not a musical and it thus will not need a dance director."

"2. In the 'Bloomer Girl' agreement, in Articles 29 and 32, you were given certain director and screenplay approvals and you had preapproved certain matters. Since there simply is insufficient time to negotiate with you regarding your choice of director and regarding the screenplay and since you already expressed an interest in performing the role in 'Big Country, Big Man,' we must exclude from our offer of employment in 'Big Country, Big Man' any approval rights as are contained in said Articles 29 and 32; however, we shall consult with you respecting the director to be selected to direct the photoplay and will further consult with you with respect to the screenplay and any revisions or changes therein, provided, however, that

Plaintiff was given one week within which to accept; she did not and the offer lapsed. Plaintiff then commenced this action seeking recovery of the agreed guaranteed compensation.

Defendant in its answer admits the existence and validity of the contract, that plaintiff complied with all the conditions, covenants, and promises and stood ready to complete the performance, and that defendant breached and "anticipatorily repudiated" the contract. It denies, however, that any money is due to plaintiff either under the contract or as a result of its breach, and pleads as an affirmative defense to both causes of action plaintiff's allegedly deliberate failure to mitigate damages, asserting that she unreasonably refused to accept its offer of the leading role in "Big Country."

Plaintiff moved for summary judgment under Code of Civil Procedure § 437c, the motion was granted, and summary judgment for $750,000 plus interest was entered in plaintiff's favor. This appeal by defendant followed.

The familiar rules are that the matter to be determined by the trial court on a motion for summary judgment is whether facts have been presented which give rise to a triable factual issue. The court may not pass upon the issue itself. Summary judgment is proper only if the affidavits or declarations in support of the moving party would be sufficient to sustain a judgment in his favor and his opponent does not by affidavit show facts sufficient to present a triable issue of fact. The affidavits of the moving party are strictly construed, and doubts as to the propriety of summary judgment should be resolved against granting the motion. Such does not become a substitute for the open trial method of determining facts.

The moving party cannot depend upon allegations in his own pleadings to cure deficient affidavits, nor can his adversary rely upon his own pleadings in lieu or in support of affidavits in opposition to a motion; however, a party can rely on his adversary's pleadings to establish facts not contained in his own affidavits. Also, the court may consider facts stipulated to by the parties and facts which are properly the subject of judicial notice.

As stated, defendant's sole defense to this action which resulted from its deliberate breach of contract is that in rejecting defendant's substitute offer of employment plaintiff unreasonably refused to mitigate damages.

The general rule is that the measure of recovery by a wrongfully discharged employee is the amount of salary agreed upon for the period of service, less the amount which the employer affirmatively proves the employee has earned or with reasonable effort might have earned from other employment. However, before projected earnings from the employment opportunities not sought or accepted by the discharged employee can be applied in mitigation, the employer must show that the other employment was comparable, or substantially similar, to that of which the employee has been deprived; the employee's rejection of or failure to seek other available employment of a different or inferior kind may not be resorted to in order to mitigate damages.

---

if we fail to agree . . . the decision of . . . [defendant] with respect to the selection of a director and to revisions and changes in the said screenplay shall be binding upon the parties to said agreement."

In the present case defendant has raised no issue of *reasonableness of efforts* by plaintiff to obtain other employment; the sole issue is whether plaintiff's refusal of defendant's substitute offer of "Big Country" may be used in mitigation. Nor, if the "Big Country" offer was of employment different or inferior when compared with the original "Bloomer Girl" employment, is there an issue as to whether or not plaintiff acted reasonably in refusing the substitute offer. Despite defendant's arguments to the contrary, no case cited or which our research has discovered holds or suggests that reasonableness is an element of a wrongfully discharged employee's option to reject, or fail to seek, different or inferior employment lest the possible earnings therefrom be charged against him in mitigation of damages.

Applying the foregoing rules to the record in the present case, with all intendments in favor of the party opposing the summary judgment motion — here, defendant — it is clear that the trial court correctly ruled that plaintiff's failure to accept defendant's tendered substitute employment could not be applied in mitigation of damages because the offer of the "Big Country" lead was of employment both different and inferior, and that no factual dispute was presented on that issue. The mere circumstance that "Bloomer Girl" was to be a musical review calling upon plaintiff's talents as a dancer as well as an actress, and was to be produced in the City of Los Angeles, whereas "Big Country" was a straight dramatic role in a "Western-type" story taking place in an opal mine in Australia, demonstrates the difference in kind between the two employments; the female lead as a dramatic actress in a Western-style motion picture can by no stretch of imagination be considered the equivalent of or substantially similar to the lead in a song-and-dance production.

Additionally, the substitute "Big Country" offer proposed to eliminate or impair the director and screenplay approvals accorded to plaintiff under the original "Bloomer Girl" contract (see fn. *ante*), and thus constituted an offer of inferior employment. No expertise or judicial notice is required in order to hold that the deprivation or infringement of an employee's rights held under an original employment contract converts the available "other employment" relied upon by the employer to mitigate damages, into inferior employment which the employee need not seek or accept. Statements found in affidavits submitted by defendant in opposition to plaintiff's summary judgment motion, to the effect that the "Big Country" offer was not of employment different from or inferior to that under the "Bloomer Girl" contract, merely repeat the allegations of defendant's answer to the complaint in this action, constitute only conclusionary assertions with respect to undisputed facts, and do not give rise to a triable factual issue so as to defeat the motion for summary judgment. . . .

The judgment is affirmed.

(Opinion by B̶u̶r̶k̶e̶,̶ ̶J̶.̶, with McCOMB, PETERS, and TOBRINER, JJ., and KRAUS and ROTH, JJ., concurring. Separate dissenting opinion by SULLIVAN, ACTING C.J.)

SULLIVAN, ACTING C.J.

The basic question in this case is whether or not plaintiff acted reasonably in rejecting defendant's offer of alternate employment. The answer depends upon whether that offer (starring in "Big Country, Big Man") was an offer of work that was substantially similar to her former employment (starring in "Bloomer Girl") or of work that was of a different or inferior kind. To my mind this is a factual issue which the trial court should not have determined on a motion for summary judgment. The majority have not only repeated this error but have compounded it by applying the rules governing mitigation of damages in the employer-employee context in a misleading fashion. Accordingly, I respectfully dissent.

The familiar rule requiring a plaintiff in a tort or contract action to mitigate damages embodies notions of fairness and socially responsible behavior which are fundamental to our jurisprudence. Most broadly stated, it precludes the recovery of damages which, through the exercise of due diligence, could have been avoided. Thus, in essence, it is a rule requiring reasonable conduct in commercial affairs. This general principle governs the obligations of an employee after his employer has wrongfully repudiated or terminated the employment contract. Rather than permitting the employee simply to remain idle during the balance of the contract period, the law requires him to make a reasonable effort to secure other employment.[19] He is not obliged, however to seek or accept any and all types of work which may be available. Only work which is in the same field and which is of the same quality need be accepted.[20]

The relevant language excuses acceptance only of employment which is of a *different kind*. It has never been the law that the mere existence of *differences between two jobs in the same field* is sufficient, as a matter of law, to excuse an employee wrongfully discharged from one from accepting the other in order to mitigate damages. Such an approach would effectively eliminate any obligation of an employee to attempt to minimize damage arising from a wrongful discharge. The only alternative job offer an employee would be required to accept would be an offer of his former job by his former employer.

Although the majority appear to hold that there was a difference "in kind" between the employment offered plaintiff in "Bloomer Girl" and that offered in "Big Country," an examination of the opinion makes crystal clear that the majority merely point out differences between the two *films* (an obvious circumstance) and then apodictically assert that these constitute a difference in the *kind* of *employment*. The entire rationale of the majority boils down to this: that the "*mere circumstances*" that "Bloomer Girl" was to be a musical revue while "Big Country"

---

[19] [1] The issue is generally discussed in terms of a duty on the part of the employee to minimize loss. The practice is long-established and there is little reason to change despite Judge Cardozo's observation of its subtle inaccuracy. "The servant is free to accept employment or reject it according to his uncensored pleasure. What is meant by the supposed duty is merely this, that if he unreasonably reject, he will not be heard to say that the loss of wages from then on shall be deemed the jural consequence of the earlier discharge. He has broken the chain of causation, and loss resulting to him thereafter is suffered through his own act." McClelland v. Climax Hosiery Mills, 252 N.Y. 347, 359, 169 N.E. 605, 609 (1930), concurring opinion.

[20] [2] This qualification of the rule seems to reflect the simple and humane attitude that it is too severe to demand of a person that he attempt to find and perform work for which he has no training or experience. Many of the older cases hold that one need not accept work in an inferior rank or position nor work which is more menial or arduous. This suggests that the rule may have had its origin in the bourgeois fear of resubmergence in lower economic classes.

was a straight drama "demonstrates the difference in kind" since a female lead in a Western is not "the equivalent of or substantially similar to" a lead in a musical. This is merely attempting to prove the proposition by repeating it. It shows that the vehicles for the display of the star's talents are different but it does not prove that her employment as a star in such vehicles is of necessity different *in kind* and either inferior or superior.

I believe that the approach taken by the majority (a superficial listing of differences with no attempt to assess their significance) may subvert a valuable legal doctrine.[21] The inquiry in cases such as this should not be whether differences between the two jobs exist (there will always be differences) but whether the differences which are present are substantial enough to constitute differences in the *kind* of employment or, alternatively, whether they render the substitute work employment of an *inferior kind*.

It seems to me that *this* inquiry involves, in the instant case at least, factual determinations which are improper on a motion for summary judgment. Resolving whether or not one job is substantially similar to another or whether, on the other hand, it is of a different or inferior kind, will often (as here) require a critical appraisal of the similarities and differences between them in light of the importance of these differences to the employee. This necessitates a weighing of the evidence, and it is precisely this undertaking which is forbidden on summary judgment.

This is not to say that summary judgment would never be available in an action by an employee in which the employer raises the defense of failure to mitigate damages. No case has come to my attention, however, in which summary judgment has been granted on the issue of whether an employee was obliged to accept available alternate employment. Nevertheless, there may well be cases in which the substitute employment is so manifestly of a dissimilar or inferior sort, the declarations of the plaintiff so complete and those of the defendant so conclusionary and inadequate that no factual issues exist for which a trial is required. This, however, is not such a case.

It is not intuitively obvious, to me at least, that the leading female role in a dramatic motion picture is a radically different endeavor from the leading female role in a musical comedy film. Nor is it plain to me that the rather qualified rights of director and screenplay approval contained in the first contract are highly significant matters either in the entertainment industry in general or to this plaintiff in particular. Certainly, none of the declarations introduced by plaintiff in support of her motion shed any light on these issues. Nor do they attempt to explain why she declined the offer of starring in "Big Country, Big Man." Nevertheless, the trial court granted the motion, declaring that these approval rights were "critical" and that their elimination altered "the essential nature of the employment."

---

[21] [5] The values of the doctrine of mitigation of damages in this context are that it minimizes the unnecessary personal and social (e.g., nonproductive use of labor, litigation) costs of contractual failure. If a wrongfully discharged employee can, through his own action and without suffering financial or psychological loss in the process, reduce the damages accruing from the breach of contract, the most sensible policy is to require him to do so. I fear the majority opinion will encourage precisely opposite conduct.

The plaintiff's declarations were of no assistance to the trial court in its effort to justify reaching this conclusion on summary judgment. Instead, it was forced to rely on judicial notice of the definitions of "motion picture," "screenplay," and "director" and then on judicial notice of practices in the film industry which were purportedly of "common knowledge."

Use of judicial notice was never intended to authorize resort to the dictionary to solve essentially factual questions which do not turn upon conventional linguistic usage.

The majority do not confront the trial court's misuse of judicial notice. They avoid this issue through the expedient of declaring that neither judicial notice nor expert opinion (such as that contained in the declarations in opposition to the motion)[22] is necessary to reach the trial court's conclusion. *Something*, however, clearly *is* needed to support this conclusion. Nevertheless, the majority make no effort to justify the judgment through an examination of the plaintiff's declarations. Ignoring the obvious insufficiency of these declarations, the majority announce that "the deprivation or infringement of an employee's rights held under an original employment contract" changes the alternate employment offered or available into employment of an inferior kind.

I cannot accept the proposition that an offer which eliminates *any* contract right, regardless of its significance, is, as a matter of law, an offer of employment of an inferior kind. Such an absolute rule seems no more sensible than the majority's earlier suggestion that the mere existence of differences between two jobs is sufficient to render them employment of different kinds. Application of such *per se* rules will severely undermine the principle of mitigation of damages in the employer-employee context.

I remain convinced that the relevant question in such cases is whether or not a particular contract provision is so significant that its omission creates employment

---

[22] [8] Fox filed two declarations in opposition to the motion; the first is that of Frank Ferguson, Fox's chief resident counsel. It alleges, in substance, that he has handled the negotiations surrounding the "Bloomer Girl" contract and its breach; that the offer to employ plaintiff in "Big Country" was made in good faith and that Fox would have produced the film if plaintiff had accepted; that by accepting the second offer plaintiff was not required to surrender any rights under the first (breached) contract nor would such acceptance have resulted in a modification of the first contract; that the compensation under the second contract was identical; that the terms and conditions of the employment were substantially the same and not inferior to the first; that the employment was in the same general line of work and comparable to that under the first contract; that plaintiff often makes pictures on location in various parts of the world; that article 2 of the original contract which provides that Fox is not required to use the artist's services is a standard provision in artists' contracts designed to negate any implied covenant that the film producer promises to play the artist in or produce the film; that it is not intended to be an advance waiver by the producer of the doctrine of mitigation of damages.

The second declaration is that of Richard Zanuck. It avers that he is Fox's vice president in charge of production; that he has final responsibility for casting decisions; that he is familiar with plaintiff's ability and previous artistic history; that the offer of employment for "Big Country" was in the same general line and comparable to that of "Bloomer Girl"; that plaintiff would not have suffered any detriment to her image or reputation by appearing in it; that elimination of director and script approval rights would not injure plaintiff; that plaintiff has appeared in dramatic and Western roles previously and has not limited herself to musicals; and that Fox would have complied with the terms of its offer if plaintiff had accepted it.

of an inferior kind. This question is, of course, intimately bound up in what I consider the ultimate issue: whether or not the employee acted reasonably. This will generally involve a factual inquiry to ascertain the importance of the particular contract term and a process of weighing the absence of that term against the countervailing advantages of the alternate employment. In the typical case, this will mean that summary judgment must be withheld.

In the instant case, there was nothing properly before the trial court by which the importance of the approval rights could be ascertained, much less evaluated. Thus, in order to grant the motion for summary judgment, the trial court misused judicial notice. In upholding the summary judgment, the majority here rely upon *per se* rules which distort the process of determining whether or not an employee is obliged to accept particular employment in mitigation of damages.

I believe that the judgment should be reversed so that the issue of whether or not the offer of the lead role in "Big Country, Big Man" was of employment comparable to that of the lead role in "Bloomer Girl" may be determined at trial.

Appellant's petition for a rehearing was denied October 28, 1970. Mosk, J., did not participate therein. Sullivan, J., was of the opinion that the petition should be granted.

NOTES AND QUESTIONS

1. **Case analysis:** *Parker v. Twentieth Century-Fox* is the first case you have read in this course. It is appropriate to introduce some techniques of case analysis at this point. You have read a majority and dissenting opinion of the Supreme Court of California. That court reviewed decisions in this case by the trial court and the District Court of Appeal.[23] California, as many states, has a system whereby appeals go to one of many intermediate appellate courts. Only cases presenting issues of general importance then go to the highest court in the state. There is no right to take civil cases to the Supreme Court; that court has discretion as to what civil cases to hear.

One District Court of Appeal does not have to follow the decisions of another. The supreme court of the state is not bound by decisions of an intermediate court. If decisions of two or more intermediate appellate courts conflict, the supreme court decides what the law should be. However, decisions of intermediate courts of appeal are *persuasive authority*. Absent good reason to the contrary, other courts of appeal and the highest court will follow them or interpret them so they are

---

[23] The intermediate appellate court's opinion is reported at 81 Cal. Rptr. 221 (1969). The District Court of Appeal, in a carefully written decision, sustained the trial court. In summarizing the issue, the District Court wrote:

> Plaintiff had been employed in Los Angeles, to appear in a musical, based on a stage play of established reputation, under the direction of a director in whom she had confidence, using a script she had approved. She was offered employment in a foreign country, to appear in a non-musical, under a director whom she did not know or trust, and using a script which (so far as defendant's affidavits show) she had read only once and as to which she had indicated, at the most, only a general approval and not a detailed one. Those differences were substantial within the meaning of the cases in the field.

consistent with the pattern of decisions adopted in the state.

Under common theories of precedent, courts are bound only by holdings in past cases. Most narrowly, a case only "holds" what was absolutely necessary to decide to reach its result. Anything beyond that necessary minimum is dicta and does not become precedent.

Can lawyers ignore mere dicta? Not necessarily. Suppose a Justice of the Supreme Court of California writes an opinion for the court in which she comments far beyond what was necessary to decide the case. The opinion is published this week, and you are scheduled to argue before the same judges next week. You would be foolish to dismiss anything in such an opinion as "mere dicta." Moreover, even if all lawyers would agree that a particular discussion was not needed to decide the precise case before an appellate court, the members of another court might read the passage and decide that it was a powerful argument for what the law ought to be. Whatever the formal precedential standing of a passage in a judicial opinion, lawyers are more comfortable when they are able to indicate that some judge, somewhere and sometime, bought an argument they are trying to make.

When the lawyers argued the *Parker* case before the trial and intermediate appellate courts, both sides devoted attention to *de la Falaise v. Gaumont-British Picture Corp.*[24] In that case, Constance Bennett de la Falaise, a famous actress in the 1930s, contracted with Gaumont-British Picture Corporation (GBP). She was to make two motion pictures, "Everything is Thunder" and "The Hawk." GBP was to pay her 10 percent of the United States gross distribution receipts or $35,000 per picture, whichever was more. Both pictures were to be made in London, England. She was to work no more than eight weeks on each. "Everything is Thunder" was filmed, and GBP paid her $35,000.

The contract called for production of "The Hawk" to begin between September 1, 1936, and November 14, 1936. Constance Bennett was to receive notice of the precise date no later than August 1, 1936. She did not receive timely notice of the starting date, and the picture was never made. The trial court found that GBP had breached the contract. This decision was affirmed by the District Court of Appeal.

Mitigation of damages was an issue on appeal. The appellate court reported that de la Falaise's agent

> . . . made diligent attempts to secure employment for her as a motion picture actress but . . . received no offers of employment and no compensation for her services in motion pictures between September 1, 1936, and January 1, 1937. However, she did receive the sum of $4,000 for two radio engagements on September 5 and 17, 1936, which took place in the evening at half past five and nine o'clock, respectively.

The court's opinion says nothing about the point, but if we assume that Constance Bennett de la Falaise performed in two American radio dramas, almost all such broadcasts at the time originated either in New York City or Los Angeles. She could not have been making a picture in London and simultaneously act in the radio dramas in New York or Los Angeles on September 5th and 17th. (Remember

---

[24] 39 Cal. App. 461, 103 P.2d 447 (1940).

Couldn't do radio shows if she had been making the movie ←

that passenger jet aircraft did not cross the Atlantic then.) The trial court awarded de la Falaise damages of $35,000, less the $4000 she earned for the two radio broadcasts.

The District Court of Appeal affirmed the trial court's decision that the $4000 was to be deducted from Constance Bennett de la Falaise's recovery. It quoted an earlier California decision as establishing that measure of damages for breach of an employment contract is the salary "less the amount which the servant has earned or with reasonable effort might have earned from other employment." The court said that the " 'other employment' which the discharged employee is bound to seek is employment of a character substantially similar to that of which he has been deprived; he need not enter upon service of a different or inferior kind." The appellate court then said that while radio engagements "might be denominated different in character from [the work] required of a moving picture actress, it cannot be said to be inferior thereto."

(a) Suppose you represented Twentieth Century-Fox in the *Parker* case. How would you argue that *de la Falaise v. Gaumont-British Picture Corp.* establishes California law in a way that would help your client's position?

(b) Suppose you represented Shirley MacLaine Parker. How would you distinguish the *de la Falaise* case?

2. *Summary judgment:* To understand many contracts cases, you have to understand something of procedure and evidence, too. Though you will explore these subjects at great length elsewhere in law school, we offer a simplified introduction.

There are several procedural devices designed to avoid unnecessary trials. Suppose I sue you but I have a very weak case. Even the simplest trial takes valuable judicial time. Lawmakers have fashioned rules to limit the burdens imposed by groundless litigation. In the older common law procedure, one device was called a "demurrer." In essence, a defendant who demurs says, "For purposes of this procedural argument only, I admit all the facts the plaintiff alleges. Even treating all these facts as true, I should win because they do not add up to a cause of action." Plaintiffs could also use demurrers against defendants' answers. Here, the motion would say, in substance, "Even if defendant proves all that he or she alleges, that is not a defense to my cause of action." Under modern procedure we no longer speak of demurrers but motions to dismiss for failure to state a cause of action or a defense. Nonetheless, you will often encounter the term *demurrer.*

While a complaint or answer may allege enough to escape being thrown out on a motion to dismiss for failure to state a cause of action or a defense, there may be no real legally relevant controversy between the parties. In such cases, lawyers use motions for "summary judgment." Suppose that Shirley MacLaine Parker's case were as follows: she signed a contract with the studio to star in "Bloomer Girl," a story that features the female lead. When Twentieth Century-Fox decided it did not want to make "Bloomer Girl," it offered her the part of, say, "Daisy" in "Big Country, Big Man." Daisy was on the screen less than two minutes out of a two-hour picture, and she was but a minor character among many. Furthermore, the actual contract tendered to the actress for "Big Country, Big Man" called for Fox to pay her only one-tenth of the salary it promised her for appearing in "Bloomer Girl." Finally, in the movie business when a star takes a minor role, except in unusual circumstances, it shows that he or she has lost popularity, and as a result, it is harder to get starring roles in the future.

Shirley MacLaine Parker's lawyer could move for summary judgment, and attach sworn affidavits from those who would testify to all of these facts, as well as copies of the written contracts, the scripts, and any other relevant documents. Twentieth Century-Fox would have to respond to this motion to avoid losing the case on summary judgment. If its affidavits did not deny the sworn statements supporting her motion, the judge would grant summary judgment and Parker would win.

On the other hand, suppose Fox offered an affidavit that Shirley MacLaine Parker had been offered the role of "Jane" in "Big Country, Big Man," and Jane was the featured part in the whole story. It offered another affidavit in which an official of the studio swore that she had been offered a contract calling for an increase in salary and had expressed interest in taking the part. A third affidavit indicated the studio was willing to shoot her scenes in California, and include a dance-hall scene in which she would be featured. In the face of such affidavits, the court would likely deny the motion for summary judgment since there would seem to be several real issues of fact between the parties. Summary judgment, then, forces parties to take a stand on what evidence they are going to offer. If the sworn affidavits show that there really is no argument about the facts, and if those facts establish the existence or absence of a cause of action or a defense, then a costly trial can be avoided.

In ruling on a motion for summary judgment, as well as making many other decisions, courts can take "judicial notice" of generally accepted facts. There is no question that they can take judicial notice that January 4, 2010, was a Monday, that in the usual system found in the United States there are 24 hours in a day and 60 minutes in an hour, that the sun sets in the west, that the Japanese bombed Pearl Harbor on December 7, 1941, and the like. Obviously, forcing people to prove such facts would be a waste of time.

However, judges are concerned about how far they should go in adding to what a party has proved or offered by way of affidavit on a preliminary motion. Suppose, for example, a party asked a court to take judicial notice that President Roosevelt knew that the Japanese were going to bomb Pearl Harbor but did not notify the military leaders in command there because he wanted to bring America into World War II in the face of a strong antiwar movement. One could cite several books making this assertion on the basis of historical records. One could cite a number of other books, as well as many book reviews, contesting this argument. Clearly, this is no place for judicial notice. Yet it is far easier to offer examples of extreme situations than to state a test that will decide most or all cases. How much is the majority of the Supreme Court of California filling in on the basis of generally accepted facts in *Parker v. Twentieth Century-Fox*? Is the majority taking judicial notice that the role in "Big Country, Big Man" is not comparable to the lead in "Bloomer Girl"? If so, is that more like the date on which Pearl Harbor was bombed or more like President Roosevelt's knowledge and motive concerning the Japanese attack?

Finally, judges bring their own experience with them to the bench. When they encounter a case from an area in which they specialized in practice, they are likely to make judgments based on their experience, adding to and interpreting the evidence. Even a judge who tried to avoid any bias produced by her experience would have difficulty putting such an interpretive framework aside. If the bias is too great — for example, where the judge is the defendant's parent — we expect the judge to decline to hear the case, but this solution only works in extreme situations. While we have no reason to think that this was the case, suppose Justice Burke, the author of the majority opinion in the *Parker* case, had been a specialist in entertainment law when he was a practicing lawyer. Would he have been justified in looking at the role and contract for "Big Country, Big Man," seeing that anyone in the industry would know it was inferior, and then writing the opinion he did?

3.   *MacLaine's goals and constraints:* One of our former students interviewed two of Shirley MacLaine Parker's agents and one of her lawyers in 1979, about nine years after the Supreme Court of California's opinion. All answered questions on the basis of what they remembered without checking files. One agent said that Ms. MacLaine had been willing to settle throughout the trial and the appeal. He pointed out that in the motion picture industry there were only five major employers, not counting independent studios, and it is in a performer's best interest to maintain good relations with all of the major producers of motion pictures. Another agent said that he had worked out a tentative settlement with the head of the Fox studio, but the corporate board rejected it because Fox's legal department wanted to go to court since they felt their case was so strong. MacLaine's lawyer did not think that Fox's lawyers were so anxious to go to court. He remembered MacLaine asking about $600,000 and Fox offering $400,000 to settle, but neither was willing to move closer to the other's figure. MacLaine had turned down a $1 million contract to make "Casino Royale" for Columbia Pictures because she was under contract to do "Bloomer Girl." The lawyer thought this affected MacLaine's advisors' judgment about what would be a fair settlement.

4.   *Objective versus subjective interests:* Suppose the case had gone to trial. Would evidence of the following facts have been relevant to the issue of the comparability of roles in the two movies? MacLaine was married to a film producer in Japan; she often traveled to various parts of the world to meet him, and to make films on location. MacLaine has long been active in liberal causes. She participated in the civil rights movement of the 1960s. She was a delegate for Robert Kennedy at the 1968 Democratic Party convention. She was active in the McGovern campaign four years later. She took stands against the war in Vietnam, and feminist issues interest her. "Bloomer Girl" was a popular musical produced in 1944 which had a theme likely to appeal to MacLaine. The story takes place in 1861. Dolly Bloomer advocates that women wear loose trousers fastened at the ankles instead of the fashionable hoop skirts, which symbolize the subjugation of women.[25] She also is an abolitionist who participates in the Underground Railroad, which helps slaves move to free states to escape their masters. Dolly's brother (the wicked capitalist) is a

---

[25] The story is loosely based on the career of Amelia Bloomer. She was an associate of Elizabeth Cady Stanton in 1848, and they championed equal rights and the vote for women. She founded *The Lily*, a temperance journal. Bloomer was noted for wearing a short black shirt and black satin trousers which were much more suited for an active life than long heavy hoop skirts.

wealthy hoop skirt manufacturer. Her niece, Evelina, rebels against her father, and she accepts her aunt's progressive ideas. However, Evelina falls in love with Jeff Calhoun, a Southerner who has come North to find his runaway slave, Pompey. Pompey is the slave who Aunt Dolly has been hiding. At the end of the story, Jeff has a change of heart. He frees Pompey and marries Evelina to provide the happy ending.[26]

Shirley MacLaine was to play Evelina. It was a good part in a well-crafted musical. Harold Arlen composed the music for "Bloomer Girl," and E.Y. (Yip) Harburg wrote the lyrics. Both were exceptionally talented; "Over the Rainbow" from "The Wizard of Oz" is just one of their many famous songs. The critics praised the score, lyrics, and choreography.

We know nothing about "Big Country, Big Man." Fox never produced it. Nevertheless, the title suggests it was a common Western. Men do things; women only talk or react. They try to keep men from getting killed by advocating cowardly retreat, or they admire male heroism. Sometimes they are just objects. They serve as fair princesses rescued by heroes. In the last act, they serve as the reward when the hero gets the girl.

Moreover, liberals would view the politics of many vintage Westerns as decidedly right-wing. The good man was self-reliant. Men with guns defended honor and property. Organized society was weak or corrupt. Moral questions had simple answers. These films accepted or justified violence as the solution to important problems. Heroes were white; villains were often Mexicans or Indians (they were not called Native Americans). Killing them was often treated as killing threatening wild animals. Of course, Westerns do not have to be written this way, but assume that "Big Country, Big Man" was the kind of film that would offend Shirley MacLaine's political beliefs.

You might ask why Fox decided not to produce "Bloomer Girl." Darryl F. Zanuck was one of the last of the great movie kings. He and his son, Richard, ran Twentieth Century-Fox. Richard's strategy was to make blockbuster films such as "The Sound of Music," "Patton," and "M*A*S*H." These pictures cost four to five times more than ordinary films, but the return could be much greater. In the mid-1960s, he was very successful. The 1966 gross income was the highest in the company's history. In 1967, seven blockbuster films were in production or planned. However, many Fox executives and bankers were worried about the risks involved in Richard Zanuck's strategy. They pressed for restraint. Fox notified Shirley MacLaine in April of 1966 that it would not film "Bloomer Girl." Fox pointed to script problems and high cost estimates.

Richard Zanuck resigned in January of 1971. The studio had produced too many costly failures such as "Tora! Tora! Tora!", "Dr. Dolittle," "Hello Dolly," and

---

[26] The play on which the musical was based was "the product of a [Communist] Party-endorsed workshop on women's rights. . . . The . . . [authors] worked on several drafts of the book and then were joined by two more experienced librettists, who made more room for song and dance by planning away the dialectic." John Gregory Dunne, *The Secret of Danny Santiago*, NEW YORK REVIEW OF BOOKS, August 16, 1984, at 17. The solution offered for racism and sexism by the musical is liberal rather than communist — attitude change rather than socialization of the means of production.

"Beyond the Valley of the Dolls." It lost $25 million in 1969 and $21 million in the first nine months of 1970, and its bankers demanded changes. Anything Fox had to pay to end its mistaken "Bloomer Girl" venture only added to these losses.

Does any of this affect your judgment about the proper result in our hypothetical case about the comparability of the female lead in "Big Country, Big Man" and in "Bloomer Girl"? Can courts make intelligent judgments about the comparability of two jobs in light of subjective preferences of employees? Is the difficulty of deciding such issues of comparability reason enough for courts to limit the question to the economic or financial aspects of a substitute job which an employer asserts the employee should have accepted? If you accept this argument, have you necessarily rejected the idea that the law of contract rests on freedom and choice?

5. _Interpretation of the_ Parker _case in later decisions:_ As of 2015, the Supreme Court of California had not reconsidered the problem raised by the *Parker* case. However, one way a case takes on meaning is by the way other courts interpret it over time. Of course, the supreme court of a state could always reject the accepted interpretation by other courts, but after time passes it is less likely to do this.

Parker v. Twentieth Century-Fox is a well-known case and has been cited and discussed by courts applying California law as well as other courts. We will briefly discuss three such decisions.

In *California School Employees Ass'n v. Personnel Comm'n*,[27] a school bus driver had been fired without cause. The driver did not take other jobs driving school buses. The jobs were in the same locale and the employee would not have had to move. There was only a few cents per hour difference in the pay and there was little variation in vacation and sick leave time among school districts. Unlike the school system that had terminated the employee without cause, the other school districts did not have a "merit system for classified employees." Probably, in the alternative school bus driving jobs, all employees within a particular classification received the same pay. In a merit system, supervisors could single out some employees and reward them for their better performance. Without discussing the issue, the District Court of Appeal said that lack of such a system was not enough to make the available jobs inferior, and the employee had failed to mitigate damages.

In *Boehm v. American Broadcasting Co.*,[28] a vice-president was wrongfully discharged and then later offered another position with ABC doing related work at the same salary. Plaintiff declined the new job, which would have required him to report to the person who had replaced him. Applying California law, the court affirmed a jury determination that the jobs were not "substantially similar." Plaintiff's objections to working under his replacement probably played an important role in the jury's decision.

In a non-California case, *Manuma v. Blue Hawaii Adventures*,[29] the plaintiff had

---

[27] 30 Cal. App. 3d 241, 106 Cal. Rptr. 283 (1st Dist. 1973).

[28] 929 F.2d 482 (9th Cir. 1991).

[29] 59 P.3d 958 (Table, unpublished decision 2002), text in 2002 Haw. App. LEXIS 369 (Dec. 6, 2002).

a one-year contract to be the "entertainment director/musician" on daily dinner cruises. Plaintiff was dismissed after eight months. The employer then offered him two positions, one involving manual labor at a shipyard and the other involving light maintenance on a yacht. Plaintiff declined both positions. The appellate court overturned the trial court's decision that plaintiff's refusal of the alternative positions was unreasonable, holding that the alternative positions were not substantially similar as a matter of law.

What do you conclude from these cases? Can we say that the law benefits upper-middle and middle-class employees more than working-class employees? Why do the courts seem to assume that one school bus driving job is like another, but that "Big Country, Big Man" is not like "Bloomer Girl" or that being an entertainment director is not the same as doing light maintenance on a yacht? Isn't the result that Shirley MacLaine could have devoted her time to peace and environmental activism during the time "Bloomer Girl" was to have been made, but that the school bus driver does not have the same luxury? Is this an unfair reading of these cases?

6. *Mitigation in sale of goods cases:* We explore the mitigation doctrine in the context of employment cases, where the doctrine presents some of its most difficult applications. However, reducing recovery by subtracting losses that the non-breaching party could reasonably have avoided (or "mitigated") is a general rule of contract damages. In the context of sale of goods cases, the rule is reflected in the "contract less resale" or "contract less market price" difference measures, which we explored in the hypothetical problems in section A.2. of this chapter, *supra*. As the next case illustrates, however, it is not always possible for a seller to mitigate losses from breach simply by reselling the goods.

NERI v. RETAIL MARINE CORP.
New York Court of Appeals
30 N.Y.2d 393, 334 N.Y.S.2d 165, 285 N.E.2d 311 (1972)[30]

Gibson, J.

The appeal concerns the right of a retail dealer to recover loss of profits and incidental damages upon the buyer's repudiation of a contract governed by the Uniform Commercial Code. This is, indeed, the correct measure of damage in an appropriate case and to this extent the code (§ 2-708, subsection [2]) effected a substantial change from prior law, whereby damages were ordinarily limited to "the difference between the contract price and the market or current price." Upon the record before us, the courts below erred in declining to give effect to the new statute and so the order appealed from must be reversed.

[Margin note, handwritten: Decline of new statute and ordered reverse]

The Hawaii Intermediate Appellate Court that decided this case designated its opinion as an unpublished disposition, meaning that the case is not to be cited as precedent even though there is a written opinion.

[30] [Eds. note: With experience, lawyers learn to know by reading the case citation which court rendered the decision. This opinion was rendered by the New York Court of Appeals. In most states this would suggest an intermediate appellate court. In New York, however, the Court of Appeals is the state's highest court, and the Supreme Court (in most states the highest court) is a lower court.]

The plaintiffs contracted to purchase from defendant a new boat of a specified model for the price of $12,587.40, against which they made a deposit of $40. They shortly increased the deposit to $4,250 in consideration of the defendant dealer's agreement to arrange with the manufacturer for immediate delivery on the basis of "a firm sale," instead of the delivery within approximately four to six weeks originally specified. Some six days after the date of the contract plaintiffs' lawyer sent to defendant a letter rescinding the sales contract for the reason that plaintiff Neri was about to undergo hospitalization and surgery, in consequence of which, according to the letter, it would be "impossible for Mr. Neri to make any payments." The boat had already been ordered from the manufacturer and was delivered to defendant at or before the time the attorney's letter was received. Defendant declined to refund plaintiffs' deposit and this action to recover it was commenced. Defendant counterclaimed, alleging plaintiffs' breach of the contract and defendant's resultant damage in the amount of $4,250, for which sum defendant demanded judgment. Upon motion, defendant had summary judgment on the issue of liability tendered by its counterclaim; and Special Term directed an assessment of damages, upon which it would be determined whether plaintiffs were entitled to the return of any portion of their down payment.

Upon the trial so directed, it was shown that the boat ordered and received by defendant in accordance with plaintiffs' contract of purchase was sold some four months later to another buyer for the same price as that negotiated with plaintiffs. From this proof the plaintiffs argue that defendant's loss on its contract was recouped, while defendant argues that but for plaintiffs' default, it would have sold two boats and have earned two profits instead of one. Defendant proved, without contradiction, that its profit on the sale under the contract in suit would have been $2,579 and that during the period the boat remained unsold incidental expenses aggregating $674 for storage, upkeep, finance charges, and insurance were incurred. Additionally, defendant proved and sought to recover attorney's fees of $1,250.

The trial court found "untenable" defendant's claim for loss of profit, inasmuch as the boat was later sold for the same price that plaintiffs had contracted to pay; found, too, that defendant had failed to prove any incidental damages . . . and . . . awarded . . . defendant $500 upon its counterclaim[31] and directed that plaintiffs recover the balance of their deposit, amounting to $3,750. The ensuing judgment was affirmed, without opinion, at the Appellate Division and defendant's appeal to this court was taken by our leave.

The issue is governed in the first instance by § 2-718 [(2) and (3)] of the Uniform Commercial Code which provides, among other things, that the buyer, despite his breach, may have restitution. . . . Section 2-718, however, establishes . . . [t]he buyer's right to restitution is subject to offset to the extent that the seller establishes a right to recover damages under the provisions of this Article. . . .

Among the provisions of this Article . . . are those to be found in § 2-708, which the courts below did not apply. Subsection (1) of that section provides that "the measure of damages for non-acceptance or repudiation by the buyer is the

---

[31] [Eds. note: See UCC § 2-718(2) regarding the origin of the $500 award.]

difference between the market price at the time and place for tender and the unpaid contract price together with any incidental damages provided in this Article (§ 2-710), but less expenses saved in consequence of the buyer's breach." However, this provision is made expressly subject to subsection (2), providing: "(2) If the measure of damages provided in subsection (1) is inadequate to put the seller in as good a position as performance would have done then the measure of damages is the profit (including reasonable overhead) which the seller would have made from full performance by the buyer, together with any incidental damages provided in this Article (§ 2-710), due allowance for costs reasonably incurred and due credit for payments or proceeds of resale."

Prior to the code, the New York cases "applied the 'profit' test, contract price less cost of manufacture, only in cases where the seller [was] a manufacturer or an agent for a manufacturer." *1955 Report of N.Y. Law Rev. Comm.*, vol. 1, p. 693. Its extension to retail sales was "designed to eliminate the unfair and economically wasteful results arising under the older law when fixed price articles were involved. This section permits the recovery of lost profits in all appropriate cases, which would include all standard priced goods." Official Comment 2, *McKinney's Cons. Laws of N.Y.*, Book 62 1/2, Part 1, p. 605, under Uniform Commercial Code, § 2-708. Additionally, and "[i]n all cases, the seller may recover incidental damages." *Id.*, Comment 3. The buyer's right to restitution was established at Special Term upon the motion for summary judgment, as was the seller's right to proper offsets; and, as the parties concede, the only question before us, following the assessment of damages at Special Term, is that as to the proper measure of damage to be applied. The conclusion is clear from the record — indeed with mathematical certainty — that "the measure of damages provided in subsection (1) is inadequate to put the seller in as good a position as performance would have done" (Uniform Commercial Code, § 2-708, subsection [2]) and hence — again under subsection (2) — that the seller is entitled to its "profit (including reasonable overhead) . . . together with any incidental damages . . . due allowance for costs reasonably incurred and due credit for payments or proceeds of resale."

It is evident, first, that this retail seller is entitled to its profit and, second, that the last sentence of subsection (2), as hereinbefore quoted, referring to "due credit for payments or proceeds of resale" is inapplicable to this retail sales contract.[32]

Closely parallel to the factual situation now before us is that hypothesized by Dean Hawkland as illustrative of the operation of the rules: "Thus, if a private party agrees to sell his automobile to a buyer for $2,000, a breach by the buyer would cause the seller no loss (except incidental damages, i.e., expense of a new sale) if the

---

[32] [2] The concluding clause, "due credit for payments or proceeds of resale," is intended to refer to "the privilege of the seller to realize junk value when it is manifestly useless to complete the operation of manufacture." *Supp. No. 1 to the 1952 Official Draft of Text and Comments of the Uniform Commercial Code, as Amended by the Action of the American Law Institute of the National Conference of Commissioners on Uniform Laws* [1954], p.14. The commentators who have considered the language have uniformly concluded that "the reference is to a resale as scrap under . . . § 2-704." *1956 Report of N.Y. Law Rev. Comm.*, p. 397; *1955 Report of N.Y. Law Rev. Comm.*, vol. 1, p. 761; *New York Annotations, McKinney's Cons. Laws of N.Y.*, Book 62 1/2, Part 1, p. 606, under Uniform Commercial Code, § 2-708; 1 William Willier and Frederick Hart, Bender's Uniform Commercial Code Service, § 2-708, pp. 1-180, 1-181. . . .

seller was able to sell the automobile to another buyer for $2,000. But the situation is different with dealers having an unlimited supply of standard-priced goods. Thus, if an automobile dealer agrees to sell a car to a buyer at the standard price of $2,000, a breach by the buyer injures the dealer, even though he is able to sell the automobile to another for $2,000. If the dealer has an inexhaustible supply of cars, the resale to replace the breaching buyer costs the dealer a sale, because, had the breaching buyer performed, the dealer would have made two sales instead of one. The buyer's breach, in such a case, depletes the dealer's sales to the extent of one, and the measure of damages should be the dealer's profit on one sale. Section 2-708 recognizes this, and it rejects the rule developed under the Uniform Sales Act by many courts that the profit cannot be recovered in this case." Dean Hawkland, Sales and Bulk Sales, 153–154 (1958 ed.); see also Comment, 31 Fordham L. Rev. 749, 755–756.

The record which in this case establishes defendant's entitlement to damages in the amount of its prospective profit, at the same time confirms defendant's cognate right to "any incidental damages provided in this Article (§ 2-710)" (Uniform Commercial Code, § 2-708, subsection [2]). From the language employed it is too clear to require discussion that the seller's right to recover loss of profits is not exclusive and that he may recoup his "incidental" expenses as well. *Procter & Gamble Distr. Co. v. Lawrence Amer. Field Warehousing Corp.*, 16 N.Y.2d 344, 354. . . .

[T]here was an explicit finding "that defendant completely failed to show that it suffered any incidental damages." We find no basis for the court's conclusion with respect to a deficiency of proof inasmuch as the proper items of the $674 expenses (being for storage, upkeep, finance charges, and insurance for the period between the date performance was due and the time of the resale) were proven without objection and were in no way controverted, impeached, or otherwise challenged, at the trial or on appeal. Thus the court's finding of a failure of proof cannot be supported upon the record and, therefore, and contrary to plaintiffs' contention, the affirmance at the Appellate Division was ineffective to save it.

The trial court correctly denied defendant's claim for recovery of attorney's fees incurred by it in this action. Attorney's fees incurred in an action such as this are not in the nature of the protective expenses contemplated by the statute (Uniform Commercial Code, § 1-106, subd. [1]; § 2-710; § 2-708, subsection [2]) and by our reference to "legal expense" in *Procter & Gamble Distr. Co. v. Lawrence Amer. Field Warehousing Corp.*, upon which defendant's reliance is in this respect misplaced.

It follows that plaintiffs are entitled to restitution of the sum of $4,250 paid by them on account of the contract price less an offset to defendant in the amount of $3,253 on account of its lost profit of $2,579 and its incidental damages of $674.

The order of the Appellate Division should be modified, with costs in all courts, in accordance with this opinion, and, as so modified, affirmed. . . .

NOTES AND QUESTIONS

1. *When would Section 2-708(2) apply as written?* Apply §§ 2-708(2) and 2-704(2) to the following problem:

> Seller contracts with Buyer to build a custom-made car for $22,000. When the car is about half completed, Buyer tells Seller that he will neither accept delivery of the car nor pay for it. This breaches their contract. At this point, Seller has spent $12,000 in labor and materials building the partially completed car. Seller estimates that it would cost $6000 to complete the car, and the current salvage value of the partially built car (together with unincorporated materials acquired specifically for this car) is $2000. It would be very difficult to sell the completed car to anyone other than Buyer because Buyer had many peculiar features designed into the car. Seller stops work on the car and sells it as salvage.

What remedies under the Uniform Commercial Code might the seller seek with a chance of success? Does § 2-708(2), as written, reach a result consistent with the expectation principle in this kind of case?

2. *Questions of technique:* Does the court's opinion in the *Neri* case suggest that we should ignore the last two phrases of § 2-708(2)? If so, is that consistent with the appropriate functions of courts and legislatures? Assume we accept some version of the idea that elected representatives make the law while judges play a more limited role. Didn't the Court of Appeals make new law to correct what it viewed as a legislative mistake in the *Neri* case? Hasn't it then usurped the New York Legislature's functions?[33]

Is there another way the court might have interpreted § 2-708(2) to reach the same result while keeping closer to traditional notions of a legislative role in creating law and a judicial role in interpreting and applying it? Look at UCC § 2-708(2) again. Suppose, for example, the Court of Appeals had said that there had been no "resale" in the *Neri* situation, and thus there was nothing to deduct. Alternatively, suppose the Court of Appeals had said that credit for the proceeds of resale were not "due" in this case. Could either of these statements be argued to be a proper application of § 2-708(2) to this case? How?

3. *History of Section 2-708(2):* The following account of the drafting history of UCC § 2-708(2) was prepared by Richard Danzig. Does his explanation help justify the Court of Appeals' interpretation of that section in *Neri v. Retail Marine*? Danzig reports:[34]

> The Chief Reporter for the Uniform Commercial Code as a whole, and the principal draftsman of Article 2 in particular, was Prof. Karl Llewellyn, then at Columbia Law School. . . .

---

[33] Of course, a state legislature can overturn a decision construing a statute by passing another statute. Is it enough that legislatures have this ultimate power? Does it protect the *Neri* court from criticism that it has usurped legislative authority?

[34] Unpublished manuscript, copyright © 1978 by Richard Danzig. Reprinted by permission.

In all critical respects, Llewellyn intended § 2-708 merely to continue the case law which had developed under § 64 of the Uniform Sales Act. When asked in open session by the President of the American Law Institute 'Anything new here?', Llewellyn replied in the negative. With a minor alteration, this section, he said, could be taken 'as standard law, sir.' 21 ALI Proceedings 209–210 (1944).

The 'standard law' under § 64 was confused in one critical respect, however. Section 64 had not dealt adequately with the problem of the lost volume seller. The key provision of § 64, its subsection (3), promulgated a difference money measure [contract price less resale price] as the general expectation standard and at the same time announced two exceptions to it:

> § 64(3): Where there is an available market for the goods in question, the measure of damages is, in the absence of special circumstances showing proximate damage of a greater amount, the difference between the contract price and the market price or current price at the time or times when the goods ought to have been accepted.

Later, in the authoritative treatise Williston published to explain the Sales Act, . . . Williston did not . . . explain the second exception, 'the special circumstances' proviso in § 64(3). It is not clear, in fact, that he thought it had any particular meaning. Williston had not written the phrase in his original draft of § 64(3). Perhaps later in the drafting process the phrase was copied out of the buyer's remedies section and inserted into the seller's remedies section simply to achieve symmetry between the two sections. . . .

A third exception to the difference money measure of § 64(3) was provided in § 64(4). Here a special rule dealt with the situation in which a seller had not finished the goods ordered by a breaching buyer. It implied that a seller might finish the goods and sell them on the open market, recovering the difference between the original contract price and the ultimate market price, but it explicitly said that in such a transaction 'the buyer shall be liable to the seller for no greater damages than the seller would have suffered if he did nothing towards carrying out the contract or the sale after receiving notice of the buyer's repudiation or countermand. The profit the seller would have made if the contract or the sale had been fully performed shall be considered in estimating such damages.'

In the years after the promulgation of the Uniform Sales Act and the publication of the first edition of Williston's treatise on the act, the courts found a use for the 'special circumstances' exception which Williston had apparently not anticipated. They conscripted it to deal with the lost volume seller. In the second (1924) edition of his [treatise], Williston spliced in a new section (§ 583a) to deal with this new development.

The 'special circumstances' proviso, Williston now explained, covered the situation in which a seller injured by a buyer's breach has the goods and may resell them at the market price, but 'by so doing he diminished his capacity to make other sales of his product unless the full possible output of his plant can be sold at that price.' Williston reported in such instances 'either because of the ease of applying a general rule or from fear that the seller may make an unfair profit courts enforce the general test of market value.' He suggested, however, that some other standard, perhaps the cost of manufacturing the goods . . . would be more appropriate. Not until McCormick's 1935 *Hornbook of Law of Damages* was the modern idea of the proper measure of damages in these cases articulated in a treatise and even there the articulation was imperfect. McCormick wrote:

> Not infrequent are cases of actions by dealers against customers for refusal to accept automobiles purchased. Neither the "resale price" nor the "market value" standard gives any adequate relief, since the dealer would ordinarily resell at the regular retail list price and since the "market value," if there can be said to be any, is the same as the contract price. The just solution, adopted in some recent cases, is to allow the dealer his profit; this is, the difference between the cost of the car to him, that is, the manufacturer's or wholesaler's delivered price, and the contract price. This may be rationalized either as resting on a "special circumstance" under [§ 64(3)] of the Sales Act or as a case where there is no "available," that is, immediate, "market" but only an eventual market costing time and effort to capture. C. McCormick, *Handbook on the Law of Damages* 661 (1935).

By the time of the UCC, the new draftspeople seemed determined to make everything neater. . . . They set out the difference money damages rule in § 2-708(1). Finally, they provided for a profit recovery by the lost volume seller in § 2-708(2).

The first draft of § 2-708 was perfectly clear. A seller injured by a buyer's breach recovered the difference between contract price and market price, 'except that if the foregoing measure of damages is inadequate' to put the seller in as good a position as performance would have done then the measure of damages is the profit the seller would have made from full performance by the buyer.' . . .

Section 2-708 remained clear until 1954. Then, after the Code had been favorably voted on in Pennsylvania and while it was being considered in New York, a new draft added the phrase 'with due allowance for costs reasonably incurred and due credit for resale.' Though the official comments and the debates cast no light on the change, it appears that the notion of 'due credit for resale' was introduced because some new reader undertook to compare § 2-708(2) with the section (§ 64) of the Uniform Sales Act it was supposedly replacing. A superficial comparison must have suggested that just as § 2-708(1) was intended to restate § 64(3), § 2-708(2) must have been intended to restate § 64(4). (Remember, the issue which § 2-708(2) dealt with was not at all apparent on the face of § 64.)

As a remedy for the unfinished goods problem, § 2-708(2) would indeed have been miscast, because it made no provision for crediting the breaching buyer with the benefit of a seller's resale of unfinished goods for scrap.

Therefore it must have seemed important to insert the unfortunate final clause, 'with due allowance for costs reasonably incurred and due credit for any resale.' A drafter's note explained:

> The main purpose of the change is to clarify the privilege of the seller to realize junk value when it is manifestly useless to complete the operation of manufacture.

Why wasn't this unfortunate change spotted and revoked? One can only guess, but a guess might be suggested by the fact that a blizzard of changes were proposed by the New York Law Revision Commission around this time and that also at this time the legislature of New York rejected the Code in a form without these changes. New York's rejection and the Commission's proposals precipitated a crisis resolved only through extended and intermittently fierce debates. In this circumstance, § 2-708(2), which had been approved by the N.Y. Law Revision Commission and which had so little pretension to doing anything beyond restating 'standard law,' probably received little attention. When the dust settled and New York accepted the Code, most state legislatures merely followed suit. The Code was too complex and faith in the arduous proceedings to date, too great, to warrant picking it apart again.

In sum, then, it appears that the misdrafting of § 2-708(2) was a consequence first of an oversight in § 64, then of a new and unfamiliar hand intruding at the last moment and simplistically comparing § 2-708(2) with § 64, and then from a combination of confusion, complexity, and complacency which led those who enacted the Code to overlook even so glaring a flaw as this one.

Here, as elsewhere, fully to understand the law it is necessary to understand the procedures, the purpose, and the failings of its drafters.

4. *Debate about* Neri: The position of the "lost volume" seller under the Uniform Commercial Code has been the subject of considerable academic controversy. Most commentators agree with the result reached by the New York Court of Appeals in *Neri v. Retail Marine. See, e.g.,* JAMES WHITE & ROBERT SUMMERS, UNIFORM COMMERCIAL CODE §§ 8–9 (West 6th ed. 2010). For a contrary view, see Charles Goetz and Robert Scott, *Measuring Sellers' Damages: The Lost-Profits Puzzle,*[35] and Morris Shanker, *The Case for a Literal Reading of UCC § 2-708(2).*[36] Among other things, Goetz, Scott, and Shanker argue that since there are so few true lost volume sellers in the world, it is not worth a court's time to listen to evidence attempting to establish that a particular seller is one.

Whether the *Neri* interpretation of § 2-708(2) was proper has not been a major issue before the courts. Typically, the decisions just cite *Neri* and turn to a more difficult problem: How does one establish that he or she is a "lost volume seller" when a buyer breaches? And which party carries the burden of proof on that issue? Those remain the questions about which there is controversy. The following case in

---

[35] 31 STAN. L. REV. 323 (1979).

[36] 24 CASE W. RES. L. REV. 697 (1974).

this casebook, *Jordan v. WorldCom*, deals with those issues.

5. *Briefs and record:* Professor Robert Gordon of Stanford Law School examined the record in the *Neri* case and his observations raise a number of questions about the decision. We can summarize them by asking whether *Neri v. Retail Marine* was a good example of a *Neri* case.

Tony Neri took the purchase price of the boat, a 1970, 31-foot Broadwater "Bay Breeze," out of his pension. However, the day after he signed the contract, he learned that he had to be hospitalized. The Bay Breeze was delivered to Retail Marine's showroom in early May 1970, a few days after Neri tried to back out of the contract. Retail Marine nonetheless installed all the accessories he had ordered. The Bay Breeze finally was sold in September to a Mr. Olsen, at the same price of $11,988 (plus 5 percent New York sales tax of $599.40) for a total of $12,587.40. Mr. Olsen did, however, receive a trade-in allowance of $2988 for his 1969 Super Craft.

It is apparent from pretrial documents that Retail Marine went into the case with a different legal theory than that which the New York Court of Appeals used to explain its decision. An affidavit of Mr. Meere, Retail Marine's vice president, contended:

> As a result of the discount that was given to the new purchasers [Olsen] by way of an inflated trade allowance, and taking into consideration the additional expenses which accrued, such as interest on the financing of the boat; the second commission to the salesman; and extra insurance, storage, and upkeep, the defendant sustained damages in excess of $2,000, which does not contemplate any attorney's fees, which the defendant is going to be required to pay to defend this action.

By the time the case got to trial, Mr. Miller, Retail Marine's counsel, looked at it differently. He did not ask about the trade-in allowance on the sale to Olsen. He argued that the sale to Olsen was irrelevant, and when he asked Mr. Meere to compute Marine's incidental damages, there was no mention of a second salesman's commission. He did bring out that Retail Marine was the largest Broadwater boat dealer in the United States. Miller computed incidental damages as follows: storage and upkeep for the boat, $200; finance charges before resale, $375; and insurance, $99.

Mr. Razis, Neri's attorney, asked Meere about the Olsen sale:

> Q. When did you sell this boat, September? Isn't it rather unusual that it took you from May, June, July, August, and September to sell a boat?
>
> A. No, sir. . . .
>
> Q. When is the best time to sell this boat?
>
> A. It is a very slow mover. There is no good time for it. [After Neri's repudiation] every sales person at our location was offered an additional commission to sell that boat.
>
> Q. Did you advertise it?

A. Yes, we did. In the *New York Times, Newsday.*

Meere also testified that the 1971 models of the Broadwater boats came out in June 1970.

Retail Marine's records of the Olsen sale, to which neither party referred at trial, tend to support the contention in Meere's affidavit that Marine took a lower profit on this sale of the boat originally ordered by Neri. Their "Dealer Advice Trade-In" form lists a "Trade overallowance" of $988.

The briefs on appeal are short and unilluminating on the lost volume seller issue. Neither brief attempted to interpret the clause in § 2-708 about "due credit for payments or proceeds of resale." The judges on the Court of Appeals and their law clerks must have done most of the research for its opinion, rather than ordering the lawyers for both sides to rebrief the case in light of the lost volume seller theory. In view of what we learn from the briefs and record on appeal, does it seem likely that Olsen would have purchased a different boat from Retail Marine if he had not bought the Bay Breeze originally ordered for Neri? If he would not have bought a different boat, what recovery would have been proper?

All in all, it appears that Retail Marine set out to offset Tony Neri's attempt to recover his down payment by seeking its actual losses ($988 on the "overallowance" on Mr. Olsen's trade-in, $250 on the second salesman's commission it had to pay when the Bay Breeze was sold to Olsen, and $674 in interest, storage, and insurance charges between the sales, or a total of $1912) incurred from having to sell a slow-moving boat three months after the next year's models were out, plus its attorney's fees. Mr. Miller, Retail Marine's counsel, was asked at trial to estimate what his fees would be. He guessed $1250, but of course this was before the case went through two appeals. Retail Marine was awarded $2579 in lost profits on the lost volume seller theory adopted by the Court of Appeals as well as $674 for incidental damages, or a total of $3253. Nonetheless, if you add the likely additional legal expenses in taking the appeals to the costs we know about ($1912 + $1250 = $3162), Retail Marine almost certainly ended with a net loss. However, it did keep Neri from recovering much of his down payment, and it did establish a rule of law helpful to automobile and boat dealers.

6. ***Down payments and cancellations:*** Tony Neri bought a boat, but then he discovered that he could not use it. He tried to back out before the boat was delivered. Why can't Neri cancel his order without legal liability?

We must distinguish the legal situation from everyday practice. Once consumer and retailer make a legally enforceable contract, neither can back out free of liability without the consent of the other absent a legally recognized excuse. As we know, many stores will let customers cancel orders or return goods and refund what the customers have paid. Does this practice suggest that the law should not hold consumers to contracts unless the seller has relied in some unusual way? Or should retailers have the option to release some customers who have cancelled while holding others (like Neri) to their contracts?

John Miller and William Ross, students of Professor Wallace Loh when he taught at the University of Washington Law School, surveyed 16 new car dealers in Seattle, Bellevue, and Renton. Most dealers were unaware that they might be able to sue buyers who canceled orders for lost profits. "All the dealers we talked to thought that the idea of recovering lost profits was, from a practical standpoint, 'ludicrous.' As one dealer put it: 'Realistically, how long could a dealer who sues customers for lost profits last in a competitive market? Once the word got out, such a reputation would drive customers away.'"

Almost all dealers required a customer to make a deposit before they would order a car with particular features for the customer. "The refundability of the 'deposit' varied among dealers. Ten of the dealers said they would refund the deposit if the buyer canceled the order. Four of the dealers said they would not refund the deposit; two dealers said they would not refund only on special factory-ordered cars or on slow-selling cars." Miller and Ross commented that they "got the sense . . . that if the customer is adamant in demanding a refund, and the customer has legitimate reasons for backing out, . . . these nonrefunding dealers will grudgingly refund [the money]."

Miller and Ross did not interview a representative sample of dealers in the Puget Sound area, and we cannot be sure that practices there match practices elsewhere. Nonetheless, their work should prompt us to ask who is likely to use the rights created by the *Neri* case and when. Is it possible that Retail Marine sued Tony Neri only because he had become ill and was unlikely to purchase another boat from Retail Marine in the future? If most sellers allow regular customers to cancel an "order" without consequence, is it fair to allow the seller to sue the occasional buyer for lost profits?

7. *Lawyer's fees for the winner:* The Court of Appeals follows the usual American rule when it refuses to allow the winning party to recover attorney's fees in a breach of contract action. The American rule stands in sharp contrast to the so-called "English rule," in which the loser must pay the winner's costs of litigation, including attorney's fees. In practice English winners recover not their actual fees, but "reasonable legal costs" as assessed by a court official. Similar "loser pays" rules are prevalent throughout much of the world. Such "fee-shifting" rules can have profound effects on the incentives to pursue, avoid, or settle litigation. To encourage claimants to come forward, many American statutes in such areas as consumer protection and civil rights authorize courts to award attorney's fees to successful plaintiffs. Such "one-way fee shifting" is regarded as an exception to the American tradition of each side bearing its own costs. Critics concerned with excessive litigation propose the general introduction of "loser pays" to inhibit "frivolous litigation." Opponents are concerned about the chilling effect on claims that are not cut-and-dried. What effect, if any, might a "loser pays" rule have had on Neri's decision to sue? On Retail Marine's strategy in defending?[37]

8. *Incidental damages:* UCC § 2-710 provides for recovery of incidental damages. The section speaks about "reasonable charges . . . incurred . . . *after the buyer's breach*" (emphasis added). Normally incidental damages are limited to recovery of *post-breach* expenditures by the non-breaching party. What incidental damages were allowed in this case? Was recovery of these amounts consistent with

---

[37] For an overview of these issues, see Herbert M. Kritzer, *The English Rule*, 78 A.B.A. J. 54 (Nov. 1992).

the expectation principle? Can you think of other post-breach expenditures by Retail Marine that it could have requested as incidental damages but did not?

9. *Questions of overhead:* When a retailer (like Retail Marine) sells a product (like a boat), they receive an amount of money (revenue), which can be seen as consisting of three parts. First, part of the revenue can be allocated to cover the direct costs associated with the sale — such as the wholesale cost of the product and any commission paid the salesperson. Second, in order for the business to be profitable in the long run, some portion of the revenue must be allocated to cover the indirect costs of selling this and other products — such as rent, utilities, interest on loans, and so forth. This is often called overhead. Overhead expenses are expenses associated with running the business that are not clearly related to any particular transaction. Finally, any amount left after recovering *all* costs, both direct and indirect, represents the *net profit* on the transaction.

It is, unfortunately, common for retailers and others to refer to the difference between revenue from the sale and wholesale cost as "profit." It is unfortunate because the use of the unmodified word *profit* creates the risk of confusing net and gross profit. Gross profit is the difference between revenue and direct costs. Or, to look at it another way, gross profit is the sum of net profit plus overhead. Net profit, on the other hand, is the difference between revenue and all costs, both direct and indirect.

The question for us is this: when a legal rule awards "profits," does it provide for an award of net or gross profit? Or, in other words, if a plaintiff is entitled to recover profits does this recovery include overhead? The UCC, in § 2-708(2), provides (at one level) an easy answer to the question since it provides that the seller is entitled to "the profit (including reasonable overhead) which the seller would have made."

In allowing gross profits to the lost volume seller, are we being consistent with the expectation principle? *Vitex Mfg. Corp. v. Caribtex Corp.* provides a rationale for the Code's approach.[38] Seller closed its plant, but then it negotiated a contract with buyer to process woolen material. Seller reopened its plant, ordered the necessary chemicals, and recalled its work force. Buyer then breached. The trial court found that seller's gross revenues would have been $31,250, its direct costs $10,136, and so its damages were $21,114. Buyer argued that the trial court had erred by not subtracting seller's overhead expenses from the contract price in determining lost profits. The Third Circuit upheld the trial court:[39]

> Although there is authority to the contrary, we feel that the better view is that normally, in a claim for lost profits, overhead should be treated as a part of gross profits and recoverable as damages, and should not be considered as a part of the seller's costs. A number of cases hold that since overhead expenses are not affected by the performance of the particular contract, there should be no need to deduct them in computing lost profits. . . .

---

[38] 377 F.2d 795 (3d Cir. 1967).

[39] *Id.* at 798–99.

[Buyer] may argue that this view ignores modern accounting principles, and that overhead is as much a cost of production as other expenses. It is true that successful businessmen must set their prices at sufficient levels to recoup all their expenses, including overhead, and to gain profits. Thus, the price the businessman should charge on each transaction could be thought of as that price necessary to yield a *pro rata* portion of the company's fixed overhead, the direct costs associated with production, and a "clear profit." Doubtless this type of calculation is used by businessmen and their accountants. . . . However, because it is useful for planning purposes to allocate a portion of overhead to each transaction, it does not follow that this allocated share of fixed overhead should be considered a cost factor in the computation of lost profits on individual transactions. . . .

. . . .

By the very nature of this allocation process, as the number of transactions over which overhead can be spread becomes smaller, each transaction must bear a greater portion or allocated share of the fixed overhead cost. Suppose a company has fixed overhead of $10,000 and engages in five similar transactions; then the receipts of each transaction would bear $2000 of overhead expense. If the company is now forced to spread this $10,000 over only four transactions, then the overhead expense per transaction will rise to $2500, significantly reducing the profitability of the four remaining transactions. Thus, where the contract is between businessmen familiar with commercial practices, as here, the breaching party should reasonably foresee that his breach will not only cause a loss of "clear" profit, but also a loss in that the profitability of other transactions will be reduced. . . . Therefore, this loss is within the contemplation of "losses caused and gains prevented," and overhead should be considered to be a compensable item of damage.

Interesting

How easy is it to calculate overhead so that it can be added to profits? Any accountant can tell you that adding up all overhead expenses and then allocating them *pro rata* to individual contracts can be a nightmare. Fortunately, there is an easier way to apply § 2-708(2). As stated above, gross profits are revenues (for a seller, usually the contract price) less direct costs. Direct costs are normally much easier to determine than overhead properly allocable to a particular contract. So another way to think of the formula in § 2-708(2) is to remember that normally "profits (including reasonable overhead)" — that is, gross profits — is the same as contract price less direct costs.

In the *Neri* case itself, there is no discussion of overhead, although § 2-708(2) specifically refers to it. There are many possible reasons for that, but one could be that the court used a "gross profit" idea when determining the profits it awarded to Retail Marine. The Court stated: "Defendant proved, without contradiction, that its profit on the sale under the contract in suit would have been $2,579." Perhaps that number was determined by subtracting defendant's cost of acquiring the boat from its manufacturer from the contract price. If so, the resulting figure would have been a gross profit figure, and to have added overhead to this figure would have allowed Retail Marine to recover more than the appropriate *pro rata* portion of overhead allocable to Neri's contract. If you understand all that has been said in this note, you will understand why.

IN RE WORLDCOM (JORDAN v. WORLDCOM)
United States Bankruptcy Court, Southern District of New York
361 B.R. 675 (2007)

*World com
=
Parent MCI*

GONZALEZ, J. BANKRUPTCY JUDGE.

[This breach of contract action, by Michael Jordan against WorldCom, was litigated in bankruptcy court. WorldCom was the parent company of MCI, a major telecommunications company in the late 20th century, specializing in offering long-distance services in the age before cell phones became ubiquitous. WorldCom filed for bankruptcy reorganization before it breached its contract with Jordan. Creditors of a debtor in bankruptcy may file with the bankruptcy court what is called a "proof of claim." Michael Jordan filed such a claim in the bankruptcy proceedings of WorldCom. Successful claimants share the available assets of the debtor. However, the debtor (or others in some cases) may dispute the validity of the claim, as WorldCom did in this case. In that event, the bankruptcy court holds a trial to adjudicate the claim's validity. The bankruptcy court normally applies whatever state law would have applied if the trial had taken place in the absence of bankruptcy. In this case, the Court determined that it should apply the law of the District of Columbia. But because the Court could find few, if any, relevant precedents in D.C., it looked extensively to the law of other jurisdictions for guidance on the law. (Of course, the precedents from other jurisdictions were not binding on the Court. They were what we call "persuasive" precedent.)

both Applied for Summary judgment — neither got it

Both Jordan and WorldCom filed motions for summary judgment. This opinion disposes of those motions. In editing the opinion, we have omitted most citations.]

BACKGROUND

*10 yr deal
$5mil sign bonus
2 mil annual after*

On or about July 10, 1995, Jordan and the Debtors entered into an endorsement agreement (the "Agreement"). At that time, Jordan was considered to be one of the most popular athletes in the world. The Agreement granted MCI a 10-year license to use Jordan's name, likeness, "other attributes," and personal services to advertise and promote MCI's telecommunications products and services, beginning in September 1995 and ending in August 2005. The Agreement did not prevent Jordan from endorsing most other products or services, although he could not endorse the same products or services that MCI produced. In addition to a $5 million signing bonus, the Agreement provided an annual base compensation of $2 million for Jordan. The Agreement provided that Jordan would be treated as an independent contractor and that MCI would not withhold any amount from Jordan's compensation for tax purposes. The Agreement provided that Jordan was to make himself available for four days, not to exceed four hours per day, during each contract year to produce television commercials and print advertising and for promotional appearances. The parties agreed that the advertising and promotional materials would be submitted to Jordan for his approval, which could not be unreasonably withheld, 14 days prior to their release to the general public. From 1995 to 2000, Jordan appeared in several television commercials and a large number of print ads for MCI.

On July 1, 2002, MCI commenced a case under [the Bankruptcy Code] in the Bankruptcy Court for the Southern District of New York. On July 18, 2003, the Debtors rejected the Agreement . . . Following that rejection of the Agreement, Jordan filed Claim No. 36077 (the "Claim") in the amount of $8 million — seeking $2 million for each of the payments that were due in June of 2002, 2003, 2004, and 2005. MCI does not object to the Claim to the extent Jordan seeks $4 million for the 2002 and 2003 payments under the Agreement. As of the rejection in July 2003, two years remained under the Agreement.

MCI asserts . . . [that] as a result of Jordan's failure to mitigate damages following the Debtors' rejection, the Claim should be reduced to $4 million. MCI argues that it is under no obligation to pay Jordan for contract years 2004 and 2005. . . .

DISCUSSION

A. *Summary Judgment Standard*

Under Federal Rule of Civil Procedure 56(c), summary judgment is only appropriate where the record shows that "there is no genuine issue as to any material fact and that the moving party is entitled to judgment as a matter of law." . . . A genuine issue of material fact exists where "there is sufficient evidence favoring the nonmoving party for a jury to return a verdict for that party." . . . In determining whether such an issue exists, "the court is required to resolve all ambiguities and draw all permissible factual inferences in favor of the party against whom summary judgment is sought." . . . The court's role is "not to weigh the evidence or make determinations of credibility but to 'determine whether there is a genuine issue for trial.' " . . . It is well established that a party opposing a motion for summary judgment "may not rest upon mere conclusory allegations or denials."

. . . .

C. *Mitigation*

The doctrine of avoidable consequences, which has also been referred to as the duty to mitigate damages, "bars recovery for losses suffered by a non-breaching party that could have been avoided by reasonable effort and without risk of substantial loss or injury." . . . The burden of proving that the damages could have been avoided or mitigated rests with the party that committed the breach. The efforts to avoid or mitigate the damages do not have to be successful, as long as they are reasonable.

Jordan argues that as a "lost volume seller" he was under no obligation to mitigate damages. Alternatively, Jordan argues that MCI failed to establish that Jordan could have entered a "substantially similar" endorsement contract and that Jordan acted reasonably in not entering another endorsement agreement after

MCI's breach. MCI counters that Jordan is not a lost volume seller and that MCI has shown that Jordan failed to take reasonable steps to mitigate damages.

1. Whether Jordan Was a "Lost Volume Seller"

Jordan argues that MCI's mitigation defense does not apply here because Jordan is akin to a "lost volume seller." Jordan points to testimony demonstrating that he could have entered into additional endorsement contracts even if MCI had not rejected the Agreement. Thus, he argues, any additional endorsement contracts would not have been substitutes for the Agreement and would not have mitigated the damages for which MCI is liable.

"A lost volume seller is one who has the capacity to perform the contract that was breached in addition to other potential contracts due to unlimited resources or production capacity. . . . A lost volume seller does not minimize its damages by entering into another contract because it would have had the benefit of both contracts even if the first were not breached. . . . The lost volume seller has two expectations, the profit from the breached contract and the profit from one or more other contracts that it could have performed at the same time as the breached contract." See *Snyder v. Herbert Greenbaum & Assocs.*, 38 Md. App. 144, 380 A.2d 618, 624–25 (1977) (under this theory, "the original sale and the second sale are independent events").

The lost volume seller theory is recognized in the Restatement (Second) of Contracts, §§ 347, 350 (1981).[40] The lost volume seller theory applies to contracts for services as well as goods. See Restatement (Second), § 347, ill.16 . . .[41]

This case offers a twist on the typical lost volume seller situation. In what the Court regards as the typical situation, the non-breaching seller has a near-inexhaustible supply of inventory . . . In the typical situation, when a buyer breaches an agreement to buy a good or service from the seller, the item is returned

---

[40] [8] Comment F to § 347 states in part:

Whether a subsequent transaction is a substitute for the broken contract sometimes raises difficult questions of fact. If the injured party could and would have entered into the subsequent contract, even if the contract had not been broken, and could have had the benefit of both, he can be said to have "lost volume" and the subsequent transaction is not a substitute for the broken contract. The injured party's damages are then based on the net profit that he has lost as a result of the broken contract.

Comment D to § 350 states in part:

The mere fact that an injured party can make arrangements for the disposition of the goods or services that he was to supply under the contract does not necessarily mean that by doing so he will avoid loss. If he would have entered into both transactions but for the breach, he has "lost volume" as a result of the breach. See Comment F to § 347. In that case the second transaction is not a "substitute" for the first one.

[41] [Eds. note: Illustration 16 reads as follows:

16. A contracts to pave B's parking lot for $10,000. B repudiates the contract and A subsequently makes a contract to pave a similar parking lot for $10,000. A's business could have been expanded to do both jobs. Unless it is proved that he would not have undertaken both, A's damages are based on the net profit he would have made on the contract with B, without regard to the subsequent transaction.]

to inventory and the lost volume seller continues in its efforts to sell its goods or services. However, the transactions that occur following the breach are not necessarily the result of the breach but fundamentally the result of the seller's continuing efforts to market its goods and services. It is this continuous effort, coupled with a virtually limitless supply, that warrants the lost volume exception to mitigation. As stated above, the transactions that may occur after the breach would, in the context of the lost volume seller, have occurred independent of the breach. Here, Jordan lacked a nearly limitless supply and had no intention of continuing to market his services as a product endorser.[42]

Although not addressed by a D.C. court, the majority of cases hold that Jordan bears the burden of proving that he is a lost volume seller. See generally *Snyder*, 380 A.2d at 624; *Ullman-Briggs, Inc. v. Salton, Inc.*, 754 F. Supp. 1003, 1008–09 (S.D.N.Y. 1991); *R.E. Davis Chemical Corp. v. Diasonics, Inc.*, 826 F.2d 678, 684 (7th Cir.1987) . . . To claim lost volume seller status, Jordan must establish that he would have had the benefit of both the original and subsequent contracts if MCI had not rejected the Agreement. . . .

In his arguments, Jordan focuses primarily on his capacity to enter subsequent agreements, arguing that . . . MCI's 16-hour annual time commitment hardly affected his ability to perform additional endorsement services. On this prong alone, Jordan likely would be considered a lost volume seller of endorsement services because he had sufficient time to do multiple endorsements. Although he does not have the "infinite capacity" that some cases discuss, a services provider does not need unlimited capacity but must have the requisite capacity and intent to perform under multiple contracts at the same time. See *Gianetti v. Norwalk Hospital*, 266 Conn. 544, 561–62; 833 A.2d 891 (2003) (plastic surgeon could be considered a lost volume seller if it were determined that he had the capacity and intent to simultaneously work out of three or four hospitals profitably).

Contrary to Jordan's analysis, courts do not focus solely on the seller's capacity. The seller claiming lost volume status must also demonstrate that it would have entered into subsequent transactions. . . . Jordan has not shown he could and would have entered into a subsequent agreement. Rather, the evidence shows that Jordan did not have the "subjective intent" to take on additional endorsements. The testimony from Jordan's representatives establishes that although Jordan's popularity enabled him to obtain additional product endorsements in 2003, Jordan desired to scale back his level of endorsements.

Jordan's financial and business advisor, Curtis Polk, testified that at the time the Agreement was rejected, Jordan's desire was "not to expand his spokesperson or pitchman efforts with new relationships . . . " Polk testified that had Jordan wanted to do additional endorsements after the 2003 rejection, he could have obtained additional deals. Jordan's agent, David Falk, testified that "there might

---

[42] [10] On one hand, the "lost volume seller" exception does not appear to be available to a product endorser because of the understandable concern over dilution through overexposure. However, if an endorser has not approached what would be his or her endorsement limit prior to dilution, it would seem that the continuous effort then to obtain more endorsements would be akin to the traditional lost volume seller, and the defense then available. As will be discussed herein, Jordan's situation is not indicative of a lost volume seller under any analysis.

have been 20 more companies that in theory might have wanted to sign him," but that Jordan and his representatives wanted to avoid diluting his image. Jordan's Memorandum for Summary Judgment stated that at the time the Agreement was rejected, Jordan had implemented a strategy of not accepting new endorsements because of a belief that new deals would jeopardize his ability to achieve his primary goal of National Basketball Association ("NBA") franchise ownership. . . .

Here, if Jordan had been seeking additional endorsement agreements independent of the Agreement's rejection, the Court could conclude that Jordan was a lost volume seller and irretrievably lost the money from the MCI Agreement. However, given Jordan's planned limitation on his endorsement activity based upon a desire to cultivate an image he perceived more compatible with that of an owner of an NBA team, rather than to continue to market his celebrity athlete image, the Court cannot make that conclusion.

One of the classic examples of the lost volume seller is found in [a hypothetical stated in] *Neri v. Retail Marine Corp* . . .

> [I]f a private party agrees to sell his automobile to a buyer for $2,000, a breach by the buyer would cause the seller no loss (except incidental damages, i.e., expense of a new sale) if the seller was able to sell the automobile to another buyer for $2,000. But the situation is different with dealers having an unlimited supply of standard-priced goods. Thus, if an automobile dealer agrees to sell a car to a buyer at the standard price of $2,000, a breach by the buyer injures the dealer, even though he is able to sell the automobile to another for $2,000. If the dealer has an inexhaustible supply of cars, the resale to replace the breaching buyer costs the dealer a sale, because, had the breaching buyer performed, the dealer would have made two sales instead of one. The buyer's breach, in such a case, depletes the dealer's sales to the extent of one, and the measure of damages should be the dealer's profit on one sale.

This example would surely have a different result if the car dealership was winding down its business and had agreed to sell one of its last cars to a buyer. If that buyer subsequently breached the contract and did not purchase the car, the dealership could hardly be expected to recover lost profits damages if the dealer put the car back onto a deserted car lot, made no attempts to sell it, and kept the dealership shuttered to new customers. Those modifications are analogous to Jordan's situation, with his stated desire to withdraw his services from the endorsement marketplace, and the lost volume seller theory accordingly does not apply to his circumstances. . . .

[I]f Jordan had entered into a subsequent agreement or agreements, and if he had showed both the capacity and the intent to make subsequent sales, that might have had the effect of helping him to establish his status as a lost volume seller, which generally would relieve him of the duty to mitigate. This would not be a novel situation, but it ignores the fact that he did not do so . . . . Because the evidence establishes, among other things, that Jordan would not have entered into subsequent agreements, Jordan has not established that he is a lost volume seller. This theory thus does not relieve Jordan from the duty to mitigate damages.

2. Whether Jordan Made Reasonable Efforts to Mitigate

Jordan argues at length that MCI must show that Jordan could have entered a "substantially similar" endorsement contract in order to mitigate damages. However, this is not the law of the mitigation of damages or the avoidable consequences theory. This language stems from federal employment cases concerning back pay and mitigation, which this case, while similar in many respects, is not. See, e.g., *Ford Motor Co. v. E.E.O.C.*, 458 U.S. 219, 231–32; 102 S. Ct. 3057, 3065–66 (1982) (the duty to mitigate damages, "rooted in an ancient principle of law, requires the claimant to use reasonable diligence in finding other suitable employment. Although the . . . claimant need not go into another line of work, accept a demotion, or take a demeaning position, he forfeits his right to back pay if he refuses a job substantially equivalent to the one he was denied.")[43]

Several of the justifications for the "substantially similar or equivalent" standard of employment law, aside from the general remedial policy of making the non-breaching party whole for losses caused by the breaching party, show why there is less concern here regarding a "substantially equivalent" opportunity: [because] Jordan was not an employee of MCI. For one, the standard exists in part to ensure the employee's future advancement by mandating that the employee's promotional opportunities and status should be virtually identical to the prior position. . . . Since Jordan was never an employee of MCI, this is not relevant. . . . The main case relied on by Jordan for this argument regarding a "substantially similar" opportunity is a case analyzed under employment law and one that presented a completely different factual and procedural background. See *Parker v. Twentieth Century-Fox Film Corp.*[44]

More accurately, MCI must show the absence of reasonable efforts by Jordan to avoid consequences or minimize his damages. Since reasonable efforts in the form of affirmative steps are required to mitigate damages, MCI carries its burden by showing that Jordan has not taken affirmative steps to mitigate damages. Jordan admits in his brief that at the time of the rejection of the Agreement, he "had already implemented a business strategy of not accepting new endorsements." Falk

---

[43] [Eds. note: The E.E.O.C. is the Equal Employment Opportunity Commission, a federal agency charged with the enforcement of Title VII of the Federal Civil Rights Act, which prohibits discrimination in employment on the basis of race, gender, and a number of other factors. When an employee is found to have been wrongfully discharged under Title VII, one remedy is to award him or her lost wages (back pay), but the statute imposes a mitigation principle. The duty to mitigate damages in this context is considered to be statutory in origin, but in substance the duty mirrors the duty to mitigate damages at common law that arises when an employment contract is breached.]

[44] [11] Even if the "substantially similar opportunity" element from employment cases was the standard here, Jordan's efforts would still be found wanting by the Court. For one, MCI has submitted evidence that similar opportunities apparently existed. MCI's expert stated that similar endorsement opportunities existed between 2003 and 2005 had Jordan chosen to pursue them, based on a measure of Jordan's popularity and familiarity with the public. . . . Polk testified that had Jordan wanted to do product endorsements during 2003 and after, he could have obtained such deals. . . . Second, under this standard, if MCI demonstrates that Jordan did not make reasonable efforts to obtain work, which the Court holds that it has, MCI does not have to demonstrate the availability of substantially similar employment. *See, e.g.,* Greenway v. Buffalo Hilton Hotel, 143 F.3d 47, 54 (2d Cir. 1998) (adopting rule from other circuits that an employer "is released from the duty to establish the availability of comparable employment if it can prove that the employee made no reasonable efforts to seek such employment").

testified that a replacement telecommunications company was not approached. . . . Polk testified that Jordan did not return to the endorsement marketplace to try and replace the revenue he was to be paid under the Agreement. . . . Polk explained that Jordan did not wish to expand his "pitchman efforts with new relationships" because of his primary goal of becoming the owner of an NBA team. . . .

Based on the foregoing, and drawing all permissible factual inferences in favor of Jordan, the Court determines that MCI has established that Jordan did not take affirmative steps to mitigate damages.

3. Whether Jordan's Beliefs That Another Endorsement Would Dilute His Impact as an Endorser or Harm His Reputation Were Reasonable Justifications for Not Mitigating Damages

Jordan cites the risk that entering another endorsement contract could dilute his impact as an endorser or damage his reputation or business interests.

a. Dilution

Jordan's dilution argument is not convincing. Jordan's agent Falk testified that although there were no "fixed numbers" for the amount of endorsements, Jordan and his representatives were wary about dilution and sensitive about "protecting the brand" of Jordan. Jordan does not set forth any facts showing that Jordan's image was at risk of dilution. MCI convincingly responds that adding an agreement to replace a lost one is merely maintaining the status quo, not a dilution of Jordan's impact by addition. MCI's expert stated that Jordan had previously had 16 endorsement agreements in place, which further weakens Jordan's dilution argument. . . . While the Court recognizes that Jordan's image is the true commodity here and its market value could be diluted from overexposure, MCI has shown that Jordan's image was not at risk of dilution by replacing the MCI endorsement agreement with another one. The only statements Jordan offers to support his argument that he behaved reasonably by not seeking another endorsement in 2003 because of a concern with diluting his image are conclusory in nature and contradicted by the available evidence. . . . There is no genuine issue of material fact that dilution did not excuse Jordan's duty to mitigate damages.

b. Risk to Reputation

[Eds. note: This part of the Court's opinion is omitted. The Court held that MCI had offered unrefuted expert evidence that "an additional endorsement agreement would not have harmed Jordan's reputation."]

. . . .

4. Whether Focusing on NBA Ownership Was a Reasonable Decision

Jordan cites his goal of owning an NBA team as a reasonable justification for his decision not to enter additional endorsement agreements.

In support, Jordan cites cases that hold if a non-breaching plaintiff chooses a reasonable course of action despite the existence of another course of action that, in hindsight, would have been better at lessening harm, the plaintiff's damages are not reduced. A closer examination of such cases reveals that they are not applicable to Jordan's situation. Cases that Jordan cites, such as *Novelty Textile Mills, Inc. v. C.T. Eastern, Inc.*, 743 F. Supp. 212 (S.D.N.Y. 1990) . . . share a common theme not present in the instant matter: the non-breaching party faced a choice between two reasonable courses of action right after the breach or tort that inflicted the damage, and made a choice to lessen the damage that appeared reasonable at the time. Jordan's choice to focus on NBA team ownership, in contrast, was not done to lessen the damage from MCI's rejection, but was done for other, unrelated business reasons.

J's decision had nothing to do w/ mitigating

In *Novelty Textile Mills*, the plaintiff hired the defendant to ship its fabric, but while the defendant had the fabric in its possession, a liquid contaminant damaged the goods. . . . The court held that, given the circumstances, the plaintiff's decision to salvage the damaged goods rather than attempting to clean them was reasonable. The court considered factors such as the resale cost, the low value of the goods, and that the goods were no longer fit for their intended use.

Those cases demonstrate that a court will not sharply second-guess the decisions made by a non-breaching party when it attempts to mitigate the damages caused by the breaching party. The cases differ from Jordan's situation because his decision to focus on NBA team ownership was independent of MCI's rejection and was not contemplated as one that would lessen the harm of that rejection. Such a decision was unrelated to the duty to mitigate damages resulting from a rejected agreement as a product endorser. In short, the argument that Jordan acted reasonably by focusing solely on his efforts to become an NBA team owner is a red herring. It may have been reasonable for Jordan to focus on becoming an NBA team owner in the scope of Jordan's overall future desires, but that does not mean it can support a determination that he was relieved of his obligation to mitigate damages in response to MCI's rejection of the Agreement.

Furthermore, Jordan did not have to pursue any endorsement, such as one that would be beneath a celebrity of Jordan's stature, e.g., endorsing a product likely to be distasteful to Jordan or his fans. Jordan had the duty to take reasonable efforts to mitigate, such as by seeking another endorsement for an established, reputable company for compensation near to what he received from MCI. MCI has established that there is no genuine issue as to whether Jordan made reasonable efforts to do so. The Court finds that as a matter of law Jordan has failed to mitigate damages.

Concl. 4 is yes reasonable dec but not for this case

D. *The Need for a Further Determination of Damages*

. . . .

In this case, there has been no determination and no evidence presented of what Jordan could have reasonably earned had he fulfilled his obligation to mitigate damages by entering the endorsement marketplace following MCI's rejection of the Agreement. It is not clear that Jordan could have found an endorsement agreement in 2003 that paid him $2 million a year for the contract years 2004 and 2005. It is also unlikely that Jordan would have been obligated to accept a large number of endorsements of smaller value to make up the $2 million, due to the dilution effect such a number would have, because such efforts would likely be unreasonable. However, the facts may reveal that one or more endorsements could have been found without "diluting" his image, partially or completely mitigating the damages. Although MCI's expert stated that he believed that Jordan could have easily earned $2 million from an additional endorsement in 2003 . . . that opinion was not presented with any objective evidence of the marketplace, such as what other celebrity endorsers of Jordan's stature earned that year and which companies were in the market for an endorser of Jordan's stature. Although the Court finds that as a matter of law Jordan has not mitigated damages, there must be an evidentiary hearing on how much his claim should be reduced to reflect what portion would have been mitigated had he used reasonable efforts to do so.

[handwritten: Basically MCI has to produce EVIDENCE regarding how Jordan could've "easily" made the 2 mil w/out dillusion. THEREFOR ruling for evidentary hearing]

NOTES AND QUESTIONS

1. **Who is Michael Jordan?** As most readers will know, Michael Jordan was a famous professional basketball player. Frequently described as "the greatest basketball player of all time," Jordan retired as a player in 2003. Wikipedia describes Jordan as "one of the most effectively marketed athletes of his generation . . . noted for his product endorsements." en.wikipedia.org/wiki/Michael_Jordan.

2. **The American Law Institute and the Restatement of Contracts:** The opinion cites several sections from the Restatement (Second) of Contracts. Students sometimes have difficulty understanding what the American Law Institute's Restatements are. It is tempting to take them as an accurate statement of "the law," but lawyers can never safely assume that this is the case. Restatements have been prepared for many areas of law, including contracts. They represent an effort by a committee of legal scholars, judges, and lawyers, acting under the auspices of the American Law Institute (ALI), to summarize and refine basic principles of common law as developed by courts. These principles are set forth in numbered sections followed by explanatory notes and illustrations. While at first glance, they may look like the Uniform Commercial Code in form, they differ in fundamental purpose. The UCC is a statute passed by legislators; its text is the law. The Restatements purport to be descriptions and refinements of court decisions. They are not law but suggestions of common law rules that courts have used in the past and could use in future cases. Only when courts accept the suggestion and follow a Restatement provision does it become a governing precedent for the court that adopted it.

The first Restatement of Contracts was published in 1932. It reflected a compromise of the views of the leading scholars of its day. It has been very successful in prompting citations to itself by judges. Notice, however, that we cannot be sure whether a judge cites a Restatement to indicate that it caused her decision, or whether it was only part of the process of rationalizing that decision. A revised Restatement (Second) of Contracts was begun in 1962 and finally appeared in 1981. It, too, represents a compromise of the views of leading scholars of the 1950s, '60s and '70s, filtered through the elaborate committee process of the American Law Institute.

One tension in the Restatement process involves the conflict between the prescriptive and the descriptive. The ALI's presentation of its efforts stresses describing the law as fashioned by the courts. Nonetheless, the drafters face conflicting lines of authority and must make choices. Rarely does one find a section of the Restatement that frankly acknowledges that different rules are followed in different jurisdictions, though that is often the case. And occasionally, the Restatement drafters explicitly innovate.

Another tension involves the ALI's image of apolitical neutrality when its work involves significant choices between competing norms. Left-wing radicals, right-wing religious fundamentalists, and personal-injury plaintiffs' lawyers are likely to be underrepresented on the American Law Institute committees. Perhaps this makes no difference. Nonetheless, students should always remember that *individuals* write and revise restatements. They must be influenced by what passes for common sense in their time. Students would waste their time challenging the good faith and intelligence of those involved, but should feel free to challenge the assumptions and value judgments implicit in these documents.

3.   *Summary judgment:* This opinion is a ruling on cross-motions for summary judgment. Summary judgment procedure is discussed in Note 2 following *Parker v. Twentieth Century-Fox*, *supra*. In summary judgment proceedings there is no testimony in court. Nonetheless, throughout this opinion there is reference to testimony by various people, particularly Curtis Polk and David Falk, both advisors/agents for Jordan. This testimony comes from affidavits or from depositions that were attached to the summary judgment motions. Extensive pretrial depositions of potential witnesses is commonplace in cases where the potential damages are as large as they were in this case.

4.   *Who is a lost volume seller?* This opinion addresses specifically what a seller must show to establish himself/herself/itself to be a "lost volume seller." The test the court applies is sometimes called the "objective/subjective" test. Placing the burden of proof on the seller, it requires that the seller demonstrate first a "capacity" to be a lost volume seller by showing that it was possible to undertake additional business. This is considered the "objective" part of the test. But the seller is also required to show that it would have tried and would have been able to obtain additional business even if the defendant had not breached. This "subjective" branch of the test is often met by showing that the seller was seeking additional business prior to the breach, and that there is no reason to suspect that the ultimate purchaser would not have closed a sale with the plaintiff in the absence of breach.[45]

Some courts appear to require the seller to meet only the objective part of the test by showing that it had the "capacity" to make an extra sale.[46] This was Jordan's

---

[45] An often-cited case applying the "objective/subjective" test is *Davis Chemical Corp. v. Diasonics*, 826 F.2d 678 (7th Cir. 1987) and 924 F.2d 709 (7th Cir. 1991) (applying Illinois law). The breached contract in that case was for the purchase of medical diagnostic equipment costing several hundred thousand dollars. After breach, the equipment intended for defendant was resold to another medical provider. Plaintiff successfully recovered lost profits rather than the contract less resale price difference, having met its burdens under the "objective/subjective" test.

[46] *E.g.*, Nederlandse Draadindustrie NBI B.V. v. Grand Pre-Stressed Corp., 466 F. Supp. 846 (E.D.N.Y. 1979).

position. The court in *Neri v. Retail Marine Corp.* found that Retail Marine was a lost volume seller and allowed lost profits as a measure of recovery. But the court did not specifically address what a seller must show to establish its eligibility for this more generous measure. Do you think that the court had an "objective/ subjective" test in mind in coming to this conclusion? If it had, would it have been appropriate for the court to have come to a final decision in the case? Or would it have been more appropriate for the court to have remanded the case to the trial court for further findings? If the latter, what additional trial court findings would you like? In answering these questions, consider the results of Professor Gordon's research into the record in *Neri v. Retail Marine*, which are discussed in Note 5 following that case.

5. *Should there be a different rule for used (or pre-owned) goods?* Retail Marine contracted to sell a new boat to Tony Neri. Should the result in the case have been different if the boat had been "pre-owned"? Consider an English case, *Lazenby Garages v. Wright*, involving the sale of a pre-owned car by a used car dealer. The plaintiff dealer had acquired the vehicle (a BMW 2002) in 1974, for £1,325, and five days later signed a contract to sell the vehicle to the defendant for £1,670, representing a gross profit of £345. The defendant reneged on the contract the very next day, and six weeks later the dealer resold the BMW 2002 to a different buyer for £1,770 (more than the original contract price). Claiming to be a lost volume seller, the dealer claimed lost profits of £345. In an opinion by Lord Denning, one of the most famous English judges of his day, the court held:[47]

> The cases show that if there are a number of new cars, all exactly the same kind, available for sale, and the dealers can prove that they sold one car less than they otherwise would have done, they would be entitled to damages amounting to their loss of profit on the one car. . . . But it is entirely different in the case of the secondhand car. Each secondhand car is different from the next, even though it is the same make. The sales manager of the plaintiffs admitted in evidence that some secondhand cars, of the same make, even of the same year, may sell better than others of the same year. Some may sell quickly, others may be sluggish. You simply cannot tell why. But they are all different.

> In the circumstances the cases about new cars do not apply. . . . Seeing that these plaintiffs resold this very car for £100 more than the sale to [the defendant], they clearly suffered no damage at all.

The opinion did not reference *Neri v. Retail Marine*, decided only four years previously, though in a different country. Do you think the two cases are consistent with each other in principle? Would the plaintiff in *Lazenby Garages* have also been denied damages in New York? And if the cases are inconsistent, which result do you favor as a matter of policy? Be prepared to defend your position.

6. *Burden of proof on mitigation issues:* On mitigation issues, the burden of proof is normally on the defendant. This means that the defendant must offer some credible evidence that the plaintiff could have mitigated damages before the plaintiff is required to offer evidence about anything other than breach and lost

---

[47] Lazenby Garages v. Wright, [1976] 1 W.L.R. 459 (Ct. App.).

wages. In *Parker v. Twentieth Century-Fox, supra,* there is no discussion of whether the plaintiff made reasonable efforts to mitigate her damages by looking for suitable employment opportunities. (The entire discussion was about whether the proposed movie "Big Country, Big Man" was a suitable mitigating opportunity.) Presumably this was because defendant did not offer any evidence suggesting that plaintiff had failed to make reasonable search efforts.

7. ***Reasonable search efforts, the burden of proof, and the "substantially similar" test:*** If an issue about reasonable search opportunities had arisen in the *Parker* case, the question arises whether the defendant would have carried the burden of showing *both* that the plaintiff had not made reasonable efforts *and* that such efforts would have uncovered mitigating opportunities that were "substantially similar." The judge in the *Jordan* case suggests in the opinion's footnote 11, *supra,* that if the defendant shows that the plaintiff did not make a reasonable search, it does not have to show what a reasonable search would have turned up. Many courts, however, have required the defendant to carry both burdens.

8. ***What did the court really hold about mitigation? And what happened on remand?*** The court held that WorldCom, by pointing to Jordan's admission that he had made no effort to mitigate his damages, had met its burden of showing that Jordan had not mitigated his damages. But then the court held that MCI must offer evidence about how much money Jordan could have earned if he had looked for and found other endorsement opportunities. How easy would it have been for MCI to offer such evidence? Must alternative endorsement opportunities be "substantially similar" under this holding? Note that on remand MCI would have had to provide evidence about what endorsement contracts Jordan could have obtained in 2004 and 2005, but any hearing would have taken place in 2007 or later.

In fact, no hearing ever took place on remand. The case was settled for $1,925,000 for Jordan's claims respecting 2004 and 2005, representing about 50 percent of the contract amount.

C. THE EXPECTATION INTEREST: PERFORMANCE RATHER THAN DAMAGES

COPYLEASE CORP. OF AMERICA v. MEMOREX CORP.
United States District Court, Southern District of New York
408 F. Supp. 758 (1976)

[Memorex manufactures supplies for photocopiers. Copylease, a distributor of these supplies, made a contract with Memorex for three types of toner, a chemical used in copiers. Copylease promised to buy specified minimum quantities of these products. Memorex, in return, granted Copylease a favorable price and an exclusive dealership[48] for Memorex toners in a specified geographical area in the Midwest.

---

48 [Eds. note: An exclusive dealership can be "exclusive" on the seller side, the buyer side, or both. This one was exclusive only on the seller side, meaning that Memorex agreed to refrain from selling toner to competitors of Copylease within the specified geographical area. Copylease, however, was free to purchase toners manufactured by other companies than Memorex.]

Soon after they signed a contract, Memorex's officials expressed dissatisfaction with various terms, which they considered unduly favorable to Copylease. Memorex was particularly concerned that Copylease was selling toners that competed with Memorex toners. Negotiations for modification of the contract followed. Though happy with the contract, Copylease was willing to consider changes if Memorex offered an attractive incentive. The negotiations, however, became quite heated, and officials of both firms exhibited great ill feeling. Memorex then notified Copylease that it was unilaterally altering the terms of their relationship. Memorex would no longer recognize Copylease as its exclusive dealer and it would no longer offer Copylease favorable prices. It would continue to sell Memorex toner to Copylease on the same terms offered to other dealers in Copylease's area. Copylease sued for breach of contract. It sought specific performance of the exclusive dealership as well as damages for losses suffered between the time Memorex took action and when a court entered an order.]

LASKER, J.

By Memorandum Opinion dated November 12, 1975, 403 F. Supp. 625, we determined that Memorex Corporation (Memorex) breached its contract with Copylease Corporation of America (Copylease) for the sale of toner and developer and directed the parties to submit proposed judgments with supporting documentation relating to the availability of injunctive relief, or, more precisely, specific performance. We have studied the submissions and conclude that further testimony is necessary to determine the propriety of such relief. Memorex takes the position that under California law Copylease is not entitled to specific performance of this contract. Copylease argues that the remedy is available — if not under California law, then under our general federal equitable powers.

It is not settled whether a federal court in a diversity case may grant equitable relief which is unavailable under the law of the state governing the substantive rights of the parties.

The view that state law controls is vigorously advocated by Professor James Moore as the only result consistent with the Erie Doctrine, 2 J. Moore, *Federal Practice*, Par. 2.09, at 451–56 (2nd ed. 1975), and Professors Charles A. Wright and Arthur R. Miller agree at least that where the remedy sought is "inextricably interwoven with the substantive right being sued upon," the federal court should be bound by state law. 11 C. Wright & A. Miller, *Federal Practice and Procedure*: Civil § 2943, at 389 (1973). On the strength of the foregoing authority we are inclined to agree with Memorex that the law of California controls the issuance of the equitable relief sought here by Copylease.

We also agree with Memorex that the provision in the contract granting Copylease an exclusive territory, on which Copylease places primary reliance in its request for specific performance, is not in itself an adequate basis under California law for an award of such relief. *Long Beach Drug Co. v. United Drug Co.*, 13 Cal. 2d 158, 88 P.2d 698, 89 P.2d 386 (1939). California law does not consider a remedy at law inadequate merely because difficulties may exist as to precise calculation of damages. *Hunt Foods, Inc. v. Phillips*, 248 F.2d 23, 33 (N.D. Cal. 1957) (applying California law); *Thayer Plymouth Center, Inc. v. Chrysler Motors Corp.*, 255 Cal.

App. 2d 300 (4th Dist. Ct. App. 1967) and cases cited there. *Long Beach Drug* and *Thayer Plymouth* also demonstrate the more fundamental refusal of California courts to order specific performance of contracts which are not capable of immediate enforcement, but which require a "continuing series of acts" and "cooperation between the parties for the successful performance of those acts." *Thayer Plymouth Center, Inc. v. Chrysler Motors Corp., supra*, 255 Cal. App. 2d at 303; *Long Beach Drug Co. v. United Drug Co., supra*, 13 Cal. 2d 158, 88 P.2d 698, 703–05, 89 P.2d 386. Absent some exception to this general rule, therefore, Copylease will be limited to recovery of damages for the contract breach.

An exception which may prove applicable to this case is found in California UCC § 2716(1). That statute provides that in an action for breach of contract a buyer may be entitled to specific performance "where the goods are unique or in other proper circumstances." Cal. UCC § 2716(1) (West 1964). In connection with its claim for interim damages for lost profits from the time of the breach, Copylease argues strongly that it could not reasonably have covered by obtaining an alternative source of toner because the other brands of toner are distinctly inferior to the Memorex product. If the evidence at the hearing supports this claim, it may well be that Copylease faces the same difficulty in finding a permanent alternative supplier. If so, the Official Comment to § 2716 suggests that a grant of specific performance may be in order:

> Specific performance is no longer limited to goods which are already specific or ascertained at the time of contracting. The test of uniqueness under this section must be made in terms of the total situation which characterizes the contract. Today, output and requirements contracts involving a particular or peculiarly available source or market present the typical commercial specific performance situation . . . However, uniqueness is not the sole basis of the remedy under this section, for the relief may also be granted "in other proper circumstances" and *inability to cover is strong evidence of "other proper circumstances."* Cal. UCC § 2716, Comment 2 (West, 1964). (emphasis added)

If Copylease has no adequate alternative source of toner, the Memorex product might be considered "unique" for purposes of § 2716, or the situation might present an example of "other proper circumstances" in which specific performance would be appropriate.

If such a showing is made it will be necessary to reconcile California's policy against ordering specific performance of contracts which provide for continuing acts or an ongoing relationship with § 2716 of the Code. Although we recognize that the statute does not require specific performance, the quoted portion of the Official Comment seems clearly to suggest that where a contract calls for continuing sale of unique or "noncoverable" goods, this provision should be considered an exception to the general proscription. Output and requirements contracts, explicitly cited as examples of situations in which specific performance may be appropriate, by their nature call for a series of continuing acts and an ongoing relationship. Thus, the drafters seem to have contemplated that at least in some circumstances specific performance will issue, contrary to the historical reluctance to grant such relief in these situations. If, at the hearing, Copylease makes a showing that it meets the requirements of § 2716, the sensible approach would be to measure, with the particulars of this contract in mind, the uniqueness or degree of difficulty in covering against the difficulties of enforcement which have caused courts to refrain from granting specific performance. It would be premature to speculate on the outcome of such analysis in this case.

NOTES AND QUESTIONS

1.   *Diversity of citizenship jurisdiction:* The United States is a federal system, and there are both federal and state courts. For the most part, problems involving contracts, torts, and property are matters of state law, while federal courts deal with statutes enacted by Congress. However, when the Thirteen Colonies became the United States, some worried that state courts might be unfair when one party was not a resident of the state where a trial was to be held. As a result, Congress gave federal courts jurisdiction over cases that parties otherwise would try in state courts where there was "diversity of citizenship." Large corporations today are often incorporated in states such as Delaware to take advantage of their favorable laws. Under a legal fiction, they are citizens of those states. Thus, diversity is very common when one of the parties is a corporation doing business nationally.

In a diversity case tried in a federal court, what law does the court apply? Federal courts apply their own rules of procedure. However, they are supposed to apply the substantive law that would be applied in the courts of the state in which they sit. Often state law is unclear, and a federal court must do its best to determine what a state court would have done had the case been tried before it.

In the *Copylease* case, the United States District Court first had to decide whether awarding an injunction or a decree of specific performance was a matter of substance or procedure. If it were but a matter of procedure, then a federal law would apply. However, the court decided that it had to follow state practice in this matter. But which state law should apply in a case being tried before a federal court sitting in New York between two "foreign" (to New York) corporations about a contract to be performed mostly in the Midwest? The written contract itself said that the law of California would apply, and the court decided to follow the choice of the parties since the "transaction bears a reasonable relation to" California.[49]

2.   *"Law" and "Equity":* Specific performance is one of a number of "equitable" remedies a court has at its disposal. An "equitable remedy" requires a person to do, or refrain from doing, something. For example, one can be told to perform a contract or told not to compete against her former employer. A "legal" remedy awards a judgment calling for payment of damages. Typically, a person bringing a lawsuit can request damages. Equitable remedies, on the other hand, are available

---

[49] Presumably Memorex manufactured or distributed its toner from California. See UCC § 1-301(a), a provision typically considered in courses on Conflict of Laws. While we will give this problem no further attention in this course, you should be aware that those who draft contracts often do specify the applicable law, and there is some limitation on their freedom to shop for a law favorable to their interests. *See* William J. Woodward Jr., *Constraining Opt-Outs: Shielding Local Law and Those It Protects from Adhesive Choice of Law Clauses*, 40 Loy. L.A. L. Rev. 9 (2006) (discussing the conflict between public ordering and private ordering involved in letting parties choose their own rules of law rather than those that would otherwise apply under the democratic process).

only in special situations at the discretion of the court.

When will courts award specific performance? (1) A court will almost always order a defaulting party to carry out a contract to convey land. (2) A court will also almost always order specific performance when a contract calls for a seller to deliver a "unique good," such as a painting by a famous artist. (3) On the other hand, an employer will almost never be able to compel an employee to carry out a contract. An employer may sometimes be able to convince a court to order the employee not to compete with the employer by performing the same services for another, or by opening a competing business.

Why do English and American courts award damages rather than order performance in ordinary situations? Part of the explanation is historical, but, as always, history is a better explanation of why something started than why it continued and was not changed. Law and equity arose as two separate branches of the English legal system long before there was a United States. Each system had its own sphere of authority, rules, and remedies. The English common law system developed first from *writs* issued directly by the King and later by the King's courts. A person who felt that he had been wronged would petition for relief. A writ could be issued ordering the alleged wrongdoer to appear before one of the King's judges and explain why the wrongdoer should not be required to give a remedy to the person injured. The court might issue a writ ordering an alleged wrongdoer to appear and show cause why a sheriff or other legal official should not carry out some action.

As this procedure became more common, the King's officials developed certain standard writs. They were used for particular types of actions. The system was frozen in the 13th century, and thereafter, for a long time, no new writs were developed, and courts did not allow parties to modify the standard language of the writs to fit their particular situations. If a wrong did not fit neatly into one of the writs, the victim had no remedy "at law." English law was narrow and technical; the King's judges could not be accused of usurping his powers.

Many people who thought they had been wronged were left without remedy by the common law courts. Those with access began to petition the King directly for the relief which the law courts would not give them. The King then referred these petitions to his Chancellor. The Chancellor could order the parties to appear before him, and if he found that a wrong had been done, he would fashion a remedy to meet the situation. A system of courts, called "chancery" or "equity" courts, grew up to handle these exceptional cases. This system functioned alongside the common law court system, but equity was wholly separate, with its own personnel, its own rules of procedure, and different substantive policies.

Equity courts claimed that their function was to see that justice was done where a legal remedy would be inadequate. At the outset their concern was for substantive justice rather than technical legal reasoning. However, equitable remedies were extraordinary and reserved for cases where some defect was perceived in what was available from the law courts. One had no right to demand equitable relief. It was given only by the grace of the King. The Chancellor exercised discretion in using the King's powers, on the King's behalf.

By the 17th century, the English legal system had institutionalized courts of equity. Written reports of decisions of the equity courts were published, and the equity judges came to rely on precedents and a formalized body of law rather than exercise discretion case by case. Equity and common law courts were rivals. Each sought to expand its jurisdiction at the expense of the other. Both systems changed by using legal fictions and tricky reasoning. They began to fall into a common pattern with a rough division of labor. Finally, the two systems were merged in England by the Common Law Procedure Act of 1854 and the Judicature Act of 1873. In the United States, merger of the courts of law and equity first came when New York adopted the Field Code of 1848. Today, all but a very few states have one court system. Judges have all the old powers of the courts of law as well as those of the courts of equity.

We can still find evidence of the old dual court system in modern American law even after merger.[50] For instance, a court will often not grant an equitable remedy unless it finds there is no adequate legal remedy, a common law rule referred to by the opinion in *Copylease*. A great amount of litigation has occurred about what makes a legal remedy "inadequate," and the cases are far from consistent.

A potentially important consideration in determining whether a remedy at law is inadequate is the different methods for enforcing law judgments and equitable decrees. A judgment for damages gives the successful plaintiff the right to ask a sheriff to seize the defendant's non-exempt property. The sheriff then sells it at a foreclosure sale, and pays the judgment out of the proceeds of the sale. If the defendant has little non-exempt property, then he is "judgment-proof." The victory before the court is worthless. However, one refusing to obey an equitable decree (ordering a person to do or not to do something) may be found in contempt and imprisoned, either as punishment or until she performs as ordered. In some situations a judge exercising equitable powers can carry out the order directly. For example, if defendant breaches a contract by failing to convey real property, the court's decree, in most states, can be recorded with the same effect as a conveyance. The court may "reform" a legal document because of fraud or mistake, and the court's decree can be recorded as a substitute for the original one. Of course, in most instances the threat is enough; most of those subject to equitable decrees comply and obey them.

3. *California law, specific performance, and the long-term relationship:* The federal court considering the *Copylease* case discussed California common law concerning specific performance of a contract. It referred to the customary rule that the legal remedy (i.e., monetary damages) must be inadequate, but it turned to a different California common law rule concerning the availability of specific performance. California courts had decided two important cases before the Uniform Commercial Code went into effect that showed a great reluctance to award specific performance of a continuing contract of any complexity.

---

[50] A very important remaining difference between law and equity is that one has a right to a jury trial in an action that, before merger, would have been brought in the law courts. One has no such right in what would have been an equitable action.

The first was *Long Beach Drug Co. v. United Drug Co.*[51] There, the parties entered a contract in 1909, appointing the plaintiff the exclusive sales agent in Long Beach, California, for Rexall drug products. The contract was to last as long as plaintiff performed according to its terms, and one of the most important was that it sell only at prices established by defendant for Rexall products. In 1909, Long Beach had a population of 18,000, and plaintiff's store was centrally located. By 1930, Long Beach had grown to a population of 142,000, and plaintiff's store was no longer centrally located. In the early 1930s, the chain store, a new form of retailing, became popular. In 1936, United Drug signed a contract with the Owl Drug Company, which ran stores throughout Los Angeles County, including four in Long Beach. In about 14 months, the four Owl stores in Long Beach sold about $10,600 worth of Rexall products, nearly four times the sales of plaintiff. At that point, United Drug stopped doing business with plaintiff.

Long Beach Drug Company sued for an injunction ordering United Drug to stop supplying other drug stores in Long Beach. The trial court granted the injunction. The Supreme Court of California reversed this order. "Equity will not decree specific performance of contracts which by their terms stipulate for a succession of acts whose performance cannot be consummated by one transaction, but will be continuous and require protracted supervision and direction." Justice Shenk explained that to "undertake to compel defendant to sell to plaintiff, and plaintiff to purchase from defendant and to uphold all products to the full list retail price set by defendant, over an indefinite term, would impose upon the court a duty well nigh impossible of performance." The court left plaintiff to seek whatever damages it could prove for what was clearly a breach of contract.

The *Long Beach Drug* case was followed in *Thayer Plymouth Center, Inc. v. Chrysler Motors Corp.*[52] Chrysler terminated a Plymouth dealer's franchise. The parties disputed whether Chrysler's action was justified. The trial court granted the dealer a preliminary injunction pending trial to keep the business alive until it could hear the case. The District Court of Appeal reversed. The decree "would impose upon the court the impossible task of supervising continuous performance by the parties." The dealer's difficulty in proving the amount of damages did not make the legal remedy inadequate.

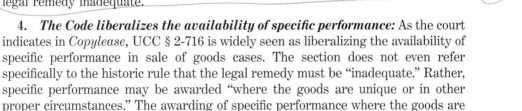

4. *The Code liberalizes the availability of specific performance:* As the court indicates in *Copylease*, UCC § 2-716 is widely seen as liberalizing the availability of specific performance in sale of goods cases. The section does not even refer specifically to the historic rule that the legal remedy must be "inadequate." Rather, specific performance may be awarded "where the goods are unique or in other proper circumstances." The awarding of specific performance where the goods are unique is consistent with a tradition limiting specific performance to situations in which damages are inadequate, but what does "in other proper circumstances" mean? Does it seem that the drafters of the Code deliberately set about to create some uncertainty about when to award specific performance? Were they trying to promote more use of this remedy?

---

[51] 13 Cal. 2d 158, 88 P.2d 698 (1939).

[52] 255 Cal. App. 2d 300, 63 Cal. Rptr. 148 (4th Dist. 1967).

In the context of the *Copylease* case, much of the ambiguity about the meaning of "in other proper circumstances" can be removed if a court is willing to rely on Official Comment 2, which is quoted extensively in the opinion. The context refers to outputs and requirements contracts as sometimes presenting "the typical commercial specific performance situation." Requirements contracts are contracts where the quantity term is determined by the buyer's orders or requirements, and they are commonplace. In the *Copylease* case, under the contract Memorex was required to meet Copylease's "requirements" of Memorex brand toner. Outputs contracts are contracts where the quantity is determined by the seller's production. They are less frequent, but nevertheless common, in the agricultural sector, where a farmer will often agree in advance to sell his production (*e.g.*, of milk) over a stated time period to a particular buyer. What characterizes both requirements and output contracts is that necessarily they require many different performances over the course of the contract. If the Official Comment is to be followed, necessarily it means abandonment of the common law's historic reluctance to award specific performance in that situation — see *Long Beach Drug Co.*, discussed in Note 3, *supra*.

The UCC may be influencing the common law, as applied to transactions not subject to Article 2. In a recent California case concerning a fact situation similar to the *Thayer Plymouth Center* case (discussed in Note 3, *supra*), the court enjoined the defendant (McDonald's Corp.) from non-renewing the plaintiff's franchises, which would have been a breach of contract. In a footnote, the court said about the earlier California cases discussed in Note 3:

> *Thayer Plymouth Center, Inc. v. Chrysler Motors Corp.* (citation omitted), relied upon by McDonald's, is . . . unpersuasive. . . . Thayer exemplifies the 'archaic doctrine' that contracts requiring court supervision must be denied specific performance, which has been superseded by modern case law recognizing that specific performance is available whenever it is practically feasible. . . . *Long Beach Drug Co. v. United Drug Corp.* (citation omitted), also cited by McDonald's, is rooted in the same archaic principle.[53]

5. Why liberalize the availability of specific performance? The Official Comments to § 2-716 do not offer any policy rationale for making specific performance more easily available. Perhaps the drafters' views were similar to the views of contemporary scholars who have advocated that courts order specific performance more often.[54] These writers point out that the reality of the American legal system in action is "bargaining in the shadow of the law." Judicial visions of courts supervising performance between angry and unwilling parties are unrealistic. A court's order for specific performance often changes only the bargaining position of the parties; it seldom forces an unwilling party to perform or to accept an unwanted

---

[53] Husain v. McDonald's Corp., 205 Cal. App. 4th 860, 871 n.5, 140 Cal. Rptr. 3d 370, 378 n.5 (Ct. App. 2012).

[54] *See, e.g.*, Anthony Kronman, *Specific Performance*, 45 U. Chi. L. Rev. 351 (1978); Alan Schwartz, *The Case for Specific Performance*, 89 Yale L.J. 271 (1979); Douglas Laycock, *The Death of the Irreparable Injury Rule*, 103 Harv. L. Rev. 687 (1990).

[handwritten margin note: Settle rather than actually forcefully perform]

performance. The parties will negotiate a settlement to solve the problem in light of the court's action.

For example, we learn from an earlier opinion in the *Copylease* case[55] that the dispute between the parties was caused by Memorex officials' dissatisfaction with the terms of the underlying contract. Officers and lawyers for both sides argued heatedly at a meeting. After several proposals for revising the contract were rejected by Copylease, Memorex unilaterally terminated Copylease's exclusive dealership, though it continued to offer to sell product — at regular rather than favorable prices — to Copylease as an "ordinary" dealer.

Copylease sought a preliminary injunction, requiring Memorex to honor Copylease's contract rights pending trial. Memorex made a cross-motion for summary judgment, challenging the validity of the contract. This prompted an early trial on the merits, which took only one day. Judge Lasker wrote an opinion finding the contract to be valid and Memorex to have breached. He wrote a second opinion (which you have read), suggesting that Copylease might be able to win a decree of specific performance after a further hearing.

What happened then? There was no hearing. A Copylease lawyer said that shortly after Judge Lasker issued his opinion, Memorex executives suggested negotiations. They blamed the lawyers on both sides for having caused the trouble. The executives on both sides handled the negotiations without the presence of the lawyers who had excited so much bad feeling at their earlier meeting and reached a settlement under which Memorex made a substantial monetary payment to Copylease, and they rewrote the contract more to Memorex's liking. The parties then continued to do business amicably under the revised contract until Copylease decided to go out of the toner business in 1978. Is it likely that a settlement on similar terms would have been reached if Judge Lasker had ruled that damages was Copylease's only remedy? *[handwritten: Prolly not]*

[handwritten margin note: Ended up settling up out of court. rewrote for M and M paid off Copylease]

The authors cited earlier in this note, and others, argue that bargained settlements typically follow orders for specific performance. The functions of the decree are, largely, to increase the cost that the one dissatisfied with a contract must pay to get out. This suggests that if Long Beach Drug Company had won their order for specific performance, the result would have been to increase the price it could charge to settle the case and give up its exclusive distributorship. But there are limits to how much the non-breaching party can demand to let the other party out of the contract, since the breaching party retains the option of just performing. When will the non-breaching party prefer a settlement to performance of a specific performance order?

As attractive as this argument for specific performance may seem, it is important to remember that there are real practical limits to the specific performance remedy. Most importantly, the buyer may prefer some kind of self-help remedy, like finding an alternative source of supply, precisely because it always takes time to get a specific performance order from a court. In such circumstances, the buyer will request damages, not specific performance, as a remedy. Later in these materials we will discuss other practical limitations on the specific performance remedy.

---

[55] 403 F. Supp. 625 (S.D.N.Y. 1975).

6. ***The buyer's damage remedies under the UCC:*** If specific performance were not allowed or not requested in the *Copylease* case, then the buyer's remedy would be in money damages. A general map of *buyers'* remedies, where the buyer has not accepted goods, appears in UCC § 2-711. This section is roughly the mirror image of the provisions on *sellers'* remedies in § 2-703. The law seeks to influence both aggrieved sellers and aggrieved buyers to find substitute contracts; this minimizes losses. Difference measures are used to compensate for having to sell at a loss or buy above the contract price. More particularly, a buyer may cover its needs (that is, buy them from someone else) and get the difference between the contract price and cover price under § 2-712. A buyer also may recover the difference between the market price and the contract price under § 2-713. Section 2-714 deals with the buyer's remedies where it has accepted goods but something is wrong with the seller's performance. Sections 2-712, 2-713, and 2-714, in turn, all say that a buyer can recover consequential damages in a proper case as defined by § 2-715(2). The term "consequential damages" is not defined in the UCC, but it would include Copylease's reduced profits on its resales because of Memorex's breaches.

7. ***A specific performance problem and the seller's suit for the price:*** Consider the following problems in light of §§ 2-709, 2-716, and 1-305. Assume for purposes of this exercise that the jurisdiction's courts have decided no cases relevant to the problems.

Seller, located in Metropolis, supplies meat to restaurants. It makes a contract with Resort 90 miles away to supply 100 prime-grade, aged sirloin steaks at a specified price to Resort each day for the entire tourist season. A truck takes about three hours for the round trip from Metropolis to Resort and back, plus time to load and unload. Seller buys meat for its entire business and does not identify specific steaks as those intended for the resort until they are wrapped the night before deliveries are to be made.

Other businesses able to supply this quantity and quality of meat are located in Metropolis and in City (four hours from Resort, but in a different direction and jurisdiction) but nowhere else nearer Resort. These other suppliers are unwilling to make the four-hour (or more) round trip to supply only one customer. Seller has been willing to do so because it has also supplied another restaurant not far from Resort.

(a) On June 1st, Seller's president announces that she will no longer perform the contract with Resort. Make an argument that a court should grant specific performance. Would, or should, it matter whether Seller repudiates in order to use its truck to deliver the meat to a new customer who has agreed to a higher price, or whether it merely wishes to withdraw from long-distance deliveries?

(b) Suppose Resort is the one that refuses to proceed with the contract. Can Seller's lawyer make a strong argument that a court should award it the contract price? Would, or should, it matter whether Resort repudiates because it has found a more attractive contract with a meat supplier in City, or has lost the chef whose specialty was making sauces that made these steaks so popular with Resort's customers? Assume that these factors don't excuse performance of the contract.

8. *The Convention on the International Sale of Goods and specific performance:* Generally, the Convention on the International Sale of Goods (CISG)[56] provides an even more liberal specific performance remedy for both buyers and sellers than does the UCC. This is consistent with the practice in much of the rest of the world, where specific performance is the preferred remedy. CISG Article 46(1) provides that "the buyer may require performance by the seller of his obligations unless the buyer has resorted to a remedy which is inconsistent with such requirements." CISG Article 62, a parallel provision for sellers, provides: "The seller may require the buyer to pay the price, take delivery, or perform his other obligations, unless the seller has resorted to a remedy which is inconsistent with this requirement." It is also important to note, however, that in order to "ease the position of those States whose courts [regard] specific performance as an exceptional rather than a usual remedy,"[57] CISG Article 28 *permits* (but does not require) a court to refuse specific performance if it would refuse specific performance for a contract governed under its own law. In *Magellan International Corporation v. Salzgitter Handel*, the court interpreted Article 28 to mean that in the United States, the availability of specific performance in sale of goods cases is governed by the UCC.[58]

D.   THE EXPECTATION INTEREST: BREACH DETERRENCE VERSUS LIQUIDATED DAMAGES

LAKE RIVER CORP. v. CARBORUNDUM CO.
United States Court of Appeals, Seventh Circuit
769 F.2d 1284 (1985)

Posner, J.

[Eds. note: We have omitted many citations in editing this opinion.] This diversity suit between Lake River Corporation and Carborundum Company requires us to consider questions of Illinois commercial law, and in particular to explore the fuzzy line between penalty clauses and liquidated-damages clauses.

Carborundum manufactures "Ferro Carbo," an abrasive powder used in making steel. To serve its midwestern customers better, Carborundum made a contract with Lake River by which the latter agreed to provide distribution services in its warehouse in Illinois. Lake River would receive Ferro Carbo in bulk from Carborundum, "bag" it, and ship the bagged product to Carborundum's customers. The Ferro Carbo would remain Carborundum's property until delivered to the customers.

Carborundum insisted that Lake River install a new bagging system to handle

---

[56] The CISG is discussed in Section A.1. of this chapter, *supra*.

[57] *Summary Records of Committee Meetings of the Vienna Conference*, quoted in Albert Kritzer, Guide to the Practical Applications of the United Nations Convention on Contracts for the International Sale of Goods 213 (Springer 1989).

[58] 76 F. Supp. 2d 919 (N.D. Ill. 1999).

the contract. In order to be sure of being able to recover the cost of the new system ($89,000) and make a profit of 20 percent of the contract price, Lake River insisted on the following minimum-quantity guarantee:

> In consideration of the special equipment [i.e., the new bagging system] to be acquired and furnished by LAKE-RIVER for handling the product, CARBORUNDUM shall, during the initial three-year term of this Agreement, ship to LAKE-RIVER for bagging a minimum quantity of [22,500 tons]. If, at the end of the three-year term, this minimum quantity shall not have been shipped, LAKE-RIVER shall invoice CARBORUNDUM at the then prevailing rates for the difference between the quantity bagged and the minimum guaranteed.

If Carborundum had shipped the full minimum quantity that it guaranteed, it would have owed Lake River roughly $533,000 under the contract.

After the contract was signed in 1979, the demand for domestic steel, and with it the demand for Ferro Carbo, plummeted, and Carborundum failed to ship the guaranteed amount. When the contract expired late in 1982, Carborundum had shipped only 12,000 of the 22,500 tons it had guaranteed. Lake River had bagged the 12,000 tons and had billed Carborundum for this bagging, and Carborundum had paid, but by virtue of the formula in the minimum-guarantee clause Carborundum still owed Lake River $241,000 — the contract price of $533,000 if the full amount of Ferro Carbo had been shipped, minus what Carborundum had paid for the bagging of the quantity it had shipped.

When Lake River demanded payment of this amount, Carborundum refused, on the ground that the formula imposed a penalty. At the time, Lake River had in its warehouse 500 tons of bagged Ferro Carbo, having a market value of $269,000, which it refused to release unless Carborundum paid the $241,000 due under the formula. Lake River did offer to sell the bagged product and place the proceeds in escrow until its dispute with Carborundum over the enforceability of the formula was resolved, but Carborundum rejected the offer and trucked in bagged Ferro Carbo from the East to serve its customers in Illinois, at an additional cost of $31,000.

Lake River brought this suit for $241,000, which it claims as liquidated damages. Carborundum counterclaimed for the value of the bagged Ferro Carbo when Lake River impounded it and the additional cost of serving the customers affected by the impounding. The theory of the counterclaim is that the impounding was a conversion, and not as Lake River contends the assertion of a lien.[59] The district judge, after a bench trial, gave judgment for both parties. Carborundum ended up

---

[59] [Eds. note: A "conversion" is the legal term for the civil wrong of taking possession without the right to do so. The crime of theft may involve the tort, or civil wrong, of conversion.

Not all conversions, of course, are crimes. Sometimes one has a privilege to take possession against the wishes of the owner. One such case arises when a creditor is granted a *lien* against the property; the holder of a lien has a right to demand that the property subject to the lien be sold and the proceeds used to pay the debt to the creditor. You may have heard of a "mechanic's lien"; statutes often grant garages, for example, a right to retain possession of a repaired car until the bill is paid. Lake River, in this case, was claiming it had a right analogous to a mechanic's lien.]

roughly $42,000 to the good: $269,000 + $31,000 − $241,000 − $17,000, the last figure representing prejudgment interest on Lake River's damages. (We have rounded off all dollar figures to the nearest thousand.) Both parties have appealed.

The only issue that is not one of damages is whether Lake River had a valid lien on the bagged Ferro Carbo that it refused to ship to Carborundum's customers — that, indeed, it holds in its warehouse to this day. Although Ferro Carbo does not deteriorate with age, the domestic steel industry remains in the doldrums and the product is worth less than it was in 1982 when Lake River first withheld it. If Lake River did not have a valid lien on the product, then it converted it, and must pay Carborundum the $269,000 that the Ferro Carbo was worth back then.

It might seem that if the minimum-guarantee clause was a penalty clause and hence unenforceable, the lien could not be valid, and therefore that we should discuss the penalty issue first. But this is not correct. If the contractual specification of damages is invalid, Lake River still is entitled to any actual damages caused by Carborundum's breach of contract in failing to deliver the minimum amount of Ferro Carbo called for by the contract. The issue is whether an entitlement to damages, large or small, entitles the victim of the breach to assert a lien on goods that are in its possession though they belong to the other party.

[The court rejected Lake River's claim that it was entitled to assert a lien on the Ferro Carbo in its possession, noting:

> When as a practical matter the legal remedy may be inadequate because it operates too slowly, self-help is allowed. But we can find no case recognizing a lien on facts like these, no ground for thinking that the Illinois Supreme Court would be the first court to recognize such a lien if this case were presented to it, and no reason to believe that the recognition of such a lien would be a good thing. It would impede the marketability of goods without responding to any urgent need of creditors.

The court then turned to the question of the validity of the liquidated damages clause.]

The hardest issue in the case is whether the formula in the minimum-guarantee clause imposes a penalty for breach of contract or is merely an effort to liquidate damages. Deep as the hostility to penalty clauses runs in the common law, see William Loyd, *Penalties and Forfeitures*, 29 HARV. L. REV. 117 (1915), we still might be inclined to question, if we thought ourselves free to do so, whether a modern court should refuse to enforce a penalty clause where the signator is a substantial corporation, well able to avoid improvident commitments. Penalty clauses provide an earnest of performance. The clause here enhanced Carborundum's credibility in promising to ship the minimum amount guaranteed by showing that it was willing to pay the full contract price even if it failed to ship anything. On the other side it can be pointed out that by raising the cost of a breach of contract to the contract breaker, a penalty clause increases the risk to his other creditors; increases (what is the same thing and more, because bankruptcy imposes "deadweight" social costs) the risk of bankruptcy; and could amplify the business cycle by increasing the number of bankruptcies in bad times, which is when contracts are most likely to be broken. But since little effort is made to prevent businessmen from assuming risks, these reasons are no better than makeweights.

A better argument is that a penalty clause may discourage efficient as well as inefficient breaches of contract. Suppose a breach would cost the promisee $12,000 in actual damages but would yield the promisor $20,000 in additional profits. Then there would be a net social gain from breach. After being fully compensated for his loss the promisee would be no worse off than if the contract had been performed, while the promisor would be better off by $8,000. But now suppose the contract contains a penalty clause under which the promisor if he breaks his promise must pay the promisee $25,000. The promisor will be discouraged from breaking the contract, since $25,000, the penalty, is greater than $20,000, the profits of the breach; and a transaction that would have increased value will be foregone.

On this view, since compensatory damages should be sufficient to deter inefficient breaches (that is, breaches that cost the victim more than the gain to the contract breaker), penal damages could have no effect other than to deter some efficient breaches. But this overlooks the earlier point that the willingness to agree to a penalty clause is a way of making the promisor and his promise credible and may therefore be essential to inducing some value-maximizing contracts to be made. It also overlooks the more important point that the parties (always assuming they are fully competent) will, in deciding whether to include a penalty clause in their contract, weigh the gains against the costs — costs that include the possibility of discouraging an efficient breach somewhere down the road — and will include the clause only if the benefits exceed those costs as well as all other costs.

On this view the refusal to enforce penalty clauses is (at best) paternalistic — and it seems odd that courts should display parental solicitude for large corporations. But however this may be, we must be on guard to avoid importing our own ideas of sound public policy into an area where our proper judicial role is more than usually deferential. The responsibility for making innovations in the common law of Illinois rests with the courts of Illinois, and not with the federal courts in Illinois. And like every other state, Illinois, untroubled by academic skepticism of the wisdom of refusing to enforce penalty clauses against sophisticated promisors, *see, e.g.*, Goetz & Scott, *Liquidated Damages, Penalties and the Just Compensation Principle*, 77 COLUM. L. REV. 554 (1977), continues steadfastly to insist on the distinction between penalties and liquidated damages. . . . To be valid under Illinois law a liquidation of damages must be a reasonable estimate at the time of contracting of the likely damages from breach, and the need for estimation at that time must be shown by reference to the likely difficulty of measuring the actual damages from a breach of contract after the breach occurs. If damages would be easy to determine then, or if the estimate greatly exceeds a reasonable upper estimate of what the damages are likely to be, it is a penalty. . . .

The distinction between a penalty and liquidated damages is not an easy one to draw in practice but we are required to draw it and can give only limited weight to the district court's determination. Whether a provision for damages is a penalty clause or a liquidated-damages clause is a question of law rather than fact, and unlike some courts of appeals we do not treat a determination by a federal district judge of an issue of state law as if it were a finding of fact, and reverse only if

Most imp rule

persuaded that clear error has occurred, though we give his determination respectful consideration. . . .

Mindful that Illinois courts resolve doubtful cases in favor of classification as a penalty, we conclude that the damage formula in this case is a penalty and not a liquidation of damages, because it is designed always to assure Lake River more than its actual damages. The formula — full contract price minus the amount already invoiced to Carborundum — is invariant to the gravity of the breach. When a contract specifies a single sum in damages for any and all breaches even though it is apparent that all are not of the same gravity, the specification is not a reasonable effort to estimate damages; and when in addition the fixed sum greatly exceeds the actual damages likely to be inflicted by a minor breach, its character as a penalty becomes unmistakable. . . . This case is within the gravitational field of these principles even though the minimum-guarantee clause does not fix a single sum as damages.

Suppose to begin with that the breach occurs the day after Lake River buys its new bagging system for $89,000 and before Carborundum ships any Ferro Carbo. Carborundum would owe Lake River $533,000. Since Lake River would have incurred at that point a total cost of only $89,000, its net gain from the breach would be $444,000. This is more than four times the profit of $107,000 (20 percent of the contract price of $533,000) that Lake River expected to make from the contract if it had been performed: a huge windfall.

Next suppose (as actually happened here) that breach occurs when 55 percent of the Ferro Carbo has been shipped. Lake River would already have received $293,000 from Carborundum. To see what its costs then would have been (as estimated at the time of contracting), first subtract Lake River's anticipated profit on the contract of $107,000 from the total contract price of $533,000. The difference — Lake River's total cost of performance — is $426,000. Of this, $89,000 is the cost of the new bagging system, a fixed cost. The rest ($426,000 − $89,000 = $337,000) presumably consists of variable costs that are roughly proportional to the amount of Ferro Carbo bagged; there is no indication of any other fixed costs. Assume, therefore, that if Lake River bagged 55 percent of the contractually agreed quantity, it incurred in doing so 55 percent of its variable costs, or $185,000. When this is added to the cost of the new bagging system, assumed for the moment to be worthless except in connection with the contract, the total cost of performance to Lake River is $274,000. Hence a breach that occurred after 55 percent of contractual performance was complete would be expected to yield Lake River a modest profit of $19,000 ($293,000 − $274,000). But now add the "liquidated damages" of $241,000 that Lake River claims, and the result is a total gain from the breach of $260,000, which is almost two and a half times the profit that Lake River expected to gain if there was no breach. And this ignores any use value or salvage value of the new bagging system, which is the property of Lake River — though admittedly it also ignores the time value of money; Lake River paid $89,000 for that system before receiving any revenue from the contract.

To complete the picture, assume that the breach had not occurred till performance was 90 percent complete. Then the "liquidated damages" clause would not be so one-sided, but it would be one-sided. Carborundum would have paid $480,000 for bagging. Against this, Lake River would have incurred its fixed cost of $89,000 plus 90 percent of its variable costs of $337,000, or $303,000. Its total costs would thus be $392,000, and its net profit $88,000. But on top of this it would be entitled to "liquidated damages" of $53,000, for a total profit of $141,000 — more than 30 percent more than its expected profit of $107,000 if there was no breach.

The reason for these results is that most of the costs to Lake River of performing the contract are saved if the contract is broken, and this savings is not reflected in the damage formula. As a result, at whatever point in the life of the contract a breach occurs, the damage formula gives Lake River more than its lost profits from the breach — dramatically more if the breach occurs at the beginning of the contract; tapering off at the end, it is true. Still, over the interval between the beginning of Lake River's performance and nearly the end, the clause could be expected to generate profits ranging from 400 percent of the expected contract profits to 130 percent of those profits. And this is on the assumption that the bagging system has no value apart from the contract. If it were worth only $20,000 to Lake River, the range would be 434 percent to 150 percent. . . .

Compare the liquidated-damages clause in this case with the penalty clause in *Arduini v. Board of Education*, 92 Ill. 2d 197, 441 N.E.2d 73 (1982), which is representative of such clauses upheld in Illinois. The plaintiff was a public school teacher whose contract provided that if he resigned before the end of the school year he would be docked 4 percent of his salary. This was a modest fraction of the contract price. And the cost to the school of an untimely resignation would be difficult to measure. Since that cost would be greater the more senior and experienced the teacher was, the fact that the liquidated damages would be greater the higher the teacher's salary did not make the clause arbitrary. Even the fact that the liquidated damages were the same whether the teacher resigned at the beginning, the middle, or the end of the school year was not arbitrary, for it was unclear how the amount of actual damages would vary with the time of resignation. Although one might think that the earlier the teacher resigned the greater the damage to the school would be, the school might find it easier to hire a replacement for the whole year or a great part of it than to bring in a replacement at the last minute to grade the exams left behind by the resigning teacher. Here, in contrast, it is apparent from the face of the contract that the damages provided for by the "liquidated damages" clause are grossly disproportionate to any probable loss and penalize some breaches much more heavily than others regardless of relative cost. . . .

The fact that the damage formula is invalid does not deprive Lake River of a remedy. The parties did not contract explicitly with reference to the measure of damages if the agreed-on damage formula was invalidated, but all this means is that the victim of the breach is entitled to his common law damages. . . . In this case that would be the unpaid contract price of $241,000 minus the costs that Lake River saved by not having to complete the contract (the variable costs on the other 45 percent of the Ferro Carbo that it never had to bag). The case must be remanded to the district judge to fix these damages.

Two damage issues remain. The first concerns Carborundum's expenses of delivering bagged Ferro Carbo to its customers to replace that impounded by Lake River . . .

[Eds. note: The rest of this opinion is not reproduced. The Court rejected Carborundum's claim for these damages. It also rejected Lake River's claim that Carborundum could have mitigated its losses from the conversion by accepting Lake River's offer to deliver the bagged product and place the proceeds in escrow.]

The judgment of the district court is affirmed in part and reversed in part, and the case is returned to that court to redetermine both parties' damages in accordance with the principles in this opinion. The parties may present additional evidence on remand, and shall bear their own costs in this court.

Affirmed in part, reversed in part, and remanded.

NOTES AND QUESTIONS

1. **The UCC and the Restatement of Contracts on penalties and liquidated damages:** Compare UCC § 2-718(1), with Restatement (Second) of Contracts § 356(1), which provides:

> Damages for breach by either party may be liquidated in the agreement but only at an amount that is reasonable in the light of the anticipated or actual loss caused by the breach and the difficulties of proof of loss. A term fixing unreasonably large liquidated damages is unenforceable on grounds of public policy as a penalty.

How, if at all, do these statements differ from the Illinois common law rule applied in the case? How, if at all, do they differ from each other? Are any differences likely to matter practically?

2. **Calculating expectation damages:** The court compares Lake River's recovery under the agreed remedy clause in the contract with expectation damages. In calculating projected expectation damages, the court assumes, without explanation, that Lake River could not mitigate any of its losses from Carborundum's breach. We speculate that the reason is that Lake River kept the bagging machine available to Carborundum for the entire three-year contract period, and that it was not practical to use the machine to bag other products while keeping it ready for any Ferro Carbo that Carborundum might ship.[60]

The formula the court suggests for calculating expectation damages is contract price less costs saved by the breach. This formula is basically the same as lost profits plus costs reasonably incurred plus overhead, for reasons discussed in Note 9 following *Neri v. Retail Marine, supra.* Do you see why?

3. **Stipulated damages and economic efficiency:** Judge Posner often casts his arguments in terms of advancing "economic efficiency." He raises questions in his opinion as to whether the law of stipulated damages is consistent with the operation of an efficient market. Students of welfare economics would recognize some of

---

[60] For further discussion of this and other issues, see Victor Goldberg, *Cleaning Up Lake River*, 3 VA. L. & BUS. REV. 427 (2008).

Posner's argument as pointing toward a *Pareto optimal* situation. Many writers tell us that the law should promote Pareto optimal transactions. When a particular activity makes at least some people better off while making no one worse off, the activity is in the general social interest. It enhances total social wealth. As a result, so-called efficient breaches of contract should be encouraged. This is the usual contemporary justification for refusing to enforce penalty clauses. They get in the way of efficient breach.

We can question this efficiency analysis in several ways. We might ask whether it takes account of the interests of all those potentially affected by a breach. What, for example, of the interests of persons other than the parties to the contract? What of the interests of employees? People who are not parties to the agreement itself may have relied on it, by taking jobs with the victim of the breach, for example. Furthermore, the analysis is most powerful when we assume that the victim's damages are easy to determine. When the amount of the damages is uncertain, we cannot be sure that a damages award will put the victim where it would have been had the contract been performed. There is a chance that the victim will be worse off after breach and a damages award, and in that situation a breach will not be Pareto optimal.

Moreover, since the 1970s some writers have argued that it is not necessary to hold some stipulated remedy clauses unenforceable to prompt efficient breaches. They contend that if a party would make an efficient breach if there were no stipulated remedy clause, then when faced with a stipulated remedy clause the party wanting to breach would approach the other party and seek to negotiate an agreed cancellation of the clause. The party seeking release from the stipulated remedy clause would offer to share the benefits of an efficient breach in return for the release. The stipulated remedy provision in the contract would serve only as a bargaining entitlement. Writers who suggest this hypothetical negotiation urge courts to enforce stipulated remedy clauses in most circumstances where such clauses are the product of free agreement. They argue that once the negotiations have concluded with a deal, the parties will behave in a "Pareto optimal" manner — that is, breaches that are "efficient" will happen. Furthermore, this position avoids the difficulties that courts have long faced in distinguishing valid liquidated damages provisions from unenforceable penalty clauses.[61]

This analysis can be illustrated using the facts of *Lake River*. Judge Posner reasons that Lake River would have made a profit of $260,000 if the stipulated remedy clause had been enforced, whereas it anticipated a profit of only $107,000 if there had been no breach. If Carborundum anticipated that the stipulated remedy clause would have been enforced, it would have made sense to offer Lake River, before any breach, a lump sum considerably less than the stipulated remedy clause to induce them to tear up the contract. Suppose, for example, Carborundum offered Lake River $100,000 to terminate the contract. On Judge Posner's analysis, Lake River would still have made an overall profit of $119,000, which is more than its

---

[61] *See* Kenneth Clarkson, Roger Miller, & Timothy Muris, *Liquidated Damages v. Penalties: Sense or Nonsense*, 1978 Wis. L. Rev. 351; Charles Goetz & Robert Scott, *Liquidated Damages, Penalties and the Just Compensation Principle: Some Notes on an Enforcement Model and a Theory of Efficient Breach*, 77 Colum. L. Rev. 554 (1977).

anticipated profit from complete performance of $107,000. Even if Lake River believed that Carborundum would continue with performance if its offer were declined, it would be in Lake River's self-interest to accept the $100,000 offer. Then the efficient breach would have occurred even if the law enforced all stipulated remedy clauses — even ones now considered penalties.

Do you agree? Consider the next note and question before you reach a final conclusion.

4. ***"A pound of flesh," popular culture, and the law:*** Shakespeare's *The Merchant of Venice*, first produced in 1600, is the source of a vivid and influential image that to this day colors our culture's responses to forfeitures and penalty clauses — the pound of flesh.[62] In the play, the law's reluctance to allow parties to deter breach by making the consequences for the breacher highly undesirable resonates with profound themes of hostility to outsiders. In *The Merchant of Venice* it is amplified by the long-established demonization of Jews,[63] but such hostility may be aroused by any outsider with whom one has economic relations but not shared communal fellowship. Does the play also suggest other reasons for the law's refusal to enforce what we call "penalty clauses" today?

Shakespeare's play begins with Bassanio in need of money so he might seek the hand of Portia, an heiress from Belmont. Bassanio is something of a spendthrift, constantly in debt. Most is owed to his friend Antonio, a merchant of Venice. Antonio, however, gives freely of his wealth and is willing to finance Bassanio, but there is a problem. All Antonio's money is tied up at present, his ships still at sea. Antonio sends Bassanio out into Venice to seek a loan using Antonio's credit rating for collateral. Bassanio goes to Shylock, a rich Jewish merchant of Venice, to seek three thousand ducats. Shylock agrees. Antonio, who has reviled Shylock, comes to close the deal. There being no love lost between the two merchants, an unusual contract is finally struck.

---

[62] Lawrence W. Levine notes that "like the Elizabethans, a substantial portion of nineteenth-century American audiences knew their Shakespeare well."

> Although nineteenth-century Americans stressed the importance of literacy . . . theirs remained an oral world in which the spoken word was central. In such a world Shakespeare had no difficulty finding a place. Nor was Shakespearean oratory confined to the professional stage; it often was a part of life. . . . In the 1850s Mark Twain worked as an apprentice to the pilot-master George Ealer on the steamboat Pennsylvania: "He would read Shakespeare to me; not just casually, but by the hour, when it was his watch, and I was steering. . . . He did not use the book, and did not need to; he knew his Shakespeare as well as Euclid ever knew his multiplication table." Shakespeare became elite culture only toward the end of the nineteenth century and the beginning of the twentieth.

Lawrence Levine, *William Shakespeare and the American People: A Study in Cultural Transformation*, 89 AM. HIST. REV. 34 (1984).

[63] In a comprehensive review of the Shylock legend, English critic John Gross observes that "behind the usurer enforcing his bond there looms that ultimate bogeyman, the Jew intent on shedding Christian blood for its own sake." JOHN GROSS, SHYLOCK: A LEGEND AND ITS LEGACY 29 (Touchstone Books 1994). In the Middle Ages, the Roman Catholic Church banned lending at interest and sanctioned the practice with excommunication. Jews were not subject to this method of enforcement, and Christians could get loans in Europe because Jews provided them. But Christians also vilified Jews as immoral moneylenders, and Shakespeare made use of this sort of resentment in his play. *See* James M. Ackerman, *A History of Usury*, 27 ARIZ. STATE. U. L. REV. 61 (1981).

> Shylock: *This kindness will I show.*
> *Go with me to a notary, seal me there*
> *Your single bond; and, in a merry sport,*
> *If you repay me not on such a day,*
> *In such a place, such sum or sums as are*
> *Express'd in the condition, let the forfeit*
> *Be nominated for an equal pound*
> *Of your fair flesh, to be cut off and taken*
> *In what part of your body pleaseth me.*

> Antonio: *Content, in faith; I'll seal to such a bond,*
> *And say there is much kindness in a Jew.*

Shortly thereafter Shylock's reason for demanding the penalty clause becomes evident. He is asked why he wants a pound of flesh: "what's that good for?" He rages:

> Shylock: *To bait fish withal: If it will feed nothing else,*
> *it will feed my revenge. He hath disgraced me, and*
> *hindered me half a million, laughed at my losses,*
> *mocked at my gains, scorned my nation, thwarted my*
> *bargains, cooled my friends, heated mine*
> *enemies; and what's his reason? I am a Jew. Hath*
> *not a Jew eyes? Hath not a Jew hands, organs,*
> *dimensions, senses, affections, passions? fed with*
> *the same food, hurt with the same weapons, subject*
> *to the same diseases, healed by the same means,*
> *warmed and cooled by the same winter and summer, as*
> *a Christian is? If you prick us, do we not bleed?*
> *if you tickle us, do we not laugh? if you poison*
> *us, do we not die? And if you wrong us, shall we not*
> *revenge? If we are like you in the rest, we will*
> *resemble you in that. If a Jew wrong a Christian,*
> *what is his humility? Revenge. If a Christian*
> *wrong a Jew, what should his sufferance be by*
> *Christian example? Why, revenge. The villainy you*
> *teach me I will execute, and it shall go hard but I*
> *will better the instruction.*

The inevitable occurs; Antonio's ships do not come in. Bassanio has better fortune as he has succeeded in courting the heiress. The trial nears, and Antonio and a friend discuss the legalities involved.

> Solanio: *I am sure the duke [the judge]*
> *Will never grant this forfeiture to hold.*

> Antonio: *The duke cannot deny the course of law:*
> *For the commodity that strangers have*
> *With us in Venice, if it be denied,*
> *Will much impeach the justice of the state;*
> *Since that the trade and profit of the city*

Consisteth of all nations. Therefore, go:
These griefs and losses have so bated me,
That I shall hardly spare a pound of flesh
To-morrow to my bloody creditor.

Antonio's friends offer Shylock more than three thousand ducats if he agrees to waive the bond. However, settlement attempts fail. The matter is now in the hands of the Court. The duke calls Shylock to open court. The duke seeks to persuade Shylock to have pity and not take his pound of flesh.

Shylock, undeterred, responds,

I have possess'd your Grace of what I purpose;
And by our Holy Sabbath have I sworn
To have the due and forfeit of my bond:
If you deny it, let the danger light
Upon your charter and your city's freedom.
You'll ask me, why I rather choose to have
A weight of carrion flesh than to receive
Three thousand ducats: I'll not answer that:
But say it is my humour: is it answer'd?
What if my house be troubled with a rat,
And I be pleas'd to give ten thousand ducats
To have it ban'd? What, are you answer'd yet?
Some men there are love not a gaping pig:
Some, that are mad if they behold a cat;
And others, when the bagpipe sings i' the nose,
Cannot contain their urine: for affection,
Master of passion, sways it to the mood
Of what it likes, or loathes. Now, for your answer:
As there is no firm reason to be render'd,
Why he cannot abide a gaping pig;
Why he a harmless necessary cat;
Why he, a woolen bagpipe; — but of force
Must yield to such inevitable shame
As to offend, himself being offended;
So can I give no reason, nor will I not,
More than a lodg'd hate and a certain loathing
I bear Antonio, that I follow thus
A losing suit against him. Are you answer'd?

Stay tuned. What happens next will be reported in Chapter 4 of these materials.

5. ***"Pay or play" clauses and "golden parachutes": penalties or something different?*** Professor Victor Goldberg argues that *Parker v. Twentieth Century-Fox* came to the right result for the wrong reason.[64] In that case, Shirley MacLaine's contract contained a "pay or play" clause: "We [the studio] shall not be obligated to utilize your services . . . [O]ur sole obligation, subject to the terms and conditions

---

[64] Victor Goldberg, *Bloomer Girl Revisited or How to Frame an Unmade Picture*, 1998 Wis. L. Rev. 1051.

of this Agreement, being to pay you the guaranteed compensation herein provided for." If Fox decided to replace her in the film or to abandon the project, they would be obligated to pay her the $750,000. Goldberg argues that this result would be appropriate even if Parker could have mitigated damages. In his view when there is a "pay or play" clause, there is no breach if the studio cancels the film; the studio's promise was to pay $750,000 or to make the film (in which case Parker would be compensated on a somewhat different and potentially more lucrative formula).[65] They are alternative ways of performing. In effect, Parker's suit is not for damages for breach, but for specific performance (i.e., payment of the $750,000). He continues: "There is no reason for wooden application of the rule barring penalty clauses. Shirley MacLaine is no Shylock. The studios are not being put upon by her or other artists; they include pay-or-play clauses in their contracts (and these are, after all, the studio's contracts) for good reason. The pay-or-play clause is a nuanced balancing of the studio's need for flexibility against the artist's reliance."[66]

Professor Goldberg's "pay-or-play" interpretation of the *Parker* case is but an example of a broader doctrine which creates an important exception to the penalty rule. Contracts are sometimes interpreted as calling for "alternative performances," one of which is the payment of money, rather than a single performance together with stipulated damages for breach. If the contract is interpreted as providing for the former, then a suit for the agreed amount is not subject to the penalty rule, and the prevailing freedom of contract principle prevails. If the contract is interpreted as providing for a single performance together with stipulated damages for breach, then the stipulated amount will be reviewed by the court for its reasonableness and will be labeled a penalty if excessive. There is no clear rule for when a court will consider an agreement to be providing for alternative performances rather than a single performance together with damages for breach.[67]

One important group of contracts that are often interpreted as providing for alternative performances are "golden parachutes." A "golden parachute," sometimes called a termination agreement, is an agreement between a corporate employer and a management-level employee providing for severance pay upon dismissal of the employee not for cause,[68] with the severance pay not limited by the employee's ability to mitigate damages by finding other employment. The severance pay can be quite generous; severance pay equal to twice the employee's annual pay is common for top corporate executives. Where the golden parachute is regarded as providing for alternative performances, then the severance pay will not be subjected to the kind of analysis about reasonableness that the court applied to the stipulated

---

[65] If the "Bloomer Girl" film had been made, Parker was to receive 10 percent of the gross or the $750,000 guaranteed payment, whichever was greater. *Id.* at 1055.

[66] *Id.* at 1085. In a footnote, Goldberg comments: "Part of the problem, I suspect, is the notion held by many contracts professors that $750,000 (in 1965 dollars) is too much to pay Shirley MacLaine for 'doing nothing.' . . . Of course, . . . [performers holding rights under a pay-or-play contract] are not doing nothing — [as one judge said], 'they also serve who only sit and wait.' " *Id.* at 1085, n.106.

[67] *See* 11 CORBIN ON CONTRACTS §§ 58.17, 58.18.

[68] Often the term *golden parachute* is limited to agreements providing for such severance payments when there is a change in corporate control, such as a merger of one corporation with another. In other circumstances the severance payment would be called a *termination agreement*.

damages clause in *Lake River*.[69] Particularly where the employee quickly finds alternative employment, the employee will receive far more as salary plus severance payment than she would have received as wages if there had been no termination of employment.

6. *A special stipulated damages standard for employee severance payments?* Wisconsin is one of a minority of jurisdictions that apply the traditional penalty rule to golden parachutes and other employee termination agreements. In *Wassenaar v. Panos*,[70] an employer hired plaintiff to manage a hotel for three years. The employer drafted a written contract, which both signed. It provided that in case of termination without cause the employer would be "responsible for fulfilling the entire financial obligation as set forth within this agreement for the full period of three years." The employer fired plaintiff without cause about 21 months before the contract expired. He was out of work for about two and a half months, and then another hotel hired him.

The Supreme Court of Wisconsin affirmed the trial court's finding that this was a liquidated damages clause and not a penalty. The employer argued that the stipulated damages clause in the case was void as a penalty because the harm to the employee was capable of estimation when the contract was made and was relatively easy to prove at trial. Justice Abrahamson noted:

> The standard calculation of damages after breach, however, may not reflect the actual harm suffered because of the breach. In addition to the damages reflected in the black-letter formulation, an employee may suffer consequential damages, including permanent injury to professional reputation, loss of career development opportunities, and emotional distress. . . . The usual arguments against allowing recovery for consequential damages — that they are not foreseeable and that no dollar value can be set by a court — fail when the parties foresee the possibility of such harm and agree on an estimated amount.

The clause passed the difficulty of estimation test. The employer also argued that since the employee obtained another job within a short time, this showed that the clause was unreasonable. Justice Abrahamson responded there was no evidence in the record showing that the stipulated amount was grossly disproportionate to the actual harm suffered. The employer had the burden of establishing this to overturn the clause once there was evidence that the employee had suffered some loss.

Are the *Lake River* and *Wassenaar* cases consistent? If the contract in *Wassenaar* had not included a termination clause, could the plaintiff employee have recovered, as damages for breach, all his wages until the end of the contract term? Could he have recovered damages for "permanent injury to professional reputation,

---

[69] There may still be legal limitations on the size of the severance pay. Corporate law establishes some limits, so that a corporate board of directors that authorizes payment of an excessive amount to a former executive pursuant to a golden parachute may be liable to shareholders for waste of corporate resources. *See* International Insurance Co. v. Johns, 874 F.2d 1447 (11th Cir. 1989). Tax law imposes special tax obligations on corporations that, pursuant to a golden parachute, pay more than three times annual pay to an executive upon severance. I.R.C. § 280G.

[70] 111 Wis. 2d 518, 331 N.W.2d 357 (1983).

loss of career development opportunities, and emotional distress"? If not, then enforcement of the stipulated remedy clause left the employee in a better position than expectation damages would have.[71] And is it possible that the plaintiff in *Lake River* suffered reputational injuries from the defendant's breach?

7. ***The Convention on the International Sale of Goods and stipulated damages:*** CISG does not address the question of penalty clauses. This means that the parties will be able to enforce penalty clauses if the gap-filling law (see CISG Article 7(2)) is the law of a jurisdiction that permits enforcement — which civil law countries generally do. On the other hand, if the gap-filling law is the law of the United States, for example, the U.S. law of liquidated damages would be applied.

[handwritten margin note: Civ law countries usually allow for punishment]

E.   THE EXPECTATION INTEREST: LOST ANTICIPATED PROFITS AND CONSEQUENTIAL DAMAGES

Recovery of "consequential damages" by a buyer is provided by UCC § 2-715(2), and the same term is also often used in common law cases. But what are consequential damages? There is no authoritative definition of this term, either in the UCC or elsewhere. One type of potential injury to a buyer upon breach that is always considered consequential damages is lost profits resulting from non-performance by a seller of goods or services. In these cases, the seller's breach prevents the buyer from fulfilling other contracts which would have earned profits for the buyer. For example, in the *Copylease* case, Memorex's breach allegedly prevented Copylease from making as many sales to its customers, resulting in a loss of profits. In this section we consider rules that can make it difficult for the buyer to recover this kind of consequential damages.

1.   The Foreseeability Test

HADLEY v. BAXENDALE
Court of the Exchequer
9 Ex. 341, 156 Eng. Rep. 145 (1854)

[As with most old English appellate cases, the account begins with a "headnote" by the Court Reporter describing the "facts" as they are revealed by the pleadings, and summarizing the proceedings below.]

. . . At the trial before CROMPTON, J., at the last Gloucester Assizes, it appeared that the plaintiffs carried on an extensive business as millers at Gloucester; and that, on the 11th of May, their mill was stopped by a breakage of the crank shaft by which the mill was worked. The steam engine was manufactured by Messrs. Joyce & Co., the engineers, at Greenwich, and it became necessary to send the shaft as a

---

[71] The *Wassenaar* case was followed by the Wisconsin Supreme Court two years later in *Koenings v. Joseph Schlitz Brewing Co.*, 126 Wis. 2d 349, 377 N.W.2d 593 (1985). In that case the employee, a lawyer, had found alternative employment at a higher salary before leaving Joseph Schlitz Brewing Company but was still allowed to collect his full salary until the end of the contract term. The Court emphasized the possibility of reputational injury to the plaintiff in changing jobs. Another case from a different jurisdiction but applying a similar analysis, and citing *Wassenaar*, is *Guiliano v. CLEO, Inc.*, 995 S.W.2d 88 (Tenn. 1999).

pattern for a new one to Greenwich. The fracture was discovered on the 12th, and on the 13th the plaintiffs sent one of their servants to the office of the defendants, who are the well-known carriers trading under the name of Pickford & Co., for the purpose of having the shaft carried to Greenwich. The plaintiff's servant told the clerk that the mill was stopped and that the shaft must be sent immediately; and in answer to the inquiry when the shaft would be taken, the answer was, that if it was sent by twelve o'clock any day, it would be delivered at Greenwich on the following day. On the following day the shaft was taken by the defendants, before noon, for the purpose of being conveyed to Greenwich, and the sum of 2£. 4s. was paid for its carriage for the whole distance; at the same time the defendants' clerk was told that a special entry, if required, should be made to hasten its delivery. The delivery of the shaft at Greenwich was delayed by some neglect; and the consequence was, that the plaintiffs did not receive the new shaft for several days after they would otherwise have done, and the working of their mill was thereby delayed, and they thereby lost the profits they would otherwise have received.

On the part of the defendants, it was objected that these damages were too remote, and that the defendants were not liable with respect to them. The learned Judge left the case generally to the jury, who found a verdict [of £50] . . .

Whateley, in last Michaelmas Term, obtained a *rule nisi* for a new trial, on the ground of misdirection. . . .

The judgment of the Court was now delivered by:

ALDERSON, B.

We think that there ought to be a new trial in this case; but, in so doing, we deem it to be expedient and necessary to state explicitly the rule which the Judge, at the next trial, ought, in our opinion, to direct the jury to be governed by when they estimate the damages.

It is, indeed, of the [greatest] importance that we should do this; for, if the jury are left without any definite rule to guide them, it will in such cases as these, manifestly lead to the greatest injustice. . . .

Now we think the proper rule in such a case as the present is this: — Where two parties have made a contract which one of them has broken, the damages which the other party ought to receive in respect of such breach of contract should be such as may fairly and reasonably be considered either arising naturally, *i.e.*, according to the usual course of things, from such breach of contract itself, or such as may reasonably be supposed to have been in the contemplation of both parties, at the time they made the contract, as the probable result of the breach of it. Now, if the special circumstances under which the contract was actually made were communicated by the plaintiffs to the defendants, and thus known to both parties, the damages resulting from the breach of such a contract, which they would reasonably contemplate, would be the amount of injury which would ordinarily follow from a breach of contract under these special circumstances so known and communicated. But, on the other hand, if these special circumstances were wholly unknown to the party breaking the contract, he, at the most, could only be supposed to have had in his contemplation the amount of injury which would arise generally, and in the great multitude of cases not affected by any special circumstances from such a breach of contract. For, had the special circumstances been known the parties might have specially provided for the breach of contract by special terms as to the damages in the case; and of this advantage it would be very unjust to deprive them. Now the above principles are those by which we think the jury ought to be guided in estimating the damages arising out of any breach of contract. . . . Now, in the present case, if we are to apply the principles above laid down, we find that the only circumstances here communicated by the plaintiffs to the defendants at the time the contract was made, were, that the article to be carried was the broken shaft of a mill, and that the plaintiffs were the millers of that mill. But how do these circumstances shew reasonably that the profits of the mill must be stopped by an unreasonable delay in the delivery of the broken shaft by the carrier to the third person? Suppose the plaintiffs had another shaft in their possession put up or putting up at the time, and that they only wished to send back the broken shaft to the engineer who made it; it is clear that this would be quite consistent with the above circumstances, and yet the unreasonable delay in the delivery would have no effect upon the intermediate profits of the mill. Or, again, suppose that, at the time of the delivery to the carrier, the machinery of the mill had been in other respects defective, then, also, the same results would follow. Here it is true that the shaft was actually sent back to serve as a model for a new one, and that the want of a new one was the only cause of the stoppage of the mill, and that the loss of profits really arose from not sending down the new shaft in proper time, and that this arose from the delay in delivering the broken one to serve as a model. But it is obvious that, in the great multitude of cases of millers sending off broken shafts to third persons by a carrier under ordinary circumstances, such consequences would not, in all probability, have occurred; and these special circumstances were here never communicated by the plaintiffs to the defendants. It follows, therefore, that the loss of the profits here cannot reasonably be considered such a consequence of the breach of contract as could have been fairly and reasonably contemplated by both the parties when they made this contract. For such loss would neither have flowed naturally from the breach of this contract in the great multitude of such cases occurring under ordinary circumstances, nor were the special circumstances, which, perhaps, would have made it a reasonable and natural consequence of such breach of contract, communicated to or known by the defendants. The Judge ought, therefore, to have told the jury, that, upon the facts before them, they ought not to take the loss of profits into consideration at all in estimating the damages. There must therefore be a new trial in this case.

Rule absolute.

NOTES AND QUESTIONS

1. **The buyer's remedies under the UCC:** Sections 2-712, 2-713, and 2-714 all say that a buyer can recover consequential damages in a proper case as defined by § 2-715(2). One requirement is that the consequential loss "could not reasonably be prevented by cover or otherwise." The other is the Code's version of *Hadley v. Baxendale. See* Official Comments 2, 3. The form of the test differs from that found in the *Hadley* opinion, but is the Code rule different in substance? How are we to determine when a seller "had reason to know" "at the time of contracting" of

"general or particular requirements and needs" of the buyer?

2. *The seller's consequential damages under the UCC:* There is no provision in the UCC giving *sellers* a right to consequential damages. Normally, when a buyer breaches a contract the seller loses the gains it would have made from receiving money. Had the drafters of the Code written a consequential damages section for sellers, sellers would seldom recover under any provision that incorporated the ideas of *Hadley v. Baxendale.*

Sellers might do many things with money. It would be hard to foresee what a seller might be planning to do with the proceeds from any particular contract. The typical common law approach was to award an aggrieved seller the difference between the contract price and the resale or market price. In addition, sellers can usually recover interest for the delayed payment.

However, sometimes as a consequence of a breach a seller suffers losses on transactions other than the one breached. In *Nobs Chemical, U.S.A., Inc. v. Koppers Co.,*[72] Nobs agreed to sell Koppers cumene, an additive for high-octane motor fuel. Nobs then ordered a large quantity of cumene from a Brazilian supplier, including some which it planned to supply to Koppers under their contract. The large quantity meant it was entitled to a volume discount. When Koppers canceled, Nobs had to pay the Brazilian supplier an extra $25 per ton on its (now smaller) order since it no longer qualified for a quantity discount. This resulted in reduced profits on other contracts. The court said that the lost quantity discount was a consequential rather than an incidental damage, and it did not allow any recovery for these reduced profits on other sales. "The Code does not provide for recovery of consequential damages by a seller."[73] The court did not discuss whether the loss in the quantity discount was foreseeable to the buyer at the time the contract was made.

3. *Some background on this famous case:* *Hadley v. Baxendale* is perhaps the best known common law contracts case of all time. Though an English case in origin, the foreseeability rule it established is now part of the law of every common law jurisdiction in the world. Commentators often assume that the case concerned a rather small flour mill from the pre-industrial world, but nothing could be farther from the truth. In 1850 the Hadley brothers established the City Flour Mills as a major industrial enterprise located in what was then England's most important western port, Gloucester. The new enterprise milled imported grain from other countries, which arrived by ship. The mill was immediately successful. In 1853 the Hadley brothers decided to construct a second mill adjacent to the original one. It was a shaft for the steam engine at the second mill that broke. The delay in its shipment caused the second mill to remain closed for longer than otherwise, but the first mill remained open throughout.[74]

---

[72] 616 F.2d 212 (5th Cir. 1980).

[73] *Id.* at 216.

[74] This information comes from Hugh Conway-Jones, *The Historical Setting for* Hadley v. Baxendale, 11 Tex. Wesleyan L. Rev. 243 (2005). For a further account of the historical setting of this famous case, including a good deal of information about Baron Alderson and the judges who set this famous precedent,

Professor John Kidwell, in an interesting article,[75] has raised the question of what damages would have been recoverable by the Hadleys, assuming that they were foreseeable at the time of contract (perhaps because Hadley had supplied Pickford & Co. the necessary information at the time of contract). The jury awarded £50 as lost profits. What assumptions do we need to make about the operation of the Hadleys' business to justify those damages under today's law of contract remedies? Remember that the broken shaft forced closure of only one of the Hadleys' two mills. And the shipment delay extended the closure of the second mill by approximately only one week.

4. Changing definitions of "foreseeability" — the "tacit agreement" rule and subsequent developments: Before passage of the Uniform Commercial Code, many states interpreted *Hadley v. Baxendale* to require that sellers of goods or services make a "tacit agreement" to pay consequential damages if they did not perform. Courts and writers often quoted Judge Learned Hand's statement of the doctrine: "We know of no test other than the loose one that the loss must be such that, had the promisor been originally faced with its possibility, he would have assented to its inclusion in what he must make good."[76] Courts following the tacit agreement rule often balanced the benefits of the contract against the burdens of the damages sought. For example, in *Hooks Smelting Co. v. Planters' Compress Co.*,[77] the court said:

> . . . the profits which the plaintiff might reasonably have expected to make on this contract did not probably exceed one or two hundred dollars. . . . And yet for the failure to properly perform this contract plaintiff is subjected to damages nearly ten times greater than the gross amount to be paid it for all the materials it furnished.

Official Comment 2 to UCC § 2-715 states: "The 'tacit agreement' test for the recovery of consequential damages is rejected." Consistent with this statement, today the rule of *Hadley v. Baxendale* is widely seen as a less strict limitation on contract damages in both Code and common law cases. Two famous English decisions, *Victoria Laundry (Windsor) Ltd. v. Newman Industries Ltd.*[78] and *The Heron II*,[79] have relaxed the strictness of the *Hadley* rule in that country as well. Both decisions contain extensive discussion of the English case law applying the *Hadley* rule in the century following its creation.

The most important recent English decision, *Transfield Shipping v. Mercator Shipping (The Achilleas)*, a 2008 decision by the House of Lords (at that time, the United Kingdom's highest court), signaled a possible new direction.[80] The defendant, a ship charterer (a lessee) returned the ship, *The Achilleas*, nine days after

---

see Richard Danzig, Hadley v. Baxendale: *A Study in the Industrialization of the Law*, 4 J. LEGAL STUD. 249 (1975).

[75] John Kidwell, *Extending the Lessons of* Hadley v. Baxendale, 11 TEX. WESLEYAN L. REV. 421 (2005).

[76] Stamford Extract Mfg. Co. v. Oakes Mfg. Co., 9 F.2d 301, 303 (2d Cir. 1925).

[77] 72 Ark. 275, 283, 79 S.W. 1052 (1904).

[78] Victoria Laundry (Windsor) Ltd. v. Newman Industries Ltd., [1949] 2 K.B. 528.

[79] The Heron II, [1969] 1 A.C. 350.

[80] [2008] UKHL 48, 3 W.L.R. 345.

the termination of the charter (i.e., the lease). In anticipation of a timely return of the ship, the owner had already rechartered the ship for a six-month period to a second charterer. In the time period between the owner's contract to recharter the ship and the defendant's breach, market prices declined dramatically for ship charters. Because of the delay, the second charterer was entitled to rescind the charter agreement. The owner agreed to reduce the charter rate by approximately $8000 per day, a total of over $1.3 million in U.S. dollars. The owner sued defendant for this amount as damages, as lost profits, for breach in returning *The Achilleas* nine days late. The court unanimously disallowed the claim, on the authority of *Hadley v. Baxendale*, but judges' interpretations varied. Some judges held that the market volatility was not reasonably foreseeable and therefore the damages resulting from the market volatility were unrecoverable under *Hadley*. This rationale, however, seems to conflict with the House of Lords decision in *The Heron II*, which upheld a lost profits recovery in apparently similar circumstances. Other judges called for reinterpretation of the rule of *Hadley* to return to something like the previously prevailing tacit agreement interpretation of the rule. At the time this note is written, it appears that these later judges' views will not prevail in England, at least in the short term.[81] But the history of *Hadley v. Baxendale* is very much one of changing interpretations over time, and there is no guarantee that these intepretations will not at some time return to those prevailing a century ago.

5.   *Disclaimers of consequential damages:* Another reason that the rule of *Hadley v. Baxendale* has a lesser impact on damage recoveries today is that many business forms used by sellers contain a clause disclaiming any liability for consequential damages. For example, Federal Express's 2012 Airbill[82] provides in small type on the front of the sender's copy:

> By using this Airbill you agree to the service conditions on the back of this Airbill and in the current FedEx Service Guide,[83] including terms that limit our liability.

On the back of the airbill, in gray ink (which is somewhat difficult to read), it says:

Limitations On Our Liability And Liabilities Not Assumed

> • Our liability in connection with this shipment is limited to the lesser of your actual damages or $100, unless you declare a higher value, pay an additional charge, and document your actual loss in a timely manner. You may pay an additional charge for each additional $100 of declared value. The declared value does not constitute, nor do we provide, cargo liability insurance.

---

[81] For good, yet contrasting, interpretations of the decision in *The Achilleas*, see Adam Kramer, *The New Test of Remoteness in Contract*, 125 L.Q.R. 408 (2009) (in favor of an interpretation akin to the tacit agreement test) and Edwin Peel, *Remoteness Re-visited*, 125 L.Q.R. 6 (2009) (in favor of a narrower interpretation).

[82] Federal Express uses slightly different forms for different kinds of packages. The wording and fonts used vary slightly from form to form.

[83] The FedEx Service Guide is a book that provides information about the company's services, rates, and terms and conditions.

> • *In any event, we will not be liable for any damage, whether direct, incidental, special, or consequential, in excess of the declared value of a shipment, whether or not FedEx had knowledge that such damages might be incurred, including but not limited to loss of income or profits.* [emphasis added]

Assuming this contract provision is enforceable as written, the italicized clause renders irrelevant any consideration of *Hadley v. Baxendale*. Why?

In Chapter 4 of these materials we will study judicial regulation of terms hidden in fine print in standard form contracts. You should wait until after studying those materials before concluding that the Federal Express clause would be enforced. But assuming that it is enforceable, what does that say about the contemporary relevance of *Hadley v. Baxendale*? Is its significance limited to cases in which there has been a failure of contract planning by a seller?

6. Hadley *as a penalty default rule:* Much contract writing has dealt with default rules. Most, if not all, contracts will be incomplete. The parties will say nothing about various subjects. Often these gaps exist concerning issues that are not central to the negotiations, but sometimes they reflect just what goes without saying. Many writers argue that a major part of contract law is and ought to be filling such gaps with predictable rules. If those bargaining know or can find out easily what the default rule is, and if it is more or less acceptable, they do not have to spend time and resources bargaining about it.

Although the vocabulary is fairly new, contract law has long supplied many default rules. Article 2 of the Uniform Commercial Code, for example, is filled with them. The harder question is: on what basis should we fashion default rules? We could attempt to fill gaps by turning to the custom of the industry in which the parties operate. Professor Lisa Bernstein, on the basis of a large empirical research project, cautions us that there may be fewer clear customs than we might expect to find.[84] Customs often conflict, and they often are vague and little more than the expectation that parties will behave reasonably and in good faith. Others argue that contract law ought to set defaults to achieve good purposes. Ian Ayres and Robert Gertner, for example, explain *Hadley v. Baxendale* as what they call a "penalty default."[85] The default rule is that you do not get consequential damages based on plans and projections that you kept secret from the other party. The rule operates to give a party an incentive to disclose information. If the consequences of a breach would be significant, the other party must know about it. Then the other party can decide whether s/he wants to take the risk, charge more to do so, or decline to bargain.

Other writers advocate fashioning default rules to carry out efficiency. "Defaults should mimic the terms that would be chosen by *idealized* contracting parties who

---

[84] *See* Lisa Bernstein, *Merchant Law in a Merchant Court: Rethinking the Code's Search for Immanent Business Norms*, 144 U. Pa. L. Rev. 1765 (1996); Bernstein, *The Questionable Empirical Basis of Article 2's Incorporation Strategy: A Preliminary Study*, 66 U. Chi. L. Rev. 710 (1999).

[85] *See* Ian Ayres & Robert Gertner, *Filling Gaps in Incomplete Contracts: An Economic Theory of Default Rules*, 99 Yale L.J. 87 (1989); Ayres & Gertner, *Strategic Contractual Inefficiency and the Optimal Choice of Legal Rules*, 101 Yale L.J. 729 (1992).

enjoy perfect information, face zero transaction costs, and seek to maximize their joint gains."[86] Some writers doubt whether judges in the context of a dispute between two parties would be equipped "to undertake the sort of sophisticated economic analysis that may well be necessary to discover the appropriately efficient rule."[87] In any event, as we work through the course, we will identify existing default rules and look for places where courts or legislatures might fashion others. However, insofar as the analysis rests on the idea that parties will know the default rules and then bargain in light of this knowledge, we should remain skeptical. We can presume that when those negotiating are represented by lawyers, the information will be at hand. But many important contracts are made without participation by lawyers. It is unclear whether business people know the rule of *Hadley v. Baxendale*. Yet interviews tell us that many business people think that one can cancel at least some kinds of contracts with only an obligation to pay the other side's out-of-pocket costs. Perhaps many know enough to be put on guard if the other party discloses what is riding on the deal.

2.   Proof of Damages with Reasonable Certainty: Of New Businesses and Experts

In this section we will study the rule that requires damages to be proved "with reasonable certainty." We will see a common legal problem — do we spend the time and effort attempting to establish something hard to prove or do we adopt a *per se* rule? On one hand, Official Comment 4 to UCC § 2-715 provides:

> The burden of proving the extent of loss incurred by way of consequential damage is on the buyer, but the section on liberal administration of remedies rejects any doctrine of certainty which requires almost mathematical precision in the proof of loss. Loss may be determined in any manner which is reasonable under the circumstances.

Official Comment 1 to UCC § 1-305 says: "Compensatory damages often are at best approximate: they have to be proved with whatever definiteness and accuracy the facts permit, but no more."

On the other hand, most states *once* followed a "new business" rule. As one court put it: "Prospective profits are not recoverable for a newly established business or for a business which has operated at a loss."[88] As the following case indicates, this rule has fallen out of fashion. According to a leading authority:[89]

> Most recent cases reject the once generally accepted rule that lost profits damages for a new business are not recoverable. The development of the law has been to find damages of an unestablished business recoverable when they can be adequately proved with reasonable certainty. The earlier

[handwritten margin note: not accepted by most states anymore]

---

[86] Christopher A. Riley, *Designing Default Rules in Contract Law: Consent, Conventionalism, and Efficiency*, 20 OXFORD J. LEGAL STUD. 367, 383 (2000). The Riley article is an excellent introduction to this area.

[87] *Id.* at 388.

[88] Keener v. Sizzler Family Steak Houses, 597 F. 2d 453, 458 (5th Cir. 1979).

[89] ROBERT DUNN, RECOVERY OF DAMAGES FOR LOST PROFITS § 4.3 (5th ed., Lawpress Corporation 1998).

cases are either ignored or rationalized as having been based on a finding that on those particular facts the evidence was inadequate as a matter of law to support a judgment for the plaintiff. What was once a rule of law has been converted into a rule of evidence.

After reading the next case, ask yourself whether this doctrinal change has been wise.

CHUNG v. KAONOHI CENTER CO.
Hawaii Supreme Court
62 Haw. 594, 618 P.2d 283 (1980)

RICHARDSON, C.J.

This case arises out of a contract to lease concession space for a fast-food Chinese kitchen in the Pearlridge Mall. Plaintiffs-appellees, Farrant Chung, Jordon Y. S. Lum, and J & C Company, a partnership consisting of Chung and Lum, brought a successful breach of contract action in the Circuit Court of the First Circuit against defendants-appellants, Kaonohi Center Company, a Hawaii general partnership. . . . We affirm.

In September 1971, plaintiffs negotiated with William Prosser, defendants' agent, for a 10-year lease on a Chinese fast-food outlet as one component of an international kitchen to be constructed by defendants at the Pearlridge Mall. At that time, plaintiff Chung was a stockbroker and plaintiff Lum owned and operated the House of Dragon, a Chinese restaurant in the Pearl City Shopping Center.[90] As a result of the negotiations, a contract to lease the Chinese kitchen was executed on January 17, 1972. On January 20, 1972, plaintiffs paid defendants a $1,666 deposit on the lease. In anticipation of operating the Chinese kitchen, plaintiffs arranged for financing, ordered equipment and furnishings, hired chefs and workers, advertised in the yellow pages of the telephone book for the to-be-built kitchen, and incurred other expenses.

Plaintiffs were in frequent contact with defendants after the lease was signed and the record shows voluminous correspondence between the parties concerning the design and operation of the fast-food Chinese kitchen. Whenever plaintiffs inquired about an opening date, they were told to be patient and were assured that they would be notified as soon as a firm date was set. During this period, defendants were negotiating with other parties about leasing the Chinese kitchen. Defendants had given a right of first refusal to a Ms. Liza Chong and were also negotiating with a Mr. Sergio Battistetti, whose partnership eventually obtained the lease on the entire international kitchen operation. Plaintiffs were never informed of these other negotiations. . . .

In early June 1973, Prosser sent a letter to plaintiffs informing them that the landlords of Pearlridge Shopping Center had decided not to pursue plaintiffs' lease

---

[90] [2] Prior to September 1971, plaintiff Lum also signed a lease with defendants to open another Chinese restaurant, the House of Pearl, at Pearlridge Mall. That restaurant opened in October 1972.

of the Chinese kitchen. A check for $1,666, the amount of plaintiffs' deposit, was enclosed.

In the trial court, plaintiffs sought specific performance of the lease agreement, contract damages including damages for emotional distress and loss of future profits, and punitive damages for fraudulent, malicious, and intentional misrepresentation and acts. The trial judge denied plaintiffs' request for an instruction on punitive damages,[91] but allowed instructions on damages for emotional distress and lost profits. The jury returned a special verdict awarding $50,000 for emotional distress and $175,000 for lost profits. Defendants then moved for judgment notwithstanding the verdict or, in the alternative, for a new trial. The motion was denied and this appeal followed.

On appeal, appellants do not challenge the jury's finding with respect to liability . . . [T]his appeal is premised entirely upon the jury's award of $225,000 in contract damages. The issues which appellants raise and the order in which they will be discussed are:

> I. Whether the trial court erred in denying defendants' motion for a mistrial, which was based upon testimony by plaintiff Lum that his wife had suffered miscarriages as a result of the contract breach. [Eds. note: Discussion of this issue has been omitted.]

> II. Whether the trial court erred in giving a jury instruction allowing damages for emotional distress for breach of a commercial contract.

> III. Whether the trial court erred in giving a jury instruction allowing damages for loss of anticipated profits in an unestablished business.

> IV. Whether the trial court erred in submitting to the jury a special verdict form, which contained spaces for damages for emotional distress and lost profits. [Eds. note: Discussion of this issue has been omitted.]

II. Damages for Emotional Distress and Disappointment.

Appellants argue that the trial court erred in giving Plaintiffs' Instruction No. 11, which read:

> If you find in favor of the plaintiffs, plaintiffs have a right to recover all damages which they have suffered and which the defendants or a reasonable person in the defendants' position should have foreseen would result from their acts or omissions. Such damages may include reasonable compensation for emotional distress and disappointment, if any, which plaintiffs have suffered as a proximate result of the defendants' conduct. There is no precise standard by which to place a monetary value on emotional distress and disappointment, nor is the opinion of any witness required to fix a reasonable amount. In making an award of damages for emotional distress and disappointment, you should determine an amount which your own experience and reason indicates would be sufficient in light of all of the evidence.

---

[91] [4] On appeal, the ruling on punitive damages is not challenged by plaintiffs.

In the trial court, appellants objected to the instruction on the grounds that "such emotional distress is recoverable only under special circumstances and not in an ordinary commercial contract such as we have here today." Appellants also urged this same contention in the briefs filed on appeal. . . .

The seminal case in this jurisdiction on damages for emotional distress and disappointment arising from breach of a contract is *Dold v. Outrigger Hotel*, 54 Haw. 18, 501 P.2d 368 (1972). In *Dold*, plaintiffs, who were visitors from the mainland, had booked hotel accommodations at the Outrigger Hotel. Upon arriving at the hotel, plaintiffs were refused accommodations and transferred to another hotel of lesser quality because the Outrigger lacked available space. We upheld a jury instruction allowing damages for emotional distress and disappointment, stating that "where a contract is breached in a wanton or reckless manner as to result in a tortious injury, the aggrieved person is entitled to recover in tort."

Appellants urge us to adopt a rule limiting the holding of *Dold* to "personal" contracts such as contracts of marriage, contracts of burial, and contracts to deliver personal messages. They argue that under traditional contract law, damages are allowable only for those injuries which are reasonably foreseeable at the time the contract was made. Since the primary objective of a "personal" contract is that of comfort, happiness, or well-being, emotional distress is a foreseeable injury which could result from a contract breach. Appellants reason that, unlike a personal contract, a commercial contract has as its primary objective financial gain and it is not reasonably foreseeable that the breach of such a contract could cause emotional distress and disappointment.

In several recent cases . . . we have implied that damages for emotional distress and disappointment may be recoverable when the relationship between the parties is based on a commercial contract. We now expressly so hold. We do not think that the dispositive factor in allowing damages for emotional distress is the nature of the contract. The dispositive factor is, rather, the wanton or reckless nature of the breach. The basis of our holding in *Dold* was our recognition that "certain situations are so disposed as to present a fusion of the doctrines of tort and contract."

The facts in this case present an ideal situation for application of the *Dold* rule. Appellants negotiated with three separate parties, including appellees, for the lease of the Chinese kitchen. At the time appellants signed the contract to lease to appellees, they had already given a right of first refusal to Liza Chong. During the year and a half after the contract to lease the kitchen was signed, appellants' agent, William Prosser, made numerous representations to appellees that they had secured the lease. Prosser and Sheldon Gordon, one of the general partners of Kaonohi Center Company, were also well aware of the effort and funds expended by appellees in reliance on the lease and allowed appellees to continue to believe that they had secured the lease. . . . The actions of appellants in this case were reprehensible and clearly amounted to wanton and/or reckless conduct sufficient to give rise to tort liability.

. . . .

III. Damages for Loss of Anticipated Profits.

We turn now to appellants' contention that damages for loss of anticipated profits should not have been allowed. . . . Appellants argue that, as a matter of law, expected profits from a new or unestablished business are too speculative to warrant recovery. Alternatively, they contend that even if this court should hold such profits recoverable, the proof in this case failed to meet the standard of reasonable certainty.

The general rule with regard to damages in a breach of contract action is that "when one sustains loss by breach of a contract, he is entitled to have just compensation commensurate with his loss." *Ferreira v. Honolulu Star-Bulletin*, 44 Haw. 567, 573–74; 356 P.2d 651, 655 (1960). In *Ferreira*, plaintiff sought damages for loss of profits which would have been realized had defendant, the *Honolulu Star-Bulletin*, fulfilled its contract to print an advertisement for an upcoming attraction at plaintiff's theater. We recognized that future profits may be an appropriate element of contract damages, but found the proof offered in the case insufficient to establish profits with reasonable certainty. We stated:

> [A] distinction is made in the law between the amount of proof required to establish the fact that the injured party has sustained some damage and the measure of proof necessary to enable the jury to determine the amount of damage. It is now generally held that the uncertainty which prevents a recovery is uncertainty as to the fact of damage and not as to its amount. However, the rule that uncertainty as to the amount does not necessarily prevent recovery is not to be interpreted as requiring no proof of the amount of damage. The extent of plaintiff's loss must be shown with reasonable certainty and that excludes any showing or conclusion founded upon mere speculation or guess. [Citations omitted.]

While *Ferreira* recognized that lost profits may be awarded in a contract action, we have never ruled directly on whether future profits in an [un]established or new business are allowable. Other courts, when faced with this question, have precluded recovery as a matter of law, reasoning that absence of prior income and expense experience renders anticipated profits too speculative to meet the standard of reasonable certainty. See, e.g., *China Doll Restaurant, Inc. v. Schweiger*, 119 Ariz. 315, 580 P.2d 776 (Ct. App. 1978); *Evergreen Amusement Corp. v. Milstead*, 112 A.2d 901 (Md. Ct. App. 1955).

Recent cases in several jurisdictions, however, have rejected a *per se* rule based upon the classification of a business as new or unestablished and focused instead upon whether a plaintiff can prove lost profits with reasonable certainty. . . . See *Remedies — Lost Profits as Contract Damages for an Unestablished Business: The New Business Rule Becomes Outdated*, 56 N.C. L. Rev. 693 (1978). We find the reasoning of this latter line of cases persuasive and reject the harsh rule which forecloses recovery merely because a business is new or unestablished. In our opinion, it would be grossly unfair to deny a plaintiff meaningful recovery for lack of a sufficient "track record" where the plaintiff has been prevented from establishing such a record by defendant's actions. Thus, we hold that where a plaintiff can show future profits in a new or unestablished business with reasonable certainty, damages for loss of such profits may be awarded.

Of course, the evidence necessary to show future profits with reasonable certainty depends on the circumstances of each individual case. While absolute certainty is not required, the court or jury must be guided by some rationale standard in making an award for loss of future profits.

We look now at the evidence of future profits in this case to determine whether it met the standard of reasonable certainty. Plaintiffs' key witness on anticipated profits was Don Voronaeff, a real estate and business appraiser. Voronaeff valued the proposed Chinese kitchen using three different valuation approaches — a reproduction cost analysis,[92] a comparative market analysis,[93] and an income stream analysis.[94] In reaching a final valuation figure, Voronaeff relied primarily on his income stream analysis, but included both the reproduction cost analysis and comparative market analysis as a check on that figure.

While appellants do not challenge the different valuation approaches utilized by Voronaeff, they do challenge the basis for his figures. They particularly focus on his assumptions regarding costs and expenses of plaintiffs' proposed operation. In order to evaluate plaintiffs' evidence, we must examine in some detail Voronaeff's income stream analysis.

An income stream analysis requires that an appraiser have a fairly accurate estimate of the projected net income of the business. The net income is derived by estimating the future gross profits of the business and subtracting the reasonably expectable expenses and cost of goods. The resulting net income is then capitalized at a rate reflecting the risk involved in the operation over an appropriate period of time, in this case over the 10-year life of the lease.

In his analysis, Voronaeff used $420,000 as the gross income for the first year of operation. . . . Voronaeff testified that he arrived at this figure by looking at the actual gross income of the Chinese kitchen in the Pearlridge International Kitchen run by Mr. Battistetti. The first year's gross income of that operation was $417,000. A person employed by Voronaeff also conducted a one-day count of customers and gross receipts of the existing Chinese kitchen which, when projected over a year, indicated a gross income of $666,041. That survey figure, Voronaeff stated, supported the gross income figure from the Battistetti operation and, based on Battistetti's gross income and gross income figures from other Chinese restaurants, a $420,000 gross income was reasonable.

Appellants object to the gross income figure utilized by plaintiffs' expert since it was based on an existing operation not run by plaintiffs. We reject this argument for obvious reasons. Appellants' contract breach prevented appellees from establishing a profit and loss record on which to base a gross income figure. The restaurant most

---

[92] [7] The cost, based on current prices, of reproducing the assets of the business is determined; this method produced an appraisal of $78,471.

[93] [8] Recently sold businesses of a similar nature are compared by both gross and net income to the subject business to indicate a fair market value; this method produced an appraisal according to gross income of $331,800 and an appraisal according to net income of $385,365.

[94] [9] The net income the business will produce over its life is determined and capitalized at a rate reflecting an appropriate rate of return to the investor and the risk involved in the business venture. See discussion in text.

nearly approximating plaintiffs' proposed kitchen was Battistetti's Chinese kitchen. It was in the identical location and served the same type of food to the same type of clientele as plaintiffs' proposed restaurant. Further, plaintiffs' expert also testified that he considered the gross income from other Chinese restaurants and ran an independent survey of the Battistetti operation as a check on the gross income figure. Under these circumstances, we find no error in allowing Mr. Voronaeff to use $420,000 as the first-year gross income of plaintiffs' proposed business.

The next stage in Voronaeff's analysis was estimating the cost of goods and expenses and subtracting them from the gross income to reach a net income figure. While plaintiffs' expert relied primarily on the Battistetti operation in establishing a gross income figure, he did not use the actual expenses and cost of goods from Battistetti's Chinese kitchen. Instead, he subtracted estimates which he testified were based on industry standards. Voronaeff extensively detailed the cost of goods and other expenses in his testimony and on cross-examination stated that the expenses he had subtracted "covered everything that you should cover in operating a business." Some expenses, he stated, like rent, taxes, insurance, and salaries, were actual, in the sense that they were reasonably fixed. Other expenses, such as cost of goods, were estimates based on Voronaeff's knowledge of the industry and projected rise in prices. After subtracting each expense, Voronaeff derived a net income figure of $67,608 for the first year of operation. He then capitalized that net income figure at a rate of 20 percent over the 10-year life of the lease to reach a final value of approximately $225,000.[95]

Appellants argue that Voronaeff's testimony as to cost of goods and expenses was speculative and lacked a factual basis. Thus, they contend, the net income on which Voronaeff based his income stream analysis was highly conjectural and the resulting valuation inaccurate. . . .

In the instant case, plaintiffs' expert testified in great detail on estimated expenditures, explaining the amount of money to be spent in each category. These estimates were based on his appraisal experience and his examination of other restaurant operations. Once a witness is qualified as an expert appraiser, he or she should be permitted to give an opinion using any of the accepted methods of valuation. Weaknesses in reaching the valuation go to the weight of such testimony. It is incumbent on the opposing party to bring out any such weaknesses on cross-examination or through presentation of counter-evidence.

Appellants had sufficient opportunity at trial to bring to the jury's attention any fallacies in Voronaeff's appraisal. Our examination of the record shows that appellants' counsel vigorously cross-examined Voronaeff on his expense and cost assumptions. It was made clear to the jury that some of Voronaeff's cost and expense figures were estimates. Appellants' witness, Sergio Battistetti, a partner in

---

[95] [11] In explaining this method, Voronaeff stated, "What we're saying is that someone would pay $225,000 to obtain an annual net income of $67,000 and they'd be getting a 20 percent return to their investment."

In a separate analysis, Voronaeff also calculated the net income of the restaurant for a 10-year period by projecting an increase of 10 percent in both gross income and expenses. He concluded that the total net income would be $1,077,000, which discounted to present-day net value would be $419,000.

the International Kitchens operation, testified that the existing Chinese fast-food kitchen had lost $13,962 in its first year of operation and was expected to net only $4,042 in its second year of operation. Dr. Lewis Freitas, a business and finance expert testifying for defendants, discredited use of the income stream approach in valuing the proposed business. He stated that that approach "requires that the income that's generated be constant and last for at least 20 or 30 years." Using the actual income and expenses of the existing operation, projected out over a ten-year period, Freitas set a present value on the Battistetti operation of between $35,000 and $40,000. The method by which that valuation was reached was clearly explained to the jury.

This was not the only information the jury had before it. It also knew that plaintiff Lum owned and operated two Chinese restaurants, one of which was located at Pearlridge Mall. The profit and expense sheets from at least one of these restaurants was introduced into evidence, so the jury could reasonably have estimated the effectiveness of plaintiff Lum's management.[96] The jury might well have concluded that the fast-food Chinese kitchen under plaintiffs' management would have been more efficient because of Lum's previous experience and his ability to share resources with his other restaurant at Pearlridge.

The jury, as fact-finder, had the responsibility of judging the credibility of the witnesses, resolving conflicting evidence, and assessing the weight of the expert's testimony. We are of the opinion that, on the whole, the jury had sufficient data from which to make a rational judgment as to the loss of future profits and on which to base its award.

. . . .

On appeal, appellants have failed to cite any cases to support their contention, relying instead upon their arguments that neither lost profits nor emotional distress damages should have been allowed. We have fully disposed of those arguments above. Further, we note that the trial court instructed the jury as follows with regard to speculative damages:

> You are not permitted to award a party speculative damages, which means compensation for loss or harm which, although possible, is conjectural or not reasonably certain. However, if you determine that a party is entitled to recover, you should compensate him for loss or harm which is reasonably certain to be suffered by him as a proximate result of the injury in question.

It is clear from this instruction that the jury was aware that it could only award damages for reasonably certain harm or loss proximately resulting from the contract breach. . . . In light of appellants' total failure on appeal to support their claim and the above jury instruction, we find no error.

Affirmed.

---

[96] [14] Appellants introduced the profit and loss sheet from the House of Dragon, which showed that plaintiff Lum's profits ranged between 4.1 percent and 11.4 percent over a five-and-a-half year period. It should be noted that the profit projected by Voronaeff for the fast-food Chinese kitchen was 15.9 percent, substantially higher than that realized in the House of Dragon operation. However, there was testimony to the effect that construction near the House of Dragon may have had a detrimental effect on business.

NOTES AND QUESTIONS

1. ***Recovery for emotional loss:*** The Hawaii Supreme Court has explicitly overruled *Chung* with respect to the recovery for emotional injury arising from "wanton and/or reckless" breach of contract.[97] Since that decision, recovery for emotional injury arising from breach of contract is allowed only "where the parties specifically provide for them in the contract or where the nature of the contract clearly indicates that such damages are within the parties' contemplation or expectation in the event of breach of contract." The court suggested as an example of the latter a contract for services, later breached, in connection with a marriage or funeral service. Recovery for emotional injury, as well as punitive damages, is also still available if the defendant's conduct, in addition to being a breach of contract, "violates a duty that is independently recognized by principles of tort law."

In justifying the overruling of the *Chung* and *Dold* precedents, the Hawaii Court reasoned as follows:[98]

> Presently, contract law allows — and at times even encourages — intentional breaches of contract. . . . Whereas society views intentional torts as reprehensible, many people have argued that intentional breaches of contract are morally neutral. Proponents of this amoral view forcefully argue that "efficient" breaches of contract, *i.e.*, breaches where the gain to the breaching party exceeds the loss to the party suffering breach, actually result in a net benefit to society because such breaches allow resources to move to their more optimal use. . . . Even Justice Holmes recognized, over 100 years ago, that breaching a contract constitutes a morally neutral act, stating that "[t]he duty to keep a contract at common law means a prediction that you must pay damages if you do not keep it — *and nothing else.*" Oliver Wendell Holmes, *The Path of the Law,* 10 HARV. L. REV. 457, 462 (1897) (emphasis added).

> Based on these policy considerations and the compensatory objectives of contract law, many courts — including the courts of this jurisdiction — focus on the loss to the non-breaching party rather than whether the breach was intentional. . . . There is simply no principled way to distinguish "intentional" breaches from "willful" or "wanton" breaches. . . .

Are these arguments persuasive to you? As the court suggests, most courts do not allow recovery of emotional distress damages for breach of contract, except possibly for some contracts for services of a personal nature. However, recovery for emotional injury is common in tort.

2. ***Can an expert provide enough certainty respecting lost profits?*** As most courts have today, the Hawaii Court rejected the historic new business rule, suggesting that experts can provide a "rational" basis to support the jury award. But how reliable were Mr. Voronaeff's estimates of lost profits? Could you construct a policy argument against allowing lost profits in this case, based on the same policy arguments the court made against allowance of damages for emotional distress? Is

---

[97]   Francis v. Lee Enterprises, 89 Haw. 234, 971 P.2d 707 (1999).

[98]   *Id.* at 243, 971 P. 2d at 716.

it possible that Kaonohi Center was attempting an "efficient breach" in reassigning the lease from the plaintiffs to Mr. Battistetti? Would you favor the restoration of the new business rule?

3. *Conflict between experts:* Note that the defendant introduced its own expert testimony, with its experts suggesting much lower lost profits than Mr. Voronaeff. Conflicts in testimony between experts about lost profits are quite common in cases where the amount in controversy is sufficient to justify investment in expert testimony by each side. The case of *Eastern Airlines, Inc. v. McDonnell Douglas Corp.*[99] provides a vivid example. This case involved the late delivery by McDonnell Douglas of 90 passenger jets to Eastern Airlines. Eastern's expert testified that the delay caused the airline to lose $23,400,000 in profits. McDonnell's expert, on the other hand, testified that the delay actually *saved* Eastern $1,294,000 because the tardy delivery reduced financing costs. In its decision remanding the case to the District Court for further proceedings, the Fifth Circuit suggested that the trial court consider calling its own expert witness, as it can do, in order to provide a more independent source of testimony on the damages question. Would that be a good solution in all cases?

4. *A court allowing but limiting lost-profit recovery by a new business:* In *Mid-America Tablewares, Inc. v. Mogi Trading Co., Ltd.*,[100] an American distributor of tablecloths, napkins, plates, and cups ordered dinnerware from a Japanese manufacturer. The contract contained detailed provisions about the lead composition of the glaze so that it would comply with American regulations. The dinnerware delivered by the defendant (Mogi) failed to comply with the contract standard and could not be sold in the United States. Mid-America had never sold dinnerware before. It sought the profits it would have made selling the product that Mogi was to supply.

Applying Wisconsin law, the Seventh Circuit found that the best available evidence under the circumstances supported a reasonable finding that there would have been future profits. It stated:

> First and foremost, the evidence established that a number of buyers from some of the country's largest retail chains embraced the Harvest Festival dinnerware with enthusiasm and uniformly believed that it would be a success. Although, as Mogi successfully brought out during cross-examination, the only way anyone could know with absolute certainty whether the line would have been successful in the marketplace would be if the line actually made it onto the shelves for an adequate period of time to gauge consumers' reaction, the law does not require this sort of absolute certainty.

While upholding the recovery of lost profits in principle, the court overturned the jury verdict, which was based largely on the expert testimony of a University of Wisconsin School of Business professor. The jury had awarded lost profits of $311,353 for the first year and $2,655,752 for subsequent years. The court

---

[99] 532 F.2d 957 (5th Cir. 1976).

[100] 100 F.3d 1353 (7th Cir. 1996).

characterized the latter award as "monstrously excessive" and based on an "extreme degree of speculation." The court remanded the case for a new trial on damages after the first year, but it was not clear what additional evidence a new jury could hear. We learned from the lawyer for the plaintiff that in fact the case was settled and no new trial ever took place.

If a court is willing to allow a jury to find lost profits for a new business that has no track record to go on, is it ever appropriate to overturn a verdict as excessive? Provided that the jury verdict is consistent with expert testimony, as it was in *Mid-America Tablewares*, can a court's judgment about what is excessive ever be superior to the jury's?

5.   *What role for mitigation?* In both *Chung* and *Mid-America Tablewares*, the court allowed recovery for lost profits beyond the first year after breach. Could the plaintiffs have mitigated those losses? Apparently the defendant in neither case raised the mitigation issue, though we are not sure why. Compare *In re WorldCom*, *supra*.

6.   *Specific performance as an alternative to damages:* The plaintiffs in *Chung* requested specific performance as an alternative to damages. The claim for specific performance seems to have been abandoned early in the litigation. It took over two and a half years from the filing of the complaint (on June 29, 1973 — only six days after breach) to the trial (January 1976). Perhaps in the interval, plaintiffs abandoned their desire for specific performance. But suppose it had been possible for plaintiffs to get a specific performance award early in the litigation. Would that have been a superior resolution to their controversy? If a specific performance award had been made, do you think that it would have been performed? Or would the defendant (Kaonohi Center) have then offered plaintiffs an attractive settlement? How much do you think defendant would have had to offer plaintiffs to get them to accept a settlement in lieu of specific performance?

7.   *Alternative measures of damages:* Suppose the court in *Chung* had concluded that the proof was too uncertain to justify any recovery of lost profits. Should the plaintiffs have been allowed to recover their expenditures in preparation for performance (they hired chefs and workers, advertised in the yellow pages, etc.) in addition to the return of their deposit? Return to this question after studying the next two cases (*Security Stove v. Railway Express* and *L. Albert & Son v. Armstrong Rubber*).

F.   THE EXPECTATION INTEREST: SOME CONCLUDING PERSPECTIVES

1.   Should the Expectation Interest Always Be Fully Protected?

According to conventional contracts talk, if there is an unexcused material breach of contract, the law should, and does, seek to put the aggrieved party in the position she would have been in had the contract been performed. (Notice that this is both a normative and an empirical claim. And the empirical claim rests on the idea that an abstract law can ensure that parties are "made whole," regardless of the particular circumstances.) If this is so, the law should prevent anyone from being harmed by a breach of contract — and, indeed, should generally deter parties from breaching insofar as they still have to provide compensation for any conceivable harms.

This account omits some crucial contextual, "on-the-ground" factors. Professor David Campbell points out that rules of contract damages as they are usually applied do not often seek to put the aggrieved party where she would have been had the contract been performed. He says: "Far from it being the function of the law of contract to (so far as possible) prevent breach, the function of that law is to make breach possible although on terms which the law regulates."[101] This is a most unorthodox position. Nonetheless, it has great plausibility.

First of all, even under formal law, in all but a limited group of cases, a seller who names a fixed price for a performance is only taking a zone of risk and not committing his or her firm to foolish, if heroic, measures to carry out the deal precisely as written. Contract law reflects this in its highly uncertain rules about impracticability, frustration of purpose, and mutual and unilateral mistake. Courts also construe the contract's statement of what it is that the seller promised to do, and sometimes judges limit what appear literally to be absolute obligations. Secondly, empirical research shows that at least in many transactions, buyers go to great lengths to help suppliers who face difficulties outside of the ordinary zone of risk assumed in their deal.[102]

Campbell points out that the law of contract remedies reflects this sharing of the risks of loss. The law rarely grants specific performance. The law, moreover, demands that a buyer mitigate any potential loss by covering her needs through a substitute contract with one of the seller's competitors if this can be done. The difference between contract price and cover price is the basic formal remedy in such cases. If buyers have to pay more to get substitute goods, sellers have to compensate them for the additional costs. Rarely will this difference be great enough to warrant litigation, but even then the aggrieved buyer will have to worry that litigation may push the supplier into bankruptcy.

When they cannot find substitute goods, buyers can seek consequential damages, but here the formal law establishes additional limitations — you have studied *Hadley v. Baxendale* and proof of damages with reasonable certainty. In all but a few situations, these are high hurdles to jump, and most buyers must consider the risk that they will be unable to succeed in the real world of litigation. Thus, the delivery of legal remedies on the ground becomes part of any calculus, and this is not a matter that can be predicted easily in a single formula for all disputes. At a general level, Campbell argues that the net effect of legal rules is to push parties to compromise and settle. The structure of the law as applied in real

---

[101] David Campbell, *The Relational Constitution of Remedy: Co-Operation as the Implicit Second Principle of Remedies for Breach of Contract*, 11 TEX. WESLEYAN L. REV. 455, 456 (2005).

[102] There is a world of *pacta sunt servanda* ("agreements must be kept") in which a deal is a deal, but it is a very limited one.

cases introduces uncertainty, and the parties can rarely be sure of the costs or outcomes.

This insight can be taken even further.[103] We can turn to law in action to add to the reasons why bringing a suit for contract damages will seldom be a winning proposition. Parties often deal on the basis of standard form contracts, and in such situations the seller's form is commonly the one that is used. Not surprisingly, these sellers' forms frequently have *force majeure* clauses that offer broad excuses. One lawyer put it that the typical seller's clause excuses performance if there is a cloud in the blue sky. Additionally, sellers' forms usually limit the buyer's recovery to replacement or repair, and disclaim consequential damages.

Except in a very few jurisdictions, a buyer who wins a contracts action does not recover her lawyer's fees from the losing seller. Even establishing that the seller is in default is often very difficult. Performance may not be defined precisely in the contract, and experts can battle about just what the seller did do in many cases. Litigation drags executives and engineers away from making money for the company and puts them in a setting that many of them hate. Many businesspeople make terrible witnesses because they are unaccustomed to being challenged by lawyers, and they may prejudice their claim by the way they respond to questions in a deposition. Judges and clerks of court often work hard to push disputing parties in a contracts action to settle the case during pretrial procedures. An entire issue of the *Journal of Empirical Studies* was devoted to the concept of the "vanishing trial" in the United States.[104] A general consensus emerged: the numbers show that we have had a sharp decline in the overall number of trials. In the special issue, 12 articles seek to explain why this is so and appraise the consequences.

Thus, a first glance at the more specific contexts seems to offer the same answer that Campbell reached — that the actual current system of delivery of legal remedies pushes parties toward a settlement rather than litigation. However, while most cases are settled, we should note that there is always a chance that the buyer could sue and recover a large sum as consequential damages. It may be unlikely, but it is still possible in the right circumstances. This possibility may reinforce all of the relational norms and sanctions that push sellers to perform. In Professor Samuel Gross's words:

> [N]orms . . . [such as trust, reputation, civility, etc.] may operate very well in practice, and yet be too vague, too complex, too changeable, or too personal to enact as laws, or even fully to articulate. Nor would it help for

---

[103] *See* Stewart Macaulay, *Renegotiations and Settlements: Dr. Pangloss's Notes on the Margins of David Campbell's Papers*, 29 Cardozo L. Rev. 261 (2007).

[104] *See* Marc Galanter, *The Vanishing Trial: An Examination of Trials and Related Matters in Federal and State Courts*, 1 J. Empirical Legal Stud. 459 (2004), and the articles that followed in that issue. *But see* John Lande, *Shifting the Focus from the Myth of "The Vanishing Trial" to Complex Conflict Management Systems, or I Learned Almost Everything I Need to Know about Conflict Resolution from Marc Galanter*, 6 Cardozo J. of Conflict Resol. 191, 211 (2005) ("Before becoming horrified at the possible demise of the trial in general, we should have a clearer picture of the actual changes and their consequences. In the meantime, the insights of legal pluralism can help provide a balanced analysis by recognizing that much adjudication occurs before trial and outside the courts.").

Sellers act, in part, b/c threat of buyer to sue even tho rarely do

the legal system to opt out of an area of behavior entirely and give informal norms free rein: a coercive option, but one that is rarely used, is necessary as a boundary, to keep the normative system intact. A separate but inefficient system of legal rules may strike just the right balance.[105]

Some businesspeople know or learn about the law and the odds of the aggrieved party winning big. Others just know that litigation is painful and something to be avoided. Thus, the possibility of litigation may remain an important part of the operating system of coping with contract disputes, even if it is rarely invoked.[106]

To be sure, empirical research has established that almost all contracts disputes are settled. For some scholars, this ends the inquiry. They seem to assume that settlements are a good thing, our system encourages them, and all is for the best. However, there is still a leap from the "is" to the "ought" here. Without a good deal of further research, we cannot be sure that settlements are good, efficient, and something to applaud.[107] It is an empirical question in each case.

Usually, in cases that are settled, there is still a loss, and the parties must divide it in some fashion. If the seller wants to back out because the market price has gone up, the buyer could just abandon the deal and find another source of supply. (Of course, the buyer is likely to remember what happened the next time she needs to purchase this product.) Alternatively, the buyer could agree to pay the original supplier an amount somewhere between the contract price and the market price, as an adjustment, if this is enough to allow the seller to perform. Finally, the parties could work out a more complex settlement wherein the seller gets relief now, but the buyer gets benefits in the future beyond the present contract.

We can see an example of this more complex kind of arrangement in a case involving Scandinavian Airlines (SAS). In October 2007, SAS announced that it had had three landing gear accidents involving its Bombardier Dash 8 Q400 turboprop aircraft in less than two months. None of the passengers or crew was injured in these accidents. However, SAS withdrew its entire fleet — 27 of these planes — from service, and the airline said that it might ask for compensation.[108] John Dueholm, SAS deputy chief executive, said that "the Dash 8 Q400 has given rise to repeated quality-related problems," and that there was "a risk that use of the Dash

---

[105] Samuel R. Gross, *The American Advantage: The Value of Inefficient Litigation*, 85 MICH. L. REV. 734, 756 (1987).

[106] The preference for informal over formal solutions to business disputes is not unique to the United States. *See* Erhard Blankenburg, *The Infrastructure for Avoiding Civil Litigation: Comparing Cultures of Legal Behavior in the Netherlands and Germany*, 28 LAW & SOC. REV. 789 (1994). *See also* Kathryn Hendley, Peter Murrell, & Randi Ryterman, *Law, Relationships and Private Enforcement: Transactional Strategies of Russian Enterprises*, 52 EUROPE-ASIA STUD. 627, 644 n.52 (a survey of over 300 factories found that "for every 100 transactions, 24 experience potential disputes. Of these, 16 are resolved through informal complaints, seven are resolved through threats of litigation and/or penalties, and one will be litigated.").

[107] Law professors debate about the virtues and vices of settlement rather than litigation. For an overview, see the articles in the symposium issue of the 2009 *Fordham Law Review*, reflecting on the seminal 1984 article by Owen Fiss, *infra* Chapter 3, note 194. *See also* Ben Depoorter, *Law in the Shadow of Bargaining: The Feedback Effect of Civil Settlements*, 95 CORNELL L. REV. 957 (2009–10). However, little of this debate seems to penetrate scholarship in the various substantive areas.

[108] Kevin Done, *SAS Acts on Q400 Aircraft*, FINANCIAL TIMES, Oct. 29, 2007, at A20.

8 Q400 could eventually damage the SAS brand."[109]

Nonetheless, in March 2008, the airline and the manufacturer reached a settlement.[110] Under the agreement, SAS would receive more than $163 million in compensation, but it would also place a sizable new order with Bombardier. The new order, valued at $883 million, was for a further 27 aircraft and included CRJ-900 jets as well as a new version of the Q400. The airline had options on another 24 aircraft from the Canadian manufacturer.

It seems as if there was something for both sides in this settlement. Occasionally, parties may reach a settlement like this one that makes both even better off than if the contract had been performed, but this is not always possible. Such settlements are easier when there is a good reason to continue the relationship in the future.[111] Thus, the outcomes of these disputes depend on a variety of factors, including the shadow of the formal law, permitting a lawsuit if the parties cannot reach a settlement; the real context within which that lawsuit would have to take place; and the details of the ongoing relationship between the parties.

If we rely on single anecdotes and case examples like this one, we may be tempted to conclude that all is for the best. Settlement, after all, allows parties to continue their relationships or work out equitable arrangements to break them up. However, these kinds of examples cannot substitute for careful examination of many kinds of cases and situations.[112] It may make a difference that one party has a lot more clout than the other. Settlements can be good, bad, or indifferent. Drawing hasty conclusions based on limited empirical knowledge may impair our chances of finding out more about when, where, and how good results were actually reached. And settlements are particularly hard to study. For various reasons, the parties often agree to keep the details of their settlement secret.

---

[109] *Id. See also* Brent Jang, *Bombardier, SAS Mend Fences with Plane Order*, THE GLOBE AND MAIL, March 11, 2008, at B4.

[110] Bernard Simon, *Bombardier and SAS End Dispute Over Turbo-Props*, FINANCIAL TIMES, March 11, 2008, at 27.

[111] Another, more recent example also makes this point. In November 2010, a midair engine explosion forced a Qantas Airlines Airbus A380 to make an emergency landing in Singapore and then to ground its fleet of A380 aircraft. In December, Qantas sued Rolls-Royce, the engine manufacturer, seeking damages covering its loss of business. In June 2011, the parties announced a settlement but did not reveal the details. Rolls-Royce commented that Qantas was "a valued customer," and that Rolls was pleased the matter had been resolved. *See* FINANCIAL TIMES, June 23, 2011.

[112] *See* Jacqueline Macaulay, *Some Barriers to Drawing Conclusions from Social Science Research* (Jan. 1979), *available at* law.wisc.edu/facstaff/macaulay/papers/barriers.pdf. Despite its age, the report is still well worth reading. Jacqueline Macaulay notes:

> The problem may not be intrinsic to the reports themselves but rather may stem from the natural tendency to generalize from a few cases or a specific situation to a whole population. An ethnographic report may be accurate, subtle and insightful but the cases covered may represent atypical rather than typical situations. . . . The most highly visible, vivid, poignant or arresting examples . . . are probably exceptions rather than the rule. The use of . . . vignettes and snapshots properly lies in exemplification, not proof. They are valid examples of what can come about but not reliable bases for generalizations about an entire group.

NOTES AND QUESTIONS

1. ***Specific performance and mitigation:*** Compare Campbell's views, as summarized above, with the views of the scholars who favor more liberal availability of specific performance. The views of the latter are discussed in Note 5 following *Copylease v. Memorex, supra.* Do you think Campbell would support the granting of specific performance in the *Copylease* case? (Is a right to specific performance inconsistent with an expectation that the parties will share losses in the event of hardship?) And what do you imagine Campbell would think about the result in *Parker v. Twentieth Century-Fox?* (Do we have loss-sharing here?)

2. ***Sellers helping buyers:*** Professor Campbell emphasizes the desirability of buyers helping out sellers in difficulty, a goal facilitated by various rules limiting buyers' remedies. Suppose the shoe is on the other foot and it is the buyer who is in difficulty and wants out of a contract. Perhaps the buyer no longer has any use for goods that have been ordered and those goods cannot readily be resold by the buyer at the contract price. Does the seller have an obligation to help out the buyer?

We have already suggested, in Note 7 following *Neri v. Retail Marine, supra,* that as a matter of practice consumer buyers can commonly cancel contracts without liability. Others have observed that in the commercial world, cancellation of orders by buyers, with no or limited liability, is a common practice. Professor Stewart Macaulay reported in a famous article on a survey of businesspeople about contracting practices:[113]

> [A]ll 10 of the purchasing agents asked about cancellations of orders once placed indicated that they expected to be able to cancel orders freely, subject to only an obligation to pay for the seller's major expenses, such as scrapped steel. All 17 sales personnel asked reported that they often had to accept cancellation. One said, "You can't ask a man to eat paper [the firm's product] when he has no use for it." A lawyer with many large industrial clients said:
>
>> Often businessmen do not feel they have "a contract" — rather they have "an order." They speak of "cancelling the order" rather than "breaching our contract." When I began practice I referred to order cancellations as breaches of contract, but my clients objected since they do not think of cancellation as wrong.

While cancellation of orders may be a common business practice, legally, of course, it is commonly a breach of contract.[114] And the law of contract protects the seller's expectation interest. While a seller has an obligation to resell the product (UCC § 2-706) and can rarely sue for the price (UCC § 2-709), if the seller is a lost volume seller it can sue for lost profits (UCC § 2-708(2)). See *Neri v. Retail Marine,*

---

[113] Stewart Macaulay, *Non-Contractual Relations in Business: A Preliminary Survey,* 28 AM. SOC. REV. 1, 10 (1963).

[114] In the commercial world, negotiated contracts on major purchases (e.g., airliners) will sometimes contain detailed provisions governing cancellation of orders, providing remedies to the seller in some circumstances. However, many orders are made verbally or by preprinted order forms that do not contain such provisions. In those circumstances there is commonly an enforceable contract, breached by a cancellation.

supra. If a seller is unable to prove its lost profits, damages may be limited to reliance expenditures (such as the costs of beginning to perform) that cannot be mitigated. Moreover, if the seller must resort to law to collect damages, it is not allowed to recover its attorney's fees, unless the contract specifically provides otherwise or there is an applicable statute providing for attorney's fees.

2.   Does It Make Any Difference Whether the Law Protects the Expectation Interest?

There seems to be some disparity between prevailing business practices, which in general do not respect the expectation interest, and the law of contract damages, which emphasizes the importance of the expectation interest, albeit with many exceptions and limitations. Why do you think there is a disparity between the law and customary practices?

On the other hand, how much does it really matter what the legal rules are that govern damages? As Professor Campbell suggests, most contract disputes, and particularly disputes between two business entities that expect to do further business, are settled. Consider the following excerpts from articles by Professor Karl Llewellyn and Professor Stewart Macaulay:

Karl N. Llewellyn, *What Price Contract? — An Essay In Perspective*
40 YALE L.J. 704, 718–22 (1931)[115]

Is the Law of Contract Necessary?

All of which, however, begs the question of why there need be any *legal* machinery at all for the purposes mentioned, other than mere protection of the factual results of accomplished bargains, work, deliveries, and payments. The peace, and more dubiously the law of alienability and of ownership, at least as against persons entrusted with possession — what more is needed? As one puts such a question, one recalls first how seldom law touches *directly* any case in which a promise has been performed, or in which an inadequate performance has been received in satisfaction. Promise, performance, and adjustment are in this sense primarily extra-legal. It needs no argument that if they did not normally occur without law's intervention, no regime of future dealings would be possible. The lawyer's idea of "contract," applied to these normal cases, where performance and informal business adjustments proceed to occur, is thus a conceptual projection of trouble and the legal spawn of trouble upon the untroubled in fact. Applied to such cases, the lawyer's idea of "contract" is unreal in genesis and misleading in implication — unless, which is the matter of inquiry, what the courts may do in the possible case of trouble is a needed factor, or at least a factor, in promise, or in performance, or in adjustment . . .

[A]s the specialization and credit, and particularly the industrial, aspects of an economy gain ground, it becomes hard to escape the positive case for utility of legal

---

enforcement of promises. Credit or reliance on a purely customary or self-interest basis presupposes for effectiveness either permanence of dealings involving long-run mutual dependence, or an ingrained traditional morality covering the point, or dealings within a face-to-face community (or its equivalent, a close-knit though wandering guild-like interest group such as the early medieval merchants seem to have made up) in which severe group pressure on delinquent promisors is available. These types of sanction fail in a society mobile as to institutions, mobile as to residence, mobile as to occupation; they fail increasingly as the market expands spatially and in complexity. They fail, in a word, as to long-run, long-range, impersonal bargains, as also in cases where death, or transfer of rights, removes from the relation what may at the outset have been a personal aspect.

Frequently enough no other sanction than the legal exists at all. Where other sanctions do exist (*e.g.*, desire for continued dealings, or for a business reputation) they show an unfortunate tendency to fail precisely where most needed, *i.e.*, when stress of loss (or gain: management manipulation of the market or merger of the debtor) is strong. Max Weber cogently remarks that expediency-founded ethics are less reliable factors in performance than are those founded in tradition. It results that even to some extent in short-run face-to-face dealings, and *a fortiori* and importantly in long-run ones, legal enforceability figures as an element of added security in credit matters; a partial insurance against the very case of need: when credit-judgment was misguided, or in case of death or assignment, or where supervening troubles disrupt either willingness or power to perform.

Stewart Macaulay, *The Use and Non-Use of Contracts in the Manufacturing Industry*
9 PRAC. LAW. 14 (Nov. 1963)[116]

Some businessmen say their firms carefully plan everything and arrange their agreements so they are legally enforceable contracts. But even these firms seldom use their legal rights openly. They are not going to sue anyone or threaten to do so, except in extraordinary situations. The contract remains in the background as a handy club to hold in reserve, in case it is necessary.

However, most firms I've seen do not plan this carefully, except in rare situations, and most are not concerned with legal sanctions. Important agreements often are worked out by the businessmen representing the buyer and the seller. Then an attorney is called in and told to draft something. He is given an hour or an afternoon for what should be several days' careful work. He is told, or he understands without being told, that he is not to "make it complicated." He is not going to be popular if he tries to make the businessmen "work out all the details." Too often the attorney discovers that the businessmen really have not reached agreement on the difficult issues, but have ignored them to avoid argument. If he wakes these sleeping dogs, he may cause his client to lose a bargain that his client thinks is a good one. If he drafts an ambiguous document avoiding hard issues, he exposes his client to serious risks, and his client will hold him responsible if any of the risks should materialize.

---

[116] 9 PRACTICAL LAWYER 14, 14–18 (Nov. 1963). Reprinted with permission from the American Law Institute — American Bar Association.

Alternatively, an attorney is not consulted at all at the planning stage. One businessman may write a letter with a proposal that is accepted by the other businessman. The letter will cover anything directly and immediately related to money, but little else. Or the businessmen may agree orally, and one may write a confirming letter stating his interpretation of their agreement. Often the one receiving such a letter remains silent, thus manifesting either acceptance of the interpretation in the confirmation, or complete disagreement and a refusal even to continue negotiations. Even when it is clear that the confirmation has been accepted, such letters are often terse and ambiguous. . . .

When disputes occur, there is a hesitancy to use legal sanctions or even to refer to the contract. Businessmen try to "work things out without bringing lawyers into it." Contract lawsuits and appellate cases concerning contract problems are relatively rare.

Why Business Can and Does Ignore Contract

Businessmen can deal without contract for obvious reasons. They have little, if any, trouble, even if they run risks of trouble. It is in the interest of everyone to perform agreements. There are personal relationships between buyers and sellers on all levels of the two corporations. Purchasing agents know salesmen, corporate presidents know corporate presidents, and so forth. This creates an incentive to get along in a continuing relationship. Most importantly, the two businesses want to do business in the future. You don't get repeat orders from unsatisfied customers, and one's reputation can influence future business if word gets around. And word does get around.

Using contract, of course, can have a number of disadvantages. If, in planning a business transaction, one is going to mention all the horrible things that can happen, he may scare off the other side so that the deal is lost. If one does set up a contractual relationship, there is some risk that one will get only performance to the letter of the contract most narrowly construed. Conversely, there is also a risk that one will be held to the letter of the contract and lose "flexibility." Using legal sanctions for breach of contract to settle disputes is costly. Usually it ends the business relationship between the parties. Furthermore, I need not tell you that lawsuits and lawyers cost money.

Of course, there is some use of legal sanctions. Typically, this occurs when someone with power thinks the gains from proceeding this way outweigh the costs. Often this is the lawyer's view, but lawyers do not always get to run their clients' affairs in the way lawyers might wish to run them.

G.   THE RELIANCE INTEREST

Contract remedies could, and sometimes do, seek to protect the _reliance interest_. Rather than trying to put aggrieved parties where they would have been had their contracts been performed, judges applying contract law might seek to compensate victims of breach for out-of-pocket losses. That is, rather than trying to approximate the situation had there been no breach, a court could instead seek to compensate for losses caused by reliance on the contract.

Suppose, for example, Buyer, thinking he has a contract with Seller, makes expenditures in order to *unlock the value* of Seller's performance. Seller is to supply a machine tool that will produce a widget. Buyer orders a special type of steel which the machine will process. When Seller defaults, Buyer has to pay for the steel. However, Buyer now has no machine with which to turn it into something that can be sold (and cannot readily obtain a substitute machine). If Buyer must pay to cancel the contract with the steel supplier or if Buyer must resell steel that has been delivered at a loss, Buyer has suffered financial injury. This injury would be considered a reliance loss.

Finally, there is another kind of reliance loss that is a necessary consequence of most contracts. Buyer, thinking he has a contract with Seller, does not continue to seek contracts to supply his need from other sellers. (Recall that Shirley MacLaine gave up the chance to make a million-dollar deal to star in *Casino Royale* for Columbia because she had a contract with Twentieth Century-Fox to play Evelina in *Bloomer Girl*). This costs the buyer the chance to find out whether other suppliers would produce the machine or, indeed, supply a better one more cheaply. This kind of reliance loss is often called the reliance of lost opportunities. In most cases whether there is such a reliance loss, as well as its extent, is not susceptible to exact proof.

To what extent, if at all, does American law protect the reliance interest? If one had asked the question in the early 1930s, she would discover that American law had no theory that directly protected the reliance interest as such. Of course, a remedy protecting the expectation interest often compensates for some kinds of reliance loss. Suppose a court awards a builder, for example, damages which consist of his lost net profit plus what he has spent trying to perform before the owner's breach. This remedy covers at least some of the builder's reliance loss as part of protecting his expectation interest.[117] However, many American lawyers before the mid-1930s would have seen compensation solely for reliance losses as applying a *tort* measure of damages to a *contracts* action, something illogical and foreign to the common law.

In 1936, Professors Lon L. Fuller and William Perdue published *The Reliance Interest in Contracts Damages.*[118] To simplify only a little, they looked at continental European legal systems and found that they often protected losses in reliance on contracts. They then looked at the common law and asked to what extent it offered such protection directly or indirectly. They were able to find some cases where our courts protected the reliance interest, although many seemed to involve instances where courts had just acted without analyzing what they were doing very carefully. Fuller and Perdue also argued that the law ought to protect the reliance

---

[117] We can illustrate this by assuming a contract to construct a building for $100,000. After the builder has spent $40,000 performing, the owner breaches the contract by stopping construction. Had the builder completed the structure, he would have spent an additional $35,000 for a total of $75,000 to complete the job. A court protects the expectation interest by awarding the builder the contract price less the cost of completion ($100,000 − $35,000 = $65,000). This award gives the builder the equivalent of the net profit he would have made ($100,000 − [$40,000 + $35,000 = $75,000] = $25,000) plus what he has lost relying on the contract and trying to perform it ($40,000). The $40,000 is a reliance loss included within the expectation recovery.

[118] 46 YALE L.J. 52 (1936–37).

interest in many situations, but it should do so openly by creating a new theory of contracts damages.

Fuller and Perdue's article has been very influential.[119] Many contracts scholars accept their classification. The Restatement (Second) of Contracts states the argument of the article in code-like form. Law students have been taught the vocabulary of the article. Courts have begun to accept this part of the legal culture. However, recovery of reliance damages has been limited to out-of-pocket expenditures by the non-breaching party. There are no cases allowing recovery, as reliance damages, of the value of opportunities foregone in reliance on a contract that was later breached.

In the next few pages we will examine the idea of the reliance interest so we can understand the concept, considering what we can say for and against offering legal protection for some or all of the reliance interest. Why does protecting the reliance interest matter, and to whom? Are the courts likely to limit reliance recovery?

SECURITY STOVE & MANUFACTURING CO. v. AMERICAN RAILWAYS EXPRESS CO.
Missouri Court of Appeals
51 S.W.2d 572 (1932)

BLAND, J.

This is an action for damages for the failure of defendant to transport, from Kansas City to Atlantic City, New Jersey, within a reasonable time, a furnace equipped with a combination oil and gas burner. The cause was tried before the court without the aid of a jury, resulting in a judgment in favor of plaintiff in the sum of $801.50 and interest, or in a total sum of $1000. Defendant has appealed.

The facts show that plaintiff manufactured a furnace equipped with a special combination oil and gas burner it desired to exhibit at the American Gas Association Convention held in Atlantic City in October, 1926. The president of plaintiff testified that plaintiff engaged space for the exhibit for the reason "that the Henry L. Dougherty Company was very much interested in putting out a combination oil and gas burner; we had just developed one, after we got through, better than anything on the market and we thought this show would be the psychological time to get in contact with the Dougherty Company"; that "the thing wasn't sent there for sale but primarily to show"; that at the time the space was engaged it was too late to ship the furnace by freight so plaintiff decided to ship it by express, and, on September 18, 1926, wrote the office of the defendant in Kansas City, stating that it had engaged a booth for exhibition purposes at Atlantic City, New Jersey, from the

---

[119] Professor Richard Craswell has mounted an attack on Fuller and Perdue's article, arguing that it is not actually very helpful analytically, and doesn't accurately reflect the pattern of judicial decisions. *See* Richard Craswell, *Against Fuller and Perdue*, 67 U. CHI. L. REV. 99 (2000); *see also Symposium: W(h)ither the Reliance Interest?*, 38 SAN DIEGO L. REV. 1–230 (2001). While we found Craswell's attempt stimulating, we were unconvinced. But the fact that such an icon of scholarship can be challenged is an important reminder of the fact that contract scholarship, like all legal scholarship, presents endless opportunities for argument and re-examination.

American Gas Association, for the week beginning October 11th; that its exhibition consisted of an oil-burning furnace, together with two oil burners which weighed at least 1500 pounds; that, "In order to get this exhibit in place on time it should be in Atlantic City not later than October the 8th. What we want you to do is to tell us how much time you will require to assure the delivery of the exhibit on time."

Mr. Bangs, chief clerk in charge of the local office of the defendant, upon receipt of the letter, sent Mr. Johnson, a commercial representative of the defendant, to see plaintiff. Johnson called upon plaintiff taking its letter with him. Johnson made a notation at the bottom of the letter giving October 4th as the day that defendant was required to have the exhibit in order for it to reach Atlantic City on October 8th.

On October 1st, plaintiff wrote the defendant at Kansas City, referring to its letter of September 18th, concerning the fact that the furnace must be in Atlantic City not later than October 8th, and stating what Johnson had told it, saying: "Now, Mr. Bangs, we want to make doubly sure that this shipment is in Atlantic City not later than October 8th and the purpose of this letter is to tell you that you can *have your truck call for the shipment between 12 and 1 o'clock on Saturday, October 2nd for this.*" (Italics plaintiff's.) On October 2nd, plaintiff called the office of the express company in Kansas City and told it that the shipment was ready. Defendant came for the shipment on the last mentioned day, received it, and delivered the express receipt to plaintiff. The shipment contained twenty-one packages. Each package was marked with stickers backed with glue and covered with silica of soda, to prevent the stickers being torn off in shipping. Each package was given a number. They ran from one to twenty-one.

Plaintiff's president made arrangements to go to Atlantic City to attend the convention and install the exhibit, arriving there about October 11th. When he reached Atlantic City he found the shipment had been placed in the booth that had been assigned to plaintiff. The exhibit was set up, but it was found that one of the packages shipped was not there. This missing package contained the gas manifold, or that part of the oil and gas burner that controlled the flow of gas in the burner. This was the most important part of the exhibit and a like burner could not be obtained in Atlantic City.

Wires were sent and it was found that the stray package was at the "over and short bureau" of defendant in St. Louis. Defendant reported that the package would be forwarded to Atlantic City and would be there by Wednesday, the 13th. Plaintiff's president waited until Thursday, the day the convention closed, but the package had not arrived at the time, so he closed up the exhibit and left. About a week after he arrived in Kansas City, the package was returned by the defendant.

Bangs testified that the reasonable time for a shipment of this kind to reach Atlantic City from Kansas City would be four days; that if the shipment was received on October 4th, it would reach Atlantic City by October 8th; that plaintiff did not ask defendant for any special rate; that the rate charged was the regular one; that plaintiff asked no special advantage in the shipment; that all defendant, under its agreement with plaintiff, was required to do was to deliver the shipment at Atlantic City in the ordinary course of events; that the shipment was found in St. Louis about Monday afternoon or Tuesday morning; that it was delivered at Atlantic City at the Ritz Carlton Hotel, on the 16th of the month. There was evidence on plaintiff's part that the reasonable time for a shipment of this character to reach Atlantic City from Kansas City was not more than three or four days. . . .

Plaintiff asked damages, which the court in its judgment allowed as follows: $147 express charges (on the exhibit); $45.12 freight on the exhibit from Atlantic City to Kansas City; $101.39 railroad and Pullman fares to and from Atlantic City, expended by plaintiff's president and a workman taken by him to Atlantic City; $48 hotel room for the two; $150 for the time of the president; $40 for wages of the plaintiff's other employee, and $270 for rental of the booth, making a total of $801.51.

Defendant contends that its instructions in the nature of demurrers to the evidence should have been given for the reason that the petition and plaintiff's evidence show that plaintiff has based its cause of action on defendant's breach of a promise to deliver the shipment at a specified time and that promise is non-enforceable and void under the Interstate Commerce Act; that the court erred in allowing plaintiff's expenses as damages; that the only damages, if any, that can be recovered in cases of this kind, are for loss of profits and that plaintiff's evidence is not sufficient to base any recovery on this ground. It is well established that a shipper cannot recover on a special contract to move a shipment within a specified time, for such would work an unjust discrimination among shippers. The only duty that the carrier is under is to carry the shipment safely and to deliver it at its destination within a reasonable time.

While the petition alleges that defendant agreed to deliver the shipment at Atlantic City on or before October 8, 1926, it also alleges that this was the reasonable and proper time necessary to transport said shipment to Atlantic City. Therefore, giving the petition a liberal construction, it would appear that all that plaintiff was contending therein was that defendant had agreed to transport the shipment within a reasonable time, and that delivery on or before October 8th was necessary to comply with the agreement. . . .

There is nothing in the evidence tending to show any unjust discrimination between shippers in the agreement had between plaintiff and defendant. Boiled down to its last analysis, the agreement was nothing more than that the shipment would be transported within the ordinary time. Plaintiff sought no special advantage, was asking nothing that would be denied any other shipper, was asking no particular route, no particular train, nor for any expedited service. It was simply seeking the same rights any other shipper could have enjoyed on the same terms. No special instructions were given or involved in the case.

We think, under the circumstances in this case, that it was proper to allow plaintiff's expenses as its damages. Ordinarily the measure of damages where the carrier fails to deliver a shipment at destination within a reasonable time is the difference between the market value of the goods at the time of the delivery and the time when they should have been delivered. But where the carrier has notice of peculiar circumstances under which the shipment is made, which will result in an unusual loss by the shipper in case of delay in delivery, the carrier is responsible for the real damage sustained from such delay if the notice given is of such character, and goes to such extent, in informing the carrier of the shipper's situation, that the carrier will be presumed to have contracted with reference thereto.

In the case at bar defendant was advised of the necessity of prompt delivery of the shipment. Plaintiff explained to Johnson the "importance of getting the exhibit there on time." Defendant knew the purpose of the exhibit and ought to respond for its negligence in failing to get it there. As we view the record this negligence is practically conceded. The undisputed testimony shows that the shipment was sent to the over and short department of the defendant in St. Louis. As the packages were plainly numbered this, *prima facie*, shows mistake or negligence on the part of the defendant. No effort was made by it to show that it was not negligent in sending it there, or not negligent in not forwarding it within a reasonable time after it was found.

There is no evidence or claim in this case that plaintiff suffered any loss of profits by reason of the delay in the shipment. In fact defendant states in its brief:

> The plaintiff introduced not one whit of evidence showing or tending to show that he would have made any sales as a result of his exhibit but for the negligence of the defendant. On the contrary Blakesley testified that the main purpose of the exhibit was to try to interest the Henry L. Dougherty Company in plaintiff's combination oil and gas burner, yet that was all the evidence that there was as to the benefit plaintiff expected to get from the exhibit.

> As a matter of evidence, it is clear that the plaintiff would not have derived a great deal of benefit from the exhibit by any stretch of the imagination. . . .

> Nowhere does plaintiff introduce evidence showing that the Henry L. Dougherty Company in all probability would have become interested in the combination oil and gas burner and made a profitable contract with the plaintiff.

There is evidence that the exhibit was not sent to make a sale.

In support of its contention that plaintiff can sue only for loss of profit, if anything, in a case of this kind, defendant, among other cases, cites that of *Adams Exp. Co. v. Egbert*, 36 Pa. 360 (1860). That case involved the shipment of a box containing architectural drawings or plans for a building, to a building committee of the Touro Aimshouse, in New Orleans. This committee had offered a premium of $500 to the successful competitor. These plans arrived after the various plans had been passed upon and the award made to another person. It was sought in that case to recover the value of the plans. The evidence, however, showed that the plans would not have won the prize had they arrived on time. The court held that the plans, under the circumstances, had no appreciable value and recovery could not be had for them and there was no basis for recovery for loss of the opportunity to compete for the prize. . . .

Defendant contends that plaintiff "is endeavoring to achieve a return of the *status quo* in a suit based on a breach of contract. Instead of seeking to recover what he would have had, had the contract not been broken, plaintiff is trying to recover what he would have had, had there never been any contract of shipment"; that the expenses sued for would have been incurred in any event. It is no doubt, the general rule that where there is a breach of contract the party suffering the loss can recover only that which he would have had, had the contract not been broken, and this is all the cases decided upon which defendant relies. . . . But this is merely a general statement of the rule and is not inconsistent with the holdings that, in some instances, the injured party may recover expenses incurred in relying upon the contract, although such expenses would have been incurred had the contract not been breached.

In *Sperry et al. v. O'Neill-Adams Co.*, 185 Fed. 231, the court held that the advantages resulting from the use of trading stamps as a means of increasing trade are so contingent that they cannot form a basis on which to rest a recovery for a breach of contract to supply them. In lieu of compensation based thereon the court directed a recovery in the sum expended in preparation for carrying on business in connection with the use of the stamps. The court said:

> Plaintiff in its complaint had made a claim for lost profits, but, finding it impossible to marshal any evidence which would support a finding of exact figures, abandoned that claim. Any attempt to reach a precise sum would be mere blind guesswork. Nevertheless a contract, which both sides conceded would prove a valuable one, had been broken and the party who broke it was responsible for resultant damage. In order to carry out this contract, the plaintiff made expenditures which otherwise it would not have made. . . . The trial judge held, as we think rightly, that plaintiff was entitled at least to recover these expenses to which it had been put in order to secure the benefits of a contract of which defendant's conduct deprived it. . . .

The case at bar was not to recover damages for loss of profits by reason of the failure of the defendant to transport the shipment within a reasonable time, so that it would arrive in Atlantic City for the exhibit. There were no profits contemplated. The furnace was to be shown and shipped back to Kansas City. There was no money loss, except the expenses, that was of such a nature as any court would allow as being sufficiently definite or lacking in pure speculation. Therefore, unless plaintiff is permitted to recover the expenses that it went to, which were a total loss to it by reason of its inability to exhibit the furnace and equipment, it will be deprived of any substantial compensation for its loss. The law does not contemplate any such injustice. It ought to allow plaintiff, as damages, the loss in the way of expenses that it sustained, and which it would not have been put to if it had not been for its reliance upon the defendant to perform its contract. There is no contention that the exhibit would have been entirely valueless and whatever it might have accomplished, defendant knew of the circumstances and ought to respond for whatever damages plaintiff suffered. In cases of this kind the method of estimating the damages should be adopted which is the most definite and certain and which best achieves the fundamental purpose of compensation.

Had the exhibit been shipped in order to realize a profit on sales and such profits could have been realized, or to be entered in competition for a prize, and plaintiff failed to show loss of profits with sufficient definiteness, or that he would have won the prize, defendant's cases might be in point. But as before stated, no such situation exists here.

While it is true that plaintiff already had incurred some of these expenses, in that it had rented space at the exhibit before entering into the contract with defendant for the shipment of the exhibit and this part of plaintiff's damages, in a sense, arose out of a circumstance which transpired before the contract was even entered into, yet, plaintiff arranged for the exhibit knowing that it could call upon defendant to perform its common law duty to accept and transport the shipment with reasonable dispatch. The whole damage, therefore, was suffered in contemplation of defendant performing its contract, which it failed to do, and would not have been sustained except for the reliance by plaintiff upon defendant to perform it. It can, therefore, be fairly said that the damages or loss suffered by plaintiff grew out of the breach of the contract, for had the shipment arrived on time, plaintiff would have had the benefit of the contract, which was contemplated by all parties, defendant being advised of the purpose of the shipment.

The judgment is affirmed. All concur.

NOTES AND QUESTIONS

1. *The briefs and record in the* Security Stove *case:* Both sides spent a great deal of time on research and argued their positions in the *Security Stove* case very well. This is, perhaps, surprising in view of the small stakes involved. The court awarded $800 damages plus interest, bringing the judgment to $1000. American Railways Express filed a brief and summary of the record of 104 pages; Security Stove responded with a 44-page brief; and American Railways Express's reply brief was 12 pages.

Security Stove was organized in 1926, the year the Express Company delayed the essential part of the shipment. Thus, Security Stove was a classic new business. The novel idea in Security Stove's furnace was that "it was so designed that by pulling a switch you could change from oil to gas or back from gas to oil." The gas manifold was the part that controlled the flow of natural gas in the burner. It was the key piece that did not arrive in Atlantic City for the trade show.

American Railways Express argued that Security Stove was suing on a special contract to deliver on time, and the Interstate Commerce Commission's rules specifically barred such contracts. These rules prevented a "common carrier," such as Railways Express, from offering services to one customer that were not available at similar prices to the general public. Security Stove responded by denying it was seeking to enforce a special contract. "Plaintiff asked for no service not open to all. . . ." Rather, it sued on the common law duty of a carrier to carry all goods with reasonable dispatch and without delay, a rule not changed by the Interstate Commerce Act. There was no agreement to rush its shipment, no special instruction.

On the issue of damages, the American Railways Express lawyers argued, "Blakesley [Security Stove's president] himself admitted that he would have had to pay these expenses [which Security Stove recovered as damages] anyway if there had been no breach of contract. . . . Instead of seeking to recover what he would have had, had the contract not been broken, plaintiff is trying to recover what he would have had, had there never been any contract of shipment. . . . " In its reply brief, the American Railways Express lawyers made the same point in different words: "[The] items of damage which plaintiff seeks to recover are not proper items of damage because the plaintiff did not incur its expenses by reason of the breach of contract. . . . [T]he only thing the plaintiff can recover in an action like this one is the loss of profits." American Railways went on to argue that there was no evidence that Railway Express would have made any profits from the exhibit.

> Nowhere does plaintiff introduce evidence showing that the Henry L. Dougherty Company in all probability would have become interested in the combination oil and gas burner and made a profitable contract with the plaintiff. . . . What the plaintiff actually lost as a result of defendant's breach of contract to deliver on or before October 8 was the benefit of the exhibit, but the plaintiff introduces no evidence whatsoever to determine as a matter of law just what that benefit was. There is absolutely no evidence beyond a mere possibility tending to show that the plaintiff would have made $800 out of the exhibit but for the defendant's breach of contract.

Security Stove's lawyers argued that it was not established that Security Stove's exhibit would have been valueless:

> Clearly, had Mr. Blakesley known that he could not have made his exhibit, he would not have gone to Atlantic City. Neither would he have sent Mr. Lundgren to Atlantic City. The chance to make the exhibit was ruined by the failure of the defendant to perform the duty imposed upon it by law, to wit: To deliver the shipment within a reasonable time. They had ample notice that special damages would result from their failure to deliver within a reasonable time.

2. *Reliance damages and disclaimers:* Had the events in the *Security Stove* case taken place today, Security Stove might have shipped its exhibit by a small package air freight service such as Federal Express. The terms on Federal Express's 2012 airbill (in Note 5 following *Hadley v. Baxendale*) disclaim liability for consequential damages. If there had been such a clause in American Railways Express's contract, and the clause was enforceable as written, would it have changed the result in the case?

3. *Is* **Security Stove** *the law? Where?* The *Security Stove* case's history is odd. It is a decision by a relatively obscure court. Judges and lawyers might give some extra weight to a commercial law decision by the United States Court of Appeals for the Second Circuit, the Court of Appeals of New York, or, perhaps, the Supreme Court of California. However, few who practice outside of Missouri (and perhaps even few who practice in Missouri but not in Kansas City) pay much attention to the Kansas City Court of Appeals. According to Shepard's Citator, the *Security Stove* decision has been cited in only 10 other cases as of September 2015. The most recent citation is in *Westfed Holdings, Inc. v. United States*, 52 Fed. Cl. 135 (2002).

On the other hand, when we turn to the law of the law schools, the picture changes. Of 14 contracts casebooks we checked in 1993, the case was a principal case in four, and a note case in four more. As of 2015 it had been cited in 27 law review articles. Indeed, it even appears in Ian Macneil, *Contracts: Instruments for Social Cooperation — East Africa* (1968), a casebook written for use in East Africa. The case appears to have been the discovery of Fuller and Perdue in their influential article *The Reliance Interest in Contracts Damages: 1.*[120] What, if anything, is the significance of academic contract law? Does it matter to anyone who is not a law professor or a law student? In what ways and to what extent?

L. ALBERT & SON v. ARMSTRONG RUBBER CO.
United States Court of Appeals, Second Circuit
178 F.2d 182 (1949)

L. HAND, C.J.

Both sides appeal from the judgment in an action brought by the Albert Company, which we shall speak of as the Seller, against the Armstrong Company, which we shall call the Buyer. The action was to recover the agreed price of four "Refiners," machines designed to recondition old rubber; the contract of sale was by an exchange of letters in December, 1942, and the Seller delivered two of the four Refiners in August, 1943, and the other two on either August 31st or September 8th, 1945. Because of the delay in delivery of the second two, the Buyer refused to accept all four in October, 1945 — the exact day not being fixed — and it counterclaimed for the Seller's breach. The judge dismissed both the complaint and the counterclaim; but he gave judgment to the Seller for the value without interest of a part of the equipment delivered — a 300-horsepower motor and accessories — which the Buyer put into use on February 20th, 1946. On the appeal the Seller's position is that its delay was not too long; that in any event the Buyer accepted delivery of the four Refiners; and that they were in accordance with the specifications. As an alternative it insists that the Buyer is liable, not only for the value of the motor, but for interest upon it; and, as to the counterclaim, that the Buyer proved no damages, assuming that there was a breach. The judge found that all four Refiners conformed to the specifications, or could have been made to do so with slight trouble and expense; that the contract was inseparable and called for four, not two and two; that the delivery of the second two was too late; and that, as the Buyer rejected all four, it was not liable on the contract at all. On the other hand, as we have said, he found that the Buyer's use for its own purposes of the motor, although not an acceptance of the Refiners, made it liable for the value of the motor in quasi-contract, but without interest. He dismissed the Buyer's counterclaim because it had failed to prove any damages.

The first issue is whether the Seller's delivery of the second two Refiners was too late, and justified the Buyer's rejection of all four in October of that year. [Eds. note: We have omitted discussion of this issue. The Court upheld the trial court's determination.]

Upon the Seller's appeal there remains only the question whether it was entitled to interest upon the value of the motor and its accessories, which the judge denied. The Buyer's use of his property was indeed a conversion, for which the Seller might sue in quasi-contract, as it did; and the judge found that the motor, although it was secondhand machinery originally, had a "fair market value of $4,590." We follow the law of Connecticut upon the point, and we read *Regan v. New York & New England*

---

[120] 46 YALE L.J. 52, 88 n.57, 91 n.63 (1936).

Ry. Co. and *Healy v. Fallon* as establishing the principle that, when the value of goods can be "ascertained with reasonable certainty as of a definite time," interest should be recovered, *Regan v. New York & New England Ry. Co.*, 60 Conn. 124, 22 A.503, 25 Am. St. Rep. 306; *Healy v. Fallon*, 69 Conn. 228, 37 A.495. Hence we hold that the Seller should have been awarded interest on the value of the motor and its accessories from the date of the Buyer's appropriation — February 20th, 1946.

Coming next to the Buyer's appeal, it does not claim any loss of profit, but it does claim that expenses which it incurred in reliance upon the Seller's promise. These were of three kinds: its whole investment in its "reclaim department," $118,478; the cost of its "rubber scrap," $27,555.63; the cost of the foundation which it laid for the Refiners, $3,000. The judge in his opinion held that the Buyer had not proved that "the lack of production" of the reclaim department "was caused by the delay in delivery of plaintiff's refiners"; but that that was "only one of several possible causes. Such a possibility is not sufficient proof of causation to impose liability on the plaintiffs for the cost of all machinery and supplies for the reclaim department." The record certainly would not warrant our holding that this holding was "clearly erroneous"; indeed, the evidence preponderates in its favor. The Buyer disposed of all its "scrap rubber" in April and May, 1945; and, so far as appears, until it filed its counterclaim in May, 1947, it never suggested that the failure to deliver two of the four Refiners was the cause of the collapse of its "reclaim department." The counterclaim for these items has every appearance of being an afterthought, which can scarcely have been put forward with any hope of success.

The claim for the cost of the foundation which the Buyer built for the Refiners stands upon a different footing. Normally a promisee's damages for breach of contract are the value of the promised performance, less his outlay, which includes, not only what he must pay to the promisor, but any expenses necessary to prepare for the performance; and in the case at bar the cost of the foundation was such an expense. The sum which would restore the Buyer to the position it would have been in, had the Seller performed, would therefore be the prospective net earnings of the Refiners while they were used (together with any value they might have as scrap after they were discarded) less their price — $25,500 — together with $3,000, the cost of installing them. The Buyer did not indeed prove the net earnings of the Refiners or their scrap value; but it asserts that it is nonetheless entitled to recover the cost of the foundation upon the theory that what it expended in reliance upon the Seller's performance was a recoverable loss. In cases where the venture would have proved profitable to the promisee, there is no reason why he should not recover his expenses. On the other hand, on those occasions in which the performance would not have covered the promisee's outlay, such a result imposes the risk of the promisee's contract upon the promisor. We cannot agree that the promisor's default in performance should under this guise make him an insurer of the promisee's venture; yet it does not follow that the breach should not throw upon him the duty of showing that the value of the performance would in fact have been less than the promisee's outlay. It is often very hard to learn what the value of the performance would have been; and it is a common expedient, and a just one, in such situations to put the peril of the answer upon that party who by his wrong had made the issue relevant to the rights of the other. [Footnote omitted.] On principle therefore the proper solution would seem to be that the promisee may recover his outlay in preparation for the performance, subject to the privilege of the promisor to reduce it by as much as he can show that the promisee would have lost, if the contract had been performed.

The decisions leave much to be desired. There is language in *United States v. Behan* which, read literally, would allow the promisee to recover his outlay in all cases: the promisor is said to be "estopped" to deny that the value of the performance would not equal it. 110 U.S. 338, 345–46, 4 S. Ct. 81, 28 L. Ed. 168 (1884). We doubt whether the Supreme Court would today accept the explanation, although the result was right under the rule which we propose. Moreover, in spite of the authority properly accorded to any decision of that court, we are here concerned only with Connecticut law; and the decisions in that state do not seem to be in entire accord. In the early case of *Bush v. Canfield*, the buyer sued to recover a payment of $5,000 made in advance for the purchase of 2,000 barrels of flour at $7.00 a barrel. 2 Conn. 485 (1818). Although at the time set for delivery the value of the flour had fallen to $5.50, the seller for some undisclosed reason failed to perform. The . . . court, HOSMER, J., dissenting, allowed the buyer to recover the full amount of his payment over the seller's objection that recovery should be reduced by the buyer's loss. The Chief Justice gave the following reason for his decision which we take to be that of the court, 2 Conn. at 488: "The defendant has violated his contract; and it is not for him to say that if he had fulfilled it, the plaintiffs would have sustained a great loss, and that this ought to be deducted from the money advanced." If there is no difference between the recovery of money received by a promisor who later defaults, and a promisee's outlay preparatory to performance, this decision is in the Buyer's favor. However, when the promisor has received any benefit, the promisee's recovery always depends upon whether the promisor has been "unjustly enriched"; and, judged by that nebulous standard, there may be a distinction between imposing the promisee's loss on the promisor by compelling him to disgorge what he has received and compelling him to pay what he never has received. It is quite true that the only difference is between allowing the promisee to recover what he has paid to the promisor and what he has paid to others; but many persons would probably think that difference vital.

In any event, unless this be a valid distinction, it appears to us that *Santoro v. Mack*, 108 Conn. 683, 145 A.273 (1929), must be read as taking the opposite view. The plaintiff, the vendee under a contract for the sale of land, had paid an electrician and an architect whom he had employed in reliance upon the promised conveyance. These payments he sought to recover, and was unsuccessful on the ground that they had not benefited the vendor, and that they had been incurred without the vendor's knowledge or consent. Yet it would seem that such expenses were as much in reasonable preparation for the use of the land, as the cost of the foundation was for the use of the Refiners. The point now before us was apparently not raised, but the decision, as it stands, seems to deny any recovery whatever. . . .

The result is equally inconclusive if we consider the few decisions in other jurisdictions. The New Jersey Court of Errors and Appeals in *Holt v. United Security Life Insurance & Trust Co.*, 76 N.J.L. 585, 72 A.301 (1909), recognized as the proper rule that, although the promisor had the burden of proving that the value of the performance was less than the promisee's outlay, if he succeeded in doing so, the recovery would be correspondingly limited. In *Bernstein v. Meech*, 130 N.Y. 354,

360, 29 N.E. 255, 257 (1891), the promisee recovered his full outlay, and no limitation upon it appears to have been recognized, as may be inferred from the following sentence: "it cannot be assumed that any part of this loss would have been sustained by the plaintiff if he had been permitted to perform his contract." In *Reynolds v. Levi*, 122 Mich. 115, 80 N.W. 999 (1899), the promisee was a well digger, who had made three unsuccessful efforts to reach water, and the promisor — a farmer — stopped him before he had completed his fourth. The court limited the recovery to the amount earned on the fourth attempt, but for reasons that are not apparent. It appears to us therefore that the reported decisions leave it open to us to adopt the rule we have stated. Moreover, there is support for this result in the writings of scholars. The Restatement of Contracts, § 333(d), allows recovery of the promisee's outlay "in necessary preparation" for the performance, subject to several limitations, of which one is that the promisor may deduct whatever he can prove the promisee would have lost, if the contract had been fully performed. Professor McCormick thinks that "the jury should be instructed not to go beyond the probable yield" of the performance to the promisee, but he does not consider the burden of proof. McCormick, Damages, § 142, p. 584. Much the fullest discussion of the whole subject is Professor Fuller's in the *Yale Law Journal*.[121] The situation at bar was among those which he calls cases of "essential reliance," and for which he favors the rule we are adopting. It is one instance of his "very simple formula: We will not in a suit for reimbursement of losses incurred in reliance on a contract knowingly put the plaintiff in a better position than he would have occupied, had the contract been fully performed."

The judgment will therefore be affirmed with the following modifications. To the allowance for the motor and accessories will be added interest from February 20th, 1946. The Buyer will be allowed to set off $3,000 against the Seller's recovery with interest from October, 1945, subject to the Seller's privilege to deduct from that amount any sum which upon a further hearing it can prove would have been the buyer's loss upon the contract, had the Refiners been delivered on or before May 1st, 1945.

Judgment modified as above, and affirmed as so modified.

NOTES AND QUESTIONS

1.   *Judge Hand and the law of Connecticut:* Once again we read an opinion of a federal court deciding a case brought to it under diversity of citizenship jurisdiction. Under *Erie Railroad Co. v. Tompkins*, 304 U.S. 64 (1938), the federal court should apply state law. In his *L. Albert & Son* opinion, Judge Hand discusses *Bush v. Canfield* and *Santoro v. Mack* in some detail. He concludes: "It appears to us . . . that the reported decisions leave it open to us to adopt the rule we have stated." Has Judge Hand successfully distinguished *Bush v. Canfield* and *Santoro v. Mack* from the case he was deciding? Can you think of distinctions he might have suggested but did not? Consider *Hadley v. Baxendale, supra.*

2.   *The Restatement view:* The Restatement (Second) appears to embody the

Learned Hand limitation on recovery of reliance expenses as set out in the *L. Albert* case:

Restatement (Second) of Contracts

§ 349. Damages based on reliance interest.

As an alternative to the measure of damages stated in § 347 [essentially, protection of the expectation interest], the injured party has a right to damages based on his reliance interest, including expenditures made in preparation for performance or in performance, less any loss that the party in breach can prove with reasonable certainty the injured party would have suffered had the contract been performed.

Illustrations:

4. A contracts to sell his retail store to B. After B has spent $100,000 for inventory, A repudiates the contract and B sells the inventory for $60,000. If neither party proves with reasonable certainty what profit or loss B would have made if the contract had been performed, B can recover as damages the $40,000 loss that he sustained on the sale of the inventory.

3. *Judge Hand and causation:* Judge Hand says that there was no merit in buyer's claim for its investment in the "reclaim department" and for the rubber scrap. What is his reasoning? Is Judge Hand consistent in his denial of recovery of these items while allowing recovery for buyer's investment in the foundation, subject to seller's right to show that the investment would have been a loss if there had been no breach? Does Judge Hand seem to impose *on the buyer* the burden of proof of showing that the investment in the "reclaim department" and the rubber scrap would not have been lost if there had been no breach, whereas with respect to the foundation he imposes that burden on the seller?

In thinking about these questions, it might be helpful to ask whether if there had been no contract at all buyer would have made the investment in (1) the reclaim department, (2) the rubber scrap, or (3) the foundations. Suppose the investment in (1) and (2) would have been made even if seller had refused to enter into any contract at all with buyer, whereas the investment in (3) was made only because of the contract. Then one could argue that the investments in (1) and (2) were not "caused" by the contract, whereas the investment in (3) would not have been made but for the contract. Should that have any bearing on the decision in this case? It is still possible, of course, that but for the contract, the buyer would have made some other deal to acquire machines to process rubber scrap that would have enabled it to make an overall profit on its total investment.

Some World War II history may provide some context for answering these questions. When the Japanese won their early victories in Southeast Asia, they cut off most American supplies of natural rubber. While German technology had developed synthetic rubber, the United States was far behind in developing it. Reclaimed rubber was a costly way to produce an inferior substitute. As the war went on, American technology developed synthetic rubber. As Allied victories pushed the Japanese back from Southeast Asia, America regained supplies of natural rubber. Thus, had the seller delivered the machines on time, what would have been the likely position of the buyer toward the end of the war? There was a market for reclaimed rubber both before and after World War II, but the demand was nothing like that in the early wartime period.

The seller's brief tells us more about this issue:

> From the evidence, largely out of the mouths of the defendant's own officers, it appeared that the defendant did not try very hard to put its reclaiming department in operation. It had just a few men working on one shift, while the rest of its factory was working 24 hours a day. After a small experimental output, the department was disbanded. While the defendant originally relied upon getting the refiners from the plaintiff to start production in this department, it duplicated its order by securing the four so-called Stuart-Bolling refiners from another party. If it really wanted to reclaim rubber, it had all the equipment it needed. . . . No witness ever intimated that the Stuart-Bolling refiners were not suitable for the purpose.

4. *Reliance damages, the UCC, and the paucity of cases:* If a court decided *L. Albert & Son v. Armstrong Rubber* today, Article 2 of the Uniform Commercial Code would apply. What result would it reach?

Perhaps the first question that should be asked is whether reliance expenditures that buyer sought to recover could be considered "consequential damages" under § 2-715(2)? There is no explicit definition of "consequential damages" in Article 2, but it is hard to imagine what else reliance damages could be.[122] If they were consequential damages, would the result in the case be the same as the result reached by Judge Hand? In particular, under the Code would the seller have the option of showing that the foundation expenditures would have been losses even if there had been no breach?

This question points to one of the more curious features of the remedies provisions of Article 2 — its failure to mention or provide specifically for recovery of reliance damages. Professor Michael T. Gibson studied all of the records of the American Law Institute dealing with the drafting of Article 2 of the UCC as well as Professor Llewellyn's papers related to Article 2.[123] There is no mention of reliance damages in either place, even though there is correspondence between Fuller and Llewellyn where they debated the arguments in Fuller's famous article, *The Reliance Interest in Contracts Damages.* Perhaps the explanation lies in the fact that there just are not very many cases in which a buyer sues only for reliance damages.[124] Suits for lost profits as consequential damages are much more

---

[122] It would not be appropriate to consider reliance damages like those claimed in *L. Albert & Son* to be incidental damages, as incidental damages are generally limited to post-breach expenditures for purposes of minimizing loss. Furthermore, UCC § 2-715(1), allowing recovery of incidental damages, does not establish any *Hadley v. Baxendale* limitations on recovery, whereas UCC § 2-715(2), allowing recovery of consequential damages, does contain such a limitation. It is clear there should be a foreseeability limitation on the recovery of reliance damages.

[123] Michael Gibson, *Reliance Damages in the Law of Sales Under Article 2 of the Uniform Commercial Code*, 29 ARIZ. ST. L.J. 909 (1997).

[124] Gibson found only 14 cases in which reliance damages were awarded, after studying 467 cases

common.

No case has yet addressed whether the UCC includes the limitation on reliance damages laid down in *L. Albert & Son* and endorsed by Restatement (Second), § 349 ("less any loss that the party in breach can prove with reasonable certainty the injured party would have suffered had the contract been performed"). Perhaps the limitation will be found implied by § 2-715(2)'s reference to "consequential damages *resulting from* the seller's breach" (emphasis added). If the reliance expenditures would have been losses notwithstanding the breach, perhaps they are not damages "resulting from" the breach. Alternatively, a court might imply such a limitation on reliance damages from UCC § 1-305(a), prohibiting the awarding of "penal" damages unless specifically authorized by the Code. There is no statutory definition of "penal" damages in the Code. Can you make an argument that to award recovery of reliance expenditures that would have been losses if there had been no breach is to award a "penal" recovery?

H. RESTITUTION AND EXIT AS ALTERNATIVE CONTRACT REMEDIES

1. Introduction

When the other party breaches your contract, you may want nothing more than to forget the whole thing. You may decide that the deal was not that good or another is better. You may think the costs of litigation will be too great. However, are you free to forget the whole thing? Sometimes yes, sometimes no. Much complicated law governs the right to exit. Here we introduce the problem and show some of the main approaches; in Volume II, Chapter 5, we return to this topic and cover it in much greater depth.

There is another closely related problem. You may want to forget the contract. However, you, as buyer, may have made a down payment or, as seller, delivered some or all of the goods. You want your money or your property back. Not surprisingly, there are legal remedies designed to get them back. Occasionally, these remedies may be more valuable than contract damages. For example, suppose you have sold what you thought was just an old book to someone for $5. However, the buyer fails to pay the $5. Then you discover that the book is a rare first edition of a classic. You may want to get the book back rather than be put where you would have been had the contract been performed. Can you do this?

Here we encounter the third and last of Fuller and Perdue's interests protected by contract remedies — the *restitution interest*. Restitution means, roughly, "to give back" or "to restore to a previous position." Fuller and Perdue note that we can see the restitution interest as a special case of the reliance interest. However, lawyers think the restitution situation often presents a stronger argument for relief. You, the breacher, are "unjustly enriched." I have relied on the contract and money or other assets have left my pocket. Moreover, they have ended up in your pocket. You have a gain while I have a loss. Restitutionary remedies are available in

---

involving the fact patterns most likely to produce reliance damages. *Id.* at 996.

many situations other than contract breaches. For example, I have a remedy to recover property from a thief, from one who has defrauded me, or from a trustee who has misused property which the trustee was to hold for my benefit. While all restitution situations are similar in some ways, they also differ. Restitution is a potential alternative remedy in many situations: breach of contract, mutual mistake, fraud, breach of fiduciary duty, and so on. But in each of these situations, the rules governing restitution may differ importantly.

We can illustrate some of the interplay between the expectation, reliance, and restitution interests with a simplified example. Suppose Seller contracts to deliver 3000 bushels of apples to Buyer for $8000. Buyer pays $1000 as a down payment. In anticipation of delivery Buyer hires two laborers to unload the apples, paying them $100 each in advance for their time. At the time for delivery, Buyer is ready and willing to pay the remaining $7000 to Seller, but Seller breaches the contract by refusing to deliver. The market price when Buyer learned of the breach is $9000. Buyer has no other work for the laborers to do, and sends them home. Buyer then arranges for purchase of more apples (at $9000), to replace those she did not obtain from Seller, and makes new arrangements to have them unloaded, but this time must pay two laborers $125 each. Buyer sues Seller.

(a) What recovery would protect Buyer's expectation interest? Her reliance interest? Her restitution interest? Are the interests mutually exclusive? Are they cumulative?

(b) What would Buyer recover under the Uniform Commercial Code? *See* §§ 2-711(1), 2-712.

(c) What would Buyer recover under the Uniform Commercial Code if the market price of apples had been $6000 at the time the Buyer learned of the breach, and the Buyer had purchased replacement apples for $6000? Recall Judge Hand's discussion of *Bush v. Canfield* in his *L. Albert & Son v. Armstrong Rubber Co.* opinion. Does this recovery protect the expectation, the reliance, or the restitution interest — or some combination of them? Compare UCC § 2-706(6), governing cases where the seller resells goods for more than the contract price. What if the buyer had chosen not to buy any replacement apples?

(d) What recovery in (c) if the buyer had chosen not to buy any replacement apples (but the facts are otherwise the same)?

2.   Walking Away From a Deal: Exit and Restitution

a.   Sales of goods

Exit and restitution are important remedies. Buyers often find exit and restitution important when they question a seller's performance. Even if the buyer finds that it would not pay to sue for the difference between the contract and cover price as damages, the right to exit allows him to avoid or minimize loss and go on about his business. Sellers, too, may value the right to walk away from a buyer who fails to make payments. Furthermore, parties may be able to threaten to cancel a contract as a tactic in negotiating settlements.

However, the law limits the use of these remedies. If a failure to perform is not important, then calling off a deal is a drastic therapy. Normally we expect, for example, a buyer to accept goods and deal with a minor defect in any of a number of ways. He can ask the seller to fix the defect. He can deduct a sum representing the cost of fixing the defect from his payment. He can accept all the good items and reject only the few bad ones. Indeed, if a buyer tries to exit when a seller's default is only trivial, we can suspect that defective performance is only a pretext. A book by Bertell Ollman, *Class Struggle is the Name of the Game*, illustrates the tactical advantages of exit and restitutionary remedies as well as suggesting why courts have not granted these remedies freely.

Ollman, a professor of politics, devised "Class Struggle," a board game designed to teach a Marxist perspective about capitalism. However, he and his friends who backed the game found that it had to be marketed through the capitalist system. In order to teach revolution, they had to play the role of entrepreneur. Initially, the game was a success. They sold more than 25,000 games in the first six months. Ollman and his friends then ordered 50,000 games from Bill Finn's company, which manufactured the board, the game pieces, and the boxes. They agreed to pay $160,000 and made a $65,000 down payment. This was a mistake. A lender decided that their accounts receivable did not warrant a loan, stores were slow in paying for games they had bought, Bloomingdale's in New York decided not to feature the game, and a customer in Holland who had asked for 5,000 games changed his mind. Finn demanded payment of the $95,000 balance due, but they did not have enough to pay him. "The whole business was about to come crashing down on our heads. Class Struggle was on the verge of bankruptcy."

Ollman, in the extract presented below, has just finished preparing the board of directors for the news that they would have to declare bankruptcy.

BERTELL OLLMAN, CLASS STRUGGLE IS THE NAME OF THE GAME: TRUE CONFESSIONS OF A MARXIST BUSINESSMAN
172–81, 201 (1983)[125]

But before I could continue, Paul interrupted. "Not yet. First, take a look at this." With that, he opened up a Class Struggle game box he was carrying, and took out two game boards. He pointed to the low ridge that followed the fold in the middle of the board. "These are the new boards. I picked them up in the factory today. The ridge in the middle is so high it disfigures the board. I also think these boards are a little lighter than the ones we got last time. Wasn't Finn supposed to give us the same board?" . . .

"Are they really that bad?" I asked. I could see what Paul was talking about, but the difference between the boards seemed to be very slight.

"I think so," Howard said angrily. "If I was a customer, I wouldn't buy a board like this."

"No, the real problem is not with customers," Paul corrected him, "but with store

---

[125] Copyright © 1983 by Bertell Ollman. Reprinted by permission of Harper Collins Publishers, William Morrow.

buyers. Some of them look the game over very carefully. They may be indifferent to its politics, but they want it to be well made. This sloppy manufacturing is going to turn them off." Paul spoke with great certainty, and then more tentatively. "A few of them, anyway."

"But they're already made, all fifty thousand of them." Ed shook his head in disgust.

"And we haven't paid for them." Howard finally spoke the words that we had all begun to think. "Izzy, what does our agreement with Finn say, I mean about this new edition?"

"That he produce the same game he did the last time. Yes," Izzy specified, noting the question in our eyes, "that means exactly the same."

"And if he doesn't?" Milt broke in before Izzy had a chance to finish.

"If he doesn't," Izzy continued, "I guess that means he is in breach of contract."

"Finn's about to sue us for the ninety-five thousand dollars we still owe him," I interjected. "That's the good news I was saving for tonight's meeting."

"Sue us? Sue us?" Howard shouted. "That bastard has just about destroyed our business by giving us a shoddy game. We should sue him for . . . for a million dollars." . . .

It was as if a great natural force, a hurricane or a river of lava, that was about to engulf us all had been stopped dead by Howard's words, and had now begun to recede. My tiredness, the tiredness of months, had given way to an energy, indeed an exhilaration. I thought I'd lost. This was, as they say, a new ball game. Finn had outsmarted himself. . . . He had given us something other than what we had contracted for. Whether customers were actually pressing us for games at this time was irrelevant. He had our sixty-five thousand dollars, and we had received nothing. . . .

The next day, Howard and I went to see Finn. . . . [They showed him the defect.]

"Look . . ." Finn shot back. "I've been making game boards for twenty years. I'm telling you there is nothing wrong with this board."

"The feel of a game, how heavy it is — and that includes how heavy the board is — all enter into the consciousness of a buyer." I said. "It's related to quality. The buyer for Toys-R-Us made a big point of this."

Finn's original defensiveness was now turning into annoyance. "This board is no lighter than the boards I make for Scrabble."

"Maybe so," Howard replied. "But as you can see, it is lighter than the board you made for the last edition of Class Struggle, and therefore it is lighter than the board you contracted to make this time."

With the mention of our contract, Finn flushed, stopped all movement, and looked at us long and hard.

Howard was the first to break the silence, but Finn had already understood. "As it stands, we don't think we can use these games. So. . . ."

"You guys are really something. You can't pay for what you ordered, so you decide after they're made that you don't want them. It isn't my fault that you're having a lousy Christmas. Where did you professors learn how to do business?" His face had turned deep red.

Finn's barbs contained enough half-truths to hurt. "Look, Bill, it's nobody's fault," I intoned without much conviction. "And business isn't bad — we really could use the games. But if we feel we can't sell them or that selling them will damage our reputation, then we have to take some action to protect ourselves. We want new game boards, just like the ones we had last time, just like the ones we ordered this time."

"There is also the matter of the damage done to our business," Howard added gravely, "due to the delay this will cause in getting games with acceptable boards. We will probably lose a lot of orders."

Finn had heard enough. The lines were now drawn. He would sue us for the money we owed him "and collect to the last penny," he promised, hissing the words out between his teeth. Straining to keep our cool, we replied that we would be suing him for breach of contract, asking for our sixty-five thousand dollars back and damages.

On leaving his office, something in me rebelled against the strictures of my new role. Finn wasn't a bad sort. We had shared some hopes and laughs together about his business as well as mine. On my last visit, he had talked about a daughter who was having a serious operation. "I hope your daughter recovers quickly, Bill," I said, turning toward him. I don't know why but I held out my hand. No, I do know why, but it made no difference. Finn put his hands behind his back and just glared at me.

Business. Wasn't I just being a good businessman? We had to protect our investment. Finn, too, was just trying to be a good businessman. I mustn't let any human feelings interfere with what business required. That is being a bad businessman. Unless those human feelings clear the way for more and better business, and that was not the case here. . . .

We received court papers announcing Finn's suit, and sent him court papers announcing ours. But Finn knew that suing us would take years, during which he would be stuck with a lot of games he couldn't use or sell, and that even if he won his suit, all that would happen was that he would force us into bankruptcy. Only a quick settlement offered him any hope of recuperating part of his investment. A few weeks went by when his lawyer, Herbert Jason, Jr., called our lawyer, Izzy, and asked whether something couldn't be worked out. "Like what?" Izzy asked. After several more calls, an appointment was made for Izzy and me to meet with Finn and Jason at the latter's office.

The evening before, the board met to hammer out a bargaining position. We had practically run out of games. If we were to stay in business, we needed more and we needed them quickly. We also reached an uneasy consensus that we could sell the new games despite the inferior board. Paul was unhappy with this decision, but eventually he, too, agreed. We would conduct business as usual, but if a customer complained, we would refund his or her money. Before he halted production, Finn had finished twenty-two thousand games, and he had the parts on hand to produce another twenty-eight thousand. The key question was how much was all this worth above the sixty-five thousand dollars we had already paid.

Izzy met me at Jason's plush Park Avenue office wearing the kind of three-piece tailored suit he puts aside for occasions such as this. . . .[126] Jason began by announcing rather formally that Mr. Finn wanted ninety-five thousand dollars that was owed him for producing fifty thousand games for Class Struggle, Inc. Whereupon, Izzy responded just as formally that Class Struggle, Inc., wanted its sixty-five thousand dollars back, as well as a half-million dollars for damages to our business firm. He could keep the damaged games. Then, less formally, Jason said, "But there does seem to be some room for a compromise." When Izzy asked what he suggested, Jason responded that Mr. Finn would kindly extend the length of time for paying the money which we owed. Jason then asked Izzy what we had in mind, to which Izzy responded that we might consider dropping our suit for damages to the business if Mr. Finn returned our sixty-five thousand dollars and gave us all the finished games. This was one of the occasions on which Finn shot me a particularly hostile glance.

From these two extreme positions, both lawyers began to edge toward a common center. Each lawyer would introduce his "last best offer" by turning to his client to make sure he had not gone too far. Every now and then Finn would put on a show of total opposition, and once he even stalked from the room. Each time Jason would soothe him, saying that such an act of generosity and statesmanship on his part would surely bring Class Struggle to settle the matter right here. After witnessing this imaginative charade a couple of times, I decided to include it in my own act. Feigning outrage at their offer, I blew up. Izzy caught on, and gave me a chance to appear as the generous statesman. Business has provided me with the occasion for many kinds of acting — comedy, farce, adventure — but this was my first essay into Shakespearean tragedy.

After an hour and a half, we had crawled to offering them fifteen thousand dollars on top of the sixty-five thousand dollars they had for the games already produced and all the raw materials (estimating it would take another fifteen thousand to twenty thousand dollars to produce twenty-eight thousand more games from these materials); and Finn had reduced his demand to thirty thousand dollars for everything. But I had already gone higher than I had been authorized by the board to go, and Finn had been more conciliatory than he had expected to be. Finn's temper was flaring more frequently now. No further progress could be made today. I had received his very last offer, and he took note of mine. The lawyers agreed to keep in touch. . . .

---

[126] [Eds. note: Why did the meeting take place at a "plush Park Avenue office"? Why did Izzy, Class Struggle, Inc.'s lawyer, wear a costume to the performance?]

NOTES AND QUESTIONS

1. ***The end of the story:*** Class Struggle, Inc., and Finn finally settled their dispute. Class Struggle agreed to pay Finn $20,000 more. Finn agreed to hand over 22,000 finished games and the parts for 28,000 others.[127]

2. ***The human side of playing "hardball":*** The chance that Class Struggle, Inc., might have been able to exit from the transaction without any legal obligation to Finn had great tactical value in the negotiations. Finn, however, was angry. Why? Ollman reports his own doubts about his part in dealing with Finn. Why did he have doubts? Isn't it the American norm that "all's fair in love, war, and business?"

Professor Stewart Macaulay, drawing on the ideas of Niklas Luhmann, comments:[128]

> There are different normative vocabularies, and when I speak in one it calls for a response in kind from you.
>
> The legal theme has specific characteristics. It asserts that I am right and you are wrong. It threatens to mobilize the power of the state to force you to live up to your obligations. "Whoever is, or claims to be, in the right in this fashion no longer needs to communicate, no longer needs to rely on a local suspension of doubt, no longer needs to present himself as being prepared to take up and respond to the other's communication; he is not even willing to argue."[129]
>
> There are barriers to shifting to a legal style of debate. "The comfortable consensus that can be normally assumed in living and acting together will be shattered."[130] It becomes harder to continue a relationship. "Starting a legal discussion usually means going beyond a point of no return: one defines oneself for the future as prepared to stand up and actively defend one's rights."[131] The other party is pushed to respond in kind. Turning to a legal discussion initiates a chain of events out of the control of the parties and introduces uncertainty. American cultures — and likely other cultures too — mark appropriate occasions for turning to legal themes. Other people, and our own consciences, seldom approve a legal attack against one who genuinely is trying to cooperate in good faith.

3. ***A legislative proposal:*** The common law of contracts has long embraced a substantial performance rule, limiting a non-breacher's right to cancel a transaction and refuse a performance to situations in which the deficiency in the other party's

---

[127] For a critical review of Ollman's book, see Zukin, *Book Review*, 14 THEORY & SOC'Y 247 (1985) ("As a board game, 'Class Struggle' was neither well designed nor well crafted, and people who played it reported that the rules were complex, it took too long to play, and playing it wasn't very much fun.").

[128] Stewart Macaulay, *Organic Transactions: Contract, Frank Lloyd Wright and the Johnson Building*, 1996 WIS. L. REV. 75, 114.

[129] Niklas Luhmann, *Communication About Law in Interaction Systems, in* ADVANCES IN SOCIAL THEORY AND METHODOLOGY 234 (Karin Knorr-Cetina & Aaron V. Cicourel eds., Routledge & Kegan Paul 1981).

[130] *Id.* at 244.

[131] *Id.* at 241.

performance is "substantial" or "material." Professor Karl Llewellyn's original draft of what became Article 2 of the Uniform Commercial Code proposed a substantial performance rule for merchant buyers in sale of goods transactions. This meant that buyers could not refuse to accept a tender of goods unless there were important defects in them. (They would, however, have been able to sue for damages to cover defects which were not substantial.) Llewellyn tried to avoid giving a buyer a right to get out of a contract when his real motive was to take advantage of a falling market. (Professor Ollman and his colleagues might not have been able to use the defects in the game boards to ward off bankruptcy, either.) Consumer buyers, however, could insist on exact performance.

The New York Merchants' Association objected.[132] The merchants worried about a substantial performance rule in the hands of judges and juries. The Merchants' Association representative said,

> Now, one merchant I was speaking [to], an officer of R.H. Macy & Company and a lawyer, said, "My Lord, what a chance for sellers to unload all their shopworn and defective goods and then let a jury decide whether they can't do it. It's wonderful."

Merchants thought they could solve the problem that concerned Llewellyn by "relational sanctions"; that is, by threatening or using the informal sanctions that accompany any long-term relationship, such as declining to enter into future transactions, or withholding cooperation in situations in which cooperation is not legally required, but is necessary as a practical matter.

The provisions of the UCC as enacted are a compromise. In general, no distinctions here are made between merchant and consumer buyers. Under § 2-601, a buyer may reject goods that "fail in any respect to conform to the contract." However, after a rejection, § 2-508 gives sellers a right to cure defective tenders of goods, subject to a number of qualifications. Once a buyer accepts goods, then § 2-608 says that the buyer may revoke his acceptance only in certain limited situations. One important limitation is that the "non-conformity [of the goods] must substantially impair [their] value to him." Different rules apply to installment contracts. Under § 2-612, a buyer may reject an installment "if the non-conformity substantially impairs the value of that installment. . . ." A buyer may call off the entire installment contract when a default "substantially impairs the value of the whole contract."

As so often is the case, compromises yield complexity. Complexity gives lawyers on both sides good arguments. It seldom gives them answers.

---

132 Zipporah Wiseman, *The Limits of Vision: Karl Llewellyn and the Merchant Rules*, 100 Harv. L. Rev. 465, 526 (1987).

COLONIAL DODGE, INC. v. MILLER
Michigan Court of Appeals
116 Mich. App. 78, 322 N.W.2d 549 (1982)

DEMING, J.

On May 28, 1976, Clarence R. Miller went to the plaintiff's dealership to pick up his new Dodge station wagon. He signed one form and drove the vehicle a short distance, exchanging cars with his wife. Mr. Miller drove an older car to work while Mrs. Miller returned home with the new car at about 3:00 P.M. When Mr. Miller returned home his wife informed him that the new car had no spare tire. Because Miller worked the night shift and the dealership was not open when he received word that his new car had no spare tire, Miller waited until the next morning to phone the salesman who had sold him the car. When Mr. Miller expressed dissatisfaction, the salesman informed him that he knew that the car had no spare tire because of a tire strike but that he (the salesman) had other things on his mind.

When Mr. Miller reiterated that he drove long distances to and from work on Detroit area expressways, up to 170 miles per day, and that he had paid extra money for high quality steel-belted radial tires, he received no satisfactory answer. Miller then told the salesman to come and get the car and that he didn't want it and that he was going to stop payment on two checks given in payment for the automobile.[133]

After Miller stopped payment on the checks, he parked the automobile in front of his house, later refusing receipt of license plates for the car. When the temporary vehicle registration expired, 10 days after the car was purchased, police officers towed the new car and impounded it.

The plaintiff concedes that the automobile did not have a spare tire but argues that one finally did arrive after the tire strike ended. Plaintiff also concedes that it is reasonable to expect, and that defendant in fact paid for, five tires with the car that he purchased.

Plaintiff sued defendant Miller for the purchase price of the car. Miller defended on the basis that he had either never accepted the car or had properly revoked acceptance under provisions of the Uniform Commercial Code. The trial court found that plaintiff was entitled to the contract price of the vehicle, less what it would have received from resale of the car within a reasonable period after the defendant breached the sales contract. Judgment was entered for $1,342.31. The plaintiff appeals.

At issue is whether Mr. Miller ever accepted the automobile within the meaning of M.C.L. § 440.2606; M.S.A. § 19.2606, and, if so, whether that acceptance was properly revoked pursuant to M.C.L. § 440.2608; M.S.A. § 19.2608. . . .

It is clear that, under the Code, delivery does not in and of itself constitute

---

[133] [1] We take judicial notice of the fact that Detroit area freeways and expressways have been the scene of violent crime and that many citizens justifiably fear automobile breakdowns while traveling on the expressways and the danger attendant thereto.

acceptance. In White & Summers, *Handbook of the Law Under the Uniform Commercial Code* (2nd ed.), § 8-2, p. 296, the concept of acceptance as within the meaning of § 2-606 is discussed. The authors point out that, because acceptance is a term of art which must be sharply distinguished from a variety of other acts which a buyer might commit, the Code first distinguishes and separates title problems from the problem of acceptance. Secondly, acceptance is only tangentially related to a buyer's possession of the goods, and in the usual case the buyer will have had possession of the goods for some time before he has accepted them within the meaning of the Code.

The mere taking of possession of goods by a delivery of goods to a buyer does not equal automatic acceptance, for the UCC makes an important and just allowance of a "reasonable opportunity" to inspect goods. M.C.L. § 440.2606(1)(a), (b); M.S.A. § 19.2606(1)(a), (b) . . .

In *Zabriskie Chevrolet, Inc. v. Smith*, 99 N.J. Super. 441, 240 A.2d 195 (1968), the court viewed a similar circumstance. Plaintiff sold defendant a new Chevrolet automobile. After driving it a short distance, the automobile became inoperable. Defendant phoned the dealership, "canceled" the sale, and stopped payment on the check written in purchase of the automobile. The dealer thereafter sued for the purchase price of the car. Plaintiff repaired the vehicle and notified defendant that the automobile was now operable. The car that the Smiths purchased remained in storage for a lengthy period of time.

In *Zabriskie*, as here, plaintiff argued strongly that UCC § 2-607(1) applied and that, having accepted the vehicle, defendant was bound to pay for it according to the terms of the contract. In specifically rejecting plaintiff's argument, the *Zabriskie* court said:

> It is clear that a buyer does not accept goods until he has had a "reasonable opportunity to inspect." Defendant sought to purchase a new car. He assumed that every new car buyer has a right to assume and, indeed, has been led to assume by the high-powered advertising techniques of the auto industry — that his new car, with the exception of very minor adjustments, would be mechanically new and factory-furnished, operate perfectly, and be free of substantial defects. The vehicle delivered to defendant did not measure up to these representations. Plaintiff contends that defendant had "reasonable opportunity to inspect" by the privilege to take the car for a typical "spin around the block" before signing the purchase order. If by this contention plaintiff equates a spin around the block with "reasonable opportunity to inspect," the contention is illusory and unrealistic. To the layman, the complicated mechanisms of today's automobiles are a complete mystery. To have the automobile inspected by someone with sufficient expertise to disassemble the vehicle in order to discover latent defects before the contract is signed, is assuredly impossible and highly impractical. . . . Consequently, the first few miles of driving become even more significant to the excited new car buyer. This is the buyer's first reasonable opportunity to enjoy his new vehicle to see if it conforms to what it was represented to be and whether he is getting what he bargained for. How long the buyer may drive the new car under the guise of inspection of new

goods is not an issue in the present case. It is clear that defendant discovered the nonconformity within 7/10 of a mile and minutes after leaving plaintiff's showroom. Certainly this was well within the ambit of 'reasonable opportunity to inspect.' " *Id.* 452–453, 240 A.2d 195.

Moreover, the court specifically recognized the "perfect tender" rule of § 2-601, specifically rejecting pre-code cases which held that substantial compliance with contract terms entitled the seller to force a buyer to accept nonconforming goods and pay for them.

We conclude that the trial court's finding that defendant Miller had accepted the automobile is clearly erroneous. Acceptance, as that term is used in the Uniform Commercial Code, is much more than taking delivery. Acceptance cannot occur, as a matter of law, unless and until the buyer has had a "reasonable" opportunity to inspect the purchased goods. . . .

Since Mr. Miller did not have a reasonable opportunity to inspect the automobile and did not act inconsistently with the seller's ownership after the hidden defect was in fact found, we hold that he had an absolute right to reject the automobile because it failed to conform to the contract, *i.e.*, it did not have five tires. . . .

Having concluded that Mr. Miller never accepted the vehicle, we turn to the facts surrounding his rejection. It is undisputed that on the morning after taking delivery of the station wagon, Mr. Miller phoned the dealership, discussed the absence of the spare tire, and, after receiving no satisfactory explanation orally rejected the automobile as not conforming to the purchase contract. He told the dealer's agent to come and pick up the car because he refused to drive it at all without a spare tire.

At issue is the propriety of defendant's rejection. M.C.L. § 440.2602; M.S.A. § 19.2602 requires a nonmerchant buyer who has rightfully rejected goods to seasonably inform the seller of the fact of rejection. Thereafter, the buyer has no further obligations with regard to goods rightfully rejected. . . . The duty of the seller to remove or repossess the nonconforming goods is universally recognized. . . .

Nor do we find that defendant's method of notice, the telephone, was inappropriate under these circumstances. There is no dispute concerning the unequivocal nature of Mr. Miller's rejection of the automobile or the reason for the rejection. . . .

Having properly rejected nonconforming goods, defendant Miller had no other obligation and properly parked the vehicle in front of his house. . . . However, we direct that, on remand, Mr. Miller execute whatever documents are required to vest legal title in the plaintiff, forthwith.

Reversed and remanded. Costs to appellee. [BRENNAN, J., concurred.]

CYNAR, J. (dissenting).

Defendant Miller entered into a special purchase order with plaintiff for the purchase of a station wagon specified as a "Heavy Duty Trailer Package" which included "heavy-duty oversized tires." The specially ordered station wagon was delivered to plaintiff and Miller picked up the vehicle after Miller executed an application for Michigan title and made payment for the vehicle with checks. The invoice indicated that the spare tire was not included in the delivery and would be shipped later, the delay being attributed to a nationwide tire strike. The following day Miller called plaintiff and complained about the missing tire, stopped payment on the checks, and advised plaintiff to pick up the station wagon, which was parked in front of his home. Plaintiff advised Miller when the replacement tire became available.

In *Zabriskie Chevrolet, Inc. v. Smith*, 99 N.J. Super. 441, 240 A.2d 195 (1968), an automobile became inoperable 7/10 of a mile and minutes after leaving the dealer's showroom. The court decided that the buyer had a right to assume that his new car, with the exception of very minor adjustments, would be mechanically new, factory-furnished, operate perfectly, and be free of substantial defects. While I am in total agreement with the *Zabriskie* decision, it must be pointed out that the facts in the matter submitted for our decision are not similar.

[handwritten margin note: Agree w/ precedent case of majority just says doesn't fit this situation]

A buyer may properly revoke acceptance where the nonconformity substantially impairs its value. The existence of such nonconformity depends on the facts and circumstances of each case. . . . The determination of substantial impairment has been made from the buyer's subjective view, considering particular needs and circumstances. . . . An objective approach was utilized in *Fargo Machine & Tool Co. v. Keaney & Trecker Corp.*, 428 F. Supp. 364 (E.D. Mich., 1977), and an objective and subjective test was employed in *Jorgensen v. Pressnall*, 274 Or. 285, 545 P.2d 1382 (1976). The purpose of the requirement of substantial impairment of value is to preclude revocation for trivial defects or defects which may be easily corrected. *Rozmus v. Thompson's Lincoln-Mercury Co.*, 209 Pa. Super. 120, 224 A.2d 782 (1966).

The trial judge's determination that the temporarily missing spare tire did not constitute a substantial impairment in value under either the subjective or objective test was not clearly erroneous. I therefore disagree with the majority finding that defendant Miller properly rejected the vehicle, and I would affirm the trial court's finding in that regard.

Having determined that defendant Miller wrongfully revoked acceptance in this case, the trial court found that the vehicle would have been resold for $1,000 less, on or about September 1, 1976, than the sales price to defendant Miller and therefore this was the amount of damages the plaintiff was entitled to recover. With this determination, I must disagree. . . . [T]he trial court should have awarded the full contract price to plaintiff.

NOTES AND QUESTIONS

1. *Two approaches:* What is it that separates the majority and the dissent? Do they disagree about the facts? The legal standard to be applied? The application of that legal standard to the facts?

2. *Act Two:* The Michigan intermediate appellate court granted a rehearing. It seems that Brennan must have had second thoughts. We offer the second opinion for your consideration. (In the notes after the opinion that follows you will learn that

there was a third, and final, act in this drama.)

COLONIAL DODGE, INC. v. MILLER
Michigan Court of Appeals
328 N.W.2d 678 (1982)

Before CYNAR, P.J., and BRENNAN and DEMING, JJ. (On Rehearing of 116 Mich. App. 78, 322 N.W.2d 549)

PER CURIAM.

A judgment was entered on January 18, 1981, awarding damages in favor of plaintiff against defendant Clarence R. Miller in the amount of $1,000, together with costs entered in the amount of $342.31. Plaintiff, Colonial Dodge, Inc., appeals as of right.

. . . [P]laintiff sought damages for breach of a sales contract to purchase a new automobile. In a nonjury trial, the trial judge determined that plaintiff was entitled to the contract price of the motor vehicle less the amount plaintiff could have received from a resale of the vehicle within a reasonable period of time after the breach. . . .

The issues . . . concern whether plaintiff is entitled to the full contract price of the vehicle purchased by Miller and whether the trial court properly awarded damages to plaintiff. Miller did not file a cross-appeal.

On April 19, 1976, Miller executed a purchase order to buy a 1976 Dodge Royal Monaco station wagon from plaintiff for $5,677. The order was submitted to Chrysler Corporation (Chrysler) for special equipment, including a heavy trailer towing package with extra-large tires. Plaintiff received an invoice from Chrysler pursuant to Miller's order; the invoice indicated that the spare tire was omitted from the delivery and would be shipped later.

On May 28, 1976, the specially ordered station wagon was picked up by Miller. Miller drove the car to a nearby expressway and exchanged cars with his wife. He drove the old car to work, and she drove the new car home. Upon getting the new vehicle home, Mrs. Miller discovered that the spare tire was missing. Miller called plaintiff the next day and spoke to Donald Diem, a salesman, about the missing spare tire. Both persons were distraught at the time of the call. Diem was under stress due to the serious surgery his wife was about to undergo. Diem offered no explanation for the missing spare tire but offered his own spare tire which turned out to be the wrong size. Miller told Diem that he would stop payment on the money orders unless he received the tire. Miller stopped payment on the two money orders, parked the vehicle in front of his home, and advised Diem to pick up the vehicle.

The tire was not delivered with the vehicle when it was received by plaintiff from the manufacturer because of a national tire shortage due to a labor strike. When the tire arrived, a notice was sent to Miller informing him of the tire's arrival and requesting that he make an appointment for its mounting on the vehicle's spare wheel located in the vehicle. There was no dispute that Miller was entitled to five tires with the purchase of the car.

On the day Miller picked up the car, he executed an application for a Michigan title. Plaintiff made application to the Secretary of State for a new title, license plates, and a certificate of registration in the name of the purchaser. After the parties executed the application for Michigan title, a temporary 10-day registration sticker was affixed to the vehicle. After the sticker had expired, the car was towed from in front of Miller's home by the St. Clair police department for storage in the Kuhn Bros. dealership in St. Clair. Defendant refused to accept the license plates when they were sent to him.

According to the trial court's opinion, the parties agreed that defendant Miller had made a valid acceptance of the station wagon under § 2606 of the Uniform Commercial Code (UCC), M.C.L. § 440.2606; M.S.A. § 19.2606. Their dispute concerned whether Miller's revocation of acceptance was valid under M.C.L. § 440.2608; M.S.A. § 19.2608, the section providing that a buyer may revoke acceptance of a commercial unit where the nonconformity "substantially impairs its value to him."

The trial court noted, in interpreting this section of the code, that the court in *Fargo Machine & Tool Co. v. Kearney & Trecker Corp.*, 428 F. Supp. 364 (E.D. Mich., 1977), utilized a modified standard in determining substantial impairment by making it a factual question to be determined by objective evidence rather than the buyer's personal position. The trial court ruled that the missing spare tire did not substantially impair the value of a new automobile under either the objective or the subjective test in this case and that the defendant wrongfully revoked acceptance. . . .

In *Zabriskie Chevrolet, Inc. v. Smith*, 99 N.J. Super. 441, 240 A.2d 195 (1968), the automobile became inoperable 7/10 of a mile and minutes after leaving the dealer's showroom. The disposition of *Zabriskie* was premised on the finding that there was no acceptance. The facts in *Zabriskie* are clearly distinguishable on the basis that the car was inoperable; whereas here the sole nonconformity was the temporary absence of a spare tire due to a nationwide strike in the tire industry.

[handwritten margin note: now admits it's a diff case]

A buyer may properly revoke acceptance of a commercial unit where the nonconformity substantially impairs its value. The existence of such nonconformity depends on the facts and circumstances of each case. *Jorgensen v. Pressnall*, 274 Or. 285, 545 P.2d 1382 (1976). The determination of substantial impairment is made from an objective view or from the buyer's subjective view, considering the particular needs and circumstances. *See* White & Summers, *Uniform Commercial Code* (2nd ed.), § 8-3, p. 308, and M.C.L. § 440.2608, Comment 2; M.S.A. § 19.2608, Comment 2. The objective approach was utilized in *Fargo Machine & Tool Co.* In *Jorgensen*, both the objective and subjective tests were used in the determination.

The trial judge determined that the missing spare tire did not constitute a substantial impairment in value under either the subjective or objective test.

The purpose of the requirement of substantial impairment of value is to preclude revocation for trivial defects or defects which may be easily corrected. *Rozmus v. Thompson's Lincoln-Mercury Co.*, 209 Pa. Super. 120, 224 A.2d 782 (1966).

The trial judge's determination that the temporarily missing spare tire did not constitute a substantial impairment in value under either the subjective or objective test was not clearly erroneous. We affirm the trial court's finding in that regard.

Having determined that Miller wrongfully revoked acceptance in this case, the trial court found that the vehicle could have been resold on or about September 1, 1976, for $1,000 less than the sales price to Miller, and, therefore, that this is the amount of damages plaintiff is entitled to recover. . . .

The trial court stated that "an implied duty on the part of the seller arose to retain the property and hold it for resale." Miller stopped payment on the money orders, parked the vehicle in front of his home, and advised plaintiff to pick up the vehicle. Plaintiff did not have a security interest or lien on the vehicle. The vehicle was registered and titled in Miller's name. Based on the record, plaintiff could not have transferred good title, contrary to the trial court's opinion.

M.C.L. § 440.2709; M.S.A. § 19.2709 provides:

> "(1) When the buyer fails to pay the price as it becomes due the seller may recover, together with any incidental damages under the next section, the price . . . (a) of goods accepted . . .

> It is not disputed that plaintiff sold Miller a car for $5,697; that Miller paid for the car in full with two money orders; that Miller took delivery of the car; that Miller stopped payment on the money orders which were tendered in payment of the car; that Miller wrongfully revoked acceptance and breached his contract.

Because plaintiff is entitled to the full contract price of $5,697 for the vehicle purchased by Miller, the judgment of the trial court relating to damages is clearly erroneous and set aside, and plaintiff is awarded the contract price.

DEMING, J. (dissenting).

I respectfully dissent. . . .

I do not accept the finding by the trial court that Mr. Miller accepted the vehicle within the meaning of the Uniform Commercial Code. The parties certainly did not agree on this point and there is absolutely nothing in the record which would support such a finding. . . . Because acceptance is a term of art as it is used in the UCC, and because acceptance has broad legal ramifications, including the duty to pay for the goods, the finding of the trial court was clearly erroneous and should be reversed. As one notes, taking delivery is not acceptance, because the UCC provides that the buyer has a reasonable time to inspect prior to accepting within the meaning of the code. . . .

The right to reject nonconforming goods prior to acceptance is nearly absolute. The UCC plainly and unequivocally rejects the notion of substantial compliance by a seller, insisting on a rule of perfect tender . . . The UCC limits the perfect tender rule only by express delineation found in § 2-612, pertaining to installment contracts, and §§ 2-718 and 2-719, which allow contractual limitations on remedies.

In some cases, the UCC also limits a buyer's right to reject for nonconformity.

Section 2-508 gives the seller a right to cure the nonconforming defect. Here the buyer asked for, then demanded a cure, but was met with refusal, then a claim that cure was not possible because of a tire strike. The UCC places the burden of cure on the seller, not the buyer. Failure to cure within a reasonable time is a risk of the seller, not the risk of the buyer. I conclude that this risk is one the plaintiff chose to take.

Since the majority opinion speaks to the matter of an acceptance, this I will address. If there has been an acceptance, it may be revoked for reasons found in § 2-608, M.C.L. § 440.2608; M.S.A. § 19.2608. At issue is whether the missing spare tire constituted a substantial impairment to the value of the automobile. The majority cites *Rozmus v. Thompson's Lincoln-Mercury Co.*, 209 Pa. Super. 120, 224 A.2d 782 (1966), for the proposition that § 2-608 precludes revocation after acceptance for trivial matters that are easily corrected. I accept that as a valid statement of the law; however, in this case, the missing tire was not trivial or unimportant to defendant Miller. The dealer had specific knowledge of the buyer's requirement of a spare tire, and a specific good was ordered. Therefore, the lack of such tire was not trivial.

Functional tires, including an adequate spare, are an integral part of the safety equipment of every automobile purchased, anywhere. As I pointed out in my original opinion, one would be foolish or suicidal, in light of recent events on Detroit area expressways, to venture forth in an improperly equipped automobile. . . .

Also at issue is the propriety of defendant's rejection. M.C.L. § 440.2602; M.S.A. § 19.2602 requires a nonmerchant buyer who has rightfully rejected goods to inform the seller of the fact of rejection. Thereafter, the buyer has no further obligation to goods rightfully rejected. M.C.L. § 440.2602(2)(c); M.S.A. § 19.2602(2)(c). The duty of the seller to remove or repossess the nonconforming goods is universally recognized. . . . I find that defendant's method of notice, the telephone, was appropriate under these circumstances. There is no dispute concerning the unequivocal nature of Mr. Miller's rejection of the automobile or the reason for the rejection. Moreover, there is no doubt that Mr. Miller did not use the car after he told the plaintiff's agent to come and pick it up. The cases holding that oral notice is not sufficient are not applicable here. . . . Rather, I would opt for the UCC rule that any notice must be "reasonable" — a notice that reasonably tells the seller of the fact of rejection and the reason therefore. . . .

I would hold that if there was an acceptance, and I think that there was not, then Miller's rejection was both appropriate and timely. . . .

The majority concludes that the plaintiff-seller is entitled to the full purchase price of the automobile. This result is not only unconscionable on these facts but wrong as a matter of law. It was the seller who breached the contract. It has no right to damages whatsoever on its own breach because the law gives it no such right, absent a wrongful rejection on the part of the buyer. . . .

I would reverse.

NOTES AND QUESTIONS

1. *Reaching a "fair" result:* In the second opinion, the court notes that Colonial Dodge's salesman "was under stress due to the serious surgery his wife was about to undergo." It also points out that the salesman offered his own spare tire, which turned out to be the wrong size. Furthermore, the dealer had an understandable reason for delivering a car without a spare tire. Why is this information relevant to the buyer's rights under § 2-608? Under the majority's view, was there any breach at all, even if minor, by Colonial Dodge? If so, what remedy, if any, for the Millers? Study § 2-714.

2. *The right to cure:* Suppose the buyer had noticed the lack of a spare tire before he took possession of the car and had refused to accept delivery. Suppose further that the salesman had then offered his own spare tire, which was the right size. Would Miller have been obligated to accept delivery? Study UCC § 2-508.

3. *Act Three — and final curtain:* The Supreme Court of Michigan, by a four-to-three vote, reversed the Court of Appeals in *Colonial Dodge, Inc. v. Miller*, 420 Mich. 452, 362 N.W.2d 704 (1985). The Supreme Court first said: "We are not persuaded that, had the matter been contested in the trial court, a finding of acceptance would be warranted on this record. However, since defendant did not submit the question to the trial judge, but in effect stipulated to acceptance, we will treat the matter as though there was acceptance." It then found, however, that the failure to include the spare tire was a substantial impairment in value to Mr. Miller, and so he could properly revoke his acceptance. The court noted:

> The defendant's occupation demanded that he travel extensively, sometimes in excess of 150 miles per day on Detroit freeways, and often in the early morning hours. Mr. Miller testified that he was afraid of a tire going flat on a Detroit freeway at 3 A.M. Without a spare, he testified, he would be helpless until morning business hours. The dangers attendant upon a stranded motorist are common knowledge, and Mr. Miller's fears are not unreasonable.

The dissent argued that the impairment of value must be substantial. "It is not sufficient that the nonconformance be worrisome, aggravating, or even potentially dangerous. It must be a nonconformity which diminishes the value of the goods to the buyer to a substantial degree." It found the possibility of Mr. Miller being stranded in an unsafe area to be unlikely. Moreover, it was a temporary deficiency easily remedied.

4. *What finally happened:* The *National Law Journal* reported that the 1976 Dodge station wagon had logged less than 400 miles when the Millers attempted to call off the transaction.[134] Mr. Miller parked the car in front of his house and told the dealer to pick it up, the dealer refused, and the police towed the car to another dealership. Either the police or this second dealer placed the car in storage, where it remained for nine years pending the course of the litigation. Title remained in Mr. Miller's name.

----

[134] Nat'l L.J., Feb. 11, 1985.

The resale value of the 1976 Dodge station wagon obviously declined during the nine years it was in storage. Who bears that loss?

5.   *Reasons for litigation:* Why did the dealer resist the buyers' claims? Usually reliable sources tell us that Chrysler Corporation urged Colonial Dodge, Inc. to fight, and the Chrysler legal staff participated in the litigation and appeals. Chrysler's officials thought that the Millers must have known that their car would be delivered without a spare tire. The Detroit newspapers and television gave great coverage to the tire workers' strike and the automobile industry's response to it. Newspapers and television reports discussed the industry's decision to deliver new cars with only four tires and a promise to deliver another when the strike ended. Moreover, Colonial Dodge tried to show that the car had been driven over 400 miles before the Millers called to complain. Both Chrysler and Colonial Dodge officials saw the Millers' reasons for revoking acceptance as a mere pretext. Suppose Chrysler and Colonial Dodge could show that another Dodge dealer had offered Mr. Miller a similar Dodge station wagon at a lower price? Suppose they could show that the Millers could not afford to make the monthly payments on the station wagon and only realized this after they had promised to buy the car? Should a court insist that a seller resisting a revocation of acceptance prove some bad faith reason for trying to back out? In other words, to what extent does § 2-608 reflect ideas about good faith in settling contract disputes?

6.   *Applying the UCC to Class Struggle:* What would the result have been in the dispute involving *Class Struggle* if the matter had been litigated, and the UCC applied?

7.   *Flow chart for buyer's options:* The diagram on the next page shows the buyer's options on the seller's tender of goods which fail to conform to the contract.

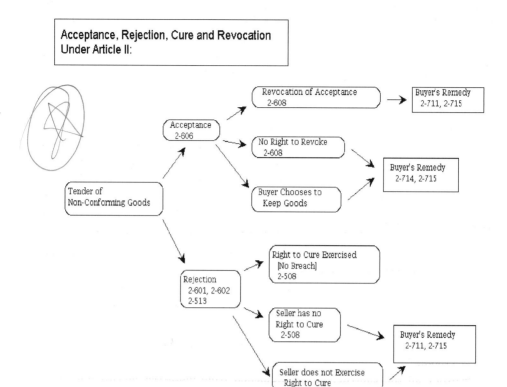

Acceptance, Rejection, Cure and Revocation Under Article II:

Tender of Non-Conforming Goods

Acceptance 2-606
- Revocation of Acceptance 2-608 → Buyer's Remedy 2-711, 2-715
- No Right to Revoke 2-608 → Buyer's Remedy 2-714, 2-715
- Buyer Chooses to Keep Goods → Buyer's Remedy 2-714, 2-715

Rejection 2-601, 2-602 2-513
- Right to Cure Exercised [No Breach] 2-508
- Seller has no Right to Cure 2-508 → Buyer's Remedy 2-711, 2-715
- Seller does not Exercise Right to Cure → Buyer's Remedy 2-711, 2-715

b. Substantial performance in building contracts

As a remedy, exit presents special difficulties in the real estate context. If the owner (in the position of the buyer) finds the builder's performance lacking, the owner is unable to return the work already completed because it is affixed to the owner's land. Under the law of property, the building, as imperfect as it is, still belongs to the owner. Courts nonetheless apply the general contract rules. If the builder has not "substantially performed," the owner is entitled to "rescind" the contract (essentially an exit remedy) and the builder can no longer sue for the contract price. The builder may nonetheless be entitled to recover something for the work performed, which now belongs to the owner, but that remedy will be in restitution for a plaintiff in default — a topic we cover later.[135]

For example, in *Plante v. Jacobs*,[136] Frank and Carol Jacobs contracted with Plante in 1956. Plante was to build a house upon their lot in Brookfield according to plans and specifications. They were to pay him $26,765 as construction progressed. They paid him a total of $20,000 in several installments. The Jacobses ultimately became unhappy with the quality of Plante's work. They failed to make their last

---

[135] *See* Section I of this chapter, *infra.*

[136] 10 Wis. 2d 567, 103 N.W.2d 296 (1960).

payment, Plante sued for it, and then the Jacobses detailed everything they could call a defect. There were 24 entries in their "schedule of items not performed or not properly performed." They estimated that the most expensive to remedy was a misplaced wall between the living room and the kitchen. It narrowed the living room and expanded the kitchen by about one foot. The Jacobses offered evidence that it would cost $4,000 to tear down this wall and rebuild it according to the plans and specifications.

The trial court said, "Based on the testimony of the defendants' witness Harrigan and the plaintiff's witness Ruby, the Court will find that the misplacing of this wall caused no damage to the defendants." Since the wall and the other defects were not a material failure to perform, Plante had substantially performed his side of the deal. This meant he was entitled to the contract price minus any damages that the Jacobses could prove with respect to other defects. They had no right to withhold the last payment because of Plante's failure to follow plans and specifications.

Justice Hallows wrote the opinion for the Supreme Court of Wisconsin affirming the trial court's decision. He observed: "The record is not clear why and when this wall was misplaced, but the wall is completely built and the house decorated and the defendants [i.e, the Jacobses] are living therein." With respect to the substantial breach claim, the opinion continued:

> The defendants rely on *Manitowoc Steam Boiler Works v. Manitowoc Glue Co.* (1903), 120 Wis. 1, 97 N.W. 515, for the proposition that there can be no recovery on the contract as distinguished from *quantum meruit* unless there is substantial performance. This is undoubtedly the correct rule at common law. For recovery on *quantum meruit*, see *Valentine v. Patrick Warren Construction Co.* (1953), 263 Wis. 143, 56 N.W.2d 860. The question here is whether there has been substantial performance. The test of what amounts to substantial performance seems to be whether the performance meets the essential purpose of the contract. . . .

> Substantial performance as applied to construction of a house does not mean that every detail must be in strict compliance with the specifications and the plans. Something less than perfection is the test of specific performance unless all details are made the essence of the contract. This was not done here. There may be situations in which features or details of construction of special or of great personal importance, if not performed, would prevent a finding of substantial performance of the contract. In this case the plan was a stock floor plan. No detailed construction of the house was shown on the plan. . . . Many of the problems that arose during the construction had to be solved on the basis of practical experience. No mathematical rule relating to the percentage of the price, of cost of completion, or of completeness can be laid down to determine substantial performance of a building contract. Although the defendants received a house with which they are dissatisfied in many respects, the trial court was not in error in finding the contract was substantially performed.

NOTES AND QUESTIONS

1. *How important is the timing of owners' substantial breach claim?* Justice Hallows observed that at the time the Jacobses asserted their claim, they were already living in the house. Suppose the Jacobses had asserted a substantial breach claim at the first time it was possible to observe that Plante had misplaced the living room wall. Would or should the result have been different? Note that if the Jacobses had properly claimed substantial breach at that time, they would have been within their rights in dismissing Plante and hiring a different builder to complete the house.

At trial Frank M. Jacobs, the owner of the house, testified:

> The living room is now 15 x 32 feet instead of 16 x 32 feet. Such narrowness of the living room of course has changed our plans so far as what we could do in decorating the room and the access to the west end of the room through the kitchen door. We had a custom-built davenport and you can't cut a foot off to give proper walking space. If another chair is at the end as it should be that is a group. The kitchen is a foot wider than the plans called for. That makes a larger kitchen so far as walking back and forth in it is concerned.

[handwritten margin note: Still can deduct damages they can PROVE even though Plante substantially performed]

2. *What remedy exists for the owner when there is not a substantial breach?* Although the court held that Plante had substantially performed, and hence was entitled to sue for the balance of the purchase price, the Jacobses were entitled to deduct from that balance damages for the defects that they proved. This part of the court's opinion will be discussed later, in Note 7 after *Peevyhouse v. Garland Coal, infra* in Section J of this chapter.

3. *Recovery in* **quantum meruit:** Justice Hallows indicates that if Plante had not substantially performed, he still could have recovered something in *quantum meruit.*[137] The next section of these materials considers this remedy. Note, however, that since Plante would have been suing as a plaintiff in default (i.e., in substantial breach), he could not have recovered more than the contract price as *quantum meruit* damages. Where the plaintiff is not in substantial breach, this is not always the case. *See United States ex rel. Coastal Steel Erectors v. Algernon Blair, infra* in this section, and the subsequent Notes and Questions.

[handwritten margin note: New Concept]

3. Restitution and *Quantum Meruit* as an Alternative Remedy for Breach of Contract

a. The remedy and its impact

We have already seen that exit and restitution may be a better remedy for a nonbreaching party than remedies that protect either the expectation or the reliance interests. Restitution's most controversial form, however, occurs when the nonbreaching plaintiff has performed and handed over goods and services to the

---

[137] The term *quantum meruit* is often italicized, as are most Latin terms incorporated into the common law, but as we will see, this is not a consistent practice. In this casebook, we italicize the term except when included in quoted material (such as a court's opinion) where the term was not italicized.

defendant pursuant to a contract, and those goods or services cannot be readily returned. In that circumstance, the plaintiff sometimes seeks a remedy in "*quantum meruit.*" The following two cases explore this remedy. In the first case, the court defines the *quantum meruit* measure of recovery and distinguishes it from "unjust enrichment." The recovery perhaps should not be considered a form of restitution at all. In the second case, however, the court allows recovery in *quantum meruit* as a form of restitution.

PAFFHAUSEN v. BALANO
Maine Supreme Judicial Court
1998 ME 47, 708 A.2d 269

CLIFFORD, J.

David Paffhausen appeals from an order entered in the Knox County Probate Court rejecting his *quantum meruit* claim against the estate of Elizabeth Balano but allowing recovery for unjust enrichment. Because we conclude that David was entitled to recover pursuant to the theory of *quantum meruit*, we vacate the judgment.

In March 1990, David, who is a carpenter and an artist, asked Elizabeth Balano for permission to renovate a building owned by her. David had hoped to convert the building into a fine art print shop. The evidence shows that Elizabeth approved David's request, with the understanding that he would pay her $60.00 per month after he "got the business up and running." Over the course of David's extensive renovations,[138] Elizabeth at various times signed notes to various town authorities approving his work and allowing him to procure permits. She also gave him a signed note on December 11, 1991, stating: "To Whom it may Concern — David can use my house as long as he needs it."[139]

The building was revamped sufficiently to allow David to host two art shows in 1994 and 1995. After Elizabeth's death in October of 1995, her personal representatives offered David one year of free rent, after which his rent would be $60 per month, but for no definite term. David rejected the offer, presumably because beyond one year he would be a tenant at will, subject to eviction. Throughout the period of David's renovation of the property, Elizabeth or her estate paid all real estate taxes and insurance premiums, and David has paid no rent.

In 1996 David filed a claim against Elizabeth's estate. The estate disallowed the

---

[138] [1] The Probate Court found:

> Petitioner did improve the property; he cleaned it up and hauled many loads of trash to the dump; he shored up the building; he built up forms, he rebuilt the foundation; he removed contaminated soil from around the building; he had the chimney rebuilt; he installed a wastewater system. . . .

These findings were well-supported by the record.

[139] [2] David testified that in April of 1993, he again approached Elizabeth for more formal assurances as to his investment in the building to which she replied: "Don't worry, the building is yours." Her close friend, Jane Scarpino, testified that Elizabeth had said to her that "this young man was going to . . . take the place" and renovate it.

claim. . . . David filed a petition to resolve a disputed claim in the Probate Court. After a hearing, the court rejected David's theory of *quantum meruit*, but did allow David to recover $12,300 as unjust enrichment based on what the court found to be the value of the improvements to the building.

David contends the court erred in concluding that he failed to prove the elements of *quantum meruit*. David argues that he and Elizabeth had an understanding that for the renovations he made to the building he reasonably expected to receive, and Elizabeth promised to give, "the use of the building at no or nominal rent" for as long as he needed it, and that this understanding entitles him to recover from the estate in *quantum meruit*. On appeal, we defer to the trial court on its findings of fact, but review de novo the application of the law to those facts. . . .

We have recently explained the difference between *quantum meruit* and unjust enrichment. *Quantum meruit*, also sometimes labeled "contract implied in fact," involves recovery for services or materials provided under an implied contract. *See Aladdin Elec. Assoc. v. Old Orchard Beach*, 645 A.2d 1142, 1145 (Me. 1994). *See also United States ex rel. Modern Elec., Inc. v. Ideal Elec. Sec. Co.*, 81 F.3d 240, 246 (D.C. Cir. 1996) ("Quantum meruit . . . rests on a contract implied in fact, that is, a contract inferred from the conduct of the parties."). Unjust enrichment describes recovery for the value of the benefit retained when there is no contractual relationship, but when, on the grounds of fairness and justice, the law compels performance of a legal and moral duty to pay, the "damages analysis is based on principles of equity, not contract." *Aladdin Elec. Assoc.*, 645 A.2d at 1145.[140]

---

[140] [3] We have made an effort to overcome considerable confusion between unjust enrichment and *quantum meruit. See A.F.A.B., Inc. v. Old Orchard Beach*, 639 A.2d 103, 105 n.3 (Me. 1994) ("terms are often used synonymously [but] the distinction between them is legally significant") . . . *See also* 66 Am. Jur. 2d, *Restitution and Implied Contracts* § 166 (1973) ("Quantum meruit is an ambiguous term. It may mean that there is a contract implied in fact to pay the reasonable value [of the goods or services furnished], or that to prevent unjust enrichment the claimant may recover on a quasi-contract for that reasonable value.").

Further confusion has resulted from our use of the term "quasi-contract" both to describe unjust enrichment . . . and to describe *quantum meruit. See Bowden v. Grindle*, 651 A.2d 347, 350 n.2 (a claim of *quantum meruit* is more appropriately described as a claim of quasi-contract. . . . The expression "*quantum meruit*" means "as much as deserved" and describes the extent of liability on a contract *implied by law*, or "quasi contract.") . . . *Cf. Johnson Group, Inc. v. Grasso Bros., Inc.*, 939 S.W.2d 28, 30 (Mo. Ct. App. 1997) ("In Missouri there exist [ ] two separate remedies for a recovery based upon quasi-contract: unjust enrichment and quantum meruit.").

The association of quasi-contract and *quantum meruit*, as in *Bowden*, is not helpful, because it suggests that the *quantum meruit* recovery is not based upon contract principles, as we have said that it must be. . . . *Cf. Restatement (Second) of Contracts* § 4 com. b (1981) ("Unlike true contracts, quasi-contracts are not based on the apparent intention of the parties to undertake the performances in question, nor are they promises. They are obligations created by law for reasons of justice.").

The Restatement definition of quasi-contract is historically accurate, because it reflects the common law's gradual acceptance of the essentially contractual writ of assumpsit even for debts arising out of non-contractual transactions where no express or tacit promise existed. *See 1 Corbin on Contracts* § 1.18(a) (rev. ed. 1993) ("The legal duties that were enforced by use of this fictitious promise have come to be described as quasi-contractual. In other words, a promise 'implied in law' is a *constructive* promise, a term that denotes a set of facts that will be treated *as if* a promise is made."). The probable historical cause for associating *quantum meruit* with quasi-contract is that at common law *quantum meruit* recoveries for the reasonable value of services provided were deemed, "in the tortured logic of

Damages in unjust enrichment are measured by the value of what was inequitably retained. In *quantum meruit*, by contrast, the damages are not measured by the benefit realized and retained by the defendant, but rather are based on the value of the services provided by the plaintiff. . . .

A valid claim in *quantum meruit* requires: "that (1) services were rendered to the defendant by the plaintiff; (2) with the knowledge and consent of the defendant; and (3) under circumstances that make it reasonable for the plaintiff to expect payment." . . . While the formalities of an express contract are not a prerequisite to recovery in *quantum meruit*, there must be a reasonable expectation on the part of the claimant to receive compensation for his services and a "concurrent intention" of the other party to compensate him. . . . Similarly, we have said that an implied promise is made to a person "when the surrounding circumstances make it reasonable for him to believe that he will receive payment . . . from the other." . . . It must appear that the one who rendered the services expected compensation and that the one who received or benefited from the services so understood, and by her words or conduct justified the expectation. . . . *Quantum meruit* may lie when "there was not a clear accession on both sides to one and the same terms," if services are provided "under circumstances that negative the idea that the services were gratuitous." . . . When such a party to whom services are rendered "knows it and permits it and accepts the benefit, he is bound to pay a reasonable compensation therefor." . . .

Although the decision of the Probate Court reflects thoughtful attention to the details of the case, the court nevertheless erred in its application of the law of *quantum meruit* to its factual findings and in its conclusion that the evidence does not support a recovery in *quantum meruit*. . . . The court did find that extensive services were rendered by David to renovate the building, and that Elizabeth "approved of his desire to transform her building into a print shop/art gallery." The court, however, erroneously concluded that David failed to show a reasonable expectation of payment. The court determined that there was no "contemporaneous understanding between the parties," and concluded there was no evidence that Elizabeth intended to reimburse David for his expenses. The court would not allow David recovery in *quantum meruit* unless he proved *Elizabeth's intention* to compensate him fully for all of his labor and expenses to convert the building either through cash reimbursement or use of the building for as long as he wished for a nominal rent. All that the law of *quantum meruit* requires David to prove, however, is that he had a reasonable expectation that his work was not gratuitous and that Elizabeth *by her words or conduct* justified this expectation. . . .

Elizabeth's note that "David can use my house as long as he needs it" falls short of an express contract. Yet the court's findings of Elizabeth's "full consent and support" for David's renovations, and that Elizabeth told David that "when he had it functioning as a print shop he could pay her $60.00 a month rent," and the other

---

yesteryear," to rest on a contract implied in law even when an express or implied contract existed. *Id.* at § 1.18(b).

Given the relative clarity that we have achieved in our distinction between *quantum meruit* and unjust enrichment, *see Aladdin*, 645 A.2d at 1145, and the ambiguity inherent in the term "quasi-contract," the latter term may have limited usefulness in our analytical framework.

evidence, including Elizabeth's written statement that David could "use my house as long as he needs it," compel a finding that "services were rendered under circumstances consistent with contract relations." . . . David's reasonable expectation of a right to use the building for at least a substantial period of time for a below-market rental in exchange for the improvements to the building that he made with Elizabeth's approval is different in kind from the legal and moral duty to pay for the value of improvements that equity imposes in the unjust enrichment context.[141] The evidence as found by the court supports David's claim that he is entitled to recover in *quantum meruit* for the reasonable value of his labor and the materials that went into the improvements to the building.

On remand, the court must determine the *reasonable* value of David's labor and the materials that were used to renovate and improve the building, . . . offset by the value of David's use of the building.

Judgment vacated. Remanded to Probate Court for further proceedings consistent with the opinion herein.

NOTES AND QUESTIONS

1. *Why not expectation damages?* The court concludes that the decedent's (Elizabeth's) note "falls short of an express contract." Why? The court does not say. We will learn, in Chapter 3 of these materials, that contracts involving a transfer of an interest in real estate, including long-term leases, must normally be in writing; but Elizabeth's note *was* in writing. We suspect that the court invoked a common law rule that is sometimes applied, stating that contracts which are too indefinite with respect to key terms are not enforceable. Here the indefiniteness was with respect to the term of the lease. The indefiniteness presents obvious problems in enforcing an expectation interest. Suppose David had sought, as a remedy, monetary damages for deprivation of the leasehold interest he had been promised. Without knowing the term of the lease, how could the court measure these damages?

2. *How is* quantum meruit *different from unjust enrichment?* The court distinguishes *quantum meruit* from "unjust enrichment." How would you determine the amount of "unjust enrichment"? Presumably the amount was less than the *quantum meruit* amount, since David appealed.

3. *Some other nuances in the law of* quantum meruit *and unjust enrichment: drawing fine distinctions:* The court emphasizes that if David's services were provided with a reasonable expectation of compensation, then *quantum meruit* recovery is available. The opinion might be read as implying that if David did not have a reasonable expectation of compensation, he might nonetheless recover

---

[141] [6] Compare *Commerce Partnership 8098 Limited Partnership v. Equity Contracting Co.*, 695 So. 2d 383, 387 (Fla. Dist. Ct. App. 1997) ("[A] common form of contract implied in fact is where one party has performed services at the request of another without discussion of compensation. These circumstances justify the inference of a promise to pay a reasonable amount for the service. The enforceability of this obligation turns on the implied promise, not on whether the defendant has received something of value.") with *Reeves v. Alyeska Pipeline Serv. Co.*, 926 P.2d 1130, 1143 (Alaska 1996) (the "obligation to make restitution that arises in [unjust enrichment] is not based upon any agreement between the parties, objective or subjective").

for unjust enrichment. However, the Restatement (Third) of Restitution and Unjust Enrichment, § 2 (3) (2011), provides: "There is no liability in restitution for an unrequested benefit voluntarily conferred, unless the circumstances of the transaction justify the claimant's intervention in the absence of contract." Providers of unrequested benefits are sometimes called "volunteers" or "intermeddlers" in discussions of restitution law. To require compensation of benefits conferred would impinge on the free choice of the recipient, who may prefer not to receive the benefit or enrichment if there is a cost. Nonetheless, compensation measured by unjust enrichment may be available if benefits are not returned when they could be, or even used and enjoyed.

All this suggests that there is a very fine line between benefits conferred in expectation of compensation, as the court finds in the principal case, and benefits conferred in circumstances entitling the provider to recovery in restitution or unjust enrichment.

4. *Is* quantum meruit *different from reliance?* Suppose the plaintiff had sought and obtained reliance damages, per *L. Albert & Son v. Armstrong Rubber, supra.* How, if at all, would his recovery have been different?

5. *What happened next?* The Maine Supreme Court remanded the case to determine the *quantum meruit* value of the plaintiff's work, to be offset by the value of his use of the building. On remand, the trial court valued Paffhausen's work at $44,240, but offset that amount by $24,700, representing the rental value of the building during the nearly eight-year period the plaintiff occupied it (mostly doing repairs and storing construction equipment). The trial court's finding on the rental value of the building was based on what the decedent (Elizabeth Balano) could have earned as rent if Paffhausen had not occupied the building. This amount included the higher estimated rental value after Paffhausen replaced the foundation, making the building usable for more valuable uses (e.g., a gallery or office space). Paffhausen appealed to the Maine Supreme Court once again, arguing that the offset from the *quantum meruit* value of his work should have been determined by the rental value of the building for the period that he used it as an art gallery (less than four months), not the entire time he occupied it in order to do the repairs. The Maine Supreme Court upheld the trial court's valuations, finding that the trial court's determination was not "clearly erroneous."[142]

Paffhausen ended up with a judgment for $19,540. Before the first appeal Paffhausen had a verdict of $12,300, as "unjust enrichment." In other words, two appeals to the Maine Supreme Court netted Paffhausen $7240. One wonders why a case of this nature was not settled. One of the authors has briefly discussed the litigation with the parties' lawyers and learned that settlement talks were attempted but were unsuccessful. Apparently the litigation was initiated after discussions occurred between plaintiff and the defendants (the executors of Elizabeth Balano's estate, who were her offspring) about how long Paffhausen could remain in the building while paying only a nominal rent. The defendants would not agree to extend a low-rent arrangement for an indefinite period of time, and plaintiff did not have a trustful relationship with them, as he had previously had with the

---

[142] Paffhausen v. Balano, 1999 ME 169, 740 A.2d 981 (1999).

decedent. At that point Paffhausen decided not to invest more money in the restoration of the building and moved his belongings out of the building; the litigation ensued.

UNITED STATES EX REL. COASTAL STEEL ERECTORS v. ALGERNON BLAIR, INC.
United States Court of Appeals, Fourth Circuit
479 F.2d 638 (1973)

CRAVEN, Circuit Judge.

May a subcontractor, who justifiably ceases work under a contract because of the prime contractor's breach, recover in quantum meruit the value of labor and equipment already furnished pursuant to the contract irrespective of whether he would have been entitled to recover in a suit on the contract? We think so, and, for reasons to be stated, the decision of the district court will be reversed.

The subcontractor, Coastal Steel Erectors, Inc., brought this action under the provisions of the Miller Act, 40 U.S.C.A. § 270a et seq.,[143] in the name of the United States against Algernon Blair, Inc., and its surety, United States Fidelity and Guaranty Company. Blair had entered a contract with the United States for the construction of a naval hospital in Charleston County, South Carolina. Blair had then contracted with Coastal to perform certain steel erection and supply certain equipment in conjunction with Blair's contract with the United States. Coastal commenced performance of its obligations, supplying its own cranes for handling and placing steel. Blair refused to pay for crane rental, maintaining that it was not obligated to do so under the subcontract. Because of Blair's failure to make payments for crane rental, and after completion of approximately 28 percent of the subcontract, Coastal terminated its performance. Blair then proceeded to complete the job with a new subcontractor. Coastal brought this action to recover for labor and equipment furnished.

The district court found that the subcontract required Blair to pay for crane use and that Blair's refusal to do so was such a material breach as to justify Coastal's terminating performance. This finding is not questioned on appeal. The court then found that under the contract the amount due Coastal, less what had already been paid, totaled approximately $37,000. Additionally, the court found Coastal would have lost more than $37,000 if it had completed performance. Holding that any amount due Coastal must be reduced by any loss it would have incurred by complete performance of the contract, the court denied recovery to Coastal. While the district court correctly stated the "'normal' rule of contract damages," . . . we think

---

[143] [Eds. note: The Miller Act is a federal statute protecting the interests of subcontractors dealing with general contractors who have successfully bid to construct a building or other facility for the United States government. Under the Miller Act, the subcontractor can sue in federal court in the name of the United States. However, the United States is not represented by separate counsel. The litigation expenses for the plaintiff are borne by the subcontractor, whose name also appears in the citation of the case.]

Coastal is entitled to recover in quantum meruit.[144]

In *United States ex rel. Susi Contracting Co. v. Zara Contracting Co.*, 146 F.2d 606 (2d Cir. 1944), a Miller Act action, the court was faced with a situation similar to that involved here — the prime contractor had unjustifiably breached a subcontract after partial performance by the subcontractor. The court stated:

> For it is an accepted principle of contract law, often applied in the case of construction contracts, that the promisee upon breach has the option to forego any suit on the contract and claim only the reasonable value of his performance.

146 F.2d at 610. . . . Quantum meruit recovery is not limited to an action against the prime contractor but may also be brought against the Miller Act surety, as in this case.[145] Further, that the complaint is not clear in regard to the theory of a plaintiff's recovery does not preclude recovery under quantum meruit. . . . A plaintiff may join a claim for quantum meruit with a claim for damages from breach of contract. . . .

In the present case, Coastal has, at its own expense, provided Blair with labor and the use of equipment. Blair, who breached the subcontract, has retained these benefits without having fully paid for them. On these facts, Coastal is entitled to restitution in quantum meruit. . . .

The impact of quantum meruit is to allow a promisee to recover the value of services he gave to the defendant irrespective of whether he would have lost money on the contract and been unable to recover in a suit on the contract. *Scaduto v. Orlando*, 381 F.2d 587, 595 (2d Cir. 1967). The measure of recovery for quantum meruit is the reasonable value of the performance, Restatement of Contracts § 347 (1932); and recovery is undiminished by any loss which would have been incurred by complete performance. 12 *Williston on Contracts* § 1485, at 312 (3d ed. 1970). While the contract price may be evidence of reasonable value of the services, it does not measure the value of the performance or limit recovery.[146] Rather, the standard for measuring the reasonable value of the services rendered is the amount for which such services could have been purchased from one in the plaintiff's position at the time and place the services were rendered.

Since the district court has not yet accurately determined the reasonable value of the labor and equipment use furnished by Coastal to Blair, the case must be

---

[144] [2] Where there is a distinction between federal and state substantive law, federal law controls in actions under the Miller Act. *United States ex rel. Astro Cleaning & Packaging Co. v. Jamison Co.*, 425 F.2d 1281, 1282 n.1 (6th Cir. 1970). But in this case the result would be the same, we think, under either state or federal law. Compare *United States ex rel. Susi Contracting Co. v. Zara Contracting Co.*, 146 F.2d 606 (2d Cir. 1944), with *Gantt v. Morgan*, 199 S.C. 138, 18 S.E.2d 672 (1942).

[145] [4] . . . This is consistent with the liberal construction which is given to the Miller Act to effectuate its protective purposes . . .

[146] [7] *Scaduto v. Orlando*, 381 F.2d 587, 595–96 (2d Cir. 1967) . . . *United States for Use of Susi Contracting Co. v. Zara Contracting Co.*, 146 F.2d 606, 610–11 (2d Cir. 1944). It should be noted, however, that in suits for restitution there are many cases permitting the plaintiff to recover the value of benefits conferred on the defendant, even though this value exceeds that of the return performance promised by the defendant. In these cases it is no doubt felt that the defendant's breach should work a forfeiture of his right to retain the benefits of an advantageous bargain. . . .

remanded for those findings. . . . When the amount has been determined, judgment will be entered in favor of Coastal, less payments already made under the contract. Accordingly, for the reasons stated above, the decision of the district court is

Reversed and remanded with instructions.

NOTES AND QUESTIONS

1. ***Might*** quantum meruit ***deter an efficient breach?*** Is the result in this case consistent with the policy underlying the rule prohibiting enforcement of stipulated damages clauses that are deemed to be a "penalty"? *See Lake River v. Carborundum, supra* in Section D of this chapter. We do not know the reasons Algernon Blair breached its contract with Coastal Steel Erectors. Might it have been attempting an efficient breach — that is, a breach that did not really harm the plaintiff, since it would lose money on the contract anyway, while benefiting the defendant?

2. ***What is a benefit?*** Traditionally, a person recovers "benefits conferred" in a restitution action. We could say that you benefit me when you do what I want you to do. We then could value my benefit by what it would cost to get someone else to do what I asked you to do. This is what we attempt to measure when the *quantum meruit* formula is applied. On the other hand, we could insist on finding an actual increase in my assets before concluding there is a benefit. This would be an attempt to measure how much I was enriched by your performance. While in many cases the two measures will amount to the same thing, in others there will be a difference. Consider the contrasting measures of restitution provided by § 371 of the Restatement (Second) of Contracts.

§ 371. Measure of Restitution Interest

If a sum of money is awarded to protect a party's restitution interest, it may as justice requires be measured by either

(a) the reasonable value to the other party of what he received in terms of what it would have cost him to obtain it from a person in the claimant's position, or

(b) the extent to which the other party's property has been increased in value or his other interests advanced.

Illustrations: . . .

2. A, a surgeon, contracts to perform a series of emergency operations on B for $3000. A does the first operation, saving B's life, which can be valued in view of B's life expectancy at $1,000,000. The market price to have an equally competent surgeon do the first operation is $1800. A's restitution interest is equal to the benefit conferred on B. That benefit is measured by the reasonable value to B of A's services in terms of the $1800 it would have cost B to engage a similar surgeon to do the operation regardless of the rule on which restitution is based.

3. ***Limiting restitution to the contract price or rate:*** The Restatement (Second) of Contracts originally proposed another major change but then dropped it. Section 373 states the traditional rule that a plaintiff may choose restitution as

a remedy instead of expectation or reliance recoveries. At one time § 373(2) provided that, where the benefits conferred on the breaching party were goods or services provided pursuant to a contract, the plaintiffs could recover no more than the amount they would have received had the parties performed their contract. The reform was deleted when the American Law Institute published the final version of the Restatement. The Comment states now:

> In the case of a contract on which he [an injured party] would have sustained a loss instead of having made a profit . . . his restitution interest may give him a larger recovery than would damages on either basis. The right of the injured party under a losing contract to a greater amount in restitution than he could have recovered in damages has engendered much controversy. The rules stated in this Section give him that right.

In 2011, the American Law Institute published the Restatement (Third) of Restitution and Unjust Enrichment. In § 38, it provided differently with respect to the ability of the nonbreaching plaintiff to collect more than the contract rate or price using the *quantum meruit* formula. Section 38 reads in part:

§ 38 Performance-Based Damages

(1) As an alternative to damages based on the expectation interest (Restatement, Second, Contracts § 347), a plaintiff who is entitled to a remedy for material breach or repudiation may recover damages measured by the cost or value of the plaintiff's performance.

(2) Performance-based damages are measured by

> (a) uncompensated expenditures made in reasonable reliance on the contract, including expenditures made in preparation for performance or in performance, less any loss the defendant can prove with reasonable certainty the plaintiff would have suffered had the contract been performed (Restatement, Second, Contracts § 349); or

> (b) the market value of the plaintiff's uncompensated contractual performance, not exceeding the price of such performance as determined by reference to the parties' agreement.

An illustration to this section makes clear that the limitation of *quantum meruit* recovery provided in § 38(2)(b) is intended to be more severe than the limitation once proposed (but later abandoned) for the Restatement (Second) of Contracts § 373(2), because it is based on contract rate for the work performed, not the total contract price.

> *Illustration 11.* A promises to build a barn for $60,000. A is wrongfully discharged after completing part of the work and receiving $20,000 in progress payments. The court finds that the cost reasonably incurred by A in partial performance has been $30,000, and that the reasonable cost of completion (by A or anyone else) will be $45,000. On this basis the court calculates that A has performed 40 percent of the work covered by the contract; the price of this work at the contract rate is $24,000. A's claim to damages by the rule of § 38(2)(b) is $4,000 (representing the ratable portion of the contract price less $20,000 already paid).

In the Reporter's Notes to § 38(2)(b), the Reporter acknowledges that the section does not reflect the majority rule among U.S. jurisdictions currently, but claims that the section is consistent with the position advocated by the vast majority of academic commentary. The rule would of course require a different result in *United States v. Algernon Blair*. It remains unclear whether § 38(2)(b) of the Restatement (Third) of Restitution and Unjust Enrichment will persuade courts to limit *quantum meruit* recovery in losing contract cases.

4. **Comparing reliance and quantum meruit:** Refer to Illustration 11 in the preceding note. What recovery under the Restatement (Third) of Restitution and Unjust Enrichment § 38(2)(a)? If it is different from the recovery provided by § 38(2)(b), what accounts for the difference?

5. **What's the right rule?** Modern writers on contracts have challenged the conventional rescission and restitution to the losing building contract as inconsistent with the policy of allowing owners to breach and pay damages where breach is "efficient."[147] Professor John Kidwell suggests that, despite their wooden reasoning, cases allowing restitution — as measured by *quantum meruit* — may reach the right result.[148]

> The principle that allows the parties to allocate risk does facilitate planning and serves to support the market, and *is* deeply imbedded in the law of contracts. The principle that exchanges should be *fair*, I argue, is also an indispensable part of contract law. The fairness principle is, however, not normally stated so boldly; but it lurks beneath the surface in the rules of duress, capacity, unconscionability, mistake, impossibility, frustration, and even in the law of consideration.[149] If the contracting parties have expressly allocated a risk, the freedom of contract / expectation principle will be honored even though it results in recognizing the expectations of a contracting party that involved an unequal exchange. In the preceding sentence I referred to an *unequal* exchange. The idealized, archetypical aspiration that lies behind contract law is a *fair exchange* and that is thought, in the absence of special circumstances, to mean an exchange of equal values. This does not mean *precisely* equal, but generally equal, in light of the incomparability of individual preferences *and* in light of the risks contemplated by the parties. . . .

> And in a case like *Boomer v. Muir*[150] the court may simply be signaling that one who wishes to have the benefit of the expectation principle in the case of a dramatically unequal exchange must have scrupulously complied with the formal requirements of contract law. The court may have believed that the owner was trying to take unfair advantage of the contractor; and it may

---

[147] *E.g.*, Andrew Kull, *Restitution as a Remedy for Breach of Contract*, 67 S. Cal. L. Rev. 1465 (1994).

[148] Excerpts from John Kidwell's remarks in the Association of American Law Schools' *Section on Remedies Newsletter* (1981).

[149] [Eds. note: Most of these rules will be considered later in these materials.]

[150] 24 P.2d 570 (Cal. App. 1933), an older case reaching the same result as the principal case in this section.

have simply employed a convenient escape hatch to reach what it found the preferable result. . . .

The principle of fair exchange presumes a certain equality of value. It is very nearly as central to the law of contracts as the expectation principle. The cases in which unjust enrichment principles are applied in contract cases are *not* inconsistent with contract law; they are merely cases in which the expectation principle has appropriately been subordinated to fair exchange.

Writing recently, Professor William Woodward reviews the attempt of the Restatement (Third) of Restitution and Unjust Enrichment § 38(2) to change the historic rule, applied in *United States ex rel. Coastal Steel Erectors v. Algernon Blair* and endorsed by the Restatement (Second) of Contracts § 373.[151] He concluded:

> This examination of the losing contract rules — the traditional one found in the Restatement, Second, of Contracts and the new one found in the new Restatement, Third, of Restitution — . . . has suggested that normative case for the new rule is, ultimately, contingent on behavioral predictions that may be false, and on an idea of contract law that is debatable and perhaps ideological. On this basis, one could argue that the proponents of change have not met their normative burden, and that the courts who have worked in the thicket of relational contracts are more likely to have got it "right" than have the theorists.

> The new complexity that the added rules contribute to predicting legal outcomes may have the effect of dampening party enthusiasm for ending their contracts and, instead, prompting them to work things out rather than resort to litigation. However one views that as an outcome, it may mean that we will not know for a long time whether the new rule will be well-received or rejected in the courts.

6.   *Restitution for lawyer's services:* Suppose a client hires a lawyer to do a certain task for $5000. After the lawyer has worked but has not completed the job, the client discharges him without cause. The client then hires a second lawyer who agrees to do the task for $6000. The second lawyer is unable to make use of any of the first lawyer's work. She completes the task and is paid $6000. The first lawyer then sues the client for the reasonable value of his work. Many courts have allowed him to recover the *quantum meruit* value of his services. The recovery is said to be based in restitution, under a principle like that stated in Restatement (Second) of Contracts § 371(a). But has the client received a "benefit"? If the lawyer received nothing for his/her work, could it be said that the client is unjustly enriched? Is this just another example of what Fuller and Perdue would call "the reliance interest"?

The Supreme Court of California, in *Fracasse v. Brent*,[152] decided that a client could

---

[151]   William Woodward Jr., *Restitution Without Context: An Examination of the Losing Contract Problem in the Restatement (Third) of Restitution* in J. Braucher, J. Kidwell, & W. Whitford, Revisiting the Contracts Scholarship of Stewart Macaulay 347, 374 (2013).

[152]   100 Cal. Rptr. 385, 494 P.2d 9 (1972).

discharge an attorney at any time with or without cause. In either case, the attorney was entitled to recover only the reasonable value of his or her services. A basic term of the contract between attorney and client will be implied by law, making it terminable by the client at will. Thus, the attorney may not sue for damages for breach of contract measured by the expectation interest even when discharged without cause. The court explained the new rule by saying, "The relation of attorney and client is one of special confidence and trust and the dignity and integrity of the legal profession demand that the interests of the client be fully protected. The right to discharge is of little value if the client must risk paying the full contract price for services not rendered upon a determination by a court that the discharge was without legal cause."

If we were to extend the logic of this policy concern, we would expect a court to refuse to award restitution damages for lawyer services in excess of the contract price. To rule otherwise would encourage a client to stay in a relationship with an attorney in whom they had lost confidence. However, the policy underlying the *Fracasse* case has not yet been extended to this circumstance.

I. RESTITUTION FOR THE PLAINTIFF IN DEFAULT

To this point, we considered the aggrieved party who suffers a breach by the other. Now we look at matters from the other side. Particularly in a long-term contract, one may invest much trying to perform, produce clear benefits to the other party, but then be unable to complete the job. Clearly, a party in default must often pay damages to the other party. However, may she recover any balance of benefits conferred over damages suffered in her favor?

Some 19th-century cases denied recovery. The typical case involved a farm laborer who contracted to work for a year. The farmer agreed to supply room and board and then to pay the laborer a sum of money at the end of the term. The laborer worked ten or eleven months and then quit. Could he recover compensation for his work? In *Hansell v. Erickson*, the Supreme Court of Illinois denied recovery, saying that the "special contract must govern."[153] The court thought the "principles involved in this case have been so long settled that it seems a waste of time to argue upon them." Its reaction to the claim speaks loudly of the assumptions about farming, work, and immigration held by those likely to rise to the appellate bench at that time:

> The pretext that appellee was a Swede, and did not understand our language, is too flimsy to deserve notice. He made the contract — it is abundantly proved, and he must abide by it. He left his employer in the midst of his harvest, probably under the promise, from some meddlesome person, to give him higher wages. This is contrary to justice and good morals, and cannot be tolerated.

Britton v. Turner[154] is a famous decision reaching the opposite result on similar facts. The New Hampshire court said: "[W]e have abundant reason to believe, that

---

[153] 28 Ill. Rep. 257 (1862).

[154] 6 N.H. 481 (1834).

the general understanding of the community is, that the hired laborer shall be entitled to compensation for the service actually performed, though he does not continue the entire term contracted for." The opinion concluded:

> This rule, by binding the employer to pay the value of the service he actually receives, and the laborer to answer in damages where he does not complete the entire contract, will leave no temptation to the former to drive the laborer from his service, near the close of his term, by ill treatment, in order to escape from payment; nor to the latter to desert his service before the stipulated time, without a sufficient reason. . . .

For many reasons, this problem has vanished from our appellate courts. However, the treatment of the plaintiff in default remains alive and troublesome in other areas. Obviously, when a party to a contract risks forfeiting what he has done trying to perform, this is an incentive to complete performance. Moreover, forfeitures can be rough surrogates for the damages actually suffered but difficult to prove. On the other hand, breaches of contracts are not always the result of morally bad conduct. Particularly in long-term contracts, one may encounter unexpected trouble only remotely related to one's own actions. Some writers see no reason to perform contracts if there is a better use for resources elsewhere. If you hold this view, you will want to minimize the costs of breach. As we turn to several areas, you might want to consider whether there should be one rule for all types of cases. Or do the interests of a party in default differ in employment, real estate, sales, and other types of contracts?

DE LEON v. ALDRETE
Texas Court of Appeals
398 S.W.2d 160 (1965)

CADENA, J.

This case involves the rights of a defaulting purchaser under a contract for the sale of land. The parties will be referred to according to the designations they carried in the trial court.

On May 30, 1960, plaintiff, Cristobal P. Aldrete, and defendants, Dario De Leon and wife, Felicitas De Leon, entered into a written contract wherein plaintiff agreed to purchase and defendants agreed to sell a tract of land in the City of Del Rio. The purchase price was $1,500.00, payable in installments according to a schedule which called for the last payment to be made on April 1, 1961. Plaintiff did not make a single payment on time, and on April 1, 1961, when, according to the contract, the full price should have been paid, plaintiff had made payments totalling less than one-half of the purchase price. Thereafter, he made partial payments totalling $350.00. On July 6, 1961, the date of the last payment made by plaintiff, he had paid only $1,070.00, leaving a balance of $430.00 unpaid and overdue since April 1, 1961.

On February 1, 1962, defendants, by general warranty deed, conveyed the land in question to Guillermo Hernandez for a cash consideration of $1,300.00. The case has been tried on the theory that, since the contract between plaintiff and defendants was unrecorded and since plaintiff did not take possession of the land,

Hernandez qualified as a bona fide purchaser and took the land free of any claims which plaintiff might assert under his contract of sale.

The trial court entered judgment for plaintiff in the sum of $1,512.60. This amount represented the total payments which plaintiff had made under the contract, $1,070.00, with interest thereon from February 21, 1962, to the date of judgment, and $250.00 which plaintiff had expended in payment of architect's fees incurred in preparation for the construction of a residence on the land. Defendants contend that there was no evidence to support the judgment. They further assert that, in any event, the trial court erred in allowing plaintiff to recover interest on the installments paid by him from February 21, 1962, to the date of judgment.

1. Plaintiff's Right to Restitution

Defendants' theory is that, because of plaintiff's failure to make the payments called for in the contract, they had the right to, and did, "rescind" the contract of sale and that, therefore, plaintiff had no right to recover the payments made by him prior to such "rescission." It is clear that defendants do not contemplate, by the use of the term "rescission," a nullification of the contract *ab initio*, with consequent rights of full restitution. What defendants assert here is the right of forfeiture.

A vendor, after breach of a contract for the sale of land by a purchaser, has the power to terminate the contract, thus ending the purchaser's interest in the land and freeing himself from the obligations imposed on him by such contract. . . . The conveyance of the land by defendants to Hernandez was an effective exercise by them of their power to terminate the contract. . . .

Where a vendor thus exercises the power of termination created in him by the purchaser's default, the question arises as to the right of the defaulting purchaser to obtain restitution of payments made by him prior to such termination. There are literally innumerable cases dealing with this problem and, as might be expected, the factual situations involved in these cases vary greatly. Attempts to state dogmatic rules without considering the factual distinctions reflected in the cases have resulted in much doctrinal confusion. . . .

What is generally described as the majority rule in this country is that a defaulting purchaser cannot recover any money paid by him under the contract to the vendor even though, as a result of the purchaser's breach, the vendor has abandoned all idea of further performance and retains the money, not for application on the purchase price, but as forfeited. . . .

The Texas decisions contain some broad general language which, if accepted at face value, would indicate that our courts are committed to the majority or "forfeiture" rule. *Tom v. Wollhoefer*, 61 Tex. 277 (1884); *Estes v. Browning*, 11 Tex. 237 (1853); *Magruder v. Poulton*, 257 S.W. 533 (Tex. Com. App., 1924). However, it is apparent that the Texas courts have not adopted a dogmatic rule of forfeiture but, instead, have embraced the more salutary rule that the vendor must make restitution if the principles of equity so require. The following language by our Supreme Court in *Lipscomb v. Fuqua*, 103 Tex. 585, 131 S.W. 1061, 1064, is pertinent:

Whether the vendor who rescinds an executory contract for the sale of land shall return the purchase money paid depends upon the equities of each case. If it would be inequitable for such rescission to occur without restoration of money paid, then it must be restored.

In *Lipscomb*, the Supreme Court properly denied restitution to the purchaser. . . . Since the damages which the vendor might suffer were uncertain and since it did not appear that the amount which the vendor sought to retain was unreasonable as an estimate of such damages, the purchaser had shown no equities which would support his claim for restitution.

The approach of our Supreme Court in *Lipscomb* is best calculated to achieve justice. Dogmatic application of the majority rule leads to indefensibly absurd results. Under that rule of forfeiture the amount of the forfeiture will always and necessarily depend simply on the stage to which the purchaser's performance has progressed, with complete disregard of the amount of damages suffered by the vendor. The surprising result is that a purchaser who pays a substantial portion of the purchase price before defaulting is in a much worse position than the purchaser who pays nothing. In the latter case, the vendor would receive only compensation for his actual losses. In the former case, a strict application of the forfeiture rule would allow the vendor to get much more, in some cases, than compensation for the loss caused him by the purchaser's default. A rule which leads to the result that the purchaser's loss increases as the seriousness of his breach decreases is so unreasonable that it does not deserve serious consideration.

One of the most popular rationalizations of the forfeiture rule is that one should not be permitted to create a cause of action in himself by his own breach of his contractual obligations. See *Estes v. Browning, supra*, 11 Tex. at 243, where our Supreme Court observed that "it would be an alarming doctrine that parties might violate their contracts because they chose to do so, and make their own infraction the basis for an action for money had and received."

This explanation and justification of what is obviously a "harsh and stringent" rule (*Tom v. Willhoeffer, supra*, 61 Tex. at 281) is singularly unpersuasive. It assumes, erroneously, that a purchaser who defaults would, as a consequence of that act alone, be entitled to recover what he has paid. No one would suppose that the purchaser's breach, standing alone, would have the effect of terminating the contract or the vendor's rights thereunder. It merely creates in the vendor a power to terminate the contract. Until he exercises such power, the vendor, apart from his right to damages, has the remedy of specific performance. If, for some reason, that remedy is unavailable, he may obtain its equivalent through enforcement of his lien (so-called foreclosure of the contract) by sale of the land and application of the proceeds to the unpaid purchase price. Patently, then, the purchaser's breach does not of itself create a cause of action in the purchaser. His right to restitution cannot arise unless and until the vendor elects to reject the remedies the law has provided for obtaining the stipulated price and chooses, instead, to abandon the contract for all purposes except that of retaining the money and enjoying the cake which he had previously eaten.

A rule which makes the right of the purchaser depend on the equities of each case leaves room for the consideration of all relevant factors, especially the all-important considerations of the amount which the purchaser has paid and the extent to which the vendor has been injured by the breach. Unless it appears that the amount paid by the purchaser exceeds the injury suffered by the vendor, restitution will not be allowed. In no event will the vendor go uncompensated for his injury.

At least in the absence of a forfeiture clause, the obvious intent of the parties to the contract is that all payments made by the purchaser are to be treated simply and only as payments on the purchase price. Where, as here, the vendor has disabled himself from performing his obligations under the contract, so that it is no longer possible to carry out the intention of the parties by applying the purchaser's payments to the purchase price, it is only equitable to regard the vendor as holding the money paid to the use of the purchaser, subject to allowance of proper damages to the vendor.

In the case before us, plaintiff had paid in excess of 70 percent of the purchase price. The damages which defendants suffered as a result of plaintiff's breach are definite and ascertainable from the evidence by resort to simple mathematical calculation. Had plaintiff fully performed, defendants would have received $1,500.00 for their land. Because of such breach, they received only $1,300.00. Plaintiff makes no contention that this was not a fair price. Clearly, in order to prevent defendants from suffering as a result of plaintiff's default, it is only necessary to allow them to retain, from the amount paid by plaintiff, the sum of $200.00. To allow them to retain the $1,070.00 paid by plaintiff, after they had received $1,300.00 as a result of their termination of the contract and sale of the land to a third party, would result in a situation where defendants would be unjustly enriched in the amount of $870.00. This result can be justified only if we are prepared to hold that plaintiff must be punished for his breach. Punitive damages are alien to the law of contract. The fundamental principle of our law concerning the liability of one who breaches his contract is the principle of compensation. This principle contemplates that the liability to respond in compensatory, as distinguished from punitive, damages will afford sufficient protection to the innocent party, and this is the only interest, absent extraordinary circumstances which are not present here, which the social welfare demands should be the subject of judicial solicitude. *Norris v. Letchworth*, 167 Mo. App. 553, 152 S.W. 421.

To restore to plaintiff the amount which he has paid, less the amount required to make defendants whole, will in no way affect the stability of contracts or reward the contract breaker. Plaintiff has lost $200.00 because of his breach. Defendants will have received $1,500.00, which is all they would have realized had plaintiff rendered faithful performance.

From what has been said, it is apparent that the trial court erred in allowing plaintiff to recover $1,070.00, the full amount of the payments he had made. Defendants should have been allowed to retain, as compensation for the damages resulting from plaintiff's breach, the sum of $200.00, allowing plaintiff a recovery of $870.00.

2. Plaintiff's Right to Recover Interest

The result of our holding is that, as of February 21, 1962, defendants were holding the amount previously paid by plaintiff, subject to an allowance for their damages, for the use and benefit of plaintiff. The sum due from defendants to plaintiff was sufficiently definite as of that date to enable them to ascertain the amount owed by them. Where the amount due is ascertainable by application of fixed rules of evidence and known standards of value, interest is recoverable from the date of the accrual of the cause of action. *Statler Hotels v. Herbert Rosenthal Jewelry Corp.*, Tex. Civ. App., 351 S.W.2d 579; Restatement, Restitution, § 356 (1937). Under such circumstances, the purchaser who is entitled to restitution is entitled to interest on the amount due him. *Phillips v. Herndon*, 78 Tex. 378, 14 S.W. 857 (1890).

Defendants present no point challenging that portion of the judgment which allows plaintiff to recover the sum of $250.00 for architect's fees.

The judgment of the trial court is modified so as to allow plaintiff to recover the sum of $870.00, with interest thereon at the rate of 6 percent from February 21, 1962, to March 3, 1963, the date of the judgment below, and, in addition, the sum of $250.00 for architect's fees. As so modified, the judgment of the trial court is affirmed.

NOTES AND QUESTIONS

1. ***Other approaches to the problem:*** Some states distinguish the rights of a defaulting party in contracts to buy land and those who have entered land contracts. The two phrases can be confusing, but they refer to distinct parts of a real estate sales transaction. All real estate sales begin with a contract to sell (or buy) land, formed in the conventional way after an offer and an acceptance. Later an event called "closing" occurs. Normally at closing, the seller transfers the deed to the real estate and the buyer pays whatever part of the agreed price had not been earlier paid as a down payment or escrow payment. Sometimes, however, the seller agrees to allow the buyer some additional number of years after closing to pay the balance of the purchase price. If so, at closing the parties enter into a second contract, called a land contract, in which the buyer agrees to pay the unpaid purchase price within an agreed-upon time period and the seller receives the right to reacquire title to the land upon default.

Wisconsin, for example, follows the "forfeiture" rule in land contract cases. If the buyer fails to make timely payments, the seller has the option to sue in "strict foreclosure." The seller establishes the contract and the buyer's failure to pay. The seller retains title to the real estate and any amounts already paid by the buyer are forfeited; the buyer loses any interest it had in the property (though the buyer has certain rights to redeem the property during a grace period). The seller is free to deal with the property in any way. The seller may use it herself rather than resell it. If she does resell it to a third party for more than the unpaid portion of the defaulting buyer's contract price, the "profit" inures solely to the seller's benefit. Of course, sellers have practical reasons in some situations to wait for a defaulting buyer to perform rather than asserting their rights.[155]

In a strict foreclosure action, a Wisconsin court may delay foreclosure for a reasonable time to permit the buyer to pay the entire remaining contract balance. However, once there has been a default, only payment of the entire balance will forestall forfeiture of the buyer's rights under the land contract. Payment of only past due amounts will not prevent foreclosure. In setting a time by which buyer may prevent foreclosure by paying the contract balance, the court "must bear in mind that in fairness the vendor should not be deprived of his land for any considerable length of time, unless there appears to be a reasonable possibility for the vendee to redeem."[156]

   2. *Plaintiff in default under the UCC:* Mr. Neri, as you will recall, began his famous case with a claim for a return of his $4250 down payment. *See Neri v. Retail Marine Corp., supra.* What is his entitlement to that down payment under UCC § 2-718(2) and (3)? How, if at all, would the answer be different if instead of a cash down payment Neri had received a trade allowance of $4250 on his old boat? *See* UCC § 2-718(4).

J.   MEASURING DAMAGES FOR SUBJECTIVE LOSSES

   Fuller and Perdue's categories — the expectation, the reliance, and the restitution interests — have advanced thinking about contract law. As is true of all analytic categories, they cannot explain everything.[157] We have already seen some of the difficulties with the expectation, reliance, and restitution interest scheme. However, our emphasis to this point has been on understanding Fuller and Perdue and the extent to which the law attempts to further the three interests. In this section, we bring the difficulties front and center. We will emphasize such things as normative conflict. How do judges manipulate contract remedies when they recognize that a problem involves two or more valued but inconsistent objectives? We will talk about the symbolic functions of law. Contract rules may declare something to be good, true, and beautiful but may do little directly to bring about that something. We will stress a bottom-up or consumer perspective on contract remedies. Whatever appellate opinions and law professors say, does contract law as delivered through the American legal system come close to protecting the expectation, reliance, and restitution interests of all or some citizens? Our goal is not to

------

   [155] The foregoing rule applies only to strict foreclosures of land contracts. *Schwartz v. Syver*, 264 Wis. 526, 59 N.W.2d 489 (1953), says that a vendee in a contract to purchase land can recover that amount of his down payment or earnest money that he can prove is over and above the vendor's damages. There is no indication that the Supreme Court of Wisconsin has considered why one rule should apply to formal land contracts and another to contracts to buy real estate where earnest money is paid to close the deal.

   [156] Kallenbach v. Lake Publications, Inc., 30 Wis. 2d 647, 658, 142 N.W.2d 212 (1966).

   [157] In order to make sense of a complicated and messy world, people must simplify and make a number of unexamined assumptions. In Roberto Unger's words, "the more [we make our premises faithful to the social reality we want to apprehend], the higher the risk that our conjectures will degenerate into a series of propositions so qualified and complicated that we are just as well off with our common sense impressions." ROBERTO MANGABEIRA UNGER, LAW IN MODERN SOCIETY: TOWARD A CRITICISM OF SOCIAL THEORY 11–12 (Free Press 1976).

undercut or destroy Fuller and Perdue, but to teach both the values and limitations of their analysis.

We will look at three cases which should serve to review what you have studied as well as to raise a number of these problems. Some students object that these are three freak cases, atypical of American business transactions in the first quarter of the 21st century. However, before you dismiss this section on that ground, you must ask whether a primary function of contract law is to deal with what are in some sense "freak cases." Ordinary business deals are performed or defaults are written off as parties go on to the next transaction. Disputes worth litigating come in unusual situations. However, our contract law may be fashioned to cope with certain kinds of transactions and may not fit others very well. It may be impossible to fashion a general contract law that applies the same principles to sales of machines, to business and to consumer products, to employment contracts involving famous actresses and to ordinary employees, to sales of condominiums and houses, and to complex real estate development schemes or the exploitation of mineral rights, and so on. Each situation has its own particular nature, and we generalize only by denying particularity.

PEEVYHOUSE v. GARLAND COAL & MINING CO.
Oklahoma Supreme Court
382 P.2d 109 (1962)

Jackson, J.

In the trial court, plaintiffs Willie and Lucille Peevyhouse sued the defendant, Garland Coal and Mining Company, for damages for breach of contract. Judgment was for plaintiffs in an amount considerably less than was sued for. Plaintiffs appeal and defendant cross-appeals.

In the briefs on appeal, the parties present their argument and contentions under several propositions; however, they all stem from the basic question of whether the trial court properly instructed the jury on the measure of damages.

Briefly stated, the facts are as follows: plaintiffs owned a farm containing coal deposits, and in November, 1954, leased the premises to defendant for a period of five years for coal mining purposes. A "strip-mining" operation was contemplated in which the coal would be taken from pits on the surface of the ground, instead of from underground mine shafts. In addition to the usual covenants found in a coal mining lease, defendant specifically agreed to perform certain restorative and remedial work at the end of the lease period. It is unnecessary to set out the details of the work to be done, other than to say that it would involve the moving of many thousands of cubic yards of dirt, at a cost estimated by expert witnesses at about $29,000.00. However, plaintiffs sued for only $25,000.00.

During the trial, it was stipulated that all covenants and agreements in the lease contract had been fully carried out by both parties, except the remedial work mentioned above; defendant conceded that this work had not been done.

Plaintiffs introduced expert testimony as to the amount and nature of the work to be done, and its estimated cost. Over plaintiffs' objections, defendant thereafter introduced expert testimony as to the "diminution in value" of plaintiffs' farm resulting from the failure of defendant to render performance as agreed in the contract — that is, the difference between the present value of the farm, and what its value would have been if defendant had done what it agreed to do.

At the conclusion of the trial, the court instructed the jury that it must return a verdict for plaintiffs, and left the amount of damages for jury determination. On the measure of damages, the court instructed the jury that it might consider the cost of performance of the work defendant agreed to do, "together with all of the evidence offered on behalf of either party."

It thus appears that the jury was at liberty to consider the "diminution in value" of plaintiffs' farm as well as the cost of "repair work" in determining the amount of damages.

It returned a verdict for plaintiffs for $5000.00 — only a fraction of the "cost of performance," *but more than the total value of the farm even after the remedial work is done.*

On appeal, the issue is sharply drawn. Plaintiffs contend that the true measure of damages in this case is what it will cost plaintiffs to obtain performance of the work that was not done because of defendant's default. Defendant argues that the measure of damages is the cost of performance "limited, however, to the total difference in the market value before and after the work was performed."

It appears that this precise question has not heretofore been presented to this court. In *Ardizonne v. Archer*, 72 Okl. 70, 178 P. 263, this court held that the measure of damages for breach of a contract to drill an oil well was the reasonable cost of drilling the well, but here a slightly different factual situation exists. The drilling of an oil well will yield valuable geological information, even if no oil or gas is found, and of course if the well is a producer, the value of the premises increases. In the case before us, it is argued by defendant with some force that the performance of the remedial work defendant agreed to do will add at the most only a few hundred dollars to the value of plaintiffs' farm, and that the damages should be limited to that amount because that is all plaintiffs have lost.

Plaintiffs rely on *Groves v. John Wunder Co.*, 205 Minn. 163, 286 N.W. 235, 123 A.L.R. 502. In that case, the Minnesota court, in a substantially similar situation, adopted the "cost of performance" rule as opposed to the "value" rule. The result was to authorize a jury to give plaintiff damages in the amount of $60,000, where the real estate concerned would have been worth only $12,160, even if the work contracted for had been done.

It may be observed that *Groves v. John Wunder Co.* is the only case which has come to our attention in which the cost of performance rule has been followed under circumstances where the cost of performance greatly exceeded the diminution in value resulting from the breach of contract. Incidentally, it appears that this case was decided by a plurality rather than a majority of the members of the court.

Defendant relies principally upon *Sandy Valley & E. R. Co. v. Hughes*, 175 Ky. 320, 194 S.W. 344; *Bigham v. Wabash-Pittsburg Terminal Ry. Co.*, 223 Pa. 106, 72 A.

318; and *Sweeney v. Lewis Const. Co.*, 66 Wash. 490, 119 P. 1108. These were all cases in which, under similar circumstances, the appellate courts followed the "value" rule instead of the "cost of performance" rule. Plaintiff points out that in the earliest of these cases (*Bigham*) the court cites as authority on the measure of damages an earlier Pennsylvania *tort* case, and that the other two cases follow the first, with no explanation as to why a measure of damages ordinarily followed in cases sounding in tort should be used in contract cases. Nevertheless, it is of some significance that three out of four appellate courts have followed the diminution in value rule under circumstances where, as here, the cost of performance greatly exceeds the diminution in value.

The explanation may be found in the fact that the situations presented are artificial ones. It is highly unlikely that the ordinary property owner would agree to pay $29,000 (or its equivalent) for the construction of "improvements" upon his property that would increase its value only about $300. The result is that we are called upon to apply principles of law theoretically based upon reason and reality to a situation which is basically unreasonable and unrealistic.

In *Groves v. John Wunder Co.*, in arriving at its conclusions, the Minnesota court apparently considered the contract involved to be analogous to a building and construction contract, and cited authority for the proposition that the cost of performance or completion of the building as contracted is ordinarily the measure of damages in actions for damages for the breach of such a contract.

In an annotation following the Minnesota case beginning at 123 A.L.R. 515, the annotator places the three cases relied on by defendant (*Sandy Valley*, *Bigham* and *Sweeney*) under the classification of cases involving "grading and excavation contracts."

We do not think either analogy is strictly applicable to the case now before us. The primary purpose of the lease contract between plaintiffs and defendant was neither "building and construction" nor "grading and excavation." It was merely to accomplish the economical recovery and marketing of coal from the premises, to the profit of all parties. The special provisions of the lease contract pertaining to remedial work were incidental to the main object involved.

Even in the case of contracts that are unquestionably building and construction contracts, the authorities are not in agreement as to the factors to be considered in determining whether the cost of performance rule or the value rule should be applied. The American Law Institute's Restatement of Contracts, §§ 346(1)(a)(i) and (ii), submits the proposition that the cost of performance is the proper measure of damages "if this is possible and does not involve *unreasonable economic waste*"; and that the diminution in value caused by the breach is the proper measure "if construction and completion in accordance with the contract would involve *unreasonable economic waste*." (Emphasis supplied.) In an explanatory comment immediately following the text, the Restatement makes it clear that the "economic waste" referred to consists of the destruction of a substantially completed building or other structure. Of course no such destruction is involved in the case now before us.

On the other hand, in McCormick, *Damages*, § 168, it is said with regard to building and construction contracts that "in cases where the defect is one that can be repaired or cured without *undue expense*" the cost of performance is the proper measure of damages, but where "the defect in material or construction is one that cannot be remedied without *an expenditure for reconstruction disproportionate to the end to be attained*" (emphasis supplied) the value rule should be followed. The same idea was expressed in *Jacob & Youngs, Inc. v. Kent*, 230 N.Y. 239, 129 N.E. 889, 23 A.L.R. 1429, as follows:

> The owner is entitled to the money which will permit him to complete, unless the cost of completion is grossly and unfairly out of proportion to the good to be attained. When that is true, the measure is the difference in value.

It thus appears that the prime consideration in the Restatement was "economic waste"; and that the prime consideration in McCormick, *Damages*, and in *Jacob & Youngs, Inc. v. Kent*, was the relationship between the expense involved and the "end to be attained" — in other words, the "relative economic benefit."

In view of the unrealistic fact situation in the instant case, and certain Oklahoma statutes to be hereinafter noted, we are of the opinion that the "relative economic benefit" is a proper consideration here. This is in accord with the recent case of *Mann v. Clowser*, 190 Va. 887, 59 S.E.2d 78, where, in applying the cost rule, the Virginia court specifically noted that "the defects are remediable from a practical standpoint and the costs *are not grossly disproportionate to the results to be obtained*." (Emphasis supplied.)

23 O.S. 1961 §§ 96 and 97 provide as follows:

> § 96. . . . Notwithstanding the provisions of this chapter, no person can recover a greater amount in damages for the breach of an obligation, than he would have gained by the full performance thereof on both sides . . .

> § 97. . . . Damages must, in all cases, be reasonable, and where an obligation of any kind appears to create a right to unconscionable and grossly oppressive damages, contrary to substantial justice, no more than reasonable damages can be recovered.

Although it is true that the above sections of the statute are applied most often in tort cases, they are by their own terms, and the decisions of this court, also applicable in actions for damages for breach of contract. It would seem that they are peculiarly applicable here where, under the "cost of performance" rule, plaintiffs might recover an amount about nine times the total value of their farm. Such would seem to be "unconscionable and grossly oppressive damages, contrary to substantial justice" within the meaning of the statute. Also, it can hardly be denied that if plaintiffs here are permitted to recover under the "cost of performance" rule, they will receive a greater benefit from the breach than could be gained from full performance, contrary to the provisions of § 96.

An analogy may be drawn between the cited sections and the provisions of 15 O.S. 1961 §§ 214 and 215. These sections tend to render void any provisions of a contract which attempt to fix the amount of stipulated damages to be paid in case of a breach, except where it is impracticable or extremely difficult to determine the actual damages. This results in spite of the agreement of the parties, and the obvious and well known rationale is that insofar as they exceed the actual damages suffered, the stipulated damages amount to a penalty or forfeiture which the law does not favor.

23 O.S. 1961 §§ 96 and 97 have the same effect in the case now before us. *In spite of the agreement of the parties*, these sections limit the damages recoverable to a reasonable amount not "contrary to substantial justice"; they prevent plaintiffs from recovering a "greater amount in damages for the breach of an obligation" than they would have "gained by the full performance thereof."

We therefore hold that where, in a coal mining lease, lessee agrees to perform certain remedial work on the premises concerned at the end of the lease period, and thereafter the contract is fully performed by both parties except that the remedial work is not done, the measure of damages in an action by lessor against lessee for damages for breach of contract is ordinarily the reasonable cost of performance of the work; however, where the contract provision breached was merely incidental to the main purpose in view, and where the economic benefit which would result to lessor by full performance of the work is grossly disproportionate to the cost of performance, the damages which lessor may recover are limited to the diminution in value resulting to the premises because of the non-performance.

We believe the above holding is in conformity with the intention of the Legislature as expressed in the statutes mentioned, and in harmony with the better-reasoned cases from the other jurisdictions where analogous fact situations have been considered. It should be noted that the rule as stated does not interfere with the property owner's right to "do what he will with his own" (*Chamberlain v. Parker*, 45 N.Y. 569), or his right, if he chooses, to contract for "improvements" which will actually have the effect of reducing his property's value. Where such result is in fact contemplated by the parties, and is a main or principal purpose of those contracting, it would seem that the measure of damages for breach would ordinarily be the cost of performance.

The above holding disposes of all of the arguments raised by the parties on appeal.

Under the most liberal view of the evidence herein, the diminution in value resulting to the premises because of non-performance of the remedial work was $300.00. After a careful search of the record, we have found no evidence of a higher figure, and plaintiffs do not argue in their briefs that a greater diminution in value was sustained. It thus appears that the judgment was clearly excessive, and that the amount for which judgment should have been rendered is definitely and satisfactorily shown by the record.

We are asked by each party to modify the judgment in accordance with the respective theories advanced, and it is conceded that we have authority to do so. 12 O.S. 1961 § 952; *Busboom v. Smith*, 199 Okl. 688, 191 P.2d 198; *Stumpf v. Stumpf*, 173 Okl. 1, 46 P.2d 315.

We are of the opinion that the judgment of the trial court for plaintiffs should be, and it is hereby, modified and reduced to the sum of $300.00, and as so modified it is affirmed.

WELCH, DAVISON, HALLEY, and JOHNSON, JJ., concur. WILLIAMS, C.J., BLACKBIRD, V.C.J., and IRWIN and BERRY, JJ., dissent.

IRWIN, J. (dissenting).

By the specific provisions in the coal mining lease under consideration, the defendant agreed as follows:

. . .

7b. Lessee agrees to make fills in the pits dug on said premises on the property line in such manner that fences can be placed thereon and access had to opposite sides of the pits.

7c. Lessee agrees to smooth off the top of the spoil banks on the above premises.

7d. Lessee agrees to leave the creek crossing the above premises in such a condition that it will not interfere with the crossings to be made in pits as set out in 7b.

. . .

7f. Lessee further agrees to leave no shale or dirt on the high wall of said pits. . . .

Following the expiration of the lease, plaintiffs made demand upon defendant that it carry out the provisions of the contract and to perform those covenants contained therein.

Defendant admits that it failed to perform its obligations that it agreed and contracted to perform under the lease contract, and there is nothing in the record which indicates that defendant could not perform its obligations. Therefore, in my opinion defendant's breach of the contract was willful and not in good faith.

Although the contract speaks for itself, there were several negotiations between the plaintiffs and defendant before the contract was executed. Defendant admitted, in the trial of the action, that plaintiffs insisted that the above provisions be included in the contract and that they would not agree to the coal mining lease unless the above provisions were included.

In consideration for the lease contract, plaintiffs were to receive a certain amount as royalty for the coal produced and marketed and in addition thereto their land was to be restored as provided in the contract.

Defendant received as consideration for the contract, its proportionate share of the coal produced and marketed and in addition thereto, the *right to use* plaintiffs' land in the furtherance of its mining operations.

The cost for performing the contract in question could have been reasonably approximated when the contract was negotiated and executed and there are no conditions now existing which could not have been reasonably anticipated by the parties. Therefore, defendant had knowledge, when it prevailed upon the plaintiffs to execute the lease, that the cost of performance might be disproportionate to the value or benefits received by plaintiff for the performance.

Defendant has received its benefits under the contract and now urges, in substance, that plaintiffs' measure of damages for its failure to perform should be the economic value of performance to the plaintiffs and not the cost of performance.

If a peculiar set of facts should exist where the above rule should be applied as the proper measure of damages (and in my judgment those facts do not exist in the instant case), before such rule should be applied, consideration should be given to the benefits received or contracted for by the party who asserts the application of the rule.

Defendant did not have the right to mine plaintiffs' coal or to use plaintiffs' property for its mining operations without the consent of plaintiffs. Defendant had knowledge of the benefits that it would receive under the contract and the approximate cost of performing the contract. With this knowledge, it must be presumed that defendant thought that it would be to its economic advantage to enter into the contract with plaintiffs and that it would reap benefits from the contract, or it would have not entered into the contract.

Therefore, if the value of the performance of a contract should be considered in determining the measure of damages for breach of a contract, the value of the benefits received under the contract by a party who breaches a contract should also be considered. However, in my judgment, to give consideration to either in the instant action, completely rescinds and holds for naught the solemnity of the contract before us and makes an entirely new contract for the parties.

In *Goble v. Bell Oil & Gas Co.*, 97 Okl. 261, 223 P. 371, we held:

> Even though the contract contains harsh and burdensome terms which the court does not in all respects approve, it is the province of the parties in relation to lawful subject matter to fix their rights and obligations, and the court will give the contract effect according to its expressed provisions, unless it be shown by competent evidence that the written agreement as executed is the result of fraud, mistake, or accident.

In *Cities Service Oil Co. v. Geolograph Co. Inc.*, 208 Okl. 179, 254 P.2d 775, we said:

> While we do not agree that the contract as presently written is an onerous one, we think the short answer is that the folly or wisdom of a contract is not for the court to pass on.

In *Great Western Oil & Gas Co. v. Mitchell, Okl.*, 326 P.2d 794, we held:

> The law will not make a better contract for parties than they themselves have seen fit to enter into, or alter it for the benefit of one party and to the detriment of the others; the judicial function of a court of law is to enforce a contract as it is written.

I am mindful of Title 23 O.S. 1961 § 96, which provides that no person can recover a greater amount in damages for the breach of an obligation than he could have gained by the full performance thereof on both sides, except in cases not applicable herein. However, in my judgment, the above statutory provision is not applicable here.

In my judgment, we should follow the case of *Groves v. John Wunder Company* . . . which defendant agrees "that the fact situation is apparently similar to the one in the case at bar," and where the Supreme Court of Minnesota held:

> The owner's or employer's damages for [a willful breach] are to be measured, not in respect to the value of the land to be improved, but by the reasonable cost of doing that which the contractor promised to do and which he left undone.

The . . . breach referred to states that where the contractor's breach of a contract is willful, that is, in bad faith, he is not entitled to any benefit of the equitable doctrine of substantial performance.

In the instant action defendant has made no attempt to even substantially perform. The contract in question is not immoral, is not tainted with fraud, and was not entered into through mistake or accident and is not contrary to public policy. It is clear and unambiguous and the parties understood the terms thereof, and the approximate cost of fulfilling the obligations could have been approximately ascertained. There are no conditions existing now which could not have been reasonably anticipated when the contract was negotiated and executed. The defendant could have performed the contract if it desired. It has accepted and reaped the benefits of its contract and now urges that plaintiffs' benefits under the contract be denied. If plaintiffs' benefits are denied, such benefits would inure to the direct benefit of the defendant.

Therefore, in my opinion, the plaintiffs were entitled to specific performance of the contract and since defendant has failed to perform, the proper measure of damages should be the cost of performance. Any other measure of damage would be holding for naught the express provisions of the contract; would be taking from the plaintiffs the benefits of the contract and placing those benefits in defendant which has failed to perform its obligations; would be granting benefits to defendant without a resulting obligation; and would be completely rescinding the solemn obligation of the contract for the benefit of the defendant to the detriment of the plaintiffs by making an entirely new contract for the parties.

I therefore respectfully dissent to the opinion promulgated by a majority of my associates.

NOTES AND QUESTIONS

1. *Rehearing and vote switching:* Following the Supreme Court of Oklahoma's decision, the Peevyhouses' lawyer petitioned for a rehearing. Ten highly regarded lawyers and academics from Oklahoma City filed an amicus curiae brief in support of the Peevyhouses,[158] arguing for the sanctity of contracts:

---

[158] This information, as well as much of the other information about this case reported in these notes, comes from Professor Judith Maute, Peevyhouse v. Garland Coal and Mining Co. *Revisited: The Ballad of Willie and Lucille*, 89 Nw. U. L. Rev. 1341, 1352–53, 1368–70, 1405–06 (1995) (hereinafter cited as Maute). Copyright © Judith Maute. Reprinted by permission. Another version of this article appears as Judith Maute, *The Unearthed Facts of* Peevyhouse v. Garland Coal and Mining Co., *in* Contracts Stories 265 (Douglas Baird ed., Foundation Press 2007). Materials from this article were also used in a movie,

[T]he express and unambiguous terms of contracts entered into by private individuals . . . cannot . . . be abrogated. . . . [W]hen contractual promises are broken, this Court should lend its aid to promisees relying on the promises of competent promisors and lend its most vigorous sanction, to insure to future promisees that the aid of this Court is certain and unwavering, particularly being mindful of the interests sought to be safeguarded by the promisee in stipulating for terms, and not alone the objective of the promisor.

The Oklahoma Supreme Court denied the petition for rehearing, but there was a vote switch. The vote on the original decision was 5-3, with Justice Welch not participating. On rehearing Justice Williams switched his vote, resulting in a 4-4 split among the participating justices. However, Justice Welch then decided to vote on the side of Garland and the rehearing petition was denied 5-4. Later the official report was amended to reflect the votes of Justices Williams and Welch after rehearing.

2. **Strip mining:** Strip mining has been defined as follows:

After the exposed coal is removed, the operator makes a second, parallel cut with the overburden placed as spoil material into the first cut. The operator continues with successive cuts until the remaining coal lies too deep below the overburden to be mined economically. The last cut leaves a pit, or open trench bounded on one side by the last spoil bank, and on the other side by the highwall. . . . If the bottom of the last cut is beneath the water table, the pit eventually fills with water, and is euphemistically called the "pond."[159]

At the time of this case, environmental regulations did not require restoration of the Peevyhouse land after the strip mining, as they often do today. Hence, the Peevyhouses' only legal claim was for breach of contract. Should the decision of the Oklahoma Supreme Court nonetheless have been influenced by environmental concerns?

3. **Background of the case:** The briefs in the *Peevyhouse* case throw some light on the facts. The following excerpt from the transcript, taken from plaintiffs' brief, reveals some of the circumstances surrounding the negotiation of the contract. The testimony is by Burl Cumpton, who admitted negotiating and executing the contract on behalf of Garland Coal and Mining Company.

Q. Isn't it true that Mr. Peevyhouse insisted upon those provisions being included in the lease?

A. That's true.

Q. Before he agreed to sign it?

A. That's right. . . .

The Ballad of Willie and Lucille: Disappointed Expectations of Contract Law and the Legal System, © 2008.

[159] Maute, *supra* note 158, at 1352–53.

Q. Mr. Cumpton, when you negotiated and obtained that lease from the Peevyhouses did you intend to comply with the terms of that contract, those specific terms of the lease that are included in there?

A. Yes, we did.

Q. Your company hasn't complied with them?

A. No, that's right.

Q. Could you, with the equipment you have, could you have complied with those terms of that lease?

A. Yes, we could, but I want to qualify that statement. . . .

The Court: You can bring it [the qualification] out on cross-examination.

The following excerpt, taken from plaintiffs' reply brief, may explain why plaintiffs wanted the remedial work done:

> From the terms of the mining lease it is clearly apparent that plaintiffs insisted upon the insertion of the terms . . . [because] they wanted to assure their continued right to the use of their land in connection with their stock farming operations. I am sure that this Court is cognizant of what effect the bisecting of a tract of land by a deep, east-west, 45-foot water-filled pit, rendering inaccessible the northern portion of plaintiffs' lands [Eds. note: about seven acres] along with 80 acres of leased land, would have on a stockman. It is quite obvious from the facts of this case that when the contract was executed between the parties that the plaintiffs had in mind only the assurance of the continued future use of their land as a stock farm and that the defendant was thoroughly cognizant of these desires and agreed to them.

Professor Judith Maute has done an extensive study of the *Peevyhouse* case, including extensive interviews with the Peevyhouses themselves. She describes Garland's failure to perform the remedial work in the following terms:

> Actual mining on the Peevyhouse land was short-lived. Garland began coal removal in February, 1957 and ended sometime that spring. Exceptionally heavy spring rains broke a six-year drought. . . . The flood conditions must have resolved any doubts Garland had about continuing to mine at this location. Garland pulled the dragline from the worksite and resumed mining at a higher and drier site. . . .
>
> Garland had no contractual duty to remove a specific quantity of coal from Peevyhouse land. . . . Nonperformance of the remedial work was the only breach. . . . As Garland prepared to leave the site, Burl Cumpton and Willie discussed the remedial work. . . . A bulldozer spent one day smoothing off the sharp peaks on the spoil banks and building a dirt levee across the pit. More heavy rains interrupted these makeshift efforts. When saturated ground caused unstable conditions that endangered workers, Garland ceased all remedial efforts. Willie then offered to accept $500 so he could hire a bulldozer and level the ground himself. Garland refused. Willie then told Cumpton that the price of the settlement would increase $500

each time he returned to Garland's Stigler office about the matter. Six fruitless visits later brought the settlement demand to $3000. Finally, Garland presented a check for $3000 conditioned on the Peevyhouses signing a release.

The Peevyhouses knew of Woodrow McConnell[160] because he was from Stigler and had represented their neighbor, Clifton Few, in a pending tort claim against Garland. The Peevyhouses went to Oklahoma City to discuss the proposed settlement with McConnell. He advised them against signing the release unless a certain paragraph was deleted. They recall his explanation: "If you sign [this], you take full responsibility to your neighbors [for damage being done to their land from the creek], and your neighbors will look to you." Settlement discussions ended when Garland refused to delete the objectionable paragraph.[161]

Professor Maute described the condition of the Peevyhouse farm as of 1995. Apparently the dirt levee constructed by Garland quickly washed out. There have been no crossings across the pit since then, and the pit is filled with water. Professor Maute continues:

> Willie and Lucille Peevyhouse still live on the land located outside Stigler. The land they leased to Garland has changed little from when the mining stopped more than 35 years ago. The rough, rocky surface on the high wall and spoil banks is sparsely vegetated. About half of the leased acreage remains unusable. . . . Lucille is bitter and distrustful of the legal system. She wants to move into the town of Stigler, leaving behind the scarred land and her memories of the legal dispute. Willie still wants the land fixed: "It's just not right to do something with land that makes it useless for the future." . . . [A]pproximately thirty acres are practically worthless to the Peevyhouses.[162]

4. *Other possible outcomes:* The Oklahoma Supreme Court analyzed the case as if the only possible outcomes were either to award the cost of performance or the diminution in value of the land. Both of these damages formulas reflect the expectation principle: they constitute different methods of estimating the position of the plaintiff if the contract had not been breached. In *Peevyhouse* the Oklahoma Supreme Court did not discuss possible damages calculations reflecting reliance or restitution principles. What possibilities can you construct? Consider the following additional information about the case. (Much of this information comes from Professor Maute's study of the case and was not included in the trial record because the lawyer for the Peevyhouses did not introduce it at trial.)

(a) It is unclear how much Garland expected the remedial work to cost at the time it signed the contract. Normally Garland paid landowners a surface damage payment in addition to royalties. In the Peevyhouses' situation, that payment would have been $3000, but it was not included in the contract because Garland agreed to

---

[160] [Eds. note: McConnell would become their attorney.]

[161] Maute, *supra* note 158, at 1368–70.

[162] *Id.* at 1405–06.

the remedial work. On the other hand, the Peevyhouses negotiated a 20-cents-per-ton royalty for mined coal instead of the normal 15 cents per ton in Garland contracts. Undoubtedly the cheapest way to do the remedial work would have been for Garland to do it when its earth-moving equipment was on site, but as indicated above, the soil was so waterlogged at the time Garland decided to quit the site that the work could not practically be done. The $29,000 estimate of the cost of doing the remedial work at a later time, which is mentioned in the court's opinion, comes from testimony at trial by an expert witness for the Peevyhouses. At trial, Garland's lawyer challenged the basis of this estimate. An expert for Garland testified that the cost of doing the work at the time of trial would have been only $8500. Writing in 1994, Professor Maute concluded that the best guess she could make about the cost of doing the remedial work at the time of the trial in this case was $18,000.[163]

(b) Garland was especially anxious to sign a contract with the Peevyhouses because it needed to divert the creek. Diversion of the creek was necessary so that the water from the creek would not run into the various "cuts" Garland would make, not only on the Peevyhouses' land but also the land of neighbors with whom Garland signed contracts. Because of the topography of the land, the most practical place to divert the creek was through the Peevyhouses' land.

(c) The Peevyhouses received $2500 in royalties under the Garland contract. Professor Maute's estimate of Garland's profits from the coal mined from the Peevyhouses' land is between $25,000 and $34,000.

(d) If the fills had been made in the pits as promised in the contract, Willie Peevyhouse would have had access to approximately 4.5 acres of unspoiled land that he owned and which was separated from the rest of the land. The fills would also have provided access to leased land. If in addition the spoil banks had been leveled, Peevyhouse would have regained nearly seven acres of pasture land. At the time, undisturbed land in the area had a market value of about $50 per acre.

5. *Specific performance:* Some have argued that the ideal solution in cases such as *Peevyhouse v. Garland Coal & Mining Co.* would be an order of specific performance requiring Garland to do the remedial work. If a court issued such an order, what do you think would have been the likely consequence? Would the pits on the Peevyhouses' land have been filled in?

James Young v. Old Ben Coal Company[164] involves a plaintiff's ultimately unsuccessful effort to get specific performance of a restoration provision in an oil and gas lease. Although there were several alternative grounds for refusing relief, the Seventh Circuit, in an opinion by Judge Posner, cited both *Peevyhouse* and *Groves v. John Wunder* (the case relied on by plaintiffs in *Peevyhouse*). Posner notes that the plaintiff in this case was seeking to require the defendant to "restore" some wells to the condition they were in before strip-mining the land in a situation in which those wells were no longer producing valuable oil or gas. He concludes:

> Breach of a duty to restore the wells to their mint operating condition would impose no loss on the owner of the oil and gas estate in the land . . . ,

---

[163] *Id.* at 1398.

[164] 243 F.3d 387 (7th Cir. 2001).

because there is no oil left in the ground and so no value to be obtained from oil wells. And one would expect the risk of the oil running out to be borne by the owner of the oil and gas estate, who has the reversionary interest in any oil that is left after the oil lease has terminated, rather than by a coal company. The owner of the oil and gas estate gains if there is oil left in the ground after the oil lease runs out, and so he should lose if there is no oil left.

This case is actually worse for the plaintiff than *Groves*, because [plaintiff] is seeking, but not wanting, specific performance. If he obtained the relief he is seeking, that would just be a prelude to a further negotiation with Old Ben. [Plaintiff] does not want nonproducing wells; he wants money to compensate him for a loss that he has not sustained, since the restoration of the wells would have value for him only if there were oil left in the ground. The essentially extortionate transaction, a source of transaction costs not offset by any social benefit, for which an order of specific performance would have set the stage, is another compelling objection, though less to the claim underlying the suit than to the relief sought, the grant of which would be inequitable. [Citations omitted.]

How does Judge Posner's comment influence your judgment about the appropriateness of specific performance in *Peevyhouse*?

6. *The authority of* Peevyhouse: A year after the *Peevyhouse* decision there was a scandal involving the Supreme Court of Oklahoma.[165] Several of its members were accused of taking bribes to decide cases, but they were *not* accused of taking a bribe in *Peevyhouse v. Garland Coal & Mining Co.* Two of the justices who concurred in the majority opinion in that case were implicated. One resigned and one was impeached. An Oklahoma Bar Association Committee investigated, and said that the other seven justices "were proved to be honest men and have not been paid, nor have they received any bribe in any case."[166] Could a lawyer in Oklahoma use this scandal as a basis for attacking the *Peevyhouse* decision? Could a lawyer in another state use it to argue that her highest court should not follow the decision? Does the fact that a judge was bribed in one case necessarily indicate there is something wrong with his or her decision in another one?

The Peevyhouses' lawyer was a solo practitioner, based in Oklahoma City. They had learned of him because he was originally from Stigler and had represented some neighbors in lawsuits against Garland. Garland was represented by one of Oklahoma City's largest law firms.

Many persons question some of the decisions made by the Peevyhouses' lawyer. He chose not to introduce much potentially relevant evidence, including the Peevyhouses' waiver of a surface damage payment in exchange for the remedial clauses. He chose to appeal the jury verdict of $5000 even though Garland probably would have settled for that amount,[167] with the result that Garland cross-appealed

---

[165] JOHN H. JACKSON, CONTRACT LAW IN MODERN SOCIETY 44 (West 1973).

[166] 36 OKLA. B. ASS'N J. 1507 (1965).

[167] This is the conclusion reached by Professor Maute. Maute, *supra* note 158, at 1386.

and obtained a significant reduction in the size of the judgment. Is the authority of the *Peevyhouse* decision lessened because the Peevyhouses' lawyer made decisions that with the advantage of hindsight seem clearly unfortunate?

7. *Revisiting* Plante v. Jacobs: Refresh your memory of *Plante v. Jacobs*, a note case in section H.2.b. of this chapter, *supra*. After the court concluded that there had been substantial performance, entitling the builder (Plante) to the unpaid contract price less any damages owing to the owner (Jacobs) for acknowledged deficiencies, it addressed the measure of those damages. Jacobs sought the cost of repair, including relocating the misplaced living room wall. Jacobs testified that the change in the living room dimensions (from 16 x 32 feet, as designed, to 15 x 32 feet, as built) had forced the Jacobses to change their plans for locating furniture and had made a custom-built davenport less useful than planned. A witness for the Jacobses, an architect, testified:

> As an architect it is my opinion that it was a serious error in narrowing the living room and widening the kitchen. I would say it would make the house less desirable to live in and to own. . . . It is standard practice in construction where an error of this magnitude occurs that the wall would be ordered to be removed and placed in the position indicated on the plans.

Two local real estate brokers testified for Plante and gave their professional opinion that the relocation of the living room wall would neither increase nor decrease the market value of the house.

In affirming the trial court's decision to allow no damages for the misplacement of the living room wall, Justice Hallows of the Wisconsin Supreme Court stated that the measure of damages was the cost of repair for items that did not involve "an unreasonable economic waste." However, this measure is inappropriate when repair would involve such waste. Then all a plaintiff can recover is the "difference in value of the house as it stands with faulty and incomplete construction and the value of the house if it had been constructed in strict accordance with the plans and specifications." The court said:

> To tear down the wall now and rebuild it in its proper place would involve a substantial destruction of the work, if not all of it, which was put into the wall and would cause additional damage to other parts of the house and require replastering and redecorating the walls and ceilings of at least two rooms. Such economic waste is unreasonable and unjustified.

Justice Hallows explained: "There may be situations in which features or details of construction of special or of great personal importance [exist] which, if not performed, would prevent a finding of substantial performance." Nevertheless, in the *Plante* case, "the plan was a stock floor plan . . . there were no blueprints . . . many of the problems that arose during the construction had to be solved on the basis of practical experience."

Do you infer that a court would require a builder to come closer to the plans to substantially perform a contract to build an architect-designed house with artistic features? If so, is the court's decision an example of the law favoring the wealthy over the middle and working class?

8. **Subsequent decisions:** There have been many cases in other states discussing which approach to measuring expectation damages is most appropriate. Some of these cases are discussed in the *Peevyhouse* opinion. Another is *Plante v. Jacobs*. A very famous opinion by Justice Cardozo is in *Jacob & Youngs v. Kent* (discussed in the *Peevyhouse* majority opinion). In that case, which raised a similar issue, Justice Cardozo applied a diminution in value measure.

In *Hancock v. Northcutt*,[168] the Alaska Supreme Court held that homeowners could recover the cost of demolishing and rebuilding a defectively constructed earth-sheltered home, even though the market value of a properly constructed earth-sheltered home was far less than that, providing a jury found that "the plaintiffs are more likely than not to demolish and rebuild the house" if they recovered the cost of doing so. What recovery would there be in *Peevyhouse* if the court had applied a similar test? What recovery in *Plante v. Jacobs*?

There have been a number of subsequent decisions in Oklahoma discussing the current status of the *Peevyhouse* holding.

(a) A 1983 10th Circuit decision in the case of *Rock Island Improvement Co. v. Helmerich & Payne, Inc.*[169] raised the same issue as that posed in the *Peevyhouse* case. A mining company leased the right to mine coal on two tracts of land in Oklahoma. The lease required that the surface be restored to its condition prior to the mining operations. The tracts of land were strip mined but not reclaimed. The parties stipulated that the value of the land was $6797 less after the mining than it would have been had the reclamation been carried out. Expert testimony established that restoring the land as called for by the lease would cost $375,000. The jury awarded the land owner $375,000. The 10th Circuit noted that there was a strong dissent in *Peevyhouse* and that since the *Peevyhouse* decision, the public policy of the state had changed as expressed by the adoption of a law regulating reclamation of open-cut mines. The court felt that it was unlikely that the Oklahoma Supreme Court would follow its decision in *Peevyhouse* and thus the court indicated that it need not adhere to the decision. The federal court found that the parties expressly included the reclamation clause, which required the lessee to bear the cost of reclamation, and the court felt that the parties' agreement should be given force. The court said nothing about the likelihood that the $375,000 (less attorney's fees) would be spent on reclamation or the wisdom of spending that much to produce an economic benefit of $6797.

(b) A year later the Oklahoma Court of Appeals decided *Thompson v. Andover Oil Co.*[170] In this case, plaintiffs brought a nuisance action against holders of an oil and gas lease for damages to the land surface resulting from oil and gas operations. The plaintiff testified that the diminution in the value of the land was $50,000. Expert testimony indicated that the cost of restoring the land was $70,000. The jury awarded $50,000. The Oklahoma Court of Appeals upheld the jury's award. The court reasoned that damages must be limited to the cost of restoring the land but twice noted that they cannot exceed the depreciated value of the land itself; the

---

[168]   808 P.2d 251 (Alaska 1991).

[169]   698 F.2d 1075 (10th Cir. 1983).

[170]   691 P.2d 77 (Okla. Ct. App. 1984).

court cited *Peevyhouse* for this proposition and made no mention of the 10th Circuit's decision in *Rock Island*.

(c) *Davis v. Shell Oil Co.*[171] was decided by the Federal District Court for the Western District of Oklahoma in 1992. In discussing the amount of damages that the plaintiff could claim, the court rejected defendant's claim that damages must be limited to diminution in value. The court cited *Rock Island* as if it held that courts in Oklahoma do not follow *Peevyhouse*. The court also noted that the citation of *Peevyhouse* in *Thompson* was in dicta and characterized *Thompson* as unpersuasive authority.

(d) In *Schneberger v. Apache Corp.*, the Oklahoma Supreme Court addressed the continuing vitality of the *Peevyhouse* rule.[172] Apache agreed to clean up ground water contaminated by drilling for oil and gas wells. They abandoned their cleanup efforts. Plaintiff's estimate of the cost of completing the cleanup was $1.3 million. Apache's experts estimated the diminution in market value of the land because of ground water contamination was $5175. The court held that damages would be limited to the diminution in value. The court held that the *Peevyhouse* rule was not limited to cases where the remedial work was "incidental to the main purpose of the contract."

HAWKINS v. McGEE
New Hampshire Supreme Court
84 N.H. 114, 146 A. 641 (1929)

NHSC

[George Hawkins sued Dr. McGee for negligence and for breach of contract after unsuccessful plastic surgery. The claim of negligence was dismissed without objection by Hawkins. Regarding the failure to perform the contract, Hawkins alleged that Dr. McGee breached a warranty guaranteeing the success of the operation. McGee moved for a directed verdict on this issue and the trial court denied the motion. Dr. McGee's requested jury instructions were not read to the jury. The jury returned a verdict for Hawkins. McGee moved to set the verdict aside on the grounds that it was contrary to the weight of the evidence and the law. Dr. McGee also argued that the damages awarded were excessive. The trial court found that the verdict was not contrary to the evidence or the law but that the damages awarded were excessive. The trial court ordered the verdict set aside unless Hawkins agreed to remit the damages in excess of $500. Hawkins refused to do so and the trial court set aside the verdict as "excessive and against the weight of the evidence." Hawkins objected and the case was transferred by the trial court judge to the Supreme Court of New Hampshire.]

BRANCH, J.

1. The operation in question consisted in the removal of a considerable quantity of scar tissue from the palm of the plaintiff's right hand and the grafting of skin taken from the plaintiff's chest in place thereof. The scar tissue was the result of a

---

[171] 795 F. Supp. 381 (W.D. Okla. 1992).

[172] 890 P.2d 847 (Okla. 1994).

severe burn caused by contact with an electric wire, which the plaintiff received about nine years before the time of the transactions here involved. There was evidence to the effect that before the operation was performed the plaintiff and his father went to the defendant's office and that the defendant in answer to the question, "How long will the boy be in the hospital?", replied, "Three or four days, . . . not over four; then the boy can go home, and it will be just a few days when he will be able to go back to work with a perfect hand." Clearly this and other testimony to the same effect would not justify a finding that the doctor contracted to complete the hospital treatment in three or four days or that the plaintiff would be able to go back to work within a few days thereafter. The above statements could only be construed as expressions of opinion or predictions as to the probable duration of the treatment and plaintiff's resulting disability, and the fact that these estimates were exceeded would impose no contractual liability upon the defendant. The only substantial basis for the plaintiff's claim is the testimony that the defendant also said before the operation was decided upon, "I will guarantee to make the hand a hundred per cent perfect hand" or "a hundred per cent good hand." The plaintiff was present when these words were alleged to have been spoken, and if they are to be taken at their face value, it seems obvious that proof of their utterance would establish the giving of a warranty in accordance with his contention.

The defendant argues, however, that even if these words were uttered by him, no reasonable man would understand that they were used with the intention of entering into any "contractual relation whatever," and that they could reasonably be understood only "as his expression in strong language that he believed and expected that as a result of the operation he would give the plaintiff a very good hand." It may be conceded, as the defendant contends, that before the question of the making of a contract should be submitted to a jury, there is a preliminary question of law for the trial court to pass upon, *i.e.* "whether the words could possibly have the meaning imputed to them by the party who founds his case upon a certain interpretation," but it cannot be held that the trial court decided this question erroneously in the present case. It is unnecessary to determine at this time whether the argument of the defendant based upon "common knowledge of the uncertainty which attends all surgical operations" and the improbability that a surgeon would ever contract to make a damaged part of the human body "one hundred per cent perfect" would, in the absence of countervailing considerations, be regarded as conclusive, for there were other factors in the present case which tended to support the contention of the plaintiff. There was evidence that the defendant repeatedly solicited from the plaintiff's father the opportunity to perform this operation, and the theory was advanced by plaintiff's counsel in cross-examination of defendant, that he sought an opportunity to "experiment on skin grafting," in which he had had little previous experience. If the jury accepted this part of plaintiff's contention, there would be a reasonable basis for the further conclusion that if defendant spoke the words attributed to him, he did so with the intention that they should be accepted at their face value, as an inducement for the granting of consent to the operation by the plaintiff and his father, and there was ample evidence that they were so accepted by them. The question of the making of the alleged contract was properly submitted to the jury.

2. The substance of the charge to the jury on the question of damages appears in the following quotation: "If you find the plaintiff entitled to anything, he is entitled to recover for what pain and suffering he has been made to endure and what injury he has sustained over and above the injury that he had before." To this instruction the defendant seasonably excepted. By it, the jury was permitted to consider two elements of damage, (1) pain and suffering due to the operation, and (2) positive ill effects of the operation upon the plaintiff's hand. Authority for any specific rule of damages in cases of this kind seems to be lacking, but when tested by general principle and by analogy, it appears that the foregoing instruction was erroneous.

"By 'damages' as that term is used in the law of contracts, is intended compensation for a breach, measured in the terms of the contract." *Davis v. New England Cotton Yarn Co.*, 77 N.H. 403, 404. The purpose of the law is to "put the plaintiff in as good a position as he would have been in had the defendant kept his contract." 3 Williston on Contracts, § 1338; *Hardie-Tynes Manufacturing Co. v. Easton Cotton Oil Co.*, 150 N.C. 150. The measure of recovery "is based upon what the defendant should have given the plaintiff, not what the plaintiff has given the defendant or otherwise expended." 3 Williston on Contracts, § 1341. "The only losses that can be said fairly to come within the terms of a contract are such as the parties must have had in mind when the contract was made, or such as they either knew or ought to have known would probably result from a failure to comply with its terms." *Davis v. New England Cotton Yarn Co.*, 77 N.H. 403, 404 (1914); *Hurd v. Dunsmore*, 63 N.H. 171 (1884).

The present case is closely analogous to one in which a machine is built for a certain purpose and warranted to do certain work. In such cases, the usual rule of damages for breach of warranty in the sale of chattels is applied and it is held that the measure of damages is the difference between the value of the machine if it had corresponded with the warranty and its actual value, together with such incidental losses as the parties knew or ought to have known would probably result from a failure to comply with its terms.

The rule thus applied is well settled in this state. "As a general rule, the measure of the vendee's damages is the difference between the value of the goods as they would have been if the warranty as to quality had been true, and the actual value at the time of the sale, including gains prevented and losses sustained, and such other damages as could be reasonably anticipated by the parties as likely to be caused by the vendor's failure to keep his agreement, and could not by reasonable care on the part of the vendee have been avoided." *Union Bank v. Blanchard*, 65 N.H. 21, 23; *Hurd v. Dunsmore, supra*; *Noyes v. Blodgett*, 58 N.H. 502. We therefore conclude that the true measure of the plaintiff's damage in the present case is the difference between the value to him of a perfect hand or a good hand, such as the jury found the defendant promised him, and the value of his hand in its present condition, including any incidental consequences fairly within the contemplation of the parties when they made their contract. 1 Sutherland, *Damages*, (4th ed.), § 92. Damages not thus limited, although naturally resulting, are not to be given.

The extent of the plaintiff's suffering does not measure this difference in value. The pain necessarily incident to a serious surgical operation was a part of the contribution which the plaintiff was willing to make to his joint undertaking with the defendant to produce a good hand. It was a legal detriment suffered by him which constituted a part of the consideration given by him for the contract. It represented a part of the price which he was willing to pay for a good hand, but it furnished no test of the value of a good hand or the difference between the value of the hand which the defendant promised and the one which resulted from the operation.

Pain was part of price

It was also erroneous and misleading to submit to the jury as a separate element of damage any change for the worse in the condition of the plaintiff's hand resulting from the operation, although this error was probably more prejudicial to the plaintiff than to the defendant. Any such ill effect of the operation would be included under the true rule of damages set forth above, but damages might properly be assessed for the defendant's failure to improve the condition of the hand even if there were no evidence that its condition was made worse as a result of the operation.

It must be assumed that the trial court, in setting aside the verdict, undertook to apply the same rule of damages which he had previously given to the jury, and since this rule was erroneous, it is unnecessary for us to consider whether there was any evidence to justify his finding that all damages awarded by the jury above $500 were excessive.

3. Defendant's requests for instructions were loosely drawn and were properly denied. A considerable number of issues of fact were raised by the evidence, and it would have been extremely misleading to instruct the jury in accordance with defendant's request number 2, that "The only issue on which you have to pass is whether or not there was a special contract between the plaintiff and the defendant to produce a perfect hand." Equally inaccurate was defendant's request number 5, which reads as follows: "You would have to find, in order to hold the defendant liable in this case, that Dr. McGee and the plaintiff both understood that the doctor was guaranteeing a perfect result from this operation." If the defendant said that he would guarantee a perfect result and the plaintiff relied upon that promise, any mental reservations which he may have had are immaterial. The standard by which his conduct is to be judged is not internal but external. Defendant's request number 7 was as follows: "If you should get so far as to find that there was a special contract guaranteeing a perfect result, you would still have to find for the defendant unless you further found that a further operation would not correct the disability claimed by the plaintiff." In view of the testimony that the defendant had refused to perform a further operation, it would clearly have been erroneous to give this instruction. The evidence would have justified a verdict for an amount sufficient to cover the cost of such an operation, even if the theory underlying this request were correct. . . .

New trial.   *Decision*

NOTES AND QUESTIONS

1. ***The hairy hand case:*** *Hawkins v. McGee* is a case that generations of law students have referred to as "the hairy hand case." It was well known, because of its appearance in casebooks, long before it was used as the first case Mr. Hart was asked to state, by the notorious Professor Kingsfield, in the movie *The Paper Chase*.

Many have wondered what became of the case. Dr. McGee settled the case for $1400 just before the date for a new trial. He agreed to this settlement once his malpractice insurer refused to defend the action because the policy only covered his liability for torts and not for contract breach. Dr. McGee did not recover from the insurer.[173]

Jorie Roberts, writing in the *Harvard Law Record*,[174] investigated the impact of the case on George and his family.

Jorie Roberts, Hawkins *Case: A Hair-Raising Experience*
66 Harv. L. Rec., Mar. 17, 1978[175]

Perhaps nothing is more hair-raising for 1Ls [first-year Harvard law students] than the famed "case of the hairy hand."

Many first-year law students initially encounter the different contract and tort damage principles in the tragic case of *Hawkins v. McGee* (84 N.H. 114, 146 A. 641, 1929). The case originated in 1922 in Berlin, New Hampshire, a small mill town near the Canadian border, when Dr. Edward McGee, a general practitioner, promised to restore George Hawkins' slightly scarred hand to "perfect condition" through surgery. Instead, Hawkins' hand was permanently disfigured and crippled.

. . . [Casebooks provide] a limited view of the case with discussions of the possible ways to ascertain Hawkins' monetary damages for the injury. But, the *Record* has delved into the human aspects behind *Hawkins v. McGee* through interviews and correspondence with George Hawkins' brother and sister-in-law, Howard J. and Edith Hawkins; his sister, Dorothy Hawkins St. Hilaire; and [his] Berlin lawyer . . . Arthur J. Bergeron . . .

A Small Pencil-Size Scar

George Hawkins was born in January, 1904 — the second of Rose Wilkinson and Charles Augustus Hawkins' six children. Rose Hawkins was originally from England, while Charles Hawkins hailed from Canada. In Berlin, Charles Hawkins first worked as a manual laborer, then became night superintendent at a local factory.

One morning in 1915, 11-year-old George burned his right hand while preparing breakfast on the family's woodburning stove. At the time, George was trying to turn on the kitchen light to illuminate the stove, but an electrical storm the night before had damaged the wiring so that George received a severe shock. One of George's younger brothers, Howard Hawkins, now an insurance agent in Berlin, described George's initial scar as a "small pencil-size scar" which did not substantially affect his use of the hand. Nevertheless, Charles Hawkins took his son George to skin special-

---

[173] McGee v. United States Fidelity & Guaranty Co., 53 F.2d 953 (1st Cir. 1931).

[174] The *Harvard Law Record* is the student newspaper of the Harvard Law School.

[175] Reprinted by permission.

ists in Montreal after the accident; but there the doctors advised the Hawkinses against doing anything to restore the hand.

During this period, the family physician, Edward McGee, while treating one of George's younger brothers for pneumonia, also became aware of George's scarred hand. Later, in 1919, after returning from several years of medical service in Europe during World War I, McGee requested George and his parents to let him operate on the hand in order to restore it to "perfect" condition.

According to Dorothy St. Hilaire, George's younger sister, McGee claimed to have done a number of similar skin grafts on soldiers in Germany during the war, although he later admitted that he had really only observed such operations.

St. Hilaire recollects that McGee, in persuading George to undergo the surgery, emphasized the social problems which his scarred hand might create. McGee encouraged the Hawkinses to allow him to operate on the hand for three years, until George finally agreed shortly after his 18th birthday. St. Hilaire remembers that, while her parents had strong doubts about the operation, they trusted McGee's judgment and were hesitant to oppose George's decision and the physician's advice.

In the Throes of Death

McGee operated on George's hand in the St. Louis Hospital in Berlin in March of 1922. The skin graft operation was supposed to be quick, simple, and effective, and to require only a few days of hospitalization. Instead, St. Hilaire recalls that her brother bled very badly for several days; the sight of the saturated surgical dressings caused her mother to faint when they first visited George at the hospital after what they thought to be minor surgery.

Moreover, while McGee had earlier stated that the skin for the graft was to come from George's thigh, Mrs. Hawkins and Dorothy, then age 13, saw that George's hand was bandaged to his chest. George was, in the words of his brother Howard, "in the throes of death" for quite a while after the operation because of his extensive bleeding and the ensuing infection. Moreover, the post-operation scar covered his thumb and the two fingers and was densely covered with hair. Howard Hawkins remembers that George's hand was partially closed up and continued to bleed periodically throughout his life. St. Hilaire, in describing the skin on George's chest from where McGee had taken the graft, compared it to thin onion skin.

After the operation failed so completely to give George the "100 percent perfect hand" which McGee had promised, Ovide Coulombe, a lawyer friend of the Hawkins and the mayor of Berlin, encouraged the Hawkinses to take the case to court. He represented the Hawkinses, while McGee engaged three lawyers from Concord.

The jury only awarded the Hawkins $3,000 for damages, and the final settlement was for $1,400 and lawyer's fees. St. Hilaire believes the jurors, while at heart solidly behind the Hawkinses' cause, were afraid to return heavier damages against McGee because he was one of the more prominent physicians in the area. Charles Hawkins took the $1,400 and his injured son back to Montreal to see if any subsequent operations would alleviate George's deformity, but the doctors there said that the grafted skin was so tough that nothing more could be done.

Never Spoke Again

Although McGee had been the Hawkinses' family physician for a number of years prior to the operation, post-operation relations between the Hawkinses and McGee were understandably cool. As far as Howard Hawkins and St. Hilaire remember, George Hawkins never spoke to McGee again. Dorothy recalls that she and her mother went to McGee's office right after their first visit to see George in the hospital and that McGee asserted then that he had nothing at all to say to the Hawkinses concerning the operation. The Hawkinses then engaged another doctor to handle George's post-operative case.

Apparently, the unsuccessful operation did not significantly reduce McGee's business. According to Arthur Bergeron, a Berlin lawyer, McGee's medical practice grew and he and two other doctors formed a clinic in Berlin. Bergeron recalls that McGee was popular in Berlin and even served as mayor of the town. He was also very musically inclined and directed McGee's Symphony Orchestra, which performed around northern New Hampshire, as a hobby.

Hawkins' crippled hand affected his employment and outlook throughout his lifetime. After the operation, George Hawkins never returned to high school, even though, in Howard's opinion, "George was very bright, learned quickly, and had a pleasing personality." He was encouraged by his parents to finish school, but would not because, in his siblings' view, he was embarrassed by his hand.

George also gave up tennis and riflery after the operation, although previously he had won several medals as a marksman for the State Home Guard. Because of his hand, George was unable to perform any heavy manual labor or learn to type. He worked for many years in the printing division of the Brown Company, a pulp and paper manufacturer in Berlin, and later in a tire store. He then entered military service for a short time in 1943, where he was stationed at Fort Devens in eastern Massachusetts.

Unaware of Fame

George married late in life and never had any children. He and his wife worked as a chauffeur-maid team for a wealthy couple in Massachusetts for several years, then returned to Berlin in 1952. After George died of a heart attack in 1958, his widow went back to North Conway, New Hampshire. According to his family members, George was always very sensitive about his hand and suffered lifelong emotional distress. His parents also grieved until their deaths because of the tragic and unnecessary crippling of their son's hand.

The Hawkins family was unaware of the widespread study of *Hawkins v. McGee* in law schools until, in 1964, Howard and Edith Hawkins' daughter Gail encountered the case early in her contracts course at Boston University Law School. Moreover, the Hawkins family did not know about the case's use in the "Paper Chase" contracts class scene until Edith Hawkins happened to see the 1972 movie during its first run.

Howard Hawkins, however, believes that George was somewhat aware of the case's importance before his 1958 death. Howard states: "I think he became aware of the importance of the case through a lawyer friend, an O. [Ovide] J. Coulombe. I think it gave him a sense of importance, in that this was bringing the facts out in the public eye, but this was only temporary, as he really lived with his incapacity all his life, and he did suffer mentally as well as physically."

Suppose Jorie Roberts and the editors of the *Harvard Law Record* had been able to talk with some of Dr. McGee's surviving relatives and friends. Might they tell a different story almost 50 years after the event? If so, how could we tell who was right?

2. ***The record:*** The following is from the record in *Hawkins v. McGee*:

Charles A. Hawkins. . . .

A. I took the boy up there one day to Dr. McGee's office, and I asked the doctor what he could do in regard to taking off that scar, and the doctor looked at the hand, and he says "That is only a simple matter," but he says "I am not doing any surgical work right now, but," he says, "you take him down to Dr. Pulsifer and he will do the job for you." . . .

Q. [D]id you have some talk after that with Dr. McGee?

A. Yes. I was going to the doctor's office about once in every two weeks for treatment for myself, and the doctor asked me, he says, "What about that boy's hand," he says, "You going to have it operated on?" I says "No, I guess not, doctor; the hand don't bother the boy any, and I don't see any need of having it done now." So I went there that summer before the operation, and every time I would go, Dr. McGee would ask me about this operation on the boy's hand, and at last the doctor says, — well, he says, "You ought to have that done because when the boy grows up he will be ashamed of that scar on his hand," and — well, I talked with the doctor about the operation, and asked him what kind of an operation it would be, and he says, "It is a very simple matter to take that scar off." Before this he says, "Bring that boy up; I want to see the hand again," and I took the boy up, — that is, before the operation; and he looked at it, and he says, "I would advise you to have it done; have the scar taken off," and well, I didn't want to have — the boy was working every day, and he was earning around about $35 a week, and he was a big help to me, and I didn't want to lay the boy up, because he never uttered no complaint about the hand at all; he was perfectly contented, and

I didn't want to lay the boy up. Well, I told the doctor then I thought probably, — naturally you would think a doctor or anybody else that worked for money, that is what we are all after, and I says to Dr. McGee, "I hain't got the money to have it done now," and Dr. McGee says "You need not bother about the money," he says, "Pay me whenever you like." And then I didn't give my consent to have it done. Then he says "Why do you hesitate? I am sure of myself. I know just what I am doing. I will cut that scar off, smooth the hand up, and I will guarantee to make the hand a hundred percent perfect hand." I says "Doctor, how long will the boy be in the hospital?" He says "Three or four days, not over four; then the boy can go home, and it will be just a few days when he will go back to work with a good hand." . . .

George Hawkins. . . .

Q. What did he [Dr. McGee] do?

A. . . . [T]he scar wasn't taken off as he said he was going to take it off. . . . [H]e dressed the hand, and I hadn't seen it, — I wouldn't look at it until two or three days after . . . and of course I was anxious to go home, because I had expected to go home in two or three days, and when I inquired whether or not I could go home, then he mentioned skin graft. . . .

Q. Were you able to move your hand away from the chest?

A. I couldn't move it an inch.

Q. How long did you remain in that condition?

A. I should say approximately three weeks. . . .

Q. Suffer any pain?

A. Yes, I did. . . .

Q. Now this hand, embarrassing to you at some times?

A. It is. . . . [I]f I was introduced to somebody I had never known before, and go to shake hands with him, — and especially a woman, they want to know what is in my hand.

Q. Is it embarrassing?

A. . . . The fellows have a good time making jokes about it.

Dr. McGee. . . .

Q. Had you explained to [Hawkins' father] what you had got to do?

A. Yes sir. . . . I told him that possibly the graft might not take; might not heal. . . . You can't tell whether they are going to grow or not. . . . That is one of the reasons that I advised him in the first place to go to Boston or New York. . . .

Q. Was anything said at that time about a guarantee?

A. No, sir; there was not.

Q. Did you ever guarantee a case in your life? . . .

A. No, sir; I didn't. . . .

Q. Doctor, did you ever know of any doctor in this community guaranteeing the result of his operations?

A. No, sir. . . .

Q. Did you ever tell Mr. Hawkins or his son that he would be out of the hospital in three or four days, not over four?

A. No, sir; I did not.

Q. . . . [W]ould it be possible, doctor, for anybody doing that operation to be out in that length of time?

A. No, sir; it would not; no, sir. . . .

Q. What did you tell him about the time it would take to complete the operation?

A. I told him I didn't know; it might take several operations, and I didn't know how long it would take; couldn't tell. I told him in the first place it might not heal at all; these grafts might not heal. I couldn't tell. You can't tell how many days it is going to take any wound to heal. . . .

3. *Choice and formation of contract:* Contract, it is often said, is based on free choice. Suppose that Dr. McGee did not intend to guarantee the success of the operation or the length of time during which George Hawkins would be away from work. Would that mean that the doctor could not be held to contractual liability? Suppose, further, that appellate judges are not sure that any doctor would ever make the kind of contract alleged in this case. Could they deal with their discomfort about the formation of a contract by minimizing liability under the rules of damages? How might they do this? The next case may be suggestive.

SULLIVAN v. O'CONNOR
Massachusetts Supreme Judicial Court
363 Mass. 579, 296 N.E.2d 183 (1973)

KAPLAN, J.

The plaintiff patient secured a jury verdict of $13,500 against the defendant surgeon for breach of contract in respect to an operation upon the plaintiff's nose. The substituted consolidated bill of exceptions presents questions about the correctness of the judge's instructions on the issue of damages.

The declaration was in two counts. In the first count, the plaintiff alleged that she, as patient, entered into a contract with the defendant, a surgeon, wherein the defendant promised to perform plastic surgery on her nose and thereby to enhance her beauty and improve her appearance; that he performed the surgery but failed to achieve the promised result; rather the result of the surgery was to disfigure and deform her nose, to cause her pain in body and mind, and to subject her to other damage and expense. The second count, based on the same transaction, was in the conventional form for malpractice, charging that the defendant had been guilty of negligence in performing the surgery. Answering, the defendant entered a general denial.

On the plaintiff's demand, the case was tried by jury. At the close of the evidence, the judge put to the jury, as special questions, the issues of liability under the two counts, and instructed them accordingly. The jury returned a verdict for the plaintiff on the contract count, and for the defendant on the negligence count. The judge then instructed the jury on the issue of damages.

As background to the instructions and the parties' exceptions, we mention certain facts as the jury could find them. The plaintiff was a professional entertainer, and this was known to the defendant. The agreement was as alleged in the declaration. More particularly, judging from exhibits, the plaintiff's nose had been straight, but long and prominent; the defendant undertook by two operations to reduce its prominence and somewhat to shorten it, thus making it more pleasing in relation to the plaintiff's other features. Actually the plaintiff was obliged to undergo three operations, and her appearance was worsened. Her nose now had a concave line to about the midpoint, at which it became bulbous; viewed frontally, the nose from bridge to midpoint was flattened and broadened, and the two sides of the tip had lost symmetry. This configuration evidently could not be improved by further surgery. The plaintiff did not demonstrate, however, that her change of appearance had resulted in loss of employment. Payments by the plaintiff covering the defendant's fee and hospital expenses were stipulated at $622.65.

The judge instructed the jury, first, that the plaintiff was entitled to recover her out-of-pocket expenses incident to the operations. Second, she could recover the damages flowing directly, naturally, proximately, and foreseeably from the defendant's breach of promise. These would comprehend damages for any disfigurement of the plaintiff's nose — that is, any change of appearance for the worse — including the effects of the consciousness of such disfigurement on the plaintiff's mind, and in this connection the jury should consider the nature of the plaintiff's profession. Also consequent upon the defendant's breach, and compensable, were the pain and suffering involved in the third operation, but not in the first two. As there was no proof that any loss of earnings by the plaintiff resulted from the breach, that element should not enter into the calculation of damages.

By his exceptions the defendant contends that the judge erred in allowing the jury to take into account anything but the plaintiff's out-of-pocket expenses (presumably at the stipulated amount). The defendant excepted to the judge's refusal of his request for a general charge to that effect, and, more specifically, to the judge's refusal of a charge that the plaintiff could not recover for pain and suffering connected with the third operation or for impairment of the plaintiff's appearance and associated mental distress.

The plaintiff on her part excepted to the judge's refusal of a request to charge that the plaintiff could recover the difference in value between the nose as promised and the nose as it appeared after the operations. However, the plaintiff in her brief expressly waives this exception and others made by her in case this court overrules the defendant's exceptions; thus she would be content to hold the jury's verdict in her favor.

We conclude that the defendant's exceptions should be overruled.

It has been suggested on occasion that agreements between patients and physicians by which the physician undertakes to effect a cure or to bring about a given result should be declared unenforceable on grounds of public policy. . . . But there are many decisions recognizing and enforcing such contracts, see annotation, 43 A.L.R.3d 1221, 1225, 1229–1233, and the law of Massachusetts has treated them as valid. . . . [citations omitted] These causes of action are, however, considered a little suspect, and thus we find courts straining sometimes to read the pleadings as sounding only in tort for negligence, and not in contract for breach of promise, despite sedulous efforts by the pleaders to pursue the latter theory. See . . . annotation, 43 A.L.R.3d, *supra*, at 1225, 1238–1244.

It is not hard to see why the courts should be unenthusiastic or skeptical about the contract theory. Considering the uncertainties of medical science and the variations in the physical and psychological conditions of individual patients, doctors can seldom in good faith promise specific results. Therefore it is unlikely that physicians of even average integrity will in fact make such promises. Statements of opinion by the physician with some optimistic coloring are a different thing, and may indeed have therapeutic value. But patients may transform such statements into firm promises in their own minds, especially when they have been disappointed in the event, and testify in that sense to sympathetic juries.[176] If actions for breach of promise can be readily maintained, doctors, so it is said, will be frightened into practicing "defensive medicine." On the other hand, if these actions were outlawed, leaving only the possibility of suits for malpractice, there is fear that the public might be exposed to the enticements of charlatans, and confidence in the profession might ultimately be shaken. See Miller, *The Contractual Liability of Physicians and Surgeons*, 1953 Wash. L.Q. 413, 416–423. The law has taken the middle-of-the-road position of allowing actions based on alleged contract, but insisting on clear proof. Instructions to the jury may well stress this requirement and point to tests of truth, such as the complexity or difficulty of an operation as bearing on the probability that a given result was promised. See annotation, 43 A.L.R.3d 1225, 1225–1227.

If an action on the basis of contract is allowed, we have next the question of the measure of damages to be applied where liability is found. Some cases have taken the simple view that the promise by the physician is to be treated like an ordinary commercial promise, and accordingly that the successful plaintiff is entitled to a standard measure of recovery for breach of contract — "compensatory" ("expectancy") damages, an amount intended to put the plaintiff in the position he would be in if the contract had been performed, or, presumably, at the plaintiff's election, "restitution" damages, an amount corresponding to any benefit conferred

---

[176] [2] Judicial skepticism about whether a promise was in fact made derives also from the possibility that the truth has been tortured to give the plaintiff the advantage of the longer period of limitations sometimes available for actions on contract as distinguished from those in tort or for malpractice. *See* Richard Lillich, *The Malpractice Statute of Limitations in New York and Other Jurisdictions*, 47 Cornell L. Q. 339; annotation, 80 A.L.R.2d 368.

by the plaintiff upon the defendant in the performance of the contract disrupted by the defendant's breach. See Restatement of Contracts § 329 and Comment A, §§ 347, 384(1). Thus in *Hawkins v. McGee*, 84 N.H. 114, 146 A. 641, the defendant doctor was taken to have promised the plaintiff to convert his damaged hand by means of an operation into a good or perfect hand, but the doctor so operated as to damage the hand still further. The court, following the usual expectancy formula, would have asked the jury to estimate and award to the plaintiff the difference between the value of a good or perfect hand, as promised, and the value of the hand after the operation. (The same formula would apply, although the dollar result would be less, if the operation had neither worsened nor improved the condition of the hand.) If the plaintiff had not yet paid the doctor his fee, that amount would be deducted from the recovery. There could be no recovery for the pain and suffering of the operation, since that detriment would have been incurred even if the operation had been successful; one can say that this detriment was not "caused" by the breach. But where the plaintiff by reason of the operation was put to more pain . . . [than] he would have had to endure, had the doctor performed as promised, he should be compensated for that difference as a proper part of his expectancy recovery. It may be noted that on an alternative count for malpractice the plaintiff in the *Hawkins* case had been nonsuited; but on ordinary principles this could not affect the contract claim, for it is hardly a defense to a breach of contract that the promisor acted innocently and without negligence. . . .

Other cases, including a number in New York, without distinctly repudiating the *Hawkins* type of analysis, have indicated that a different and generally more lenient measure of damages is to be applied in patient-physician actions based on breach of alleged special agreements to effect a cure, attain a stated result, or employ a given medical method. This measure is expressed in somewhat variant ways, but the substance is that the plaintiff is to recover any expenditures made by him and for other detriment (usually not specifically described in the opinions) following proximately and foreseeably upon the defendant's failure to carry out his promise. . . . [citations omitted] This, be it noted, is not a "restitution" measure, for it is not limited to restoration of the benefit conferred on the defendant (the fee paid) but includes other expenditures, for example, amounts paid for medicine and nurses; so also it would seem according to its logic to take in damages for any worsening of the plaintiff's condition due to the breach. Nor is it an "expectancy" measure, for it does not appear to contemplate recovery of the whole difference in value between the condition as promised and the condition actually resulting from the treatment. Rather the tendency of the formulation is to put the plaintiff back in the position he occupied just before the parties entered upon the agreement, to compensate him for the detriments he suffered in reliance upon the agreement. This kind of intermediate pattern of recovery for breach of contract is discussed in the suggestive article by Fuller and Perdue, *The Reliance Interest in Contracts Damages*,[177] where the authors show that, although not attaining the currency of the standard measures, a "reliance" measure has for special reasons been applied by the courts in a variety of settings, including noncommercial settings.

For breach of the patient-physician agreements under consideration, a recovery

---

[177] [Eds. note: This article is cited and discussed in the introduction to Chapter 2, *supra*.]

limited to restitution seems plainly too meager, if the agreements are to be enforced at all. On the other hand, an expectancy recovery may well be excessive. The factors, already mentioned, which have made the cause of action somewhat suspect, also suggest moderation as to the breadth of the recovery that should be permitted. Where, as in the case at bar and in a number of the reported cases, the doctor has been absolved of negligence by the trier, an expectancy measure may be thought harsh. We should recall here that the fee paid by the patient to the doctor for the alleged promise would usually be quite disproportionate to the putative expectancy recovery. To attempt, moreover, to put a value on the condition that would or might have resulted, had the treatment succeeded as promised, may sometimes put an exceptional strain on the imagination of the fact-finder. As a general consideration, Fuller and Perdue argue that the reasons for granting damages for broken promises to the extent of the expectancy are at their strongest when the promises are made in a business context, when they have to do with the production or distribution of goods or the allocation of functions in the market place; they become weaker as the context shifts from a commercial to a noncommercial field. . . .

There is much to be said, then, for applying a reliance measure to the present facts, and we have only to add that our cases are not unreceptive to the use of that formula in special situations. We have, however, had no previous occasion to apply it to patient-physician cases.

The question of recovery on a reliance basis for pain and suffering or mental distress requires further attention. We find expressions in the decisions that pain and suffering (or the like) are simply not compensable in actions for breach of contract. The defendant seemingly espouses this proposition in the present case. True, if the buyer under a contract for the purchase of a lot of merchandise, in suing for the seller's breach, should claim damages for mental anguish caused by his disappointment in the transaction, he would not succeed; he would be told, perhaps, that the asserted psychological injury was not fairly foreseeable by the defendant as a probable consequence of the breach of such a business contract. See Restatement of Contracts, § 341, and Comment A. But there is no general rule barring such items of damage in actions for breach of contract. It is all a question of the subject matter and background of the contract, and when the contract calls for an operation on the person of the plaintiff, psychological as well as physical injury may be expected to figure somewhere in the recovery, depending on the particular circumstances. . . . Suffering or distress resulting from the breach going beyond that which was envisaged by the treatment as agreed, should be compensable on the same ground as the worsening of the patient's condition because of the breach. Indeed it can be argued that the very suffering or distress "contracted for" — that which would have been incurred if the treatment achieved the promised result — should also be compensable on the theory underlying the New York cases. For that suffering is "wasted" if the treatment fails. Otherwise stated, compensation for this waste is arguably required in order to complete the restoration of the status quo ante.[178]

---

[178] [6] Recovery on a reliance basis for breach of the physician's promise tends to equate with the usual recovery for malpractice, since the latter also looks in general to restoration of the condition before the injury. But this is not paradoxical, especially when it is noted that the origins of contract lie in tort.

holdings

In the light of the foregoing discussion, all the defendant's exceptions fail: the plaintiff was not confined to the recovery of her out-of-pocket expenditures; she was entitled to recover also for the worsening of her condition, and for the pain and suffering and mental distress involved in the third operation. These items were compensable on either an expectancy or a reliance view. We might have been required to elect between the two views if the pain and suffering connected with the first two operations contemplated by the agreement, or the whole difference in value between the present and the promised conditions, were being claimed as elements of damage. But the plaintiff waives her possible claim to the former element, and to so much of the latter as represents the difference in value between the promised condition and the condition before the operations.

NOTES AND QUESTIONS

1. *The judge's charge:* Examine the trial judge's charge to the jury. Is this charge entirely consistent with either an expectation or a reliance measure of damages? Or is it inconsistent with respect to the proper measure of damages? If the latter, why was the case not remanded to the trial court for retrial after a proper charge with respect to damages?

2. *The jury's decision:* An extensive excerpt from the trial transcript in this case appears in Richard Danzig & Geoffrey Watson, The Capability Problem in Contract Law at 33–44 (2d ed. 2004). Those excerpts suggest that while Alice Sullivan's post-operative nose did not meet her expectations, its appearance was not appreciably worse than her pre-operative nose. They also suggest that there was no appreciable pain and suffering with respect to the third operation, which was aborted almost as soon as it began and required only one stitch. If the jury accepted that testimony, could they have properly awarded $13,500 in damages under the trial judge's charge? Do you think that juries usually pay close attention to a judge's charge on measure of damages?

K. SOME REVIEW PROBLEMS

Here, for your convenience, are some review problems. You may find that reviewing the material by using these problems helps you to understand Chapter 2. They range from some that are very easy to some with wicked and nasty twists and turns. Some of them cannot be "answered" at all; the best anyone can do is offer plausible arguments for both plaintiff *and* defendant. Different professors empha-

---

See E. Allan Farnsworth, *The Past of Promise: An Historical Introduction to Contract*, 69 Colum. L. Rev. 576, 594–596; Breitel, J. in Stella Flour & Feed Corp. v. National City Bank, 285 App. Div. 182, 189, 136 N.Y.S.2d 139 (dissenting opinion). A few cases have considered possible recovery for breach by a physician of a promise to sterilize a patient, resulting in birth of a child to the patient and spouse. If such an action is held maintainable, the reliance and expectancy measures would, we think, tend to equate, because the promised condition was preservation of the family status quo. *See* Custodio v. Bauer, 251 Cal. App. 2d 303, 59 Cal. Rptr. 463; Jackson v. Anderson, 230 So. 2d 503 (Fla. App.). . . . See also annotation, 27 A.L.R.3d 906. It would, however, be a mistake to think in terms of strict "formulas." For example, a jurisdiction which would apply a reliance measure to the present facts might impose a more severe damage sanction for the willful use by the physician of a method of operation that he undertook not to employ.

size different things, and some of these problems fit one teaching style better than others. In every case you should try to ask yourself both what is the answer and *why* it is the answer. Furthermore, you should remember that the "whys" always involve at least two levels of analysis: (1) *what rule* of law, *interpreted* in which way, yields an answer or possible answers, and (2) why do we have such a rule of law, and what impact is it likely to have on what kinds of people?

Each subpart of a question is independent of the other subparts. S means seller and B means buyer. Assume the Uniform Commercial Code is in force in the jurisdiction, *but* it has been interpreted as not applying to building contracts. You should assume that there is no evidence of incidental expenses, unless such expenses are explicitly mentioned in the problem.

1. Imagine a contract to purchase lettuce. The contract price is $8000. The market value of the designated quantity of lettuce at the delivery date is $8400.

    a.   S breaches. What are B's damages?

    b.   B breaches. What are S's damages?

2. Imagine a contract to purchase lettuce. The contract price is $8000. The market value of the designated quantity of lettuce at the delivery date is $7500.

    a.   S breaches. What are B's damages?

    b.   B breaches. What are S's damages?

    c.   B breaches. S resells the lettuce for $8000. What are S's damages?

3. Imagine a contract to purchase lettuce. The contract price is $8000. B pays $500 as a down payment when the contract is made. The market value of lettuce at the delivery date is $8400.

    a.   S breaches. What are B's damages?

    b.   B breaches. What are S's damages? Can B recover any of its down payment? (Some people answer this question too hastily.)

4. Builder agrees to build a house for Owner on Owner's lot for a contract price of $120,000. Builder can build the house at a total cost to him of $110,500. The only other contractor available to build the house bid $120,800. No work has yet begun.

    a.   Builder breaches. What are Owner's damages?

    b.   Owner breaches. What are Builder's damages?

5. Builder contracts to build a house for Owner on Owner's lot, and Owner agrees to pay $120,000 for it, all of the money to be paid on completion of construction. Builder can build the house at a total cost to him of $115,000. The only other contractor available to build the house bid $120,800. Builder commences work and spends $30,000 on it. At this point it would cost Builder $85,000 to complete the work, but it would cost Owner $94,000 to have the work completed by the only other contractor available. Owner has paid nothing to Builder.

    a.   Builder breaches. How much can Owner recover as a victim of a breach of contract? Can Builder recover on a restitution theory?

    b.   Owner breaches. How much can Builder recover as a victim of a breach of contract? On a restitution theory?

6. Builder agrees to build a house for Owner on Owner's lot, and Owner agrees to pay $100,000 for it. Builder begins work on the house. Before Owner has made any payment to Builder, Owner breaches the contract by preventing Builder from doing further work on the house. At the time of breach, Builder had spent $50,000 for labor and for materials actually incorporated into the structure. In addition, Builder spent $10,000 to rent machinery needed to construct the house. Although this machinery can be returned to the lessor earlier than planned, due to Owner's breach, Builder is not entitled to any reduction in the rental cost. Builder's reasonable estimate of the cost of completing the job had Owner not breached is $60,000. This figure does not include any of the expenses already listed. A real estate appraiser estimates that the value of Owner's land, together with the partially completed structure, is $20,000 more than it would be had Builder done no work at all.

    a. What recovery would Builder be entitled to if the goal is to protect Builder's expectation interest? [*See* Restatement (Second) of Contracts § 347.]

    b. What recovery would Builder be entitled to if the goal is to protect Builder's reliance interest? [*See* Restatement (Second) of Contracts § 349.]

    c. According to the Restatement (Second) of Contracts, §§ 370, 371, and 373, what recovery would Builder be entitled to if the goal is to protect Builder's restitution interest?

    d. According to the Restatement (Third) of Restitution and Unjust Enrichment, § 38, what recovery would Builder be entitled to if the goal is to protect Builder's expectation interest?

    e. Which recovery would be the most just? Why?

7. Imagine a contract for the sale of a widget, a movable good, for $5000. B pays $2000 when the contract is signed. The balance is due on delivery. The contract requires delivery to XYZ Transport Company on June 1. The expected shipping time by XYZ to B's factory is three days.

    a. S fails to deliver the widget to XYZ on June 1. B purchases a substitute widget on June 6 for $6000. However, the market price on June 1 was $5000. B, however, did not learn of S's failure to deliver until June 4. On June 4 the market price of the widget was $5500. What recovery, if any, for B?

    b. B breaches and S retains possession of the widget. S resells the widget for $5000. S's expenses of resale are $200. To what extent, if at all, can B recover his down payment?

8. Peter Pitch is a piano tuner. On Monday Toni Tonedeaf entered a contract to have Peter tune her piano for $50. Peter agreed to come to her house the next Saturday morning at 10:00 A.M. On Wednesday, Toni called Peter and told him not to come. This was a breach of their contract. On Thursday Peter arranged to tune Arthur Artiste's piano for $50 at 10:00 on Saturday morning, the time originally scheduled for Toni's piano. Is Peter entitled to any damages as a result of Toni's breach?

9. Pearl had inherited a Guarnerius violin from her father, a well-known concertmaster. She decided to sell the violin. She believed it was worth $60,000. She planned to invest $50,000 of the proceeds in the stock of ARA, Inc., a local manufacturing company. She contacted a musical instrument dealer who agreed to try to arrange a sale for her in exchange for a 5 percent commission. The broker, Saul Smith, believed he knew of a musician who was particularly interested in acquiring a Guarnerius. Sure enough, 10 days later Saul reported that Dennis Darcy had offered to buy the violin for $62,000. Pearl knew Darcy, and accepted the offer. The written agreement provided that Pearl was to personally deliver the violin to Darcy on September 1, in Los Angeles. Pearl paid Saul Smith the $3100 commission for arranging the sale.

She flew to Los Angeles (at a cost of $600 for the round trip) to deliver the violin. When she arrived, Darcy examined the violin and refused to accept it. He alleged that it had been cracked and repaired, and was not worth the amount which he had agreed to pay. However, it had in fact never been cracked. Darcy apparently refused to buy the violin because friends had persuaded him that the price was too high, and so he fabricated the story about the crack. Pearl returned to Madison. She contacted Saul Smith who, upon hearing the tale, returned $1550 of the commission to her. Smith was not legally obligated to do this under his contract with Pearl.

Pearl then flew to New York (at a round-trip cost of $400) and left the violin with an auctioneer who was about to conduct an auction of musical instruments. The auction was held each year and was widely publicized. The auctioneer was entitled to a commission of seven percent. The violin was sold on October 15 for $58,000. Pearl received a check for $53,940. She invested $50,000 of the proceeds in the ARA stock the next day. The stock had risen in value since September — in fact, $50,000 of stock in ARA on September 1 would have been worth $58,000 on October 15.

How much can Pearl recover?

10. This last summer Paula decided to start a printing/advertising business in Metro, to publish newsletters for regional companies and charitable organizations. She concluded that to be successful she needed a professional artist on her staff. She contacted Employment Agency. She agreed to pay them a fee of $500 if they identified an artist whom she subsequently signed to an employment contract. Agency arranged for Dave to interview with Paula, and on August 10 Dave signed an employment contract with Paula. The contract was for one year, to begin on October 1, and provided that Dave was to be paid $24,000 plus $800 (in advance) for moving expenses.

On September 29 Dave called Paula and said that he would not be able to take the job. He had decided that he couldn't leave Cleveland. Dave explained further that he had already shipped a load of furniture to Metro, and so he couldn't return the $800 moving expenses.

Paula desperately needed the services of an artist since, in anticipation of having an artist on board by October 1, Paula had taken on a project with an October 30 deadline. Paula contacted the Agency again and, for a fee of $600, they located another artist, Rachel, who agreed to quit her existing job and begin work for Paula on October 15. Somewhat ironically, Rachel lived in Suburb, a town just a few miles from Metro, and hadn't been identified in the earlier search because of a computer-coding error. On October 10, Paula signed a one-year contract with Rachel providing for an annual salary of $25,000. Rachel also demanded a bonus of $1500 because of having to change jobs on such short notice in order to work on the special project due October 30.

You should also know that Paula had previously arranged to make a presentation to a prospective client on October 6. The presentation was made but did not lead to a contract. Paula is convinced that this was because the client wanted to meet Paula's staff artist. This was impossible since Dave had repudiated and Rachel hadn't been hired yet. Paula believes, based on conversations with a friend who worked in the office of the potential client, that had an artist been available she would have landed the job and made an $11,000 profit.

Paula has come to you and asked you to represent her in a suit against Dave. Please write a memo to the file in which you evaluate all aspects of the claim which Paula could make against Dave. Discuss all credible arguments that you can make for both Paula and Dave.

Chapter 3

CONTRACT AND CONTINUING RELATIONS

A. INTRODUCTION

The organization of this chapter is complex. Sometimes it may be hard to follow because we are trying to teach several things at once. Chapter 2 was an overview of the legal and practical protections given by the private law remedy system for breach of voluntarily assumed obligations. Most, but not all, of the materials in that chapter dealt with relatively simple kinds of agreements — one-shot deals or transactions in which the relationship of the parties began when they entered their agreement and ended when they performed or breached it. (*Copylease v. Memorex*, of course, was an exception.) Chapter 3 develops many of the ideas found in Chapter 2, but in complex social and economic contexts. Here we consider what, if anything, the law has to offer to support such relationships. We ask whether the legal system can offer more than salvage when they are wrecked. We ask whether turning to contract law or restitution might have costs that society does not want to pay.

This chapter develops the ideas found in the previous one in new contexts. As long ago as 1934, Professor Harold Havighurst organized a contracts casebook functionally.[1] He argued that contracts dealing with such things as sales of goods, real estate, insurance, employment, and services raise problems distinct to each functional area and provoke the development of contract rules suited to that context. The rules may be stated as if they applied uniformly to all contracts, but their application may differ in various settings. We will continue to consider this insight throughout the rest of this casebook.

Contracts can be sorted in other ways as well. There are three clusters of parties to contracts and each cluster may exhibit distinct features: Deals can be (1) person-to-person; (2) person-to-organization; and (3) organization-to-organization. Much of our thinking about contracts focuses primarily on the first of these. Daniel Markovits argues that the philosophical foundation of contract is the "collaborative view": Contracting parties form respectful communities of collaboration where contractors treat each other as ends in themselves and refrain from treating each other as mere instrumentalities.[2] Whatever our beliefs tell us about the first type of

[handwritten margin note: 3 clusters of parties to K's]

---

[1] HAROLD HAVIGHURST, A SELECTION OF CONTRACT CASES AND RELATED QUASI-CONTRACT CASES (Lawyer's Cooperative Publishing Co. 1934).

[2] Daniel Markovits, *Contract and Collaboration*, 113 YALE L.J. 1417 (2004). Ethan Leib, in his article *On Collaboration, Organizations, and Conciliation in the General Theory of Contract*, 24 QUINNIPIAC L. REV. 1 (2005), notes that the typology has roots in Meir Dan-Cohen, *Rights, Persons, and Organizations: A Legal Theory for Bureaucratic Society* 82–84 (University of California Press 1986). Leib points out that Markovits's theory only addresses the first type of contract.

contract (person-to-person deals), this view of the interdependence of contracting parties does not always fit the second and third types as well, and as a result courts and legislatures sometimes respond differently to them. Indeed, Alan Schwartz and Robert E. Scott fashion a contract theory aimed primarily at the third type, and they seek efficiency as the major goal.[3] We will ask again and again whether ideas that fit one of these types of contracts also serve the others well.

We can sort contracts another way. Some transactions are fairly "discrete." The parties deal for the first time, and they have no reason to think that they may deal again. The bargain consists of the express terms agreed upon and little more. For example, a traveler with out-of-state license plates has a flat tire while driving on an interstate highway. He installs the spare tire on his car. He leaves the highway and drives to the nearest small town to seek someone who can repair his tire. It is very likely that both the traveler and the person at the local tire repair business have had no prior dealings on a personal or a business level, and they have little reason to expect that they will have more dealings in the future. The tire repair person might hold ethical ideas about helping travelers in need, or he might see the traveler as someone in a dependent and vulnerable position who can be exploited and charged "what the traffic will bear."

Consider the same tire repair transaction, but change the relationship between the parties. Now the traveler is returning to his home town from a trip, and he went to high school and played on the football team with the repair person. The repair shop regularly services the automobile owner's tires and sells him replacements when they are needed. These two people tell each other jokes, call each other by their first names, and complain to each other about their favorite sports teams. The regular customer who lives in the same community expects to be treated well, and he can take his business elsewhere if he feels that he hasn't been treated right. This is a "relational" contract. Long-term continuing relations are embedded in a field of norms and sanctions, most of which are not legal but social. Notice, too, that in the categories we mention in the third paragraph of this introduction, organization-to-organization contracts can be discrete or highly relational. The vice president in charge of sales of a major manufacturer of commercial aircraft may have dealt over the course of many years with the officials of a major airline who are in charge of buying new aircraft. Any particular sale usually has a past history of prior purchases and at least the prospect of dealing in the future after the present contract has been performed. Discrete contracts can have the potential of turning into relational ones.

Contracts do not fall neatly into either discrete or relational categories. Rather, there is a range of relational elements that may be involved. Consider the following situations:

(1) Company Executive rents a car from a local firm for a business trip, in a place she has never been before and never expects to be again.

(2) Company regularly calls on Rent-A-Car, a national organization, whenever Company's officials need a car. Company has seasonal needs, requests for different

---

[3] Alan Schwartz & Robert E. Scott, *Contract Theory and the Limits of Contract Law*, 113 YALE L.J. 541 (2003).

car types for different jobs, and so on. Rent-A-Car makes a special effort to fill Company's orders to keep its goodwill. Rent-A-Car assigns particular employees to service the Company account, and they form personal relationships with Company executives and employees who deal with rental automobiles and trucks.

(3) Company leases a whole fleet of cars from Rent-A-Car, and Rent-A-Car agrees to service them and replace them after they have traveled a certain number of miles. Rent-A-Car employees now regularly work at Company's headquarters and divisional offices in connection with maintaining this fleet.

(4) Company decides to integrate a fleet of cars into its own organization. It ends the agreement with Rent-A-Car and takes on the former Rent-A-Car employees who serviced its account as its own employees.

These arrangements illustrate points along the spectrum from discrete transaction to relational. The first three will use what we can call a "contract," a more or less formal statement of the terms of the agreement. However, as the arrangements become more relational, the formal contract will be a less adequate description of the parties' actual expectations. These develop through experience and personal contact. Rent-A-Car's employees assigned to the Company account will develop special working relationships with Company's people, a specialized knowledge about Company's problems, and an interest in solving them. Rent-A-Car employees and Company employees are likely to become involved in a network of exchanging favors and information. Indeed, some employees of both concerns may find their loyalties unclear. A particular Company employee may become Rent-A-Car's informal advocate within Company. The reputation and status of the employee who selected Rent-A-Car, and recommends continuing to do business with it, may turn on Rent-A-Car's performance. The employee and Rent-A-Car's representatives may work closely to keep everyone satisfied with its performance and repair, or even cover up, any failures to perform.

We also can see the final stage where Company absorbs the car fleet as a contract. The elaborate transaction may be affected by one or more labor unions' collective bargaining agreements with Company and Rent-A-Car. There is likely to be some internal organizational plan of Company's. If Company is big enough, it may decide to treat its own divisions as independent units and make arrangements resembling contracts with them to supply its needs. It may even make them compete with real outside contractors for its business.

Robert Gordon, in an often-quoted passage, tells us that in relational contracts:

> [P]arties treat their contracts more like marriages than like one-night stands. Obligations grow out of the commitment that they have made to one another, and the conventions that the trading community establishes for such commitments; they are not frozen at the initial moment of commitment, but change as circumstances change; the object of contracting is not primarily to allocate risks, but to signify a commitment to cooperate . . .

and the sanction for egregiously bad behavior, is always, of course, refusal to deal again.[4]

What difference does the degree of relationalness of a contract make to contract law?[5]

Are there some kinds of relational agreements between people in close inter-personal relationships that should not be subject to contract law, litigation, and judicial sanctions? Relational norms and sanctions exist and are often very powerful. Are legal sanctions also needed?[6] Might the presence of legal norms and sanctions "crowd out" ethical, moral, and relational norms and sanctions such as guilt and loss of self-esteem or damage to or loss of an important relationship?[7]

We will ask continually whether there are relationships that might be hurt if they are subject to legal regulation or too much legal regulation. Law is only one social institution and only one of many normative systems. Sometimes law is central; sometimes it stands at the margins of the other institutions and norms — exerting, at best, a subtle and indirect influence. It is possible that there is more risk of law crowding out other norms and sanctions in some situations than in others, but, on the other hand, law could sometimes reinforce rather than undermine trust.[8]

 The materials in this chapter deal mostly with agreements falling toward the relational side of the spectrum. We start with family rather than business relationships. This choice makes sense because all our readers have some experi-ence in families, but only a few know much about business relations. Also, regulation of family relations often is not very different from regulation of business relations in the problems it poses for the legal system. In fact, businesspeople sometimes describe partnerships as a kind of "marriage," and the relationship of those working face to face over time may take on aspects of family relations. After working through contract and the family, we will turn to employment and other business relationships. We will ask many times whether the presence or absence of relational

---

4 Robert Gordon, *Macaulay, Macneil, and the Discovery of Solidarity and Power in Contract Law*, 1985 WIS. L. REV. 565, 569.

5 Elizabeth Mertz, *An Afterword: Tapping the Promise of Relational Contract Theory — "Real" Legal Language and A New Legal Realism*, 94 NW. U. L. REV. 909, 914–15 (2000) (making the point that relational versus discrete contract is not a rigid categorization; rather the inquiry is whether relational aspects of a contract require contextual analysis).

6 *See* Dori Kimel, *The Choice of Paradigm for Theory of Contract: Reflections on the Relational Model*, 27 OXFORD J. LEGAL STUD. 233, 247–48 (2007) (arguing that an enforceable, stable core of relatively clear contract terms may help relationships develop by providing a modicum of reassurance concerning what rights exist if the relationship later breaks down).

7 *See, e.g.*, Robert E. Scott, *The Case for Formalism in Relational Contract*, 94 NW. U. L. REV. 847, 852 (2000) ("[A]ny effort to judicialize" relational norms may "destroy the very informality that makes them so effective in the first instance."); *see also* Iris Bohnet et al., *More Order with Less Law: On Contract Enforcement, Trust, and Crowding*, 95 AM. POL. SCI. REV. 131 (2001); Larry E. Ribstein, *Law v. Trust*, 81 B.U. L. REV. 553, 568–71 (2001).

8 *See* Ethan J. Leib, *Friendship & The Law*, 54 UCLA L. REV. 631 (2007); Leib, *Friends as Fiduciaries*, 86 WASH. U. L.R. 665 (2009) (acknowledging the crowding-out possibility but arguing that there are so many other incentives for friendship that legal responsibilities among friends are seldom likely to deter people from entering such relationships).

elements in a transaction does or should matter as legal agencies fashion and apply contract law.

One purpose of this chapter is simply to take another look at the whole battery of contract remedies from Chapter 2 — expectation damages, reliance, restitution, specific performance, and all the rest — in this new context of complex ongoing relations. As we saw in Chapter 2, seeking vindication through civil litigation processes is far from costless in money, time, and emotional energy. Even winners often wonder whether their victory was worth the price. The costs usually increase when people involved in a long-term continuing relationship take disputes to courts. You will have an opportunity here to compare the effectiveness and fairness of contract litigation to some alternatives — including such non-judicial means of dispute processing as arbitration, mediation, and private sanctions devised and imposed by the parties themselves.

A second purpose of Chapter 3 is to consider legal enforcement and regulation of contract relations as a form of official intervention into the lives and dealings of parties. To simplify considerably, someone asks an agency — court, regulatory body, or arbitration panel — to intervene in a set of contract relations. The agency has a choice of three basic responses: (i) it can intervene primarily to facilitate the relationship according to the wishes of the parties; (ii) it can regulate the relationship, imposing on it notions of policy not derived from the interests of the immediate parties; or (iii) it can abstain because the parties' problems are beyond the agency's competence or concern or because the parties' freedom to do as they please is itself an important value.

We will be considering two different perspectives about how legal agencies make these choices:

(a) We will look at contract doctrine. Contract law has a number of standards to help legal officials decide when and how to intervene. We have encountered some of them already. For example, many writers claim that the expectation principle of contract damages facilitates planning and risk assumption. The courts' refusal to enforce penalty clauses is regulatory. The refusal to award speculative damages is a doctrine of abstention.

In this chapter we consider a collection of doctrines that common-law judges and treatise-writers developed in the "classical" period of contract law in the late 19th century. Judges and scholars said that these rules drew lines between situations in which courts would enforce contracts and those in which they had to abstain — doctrines marking off "enforceable" from "unenforceable" transactions. This "classical" 19th century doctrine is still with us in some form, but it now coexists with a whole set of rules fashioned in the mid-20th century that add to, qualify, and frequently contradict the traditional learning. Part of our task, of course, is to get a sense of when the old-fashioned contracts religion will hold sway and when judges and lawyers will use these newer ideas.

(b) However, we view legal doctrine as little more than a set of tools used in the service of substantive social policies. Conflict in the rules reflects conflict in larger social values. The major focus of this chapter will be on these social policies, and we will look at doctrine as means to ends.

Doctrine may serve another function. The way we state legal rules may limit the way we see problems and solutions. We can become so accustomed to certain rules that they just seem to reflect common sense. Yet that common sense may reflect a distinct way of looking at the world that is questionable. We will try to look behind and within legal rules to make these assumptions explicit so we can ask whether we want to accept them. Professor Jay Feinman asserts: "The ideological function of contract law is to conceal . . . choices, to make results seem determinate when they are not."[9] He continues: "As contract law is one realm of elite ideology, the concealment it produces typically legitimates the status quo."[10] We will test his assertions in the materials that follow.

1. The Vocabulary of Contract Formation

At the beginning of Chapter 2, we offered a relatively extended "digression" on the history of the development of the UCC. We felt that this was necessary background for a discussion of the expectation principle, its role in contract doctrine, and its codification in the Uniform Commercial Code. We now offer another digression[11] from our main objective. This "digression" is more controversial, at least to label it as a digression. We are convinced, however, that we can familiarize you with most of the formation rules in just a few pages, with little loss to your capacity to solve the puzzles that these rules are designed to solve. We then introduce you to the ins and outs of the rules that govern whether agreements need to be in writing in much the same way, with an emphasis on descriptive textual notes rather than on appellate opinions. Finally, we return to many of the formation rules with a focus on exposing policy conflicts rather than doctrinal explication. In the long run, we believe that you will have a richer understanding of both doctrine and policy. In addition, you will have plenty of practice in dissecting appellate opinions.

You should regard the summary of doctrine that follows as you would the vocabulary list at the beginning of a lesson in the grammar of a foreign language. In the foreign language course your principal objective is to learn the grammar of the language, although you need a vocabulary to do this and must inevitably learn both grammar and vocabulary simultaneously. Read the note that follows as you would that vocabulary list — as an essential, but subordinate, part of the lessons of Chapter 3.

a. An introduction to the rules of offer and acceptance

A Doctrinal Note — Contract Formation

Offer-and-acceptance doctrine is a late development in the common law of contract. It did not become a separate topic in the law until the classical period of the mid- to late 19th century. Before then, lawyers were only trained to ask whether

---

[9] Jay M. Feinman, *The Significance of Contracts Theory*, 41 U. CIN. L. REV. 1283 (1989).

[10] *Id.*

[11] You should not be surprised if your teacher asks you to read this essay on your own, read it later in the course, or even skip it entirely.

defendant had made, and broken, a *promise* of some type that was "actionable," i.e., one they could make the basis of a lawsuit under the writs available. The classical lawyers changed the question from "Was there an actionable promise?" to "Was there a *contract*?" They said that a contract required (1) an offer, (2) an acceptance of the terms of that offer, and (3) consideration. (We will explore later what remains of the consideration doctrine in modern contract law.)

Once the problem was put this way, academic writers and judges put an enormous amount of energy into elaborating the new topic. Almost half of the first American treatise on contract law, Langdell's *Cases and Summary of the Law of Contracts* (1871), deals with offer and acceptance (the rest deals with consideration and the Statute of Frauds). The writers and judges wanted to develop rules that would fix the *exact moment* that parties created a contract. Before this instant, the parties were still completely free to alter their negotiating positions or back out entirely. After formation, they lost this power and were bound to a contract.

Contracts scholars said that offer-and-acceptance law served to (1) enable the court to mark off a dividing line between "preliminary negotiations" toward a deal and the closing of a bargain; (2) ensure that the parties had agreed on some minimum quantity of sufficiently defined terms so that a court could find that they actually *had* made a deal; and (3) give the court a reliable method to determine the content of their deal.

We can imagine these scholars' ideal world. The offeror says during the negotiations: "I offer you the following terms, and if you accept, there is a deal." Then the offeror states all the essential terms unambiguously. The offeree responds: "I accept your offer." At this moment (assuming consideration), their actions would form a contract, and a court could easily determine its existence and the content of its terms.

Real life, unfortunately, is messy. It frequently produces situations that do not look anything like a neat offer followed by a clear acceptance. For example, parties may be negotiating even after they start performing. We cannot be sure whether they are in or out of the contract. They may leave the content of the deal to be worked out as the relationship develops. Instead of a one-shot, comprehensive offer, they will make a long, strung-out series of proposals and adaptations. They cannot determine precisely the content of their contract until they have fully performed. This is likely to be the case with the highly relational contracts dealt with in Chapter 3 of these materials. Furthermore, real-life communication must rely on language and silence. It is riddled with ambiguities and potential for misunderstanding. When I hear the words of your "offer," and say, "I accept," what is our deal? Am I consenting to the deal you thought you were proposing or the one I thought I heard, or something else? Notice also that there may be a big difference between what we said and what we can prove at trial.

In the face of all this indeterminacy, classical courts and commentators none-theless went sturdily ahead. They tried to find a magic moment at which the parties had manifested their intention to be bound contractually. To cover the bewildering variety of human contracting behavior, this effort rapidly produced a complex body of rules. It would have been a miracle had they been consistent. The miracle did not occur.

One result was that, as with any technically intricate body of law, offer-and-acceptance became something of a Law of Loopholes. Much of this law today serves as a collection of ploys used by lawyers to get their clients out of perfectly good contracts — in the sense that the parties intended a deal — that have gone sour.[12] It may be enough for a lawyer to assert a barely plausible offer-and-acceptance theory which would let his or her client escape contractual liability. Often the other party will not think it worth debating fine points of arcane law. Faced with the threat of litigation, a person may decide to drop the whole matter or offer or accept a token settlement. Courts have frequently exploited the technicality of these rules for regulatory purposes — they use them to punish bad-faith conduct and protect good-faith reliance.

The other result of the complexity of these rules is that, to a large extent, they have collapsed of their own weight. Many courts and writers saw the technicality of these rules as leading either to contradictory results or results that were bothersome to common sense. As elsewhere in the law, writers exposed that the rules did not work, and they built a climate of opinion supporting reform. Some courts have been willing to use doctrines such as the Restatement (Second) of Contracts § 90 to protect reliance even where the formation rules have not been satisfied. Article 2 of the Uniform Commercial Code swept away nearly all of the fine points of classic offer and acceptance and much of consideration. For example, UCC § 2-204 repeals rules that require courts to find a precise instant when parties made a contract. It says:

> (1) A contract for sale of goods may be made in any manner sufficient to show agreement, including conduct by both parties which recognizes the existence of such a contract.
>
> (2) An agreement sufficient to constitute a contract for sale may be found even though the moment of its making is undetermined.
>
> (3) Even though one or more terms are left open a contract for sale does not fail for indefiniteness if the parties have intended to make a contract and there is a reasonably certain basis for giving an appropriate remedy.

Furthermore, the Restatement (Second) of Contracts invites courts to abandon the old religion and follow the Code's approach in areas other than sales of goods where Article 2 applies.

Having said all this, you need to learn something about formation of contracts. While this law may be very ill, it is not dead. In a particular case before a particular judge, you could find it necessary to be a master of its rhetoric and the tricks used by the profession to work with it. Classic contracts courses began with offer and acceptance. Many of the problems fondly remembered by lawyers from their law school days almost never occur today. Nonetheless, this odd body of law constitutes a vocabulary and common culture of the bar. Occasionally, a lawyer will seize on

---

[12] A major reason for using formation rules to bail out of a deal is to avoid the law governing performance of contracts. Performance law is highly qualitative and uncertain. For example, I need not continue to perform if you have failed "to substantially perform." I need not continue to perform if something has happened "the non-occurrence of which was a basic assumption on which the contract was made." We cannot blame lawyers for trying to avoid wading in these dismal swamps.

some part of it and twist a client's case so that it falls within it. Great treatises and law review articles lovingly treat all these issues in exhaustive detail. Thus, help is at hand in walking through the minefield if you recognize in time that you are about to enter it. We address some contemporary, and more lively, formation problems in Volume II of these materials.

The standard of interpretation — a meeting of the minds versus objective signs of agreement: Throughout most of the 19th century, judges said contract rested on the "intention of the parties," and there had to be a "meeting of the minds." The requirement that there be a subjective union of the wills of the parties became not just a metaphor representing an idealized vision of agreement, but a legal standard. The rhetoric links theories of individual autonomy and liability based on choice. At the extreme, it suggests that I am not bound to any contract that I did not *intend* to make. While intellectual developments of the late 19th and early 20th century attacked the requirement that the parties must simultaneously share an actual intention to make legally binding promises, the residue of the idea still remains as a tool occasionally called on by courts to rationalize, if not motivate, decision. Lawyers and judges still speak lovingly of "a meeting of the minds" as a term of art in the technical vocabulary of the bar.

Writers such as Oliver Wendell Holmes Jr. and Professor Samuel Williston campaigned for an "objective theory of contract." They argued that actual intention and real choice is irrelevant; liability rests on outward objective manifestations. If I look as if I am making a promise, I have made one. I can commit a contract that I did not intend to make. Does this mean that two actors in a stage play who exchange promises have made a contract because they appear to be doing so? Of course not — because the context of their behavior includes the fact that they are actors in a play and, once one broadens the context, they can no longer objectively be said to manifest agreement.

Professor Malcolm Sharp rationalized the imposition of liability a bit differently. Drawing on some ideas usually associated with tort law, he suggested that parties are held liable for intentional or negligent communication that causes loss. I am responsible for your reasonable interpretations of my behavior. Instead of concepts of individual choice, contract turns on either fault-based, or strict, liability. This position promotes easy reliance on promises and protects plans and risk-taking. It avoids problems that would arise if contract were really based on subjective choice. For example, I can fail to read (or misunderstand) a printed form contract that I sign and still be bound by it. I may be bound to a contract that I would not have accepted if I had understood the terms. I am not bound because I choose to make a promise, but because I behaved in a way that could reasonably lead another to rely on my apparent promise to perform, to that other's injury.

Applying the principle of objectivity, courts hold people to offers made as a joke if the offeree has no reason to see the humor of the situation. Similarly, one who has reason to know that raising his or her hand is a symbol meaning "I raise the bid" or "I accept" has symbolized just that, and is bound, although she forgot the code or did not intend the gesture to have that meaning.

Many treatises and judicial opinions state that advertisements are not offers. The principle of objective interpretation may explain why some advertisements are not offers. The advertisement may be so uncertain that a reasonable person could not read it as a commitment to supply any and all with an unlimited quantity of the thing publicized. However, some very specific advertisements have been held to make offers that buyers can accept and create a contract. If you made an inquiry about a product and I responded by sending you a clipped advertisement, the circumstances might lead a court to say that the clipped newspaper ad *was* an offer, even though the same ad would *not* constitute an offer to those who read it in *The Daily News*. Moreover, federal and state consumer protection statutes often hold the merchant responsible for false and misleading ads. Professors Jay Feinman and Stephen Brill argue that statements that ads are not offers are wrong and misleading. These consumer protection statutes enable potential customers to have broad rights to avoid "bait-and-switch" tactics whereby a merchant advertises a low price to lure buyers to his store and then "switches" them to more expensive models of the item.[13] Advertisements of rewards may be construed as offers, which ripen into contracts by doing the requested action. This may be because reward offers don't generally create a risk of excessive acceptances.[14]

Courts interpret contracts in context in terms of what a reasonable person should understand from the communication. Secret reservations and private meanings of words do not control; I can't avoid being bound by my promise even though I cross my fingers behind my back, and have a witness. *Shared* special meanings and usages and customs of a shared trade, however, may color or even alter the meaning of the words. If a court believes that you and I have agreed that "I am not interested" means "I accept your offer" (to confuse competitors, for example), then the court will respect our private meaning, and find that we created a contract. But notice the problems of proving it: how do I establish that you and I shared an unusual meaning of a word or a phrase?

Silence in the face of an offer: Silence in response to an offer is not an acceptance, except when it is. Suppose S writes to B, "Unless I hear from you in two days, you will be deemed to have accepted my offer." Generally, B is free to ignore S's statement. Doing nothing does not create contractual liability. This rule protects free choice and avoids what could be a burdensome commercial practice — responding to ward off liability. *However*, in a continuing relationship, the parties can agree that renewals of their arrangement will take place automatically unless one party gives notice of a desire to cancel it. This agreement can be implied from custom and past practice. (Examples are book and music clubs where customers agree to accept the monthly selection unless they send notice before a specified time.) This means that if S and B had often done business in the past, and B had accepted that it was reasonable for S to treat B's silence as an acceptance, then B could be bound to a contract.

---

[13] Rules prohibit making deliberately false statements in advertisements, using "bait and switch" techniques, and so forth. But to the classical lawyer, these are not seen as rules of contract law. They are rules governing unfair trade practices. Such classifications can make statements such as "an ad is not an offer" very misleading. *See* Jay M. Feinman & Stephen R. Brill, *Is an Advertisement an Offer? Why It Is, and Why It Matters*, 58 HASTINGS L.J. 61 (2006).

[14] Reward offers also pose special conceptual problems insofar as revocation of them is concerned. How do you revoke an offer when you don't know who may have seen it and relied on it? The problem isn't important enough to go into here, but you might ask yourself how the courts may have responded.

There are difficult cases involving B's reliance on S's statements about silence as acceptance. Most are older decisions involving purchases of insurance where an agent represents that the customer is covered *unless* the customer is notified otherwise by the insurance company. The courts usually found a way in which to protect the customer who had relied in such cases, sometimes using the theory of estoppel to bar proof that there had been no acceptance — this is a trick used to preserve the doctrine while not applying it. The court might say that the conduct of the agent "raised an estoppel" and that the company was forbidden to assert that no contract arose, even though *theoretically* there was no contract. The modern practice of agent's binders has arisen to deal with the problem of coverage while awaiting a decision by the home office. A few cases involve reliance by a retailer on a "silence as acceptance" practice of a wholesaler. A retailer orders "subject to acceptance at the home office," the time to order elsewhere for the season passes, and the wholesaler refuses to fill the order. Some courts have strained to find any communication from the seller to be an acceptance to protect the reliance.

The duration of offers: People must accept offers in order to create conventional contracts, but they cannot accept them after they have expired. An offer lasts only to any limit specified in its terms — if it says "this offer will lapse next Wednesday," one cannot accept it on Thursday.

Offers that specify no expiration time, but are on their face unlimited, are, nevertheless, open only for a reasonable time. How long is reasonable depends on the circumstances. In a rapidly fluctuating market this might be as short as the time to place a telephone call or send an e-mail. On the other hand, an offer to sell a business or a vacant lot might remain open for weeks.

Sometimes the question is not whether the offer has expired, but whether it has been revoked. Generally, an offeror can revoke an offer until it has been accepted. Can an offeror revoke an offer before the time it is set to expire? Suppose S offers to sell a house to B and promises to hold the offer open until next Wednesday. On Tuesday, S gets a much better proposal from T. Can S revoke the offer to B and sell to T without liability to B? The answer provided in classical doctrine might surprise you. Traditionally, an offeror could revoke at any time before acceptance *despite* a promise not to do this. The explanation lies in another formation doctrine. As we will see shortly, a promise not to revoke lacks consideration (and so is not binding) since the buyer gave nothing for it, and so that promise was not enforceable. There is a way for B to secure an irrevocable offer under classical doctrine. B could buy an option by giving S consideration for the promise not to revoke, and then the promise would be enforceable.

Some courts have applied Restatement of Contracts § 90 to irrevocable, or "firm" offers. Once there is reliance on the promise not to revoke, the offeror loses his or her power *not* to revoke. Many of these cases involve subcontractors' bids on work (that is, offers) to general contractors, who use the sub's bid in making their own bid. Most modern cases hold that the sub's bid cannot be revoked. In many instances, the sub's bid is not accompanied by an express promise not to revoke, but courts imply such a promise. Then they protect reliance on the promise they have fashioned. UCC § 2-205 explicitly repudiates the common-law rule requiring consideration to create irrevocable offers and says that a merchant can make an irrevocable offer in writing, which will stay open despite the absence of consideration or any proof of actual reliance. The statute limits the duration of such an offer.

The manner of acceptance: One must use a reasonable means to communicate his or her acceptance. For example, it usually is safer to accept by email when an offer was made by email, since the use of an email suggests the need for quick action. In some circumstances one might not need to respond by a rapid means of communication. Suppose, for example, it is clear from the circumstances that an offeror used an email only to attract attention, and the market is not a fluctuating one. Probably a letter would still be a reasonable means of acceptance.

Under classical doctrine, one must accept the precise offer made to create a contract. "The offeror is master of the offer," as the saying goes. For example, one cannot accept an offer to sell a five-year-old Ford for $10,000 by saying "I accept your offer to sell a four-year-old Chevrolet for $5000." Could you accept the offer to sell the five-year-old Ford by saying, "I accept your offer to sell the five-year-old Ford for $10,000, and I will give you a personal check next Monday?" That would depend on whether the court would interpret the offer as requiring payment in cash; some courts might do so, and see the statement as proposing payment by check as an imperfect acceptance or a counteroffer. However, UCC § 2-511(2) says: "Tender of payment is sufficient when made by any means or in any manner current in the ordinary course of business unless the seller demands payment in legal tender and gives any extension of time reasonably necessary to procure it."

It is useful to distinguish between the revocation of an offer, which is what an offeror does to terminate one that she has made, and a rejection, which is what an offeree does when she refuses to go along with a deal that the offeror has proposed. The offeree rejects an offer by expressly or impliedly communicating a lack of interest. And, importantly, a counteroffer is treated as a rejection. This means that in our hypothetical case in the preceding paragraph involving the five-year-old Ford, *if* the proposal to pay by check was treated as a counteroffer, the buyer could no longer accept the offer even if she later agreed to pay cash. In other words, if you offer to sell your car to me for $10,000, and I respond, "Would you take $9500?" I have rejected your offer by making a counteroffer and I have terminated my power to accept it even on the original terms.

Business practice is often inconsistent with the old rule requiring the acceptance to mirror the offer — which creates a problem called "the battle of the forms." The parties exchange business documents with different or conflicting terms, but both think they have a deal. For example, the buyer uses a *purchase order* with terms printed on the back. One of these terms grants a right to cancel for any delay. Seller accepts on its own *acknowledgment of order* form, which also has printed terms on the back. One term says that delivery dates are only approximate and seller will satisfy the contract if it delivers goods within a reasonable time. At common law, there was no contract at this point because of the failure of seller's acceptance to mirror the terms of the buyer's offer. However, if seller shipped goods and buyer accepted them, courts might say that seller's "acknowledgment of order" form (which looked like an acceptance) was in law a counteroffer. This counteroffer was accepted by buyer's action of accepting the goods when they were shipped to it. Buyer could not return the goods on the ground that its form said it could cancel for any delay; its form was treated by the law as altogether irrelevant.

The Uniform Commercial Code has done a major remodeling job on the classical law governing inconsistent forms. Under UCC § 2-207, if there is a "definite and seasonable expression of acceptance," there is a contract. There are elaborate provisions on how courts will fashion the terms, which are considered in detail in Volume II of this book. If there is no such expression of acceptance, the parties' conduct may create a contract, the terms of which will be all those upon which their writings agree plus, where they disagree, the provisions of the UCC. The section is complex and has prompted a great deal of litigation.

The acceptance-when-mailed rule: Generations of law students have cut their legal teeth on "the mailbox rule." Suppose the following sequence:

(1) An offer is mailed on November 10th at 1:00 P.M., and it arrives on November 12th at 2:00 P.M.

(2) A letter of acceptance, properly addressed, is deposited in a mailbox on November 12th at 3:00 P.M. It arrives on November 14th at 1:00 P.M., *or* there is an airplane crash and the letter never arrives at all.

(3a) The offeror telephones the offeree on November 12th at 3:05 P.M. and says, "I revoke my offer." *Or:*

(3b) The offeree telephones the offeror at that time and says, "Disregard the letter you will get. I do not want to buy the goods, and I call off my acceptance."

Although there are very few cases, writers said that a contract was formed when a letter of acceptance was placed in the mail. As a result, neither attempt to back out by telephone call is effective. (Of course, the other party always could consent to calling off the deal, but she does not have to do this.)

Writers have attacked the rule as an over-generalization, and have suggested that it may be appropriate to find a contract in one case (3a) but not in the other (3b). We can defend the general rule binding the offeror once the offeree deposits a letter of acceptance, since the offeree is likely to rely from that point. At the least, the offeree won't look for other deals from then on. It may be that an efficient economy results when offerees can begin to rely at once, without needing to wait for a confirmation that their acceptance has been received by the offeror. On the other hand, it is harder to build a case for binding the offeree when the first thing that the offeror hears from the offeree is the message that the offeree doesn't want a deal. There would be, of course, no reliance by the offeree who has changed her mind. And the letter of acceptance, though posted by the offeree, cannot prompt reliance because the offeror doesn't see it before she knows that the offeree wants it disregarded. Nonetheless, most courts have opted for a flat rule; both are bound, at least insofar as the rules of offer and acceptance are concerned, when the letter is posted.

For a time it appeared that the practical significance of the "mailbox rule" was likely to decline to the vanishing point; the rule is important only in an era in which communications are sequential, and not simultaneous. As telephones became the dominant method of business communication, the kinds of problems created by telegrams and forms bearing small print sent by "snail mail" were less likely to occur. But email, texts, and the like can obviously present some of the same kinds of problems as the telegram once did, especially in the context of volatile markets in which prices and conditions can change very rapidly.

The requirement of certainty: Finally, contracts must be reasonably certain to be enforceable. How certain is certain enough is hard to say. A contract to sell a named product, "quantity and price to be agreed," would not be definite enough at common law. Even an open price term probably would be enough to prevent a contract from being formed under classical rules. Once again, the Uniform Commercial Code has liberalized the standard, seeking to ratify common commercial practices. UCC § 2-204(3) expresses the standard as "a contract does not fail for indefiniteness if the parties have intended to make a contract and there is a reasonably certain basis for giving an appropriate remedy." Section 2-305 governs "open price terms" and provides that "the parties if they so intend can conclude a contract for sale even though the price is not settled. In such a case the price is a reasonable price at the time for delivery if (a) nothing is said as to price; or (b) the price is left to be agreed by the parties and they fail to agree; or (c) the price is to be fixed in terms of some agreed market or other standard as set or recorded by a third person and it is not so set or recorded. . . . " Subsection (4), however, provides: "Where, however, the parties intend not to be bound unless the price be fixed or agreed and it is not fixed or agreed there is no contract. . . . "

A great deal more could be said about offer-and-acceptance rules. We will explore some of the finer points of formation doctrine in the pages that follow. But the summary you have just read embodies much of the content of the doctrine that occupies some law students for several weeks. We might add at this point that there is nothing wrong with using formation rules as the subject of study in a basic contracts course. Usually, we suspect that the real agenda in an extensive study of the mailbox rule and other chestnuts of offer-and-acceptance law, is not the content of the rules themselves. Rather, it is legal analysis. We simply believe that the analysis of different rules, ones that address modern problems, is just as effective in teaching the general skill of analysis and more meaningful as far as substantive knowledge is concerned.

b. Some practice problems

In order to encourage you to think about this material by facing the difficulties involved in applying it, we offer the following review problems. In thinking about these problems you should remember that many formation issues turn not on the application of legal rules, but rather on thoughtful interpretation of the language used by the parties in communicating or miscommunicating with each other.

1. Rodney Brown began working as an employee for Acme International (AI), a Fortune 500 company, in September 2013. When he was hired, he went through a formal orientation organized by the human resources department. At that time, he received a 20-page handbook detailing the rights of AI employees, which was silent on the question of how disputes between AI and its employees would be handled. On April 30, 2014, AI sent an email message to all of its employees. The email came from "Webmaster AI. webmaster@AI.com." The subject line of the email was "M.

Wooten — New Dispute Resolution Policy." Michael Wooten was the president of AI. Nowhere in the email's heading was any indication given that the email was of critical importance or that it was intended to alter employees' legal rights.

The text of the message was in the form of a letter addressed "Dear Fellow Employee:". Its length was the equivalent of one full page, single-spaced. The first two of the email's eight paragraphs made no mention of the dispute resolution policy (DRP). The paragraphs were instead innocuous descriptions of AI as "a leader in a very competitive marketplace." The first mention of the DRP came in the third paragraph: "We have developed the Dispute Resolution Policy (DRP) to address legal issues raised either by an employee or by Acme International." The DRP was again mentioned in the fifth paragraph, where it was described as "an essential element of the [employee's] employment relationship." No other reference — implicit or explicit — was made in the text of the message to the fact that AI expected its employees to be bound by the DRP if they continued working there.

The email message included two links at the bottom of the page — to dispute_resolution.htm and DRP_Handbook_2.doc — located on AI's internal website, which employees could access by clicking on either link. The first link sent employees to a two-page flyer, which set out key provisions of the DRP in plain language in a question-and-answer format. In bold, highlighted text, the flyer informed employees that the DRP required all disputes to be arbitrated. It further provided that the DRP is "the exclusive means of resolving workplace disputes involving legally protected rights." Other sections of the flyer informed employees that the DRP would apply to all employees who "continue [their] employment after the effective date of the DRP's adoption," and that "employment discrimination and harassment claims, based on, for example . . . disability" are governed by the DRP.

The second link sent employees to a 26-page handbook, which detailed the provisions of the DRP in lawyer-written language. AI did nothing more to inform its employees of the DRP than send this message and provide these links.

Brown does not remember having received the email. Yet AI's webmaster can present evidence from its internal tracking log showing that Brown both received and opened the email at 1:56 p.m. on April 30, 2014. (The email was sent at 1:54 p.m. that same day.) AI's evidence does not indicate whether Brown actually read the text of the email or whether he clicked on either link. Rodney Brown is an active user of email. He receives 20 to 100 messages a day. He often scans the text of messages and deletes those of little interest to him.

On September 15, 2015, Brown was discharged by AI after his supervisor found him napping on the job on numerous occasions. Brown believes that his discharge violates the Americans with Disabilities Act and wants to sue AI. He has long suffered from sleep apnea, a condition that can disturb sleep, make it almost impossible to wake up in the morning, and cause episodes of sleep during the day.

Brown is a client of your law firm. He is determined to have his day in court and argues that he never affirmatively opted for arbitration.[15] Your boss has given you

---

[15] Brown's concern arises from his unfamiliarity with arbitration. We will consider the differences between litigation and arbitration later in these materials.

No cosideration
Not reasonable acceptance if at all

a summary of the facts and has asked you whether Brown is bound by the DRP. Think through the best argument for Brown, and how AI will counter it.

2. Pepsico, Inc., sponsored a television commercial that was broadcast many times. A court described the commercial as follows:

The commercial opens upon an idyllic, suburban morning, where the chirping of birds in sun-dappled trees welcomes a paperboy on his morning route. As the newspaper hits the stoop of a conventional two-story house, the tattoo of a military drum introduces the subtitle, "MONDAY 7:58 A.M." The stirring strains of a martial air mark the appearance of a well-coiffed teenager preparing to leave for school, dressed in a shirt emblazoned with the Pepsi logo, a red-white-and-blue ball. While the teenager confidently preens, the military drumroll again sounds as the subtitle "T-SHIRT 75 PEPSI POINTS" scrolls across the screen. Bursting from his room, the teenager strides down the hallway wearing a leather jacket. The drumroll sounds again, as the subtitle "LEATHER JACKET 1450 PEPSI POINTS" appears. The teenager opens the door of his house and, unfazed by the glare of the early morning sunshine, puts on a pair of sunglasses. The drumroll then accompanies the subtitle "SHADES 175 PEPSI POINTS." A voice-over then intones, "Introducing the new Pepsi Stuff catalog," as the camera focuses on the cover of the catalog.

The scene then shifts to three young boys sitting in front of a high school building. The boy in the middle is intent on his Pepsi Stuff Catalog, while the boys on either side are each drinking Pepsi. The three boys gaze in awe at an object rushing overhead, as the military march builds to a crescendo. The Harrier Jet is not yet visible, but the observer senses the presence of a mighty plane as the extreme winds generated by its flight create a paper maelstrom in a classroom devoted to an otherwise dull physics lesson. Finally, the Harrier Jet swings into view and lands by the side of the school building, next to a bicycle rack. Several students run for cover, and the velocity of the wind strips one hapless faculty member down to his underwear. While the faculty member is being deprived of his dignity, the voice-over announces: "Now the more Pepsi you drink, the more great stuff you're gonna get."

The teenager opens the cockpit of the fighter and can be seen, helmetless, holding a Pepsi. Looking very pleased with himself, the teenager exclaims, "Sure beats the bus," and chortles. The military drumroll sounds a final time, as the following words appear: "HARRIER FIGHTER 7,000,000 PEPSI POINTS." A few seconds later, the following appears in more stylized script: "Drink Pepsi — Get Stuff." With that message, the music and the commercial end with a triumphant flourish.

Part of the Pepsi Stuff promotion includes a catalog, available on request. The catalog specifies the number of Pepsi Points required to obtain promotional merchandise and includes an Order Form listing 53 items of Pepsi Stuff merchandise redeemable for Pepsi Points. The list does not include a Harrier Jet. The amount of Pepsi Points required to obtain the listed merchandise ranges from 15 for a jacket patch to 3,300 for a mountain bike. The catalog contains directions for redeeming Pepsi Points for merchandise. The directions note that merchandise may be ordered "only" with the original order form. The catalog notes that in the event that a consumer lacks enough Pepsi Points to obtain a desired item, additional Pepsi Points may be purchased for 10 cents each; however, at least 15 original Pepsi Points must accompany each order.

A client has asked whether he can accept Pepsi's offer for a Harrier Jet Fighter by tendering $700,008.50 and 15 original Pepsi Points.[16]

No, advertisement not usually considered offer [handwritten]

2. A Policy Approach to Judicial Intervention

Finally, we return to explore the main theme of this chapter. What factors should a court or other legal agency consider in deciding how to respond to a request to intervene in a relationship? Should the agency help or regulate the relationship? Or should it stand aside and leave parties where it finds them when one asks for help? We often will repeat this question in specific contexts. However, for now, you may find it useful to consider some general observations that Professor Zechariah Chafee made long ago.[17] Chafee identified four policies that he thought should govern the decision to intervene — the first favors intervention, and the last three oppose it. Chafee was writing about legal intervention in the affairs of not-for-profit organizations, but you will soon see that his ideas about the policies involved also apply to many types of contracts.

(1) *The "Stranglehold" Policy.* Sometimes a relationship is so important to the parties that changing or leaving it would have unusually serious consequences for their lives. It is not easy for them to "exit" if the relationship goes wrong. They can't pack up and go elsewhere. (Chafee gives as examples workers expelled from unions, doctors from medical societies, or brokers from stock exchanges.) In such cases, only outside intervention may prevent or compensate what we see as serious harm. The fact that one party holds the other in a stranglehold is a reason for intervention. *Stranglehold policy* [handwritten]

(2) *The "Dismal Swamp" Policy.* The agency may be getting in over its head. It may not be able to sort out conflicting claims of right and wrong in a complex relationship. The relationship has its own unique history, specialized vocabulary, power hierarchies, personal animosities, and implicit understandings. (The obvious example is the difficulty faced by courts asked to decide contending claims to church property among schismatic factions. Each asserts that it, and it alone, represents the true religion of the church. It is easy to see why courts are reluctant to intervene.) *Dismal Swamp* [handwritten]

(3) *The "Hot Potato" Policy.* If most of the parties think that outside intervention is undesirable and would be an uncalled-for interference in their affairs, the agency's attempt to intervene may simply cause resentment and resistance. This is particularly true if the legal agency operates as a court and uses *Hot Potatoe* [handwritten]

---

[16] $699,998.50 plus 15 original Pepsi Points (worth $1.50), plus a $10.00 shipping and handling fee. *See* Leonard v. Pepsico, Inc., 88 F.Supp. 2d 116 (S.D.N.Y. 1999), *aff'd*, 210 F.3d 88 (2d Cir. 2000).

[17] Zechariah Chafee, *The Internal Affairs of Associations Not for Profit*, 43 Harv. L. Rev. 993, 1021–29 (1930).

an adversarial procedure. Such procedures invite parties to show their opponents in the worst possible light. When a plaintiff charges a defendant with wrongful conduct, it may aggravate an already difficult relationship. As a result, parties may not cooperate in fact-finding, settlement, or enforcement processes.

(4) *The "Living Tree" Policy.* The autonomy of the relationship itself may be independently valuable. Chafee says that the "health of society will usually be prompted if the groups within it which serve the industrial, mental, and spiritual needs of citizens are genuinely alive. . . . Legal supervision must often be withheld for fear that it may do more harm than good."[18] If parties "legalize" their relationship, and structure it with a view toward invoking outside legal regulation to enforce their demands, they may sacrifice cooperation.

Chafee's list of policies obviously is not exhaustive. Moreover, the list seems to emphasize passive virtues rather than legal action to carry out valued goals. Chafee's legal agencies would be cautious. Perhaps he is right, but you do not have to accept this view. You may want those you see as wise judges to be given a roving commission to do good. You may see Chafee's statement of the policies as a useful way to hide legal support for power as it exists in the society. Chafee's article does not justify active intervention in relationships to carry out values that you may see as fundamental.

Nonetheless, Chafee is descriptively accurate. Legal agencies recognize the four policies he identifies, although they seldom offer such colorful names. You should keep the four policies in mind, along with further policies thought important by the judges you read, as you consider the cases that follow. You should also remember them when we move from contract in the family setting to employment and other business contexts.

B.   CONTRACT IN THE FAMILY SETTING

1.   Which Promises Should the Law Enforce? Illustrations and Issues

Should the courts, as the arm of the state, enforce every statement made in the form of a promise? The courts have never thought so. But as soon as we accept the need to divide the enforceable from the unenforceable, we encounter the difficult task of articulating the criteria for deciding which is which.

a.   Courts and contracts between husband and wife

Husbands and wives can make contracts with each other. For example, the wealthy often come to marriages, particularly second or third marriages, agreeing to keep their property separate. One spouse may wish to buy the land, or artwork, or automobile of the other spouse. One agrees to buy, the other to sell. If we assume that the transaction meets the general rules of contract, this contract would be as enforceable as if they were strangers. But husbands and wives make many promises

---

[18] *Id.* at 1027.

to each other of a different character. Some are trivial; some are serious. They can range from agreements about who will pick up the wine and who will shop for what is needed to make the meal at a dinner party, to whether his elderly father will be invited to live with them in the family home. We can think of almost all human interaction as contractual, but this does not mean that all human interaction will be transformed into contracts legally enforceable by courts.

We will begin with a traditional view. You may not like it, but it is a view that still may appeal to some people.

BALFOUR v. BALFOUR
King's Bench Court of Appeal
2 K.B. 571 (1919)

[Mrs. Balfour sued her husband for breach of contract. Mr. and Mrs. Balfour had lived together in Ceylon for 15 years. He was given leave from his position with the Government of Ceylon, and the Balfours returned to England for an eight-month vacation. They were to return to Ceylon on August 8, 1916, but Mrs. Balfour was suffering from rheumatic arthritis and her doctor advised her to remain in England for another three months. Before Mr. Balfour sailed on August 8, 1916, he gave his wife a check for £24, and he promised to give her £30 a month until she returned to Ceylon. Afterward, Mr. Balfour wrote his wife suggesting that they remain apart. He did not send the £30 each month, and Mrs. Balfour sued for the balance due. The trial judge held that Mr. Balfour was under an obligation to support his wife, and her consent to define that obligation as £30 monthly was consideration to support a contract. He awarded Mrs. Balfour judgment. The Court of Appeal reversed.]

WARRINGTON, L.J. . . .

The matter really reduces itself to an absurdity when one considers it, because if we were to hold that with regard to all the more or less trivial concerns of life where a wife, at the request of her husband, makes a promise to him, that is a promise which can be enforced in law. . . . The husband expressed his intention to make this payment, and he promised to make it, and was bound in honour to continue it so long as he was in a position to do so. The wife, on the other hand, so far as I can see, made no bargain at all. . . .

DUKE, L.J. . . .

The proposition that the mutual promises made in the ordinary domestic relationship of husband and wife of necessity give cause for action on a contract seems to me to go to the very root of the relationship, and to be a possible fruitful source of dissension and quarrelling. I cannot see that any benefit would result from it to either of the parties, but on the other hand it would lead to unlimited litigation in a relationship which should be obviously as far as possible protected from possibilities of that kind. . . .

ATKIN, L.J. . . .

The defence to this action on the alleged contract is that the defendant, the husband, entered into no contract with his wife, and for the determination of that it is necessary to remember that there are agreements between parties which do not result in contracts within the meaning of that term in our law. The ordinary example is where two parties agree to take a walk together, or where there is an offer and acceptance of hospitality. . . . [O]ne of the most usual forms of agreement which does not constitute a contract appears to me to be the arrangements which are made between husband and wife. It is quite common, and it is the natural and inevitable result of the relationship of husband and wife, that the two spouses should make arrangements between themselves . . .

To my mind those agreements, or many of them, do not result in contracts at all, and they do not result in contracts even though there may be what as between other parties would constitute consideration for the agreement. The consideration, as we know, may consist either in some right, interest, profit, or benefit accruing to one party, or some forbearance, detriment, loss, or responsibility given, suffered, or undertaken by the other. That is a well-known definition, and it constantly happens, I think, that such arrangements made between husband and wife are arrangements in which there are mutual promises, or in which there is consideration in form within the definition that I have mentioned. Nevertheless they are not contracts, and they are not contracts because the parties did not intend that they should be attended by legal consequences.

To my mind it would be of the worst possible example to hold that agreements such as this resulted in legal obligations which could be enforced in the Courts. It would mean this, that when the husband makes his wife a promise to give her an allowance of 30 shillings or £2 a week, whatever he can afford to give her, for the maintenance of the household and children, and she promises so to apply it, not only could she sue him for his failure in any week to supply the allowance, but he could sue her for non-performance of the obligation, express or implied, which she had undertaken upon her part. All I can say is that the small Courts of this country would have to be multiplied one hundred fold if these arrangements were held to result in legal obligations. They are not sued upon, not because the parties are reluctant to enforce their legal rights when the agreement is broken, but because the parties, in the inception of the arrangement, never intended that they should be sued upon. Agreements such as these are outside the realm of contracts altogether. The common law does not regulate the form of agreements between spouses. Their promises are not sealed with seals and sealing wax. The consideration that really obtains for them is that natural love and affection which counts for so little in these cold Courts. The terms may be repudiated, varied, or renewed as performance proceeds or as disagreements develop, and the principles of the common law as to exoneration and discharge and accord and satisfaction are such as find no place in the domestic code. The parties themselves are advocates, judges, Courts, sheriff's officer, and reporter. In respect of these promises each house is a domain into which the King's writ does not seek to run, and to which his officers do not seek to be admitted. The only question in this case is whether or not this promise was of such a class or not. For the reasons given by my brethren it appears to me to be plainly established that the promise here was not intended by either party to be attended by legal consequences. I think the onus was upon the plaintiff, and the plaintiff has not established any contract. The parties were living together, the wife intending to return. The suggestion is that the husband bound himself to pay £30 a month under all circumstances, and, although she was in ill-health and alone in this country, that out of that sum she undertook to defray the whole of the medical expenses that might fall upon her, whatever might be the development of her illness, and in whatever expenses it might involve her. To my mind neither party contemplated such a result . . .

NOTES AND QUESTIONS

1.   *Mrs. Balfour's tactics:* Sometime in 1918, Mrs. Balfour obtained a legal separation and an order for alimony. Stephen Hedley tells us: "It is unclear what advantage Mrs. Balfour was seeking by exercising both contractual and matrimonial rights. The only plausible explanation seems to be that she wanted alimony plus £30 per month; I am informed that maintenance awards at that date were not generous."[19]

2.   *Intent to create legal relationships:* Hedley comments on the *Balfour* case and the requirement that parties intend to create legal relationships. He says, "A marriage run on the common law principles designed for businesses would indeed be a sorry affair, but so would a business run on those same principles. Willing co-operation without reference to legal entitlements is normal (and indeed, essential) in both spheres." He continues, "[S]ince there are such obvious differences between the two, there must be something very wrong with a theoretical approach that claims to distinguish them only by reference to a presumed, unquantifiable, and highly questionable difference in willingness to sue." Hedley concludes that "the modern law of 'intent to create legal relations' essentially reduces to this: that where the parties were dealing at arms' length, promises will generally be enforced; but in domestic contexts, contractual liability will be imposed only if the party seeking enforcement has already performed one side of the bargain and is simply seeking reciprocity. The courts will not enforce an executory agreement [in a domestic context]. Beyond this, I argue, there is no requirement of an agreement of an 'intention to create legal relations.' "[20]

Assume Hedley's reading of the English cases is correct. Can we explain this result by those courts' judgments about the importance of domestic promises measured against the costs of judicial action? Do you find any support for this explanation in the *Balfour* decision?

Professors Mary Keyes and Kylie Burns are very critical of a test that rests on an intention to make a legally binding contract in a family context. It "makes no sense as the parties are unlikely to have considered this question."[21] They point out that under modern statutes, some contracts in a family setting are enforced. They

---

[19]   Stephen Hedley, *Keeping Contract in its Place* — Balfour v. Balfour *and the Enforceability of Informal Agreements*, 5 OXFORD J. LEGAL STUD. 391, 392 n.4 (1985).

[20]   Hedley, *id.* at 391, 393, 396–97 (1985).

[21]   Mary Keyes & Kylie Burns, *Contract and the Family: Whither Intention?* 26 MELBOURNE U. L. REV. 577, 595 (2002).

They argue this is the intention to not impose legal contract

Issue/ what's impose have legal contract

see the problem as fashioning appropriate limitations on both the procedures for making contracts and the fairness of those bargains that are made.

ANSIN v. CRAVEN-ANSIN
Massachusetts Supreme Judicial Court
457 Mass. 283, 929 N.E.2d 955 (2010)

Way more recent and prob relevant

MARSHALL, C.J.

Married 21 yrs, got written agreement in '04, Divorce filed by husband '06, he looks to enforce

We granted direct appellate review in this divorce proceeding to determine whether so-called "postnuptial" or "marital" agreements are contrary to public policy and, if not, whether the marital agreement at issue is enforceable. The dispute is between Kenneth S. Ansin (husband) and Cheryl A. Craven-Ansin (wife) concerning the validity of their 2004 written agreement "settling all rights and obligations arising from their marital relationship" in the event of a divorce. Two years after the agreement was executed, in November 2006, the husband filed a complaint for divorce and sought to enforce the terms of the agreement. At the time of the complaint, the parties had been married for 21 years and had two sons.

A judge in the Probate and Family Court upheld the agreement, finding that it was negotiated by independent counsel for each party, was not the product of fraud or duress, and was based on full financial disclosures by the husband, and that the terms of the agreement were fair and reasonable at the time of execution and at the time of divorce. Judgment [was] entered enforcing the marital agreement.

Marital agreement upheld

Judge enforced agreement, ct.

The wife appealed, and we granted both parties' applications for direct appellate review. We now affirm.

Facts. . . . The parties were married in July 1985. The execution of their marital agreement 19 years later was precipitated by marital problems that began toward the end of 2003. . . . The parties separated . . . for some six weeks. While the parties were separated, the husband promised his wife that he would recommit to the marriage if she would sign a marital agreement. She agreed to do so, she said, in an attempt to preserve the marriage and the family. The parties resumed living together and went on a "second honeymoon."

In April 2004, they began negotiating the terms of the agreement . . . . Each retained counsel. . . . Several draft agreements were exchanged. The judge found that in the course of the negotiations the wife was "fully informed" of the marital assets . . . . [W]ith the assistance of their respective counsel, the parties reached an agreement; it was signed in July 2004. . . .

The agreement sets forth the parties' intent that, in the event of a divorce, the terms of the agreement are to be "valid and enforceable" against them, and "limit the rights" that "otherwise arise by reason of their marriage." . . . As for the distribution of property in the event of a divorce, the agreement states that the wife "disclaims any and all interest she now has or ever may have" in the husband's interest in the Florida real estate and other marital assets. [Eds. note: the husband brought these assets to the marriage.] The husband agreed to pay the wife $5 million, and 30 percent of the appreciation of all marital property held by the couple from the time of the agreement to the time of the divorce. . . .

On execution of the marital agreement, the relationship between the husband and wife took on, in the judge's words, a "light and optimistic tone" and both were "looking forward to strengthening their marriage." The two engaged in numerous activities together, including training for a marathon and traveling. . . . [T]he husband applied for and was accepted to Harvard University's Kennedy School of Government; his decision to enroll as a student there was not supported by his wife. The wife began to increase her consumption of alcohol, leading to more arguments with her husband. In June 2005, at the wife's request, the husband moved out of the house. . . . In November 2006, the husband filed a petition for divorce.

Validity of marital agreement. Whether a marital agreement should be recognized in Massachusetts is a long-deferred question of first impression. Consistent with the majority of States to address the issue, *see Bratton v. Bratton*, 136 S.W.3d 595, 599–600 (Tenn. 2004), we conclude that such agreements may be enforced. Our decision is consistent with our established recognition that a marital relationship need not vitiate contractual rights between the parties. We have, for example, recognized the validity of premarital agreements, *Osborne v. Osborne*, 384 Mass. 591, 598, 428 N.E.2d 810 (1981), and separation agreements, *Knox v. Remick*, 371 Mass. 433, 436, 358 N.E.2d 432 (1976), reasoning that it was important to respect the parties' "freedom to contract" and that such agreements may serve a "useful function" in permitting the parties to arrange their financial affairs "as they best see fit." . . .

The wife argues that marital agreements are different in kind and should be declared void against public policy because they are "innately coercive," "usually" arise when the marriage is already failing, and may "encourage" divorce. The wife provides no support for, and we reject, any assumption that marital agreements are typically executed amid threats of divorce or induced by illusory promises of remaining in a failing marriage. Marital contracts are not the product of classic arm's-length bargaining, but that does not make them necessarily coercive. . . .

Judicial review of a marital agreement. A marital agreement stands on a different footing from both a premarital and a separation agreement. Before marriage, the parties have greater freedom to reject an unsatisfactory premarital contract. . . .

A separation agreement, in turn, is negotiated when a marriage has failed and the spouses "intend a permanent separation or marital dissolution." . . . The family unit will no longer be kept intact, and the parties may look to their own future economic interests. . . . The circumstances surrounding marital agreements in contrast are "pregnant with the opportunity for one party to use the threat of dissolution 'to bargain themselves into positions of advantage.' " *Pacelli v. Pacelli*, 319 N.J. Super. 185, 195, 725 A.2d 56 (App. Div. 1999), quoting *Mathie v. Mathie*, 12 Utah 2d 116, 121, 363 P.2d 779 (1961).

For these reasons, we join many other States in concluding that marital agreements must be carefully scrutinized. *See, e.g., Casto v. Casto*, 508 So. 2d 330, 334 (Fla. 1987) (court "must recognize that parties to a marriage are not dealing at arm's length, and, consequently, trial judges must carefully examine the circumstances to determine the validity of [marital] agreements") . . .

Before a marital agreement is sanctioned by a court, careful scrutiny by the judge should determine at a minimum whether (1) each party has had an opportunity to obtain separate legal counsel of each party's own choosing;[22] (2) there was fraud or coercion in obtaining the agreement; (3) all assets were fully disclosed by both parties before the agreement was executed; (4) each spouse knowingly and explicitly agreed in writing to waive the right to a judicial equitable division of assets and all marital rights in the event of a divorce; and (5) the terms of the agreement are fair and reasonable at the time of execution and at the time of divorce. Where one spouse challenges the enforceability of the agreement, the spouse seeking to enforce the agreement shall bear the burden of satisfying these criteria. . . .

As with contracts generally, marital agreements are not enforceable if tainted by fraud or coercion. . . . We agree with those States that have held that the spouse seeking to enforce a marital agreement, in contrast to the enforcement of contracts generally, must establish that the other spouse's consent was not obtained through coercion or fraud. . . . [W]e see no reason to question [the trial judge's] ultimate finding that the marital agreement was not the product of coercion or fraud. The agreement was the product of lengthy negotiations between the parties, each represented by separate, experienced counsel. The wife's attorney testified that, consistent with the instructions of her client, she intended to negotiate an enforceable marital agreement. . . . The evidence is clear that the wife made an informed, voluntary choice to sign the agreement.[23] . . . [Eds. note: The court used similar reasoning to conclude that the wife had knowingly waived her legal rights and that full disclosure of assets had been made.]

In evaluating whether a marital agreement is fair and reasonable at the time of execution, a judge should [] consider the entire context in which the agreement was reached, allowing greater latitude for agreements reached where each party is represented by separate counsel of their own choosing. A judge may consider "the magnitude of the disparity between the outcome under the agreement and the outcome under otherwise prevailing legal principles," whether "the purpose of the agreement was to benefit or protect the interests of third parties (such as the children from a prior relationship)," and "the impact of the agreement's enforcement upon the children of the parties." American Law Institute Principles of Family Dissolution, §7.05(3)(a), (c), (d) (2002). Other factors may include the length of the marriage, the motives of the contracting spouses, their respective bargaining

---

[22] [9] We do not require, as do some other States, that a marital agreement will be enforceable only if each spouse is represented by separate counsel. *See, e.g.*, Minn. Stat. Ann. § 519.11 (1a) (c) (2006). . . . Reliance on the advice of experienced, independent legal counsel, however, will go a long way toward ensuring the enforceability of an agreement.

[23] [13] The wife suggests that because the parties' younger son suffers from an illness, she was pressured into signing the agreement to preserve her son's "happiness and stability." The judge made no findings concerning the son's illness or its effect on the wife's decision to sign the marital agreement. The wife made no request for additional findings on those points, and we do not consider them. It may be that in some circumstances evidence that a spouse agrees to a marital agreement because of concern for the illness of a child and evidence that the child will be harmed by a divorce will be sufficient to establish coercion or duress.

positions, the circumstances giving rise to the marital agreement, the degree of the pressure, if any, experienced by the contesting spouse, and other circumstances the judge finds relevant. . . .

The gravamen of the wife's complaint is that she will be left with a disproportionately small percentage of the couple's marital assets. A marital agreement need not provide for an equal distribution of assets, as long as a judge has concluded that the agreement is fair and reasonable. . . .

Conclusion. Enforcement of a marital agreement is not contrary to public policy. We agree with the [trial] judge . . . that the marital agreement in this case should be specifically enforced.

NOTES AND QUESTIONS

1.   ***Towards a general rule on postnuptial agreements?*** A 2012 law review note categorized the *Ansin* court's approach as "moderate as compared to other states' approaches."[24] At one end of the spectrum are states like Utah[25] and Wisconsin,[26] which do not distinguish between prenuptial and postnuptial contracts. At the other end are states like Ohio[27] and Iowa,[28] which summarily reject the application of a contract law framework to agreements between married couples.

In *Miller v. Miller*, a 19th-century case from Iowa, a wife sued her husband for breach of a written contract.[29] The written contract began: "This agreement, made this fifth day of August, 1885, between the undersigned, husband and wife, in the interests of peace and for the best interests of each other and of their family, is signed in good faith by each party, with the promise, each to the other, and to their children, that they will each honestly promise to help each other to observe and keep the same, which is as follows, to wit: All past causes and subjects of dispute . . . shall be absolutely ignored and buried, and no allusion thereto by word or talk to each other or any one else shall ever be made." The contract provided that the husband would pay the wife $16.66 per month "so long as Mrs. Miller shall faithfully observe the terms and conditions of their contract." She had promised to refrain from "scolding, fault-finding and anger insofar as relates to the future . . . " She was to "keep her home and family in a comfortable and reasonably good condition . . . " Finally, "[t]hey agree to live together as husband and wife and observe faithfully the marriage relation, and each to live virtuously with the other." Mrs. Miller's petition alleged, and for purposes of the demurrer it was taken as true, that Mr. Miller "while improperly spending money upon other women, refused to furnish

---

[24]   Stephanie A. Bruno, *Insuring the Knot: The Massachusetts Approach to Postnuptial Agreements*, 45 Suffolk U.L. Rev. 397, 399 (2012).

[25]   *See* Reese v. Reese, 984 P.2d 987 (Utah 1999).

[26]   Wis. Stat. Ann. § 766.58 (6) (LexisNexis 2005).

[27]   Ohio Rev. Code. Ann. § 3103.06 (LexisNexis 2008) (allows only postnuptial agreements providing for immediate separation).

[28]   *See* Hussemann v. Hussemann, 847 N.W.2d 219, 224 (Iowa 2014).

[29]   78 Iowa 177, 35 N.W. 464 (1889), *aff'd*, 42 N.W. 641 (1889).

the plaintiff with necessary clothing, and she had been compelled to furnish it herself by her personal earnings."

The trial court sustained the husband's demurrer, and the Supreme Court of Iowa affirmed this judgment. It found that enforcing such a contract would be against public policy. It explained that in order to enforce the husband's promise, a court would have to decide whether the wife had carried out her part of the bargain. "[J]udicial inquiry into matters of that character, between husband and wife, would be fraught with irreparable mischief, and forbidden by sound considerations of public policy." A court would have to ask, "Was she not at some time angry? Has she kept the family in a comfortable condition? . . . [S]uch inquiries in public would strike at the very foundations of domestic life and happiness. . . . An effort at compulsory payment would almost certainly bring before the courts allegations of misconduct, based upon incidents of little moment, to be magnified or belittled in the interest of success in court."

In 2009, the Supreme Court of Iowa revisited and reaffirmed *Miller v. Miller*.[30] After 28 years of marriage, Vergestene Cooper discovered her husband was having an affair with another woman. Bernard Cooper promised to break off the relationship and agreed to make generous support payments "if any of my indiscretions lead to and/or are [the] cause of a separation or divorce."[31] The agreement between the couple was committed to paper and signed by both of them. Five years later, upon learning that the affair had continued, Vergestene filed for divorce and sought to enforce the agreement. Although the trial court acceded, the Supreme Court reversed. Comparing the situations of the two couples, the court noted the greater specificity of the Coopers' agreement, but nonetheless held it to be unenforceable as a matter of public policy. The court was troubled by the fact that Bernard's sexual conduct triggered the agreement. Much like their 19th-century counterparts, the justices did not want to insert themselves into the dismal swamp of marital relations. "The relationship between spouses cannot be regulated by contracts . . . as if the matter involved the timely delivery of a crate of oranges. We do not wish to create a bargaining environment where sexual fidelity or harmonious relationships are key variables."[32] The case was remanded, with instructions to divide the marital assets equitably, without regard to the reconciliation agreement.[33]

As *Ansin* reminds us, an openness to enforcing postnuptial agreements does not constitute *carte blanche*. The contract must still be free of fraud and coercion and state fair and reasonable terms. Courts look askance at postnuptial agreements that, when triggered, leave one spouse empty-handed. For example, in *In re Marriage of Mehren & Dargan*, the husband, who had struggled with cocaine addiction for many years, agreed to give up his interest in any community property if he relapsed. The couple committed their agreement to paper and signed it before a notary public. When he began using drugs again, his wife filed for divorce and

---

[30] In re Marriage of Cooper, 769 N.W.2d 582 (Iowa 2009).

[31] *Id.* at 584.

[32] *Id.* at 586.

[33] *Id.* at 587.

sought to enforce the contract. The California Court of Appeal found that it violated public policy, arguing that "[b]ecause the conduct of one spouse would affect the division of community property, the agreement frustrates the statutory policy favoring no-fault divorce. . . . [T]he very issue determining whether she [the wife] was entitled to the property would necessarily involve a judicial determination concerning husband's drug use, a factual adjudication of fault that the no-fault statute seeks to avoid."[34]

The court contrasted marital contracts with commercial contracts: "Commercial contracts have a specific object, and parties to such contracts generally enter into them intending that the objects be achieved. Marital contracts, on the other hand, are generally entered into in the expectation that they will never be invoked."[35] Do you agree? Did the couples in these cases actually intend their agreements to be legally enforceable? Who do you think drafted their contracts? Why did they want such documents?

Are the factual determinations suggested by the court more difficult than those involved in a complex long-term commercial contract? Which of the policies identified by Professor Chafee did the court draw on? Does the case reflect a concern about legal norms "crowding out" the norms of a family relationship? There are some studies in cognitive psychology showing that people who reciprocate because of a psychological inclination to do so will be less willing if failure to reciprocate is punishable by formal sanctions. Formal sanctions undercut a person's ability to show a willingness to cooperate, and they may imply that the situation itself does not call for interpersonal cooperation.

Professors Robert and Elizabeth Scott tell us that "extralegal mechanisms are used to ensure performance in the intact marriage, and legal enforcement is seldom available."[36] Legal mechanisms can undermine the informal mechanisms that generally promote cooperation in intact relationships. Or, as Niklas Luhmann noted, "Starting a legal discussion usually means going beyond a point of no return: one defines oneself for the future as prepared to stand up and actively defend one's rights." As a result, "the comfortable consensus that can normally be assumed in living and acting together will be shattered."[37] In the *Mehren* case, the agreement under which the wife reconciled with her drug-addicted husband specified a large sanction if he resumed using cocaine. Is it likely that this legal responsibility undercut all of the other social incentives not to disappoint the wife and "crowded them out" of the picture? Might the husband's disappointments and frustrations have created a perceived need for cocaine great enough to be worth the price of giving up his share of community property, or allow him to ignore any guilt for disappointing his wife? Do you find this story likely?

---

[34] 118 Cal. App. 4th 1167, 1171–72, 13 Cal. Rptr. 3d 522 (2004). The court also found, given that the husband's promise to forego cocaine, an illegal drug, was itself a crime, the contract lacked consideration.

[35] *Id.* at 1170.

[36] Elizabeth S. Scott & Robert E. Scott, *Marriage as Relational Contract*, 84 Va. L. Rev. 1225, 1303 (1998).

[37] Niklas Luhmann, *Communication About Law in Interaction Systems*, in Advances in Social Theory and Methodology 234 (Karin Knorr-Cetina & Aaron V. Cicourel eds., 1981).

2. *Cultural norms:* We suggest that Chafee's "living tree" and "dismal swamp" policies are not value-neutral in their impact. Consideration and public policy doctrines are not simply technical exercises in applying general rules. They reflect assumptions of judges and lawyers arguing to them about particular relationships and transactions. For example, Professor Kathryn Powers points out that legal regulation can have an indirect discriminatory effect.[38] It may confirm social practices that appear neutral and nondiscriminatory, but that in fact perpetuate the exclusion of a particular group that has been subject to discrimination in the past. American law offered ideals of equality and justice, but women had a subordinate status. To rationalize this contradiction, "a legal tradition evolved which recognized a world split into public and private spheres and segregated women into the private sphere where such legal ideals did not apply." Powers adds, "The public sphere is the official world of the workplace, the marketplace, and the government, and is predominantly male. The private sphere is the domestic world of family, child rearing, and household maintenance, and is almost exclusively female."

Law left most aspects of private life unregulated. "By refusing to substantially regulate the private sphere, the legal order left the resolution of . . . disputes to the parties and thereby permitted custom to dictate the appropriate conduct for marital parties." Could we defend the *Balfour* position by arguing persuasively that it protects women as a group? Any contract necessarily reflects the power position of the parties. In most instances, men are more powerful than women because men have historically controlled economic wealth. Thus, most contracts between husbands and wives will be unfavorable to wives. Cost barriers to litigation will block access to the courts in most cases that do not involve the wealthy. The best that the courts could do is refuse to enforce all of these contracts that affect ongoing marital relationships. In most instances, this will avoid adding judicial power to that which husbands have as a result of their economic position. Courts leave the parties to the legal regulation that is involved in the law of divorce, child custody, and property division. Usually, wives do better under this body of law than husbands do. Would you accept the assumptions on which this argument rests? Would it better reflect the situation in, say, 1960 than in the 21st century?

3. *Premarital agreements:* Until the 1960s, American courts found premarital contracts that encouraged or facilitated divorce to be against public policy. Courts believed divorce would be encouraged by enforcement of agreements purporting to protect income and property of one spouse from the other spouse's claims upon divorce. Typically, this view refused to allow the parties to use a contract to undercut legislation that protected the woman's economic position. In *Posner v. Posner*, decided in 1970, the Supreme Court of Florida decided that premarital agreements that dealt with property division upon divorce were no longer necessarily against public policy.[39] The court pointed to no-fault divorce and the changing roles of women.

In 1983, the National Conference of Commissioners on Uniform State Laws (now the Uniform Law Commission [ULC]) published its model Uniform Premarital

---

[38] Kathryn Powers, *Sex Segregation and the Ambivalent Directions of Sex Discrimination Law,* 1979 Wis. L. Rev. 1.

[39] 233 So. 2d 381 (Fla. 1970).

Agreement Act (UPAA). It treated a premarital agreement almost as an ordinary contract. Section 2 stated: "A premarital agreement must be in writing and signed by both parties. It is enforceable without consideration." Section 3 allows parties to agree about matters such as "the rights and obligations of each of the parties to any of the property of either or both of them whenever and wherever acquired or located." Under the act, parties can agree to the "modification or elimination of spousal support." They can also deal with "any other matter, including their personal rights and obligations, not in violation of public policy or a statute imposing a criminal penalty." One limitation was that "[t]he right of a child to support may not be adversely affected by a premarital agreement." The spouse seeking to overturn an agreement could show under Section 6 either that it had not been entered into "voluntarily" or that it was both unconscionable *and* the other party had failed to disclose all of his or her assets. The proposed statute proved to be very popular. Between 1985 and 2015, 26 states and the District of Columbia enacted the UPAA.[40]

Even in some states that have not passed the UPAA, courts will now enforce premarital agreements if they are not unconscionable. These courts do not see a premarital agreement as just another contract, but they find a state interest in the consequences of divorce. For example, the Supreme Court of Kentucky applied a test much broader than that found in the UPAA in *Lane v. Lane.*[41] At the time of their marriage, Paula Lane was 29, and she worked as a night desk clerk in a hotel for $19,000 a year, while David Lane, who was 26, was a successful stockbroker, earning $166,000 a year. Three days before their marriage, they executed a prenuptial agreement. Among other things, it waived maintenance if the parties divorced. By the time of the divorce after nine and a half years of marriage, David was earning approximately one million dollars a year, and he was a partner in his firm. Paula had given birth to two children and did not work outside the home. The court noted: "While a significant disparity in the parties' incomes existed at the time of the marriage, this disparity grew exponentially during the marriage in large part because the husband was able to concentrate on his career while the wife stayed home to care for the children and the home." The trial court found the contractual waiver of maintenance to be unconscionable; the Court of Appeals reversed, but the Supreme Court affirmed the trial court's finding. The Supreme Court noted that "appropriate disclosures were made and the underlying validity of the agreement is not at issue herein." The problem was caused by the changed situation after a nine-and-a-half year marriage and the birth of two children, making the agreement unconscionable. It seems clear that if Kentucky were a state that had passed the UPAA, Paula Lane would not have been able to overturn the contract provision that denied her maintenance because David had appropriately disclosed his assets before the marriage at the time the agreement was made.[42]

---

[40] *See* uniformlaws.org/Act.aspx?title=Premarital%20Agreement%20Act. Some of these states enacted their own modifications of various provisions of the UPAA. It is not enough to know that a state has enacted a uniform act; a lawyer must always check to see whether a particular legislature played variations on the theme composed by ULC.

[41] 202 S.W.3d 577 (Ky. 2006). Compare *Button v. Button*, 131 Wis. 2d 84, 388 N.W.2d 546 (1986), where the court construed Wisconsin statutes to require an appraisal of the fairness of a premarital agreement at the time when the parties seek to invoke it.

[42] Professor Judith T. Younger is very critical of both premarital and postmarital contracts. She says:

California originally passed the UPAA. Then a high-profile case captured many headlines, and this provoked a major change in California law. Barry Bonds, a famous baseball player, sought to enforce a prenuptial agreement against his former wife, Sun, when they divorced. It denied Sun a share of Barry's earnings accumulated during the time that they were married. She had arrived in the United States from Sweden in 1985 and met Bonds in 1987. They were to marry in January of 1988. The night before the wedding, Sun signed the prenuptial agreement, and she did not have separate counsel. The trial court believed Barry Bonds's witnesses and found that Sun entered the agreement "free from the taint of fraud, coercion, and undue influence." The Court of Appeals reversed.[43] It found that the trial court failed to give enough weight to Sun's lack of her own lawyer when Bonds had two as well as an agent. Moreover, it stressed her lack of income, dependence on Barry Bonds, and her situation as a young person who had come to the United States from another country. The Supreme Court of California reversed and reinstated the trial court's decision. Lack of an independent lawyer was only a factor to consider, rather than a requirement. The evidence indicated that she entered the agreement voluntarily. Sun could have refused to go ahead with the wedding because it was only an informal affair with few guests invited. Prospective spouses do not owe each other strict fiduciary duties.

A woman who was a member of the California legislature pushed a bill to respond to the *Bonds* decision, and it won broad support and was enacted. Under this amendment of the Uniform Premarital Agreement Act, "it shall be deemed that a premarital agreement was not executed voluntarily unless the court finds . . . all of the following:"

(1) The party against whom enforcement is sought was represented by independent legal counsel at the time of signing the agreement or, after being advised to seek independent legal counsel, expressly waived, in a separate writing, representation by independent legal counsel.

(2) The party against whom enforcement is sought had not less than seven calendar days between the time that party was first presented with the agreement and advised to seek independent legal counsel and the time the agreement was signed.

(3) The party against whom enforcement is sought, if unrepresented by legal counsel, was fully informed of the terms and basic effect of the agreement as well as the rights and obligations he or she was giving up by signing the agreement, and was proficient in the language in which the explanation of the party's rights was conducted and in which the agreement was written. The explanation of the rights and obligations relinquished

---

"By enforcing them the courts are enabling the dominant party to acquire financial advantages and to shift the risk of a failed relationship from him, even though he can afford to bear it, to her, the weaker party who cannot easily bear such a burden." Judith T. Younger, *Lovers' Contracts in the Courts: Forsaking the Minimum Decencies*, 13 Wm. & Mary J. Women & L. 349, 427 (2007). She thinks that the law should be improved so that courts "ensure that minimum decencies for these contracts are observed." *Id. See also* Younger, *Antenuptial Agreements*, 28 Wm. Mitchell L. Rev. 697, 698–702 (2001).

[43] *In re* Marriage of Bonds, 83 Cal. Rptr. 2d 783 (Cal. Ct. App. 1999), *rev'd in part*, 5 P.3d 815 (Cal. 2000).

shall be memorialized in writing and delivered to the party prior to signing the agreement. The unrepresented party shall, on or before the signing of the premarital agreement, execute a document declaring that he or she received the information required by this paragraph and indicating who provided that information.

(4) The agreement and the writings executed pursuant to paragraphs (1) and (3) were not executed under duress, fraud, or undue influence, and the parties did not lack capacity to enter into the agreement.

(5) Any other factors the court deems relevant.[44]

Max Gutierrez Jr. was a partner at a large San Francisco law firm. He argued that the California amendment to the Uniform Premarital Agreement Act created great uncertainty. He pointed to the phrase "any other factors the court deems relevant." "How will we ever know what the court might deem relevant?" He also pointed out that "having independent counsel is not insurance of the prenup being enforceable but not having one is insurance that it's not going to be enforceable."[45] Could you argue that this uncertainty would likely produce better results than the UPAA in cases where there were disputes about property division after a divorce?

Substantive review of premarital contracts is typically justified on ideas of cognitive limitations and bounded rationality.[46] These ideas are often criticized as paternalistic. It can be argued instead that substantive review of these contracts is more effectively defended on the grounds of the public interest in marriage.[47]

Does the material on prenuptial and postnuptial agreements suggest the difficulties that arise when the legal system confronts relational contracts that rest on some measure of trust and which demand that parties, to protect themselves, must have great skill in predicting the future? Marriage may be particularly socially and economically important, but to what extent would similar concerns exist in such relationships as employment or the purchase of expensive items such as houses or automobiles?

---

[44] CAL. FAM. CODE § 1615(c) (2015).

[45] Catherine Bigelow, *Marriage, American-Style: The Modern Prenup — Who Gets Them and Who Needs Them?* SAN FRANCISCO CHRONICLE, Jan. 19, 2003, Magazine Section at 24.

[46] Lynn A. Baker & Robert E. Emery, *When Every Relationship is Above Average: Perceptions and Expectations of Divorce at the Time of Marriage*, 17 LAW & HUM. BEHAV. 439 (1993), surveyed marriage license applicants and law students about their knowledge of the law of divorce, statistics about divorce rates, and expectations for their own marriage. The subjects had "thoroughly idealistic expectations about both the longevity of their own marriages and the consequences should they personally be divorced." *Id.* at 446. This meant that both men and women see the possibility of divorce as irrelevant and are unlikely to engage in prenuptial contracting.

[47] Karen Servidea, Note, *Reviewing Premarital Agreements to Protect the State's Interest in Marriage*, 91 VA. L. REV. 535, 576–78 (2005) (arguing, "Antenuptial agreements governing alimony and property division implicate the state's interest because such agreements might leave one spouse a public charge, reduce the standard of living of children, and alter incentives to invest in and exit from marriage. . . . Even the most knowing and voluntary waiver of a spouse's marital rights cannot adequately protect the state's interest.") *Compare* Allison A. Marston, *Planning for Love: The Politics of Prenuptial Agreements*, 49 STAN. L. REV. 887 (1997).

b. Marriage and cohabitation contracts

Many feminist writers have attacked traditional marriage. While some argued that freedom for women requires the abolition of marriage, others thought that marriage contracts, freely negotiated, could reform the institution. During the 1980s, there were reports that many engaged couples were entering into these contracts.[48] How widespread do you believe such agreements are today? What is the basis for your belief?

One publicized agreement in the early 1970s was between Alix Kates Shulman and her husband, drafted after two children had been born.[49] The contract focuses primarily on the allocation of domestic duties. A part entitled "Children" consists of many paragraphs assigning tasks connected with mornings, transportation, helping with homework, personal questions and explaining things, nighttime, babysitters, sick care, and weekends. "Housework" deals with cooking, shopping, cleaning, and laundry. The allocations are detailed and specific. For example, he is to deal with children at night (baths, stories, bed routine, and waking up in the middle of the night) three nights a week; she does it three other nights, and they use Friday to compensate the one who has done extra work during the week. Should, or would, courts enforce this contract or should, or would, the rule in the *Balfour* case apply?

Changes in the law often mirror changes in the larger society. Views about sexuality and marriage have changed in the past 40 or 50 years. Of course, not everyone accepts the new lifestyles and the challenges to traditional marriage. The following materials report two distinct judicial reactions to social change. As you read them, remember writers such as Chafee and Powers. Notice, too, that common-law ideas provide rationalizations and rhetoric for all sides in the debate.

MARVIN v. MARVIN
California Supreme Court
18 Cal. 3d 660, 134 Cal. Rptr. 815, 557 P.2d 106 (1976)

Tobriner, J.

During the past 15 years, there has been a substantial increase in the number of couples living together without marrying.[50] Such nonmarital relationships lead to legal controversy when one partner dies or the couple separates. Courts of Appeal, faced with the task of determining property rights in such cases, have arrived at conflicting positions: two cases (*In re Marriage of Cary*, 34 Cal. App. 3d 345 [1973]; *Estate of Atherley*, 44 Cal. App. 3d 758 [1975]) have held that the Family Law Act

---

[48] *See, e.g.,* Wall Street Journal, July 23, 1986, at 23, col. 4. ("Such pacts used to be largely the domain of the rich and famous, but lawyers now estimate that the number of couples using them has risen as much as 50 percent in some places since the early 1980s.") *See also* Deutsch, *More Couples Are Taking No Chances on Love*, New York Times, August 13, 1995, sec. 3, at 10, which makes a similar point 10 years later. It, too, relies on the opinions of lawyers who practice in the family law area.

[49] The contract appears in Ms. Magazine 66, 72 (Spring 1972).

[50] [1] "The 1970 census figures indicate that today perhaps eight times as many couples are living together without being married as cohabited ten years ago." (Comment, In re Cary: *A Judicial Recognition of Illicit Cohabitation*, 25 Hastings L.J. 1226 [1974].)

(Civ. Code §§ 4000 *et seq.*) requires division of the property according to community property principles, and one decision (*Beckman v. Mayhew*, 49 Cal. App. 3d 529 [1975]) has rejected that holding. We take this opportunity to resolve that controversy and to declare the principles which should govern distribution of property acquired in a nonmarital relationship.

We conclude: (1) The provisions of the Family Law Act do not govern the distribution of property acquired during a nonmarital relationship; such a relationship remains subject solely to judicial decision. (2) The courts should enforce express contracts between nonmarital partners except to the extent that the contract is explicitly founded on the consideration of meretricious sexual services. (3) In the absence of an express contract, the courts should inquire into the conduct of the parties to determine whether that conduct demonstrates an implied contract, agreement of partnership or joint venture, or some other tacit understanding between the parties. The courts may also employ the doctrine of *quantum meruit*, or equitable remedies such as constructive or resulting trusts, when warranted by the facts of the case.

In the instant case plaintiff and defendant lived together for seven years without marrying; all property acquired during this period was taken in defendant's name. When plaintiff sued to enforce a contract under which she was entitled to half the property and to support payments, the trial court granted judgment on the pleadings for defendant, thus leaving him with all property accumulated by the couple during their relationship. Since the trial court denied plaintiff a trial on the merits of her claim, its decision conflicts with the principles stated above, and must be reversed.

1. The factual setting of this appeal.

Since the trial court rendered judgment for defendant on the pleadings, we must accept the allegations of plaintiff's complaint as true, determining whether such allegations state, or can be amended to state, a cause of action. We turn therefore to the specific allegations of the complaint.

Plaintiff avers that in October of 1964 she and defendant "entered into an oral agreement" that while "the parties lived together they would combine their efforts and earnings and would share equally any and all property accumulated as a result of their efforts whether individual or combined." Furthermore, they agreed to "hold themselves out to the general public as husband and wife" and that "plaintiff would further render her services as a companion, homemaker, housekeeper, and cook to . . . defendant."

Shortly thereafter plaintiff agreed to "give up her lucrative career as an entertainer [and] singer" in order to "devote her full time to defendant . . . as a companion, homemaker, housekeeper, and cook;" in return defendant agreed to "provide for all of plaintiff's financial support and needs for the rest of her life."

Plaintiff alleges that she lived with defendant from October of 1964 through May of 1970 and fulfilled her obligations under the agreement. During this period the parties as a result of their efforts and earnings acquired in defendant's name substantial real and personal property, including motion picture rights worth over

$1 million. In May of 1970, however, defendant compelled plaintiff to leave his household. He continued to support plaintiff until November of 1971, but thereafter refused to provide further support.

On the basis of these allegations plaintiff asserts two causes of action. The first, for declaratory relief, asks the court to determine her contract and property rights; the second seeks to impose a constructive trust[51] upon one-half of the property acquired during the course of the relationship.

Defendant demurred unsuccessfully, and then answered the complaint. Following extensive discovery and pretrial proceedings, the case came to trial. Defendant renewed his attack on the complaint by a motion to dismiss. Since the parties had stipulated that defendant's marriage to Betty Marvin did not terminate until the filing of a final decree of divorce in January 1967, the trial court treated defendant's motion as one for judgment on the pleadings augmented by the stipulation.

After hearing argument the court granted defendant's motion and entered judgment for defendant. Plaintiff moved to set aside the judgment and asked leave to amend her complaint to allege that she and defendant reaffirmed their agreement after defendant's divorce was final. The trial court denied plaintiff's motion, and she appealed from the judgment.

2. Plaintiff's complaint states a cause of action for breach of an express contract.

In *Trutalli v. Meraviglia*, 215 Cal. 698, 12 P.2d 430 (1932), we established the principle that nonmarital partners may lawfully contract concerning the ownership of property acquired during the relationship. We reaffirmed this principle in *Vallera v. Vallera*, 21 Cal. 2d 681, 685, 134 P.2d 761 (1943), stating that "If a man and woman [who are not married] live together as husband and wife under an agreement to pool their earnings and share equally in their joint accumulations, equity will protect the interests of each in such property."

In the case before us plaintiff, basing her cause of action in contract upon these precedents, maintains that the trial court erred in denying her a trial on the merits of her contention. Although that court did not specify the ground for its conclusion that plaintiff's contractual allegations stated no cause of action, defendant offers some four theories to sustain the ruling; we proceed to examine them.

Defendant first and principally relies on the contention that the alleged contract is so closely related to the supposed "immoral" character of the relationship between plaintiff and himself that the enforcement of the contract would violate public policy.[52]

---

[51] [Eds. note: A constructive trust is a remedy that is imposed to avoid unjust enrichment. One person, who holds legal title to property, is ruled to hold that property for the benefit of another. Many kinds of circumstances might cause a court to impose a constructive trust. Constructive trusts are part of the substantive law of restitution. Constructive trusts are not true trusts, any more than quasi-contracts are true contracts. Some would argue that the constructive trust is the equitable equivalent of quasi-contract. In each case, a court treats something that is not a true trust or contract as if it were one or the other in order to reach a just result.]

[52] [4] Defendant also contends that the contract was illegal because it contemplated a violation of

A review of the numerous California decisions concerning contracts between nonmarital partners, however, reveals that the courts have not employed such broad and uncertain standards to strike down contracts. The decisions instead disclose a narrower and more precise standard: a contract between nonmarital partners is unenforceable only *to the extent* that it *explicitly* rests upon the immoral and illicit consideration of meretricious sexual services.

Numerous cases have upheld enforcement of agreements between nonmarital partners in factual settings essentially indistinguishable from the present case.[53]

Although the past decisions hover over the issue in the somewhat wispy form of the figures of a Chagall painting, we can abstract from those decisions a clear and simple rule. The fact that a man and woman live together without marriage, and engage in a sexual relationship, does not in itself invalidate agreements between them relating to their earnings, property, or expenses. Neither is such an agreement invalid merely because the parties may have contemplated the creation or continuation of a nonmarital relationship when they entered into it. Agreements between nonmarital partners fail only to the extent that they rest upon a consideration of meretricious sexual services. Thus the rule asserted by defendant, that a contract fails if it is "involved in" or made "in contemplation" of a nonmarital relationship, cannot be reconciled with the decisions.

The . . . cases cited by defendant which have *declined* to enforce contracts between nonmarital partners involved consideration that was expressly founded upon illicit sexual services. . . .

The decisions in [these] . . . cases thus demonstrate that a contract between nonmarital partners, even if expressly made in contemplation of a common living arrangement, is invalid only if sexual acts form an inseparable part of the consideration for the agreement. In sum, a court will not enforce a contract for the pooling of property and earnings if it is explicitly and inseparably based upon services as a paramour. . . . [E]ven if sexual services are part of the contractual consideration, any *severable* portion of the contract supported by independent consideration will still be enforced.

---

former Penal Code § 269(a), which prohibited living "in a state of cohabitation and adultery." [§ 269(a) was repealed by Stats. 1975, ch. 71, eff. Jan. 1, 1976.] Defendant's standing to raise the issue is questionable because he alone was married and thus guilty of violating § 269(a). Plaintiff, being unmarried, could neither be convicted of adulterous cohabitation nor of aiding and abetting defendant's violation. The numerous cases discussing the contractual rights of unmarried couples have drawn no distinction between illegal relationships and lawful nonmarital relationships. Moreover, even if we were to draw such a distinction — a largely academic endeavor in view of the repeal of § 269(a) — defendant probably would not benefit; his relationship with plaintiff continued long after his divorce became final, and plaintiff sought to amend her complaint to assert that the parties reaffirmed their contract after the divorce.

[53] [5] Defendant urges that all of [these cases] . . . can be distinguished on the grounds that the partner seeking to enforce the contract contributed either property or services additional to ordinary homemaking services. No case, however, suggests that a pooling agreement in which one partner contributes only homemaking services is invalid. . . . A promise to perform homemaking services is, of course, a lawful and adequate consideration for a contract (*see* Taylor v. Taylor, 66 Cal. App. 2d 390, 398, 152 P.2d 480 [1954]) — otherwise those engaged in domestic employment could not sue for their wages — and defendant advances no reason why his proposed distinction would justify denial of enforcement to contracts supported by such consideration.

The principle that a contract between nonmarital partners will be enforced unless expressly and inseparably based upon an illicit consideration of sexual services not only represents the distillation of the decisional law, but also offers a far more precise and workable standard than that advocated by defendant. Our recent decision in *In re Marriage of Dawley*, 17 Cal. 3d 342, 131 Cal. Rptr. 3, 551 P.2d 323 (1976) offers a close analogy. Rejecting the contention that an antenuptial agreement is invalid if the parties contemplated a marriage of short duration, we pointed out in *Dawley* that a standard based upon the subjective contemplation of the parties is uncertain and unworkable; such a test, we stated, "might invalidate virtually all antenuptial agreements on the ground that the parties contemplated dissolution . . . but it provides no principled basis for determining which antenuptial agreements offend public policy and which do not." *Dawley*, 17 Cal. 3d at 352.

Similarly, in the present case a standard which inquires whether an agreement is "involved" in or "contemplates" a nonmarital relationship is vague and unworkable. Virtually all agreements between nonmarital partners can be said to be "involved" in some sense in the fact of their mutual sexual relationship, or to "contemplate" the existence of that relationship. Thus defendant's proposed standards, if taken literally, might invalidate all agreements between nonmarital partners, a result no one favors. Moreover, those standards offer no basis to distinguish between valid and invalid agreements. By looking not to such uncertain tests, but only to the consideration underlying the agreement, we provide the parties and the courts with a practical guide to determine when an agreement between nonmarital partners should be enforced.

[The court rejected a second contention by defendant that enforcement of the 1964 contract would impair the community property rights of Betty Marvin, defendant's lawful wife, and so violated public policy.]

In summary, we base our opinion on the principle that adults who voluntarily live together and engage in sexual relations are nonetheless as competent as any other persons to contract respecting their earnings and property rights. Of course, they cannot lawfully contract to pay for the performance of sexual services, for such a contract is, in essence, an agreement for prostitution and unlawful for that reason. But they may agree to pool their earnings and to hold all property acquired during the relationship in accord with the law governing community property; conversely they may agree that each partner's earnings and the property acquired from those earnings remains the separate property of the earning partner. So long as the agreement does not rest upon illicit meretricious consideration, the parties may order their economic affairs as they choose, and no policy precludes the courts from enforcing such agreements.

In the present instance, plaintiff alleges that the parties agreed to pool their earnings, that they contracted to share equally in all property acquired, and that defendant agreed to support plaintiff. The terms of the contract as alleged do not rest upon any unlawful consideration. We therefore conclude that the complaint furnishes a suitable basis upon which the trial court can render declaratory relief.

The trial court consequently erred in granting defendant's motion for judgment on the pleadings.

Holding

3. Plaintiff's complaint can be amended to state a cause of action founded upon theories of implied contract or equitable relief.

As we have noted, both causes of action in plaintiff's complaint allege an express contract; neither assert any basis for relief independent from the contract. In *In re Marriage of Cary, supra,* however, the Court of Appeal held that, in view of the policy of the Family Law Act, property accumulated by nonmarital partners in an actual family relationship should be divided equally. Upon examining the *Cary* opinion, the parties to the present case realized that plaintiff's alleged relationship with defendant might arguably support a cause of action independent of any express contract between the parties. The parties have therefore briefed and discussed the issue of the property rights of a nonmarital partner in the absence of an express contract. Although our conclusion that plaintiff's complaint states a cause of action based on an express contract alone compels us to reverse the judgment for defendant, resolution of the *Cary* issue will serve both to guide the parties upon retrial and to resolve a conflict presently manifest in published Court of Appeal decisions.

Both plaintiff and defendant stand in broad agreement that the law should be fashioned to carry out the reasonable expectations of the parties. Plaintiff, however, presents the following contentions: that the decisions prior to *Cary* rest upon implicit and erroneous notions of punishing a party for his or her guilt in entering into a nonmarital relationship, that such decisions result in an inequitable distribution of property accumulated during the relationship, and that *Cary* correctly held that the enactment of the Family Law Act in 1970 overturned those prior decisions. Defendant in response maintains that the prior decisions merely applied common law principles of contract and property to persons who have deliberately elected to remain outside the bounds of the community property system.[54] *Cary,* defendant contends, erred in holding that the Family Law Act vitiated the force of the prior precedents.

As we shall see from examination of the pre-*Cary* decisions, the truth lies somewhere between the positions of plaintiff and defendant. The classic opinion on this subject is *Vallera v. Vallera, supra.* Speaking for a four-member majority, Justice Traynor posed the question: "whether a woman living with a man as his wife but with no genuine belief that she is legally married to him acquires by reason of cohabitation alone the rights of a co-tenant in his earnings and accumulations during the period of their relationship." *Id.* at 684.

---

[54] [11] We note that a deliberate decision to avoid the strictures of the community property system is not the only reason that couples live together without marriage. Some couples may wish to avoid the permanent commitment that marriage implies, yet be willing to share equally any property acquired during the relationship; others may fear the loss of pension, welfare, or tax benefits resulting from marriage. Others may engage in the relationship as a possible prelude to marriage. In lower socio-economic groups the difficulty and expense of dissolving a former marriage often leads couples to choose a nonmarital relationship; many unmarried couples may also incorrectly believe that the doctrine of common-law marriage prevails in California, and thus that they are in fact married. Consequently we conclude that the mere fact that a couple have not participated in a valid marriage ceremony cannot serve as a basis for a court's inference that the couple intend to keep their earnings and property separate and independent; the parties' intention can only be ascertained by a more searching inquiry into the nature of their relationship.

Vallera explains that "Equitable considerations arising from the reasonable expectation of the continuation of benefits attending the status of marriage entered into in good faith are not present in such a case." *Id.* at 685. In the absence of express contract, *Vallera* concluded, the woman is entitled to share in property jointly accumulated only "in the proportion that her funds contributed toward its acquisition." *Id.* at 685. Justice Curtis, dissenting, argued that the evidence showed an implied contract under which each party owned an equal interest in property acquired during the relationship.

The majority opinion in *Vallera* did not expressly bar recovery based upon an implied contract, nor preclude resort to equitable remedies. But *Vallera*'s broad assertion that equitable considerations "are not present" in the case of a nonmarital relationship . . . led the Courts of Appeal to interpret the language to preclude recovery based on such theories. . . .

This failure of the courts to recognize an action by a nonmarital partner based upon implied contract, or to grant an equitable remedy, contrasts with the judicial treatment of the putative spouse. Prior to the enactment of the Family Law Act, no statute granted rights to a putative spouse. The courts accordingly fashioned a variety of remedies by judicial decision. Some cases permitted the putative spouse to recover half the property on a theory that the conduct of the parties implied an agreement of partnership or joint venture. . . . Others permitted the spouse to recover the reasonable value of rendered services, less the value of support received. Finally, decisions affirmed the power of a court to employ equitable principles to achieve a fair division of property acquired during putative marriage.[55]

Thus in summary, the cases prior to *Cary* exhibited a schizophrenic inconsistency. By enforcing an express contract between nonmarital partners unless it rested upon an unlawful consideration, the courts applied a common law principle as to contracts. Yet the courts disregarded the common law principle that holds that implied contracts can arise from the conduct of the parties. Refusing to enforce such contracts, the courts spoke of leaving the parties "in the position in which they had placed themselves," just as if they were guilty parties *in pari delicto. Oakley v. Oakley*, 82 Cal. App. 2d 188, 192.

Justice Curtis noted this inconsistency in his dissenting opinion in *Vallera*, pointing out that "if an express agreement will be enforced, there is no legal or just reason why an implied agreement to share the property cannot be enforced." . . .

Still another inconsistency in the prior cases arises from their treatment of property accumulated through joint effort. To the extent that a partner had contributed *funds* or *property*, the cases held that the partner obtains a proportionate share in the acquisition, despite the lack of legal standing of the relationship. *Vallera v. Vallera, supra*, 21 Cal. 2d at 685; see *Weak v. Weak*, 202 Cal. App. 2d 632,

---

[55] [15] The contrast between principles governing nonmarital and putative relationships appears most strikingly in *Lazzarevich v. Lazzarevich*, 88 Cal. App. 2d 708. When Mrs. Lazzarevich sued her husband for divorce in 1945, she discovered to her surprise that she was not lawfully married to him. She nevertheless reconciled with him, and the Lazzareviches lived together for another year before they finally separated. The court awarded her recovery for the reasonable value of services rendered, less the value of support received, until she discovered the invalidity of the marriage, but denied recovery for the same services rendered after that date.

639. Yet courts have refused to recognize just such an interest based upon the contribution of *services*. As Justice Curtis points out, "Unless it can be argued that a woman's services as cook, housekeeper, and homemaker are valueless, it would seem logical that if, when she contributes money to the purchase of property, her interest will be protected, then when she contributes her services in the home, her interest in property accumulated should be protected." . . .

Thus as of 1973, the time of the filing of *In re Marriage of Cary*, *supra*, the cases apparently held that a nonmarital partner who rendered services in the absence of express contract could assert no right to property acquired during the relationship. The facts of *Cary* demonstrated the unfairness of that rule.

Janet and Paul Cary had lived together, unmarried, for more than eight years. They held themselves out to friends and family as husband and wife, reared four children, purchased a home and other property, obtained credit, filed joint income tax returns, and otherwise conducted themselves as though they were married. Paul worked outside the home, and Janet generally cared for the house and children.

In 1971 Paul petitioned for "nullity of the marriage." Following a hearing on that petition, the trial court awarded Janet half the property acquired during the relationship, although all such property was traceable to Paul's earnings. The Court of Appeal affirmed the award.

Reviewing the prior decisions which had denied relief to the homemaking partner, the Court of Appeal reasoned that those decisions rested upon a policy of punishing persons guilty of cohabitation without marriage. The Family Law Act, the court observed, aimed to eliminate fault or guilt as a basis for dividing marital property. But once fault or guilt is excluded, the court reasoned, nothing distinguishes the property rights of a nonmarital "spouse" from those of a putative spouse. Since the latter is entitled to half the "quasi-marital property," Civ. Code § 4452, the Court of Appeal concluded that, giving effect to the policy of the Family Law Act, a nonmarital cohabitator should also be entitled to half the property accumulated during an "actual family relationship." 34 Cal. App. 3d at 353.

If *Cary* is interpreted as holding that the Family Law Act requires an equal division of property accumulated in nonmarital "actual family relationships," then we agree with *Beckman v. Mayhew* that *Cary* distends the act. No language in the Family Law Act addresses the property rights of nonmarital partners, and nothing in the legislative history of the act suggests that the Legislature considered that subject. The delineation of the rights of nonmarital partners before 1970 had been fixed entirely by judicial decision; we see no reason to believe that the Legislature, by enacting the Family Law Act, intended to change that state of affairs.

But although we reject the reasoning of *Cary*, we share the perception of the *Cary* courts that the application of former precedent in the factual setting of those cases would work an unfair distribution of the property accumulated by the couple. We should not, therefore, reject the authority of *Cary* without also examining the deficiencies in the former law which led to those decisions.

The principal reason why the pre-*Cary* decisions result in an unfair distribution of property inheres in the court's refusal to permit a nonmarital partner to assert rights based upon accepted principles of implied contract or equity. We have examined the reasons advanced to justify this denial of relief, and find that none have merit.

First, we note that the cases denying relief do not rest their refusal upon any theory of "punishing" a "guilty" partner. Indeed, to the extent that denial of relief "punishes" one partner, it necessarily rewards the other by permitting him to retain a disproportionate amount of the property. Concepts of "guilt" thus cannot justify an unequal division of property between two equally "guilty" persons.[56]

Other reasons advanced in the decisions fare no better. The principal argument seems to be that "[e]quitable considerations arising from the reasonable expectation of . . . benefits attending the status of marriage . . . are not present [in a nonmarital relationship]." *Vallera v. Vallera, supra,* 21 Cal. 2d at 685. But, although parties to a nonmarital relationship obviously cannot have based any expectations upon the belief that they were married, other expectations and equitable considerations remain. The parties may well expect that property will be divided in accord with the parties' own tacit understanding and that in the absence of such understanding the courts will fairly apportion property accumulated through mutual effort. We need not treat nonmarital partners as putatively married persons in order to apply principles of implied contract, or extend equitable remedies; we need to treat them only as we do any other unmarried persons.[57]

The remaining arguments advanced from time to time to deny remedies to the nonmarital partners are of less moment. There is no more reason to presume that services are contributed as a gift than to presume that funds are contributed as a gift; in any event the better approach is to presume, as Justice Peters suggested, "that the parties intend to deal fairly with each other."

The argument that granting remedies to the nonmarital partners would discourage marriage must fail. . . . Although we recognize the well-established public policy to foster and promote the institution of marriage . . . perpetuation of judicial rules which result in an inequitable distribution of property accumulated during a

---

[56] [21] Justice Finley of the Washington Supreme Court explains: "Under such circumstances [the dissolution of a nonmarital relationship], this court and the courts of other jurisdictions have, in effect, sometimes said, 'We will wash our hands of such disputes. The parties should and must be left to their own devices, just where they find themselves.' To me, such pronouncements seem overly fastidious and a bit fatuous. They are unrealistic and, among other things, ignore the fact that an unannounced (but nevertheless effective and binding) rule of law is inherent in any such terminal statements by a court of law. The unannounced but inherent rule is simply that the party who has title, or in some instances who is in possession, will enjoy the rights of ownership of the property concerned. The rule often operates to the great advantage of the cunning and the shrewd, who wind up with possession of the property, or title to it in their names, at the end of a so-called meretricious relationship. So, although the courts proclaim that they will have nothing to do with such matters, the proclamation in itself establishes, as to the parties involved, an effective and binding rule of law which tends to operate purely by accident or perhaps by reason of the cunning, anticipatory designs of just one of the parties." West v. Knowles, 50 Wn. 2d 311, 311 P.2d 689, 692 (1957) (concurring opinion).

[57] [22] In some instances a confidential relationship may arise between nonmarital partners, and economic transactions between them should be governed by the principles applicable to such relationships.

nonmarital relationship is neither a just nor an effective way of carrying out that policy.

In summary, we believe that the prevalence of nonmarital relationships in modern society and the social acceptance of them, marks this as a time when our courts should by no means apply the doctrine of the unlawfulness of the so-called meretricious relationship to the instant case. As we have explained, the nonenforceability of agreements expressly providing for meretricious conduct rested upon the fact that such conduct, as the word suggests, pertained to and encompassed prostitution. To equate the nonmarital relationship of today to such a subject matter is to do violence to an accepted and wholly different practice.

We are aware that many young couples live together without the solemnization of marriage, in order to make sure that they can successfully later undertake marriage. This trial period,[58] preliminary to marriage, serves as some assurance that the marriage will not subsequently end in dissolution to the harm of both parties. We are aware, as we have stated, of the pervasiveness of nonmarital relationships in other situations.

The mores of the society have indeed changed so radically in regard to cohabitation that we cannot impose a standard based on alleged moral considerations that have apparently been so widely abandoned by so many. Lest we be misunderstood, however, we take this occasion to point out that the structure of society itself largely depends upon the institution of marriage, and nothing we have said in this opinion should be taken to derogate from that institution. The joining of the man and woman in marriage is at once the most socially productive and individually fulfilling relationship that one can enjoy in the course of a lifetime.

We conclude that the judicial barriers that may stand in the way of a policy based upon the fulfillment of the reasonable expectations of the parties to a nonmarital relationship should be removed. As we have explained, the courts now hold that express agreements will be enforced unless they rest on an unlawful meretricious consideration. We add that in the absence of an express agreement, the courts may look to a variety of other remedies in order to protect the parties' lawful expectations.[59]

The courts may inquire into the conduct of the parties to determine whether that conduct demonstrates an implied contract or implied agreement of partnership or joint venture . . . or some other tacit understanding between the parties. The courts may, when appropriate, employ principles of constructive trust . . . or resulting trust. Finally, a nonmarital partner may recover in *quantum meruit* for the reasonable value of household services rendered less the reasonable value of

---

[58] [23] ALVIN TOFFLER, FUTURE SHOCK 253 (Bantam Books 1971).

[59] [24] We do not seek to resurrect the doctrine of common-law marriage, which was abolished in California by the statute in 1895. *See* Norman v. Thomson, 121 Cal. 620, 628, 54 P. 143 (1898); Estate of Abate, 166 Cal. App. 2d 282, 292, 333 P.2d 200 (1958). Thus we do not hold that plaintiff and defendant were "married," nor do we extend to plaintiff the rights which the Family Law Act grants valid or putative spouses; we hold only that she has the same rights to enforce contracts and to assert her equitable interest in property acquired through her effort as does any other unmarried person.

support received if he can show that he rendered services with the expectation of monetary reward.[60]

Holding / Final Reasoning

Since we have determined that plaintiff's complaint states a cause of action for breach of an express contract, and, as we have explained, can be amended to state a cause of action independent of allegations of express contract,[61] we must conclude that the trial court erred in granting defendant a judgment on the pleadings.

The judgment is reversed and the cause remanded for further proceedings consistent with the views expressed herein.

WRIGHT, C.J., McCOMB, J., MOST, J., SULLIVAN, J., and RICHARDSON, J., concurred.

CLARK, J., Concurring and Dissenting.

The majority opinion properly permits recovery on the basis of either express or implied in fact agreement between the parties. These being the issues presented, their resolution requires reversal of the judgment. Here, the opinion should stop.

This court should not attempt to determine all anticipated rights, duties, and remedies within every meretricious relationship — particularly in vague terms. Rather, these complex issues should be determined as each arises in a concrete case.

The majority broadly indicate that a party to a meretricious relationship may recover on the basis of equitable principles and in *quantum meruit*. However, the majority fail to advise us of the circumstances permitting recovery, limitations on recovery, or whether their numerous remedies are cumulative or exclusive. Conceivably, under the majority opinion a party may recover half of the property acquired during the relationship on the basis of general equitable principles, recover a bonus based on specific equitable considerations, and recover a second bonus in *quantum meruit*.

The general sweep of the majority opinion raises but fails to answer several questions. First, because the Legislature specifically excluded some parties to a meretricious relationship from the equal division rule of Civil Code § 4452, is this court now free to create an equal division rule? Second, upon termination of the relationship, is it equitable to impose the economic obligations of lawful spouses on meretricious parties when the latter may have rejected matrimony to avoid such obligations? Third, does not application of equitable principles — necessitating examination of the conduct of the parties — violate the spirit of the Family Law Act of 1969, designed to eliminate the bitterness and acrimony resulting from the former fault system in divorce? Fourth, will not application of equitable principles reimpose upon trial courts the unmanageable burden of arbitrating domestic

---

[60] [25] Our opinion does not preclude the evolution of additional equitable remedies to protect the expectations of the parties to a nonmarital relationship in cases in which existing remedies prove inadequate; the suitability of such remedies may be determined in later cases in light of the factual setting in which they arise.

[61] [26] We do not pass upon the question whether, in the absence of an express or implied contractual obligation, a party to a nonmarital relationship is entitled to support payments from the other party after the relationship terminates.

disputes? Fifth, will not a *quantum meruit* system of compensation for services — discounted by benefits received — place meretricious spouses in a better position than lawful spouses? Sixth, if a *quantum meruit* system is to be allowed, does fairness not require inclusion of all services and all benefits regardless of how difficult the evaluation?

When the parties to a meretricious relationship show by express or implied in fact agreement they intend to create mutual obligations, the courts should enforce the agreement. However, in the absence of agreement, we should stop and consider the ramifications before creating economic obligations which may violate legislative intent, contravene the intention of the parties, and surely generate undue burdens on our trial courts.

By judicial overreach, the majority perform a *nunc pro tunc* marriage, dissolve it, and distribute its property on terms never contemplated by the parties, case law, or the Legislature.

NOTES AND QUESTIONS

1. ***The background of the case:*** According to newspaper accounts, Michelle Triola started singing professionally in nightclubs in Hollywood after she graduated from high school. She then went on the Playboy Club circuit. When she was 20, she was a dancer featured in Las Vegas and Reno. In 1963, she went to Europe and sang in nightclubs for $300 to $1000 a week. She returned the next year and joined the cast of the film "Ship of Fools." She met Lee Marvin, one of the stars of the picture. After a few weeks of dating, Lee moved into Michelle's Hollywood Hills apartment. They spent the next six years together. She spent most of her time decorating the couple's $250,000 Malibu beach house and entertaining show business friends. In 1970, she changed her last name legally to Marvin. A few months later, Lee Marvin left to marry his high school sweetheart.

Michelle Marvin tried to resume her career, but no one was interested in a 37-year-old singer who had not performed often in years. Lee Marvin promised to give her $833 a month for five years. He stopped payments after 14 months because he thought she had told a Hollywood gossip columnist that his new marriage was failing. She supported herself by watering plants, typing scripts, and doing odd jobs for friends. Finally, she found a $125-a-week secretarial position at the William Morris Agency in Beverly Hills.[62]

Marvin Mitchelson, Michelle's lawyer, wrote a book called *Made in Heaven, Settled in Court*.[63] He said that Michelle came to him broke, frightened, and miserable. She was seeking some way to make Lee Marvin resume making the promised payments of $833 a month for four more years. He told her:

---

[62] For comparative purposes, it is useful to consider the amounts at issue in 2015 dollars. Michelle's weekly payment for nightclub singing would be between $2300 and $7700. The beach house would be worth almost $2 million. The monthly fee promised by Lee would amount to about $5000, and Michelle's secretarial position would yield $730 per week.

[63] (Warner Books 1979).

[S]he was entitled to a great deal more. . . . I felt that she had a right to half of the assets acquired during the time they lived together as "man and wife." Anything less would not only be an injustice but, I strongly felt, probably unconstitutional as well. . . .

I explained my beliefs on the subject to Michelle, and she agreed it was very important that some precedents be set in this particular area of the law. She remained willing to test it even after I told her we'd probably lose in the lower courts, and any hope of a voluntary financial settlement might be ruined by the very act of raising the issue at all.

2. ***The impact of* Marvin v. Marvin *on those involved:*** The Supreme Court of California said that the facts alleged by Marvin Mitchelson for Michelle Marvin stated a cause of action. This clearly was a victory in terms of creating new law. However, Michelle Triola Marvin still had to prove her case. She had to establish an express or implied contract to share property. Or she had to prove facts establishing some other theory of relief found within the Supreme Court's opinion. A much publicized trial took 11 weeks and featured the testimony of many famous people from the film industry about the couple's relationship. Michelle was her own chief witness, and Lee's lawyer cross-examined her at length. He developed inconsistencies in her testimony. Lee Marvin told a very different story about their relationship.

The trial judge, sitting as trier of fact, found that Michelle Marvin had not proved that a contract to share property existed. He wrote that the

> basic statement on which plaintiff relies is the one which she says (and defendant denies) was made by defendant at San Blas — "What I have is yours and what you have is mine." Considering the circumstances from which it allegedly sprung, the lack of intent to make a contract is immediately apparent. In 1964–1965 defendant was married; he had considerable unresolved financial problems; he had repeatedly informed plaintiff that he did not believe in marriage because of the property rights which a wife thereby acquires. Plaintiff could not have understood that phrase to accord the same rights to one who was not defendant's wife.

The judge pointed out that it was not clear what they were to share over what period. During the time Lee and Michelle lived together, he deposited his salary into his separate bank account. He always bought and sold property in his name. Michelle had her own bank account. She deposited into it an allowance Lee gave her as well as the sums she earned as a singer. Lee created joint bank accounts when they were "on location" making a motion picture, but when the pictures were finished Lee withdrew the remaining balances and deposited them back into his separate account. She could not show that she had given up her career at his request. Indeed, he had done several things to further her career as a singer while they lived together. It was unclear whether she would have had a successful career as a singer had she never lived with Lee Marvin.

The *National Law Journal* reported that Marvin Mitchelson, Michelle's lawyer, said that she did not have a perfect *Marvin* case. "There are better witnesses than Michelle. . . . She is not as good an actor as Lee, but then he won an Academy

Award. I think she told the truth about the relationship as she remembered it." He also said that if Ms. Marvin had had greater financial resources, he might have done more pre-trial investigation. The *Los Angeles Times News Service* reported: "Mitchelson lost the almost $100,000 it cost to try the case."[64]

In its *Marvin* opinion, the Supreme Court of California suggested the possibility of other theories of recovery that might be applicable when unwed couples lived together. For example, if a couple produced property through "mutual effort," it should be divided even though there was no contract. However, the trial court said:

> [W]here both wanted to be free to come and go without obligation, the basis for any division of property surely cannot be her "giving up" her career for him. It then can only be her work as cook, homemaker, and companion that can be considered as plaintiff's contribution to the requisite "mutual effort." Yet, where $72,000 has been disbursed by defendant on behalf of plaintiff in less than six years, where she has enjoyed a fine home and travel throughout the world for about 30 months, where she acquired whatever clothes, furs, and cars she wished and engaged in a social life amongst screen and stage luminaries, such services as she has rendered would appear to have been compensated.

Finally, in the last two paragraphs of his opinion, the trial judge awarded Michelle Marvin $104,000 "for rehabilitation purposes so that she may have the economic means to reeducate herself and to learn new, employable skills or to refurbish those utilized, for example, during her most recent employment and so that she may return from her status as companion of a motion picture star to a separate, independent but perhaps more prosaic existence." The judge noted that it was unlikely that Michelle could resume her career as a singer, and she was supporting herself by unemployment insurance benefits. Lee Marvin owned property worth more than a million dollars. The judge explained that $104,000 would be about equivalent to the highest rate that she had ever earned as a singer, $1000 per week, for the two years he estimated that she would need to rehabilitate herself.

In August 1981, a three-judge panel of the Court of Appeal of California reversed the trial court's award of $104,000 for rehabilitation.[65] The vote was two to one. The majority said that the award was without support in either equity or law. The rehabilitation remedy had to rest on some recognized cause of action, and the trial court's award did not. Michelle noted that the two men on the court had voted against her while the one woman voted to remand for additional findings. Marvin Mitchelson promised to take the case to the Supreme Court of California, but less than a month later it refused to hear the case. The battle had ended after 11 years.

Michelle Marvin received nothing from her suit but publicity. Many saw her as a feminist heroine. She said that she had gained real satisfaction in establishing the rights of women living in relationships with men other than marriage. Marvin

---

[64] *See* Oliver, *Mitchelson Got Rich as a Result of Marvin*, Milwaukee Journal, Feb. 4, 1986, Green Sheet, at 1. Recalculated in 2015 dollars, Mitchelson's losses would be over $415,000.

[65] Marvin v. Marvin, 122 Cal. App. 3d 871, 176 Cal. Rptr. 555 (Dist. Ct. App. 1981). The amount awarded would be worth over $432,000 in 2015 dollars.

Mitchelson, her lawyer, called her "the Joan of Arc of live-in women." The *Los Angeles Times News Service* reported in 1986, "Michelle Triola Marvin, 48, now works in public relations and lives in the Los Angeles area with comedian Dick Van Dyke.[66] She continued to live with Van Dyke, her partner of 30 years, until her death at age 76 from lung cancer in October 2009.

Lee Marvin, however, continued to earn large sums as an actor until his death in 1987. He saw the case as a cause, and he was determined not to pay Michelle anything. His lawyer said that his client was fighting the case because he was highly principled, and he wanted to erase from the public mind the "grand illusion that merely living together generates some rights." Ten years later Marvin said, "It was a comedy. . . . I didn't have anything else to do that year. I enjoyed it. It probably disturbed my wife and family, but it didn't bother me. It was a learning experience. I learned how little truth there is in court."[67]

Marvin Mitchelson, Michelle's lawyer, became famous and gained many clients in the divorce and family law areas. Newspaper accounts say that in 1982, he charged $200 an hour but preferred taking a $15,000 retainer for cases in California and $25,000 to $50,000 for cases elsewhere. Some large cases involve much more.

Family law experts have praised his effort in *Marvin v. Marvin.* Lee Marvin's lawyer credited Mitchelson with "tenacity and persistence" in pushing a case that no other lawyer would have taken.

Recall Mitchelson's comments about the *Marvin* case in his book. Michelle came to him in a dependent situation; she was hardly an arm's-length bargainer. She regarded Mitchelson as a professional expert. He told her that he thought "she was entitled to a great deal more" than the $833-per-month payments. He felt that she "had a right" to half the assets. Was he defining the expectation in their lawyer-client undertaking? Was he promising her the equivalent of a "perfect hand" or a more pleasing nose? If so, is there a contract remedy for failure to deliver on such a promise? Mitchelson apparently induced Michelle to forego pursuit of the $38,318 ($833 x 46 months remaining of the 60 months Marvin had promised to pay) in remaining promised monthly support payments.[68] Could she recover this sum under a reliance theory of contract damages if it were recognized in California?

3. ***Implied contracts between those who cohabitate:*** The *Marvin* case held that parties who cohabited could make express or implied contracts dealing with property or other matters involved in their relationship. However, Michelle Marvin was unable to prove that there was an implied contract to share income based on how the parties had lived together.

---

[66] *See* Oliver, *Promises, Promises*, MILWAUKEE JOURNAL, Feb. 4, 1986, Green Sheet, at 1.

[67] Seligson, *How Getting Shot Saved Lee Marvin's Life*, PARADE MAGAZINE, April 27, 1986, at 4, 5.

[68] Mitchelson's complaint could have asked for the $38,318 in one count and then, alternatively, demanded the half share of the assets in another count. Some lawyers think it bad tactics to suggest an alternative theory in a complaint that would produce a much smaller recovery than one's main cause of action.

Friedman v. Friedman suggests that establishing an implied contract is very difficult in California.[69] Terri and Elliott Friedman had lived together for 21 years but were never married. They took title to real property as husband and wife, filed joint tax returns, and lived as if they were married. They had two children, and Elliott went to law school and then went into a successful practice. Terri had major back problems, and she became physically disabled. The couple separated. Elliott paid Terri approximately $190,000 in monthly support payments following their separation. The trial court found an implied contract to pay Terri support. Terri testified that Elliott and she had discussed what would happen if their relationship ended on one or two occasions, and Elliott said she should "not worry about support." Elliott testified that he did nothing to lead Terri to believe that he would provide support if they separated.

The appellate court reversed by a two-to-one vote. The majority found that the record failed to disclose conduct on the part of the parties from which it could be implied that the parties specifically intended that Terri would be supported in the same manner as if she and Elliott had actually been married when the relationship ended. It would be bad policy to look to the post-termination payments as evidence of such an implied contract because "those who might otherwise voluntarily provide financial assistance to another in need would be discouraged from doing so." How likely is it that cohabiting couples will think about their specific obligations to each other if and when they break up? Are they likely to do more than just assume that each will treat the other fairly?

4. ***The impact of* Marvin v. Marvin *on the law outside California:*** Almost every state now recognizes express contracts between cohabitants, especially if they are written.[70] A few have gone further and enforced agreements even where sexual relations were part of the agreement. Many bills were introduced in state legislatures to require that legally enforceable agreements between unmarried cohabitants be in writing, although ultimately only Texas and Minnesota passed laws requiring a writing.[71] During the 1960s and 1970s, the number of couples living in such relationships increased in all parts of the United States. Recognition of the cohabitant relationship opens all kinds of legal questions, as so many statutes are written to give rights and duties to spouses. Do these same rights and duties apply to those cohabiting who are not married?

Professor Cynthia Grant Bowman describes the approach of the courts in the state of Washington:[72]

> Its approach . . . confers rights generally upon couples in what it calls a "meretricious relationship," defined as "a stable, marital-like relationship where both parties cohabit with knowledge that a lawful marriage between them does not exist." . . . Upon dissolution or death, property of individuals

---

[69] 20 Cal. App. 4th 876, 24 Cal. Rptr. 2d 892 (1st Dist. 1993).

[70] Cynthia Grant Bowman, *Legal Treatment of Cohabitation in the United States*, 26 Law & Pol'y 119, 126 (2004) (stating that the exceptions are Illinois, Georgia, and Louisiana).

[71] *See* Tex. Fam. Code § 1.108 (1997); Minn. Stat. § 513.075 (1980).

[72] *Id.* at 129–30, 131–32. Reprinted with permission of John Wiley and Sons.

in such relationships which would have been community property if they were married is to be divided between them in a just and equitable distribution. . . .

Unlike a contract-based system, the Washington approach, rather than assuming (and encouraging) individual autonomy, presumes that a couple in such a relationship is in fact a joint economic unit, thus encouraging the type of sharing behavior typical of marriage. If a couple in a long-term unmarried relationship do not wish to pool their income and undertake economic responsibility for one another, they need to contract *out* of such obligations in the state of Washington, unlike in California and other states following *Marvin*, where such obligations are undertaken by contracting *in*. Because registration is not required, Washington residents who are not well-versed in the law may have an unpleasant surprise upon ending their relationships.

Evaluating the status-based approach taken in Washington from the touchstone of protection for vulnerable parties, it clearly improves upon contract schemes in this respect, imposing upon cohabitants who have become interdependent an obligation to share their property upon termination of the relationship without the necessity of proving a contract. . . .

The Washington scheme for meretricious relationships . . . is limited to property distribution and does not include provision for postrelationship support if there is no property to distribute . . .

Although it was ultimately reversed, the trial court in the *Marvin* case fashioned the unique rehabilitation remedy. Most courts, however, have used more conventional contract or family law remedies in enforcing agreements between unmarried couples. For example, in *McCullon v. McCullon*,[73] a New York court ordered Mr. McCullon to pay Ms. McCullon alimony of $50 per week and child support of $50 per week. They had lived together for 28 years without marriage. He had promised to support her for life in exchange for her implied promise to perform household services for him. In a similar case, *Kozlowski v. Kozlowski*,[74] the New Jersey Superior Court awarded Ms. Kozlowski a lump sum equal to the present value of an annuity to support her for the rest of her life. The court refused to compensate her for past services and lost opportunities. Mr. Kozlowski had fulfilled his obligation by supporting Ms. Kozlowski for the previous 15 years.

Other courts have been unwilling to require people to provide future support to others with whom they have cohabited. However, they have ordered that property accumulated during the term of the relationship be partitioned between the two parties. In deciding these cases, courts usually begin by solemnly declaring that the intentions of the parties are the key to the matter. However, in most cases there is perilously little evidence of any actual intention about the rights to property when the unimaginable — the breakup of a wonderful relationship — happens. Courts

---

[73] 419 N.Y.S. 2d 226 (1979).

[74] 395 A.2d 913 (1978).

often presume that parties intended to divide property that was accumulated during the course of the relationship equally.[75]

Appellate decisions offer other possible remedial theories based on the law dealing with partnership, joint ventures, constructive trusts, and general principles of equity. The remedy chosen will depend on the rules in particular jurisdictions, the relative importance of partitioning property compared to support for the aggrieved party, and some rough judgment about the responsibility for creating reasonable expectations and defeating those expectations by failing to perform. It is an area where the imagination and persuasiveness of the lawyers is likely to have real impact.

While couples who live together without marriage often talk about a free and easy arrangement, breaking up any relationship is difficult. Many troubled cohabiting couples seek counseling when they find they have a marriage in substance if not in form. Lawyers find they face real difficulties in working out terminations. Joseph Summers, a St. Paul, Minnesota, Family Court judge, says a typical situation involves a young man who moves out of his girlfriend's apartment in anger. He returns to claim his waterbed. She refuses to return it, presenting him with a bill for her money spent for payments on his car. Also, the judge says "what was a gift when it was given often turns into a loan after a couple breaks up." There has been a great growth in mediation, attempting to lead parties to agree about ending relationships, paying past debts, and dividing property. Litigation is seen as a bad, but sometimes necessary, technique for dealing with such questions. While there are folk norms about washing dirty linen in public, people do seem willing today to take family cases before judges. The threat that one party might go to court may play a role in persuading the other to negotiate or accept mediation.

The U.S. Census for 2012 reported 7.8 million unmarried couples living together, an increase of 60 percent over 1996 levels. Researchers say that two-thirds of couples married in 2012 lived together for more than two years before their marriage.[76] An article published in 2009 says: "Most couples didn't consciously decide to live together; two-thirds of cohabitors said they either 'slid into it' or 'talked about it, but then it just sort of happened.' Just one-third talked about it and made a decision to live together."[77] What are the implications of this information? How do you suppose these numbers compare to, say, 1949? 1969?

 5. *Not all states follow* **Marvin v. Marvin.** Throughout the 1960s and 1970s, there was a great change in the laws of many states related to sexuality, marriage, and cohabitation by unwed couples. Many state supreme courts seemed eager to recognize *Marvin v. Marvin* or go beyond it. However, not everyone in the United States welcomed these changes. Defense of traditional marriage, the family, and sex roles were adopted as symbols by a number of groups. Some of this thinking,

---

[75] *See* Carlson v. Olson, 256 N.W.2d 249 (Minn. 1977); Beal v. Beal, 577 P.2d 507 (Or. 1978).

[76] Lauren Fox, *The Science of Cohabitation: A Step Toward Marriage, Not a Rebellion*, THE ATLANTIC, March 20, 2014.

[77] Sharon Jayson, *Couples Study Debunks "Trial Marriage" Notion; Most Say They Cohabit Just to Be Together*, USA TODAY, July 9, 2009, at 7D.

perhaps, can be found in *Hewitt v. Hewitt.*[78] It is a major victory for those opposed to *Marvin v. Marvin* and the cluster of ideas for which it stands. Victoria Hewitt alleged she lived with Robert Hewitt "from 1960 to 1975 in an unmarried, family-like relationship to which three children have been born." She sued to recover "an equal share of the profits and properties accumulated by the parties" during that period. The trial court dismissed her complaint, but the Appellate Court reversed. It adopted the rule of *Marvin v. Marvin*, at least for situations where the parties had lived "a most conventional, respectable, and ordinary family life." The court noted that fornication was an offense in Illinois only when it is "open and notorious."

Victoria Hewitt had an appealing case. In June of 1960, when Victoria and Robert were students at Grinnell College, she became pregnant. Robert told her that they were husband and wife, and no formal ceremony was necessary. He would "share his life, his future, his earnings, and his property" with her. Victoria and Robert told their parents they were married, and they lived as if they were. She devoted efforts to Robert's professional education and establishing his practice of pedodontia. She obtained financial assistance from her parents to support the practice in its early days, and she worked to create and maintain the business records of the practice. The practice paid her for services in the office, but she deposited her checks into their joint account. Robert owned nothing when they began living together. He now earned over $80,000 a year and owned much property. She alleged she had given him every assistance a wife and mother could. She organized and participated in social and community activities designed to enhance his professional reputation.

The Supreme Court of Illinois unanimously reversed the Appellate Court, affirming the trial court's decision dismissing Victoria Hewitt's complaint. One should compare the kinds of arguments made in the *Hewitt* opinion with those offered by Justice Tobriner in the *Marvin* case.

What follows is taken from the Supreme Court of Illinois's opinion:[79]

> The issue of unmarried cohabitants' mutual property rights . . . cannot appropriately be characterized solely in terms of contract law, nor is it limited to considerations of equity or fairness as between the parties to such relationships. There are major public policy questions involved in determining whether, under what circumstances, and to what extent it is desirable to accord some type of legal status to claims arising from such relationships. Of substantially greater importance than the rights of the immediate parties is the impact of such recognition upon our society and the institution of marriage. Will the fact that legal rights closely resembling those arising from conventional marriages can be acquired by those who deliberately choose to enter into what have heretofore been commonly referred to as "illicit" or "meretricious" relationships encourage formation of such relationships and weaken marriage as the foundation of our family-based society? . . .

---

[78]   77 Ill. 2d 49, 394 N.E.2d 1204 (1979).

[79]   394 N.E.2d, at 1207–11.

Hewitt Case: Circ Ct. says Deny cla...
Appellate Ct.: were behind the times / Lets reinter...
ILSC: No, can't do that, we agree w/ Circ ct.

B.   CONTRACT IN THE FAMILY SETTING   271

The real thrust of plaintiff's argument here is that we should abandon the rule of illegality because of certain changes in societal norms and attitudes. It is urged that social mores have changed radically in recent years, rendering this principle of law archaic. It is said that because there are so many unmarried cohabitants today the courts must confer a legal status on such relationships. This, of course, is the rationale underlying some of the decisions and commentaries. . . . If this is to be the result, however, it would seem more candid to acknowledge the return of varying forms of common law marriage than to continue displaying the naiveté we believe involved in the assertion that there are involved in these relationships contracts separate and independent from the sexual activity, and the assumption that those contracts would have been entered into or would continue without that activity.

Even if we were to assume some modification of the rule of illegality is appropriate, we return to the fundamental question earlier alluded to: If resolution of this issue rests ultimately on grounds of public policy, by what body should that policy be determined? *Marvin*, viewing the issue as governed solely by contract law, found judicial policy-making appropriate. Its decision was facilitated by California precedent and that State's no-fault divorce law. In our view, however, the situation alleged here was not the kind of arm's-length bargain envisioned by traditional contract principles, but an intimate arrangement of a fundamentally different kind. The issue, realistically, is whether it is appropriate for this court to grant a legal status to a private arrangement substituting for the institution of marriage sanctioned by the State. The question whether change is needed in the law governing the rights of parties in this delicate area of marriage-like relationships involves evaluations of sociological data and alternatives we believe best suited to the superior investigative and fact-finding facilities of the legislative branch in the exercise of its traditional authority to declare public policy in the domestic relations field.

That belief is reinforced by the fact that judicial recognition of mutual property rights between unmarried cohabitants would, in our opinion, clearly violate the policy of our recently enacted Illinois Marriage and Dissolution of Marriage Act. Although the Act does not specifically address the subject of nonmarital cohabitation, we think the legislative policy quite evident from the statutory scheme. . . . [The court notes that a goal of that act is to "strengthen and preserve the integrity of marriage and safeguard family relationships." (Ill. Rev. Stat. 1977, ch. 40, par. 102.)] . . .

The Act also provides: "Common law marriages contracted in this State after June 30, 1905, are invalid." . . .

> [W]e believe that these questions are appropriately within the province of the legislature, and that, if there is to be a change in the law of this State on this matter, it is for the legislature and not the courts to bring about that change.

We accordingly hold that plaintiff's claims are unenforceable for the reason that they contravene the public policy implicit in the statutory scheme of the Illinois Marriage and Dissolution of Marriage Act, disfavoring the grant of mutually enforceable property rights to knowingly unmarried cohabitants. The judgment of the appellate court is reversed and the judgment of the circuit court of Champaign County is affirmed.

In a 2014 case, *Blumenthal v. Brewer*,[80] an Illinois appellate court questioned the continued viability of *Hewitt*, noting that since the case was decided, "Illinois' public policy toward nonmarital relationships . . . has changed significantly."[81] Jane Blumenthal and Eileen Brewer became domestic partners in 1981, remaining together and raising three children together until 2008, when Blumenthal unilaterally ended the relationship by moving out of the family home. At no time during their 26-year relationship did the couple have the right to marry in Illinois.[82] They took a series of steps to document their commitment to one another, including cross-adopting their three children, registering with the Domestic Partner Registry in Cook County in 2003, and signing an affidavit confirming their status as "each other's sole domestic partner."[83] When their children were young, the couple decided that Brewer would stay at home and Blumenthal would become the family's primary breadwinner by pursuing her medical career. When Brewer, an attorney, returned to the workplace, she sought out jobs in the public sector that had predictable working hours (eventually culminating in her being elected as a judge of the Cook County Circuit Court in 2002), but at lower pay than she could have earned in a private law firm. As a result, Blumenthal came to earn several times more than Brewer. The couple commingled their earnings in the purchase of the family home, though the bulk of the money came from Blumenthal.

When the relationship unraveled, Brewer became financially responsible for the family home, paying the mortgage, taxes, and insurance. She estimated that she spent at least 15 hours per week on the upkeep of the house. Brewer worried that when the house was sold, her contributions would be given short shrift. Following the reasoning of *Marvin v. Marvin*, she argued that the day-to-day reality of her relationship with Blumenthal had given rise to an implied contract. She asked the court to impose "a constructive trust over the [family home] to prevent unjust enrichment arising from Blumenthal's greater net worth at the end of the relationship or, in the alternative, a partition which adjusts for Brewer's sole financial liability for the property since [the breakup,] and which adjusts for the value of Brewer's personal hours improving the property since [the breakup,] based on the theory of *quantum meruit*."[84]

In response to Brewer's arguments, Blumenthal reminded the court of Illinois's abolition of common-law marriage and charged that Brewer was trying to resurrect it. She also relied on *Hewitt*, claiming that it "does not allow for implied contract

---

[80] 24 N.E.3d 168, 2014 Ill. App. LEXIS 904 (Ill. App. 2014).

[81] *Id.* at 176.

[82] Same-sex couples gained the right to marry in Illinois as of June 1, 2014 (750 ILL. COMP. STAT. 80/1 *et seq.* (LEXIS 2014).

[83] *Blumenthal*, 24 N.E.3d 168, at 171.

[84] *Id.* at 172.

claims based on nonmarital cohabitation."[85] The trial court agreed with her, dismissing Brewer's case. The appellate court disagreed, concluding that changes in the law and social norms had corroded *Hewitt*'s foundation. The court found that "the public policy to treat unmarried partnerships as illicit no longer exists, that Brewer's suit is not an attempt to retroactively create a marriage, and that allowing her to proceed with her claims against her former domestic partner does not conflict with this jurisdiction's abolishment of common-law marriage."[86]

The court further noted that "the legal doctrine of unjust enrichment describes a recovery for the value of a benefit retained to the loss of another when there is no contractual relationship between them, but when 'on the grounds of fairness and justice, the law compels the performance of a legal and moral duty to pay' for that benefit. Put another way, the doctrine does not require that there be any express promise between the parties. Instead, unjust enrichment implies a contract between the parties so that one party is not allowed to unfairly enrich herself at the expense of the other party. Terminology such as fairness and justice may suggest that the doctrine provides an equitable remedy, however, an unjust enrichment claim is an action at law and is sometimes known as a contract implied at law, a quasi-contract, [or] restitution. . . . "[87]

The court was also mindful of the Illinois Supreme Court's reluctance to insert itself into issues best left to the legislature, as expressed in *Hewitt*. "After having reviewed the legislation that was enacted during the years that Brewer and Blumenthal were together, buying a house, having children, dividing up their domestic responsibilities, and pursuing their legal and medical careers, we conclude that although Brewer and Blumenthal were not legally entitled to marry in this jurisdiction, the legislature no longer disfavors their 26-year cohabitation or Brewer's claims against Blumenthal. Furthermore, Brewer did not allege an agreement with Blumenthal based on illicit consideration of sex, which was the primary historical rationale for rejecting cohabitation agreements. Instead, Brewer, who never had the option of marrying Blumenthal in Illinois, alleged that the couple intentionally commingled and shared their assets based on a mutual commitment and expectation of a lifelong relationship, that they divided their domestic and work responsibilities to best provide for the three children they had together, and that neither partner intended for their decisions and family roles to leave Brewer at a financial disadvantage later in life."[88]

The appellate court remanded the case to the trial court for a hearing on the merits. Whether the parties will have their day in court remains to be seen. Blumenthal has appealed to the Illinois Supreme Court, which was scheduled to decide the case in 2015.

6. ***The cases compared:*** Contrast the *Marvin*, *Hewitt*, and *Blumenthal* cases. Consider the following statements:

---

[85] *Id.* at 173.

[86] *Id.* at 174.

[87] *Id.* at 172–73.

[88] *Blumenthal*, 24 N.E.3d 168, at 181–82.

(a) Is the position taken by the court in the *Hewitt* case an example of judicial neutrality? Do the burdens imposed by the court's position fall equally on men and women? What does it mean to defer to the legislature to make or change law?

(b) The Illinois court says that Victoria Hewitt's claims are not "totally devoid of merit," but change in the law is for the legislature. Is the legislature likely to help Victoria Hewitt or others in her position? By what process? Suppose she asks you to tell her how to go about gaining legislative relief. Who should she see and what should she say? Would a statute passed yesterday afternoon help Victoria Hewitt, or would she have to be content to help others in the future?

(c) Is it silly to accept the words of the Illinois Supreme Court explaining its decision as anything more than a cover for the real basis of its decision? *Marvin v. Marvin* represents California and 1960s and 1970s "new morality." *Hewitt v. Hewitt*, likewise, does not reflect merely an exercise of legal reasoning about the roles of legal institutions, but reflects the "traditional values" politics of Illinois when it was decided. Is this an unfair statement? In what way?

(d) Is it the place of the appellate court to effectively overrule a decision of the Supreme Court?

7.   ***The direct impact of* Marvin:** In 2001, Professor Ira Ellman, writing on the occasion of the 25th anniversary of the *Marvin* decision, noted: "[D]ecades of urging by contract enthusiasts have led few couples (married or unmarried) to make express contracts at all . . . "[89] In a footnote, Ellman asserts: "Real data on the frequency of contracting are scarce, but the basic claim is not in serious dispute." He goes on to note that one of his informants, a lawyer whose practice focuses on unmarried couples, told Ellman that the number of couples entering into written agreements is "minuscule." Those that do generally perceive their relationship to be reciprocal; they rarely regard it as contractual.

If clients are unlikely to make such agreements, and if lawyers are likely to bring very few cases under the *Marvin* theory, why then do professors teach it in one or more courses in most law schools?

8.   ***Was* Marvin *a way to deal with some of the legal issues in gay and lesbian relationships?*** Before the legalization of same-sex marriage throughout the United States in 2015, many gay and lesbian couples turned to contract as a mechanism to protect their rights. In *Jones v. Daly*, a gay man made a claim against the estate of his male partner.[90] According to the plaintiff's complaint, the two men had an oral cohabitors agreement. The complaint alleged that the plaintiff agreed to render services "as lover, companion, homemaker, traveling companion, house-keeper, and cook" to his deceased partner. The trial court's dismissal of plaintiff's complaint was affirmed. The court said the agreement's terms "clearly show that plaintiff's rendition of sexual services . . . was an inseparable part of the consid-

---

[89] Ira Mark Ellman, *Unmarried Partners and the Legacy of* Marvin v. Marvin: *Contracts Thinking Was* Marvin's *Fatal Flaw*, 76 NOTRE DAME L. REV. 1365, n.17 (2001). The trend of contracting within families (or quasi-families) extends beyond partners to agreements between parents and children, as well as co-parenting agreements. *See* Deborah Zalesne, *The Contractual Family: The Role of the Market in Shaping Family Formations and Rights*, 36 CARDOZO L. REV. 1027 (2015).

[90] 122 Cal. App. 3d 500, 176 Cal. Rptr. 130 (1981).

eration for the 'cohabitors agreement,' and indeed was the predominant consideration." If we assume that the lawyer who drafted the complaint was competent, why did s/he draft it to refer to plaintiff's services as a lover?

In *Gonzalez v. Green*, the parties had been same-sex domestic partners since 2001.[91] In 2005, they separated. Defendant's attorney drafted a separation agreement. It provided for the division of real and personal property accumulated by the parties during their time together. It also called for a one-time payment from defendant to plaintiff of $780,000 as "the only support, maintenance, or other form of payment by either party hereto to the other." The court upheld the agreement because "illicit sexual relations were not part of the consideration of the contract."

9. *How far can we change the law by using contract?* Contrast the opinion in *Marvin v. Marvin* with *In re Baby M*.[92] In the *Baby M* case, the Supreme Court of New Jersey said:

> . . . the Court is asked to determine the validity of a contract that purports to provide a new way of bringing children into a family. For a fee of $10,000, a woman agrees to be artificially inseminated with the semen of another woman's husband; she is to conceive a child, carry it to term, and after its birth surrender it to the natural father and his wife. The intent of the contract is that the child's natural mother will thereafter be forever separated from her child. The wife is to adopt the child, and she and the natural father are to be regarded as its parents for all purposes. The contract providing for this is called a "surrogacy contract," the natural mother inappropriately called the "surrogate mother."
>
> We invalidate the surrogacy contract because it conflicts with the law and public policy of this State. While we recognize the depth of the yearning of infertile couples to have their own children, we find the payment of money to be a "surrogate" mother illegal, perhaps criminal, and potentially degrading to women. Although in this case we grant custody to the natural father, the evidence having clearly proved such custody to be in the best interest of the infant, we void both the termination of the surrogate mother's parental rights and the adoption of the child by the wife/ stepparent. We thus restore the "surrogate" as the mother of the child. We remand the issue of the natural mother's visitation rights to the trial court, since that issue was not reached below and the record before us is not sufficient to permit us to decide it de novo.

Essentially, the New Jersey court said that the surrogacy agreement was an attempt to evade the adoption and child custody laws of the state. Had Michelle Marvin been able to prove the implied contract that she alleged, would it not have been an attempt to use contract to evade the marriage and community property laws of California? Is there any difference between the cases? Is there any policy involved beyond protecting the weaker party from the contract that she made? Suppose a man with an extremely painful terminal disease makes a contract calling

---

[91] 831 N.Y.S.2d 856 (S.Ct. N.Y. 2006).

[92] 109 N.J. 396, 537 A.2d 1227 (1988).

for a woman to kill him. She does this. Would, or should, her contract be a defense to a criminal action that charges the woman with homicide? How is the *Marvin* decision different?

2. Which Promises Should the Law Enforce? — The Response of Contract Doctrine and the Role of Form

a. "Bait": promises by a family member with money to influence the lives of those without it

In this section we seek to develop several ideas related to contract doctrine. For the most part, we look at promises made to family members to induce them to do things desired by the one with money. These are not commercial situations, but courts often use contract law as a tool to resolve problems that do not fit into family or property law. Although, as we shall see, there is no "typical" bait situation, there are a great many cases in which aging farmers, or other small businessmen, promise to turn their property over to one or more children in exchange for a promise by the children to support their parents for their remaining lifetimes. Later, or sometimes sooner, conflicts arise and one or the other of the parties seeks either to enforce or repudiate the bargain. A disproportionate number of well-known contract cases follow this pattern, and so it is a useful paradigm for the study of contract doctrine, the limits of judicial capability, and the advantages and disadvantages of thinking of agreements as creating relationships rather than creating transactions.

Before narrowing our focus to contract, we should briefly consider some of the other legal devices that may apply to the "bait" situation. As you will see, lawyers often press contract into service when they find these other theories don't quite work. Suppose a father is unhappy about the purposeless life of his son, who has graduated from college but has refused to follow a conventional career. The father wants the son to go to law school. However, the father also wants evidence that the son will work to the full level of his ability. Thus he writes his son:

> I will give you tuition and a reasonable allowance for books, room and board, clothes, and recreation. I will do this only if you go to State University Law School and if you pass the examinations at the end of the first semester with at least the average grade needed for graduation.

The son is admitted to law school, pays his expenses from his own money and what he can earn from a part-time job, and goes to classes. Before final examinations at the end of the first semester, his father dies. There is no provision in the father's will calling for payment of his son's law school expenses. The will leaves all of the father's money to the son's stepmother, who dislikes him. The son takes examinations and receives the highest grade average in the class. The executor of the father's estate refuses to pay any money to the son without a court order to do so. What theories might the son assert against the estate, and what chances for success would each have?

Our facts almost fit a number of conventional legal categories governing ways to transfer property in families, but they do not quite satisfy the requirements of wills, gifts, or trusts. The letter to the son would not itself serve as a *will*, or as an amendment to the original one. The letter does not purport to be a will, and the father did not sign it in the presence of two witnesses. Under some circumstances, a few states will accept a little less formality. However, the legal system demands relatively precise compliance with the formal requirements of creating wills. The transaction between father and son was not a legally effective *gift* either. To make a gift, the law insists on donative intent plus a delivery of property.[93] Whatever the father's intention, here he delivered nothing to complete a gift.

Could we call the arrangement a *trust*? Restatement (Second) of Trusts, § 2, defines a trust as "a fiduciary relationship with respect to property, subjecting the person by whom the title to the property is held to equitable duties to deal with the property for the benefit of another person." People may create trusts in several ways, including a declaration by the owner of property that he or she holds property as trustee for another. Thus, suppose X stated that he was the owner of 100 shares of AT&T stock and was holding the shares in trust for the benefit of his granddaughter until her 21st birthday. This declaration would create a trust. X would have a legal obligation to deal with the 100 shares of stock only for the benefit of his granddaughter. It is questionable whether the father's letter to this son in our case could reasonably be construed as such a declaration. The father did not state he was holding *specific property* as a trustee, ready to devote it to paying law school bills. Instead, the father stated that he would pay in the future without segregating assets for this purpose.

Contract to the rescue? Finally, can we call the transaction between father and son a *contract*? This raises the question of whether there was "consideration" for the father's promise. Was this "a bargained-for exchange between the parties," or, rather, was it no more than "a statement of intention or a promise to make a gift to the son on a certain condition?" A completed gift requires no consideration to be enforced. However, a promise to make a gift in the future — or, for that matter, a promise to make a will or create a trust — will typically be unenforceable without consideration. There are some exceptions, but we will come to them later. It is often difficult to distinguish a conditional gift from a bargain.

Legal formality: We can view the requirements for making a legally enforceable will, gift, trust, or contract as *forms*. That is, there is a necessary pattern of conduct or ceremony which people must follow to trigger a particular legal relationship. For example, wills require a writing witnessed by two people. Gifts require intent plus delivery. Trusts require a declaration to hold specific assets for another, and contracts require an exchange (and often, but not always, a writing as well). We can ask about the costs and benefits of formal requirements. This will help us understand whether the law is likely to insist firmly that there is one and only one way to make, for example, a will. Assume that our son cannot establish a will, gift, trust, or conventional contract. We will ask whether he could turn to some less formal way of having his father's promise enforced.

---

[93] The delivery requirement can sometimes be met by the delivery of a token representing the property, such as a passbook (which would represent a bank account), or a key to a locked box, which might substitute for the delivery of the box itself.

The *costs of form* are obvious. One person may clearly intend to transfer property, and the other may expect to get it and even rely on the transaction. However, if they have not met a formal requisite, the attempted transfer of rights fails. Justice is defeated by a "mere technicality." One who has purported to transfer or promise can, in bad faith and without any excuse, refuse to carry out the transaction and hide behind the legal rule. Moreover, knowledge of legal forms is not widespread, and people must hire lawyers to be sure that they achieve their purposes.

The *functions or benefits of form* may not be obvious to everyone. The persistence of formal requirements in many legal systems suggests, but does not prove, that there may be some, or a great deal of, utility in them. Professor Lon Fuller says that legal formalities have three functions — cautionary, evidentiary, and channeling.[94] Let's examine what he means.

Cautionary: If people must go through a formal ceremony to create legal relationships, it may warn them that they are doing something serious and important. Such a warning should serve to prompt thought about the commitment being made. "Do I really want to give away Grandfather's watch?" "Do I want to do it unconditionally or should I attach some strings to be sure that my son is worthy?" Many people avoid thinking about their own death. The will ceremony with witnesses (and even the usual presence of a lawyer who asks questions) may shock them into recognizing what they are doing. Handing over a valued possession in order to make a delivery for a gift should be more than just talk. Insofar as people view exchange-based bargains as serious and as slightly dangerous, a contract also serves as a form. Bargaining warns people not to be careless in the promises they make. In this view, people who make benevolent promises from which they receive only intangible satisfactions such as gratitude need protection against their own generous impulses.

Obviously, legal formalities can provide greater or lesser degrees of caution. An oral exchange of promises between business bargainers may involve more caution than an oral promise to make a gift. A signed, written promise may have more shock value. There are customs in our society about the magical impact of signing documents. All salespeople know that it is a long step from orally closing a deal to getting the papers signed. Requiring parties to put contracts in writing and then appear before a government official who cross-examines them about their understanding of what they have done seems to offer even more caution. Some legal systems require just this kind of procedure to make certain transactions legally enforceable.

---

[94] Lon L. Fuller, *Consideration and Form*, 41 COLUM. L. REV. 799 (1941). For a critical appraisal, *see* Duncan Kennedy, *From the Will Theory to the Principle of Private Autonomy: Lon Fuller's "Consideration and Form,"* 100 COLUM. L. REV. 94 (2000). The summary of Professor Kennedy's article says: "Fuller's scheme came closer to modern policy analysis than anything in the prior literature. It nonetheless achieved only a partial synthesis, denying any place to what the writers of the time called the 'social' dimension of the field and underplaying conflict among the factors he identified. These traits may be explained by the fact that he was breaking new ground and by the center-right ideological agenda he was pursuing within private law theory."

Evidentiary: Some forms give us evidence that a transaction took place while others also tell us what the terms of the transaction are. A will signed before two witnesses, apart from a risk of forgery, tells us that the testator made a will and who gets what. Contrast the situation that would exist under oral wills if the law were to recognize them. Courts would have to rely on testimony about what the deceased said and intended. Those most likely to have heard the deceased are also the likely beneficiaries, or their relatives, who would have reason to shade their stories. Written contracts serve the evidentiary function nicely, provided that the parties understand what they have signed. Oral contracts are less useful. Perhaps it is easier to believe that a person made a promise when the other party gave something in exchange for it. It is, for example, easier to believe that a person made an oral promise when the other party has performed and seeks payment.

Channeling: A legal form is important to people who want to do something with legal consequences. The law says that you have no gift if there is no intent or delivery. It also says that you can make a gift successfully if you do intend to make one and hand over property or a token representing it. If you want to be sure that you have a legally enforceable contract, it is useful to find a blueprint telling you how to build one.

Courts need channels too. The more objective the formal requirements, the easier it is for judges. Contrast two different types of legal rules. One rule says that manufacturer may sell an item without responsibility for its defects if the seller uses a certain form of words. The other rule allows disclaimers only if a buyer "should reasonably have known" that seller intended an "as is" sale. In the first case, the question is little more than did the seller use the magic words? In the second, one must weigh and balance norms and facts to determine what the buyer should have known. Moreover, the channel serves more than the judge's convenience. It is easier for others who care to predict what any judge might do if the law says that certain words and only those words are effective. This last point concerns the legitimacy of the judicial role in a society where legislatures are supposed to have primary rulemaking power. Some think that the more clearly judges are in the rule-applying rather than rulemaking business, the easier it is to defend what they do.

Consideration, Fuller says, may serve some of this channeling function. In planning a contract, a lawyer knows that she is taking far fewer risks if she casts the arrangement as an exchange. The courts can quickly sort clear-cut exchanges from all other promissory transactions, and they may refuse to act or demand strong reasons for enforcement of non-exchanges. Nonetheless, we can ask to what extent consideration is an effective form compared to the requirement that a certain type of contract be in writing. To say that a doctrine serves some formal functions does not mean that other doctrines might not serve the same functions better.

We now turn to some cases dealing with consideration, and reliance as a substitute for consideration, in the family bait situation. Remember that in all of the situations we will consider, there were other ways that the person making the promise could have structured things to make it easier to enforce the promise in question. Should we hold to form or seek substantive justice on the facts of each particular case?

New Case   CONSIDERATION / FAMILY "B.H"

HAMER v. SIDWAY

New York Court of Appeals

124 N.Y. 538, 27 N.E. 256 (1891)

The deal

The plaintiff presented a claim to the executor of William E. Story, Sr., for $5,000 and interest from the 6th day of February, 1875. She acquired it through several . . . assignments from William E. Story, 2d. The claim being rejected by the executor, this action was brought. It appears that William E. Story, Sr., was the uncle of William E. Story, 2d; that at the celebration of the golden wedding of Samuel Story and wife, father and mother of William E. Story, Sr., on the 20th day of March, 1869, in the presence of the family and invited guests, he promised his nephew that if he would refrain from drinking, using tobacco, swearing, and playing cards or billiards for money until he became 21 years of age, he would pay him the sum of $5,000. The nephew assented thereto, and fully performed the conditions inducing the promise. When the nephew arrived at the age of 21 years, on the 31st day of January, 1875, he wrote to his uncle, informing him that he had performed his part of the agreement, and had thereby become entitled to the sum of $5,000. The uncle received the letter, and a few days later, on the 6th day of February, he wrote and mailed to his nephew the following letter:

Buffalo, Feb. 6, 1875. W.E. Story, Jr. — Dear Nephew: Your letter of the 31st ult. came to hand all right, saying that you had lived up to the promise made to me several years ago. I have no doubt but you have, for which you shall have five thousand dollars, as I promised you. I had the money in the bank the day you was twenty-one years old that I intend for you, and you shall have the money certain. Now, Willie, I do not intend to interfere with this money in any way till I think you are capable of taking care of it, and the sooner that time comes the better it will please me. I would hate very much to have you start out in some adventure that you thought all right and lose this money in one year. The first five thousand dollars that I got together cost me a heap of hard work. You would hardly believe me when I tell you that to obtain this I shoved a jack-plane many a day, butchered three or four years, then came to this city, and, after three months' perseverance, I obtained a situation in a grocery store. I opened this store early, closed late, slept in the fourth story of the building in a room 30 by 40 feet, and not a human being in the building but myself. All this I done to live as cheap as I could to save something. I don't want you to take up with this kind of fare. I was here in the cholera season of '49 and '52 and the deaths averaged 80 to 125 daily, and plenty of smallpox. I wanted to go home, but Mr. Fisk, the gentleman I was working for, told me, if I left them, after it got healthy he probably would not want me. I stayed. All the money I have saved I know just how I got it. It did not come to me in any mysterious way, and the reason I speak of this is that money got in this way stops longer with a fellow that gets it with hard knocks than it does when he finds it. Willie, you are twenty-one, and you have many a thing to learn yet. This money you have earned much easier than I did, besides acquiring good habits at the same time, and you are quite welcome to the money. Hope you will make good use of it. I was ten long years getting it together after I was your age. Now, hoping this will be satisfactory, I stop. One thing more. Twenty-one years ago I bought you 15 sheep. These sheep were put out to double every four years. I kept track of them the first eight years. I have not heard of them since. You father and grandfather promised me that they would look after them till you were of age. Have they done so? I hope they have. By this time you have between five and six hundred sheep, worth a nice little income this spring. Willie, I have said much more than I expected to. Hope you can make out what I have written. To-day is the seventeenth day that I have not been out of my room, and have had the doctor as many days. Am a little better to day. Think I will get out next week. You need not mention this to your father, as he always worries about small matters. Truly yours, W.E. STORY. P.S. You can consider this money on interest.

Long letter promising to pay in future w/ interest. Nephew cool w/ it. Uncle dies 2 yrs later and never paid

The nephew . . . consented that the money should remain with his uncle in accordance with the terms and conditions of the letter. The uncle died on the 29th day of January 1887, without having paid over to his nephew any portion of the said $5,000 and interest. . . .

PARKER, J. . . .

The question which . . . lies at the foundation of plaintiff's asserted right of recovery, is whether by virtue of a contract defendant's testator, William E. Story, became indebted to his nephew, William E. Story, 2d, on his twenty-first birthday in the sum of $5,000. The trial court found as a fact that "on the 20th day of March, 1869 . . . William E. Story agreed to and with William E. Story, 2d, that if he would refrain from drinking liquor, using tobacco, swearing, and playing cards or billiards for money until he should become twenty-one years of age, then he, the said William E. Story, would at that time pay him, the said William E. Story, 2d, the sum of $5,000 for such refraining, to which the said William E. Story, 2d, agreed, and that he "in all things fully performed his part of said agreement." The defendant contends that the contract was without consideration to support it, and therefore invalid. He asserts that the promisee, by refraining from the use of liquor and tobacco, was not harmed, but benefitted; that that which he did was best for him to do, independently of his uncle's promise, — and insists that it follows that, unless the promisor was benefited, the contract was without consideration, — a contention which, if well founded, would seem to leave open for controversy in many cases whether that which the promisee did or omitted to do was in fact of such benefit to him as to leave no consideration to support the enforcement of the promisor's agreement. Such a rule could not be tolerated, and is without foundation in the law. The exchequer chamber in 1875 defined "consideration" as follows: "A valuable consideration, in the sense of the law, may consist either in some right, interest, profit, or benefit accruing to the one party, or some forbearance, detriment, loss, or responsibility given, suffered, or undertaken by the other." Courts "will not ask whether the thing which forms the consideration does in fact benefit the promisee or a third party, or is of any substantial value to any one. It is enough that something is promised, done, forborne, or suffered by the party to whom the promise is made as consideration for the promise made to him." Anson, *Cont.* 63. . . . Pollock in his work on Contracts (page 166), after citing the definition given by the exchequer chamber, already quoted, says: "The second branch of this judicial description is really the most

Def says no consideration for agreement

Basically don't care if it ACTUALLY benifitted promisor

important one. 'Consideration' means not so much that one party is profiting as that the other abandons some legal right in the present, or limits his legal freedom of action in the future, as an inducement for the promise of the first." Now, applying this rule to the facts before us, the promisee used tobacco, occasionally drank liquor, and he had a legal right to do so. That right he abandoned for a period of years upon the strength of the promise of the testator that for such forbearance he would give him $5,000. We need not speculate on the effort which may have been required to give up the use of those stimulants. It is sufficient that he restricted his lawful freedom of action within certain prescribed limits upon the faith of his uncle's agreement, and now, having fully performed the conditions imposed, it is of no moment whether such performance actually proved a benefit to the promisor, and the court will not inquire into it; but, were it a proper subject of inquiry, we see nothing in this record that would permit a determination that the uncle was not benefited in a legal sense. . . .

[T]he agreement which we have been considering was within the condemnation of the statute of frauds, because not to be performed within a year, and not in writing. But this defense the promisor could waive, and his letter and oral statements subsequent to the date of final performance on the part of the promisee must be held to amount to a waiver. . . .

[I]t must be deemed established for the purposes of this appeal that on the 31st day of January, 1875, defendant's testator was indebted to William E. Story, 2d, in the sum of $5,000; and, if this action were founded on that contract, it would be barred by the statute of limitations, which has been pleaded, but on that date the nephew wrote to his uncle . . . [O]n February 6th, the uncle replied . . . as follows: "Dear Nephew: Your letter of the 31st ult. came to hand all right, saying that you had lived up to the promise made to me several years ago. I have no doubt but you have, for which you shall have $5,000, as I promised you. I had the money in the bank the day you was 21 years old that I intend for you, and you shall have the money certain. Now, Willie, I do not intend to interfere with this money in any way till I think you are capable of taking care of it, and the sooner that time comes the better it will please me. I would hate very much to have you start out in some adventure that you thought all right and lose this money in one year. . . . W. E. STORY. P.S. You can consider this money on interest." The trial court found as a fact that "said letter was received by said William E. Story, 2d, who thereafter consented that said money should remain with the said William E. Story in accordance with the terms and conditions of said letter." And further, "that afterwards, on the 1st day of March 1877, with the knowledge and consent of his said uncle, he duly sold, transferred, and assigned all his right, title, and interest in and to said sum of $5,000 to his wife, Libbie H. Story, who thereafter duly sold, transferred, and assigned the same to the plaintiff in this action." We must now consider the effect of the letter and the nephew's assent thereto. Were the relations of the parties thereafter that of debtor and creditor simply, or that of trustee and *cestui que trust*?[95] If the former, then this action is not maintainable, because barred by lapse of time. If the latter, the result must be otherwise. No particular expressions are necessary to create a trust. Any language clearly showing the settler's intention is sufficient if the

---

[95] [Eds. note: A *cestui que trust* is the beneficiary of the trust.]

[handwritten margin notes at top: Probably would love to treat it as K instead of Trust but time barred / LD Has the money SPECIFICALLY set aside, why we are able to call it a trust]

property and disposition of it are definitely stated. . . . A person in the legal possession of money or property acknowledging a trust with the assent of the *cestui que trust* becomes from that time a trustee if the acknowledgment be founded on a valuable consideration. His antecedent relation to the subject, whatever it may have been, no longer controls. . . . If before a declaration of trust a party be a mere debtor, a subsequent agreement recognizing the fund as already in his hands, and stipulating for its investment on the creditor's account, will have the effect to create a trust. . . . It is essential that the letter, interpreted in the light of surrounding circumstances, must show an intention on the part of the uncle to become a trustee before he will be held to have become such; but in an effort to ascertain the construction which should be given to it we are also to observe the rule that the language of the promisor is to be interpreted in the sense in which he had reason to suppose it was understood by the promisee. . . . At the time the uncle wrote the letter he was indebted to his nephew in the sum of $5,000, and payment had been requested. The uncle, recognizing the indebtedness, wrote the nephew that he would keep the money until he deemed him capable of taking care of it. He did not say, "I will pay you at some other time," or use language that would indicate that the relation of debtor and creditor would continue. On the contrary, his language indicated that he had set apart the money the nephew had "earned," for him, so that when he should be capable of taking care of it he should receive it with interest. . . . Certainly the uncle must have intended that his nephew should understand that the promise not "to interfere with the money" referred to the money in the bank, which he declared was not only there when the nephew became 21 years old, but was intended for him. True, he did not use the word "trust," or state that the money was deposited in the name of William E. Story, 2d, or in his own name in trust for him, but the language used must have been intended to assure the nephew that his money had been set apart for him, to be kept without interference until he should be capable of taking care of it. . . . In this declaration there is not lacking a single element necessary for the creation of a valid trust, and to that declaration the nephew assented. . . . The order appealed from should be reversed, and the judgment of the special term affirmed, with costs payable out of the state. All concur.

NOTES AND QUESTIONS

1. ***Bargains and contingent gifts:*** What is "consideration" and how does it differ from a contingent gift (a gift with strings attached)? Does the promisor's true subjective motive matter? Consider a classic — but still influential — statement, and then the formulation of the American Law Institute; then reflect on whether either provides much practical help.

    (a) O.W. Holmes, Jr.:[96]

    It is said that consideration must not be confounded with motive. It is true that it must not be confounded with what may be the prevailing or chief motive in actual fact. A man may promise to paint a picture for five hundred dollars, while his chief motive may be a desire for fame. A consideration

---

[96] The Common Law 230 (M. Howe ed., 1963) (1881).

may be given and accepted, in fact, solely for the purpose of making a promise binding. But, nevertheless, it is the essence of a consideration, that, by the terms of the agreement, it is given and accepted as the motive or inducement of the promise. Conversely, the promise must be made and accepted as the conventional motive or inducement for furnishing the consideration. The root of the whole matter is the relation of reciprocal conventional inducement, each for the other, between consideration and promise.

(b) Drawing on *Hamer v. Sidway*, the Restatement (Second) of Contracts states:

§ 71. Requirement of Exchange; Types of Exchange

(1) To constitute consideration, a performance or a return promise must be bargained for.

(2) A performance or return promise is bargained for if it is sought by the promisor in exchange for his promise and is given by the promisee in exchange for that promise.

(3) The performance may consist of

    (a) an act other than a promise, or

    (b) a forbearance, or

    (c) the creation, modification, or destruction of a legal relation.

(4) The performance or return promise may be given to the promisor or to some other person. It may be given by the promisee or by some other person.

2. **Williston's tramp case:** In *Maughs v. Porter*,[97] the defendant advertised in a newspaper that there would be an auction of residence lots. The advertisement's heading was "NEW MODEL FORD FREE." The text said that everyone "has an equal chance at the new Ford regardless of buying or bidding. Come to the auction. . . . " Plaintiff went to the auction. She placed her name on a slip of paper in a box held by the auctioneer. Defendant drew her name as the winner of the Ford. Defendant placed an order for the car with a Ford dealer but refused to pay for it when it was ready for delivery. Defendant demurred to plaintiff's complaint. He alleged that his promise lacked consideration, and so it was unenforceable. He also argued that the drawing was an illegal lottery, and so any contract resulting from it was unenforceable.

The Supreme Court of Virginia first noted that a promise to make a gift is legally unenforceable. It remarked that it was often difficult to determine whether there was consideration. It then quoted *1 Williston on Contracts* § 112 (1920) to illustrate the difficulty and a method for resolving it:

If a benevolent man says to a tramp: "If you go around the corner to the clothing shop there, you may purchase an overcoat on my credit," no reasonable person would understand that the short walk was requested as

---

[97] 157 Va. 415, 161 S.E. 242 (1931).

the consideration for the promise, but that in the event of the tramp going to the shop the promisor would make him a gift. Yet the walk to the shop is in its nature capable of being consideration. It is a legal detriment to the tramp to make the walk, and the only reason why the walk is not consideration is because on a reasonable construction it must be held that the walk was not requested as the price of the promise, but was merely a condition of a gratuitous promise. It is often difficult to determine whether words of condition in a promise indicate a request for consideration or state a mere condition in a gratuitous promise. An aid, though not a conclusive test, in determining which construction of the promise is more reasonable is an inquiry whether the happening of the condition will be a benefit to the promisor. If so, it is a fair inference that the happening was requested as a consideration. On the other hand, if, as in the case of the tramp stated above, the happening of the condition will be not only of no benefit to the promisor but is obviously merely for the purpose of enabling the promisee to receive a gift, the happening of the event on which the promise is conditional, though brought about by the promisee in reliance on the promise, will not properly be construed as consideration. In case of doubt where the promisee has incurred a detriment on the faith of the promise, courts will naturally be loath to regard the promise as a mere gratuity and the detriment incurred as merely a condition. But in some cases it is so clear that a conditional gift was intended that even though the promisee has incurred detriment, the promise has been held unenforceable.

The court in the *Maughs* case found there was consideration for the promise of a car to the winner of the drawing. "The object of the defendant unquestionably was to attract persons to the auction sale with the hope of deriving benefit from the crowd so augmented. Even though persons attracted by the advertisement of the free automobile might attend only because hoping to draw the automobile, and with the determination not to bid for any of the lots, some of these even might nevertheless be induced to bid after reaching the place of sale." However, the court then affirmed, sustaining the demurrer, because the advertisement was for a lottery which "contravenes public policy and avoids the agreement." (We will return to consider the public policy objection at greater length in Chapter 4.)

Courts and writers have said that the law looks only for the existence and not the adequacy of consideration. However, as the *Maughs* case and the tramp illustration show, we cannot rely solely on the form of the transaction. Both situations fit neatly into the form of "if you do X, then I'll do Y." Are we interested in the subjective state of mind of the one making the promise? Williston tells us that the person talking to the tramp is "a benevolent man." Suppose that the giver of the coat is an ambitious politician who wishes to be seen, and photographed, walking with the tramp and giving him the overcoat, in order to project an image of concern and generosity to the voting public? Would this matter?

Whatever the actual motives of the benevolent person, we "just know" that a rational profit maximizer would not ordinarily give a coat to a tramp to induce him to walk around the corner. We also just know, however, that gifts tied to business deals are part of bargaining. They are economically rational gestures which help close deals. Should courts distinguish charity from business gestures? We also might view the *Maughs* cases as judicial regulation of advertising. Whatever the form of the arrangement and whatever the subjective or objective intent of the one placing the ad, it is a good thing for business to force those in the market to stand behind their representations. The only problem with this explanation is the court's decision that the drawing was an illegal lottery.

Professor Clare Dalton notes that many judges and law professors assert that consideration is principally a formal requirement. She argues that they want us to think that courts do not intervene in private bargains and make substantive judgments about what agreements should and should not be enforced. These writers insist that the law is not concerned with the adequacy of the parties' exchange but only whether the parties intended to trade one item for something else. However, when exchanges are significantly unequal, judges inevitably look behind formal rules and consider the substance of objective value. To hide this state intervention in private transactions, judges and law professors often are tempted to talk about the intention of the parties to bargain rather than the fairness of their agreement.[98] On the other hand, an answer to Dalton is that courts may openly acknowledge intervention by using either § 90 of the Restatement, addressed later in this chapter, and the doctrine of unconscionability, which we will examine in Chapter 4.

How might Dalton apply her argument to *Hamer v. Sidway* and Williston's tramp case? Why do we need a neutral, apolitical contract doctrine? Who is in the audience that applauds neutral, apolitical judging in contract cases? Suppose we find that the intentions of the parties at the time of the transaction are too unclear to answer the question of liability. Can we have a single rule resting on choice and bargain, or must we have many rules dealing with different situations in light of different policy considerations?

3. ***Promises to make gifts distinguished from trusts:*** In *Hamer v. Sidway*, the uncle sent a letter from Buffalo, telling the nephew about some sheep bought at the nephew's birth and put in the possession of the nephew's father and grandfather. The uncle's gift of the sheep created a trust. The uncle could not reclaim these sheep before the nephew reached the age of majority. If the father sold some of the sheep and invested the money in corporate securities, the courts would hold him to the fiduciary duties of a trustee. If this were an unreasonable investment or if the father were unwilling to hand over the stock or proceeds when the son reached the age of majority, the son could sue the father successfully for breach of trust. Courts protect trust beneficiaries with remedies more powerful than those used for breaches of contract. For example, the son could trace the money his father gained by selling the sheep into the corporate securities. The son could recover those securities. However, if they were now valueless, the son could recover the fair market value of the sheep misappropriated by his father, the trustee. Students consider these subjects at length in other courses. All you need to know for purposes of a contracts course is that lawyers for claimants will often want to classify a transaction as a trust rather than as a contract. The remedies differ and, as *Hamer v. Sidway* indicates, often so does the applicable statute of limitations.

---

[98] Clare Dalton, *An Essay in the Deconstruction of Contract Doctrine*, 94 YALE L.J. 997, 1094–95 (1985).

4. *Bargains as distinguished from statements of intention:* The uncle also mentioned a transaction between Mr. Fisk and himself. Suppose the uncle stayed with Fisk through the cholera epidemic but then Fisk fired him. Could the uncle sue Mr. Fisk for breach of contract successfully? How, if at all, does this transaction differ from that found to be a contract between the uncle and the nephew in *Hamer v. Sidway*?

5. *Bargains and benefits:* In *Hamer v. Sidway*, what benefit did the uncle get from his promise? How was the nephew giving up anything? Wasn't the behavior the uncle asked of the nephew for the nephew's own benefit? Suppose I tell you that I'll give you a new watch for your birthday. You smile and thank me, and I feel good. Under *Hamer v. Sidway*, would this be a bargain supported by consideration? How, if at all, does the situation differ? Suppose at the time a minor had no legal right to smoke, drink, or gamble, but many minors did these things. Would there then be consideration for the promise?

6. *Importance of the transaction:* Why does the law intervene in a transaction such as *Hamer v. Sidway* but refuse to do so in those such as *Balfour v. Balfour*? Are the questions a court must answer less difficult in the *Hamer* case? Who are the real parties in interest in the *Hamer* case — that is, who would get the money if the assignee of the nephew did not win this lawsuit? Is the court less likely to fall into a "dismal swamp" while holding a "hot potato"? Are transactions such as those between the uncle and the nephew more socially important in some way than those between husband and wife? Consider the functions of form. Does the transaction in *Hamer v. Sidway* carry out those functions while the one in *Balfour v. Balfour* fails to meet them? *Hamer* was decided in 1891 and *Balfour* in 1919. Would your answers to these questions differ if asked in 1891, 1919, or today?

The *Wall Street Journal* reported that the idea of family bait was alive and well as recently as 1999.[99] Tom Glavine, who then pitched for the Atlanta Braves baseball team, made $8 million a year. He wanted to be sure that his children worked. He created a trust that would match their earned income up to $100,000. His four-year-old daughter Amber wanted to be an animal doctor "for lions, tigers, and baby giraffes." Glavine provided $200,000 to set up a veterinary practice or any other business, as long as Amber has done well in school. However, Glavine thought there was great value in mothers staying home with their children. The trust gives her a financial reward if she does this.

A couple who had made a fortune from their Microsoft stock provided that payments from the trust they created would be curtailed if one of their children was on drugs, abusing alcohol, in a cult, or following a "beach-bum" lifestyle. This couple wanted their children to be able to make charitable donations, but they put restrictions on this: "I definitely don't want our money to go to militaristic gun-toting extremists." When we look at family bait, to what extent are we asking only whether the donor has followed legal formalities? To what extent are we asking whether the use of bait is good policy?

---

[99] Monica Langley, *Trust Me, Baby: The House, the Money — It'll All Be Yours; There's Just One Thing — Rich Parents Find a New Way to Keep Tabs on Heirs: "Family Incentive Plans" — Bonus for an At-Home Mom*, WALL STREET JOURNAL, Nov. 17, 1999, page A1.

Doctrine of Consideration

3. An Introduction to the Doctrine of Consideration

Although it has been our experience that a careful and thorough study of the *Hamer v. Sidway* case serves to reveal a great deal about the doctrine of consideration, we offer at this point another note. This one summarizes the doctrine of consideration, and we intend that you read it in the same spirit as the note summarizing the offer-and-acceptance doctrine. Some of this note repeats things you should already know; other parts of it introduce some special applications of the doctrine, as well as some exceptions. Just as with the note dealing with offer and acceptance, you should not be surprised if your teacher asks you to read it on your own, or at another point in the text.

A Doctrinal Note — Consideration

Courts, as we have already said more than once, will enforce some promises but not others. The doctrine of consideration has been one of the tools used to distinguish one kind from the other. Professor John Murray speaks of consideration as the most significant of several "validation devices" found in the law.[100] Murray also observes "the reason the doctrine of consideration is so well remembered by most lawyers, and a greater importance attributed to it than it deserves, is the difficulty which most students have in understanding it."[101] One reason for the difficulty is that consideration really is a number of rules, and it is impossible to capture it in a single, concrete statement. Most attempts are so abstract and qualified as to communicate little to one not already well-versed in contracts lore. Another reason for confusion is that consideration is a legal construct without a counterpart in human perception. Any person might see a contract as "fair" or "unfair," but only a lawyer could characterize one as "supported by consideration."

Promisee vs. Promisor when both made Promises

Someone must make a promise to another to create a contract. Often both people involved make promises to each other. For example, seller promises to deliver a car if buyer will pay $1000. Buyer in turn promises to pay $1000 if seller will deliver the car. Law professors often speak of the *promisor* — the one who makes a promise — and the *promisee* — the one who receives the promise. In our car case, seller and buyer are both promisor and promisee; each promise (and each made a promise) has both a promisor and a promisee. That is only a complicated, but conventional, way of saying that each made a promise to the other.

Consideration — a promise for an act: Suppose that a seller refused to deliver the car although the buyer had paid seller the money. Could the buyer sue the seller for damages? To succeed, the buyer would have to establish there was a legally enforceable contract which was breached. Buyer would have to prove that seller made the promise, and then show that the promise was of the kind the law enforces. One way to validate the promise is to show that buyer gave *consideration* for it. The $1000 buyer paid seller would be consideration to support enforcement of seller's promise to deliver the car. This is the easiest case. Buyer paid the money, and this was the price for the promise. Contracts scholars call this a "half-completed

---

[100] Other validation devices include the sealed instrument, particular types of promises in writing made enforceable by statutes, and certain kinds of reliance.

[101] John Murray, Contracts 139 (2d ed. 1974).

exchange," and many see it as the paradigmatic case for enforcement of a promise. Not only has buyer failed to get what he expected, but seller has his money.

Consideration — a promise for a promise: Suppose buyer had never paid the $1000 as promised. However, buyer was ready, willing, and able to do so when seller refused to deliver the car. There would still be consideration for seller's promise. Buyer's promise to pay would serve as consideration for seller's promise to deliver. *Consideration can be either an action or a promise to act.* We wrote the last sentence as we did to keep it easy to read. However, instead of promising to act, I can also promise not to act when I had a legal right to do so. That, too, works as consideration. For example, you promise to pay me $5000 in exchange for my promise not to sue you. My promise not to do something is consideration for your promise to pay.

A promise is consideration, however, only if performing it would be consideration. Suppose, in exchange for your promise to pay me $1000, I promise not to smash the windows of your store. Since I have no legal right to smash your windows, my promise is not consideration for yours. Of course, this does not mean that my promise might not be valuable if I had the power to smash your windows and the police were unlikely to protect you. Consideration is not just something you want or value. It must be something I have a legal right to withhold from you if you do not pay.

Consideration — bargained for and given in exchange: Not just any act or promise will serve as consideration. This is true even if the action or the promise was or would be very valuable to the one getting it. Consideration must be *bargained for and given in exchange.* Suppose last year Bill gave his sister, June, $5000. She needed money to pay living expenses and tuition at the university. June graduated and has a good job. June owns a vintage MGB sports car in excellent condition, which Bill has always admired. June, out of gratitude for all of Bill's previous help, promises to give the car to Bill when she takes delivery of a new car she is buying. However, before June gets the new car, Bill and June have a serious fight over politics and religion, and June refuses to carry out her promise. If Bill wishes to pursue the matter, is June's promise to transfer title to the MGB supported by consideration? (Notice, again, the potential role of other-than-legal norms and sanctions in our hypothetical situation.)

The legal question may give some students trouble. Both the $5000 and the MGB are valuable. June wanted the $5000, and Bill wants the MGB. However, the $5000 given by Bill to June is *not consideration* for her promise to give him the MGB. It was not "bargained for and given in exchange." "Bargained for" does not mean "haggled over" but rather means that paying the $5000 would have to be the inducement for her promise to transfer title to the car.

Bill's kind act in the past prompted her promise, but he gave her the money as a gift with no strings attached. If at the outset of their dealings she had said, "I will transfer title to the MGB next year *if* you now pay me $5000," and he had agreed to this deal, then there would have been consideration. But as we have posed the case, while she may have felt morally bound to her brother, she did not bargain to get the needed money. Thus, her promise would lack consideration. That is, she could back out without being liable to pay her brother damages. He could not win a specific performance action even if a court might consider the MGB unique.

Consideration — transforming gifts into bargains to make them legally enforceable: Let's change the case. Suppose June wants to promise to give her MGB to Bill. However, her good friend Fred Firstyear, a law student, told her that promises to make gifts are not legally enforceable. Bill protests that it doesn't matter, but June wants to make a legally enforceable promise to hand over the car. She asks Bill to promise to give her a paperback book regularly sold for $10, in exchange for her promise to deliver the MGB. Bill said that the whole thing was silly, but he finally agreed to go through with the ceremony to please her. Now is June's promise enforceable as supported by consideration?

Some courts have said things such as: "We look for only the presence and not the adequacy of consideration." Some have refused to look behind the form of the transaction to the real transaction. However, the Restatement of Contracts follows the bargain theory of consideration. Since the promise to deliver the book in no way induced June's promise, it says there is no consideration.

[handwritten margin note: The book wasn't actually a part of consideration]

Even here, the Restatement is not always perfectly clear. It says there would be consideration if June's motives were mixed. If she acted both to get the book because she really wanted it, *and* to express her gratitude, then there would be consideration. Suppose, for example, June needed more money because she had to pay bills that had piled up while she was in school. She agrees to sell the MGB to Bill for $500, although the market value of the car is many times that amount. She would not sell the car to anyone else for $500. However, this way she can discharge her sense of obligation and get some cash too. There would be consideration for her promise, since a material part of the inducement to hand over the MGB was the $500. In sum, courts and law book writers are not clear on how much freedom people have to transform gifts into the form of bargains while still satisfying the consideration requirement.

[handwritten margin note: However can still usually have unequal bargain under restatement You'll pretty unclear]

Consideration — policing bargains for equality? A promise and the consideration for it need not be of equal value. Remember that consideration is a legal construct and not a free-floating fairness doctrine. A prominent exception to this rule concerns an exchange of unequal sums of money. A promise to pay $100 in exchange for $5 is unenforceable for want of consideration. Courts often explain by reciting that while they will not *investigate* the adequacy of consideration, they will not enforce a bargain which on its face can be nothing but an unequal exchange. Despite the form of bargain, the transaction would be a gift of $95.

[handwritten margin note: Exception to allowing unequal transactions]

How far can we take this idea? Some have said that we cannot compare personal utility. Suppose Bob agrees to exchange a book for Ann's 15-year-old Honda automobile. Anyone can buy another copy of the book for $20. The used Honda, at the time of the transaction, was worth about $1500. Nonetheless, how do we know how much the book was worth to Ann? The statements in the cases probably reflect a genuflection in the direction of the extravagant ideas of individual autonomy prevalent in the 19th century. Courts were reluctant to attempt to regulate contracts openly. Obviously, there are very few reported cases where someone has traded a $20 book for a used automobile. Thus, we have few tests of a court's willingness to follow past declarations about disinterest in the adequacy of consideration.

So long as the consideration is sufficient to make credible the idea that it was bargained for and given in exchange, courts do not ask whether one party made a good deal and the other a very bad one. Suppose the fair market value of the old Honda was $1500, but Bob agreed to buy it for $8500. There is consideration for Bob's promise to pay $8500. The solution to this problem is to teach people such as Bob to be better shoppers and bargainers. However, at some point a disparity in value suggests that we are not looking at a bargain at all. It would be far easier, for example, to argue that the disparity in values between the $20 book and the Honda showed only a sham bargain and thus no consideration than to argue there was a true exchange.

Courts have hesitated to use the consideration doctrine openly to investigate the equality of exchanges. They will, however, refuse to enforce grossly disproportionate exchanges on the ground that they were procured by fraud, are unconscionable, or were the product of duress. But each of these attacks on the contract opens questions very different from those posed by consideration. They force us to face directly many difficult issues. How much do I have to tell you when we are bargaining? To what extent may I take advantage of your difficult circumstances which I did not create? What kinds of leverage so interfere with what we want to call free choice that we should label use of such leverage duress, and refuse to enforce the promise?

Consideration — benefit or detriment? Let's change the facts again. Suppose Ann promises to transfer title to the Honda if Bob agrees to serve as the county chairperson for a Red Cross blood drive. Ann will not benefit financially, and Bob's action will aid the community rather than Ann alone. Bob's promise is consideration for Ann's. Ann, for her own reasons, has diverted Bob's activities, and this is enough. No tangible benefit need move to the promisor. Serving as chairperson is a legal detriment to Bob. He has agreed to do something he was free not to do. This is true even though Bob finds the job rewarding and satisfying, rather than personally detrimental.

Consideration — modifications of bargains and pre-existing legal obligations: One of the standard consideration problems involves the modification of ongoing bargains. Suppose Dan Architect agrees to superintend a construction project for Bruce Builder for a $10,000 fee. During the project, Dan unjustifiably takes the plans and refuses to continue supervising the work or to make the plans available to Bruce unless Bruce pays Dan an additional $2000. Bruce promises to do so since it is cheaper to buy off Dan than do anything else. Is there consideration for Bruce's promise to pay Dan an additional $2000? No, because Dan demanded an additional amount to do no more than he originally promised. Consideration serves to protect reliance on bargains and blunt the leverage people in Dan's position get when their trading partners cannot replace them easily.

But there are good reasons to modify bargains where coercion is not a major factor. Consideration can get in the way of these modifications. Suppose Angela borrowed $500 from Julia and agreed to repay the money on December 1st. On December 1st, Angela had only $400. Julia needed money then, and so she promised to discharge the debt if Angela paid her the $400. Payment of $400 would not be consideration for Julia's promise. Angela had a pre-existing duty to pay the debt in full. She promised nothing she was not already bound to give.

Notice that as a practical matter this lack of consideration for the promise seldom presents problems. Why would Julia want to sue Angela for the balance after having made the promise to take $400 in full settlement? Most non-lawyers would not know about the consideration rule and would think themselves bound to the settlement. However, suppose Julia discovered that Angela had tricked her. Angela easily could have paid the full $500 on December 1st, but she made up a sad story to cheat Julia and pay her only part of what she owed her. Or, suppose on December 2nd, Angela learned that she had just inherited $1,000,000 from her long lost uncle Harvey. Julia might think that Angela ought to share the wealth, at least to the extent of the $100 gift that Julia was forced to give her. In either of these situations, Julia might see a lawyer who could give her the good news about the consideration doctrine.

However, there must be a pre-existing legal obligation in order to trigger the rule. Suppose Angela owes Julia $500, payable on December 1st. However, Julia needs money because of unexpected obligations. She asks Angela if she could repay her on November 25th. Angela says she has only $400, but is willing to pay that then in full satisfaction of the debt. Julia promises to discharge the debt for $400. Since Angela's payment was early, she was under no pre-existing legal obligation to pay then. The payment is consideration for Julia's promise.

How far can we push this idea to beat the consideration doctrine? Suppose Angela comes to Julia on December 1st, and tells her that she has only $400. Julia agrees to release the debt for that amount. However, Fred Firstyear, the law student, accompanies Angela. He has told her about the consideration doctrine. Angela tells Julia to agree to release the debt in exchange for the payment of the $400 plus a copy of a $3.95 paperback book which Angela has brought with her. Julia laughs but goes along with Fred's structuring of the transaction. Angela did not owe Julia $400 plus a paperback book — there was no pre-existing duty to give this performance. The Restatement (Second) of Contracts § 71 would insist that the different performance be "bargained for and given in exchange." However, many courts have accepted $1.00 thrown in to make a deal legal, and some have required only a trivial modification to find consideration.

Another question that sometimes arises in applying the pre-existing duty rule concerns the question of the nature of the pre-existing duty itself. Does there have to be a real, substantial duty? Is it enough that there might be one? Suppose Stuart thinks he has a claim against the Marx Publishing Company for infringement of copyright. Marx has published a book that Stuart thinks steals his ideas. Stuart makes a demand, and Marx offers $500 in full settlement of all claims. Stuart accepts this sum and releases his claim. Suppose we brought together a group of 1,000 copyright lawyers and asked whether Stuart had a claim against Marx. Assume 200 would say he did because of their interpretation of the law, 200 would say he did because of their interpretation of the application of the law to the facts, and 600 would say Stuart had no claim at all. Marx, of course, settled to avoid having to litigate and having a claim pending against it. There is consideration for the release. One can give up a chance to litigate a claim that is doubtful because of uncertainty about the facts or the law.

Furthermore, it is enough for some courts that the one in Stuart's position honestly believed that he had a claim even if he was wrong. The Restatement (Second) of Contracts § 74 says that it is enough that Stuart "honestly believes that his claim or defense is just and may be determined valid." Notice that this would include a situation where Stuart's lawyer told him that the cases were against him but thought there was some chance that they could get the courts to overturn their old decisions and make new law.[102] Thus, in our previous examples, if Angela had any reason to think she had a defense against Julia's claim for the $500, there would be consideration for the promise to settle for $400.

We are not yet finished with qualifications to the pre-existing duty rule. Suppose Builder promises to construct an apartment building according to plans and specifications in exchange for $750,000. However, once the excavation for the foundation is underway, Builder discovers an underground stream flowing through the property. Builder must divert the stream and use a different foundation than the one specified. Owner promises to pay three-fourths of the increased costs so Builder will go ahead. At first glance, this would seem to be an example of a pre-existing duty case, and so Owner's promised additional payment would lack consideration. However, if the unforeseen event causes a great additional expense, some courts have been willing to say that this is an exception to the consideration doctrine and enforce the promise.

Some courts have, in effect, almost abandoned the pre-existing duty rule. Some have said that the party who performs the duty for an increased payment thereby gives up her right to breach and pay damages.[103] In Wisconsin, as long as a sum certain has not become due, older cases say that the consideration from the original promise "relates forward" to support a second promise modifying the original obligation.[104]

The pre-existing duty rule is shot through with exceptions and qualifications. It is difficult to state when it will and will not apply. Section 2-209 of the Uniform Commercial Code opens with the bold statement: "An agreement modifying a contract within this Article needs no consideration to be binding." The comments say that the parties must modify their contract in "good faith." The comments invite courts to deal with extortion of modifications by using the good-faith requirement

---

[102] There is an even more extreme limitation of the pre-existing legal obligation rule. Suppose John is a skilled lawyer. He has looked into all the events surrounding his father's conveyance of property in 1939, and concluded that he has no claim and no way to upset the transaction. Mark is buying the property from its present owner who purchased it from the person John's father sold it to. Mark is very cautious. He offers John $100 if he will execute a "quitclaim deed" conveying any rights he has to the land to Mark. John agrees. Execution of the quitclaim deed is consideration for the promised $100 although John believes that he has no valid claim and a panel of expert lawyers would say that he had none. The purchaser gains documentary evidence that his title is clear, and this is enough for most courts.

[103] This offends legal technicians. One does not have a "right" to breach but only a "power" to do so. But in a tight spot the logic of the consideration doctrine often bends to the need to enforce a promise modifying a deal.

[104] Here we have a pure legal fiction. Such legal reasoning is a little like reshuffling the deck when playing solitaire and the cards do not come out the right way. Nonetheless, this is not the only example of a legal fiction being employed to make things come out the right way. *See* Lon L. Fuller, Legal Fictions (Stanford University Press 1967).

rather than the common-law pre-existing duty rule. Of course, this leaves it to the courts to work out which are good modifications and which are bad ones. Few standards exist to tell us how hard one may twist the arm of the other before crossing the line into the zone of bad faith. The Restatement (Second) of Contracts § 89 says that a promise modifying a contract is binding without consideration:

Restatement on modification

(a) if the modification is fair and equitable in view of circumstances not anticipated by the parties when the contract was made; or

(b) to the extent provided by statute; or

(c) to the extent that justice requires enforcement in view of material change of position in reliance on the promise.

Once again we have qualitative standards courts must work out in the future on a case-by-case basis. We shall have to see how far courts abandon older views and embrace the Restatement to deal with modifications.

Consideration — illusory and alternative promises: Illusory and alternative promises pose still further difficulties for the consideration doctrine. Suppose Joe makes raspberry, strawberry, and grape jam and sells it at a local farmers' market every weekend. He puts the jam into used jam/jelly containers and seals them with wax on top. He tells a local boys' club that he will pay five cents for every jar with a top they bring him. The 11-year-old president of the club says "That's great. We know where there are a lot of them. We'll do it." Shortly afterward, Joe finds a better source of used jars and does not need any more. He tells the president of the boys' club that the deal is off.

You are the parent of the disappointed 11-year-old president, and you are also a lawyer. Your son asks whether Joe made a legally binding contract with the club to buy jars from it. The answer would depend on a court's interpretation of what your son said. If it interpreted his remarks as "We have access to a supply of jars, and we promise to deliver them to you," there would be consideration. Your son would have promised to deliver the jars. Suppose, on the other hand, his words conveyed the idea "We think we can find jars, and if we still feel like gathering them, we will bring them to you." Then your son has made "an illusory promise" which would not be consideration for Joe's promise to buy. This is a statement in the form of a promise that does not limit the options open to your son. In effect, he said "I'll perform, if I feel like it." Whether a promise is illusory often turns on how we translate it. If your son committed the club to deliver jars, or not to deliver them to anyone else, then his promise would not be illusory but would limit his freedom. In that event, it would be good consideration for Joe's promise.

Illusionary promises are not consideration

It is often difficult to spot illusory promises because they are seldom as blatant as "I'll perform if I feel like it." Sometimes, for example, A may hire B to act as agent for three years. However, buried in the mass of clauses in their printed form contract is one that provides that either A or B can end the agreement at any time. As you can see, this gives either party the legal right to perform or not to perform the agency agreement. Without more, this would be an illusory promise.

Suppose you represented A, and it was important that the contract be legally binding. Many lawyers provide some period of notice before a party can end the agreement. If the contract requires notice, then both parties are bound at least until the period expires. This would be enough to make the promise real and not illusory. A court might imply such an obligation to give reasonable notice before exercising a right to cancel at will. If it were willing to do this, the implied promise would salvage the deal. Parties who overlook the illusory promise trap, however, cannot always rely on courts to bail them out.[105]

Promises enforceable without consideration: It would be nice if we could stop here, but we cannot. You must at least cast your eye over the cases that the Restatement of Contracts candidly refers to as promises enforceable *without* consideration. Some are cases where courts in the past strained to find consideration and seemed to stretch even this malleable doctrine beyond its limits. Others are pure "exceptions," fashioned to patch up unsatisfactory results yielded by a strict application of the consideration notion.

Promises to repay despite defenses to the debt: Suppose Bob owes Jane $1000, and he did not repay the money when payment was due. Then Bob discovers he has one of several defenses to the debt:

(1) He was a minor when he contracted the debt, it was not for "necessaries," and he disaffirms the debt within a reasonable time after he reaches the age of majority;

(2) The statute of limitations runs before Jane files an action to collect the debt.

Despite having one of these defenses, Bob promises Jane that she will be repaid. Jane gives no new consideration for the promise. Nonetheless, common-law courts would enforce it. They made a great deal of noise trying to square this position with orthodox notions of consideration, but all attempts seemed to be fudging the rules. Some courts used the common law's all-purpose wild card — "waiver." Others talked about "moral consideration" to support the second promise. This suggests the reason for the result. These defenses were seen as technical evasions of a real obligation to repay debts. In the society from which judges came, it was a true moral obligation.

Waiver: As we suggested, waiver is one of the wild cards in the common law. The term means that a person may lose a right when she voluntarily gives it up. Of course, she might be estopped if she misled the other party into relying on her statements such that allowing her to assert the right would be unjust. However, a waiver does not require proof of reliance. Can one waive a right without receiving consideration for giving it up? This has been the subject of some dispute. Professor Williston insisted that, with a few exceptions, consideration was necessary. However, the common-law cases did not support his position.

The Restatement (Second) of Contracts § 84 deals with promises to perform despite the nonoccurrence of a condition — the typical situation where we find waivers. For example, Bob promises to pay, but only if A, B, and C happen. A and B happen, but C does not. Bob then promises to pay anyway. The Restatement says that Bob's promise is enforceable unless the condition is material. While there are cases supporting the Restatement position, not all the decisions impose this limitation. Some just say or assume that waivers do not require consideration.

---

[105] *Compare* UCC § 2-309(3).

There is a great deal more to this problem than we can present here. For now, it is enough to recognize that this is a complex and inconsistent body of law. Your legal research in this area is likely to produce more plausible arguments than real answers.

Consideration and anti-consideration — Restatement § 90: The major exception to the consideration doctrine offered by the Restatement (Second) of Contracts is § 90. As you will learn from the cases that follow this note, courts can enforce promises without consideration on the basis of reliance on a promise that the promisor should have *expected* to induce reliance, to the extent required to prevent injustice. While the Restatement's Comments and Illustrations are suggestive, the boundaries of this idea remain open. A court could use it to cancel a great deal of the impact of consideration doctrine. The alternative reliance-on-a-promise doctrine is meant to give courts a great deal of discretion, and thus its application in a particular case is usually uncertain. Courts often talk about § 90 before applying standard consideration and offer-and-acceptance doctrine. While parties who assert reliance on a promise often lose, many states have accepted the doctrine, and courts could always develop it much more.

Consideration — conclusions: This brief essay is only a quick introduction to the complexities of consideration. The rules in any particular state would require research and difficult analysis. In many states, with regard to one or more aspects of the doctrine, there is enough contradiction that we cannot state any rule with confidence. There are good treatments of the doctrine in treatises by Corbin, Williston, Farnsworth, Calamari and Perillo, and Murray. The important thing is to recognize when you face a consideration problem so you will see that you need to research it.

In order to test your understanding of the story about consideration that you have just read, try your hand at analyzing the following problem. It comes from *United States v. Meadors*,[106] a 1985 decision that discusses *Hamer v. Sidway* at length.

Jay Judd and his wife, Harold Ducote and his wife, and Melton E. Meadors owned a lumber company. They applied for a loan from the Small Business Administration. It required a personal guarantee; it was not enough that the lumber company corporation would be liable to repay the money. SBA knew only of the five people involved in the application. SBA prepared a guarantee form that had only five lines for signatures. Before the group of borrowers executed the SBA form, Melton E. Meadors married Betty Jo. As Melton's wife, the loan to the lumber company could benefit Betty Jo in several ways. There is no indication that anyone at the SBA knew of this marriage. The five people originally involved and Betty Jo went to the closing of the loan. Each husband and wife signed the form, including Betty Jo. That is, there were six signatures on the guarantee. The loan was not repaid, and the SBA sued all who had signed, including Betty Jo Meadors. How would Betty Jo's lawyer argue that she should not be bound to her written promise to be liable if the lumber company did not repay the loan?

---

[106] 753 F.2d 590 (7th Cir. 1985).

4. The Conditional Gift Revisited

The next case revisits, for the third time, the problem of the conditional gift, but also provides a transition to our investigation of a doctrine in which post-promise reliance serves to justify enforcing a promise.

KIRKSEY v. KIRKSEY
Alabama Supreme Court
8 Ala. 131 (1845)

[handwritten: Conditional gift case / Post Promise reliance as justification for enforment.]

Assumpsit by the defendant, against the plaintiff in error. The question is presented in this court, upon a case agreed, which shows the following facts:

The plaintiff was the wife of defendant's brother, but had for some time been a widow, and had several children. In 1840, the plaintiff resided on public land, under a contract of lease, she had held over, and was comfortably settled, and would have attempted to secure the land she lived on. The defendant resided in Talladega county, some sixty or seventy miles off. On the 10th October, 1840, he wrote to her the following letter:

> Dear sister Antillico — Much to my mortification, I heard, that brother Henry was dead, and one of his children. I know that your situation is one of grief and difficulty. You had a bad chance before, but a great deal worse now. I should like to come and see you, but cannot with convenience at present. . . . I do not know whether you have a preference on the place you live on or not. If you had, I would advise you to obtain your preference, and sell the land and quit the country, as I understand it is very unhealthy, and I know society is very bad. If you will come down and see me, I will let you have a place to raise your family, and I have more open land than I can tend; and on account of your situation, and that of your family, I feel like I want you and the children to do well.

[handwritten: Told her to sell house, move w/ him → she does]

Within a month or two after the receipt of this letter, the plaintiff abandoned her possession, without disposing of it, and removed with her family to the residence of the defendant, who put her in comfortable houses and gave her land to cultivate for two years, at the end of which time he notified her to remove, and put her in a house not comfortable, in the woods, which he afterwards required her to leave.

[handwritten: After two yrs. moves her to worse house → then all togeth kicks out]

A verdict being found for the plaintiff, for two hundred dollars, the above facts were agreed, and if they will sustain the action, the judgment is to be affirmed, otherwise it is to be reversed.

ORMOND, J. The inclination of my mind, is, that the loss and inconvenience, which the plaintiff sustained in breaking up and moving to the defendant's, a distance of sixty miles, is a sufficient consideration to support the promise, to furnish her with a house, and land to cultivate, until she could raise her family. My brothers, however, think that the promise on the part of the defendant was a mere gratuity, and that an action will not lie for its breach.

[handwritten: → say its gratuity not w/ consideration]

The judgment of the Court below must therefore be reversed, pursuant to the agreement of the parties.

NOTES AND QUESTIONS

1. ***Distinctions:*** Does this case differ significantly from *Hamer v. Sidway*? In both, a relative with wealth wants to influence the behavior of a family member "for his (or her) own good." In both, the one receiving the promise had expectations and relied. Shouldn't courts decide the cases the same way?

2. ***The background of the case:*** Recent research by Professors William Casto and Val Ricks suggests that Isaac Kirksey, the defendant, wanted Antillico to move to public land to hold his place so that he could buy the land later from the U.S. government at a very low price.[107] If Isaac didn't move someone there, another squatter might occupy this land and gain the preference. Congress changed the law so that Isaac could not buy it at a discount because he already owned more than 320 acres of such land. However, this law also would have allowed Antillico to buy the land at a great discount. "Only by evicting . . . [Antillico] could Isaac hope to retain the land." Had the court discussed Isaac's plan, assuming that Professors Casto and Ricks are right about Isaac's motives, would it have found consideration? Casto and Ricks's research indicates that Isaac was a slave owner who grew cotton, and he did not need to look to Antillico and her children to provide labor. Casto and Ricks argue that Isaac wanted Antillico to move to land near his home in order to improve his claim to land previously owned by the Creek Nation that was ceded to the federal government in 1832. Congress made this land available to those occupying it.

3. ***Modern approaches:*** Is it likely, today, that courts would decide *Kirksey v. Kirksey* the same way for the same reasons? Could Sister Antillico rely on the estoppel doctrine enunciated in the next case?

RICKETTS v. SCOTHORN
Nebraska Supreme Court
57 Neb. 51, 77 N.W. 365 (1898)

SULLIVAN, J.

In the district court of Lancaster County the plaintiff Katie Scothorn recovered judgment against the defendant Andrew D. Ricketts, as executor of the last will and testament of John C. Ricketts, deceased. The action was based upon a promissory note, of which the following is a copy:

> May the first, 1891. I promise to pay to Katie Scothorn on demand, $2,000, to be at 6 per cent per annum.
>
> J.C. Ricketts.

In the petition the plaintiff alleges that the consideration for the execution of the note was that she should surrender her employment as bookkeeper for Mayer Bros. and cease to work for a living. She also alleges that the note was given to induce her to abandon her occupation, and that, relying on it, and on the annual interest, as a

[107] *See* William R. Casto & Val D. Ricks, *"Dear Sister Antillico . . . ": The Story of* Kirksey v. Kirksey, 94 GEO. L.J. 321 (2006).

means of support, she gave up the employment in which she was then engaged. These allegations of the petition are denied by the executor. The material facts are undisputed. They are as follows: John C. Ricketts, the maker of the note, was the grandfather of the plaintiff. Early in May, — presumably on the [date the note bears], — he called on her at the store where she was working. What transpired between them is thus described by Mr. Flodene, one of the plaintiff's witnesses:

> A. Well the old gentleman came in there one morning about 9 o'clock, — probably a little before or a little after, but early in the morning, — and he unbuttoned his vest and took out a piece of paper in the shape of a note; that is the way it looked to me; and he says to Miss Scothorn, "I have fixed out something that you have not got to work any more." He says, "None of my grandchildren work and you don't have to."

> Q. Where was she?

> A. She took the piece of paper and kissed him; and kissed the old gentleman and commenced to cry.

It seems Miss Scothorn immediately notified her employer of her intention to quit work and that she did soon after abandon her occupation. The mother of the plaintiff was a witness and testified that she had a conversation with her father, Mr. Ricketts, shortly after the note was executed in which he informed her that he had given the note to the plaintiff to enable her to quit work; that none of his grandchildren worked and he did not think she ought to. For something more than a year the plaintiff was without an occupation; but in September, 1892, with the consent of her grandfather, and by his assistance, she secured a position as bookkeeper with Messrs. Funke & Ogden. On June 8, 1894, Mr. Ricketts died. He had paid one year's interest on the note, and a short time before his death expressed regret that he had not been able to pay the balance. In the summer or fall of 1892 he stated to his daughter, Mrs. Scothorn, that if he could sell his farm in Ohio he would pay the note out of the proceeds. He at no time repudiated the obligation. We quite agree with counsel for the defendant that upon this evidence there was nothing to submit to the jury, and that a verdict should have been directed peremptorily for one of the parties. The testimony of Flodene and Mrs. Scothorn, taken together, conclusively establishes the fact that the note was not given in consideration of the plaintiff pursuing, or agreeing to pursue, any particular line of conduct. There was no promise on the part of the plaintiff to do or refrain from doing anything. Her right to the money promised in the note was not made to depend upon an abandonment of her employment with Mayer Bros. and future abstention from like service. Mr. Ricketts made no condition, requirement, or request. He exacted no *quid pro quo.* He gave the note as a gratuity and looked for nothing in return. So far as the evidence discloses, it was his purpose to place the plaintiff in a position of independence where she could work or remain idle as she might choose. The abandonment by Miss Scothorn of her position as bookkeeper was altogether voluntary. It was not an act done in fulfillment of any contract obligation assumed when she accepted the note. The instrument in suit being given without any valuable consideration, was nothing more than a promise to make a gift in the future of the sum of money therein named. Ordinarily, such promises are not enforceable even when put in the form of a promissory note. But it has often been held that an action on a note given to a church, college, or other like institution, upon the faith of which money has been expended or obligations incurred, could not be successfully defended on the ground of a want of consideration.

In this class of cases the note in suit is nearly always spoken of as a gift or donation, but the decision is generally put on the ground that the expenditure of money or assumption of liability by the donee, on the faith of the promise, constitutes a valuable and sufficient consideration. It seems to us that the true reason is the preclusion of the defendant, under the doctrine of estoppel, to deny the consideration. Such seems to be the view of the matter taken by the Supreme Court of Iowa in the case of *Simpson Centenary College v. Tuttle*, 71 Ia. 596, where ROTHROCK, J., speaking for the court, said: "Where a note, however, is based on a promise to give for the support of the objects referred to, it may still be open to this defense [want of consideration], unless it shall appear that the donee has, prior to any revocation, entered into engagements or made expenditures based on such promise, so that he must suffer loss or injury if the note is not paid. This is based on the equitable principle that, after allowing the donee to incur obligations on the faith that the note would be paid, the donor would be estopped from pleading want of consideration."

Under the circumstances of this case is there an equitable estoppel which ought to preclude the defendant from alleging that the note in controversy is lacking in one of the essential elements of a valid contract? We think there is. An estoppel *in pais* is defined to be "a right arising from acts, admissions, or conduct which have induced a change of position in accordance with the real or apparent intention of the party against whom they are alleged." Mr. Pomeroy has formulated the following definition: "Equitable estoppel is the effect of the voluntary conduct of a party whereby he is absolutely precluded, both at law and in equity, from asserting rights which might perhaps have otherwise existed, either of property, or contract, or of remedy, as against another person who in good faith relied upon such conduct, and has been led thereby to change his position for the worse, and who on his part acquires some corresponding right either of property, of contract, or of remedy." 2 POMEROY, EQUITY JURISPRUDENCE 804.

According to the undisputed proof, as shown by the record before us, the plaintiff was a working girl, holding a position in which she earned a salary of $10 per week. Her grandfather, desiring to put her in a position of independence, gave her the note, accompanying it with the remark that his other grandchildren did not work, and that she would not be obliged to work any longer. In effect he suggested that she might abandon her employment and rely in the future upon the bounty which he promised. He, doubtless, desired that she should give up her occupation, but whether he did or not, it is entirely certain that he contemplated such action on her part as a reasonable and probable consequence of his gift. Having intentionally influenced the plaintiff to alter her position for the worse on the faith of the note being paid when due, it would be grossly inequitable to permit the maker, or his executor, to resist payment on the ground that the promise was given without consideration. The petition charges the elements of an equitable estoppel, and the evidence conclusively establishes them. If errors intervened at the trial they could not have been prejudicial. A verdict for the defendant would be unwarranted. The judgment is right and is *Affirmed*.

He could know she may quit when made the promise and she reasonably relied → therefor no need for consideration in this case

NOTES AND QUESTIONS

1. ***Restatement § 90:*** Decisions such as the *Ricketts* case were summarized in § 90 of the Restatement of Contracts. It was perhaps the most influential single section of the 1932 effort. In 1981, the Restatement (Second) of Contracts was published. The text of § 90 was modified to address remedies, though it is questionable whether the open-ended language provides much guidance. The provision now states (with the new language italicized):

§ 90. Promise Reasonably Inducing Action or Forbearance

(1) A promise which the promisor should reasonably expect to induce action or forbearance on the part of the promisee *or a third person* and which does induce such action or forbearance is binding if injustice can be avoided only by enforcement of the promise. *The remedy granted for breach may be limited as justice requires.*[108]

2. ***Construction of § 90:*** Is serious reliance enough, or must we take the clause about "avoiding injustice" seriously? If we must apply all of the terms of the section, what does this last clause mean?[109]

(a) Suppose that before his death, John C. Ricketts discovered that Katie had left her career as a bookkeeper for Mayer Bros. and become a mass murderer or a prostitute. Could John or his executor defend against enforcement of the promise in either or both of these cases? Suppose she had become an advocate of women's suffrage or gone to law school with the plan of becoming a lawyer? Assume that her grandfather thought these were outrageous things for a woman to do.

(b) Based on the language of § 90 and the facts reported in the opinion, can you make a good argument that courts need not enforce the promise John C. Ricketts made to Katie Scothorn? That is, is *Ricketts v. Scothorn* an example of a Restatement § 90 case? What was the nature of Katie's reliance?

(c) In *Kirksey v. Kirksey*, why did the brother-in-law invite his brother's widow to live in a house on his land, give her a comfortable house, then give her a house in the woods, and finally notify her to remove? Suppose "Dear Sister Antillico" was an impossible person to live near. She complained constantly and she could not control her children. Can injustice then be avoided only by forcing the brother-in-law to pay damages based on his promise to let Antillico "have a place to raise" her family, at least until her children are grown?

Suppose instead that the brother-in-law may have been interested in Antillico sexually. She resisted his advances or he tired of her, and then he tried to get rid of her. Wouldn't such a story be relevant to avoiding injustice? However, suppose

---

[108] The original RESTATEMENT OF CONTRACTS was published in 1932. Samuel Williston, of Harvard Law School, was the Reporter, and Arthur Corbin, of Yale Law School, was the Special Adviser. The RESTATEMENT (SECOND) OF CONTRACTS was published in 1981.

[109] Proceedings of 1979 Annual Meeting, 56 A.L.I. PROC. 301, 349 (1979) (in which Professor E. Allan Farnsworth, Reporter of the RESTATEMENT (SECOND) OF CONTRACTS for the second half of the project, said of references to avoiding injustice: "It is restatementese to use this phrase when we are saying honestly that this is an instance in which we feel the court must have some discretion, and then to go on, to the extent you can in black letter, and comment to confine the discretion.")

both stories were true — she proved to be impossible to live with or be near, *and* he had tried to exploit her sexually. What now should a judge do with the case? Recall Chafee's categories in our introduction. Do you get a whiff of the smell of a dismal swamp?

(d) Suppose the grandfather or the brother-in-law tried to perform their promises but then faced a financial crisis. Each had to pay for an exceedingly expensive operation to save the lives of young children who were related to Katie and Antillico. As a result, there was no money or property left to carry out the promise. Under any or all of the doctrines we have considered which bear on the bait problem, should a court consider the merits of those who would get the money or property if the promise were not enforced? Could it do this legitimately under any of the doctrines other than Restatement of Contracts § 90?

Could a court make any of the determinations suggested in this note in a way you think proper? If anything, aren't these questions more difficult to answer than those raised in *Balfour v. Balfour* or *Miller v. Miller*? Are the interests of William E. Story 2d, Katie Scothorn, and Antillico Kirksey important enough to society to warrant spending very much judicial time in trying to cope with such issues?

3. *Of Restatements and political compromises:* The late Professor Grant Gilmore taught at the law schools at the Universities of Chicago, Yale, and Vermont. He was the author of important books on security interests in personal property, admiralty, and contracts, as well as many significant articles. His book, THE DEATH OF CONTRACT, published in 1974, became widely discussed by contracts scholars.

Gilmore wrote in THE DEATH OF CONTRACT that § 90 and the consideration requirement of the first Restatement of Contracts were inconsistent. In order to enforce a promise, there had to be consideration — something "bargained for and given in exchange." But a court might enforce a promise when there had been significant foreseeable reliance "if injustice can be avoided only by enforcement of the promise." He said: "We have become accustomed to the idea, without in the least understanding it, that the universe includes both matter and anti-matter. Perhaps what we have here is Restatement and anti-Restatement or Contract and anti-Contract."[110] Gilmore also asserted: "The one thing that is clear is that these two contradictory propositions cannot live comfortably together: in the end one must swallow the other up."[111]

He noted that § 90 offered four illustrations. "An attentive study of the four illustrations will lead any analyst to the despairing conclusion, which is of course reinforced by the mysterious text of § 90 itself, that no one had any idea what the damn thing meant."[112]

Are the sections truly contradictory? Indeed, why must one section "swallow the other up?" Is it a fair criticism that the precise boundaries of § 90 were unclear and the text of the Restatement called for a case-by-case development of the common law in the future?

---

[110] GRANT GILMORE, THE DEATH OF CONTRACT 61 (Ohio State University Press, 1974).

[111] *Id.*

[112] *Id.* at 64–65.

4. *The impact of § 90:* The language of Restatement § 90 suggests the possible breadth of its application. The provocative question is whether or not courts have taken the opportunity that this language affords. In other words, how important is § 90, really? We can get a very rough idea of the impact of § 90 if we look at reported cases that cite it. The American Law Institute has collected references in *The Restatement in the Courts* until 1976, and since then in pocket parts to the Restatement of Contracts. Of course, reported cases do not necessarily reflect the impact of any rule of law. There may be many trial court decisions that are influenced by a doctrine, but which never prompt written opinions and never get appealed. Lawyers may give advice or negotiate based on their view of what a court would or might do if the case were ever litigated and appealed. Rules may influence a folkview of what is right and wrong so that people accept a situation and do not complain. Nonetheless, reported cases are fairly easy to count, and they are the best indication we have of the impact of § 90.

From 1932 to 1978, there were about 350 cases that cited Restatement of Contracts § 90 reported in the ALI publications.[113] Only six of these cases involve bait offered by one family member to another. By far, most of the cases involve commercial situations concerning long-term continuing relationships. Jay M. Feinman surveyed cases involving Restatement of Contracts § 90 by looking at the cases reported from 1967 to 1983 in the West Digest system. He states: "Although my survey of the recent case law revealed a few . . . family promises, promissory estoppel cases now arise chiefly in commercial contracts."[114] Professors Daniel A. Farber and John H. Matheson, in another widely cited article, report: "Despite its tentative origins and its initial restriction to donative promises, promissory estoppel is regularly applied to the gamut of commercial contexts."[115]

But by the 1990s some scholars were challenging the significance of promissory estoppel. In 1997 Professor Sidney DeLong argued that § 90's story was about "a revolution that wasn't."[116] In 1998, Professor Robert Hillman joined in challenging the idea of the importance of § 90, relying on a study of all the decided promissory estoppel cases for a two-year period, beginning in July 1994.[117] He concluded that the win rate for those relying on the promissory estoppel theory was low. Although we can hardly do justice to his article in a sentence or two, he begins his conclusion by asserting:

---

[113] Professors Daniel A. Farber and John H. Matheson surveyed the § 90 cases decided from 1975 to 1985, as reported in Shepard's Citations, Restatement of the Law (1985). They found 222 cases citing § 90. They also ran a LEXIS search of cases decided from January 1, 1980, to 1985 that used the term "promissory estoppel." This produced 540 cases, but many only mentioned the doctrine without applying it. In short, case-counting is not as easy as it might seem, even aided by databases such as LEXIS. Farber and Matheson do not report the number of family promise cases because their article is about the use of the doctrine in commercial litigation. *See* Farber & Matheson, *Beyond Promissory Estoppel: Contract Law and the "Invisible Handshake,"* 52 U. Chi. L. Rev. 903 (1985).

[114] Jay M. Feinman, *Promissory Estoppel and Judicial Method,* 97 Harv. L. Rev. 678, 691 n.59 (1984).

[115] Farber & Matheson, *supra* note 113, at 907.

[116] Sidney DeLong, *The New Requirement of Enforcement Reliance in Commercial Promissory Estoppel: Section 90 as Catch-22,* 1997 Wis. L. Rev. 873.

[117] Robert A. Hillman, *Questioning the "New Consensus" on Promissory Estoppel: An Empirical and Theoretical Study,* 98 Colum. L. Rev. 580 (1998).

Analysts of promissory estoppel have predicted that the theory would "swallow up" bargain theory. Even discounting such hyperbole, the amount of ink that has been spilled by scholars analyzing promissory estoppel certainly suggests the importance, if not dominance, of the theory. Measured in terms of win rates in the courts, however, promissory estoppel may no longer be, if it ever was, a significant theory of recovery.

Professor Juliet Kostritsky, however, has offered a rebuttal of Hillman's gloomy assessment with a study of her own.[118] She studied five years of cases and concluded that if one took qualitative factors into account (which involved assessing the viability of the underlying claim), Hillman's prognosis was too pessimistic. Another scholar, Marco Jimenez, updated Kostritsky's work and agrees that promissory estoppel remains a viable claim.[119] Obviously, the jury is still out on the question of the current significance of Restatement § 90, and various answers have been given in different states. We will consider promissory estoppel in commercial contexts later in the course.

5. *Expectation or reliance remedies?* In *Hamer v. Sidway*, and *Ricketts v. Scothorn*, the courts found that family promises created liability. In both cases courts gave remedies designed to protect the expectation interest. Have the courts been too generous? Why should a family member who has relied on a nonbusiness promise recover more than compensation for his reliance?

Much of the debate about reliance remedies in family cases was prompted by the two Restatements of Contracts. The first Restatement of Contracts seemed not to recognize the possibility of reliance remedies. The Restatement (Second) of Contracts, however, does recognize this possibility. An exchange between Samuel Williston and Mr. Coudert in the course of the American Law Institute's discussion of § 90 of the first Restatement of Contracts has achieved a certain notoriety in the world of contracts teachers. Williston offered an example. An uncle promised Johnny, his nephew, $1,000 so that he could buy a car. Johnny then contracted with an auto dealer to buy a car for $1,000. Several members of the ALI, in good law teacher fashion, changed the facts to test the principle. They asked for Williston's opinion about the result under § 90 if the nephew bought a car for only $500. Williston responded, "If Johnny had done what he was expected to do, or is acting within the limits of his uncle's expectation, I think the uncle would be liable for $1000; but not otherwise." He explained, "Either the promise is binding or it is not. If the promise is binding, it has to be enforced as it is made."

Fuller and Perdue[120] argue that as a matter of policy Williston is wrong. They say that the reasons that courts measure damages for breach of contract by the expectation interest do not apply when promises are enforced only because people have relied on them.

---

[118] Juliet Kostritsky, *The Rise and Fall of Promissory Estoppel or is Promissory Estoppel Really as Unsuccessful as Scholars Say It Is: A New Look at the Data*, 37 WAKE FOREST L. REV. 531 (2002).

[119] Marco J. Jimenez, *The Many Faces of Promissory Estoppel: An Empirical Analysis Under the Restatement (Second) of Contracts*, 57 UCLA L. REV. 669 (2010).

[120] Lon L. Fuller & William R. Perdue Jr., *The Reliance Interest in Contracts Damages*, 46 YALE L.J. 52, 64–65 (1936).

The suggestion that the expectation interest is adopted as a kind of surrogate for the reliance interest because of the difficulty of proving reliance can scarcely be applicable to a situation where we actually insist on proof of reliance, and indeed, reliance of a "definite and substantial character." The notion that the expectancy is granted as compensation for foregoing the opportunity to enter other similar contracts is also without application in this situation, if for no other reason than because no contract is here "entered" at all. Finally the policy in favor of facilitating reliance can scarcely be extended to all promises indiscriminately. Any such policy must presuppose that reliance in the particular situation will normally have some general utility. Where we are dealing with "exchanges" or "bargains" it is easy to discern this utility since such transactions form the very mechanism by which production is organized in a capitalistic society. There seems no basis for assuming any such general utility in the promises coming under § 90, since they are restricted only by a negative definition — they are not bargains.

The Restatement (Second) of Contracts § 90 largely accepts Fuller and Perdue and rejects Williston on the remedy appropriate when promises are enforced on the basis of reliance. As you will recall, the major change in the revised version is the addition of a sentence — "The remedy granted for breach may be limited as justice requires." The Comment says:

> A promise binding under this section is a contract, and full-scale enforcement by normal remedies is often appropriate. But the same factors which bear on whether any relief should be granted also bear on the character and extent of the remedy. In particular, relief may sometimes be limited to restitution or to damages or specific relief measured by the extent of the promisee's reliance rather than by the terms of the promise.

Suppose courts analyzed both *Hamer v. Sidway* and *Ricketts v. Scothorn* as Restatement § 90 cases. Assume that a court concluded that the reliance in each case was of the kind justifying some remedy. How much would the nephew and granddaughter recover? Should a court attempt to value the reliance loss involved in refraining from smoking, drinking, and gambling for several years and limit recovery to that amount? Should a court consider what, if anything, the grand-daughter lost by relying on her grandfather's promise?

Professor Melvin Eisenberg argues: "[T]he issue of consideration is often merely a screen for complex issues of damages."[121] He continues: "[C]ontracts rules must reflect considerations of administrability, particularly information costs, as well as considerations of substance. An otherwise preferable rule may therefore be rejected if its application turns on facts that cannot be readily, reliably, and suitably determined in the relevant forum." He illustrates his argument by considering *Kirksey v. Kirksey*:

> It seems clear enough in theory that a relying promisee should recover the value of any reasonably foreseeable cost he incurs in reliance, financial or not. The problem in these cases is that in practice the dollar value of

---

[121] Melvin A. Eisenberg, *Donative Promises*, 47 U. Chi. L. Rev. 1 (1979). Reprinted with permission.

nonfinancial costs is very difficult to measure. Accordingly, it might be urged either that the fact-finder should measure nonfinancial costs directly, or that he should refuse to compensate these costs at all. Direct measurement, however, would often be difficult or impossible to accomplish in an objective manner, while a refusal to compensate nonfinancial costs would often be unduly hard on the promisee. For example, in *Kirksey v. Kirksey*, Antillico, a widow, had uprooted herself and her children from the land on which they were settled, and moved to the farm of her brother-in-law Kirksey, in reliance on Kirksey's promise to let her "have a place to raise [her] family" on the farm. Several years later Kirksey forced her to leave. Antillico's financial costs were probably very small. Her nonfinancial costs, however, were probably substantial, consisting not only of the emotional and physical travail of the journey to Kirksey's farm, but also the loss of an opportunity to remain in a settled existence rather than twice resettling. It would be hard not to let her recover for these costs, yet it would be very difficult to measure those costs directly in an objective manner. One solution would be to throw the issue to the fact-finder for intuitive measurement, as in personal injury cases. In those cases, however, the transaction typically is not consensual, and, partly for that reason, no objective financial measure is at hand. In contrast, where a donative promise has been relied upon, it is the promise that causes the resulting cost, and the promise can frequently provide an objective financial measure of the cost. For example, in *Kirksey v. Kirksey*, we know that the promise was sufficient to induce Antillico to relocate; we do not know that a lesser promise would have been sufficient. Rather than attempt to measure Antillico's costs intuitively, it seems preferable to measure them objectively, although indirectly, by using her financial expectation (the rental value of a place on Kirksey's farm) as a surrogate measure of her costs.

It might be objected against this technique that the promisee's financial expectation will normally exceed his anticipated costs — otherwise, he would not have changed his position. Financial expectation will not necessarily exceed *actual* costs, however, since in deciding to change his position, the promisee will probably not anticipate the costs of a breach. For example, in deciding to move to Kirksey's farm, Antillico must have anticipated the financial and emotional costs of resettling young children once. But she probably did not anticipate the costs of resettling with young children twice, since had Kirksey kept his promise, she could have lived at his farm until her children had grown up (or for life, depending on how Kirksey's promise is interpreted). . . .

Broadly speaking, expectation should be employed as a surrogate for measuring the costs of reliance only if those costs appear significant, difficult to quantify, and closely related to the full extent of the promise. An important index for determining whether this test has been met is whether the promisee was induced to make a substantial change in his life that is not easily reversible. Under this index, an expectation measure would be appropriate in *Kirksey v. Kirksey*.

New Topic

5.　The Statute of Frauds and Family "Bait" Promises

Statute of Frauds begins

Once again we turn to the family bait problem to illustrate another issue. Perhaps the best example of a formal legal requirement is the rule that certain contracts must be in writing to be enforceable.[122] Such a requirement runs counter to the way people often act. People make oral promises and rely on them. This often happens in situations where the parties are supposed to trust one another. Asking for a written contract might seem an attack on the integrity of the other party. In family transactions, particularly, people feel they should trust one another. It might seem greedy to press a relative to make a will, a conveyance, or a written detailed contract. Legislators and judges can insist on written documents to limit false claims and ease the burdens on courts. On the other hand, they can offer aid to those who have been trusting. Sometimes it looks as if they are trying to do both at once.

Def of SoF

Lawyers speak of requirements that certain contracts be in writing as "Statute of Frauds requirements." The English "Act for the Prevention of Frauds and Perjuries" was enacted in 1677. It contained 25 sections designed to control perjury by requiring written evidence of conveyances, wills, trusts, and contracts. Many of the patterns found in this early statute are still with us.

The 1677 Act provided that a person may not sue for breach of several categories of contracts "unless the agreement upon which such action shall be brought, or some memorandum or note thereof, shall be in writing, and signed by the party to be charged therewith."[123] You should notice several things. The complete contract itself does not have to be in writing. It is enough that there is a memorandum or note. One might write a letter describing an earlier oral agreement. This probably would satisfy the requirement of the statute.

Both parties do not have to sign the writing. Only "the party to be charged" need sign it. This means that the one who signed can be bound although the other is not — because he or she never signed. (You should be careful here, however, since some contemporary statutes require that both parties sign writings, at least with respect to some kinds of transactions.)

And finally, the English statute, unlike those in some American states, does not say that an oral agreement within the statute is void. It says it is unenforceable in courts. This distinction has various legal consequences. For example, Rule 8(c) of the Federal Rules of Civil Procedure provides that a litigant must raise the Statute of Frauds by way of affirmative defense. If a defendant fails to raise it, a court will enforce an oral contract even if it is within the statute.

Cool Civ Pro Connection

What contracts must be in writing? Today in most American states those contracts listed by the original English statute still must be in writing. They are:

---

[122] Many laypeople have the idea that unless they sign something they are not bound. Such a rule would be of no surprise to them. What would surprise them is just how many important agreements need not be in writing to be enforceable!

[123] A separate section established a writing requirement for sales of goods for the price of more than ten pounds sterling.

(1) a contract of an executor or administrator to answer for a duty of his or her decedent (the executor-administrator provision);

(2) a contract to answer for the duty of another (the suretyship provision);

(3) a contract made upon consideration of marriage (the marriage provision);

(4) a contract for the sale of an interest in land (the land contract provision);

(5) a contract that cannot be performed within one year from its making (the one-year provision); and

(6) a contract for the sale of goods in excess of a certain value.

The English statute has been superseded by § 2-201 of the UCC, which generally requires a writing when the contract price is $500 or more. (Proposals for a revision of Article 2 would have increased the threshold to $5000.)

The Statute of Frauds involves both the benefits and the costs of form. The statute announces that it has an *evidentiary* purpose — it is to prevent perjury. Required writings may serve to *caution* people and remind them they are making a commitment. Many people seem to believe in the magical significance of signing a writing. It is an important symbol of commitment. They may well think that if they do not sign, they are not bound. The writing requirement also may help *channel* behavior. Those who want to make a binding conveyance, will or contract of the type that must be within the statute can do so. As always, formal requirements also have costs. Not everyone knows that these contracts must be in writing. People can be fooled and rely on oral promises.

The Statute of Frauds is a statute. Virtually every American jurisdiction has legislation patterned on the 1677 English Act, and many legislatures have added writing requirements governing other contracts as well. Nonetheless, the courts have not given the usual deference to this legislation. To a great extent, they have treated the Statute of Frauds as if it were a common-law principle and developed it incrementally. The courts often have not been sympathetic to writing requirements, and they have worked hard to limit the impact of these provisions. However, at times the rule can block enforcement of an oral contract when the plaintiff has what seems a good case but for the statute.

Professor Arthur Corbin suggests the difficulty in generalizing about the Statute of Frauds:[124]

> There is much conflict and lack of uniformity. Two conflicting tendencies have been evident for the whole two hundred and seventy years. One of these is to regard the statute as a great and noble preventive of fraud and to apply it against the plaintiff with a good conscience even in cases where no doubt exists that the defendant made the promise with which he is charged. The other and much more frequent one is to enforce promises that a jury would find to have been in fact made, and if necessary to this end to narrow the operation of the statute. This narrowing of application was

---

[124] ARTHUR CORBIN, CONTRACTS 374 (one vol. ed. 1952).

sometimes accompanied by general words of encomium for the great statute; but in recent years the courts nearly always say nothing on the subject except what may be necessary to the business actually in hand, the enforcement of the promise. The narrowing process has been in part one of supposed interpretation of language and in part one of permitting the jury to determine the application of the statute by a general verdict under instructions that do not in fact hamper the jury in its effort to do "justice."

We cannot provide anything approaching a comprehensive analysis of the statute as interpreted by courts. Nonetheless, the following few pages depict some of the ironies and fine-line drawing that have resulted from the effort to offset the costs of imposing formal requirements.

Contracts not to be performed within one year: The statute calls for contracts performed over time to be in writing. How do we know if we have one? An employment contract calling for the employee to work 367 days would fall within the statute.[125] There is no way the employee can perform it in less than a year. However, courts will not look into the transaction to determine the likelihood that performance will take more than a year. It is enough that there is no legal barrier to performance within that time. For example, suppose Willie's uncle promises to pay $5000 per year to Willie for the remainder of Willie's life if Willie will run Uncle's store for the next six months. Some courts might find that this contract is not within the Statute of Frauds.[126] Courts have construed the statute to apply only to contracts which a party cannot possibly perform within a year. Although Willie is still young, it is possible that he might die within a year from the time they made the contract. If this happened, the uncle would complete his performance in less than a year.

Similarly, suppose an oral contract for the construction of a building which would be impossible for anyone to build in less than five years. This oral contract would not fall within the statute. It would be enforceable, even though oral, since legally the builder would not breach the contract if it found a way to complete it within 364 days, and the court would not consider the practical feasibility of such a pace of construction.

Contracts to answer for debts of another: The law has sought to protect sureties who agree to pay debts of others if they fail to do so. There is an important exception, however. Suppose Edward Entrepreneur's business has suffered losses. Bert Banker, to whom Edward owes $10,000, is threatening to foreclose his mortgage on Edward's factory and put him out of business. Sam Samaritan is one of Edward's major suppliers. He thinks that foreclosure will ruin Entrepreneur, cost Samaritan a good customer, and make certain that Entrepreneur will pay only a fraction of what he owes Samaritan for past deliveries. Samaritan and Banker

---

[125] We picked the number to take care of leap years. Lolz

[126] Contracts "not within" the statute are enforceable although they are not in writing. Being "within" the statute means the writing requirement must be met. If the requirement is met, lawyers usually speak of the statute being "satisfied" or "met." A contract is "outside" the statute if it need not be in writing.

orally agree that if Banker refrains from foreclosing, Samaritan will pay the debt if Entrepreneur fails to do so.

Courts have said that this oral contract is not within the statute. Samaritan would seem to have made an oral promise to answer for the debt of another. However, courts have developed an exception to this provision known as the "main purpose" or "leading object" rule. They reason that the policy of the provision is that often people promise to pay another's debt for sentimental or gratuitous purposes. Where a promisor's main purpose is his or her own economic well-being, there is less need for protection. Courts then will enforce the promise. Bert Banker can sue Sam, although Sam's promise to pay Eddie's debt was oral. Had Sam been Eddie's old army buddy, with no financial stake in Eddie's business, Sam's oral promise would have been unenforceable.

Int. and explained well

What kind of a writing will be enough, and what is a signature? Certainly, the statute is satisfied if parties prepare a document they call a "Contract," which contains all the terms of their agreement, and which they both sign at the bottom. However, how much less will do? Suppose Vera Vendor orally agrees to sell her farm, Plumacre, to Pete Purchaser for $150,000. They do not sign a written contract. One week after the agreement, Vera dictates a memorandum detailing her agreement with Pete. Her secretary transcribes it. Vera proofreads the transcribed memorandum, initials it, and places it in her files. One week later, she calls Pete to tell him that the deal is off. Pete sues Vera for specific performance and through pretrial discovery obtains a copy of the memorandum. Does it satisfy the Statute of Frauds?

This contract is one for the sale of an interest in land, and so the Statute of Frauds requires it to be in writing. Whether Vera's memorandum is enough depends on the language of the particular statute and its construction by the courts in the state. The memorandum initialed by Vera would appear to satisfy the English statute of 1677. It required either a written contract or "some note or memorandum thereof" signed by the party to be charged. Courts have held initials satisfy the requirement of a signature. However, the rule in some states would be different. For example, the Wisconsin statute governing conveyances of land requires a written instrument signed by all parties. Vera's memorandum would not be enough in Wisconsin and in other states with similar statutes.

DEPENDS

Not enough in WISCO

What must be in the memorandum? Restatement (Second) of Contracts § 131 says that the writing must (a) reasonably identify the subject matter of the contract, (b) be sufficient to indicate that the parties have made a contract with respect to that subject, and (c) state with reasonable certainty the essential terms of the unperformed promises in the contract. Often these tests leave matters uncertain. Something less than the high point of drafting will do, but how much less is unclear. A series of memoranda, taken together, might satisfy the statute.

The UETA, the ESIGN Act, and electronic documents: By the 1990s, the need for statutes to address the meaning and effect of electronic records and signatures had become apparent. The Uniform Law Commission (ULC) proposed the Uniform Electronic Transactions Act (UETA). Forty-seven states, the District of Columbia, and the U.S. Virgin Islands had adopted it as of 2015.[127] It generally seeks to make electronic "records" equivalent, for most purposes, to paper documents. Section 7 of the UETA is entitled "Legal Recognition of Electronic Records, Electronic Signatures, and Electronic Contracts," and it provides:

> (a) A record or signature may not be denied legal effect or enforceability solely because it is in electronic form.
>
> (b) A contract may not be denied legal effect or enforceability solely because an electronic record was used in its formation.
>
> (c) If a law requires a record to be in writing, an electronic record satisfies the law.
>
> (d) If a law requires a signature, an electronic signature[128] satisfies the law.

The UETA is not to be confused with UCITA, the Uniform Computer Information Transactions Act. UCITA, remember, was a substantially more ambitious, and controversial, effort to deal with transactions concerning computer information. It is approximately 10 times as long as the UETA, and begins with 65 definitions. In many respects it is as if there were a special version of Article 2 of the UCC just for software and digital content — and in fact it began life as part of a comprehensive review of Article 2. UCITA, as of 2015, had been adopted in only two states, Virginia and Maryland.[129]

In 2009, the American Law Institute completed work on a project called Principles of the Law of Software Contracts, a type of project that is intended to be more tentative than a restatement. The ALI Principles are primarily based on UCC Article 2, with a few more specific provisions designed for the software context.

The ESIGN Act is the Electronic Signatures in Global and National Commerce Act. It is a federal statute adopted in 2000 because of impatience with the 50-state enactment process for a uniform state law. It is intended to be "synchronized" with the UETA, and is generally comparable. It is applicable (since it is a federal statute) even in jurisdictions that have not passed the UETA. The ESIGN Act also seems to contain some consumer-friendly provisions that the UETA lacks.

All of these statutes have very minimal requirements for what qualifies as an electronic signature. None of them requires digital signatures that are encrypted or based on retinal patterns or fingerprints, and thus provide enhanced reliability. Section 2(8) of the UETA defines an "electronic signature" as "an electronic sound, symbol, or process attached to or logically associated with a record and executed or adopted by a person with the intent to sign the record."

---

[127] The outliers are Illinois, New York, and Washington, though each has statutes relating to electronic transactions.

[128] [Eds. note: The UETA defines "electronic signature" as an "electronic sound, symbol, or process attached to or logically associated with a record and executed or adopted by a person with the intent to sign the record."]

[129] Several states (Iowa, North Carolina, West Virginia, Vermont, and Idaho) have passed anti-UCITA statutes, sometimes referred to as "bomb shelter" laws because they prohibit the use of UCITA provisions through choice-of-law provisions.

The effect of part performance and promises to convey land: Courts often depart from the requirements of form to relieve undue hardship, and the Statute of Frauds cases are no exception. The so-called part performance doctrine is a major example. This doctrine developed in cases involving land. Not surprisingly, one area where the Statute of Frauds requires a writing is transactions concerning interests in land. Land is economically important. In England, where the rule developed, land ownership played a key role in the culture as well, often determining social rank. Given the importance of the transaction and the fact that many third parties may have an interest in who owns real estate or who has mortgages or other interests, contracts involving land seem perfect candidates for a strong formal requirement. However, at least in some situations, courts have recognized the claims of those who have relied on oral promises to convey. In fact, the Court of Chancery began to fashion the doctrine of part performance only nine years after the passage of the Statute of Frauds.[130] We will consider this way of getting around the writing requirement in this section. We will look first at some early Wisconsin cases, then at an attempt at statutory codification of the part-performance doctrine, and finally at the courts' treatment of the statute.[131]

The Rodman *case:* The first Wisconsin case we will consider is *Rodman v. Rodman*.[132] In *Rodman*, a son sought specific performance of an oral contract which he had made with his father. The son alleged that his father had promised to make a will leaving real estate to him. The trial court entered a judgment for the estate and the son appealed. The Supreme Court of Wisconsin affirmed the trial court's decision.

The facts revealed that the elder Rodman (age 67) owned a 500-acre farm. He wanted to cease active operation of the farm. In 1873, he persuaded Winfield, his 22-year-old son, to return to the farm. Winfield was to operate the farm on shares and they were to live in the homestead together. Winfield married soon after they made this arrangement. Winfield managed the farm for 22 years until his father's death in 1895. The father attempted to make a will in 1881 which would have left the farm to Winfield. The will, however, was invalid because the father did not sign it in the presence of two witnesses. Winfield testified that his father told him that if he stayed home and cared for his father, he would get the homestead. Winfield and his father had a dispute in 1886, and the father said that Winfield and his wife must

---

[130] Butcher v. Shapely, 1 Vern. 363 (1686).

[131] The material in this section does develop Wisconsin law in some detail. As is true of all examples in casebooks, it is less important if you practice in another state. However, it illustrates courts in one jurisdiction coping with the contradictory messages involved when one legal rule imposes a formal requirement and another rule tells courts to protect reliance — sometimes. You are likely to find this conflict wherever you practice law.

The Wisconsin statute and the cases struggling to apply it deal with a problem common to all jurisdictions. For example, the National Conference of Commissioners on Uniform State Laws drafted a proposed Uniform Land Transactions Act (ULTA), which it approved in 1975, but which was withdrawn from ULC's legislative action agenda in 1990 because no state had adopted it. This model act may, nevertheless, be influential in law reform in the future. The reasons why the ULTA failed are explored in a 1996 study by Professor Ronald Benton Brown. *See* Brown, *Whatever Happened to the Uniform Land Transactions Act?*, 20 Nova L. Rev. 1017 (Spring 1996).

[132] 112 Wis. 378, 88 N.W. 218 (1901).

leave the farm. Two older sons resolved the quarrel.

The trial court ruled that Winfield had not proved an oral contract to make a will. The Wisconsin Supreme Court found this finding was not against the weight of the evidence. The Supreme Court pointed out that when Winfield and his father had their dispute, Winfield did not make any claim of contractual rights. They made the alleged contract in 1873, but the father attempted to execute a will to carry out the contract eight years later. During that time, an earlier will existed with provisions inconsistent with the alleged contract.

The Supreme Court also affirmed the finding because, even if Winfield had proved an oral contract to make a will, it would have been invalid under the Statute of Frauds. The alleged contract concerned the transfer of an interest in real estate. Winfield's work on the farm for 22 years did not serve to take the case out of the provisions of the Statute of Frauds. The father had never given Winfield exclusive possession of the premises. Mere performance of services is not enough. The father remained in possession of the property until his death. The court pointed out:

> During all of this time the plaintiff and Robert L. Rodman [the father] lived upon the homestead, the plaintiff doing the work necessary to the operation of the farm and the gathering of the crops, but the father remaining the final director of farm operations, in that he dictated what kind of crops should be raised, rented parts of the farm to third persons at various times, and deeded two acres . . . to a third person. The father also made and paid for all substantial repairs and improvements in the place, and paid all taxes, except the road tax, which was worked out by the plaintiff. . . . It is true that plaintiff also lived upon the premises, but such possession as he had was subordinate to his father's superior possession and was plainly due to the sharing agreement and not to the alleged contract to will.

The **Powell** *case:* The second Wisconsin case is *Estate of Powell.*[133] Lottie and George Wilcox sued for specific performance of an oral contract to transfer a farm to them by will or by deed. The executor and beneficiaries under the deceased's will appealed. The decree for Lottie and George was affirmed.

Lottie alleged that her uncle had promised to transfer a farm to her if she and her husband would work it on shares until the uncle's death. Lottie was the child of her uncle's sister, who died when Lottie was two years old. The uncle took her into his home and reared her as his own child. Lottie "performed services in the home as great as any daughter could." The uncle's son was "demented." Lottie cared for him, attending to his personal cleanliness. She married George Wilcox, who rented on shares a large, highly improved, well-stocked farm. The uncle asked them to return to his farm, and they moved back and remained until the uncle's death nearly 20 years later.

The court observed:

> The Powell farm was ill-kept and run down; the buildings were dilapidated, except the barn which was unfinished; it was not nearly so attractive or remunerative as a renting proposition as the farm the Wilcoxes left. Powell

---

[133] 206 Wis. 513, 240 N.W. 122 (1932).

[the uncle] lived at a small hamlet a half mile from the farm, but a room was always kept ready for his use in the house on the farm. Mrs. Wilcox did his washing mostly and looked after him in a general way until his marriage eight or nine years before his death. From the time they went on the Powell farm the Wilcoxes worked and managed it as they would a farm of their own. Wilcox cleaned it and kept it clean of quack grass and Canada thistles; cleaned out fence rows; built new fences; repaired the house and kept it in repair; helped finish a barn in process of construction; built a hog pen, hen house, and other outbuildings; tore down and removed dilapidated outbuildings; did work on a silo; made a driveway; wired outbuildings for electric lights; grubbed out an old and set out a new orchard and small fruit; bred the scrub cattle into a fifteen-sixteenths and better blooded Guernsey herd; kept purebred China hogs, — all beyond the work and conduct of a tenant and without being paid for the extra work or reimbursed his expenditures. Powell paid for most of the material that went into the improvements and did some work upon them, but the evidence tends to show the aggregate value of Wilcox's work and material not paid for or reimbursed amounted to upwards of $4,000. The receipts of the farm were divided equally between Powell and Wilcox, without any strict or regular accounting. Powell's income from it was far beyond what would be realized from renting on shares to an ordinary tenant, as Wilcox was an excellent farmer.

Four disinterested people testified that Powell said, "Lottie and George would have the farm some day. . . . " "Lottie was to him a daughter, nearest and dearest to him of any one on earth. . . . " "When Powell was through with the farm it went to Lottie." Others testified, however, about statements Powell made after his marriage that the Wilcoxes had no claim to the farm. These statements were made when the new wife was suspicious of the Wilcoxes and hostile to them.

Lottie and George testified that Powell had entered into an agreement with them before they moved back to his farm. They were to repair the place as if it were their own. They went back to the farm solely because of the agreement, and they expected Powell to will the farm to her.

The Supreme Court said that a trial court should not decree specific performance of a contract unless the plaintiff establishes the promise by clear, satisfactory, and convincing proof. However, "[t]he trial judge might properly find the evidentiary facts as above stated, and we consider that their cumulative force warranted the inference of ultimate fact that a contract to transfer the farm was made." The statements made after Powell's marriage were self-serving.

Then the Supreme Court turned to the Statute of Frauds issue:

It is urged that there was no such partial performance by the respondents [Lottie and George Wilcox] as to warrant specific enforcement of the contract because the proof does not show that the respondents entered upon the land as and solely as a result of the contract. . . . But there is testimony of the respondents themselves to the precise point that they did so enter, and the circumstances indicate that they would not have gone upon the farm as mere tenants and that they did not so enter. It is urged that possession alone and that services alone do not constitute sufficient performance. While it may be that no one act or no one class of acts of the respondents would alone have constituted sufficient partial performance to warrant specific enforcement, their acts in the aggregate throughout the twenty years that were beyond the requirements of ordinary tenancy and husbandry were such that to deny them specific enforcement would operate as a fraud upon them, and the prevention of fraud is the basis of and reason for the equitable relief of specific performance.

. . . .

[I]t is to be regretted that the wishes of the testator, which were entirely reasonable and which he endeavored to place in legal and binding form, failed to become effective by reason of a failure to properly witness the will, of which he knew nothing. These matters, however, are of little moment in the consideration of the issues of this case.

The 1969 statute: In 1969, Wisconsin enacted a statute drafted by a committee of the State Bar Association of Wisconsin, presumably to clarify the extent of the rule which had emerged from cases like *Rodman* and *Powell.* The legislation stated both the writing requirement and the exceptions to protect reliance on oral promises. Wisconsin Statutes § 706.001(1) says that subject to a few exceptions, chapter 706 of the statutes "shall govern every transaction by which any interest in land is created, aliened, mortgaged, assigned, or may be otherwise affected in law or equity." The major exceptions are wills and leases for less than a year. Section 706.02(1) provides, in relevant part, as follows:

§ 706.02. Formal requisites.

(1) Transactions under § 706.001(1) shall not be valid unless evidenced by a conveyance that satisfies all of the following:

(a) Identifies the parties; and

(b) Identifies the land; and

(c) Identifies the interest conveyed . . . and

(d) Is signed by or on behalf of each of the grantors; and

(e) Is signed by or on behalf of all parties, if a lease or contract to convey . . . .

Section 706.04 states the counterrules. It says:

§ 706.04. Equitable relief.

A transaction which does not satisfy one or more of the requirements of § 706.02 may be enforceable in whole or in part under doctrines of equity, provided all of the elements of the transaction are clearly and satisfactorily proved and, in addition:

(1) The deficiency of the conveyance may be supplied by reformation in equity; or

(2) The party against whom enforcement is sought would be unjustly enriched if enforcement of the transaction were denied; or

(3) The party against whom enforcement is sought is equitably estopped from asserting the deficiency. A party may be so estopped whenever, pursuant to the transaction and in good faith reliance thereon, the party claiming estoppel has changed his or her position to the party's substantial detriment under circumstances such that the detriment so incurred may not be effectively recovered otherwise than by enforcement of the transaction, and either:

    (a) The grantee has been admitted into substantial possession or use of the premises or has been permitted to retain such possession or use after termination of a prior right thereto; or

    (b) The detriment so incurred was incurred with the prior knowing consent or approval of the party sought to be estopped.

In addition, § 706.001(3) provides: "This chapter shall be liberally construed, in cases of conflict or ambiguity, so as to effectuate the intentions of parties who have acted in good faith."

Can we say that § 706.04 merely codifies the *Rodman* and the *Powell* cases? Might the son in the *Rodman* case have made a good argument had the statute been in effect at the time of the transaction there? Would Lottie necessarily have won had the statute been in effect at the time of the transaction in the *Powell* case?

NOTES AND QUESTIONS

    1. *An example of the possession exception:* Other states have grappled with the reach of the part-performance exception to the Statute of Frauds. Consider, for example, *Seavey v. Drake.*[134] In that case, as had been alleged in *Rodman,*[135] a father made an oral promise to convey land to his son. The son took possession of part of his father's land, built a house, barn, and stable and made other improvements. He did all of this with his father's help. The father died, and the son brought a bill in equity for specific performance of an oral promise to convey the land. The son had held his father's note for $200, and he alleged that he returned the note to his father after he took possession. The executor moved to dismiss the bill because there was an oral promise to convey land not supported by consideration. The court denied the motion. Equity removes the bar of the Statute of Frauds when there has been part performance. "[I]t is a fraud for the vendor to insist upon the absence of a written instrument, when he has permitted the contract to be partly executed." The absence of consideration is not important, "for equity protects a parol gift of land equally with a parol agreement to sell it, if accompanied by possession, and the donee has made valuable improvements upon the property induced by the promise to give it." How, if at all, does *Seavey v. Drake* differ from the situation in *Rodman v. Rodman*?

    2. *Reliance on contracts unenforceable under the Statute of Frauds:* Suppose A makes an oral promise to sell or rent land to B. B incurs substantial expense

---

[134]   62 N.H. 393 (1882).

[135]   Remember, the trial court had found that the son had failed to prove the promise.

traveling to the land so he can take possession and improve it. These expenses do not enrich A. Before B can take possession and make improvements, A refuses to go through with the deal. Can B recover his or her reliance losses from A? Some courts have said no. Perhaps the most extreme example of the hard line is *Boone v. Coe*.[136] W.H. Boone and J.T. Coe, the plaintiffs, were farmers living with their families in Kentucky. In the fall of 1909, the defendant, J.F. Coe,[137] orally promised that if Boone and Coe would move to Texas and manage defendant's farm there for a year, they would receive a portion of the crops raised. Plaintiffs moved from Kentucky to Texas with their families, wagons, horses, and camping outfit. The trip took 55 days. When they arrived, the defendant would not allow them to begin performing the contract, and they returned to Kentucky. They alleged that they:

> spent in going to Texas, in cash, the sum of $150; that the loss of time to plaintiffs and their teams [of horses] in making the trip to Texas was reasonably worth $8 a day for a period of 55 days, or the sum of $440; that the loss of time to them and their teams during the period they remained in Texas was $8 a day for 22 days, or $176; that they paid out in actual cash for transportation for themselves, families and teams from Texas to Kentucky, the sum of $211.80; that the loss of time to them and their teams in making the last named trip was reasonably worth the sum of $100; that in abandoning and giving up their homes and businesses in Kentucky, they had been damaged in the sum of $150, making a total damage of $1,387.80, for which judgment was asked.

Defendant's demurrer to the petition was sustained, and the trial court's decision was affirmed on appeal. The court explained that allowing such damages would be an indirect enforcement of the oral contract, which was barred by the Statute of Frauds. Plaintiffs could sue in *quantum meruit*, but for such a recovery it "must appear that the defendant has actually received or will receive some benefit from the acts of part performance. It is immaterial that the plaintiff may have suffered a loss because he is unable to enforce his contract." "In the case under consideration, the plaintiffs merely sustained a loss. Defendant received no benefit."

Section 139 of the Restatement (Second) of Contracts provides that a promise that prompts reliance "is enforceable notwithstanding the Statute of Frauds if injustice can be avoided only by enforcement of the promise." It continues:

> (2) In determining whether injustice can be avoided only by enforcement of the promise, the following circumstances are significant:
>
> (a) the availability and adequacy of other remedies, particularly cancellation and restitution;
>
> (b) the definite and substantial character of the action or forbearance in relation to the remedy sought;

---

[136] 153 Ky. 233, 154 S.W. 900 (Ct. App. 1913).

[137] The opinion does not state his relationship to the plaintiff, J.T. Coe, but we can suspect that this is another family bait situation.

(c) the extent to which the action or forbearance corroborates evidence of the making and terms of the promise, or the making and terms are otherwise established by clear and convincing evidence;

(d) the reasonableness of the action or forbearance;

(e) the extent to which the action or forbearance was foreseeable by the promisor.

If the Wisconsin Supreme Court decided to follow § 139, would its decision in the *Rodman* case still stand? Are § 139 and Wis. Stat. § 706.04 functionally equivalent?

3. ***Restitution of benefits conferred under contracts made unenforceable by the Statute of Frauds:*** In *Montanaro Brothers Builders, Inc. v. Snow*, the court said:[138]

> It is hornbook law that a party whose agreement is unenforceable under the Statute of Frauds or because of indefiniteness is generally entitled to restitution. . . . When a landowner relies upon the Statute of Frauds as a basis for repudiating his agreement, it is unjust to permit him to retain payments or services that he has received and to transfer nothing in return. . . . The plaintiffs' claim in restitution is not a claim arising out of an express or an implied contract but invokes instead an obligation, independent of contract, "based on equitable principles to operate whenever justice requires compensation to be made."

Restatement (Second) of Contracts § 375 provides that one is not barred from restitution "because of the Statute of Frauds unless the Statute provides otherwise or its purpose would be frustrated by allowing restitution." When might the purpose of the Statute of Frauds be frustrated by restitution of benefits conferred? Why is there such a requirement? Doesn't an award of reliance-based damages under § 139 of the Restatement (Second) always frustrate the purposes of the Statute of Frauds?

Professor Charles Knapp says that "the Statute of Frauds, given three hundred years of judicial whittling-down, capped by the recent tendency to hold that the Statute bends to substantial reliance on an oral bargain" is a "rule that can be understood only in light of its exceptions." He then asks whether one should now ask "whether the exceptions together do not now make up 'the rule' with the former rule being itself relegated to the status of an exception."[139]

4. ***Professional responsibility:*** Suppose a vendor made an oral agreement to convey but did not sign a written contract. Can the vendor's lawyer ethically defend the vendor's refusal to convey by asserting the Statute of Frauds? Can the lawyer ethically *refuse* to assert the Statute of Frauds as a defense to a claim against her client? Would it depend on why the vendor wants to back out of the oral arrangement?

5. ***The expectation, reliance, and restitution interests:*** If you look back over

---

[138] 190 Conn. 481, 460 A.2d 1297 (1983).

[139] Charles L. Knapp, Book Review, 82 MICH. L. REV. 932, 944–45 (1984).

the preceding discussion of the Statute of Frauds, it should become apparent that, in addition to blowing hot and cold about the virtues of enthusiastic enforcement of the writing requirement, the courts may approach a plaintiff's claims differently depending on which of the contractual interests is being protected — the expectation, the reliance, or the restitution interest. Does separating the cases on the basis of the interest protected create a stronger sense of order? Should it? We have talked separately about the treatment the courts give to plaintiffs seeking to protect their reliance interests, or their restitution interests. What more can we say about the circumstances in which part performance of an oral agreement entitles a person to a full *expectation* interest remedy?

Let us first consider contracts for the sale of land. Once the vendor conveys the land to the purchaser, courts usually say that the statute ceases to apply and the vendor may sue for the full contract price. Payment of the price by the purchaser, on the other hand, usually does not take the transaction out of the statute. The purchaser's only remedy is restitution. But if the purchaser takes possession of the land and makes improvements to it, most courts would then allow the purchaser to get specific performance.

The Restatement (Second) of Contracts § 129 extends this idea and provides for specific performance "if it is established that the party seeking enforcement, in reasonable reliance on the contract and on the continuing assent of the party against whom enforcement is sought, has so changed his position that injustice can be avoided only by specific enforcement." While one can find support in the cases for this rule, it is not clear that all courts would follow what they would see as a striking innovation. Again, research and advocacy are necessary if it is worth seeking an answer. See also Restatement (Second) of Contracts § 139, which takes essentially the same position with respect to all cases — not just cases involving interests in land.

Courts have also applied the part performance doctrine to contracts that cannot be performed within one year. Recall the example of the oral agreement between Willie and his uncle. Willie promised to manage the store for six months. As a result, Willie's performance would take less than a year to complete. Also, the uncle, within a year, might perform his promise to pay money to Willie for the rest of his life. Willie could die within that time. Thus, the oral agreement was not covered by the statute. Suppose, instead, that Willie had promised to manage the store for two years. Now Willie could not possibly perform his side of the contract within a year, and the statute would bar enforcement of the oral agreement.

However, suppose Willie completed performance, managing the store for two years. Then his uncle died before making any payments, and his uncle's executor refused to pay. The Restatement (Second) of Contracts § 130(2) says that when Willie completes performance, although it takes more than a year, the uncle's promise to pay him $5000 annually for life becomes enforceable. Suppose, however, the uncle repudiated the agreement before Willie had finished his two-year term. What, if anything, could Willie recover under a restitution theory? Suppose Willie had paid $1200 as tuition for a retail management training course? Could he recover this amount from his uncle as a reliance expenditure under § 139? As you might imagine, questions such as this are usually settled rather than litigated, so we lack enough appellate opinions to suggest general rules.

6. ***Contracts for the sale of goods:*** "Transactions in goods" are now covered by Article 2 of the Uniform Commercial Code. Those who drafted it had a chance to consider the older writing requirement as well as the various exceptions and constructions courts had fashioned. How did the drafters respond to problems such as the tension between the virtues of form and reliance on oral contracts? In addition to reading § 2-201, you should read the Official Comments.

Section 2-201(1) requires a writing if the price of the goods is $500 or more. An oral contract within the statute "is not enforceable by way of action or defense" unless it falls within one of the exceptions. This may mean that the contract price should not be a limit on recovery in restitution where the fair market value is greater than the amount agreed to by the parties.

The writing must be "sufficient to indicate that a contract for sale has been made between the parties. . . . A writing is not insufficient because it omits or incorrectly states a term agreed upon but the contract is not enforceable under this paragraph beyond the quantity of goods shown in such writing." The writing must be signed by the defendant; not necessarily by both buyer and seller.

There are a great many more complexities that arise as one seeks to apply § 2-201 to real problems. We will return to some of them later in these materials.

7. ***CISG and the Statute of Frauds:*** The CISG in Article 11 explicitly provides that contracts of sale need not be in writing. This is in keeping with the fact that the majority of the world's countries have no Statute of Frauds requirements. But the repudiation of writing requirements is significantly undercut by the fact that Article 96 authorizes a country to make a declaration that Articles of CISG that eliminate writing requirements are inoperative when one party has a place of business in the country making the declaration. However, the United States has not made a declaration under Article 96.

8. ***Should we repeal the Statute of Frauds?*** Many jurisdictions have modified or repealed the Statute of Frauds, including the United Kingdom, New Zealand, and several Canadian provinces. Professor G.H.L. Fridman conducted a study for the Ontario Law Reform Commission. He attacked the statute and advocated repeal.[140] He charges that the courts have had to:

> engage upon casuistry and legal sophistry of the most blatant kind in order to avoid the consequences that would flow from what would otherwise be the logical and correct application of the statute's provisions. The statute has been the cause of the invention of an equitable doctrine [part performance] that, frankly and plainly, contradicts the statute and contravenes the law. . . . If there is one thing that would suggest that the present law is absurd, outdated, inconvenient, and unduly complex it is this doctrine. If the repeal of . . . the Statute of Frauds would have the result of eradicating the doctrine of part performance, that alone would justify such repeal. . . . In the end what has emerged is what might be called a

---

[140] G.H.L. Fridman, *The Necessity for Writing in Contracts Within the Statute of Frauds*, 35 U. Toronto L.J. 43 (1985). Copyright © University of Toronto Press. Reprinted with permission.

'make-do-and-mend' type of justice. Such an approach . . . cannot but encourage reasonable people to think less favorably of the law, and of a system of justice that allows, even promotes, such judicial chicanery.

Fridman asserts that the writing requirement serves no important purpose in today's world. He looks at Professor Fuller's functions of form — evidence, caution, and channeling. He concludes that the statute and its exceptions fail to attain enough of the benefits of these functions to justify its costs. We often do not gain evidence there was a contract and the nature of its terms. The statute fails to cover some important contracts which are enforceable although oral. The statute seems to cover other important contracts, but they are enforceable because they fall into one of the many exceptions to the rule.

Fridman concedes there may be something to the cautionary function, but he says that writers carry the argument too far.

> It may be true that people who have to enter into a written document take more care and pay more attention to what they are doing, but not necessarily. Every lawyer is familiar with the contracting party who signs without reading, only to find the true nature of his obligation later, if and when litigation is threatened. . . . The contracting party may not have read it . . . because he was too lazy or disinclined to attempt to understand its meaning, or because he was acting in reliance upon the word of the other party or his own recollections of what was said or what was intended. For whatever reason, there are many parties who do not take any more care about contracting because the contract is written or is contained more or less in some written form than they do or would if the contract were merely oral.

Fridman also questions the channeling function:

> Just as the fact that a contract is in writing, or is evidenced by writing, does not always lead to more careful consideration of what one is doing, so, too, the fact that there has to be some kind of writing may not necessarily bring home to a party that he is bound, or may not always and sufficiently distinguish a binding obligation from one that is not. The man in the street often has peculiar ideas about whether a contract has to be in writing. He may think that, unless there is a document, there is no contract, when — save for special situations . . . this is not the case. He may, on the other hand, regard "a man's word as his bond" and so think that he has a valid, enforceable contract when, because of the Statute of Frauds, or something else, he has not.

Moreover, the statute opens the possibility of fraud when a buyer signs a writing but the seller does not. The buyer cannot hold the seller to the contract, but the seller can hold the buyer who signed. Thus, the seller may look for a better price while having the buyer's deal to fall back on if he does not find a better purchaser. Most buyers would not be aware of what they had done, and so a seller could trick a buyer into this kind of disadvantageous situation.

Fridman concludes: "Whether the ultimate answer is to allow all contracts to be oral or to make it mandatory for all contracts to be in writing, the conclusion that is ineluctable is that the provisions of the Statute of Frauds dealing with contracts will have to be repealed."

Does Professor Fridman convince you? Whether requiring a writing promotes evidence, caution, and channeling is, in part, an empirical question. From where does Professor Fridman get his facts? Furthermore, what is wrong with a rule partially offset by a counterrule? We begin with a rule that contracts for the sale of land must be in a signed writing. Then we fashion a limited counterrule that says in exceptional cases where our writing rule would produce clearly unfair results, we might enforce an oral promise. Does this necessarily or usually lead to bad results or raise the cost of litigation unduly?

6. Family Bait: Reaching the Right Result by Manipulating Doctrines of Contract Formation

Suppose a father makes a statement that might or might not be a promise to make a gift, write a will, or create a trust. A member of his family relies on this statement. Then the father fails to act. In *Hamer v. Sidway*, we saw a court finding consideration to protect reliance where there was a plausible argument that there was no bargain. Judges can manipulate other doctrines too. Courts can construe language and conduct to fit existing legal categories so that the "right result" seems just to follow inevitably — or, on occasion, they can create a doctrinal distinction in order to rationalize treating differently two cases that seem to be quite alike.

The next case introduces such a doctrinal tool. The notes that follow speculate on its origins and discuss the intellectual history of this often-maligned contract rule.

DAVIS v. JACOBY
California Supreme Court
1 Cal. 2d 370, 34 P.2d 1026 (1934)

THE COURT.

Plaintiffs appeal from a judgment refusing to grant specific performance of an alleged contract to make a will. The facts are not in dispute and are as follows:

The plaintiff, Caro M. Davis, was the niece of Blanche Whitehead, who was married to Rupert Whitehead. Prior to her marriage in 1913 to her coplaintiff, Frank M. Davis, Caro lived for a considerable time at the home of the Whiteheads, in Piedmont, California. The Whiteheads were childless and extremely fond of Caro. The record is replete with uncontradicted testimony of the close and loving relationship that existed between Caro and her aunt and uncle. During the period that Caro lived with the Whiteheads she was treated as and often referred to by the Whiteheads as their daughter. In 1913, when Caro was married to Frank Davis, the marriage was arranged at the Whitehead home and a reception held there. After the marriage Mr. and Mrs. Davis went to Mr. Davis's home in Canada, where they have resided ever since. During the period 1913 to 1931 Caro made many visits to the

Whiteheads, several of them being of long duration. The Whiteheads visited Mr. and Mrs. Davis in Canada on several occasions. After the marriage and continuing down to 1931 the closest and most friendly relationship at all times existed between these two families. They corresponded frequently, the record being replete with letters showing the loving relationship.

By the year 1930 Mrs. Whitehead had become seriously ill. She had suffered several strokes and her mind was failing. Early in 1931 Mr. Whitehead had her removed to a private hospital. The doctors in attendance had informed him that she might die at any time or she might linger for many months. Mr. Whitehead had suffered severe financial reverses. He had had several sieges of sickness and was in poor health. The record shows that during the early part of 1931 he was desperately in need of assistance with his wife, and in his business affairs, and that he did not trust his friends in Piedmont. On March 18, 1931, he wrote to Mrs. Davis telling her of Mrs. Whitehead's condition and added that Mrs. Whitehead was very wistful:

> Today I endeavored to find out what she wanted. I finally asked her if she wanted to see you. She burst out crying and we had great difficulty in getting her to stop. Evidently, that is what is on her mind. It is a very difficult matter to decide. If you come it will mean that you will have to leave again, and then things may be serious. I am going to see the doctor, and get his candid opinion and will then write you again. . . . Since writing the above, I have seen the doctor, and he thinks it will help considerably if you come.

Shortly thereafter, Mr. Whitehead wrote to Caro Davis further explaining the physical condition of Mrs. Whitehead and himself. On March 24, 1931, Mr. Davis, at the request of his wife, telegraphed to Mr. Whitehead as follows: "Your letter received. Sorry to hear Blanche not so well. Hope you are feeling better yourself. If you wish Caro to go to you can arrange for her to leave in about two weeks. Please wire me if you think it advisable for her to go." On March 30, 1931, Mr. Whitehead wrote a long letter to Mr. Davis, in which he explained in detail the condition of Mrs. Whitehead's health and also referred to his own health. He pointed out that he had lost a considerable portion of his cash assets but still owned considerable realty, that he needed someone to help him with his wife and some friend he could trust to help him with his business affairs and suggested that perhaps Mr. Davis might come to California. He then pointed out that all his property was community property; that under his will all the property was to go to Mrs. Whitehead; that he believed that under Mrs. Whitehead's will practically everything was to go to Caro. Mr. Whitehead again wrote to Mr. Davis under date of April 9, 1931, pointing out how badly he needed someone he could trust to assist him, and giving it as his belief that if properly handled he could still save about $150,000. He then stated: "Having you [Mr. Davis] here to depend on and to help me regain my mind and courage would be a big thing." Three days later, on April 12, 1931, Mr. Whitehead again wrote, addressing his letter to "Dear Frank and Caro," and in this letter made the definite offer, which offer it is claimed was accepted and is the basis of this action. In this letter he first pointed out that Blanche, his wife, was in a private hospital and that, "she cannot last much longer . . . my affairs are not as bad as I supposed at first. Cutting everything down I figure $150,000 can be saved from the wreck." He then enumerated the values placed upon his various properties and then continued:

[M]y trouble was caused by my friends taking advantage of my illness and my position to skin me.

Now if Frank could come out here and be with me, and look after my affairs, we could easily save the balance I mentioned, provided I don't get into another panic and do some more foolish things.

The next attack will be my end, I am 65 and my health has been bad for years, so, the Drs. don't give me much longer to live. So if you can come, Caro will inherit everything and you will make our lives happier and see Blanche is provided for to the end.

My eyesight has gone back on me, I cant read only for a few lines at a time. I am at the house alone with Stanley [the chauffeur] who does everything for me and is a fine fellow. Now, what I want is some one who will take charge of my affairs and see I don't lose any more. Frank can do it, if he will and cut out the booze.

Will you let me hear from you as soon as possible, I know it will be a sacrifice but times are still bad and likely to be, so by settling down you can help me and Blanche and gain in the end. If I had you here my mind would get better and my courage return, and we could work things out.

This letter was received by Mr. Davis at his office in Windsor, Canada, about 9:30 A.M. April 14, 1931. After reading the letter to Mrs. Davis over the telephone, and after getting her belief that they must go to California, Mr. Davis immediately wrote Mr. Whitehead a letter, which, after reading it to his wife, he sent by air mail. This letter was lost, but there is no doubt that it was sent by Davis and received by Whitehead, in fact the trial court expressly so found. Mr. Davis testified in substance as to the contents of this letter. After acknowledging receipt of the letter of April 12, 1931, Mr. Davis unequivocally stated that he and Mrs. Davis accepted the proposition of Mr. Whitehead and both would leave Windsor to go to him on April 25th. This letter of acceptance also contained the information that the reason they could not leave prior to April 25th was that Mr. Davis had to appear in court on April 22nd as one of the executors of his mother's estate. The testimony is uncontradicted and ample to support the trial court's finding that this letter was sent by Davis and received by Whitehead. In fact under date of April 15, 1931, Mr. Whitehead again wrote to Mr. Davis and stated:

Your letter by air mail received this A.M. Now, I am wondering if I have put you to unnecessary trouble and expense, if you are making any money don't leave it, as things are bad here. . . . You know your business and I don't and I am half crazy in the bargain, but I don't want to hurt you or Caro.

Then on the other hand if I could get some one to trust and keep me straight I can save a good deal, about what I told you in my former letter.

This letter was received by Mr. Davis on April 17, 1931, and the same day Mr. Davis telegraphed to Mr. Whitehead: "Cheer up — we will soon be there, we will wire you from the train."

Between April 14, 1931, the date the letter of acceptance was sent by Mr. Davis, and April 22nd, Mr. Davis was engaged in closing out his business affairs, and Mrs.

Davis in closing up their home and in making other arrangements to leave. On April 22, 1931, Mr. Whitehead committed suicide. Mr. and Mrs. Davis were immediately notified and they at once came to California. From almost the moment of her arrival Mrs. Davis devoted herself to the care and comfort of her aunt, and gave her aunt constant attention and care until Mrs. Whitehead's death on May 30, 1931. On this point the trial court found: "[F]rom the time of their arrival in Piedmont, Caro M. Davis administered in every way to the comforts of Blanche Whitehead and saw that she was cared for and provided for down to the time of the death of Blanche Whitehead on May 30, 1931; during said time Caro M. Davis nursed Blanche Whitehead, cared for her, and administered to her wants as a natural daughter would have done toward and for her mother." . . .

After the death of Mrs. Whitehead, for the first time it was discovered that the information contained in Mr. Whitehead's letter of March 30, 1931, in reference to the contents of his and Mrs. Whitehead's wills was incorrect. By a duly witnessed will dated February 28, 1931, Mr. Whitehead, after making several specific bequests, had bequeathed all of the balance of his estate to his wife for life, and upon her death to respondents Geoff Doubble and Rupert Ross Whitehead, his nephews. Neither appellant was mentioned in his will. It was also discovered that Mrs. Whitehead by a will dated December 17, 1927, had devised all of her estate to her husband. The evidence is clear and uncontradicted that the relationship existing between Whitehead and his two nephews, respondents herein, was not nearly as close and confidential as that existing between Whitehead and appellants.

After the discovery of the manner in which the property had been devised was made, this action was commenced upon the theory that Rupert Whitehead had assumed a contractual obligation to make a will whereby "Caro Davis would inherit everything"; that he had failed to do so; that plaintiffs had fully performed their part of the contract; that damages being insufficient, quasi-specific performance should be granted in order to remedy the alleged wrong, upon the equitable principle that equity regards that done which ought to have been done. The requested relief is that the beneficiaries under the will of Rupert Whitehead, respondents herein, be declared to be involuntary trustees for plaintiffs of Whitehead's estate.

It should also be added that the evidence shows that as a result of Frank Davis leaving his business in Canada he forfeited not only all insurance business he might have written if he had remained, but also forfeited all renewal commissions earned on past business. According to his testimony this loss was over $8,000. . . .

The theory of the trial court and of respondents on this appeal is that the letter of April 12th was an offer to contract, but that such offer could only be accepted by performance and could not be accepted by a promise to perform, and that said offer was revoked by the death of Mr. Whitehead before performance. In other words, it is contended that the offer was an offer to enter into a unilateral contract, and that the purported acceptance of April 14th was of no legal effect.

The distinction between unilateral and bilateral contracts is well settled in the law. It is well stated in § 12 of the American Institute's Restatement of the Law of Contracts as follows:

A unilateral contract is one in which no promisor receives a promise as consideration for his promise. A bilateral contract is one in which there are mutual promises between two parties to the contract; each party being both a promisor and a promisee.

This definition is in accord with the law of California. . . .

In the case of unilateral contracts no notice of acceptance by performance is required. Section 1584 of the Civil Code provides, "Performance of the conditions of a proposal . . . is an acceptance of the proposal." . . .

Although the legal distinction between unilateral and bilateral contracts is thus well settled, the difficulty in any particular case is to determine whether the particular offer is one to enter into a bilateral or unilateral contract. Some cases are quite clear-cut. Thus an offer to sell which is accepted is clearly a bilateral contract, while an offer of a reward is a clear-cut offer of a unilateral contract which cannot be accepted by a promise to perform, but only by performance. *Berthiaume v. Doe*, 22 Cal. App. 78, 133 Pac. 515. Between these two extremes is a vague field where the particular contract may be unilateral or bilateral depending upon the intent of the offeror and the facts and circumstances of each case. The offer to contract involved in this case falls within this category. By the provisions of the Restatement of the Law of Contracts it is expressly provided that there is a *presumption* that the offer is to enter into a bilateral contract. Section 31 provides:

> In case of doubt it is presumed that an offer invites the formation of a bilateral contract by an acceptance amounting in effect to a promise by the offeree to perform what the offer requests, rather than the formation of one or more unilateral contracts by actual performance on the part of the offeree. . . .

In the comment following § 31 of the Restatement the reason for such presumption is stated as follows:

> It is not always easy to determine whether an offeror requests an act or a promise to do the act. As a bilateral contract immediately and fully protects both parties, the interpretation is favored that a bilateral contract is proposed.

While the California cases have never expressly held that a presumption in favor of bilateral contracts exists, the cases clearly indicate a tendency to treat offers as offers of bilateral rather than of unilateral contracts. . . .

Keeping these principles in mind we are of the opinion that the offer of April 12th was an offer to enter into a bilateral as distinguished from a unilateral contract. Respondents argue that Mr. Whitehead had the right as offeror to designate his offer as either unilateral or bilateral. This is undoubtedly the law. It is then argued that from all the facts and circumstances it must be implied that what Whitehead wanted was performance and not a mere promise to perform. We think this is a *non sequitur*, in fact the surrounding circumstances lead to just the opposite conclusion. These parties were not dealing at arm's length. Not only were they related, but a very close and intimate friendship existed between them. The record indisputably demonstrates that Mr. Whitehead had confidence in Mr. and Mrs. Davis, in fact that he had lost all confidence in everyone else. The record amply shows that by an accumulation of occurrences Mr. Whitehead had become desperate, and that what he wanted was the promise of appellants that he could look to them for assistance. He knew from his past relationship with appellants that if they gave their promise to perform he could rely upon them. The correspondence between them indicates how desperately he desired this assurance. Under these circumstances he wrote his offer of April 12th, above quoted, in which he stated, after disclosing his desperate mental and physical condition, and after setting forth the terms of his offer: *"Will you let me hear from you as soon as possible* — I know it will be a sacrifice but times are still bad and likely to be, so by settling down you can help me and Blanche and gain in the end." By thus specifically requesting an immediate reply Whitehead expressly indicated the nature of the acceptance desired by him — namely, appellants' promise that they would come to California and do the things requested by him. This promise was immediately sent by appellants upon receipt of the offer, and was received by Whitehead. It is elementary that when an offer has indicated the mode and means of acceptance, an acceptance in accordance with that mode or means is binding on the offeror.

Another factor which indicates that Whitehead must have contemplated a bilateral rather than a unilateral contract, is that the contract required Mr. and Mrs. Davis to perform services until the death of both Mr. and Mrs. Whitehead. It is obvious that if Mr. Whitehead died first some of these services were to be performed after his death, so that he would have to rely on the promise of appellants to perform these services. It is also of some evidentiary force that Whitehead received the letter of acceptance and acquiesced in that means of acceptance. . . .

For the foregoing reasons we are of the opinion that the offer of April 12, 1931, was an offer to enter into a bilateral contract which was accepted by the letter of April 14, 1931. Subsequently appellants fully performed their part of the contract. Under such circumstances it is well settled that damages are insufficient and specific performance will be granted. . . .

For the foregoing reasons the judgment appealed from is reversed.

NOTES AND QUESTIONS

1. *What if the Davises lose on their contract theory?* It is useful to understand what the situation would be if Frank and Caro cannot establish a contract: Rupert died first, owning one-half the estate under California's community property laws. His will left a life estate in this interest to Blanche, and then at her death, this property was to go to his nephews, Rupert Ross Whitehead and Geoff Doubble.

Blanche died after Rupert, but her will left everything she had to Rupert. Since he was dead at her death, it is as if she had no will. Some of Blanche's one-half of the property might find its way to Caro, but it is not clear if this is the case. Even if Caro took as a niece, the amount would be much less than Frank and Caro claimed under the contract.

2. *The doctrinal twists of* Davis v. Jacoby *— the legatee's argument:* The court in *Davis v. Jacoby* deals with the unilateral contract argument made by the

legatees under Rupert Whitehead's will. They attempt to defeat the Davises' claim to all of his property. The legatees conceded that Mr. Whitehead had made an offer to Caro and Frank Davis, but they argued that it had been an offer contemplating a *unilateral contract*. They said that Rupert's promise was offered for action and not for a return promise.

Their argument continued: One can accept an offer for a unilateral contract only by full performance; only then does it become a contract. Until the Davises performed the requested action, the offeror (Mr. Whitehead) was free to revoke his offer and back out without liability to the offerees (the Davises). Another rule of law says that death revokes all outstanding offers. Since the Davises had not fully performed before Mr. Whitehead committed suicide, there was no contract to make a will. The will as written stands, the legatees win, and the Davises do not get any of the Whiteheads' property as promised.

The court, of course, rejected this argument. It found that Mr. Whitehead's offer contemplated a *bilateral contract*. A contract was formed when Frank Davis sent his letter to Mr. Whitehead, promising to come to California and perform the services. Therefore, the legatees under the will take subject to this contract, and they get little or nothing.

The unilateral contract paradigm: A transaction such as that put forward by the legatees is conceivable. Suppose Rupert Whitehead had written to the Davises exactly as reported in the case. However, he also explained that he was concerned about the quality of care which Caro might give his wife and about the quality of business services which Frank might provide because of Frank's drinking problem. (Recall the sentence in Whitehead's letter: "Frank can do it, if he will and cut out the booze.") Therefore, suppose Rupert continued:

> I promise to arrange our wills so that we will leave everything we own to Caro if Caro properly cares for Blanche and if Frank properly handles the business. However, I reserve the right to revoke this offer without any need to show cause at any time before you two complete your performances. I recognize that I am asking you to move here and try to perform. You run the risk that I might be unreasonably dissatisfied with what you do and the risk that I might die before you finish the job. Nonetheless, you'll just have to trust me and take your chances.

Rupert would gain maximum leverage over Caro and Frank, if they started to perform. The more they invested in trying to perform (leaving their home and business in Ontario and providing services in California), the more they would have to lose if they displeased Rupert. As people age and are subject to business losses and the death of a spouse, they often become unreasonable and impossible to please. Thus, the risk would be real.

"Heads I win, tails you lose": There is just one difficulty with the offer we've imagined. Rupert Whitehead wants to induce Caro and Frank to tear up their lives, make a commitment to him, and to perform the services in a manner above and beyond the call of duty. How can he hope to persuade them to do this in the face of the distrust reflected in his letter and in the face of the risks he is forcing them to

take?[141] He could be relying on Caro's feeling for her aunt and offering such a high payoff that Caro and Frank would think it a good gamble. Yet the gambling aspects might well convince them to stay in Windsor, Ontario. The expression of distrust might cut against the emotional ties between Caro and her aunt which Rupert Whitehead was counting on. Many would think it improper to force family members to wager their home and business on the whims of an old man facing the loss of his wife and his wealth at the same time. And we must recall economic conditions at the time of this transaction. If Frank Davis gave up his insurance business and failed to gain from managing Rupert's business, it would not be easy to start again.

Rewards and risks: There are not many true unilateral contracts in the world. Few people are willing to place significant reliance on a promise that an offeror can revoke at any time. Of course, some reward situations fit this legal category. Suppose I offer a reward of $10,000 to anyone who captures a criminal. Suppose I offer a commission to any real estate broker who finds a buyer to whom I sell my house. In each instance, the person seeking the reward runs the risk that someone will beat her to it. In each case, the person seeking the reward can invest as much effort in trying to perform as she thinks warranted in light of the risks.

Courts often call settlement agreements unilateral contracts. They read these contracts as "I give up my right to sue you in exchange for your act of paying me, say, $10,000." This means that I do not lose my right to sue until you pay the $10,000. I do not run the risk that you will promise to pay the money, fail to do it, but then limit my claim to the amount of the settlement.

One could view most employment situations as unilateral contracts with terms very similar to those which we imagined in our hypothetical letter from Rupert to Frank. Most people have no express contract covering their job, and they are not tenured faculty, members of a civil service system, or working under a collective bargaining agreement between management and a union. One has a job as long as one pleases the boss. The boss can revoke the deal at any time for good, bad, or no reason. Of course, most assume, or hope, that it is "their job" as long as they do the work competently. Until recently this expectation has been reinforced by social rather than legal sanctions. We can express the deal as the boss's promise to pay for the employee's act of working each day.

Selective use of unilateral, bilateral, and option contracts: Different means of formation can be invoked selectively with the justice of the results in mind. Consider the following variations:

(a) In some instances, courts might allow the offeror to back out if he or she

---

[141] *See* David F. Haas & Forrest A. Deseran, *Trust and Symbolic Exchange*, 44 Soc. Psych. Q. 3 (1981) (Trust "is established in various ways, one of which is investment in expensive gestures of good faith. We have called the exchange of such tokens of good faith 'symbolic exchanges.' We have argued that the use of symbolic exchange requires the existence of a standardized vocabulary of symbolic exchange . . . [A] refusal to reciprocate . . . or indeed any violation of the canons of symbolic exchange may signify a refusal of the relationship indicated by the exchange."). Indeed, if Caro and Frank come to California after the hypothetical letter in the text, wouldn't they seem to be greedy and not motivated by the proper family spirit? *Cf.* Richard Bilder, Managing the Risks of International Agreement (University of Wisconsin Press 1981) (dealing with another situation in which trust must be created before risks will be accepted).

managed to reserve this right clearly. Suppose a couple is considering divorce. They contact a real estate broker and explain that they are thinking of selling their house, but they are not sure that they will divorce and move. They make a nonexclusive listing with the broker because, as they make clear, they plan to show it themselves. The broker shows the house to a number of people. The couple reconcile and want to keep their house. It is unlikely that the broker would have any rights because the couple managed to explain the situation. The broker had the choice in light of the situation to invest no time or only a little in trying to find a buyer. Moreover, the transaction is not unusual but rather common. The broker should not be surprised when the couple take the house off the market.

(b) The easiest solution when the facts lend themselves to it, is the one taken in *Davis v. Jacoby*. The court finds that the offeror was bargaining for a promise which the offeree made. Thus, we have a bilateral contract. The deal is closed, and the offeror can no longer back out at will. This solution is often slightly messy. Suppose, for example, Caro and Frank sent the letter promising to come to California and perform the services. They begin preparations to leave Canada, but they discover that the loss they would have to take would be fantastically large. They telephone Rupert and tell him they are not coming. Could Rupert, or his executor, sue Caro and Frank for breach of their promise to come? If you follow the logic of the court's opinion, the answer is yes. Somehow one wonders if a court would reach that result on the facts. Rupert, himself, worried that he had asked too much. One of his letters offered Caro and Frank a graceful way to back out.

(c) In *Los Angeles Traction Co. v. Wilshire*,[142] a group of citizens offered a $2000 reward if a street car line were extended to an intersection of two streets in Los Angeles. The street car company began construction but the group tired of waiting for completion and purported to revoke. The court found that the contract was "unilateral when made but became bilateral when it was acted upon" by the street railway. Thus, the offer could not be revoked at will, and the court found that there was no undue delay which would provide a defense under the contract which was formed. Clearly, this explanation fails to explain anything. The transformation from a unilateral to a bilateral contract is a form of word magic. The court offered no justification for protecting the railroad's reliance.

(d) Professor Dudley O. McGovney suggested that in a unilateral contract situation typically, but not always, there is an implied-in-fact subsidiary promise not to revoke once performance has begun.[143] The offeror must give the offeree a fair chance to do the task to earn the reward, unless expressly or by custom the offeree assumes the risk of relying only to find the offer revoked.

(e) The original Restatement of Contracts § 45 became the most commonly accepted solution to the problem of the unilateral contract. It provided:

> If an offer for a unilateral contract is made, and part of the consideration requested in the offer is given or tendered by the offeree in response thereto, the offeror is bound by a contract, the duty of immediate

---

[142] 135 Calif. 654, 67 Pac. 1086 (1902).

[143] Dudley O. McGovney, *Irrevocable Offers*, 27 HARV. L. REV. 644 (1914).

performance of which is conditional on the full consideration being given or tendered within the time stated in the offer, or, if no time is stated therein, within a reasonable time.

Professors Friedrich Kessler and Malcolm Pitman Sharp label the problem as "Unilateral Versus Bilateral Contracts: Manufactured Difficulties."[144] Professor Karl Llewellyn argued that unilateral contracts are rare and unimportant.[145] He argued that any issue which must be illustrated with hypothetical flagpole cases (in which the offeror offers a reward for climbing a flagpole but revokes the offer before the offeree reaches the top) ought to be suspect. The whole thing smells unreal. The Restatement (Second) of Contracts tries to erase the term "unilateral contract" from legal vocabulary and speaks of promises *calling for performances*, not simply promises.

3.   ***Unilateral contracts and loopholes:*** At one time the doctrine offered a possible loophole for a clever lawyer who wanted to break a contract for his client. Suppose a buyer, the client, ordered goods from seller, saying, "Please send me one model number 1000 automated thing." The seller responded by sending buyer an acknowledgment of order form, which is a promise to ship the goods. Before the goods arrive, buyer wants to back out because he has a better offer from another seller. The buyer's lawyer could send a notice revoking his client's "unaccepted offer." The lawyer would claim that the offer had been for the act of shipping goods. A promise to ship would not close the deal. The argument was just good enough to make the seller's case difficult. Many sellers would drop the whole thing and let the buyer out of his order.

Professor Llewellyn was the drafter of Article 2 of the Uniform Commercial Code. He plugged the loophole in § 2-206.[146] Restatement (Second) of Contracts § 29(2) says that essentially the same rule extends to all contracts.

4.   ***Failure to observe form versus expectation and reliance:*** What was involved in *Davis v. Jacoby*? Given the formalities of the Statute of Wills, why did Caro and Frank Davis have any claim against the estate? Rupert did request services. It was clear that he did not think he could ask for what he wanted as a gift without offering compensation. Caro and Frank performed some services. Thus, Caro, and perhaps Frank, would have a claim to restitution for the fair-market value of Caro's work in caring for Blanche and for any services that Frank offered while in California. However, they wanted much more than the fair-market value of a few weeks of nursing care. They did close a business and a house in Windsor, Ontario, and travel to California, but it is unclear what that cost them. Their reply brief contains a passage in which their lawyer addressed this question.

---

[144] FRIEDRICH KESSLER AND MALCOLM PITMAN SHARP, CASES ON CONTRACT (1953).

[145] Karl Llewellyn, *On Our Case-Law of Contract: Offer and Acceptance* (pts. 1 & 2), 48 YALE L.J. 1, 779 (1938–39).

[146] "Unless otherwise unambiguously indicated by the language or circumstances . . . (b) an order or other offer to buy goods for prompt or current shipment shall be construed as inviting acceptance either by a prompt promise to ship or by the prompt or current shipment of conforming or non-conforming goods. . . . "

While the court in finding IX stated that Plaintiffs *temporarily* closed their home, and that Frank Davis *temporarily* discontinued, but did not abandon, his business, the undisputed evidence is to the contrary. At the time of leaving Canada for California, appellants' home was permanently closed, and Frank Davis did abandon his business. The fact that after the death of both Mr. and Mrs. Whitehead, Frank Davis went back to Canada and reopened their home, and was re-employed by the insurance company, did not make the closing of their home and the abandonment of his business any less permanent. What both intended to do was to leave Canada forever or as long as necessary to carry out their contract with Whitehead. . . .

They did not wait to determine whether Rupert's death avoided their contract, or whether his death made it impossible for them fully to perform, or whether Rupert's offer to them was accepted in compliance with all technical requirements, or whether they should personally gain or lose by fulfilling their obligations. They stood not upon the order of their going, but went promptly and without question, and, by the way, at their own expense.[147]

Neither did they know whether, after fully performing their contract, they were to receive adequate or *any* compensation therefore. Rupert's affairs were in bad shape. His death prevented Frank from taking charge of them. The times were bad. Part at least of Rupert's property was mortgaged. It might be that all would be lost. Yet they did not hesitate. . . .

[T]o deny them relief now would amount to the perpetuation of a gross fraud upon them.[148]

Did Rupert make a promise to make wills to give the estate to Caro, or was his statement similar to Dr. McGee's estimate about the length of time George Hawkins would have to stay in the hospital? One can make a contract to make a will, but we can debate whether Rupert did this.[149] Does the court's opinion satisfy you when it concludes that he did? In a sense, the problem here is analogous to the one with which we began the course. There we asked if certain transactions come within Article 2 of the Uniform Commercial Code, and we found a number of situations hard to classify. Here, we are again trying to fit real-life events into legal categories designed with other kinds of transactions in mind.

Could a money judgment serve to restore Caro and Frank to the position in which they were before Rupert's letters? One California court thought that in many situations it could not:

---

[147] [Eds. note: The odd syntax in this sentence is explained by the fact that the statement is a Shakespearean allusion. *Macbeth*, Act III, Scene III.]

[148] Did this argument help the Davises' position that they made a contract with Rupert Whitehead?

[149] Instead of a promise, Rupert may have made a misrepresentation of fact concerning the dispositions in the two wills. However, as you will see in Chapter 4, in the early 1930s Caro and Frank probably would have had to prove that Rupert made a knowing misrepresentation to recover under the tort of fraud. This would not have been easy. There would also have been a question about the appropriate measure of damages at that time.

> Where the services rendered by plaintiff consisted in nursing and caring for a person enfeebled and suffering from a horrible disease, requiring constant and unceasing watchfulness, harrowing to the mind, destructive to the peace and comfort of the one performing the services, and possibly injurious to the health, it has been held that it is evident that decedent did not intend so to measure them, it is out of the power of any court, after the performance of such services, to restore the plaintiff to the situation in which he was before the contract was made or to compensate him therefore in damages.[150]

While this observation may be true in many instances, what do we learn from it? We could return to Chafee (he of the stranglehold, dismal swamp, hot potato, and living tree policies) once again and argue that the balance of factors suggests that courts should not intervene but should leave parties where they are. On the other hand, courts could attempt to reward relatives who offer care by protecting their expectation or their reliance losses. The lawyers for the legatees in *Davis v. Jacoby* threw the bilateral versus unilateral issue at the court, and the court had to play with it. Frank and Caro's lawyers worked to characterize their letters and conduct as a return promise creating a bilateral contract. Would the case have been better analyzed by using Restatement of Contracts § 90 and focusing on the amount of foreseeable substantial reliance and whether injustice could be avoided only by enforcing, in whole or in part, the promise?

Suppose you thought that Frank and Caro could not prove that they relied very substantially. They were able to reclaim their home and Frank's insurance business. Could you still make a case that after their response to Rupert's letters, their claim to the estate was far better than that of Rupert Ross Whitehead and Geoff Doubble? That is, are there some promises that courts ought to enforce apart from a return promise, performance, or reliance? Professor Mark Pettit Jr. argues that courts think this is the case, and they often use the idea of a unilateral contract to achieve the result they seek. Despite the academic attack on the idea following Llewellyn's great articles of the 1930s, Pettit says, "in fact unilateral contract never died, but is alive and thriving as never before."[151] We will see the doctrine again when we look at employment contracts.

5. ***Contracts subject to conditions of personal satisfaction:*** After considering unilateral contracts, we must examine a distinct but similar legal category into which the facts such as those in *Davis v. Jacoby* might fit. Recall our hypothetical version of the facts in the *Davis* case where we created an express unilateral contract to give Rupert leverage over the performances of Caro and Frank. Suppose, instead, Rupert had promised to will all his property to Caro in exchange for Caro and Frank's promises to perform services "to the satisfaction of Rupert Whitehead." Assume that Caro and Frank accepted this offer. The appropriate legal classification now is that the parties made a bilateral contract, *subject to the condition of Rupert's satisfaction.* That is, Rupert promises to pay, *provided that* he is satisfied with their work. Of course, this would still place a tremendous risk onto

---

[150] Walker v. Calloway, 99 Cal. App. 2d 675, 680, 222 P.2d 455 (1950).

[151] Mark Pettit Jr., *Modern Unilateral Contracts*, 63 B.U. L. Rev. 551 (1983).

Caro and Frank, but it would be somewhat different from the risks involved in a unilateral contract or from a promise enforced because of reliance under Restatement § 90.

(a) Unlike the promise of Rupert subject to enforcement under Restatement § 90, Caro and Frank would have made a promise to come to California and give services. Rupert's estate could sue them if they never left Windsor, if they came to California and then abandoned the project, or if they performed poorly.

(b) Unlike the situation under the classic unilateral contract unencumbered by reforms such as Restatement § 45, Caro and Frank would not be taking the risk of Rupert revoking his offer either by choice or by death. Their promise would form a contract, and death only revokes offers and not contracts.[152]

Of course, Rupert would have tremendous leverage under a "personal satisfaction" condition. Caro and Frank would have to satisfy him before he would have to perform his promise. Under this assumption, Rupert promised to make the will *only if he were satisfied*. Nonetheless, courts would be likely to insist that Rupert act in good faith in asserting that he was dissatisfied. They might even require that he be reasonable in his judgment, but this is not clear. Section 228 of the Restatement (Second) of Contracts adopts the view that "if it is practicable to determine whether a reasonable person in the position of the obligor would be satisfied, an interpretation is preferred under which the condition occurs if such a reasonable person in the position of the obligor would be satisfied."[153] He certainly could not call the whole thing off on a whim as he could if we were dealing with a revocable offer.

Qualitative vs. quantitative standards: Obviously, the deal is still risky for Caro and Frank. They would prefer that their performance be measured by an objective standard. If anyone could think of one, it might serve the interests of all concerned better. Yet it would not be easy to spell out just what Caro and Frank were to do. Imagine trying to write the clause concerning Frank's "laying off the booze." It might be easy to write a provision prohibiting his drinking a drop of liquor. However, it might not be easy to prove that he didn't honor the requirement. If he were willing to discuss the subject at all, Frank probably would ask for a clause speaking of drinking so much that it impaired his ability to perform business services regularly. Yet this would pose difficult questions of proof and judgment. In light of the difficulties, some contract drafters would not raise the question expressly. They would try to include language requiring adequate business services, hoping it might offer some support for negotiations if Frank's drinking became a problem.

Implied conditions of good faith and reasonable performance: Finally, suppose an older person seeking care from a younger couple does not demand an express promise to give good care. Can those in the role of Caro and Frank mistreat those

---

[152] Death may be a defense to a failure to perform a contract calling for the deceased's personal services where no one else can substitute, but it would not be a defense to a contract to convey land or pay money.

[153] The language of the Restatement seems exceptionally guarded in its phrasing; this probably reflects an underlying controversy with respect to the rule itself.

in the roles of Rupert or Blanche and still recover all of the property promised? A court would likely read the promise to make a will or to convey as subject to a condition of giving reasonable care. Then the quality of care would be an issue upon which the parties could offer proof. See *Jones v. Clark*, where a niece moved from New Hampshire to Alhambra, California, at her aunt's request.[154] The aunt promised that she would leave all her property to the niece by will. The aunt executed a codicil to her will a few weeks before her death. It declared that no property was being left to the niece because "since she has lived in Alhambra she has not helped me, nor been good to me and has disturbed me greatly by her actions toward me." Nonetheless, the court allowed the niece to prove that she had offered good care.

7. Contracts to Provide for the Old: Contract and Restitution as a Substitute for an Extended Family

Arrangements to provide for old people offer another example of the tension between legal formality and protecting reliance on promises. As people get old, they often become unable to care for themselves alone. Some need nursing care. Almost all want companionship. Spouses usually take care of spouses. But what happens when both are incapacitated or one dies? The three-generation family is a solution common throughout the world, but not one that is customary in middle-class American society.

Rich older people can hire a staff to provide care. Today upper-middle-class people can pay a great deal to segregate themselves from younger society. They move into the "Golden Years" retirement home, complete with golf course, bridge club, and staff nurse. Poorer older people who cannot take care of themselves while living on welfare, Social Security, or a pension, are also segregated from the larger society. However, the surroundings are not likely to be so architecturally pleasing. Many counties in many states have the "county old folks home." Years ago the mental hospital was often a final residence for many, though that is increasingly uncommon. Medicaid benefits may be important to many who need assistance — though the number of caregivers seems to be increasingly inadequate.

In any event, many of the old who have been stripped of friends, dignity, and family find themselves in care facilities when they become senile or bothersome. In between these extremes of wealth, older people often use the assets they have (usually their homes or farms as well as their pensions) to make arrangements so that they can live in their own homes while receiving care. These arrangements bump into the law of wills, gifts, contracts, restitution, and public benefits and produce a surprising number of disputes, litigation, and appellate opinions in every state.

These problems are less likely to develop if an older person has money. The present generation is generally better off than preceding generations. The poverty rate among people in the United States aged 65 and older was 9.5 percent in 2013,

---

[154] 19 Cal. 2d 156, 119 P.2d 731 (1941).

compared to an overall U.S. poverty rate of 14.5 percent.[155] The *Wall Street Journal* reported that in 1984 one in seven people over age 65 was below the poverty line while in 1964, one in four people was.[156] However, such problems may increase in the future as people live longer and costs of care rise.

Even older people with assets may want care from a relative and not a hired nurse. An older person may own a house or a farm plus some savings, but be uncertain that this will cover all expenses of care until death. In these cases, he or she may pursue a strategy of reward. This chapter contains several cases in which an older person promised to exchange their property for care from a relative or a friend. At the other extreme, an older person may rely on family ties so that one of his or her children will stay home or return to provide care and companionship. Often this role falls to the unmarried daughter, who, tradition would have it, has nothing better to do with her life.[157] Again, the *Wall Street Journal* says:

> Support for the very old may have to come increasingly from children approaching retirement or already retired and dealing with their own health problems. Many of the middle-aged may encounter simultaneous demands to support a parent in a nursing home and to put children through college. Daughters and daughters-in-law, the traditional caretakers of the elderly, are today far more likely to be employed, unwilling or financially unable to give up work to help an aged parent. . . .

> Divorce, remarriage, single parenthood and other changes in family patterns all are blurring lines of family responsibility. For example, the high divorce rate lessens chances that an elderly woman — men are more likely to remarry after divorce or death of a spouse — will have a helpmate when she needs one.[158]

Of course, there are many strategies to induce grown children to care for their aged parents. For example, suppose an unmarried daughter comes home to take care of Mom and Dad. She is likely to expect to be better treated in their wills than her brothers who send Christmas cards or gifts and visit whenever they find it

---

[155] *See* http://www.census.gov/hhes/www/poverty/about/overview.

[156] WALL STREET JOURNAL, July 30, 1984, p. 1, col. 1, p. 10, cols. 4–5.

[157] Some students have objected to this sentence as sexist. We think it descriptively accurate. The sexism is in the assumption that the customary role of women is their correct or only role and that it should be the model for the future. A description of what that role has been is either accurate or not. Care of the old can be a demanding and thankless job. Often there is a tremendous loss of freedom for the one giving care, since it is so difficult to leave for more than a short time. The burden most often falls on daughters who do not at the time have families or socially valued careers of their own. As so often is true, litigation of the sort described in the following sections is probably a surrogate for deeper problems in families and general social problems in dealing with our increasing lifespan. *See* Emily Abel, *Adult Daughters and Care for the Elderly*, 12 FEMINIST STUD. 479 (1986). Social science research indicates that daughters are more likely than sons to be expected to take on caregiving obligations, though this effect is somewhat blunted by other obligations. Family members' specific caregiving duties tend to be gendered, with daughters called upon to handle housework and sons handling financial matters. Jeanette A. Lawrence, Jacqueline J. Goodnow, Kerry Woods, and Gery Karantzas, *Distributions of Caregiving Tasks Among Family Members: The Place of Gender and Availability*, 16 J. OF FAM. PSYCHOL. 493 (2002).

[158] WALL STREET JOURNAL, July 30, 1984, p. 1, p. 10, cols. 4–5.

convenient. The brothers and other sisters may make financial contributions to run the household. However, neither the brother who writes the check nor the sister who cares for their aged parents wants to label her actions as motivated by a desire for gain. Aged parents, too, may want to imagine the situation as one held together by love rather than work now for pay later when the will is probated. For many people, contracts and wills along with death are taboo subjects. The law reflects this ambivalence about the true nature of the situation.

Even the hired nurse or housekeeper may become "a member of the family." She[159] may hear countless expressions of gratitude, including expressions or intimations of the idea that "you deserve more than I am paying you and I will make it right in my will." Then, too, a neighbor who assumes the duty of "just running next door to see that everything is okay" may give important services. She may provide nursing care during an older person's serious illness because no one else is available. Such a generous neighbor may expect the older person to remember her in the will, but custom dictates that she not voice this expectation while the older person is alive.

Throughout this section, we must remember that the law has provisions about wills and what happens if a person fails to make one. People have great freedom to will property to anyone. However, wills are revocable until death. One strategy sometimes recommended for older people is that they should use the leverage created by the right to make and revoke wills in order to get adult children to behave decently. Wills, however, can be attacked by charges of duress, undue influence, or lack of mental capacity on the part of the testator. Judges seek to protect those whom age has robbed of defenses from predators. Actually, those protected usually are the spouse and children who do not get "enough" under the will.

People often fail to make wills, or they have invalid ones. Statutes then divide property among relatives based on family relationships. For example, children take equally, whether or not they shared the work of caring for elderly parents. Relatives take the entire estate, although a nurse or neighbor was considered "one of the family" and did all of the dirty work. If the deceased did not leave you enough in the will, or if the deceased did not make a valid will, you must find a legal theory to justify any recovery. Contract and restitution are the most likely avenues open.

We will consider a number of common situations related to care for the elderly and the legal problems involved.

Contracts to make wills and the dead man's statute: First, suppose an older person promises to leave everything to the one giving care in exchange for services. The older person fails to execute such a will and then dies. The one who made a contract to give care may be able to get the promise enforced if they can prove that there was a valid contract. But they may run into trouble with the "dead man's statute." This doctrine prevents parties, in most instances, from testifying on their own behalf about conversations with people who are now dead. There are exceptions and qualifications to the dead man's statute in most states. Nonetheless, as a

---

[159] We think women assume this role more often than men. Again, we are describing socially defined gender roles and not asserting that it ought to be this way.

practical matter, one who gave care will have a much easier time proving his or her case if there is written evidence that a contract existed or if there is a disinterested witness who can testify to the making of an oral contract.

Payment for care when there is no express contract: Second, suppose that a person renders services with an expectation of compensation, through a will or otherwise. However, the recipient does not make a will or even an express contract to make one. For example, in *Estate of Voss*, an elderly man advertised in the newspaper for a housekeeper.[160] Plaintiff worked for him, but they never made a definite arrangement concerning wages. She lived in his house and ate food for which he paid. Plaintiff alleged that the elderly man promised to marry her, and that, as a result, she was lulled into continuing to work for him. No marriage took place, she testified, because the elderly man's son strongly opposed it. A fair wage would have been $35 per week, which was more than the value of her room and board. The plaintiff might have claimed that there was a contract implied in fact, or an obligation imposed by law to avoid unjust enrichment — which is sometimes called a contract implied in law.

The plaintiff's theory in the *Voss* case was restitution of benefits conferred. The old man accepted a benefit fully aware that it was not being offered as a gift. The court sustained plaintiff's claim. It awarded the housekeeper the going price for her services, less the value of her board and room, and not the value to the elderly man, which might have been more or less. Under this theory, the award pays her for her work, but she does not get the entire estate. After she is paid, the balance of the estate goes to the legatees under the will or to the relatives if there is no will.

Courts thus need not venture into the dismal swamp of evaluating family members' actions in time of need. Courts can avoid assessing the quality of the caregiver's services as well. The one receiving care can value contributions above and beyond the call of duty in a will. If the deceased fails to execute a will recognizing a housekeeper's work, then the caregiver is limited to the fair-market value of services rendered for which she has not been paid. Courts do not attempt to measure the intangible subjective values often involved in these relationships. Of course, this result may not please a housekeeper who is not a relative. She was there in the hour of need while the relatives did little or nothing. But, the deceased may have thought the housekeeper was paid all she had coming.

Recovery by family members: A family member who provides care for an elderly relative faces a major problem in recovering restitution of benefits conferred. Courts have long said there is a presumption that services given by one member of the family to another are gratuitous.[161] The one receiving the benefit

---

[160] 20 Wis. 2d 238, 121 N.W.2d 744 (1963).

[161] In *Estate of Steffes*, 95 Wis. 2d 490, 290 N.W.2d 697 (1980), the court considered compensation for services rendered by persons cohabiting but not related by marriage. Mary Lou Brooks and Virgil Steffes each were married to other persons. They met in a tavern where she worked, and then, at his request, she lived in his home on his farm from 1969 to 1976, when he died. She cleaned, cooked, washed, and ironed; she also picked corn, ran the combine, loaded silage, helped pour concrete walls, helped remodel the house, and paid the bills. Until 1974, Brooks and Steffes had sexual relations. In 1974, Steffes's wife died. In that same year, doctors found that Steffes had a brain tumor. Brooks gave him nursing care and drove him to a hospital for 28 consecutive days for cobalt treatments. He said that he

may not know that the person offering services expects payment for them. Thus he has not had a chance to reject services he would do without if he knew that he had to pay for them.

A family member must overcome a strong presumption to recover for benefits conferred. For example, in *Miller v. Estate of Bell*, there were four children, two sons and two daughters.[162] At the time of the litigation, the daughters were age 50 and 56 and living with families of their own. The two daughters, who lived near their parents, had cleaned and shopped for them and given them some personal care for six years before their deaths. Both parents had stated that all of the property should go to the daughters because they had taken care of them. The father made a will, giving all of his property to his wife if she survived him. If she did not, the property went to the daughters, except $100 that he left to each of the sons. The mother made no will because she told their lawyer that she had no property. Actually, she owned a half interest in most of the property, which the couple held jointly. The father died first. Since the mother survived her husband, she inherited

---

would leave her the proceeds of the sale of the farm, but he did not make such a will. She sued for the value of her services. The trial court found that she expected compensation, and that he had requested the services. The court awarded her $14,600 as compensation for the work during the last two years of Steffes's life (his gross estate was $733,644.65).

On appeal, the personal representative (Virgil Steffes's son) argued that because Virgil Steffes had treated Mary Lou Brooks as part of the family, the presumption of gratuitous services should apply. Justice Abrahamson wrote the majority opinion, which affirmed the trial court's decision. It was unnecessary to decide whether the presumption was applicable because if "a promise can be implied from the facts, then the plaintiff is entitled to compensation regardless of the fact that she rendered services with a sense of affection, devotion, and duty." Plaintiff expected payment, and the deceased expressed his intention to provide for her.

The personal representative also argued that she could not recover on an implied contract because she was living in an adulterous relationship. The trial court found that the illicit bargain was incidental to the plaintiff's performance of lawful services. It was not a condition of nor a consideration for deceased's implied promise to compensate. The majority of the Wisconsin Supreme Court accepted this finding, citing *Marvin v. Marvin*.

Justice Coffey dissented. He said "I have examined the circumstances and can only reach the conclusion that sexual intimacy, in violation of their marriage vows, was the underlying motivation for Mrs. Brooks's entry into and stay in the home of deceased."

Justice Coffey also quoted at length from *Hewitt v. Hewitt*, in which the Supreme Court of Illinois rejected the *Marvin* doctrine. He said, "I believe the majority has resorted to an unfortunate form of judicial surgery that can only serve to accelerate the growth of the self-destructive cancer of the [1970s'] 'immorality' and the decline of the family. . . . The judicial system is ill-equipped to deal with a social change of this magnitude because we are without the benefit of up-to-date economic, social, and psychological data in the field of domestic relations and the far-reaching implications of court-approved abandonment and the problems accompanying fatherless and motherless children in the decades ahead. . . . "

Note that Mary Lou Brooks sought only $29,000 from the estate, based on a restitution theory. Wisconsin had not recognized *Marvin v. Marvin* at that time. Was the vigorous (and expensive) defense raised by the estate justifiable in terms of the dollars involved? If the tone of the brief can be relied upon as capturing the motivations behind the defense, it seems that it was seen, at least in part, as a crusade against a woman who had left her family for an illicit relationship and a campaign for the old-fashioned moral high ground. The irony is that in resisting a settlement of the case, the defendants gave the Supreme Court of Wisconsin an opportunity to decide a case setting a precedent for recovery by a participant in what had been an illicit relationship. As of 2015, *Steffes* was still the governing case.

[162] 224 Wis. 593, 273 N.W. 67 (1937).

a half interest in the property under his will and had her own half interest as well. When she died without a will, all of this property went to the four children equally, and not according to the terms of her husband's will. The court rejected the daughters' restitution claim against their mother's estate since their services were presumed to have been gratuitous.[163] However, the court noted that their bequests under their father's will were more than the fair value of all their services.

One can contrast *Estate of Grossman*.[164] A daughter lived in Milwaukee where she worked as a waitress, and her parents lived in Dale, Wisconsin. Dale is about 100 miles north of Milwaukee. When her mother became seriously ill, her father asked her to return home. She cared for her mother for about six weeks until her death. A doctor testified that the daughter's services had been necessary. The daughter sacrificed an average of $8.00 per day, which she would have earned had she stayed at work in Milwaukee. The trial court allowed her claim against the estate for $4.00 per day for her services. The Supreme Court of Wisconsin affirmed, saying: "While the proof offered by claimant to overcome the presumption that the services were gratuitous is not too strong, it is considered sufficient to overcome the presumption and sustain the trial court in granting judgment. . . . "

The daughter also made trips to Dale from Milwaukee between February 1st and July 1, 1942, on September 1, 1942, and on November 22, 1945. Her father was "an aged man" with a heart condition. During her visits she cared for him and did housework. The father died on December 13, 1945. The Supreme Court disallowed a claim for these trips and services. It said:

> While claimant is to be complimented on the interest shown in her father and her desire to be helpful to him, and without doubt the father was happy to see her and such services as she rendered were helpful to him, nevertheless these trips home were no different than the trips she made home prior to the time her mother was taken sick, even though they may have been a little more frequent and the services rendered were somewhat greater. There is nothing to indicate that the father requested her to come home at the times in question, and certainly no parent would expect to pay a child for services when she occasionally drops in to visit for a day or two at a time.

Another factor, perhaps relevant, in the *Grossman* case was the disposition of the father's estate. The claimant and her brother survived the father. The brother was in the Army during the time the daughter performed the services. In 1942, the father deeded the family house to his daughter, reserving a life estate. This property was appraised at $2750. In his will, the father gave the daughter $500, and then divided the balance of his estate equally between the daughter and the son.

---

[163] In the 1980s, the daughters might have had a claim for malpractice against the lawyer who handled their parents' estates. *See* Auric v. Continental Casualty Co., 111 Wis. 2d 507, 331 N.W.2d 325 (1983). Not all states allow those who would have taken under an invalid will to sue the lawyer for negligence. The Wisconsin court said that allowing such suits would provide an incentive to exercise due care.

[164] 250 Wis. 457, 27 N.W.2d 365 (1947).

Restitution for friendly neighbors: Family members are not the only ones to face the gratuitous services problem. Neighbors and friends also help old people. They may mow the lawn, do odd jobs, visit, bring in food, and offer some household service and nursing care. Then the older person dies. May the neighbor make a claim for the reasonable value of his or her services against the estate? There is no presumption, as there is in the case of family. However, the neighbor will have difficulty establishing that the older person should have known that the neighbor expected payment. Sometimes the older person did not ask for the services and, as a practical matter, would have had difficulty rejecting them if he or she wanted to do so.

In re Goldrick's Will involved the helpful neighbor story.[165] The Wisconsin Supreme Court reversed a judgment for $500. It noted that the services were "various things that a friendly neighbor might well perform for a widow next door, whose relations to her husband and to her had always been friendly and neighborly." Consider that statement in light of the record of the trial. The neighbor's evidence concerning the work done was as follows:

> George Goldrick was buried on the 13th day of June, 1918, and after his death I performed services for Mrs. Goldrick in looking after her mortgages, insurance, taxes, collected her interest, worked around her house, looked after the building of a porch, re-roofed the house, built a cistern, cleaned the house and put in ice for her, mowed the lawn, drove her around about five thousand miles, looked after selling land, sold lots and land; looked after some trespass, and went to see town boards with reference to her assessments, and whatever business she had to do I did for her.

> Had quite a job looking after the interest. Don't think one out of twenty-five could pay the interest and pay the taxes, and had quite a lot of trouble with that. A lot of times they would come and pay twenty or thirty dollars to Mrs. Goldrick, and she would not keep track of it, and had quite a job trying to keep that straightened out. A lot of receipts were not dated, and it was pretty hard to read her writing. I made out her income reports, both state and federal, looked after the payment of all taxes at all times; attended to mortgage foreclosures and bid in the property. Went to Oshkosh for her. When the Goldrick estate was probated a forty was omitted and I had to see about going through all that again. Drove out to different farmers in regard to interest, looked after the Mattoon farm, and had to do quite a lot of chasing around. Went to Oshkosh to look over some lots which a man wanted to trade for some property in Aniwa. Went to the Town of Plover when the equalization board was in session to get her valuation down. Went to the Town of Harrison to see about getting taxes lower in that town.

> I looked after a trespass for her. When she sold 200 acres of timber I went and looked over that for her. Sold eight, ten, or twelve pieces of land for her and looked after her business in general whatever she had to do. She couldn't even sign anything, she wanted to know from me whether she should sign it or not.

---

[165] 198 Wis. 500, 224 N.W. 741 (1929).

After Goldrick's death Mr. Cady was the attorney for the estate and I sent in whatever papers I had, and perhaps once in every five or six weeks I would get a letter from him wanting to know about which or when this property was bought or that property was bought, and had a lot of trouble with the government over income tax.

Had to make good on some abstracts which Mr. Goldrick had gotten for people. Looked after the building of line fences and looked after her checking accounts. Such services were worth at least $25.00 per month.

They covered a period of eight and a half years up to the time of her death. She was seventy-four when she died. She had heart trouble and rheumatism and was not able to look after her own affairs. For the last two years she has not been just right mentally.

In addition to the work I mentioned I also helped build a cement sidewalk, helped clean the windows, cleaned the furnace, and helped set out some shrubs, filled in manure, shoveled the walks, put on screens, took off screens, attended to locks, put on the storm windows and storm doors, emptied out slop and put on and took off the screen doors and windows. Packed the ice in the ice house. Shoveled off the roads and moved the furniture, looked after moneys, mortgages and notes, made out deeds; nobody had anything to do with the property excepting myself.

The Wisconsin Supreme Court explained:

> There is undoubtedly a strong temptation to participate in the estates of deceased persons by magnifying trifling services into large claims, when the persons to whom the supposed services were rendered are dead and have no answer to make. Claimants silent in lifetime, become voluble when their pretended debtors no longer can speak. Such claims are not favored in law.

Mrs. Goldrick had remembered her neighbor in her will. The court characterized the situation as one where the neighbor expected a larger legacy than he received. The value of the estate was $88,000, and there were no children. A year before the widow died, she executed a will under which she left the friendly neighbor $9,000. Later she executed the will which was probated, under which the friendly neighbor took only $1,000. There was no evidence as to why she changed her mind.

Promises recognizing past services: Finally, it is not uncommon for elderly people to recognize that they are receiving services above and beyond the call of duty. They then promise to pay a family member or a neighbor for them. For example, *In re Estate of Tulley* involved a woman who was once a neighbor of the claimant.[166] The woman was in ill health, and the claimant helped her find and furnish an apartment. The claimant visited the woman daily and did the shopping and cleaning. The woman told her landlord that she did not know what she would do without claimant's help. On September 11, 1975, the woman gave claimant a check for $5,000 and a handwritten note. It said, "Jean I am leaving a check for you rather than putting you in the will. This way you won't have to pay tax on it. I only

---

[166] 86 Wis. 2d 593, 273 N.W.2d 329 (1979).

hope there is enough left to cover it by the time I die." The woman died on November 1, 1975. There was not enough in the bank account to cover the check, but she left an estate of about $40,000.

The Supreme Court of Wisconsin found that the $5,000 check was an invalid testamentary disposition because it failed to follow the formalities of execution prescribed by the Statute of Wills. The court said that people could make a contract and delay payment until after death. However, there was no proof that claimant ever expected compensation for her services or that they had bargained. The check and the note were not a promise to pay in exchange for the services. "[I]t was the intent of decedent to show appreciation for the kindnesses of the claimant and . . . it was the intent of claimant to render assistance to the decedent without expectation of monetary compensation."

Suppose the woman had written a slightly different note. Suppose she had said, "Jean, you have been wonderful and done so much for me. And so I promise to pay you $5,000 when I die. You can collect it by cashing this check." In other words, the older woman's promise recognizes an obligation she felt because of all Jean's kindness to her. Such a transaction would not be a bargain, and there would be no consideration for it under an orthodox view.

Recall the definition of consideration given in Restatement (Second) of Contracts § 71: "To constitute consideration, a performance or a return promise must be bargained for." Then it says, "A performance or return promise is bargained for if it is sought by the promisor in exchange for his promise and is given by the promisee in exchange for that promise."[167] The problem in our hypothetical case is there was no swap but only a recognition that Jean had done so much. You cannot bargain for a performance you already have. Reliance theories, such as Restatement (Second) of Contracts § 90, may not work either. In these cases, the claimant conferred the benefit first and not in reliance on a promise which came later. Section 90 might help if Jean could show that she had continued providing services relying on the promise. Do you see why this might be hard to prove?

Most states do recognize "past consideration" as enough to justify enforcing a promise in a narrowly limited class of cases involving commercial transactions and far from our kindly neighbor situation. Suppose you and I made a contract under which you conferred a benefit on me. However, I had or acquired a defense to your rights under that contract because:

(1) I was under the age of majority (usually 18 or 21) when I entered the agreement, or

(2) the statute of limitations had run on your claim, or

(3) I received a discharge of all my debts in bankruptcy.

Then, I, being over 18 and knowing of my defense, made a new promise to pay you for the benefit which you had conferred. Most courts would award you damages if I then failed to pay after this second promise.[168] Some courts explained the case

---

[167] The entire text of § 71 is in Note 1 after *Hamer v. Sidway.*

[168] Liability for breach of contract is not sacrosanct. A contract party who goes into bankruptcy is

as one where I waived my defense, and so you can sue on the original promise that was supported by consideration. The original Restatement of Contracts recognized these three situations as exceptions to the rule of § 75, in sections 86, 87, and 89. These sections, together with § 90, were grouped under the heading "Contracts Without Consideration." However, many of the judges who decided the cases that established these rules did not concede that promises were being enforced without consideration. They looked hard and found some. They asserted there was a moral obligation to pay any debt despite the existence of "technical" defenses (and immoral ones?) such as bankruptcy, the statute of limitations, or infancy.[169] What they called a moral obligation served as consideration for the debtor's subsequent promise to pay.

Recognition of a moral obligation as consideration: The supreme courts of Wisconsin and a very few other states have expanded this idea of a moral consideration to pay for past benefits. Some of the Wisconsin cases deal with commercial situations, but many concern promises by older people to pay family members and neighbors for care and services. See, for example, *Estate of Hatten*,[170] *Estate of Schoenkerman*,[171] and *Estate of Gerke*.[172] Yet there must be a moral obligation to pay for the services, and the court is the judge of whether or not such a moral obligation exists. For example, in *Estate of Briese*, the court found there was no such moral obligation in a case involving family services.[173] Husband promised dying First Wife to take care of her Mother, who had lived with them for more than 30 years. A year after First Wife's death, Husband remarried. Mother left in anger, although Husband did not tell her to leave. Mother sued for breach of Husband's promise to First Wife to take care of Mother. She lost. There was no consideration for Husband's promise. Moral consideration does not apply. The benefits Husband had received from First Wife (the promisee) were benefits "which it was the legal and moral duty of the promisee to confer without compensation, else any promise made by a husband to his wife becomes legally enforceable." Mother also claimed that she had furnished moral consideration to support the husband's promise to First Wife (her daughter) because she had done housework with her daughter while living with them from 1905 to 1935 and then had continued to run the house for two years until the dispute after the remarriage. The Supreme Court of Wisconsin did not respond to this argument in its opinion.

The drafters of the Restatement (Second) of Contracts accepted some part of the Wisconsin moral consideration cases and attempted to codify their view of them. Its

---

likely to be able to discharge some or all of her contract debts. The "discharge" (elimination) of contractual liability is subject to complex rules under the federal bankruptcy code if the contract party has commenced and completed a bankruptcy case. 11 U.S.C. §§ 523, 524(d), & 727(a). This tends to support Lawrence Friedman's prescient observation that "[t]he most dramatic changes touching the significance of contract law in modern life . . . came about, not through internal developments in contract law, but through developments in public policy which systematically robbed contract of its subject-matter." Lawrence Friedman, CONTRACT LAW IN AMERICA: A SOCIAL AND ECONOMIC CASE STUDY (1965).

[169] [Eds. note: We discuss the infancy doctrine in Chapter 4, *infra.*]

[170] 233 Wis. 199, 288 N.W. 278 (1940).

[171] 236 Wis. 311, 294 N.W. 810 (1940).

[172] 271 Wis. 297, 73 N.W.2d 506 (1955).

[173] 240 Wis. 426, 3 N.W.2d 691 (1942).

version provides:

§ 86. Promise for Benefit Received

(1) A promise made in recognition of a benefit previously received by the promisor from the promisee is binding to the extent necessary to prevent injustice.

(2) A promise is not binding under Subsection (1)

(a) if the promisee conferred the benefit as a gift or for other reasons the promisor has not been unjustly enriched; or

(b) to the extent that its value is disproportionate to the benefit.

Section 86 may be inconsistent with many of the Wisconsin moral consideration cases. In many of those cases "the promisee conferred the benefit as a gift . . . " in the sense that the promisee did not expect to be paid for the noble action. However, courts electing to follow § 86 will have to decide what the text means by the term *gift*. On one hand, a father may give his daughter a new stereo system for a birthday present. On the other, a daughter may care for her aged father for years out of a sense of love or familial duty. Are both of these transactions gifts within the meaning of § 86? Do you see any difference between them? For a discussion of Restatement (Second) of Contracts § 86, see Professor Stanley Henderson, *Promises Grounded in the Past: The Idea of Unjust Enrichment and the Law of Contracts.*[174]

8.   If Law Is to Intervene, What Remedies Are Appropriate?

a.   Reliance and the expectation interest in the family context

Promises enforced because of reliance and the measure of recovery: We've considered several cases where courts protected reliance on promises where there was doubt whether the transaction should be called a bargain. When we looked at *Hamer v. Sidway* (the generous uncle case), and *Ricketts v. Scothorn* (the generous grandfather case), we considered whether expectation or reliance damages should be awarded in such cases. We noted the Restatement (Second) of Contracts § 90's recognition of reliance recovery. Assuming you conclude that a plaintiff deserves something more than restitution, should he or she receive the value of full performance of the promise?

Recognition of past benefits and limited remedies: Suppose an older person makes a promise to pay for care and housekeeping services rendered in the past. Assume that the circumstances make this promise enforceable under the "moral consideration" doctrine in Wisconsin. How much can the person who performs the services recover? Will the court enforce the older person's promise or will it limit the remedy?

---

[174] 57 Va. L. Rev. 1115 (1971).

In *Estate of Hatten*, plaintiff sued on a promissory note given by an older person to pay for past services.[175] The note was for $25,000. The court stated:

Were we required to determine whether the services, meals, etc., were reasonably worth the sum of $25,000, — in other words, if this action were one to recover *quantum meruit*, we should have no hesitation in holding that they were not reasonably worth that amount.

Yet the court found the note a valid claim against the estate because "whether or not the consideration was adequate is a matter exclusively for the decision of the parties."

On the other hand, in *Estate of Gerke*,[176] the older person had promised to leave "everything" to the plaintiff upon the older person's death as compensation for past services. The court enforced the promise because of moral consideration. However, it limited plaintiff's recovery to the reasonable value of "that which the claimant furnished, in return for which the promise was made." The court explained that to "measure recovery by the value of the estate would circumvent the statute of wills . . . and will not be countenanced." Neither the briefs of the lawyers nor the opinion of the Supreme Court of Wisconsin cite *Estate of Hatten*. Can we conclude that *Estate of Hatten* is overruled by implication, or are the cases distinguishable?

Robert Braucher, the Reporter for the first part of the Restatement (Second) of Contracts, saw these cases as distinguishable. Section 86, you will recall, adopts some part of the Wisconsin "moral consideration" rule but rejects that phrase. It provides that "[a] promise made in recognition of a benefit previously received by the promisor from the promisee is binding *to the extent necessary to prevent injustice*." Comment *i* says that:

Where the value of the benefit is uncertain, a promise to pay the value is binding and a promise to pay a liquidated sum may serve to fix the amount due if in all the circumstances it is not disproportionate to the benefit. . . . A promise which is excessive may sometimes be enforced to the extent of the value of the benefit, and the remedy may be thought of as quasi-contractual rather than contractual. In other cases a promise of disproportionate value may tend to show unfair pressure or other conduct by the promisee such that justice does not require any enforcement of the promise.

There are two illustrations of Comment *i*:

12. A, a married woman of sixty, has rendered household services without compensation over a period of years for B, a man of eighty living alone and having no close relatives. B has a net worth of three million dollars and has often assured A that she will be well paid for her services, whose reasonable value is not in excess of $6,000. B executes and delivers to A a written promise to pay A $25,000 "to be taken from my estate." The promise is binding.

---

[175] 233 Wis. 199, 288 N.W. 278 (1940).

[176] 271 Wis. 297, 73 N.W.2d 506 (1955).

13. The facts being otherwise as stated in Illustration 12, B's promise is made orally and is to leave A his entire estate. A cannot recover more than the reasonable value of her services.

The Reporter's Note says that Illustration 12 is based on *Estate of Hatten* and Illustration 13 is based on *Estate of Gerke*.

Does Comment *i* satisfactorily explain the difference between the *Hatten* and *Gerke* cases as to remedy? Can courts make the determinations called for by the *Hatten*, *Gerke*, and Restatement (Second) of Contracts § 86 doctrines? On what basis? To what extent is predictability important in this area?

Suppose a daughter has taken care of her elderly father. He promises to leave everything to her under circumstances where his promise would be enforceable in Wisconsin because of the doctrine of moral consideration. Why aren't her expectations important enough to deserve full protection?

b.   Specific performance and "shotgun marriages"

Up to this point our focus has been on contracts to care for the elderly and fights between relatives and caretakers after care was given. Usually the older person has died, and then the contracts litigation is part of the process of dividing the estate. In this section, however, we return to the problems of legal intervention in ongoing relationships. To what extent, if at all, can courts police the quality of care? To what extent, if at all, can they protect the interests of the caregiver in the face of the desires of the older person to break off the relationship? These relationships are subjective and involve human feeling. They are not primarily economic. It is difficult to care for the old, and it is difficult to be old and lose independence and control after a lifetime of running things. It is easy to dismiss these situations and say that people should not run to court to cope with such problems. If, however, courts are not the place for resolving such battles, where then is the place? First, we will look at the rights of the one entitled to receive care under a contract. Then we will consider the rights of the one giving it.

The rights of the one giving care: The following cases introduce problems in running ongoing relationships. On the one hand, they force us to ask what courts could and should do when relationships of this kind are in trouble. On the other hand, they should also suggest questions related to preventing the trouble in the first place. Could lawyers have anticipated and prevented the problems that arose in these cases? One of a lawyer's tasks is to draft legal instruments such as contracts, wills, and trusts so that they are legally enforceable. However, this is hardly enough. The more important task is to plan transactions so they will work without being enforced by the courts.

BRACKENBURY v. HODGKIN
Maine Supreme Judicial Court
102 A. 106 (1917)

CORNISH, C. J.

The defendant Mrs. Sarah D. P. Hodgkin on the 8th day of February, 1915, was the owner of certain real estate — her home farm, situated in the outskirts of Lewiston. She was a widow and was living alone. She was the mother of six adult children, five sons, one of whom, Walter, is the codefendant, and one daughter, who is the coplaintiff. The plaintiffs were then residing in Independence, Missouri. Many letters had passed between mother and daughter concerning the daughter and her husband returning to the old home and taking care of the mother, and finally on February 8, 1915, the mother sent a letter to the daughter and her husband which is the foundation of this bill in equity. In this letter she made a definite proposal, the substance of which was that if the Brackenburys would move to Lewiston, and maintain and care for Mrs. Hodgkin on the home place during her life, and pay the moving expenses, they were to have the use and income of the premises, together with the use of the household goods, with certain exceptions, Mrs. Hodgkin to have what rooms she might need. The letter closed, by way of postscript, with the words, "you to have the place when I have passed away."

Relying upon this offer, which was neither withdrawn nor modified, and in acceptance thereof, the plaintiffs moved from Missouri to Maine late in April, 1915, went upon the premises described and entered upon the performance of the contract. Trouble developed after a few weeks, and the relations between the parties grew most disagreeable. The mother brought two suits against her son-in-law on trifling matters, and finally ordered the plaintiffs from the place, but they refused to leave. Then on November 7, 1916, she executed and delivered to her son, Walter C. Hodgkin, a deed of the premises, reserving a life estate in herself. Walter, however, was not a bona fide purchaser for value without notice, but took the deed with full knowledge of the agreement between the parties and for the sole purpose of evicting the plaintiffs. On the very day the deed was executed he served a notice to quit upon Mr. Brackenbury, as preliminary to an action of forcible entry and detainer which was brought on November 13, 1916. This bill in equity was brought by the plaintiffs to secure a reconveyance of the farm from Walter to his mother, to restrain and enjoin Walter from further prosecuting his action of forcible entry and detainer, and to obtain an adjudication that the mother holds the legal title impressed with a trust in favor of the plaintiffs in accordance with their contract.

The sitting justice made an elaborate and carefully considered finding of facts and signed a decree, sustaining the bill with costs against Walter C. Hodgkin, and granting the relief prayed for. The case is before the law court on the defendants' appeal from this decree.

Four main issues are raised.

1. *As to the completion and existence of a valid contract.*

A legal and binding contract is clearly proven. The offer on the part of the mother was in writing, and its terms cannot successfully be disputed. There was no need that it be accepted in words, nor that a counterpromise on the part of the plaintiffs be made. The offer was the basis, not of a bilateral contract, requiring a reciprocal promise, a promise for a promise, but of a unilateral contract requiring an act for a promise. "In the latter case the only acceptance of the offer that is necessary is the performance of the act. In other words, the promise becomes binding when the act is performed." . . . This is elementary law.

The plaintiffs here accepted the offer by moving from Missouri to the mother's farm in Lewiston and entering upon the performance of the specified acts, and they have continued performance since that time so far as they have been permitted by the mother to do so. The existence of a completed and valid contract is clear.

2. *The creation of an equitable interest.*

This contract between the parties, the performance of which was entered upon by the plaintiffs, created an equitable interest in the land described in the bill in favor of the plaintiffs. The letter of February 8, 1915, signed by the mother, answered the statutory requirement that "there can be no trust concerning lands, except trusts arising or resulting by implication of law, unless created or declared by some writing signed by the party or his attorney." . . . No particular formality need be observed; a letter or other memorandum is sufficient to establish a trust provided its terms and the relations of the parties to it appear with reasonable certainty. *Bates v. Hurd*, 65 Me. 180; *McClellan v. McClellan*, 65 Me. 500. The equitable interest of the plaintiffs in these premises is obvious, and they are entitled to have that interest protected.

3. *Alleged breach of duty on the part of the plaintiffs.*

The defendants contend that, granting an equitable estate has been established, the plaintiffs have failed of performance because of their improper and unkind treatment of Mrs. Hodgkin, and therefore have forfeited the right to equitable relief which they might otherwise be entitled to. The sitting justice decided this question of fact in favor of the plaintiffs, and his finding is fully warranted by the evidence. Mrs. Hodgkin's temperament and disposition, not only as described in the testimony of others, but as revealed in her own attitude, conduct, and testimony as a witness, as they stand out on the printed record, mark her as the provoking cause in the various family difficulties. She was "the one primarily at fault."

4. *Adequate relief at law.*

The defendants finally invoke the familiar rule that the plaintiffs have a plain and adequate remedy at law, and therefore cannot ask relief in equity.

The answer to this proposition is that this rule does not apply when the court has been given full equity jurisdiction, or has been given special statutory jurisdiction covering the case. . . . The court in equity in this state is given special statutory jurisdiction to grant relief in cases of trusts (R.S. 1903, c. 79, § 6, par. 4), and therefore the exception and not the rule must govern here.

The plaintiffs are entitled to the remedy here sought, and the entry must be: Appeal dismissed. Decree of sitting justice affirmed, with costs against Walter C. Hodgkin.

NOTES AND QUESTIONS

1. ***Background of the case:*** Dawson and Harvey, in their 1959 casebook on contracts, tell us, "Our informant learned from Mr. Brackenbury that the latter secured a transcript of the record in the equity case and 'would from time to time, read from it to the old lady.'" In their teacher's manual to that casebook, Dawson and Harvey added more details. A younger brother of Mrs. Brackenbury sided with his mother, Mrs. Hodgkin. He said that:

> Conditions got to be unbearable for my mother chiefly from Brackenbury. I have been in when they were eating and food was not passed to her, but rather thrown to her by Brackenbury. I never did hear my sister in any argument with mother, but apparently approving what her husband did. The fork which she always had to use was an old iron one with two tines broken off, fit only for the waste cart. I went into the house once when he followed with a gun and threatened to shoot me. But I did not budge.

Douglas I. Hodgkin is Sarah Hodgkin's great-grandson. Until he retired, he was a professor of political science at Bates College in Lewiston, Maine. He compiled information about the family feud that continued from 1915 to 1922.[177] The feud received extensive coverage in the local newspapers. He says, "The feud arose from the irascible personality of Sarah D. Purinton Hodgkin and the rivalries among her six living children over the family property." Professor Hodgkin continued: "The residences of the family members were in close proximity to one another. Many of Mrs. Hodgkin's sons live in homes within sight of hers and of one another. It was difficult or impossible for the combatants to avoid the others." None of Mrs. Hodgkin's sons would live with her, and she attempted to recruit her daughter Bertha and her husband Joe Brackenbury. They knew what they might face, and they insisted on a letter that made detailed promises.

Trouble flared within the first month of the Brackenburys' arrival. Joe Brackenbury and Sarah Hodgkin argued about who would decide what work needed to be done. Sarah Hodgkin went to bed at 4:30 or 5:00 P.M. during the winter, and she demanded that the house be quiet. She did not like Bertha's cooking. Sarah Hodgkin tried to get the Brackenburys to leave. Finally, she sold the property to her son Walter, and this prompted the case which you have read.

Battles continued after the decision. Joe Brackenbury cut wood on the property, and Sarah Hodgkin sued him for trespass. The jury found for Sarah Hodgkin but

---

[177] DOUGLAS I. HODGKIN, FRACTURED FAMILY: FIGHTING IN THE MAINE COURTS (2005). Professor Hodgkin dedicated his book to his siblings, who participated "in the handling of family matters in a diplomatic, peaceful, and cooperative manner."

awarded her only one cent as damages. The brothers who sided with their mother came to the house and attempted to remove a bed at her request. Bertha stopped them. Walter Hodgkin called the police and asserted that Bertha had threatened to shoot him if he tried to move the bed. The jury found Bertha not guilty. She then sued Walter for $3000 because of the embarrassment of the criminal complaint. She was awarded $212.14 in damages. Irving and Russell Hodgkin had an argument that ended when Irving hit Russell in the face. Once again the family returned to the local courts. Russell was awarded $66.71.

Sarah Hodgkin died on January 4, 1921. She left Bertha and her brother Russell nothing in her will "because I have assisted them each to a great extent in the past with financial and other assistance." Bertha and Russell contested the will, alleging undue influence and lack of testamentary capacity. The court admitted the will to probate. Joe and Bertha Brackenbury then sold the property and moved back to Independence, Missouri. Bertha died in 1961 at the age of 97. She corresponded with her nieces and nephews, but she remained estranged from her brothers for the rest of their lives.

2.   *Coerced performance and personal relationships:* Why didn't the court consider the "shotgun marriage" aspects of specific performance? The final decree provided "Sarah D.P. Hodgkin shall hold said land which shall be impressed with a trust in their [the Brackenburys'] favor and in accordance with the terms of the contract so long as the plaintiffs hereafter perform their contract according to the language and spirit thereof." Could the court have done more to police the relationship? Was it necessary to leave Mrs. Hodgkin at the mercy of Brackenbury?

Usually, courts will not grant specific performance in a personal services contract. In *Fitzpatrick v. Michael*, a Maryland court explained why: "[M]ischief likely to result from the enforced continuance of the relationship incident to the service when it has become personally obnoxious to one of the parties is so great that the best interests of society require that a remedy be refused . . . "[178]

In a few situations, courts will grant a negative injunction. At least in form, the court is not ordering someone to perform services. It just orders the defendant not to perform those services for anyone other than the plaintiff. For example, in *Warner Bros. Pictures, Inc. v. Nelson*, the actress Bette Davis was under a long-term contract with Warner Bros. Pictures that called for her to act in its motion pictures.[179] She had a dispute with the studio, and went to England and threatened to make pictures for an English studio. The court ordered her not to render "any services for or in any motion picture or stage production or productions of any person, firm, or corporation other than the plaintiffs." The indirect coercion supporting the contract worked. Bette Davis resumed making pictures for Warner Bros. Soon thereafter Davis and Warner Bros. renegotiated her contract. After winning the lawsuit, why was Warner Bros. willing to do this?

3.   *Review of themes to this point:* Consider the following situation as a way of reviewing what you should have learned to this point in the course:

---

[178]   9 A.2d 639 (1939).

[179]   [1937] I K.B. 209.

Husband and wife agree in writing that Wife will work while Husband begins law school.[180] After he finishes the second year, she will start the first year at the same law school, assuming she is admitted. After graduation, he will take a job in the area to support the two of them while she finishes law school.

They perform the agreement, and she gains admission to the law school he is attending. At graduation a law firm in San Diego, California, offers him a job. He is to begin immediately. He wants to take it. He insists that his wife come with him to San Diego. He does not want to be separated from her and their children. He argues that they cannot afford to maintain two households. She does not want to change law schools. The only law schools in the San Diego area that will accept her as a transfer student are of much lesser status than her current law school. If she transferred she would probably have fewer job opportunities at graduation. She does not want a divorce. She believes that if they can solve this problem, the marriage will survive. If there is nothing else that can be done, she will go to the San Diego area as he insists. However, she has not told him this.

You are a practicing lawyer. Wife is an old friend and you have offered her a summer job between her first and second year in law school. She asks for your advice, and suggests that she sue her husband for specific performance or for damages caused by his anticipatory breach of contract.[181] She will care for their children while she finishes law school. However, this will require both tuition and support, including money to replace the child care services that the husband would have given, as well as to pay for the expenses of finishing law school. She believes that he can borrow any money he cannot save by living very frugally in San Diego. What advice would you give the wife? Should she sue? If so, for what? Is she likely to win a decree of specific performance or a judgment for a sum of money as damages? Would filing a complaint be a good or bad bargaining strategy? Are there ways other than litigation to handle a dispute of this kind?

9.   Alternatives to Litigation in Family Matters

We have looked at relationships between husbands and wives and between families and those who care for the old. Traditionally, courts said that litigation was an inappropriate way to deal with problems between spouses. Similarly, there might be better ways than litigation to compensate meritorious services to the elderly. During the 1970s and 1980s, there was much debate about "alternatives to litigation." Critics said that American courts were crowded. Litigation was costly

---

[180] This may be an agreement that they cannot perform within one year. Many professional schools require students to be enrolled for a specified time. As a result, the contract might come within the Statute of Frauds. Absent an exception to the statute such as part performance, oral promises for performances that would take more than a year would not be legally enforceable. While we have made the promises in writing here, how likely are Husband and Wife to make this kind of arrangement in writing if they are living together?

[181] You may assume that the husband's statements about moving to San Diego would themselves breach their contract when he made them. Although the date for his performance — supporting her during her last two years of law school — may not yet have come, the law would allow her to sue now as a result of his clear repudiation of his obligations under the contract. Obviously, we are assuming away a difficult problem. In the usual situation, the husband's statements would not be so clear. You would face difficulty establishing that he had repudiated the contract at this point.

and served to enrich lawyers. Public formal adversary procedures injured or destroyed long-term relationships. Radicals saw the American legal system as part of a system of repression. Elite lawyers saw the courts being overwhelmed by an outpouring of relatively minor disputes. Both drew on the work of anthropologists and the people's courts found in socialist societies in suggesting that there should be non-adversarial ways of resolving disputes that involve long-term continuing relationships.

We will consider a sketch of one way in which a society very different from our own resolves disputes, and then we will ask to what extent we find analogous procedures in this country. Finally, we will look at the way the American legal system resolves most disputes — by a process that has been labeled "bargaining in the shadow of the law." We will ask what role the contract doctrine that you have learned might play in this process. Indeed, we will question the accuracy of the term *alternatives to litigation* and suggest that there is only one larger complex process.

a. Stories from other societies

If we didn't have our ct system this is one way it may look

Comparative approaches to law often open our eyes to the nature of our own legal system and the assumptions on which it rests. Clearly, we do not ask you to read about African tribal law because we think you are likely to make direct use of this information in your law practice.

There are a number of classic problems in comparative work. It is misleading to compare a formal, idealized version of, say, French law with the day-to-day reality of courts in Milwaukee or Chicago. Furthermore, we always have trouble defining the boundaries of what we want to call the legal system. What is part of government in a Chinese setting may be within the jurisdiction of family therapists and parish priests or rabbis in the United States. Consider the following materials in light of a broad view of American social structure, asking whether we have analogous institutions and looking for similarities as well as differences. Then ask whether it makes any difference if a social function is assigned to the public or private sector, insofar as those labels have any connection with reality.

James L. Gibbs's description of the Kpelle[182] moot proved a provocative example for those seeking to reform the American legal system's way of coping with interpersonal disputes in families and neighborhoods.[183] The Kpelle were a group of about 175,000 people who lived in Central Liberia and the adjoining regions of Guinea. They had a formal court system that was "particularly effective in settling cases such as assault, possession of illegal charms, or theft where the litigants are not linked in a relationship which must continue after trial." However, the court was "particularly inept at settling . . . matrimonial disputes because its harsh tone tends to drive spouses farther apart rather than to reconcile them."

---

[182] A student from Liberia informs us that "Pella" is the closest English pronunciation. Native speakers vocalize the "K" along with the "p" to create one new sound, but our Midwestern tongues were unequal to the task.

[183] James Gibbs, The Kpelle Moot in Law and Warfare: Studies of the Anthropology of Conflict 277–89 (Bohannan ed., 1967). First published in Africa, J. Int'l Afr. Inst. 33(1) (1963).

For cases involving such continuing relationships, the Kpelle used a moot, which was more effective than a court in many cases. Gibbs says the "genius of the moot lies in the fact that it is based on a covert application of the principles of psychoanalytic theory which underlie psychotherapy." First, the moot took place before a group that included the kin of the litigants and neighbors from the quarter in which the case was being heard. Second, it was held on Sunday, a day of rest, at the home of the complainant. Third, the complainant selected as mediator a kinsman who was a town chief or elder. Fourth, an introductory ceremony was held which focused attention on maintaining harmony and the well-being of the group. Fifth, the proceeding was informal but structured. The complainant spoke, but might be interrupted by the mediator or anyone else who wished to challenge what was said or add to it. The mediator might fine those who spoke out of turn — for example, he might order them to bring rum for all to drink. Sixth, the mediator and the others present would point out the various faults of both parties, and at the end of the proceeding, the mediator would express the consensus of the group. Seventh, the one mainly at fault would formally apologize to the other by giving token gifts, which must be accepted; the one found less at fault would return a smaller token to signify acceptance of the apology.

Gibbs points out that the process resulted in an airing of all grievances between the parties. The process took place in a familiar setting soon after the matter had come up and before positions had hardened. Both parties were required to consent to bring the matter to the moot, although there was social pressure to consent. Fault was usually attributed to both sides. Those who participated in the moot knew the parties and their history, and so they could judge behavior in its full context. They could see how what an outsider might view as trivial had significance in light of past events. Behavior was judged against traditional customary norms of the Kpelle that defined the behavior of a good wife, a good son, a good cousin who was a neighbor, and so on. Furthermore, the sanctions imposed were largely symbolic. They were not so burdensome as to prompt resentment. Both parties were re-educated by the reactions of relatives, friends, and neighbors to their attitude and conduct. For example, Gibbs reports that a husband learned that the group viewed his customary mildly paranoid sarcasm as destructive of harmony in his marriage, and it did not accept his view of the situation. Presumably, he mended his ways. Disputants were coaxed to conformity by the granting of rewards. The major one was group approval, which "goes to the wronged person who accepts an apology and to the person who is magnanimous enough to make one." Thus, successful moots involved changing attitudes and perceptions of situations as the foundation of behavior in the future. Finally, we can note that it would be difficult for a Kpelle group member to run away from his or her troubles — there was a strong sense of extended family obligation, and it was difficult to leave one's place in the social organization and find needed social and economic support.

Gibbs's conclusions include important qualifications often overlooked by Americans who advocate some version of Kpelle moots for the United States. First, Gibbs stresses:

A moot is not always successful.[184] . . . Both parties must have a genuine willingness to cooperate and a real concern about their discord. Each party must be willing to list his grievances, to admit his guilt, and to make an open apology. The moot, like psychotherapy, is impotent without well-motivated clients.

Second, Gibbs notes that courts have a complementary function to the moots. Courts declare rights. In the case of matrimonial disputes, they grant divorces, which are sometimes the appropriate remedy. Moots, by contrast, are aimed at restoring societal harmony. "The essential point is that both formal and informal dispute-settlement procedures serve significant functions in Kpelle society and neither can be fully understood if studied alone." Although Gibbs does not say so, Kpelle group members might have accepted the risks involved in going to the moot to avoid the greater risks involved in going to court.

Are Kpelle moots consistent with American or British views of individual rights and privacy? What would the judges who decided *Balfour v. Balfour* say about such institutions? People from other parts of the world might have very different norms about privacy, families, and communities. Can we say that European and American societies value privacy so greatly that people who live in them are not subject to social control by their friends and neighbors? Does the answer turn on your social class?

All of us who have attended high school or lived in group residences know that there is such a thing as social control apart from the public legal system in our society. Professor A.P.N. Nauta studied 196 women living in blocks of 12 adjoining houses in the eastern part of Amsterdam.[185] The researcher asked for details of quarrels between neighbors — who quarreled with whom, why, and what happened exactly. We could interpret almost all the quarrels as sanctions against infringements of norms. The exerter of sanctions turned out time and again to be the controlling neighbor. Most of those controlled were younger, had lived for shorter times in the block, were more permissive, and worked more outside the home. Other women felt that they were being controlled by their neighbors, although they avoided quarrels. Some withdrew from contact with neighbors, but many were dependent on their neighbors for assistance and sociability. It was easy to gossip about neighbors, and those with less restrictive views about proper conduct felt pressure to conform. You can make your own judgment about the extent to which you would find similar forms of social control in American apartment and suburban

---

[184] An analysis of moots among the Ndendeuli of Southern Tanzania reveals that they can be iterative. If the moot is initially unsuccessful, the participants (or a subset of them) may gather again. P.H. GULLIVER, DISPUTE SETTLEMENT WITHOUT COURTS, IN LAW IN CULTURE AND SOCIETY 24–68 (Nader ed., 1969).

[185] A.P.N. von Nauta, *Social Control and Norm Restrictiveness: Some Results of an Inquiry into Neighbour Relationships*, 10 SOCIOLOGIA NEERLANDICA 233 (1974). Studies of neighborhood disputes in China and Russia likewise reveal the power of local norms and a distaste for the courts. Haini Guo & Bradley Klein, *Bargaining in the Shadow of the Community: Neighborly Dispute Resolution in Beijing Hutongs*, 20 OHIO ST. J. ON DISP. RESOL. 825 (2005); Kathryn Hendley, *Resolving Problems Among Neighbors in Post-Soviet Russia: Uncovering the Norms of the Pod"ezd*, 36 LAW & SOC. INQUIRY 388 (2011).

living. Insofar as you find something of this sort, how does it differ from Kpelle moots?

b. "Alternatives" in American society

To what extent do we find institutions similar to Kpelle moots in the United States? Is it true that we can solve personal disputes only by withdrawal, violence, or litigation? Suppose a middle- or an upper-middle-class family faces marital difficulties. Is it likely that either the husband's or the wife's parents will play a role in trying to resolve the problems? Will neighbors play a role? What professionals might they call on? How might they go about coping with the problems? Might contract in some form play a part? Remember *Miller v. Miller*. Do courts and other state institutions have an informal side, in which officials behave more like mediators than their formal job descriptions would suggest?

Suppose a working-class or poor family has an ongoing dispute. What do police do with family disputes when the neighbors call them? Raymond Parnas, in a description that predated mandatory arrest laws in domestic disturbance cases and at least some greater appreciation of the significance of such behavior, told us:[186]

> If the victim and offender are both present when the police arrive and the victim has not sustained serious injury, the police, depending upon the circumstances of the incident and their own individual inclination, may use one or more of the following procedures: mediation; referral [to private or public agencies]; threats of arrest or other forms of indirect sanctions; voluntary, temporary separation of the disputants; the threat of filing cross-complaints; refusal to arrest except on a warrant.

Of course, police in a smaller city might act differently from police in a major metropolitan center. In addition, we note that expectations and procedures seem to be changing with a realization of the stakes in these cases. What differences are there in the approaches that we might expect from, on the one hand, American police, and on the other hand, from a therapist whose clients are relatively well-off people?[187]

c. Calls for new approaches and the practice of law

Apart from the many "private governments" found in American society, people often consult lawyers when they face problems. One who knew about lawyers only from the articles in the popular press might assume that all clients who enter lawyers' offices engage in bitter protracted litigation. Clearly some lawyers representing some clients do appear before juries and carry appeals to the highest available court. However, frequently this is not what happens. We will consider an example of a call for a new style of dispute resolution, and then we will turn to descriptions of the practice of law. We will raise some questions about negotiation

---

[186] Raymond I. Parnas, *The Police Response to the Domestic Disturbance*, 1967 Wis. L. Rev. 914, 932.

[187] The role of police in family disputes is controversial. Many argue that battering husbands ought to be arrested and jailed rather than subjected to slaps on the wrist. Often, however, the battered wife needs the husband's income and faces difficult choices.

and mediation. Finally, we will look at how the legal system in action often handles disputes about compensating those who care for the old.

i.   *Calls for mediation rather than adjudication*

Even if we cannot help parties find a way to continue a long-term relationship, they may need help in finding a way out of one. Much like the Kpelle, many Americans have found the formal court system to be ill-suited to handling disputes involving family, friends, and neighbors. Such disputes often do not lend themselves to complete victory for one party. Instead, they cry out for compromise solutions that are tailored to the needs of the parties. Mediation, in which the parties rely on a third party to facilitate their negotiations, has proven useful for many. It allows the parties — either directly or through their lawyers — to be actively involved in working out the problem. The mediator has no power to impose a result on the parties; her goal is to assist the parties in finding the solution themselves. She is also powerless to force the parties to participate; once they feel the process has ceased to be productive, they are free to exit.

Although mediation was originally conceived as a voluntary process, relatively few parties opt for it without a nudge from the courts. Judges encourage mediation as a way to manage their ever-expanding caseload and to divert eligible cases. In many states, so-called "mandatory" mediation has become a first step for divorcing couples and others involved in family squabbles. Of course, only *participation* in the mediation is required; courts cannot compel the parties to resolve their dispute. An analysis of such programs notes: "Critics have raised the concern that coercion *into* the mediation process translates into coercion *in* the mediation process, creating undue settlement pressures that produce unfair outcomes. In cases involving an imbalance of power, the weaker party is thought to be particularly vulnerable to such pressures. However, studies of divorce mediation that examine the effects of mandatory mediation and that explore gender differences in evaluations of the process tend not to support such concerns."[188]

The use of mediation is not limited to divorces and other family disputes. It is particularly well-suited to such disputes because the parties are typically keen to find a path forward in their relationship. But other situations can give rise to relationships that are the functional equivalent of shotgun marriages. Examples include neighbors who lack the resources to move or business partners who are devoted to their mutual venture. Mediation offers them an opportunity to go beyond the stated cause of action to explore the deeper causes of the problem, which may be rooted more in emotion than in law. While not irrelevant, law takes a back seat as the parties delve into how and why their relationship derailed. However, mediation is focused on the problem at hand; it is not a substitute for

---

[188] Roselle L. Wissler, *The Effects of Mandatory Mediation: Empirical Research on the Experience of Small Claims and Common Pleas Courts*, 33 WILLAMETTE L. REV. 565 (1997). In a more recent overview of alternative dispute resolution (ADR), Carrie Menkel-Meadow concludes that "sophisticated mediators and arbitrators are . . . sensitive to power imbalances and can be trained to 'correct' for them without endangering their 'neutrality' in the ADR process." Carrie Menkel-Meadow, *Mediation, Arbitration, and Alternative Dispute Resolution*, in INTERNATIONAL ENCYCLOPEDIA OF THE SOCIAL AND BEHAVIORAL SCIENCES (Neil J. Smelser & Paul B. Balthes eds., Elsevier Ltd. 2015).

psychotherapy and cannot change ingrained behavior that may have contributed to the dysfunctional relationship.

Mediation can also be a useful tool for parties who have no pre-existing relationship and no plans for future contact. By avoiding the courts, they save the time, money, and emotional energy required by the adversarial process. This can provide a powerful incentive to participate. Indeed, those who have participated in mediation (even when it fails) often emerge more satisfied than those who rely solely on the courts and are more likely to comply with the decision. But mediation is not a magic elixir; both parties must be motivated. Florida's foreclosure mediation program, established in the wake of the 2008 financial crisis, required all foreclosure actions between banks and owners of residential homestead property to be referred to mediation (using court-certified mediators), unless the parties agreed otherwise or mediation had already been conducted.[189] The program was ultimately terminated due to antipathy from both banks and homeowners.[190] Neither saw mediation as serving their interests. (We will return to the question of mediation in commercial transactions at the end of this chapter.)

Mediation can take many different forms, as can mediators. Mediators usually have prior training as lawyers, social workers, or psychologists. As a general rule, acting as a mediator is not considered to be engaging in the practice of law. Judges often find themselves assuming the role of mediator, trying to encourage the parties to find a compromise that will avoid a trial on the merits. When such efforts fail, there may be a danger of judges taking out their frustrations on the parties (or being perceived as doing so).

William Felstiner, one of the leading scholars of the subject, notes that conflicts of values are less likely to produce mediated agreements than conflicts over interests.[191] For example, Lee Marvin probably could have saved money by agreeing to pay Michelle the amount awarded by the trial court for rehabilitation, rather than paying his lawyer to take the case to the appellate court. However, Marvin reportedly saw the matter as a cause. He thought a woman should not have claims to money just because she had lived with a man. This suggests that mediation might not have worked between Lee and Michelle.

In light of these comments on mediation, consider the dispute between the Fusion Dance Company and Freddick Bratcher.[192] Bratcher, the former

---

[189] According to a report by the task force that established the program, its purpose was to relieve pressure on the courts; the task force noted that "[t]he enormous increase in foreclosure filings . . . represents a caseload traffic jam that the infrastructure cannot meet in a timely and efficient manner without support and traffic management." The mediation program was described as an "off-ramp" that would keep the courts functioning. FLORIDA SUPREME COURT TASK FORCE ON RESIDENTIAL MORTGAGE FORECLOSURE CASES: FINAL REPORT AND RECOMMENDATIONS ON RESIDENTIAL MORTGAGE FORECLOSURE CASES 7–9 (Aug. 17, 2009), *available at* http://www.floridasupremecourt.org/pub_info/documents/Filed_08-17-2009_Foreclosure_Final_Report.pdf.

[190] *See* Roger C. Benson, *The Residential Mortgage Foreclosure Mediation Disaster, Florida Style* (Nov. 2011), *available at* mediate.com/articles/BensonR1.cfm.

[191] William L.F. Felstiner, *The Logic of Mediation, in* TOWARD A GENERAL THEORY OF SOCIAL CONTROL (Donald Black ed., 1981).

[192] The story is told in the NEW YORK TIMES, March 31, 1980, p. C14, cols 5–6.

choreographer for Fusion, had a falling out with Fusion's president. Bratcher left the company, but sought to enjoin Fusion from performing dances he had choreographed. Shortly after the trial began, Judge Tendrich called the lawyers to the bench, strongly suggested they reach an agreement, and adjourned the proceeding. Late that afternoon, an agreement was reached and entered into the court record. The agreement provided that Bratcher was to have the right to supervise the presentation of three of his dances at a scheduled performance in Palm Beach, but that after that Bratcher was to have all rights in the works. Both sides were pleased with what one called the judge's "ceremonic intervention."

What role did the judge's "ceremonic intervention" play in the mediation efforts of the lawyers for the two factions of the Fusion Dance Company?[193] Why were they unable to resolve the matter before bringing it to court? There is no report of what happened after the hearing. Do you suppose that the rehearsals and performances of the three dances in Palm Beach were successful? Does the situation differ from demands that a court specifically enforce a long-term contract — demands which courts usually resist? Is mediation always a neutral and praiseworthy way to achieve harmony? Suppose one party is right. Does mediation undercut vindication of rights and substitute only a compromise that reflects power and the defects of the legal system?[194] Does it reflect a modern value-relativity that hesitates to find one right and the other wrong?

ii.   *Alternative dispute resolution and the practice of law*

The following material deals with areas other than family disputes. Nonetheless, it suggests that lawyers regularly play roles other than that of courtroom advocate. We can ask whether lawyers in family disputes also play the part of mediator.

---

[193] Efforts at mediation by judges are common. Often their intervention is direct rather than "ceremonic." Many judges today are proud of their skill at persuading parties to settle. *See* Judges Hubert L. Will, Robert R. Merhige Jr., & Alvin B. Rubin, *The Role of the Judge in the Settlement Process*, 75 F.R.D. 75, 203 (1977). For an assessment of the benefits and costs of this judicial activity, *see* Marc Galanter & Mia Cahill, *Most Cases Settle: Judicial Promotion and Regulation of Settlements*, 46 Stan. L. Rev. 1339 (1994).

[194] *See* Albert W. Alschuler, *Mediation With a Mugger: The Shortage of Adjudicative Services and the Need for a Two-Tier Trial System in Civil Cases*, 99 Harv. L. Rev. 1808 (1986). Alschuler argues that Americans settle too many cases for the wrong reasons. A person with a claim confronts many pressures to compromise. The legal system operates very slowly. Our courts use a cumbersome and expensive fact-finding mechanism. There is great substantive uncertainty. Judges and other court officials press the parties to settle. The system gives each party the power to drive up the other's unrecoverable costs. He concludes:

> In a more civilized society, the extensive rationing of adjudication by price and queue would not assure wrongdoers that they always could "settle" and profit from their wrongs. In this society, a right would be something that one gets, not merely something that one has. People would know that they could take their disputes to the courts and that the courts would resolve them. With this assurance, people might be less likely to take their disputes to the streets or to the subways. *Id.* at 1859.

See also Owen Fiss, *Against Settlement*, 93 Yale L.J. 1073 (1984) ("Settlement is a capitulation to the conditions of mass society and should be neither encouraged nor praised.").

Professor Stewart Macaulay studied lawyers and consumer protection laws.[195] He found that lawyers, at various times, play the following roles: the gatekeeper who teaches clients about the costs of using the legal system, the knowledgeable friend or therapist, the broker of information or coach, the go-between or informal mediator, the legal technician, and the adversary bargainer-litigator.[196] However, most lawyers would not do anything with a consumer matter beyond letting a client or potential client express anger, attempting to change the client's view of the situation, telling the client how to complain, or directing him or her to a state or local agency. Thus, lawyers play the role of gatekeeper to the legal system, filtering out potential claims.

Attorneys who become more involved in a dispute might find themselves playing the part of go-between or informal mediator. They might telephone or write the seller or creditor. The lawyer may be able to present the complaint so that it is more understandable and transform the presentation so that it is more persuasive. The complaint, restated by a lawyer, may gain legitimacy. The lawyer is saying that he or she has reviewed the buyer's or debtor's story, the assertions of fact are at least plausible, and the buyer or debtor has reason to complain if these are the facts. The lawyer is more likely than the consumer to talk to someone who has authority to do something about a problem. And a tacit threat always lurks in the background; lawyers are people who can make trouble if a settlement isn't reached.

When they talk with the seller or creditor, lawyers often learn that their clients did not tell them the whole story — there is usually another side. However, lawyers may be able to reach a settlement if they do not ask for too much. Good lawyers know how much is too much. A skillful lawyer may be able to avoid confrontation and give the seller or creditor a graceful way to agree to a settlement. Ideally, the lawyer and the seller or creditor will fashion a solution that both looks good to the client and does not hurt the seller or creditor very much.[197]

Once a lawyer obtains such an offer, the next step is to sell it to the client. The client may want to fight to the Supreme Court, but the lawyer must persuade the client that the settlement is fair and litigation would not be profitable. Often enough, the client takes the settlement but remains unhappy with the lawyer's services. The client thought he or she had rights and expected vindication. Instead, all the lawyer produced was a deal.

Why don't lawyers accept all clients who come to their offices and immediately turn to litigation? Would we expect lawyers to treat family matters much as they

---

[195] Stewart Macaulay, *Lawyers and Consumer Protection Laws*, 14 Law & Soc'y Rev. 115 (1979).

[196] We can also distinguish styles in playing these roles. For example, Gary Neustadter studied lawyers handling individuals seeking relief from debts in bankruptcy. Some lawyers sought to counsel clients and explain all options open to them. Others created a routine and mass-processed clients through the legal system as quickly as possible. *See* Neustadter, *When Lawyer and Client Meet: Observations of Interviewing and Counseling Behavior in the Consumer Bankruptcy Office*, 35 Buff. L. Rev. 177 (1986).

[197] For example, a used car dealer might offer to take back a car with which the lawyer's client is dissatisfied. However, the dealer is unlikely to offer to refund the purchase price. Rather, the dealer might offer to take the car plus an additional amount of money in exchange for another car on the dealer's lot. The net price paid by the client will be far less than the asking price for the substitute car. Nonetheless, the dealer may still be able to profit on the entire transaction.

treat consumer protection questions? Insofar as the practice of law often involves negotiating settlements, what role do legal rules and procedures play? Consider the following excerpts from Professor Marc Galanter's article, and ask why legal educators want to stress doctrine and adjudication rather than what he calls "litigotiation."

Marc Galanter, *Worlds of Deals: Using Negotiation to Teach About Legal Process*
34 J. Legal Educ. 268 (1984)[198]

[The phrase] . . . alternative dispute resolution strikes me as revealing something about the tacit picture of the legal world which permeates American legal education. It links negotiation with alternatives and implicitly juxtaposes them to something unspecified. Alternatives, we may ask, to what? To adjudication, to courts. Even while affirming that negotiation is important, the title reflects the view that negotiation (and mediation and so forth) occupies the outer edges of the legal realm — peripheral to the real thing, adjudication in courts; they are soft as opposed to the hard core of legal doctrine. Negotiation is something apart from the real law that occupies legal educators.

This picture is misleading in several ways. It implies that negotiation (and other so-called alternatives) are infrequent, new, unproven, marginal. But the gravitation to the mediative posture by judges and other decision makers armed with arbitral powers is surely one of the most typical patterns of disputing on the American scene — as an examination of our courts and administrative agencies will attest. The linking of negotiation to "alternatives" to litigation is misleading in another sense. On the contemporary American legal scene the negotiation of disputes is not an alternative to litigation. It is only a slight exaggeration to say that it *is* litigation. There are not two distinct processes, negotiation and litigation; there is a single process of disputing in the vicinity of official tribunals that we might call *litigotiation,* that is, the strategic pursuit of a settlement through mobilizing the court process. Full-blown adjudication of the dispute — running the whole course — might be thought of as an infrequently-pursued alternative to the ordinary course of litigotiation. I do not minimize its importance: adjudication remains a compelling presence even when it does not occur.

The courts are central to the litigotiation game because of the "bargaining endowments" they bestow on the parties. What might be done by (or in or near) a court, that is, gives the parties bargaining chips or counters. Bargaining chips derive from the substantive entitlements conferred by legal rules and from the procedural rules that enable these entitlements to be vindicated. But rules are only part of the endowment conferred by the law — the delay, cost, and uncertainty of eliciting a favorable determination also confer bargaining counters on the disputants. Everything that might affect outcome counts — all the outcome for the party, not just that encompassed by the rules. The ability to impose delay, costs, risk, embarrassment, publicity comes into play along with the rules. Rules are important but they interact with a host of other factors in ways that do not correspond to the neatly separated background and foreground of the law school classroom.

The settlement process is not some marginal, peripheral aspect of legal disputing in America; it is the central core. Something like 90 percent of civil cases are settled (and of course many more disputes are settled before reaching the stage of filing). Lawyers spend more time on settlement discussions than on research or on trials and appeals. Much of the other activity that lawyers engage in is articulated to the settlement process. Even in the case that departs from the standardized routines of settlement, negotiation and litigation are not separate processes, but are inseparably entwined. Negotiation, then, is not the law's soft penumbra, but the hard heart of the process. The so-called hard law turns out to be only one (often malleable) set of counters in the litigotiation game. . . .

[T]he world of negotiation [is] made up of different bargaining arenas. By this I mean some more or less bounded constellation of lawyers (and in some cases other actors, such as insurance adjusters or detectives or judges) who interact with one another in connection with the settlement (and occasional adjudication) of particular kinds of cases in a particular locality. They share (more or less) expectations and understandings about procedures, applicable norms, outcomes. In a particular locality there may be a personal injury bargaining arena, a medical malpractice bargaining arena, a family law arena, an antitrust arena, and so forth. Individual lawyers may participate in one or several; lawyers may be comfortably familiar with a certain arena or find it strange and intimidating. Such arenas may be more or less differentiated and more or less bounded. A lawyer may spend his whole working life in a single arena in which everybody knows everybody, one's reputation in the arena is a prime concern, and everybody knows what every case is worth. (I gather that criminal law in some middle-sized cities approximates this.) Or an arena may be diffuse — one may constantly encounter antagonists who are strangers, with little concern about reputation and little shared knowledge about standards and benchmarks. An arena may deal with cases that are exhaustively researched and investigated, or with cases that are too small to support much investment in generating information.

So, preparing to negotiate involves not only acquiring generalized skills, but learning to read the landscape, to dope out the features of the bargaining arena. It is crucial to know whether you are dealing with people who are concerned to deal with you again, whether deals are standardized here or custom-made, and what expectations are shared about the process and outcome.

iii.   *Compensating care for the old*

Mediation has proven to be a useful tool when adult children are faced with difficult decisions over how to manage as their parents become unable to make decisions for themselves. A 2015 *New York Times* article focused on three sisters in their fifties who had to deal with their 84-year-old mother and 53-year-old developmentally disabled brother. One sister extolled the virtues of mediation: "We wanted to stay connected as siblings, but if you don't get someone else to help you out, you kind of fall prey to your childhood antics. A mediator makes a hard job a little easier."[199] Indeed, elder mediation is a growth industry.

We talked with officials familiar with the probate and administration of estates in Dane County, Wisconsin. They told us that care for the elderly poses common problems. While they process most estates in what is essentially an administrative procedure, enough flawed wills and family situations occur so that they know the situation well. For example, a common case involves a farm estate. Suppose a farm family consists of husband and wife and five children. Four children leave the farm and go to cities to pursue careers. One brother stays and works the farm with his father. The father dies and leaves everything to the mother. She never makes a will. She lives until the child who stayed and worked the farm is in his fifties. Then she dies. Under intestate succession, all five children take equally. The four who left the farm want to sell and divide the proceeds. However, this would leave the one who worked the farm all his life with no future. Another common case involves the daughter who comes home to take care of aged parents. Trouble comes when their wills do not honor her or when they do not remember her special contribution.

Commissioners and clerks who handle probate say that they tell the lawyers that they do not want to see such cases as disputes. They hold pretrial conferences as well as informal discussions so that the lawyers do not lose the forest by concentrating on the trees. Lawyers for the estate may forget that the estate is the client rather than the executor or particular heirs. It makes no sense to spend thousands of dollars to resolve claims that lawyers could settle for much less. Ninety-five percent of these claims for caring for the old are settled for something less than the claimant asked for but for more than the law might require the estate to pay. The law may allow a lawyer to make a good case for those who cared for the old, and this is enough to justify a settlement. One always seeks to get all those with any claim to the estate to agree to these settlements so that no one later can attack the final distribution of the estate.

Lawyers learn how to handle matters sensibly. In smaller counties, the same group of lawyers handle most of the estates. Older lawyers appear most often. They have drafted the wills and outlived their clients. Dane County is relatively populous; there are many lawyers and the group who probates the estates changes over time. Senior lawyers delegate all but the very difficult ones to junior lawyers. Lawyers just out of law school get small estates as some of the first matters they see. Younger lawyers sometimes see things as all or nothing. Those who handle probate explain that one has to consider the costs to the estate and the various claimants as contrasted with what they might gain by litigation. The probate commissioners are lawyers, and so they can educate lawyers in the advantages of settling these claims.

Of course, the lawyers have to persuade their clients to settle. However, these matters involve family members who are seldom eager to battle each other if they can work out any settlement that is acceptable to everyone. Families do not want to wash their dirty linen in public. Family members may feel guilty about allowing a sister or brother to care for their elderly parent. If handled properly, lawyers can

---

[199] Abby Ellin, *Strengthening Troubled Sibling Bonds to Deal with an Aging Parent*, NEW YORK TIMES, May 30, 2015, at B4.

use this guilt in suggesting a settlement that pays for care. When there was an estate tax, if the estate was large enough, payments for services would be a deduction against the gross estate when they calculated the estate tax. The parties can see the government paying part of what extra is given to the brother or sister who cared for the elderly parent. Lawyers, themselves, can push hard for settlements. They can explain both the law and the equities of the claim in such a way that most relatives will accept that a settlement may be best for all concerned.

It would seldom pay for a lawyer to encourage taking a family fight through litigation. Few potential heirs can pay large fees, and a contingent fee would make economic sense only when there is a good chance of winning a large sum against a wealthy estate.

C. FRANCHISE AND EMPLOYMENT RELATIONS

Much of what we have seen in studying contract and family relationships returns when we look at franchises and employment. Those who hold a franchise typically must invest in their dealership. Employees may invest their training and skill, but usually employers do not require them to contribute to the costs of the place of business, machines, or inventory. Of course, as always, there are in-between cases. An employee may have gone to school to develop the skills she needs to do the job.

Automobile dealerships, fast-food restaurants, motels, dry cleaners, gas stations, and nationwide real estate firms are all examples of the franchise. A firm granting a franchise usually provides a trade name, products, and procedures. The one receiving a franchise agrees to follow the procedures and invest both labor and capital. Absent legal regulation, franchisors retain great influence over the day-to-day operations of the business. They reserve almost absolute power to end the arrangement without any need to show cause. The threat of taking away the sign that says "Mobil," "Holiday Inn," "McDonalds," or "Chevrolet" turns requests into commands.

Some franchisees may be so productive that they command real independence. In other situations, however, a franchisee resembles an employee because the franchisor exercises almost complete control of the operation. This is particularly the case where the franchisee does not invest large sums of capital at the outset, but invests his or her labor in creating a going business. Even where this is the case, franchisees may have greater incentives than most employees to work hard, and many of the statutes regulating wages and hours of employment do not apply to their efforts.

Until the 1950s, franchisees had only the rights that franchisors gave them in franchise agreements. Franchisors seemed more concerned with protecting their interests than creating systems of due process for those who ran their local retailing outlets. In increasing numbers since the mid-1930s, franchisees have often appealed to the American legal system, with mixed success.

When we considered *Copylease v. Memorex* (the photocopier-toner case in Chapter 2), we saw that California courts were no more eager to attempt to regulate ongoing franchise relationships than other courts have been to deal with contracts between husband and wife. Furthermore, the reasons offered for hesitating to venture into what Chafee called "the dismal swamp" were much the same. However, the legal system sometimes intervenes in employment and franchise relationships. Since the 1960s, those championing employees and franchisees have increasingly called for more intervention. While we can distinguish the situations at the extremes, in practice many franchises come close to employment relationships. Indeed, often the franchisor seeks both the control that an employer has over employees and the image of "running your own business" to provide incentives for hard work.

1.   The Franchise

a.   Creating the relationship

Many franchises are very valuable. A good manager, with only a little luck, can make a great deal of money being the local Toyota dealer or running a Holiday Inn. A franchisee will probably never get rich running a Mobil service station or a fast-food establishment; nonetheless, it is a chance at upward mobility for many. In 1984, the Commerce Department estimated that franchising accounted for $456.7 billion in sales, a jump of more than 270 percent from 1969, when only $112.8 billion came from franchising.[200] By 2015, industry figures indicated there were as many as 900,000 franchises in the United States, accounting for $2.1 trillion annually.[201]

However, franchisors do not hand out franchises just for the asking. Those seeking them will have to convince a franchisor's representatives that they have enough skill and capital to succeed in business. Furthermore, the person seeking a franchise will want to enter business as soon as possible after the franchisor awards it. If a local representative says that the home office will approve, the applicant may be tempted to invest in signs, inventory, and the like. Once again, courts could draw sharp lines to serve as forms. They could say that a person who has a franchise agreement signed by the franchisor has whatever rights it grants, and one who has yet to receive a signed document has nothing. Many courts have taken just this position. However, other courts have offered relief even to those who have yet to pass through the formality creating the status of franchisee.

HOFFMAN v. RED OWL STORES, INC.
Wisconsin Supreme Court
26 Wis. 2d 683, 133 N.W.2d 267 (1965)

Action by Joseph Hoffman (hereinafter "Hoffman") and wife, plaintiffs, against defendants Red Owl Stores, Inc. (hereinafter "Red Owl") and Edward Lukowitz.

The complaint alleged that Lukowitz, as agent for Red Owl, represented to and agreed with plaintiffs that Red Owl would build a store building in Chilton and stock it with merchandise for Hoffman to operate, in return for which plaintiffs were to put up and invest a total sum of $18,000; that in reliance upon the above-mentioned agreement and representations plaintiffs sold their bakery building and business

---

[200]   NEW YORK TIMES, Jan. 20, 1985, at F4, col. 3.

[201]   *See* azfranchises.com/franchisefacts.htm (giving franchise industry statistics).

and their grocery store and business; also in reliance on the agreement and representations Hoffman purchased the building site in Chilton and rented a residence for himself and his family in Chilton; plaintiffs' actions in reliance on the representations and agreement disrupted their personal and business life; plaintiffs lost substantial amounts of income and expended large sums of money as expenses. Plaintiffs demanded recovery of damages for the breach of defendants' representations and agreements. . . .

Hoffman, assisted by his wife, operated a bakery at Wautoma from 1956 until sale of the building late in 1961. The building was owned in joint tenancy by him and his wife. Red Owl is a Minnesota corporation having its home office at Hopkins, Minnesota. It owns and operates a number of grocery supermarket stores and also extends franchises to agency stores which are owned by individuals, partnerships, and corporations. Lukowitz resides at Green Bay and since September, 1960, has been divisional manager for Red Owl in a territory comprising Upper Michigan and most of Wisconsin, in charge of 84 stores. Prior to September, 1960, he was district manager having charge of approximately 20 stores.

In November, 1959, Hoffman was desirous of expanding his operations by establishing a grocery store and contacted a Red Owl representative by the name of Jansen, now deceased. Numerous conversations were made in 1960 with the idea of establishing a Red Owl franchise store in Wautoma. In September, 1960, Lukowitz succeeded Jansen as Red Owl's representative in the negotiations. Hoffman mentioned that $18,000 was all the capital he had available to invest and he was repeatedly assured that this would be sufficient to set him up in business as a Red Owl store. About Christmas time, 1960, Hoffman thought it would be a good idea if he bought a small grocery store in Wautoma and operated it in order that he gain experience in the grocery business prior to operating a Red Owl store in some larger community. On February 6, 1961, on the advice of Lukowitz and Sykes, who had succeeded Lukowitz as Red Owl's district manager, Hoffman bought the inventory and fixtures of a small grocery store in Wautoma and leased the building in which it was operated.

After three months of operating this Wautoma store, the Red Owl representatives came in and took inventory and checked the operations and found the store was operating at a profit. Lukowitz advised Hoffman to sell the store to his manager, and assured him that Red Owl would find a larger store for him elsewhere. Acting on this advice and assurance, Hoffman sold the fixtures and inventory to his manager on June 6, 1961. Hoffman was reluctant to sell at that time because it meant losing the summer tourist business, but he sold on the assurance that he would be operating in a new location by fall and that he must sell this store if he wanted a bigger one. Before selling, Hoffman told the Red Owl representatives that he had $18,000 for "getting set up in business," and they assured him that there would be no problems in establishing him in a bigger operation. The makeup of the $18,000 was not discussed; it was understood plaintiff's father-in-law would furnish part of it. By June, 1961, the towns for the new grocery store had been narrowed down to two, Kewaunee and Chilton. In Kewaunee, Red Owl had an option on a building site. In Chilton, Red Owl had nothing under option, but it did select a site to which plaintiff obtained an option at Red Owl's suggestion. The option stipulated a purchase price of $6,000 with $1,000 to be paid on election to purchase and the balance to be paid within thirty days. On Lukowitz's assurance that everything was all set, plaintiff paid $1,000 down on the lot on September 15th.

On September 27, 1961, plaintiff met at Chilton with Lukowitz and Mr. Reymund and Mr. Carlson from the home office, who prepared a projected financial statement. Part of the funds plaintiffs were to supply as their investment in the venture were to be obtained by sale of their Wautoma bakery building.

On the basis of this meeting Lukowitz assured Hoffman: "[E]verything is ready to go. Get your money together and we are set." Shortly after this meeting Lukowitz told plaintiffs that they would have to sell their bakery business and bakery building, and that their retaining this property was the only "hitch" in the entire plan. On November 6, 1961, plaintiffs sold their bakery building for $10,000. Hoffman was to retain the bakery equipment, as he contemplated using it to operate a bakery in connection with his Red Owl store. After sale of the bakery Hoffman obtained employment on the night shift at an Appleton bakery.

The record contains different exhibits which were prepared in September and October, some of which were projections of the fiscal operation of the business and others were proposed building and floor plans. Red Owl was to procure some third party to buy the Chilton lot from Hoffman, construct the building, and then lease it to Hoffman. No final plans were ever made, nor were bids let or a construction contract entered. Some time prior to November 20, 1961, certain of the terms of the lease under which the building was to be rented by Hoffman were understood between him and Lukowitz. The lease was to be for ten years with a rental approximating $550 a month. . . . At the end of the ten-year term he was to have an option to renew the lease for an additional ten-year period or to buy the property at cost on an installment basis. There was no discussion as to what the installments would be or with respect to repairs and maintenance.

On November 22nd or 23rd, Lukowitz and plaintiffs met in Minneapolis with Red Owl's credit manager to confer on Hoffman's financial standing and on financing the agency. Another projected financial statement was there drawn up entitled: "Proposed Financing For An Agency Store." This showed Hoffman contributing $24,100 of cash capital, of which only $4,600 was to be cash possessed by plaintiffs. Eight thousand was to be procured as a loan from a Chilton bank secured by a mortgage on the bakery fixtures, $7,500 was to be obtained on a 5 percent loan from the father-in-law, and $4,000 was to be obtained by sale of the lot to the lessor at a profit.

A week or two after the Minneapolis meeting, Lukowitz showed Hoffman a telegram from the home office to the effect that if plaintiff could get another $2,000 for promotional purposes the deal could go through for $26,000. Hoffman stated he would have to find out if he could get another $2,000. He met with his father-in-law, who agreed to put $13,000 into the business provided he could come into the business as a partner. Lukowitz told Hoffman the partnership arrangement "sounds fine" and that Hoffman should not go into the partnership arrangement with the "front office." On January 16, 1962, the Red Owl credit manager teletyped Lukowitz that the father-in-law would have to sign an agreement that the $13,000 was either a gift or a loan subordinate to all general creditors and that he would prepare the agreement. On January 31, 1962, Lukowitz teletyped the home office that the father-in-law would sign one or other of the agreements. However, Hoffman testified that it was not until the final meeting some time between January 26 and February 2, 1962, that he was told that his father-in-law was expected to sign an agreement that the $13,000 he was advancing was to be an outright gift. No mention was then made by the Red Owl representatives of the alternative of the father-in-law signing a subordination agreement. At this meeting the Red Owl agents presented Hoffman with the following projected financial statement:

Capital required in operation:

Cash	$5,000.00
Merchandise	$20,000.00
Bakery	$18,000.00
Fixtures	$17,500.00
Promotional Funds	$1,500.00
TOTAL	**$62,000.00**

Source of funds:

Red Owl 7-day terms: $ 5,000.00

Red Owl fixture contract (Term 5 years): $14,000.00

Bank loans (Term 9 years): Union State Bank of Chilton, $8,000.00 (secured by bakery equipment)

Other loans (Term No-pay)

   No interest

Father-in-law (Secured by None): $13,000.00

Secured by Mortgage on Wautoma Bakery Bldg.: $2,000.00

Resale of land: $6,000.00

Equity Capital: $5,000.00 cash; $17,500.00 bakery equipment

Amount owner has to invest: $22,500.00

TOTAL: $70,500.00

Hoffman interpreted the above statement to require of plaintiffs a total of $34,000 cash made up of a $13,000 gift from his father-in-law, $2,000 on the mortgage, $8,000 on the Chilton bank loan, $5,000 in cash from plaintiff, and $6,000 on the resale of the Chilton lot. Red Owl claims $18,000 is the total of the unborrowed or unencumbered cash, that is, $13,000 from the father-in-law and $5,000 cash from Hoffman himself. Hoffman informed Red Owl he could not go along with this proposal, and particularly objected to the requirement that his father-in-law sign an agreement that his $13,000 advancement was an absolute gift. This terminated the negotiations between the parties.

The case was submitted to the jury on a special verdict with the first two questions answered by the court. This verdict, as returned by the jury, was as follows:

"*Question No. 1*: Did the Red Owl Stores, Inc., and Joseph Hoffman on or about mid-May of 1961 initiate negotiations looking to the establishment of Joseph Hoffman as a franchise operator of a Red Owl Store in Chilton?" Answer: Yes. (Answered by the Court.)

"*Question No. 2*: Did the parties mutually agree on all of the details of the proposal so as to reach a final agreement thereon?" Answer: No. (Answered by the Court.)

"*Question No. 3:* Did the Red Owl Stores, Inc., in the course of said negotiations, make representations to Joseph Hoffman that if he fulfilled certain conditions that they would establish him as a franchise operator of a Red Owl Store in Chilton?" Answer: Yes.

"*Question No. 4*: If you have answered Question No. 3 'Yes,' then answer this question: Did Joseph Hoffman rely on said representations and was he induced to act thereon?" Answer: Yes.

"*Question No. 5:* If you have answered Question No. 4 'Yes,' then answer this question: Ought Joseph Hoffman, in the exercise of ordinary care, to have relied on said representations?" Answer: Yes.

"*Question No. 6:* If you have answered Question No. 3 'Yes' then answer this question: Did Joseph Hoffman fulfill all the conditions he was required to fulfill by the terms of the negotiations between the parties up to January 26, 1962?" Answer: Yes.

"*Question No. 7:* What sum of money will reasonably compensate the plaintiffs for such damages as they sustained by reason of:

(a) The sale of the Wautoma store fixtures and inventory?"

Answer: $16,735.

"(b) The sale of the bakery building?"

Answer: $2,000.

"(c) Taking up the option on the Chilton lot?"

Answer: $1,000.

"(d) Expenses of moving his family to Neenah?"

Answer: $140.

"(e) House rental in Chilton?"

Answer: $125.

Plaintiffs moved for judgment on the verdict while defendants moved to change the answers to Questions 3, 4, 5, and 6 from "Yes" to "No," and in the alternative for relief from the answers to the subdivisions of Question 7 or a new trial. On March 31, 1964, the circuit court entered the following order:

It Is Ordered in accordance with said decision on motions after verdict hereby incorporated herein by reference:

1. That the answer of the jury to Question No. 7(a) be [stricken] and the same is hereby vacated and set aside and that a new trial be had on the sole issue of the damages for loss, if any, on the sale of the Wautoma store, fixtures, and inventory.

2. That all other portions of the verdict of the jury be and hereby are approved and confirmed and all after-verdict motions of the parties inconsistent with this order are hereby denied.

Defendants have appealed from this order and plaintiffs have cross-appealed from paragraph 1, thereof.

CURRIE, C.J.

The instant appeal and cross-appeal present these questions:

(1) Whether this court should recognize causes of action grounded on promissory estoppel as exemplified by § 90 of Restatement, 1 Contracts?

(2) Do the facts in this case make out a cause of action for promissory estoppel?

(3) Are the jury's findings with respect to damages sustained by the evidence?

Recognition of a Cause of Action Grounded on Promissory Estoppel.

Section 90 of Restatement, 1 Contracts, provides:

> A promise which the promisor should reasonably expect to induce action or forbearance of a definite and substantial character on the part of the promisee and which does induce such action or forbearance is binding if injustice can be avoided only by enforcement of the promise.

The Wisconsin Annotations to Restatement, Contracts, prepared under the direction of the late Professor William H. Page and issued in 1933, [stated]:

> The Wisconsin cases do not seem to be in accord with this section of the Restatement. It is certain that no such proposition has ever been announced by the Wisconsin court and it is at least doubtful if it would be approved by the court.

> . . . Because we deem the doctrine of promissory estoppel, as stated in § 90 of Restatement (First) of Contracts, is one which supplies a needed tool which courts may employ in a proper case to prevent injustice, we endorse and adopt it.

Applicability of Doctrine to Facts of this Case.

The record here discloses a number of promises and assurances given to Hoffman by Lukowitz on behalf of Red Owl, upon which plaintiffs relied and acted upon to their detriment.

Foremost were the promises that for the sum of $18,000 Red Owl would establish

Hoffman in a store. After Hoffman had sold his grocery store and paid the $1,000 on the Chilton lot, the $18,000 figure was changed to $24,100. Then in November, 1961, Hoffman was assured that if the $24,100 figure were increased by $2,000 the deal would go through. Hoffman was induced to sell his grocery store fixtures and inventory in June, 1961, on the promise that he would be in his new store by fall. In November, plaintiffs sold their bakery building on the urging of defendants and on the assurance that this was the last step necessary to have the deal with Red Owl go through.

We determine that there was ample evidence to sustain the answers of the jury to the questions of the verdict with respect to the promissory representations made by Red Owl, Hoffman's reliance thereon in the exercise of ordinary care, and his fulfillment of the conditions required of him by the terms of the negotiations had with Red Owl.

There remains for consideration the question of law raised by defendants that agreement was never reached on essential factors necessary to establish a contract between Hoffman and Red Owl. Among these were the size, cost, design, and layout of the store building; and the terms of the lease with respect to rent, maintenance, renewal, and purchase options. This poses the question of whether the promise necessary to sustain a cause of action for promissory estoppel must embrace all essential details of a proposed transaction between promisor and promisee so as to be the equivalent of an offer that would result in a binding contract between the parties if the promisee were to accept the same.

. . . If promissory estoppel were to be limited to only those situations where the promise giving rise to the cause of action must be so definite with respect to all details that a contract would result were the promise supported by consideration, then the defendants' instant promises to Hoffman would not meet this test. However, § 90 of Restatement, 1 Contracts, does not impose the requirement that the promise giving rise to the cause of action must be so comprehensive in scope as to meet the requirements of an offer that would ripen into a contract if accepted by the promisee. Rather the conditions imposed are:

(1) Was the promise one which the promisor should reasonably expect to induce action or forbearance of a definite and substantial character on the part of the promisee?

(2) Did the promise induce such action or forbearance?

(3) Can injustice be avoided only by enforcement of the promise?

We deem it would be a mistake to regard an action grounded on promissory estoppel as the equivalent of a breach-of-contract action. . . . While the first two of the above-listed three requirements of promissory estoppel present issues of fact which ordinarily will be resolved by a jury, the third requirement, that the remedy can only be invoked where necessary to avoid injustice, is one that involves a policy decision by the court. Such a policy decision necessarily embraces an element of discretion.

We conclude that injustice would result here if plaintiffs were not granted some relief because of the failure of defendants to keep their promises which induced plaintiffs to act to their detriment.

Below line is abt Damages / Q7 i think

Damages.

Defendants attack all the items of damages awarded by the jury.

Attack sale of Bakery cuz half loss is Mrs. H → if def. forsees damage / encourges it they can recover it → Affirm $ amnt here

The bakery building at Wautoma was sold at defendants' instigation in order that Hoffman might have the net proceeds available as part of the cash capital he was to invest in the Chilton store venture. The evidence clearly establishes that it was sold at a loss of $2,000. Defendants contend that half of this loss was sustained by Mrs. Hoffman because title stood in joint tenancy. They point out that no dealings took place between her and defendants as all negotiations were had with her husband. Ordinarily only the promisee and not third persons are entitled to enforce the remedy of promissory estoppel against the promisor. However, if the promisor actually foresees, or has reason to foresee, action by a third person in reliance on the promise, it may be quite unjust to refuse to perform the promise. . . . Here not only did defendants foresee that it would be necessary for Mrs. Hoffman to sell her joint interest in the bakery building, but defendants actually requested that this be done. We approve the jury's award of $2,000 damages for the loss incurred by both plaintiffs in this sale.

Say since didn't pay the xtra 5k cant get back OG 1k → ct affirm gets 1k still

Defendants attack on two grounds the $1,000 awarded because of Hoffman's payment of that amount on the purchase price of the Chilton lot. The first is that this $1,000 had already been lost at the time the final negotiations with Red Owl fell through in January, 1962, because the remaining $5,000 of purchase price had been due on October 15, 1961. The record does not disclose that the lot owner had foreclosed Hoffman's interest in the lot for failure to pay this $5,000. The $1,000 was not paid for the option, but had been paid as part of the purchase price at the time Hoffman elected to exercise the option. This gave him an equity in the lot which could not be legally foreclosed without affording Hoffman an opportunity to pay the balance. The second ground of attack is that the lot may have had a fair market value of $6,000, and Hoffman should have paid the remaining $5,000 of purchase price. We determine that it would be unreasonable to require Hoffman to have invested an additional $5,000 in order to protect the $1,000 he had paid. Therefore, we find no merit to defendants' attack upon this item of damages.

We also determine it was reasonable for Hoffman to have paid $125 for one month's rent of a home in Chilton after defendants assured him everything would be set when plaintiff sold the bakery building. This was a proper item of damage. Plaintiffs never moved to Chilton because defendants suggested that Hoffman get some experience by working in a Red Owl store in the Fox River Valley. Plaintiffs, therefore, moved to Neenah instead of Chilton. After moving, Hoffman worked at night in an Appleton bakery but held himself available for work in a Red Owl store. The $140 moving expense would not have been incurred if plaintiffs had not sold their bakery building in Wautoma in reliance upon defendants' promises. We consider the $140 moving expense to be a proper item of damage.

Moving damage proper too ↗

We turn now to the damage item with respect to which the trial court granted a new trial, i.e., that arising from the sale of the Wautoma grocery-store fixtures and inventory for which the jury awarded $16,735. The trial court ruled that Hoffman could not recover for any loss of future profits for the summer months following the sale on June 6, 1961, but that damages would be limited to the difference between the sales price received and the fair market value of the assets sold, giving consideration to any goodwill attaching thereto by reason of the transfer of a going business. There was no direct evidence presented as to what this fair market value was on June 6, 1961. The evidence did disclose that Hoffman paid $9,000 for the inventory, added $1,500 to it and sold it for $10,000 or a loss of $500. His 1961 federal income-tax return showed that the grocery equipment had been purchased for $7,000 and sold for $7,955.96. Plaintiffs introduced evidence of the buyer that during the first 11 weeks of operation of the grocery store his gross sales were $44,000 and his profit was $6,000 or roughly 15 percent. On cross-examination he admitted that this was gross and not net profit. Plaintiffs contend that in a breach-of-contract action damages may include loss of profits. However, this is not a breach-of-contract action.

The only relevancy of evidence relating to profits would be with respect to proving the element of goodwill in establishing the fair market value of the grocery inventory and fixtures sold. Therefore, evidence of profits would be admissible to afford a foundation for expert opinion as to fair market value.

Where damages are awarded in promissory estoppel instead of specifically enforcing the promisor's promise, they should be only such as in the opinion of the court are necessary to prevent injustice. Mechanical or rule-of-thumb approaches to the damage problem should be avoided. . . .

> Enforcement of a promise does not necessarily mean specific performance. It does not necessarily mean damages for breach. Moreover, the amount allowed as damages may be determined by the plaintiff's expenditures or change of position in reliance as well as by the value to him of the promised performance. Restitution is also an 'enforcing' remedy, although it is often said to be based upon some kind of a rescission. In determining what justice requires, the court must remember all of its powers, derived from equity, law, merchant, and other sources, as well as the common law. Its decree should be molded accordingly. 1A CORBIN, CONTRACTS 221, § 200.

> The wrong is not primarily in depriving the plaintiff of the promised reward but in causing the plaintiff to change position to his detriment. It would follow that the damages should not exceed the loss caused by the change of position, which would never be more in amount, but might be less, than the promised reward. Seavey, *Reliance on Gratuitous Promises or Other Conduct*, 64 HARV. L. REV. 913, 926 (1951).

At the time Hoffman bought the equipment and inventory of the small grocery store at Wautoma he did so in order to gain experience in the grocery-store business. At that time discussion had already been had with Red Owl representatives that Wautoma might be too small for a Red Owl operation and that a larger city might be more desirable. Thus Hoffman made this purchase more or less as a temporary experiment. Justice does not require that the damages awarded him, because of selling these assets at the behest of defendants, should exceed any actual

In terms of new grocery sales, a proper trial is to give all just lost profits — [handwritten marginalia]

loss sustained measured by the difference between the sales price and the fair market value.

Since the evidence does not sustain the large award of damages arising from the sale of the Wautoma grocery business, the trial court properly ordered a new trial on this issue.

By the Court. — Order affirmed. Because of the cross-appeal, plaintiffs shall be limited to taxing but two-thirds of their costs.

NOTES AND QUESTIONS

1. ***The promise on which Hoffman relied:*** Restatement of Contracts § 90 speaks of relying on a promise. Did Red Owl make a promise to Joseph Hoffman? A great deal is known about the underlying facts because of two separate articles about the case that have been written based on studies of the trial record, and in one case on interviews with Joseph Hoffman as well.[202] There were basically three key times when Hoffman relied to his detriment. The first was in May–June 1961, when he sold the Wautoma grocery. The second was in September 1961, when he paid $1,000 for an option on the Chilton lot. And the third time was in October and November 1961, when he sold both his bakery business and the building in which it was located. The trial judge had carefully charged the jury that they were to award damages only for reliance that occurred after a "representation" had been made to Hoffman. It is evident from the jury's verdict that the jurors decided that representations had been made to Hoffman before he sold the grocery store in May–June.

Hoffman's expectations and reliance were based primarily on the conduct and statements of Edward Lukowitz, the divisional manager for Red Owl Stores. Hoffman knew that Lukowitz could not award franchises. He knew that power belonged to officials at Red Owl's home office in Hopkins, Minnesota, a suburb of Minneapolis. However, under the law of agency, Red Owl was responsible for Lukowitz's conduct in the usual course of his job.

Hoffman had had many discussions with Lukowitz before May and June. He knew that Lukowitz believed that Hoffman was qualified to be a Red Owl franchisee and would operate a franchise successfully. Hoffman also knew that Red Owl had decided that Wautoma was too small for a Red Owl franchise, but no other site had yet been determined. Hoffman expressed reluctance to sell the Wautoma grocery at the beginning of the busy summer period, but relented when Lukowitz advised that he should be free to help with site selection and other preparatory work for a new franchise. Hoffman told Lukowitz that he had only $18,000 to invest, and Lukowitz led Hoffman to believe that this amount would be sufficient. At this time, however, Hoffman had no awareness of any specific discussions between Lukowitz and officials at Red Owl's home office respecting Hoffman's qualifications as a potential franchisee.

---

[202] Robert Scott, Hoffman v. Red Owl Stores *and the Myth of Precontractual Reliance*, 69 Ohio St. L.J. 71 (2007), reprinted in Douglas Baird, Contract Stories 62–93 (2007); William Whitford & Stewart Macaulay, Hoffman v. Red Owl Stores: *The Rest of the Story*, 61 Hastings L.J. 801 (2010).

Hoffman had many discussions with Lukowitz over the summer of 1961, including visits with him to several potential locations. They decided upon Chilton, and Hoffman obtained the option on a lot that is mentioned in the opinion. Hoffman was reluctant to invest the $1,000 on the lot without further assurance that Red Owl was committed to a franchise at this location. Lukowitz advised Hoffman to hold off until after Lukowitz had an opportunity to visit Red Owl's home office. Upon his return from the home office, Lukowitz phoned Hoffman, and according to Hoffman's testimony stated: "Everything is all set. Go ahead and pick up your option."

After purchase of the option, Hoffman met with Lukowitz and officials from Red Owl's home office at the Chilton location. There were discussions of Hoffman's financial situation and what he proposed to invest. A proposed financial plan for the franchise was drafted. Later Lukowitz showed Hoffman a draft floor plan for a building to be constructed on the Chilton lot. Then in October Lukowitz telephoned Hoffman, and according to Hoffman's testimony, represented that he had conferred further with home office officials who had said "the only hitch in this thing . . . was that I had to get rid of my bakery and my bakery building." Lukowitz knew that Hoffman was reluctant to sell the bakery, as the bakery business was providing his family's support, but Hoffman and his wife decided to proceed upon Lukowitz's insistence that it was "the only hitch." After the sale, Hoffman supported the family by working as an employee in Appleton, a larger town located 60 to 70 miles from Wautoma.

When do you think Hoffman first received sufficient assurances to constitute a "promise," or what the court calls a "representation," sufficient to justify a recovery for subsequent reliance losses under § 90? Evidently the court thought that the jury could reasonably find that promises on which Hoffman might reasonably rely were made as early as May–June, 1961. Do you think the statements made to Hoffman at that time were promises, or simply encouraging advice or predictions by Lukowitz? Suppose the court had found that there was not sufficient evidence of an actionable promise before September or October. How would that have affected the calculation of damages?

rains had a doubly beneficial effect for Waushara Countians this week.

Crops were getting off to an ex-

crops not irrigated had been in need of some good soaking rainfall. This week they got it.

And the serious fire hazard that

CONFIRMING THE DEAL—With inventory and paper work completed, Joe Hoffman, left, and Ed Wrysinski shake hands on the deal they made this week in which Hoffman sold his grocery, "Joe's Red Owl", to Wrysinski.

2. *Interpreting Lukowitz's communications in light of Hoffman's background:* The record on appeal also shows that Joseph Hoffman was a high school graduate and had attended vocational school for one year, taking business courses. In November of 1956, he bought a bakery in Wautoma and ran it with his wife. He worked night and day and got so little sleep that his wife listened to all long-distance telephone conversations "to be sure he [Joe Hoffman] was wide awake and that he knew what he was doing." At the time of the trial, Hoffman was 31, and he and his wife had seven children. Assuming that Lukowitz knew all this, does it help a court and jury interpret his statements and conduct to decide if he made a promise to

Hoffman? Lukowitz himself had only a high school education. Is that relevant?

3. **The Statute of Frauds:** Why didn't the Statute of Frauds bar recovery in *Hoffman v. Red Owl*? Was the franchise contract that Hoffman and Red Owl planned to enter one that could not be performed within a year? Was it a contract for the sale of goods of a value greater than $500? If the Statute of Frauds would have applied, can we assume that compliance with the Statute of Frauds is not necessary if the circumstances are otherwise appropriate for application of promissory estoppel?

4. **Sale of the bakery business:** At trial Hoffman had tried to present evidence of a $6,000 loss on the sale of his bakery business in October. This evidence was excluded from trial because the bakery was owned by a corporation (Tasty Bakery) wholly owned by Hoffman and his wife, and the corporation had not been joined as a plaintiff in the case. The Supreme Court's opinion does not mention or discuss any possible loss from sale of the bakery business. However, before the Supreme Court's decision, Hoffman's lawyer had filed a separate suit on behalf of Tasty Bakery against Red Owl Stores. The parties agreed to postpone a trial until after the Supreme Court's decision, after which Red Owl conceded liability and the two suits were joined for ascertaining damages. After a day and half of jury trial, the parties settled. Because of the settlement, no transcript of the second trial has ever been made. The settlement was for $10,600. This amount may have been heavily influenced by evidence that the bakery business had been sold at a substantial loss, as Hoffman claimed.

5. **Impact on Hoffman and his lawyer:** Hoffman's attorney wrote the authors:

> This was certainly one of the most interesting cases I have handled even though not the most remunerative. Hoffman received $6,600. My fees were $4,000.00. Two-thirds of costs were paid by Red Owl Stores, Inc., in accordance with the Supreme Court decision.

> Shortly after Joseph Hoffman's experience with Red Owl, he started to work for Metropolitan Life Insurance Company as a salesman. He immediately won honors for highest sales and was promoted to District Manager in Milwaukee. I am informed within the next couple of months he will be transferred to Indiana in a managerial capacity.

The authors of this casebook have learned that Hoffman used the settlement proceeds to support his family during the lean years during which he started his life insurance business. He later went on to have a successful career, in a managerial capacity, with Metropolitan Life, serving as a district manager in Lafayette, Indiana, for many years, and eventually retiring as a district manager in St. Joseph, Michigan. Hoffman then joined a successful real estate business in St. Joseph that had been started by his wife. As of 2010, Hoffman and his wife still worked in this real estate business, Red Arrow Realty, though it was then owned by their son.

6. **Impact on Red Owl:** Suppose it is a few weeks after the Red Owl opinion became final. You represent Red Owl. You are asked to prepare a memorandum suggesting what the organization should do to avoid future liability under *Hoffman v. Red Owl*. Remember that your legal advice must seem practical and realistic to Red Owl's executives, who are not lawyers, or they will ignore it.

7. **Impact of** **Hoffman v. Red Owl Stores** **on the law:** Professor Jay Feinman surveyed the reported cases discussing § 90 that involved issues of what has come to be called "precontractual reliance." He reports a major difference in approach:[203]

Belief
vs.
Future-Oriented

> In circumstances that depart from the promissory norm, courts are variously strict and flexible in determining whether a manifestation of intention may furnish a basis for actionable reliance. The strict view holds that a statement that is not specifically demonstrative of an intention respecting future conduct or that is indefinite or limited cannot be the basis for promissory estoppel. Under a more flexible view, courts have held such statements to suffice.
>
> The strict view carefully distinguishes promises, which are future-oriented, from statements of belief, which concern only the present. For example, in cases involving franchisors who have made representations about the business potential that franchisees may expect or about their own policies of support for franchisees, some courts have held that such representations may not reasonably be relied upon as indications of future conduct. Courts usually view these representations, unlike promises to grant franchises, as statements of "belief" (that is, predictions or statements of current company policy) rather than intention. The statements are, therefore, not promises.
>
> The strict view also requires that the promise be definite and unequivocal. The court may determine that the promisor's expression concerning its future conduct is insufficiently certain and specific to give rise to promissory estoppel. Similarly, if the expression is made in the course of preliminary negotiations when material terms of the agreement are lacking, the degree of certainty necessary in a promise is absent. Finally, when the intention manifested is conditional, the promissory ideal is not met unless the event constituting the condition occurs. This rule holds good even when the event is within the control of the promisor, as is a condition of approval by a home office or higher official or a condition of execution of a final written agreement. The conclusion courts have drawn in all of these instances is that the facts of the case are not sufficiently compelling to invoke the limited reliance doctrine.
>
> The alternative, more flexible approach to promise allows reliance recovery in a wider variety of settings. Courts adopting this perspective hold that a promise need not be explicitly expressed but may be inferred from, for example, statements about future conduct or factual representations about a present state of affairs. The standard, consistent with the definition in § 90, is not whether the promisor clearly made a promise, but whether, given the context in which the statement at issue was made, the promisor

---

[203] Jay M. Feinman, *Promissory Estoppel and Judicial Method*, 97 HARV. L. REV. 678, 691–92 (1984). Copyright © Harvard Law Review. Reprinted with permission. *See also* Michael B. Metzger & Michael J. Phillips, *The Emergence of Promissory Estoppel as an Independent Theory of Recovery*, 35 RUTGERS L.J. 472 (1983) ("[T]he term 'PROMISSORY' estoppel" would seem an obvious misnomer. In fact, estoppel's 'reliance' component may eventually so come to dominate its 'promissory' aspect as to render the latter nugatory.").

should reasonably have expected that the promisee would infer a promise. This standard may be met not only by a particular promise or representation, but also by general statements of policy or practice, such as published plans for employee compensation or benefits. In appropriate cases of this type, the court may infer a promise even in the face of inconsistent expressions.

Does § 90 call for an exercise of judgment based on reason and intuition, rather than a strictly logical exercise that a judge can express neatly in an opinion that pleases scholars? Judges sense the appropriate answer in light of the total situation, their values and biases, and the ideas of the times. Is this a description of the approach in the *Red Owl* case? Feinman is very critical of this approach. He summarizes his objections:

> First, the courts are so distant from the actual contexts of cases that judicial application of the method is properly characterized as interpretive rather than empirical. Second, the courts' interpretive activity is not and cannot be consistently executed. Third, judicial interpretation is necessarily based on a subjective application of policies more complex than any simple preference for facilitation of commercial exchange.[204]

As you understand these three points from this brief summary, would you concede all three and still defend an intuitive approach? Compare the argument of Professors Daniel A. Farber and John H. Matheson:[205]

> Courts often resort to conclusory language in finding that a manifestation rises to the level of a promise. This is not surprising. Judges called upon to determine whether a promise has been made must look beyond the words and acts which constitute the transaction to the nature of the relationship between the parties and the circumstances surrounding their actions. But relationships and surrounding circumstances do not speak for themselves. They must be interpreted by judges on the basis of the expectations likely to arise between similarly situated parties. The conclusory tone follows because we are being told what we ought to already understand as members of the community. It is inherent in the use of an objective standard — under both traditional contract and promissory estoppel theories of obligation — to determine whether a commitment was voluntarily made.

Assume that we are members of a language community — we are lawyers and businesspeople who should understand business culture. Why should we understand what we are being told in an appellate opinion? Cases have passed through an elaborate filtering system to arrive in an appellate court. Doesn't this suggest that members of the community could translate the messages involved differently? Do Farber and Matheson answer Feinman's objections?

8. ***A more recent case and the practices of the courts:*** *Neiss v. Ehlers* did not

---

[204] Feinman, *supra* note 203, at 703.

[205] Daniel A. Farber & John H. Matheson, *Beyond Promissory Estoppel: Contract Law and the "Invisible Handshake,"* 52 U. CHI. L. REV. 903 (1985).

involve a franchise, but rather, negotiations for services combined with an owner-ship interest.[206] The Oregon Court of Appeals reviewed the decisions in various states concerning precontractual reliance. Plaintiff was an optician working in Portland, Oregon. Defendants had opened an optical business in Ashland. The parties adopted "a letter outline" of "the initial agreement." Plaintiff was to move to Ashland and work for a specified salary and benefits. (Ashland is about 290 miles south of Portland, near the Oregon-California border.) She was to get raises "in accordance with good business practices, subsequent to appropriate legal and accounting advice." Then the agreement provided: "Furthermore, in consideration of the particular skills and contributions of Violet E. Neiss to Ashland Optical Expressions, she shall be granted a one-third interest in Ashland's Optical Expressions as soon as it can be practically arranged [but in no case later than May 1, 1990] through the establishment of an S corporation and/or in a manner agreed upon by all above named parties and subsequent to appropriate legal and other necessary advice." The agreement also provided that Neiss would be employed by the business for 10 years, subject to her choosing to leave earlier.

Neiss worked in Ashland for more than two years. The parties attempted to negotiate an agreement covering both her employment and her acquisition of an ownership interest. They were unsuccessful. Neiss then returned to Portland. She sued for the wages and benefits that she would have received, for losses caused by her move to Ashland, the wages and benefits that she would have received had she stayed with the firm in Portland, and for the value of the share of the Ashland business that the defendants had promised her. The trial court granted defendants' motion for summary judgment. It found that the employment and ownership agreement were not divisible, and the parties' agreement was too indefinite to be enforced.

The Oregon Court of Appeals reversed the trial court's decision. It agreed with the trial court that the original document was an agreement to agree, which could not be enforced as a contract. It then asked whether precontractual reliance could be compensated under promissory estoppel. It considered cases from Texas, North Dakota, and Montana that said that there "can be no promissory estoppel without a real promise." Parties take the risk of any reliance that comes before there is a promise that is "clear, definite and unambiguous as to essential terms." The Oregon court then looked to a Colorado decision and an article by Professor Stanley D. Henderson that called for "the more expansive application of the doctrine."[207] The Colorado court said: "The development of the cause of action reflects an attempt by the courts to keep remedies abreast of increased moral consciousness of honesty and fair representations in all . . . dealings." The Oregon Court of Appeals also relied on *Hoffman v. Red Owl Stores, Inc.*

The Oregon court said that the better reasoning supports applying promissory estoppel to promises that are too indefinite or incomplete to enforce as contracts. Promissory estoppel remedies "are more flexible and are aimed at compensating the promisee for damages that result from actions in reliance on the promise, rather

---

[206]   135 Or. App. 218, 899 P.2d 700 (1995).

[207]   Stanley D. Henderson, *Promissory Estoppel and Traditional Contract Doctrine*, 78 YALE L.J. 343 (1969).

than providing comprehensive contract relief for the breach of the indefinite promise itself." The focus is on "the harm that results from the promisor's inducement and the promisee's actions in reliance." The Oregon court did note that "the facts of specific cases may be such that the promise is not only too indefinite for enforcement as a contract, but is so illusory that it could not have been acted on or foreseen as an inducement to action." The court decided that Neiss's case should not have been subject to summary judgment because the elements of promissory estoppel "were not conclusively negated or resolved by the evidence in the trial court proceedings."

[handwritten margin note: Shouldn't have been SJ cuz evidence needed more to determine if "illusory" or real promise]

In 2004, Professors Alan Schwartz and Robert E. Scott gathered citations to cases involving preliminary negotiations and preliminary agreements. They found 280 cases and selected every other case to produce a sample of 140 cases. The sample included cases from 29 state courts, 19 federal district courts, and seven federal courts of appeal. Thirty cases in this sample involved situations where the parties had not reached agreement but where one of the bargainers claimed reliance on the ongoing negotiations. The courts refused to find liability in 87 percent of these promissory estoppel claims because there was no "clear and unambiguous promise."[208] Does a study based on this number of reported cases necessarily tell you the full story of the impact of the § 90 theory on precontractual behavior or on disputes involving allegations of precontractual promises?

9. _The measure of recovery in promissory estoppel:_ *Hoffman v. Red Owl Stores* is often cited as limiting recovery in promissory estoppel to reliance damages. Professors Farber and Matheson surveyed 222 promissory estoppel cases decided between 1975 and 1985. Courts apply the doctrine regularly in commercial contexts. They use it as a primary basis of enforcement even where they could have applied traditional contract theory. Reliance plays little role in the determination of remedies. Farber and Matheson report: "The courts addressed the issue of the extent of recovery in 72 of the [222] cases in our data group. In only one-sixth of those cases was recovery limited explicitly to reliance damages. Full expectation recovery was granted in the remaining five-sixths of the cases."[209] Why wasn't Joseph Hoffman entitled to full expectation damages? Could you have calculated an expectation remedy for Hoffman?

[handwritten margin note: Case for limiting damages]

Judge Richard Posner wrote an opinion for the United States Court of Appeals for the Seventh Circuit, applying Wisconsin law in a diversity of citizenship case. In *Cosgrove v. Bartolotta*,[210] the plaintiff, a lawyer, agreed to make a substantial loan to finance a new restaurant in return for a promised partial ownership interest. The plaintiff then relied on the partial agreement by helping the defendant on various legal matters in setting up the restaurant, and he did not charge for doing this. The work was done outside of regular work hours, and it was not clear what the plaintiff's opportunity costs were for this expenditure of time and energy. In the end, defendant found alternative financing and did not honor the agreement by awarding the plaintiff the promised ownership interest. The jury found that there

---

[208] *See* Alan Schwartz & Robert E. Scott, *Precontractual Liability and Preliminary Agreements,* 120 Harv. L. Rev. 661, 671 (2007).

[209] Farber & Matheson, *supra* note 205, at 909 n.24.

[210] 150 F.3d 729 (7th Cir. 1998).

was no contract because details respecting the partial ownership interest remained to be negotiated. Nevertheless, the jury awarded plaintiff expectation damages (that is, the fair market value of the promised ownership interest) on a § 90 theory.

Judge Posner's opinion applies Wisconsin law. He upheld the jury verdict, including the award of expectation damages. The *Cosgrove* case tests the limits of precontractual reliance recovery both because it was not clear that the reliance was very extensive, and because it allowed expectation damages.[211] Reliance damages would have been difficult to calculate — should the lawyer be allowed to bill at his usual hourly rate when working outside of normal working hours? Reliance damages surely were less than the expectation damages awarded. Did Judge Posner apply *Hoffman v. Red Owl Stores* correctly? Does that case "hold" that a plaintiff who wins under a Restatement § 90 theory can recover only reliance damages and not an expectation measure? Was it necessary for the Wisconsin court to decide this issue under the facts of the Red Owl case?

One in which Judge Posner, int. WI law, allows exp. int. damage under Precontract

10. *A new, non-contractual duty?* Did the *Red Owl* case create a new kind of obligation — a duty to negotiate in good faith? Would seeing liability in this case as based on a violation of that duty, and not a contractual duty, avoid some of the messy conceptual problems we might otherwise face? European law generally recognizes such a duty, and some scholars have suggested that a duty to negotiate in good faith may be creeping into the law of the United States as well.[212] What are the advantages and disadvantages of such an approach?[213]

11. *What could be accomplished through restitution?* Professor Robert E. Scott questions *Hoffman v. Red Owl Stores'* § 90 solution to the problem of precontractual reliance.[214] He argues that the case provides little guidance about how to determine when a "promise" has been made — either to people bargaining or to courts appraising their conduct. Second, he tells us:

> My preferred approach . . . to look[ing] for the missing promise [is] to focus instead on quasi-contract: Here the argument was that Mr. Hoffmann had conferred a benefit on Red Owl during the period from May through November when he opened and then sold his grocery store, and thereafter sold the bakery business and building and purchased an option on a lot in Chilton. All these actions gave Red Owl valuable and beneficial information as to the kind of franchisee that Hoffmann was likely to be and the extent of his commitment to the project. Under the prevailing view, a quasi-

---

[211] In another case, a general contractor sued a subcontractor who backed out of a project after the bid was accepted, and the Nevada Supreme Court relied on § 90 to award the additional amount the general contractor had to pay a substitute subcontractor under an expectation theory. *Dynalectric Co. of Nevada v. Clark & Sullivan Constructors*, 255 P.3d 286 (Nev. 2011).

[212] Harvey L. Temkin, *When Does the "Fat Lady" Sing: An Analysis of "Agreements in Principle" in Corporate Acquisitions*, 55 FORDHAM L. REV. 125 (1987), suggests such an approach. *See also* Skycom Corporation v. Telstar Corp., 813 F.2d 810, 817 (7th Cir. 1987), for a case in which the Seventh Circuit, applying Wisconsin law, speculated that the *Hoffman* case might provide a basis for non-contractual liability.

[213] *See* E. Allan Farnsworth, *Precontractual Liability and Preliminary Agreements: Fair Dealing and Failed Negotiations*, 87 COLUM. L. REV. 217 (1987).

[214] Robert E. Scott, *Another View of* Hoffman v. Red Owl Stores, 61 HASTINGS L.J. 859 (2010).

contract claim lies either because one party wrongfully induced the other to confer the benefit in question or had the opportunity to prevent the other from conferring the benefit by mistake. This at least put the right question to a court: Was Hoffman wrongfully induced to provide this benefit to Red Owl or was he a "mere volunteer"? . . . [T]he key issue is whether Hoffmann was "wrongfully" induced to provide a benefit to Red Owl either because Red Owl officials' inducements were opportunistic or because these same officials failed to correct Hoffmann's evident misunderstanding.

Basically a theory saying pay Hoffman for benefit he gave Red Owl

If a court adopted Professor Scott's *quantum meruit* approach, how would it assess damages?

b. Ending the relationship

Those who create franchises structure their business relationships to achieve several purposes. They seek to benefit both their firms and those who hold their franchises and meet the public at the retail level. Franchisors also seek to build and guard the reputation of their product or service. A local dealer representing, for example, the Ford Motor Company gains the use of a valuable trade name, national advertising, all the efforts directed at designing and manufacturing successful products, and a great deal of training and systems of marketing. Or, to take another example, it will almost always be more profitable to run a McDonald's fast food franchise than "Joe's Eats." Franchisors want franchisees who are honest and efficient and who represent the product and trade name in their locality in a manner that enhances its reputation. The customers have an interest in good business practices, too.

Lawyers for franchisors usually draft elaborate standard form agreements to govern these relationships. In the past, these documents almost always reserved to the franchisors the right to end the relationships at will. Furthermore, franchises usually run for a specified term that is not too long. Thus, instead of termination, a franchisor could refuse to renew the arrangement when it expired. This structure aided franchisors in ending relationships when franchisees didn't perform well or when a franchisor found another person who might perform better at the same location. It also served to reinforce the power of the franchisor to gain compliance with its requests and demands. A franchisee might want a "free ride," gaining the benefits of the franchise's reputation without investing much to maintain it. The threat of cancellation or nonrenewal was always present, although when things went well the threat would be in the background and almost never mentioned.

Makes sense

Franchisees who had served long and hard often thought the arrangement poorly protected their interests. Franchisors and academics who champion their cause sometimes argue that franchisors have no reason to treat efficient franchisees poorly:

Fair enough

counter to Franchisees Bitching

The franchisor is not likely to terminate franchisees merely to confiscate their sunk investments opportunistically because franchisors must be concerned about their reputations when attempting to sell additional franchise locations.[215]

However, sometimes a franchisor makes a business judgment that profits it but injures dealers. For example, automobile manufacturers have moved to sell and service cars in fewer but larger dealerships to gain some economies of scale. This may benefit the manufacturer and perhaps many consumers, but it came at the expense of many smaller dealerships that had been in operation for years. Petroleum refiners decided to convert many gasoline stations from places where cars were repaired to convenience stores where customers pumped gasoline into their cars. This maximized the refiners' profits and benefited those dealers who could make more from a convenience store than from car repairs. However, the change was a devastating blow to those dealers who had built a reputation as experts in car service and who were poorly situated to compete in the convenience store market.

To complicate matters further, middle managers who deal with franchisees often act for their own interests. Sometimes dealers have been required to give bribes or kickbacks in order to keep their franchises. In addition, middle management might sometimes be evaluated in terms of short-term rather than long-term performance, and this might cause them to encourage franchisees to resort to questionable, or illegal, business practices. In addition, the evaluation of the performance of franchisees is often largely a matter of judgment by middle management, who may make mistakes.[216]

Just before and just after the Second World War, automobile dealers in about a third of the states successfully lobbied their legislators for statutes to defend their interests. There were a number of "atrocity stories" about manufacturers imposing unreasonable quotas on dealers and dealers being forced to bribe the manufacturers' officials who were in charge of dealers. While these statutes covered many things, an important provision prohibited a manufacturer from canceling a dealer franchise except for "just cause." Rather than continue to work state-by-state, the National Automobile and Truck Dealers' Association turned to the United States Congress and gained the "Automobile Dealers' Day in Court Act of 1956."[217] That act limits the power of manufacturers to cancel or fail to renew a dealer's franchise

---

[215] Benjamin Klein & Lester F. Saft, *The Law and Economics of Franchise Tying Contracts*, 28 J.L. & Econ. 345, 356 (1985). For a similar argument, see Steven N. Wiggins, *Franchising — A Case of Long-Term Contracts*, 144 J. Institutional Theoretical Econ. 149, 151 (1988). *See also* Klein, *The Economics of Franchise Contracts*, 2 J. Corp. Fin. 9 (1995). *But see* Uri Benoliel, *The Expectation of Continuity Effect and Franchise Termination Laws: A Behavioral Perspective*, 46 Am. Bus. L.J. 139 (2009) ("[A] good-cause requirement increases the expectation of continuity, which in turn enhances the level of relational behavior, joint action, trust, and fairness in the marketing channel.").

[216] *See* Benoliel, *supra* note 215 ("According to the model presented here, the economic calculus overlooks a significant source of efficiency: the expectation of relationship continuity."); *see also* Gillian K. Hadfield, *Problematic Relations: Franchising and the Law of Incomplete Contracts*, 42 Stan. L. Rev. 927, 992 (1990) ("[T]o interpret the franchise contract is to read it in the context of this relationship, to test the written terms against the basic sense of the relationship and the commitment problems facing both franchisee and franchisor. Only by so doing can courts ensure that the exchanges they enforce are indeed the exchanges that constitute a franchise.").

[217] 15 U.S.C. § 1222 (2013). *See* Stewart Macaulay, Law and the Balance of Power: The Automobile Manufacturers and Their Dealers (Russell Sage Foundation 1966).

[Handwritten margin note at top: "Need Good Cause to Cancel car dealer franchise"]

absent "good cause," as defined in the legislation. In 2002, Congress passed the Motor Vehicle Franchise Contract Arbitration Fairness Act, which limited and regulated the uses of arbitration clauses in automobile franchise contracts.[218]

This federal statutory scheme served to protect the dealers very well until the financial crisis of 2008. Both General Motors and Chrysler went into bankruptcy and were reorganized into new business units. As part of this process, Chrysler terminated about 790 dealerships. General Motors refused to renew dealership agreements with about 1,300 dealers and took one or more brands (such as Oldsmobile, Pontiac, Hummer, and Saab) away from about 700 others. The National Automobile and Truck Dealers' Association lobbied Congress, and several senators publicly championed dealers from their states who had been terminated. In response to the situation, section 747 of the Consolidated Appropriations Act of 2010 created an arbitration procedure whereby franchisees could seek reinstatement or readmission to the dealer network of a manufacturer. Responding to the act, General Motors offered 661 dealers an opportunity for reinstatement, and Chrysler offered such an opportunity to 86 dealers. In several cases, however, Chrysler sought to impose new requirements on dealers who had won reinstatement. Chrysler's actions were challenged in two cases.[219] We will not know the full meaning of this statute until and unless the Supreme Court of the United States construes the legislation in the future.

Retail gasoline dealers battled for legislation to protect their franchises, through the states and finally at the federal level, from the 1950s to the mid-1970s. As a result of this lobbying by gasoline dealers, some states passed general franchise protection acts, which were not limited to dealers who sold particular products such as gasoline. (These statutes did not cover automobile dealers because they had their own federal and state statutes.) Finally, the gasoline dealers succeeded in getting federal legislation passed; this federal statute preempted all state statutes that dealt with the questions that the federal act covered.[220] It limited the power of the major oil companies to *cancel* franchises without cause. However, the federal act's provisions dealing with an oil company *failing to renew* a franchise after its term had ended proved to offer gasoline dealers far less protection than the gasoline dealers' trade association officials had assumed. Some major oil companies responded by offering franchises that ran for only relatively short terms.

[Handwritten margin note: "Not a lot of protection on renewals for gas dealers, so oil companies just offered short deals"]

We will look at the Wisconsin Fair Dealership Law[221] as an example of similar statutes found in many states.[222] Section 135.03 says that no franchisor may

---

[218] 15 U.S.C. § 1226 (2013).

[219] *See* Los Feliz Ford, Inc. v. Chrysler Grp., LLC, 571 Fed. Appx. 546 (9th Cir. 2014); Chrysler Grp., LLC v. Fox Hills Motor Sales, Inc., 776 F.3d 411 (6th Cir. 2015).

[220] *See* Stewart Macaulay, *Long-Term Continuing Relations: The American Experience Regulating Dealerships and Franchises*, in FRANCHISING AND THE LAW: THEORETICAL AND COMPARATIVE APPROACHES IN EUROPE AND THE UNITED STATES 179–237 (C. Joerges ed., Nomos Verlagsgesellschaft 1991).

[221] Wis. Stat. §§ 135.01–135.07.

[222] Many states have passed statutes protecting dealers. Some of these laws protect only specific kinds of dealers, such as those who sell automobiles, gasoline, or farm equipment or those who distribute beer and wine. However, Adi Ayal and Uri Benoliel, in *Revitalizing the Case for Good Cause Statutes: The Role of Review Sites*, 19 STANFORD J.L. BUS. & FIN. 331, 334 n.8 (2014), report that 17 states have

"terminate, cancel, fail to renew or substantially change the competitive circumstances of a dealership agreement without good cause." Section 135.02(4) defines good cause as:

> (a) Failure by a dealer to comply substantially with essential and reasonable requirements imposed upon the dealer by the grantor, or sought to be imposed by the grantor, which requirements are not discriminatory as compared with requirements imposed on other similarly situated dealers either by their terms or in the manner of their enforcement; or

> (b) Bad faith by the dealer in carrying out the terms of the dealership.

The burden of proving good cause is on the franchisor. The provisions of the statute may not be varied by contract. This legislation raises many of our familiar problems related to legal intervention in long-term continuing relationships.

To understand modern developments, we must recall the legislative history of this statute. A lawyer who had handled franchise litigation in the early 1970s drafted the original bill. Governor Patrick Lucey, a Democrat, offered this draft to the Wisconsin Legislature in 1972. However, there was not enough interest to prompt hearings, and the bill died at the end of the session. The drafter tells us what happened next:[223]

> Then came the 1974 session. Battalions of gasoline dealers suffering at the hands of major and minor oil companies marched on Madison [the state capital], demanding relief. Farm implement dealers, beer wholesalers,

---

general franchise termination laws that require "good cause" for the termination of a franchise. The Wisconsin Fair Dealership Law, for example, is not limited to specific kinds of dealers, and it offers broad protections to franchisees. Ayal and Benoliel say that the "good cause" states are Arkansas, California, Connecticut, Delaware, Hawaii, Illinois, Indiana, Iowa, Michigan, Minnesota, Nebraska, New Jersey, Rhode Island, Tennessee, Virginia, Washington, and Wisconsin. Since 1992, about 30 states have considered but refused to adopt franchisee protection statutes.

Why focus on the Wisconsin statute? While there are differences in these statutes among states, the Wisconsin legislation suggests problems common to most of them. There are more judicial opinions interpreting the Wisconsin statute than that of any other state. Moreover, courts in other jurisdictions may use decisions applying the Wisconsin act as persuasive authority about how to read similar provisions in statutes passed in other states. *See, e.g.*, Kent Jenkins Sales, Inc. v. Angelo Bros. Co., 804 F.2d 482 (8th Cir. 1986), which relies on two cases interpreting the Wisconsin Fair Dealership Law to give meaning to a very similar Arkansas statute.

In 1992, Iowa passed a franchise protection act that was similar to the Wisconsin statute, but the Iowa law contained additional sections that offered even more protection to franchisees. A group representing franchisors conducted a lobbying effort before the Iowa legislature for several sessions. They were successful in provoking some changes. Nonetheless, the Iowa statute still prohibits franchisors from placing competing franchise locations "in unreasonable proximity to the existing franchisee's outlet or location," terminating a franchise except for good cause after giving the franchisee a chance to cure any default, and not renewing a franchise except for good cause or the franchisor's complete withdrawal from the geographic market served by the franchisee. *See* Iowa Code Ann. §§ 537A.10, 1–17 (Cumulative Ann. Pocket Part 2015). The Iowa statute authorizes reasonable attorney's and expert witness fees for successful franchisees. This statute remains one of the two or three strongest in favor of franchisees in the nation.

[223] William F. Nelson, *Legislative History*, in State Bar of Wisconsin, Advanced Training Seminars — Continuing Legal Education; Magna Carta for Wisconsin Businesses: The Wisconsin Fair Dealership Act (Nov. 1979). Reprinted with permission.

building supply wholesalers, and a whole myriad of small Wisconsin businessmen joined their ranks. The old franchise law, offered two years before by Governor Lucey, was retrieved from the dead issues file, dusted off [as Assembly Bill 837], and sailed through the Assembly with only slight amendment, surprisingly little debate, and by an overwhelming margin. The galleries were filled with the green and orange and white shirts of small gasoline dealers who had become its champions.

By then, it had achieved a partisan flavor. Democrats, almost to a person, supported it. Republicans were in opposition, though there were lots of defectors.

The bill arrived at the State Senate in the late winter of 1974, at a time perilously close to adjournment, considering that it needed to be scheduled for hearings and take its place on the calendar of the Senate. . . . Those who had supported its passage by the Assembly, while heady with success, recognized the almost impossible task of passing the Senate so late in the session, the Senate being controlled as it was by a narrow margin of Republicans. . . .

[I]t faced the stern and serious opposition of those who had not been fully aware of its existence until it passed the Assembly so easily. It was immediately locked in committee by the forces in opposition. The committee chairman vowed that it would never again see the light of day. It was always apparent that the Senate supported . . . [the bill] by a narrow majority vote, but that support for the bill fell far short of the two-thirds needed to suspend the rules and allow the matter to take the floor. . . . Debate on holding the bill in committee, in view of full galleries, resulted in the Senate, apparently for the first time in years, voting the bill out of committee even though hearings had never been had, since the chairman had refused to schedule them.

Suddenly the corridors of the Senate were choked with small businessmen, gasoline dealers, professional lobbyists, and business executives, all asking earnestly to be heard, pro and con, on the issues raised by Assembly Bill 837. . . . Effort after effort made by the proponents of the bill to suspend the rules and bring the bill to the floor fell painfully short of the needed two-thirds. But after each effort failed, the proponents regrouped. . . .

Finally, on April 4, 1974, the last day of the session, a motion was made to suspend the rules for the purpose of putting Assembly Bill 837 at the bottom of Consent Calendar A; sure death, because Consent Calendar A would not be reached prior to adjournment. The motion carried by far more than the needed two-thirds majority. The presiding officer of the Senate then ruled that a specific waiver of the rules to put the bill at the bottom of Consent Calendar A had the effect of a general waiver of the rules, and that the bill was now on the floor. . . . After loud protest, a vote was taken on the presiding officer's procedural ruling. It was sustained by the same simple majority of the Senate that had always favored the bill.

The bill would still die if the Senate added any amendment to it, since it was the last day of the legislative session and there was no time left to seek or receive Assembly concurrence in any amendment. Also, in normal passage of legislation, a bill must be held for a third reading, which occurs on the following day and requires a second vote on engrossment before the bill is held to have passed the Senate and be available for consideration by the Governor. For Assembly Bill 837, tomorrow would never come. It was the last day.

Nonetheless, the debate on engrossment began. Then the roll call. The bill passed! An amendment to exempt the beer industry was rejected by only one vote. After bitter and vicious debate, the bill had been engrossed without amendment, but the votes simply did not exist to suspend the rules and waive the third reading. The victory for some and the defeat for others still seemed meaningless, just a gesture.

Then a senator [the senator later became Justice Bablitch of the Supreme Court of Wisconsin] moved that the Senate vote to reconsider its original vote on engrossment. The roll call was taken and the vote came out just the same, rejecting reconsideration. Confusion reigned in the jammed galleries and halls. No one seemed to know what was going on. Then the same senator asked the chief clerk to see if there was any precedent for the effect of rejection by the Senate as a whole of a vote for reconsideration of engrossment, when that occurred on the last day of the session. The chief clerk announced that in 1937 the Senate had ruled that the effect of rejection of a motion to reconsider engrossment was to waive the rule requiring a third reading. No two-thirds vote was required. The lieutenant governor adopted the precedent, and an appeal of his ruling was affirmed by the same majority which had voted to engross the bill.

Once the bill passed, the leader of the opposition moved to make the vote unanimous and to suspend the rules, sending the act to the Governor immediately. The motion passed, and the Governor signed the bill that afternoon. The original bill strictly regulated the end of a franchisor-franchisee relationship, because those drafting and advocating the bill assumed they would have to accept amendments to weaken it. However, the opponents were unwilling to compromise because they were confident they could defeat the bill by delaying the legislative process. Thus, when it passed, it was a much stronger statute than its proponents had expected to gain.

The following case raises many of the difficulties in legal regulation of long-term continuing relationships. Walgreen Drug Stores had long operated in many states through its agency division. Agency stores could purchase Walgreen's house-brand drugs, and they could use Walgreen's trade name. Walgreen decided to close its entire agency division, and it terminated many stores in Wisconsin. However, it was not withdrawing from business in Wisconsin. It planned to remain in Wisconsin, running its own large stores in shopping centers in the best areas for high-volume sales.

Thirteen pharmacies in southern Wisconsin brought a class action suit. The Wisconsin Pharmaceutical Association helped coordinate the suit, although the

WPA remained neutral. Walgreen is a member of WPA.

Fighting a major corporation is never easy. Notice the number of difficult issues that the lawyers for the pharmacies had to brief and argue.

On Quimbee truis Walgreens to cancel dealership agreements

COLLINS DRUGS, INC. v. WALGREEN CO.[224]
United States District Court, Western District of Wisconsin
539 F. Supp. 1357 (1982)

CRABB, C.J.

These civil actions for injunctive and monetary relief under the Wisconsin Fair Dealership Law, Wis. Stat. §§ 135.01 *et seq.*, are before the court on defendant's motions for summary judgment. Both actions were begun in state court and removed here by defendant. Diversity jurisdiction is present. 28 U.S.C. § 1332. The issue in both cases is whether the Wisconsin Fair Dealership Law permits a grantor to cancel *all* of its dealership arrangements within the state for bona fide economic reasons such as a change in its manner of doing business. For the reasons that follow, I conclude that the Wisconsin Fair Dealership Law does not permit grantors to terminate dealerships for any reason other than "good cause," as that term is defined in the Act; that defendant Walgreen's termination of its dealership agreements was without good cause; and that those plaintiff-dealers whose agreements are covered under the Act are entitled to damages and to partial summary judgment in their favor, but that none of the plaintiffs is entitled to injunctive relief.

From the record, I find that there is no genuine issue with respect to the following material facts.

FACTS

Plaintiffs are pharmacies doing business in the State of Wisconsin. Defendant is a corporation organized under the laws of the State of Illinois. . . .

Defendant manufactures and sells under its own private labels a wide variety of drugs, beauty aids, and household commodities. It also sells similar products manufactured by other companies. Prior to October 1, 1980, defendant sold these products to the consuming public through a nationwide system of both company-owned and independently-owned stores.

Every independently-owned drug store which sold Walgreen brand products operated under a standard written agreement (the "Retailer's Agreement"). At the beginning of 1980, approximately 1,400 independently-owned drug stores operated throughout the United States under such agreements.

These are companies that sell Walgreen Brand along w/ name brand – but they themselves aren't Walgreens

The Retailer's Agreement governed all aspects of the contractual relationship

---

[224] On appeal, the caption for this case changed to Kealey Pharmacy & Home Care Services, Inc. v. Walgreen. This case has had several captions, but for the sake of uniformity, we will refer to it as the *Walgreen* case.

between defendant and its dealers, including such matters as the right of the independently-owned store to use the Walgreen trade name and trademark, defendant's right to locate a company-owned store near the independently-owned store, and the minimum amount of Walgreen products that the retailer must purchase each year. Paragraph "Fourth. (c)" of the Retailer's Agreement expressly provided that "[i]n the event Walgreen determines at any time to discontinue all similar Agreements, it may, at its option, terminate this agreement upon thirty days' written notice" to the dealer. Under the terms of the Retailer's Agreement, the plaintiff dealers were permitted to, and did, purchase additional goods for resale from suppliers other than defendant.

[handwritten margin note: Agreement says Walgreen can't terminate when they feel like it]

[handwritten margin note: Plaintiffs can buy non Wlgrn stuff]

On April 14, 1980, defendant's board of directors met and decided to discontinue the operations of its Agency Division, which administered the defendant's relationship with its dealers, and to terminate all of the Retailer's Agreements as of October 1, 1980, on the ground that these independently-owned drug stores were producing an inadequate rate of return.

By letter dated April 17, 1980, defendant informed plaintiffs and each of its other approximately 1,400 independent dealers that, pursuant to paragraph "Fourth. (c)" of its Retailer's Agreement, defendant had elected to terminate the agreements, effective October 1, 1980.

By letter dated April 28, 1980, defendant informed every dealer that defendant would furnish the dealer's name and address to manufacturers, wholesalers, suppliers, and vendors for the purpose of assisting the dealers in finding alternative sources of supply. Subsequently, defendant gave to other drug store companies the names and addresses of most of its dealers.

As a result of defendant's April 1980 decision to terminate the Agency Division and all of its Retailer's Agreements, the division was disbanded. Division staff was reduced from 110 persons to three; over half of the staff left defendant's employment and the remainder were transferred to other positions within the Walgreen organization. The division field personnel responsible for the dealers in the State of Wisconsin are no longer employed by defendant.

. . . .

Defendant continues to operate company-owned stores in Wisconsin.

OPINION

A. Dealership Agreements Covered by the Wisconsin Fair Dealership Law

Defendant does not contend that plaintiffs are not dealers within the meaning of that term in Wis. Stat. § 135.02. It contends, however, that not all of the plaintiffs are parties to agreements subject to the provision of the Wisconsin Fair Dealership Law, either because they were operating under agreements executed prior to the effective date of the law or because they were operating under "renewal agreements" executed prior to the effective date of the amendment to the Fair Dealership Law, which specified that the provisions of the law extended to renewal agreements. Therefore, the threshold inquiry is to determine which of the plaintiffs are parties to agreements subject to the provisions of the Wisconsin Fair Dealership Law. . . .

1. Pre-April 5, 1974, agreements.

As the Wisconsin Fair Dealership Law was originally enacted in 1974, it provided that:

> No grantor, directly or through any officer, agent or employee may terminate, cancel, fail to renew, or substantially change the competitive circumstances of a Retailer's agreement entered into after the effective date of this act (1973) [sic] without good cause.[225] The burden of proving good cause shall be on the grantor.

Wis. Stat. § 135.03. (Emphasis supplied.) It is clear from the language of the statute as it was originally enacted that pre-April 5, 1974, agreements were not entitled to coverage under the Wisconsin Fair Dealership Law. However, by an amendment enacted on November 24, 1977, the underscored language was deleted, and Wis. Stat. § 135.025 was created to provide that one of the purposes of the Wisconsin Fair Dealership Law was "to govern all dealerships, including any renewals or amendments, to the full extent consistent with the constitutions of this state and the United States." Wis. Stat. § 135.025(2)(d). By its deletion of the underscored phrase, the legislature seemed to be inviting the courts to grant coverage under the Wisconsin Fair Dealership Law to those grantees of dealership entered into prior to April 5, 1974.

In *Wipperfurth v. U-Haul Co. of Western Wisconsin, Inc.*, 101 Wis. 2d 586, 304 N.W.2d 767 (1981), the Supreme Court for the State of Wisconsin declined the legislature's invitation . . . [and held] that retroactive application of the Wisconsin Fair Dealership Law would be an unconstitutional impairment of the obligation of contract in violation of the contract clause contained in Article I, § 10 of the United States Constitution, because the legislature had failed to make the showing that retroactive application of the Act to existing contracts was reasonably necessary and exigent, and served a vital purpose of government.

In the instant case, two of the plaintiffs' complaints are controlled by *Wipperfurth*. . . . Therefore, with respect to these plaintiffs, defendant's motion for summary judgment will be granted and [the] amended complaints dismissed. . . .

2. Agreements executed after April 5, 1974, but renewed prior to November 24, 1977, by plaintiffs that had been parties to previous agreements with defendant executed prior to April 5, 1974.

Plaintiffs Kealey Pharmacy and Langmack's Drugs executed dealership agreements with defendant on August 21, 1974, and on June 7, 1976, respectively. Defendant contends that these agreements are outside the scope of the Fair Dealership Law because the agreements were renewals of earlier agreements,

---

[225] [2] The Wisconsin Fair Dealership Law became effective the day after it was published. It was published April 4, 1974.

executed before the enactment of the 1977 amendment that made explicit provision for the coverage of renewal agreements.

When it enacted the Fair Dealership Law in 1974, the legislature intended it to apply to all dealership agreements "entered into thereafter." As *Wipperfurth* makes clear, the mere continuance after April 5, 1974, of a dealership arrangement of indefinite duration does not constitute a dealership agreement "entered into after" that date. Similarly, an automatic renewal contemplated under the terms of a dealership agreement is not an agreement "entered into" so as to bring the dealership under the original terms of the Act.

Auto renewals don't count as entered into after

The new Kealey and Langmack contracts were not simply automatic renewals of the prior contracts; they represented a significant alteration of the relationship between the parties. The new contracts differed from the prior ones in several respects and, in particular, with respect to the minimum yearly purchase requirement for each dealer. Moreover, under the old contracts, defendant had no obligation to renew its agreement with either plaintiff.

Thus, when defendant negotiated the new contracts, it was making a fresh decision in each instance whether to appoint Kealey Pharmacy and Langmack's Drugs as Walgreen agencies. . . .

These ain't auto renewals

In the circumstances present in this case, I find and conclude that the Kealey and Langmack contracts were dealership agreements "entered into" after April 5, 1974, and therefore subject to the terms of the Fair Dealership Law.

B. Scope and Constitutionality of the Wisconsin Fair Dealership Law

Defendant musters two arguments against binding it to the provisions of law: the first is that the legislature never intended to make the Fair Dealership Law applicable to statewide terminations of dealerships effected for legitimate business reasons, and the second is that if the legislature did intend such a broad application of the law, it was acting unconstitutionally in violation of defendant's rights to due process and to freedom of contract.

1. Applicability of Wisconsin Fair Dealership Law to Statewide Dealership Terminations.

Section 135.03 of the Wisconsin Fair Dealership Law proscribes the termination, cancellation, failure to renew, or substantial change in the competitive circumstances of a dealership agreement "without good cause." "Good cause" is defined in § 135.02 as:

> (a) Failure by a dealer to comply substantially with essential and reasonable requirements imposed upon him by the grantor, or sought to be imposed by the grantor, which requirements are not discriminatory as compared with requirements imposed on other similarly situated dealers either by their terms or in the manner of their enforcement; or

> (b) Bad faith by the dealer in carrying out the terms of the dealership.

The statute says nothing about any circumstances in which a grantor may terminate an agreement for any reason other than the dealer's bad faith or failure to perform its obligations under the agreement. The fair inference is that any other terminations are violative of the statute. In this respect, the statute is clear and unequivocal. Ordinarily, when the language of a statute is unambiguous, judicial inquiry is at an end . . . Defendant counters, correctly, that the rules of statutory construction do not bind a court to a literal reading of a statute, where literalism would lead to a result wholly at odds with the legislature's intent . . . or where a clearly expressed legislative intention compels a construction contrary to the language of the statute itself. . . .

However, a heavy burden of persuasion rests on the party urging that a statute should be read to mean something other than what it appears to mean on its face. Two arguments may be marshalled in support of defendant's position that, despite the clear language dictating coverage, the statute should be declared inapplicable to the terminations at issue here. The first is what I will call the "fair treatment" argument; the second, I will refer to as the "omission of non-judicial remedies" argument.

[Handwritten margin note: BASICALLY if u read literally it can only terminate for "good cause" below are arguments as to def makes as to why it shouldn't be taken literally at face value]

a. Fair Treatment Argument

Relying on the statutory statement that the Wisconsin Fair Dealership Law has as one of its purposes "the continuation of dealerships on a *fair* basis," defendant suggests that the legislature's concern was directed solely at the discriminatory termination of one dealership or of a small number of dealerships without statutory good cause, and not about the nondiscriminatory, evenhanded, and impartial terminations at issue here. Defendant argues that the statutory references to fairness are evidence that the legislature never considered or addressed the possibility of wholesale dealership terminations and never intended to prohibit such terminations. This argument fails upon a reading of the statute, a review of the legislative history, and the application of logic.

First, nothing in the language of the statute compels the interpretation defendant suggests.[226] It is true that "fair" can mean evenhanded and impartial; it can also mean "just" and "equitable." THE AMERICAN HERITAGE DICTIONARY OF THE ENGLISH LANGUAGE 471 (1970). Given the legislature's expressed concern with the imbalance of power between dealers and grantors, it seems unlikely that the framers of the statute intended "fair" to refer only to evenhanded, nondiscriminatory treatment as between one dealer and another, and not to refer as well to the fairness, or equitableness, of the relationship between a grantor and its dealer. It seems even more unlikely that the legislature intended to permit a grantor to take any kind of action adverse to its dealers, provided only that it took the same action with respect to all of its dealers.

---

[226] [6] The statute's references to fairness are contained in subsections (2)(a) and (2)(b) of § 135.025, which lists the purposes of the Fair Dealership Law as the promotion of "the compelling interest of the public in fair business relations between dealers and grantors, and in the continuation of dealerships on a fair basis," § 135.025(2)(a); and the protection of "dealers against unfair treatment by grantors who inherently have superior economic power and superior bargaining power in the negotiation of dealership." Wis. Stat. § 135.025(2)(b).

Second, the legislative history of the Fair Dealership Law refutes defendant's suggestion that the legislature might not have been thinking of the possibility of statewide dealership terminations when it enacted the law. In 1973, the entire United States began to feel the effects of the concerted actions of the Organization of Petroleum Exporting Countries. Many American oil companies began reducing the number of their retail gasoline outlets in Wisconsin and, in some instances, ceased supplying gasoline altogether to their independently-operated dealerships in Wisconsin. The Wisconsin legislature was aware of this phenomenon. Indeed, one proposed version of the Fair Dealership Law, Senate Substitute Amendment 3, would have limited its scope to gasoline dealership terminations only.

Moreover, in the course of enacting the Act, the Wisconsin legislature considered, but failed to adopt, Senate Amendment 4 to 1973 Assembly Bill 837. Had it adopted the amendment, the legislature would have provided exceptions from the Fair Dealership Law for actions taken by a grantor to:

(a) vertically integrate;

(b) alter or adjust its marketing technique, scheme, or plan;

(c) withdraw from a geographic marketing area; or

(d) dispose of, through sale or lease, any parcel of real estate occupied by a dealer upon the expiration of the dealer's lease for the parcel as long as the parcel of real estate ceases to be the site of a branded outlet of the grantor.

Although the legislature's failure to enact this amendment is not dispositive of the question of its intent, it is supportive of the view that the statute should not be read in the restrictive manner urged by defendant.

Finally, logic alone would compel the conclusion that the legislature did not intend to provide an exception from the Fair Dealership Law for large-scale terminations of dealerships, any more than it intended to permit exceptions for the termination of a single dealership for a bona fide business reason. As several commentators have pointed out, the adverse impact upon a dealer of a unilateral termination of its dealership is not lessened because the grantor is acting in good faith for sound business reasons.[227] Neither is the adverse impact lessened because all other similarly situated dealers are being terminated as well.

---

[227] [7] *See, e.g.*, Ernest Gellhorn, *Limitations on Contract Termination Rights — Franchise Cancellations*, 1967 DUKE L.J. 465, 504–05:

> Analytically, the terminating party's motives are unrelated to the harshness of the bargain or of its effect. Motives have no relationship to the parties' relative bargaining power. Nor would the application of a good-faith test be affected either by whether the dominant party was misusing its power or by whether termination would have unduly harsh effects on the terminated party. Rather, its application would be determined by the extent to which such misuse was disclosed by improper motives. The assumption, in other words, seems to be that fairness can be assured (or fundamental unfairness prevented) by attention to the motives upon which a party acts. Not only is empirical support for this assumption lacking, but it also seems contrary to common sense. There is no evidence that a weaker party would be protected adequately by requiring the dominant party to exhibit proper motives in exercising the power to terminate. . . .

Reason 2 it shouldn't be read literally

b. The Absence of Non-Judicial Remedies Argument

Under the Fair Dealership Law, *all* terminations, cancellations, or failures to renew dealership agreements are violative of the statute unless they are effected for "good cause." Any dealer whose dealership is terminated in violation of the statute has one remedy only: a suit for damages or injunctive relief or both. The statute makes no provision for negotiated terminations under any circumstances and it makes no provision for protecting dealers from the loss of their investment upon termination other than by legal action.[228]

The absence of any non-judicial remedy for termination or of any provision under which a [grantor] can effect a valid termination of a dealership it no longer wants to continue suggests two possibilities. The first is that urged by defendant: the absence of these provisions demonstrates that the legislature was addressing only the discriminatory termination of individual dealerships, effected under circumstances in which the grantor remains a viable franchisor within the state, continuing to operate through independent dealerships. Surely, the argument continues, the legislature neither desired nor intended to lock every grantor into eternal dealership agreements with each of its Wisconsin dealers, despite the grantor's desire to withdraw from an entire geographic area, or to cease production of the kinds of products sold through the dealerships, or to change its entire system of marketing its products. Thus, the legislature must have intended an exception for such major changes in the grantor's method of doing business.

The flaw in this interpretation is that it is no more reasonable to assume that the legislature intended to prohibit forever the closing down of *one* of a grantor's dealerships than to assume that the legislature intended to prohibit forever the closing down of *all* of the grantor's dealerships. The defendant's interpretation ignores the fact that, just as there are instances in which a grantor has sound business reasons for closing all of its dealerships, there are instances in which a grantor has equally sound business reasons (but not the "good cause" required under the statute) for ending its relationship with a particular dealer.

The second and more plausible interpretation of the Fair Dealership Law's omission of non-judicial remedies is that the legislature was not trying to create a system of "perpetual care" dealerships, but rather that it believed that only the threat of a civil action for money damages or injunctive relief would give sufficient support to a dealer's bargaining position to allow the dealer to negotiate a fair termination agreement.

The legislature may well have concluded that when a grantor terminates a dealership for any reason other than good cause, the dealer should be reimbursed for any loss of investment caused by the termination. Having reached this conclusion, it may have decided that, rather than try to fashion a procedure that would permit terminations subject to some statutory damage formula, it would

---

[228] [8] By contrast, the federal Petroleum Marketing Practices Act permits a dealer and grantor to terminate a dealership by agreement under certain situations and permits the grantor to withdraw from a particular geographic market area, subject to certain conditions. *See* 15 U.S.C. § 2802(b)(2). Under 15 U.S.C. § 2805(c), a franchisor can "buy out" uneconomical franchises. *See generally* Brach v. Amoco Oil Co., 677 F.2d 1213 (7th Cir. 1982).

leave the task of determining a dealer's fair compensation to the courts to be determined on a case-by-case basis. Creating a cause of action for damages based on all terminations except those motivated by good cause was the most expeditious way to draft a statute which would achieve this legislative objective.

The legislature's concern was to protect dealers. It is consistent with this concern that the legislature would have provided that in any termination not undertaken for good cause, the dealer is entitled to a judicial determination of the damages it has incurred as a result of its termination and, in appropriate instances, to an injunction against the termination.

At first reading, the statutory provision of injunctive relief against invalid terminations supports the view that application of the Act to statewide dealership terminations would have the effect of prohibiting any business changes from ever occurring, an effect that the legislature could not have intended. However, a closer look at the statute reveals that the grant of injunctive relief is discretionary with the court. Section 135.06 provides that a dealer "also *may* be granted injunctive relief against unlawful termination, cancellation, nonrenewal, or substantial change of competitive circumstances." Wis. Stat. § 135.06 (Emphasis supplied.) By making the granting of injunctive relief discretionary, the legislature gave implicit recognition to the fact that there would be instances of dealership terminations where permanent injunctive relief would be wholly inappropriate.

For the foregoing reasons, I conclude that a Wisconsin court considering this issue would hold that the Wisconsin Fair Dealership Law is not limited in its application to only those terminations or other adverse actions that discriminate against one dealer in relation to other dealers; rather, a Wisconsin court would conclude that the law was intended to, and does, cover nondiscriminatory, across-the-board terminations of dealerships even if those terminations are undertaken because the grantor decides to withdraw from an entire geographic area, or to cease production of the products sold by its dealers, or to change its marketing structure, or for any other business reason.

2. Constitutionality of the Wisconsin Fair Dealership Law as Applied to Across-the-Board Dealership Terminations.

[Judge Crabb found that the application of the statute to the franchise terminations involved in the case "does not violate any constitutional right of the defendant." She explained:]

Under the Fair Dealership Law, grantors remain free to enter into dealership agreements . . . subject only to certain restrictions upon their ability to modify or cancel those agreements. The restrictions are set out in the statute, they are known in advance to the grantor, and they apply equally to all grantors. The strict prohibitions upon termination are a rational means of preventing grantors from subjecting economically weaker dealers to severe financial hardship through termination or nonrenewal of dealership agreements; they serve to redress the imbalance of bargaining power between grantor and dealer . . . .

Moreover, the legislature avoided the constitutional problem that would attend a statute that required a grantor to continue doing business forever with its

Wisconsin dealers, whatever the economic consequences, when it committed the issuance of permanent injunction relief to the court's discretion . . . .

C. Remedy.

All of the plaintiffs are seeking damages and all plaintiffs except Collins are seeking permanent injunctions forbidding defendant from terminating their dealerships.

1. Money damages.

The plaintiffs have not moved for summary judgment on the issue of defendant's liability for money damages under the Fair Dealership Law. However, it is proper for a court to enter summary judgment for non-moving parties, if no factual dispute exists and if the non-movants are entitled to summary judgment as a matter of law.

There is no dispute of fact among the parties, only a dispute as to whether on the non-disputed facts defendant has any liability to those plaintiffs covered by the provisions of the Fair Dealership Law. On that issue, plaintiffs are entitled to partial summary judgment in their favor. Defendant is liable to all plaintiffs except Genoa City Pharmacy and Bernie's Walgreen Agency for money damages resulting from the terminations of plaintiffs' dealerships effected in violation of Chapter 135, the Wisconsin Fair Dealership Law. The appropriate damages remain to be determined in a subsequent proceeding.

2. Injunctive Relief.

The basis for injunctive relief in the federal courts is irreparable harm and inadequacy of legal remedies. . . .

In addition, the court must balance the probabilities of harm to the individual parties if an injunction is or is not issued, and determine whether the public interest will be disserved by its issuance. In the cases before the court, there is no showing that the harm to plaintiffs cannot be compensated adequately by an award of damages. Moreover, I am persuaded that it would be unduly burdensome to require defendant to maintain its distribution system in Wisconsin when it has abandoned that system in every other state. Finally, societal interests are not served by prohibiting businesses from ever changing their business structures or their methods of operation. I conclude, therefore, that a grant of permanent injunctive relief is not justified in these cases, and I will grant defendant's motion for summary judgment on plaintiffs' claims for permanent injunctive relief requiring the reinstatement of the dealerships. . . .

Judge Crabb later awarded the 11 successful plaintiffs $431,182 in damages. Included in this amount were their attorneys' fees of $75,407 and costs of $15,428, which are reimbursable under Wis. Stat. § 135.06.[229] Walgreen appealed the award

---

[229] Her decision is reported at 607 F. Supp. 155 (W.D. Wis. 1985).

of damages to the United States Court of Appeals for the Seventh Circuit. It affirmed her decisions except for an award of pre-judgment interest. The Seventh Circuit's discussion about computing damages follows:[230]

> Judge Crabb awarded plaintiffs $431,182 in damages. Her division of that amount among the plaintiffs is not contested. . . .
>
> The only significant argument defendant has made with respect to damages concerns the $294,705 the district court allowed plaintiffs for lost future profits. Plaintiffs' expert witness on this subject was Donald Nichols, Chairman of the Department of Economics of the University of Wisconsin in Madison. He was formerly Deputy Assistant Secretary of Labor of the United States and served as an expert witness as to lost future profits in two WFDL cases tried in the district court for the Eastern District of Wisconsin. His testimony was summarized in [Walgreen II] and produced a present value of lost sales for the 11 stores of $3,237,872. [The lost sales amount was calculated by projecting an estimated decline in the rate of increase of gross sales for plaintiffs' stores over the 20-year estimated life of these stores, and then discounting the resulting estimate to a present value using a real interest rate of 3 percent.] He determined that their variable profit rate was 9.4 percent. Multiplying those two figures produced the $295,000 lost future profits allowed by the district court. . . . This was the most conservative of three estimates Nichols provided for plaintiffs' loss of future profits, and was the one selected by Judge Crabb as the proper amount of damages plaintiffs should recover in that category. . . .
>
> Defendant argues that plaintiffs did not present adequate evidence to support the $295,000 lost-profits figure accepted by the court. Walgreen sets forth numerous factors that bear upon the profitability of various plaintiff stores and Walgreen-owned stores which might explain the 4 percent decrease in growth rate observed by Nichols apart from the Walgreen termination decision. Defendant asserts that the court and plaintiffs' expert overlooked or ignored such factors as new competition, increased advertising, and store improvements with regard to both individual Walgreen and former Walgreen Agency stores. Both Judge Crabb and Professor Nichols, however, were aware of these factors, presented in detail below by defendant, and agreed that they demonstrated all the more clearly that Walgreen's termination caused the 1981 4 percent decline in gross sales:
>
> [T]he only event common to all the stores is the plaintiffs' termination as agency stores in October 1980. It is more probable than not that this event was the cause of the 1981 decline in the rate of annual sales growth for plaintiffs. The probability is enhanced by the evidence adduced by defendant to show that in 1981 some of the plaintiffs had increased competition, some had less; that some plaintiffs increased their advertising budgets,

---

[230] Kealey Pharmacy & Home Care Services, Inc. v. Walgreen Co., 761 F.2d 345, 351–52 (7th Cir. 1985). Although the caption for this case is different, it is a continuation of the *Walgreen* case, except that it concerns one of the other terminated stores.

some decreased them; that some plaintiffs felt the effects of the economic recession in their towns; that some plaintiffs increased their business dramatically by emphasizing a special line of products . . . or by negotiating exclusive prescription contracts with nursing homes. . . . In other words, defendant has helped show that there was no one event common to all the plaintiffs that would account for the change in behavior in their average rate of sales growth other than their termination as Walgreen agencies. . . .

Future profits are difficult to prove and an estimate of lost future profits is inherently speculative to some degree, but these problems do not preclude recovery of damages under Wisconsin law. . . . The conservative estimates utilized by the plaintiffs' expert and adopted by the district court were computed with the reasonable certainty required and were not the result of mere guesswork. . . . It is not irrelevant to our holding that despite defendant's offer of numerous observations and criticisms, both here and below, regarding the damages figure adopted by the district court, Walgreen produced no expert witness on the issue of future profits.

NOTES AND QUESTIONS

1. *Later interpretations:* The Seventh Circuit explained its *Walgreen* decision, affirming the trial court, in *Remus v. Amoco Oil Co.*[231]

[Walgreen] does not stand for the proposition that the Fair Dealership Law forbids a franchisor to make system-wide changes without the consent of every franchisee. Walgreen (we found) was trying to eliminate the dealers who had built its reputation in Wisconsin, so that it could open its own stores and appropriate the goodwill that the dealers had created. . . . This was just the sort of conduct that the Wisconsin legislature had wanted to prevent.

Is this reading of the *Walgreen* case consistent with Judge Crabb's reasoning?

In *Ziegler v. Rexnord*, a majority of the Supreme Court of Wisconsin said:[232]

The real issue is whether a grantor . . . may alter its method of doing business with its dealers . . . to accommodate its own economic problems, or whether it must subordinate those problems — regardless how real, how legitimate, or how serious — in all respects and permanently if the dealer wishes to continue the dealership. We find that the grantor's economic circumstances may constitute good cause to alter its method of doing business with its dealers, but such changes must be essential, reasonable and nondiscriminatory. . . .

Ziegler contends that a grantor may not alter a dealership for economic reasons relating to the grantor only. Thus, no matter how severe the

[231] 794 F.2d 1238, 1241 (7th Cir. 1986).

[232] 147 Wis. 2d 308, 433 N.W.2d 8 (1988).

economic crisis at PMD, Rexnord had to execute an identical contract with Ziegler when the old contract expired on June 30, 1984, or be liable for WFDL damages.

This position is unjust and unreasonable. The WFDL meant to afford dealers substantial protections previously unavailable at common law; however, the Wisconsin legislature could not have intended to impose an eternal and unqualified duty of self-sacrifice upon every grantor that enters into a distributorship agreement. . . .

Put another way, the grantor may terminate, cancel, or fail to renew a dealership if the dealer refuses to accept proposed changes in the dealership relationship provided that the changes are essential, reasonable, and not discriminatory between similarly situated dealers. In determining whether the changes are essential and reasonable, a balancing must be done. Whether the changes are essential and reasonable must also be considered in regard to the effect on the grantee. . . .

The court relied on the WFDL's statement of purpose: "To promote the compelling interest of the public in fair business relations between dealers and grantors, and in the continuation of dealerships on a fair basis." Justices Abrahamson and Heffernan dissented because "the majority's interpretation of the good cause requirement focuses on the grantor and therefore contravenes the plain language of § 135.02(4), [Wis.] Stat., which focuses entirely on the conduct of the dealer." What does the decision in the *Ziegler* case leave of Judge Crabb's opinion in the *Walgreen* case?

2. *Proof of damages with reasonable certainty:* The group claim helped the plaintiffs' lawyers and expert make a statistical case for damages. The lawyers for Walgreen were critical of Judge Crabb's acceptance of the statistical argument of the plaintiffs; they believed that the statistical summary obscured some very important differences between stores in Milwaukee and all other stores, as well as failing to account for changing competitive conditions in the stores sampled by plaintiffs.

You should not underestimate the difficulties involved in proving lost profits of a franchisee. The requirement to prove those damages with reasonable certainty is likely to be one of the most difficult challenges for plaintiffs in a franchise termination case, if they seek damages. The court in *C.A. May Marine Supply Co. v. Brunswick Corp.* discussed measuring damages under the Wisconsin Fair Dealership Law:[233]

A showing of the profits lost by the dealer as a result of the breach of contract is the usual and most common procedure to prove the damage . . . Where the business is new and the dealer goes out of business before he is able to compile an earnings record, the amount of lost profits is gauged by a "yardstick" study of the business profits of a closely comparable

---

[233] 649 F.2d 1049, 1053 (5th Cir. 1981).

business. . . . Otherwise, the dealer's profit record prior to the violation is compared with his performance subsequent thereto. This method is often called the "before and after" theory.

Loss of business value is the second major measure of damages in dealership cases. This method focuses upon the change in worth of a going concern after total or almost total destruction caused by a breach of contract. . . . Both business goodwill and future profits are computed into the "going concern" value loss. Hence, damage awards which include recovery for lost future profits and "going concern" value are impermissibly duplicitous.

Another possibility would be to award reliance losses. The Eighth Circuit in *Central Microfilm Service Corp. v. Basic/Four Corp.*,[234] suggested that where the "peculiar circumstances of the case involved" make use of an expectation measure impossible to apply accurately, an alternative measure of damages would be available.

3. *Consequences of the statute:* What can we say about the impact of the statute? Lawyers seem relatively well-informed about this statute's potential.[235] The State Bar of Wisconsin has run several Continuing Legal Education sessions focused on this act, and it has published a detailed guide to the many issues that its provisions provoke. One reason for all the interest is that the statute does authorize awards of attorney's fees for franchisees who prevail under the rights that it creates. This makes the decision to litigate a better risk for plaintiffs in many situations.

Between April 1974, when the Act became effective, and July 2015, there have been 259 reported cases dealing with the statute, or about six per year. The Supreme Court of Wisconsin has dealt with the statute in 36 cases and the state intermediate appellate courts have faced the Fair Dealership Law in 46 cases. Dealerships and franchises often involve a grantor that is incorporated in a state other than Wisconsin, and so there is often diversity of citizenship that creates federal jurisdiction. The United States Court of Appeals for the Seventh Circuit has considered the law in 67 cases. There have been 110 reported opinions from the United States District Courts that involved the statute as well.

Of course, counting citations does not reveal the impact of the statute, as lawyers advise franchisors or franchisors make decisions whether to simply terminate franchisees, or to attempt to negotiate a termination for some amount in settlement of the franchisee's rights.[236]

Section 135.02(1) defines who can claim rights under the Wisconsin Fair

---

[234] 688 F.2d 1206 (1982).

[235] *See* Michael A. Bowen & Brian E. Butler, The Wisconsin Fair Dealership Law (State Bar of Wisconsin, 4th ed. 2012).

[236] You will notice that federal courts acting under diversity of citizenship jurisdiction have made most of the decisions under the Wisconsin Fair Dealership Law. Wisconsin courts have written opinions in 82 of the 259 cases. As always, it is difficult to judge how far the Supreme Court of Wisconsin will follow this body of case law created by federal courts "applying Wisconsin law" under diversity of citizenship jurisdiction.

Dealership Act. There must be an agreement under which a person is granted rights and "in which there is a community of interest in the business of offering, selling, or distributing goods or services at wholesale, retail, by lease, agreement, or otherwise." Someone who runs a fast-food franchise is a "dealer." An ordinary employee who exchanges services for wages is not. However, there are many situations in between these extremes. Many of the cases involve people in various kinds of relationships trying to claim that they have a dealership covered by the statute. This suggests that plaintiffs' lawyers see the statute as offering real advantages to their clients that are not found in the common law of employment. The Wisconsin Supreme Court has said that a WFDL dealership is "a contract or agreement establishing a particular sort of commercial relationship that encompasses an extraordinarily diverse set of business relationships not limited to the traditional franchise."[237] There are limits to its reach, however. Courts have held that contracts between HMOs and chiropractors for the provision of chiropractic services to HMO members did not make the chiropractors dealers under the Wisconsin Fair Dealership Law.[238] Manufacturers' representatives and freight forwarders have also failed to establish the "community of interest" necessary to qualify as a dealer under the statute.[239]

Michael A. Bowen and Brian E. Butler wrote the State Bar of Wisconsin's continuing legal education text about the WFDL.[240] The authors note that many franchisors are incorporated in states other than Wisconsin. This means that often there is diversity of citizenship, and cases go to the federal courts. Bowen and Butler assert: "Judges are deeply divided on the issue of who is to be protected by the statute. Ideological clashes as to the wisdom of the legislation and its proper scope are apparent in the decisions. Although generalizations are dangerous, most judges seem hostile to the WFDL." The authors argue that the federal courts have attempted to keep the definition of those who are given rights by the act as narrow as possible. Moreover, federal judges have sought to offer relatively clear rules to make the statute more predictable. Most Wisconsin courts, however, have taken a much more case-by-case approach. They balance factors as applied to the facts of each case. The line drawn by the state courts between those given rights by the statute and those who are not is much less precise than that created by the federal courts.

Not everyone is enthusiastic about the statute's consequences. A prominent

---

[237] Baldewein Co. v. Tri-Clover, Inc. 233 Wis. 2d 57, 70, 606 N.W.2d 145 (2000).

[238] Bakke Chiropractic Clinic v. Physicians Plus Insurance, 215 Wis. 2d 605, 573 N.W.2d 542 (Ct. App. 1997).

[239] Ziegler Co., Inc. v. Rexnord, Inc., *see supra* note 232, held that there are two guideposts to aid in determining whether the necessary community of interest exists. First, there must be a continuing shared financial interest in the business. Second, there must be interdependence. One seeking the protection of the statute must "demonstrate a stake in the relationship large enough to make the grantor's power to terminate, cancel, or not renew a threat to the economic health of the person (thus giving the grantor inherently superior bargaining power)." The court established a qualitative test resting on balancing a long list of factors. The court did not comment on a Seventh Circuit decision by Judge Posner, *Moore v. Tandy Corp.*, 819 F.2d 820, 822, 844 (7th Cir. 1987), in which he speculated on why the state chose to protect dealers, but not employees.

[240] *See* Bowen & Butler, *supra* note 235.

Wisconsin lawyer commented about the consequences of the statute:

> As an aside, it is interesting to note that the WFDL has had just the opposite effect than was anticipated. Before the enactment of the WFDL, usually only the very large grantors (e.g., petroleum refiners, brewers, distillers, etc.) entered into detailed dealership agreements. Other grantors simply left the relationship with their dealers quite vague and usually did not have any written dealership agreement whatsoever. Now because the only way a relationship can normally be terminated or changed is when the grantor can *prove* that the dealer breached a dealership agreement term, it is essential that those terms be specified with excruciating detail. Today even the smallest grantors must resort to written and tight contracts in order to protect their own rights. Moreover, the WFDL has injured many good dealers as well as the general public because many grantors are now afraid to terminate marginal dealers for fear of being sued. Those marginal dealers are many times reducing the level of service normally provided by the grantor's dealers and are, in some instances, injuring the grantor's goodwill, which affects the ability of the better dealers to sell the same products and services.[241]

William Nelson, the drafter of the statute, noted that another reason for preferring WFDL actions if you are a plaintiff (and disliking them if you are a defendant-franchisor), was the non-discrimination clause in the Act. This permits plaintiffs to go through all the franchisor's records, which makes them unhappy, but is essential. In addition, as mentioned above, attorney's fees are recoverable under the WFDL, which may advantage plaintiffs with strong claims but few resources.

Adi Ayal and Uri Benoliel reported that the classic economic analysis of good cause statutes (GCS) opposes their use.[242] This approach "relies on a central argument: GCS dispute an indispensable control mechanism against franchisee free-riding, namely the ability of the franchisor to terminate any franchise contract at will." An at-will contract, these economists argue, keeps the franchisee under the constant threat of losing her business if she neglects to invest in quality premises and services. A good cause statute, on the other hand, creates an incentive for each individual franchisee to enjoy the chain's good reputation while skimping on the investment necessary to promote the national brand and ensure quality at each local venue.

Ayal and Benoliel studied a chain of nationally franchised hotels, focusing on hotels in locations less likely to rely on the repeat business of travelers. Some were located in states with good cause statutes, and others were located in states without such legislation. They found that the presence or absence of a good cause statute makes little difference in a modern context. Moreover, they found that online review sites (such as Expedia, Booking.com, Hotels.com, and Priceline.com) create a novel

---

[241] Quinn Martin, *Advising Grantors How to Structure Sales Programs to Avoid Problems Under the WFDL*, in State Bar of Wisconsin, Advanced Training Seminars — Continuing Legal Education; Magna Carta for Wisconsin Businesses: The Wisconsin Fair Dealership Act (Nov. 1979). The author, Quinn Martin, is a retired partner at one of Wisconsin's largest law firms.

[242] *See* Ayal & Benoliel, *supra* note 222.

and effective control mechanism against franchisee free-riding. Customers have sufficient motivation to write reviews and post them. Although a person seeking a hotel room may be unlikely to return to a particular location, she can go online and discover that a franchised hotel in a particular location is rated poorly by its previous customers. They will point out such things as dirty rooms, run-down premises, broken heating or air conditioning, and an understaffed front desk or housekeeping service. The evidence is that potential customers do consider online reviews when making purchasing decisions.

4. **What is "good cause" for ending a dealership?** Section 135.02(4) defines "good cause" as the failure "to comply substantially with essential and reasonable requirements" that "are not discriminatory as compared with requirements imposed on other similarly situated dealers either by their terms or in the manner of their enforcement." Notice that "substantially," "essential," "reasonable," and "discriminatory" are all qualitative terms, calling for judgment in their application in a particular case. Also remember that the burden of proof to show good cause for terminating a dealership is on the *franchisor*.

In *Al Bishop Agency, Inc. v. Lithonia-Div. of National Service Industries, Inc.*, the court applied the statutory definition of good cause.[243] One of the issues in the case was whether Lithonia was justified in terminating the plaintiff for failure to meet certain sales volume requirements. The court held that the law provided that such requirements must be both essential and reasonable. In this case the requirements met both criteria, and so defendant was justified in terminating plaintiff. The court went on, however, to find that since Lithonia had not given proper notice, or allowed cure of plaintiff's default as required, the plaintiff was entitled to an injunction prohibiting the termination of the dealership. As Bowen and Butler note: "[A] requirement imposed simultaneously with the notice of termination may be timely if the dealer can satisfy that requirement at once."[244] But the dealer must be given a reasonable time to meet the requirement.

In *JPM, Inc. v. John Deere Indust. Equip. Co.*, the Seventh Circuit found that economic duress could be the basis for finding a constructive termination of a franchise under the Wisconsin Fair Dealership Law.[245] John Deere had told its dealer in northwest Wisconsin that it had to sell its business to a particular buyer. However, the trial court granted John Deere's motion for summary judgment. The Seventh Circuit affirmed. The dealer (JPM) had not shown that the elements of economic duress were present. JPM had choices other than selling the business. JPM had not pursued the injunctive relief available to it under the WFDL, and it did not show that the damages remedies under that statute would have been insufficient to afford it relief.

5. **The continuing battle — arbitration to avoid the statute:** Lawyers for franchisors have sought ways to limit the statute's impact. One effort involved the selection of the law of another state in the franchise agreement; the Wisconsin Supreme Court ruled that Wisconsin law overrode such a provision, at least on the

---

[243] 474 F. Supp. 828 (E.D. Wis. 1979).

[244] *See* Bowen & Butler, *supra* note 235.

[245] 94 F.3d 270 (7th Cir. 1996).

facts of *Bush v. National School Studios, Inc.*[246] However, United States District Judge Barbara Crabb ruled that the Wisconsin Fair Dealership Law is subject to the Federal Arbitration Act, because of the supremacy clause in the U.S. Constitution.[247] This means that if the contract has an arbitration clause, dealers seeking to assert claims must present those claims to arbitrators, rather than courts and juries. Is there any reason for dealers to care whether their claims are heard by arbitrators or courts?

In *S+L+H S.p.A v. Miller-St. Nazianz, Inc.*,[248] the Seventh Circuit decided that the parties had made an enforceable contract to arbitrate disputes. The agency agreement that granted the dealer an exclusive territory provided that "any controversy or claim arising out of or relating to this Agreement, its execution or breach, shall be settled by arbitration in Rome under the Rules of the Italian Arbitration Association." The manufacturer failed to renew the dealership because it was dissatisfied with the low volume of sales. However, it did not give the dealer an opportunity to cure and 90 days' written notice of nonrenewal as required by the Wisconsin statute. The dealer argued that if its claims were arbitrated in Italy, it would have "no assurance that Wisconsin law will be applied and no recourse if it is not." Under the Rules of Italian Arbitration, if the parties have not specified by contract the substantive law to be applied, the arbitrator applies the rules of law he or she deems appropriate, and the arbitrator's decisions cannot be appealed. The court said that under the Federal Arbitration Act, a state statute cannot void the choice of the parties to arbitrate. In 2008, the *Wall Street Journal* reported that many franchisors have ceased using arbitration clauses in their franchise contracts. The concern is cost:

> Arbitration can involve three arbitrators, each of whom may charge $300 to $600 an hour. Some critics say there is little incentive for arbitrators to speed things up since they are paid by the hour. Some proceedings can cost upward of $100,000, depending on how complex the issues are and how long it takes both sides to testify. So these days, arbitration isn't always cheaper than going to court.[249]

On the other hand, a more systematic comparison of the use of arbitration clauses in franchise agreements found little change in their use between 1999 and 2007. Some franchisors had opted out, which might explain the anecdotal evidence of flight from arbitration, but other franchisors had opted in.[250] We will address enforcement of arbitration clauses and the pros and cons of using arbitration in more detail in Chapter 4.

---

[246] 139 Wis. 2d 635, 407 N.W.2d 883 (1987).

[247] Good(e) Business Systems, Inc. v. Raytheon Co., 614 F. Supp. 428 (W.D. Wis. 1985).

[248] 988 F.2d 1518 (7th Cir. 1993).

[249] Richard Gibson, *Pressure Grows to Rethink the Use of Mandatory Arbitration Clauses*, WALL STREET JOURNAL, June 3, 2008, at B7.

[250] Christopher R. Drahozal and Quentin R. Wittrock, *Is There a Flight from Arbitration?* 37 HOFSTRA L. REV. 71 (2008).

2. Grievance Processes Under Collective Bargaining

Contracts relating to employment are the source of many disputes. One kind of employment-related contract is the collective bargaining agreement, which is negotiated by a union on behalf of its members. Courses in labor law teach a great deal about unions, managements, and collective bargaining. Here we offer only the briefest introduction to a small part of the area.

The contracts that unions negotiate on behalf of their membership nearly always contain a procedure for processing grievances. This grievance procedure usually provides for binding arbitration if the parties cannot otherwise agree.[251] Having a brief picture of grievance arbitration provides a useful contrast with how courts deal with relationships between employer and employee in the absence of a collective bargaining agreement.

The history of unions in the United States is one of seeking to overcome great obstacles. Unions were seen as criminal conspiracies, an un-American invention of foreigners, and an attack on individual freedom of contract. Champions of unions pressed a legitimating rhetoric with some degree of success,[252] although union membership[253] has declined from 20 percent of the workforce in 1983 to 11 percent in 2014.[254]

Three characteristics of unions are worth noting. First, the idea of unions is an expression of confidence in *democracy*. Whether employees have a union and which union represents them turns on a vote of the bargaining unit.[255] Furthermore, the membership elects union officials to office. Second, we characterize union-management relations as the product of a *contract*. Organized workers gained bargaining power because of the right to strike, and that bargaining power served to produce a collective bargaining agreement. Third, norms of *industrial due process* govern the system. If union members wish to challenge management action, there are procedures to resolve disputes while at the same time ensuring that the rights of management and the convenience of the public will not be interfered with unnecessarily. Instead of strikes, we substitute orderly process.

The grievance arbitration process serves the interests both of the union and of management. Grievance systems enable unions to challenge the way management is carrying out the collective bargaining agreement. Union officials can gain the support of members by handling grievances in a satisfactory way. Management

---

[251] This "grievance arbitration" is different from the arbitration called for by statutes that mandate arbitration in setting wages between units of government and their employees.

[252] *See* Karl Klare, *Judicial Deradicalization of the Wagner Act and the Origins of Modern Legal Consciousness, 1937–1941*, 62 Minn. L. Rev. 265 (1978); Katherine Van Wezel Stone, *The Post-War Paradigm in American Labor Law*, 90 Yale L.J. 1509 (1981).

[253] The U.S. lags behind other industrialized countries in union membership. *See* Derek Thompson, *Are Unions Necessary?* The Atlantic, June 11, 2012: theatlantic.com/business/archive/2012/06/are-unions-necessary/258356.

[254] *Union Members — 2014*, U.S. Bureau of Labor Statistics, Jan. 23, 2015: http://www.bls.gov/news.release/union2.nr0.htm.

[255] Note that we speak of the idea of unions. Some unions, like all other institutions, may fail to implement successfully their own ideals.

avoids disputes that provoke strikes, and it gains information about problems in its operations. All things, of course, have costs. The system limits management's power. Systems can become bureaucratic and foreign to union members. The no-strike provision, which is usually the price management charges for a grievance arbitration procedure, limits the power of the union. We will consider some of the costs and benefits of a grievance system in the materials that follow.

a. Grievance systems

Grievance systems vary. Nonetheless, most procedures involve a filtering system that handles disputes quickly and informally. An employee who claims to have been the victim of improper application of the collective bargaining agreement must usually present the complaint to a supervisor. A worker may appeal an adverse judgment to a superintendent, who will meet with a union grievance committee. If this process does not solve the problem, then the dispute may go to the personnel department of the company. An official will deal with a representative of the regional or national office of the union. If the problem has still not been settled, most collective agreements then call for arbitration. Sometimes there is a three-person panel with representatives of the union and management as well as a neutral arbitrator. Sometimes there is a single arbitrator. There are procedures for choosing arbitrators. Some aspects of the arbitration decision are subject to review in the courts.

Most grievances relate to employee discipline. Others concern job assignments, overtime, or seniority. While problems are sometimes resolved without following the grievance procedures as set out in the collective bargaining agreement, the "duty of fair representation" has meant that members can sue their unions if they fail to process grievances correctly. In many instances it is safer to follow the book than try to work things out or attempt to screen out unwarranted or crazy claims.

The system does not always work as we might think it should. On one hand, union officials may stir up grievances for political purposes, to strengthen their chances for re-election, or to gain interpretations of the contract to trade in the collective bargaining process. On the other hand, workers do not always take their problems to the process, fearing the loss of their supervisor's goodwill or lacking faith in their local union officials. Those who support the local officials may get more effort expended in pressing their grievances than others, despite the legal duty of fair representation.[256] The international union may be pursuing policies that particular members dislike, and its officials may be seen as unlikely to press particular claims. In short, the grievance process is part of a multiparty political process. It is not just management and labor working in some technical fashion to construe the terms of a collective contract.

Management and its lawyers are not always happy with the grievance process either. The grievance process may actually foster hostility between the parties, and grievance representatives may lack skill in handling grievances. Others attack the

---

[256] *See* Mitchell H. Rubinstein, *Duty of Fair Representation Jurisprudential Reform: The Need to Adjudicate Disputes in Internal Union Review Tribunals and the Forgotten Remedy of Re-Arbitration,* 42 U. Mich. J.L. Reform 517 (2009).

grievance procedure because it places maximum value on avoiding interruption of production, even if that is at the expense of employee health and safety.

b.   Arbitration versus adjudication

To what extent, if at all, does arbitration of a grievance differ from adjudication before a court? Consider the following case. How might a court have decided the case had TWA and the flight attendant been operating under a binding employment contract and taken the case to a judge and jury?

How would it've been diff

IN RE TRANS WORLD AIRLINES, INC.

System Board of Adjustment
46 Lab. Arb. Rep. 611 (1965)

Decision of Arbitrators

WIG DEMONSTRATION

a Stewardice in 3 here

WALLEN, ARBITRATOR:

The facts of the case are fairly clear. X is a Stewardess in the International Division. She has been employed by TWA since 1956 and apparently has a clear record. The difficulties which led to her discharge grew out of a hostess grooming and appearance inspection scheduled beginning February 1, 1964. Pursuant to a posted notice, all Idlewild International-Based Hostesses were to appear for such an inspection after pre-flight briefing for their first trip in February. Particular emphasis was to be placed on personal appearance — "weight, length, color and styling of hair, complexion and make-up, as covered in the Flight Service Manual."

The Flight Service Manual, § 01.10.01 dated February 1, 1963, sets forth detailed regulations concerning their hairstyles. One regulation provides: "The hair shall be worn close to the head, and when pulled straight from the hairline at the nape of the neck, must not extend below the top of the collar when standing erect."

Another states:

> After obtaining previous supervisory approval, a wig may be worn by a Hostess if it enhances her uniform appearance. A wig may not be worn to disguise any non-conformity with standard hair regulations. A wig will be subject to inspection and must comply with standard hair regulations. The wig must be of good quality natural hair, regulation hair style, length and color and maintained in a good, clean condition. The decision as to whether the wig enhances the Hostess's uniform appearance, and complies with regulations, shall be made solely by the Supervisor.

X, scheduled out for a flight on February 15, 1964, had not yet gone through the Hostess grooming appearance inspection. She was summoned to Hangar 12 at JFK, after her pre-flight briefing, by Hostess Supervisor Elizabeth Connelly. Miss Connelly found X's general appearance — complexion, weight, uniform, and hands

— satisfactory. However, Miss Connelly knew that X had had approval as required by the regulations to wear a wig; had been told by another supervisor that she had been seen in Rome with her hair beyond regulation length; and had a year or more before flown and roomed with X and knew that in the past she had had long hair.

Against this background Miss Connelly asked X if she was wearing a wig. X said no, whereupon the supervisor asked her to lift her hair at the back of her neck in order to verify if a wig was being worn or whether, on the other hand, she was in fact observing the hostess's natural hair. It appears that if a wig was being worn, X would have been asked to remove it so that compliance with the requirement that her natural hair nonetheless not exceed regulation length could be verified.

X, however, refused to demonstrate in the manner asked that she was wigless. She left on her flight but on February 17 was interviewed by Alexander Rossi, Assistant Transportation Manager of Hostesses and Pursers, International, in the presence of Supervisor Connelly. Again she was asked if she was wearing a wig; again she said no; and again she was asked to but refused to verify her answer in the manner described earlier.

[handwritten margin note: wouldn't lift hair to show if she had a wig]

Further efforts to persuade X to submit to verification of her statement that she was not wearing a wig were unavailing. She was asked by Rossi to come in by February 21 for this purpose. When she did not do so she was placed on off-duty status and told to report to H.H. Brown, Rossi's superior. She did not so report whereupon Brown, by letter, told her to report to his office in complete uniform by March 3. When she did not appear by that date she was terminated for willful insubordination.

X's refusal to verify her claim that she was not wearing a wig, it appears, was based on her feeling that it was humiliating to be asked to raise the back of her hair; that she was being treated like a child; that she had not before been asked to make such a demonstration; that her appearance had been deemed satisfactory; and that she "did not feel it was necessary for a hostess to have to comply with these requests." She regarded the request as undignified, an invasion of privacy, and personally obnoxious. She deemed the repeated requests that she reappear for inspection harassment and of the two grievances filed, one protests such harassment while the second protests her subsequent discharge.

[handwritten margin note: Basically calls the meetings harassment and disputes in one claim, other claim is from resulting discharge]

X is a long-service hostess with an otherwise good record and while her annoyance at having to supply verification of compliance with uniform and appearance regulations is understandable, it fails to take into account the fact that human nature being what it is, such regulations are not self-enforcing. While the great majority of hostesses are mature enough to comply with regulations regarding hair length or other matters of personal appearance not observable at a glance, in a work force of 2,200 there will inevitably be a few who will try to beat the rules. If successful, they imperil the very existence of the rules, for each case of successful non-compliance breeds disrespect for the rule and undermines the will of others to comply.

Hence management must be accorded the right to verify compliance with clothing, hair length, and appearance regulations in a manner which imposes no unreasonable or undignified demands on the employee. To ask an employee to furnish such verification is neither improper nor unreasonable. On the contrary, it constitutes the kind of submission to the discipline of the workplace that all human beings inevitably encounter in a complex, closely knit economic society. To the extent that X's stance in this case was based on a refusal to submit to this kind of discipline associated with her job, it was in error.

X's supervisors plainly had a right to determine whether her natural hair was of the prescribed length, regardless of whether or not a wig was being worn. The regulations are clear on the point and they are in no sense unreasonable. In order to do so, the supervisors had to determine whether or not she was wearing a wig.

X's refusal to demonstrate that she was not wearing a wig by lifting the hair at the back of her head was based, at least in part, on the claim that such an act would subject her to an indignity. Here we enter into the realm of individual emotions. We venture to guess that many young ladies would think nothing of complying with such a request and would see in it no indignity. On the other hand, it is possible that some individuals might deem a request for such a demonstration in the impersonal surroundings of the workplace to be offensive or humiliating. And a third possibility exists — that someone who has no qualms in the matter might nonetheless invoke personal privilege to avoid verification of her natural hair length.

We are uncertain of X's motivation in her refusal to demonstrate that she was not wearing a wig. On the other hand, there is no evidence to show that she was in fact masking an evasion of the hair length rule. Hence we are constrained to accept her plea that her refusal arose out of her belief that the request offended the canons of good taste as she views them.

It might be argued that this leaves supervision in the position of being unable to verify whether a hostess authorized to wear a wig has natural hair of regulation length. We point out, however, that supervision has the right to require hostesses with approved wigs to appear at inspections, if requested, with the wig in hand so that both the wig and the natural hair may be viewed by the supervisor.

There remains the question, whether a supervisor may require a hostess to demonstrate that her natural hair is of regulation length. Since hair is sometimes curly or wavy this may not always be ascertainable by a glance. We hold that it is reasonable to infer from the regulation prescribing hair length that a supervisor may verify it by asking the hostess to demonstrate it in the course of an inspection.

As we have said, there is no evidence that X's refusal to demonstrate that she was not wearing a wig was designed to evade the hair-length rule. Inasmuch as her refusal appears to have stemmed from deeply held, though misplaced feelings in the matter, we hesitate to affirm the discharge penalty levied in her case. For this reason, all Board members concur in her reinstatement. However, we are unable to overlook her failure to accede to requests to appear for subsequent inspections on February 21 and later. Her failure to do so violated her obligations as an employee.

The Neutral Referee and the Company members are of the opinion that X was insubordinate in failing to appear for inspections by Rossi and Brown as directed and that her insistence on complete freedom from verification of compliance with appearance regulations was misplaced. Hence the majority, with the Association members dissenting on this point only, voted to direct her reinstatement without back pay as a means of pointing up her errors in these areas.

DECISION

1. The Union's grievance protesting harassment of X is denied.

2. X shall be reinstated without back pay but with seniority unimpaired.

NOTES AND QUESTIONS

1. *The case as a reflection of important history:* The TWA case was decided in 1965. While much has changed since then, an experienced labor arbitrator told us that it remains a good example of this kind of dispute resolution. TWA ceased to exist when it was bought by American Airlines in 2001. The dispute about hair length and wigs reflected an earlier day when flight attendants were called stewardesses, and the airlines had much greater control over all aspects of the job. A *New York Times* book review notes:

> The experience of flight attendants . . . illustrate[s] one of the ways our world has changed since then [the 1960s]. . . . They no longer have to be 25, size 4 and single. Sometimes they are men; sometimes they are grandmothers. When the Equal Employment Opportunity Commission was established . . . its first complainants were stewardesses. The commission's clerical staff was "still unpacking when Barbara Roads, a union leader for the flight attendants, and another stewardess arrived. . . . " This woman came up to us, two blondes in stewardess uniforms, and she said, 'What are you doing here?' Roads recalled. The two women . . . told them about the airline ban on marriage, the age discrimination, and the endless measurements to check for weight gain. 'They couldn't believe it.'"

> In a 1964 Congressional hearing, when airline executives testified that it was imperative for businessmen that attractive women light their cigars and fix drinks, Representative Martha Griffiths said, "What are you running, an airline or a whorehouse?" and the conversation began to change.[257]

The rise of feminism in the 1960s and 1970s probably had much to do with the changes in this job. By 1987, the TWA In-Flight Service Manual provided: "Hair of any length is acceptable so long as it is worn in a style not exceeding the underarm level." Also, "a natural-looking wig or hairpiece may be worn if it meets with the standard hair regulations of length, style, color, cut, and condition." A TWA Vice President in charge of labor relations told us that Ms. X, the employee in the reported case, became an official in the TWA flight attendants' union. She may have lost the battle in the reported case, but she won the larger war.

Some changes in the appearance standards were provoked by Title VII of the Civil Rights Act of 1964, 42 U.S.C. §§ 2000e *et seq.* In *Frank v. United Airlines*, the

---

[257] Amy Bloom, Book Review of GAIL COLLINS, WHEN EVERYTHING CHANGED: THE AMAZING JOURNEY OF AMERICAN WOMEN FROM 1960 TO THE PRESENT, *New York Times Review of Books*, Oct. 18, 2009, at 9.

court found that United Airlines could impose different appearance standards on men and women, but only if those standards imposed essentially equal burdens on men and women.[258] In the case under review, the court found that the weight requirements for women were more burdensome than those for men, and so were unlawful.

While more variety is allowed today than in the past, airlines remain concerned about the appearance of their flight attendants. United Airlines, for example, provides: "Tattoos must never be visible while in uniform. . . . Visible body piercing (including tongue piercing) other than earlobes is not permitted while in uniform."[259] The American Airlines 2015 appearance standards for female flight attendants provide:[260]

> Hairstyles will be clean, neat and will be maintained in a professional manner that is appropriate for business wear. . . . Hair will be styled so that it does not require frequent handling or fall into the face when bending over. Bangs will be no longer than the top of the eyebrows. Hair below the top of the shoulders will be pulled back and secured at the sides. Hair that extends more than eight inches below the top of the uniform collar will be worn back and up at all times. . . .

> If a wig or hairpiece is worn, it will be natural looking, of good quality, and appropriate for business wear. Wig and hairpiece styles will meet all criteria for hairstyles and length.

If men or women choose to color their hair, the result must be a "natural human hair shade." Cornrows and fully or partially braided hairstyles (without beads or trim) are allowed, but dreadlocks are prohibited. Men are forbidden to have ponytails. Flight attendants are cautioned that, pursuant to their collective bargaining agreement, "failure to adhere to grooming and image regulations may result in corrective action up to and including termination."

American's appearance standards have another provision that would not have been there in 1965, when the TWA case was decided: "Female maternity uniform items are available for order and can be worn by a female flight attendant only during pregnancy."

Why do airlines and flight attendants' unions draft complex provisions dealing with everything from earrings to the hairstyles of flight attendants? Would you expect to find similar appearance standards at a large law firm that represents corporate clients? Would such firms need to spell out such matters? Do law students interviewing for jobs in such firms have a good idea of how they should dress for an interview? How do they learn these norms?

2. *Functions of the three-member arbitration panel:* At least in close cases, we can expect that the union representative will usually vote for the employee, and the management representative will usually vote for the employer. The deciding

---

[258] 216 F.3d 845 (9th Cir. 2000).

[259] United Airlines Inflight Services Flight Attendant Uniform Appearance Standards (2013), *available at* http://unitedafa.org/docs/uniforms/appearance_standards.pdf.

[260] American Airlines, *Flight Attendant Image Standards* 9–10 (on file with the authors).

vote, then, is cast by the neutral member. Why do parties often want this arrangement rather than having just a single arbitrator?

3. *Arbitration contrasted with adjudication:* As with litigation, the majority of labor grievances are settled. For grievances that move forward, the procedural rules differ from litigation. If the substance of the grievance is not clear at the outset, the parties will work together to clarify it for the arbitrators. The parties may or may not be represented by lawyers. The rules of evidence are not observed formally in arbitration. Additionally, arbitrators are more concerned with following the norms of the workplace than with following precedent. For example, they look to whether the discipline meted out is consistent with prior practice and is proportionate to the misconduct. Furthermore, the process often is said to serve the "airing" functions of a Kpelle moot, which emphasizes the importance of giving the parties an opportunity to speak their piece in full. Ideally, arbitration would produce quick answers, but usually the entire grievance process works slowly.[261]

4. *Goals of labor arbitration:* There is some dispute about how far labor arbitrators should go beyond a rather literal interpretation of the language of the contract. How far should they bring a sense of the customs of the plant or industry with them in reading the language? How far should they fashion a result they think will further the ongoing relationship between the organized workers and management? How far should they attempt to give the parties the decision that "they really want" or a decision that one wants and that the other will accept? Contrast the following views:

John Phillips, a lawyer for employers who was discouraged by results in four of his cases in which arbitrators reviewed, and reversed, employee discharges, argued that arbitrators were abusing their authority and that more judicial review of arbitrators' decisions was necessary.[262] Phillips asked:

> How can it be rationally argued that, by agreeing to arbitrate grievances or by selecting a particular arbitrator, a party is bound by *any* award, no matter how contrary to the contract, unsupported by any evidence, or nonsensical? . . .

> Some commentators have lamented even minimal judicial involvement in the review process and the decline of the "golden age" of arbitration. It would appear, however, that arbitrators remain in little danger of all but the most limited judicial oversight. . . .

---

[261] Paul Zirkel reports that in the cases he studied, the "average length of time that elapsed between the filing of the grievance and the date of the first hearing was 185 days." The average length of time between the first hearing and the closing date was 22 days. The average elapsed time between the last hearing and the award was 50 days. Paul Zirkel, *A Profile of Grievance Arbitration Cases*, 38 ARB. J. 35 (1983).

[262] John Phillips, *Their Own Brand of Industrial Justice: Arbitrators' Excesses in Discharge Cases*, 10 EMP. REL. L.J. 48 (1984). Reprinted with permission from EMPLOYEE RELATIONS LAW JOURNAL, V10, N1, Summer 1984. Copyright © 1984 by Executive Enterprises, Inc., 22 West 21st Street, New York, NY 10010-6904. All Rights Reserved.

Arbitrators, generally with court approval, hold that their appointments give them the inherent right to determine if the penalty fits the offense. . . .

Why don't employers simply reject arbitration provisions? Since 97 percent of the nation's collective bargaining agreements contain such clauses and protection against strikes is dependent on them, this alternative is impractical, from both negotiations and operational standpoints. . . .

Conclusion

. . . A 1983 survey of arbitrators disclosed that nearly 60 percent equated a discharge to capital punishment in a criminal case. . . .

Awards such as those discussed above destroy confidence in the arbitration process and jeopardize industrial discipline. A recent Gallup Poll disclosed that "65 percent of Americans think the overall level of ethics in American Society has declined in the past decade." Arbitrators who reinstate employees guilty of violence, harassment, carelessness, or other misconduct promote disorder and anarchy in the workplace. It is unfortunate that employers cannot replace such offenders with the many capable workers now on the nation's unemployment rolls. How can American businesses hope to rival domestic and foreign competition when hamstrung by such "industrial justice?" How do such awards contribute to the quality of America's work life? . . .

In the final analysis, this article is a plea to arbitrators to enforce contracts and work rules as they are written, to exhibit more common sense and concern themselves less with social reform, and, in the words of the Supreme Court, to demonstrate "some minimum level of integrity" in discharge cases.

Robert Coulson, a leading figure in the development of the American Arbitration Association, responded to Phillips.[263] He began by recounting seven instances in which arbitrators had confirmed *harsh* actions by management. He went on to argue that we should not be so quick to condemn the arbitrator. The arbitrator has seen not just the summary of testimony but the testimony itself. In addition, Coulson notes that quite often management itself has signaled to the arbitrator that it would be satisfied with a suspension rather than a discharge. Coulson closes with a statement representative of the view that arbitration is more likely to respect the realities of the workplace:

The contract is not simply a piece of paper signed by the parties. It is a living relationship, defined and redefined during its term by innumerable conversations, grievance conferences, and arbitration hearings. Harsh discipline may be equally as destructive to the employer-employee relationship as the overabundance of equity that so troubles lawyer Phillips . . .

---

[263] Robert Coulson, *The Arbitrator's Role in Discharge Cases: Another Viewpoint*, 10 Emp. Rel. L J. 61 (1984).

5. ***Impact of reinstatement of an employee:*** Professor Arthur A. Malinowski studied employees reinstated with or without back pay by labor arbitrators.[264] Employers found that most employees returning to work were satisfactory and caused few disciplinary problems, but employers still viewed the arbitrator's order as unacceptable and wrong. Ten of the 73 employees ordered reinstated never returned to work, and six of them had more than 11 years' seniority. Some might have found it difficult to return after being accused of wrongdoing. Some found other jobs while waiting for the result of the grievance process, and the new job may have seemed better than the old one.

c. Judicial review of arbitration

Suppose either union or management is dissatisfied with an arbitrator's decision. The disappointed party can appeal to the courts, but what will the courts do with such a case? Notice that there are two issues: first, the parties may debate as to whether they agreed to submit a particular dispute to arbitration.[265] Second, they may debate the correctness of an arbitrator's interpretation of the collective bargaining agreement as applied to a particular case. The Supreme Court of the United States announced three opinions on the same day concerning judicial review of labor arbitration — not surprisingly, labor lawyers call these cases "the trilogy."[266] These decisions state an ideology about the relationship between the public legal system and the private mini-government of collective bargaining. Mr. Justice Douglas's views about labor arbitration recall Lord Atkin's views of the relationship of the courts and the family in *Balfour v. Balfour*.

The following is from Justice Douglas's opinion in *United Steelworkers of America v. Warrior & Gulf Navigation Co.*, one of the *Steelworkers Trilogy* cases:[267]

> But the grievance machinery under a collective bargaining agreement is at the very heart of the system of industrial self-government. Arbitration is the means of solving the unforeseeable by molding a system of private law for all the problems which may arise and to provide for their solution in a way which will generally accord with the variant needs and desires of the parties. . . .
>
> The labor arbitrator performs functions which are not normal to the courts; the considerations which help him fashion judgments may indeed be foreign to the competence of courts. . . .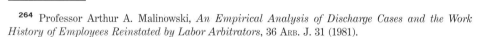

---

[264] Professor Arthur A. Malinowski, *An Empirical Analysis of Discharge Cases and the Work History of Employees Reinstated by Labor Arbitrators*, 36 ARB. J. 31 (1981).

[265] A typical clause tells an arbitrator to "resolve all disputes concerning the application or interpretation of the contract." Sometimes the clause is broader, empowering an arbitrator to resolve "any and all disputes which may arise between the parties." In other instances, the contract withdraws power from the arbitrator to deal with particular issues or otherwise attempts to limit his or her jurisdiction.

[266] The three cases are United Steelworkers of America v. American Mfg. Co., 363 U.S. 564 (1960); United Steelworkers of America v. Warrior & Gulf Navigation Co., 363 U.S. 574 (1960); United Steelworkers of America v. Enterprise Wheel and Car Corp., 363 U.S. 593 (1960).

[267] 363 U.S. 574 (1960).

The labor arbitrator's source of law is not confined to the express provisions of the contract, as the industrial common law — the practices of the industry and the shop — is equally a part of the collective bargaining agreement although not expressed in it. The labor arbitrator is usually chosen because of the parties' confidence in his knowledge of the common law of the shop and their trust in his personal judgment to bring to bear considerations which are not expressed in the contract as criteria for judgment. The parties expect that his judgment of a particular grievance will reflect not only what the contract says but, insofar as the collective bargaining agreement permits, such factors as the effect upon productivity of a particular result, its consequence to the morale of the shop, his judgment whether tensions will be heightened or diminished. For the parties' objective in using the arbitration process is primarily to further their common goal of uninterrupted production under the agreement, to make the agreement serve their specialized needs. The ablest judge cannot be expected to bring the same experience and competence to bear upon the determination of a grievance, because he cannot be similarly informed.

The Congress, however, has by § 301 of the Labor Management Relations Act, assigned the courts the duty of determining whether the reluctant party has breached his promise to arbitrate. For arbitration is a matter of contract and a party cannot be required to submit to arbitration any dispute which he has not agreed so to submit. Yet, to be consistent with congressional policy in favor of settlement of disputes by the parties through the machinery of arbitration, the judicial inquiry under § 301 must be strictly confined to the question whether the reluctant party did agree to arbitrate the grievance or did agree to give the arbitrator power to make the award he made. An order to arbitrate the particular grievance should not be denied unless it may be said with positive assurance that the arbitration clause is not susceptible of an interpretation that covers the asserted dispute. Doubts should be resolved in favor of coverage.

Not everyone agreed with Justice Douglas's approach. Professor Paul R. Hays argued that:[268]

One of the difficulties with . . . [Douglas's] . . . views of the nature of arbitration and the collective agreement is that both are still matters of contract. They still are in actual fact what the parties want them to be, whatever Mr. Justice Douglas may think they ought to be. In each of these cases, it must be remembered that one of the parties was there screaming to high Heaven that what *he* intended bore no resemblance whatever to the thing that Mr. Justice Douglas has described. . . .

Essentially, what the *United Steelworkers v. Warrior* case finds is that even the question of whether or not the parties have agreed to submit a particular issue to arbitration is, except for a few instances, for the arbitrator to decide. You can see that this suggests a broad definition of arbitrator's authority.

---

[268] Professor Paul R. Hays, *The Supreme Court and Labor Law, October Term, 1959*, 60 Colum. L. Rev. 901 (1960).

Lawyers have not been content to accept the power that the *Steelworkers Trilogy* cases seem to grant to arbitrators. They have gone to court, looking for ways around the *Steelworkers Trilogy* decisions, and they have found just enough success to keep them coming back to the courts. We must leave the topic for courses in labor law, but Professor William Gould has suggested what happened in the 30 years after the *Steelworkers Trilogy* decisions:[269]

> It is now almost thirty years since the United States Supreme Court, in its landmark *Steelworkers Trilogy* decisions, promoted both the labor arbitration process itself and the finality to be given to labor arbitration awards. But the landscape of judicial review of labor arbitration is now more reminiscent of a thirty years' war than the substitute for strife once heralded. . . .
>
> The increasing number of challenges to the finality of arbitration awards, particularly by employers, has prompted this comment from the Court of Appeals for the First Circuit:
>
>> It is a firm principle of federal labor laws that where parties agree to submit a dispute to binding arbitration, absent unusual circumstances, they are bound by the outcome of said proceedings. . . . Yet we are, with exasperating frequency, confronted by challenges to such decisions brought by parties who are apparently still under the delusion that, as a matter of course, the losing party is entitled to appeal to the courts any adverse ruling by an arbitrator.
>
> But it is more than delusion on the part of defendants that is involved. Reaffirmance of *Steelworkers Trilogy*, and indeed *expansion* of the *Trilogy's* principles, albeit with new exceptions to the rule promoting finality of arbitration awards, has only invited more litigation and judicial contests. . . .

3. Employment Relations

To what extent does, or should, the law intervene in long-term employment relationships? Here we are interested primarily in the legal response to an employer's assertion of power to hire and fire employees. We will leave to other courses the study of the many legal provisions governing minimum wages, maximum hours, health and safety on the job, and unemployment and worker's compensation, as well as federal and state laws prohibiting hiring and firing people because of their race, religion, gender, age, sexual preference, or gender identity.[270] Because employees are rarely fired for only one reason, it is often very

---

[269] *See* William B. Gould IV, *Judicial Review of Labor Arbitration Awards — Thirty Years of the Steelworkers Trilogy: The Aftermath of AT & T and Misco*, 64 NOTRE DAME L. REV. 464, 470–71, 472–75 (1989). Copyright reserved by William B. Gould IV. *See also* Gould, *Kissing Cousins? The Federal Arbitration Act and Modern Labor Arbitration*, 55 EMORY L.J. 609 (2006).

[270] *See* Cynthia Estlund, *Rebuilding the Law of the Workplace in an Era of Self-Regulation*, 105 COLUM. L. REV. 319, 330 (2005). Estlund looks at the Fair Labor Standards Act, the Social Security Act, the Occupational Safety and Health Act, and the Civil Rights Act. She notes that these laws tend to be under-enforced or unenforced. "Simply ignoring the law is an especially tempting strategy for marginal

difficult for an employee to prove that she was fired *because* of her gender, race, or age.[271] Sometimes an employee is certain that this is why she was fired, but she will find that her lawyer will consider trying to establish a contracts cause of action in addition to a discrimination claim that she cannot be sure that she can prove. Lawyers for employers who are consulted about terminating employment must be concerned by all of the potential claims an employee might make. The situations can overlap and fit under several legal theories.[272]

a. Proving employment contracts and gaining meaningful remedies

Reliance and the policies of form: Suppose an employee asserts reliance on an oral promise, either an express or an implied one, for employment for 367 days. Once again, we would face the Statute of Frauds. In most states, promises that by their terms cannot possibly be performed within one year must be in writing. In many states this means that a contract to work for 367 days must be in writing.[273] Many employment agreements are oral and most uncertain. Job applicants often, if not usually, find out how much the job pays. The newly hired worker, however, learns little more than that she is to show up for work the following morning, and she will learn what to do as she works day by day. If the job is to run for more than

---

producers at the bottom of the production chain, who have little fixed capital or stake in their reputation, who tend to operate under the regulatory radar, and who often rely heavily on undocumented immigrant workers who are too fearful or desperate to complain." Cynthia Estlund, *Who Mops the Floors at the Fortune 500? Corporate Self-Regulation and the Low-Wage Workplace*, 12 LEWIS & CLARK L. REV. 671 (2008). *Compare* Steven Greenhouse & Stephanie Rosenbloom, *Wal-Mart to Settle Suits Over Pay for $352 Million*, NEW YORK TIMES, Dec. 24, 2008 ("Wal-Mart said . . . that it would pay at least $352 million, and possibly far more, to settle lawsuits across the country claiming that it forced employees to work off the clock."); *see also* Steven Greenhouse, *Low-Wage Workers Are Often Cheated, Study Says*, NEW YORK TIMES, Sept. 2, 2009, at A11 ("The researchers said one of the most surprising findings was how successful low-wage employers were in pressuring workers not to file for workers' compensation. . . . [M]any small businesses say they are forced to violate wage laws to remain competitive.").

[271] *See* David Benjamin Oppenheimer, *Verdicts Matter: An Empirical Study of California Employment Discrimination and Wrongful Discharge Jury Verdicts Reveals Low Success Rates for Women and Minorities*, 37 U.C. DAVIS L. REV. 511 (2003) ("In termination cases generally, plaintiffs won 46 percent of the verdicts, but in race discrimination termination cases filed by non-whites, plaintiffs won only 16 percent of the time, including three of twelve (25 percent) for black plaintiffs. In sex discrimination termination cases filed by women, plaintiffs won only 25 percent of the time."). In 2013, the Supreme Court clarified that plaintiffs carry the burden of proof in discrimination termination cases, making it more difficult for them to prevail. University of Texas Southwestern Medical Center v. Nassar, 133 S. Ct. 2517, 186 L. Ed. 2d 503 (2013).

[272] A cautious employer may offer termination benefits in exchange for a release of all claims when dealing with someone who fits within a protected class and who might, in addition, fall into one of the exceptions to employment-at-will.

[273] In some states, the courts have said that an oral promise for permanent employment does not need to be in writing. These courts reason that the employee might die before a year had passed, and in this case the contract would be performed. Those who like technical details might object: death does not perform a contract; rather, it excuses performance. And so a contract for permanent performance would not be "performed" within one year. We can laugh at the technical argument, but you might find yourself facing it some time in the future. *See* JOSEPH M. PERILLO, CALAMARI & PERILLO ON CONTRACTS § 19.23 (6th ed. 2009). Some courts distinguish a promise for permanent employment from one for a stated period greater than a year. The latter falls under the Statute of Frauds, while the former does not. *See id.* at § 19.18.

one year, the agreement may not meet the demand for a writing. But can reliance outweigh the policies of form crystallized in the Statute of Frauds? Consider:

McINTOSH v. MURPHY
Hawaii Supreme Court
52 Haw. 29, 469 P.2d 177 (1970)

LEVINSON, J.

This case involves an oral employment contract which allegedly violates the provision of the Statute of Frauds requiring "any agreement that is not to be performed within one year from the making thereof" to be in writing in order to be enforceable. HRS § 656-1 (5). In this action the plaintiff-employee Dick McIntosh seeks to recover damages from his employer, George Murphy and Murphy Motors, Ltd., for the breach of an alleged one-year oral employment contract.

While the facts are in sharp conflict, it appears that defendant George Murphy was in southern California during March 1964, interviewing prospective management personnel for his Chevrolet-Oldsmobile dealerships in Hawaii. He interviewed the plaintiff twice during that time. The position of sales manager for one of the dealerships was fully discussed but no contract was entered into. In April 1964, the plaintiff received a call from the general manager of Murphy Motors informing him of possible employment within thirty days if he was still available. The plaintiff indicated his continued interest and informed the manager that he would be available. Later in April, the plaintiff sent Murphy a telegram to the effect that he would arrive in Honolulu on Sunday, April 26, 1964. Murphy then telephoned McIntosh on Saturday, April 25, 1964, to notify him that the job of assistant sales manager was open and work would begin on the following Monday, April 27, 1964. At that time McIntosh expressed surprise at the change in job title from sales manager to assistant sales manager but reconfirmed the fact that he was arriving in Honolulu the next day, Sunday. McIntosh arrived on Sunday, April 26, 1964, and began work on the following day, Monday, April 27, 1964.

As a consequence of his decision to work for Murphy, McIntosh moved some of his belongings from the mainland to Hawaii, sold other possessions, leased an apartment in Honolulu, and obviously forwent any other employment opportunities. In short, the plaintiff did all those things which were incidental to changing one's residence permanently from Los Angeles to Honolulu, a distance of approximately 2200 miles. McIntosh continued working for Murphy until July 16, 1964, approximately two and one-half months, at which time he was discharged on the grounds that he was unable to close deals with prospective customers and could not train the salesmen.

At the conclusion of the trial, the defense moved for a directed verdict arguing that the oral employment agreement was in violation of the Statute of Frauds, there being no written memorandum or note thereof. The trial court ruled that as a matter of law the contract did not come within the Statute, reasoning that Murphy bargained for acceptance by the actual commencement of performance by McIntosh, so that McIntosh was not bound by a contract until he came to work on

Monday, April 27, 1964. Therefore, assuming that the contract was for a year's employment, it was performable within a year exactly to the day and no writing was required for it to be enforceable. Alternatively, the court ruled that if the agreement was made final by the telephone call between the parties on Saturday, April 25, 1964, then that part of the weekend which remained would not be counted in calculating the year, thus taking the contract out of the Statute of Frauds. With commendable candor the trial judge gave as the motivating force for the decision his desire to avoid a mechanical and unjust application of the Statute.[274]

The case went to the jury on the following questions: (1) whether the contract was for a year's duration or was performable on a trial basis, thus making it terminable at the will of either party; (2) whether the plaintiff was discharged for just cause; and (3) if he was not discharged for just cause, what damages were due the plaintiff. The jury returned a verdict for the plaintiff in the sum of $ 12,103.40. . . . The . . . ground of appeal is whether the plaintiff can maintain an action on the alleged oral employment contract in light of the prohibition of the Statute of Frauds making unenforceable an oral contract that is not to be performed within one year.

I. Time of Acceptance of the Employment Agreement

The defendants contend that the trial court erred in refusing to give an instruction to the jury that if the employment agreement was made more than one day before the plaintiff began performance, there could be no recovery by the plaintiff. The reason given was that a contract not to be performed within one year from its making is unenforceable if not in writing. . . .

[W]e base our decision in this case on the doctrine of equitable estoppel which was properly briefed and argued by both parties before this court, although not presented to the trial court.

II. Enforcement by Virtue of Action in Reliance on the Oral Contract

In determining whether a rule of law can be fashioned and applied to a situation where an oral contract admittedly violates a strict interpretation of the Statute of Frauds, it is necessary to review the Statute itself together with its historical and modern functions. The Statute of Frauds, which requires that certain contracts be in writing in order to be legally enforceable, had its inception in the days of Charles II of England. Hawaii's version of the Statute is found in HRS § 656-1 and is substantially the same as the original English Statute of Frauds. . . .

Retention of the Statute today has . . . been justified on at least three grounds: (1) the Statute still serves an evidentiary function, thereby lessening the danger of perjured testimony (the original rationale); (2) the requirement of a writing has a

---

[274] [1] THE COURT: You make the law look ridiculous, because one day is Sunday and the man does not work on Sunday; the other day is Saturday; he is up in Fresno. He can't work down there. And he is down here Sunday night and shows up for work on Monday. To me that is a contract within a year. I don't want to make the law look ridiculous, Mr. Clause, because it is one day later, one day too much, and that one day is a Sunday, and a non-working day.

cautionary effect, which causes reflection by the parties on the importance of the agreement; and (3) the writing is an easy way to distinguish enforceable contracts from those which are not, thus channelling certain transactions into written form.[275]

In spite of whatever utility the Statute of Frauds may still have, its applicability has been drastically limited by judicial construction over the years in order to mitigate the harshness of a mechanical application.[276] Furthermore, learned writers continue to disparage the Statute, regarding it as "a statute for promoting fraud" and a "legal anachronism."[277]

Another method of judicial circumvention of the Statute of Frauds has grown out of the exercise of the equity powers of the courts. Such judicially imposed limitations or exceptions involved the traditional dispensing power of the equity courts to mitigate the "harsh" rule of law. When courts have enforced an oral contract in spite of the Statute, they have utilized the legal labels of "part performance" or "equitable estoppel" in granting relief. Both doctrines are said to be based on the concept of estoppel, which operates to avoid unconscionable injury. . . .

Part performance has long been recognized in Hawaii as an equitable doctrine justifying the enforcement of an oral agreement for the conveyance of an interest in land where there has been substantial reliance by the party seeking to enforce the contract. . . . Other courts have enforced oral contracts (including employment contracts) which failed to satisfy the section of the Statute making unenforceable an agreement not to be performed within a year of its making. This has occurred where the conduct of the parties gave rise to an estoppel to assert the Statute. . . .

It is appropriate for modern courts to cast aside the raiments of conceptualism which cloak the true policies underlying the reasoning behind the many decisions enforcing contracts that violate the Statute of Frauds. There is certainly no need to resort to legal rubrics or meticulous legal formulas when better explanations are available. The policy behind enforcing an oral agreement that violated the Statute of Frauds, as a policy of avoiding unconscionable injury, was well set out by the California Supreme Court. In *Monarco v. LoGreco*, 35 Cal. 2d 621, 623, 220 P.2d 737, 739 (1950), a case that involved an action to enforce an oral contract for the conveyance of land on the grounds of 20 years' performance by the promisee, the court said:

---

[275] [2] Lon L. Fuller, *Consideration and Form*, 41 Colum. L. Rev. 799, 800–03 (1941); Note: *Statute of Frauds — The Doctrine of Equitable Estoppel and the Statute of Frauds*, 66 Mich. L. Rev. 170 (1967).

[276] [3] Thus a promise to pay the debt of another has been construed to encompass only promises made to a creditor which do not benefit the promisor (Restatement of Contracts § 184 (1932); 3 Williston, The Law of Contracts § 452 (Jaeger ed., 1960); a promise in consideration of marriage has been interpreted to exclude mutual promises to marry (Restatement, *supra* § 192; 3 Williston, *supra* § 485); a promise not to be performed within one year means a promise not performable within one year (Restatement, *supra* § 198; 3 Williston, *supra* § 495); a promise not to be performed within one year may be removed from the Statute of Frauds if one party has fully performed (Restatement, *supra* § 198; 3 Williston, *supra* § 504); and the statute will not be applied where all promises involved are fully performed (Restatement, *supra* § 219; 3 Williston, *supra* § 528).

[277] [4] Francis M. Burdick & Evander Willis, *A Statute for Promoting Fraud*, 16 Colum. L. Rev. 273 (1916); Willis, *The Statute of Frauds — A Legal Anachronism*, 3 Ind. L.J. 427, 528 (1928).

The doctrine of estoppel to assert the Statute of Frauds has been consistently applied by the courts of this state to prevent fraud that would result from refusal to enforce oral contracts in certain circumstances. Such fraud may inhere in the unconscionable injury that would result from denying enforcement of the contract after one party has been induced by the other seriously to change his position in reliance on the contract.

In seeking to frame a workable test which is flexible enough to cover diverse factual situations and also provide some reviewable standards, we find very persuasive section [139] of the Second Restatement of Contracts.[278] That section specifically covers those situations where there has been reliance on an oral contract that falls within the Statute of Frauds. Section [139] states:

(1) A promise which the promisor should reasonably expect to induce action or forbearance on the part of the promisee or a third person and which does induce the action or forbearance is enforceable notwithstanding the Statute of Frauds if injustice can be avoided only by enforcement of the promise. The remedy granted for breach is to be limited as justice requires.

(2) In determining whether injustice can be avoided only by enforcement of the promise, the following circumstances are significant: (a) the availability and adequacy of other remedies, particularly cancellation and restitution; (b) the definite and substantial character of the action or forbearance in relation to the remedy sought; (c) the extent to which the action or forbearance corroborates evidence of the making and terms of the promise, or the making and terms are otherwise established by clear and convincing evidence; (d) the reasonableness of the action or forbearance; (e) the extent to which the action or forbearance was foreseeable by the promisor.

We think that the approach taken in the Restatement is the proper method of giving the trial court the necessary latitude to relieve a party of the hardships of the Statute of Frauds. Other courts have used similar approaches in dealing with oral employment contracts upon which an employee had seriously relied. See *Alaska Airlines, Inc. v. Stephenson*, 217 F.2d 295 (9th Cir. 1954); *Seymour v. Oelrichs*, 156 Cal. 782, 106 P. 88 (1909). This is to be preferred over having the trial court bend over backwards to take the contract out of the Statute of Frauds. In the present case the trial court admitted just this inclination and forthrightly followed it.

There is no dispute that the action of the plaintiff in moving 2200 miles from Los Angeles to Hawaii was foreseeable by the defendant. In fact, it was required to perform his duties. Injustice can only be avoided by the enforcement of the contract and the granting of money damages. No other remedy is adequate. The plaintiff found himself residing in Hawaii without a job.

It is also clear that a contract of some kind did exist. The plaintiff performed the contract for two and one-half months, receiving $3,484.60 for his services. The exact length of the contract, whether terminable at will as urged by the defendant, or for

---

[278] [Eds. note: At the time the case was decided, the RESTATEMENT (SECOND) OF CONTRACTS was in draft form and the reference was to § 217A, which became § 139 in the final version of the document.]

Basically Pages 64 abt if a year is all white noise, admit IT IS IN Statute of Frauds, don't be rediculous, we'll just get out for 139

C. FRANCHISE AND EMPLOYMENT RELATIONS 423

a year from the time when the plaintiff started working, was up to the jury to decide.

In sum, the trial court might have found that enforcement of the contract was warranted by virtue of the plaintiff's reliance on the defendant's promise. Naturally, each case turns on its own facts. Certainly there is considerable discretion for a court to implement the true policy behind the Statute of Frauds, which is to prevent fraud or any other type of unconscionable injury. We therefore affirm the judgment of the trial court on the ground that the plaintiff's reliance was such that injustice could only be avoided by enforcement of the contract.

Affirmed.

Dissenting Opinion of ABE, J., (with whom KOBAYASHI, J., joins).

The majority of the court has affirmed the judgment of the trial court; however, I respectfully dissent. . . .

As acknowledged by this court, the trial judge erred when as a matter of law he ruled that the alleged employment contract did not come within the Statute of Frauds; however, I cannot agree that this error was not prejudicial as this court intimates.

He says incorrect decision abt stat of frauds was prejudicial

On this issue, the date that the alleged contract was entered into was all-important and the date of acceptance of an offer by the plaintiff was a question of fact for the jury to decide. In other words, it was for the jury to determine when the alleged one-year employment contract was entered into and if the jury had found that the plaintiff had accepted the offer[279] more than one day before plaintiff was to report to work, the contract would have come within the Statute of Frauds and would have been unenforceable. . . .

This court holds that though the alleged one-year employment contract came within the Statute of Frauds, nevertheless the judgment of the trial court is affirmed "on the ground that the plaintiff's reliance was such that injustice could only be avoided by enforcement of the contract."

I believe this court is begging the issue by its holding because to reach that conclusion, this court is ruling that the defendant agreed to hire the plaintiff under a one-year employment contract. The defendant has denied that the plaintiff was hired for a period of one year and has introduced into evidence testimony of witnesses that all hiring by the defendant in the past has been on a trial basis. The defendant also testified that he had hired the plaintiff on a trial basis.

Here on one hand the plaintiff claimed that he had a one-year employment contract; on the other hand, the defendant claimed that the plaintiff had not been hired for one year but on a trial basis for so long as his services were satisfactory. I believe the Statute of Frauds was enacted to avoid the consequences this court is forcing upon the defendant. In my opinion, the legislature enacted the Statute of Frauds to negate claims such as has been made by the plaintiff in this case. But this

REMEMBER - if UCC there's diff rule or SoF

---

[279] [1] Plaintiff testified that he accepted the offer in California over the telephone.

court holds that because the plaintiff in reliance of the one-year employment contract (alleged to have been entered into by the plaintiff, but denied by the defendant) has changed his position, "injustice could only be avoided by enforcement of the contract." Where is the sense of justice?

Now assuming that the defendant had agreed to hire the plaintiff under a one-year employment contract and the contract came within the Statute of Frauds, I cannot agree, as intimated by this court, that we should circumvent the Statute of Frauds by the exercise of the equity powers of courts. As to statutory law, the sole function of the judiciary is to interpret the statute and the judiciary should not usurp legislative power and enter into the legislative field. . . . Thus, if the Statute of Frauds is too harsh as intimated by this court, and it brings about undue hardship, it is for the legislature to amend or repeal the statute and not for this court to legislate.

Honestly makes more sense to me

NOTES AND QUESTIONS

1. ***The policies of the Statute of Frauds:*** Undoubtedly, had there been a written contract, the parties could have avoided all of the confusion about the nature of the deal. However, in light of the usual bargaining practices of potential employers and job-seekers, why should courts place the burden of getting a written contract on the employee? What kinds of employees bring draft contracts to job interviews and ask employers to sign them? Wouldn't the dissent's rule allow agents of employers to promise anything to get employees to move to the location of the job and then, if things didn't work out, the employer could walk away from their promises without having to pay for any reliance losses? If the rule suggested by the dissenting opinion were the law, could a lawyer ethically advise an employer client how to use the Statute of Frauds to trick employees in this way? Is there any limitation on advising a client about his or her legal rights? Would you distinguish externally imposed limitations such as codes of professional responsibility from your own conscience? Can you properly withhold from a client information about his or her legal rights because you disapprove of how the client is going to use them?

2. ***The jury and the Statute of Frauds:*** Is enthusiasm (or skepticism) about the Statute of Frauds linked to attitudes about juries? You might think that the employer in this case probably made no one-year employment promise, but the jury was simply sympathetic to the plaintiff. The Statute of Frauds would allow the trial judge to keep the case away from the jury. If you believed juries systematically were too sympathetic to plaintiffs, would you support a more rigorous application of the Statute of Frauds? How could you know whether too many jurors had a pro-plaintiff bias?

3. ***Making out a defense of just cause to fire an employee:*** Even when the parties have a legally enforceable contract, an employer can still fire an employee if the employer has "just cause" to do so. In addition to the Statute of Frauds defense, Murphy and Murphy Motors mounted a "just cause" defense to the action by McIntosh "on the grounds that he was unable to close deals with prospective customers and could not train the salesmen," as the majority opinion explains. The jury returned a verdict for McIntosh.

How broad is the defense of just cause? Must the employee have performed badly, or do business reasons of the employer suffice? Also, is it enough for the employer to have a subjective or reasonable belief that there is just cause? Professor Robert Bird tells us that there are two requirements for a "just cause" defense: "(1) The employer has stated an objectively equitable, sensible, and logical reason that constitutes sufficient cause for discharge; and (2) The employer subjectively believes that sufficient evidence exists that the sufficient cause is in fact true."[280] He continues:

> Courts have accepted a number of motives as objectively sensible reasons for discharge. The most prominent of these reasons is a reduction in force. Adverse economic conditions, even if the employee is not at fault for these conditions, constitute just cause for discharge of that employee. These adverse conditions include the discontinuance of a new product line, business cutbacks, business closing, elimination of a position, and a reduction in force.

> In addition, employers have satisfied just cause requirements when the employee fails to meet performance standards, or engages in conduct that injures the employer's reputation or interests. This may include public advocacy of illegal behavior. Other just cause reasons for terminating an employee include intoxication, severe personality conflicts, criminal acts against the employer, lateness and absences, and insubordination.

But should an employer's decision about any of these matters be reviewed by a judge or a jury? The courts do not agree on the answer. The Supreme Court of Washington decided that it was enough that the employer reasonably believed that the facts constituting just cause were true.[281] Bird approves this approach and comments: "The fact-finder's role is limited to determining whether the reason for discharge is reasonably believed by the employer to be true, not necessarily whether the reason was true according to the fact-finder."[282]

Why would employers want discretion to fire rather than being satisfied with something such as the Washington "reasonable belief" version of just cause?

4.   Employment-at-Will

a.   Introduction

You have just read *McIntosh v. Murphy.* It is easy to read the case without focusing on the assumption that unless plaintiff had a contract for a definite term, he could be discharged at any time. It is important to realize, however, that job security in the United States is quite limited as compared to other industrialized nations. Most employees in the United States have far less job security than employees in most countries in Europe. Some American employees, such as

---

[280]   Robert C. Bird, *Rethinking Wrongful Discharge: A Continuum Approach*, 73 U. Cin. L. Rev. 517, 531–32 (2005).

[281]   Baldwin v. Sisters of Providence in Washington, Inc., 769 P.2d 298 (Wash. 1989).

[282]   Bird, *supra* note 280, at 536.

television personalities and presidents of major corporations, have individual employment contracts for specified terms. Many of these contracts come with "golden parachutes." If such an employee is discharged, the contract provides that she walks away with a large sum of money and other benefits. Other Americans are members of labor unions working under some degree of job security that is provided by their collective bargaining agreements and our labor laws. Civil service or tenure provisions protect others. Most Americans are, however, employees-at-will. As you will see in the following materials, they have, at best, only limited legally enforceable job security.

Until the 1970s or 1980s, most Americans who had jobs expected that these jobs would continue as long as they did not give their employers cause to fire them. People tended to be hired as beginners, and they climbed a promotion ladder within the shop, factory, or office. Some had written contracts with many provisions spelled out. But these contracts usually did not specify employment for a particular number of days, months, or years. The employer might even say that the job was "permanent" or yours "as long as you do the job." Nonetheless, courts generally construed any contract without a definite term as an employment-at-will. The American rule was that the employee could leave at any time for another job or retirement. Equality seemed to call for the rule to cut both ways. Thus, an employer might fire an employee-at-will for good, bad, or no reason, so long as the employer could not be proven to have discriminated against a member of a protected class.

More recently, the organization of work has changed in many sectors of the American economy. Work may be moved from a factory in Michigan to Alabama and then to Mexico, before it is sent to China. In many fields, there is more lateral hiring rather than strictly promoting from within. Some employees, especially those who are in the knowledge-based sectors, are not very interested in job security and plan on changing jobs frequently, expecting only that "the employer is not going to interfere with your next opportunities," as Professor Alan Hyde put it.[283]

Of course, for employees to take the perspective that Hyde describes, it may be important that there is another employer willing to hire people eager to change jobs, or that there are self-employment or consulting opportunities. During the economic troubles that began in 2007, many could not find a new job and hanging on to the old one was important.[284] However, as a result of these new patterns of employee mobility, employers sought to defend the knowledge, trade secrets, and intellectual property that employees might pick up in a few years. We began seeing more contracts with clauses saying that the employee could not compete with his former employer for a certain time. Clauses limiting the disclosure of trade secrets became more common, and other clauses called for employees who left before a certain time to pay back the costs of specialized training. We will look at attempts by the legal system to regulate and enforce such employment contract provisions in Chapter 4.

---

[283] *Economic Analysis of Labor and Employment Law in the New Economy: Proceedings of the 2008 Annual Meeting*, Association of American Law Schools, Section on Law and Economics, 12 EMPL. RTS. & EMPLOY. POL'Y J. 327 (2008). *See also* KATHERINE VAN WEZEL STONE, *infra* note 296.

[284] *See* Mark Berger, *Unjust Dismissal and the Contingent Worker: Restructuring Doctrine for the Restructured Employee*, 16 YALE L. & POL'Y REV. 1 (1997).

In many circumstances an employer is eager to persuade a potential employee to take a job or persuade an existing employee not to leave. Employers benefit from loyalty, particularly if employees come to see themselves as part of a community seeking goals rather than just people punching a time clock and putting in hours. Those who study employment often speak of "psychological contracts" that exist in business organizations.[285] Employer and employee owe each other fair treatment and hard work. Professor Robert Bird says that employment is a relational contract and "while attorneys draft legal contracts, the parties draft relational agreements."[286] But the psychological contract may be something very different from the legal contract.

b.   Development of the at-will doctrine

The United States is almost the only industrialized nation without some form of job security guaranteed by law for most workers.[287] The story of how the United States ended up in this lonely position is somewhat contested. In England, where much of the United States common law originated, the rule was that a general hiring was presumed to be for a term of one year.[288] However, according to an often-repeated story, H.G. Wood declared in his 1877 treatise on master and servant that the United States followed a different rule:[289]

> With us the rule is inflexible that a general or indefinite hiring is *prima facie* a hiring at will, and if the servant seeks to make it out a yearly hiring, the burden is upon him to establish it by proof. A hiring at so much a day, week, month, or year, no time being specified, is an indefinite hiring, and no presumption attaches that it was for a day even, but only at the rate fixed for whatever time the party may serve.

Wood's treatise was very influential. Many scholars, however, argued that Wood made this statement without adequate explanation, citing only four cases, none of which supported him. On the other hand, Professor Andrew Morriss points out that

---

[285] *See, e.g.*, Amamuel G. Tekleab & M. Susan Taylor, *Aren't There Two Parties in an Employment Relationship? Antecedents and Consequences of Organization — Employee Agreement on Contract Obligations and Violations*, 24 J. Organizational Behav. 585 (2003); Tanguy Dulac, Jacqueline A-M. Coyle-Shapiro, David J. Henderson, & Sandy J. Wayne, *Not All Responses to Breach Are the Same: The Interconnection of Social Exchange and Psychological Contract Processes in Organizations*, 51 Acad. Mgmt. J. 1079 (2008); Elaine C. Hollensbe, Shalini Khazanchi, & Suzanne S. Masterson, *How Do I Assess If My Supervisor and Organization Are Fair? Identifying the Rules Underlying Entity-Based Justice Perceptions*, 51 Acad. Mgmt. J. 1099 (2008).

[286] Robert C. Bird, *Employment as a Relational Contract*, 8 U. Pa. J. Lab. & Emp. L. 1 (2005).

[287] *See* Linda Dickens, Michael Jones, Brian Weekes & Moira Hart, *The British Experience Under a Statute Prohibiting Unfair Dismissal*, 37 Indus. & Lab. Rel. Rev. 497 (1984). They say that the "main impact of the [British] legislation, with its emphasis on the need for the employer to act reasonably in carrying out dismissal, has been the development of procedures for handling discipline and dismissal. Such procedures, usually devised and administered by management, are now almost universally accepted among small firms. These procedures usually consist of the giving of warnings (oral and then written) before dismissal and the right to appeal a dismissal decision to higher levels of management within the organization."

[288] 1 William Blackstone, Commentaries on the Law of England 423 (1979 ed.).

[289] H.G. Wood, Master and Servant (1877).

the at-will rule had been adopted by seven states before Wood published his treatise, and it was present in the first draft of the New York Civil Code, proposed in 1862.[290] Morriss sees attributing the rule to Wood as a tactic used by its critics to delegitimize it.

By the beginning of the 20th century, the at-will rule had been adopted by many American courts, albeit without much analysis. However, the at-will doctrine fit with prevailing assumptions about a limited role for government interference in private relationships. Professor Jay Feinman argued:

> Educated, responsible, and increasingly numerous, the middle level managers and agents of enterprises might have been expected to seek a greater share in the profits and direction of enterprises as the owners had to rely more heavily on them with the increasing size of business organizations. But the employment-at-will rule [ensured] that as long as the employer desired it (and as long as the employee was not irreplaceable, which was seldom the case) the employee's relation to the enterprise would be precarious.[291]

Much of Morriss's legal history of the at-will rule argues against Feinman's analysis. For example, Morriss points out that the rule spread from the West and South to the East. Moreover, the rule became that of the majority of states only after the mid-1890s, "well after many of the significant industrial struggles between capital and labor."[292] Morriss's own explanation focuses on institutional considerations. He argues that the at-will rule allows appellate courts to take a group of cases from juries. A trier of fact will have difficulty deciding whether there was cause to fire an employee. Faced with this capability problem, Morriss sees the courts serving as a gatekeeper blocking access to the legal system. He continues:

> One of the fundamental problems for the courts in evaluating these claims was the difficulty of setting a standard by which they could measure the employee's conduct. As a result, the appellate courts which developed the at-will rule realized that the ability of the courts to evaluate the termination decision was weak. The at-will rule offered a partial solution by shifting cases involving indefinite contracts.[293]

Professor Richard Bales questions Morriss's argument. Bales says that Morriss makes valid points about the first states to adopt at-will employment, but he fails to disprove any linkage between the at-will rule and industrialization. "[I]t may have been precisely because the western and southern states were underindustrialized that they were among the first to adopt the at-will rule. Underindustrialized states needed a way to attract capital, and one of their options was to offer attractive

---

[290] Andrew P. Morriss, *Exploding Myths: An Empirical and Economic Reassessment of the Rise of Employment At-Will*, 59 Mo. L. Rev. 679 (1994).

[291] Jay M. Feinman, *The Development of the Employment at Will Rule*, 20 Am. J. Legal Hist. 118, 133 (1976).

[292] Morriss, *supra* note 290, at 703.

[293] *Id.* at 753.

employment rules to capitalists deciding where to build their next factory."[294] Once this strategy started to work, the industrialized states "would have been compelled to follow suit to remain economically competitive with the early adopters."[295] Bales calls this an "interjurisdictional race to the bottom in employment standards."

As so often is the case when we look at the history of legal rules, we cannot be sure why people in earlier times acted one way and not another. We can imagine various functions certain rules might serve,[296] but we cannot know that some or all of them motivated judges, lawyers, and those influential in creating the current of opinion that was in the air at that time. It is possible that some or most of the judges were responding to the legal culture of the time. The argument from symmetry might have convinced legally trained people: employees should not be bound to employers for long terms, and so employers should be similarly unfettered.

As commonly is true in American law, there has long been a countertheme to the employment-at-will rule. Even in the rule's heyday, American courts held that a promise of permanent employment was enforceable if there was also *independent consideration* — consideration given by the employee other than just doing the work. For example, at the turn of the 19th into the 20th century, railroads often gained releases of tort claims from their employees in exchange for small payments of money and promises of permanent employment. Other employees occasionally made contributions of money to businesses in exchange for such promises. These "added benefits" were an extra or independent consideration for the promise of permanent employment. In these cases the employer would have to show cause to fire the employee. Some decisions found that if an employee gave up something of value to gain a job with the employer, this would be special added consideration that made the promise of permanent employment enforceable. For example, one might sell a business for money and a promise of permanent employment. This would be enough to offer protection. However, few courts have been willing to protect an employee whose "additional consideration" consisted of leaving a good job to take one with a new employer, relying on a promise of permanent employment. You cannot just find something that you can label as consideration and assume that a promise of permanent employment will be enforceable. This is a very limited exception to the general at-will rule. As we have seen, some courts in more recent times have been willing to turn to promissory estoppel in this situation; others have not.[297]

During the decade of reform that stretched from the late 1960s into the 1980s, courts strained against the confines of the employment-at-will rule. Cases challeng-

---

[294] Richard A. Bales, *Explaining the Spread of At-Will Employment as an Interjurisdictional Race to the Bottom of Employment Standards*, 75 TENN. L. REV. 453, 455 (2008).

[295] *Id.*

[296] Professor Katherine Van Wezel Stone offers another possibility: "If there were no at-will rule and if instead the common law gave employees some form of job security, then employers could not use job security as an inducement for loyalty, longevity, and commitment." KATHERINE VAN WEZEL STONE, FROM WIDGETS TO DIGITS: EMPLOYMENT REGULATION FOR THE CHANGING WORKPLACE 49 (Cambridge University Press 2004).

[297] *See* Hunter v. Hayes, 533 P.2d 952 (Colo. Ct. App. 1975); Worley v. Wyoming Bottling Co., Inc., 1 P.3d 615 (2000), *see infra* note 355.

ing the rule increased tenfold between 1969 and 1983.[298] In many states, courts searched for ways to limit the absolute discretion of employers without having to undertake the review of all firings of employees-at-will. A number of academic writers called for an industrial due process.[299] The courts in California took the lead.

c. Attempts to provide meaningful protections to employees-at-will

Several major legal changes have begun in California and traveled across the country eastward — no-fault divorce, *Marvin v. Marvin*, and limitations on at-will employment, for example. After the California innovations, judges in almost all states refashioned the legal treatment of at-will employment during the last quarter of the 20th century. We will look first at the story of this clear example of judicial lawmaking. Then we will offer several cases so that you can learn something about how the new rules have been applied. We will also keep asking what difference, if any, the changes made.

The California story begins with *Petermann v. International Brotherhood of Teamsters Local 96*,[300] a case that was provoked by the crusade by various legislators against the Teamsters Union after the Second World War. Petermann was a non-union employee-at-will of the Teamsters. He alleged that he had been ordered by union officials to testify falsely under oath before a California legislative committee. He testified truthfully, and he was fired. The Supreme Court of California found that to allow an employer to discharge an employee because of his refusal to commit perjury would be against public policy.

Petermann stood as an odd exception to the at-will rule until 1980. Then the Supreme Court of California expanded the limitation on at-will employment in *Tameny v. Atlantic Richfield Co.*[301] Tameny, the plaintiff, alleged that he had worked for Arco for fifteen years. He was a retail sales representative who managed relations between Arco and certain franchised gasoline dealers. The complaint stated that Tameny's supervisors told him to "threaten [and] cajole . . . the so-called 'independent' service station dealers in [his] territory to cut their gasoline prices to a point at or below a designated level specified by Arco." Had Tameny done this, it would have violated both federal and state antitrust laws as well as a consent decree that had been entered against Arco in a federal antitrust prosecution. Arco fired Tameny because of his "unsatisfactory performance." Tameny sought relief on five different theories, including both contract and tort causes of action. The trial court upheld Arco's demurrer and dismissed Tameny's case.

---

[298] Susan F. Marrinan, *Employment-At-Will: Pandora's Box May Have an Attractive Cover*, 7 Hamline L. Rev. 155, 201 (1984).

[299] *See, e.g.*, Lawrence E. Blades & Clyde W. Summers, *Employment at Will vs. Individual Freedom: On Limiting the Abusive Exercise of Employer Power*, 67 Colum. L. Rev. 1404 (1967); Summers, *Individual Protection Against Unjust Dismissal: Time for a Statute*, 62 Va. L. Rev. 481 (1976).

[300] 174 Cal. App. 2d 184, 344 P.2d 25 (1959).

[301] 27 Cal. 3d 167, 610 P.2d 1330 (1980).

The Supreme Court of California reversed the trial court's decision. The majority found that the allegations of the complaint, if true, stated a cause of action based on the *Petermann* principle. However, the majority also decided that if Tameny proved his case, he could recover compensatory tort remedies and punitive damages as well. It said that "an employer's obligation to refrain from discharging an employee who refuses to commit a criminal act reflects a duty imposed by law upon all employers in order to implement the fundamental public policies embodied in the state's penal statutes." It quoted Professor William Prosser's text on torts: "Contract actions are created to protect the interest in having promises performed. . . . Tort actions are created to protect the interest in freedom from various kinds of harm. The duties of conduct which give rise to them are imposed by law, and are based primarily upon social policy, and not necessarily upon the will or intention of the parties."[302] It concluded that an employer who fired an employee who refused to follow an unlawful order violated a basic duty imposed by law upon all employers. Thus, tort remedies were appropriate.

Just as in the *Marvin v. Marvin* case you read earlier in this chapter,[303] the majority opinion in *Tameny* was by Justice Tobriner. Justice Clark's dissent in *Tameny* raised much the same objection as he made to much of the court's action in the *Marvin* case. He said: "In the belief we know better the needs of society, we again substitute our policy judgment for that of the Legislature, not even attempting to act under constitutional or other than personal compulsion." The California Labor Code provided that employment without a specified term could be terminated at will. Other legislative provisions created two exceptions — the dismissal of an employee who was absent from work to serve as an election officer or dismissal because the employee participated in labor activities. "We err because the Legislature, by stating the general rule and *expressly* making exceptions thereto, must be deemed to intend no other exception for now."

Justice Mathew O. Tobriner was a liberal labor lawyer before Governor Pat Brown appointed him to the bench; he served on the Supreme Court of California for 20 years. Justice William P. Clark had been Governor Ronald Reagan's Executive Secretary before Reagan appointed him as a trial judge in 1969 and then to the state supreme court in 1971. In 1981, after Reagan was elected president, Clark left the California court to become Deputy Secretary of State.

Two intermediate appellate decisions in California offered other theories upon which an employee-at-will might win against her employer. In *Cleary v. American Airlines*,[304] plaintiff had worked for the airline for 18 years under an employment for an unspecified term. He alleged that the airline had fired him because of his union-organizing activities. Moreover, the airline had not followed its own internal procedures because it did not afford Cleary a fair hearing to appeal his discharge. The trial court sustained a demurrer to the complaint, but the appellate court overturned the trial court's decision. The long term of satisfactory performance and the failure to follow procedures operated "as a form of estoppel, precluding any

---

[302] WILLIAM PROSSER, LAW OF TORTS 613 (4th ed. 1971).

[303] *See* Marvin v. Marvin, *supra* Chapter 3, section B.1.b.

[304] 111 Cal. App. 3d 443, 168 Cal. Rptr. 722 (1980).

discharge of such an employee without good cause." If plaintiff carried his burden of proof, he would be entitled to recover compensatory damages in tort and "in addition, punitive damages if his proof complies with the requirements for the latter type of damages."

CASE ②

In *Pugh v. See's Candies, Inc.*,[305] Pugh had been an at-will employee for 32 years, and See's had promoted and praised him over that time. See's had announced a policy of job security "for those who did their work." The court found an implied contract limitation on termination at will. The court said that it would allow both compensatory and punitive damages for breach of this implied contract.

Basically 32 yr. history of working meant could only fire for "cause" [definition on this page]

To put these cases in a broader perspective, we should note that there was a recession in the early 1980s, and many workers who were employees-at-will lost their jobs. Many of them sued, and a group of California lawyers who specialized in wrongful termination cases developed. A 1988 Rand Institute study looked at the consequences of the changes in rules concerning wrongful discharge in California.[306] The study looked at 120 jury trials decided in that state between 1980 and 1986. Plaintiffs were victorious in 68 percent of the cases. The average initial jury verdict was more than $650,000, although some very large awards inflated this figure; the median verdict was $177,000. Except for the smallest awards, on average 40 percent of the award was for punitive damages.

As a result of post-trial motions, appeals, and settlements, the final payments to plaintiffs were approximately half of the amount initially awarded. A typical case cost $80,000 to defend. The larger the case, the higher the defense costs were likely to be. A 1987 case involving a potential award of $1.5 million would cost almost $250,000 to defend. Plaintiffs' lawyers typically charged a 40 percent contingency fee. The total legal fees, including the fees of both plaintiff and defendant, averaged $160,000 per case. What this meant was that the lawyers' fees constituted more than half of the money changing hands as a result of the litigation. Some lawyers lost their cases and recovered nothing under contingent-fee arrangements. The median employee bringing suit could expect to recover only $30,000 once losing cases, post-trial reductions, and contingency fees were taken into account. Of course, a few employees recovered much more than this and some recovered far less or nothing.

All a discussion on contingent fee lawyers

Contingent-fee litigation will generally involve lawyers taking a large portion of what is recovered. Some might accept this as a necessary cost of deterring the powerful from violating the rights of others. We could, alternatively, provide those who cannot afford lawyers with government-supplied lawyers. Or we could cut the costs of business by doing nothing to overcome the cost barriers to litigation. If you doubt the validity of most of the claims that provoke contingent-fee litigation, you might be more comfortable with ruling out contingent fees. We must remember, however, that the contingent fee is a market solution to a problem. If there were not enough claimants who wanted to use it, lawyers would seek other ways to make a living.

---

[305] 116 Cal. App. 3d 311, 171 Cal. Rptr. 917 (1981).

[306] James Dertouzos, Elaine Holland, & Patricia Ebener, *The Legal and Economic Consequences of Wrongful Termination*, Rand Institute for Civil Justice Report R-3602-ICJ (1988).

California employment-at-will law changed sharply in 1988. In 1986, the Supreme Court of California agreed to review in *Foley v. Interactive Data Corp.*[307] Foley had worked for Interactive Data [IDC] for seven years. He did not have an express employment contract for a specific term. IDC had "Termination Guidelines," which set forth a seven-step procedure for firing an employee. In January 1983, Foley told Richard Earnest, an IDC official, that Kuhne, a man hired to become Foley's supervisor, was under investigation by the FBI for embezzling from Kuhne's former employer. Earnest told Foley not to discuss rumors.[308] In March, Kuhne transferred Foley from Los Angeles, California, to Waltham, Massachusetts. A week after the transfer, Earnest told Foley that he was not doing a good job. Seven days later Earnest fired Foley.

Foley sued, asserting three claims: (1) a tort claim for a discharge that violated public policy; (2) a contract action for breach of an implied-in-fact contract to terminate only for good cause; and (3) a tort cause of action for breach of the implied covenant of good faith and fair dealing. The trial court sustained the employer's demurrer to Foley's entire complaint. The court of appeal upheld the dismissal of each of Foley's claims. The Supreme Court of California granted plaintiff a hearing. Levine suggests that given the composition of the court at the time it agreed to review the case, it is likely that the court planned to reverse the extremely narrow approach of the appellate court, which was at odds with the decisions of most of the other intermediate California appeals courts.[309] The case was argued in November 1986. However, before a decision could be rendered, three of the justices of the court were defeated for reelection to another term. Many conservatives invested a great deal of money to defeat Chief Justice Rose Bird. She was the first woman to be a justice on the Supreme Court of California. She was appointed by Governor Jerry Brown, and conservatives saw her as very liberal. However, the focus of the election battle was the death penalty. The conservatives were strongly in favor of it while the Chief Justice was opposed. Two of Chief Justice Bird's liberal colleagues on the court went down to defeat with her.

Governor George Deukmejian[310] had been the Attorney General of California, and he had advocated the death penalty while often being frustrated by the court. He appointed three new justices who would serve at least until the next election, and all three supported the death penalty. *Foley v. Interactive Data Corp.* was reargued before a much more conservative panel in April 1987. A very divided court rendered its decision on December 29, 1988, and the California law of employment-at-will changed once again.

---

[307]   47 Cal. 3d 654, 765 P.2d 373 (1988).

[308]   In September 1983, about six months after Foley's discharge, Kuhne pleaded guilty in federal court to a felony count of embezzlement.

[309]   Lawrence C. Levine, *Judicial Backpedaling: Putting the Brakes on California's Law of Wrongful Termination*, 20 Pac. L.J. 993, 1011–12 (1989).

[310]   George Deukmejian, a Republican, was a member of the California Assembly and then Attorney General before he became governor. Asked why he ran for the office of Governor, Deukmejian replied, "Attorneys General don't appoint judges — Governors do." During his eight-year term, Deukmejian appointed 1,000 judges, and by the time he left office, he had appointed the majority of California Supreme Court justices then serving on the bench. *See* http://governors.library.ca.gov/35-deukmejian. html.

The Supreme Court of California majority acknowledged the existence of a tort cause of action for terminating an employee in a situation where the termination would violate public policy. The court provided little guidance about what constitutes public policy, but it said that it had to be "substantial," "fundamental," and "basic."[311] Foley claimed that he had a duty to communicate to his employer that a prospective employee might be an embezzler. The court said: "When the duty of an employee to disclose information to his employer serves only the private interest of the employer, the rationale underlying the *Tameny* cause of action is not implicated." Thus, it upheld the trial court's ruling sustaining the demurrer to this count in Foley's complaint.

Next the court decided that Foley had pleaded facts which, if proved, might be sufficient for a jury to find an implied-in-fact contract limiting defendant's right to discharge him arbitrarily. Foley's implied contract claim was not barred by the Statute of Frauds because the contract could have been performed within one year: "[P]laintiff could have terminated his employment within that period, or defendant could have discharged plaintiff for cause." The court accepted the reasoning of *Pugh v. See's Candies, Inc.*,[312] and found that Foley's allegations of facts were sufficient to establish a cause of action for breach of an implied contract:

> First, defendant overemphasizes the fact that plaintiff was employed for "only" six years and nine months. Length of employment is a relevant consideration but six years and nine months is sufficient time for conduct to occur on which a trier of fact could find the existence of an implied contract. . . . Plaintiff here alleged repeated oral assurances of job security and consistent promotions, salary increases, and bonuses during the term of his employment contributing to his reasonable expectation that he would not be discharged except for good cause.

> Second, an allegation of breach of written "Termination Guidelines" implying self-imposed limitations on the employer's power to discharge at will may be sufficient to state a cause of action for breach of an employment contract. . . .

> Finally, . . . plaintiff alleges that he supplied the company valuable and separate consideration by signing an agreement whereby he promised not to compete or reveal any computer-related information for one year after termination.

The majority of the court refused to recognize a wrongful termination action based on tortious breach of the implied covenant of good faith and fair dealing.[313] Such an implied covenant gives rise only to a contract action because the implied covenant does not protect a generalized public interest. This meant that the remedy

---

[311] In subsequent cases, the California Supreme Court clarified that claims of public policy violations had to be grounded in the constitution, statutes, or administrative regulations that carried out statutory goals. *See* Green v. Ralee Engineering Co., 19 Cal. 4th 66, 78 Cal. Rptr. 2d 16, 960 P.2d 1046 (1998).

[312] *See supra* note 305.

[313] The court distinguished insurance cases, in which it recognized that breach of such an implied covenant gave rise to a tort action. "[T]he employment relationship is not sufficiently similar to that of the insurer and insured."

for breach of this covenant was limited to contract damages. The court said that recovery for breach of the implied covenant should be limited to contract damages because there is a need for predictability to promote commercial stability. The court rejected the approach taken by the intermediate appellate court in *Cleary v. American Airlines, Inc.*,[314] and was highly critical of that decision.

The majority said that it was neither "unaware of nor unsympathetic to claims that contract remedies for breaches of contract are insufficient because they do not fully compensate due to their failure to include attorney's fees and their restrictions on foreseeable damages." However, it noted that there are many remedies that could better be provided by the legislature, such as increasing the amounts of contract damages, awarding attorney's fees, establishing arbitration, or providing tort remedies.

Thus, the Supreme Court of California affirmed the trial court's dismissal of Foley's tort claim based on the implied covenant of good faith and fair dealing. Furthermore, in *Newman v. Emerson Radio Corp.*,[315] a majority of that court decided that the *Foley* decision was to be applied to all claims filed both before and after *Foley*. That is, *Foley* was to be applied retroactively.

Gantt v. Sentry Insurance Corp.[316] illustrates other problems with private litigation as a means of regulating the workplace. In that case, the jury found that Sentry's lawyer had attempted to coerce Gantt to testify falsely in a sexual harassment case brought against the insurance company. Soon after the hearing in the harassment case, Gantt was demoted and then left the firm. Gantt sued for tort damages for wrongful termination and recovered a jury verdict of $1.34 million that the Supreme Court of California affirmed. The case fell under the rule of the *Petermann* and *Tameny* decisions. It is likely that Gantt's lawyer was paid by a contingent fee, and the lawyer would probably have gotten anywhere from one-third to more than one-half of the amount awarded. Note, too, that the sexual harassment took place in 1980. Gantt was demoted in 1983, he won before the jury in 1986, and the Supreme Court of California affirmed his judgment at the end of 1992. In 1992, he was 50 years old and working as a junior high school math teacher. Gantt said that "co-workers accused him of betraying the company when he reported the harassment to his supervisors. . . . [E]xecutives and co-workers shrugged off the sexually offensive conduct with comments like: 'He doesn't mean anything by it.'" Sentry argued that Gantt was fired because of poor job performance.[317]

In addition to facing costs of litigation, delay and the informal sanctions of the workplace, employees who bring wrongful termination suits face still another problem. A cartoon in the *Wall Street Journal* makes the point very well.[318] A job applicant is sitting across the desk from a potential employer who is reading the applicant's résumé. The applicant says to the potential employer: "You'll notice that

---

[314] *See supra* note 304.

[315] 48 Cal. 3d 973, 772 P.2d 1059 (1989).

[316] 1 Cal. 4th 1083, 824 P.2d 680 (1992).

[317] San Francisco Chronicle, June 16, 1992, at A1.

[318] Wall Street Journal, Jan. 27, 2005, at D8.

every single one of those wrongful termination suits was decided in my favor."

CASE 4

In *Hunter v. Up-Right, Inc.*, an employee alleged that the employer told him to resign because his job was being eliminated.[319] The employee did so. However, the job was not eliminated. The Supreme Court of California said that an employee can recover for misrepresentation only if it is separate from the termination of the employment contract. The damages cannot result from the termination itself. The court said that misrepresentation claims were hard to defend, and few could be thrown out on demurrer or summary judgment. "The resultant costs and inhibition of employment decision making are precisely the sort of consequences we cited in *Foley* in disapproving tort damages for breach of the implied covenant of good faith and fair dealing."

CASE 4

In *Guz v. Bechtel Nat'l, Inc.*, the California court continued to be skeptical about an implied contract to discharge only for cause when employment documents talked of employment-at-will.[320] The court said:

All; Just starts; for a long time only; enough > Post Foley ideas

> A number of post-*Foley* California decisions have suggested that long duration of service, regular promotions, favorable performance reviews, praise from supervisors, and salary increases do not, without more, imply an employer's contractual intent to relinquish its at-will rights. . . .

> These decisions reason that such events are but natural consequences of a well-functioning employment relationship, and thus have no special tendency to prove that the employer's at-will implied agreement, reasonably understood as such by the employee, has become one that limits the employer's future termination rights. . . . A rule granting such contract rights on the basis of successful longevity alone would discourage the retention and promotion of employees.[321]

So much for an introduction to this branch of California law. What do we find when we look elsewhere? The results and reasoning of the decisions are inconsistent.

WAGENSELLER v. SCOTTSDALE MEMORIAL HOSPITAL
Arizona Supreme Court
147 Ariz. 370, 710 P.2d 1025 (1985)

FELDMAN, J.

Catherine Sue Wagenseller petitioned this court to review a decision of the court of appeals affirming in part the trial court's judgment in favor of Scottsdale Memorial Hospital and certain Hospital employees (defendants). The trial court had dismissed all causes of action on defendants' motion for summary judgment. The court of appeals affirmed in part and remanded, ruling that the only cause of action available to plaintiff was the claim against her supervisor, Kay Smith. . . .

---

[319] 6 Cal. 4th 1174, 864 P.2d 88 (1993).

[320] 24 Cal. 4th 317, 8 P.3d 1089 (2000).

[321] *Id.* at 341–42, 1104–05.

We granted review to consider the law of this state with regard to the employment-at-will doctrine. The issues we address are:

1. Is an employer's right to terminate an at-will employee limited by any rules which, if breached, give rise to a cause of action for wrongful termination?

2. If "public policy" or some other doctrine does form the basis for such an action, how is it determined?

3. Did the trial court err, in view of *Leikvold v. Valley View Community Hospital,* 141 Ariz. 544, 688 P.2d 170 (1984), when it determined as a matter of law that the terms of Scottsdale Memorial Hospital's personnel policy manual were not part of the employment contract?

4. Do employment contracts contain an implied covenant of "good faith and fair dealing," and, if so, what is the nature of the covenant? . . .

Factual Background

Catherine Wagenseller began her employment at Scottsdale Memorial Hospital as a staff nurse in March 1975, having been personally recruited by the manager of the emergency department, Kay Smith. Wagenseller was an "at-will" employee — one hired without specific contractual term. Smith was her supervisor. In August 1978, Wagenseller was assigned to the position of ambulance charge nurse, and approximately one year later was promoted to the position of paramedic coordinator, a newly approved management position in the emergency department. Three months later, on November 1, 1979, Wagenseller was terminated.

Most of the events surrounding Wagenseller's work at the Hospital and her subsequent termination are not disputed, although the parties differ in their interpretation of the inferences to be drawn from and the significance of these events. For more than four years, Smith and Wagenseller maintained a friendly, professional working relationship. In May 1979, they joined a group consisting largely of personnel from other hospitals for an eight-day camping and rafting trip down the Colorado River. According to Wagenseller, "an uncomfortable feeling" developed between her and Smith as the trip progressed — a feeling that Wagenseller ascribed to "the behavior that Kay Smith was displaying." Wagenseller states that this included public urination, defecation, and bathing, heavy drinking, and "grouping up" with other rafters. Wagenseller did not participate in any of these activities. She also refused to join in the group's staging of a parody of the song "Moon River," which allegedly concluded with members of the group "mooning" the audience. Smith and others allegedly performed the "Moon River" skit twice at the Hospital following the group's return from the river, but Wagenseller declined to participate there as well.

Wagenseller contends that her refusal to engage in these activities caused her relationship with Smith to deteriorate and was the proximate cause of her termination. She claims that following the river trip Smith began harassing her, using abusive language, and embarrassing her in the company of other staff. Other emergency department staff reported a similar marked change in Smith's behavior toward Wagenseller after the trip, although Smith denied it.

Up to the time of the river trip, Wagenseller had received consistently favorable job performance evaluations. Two months before the trip, Smith completed an annual evaluation report in which she rated Wagenseller's performance as "exceed-[ing] results expected," the second highest of five possible ratings. In August and October 1979, Wagenseller met first with Smith and then with Smith's successor, Jeannie Steindorff, to discuss some problems regarding her duties as paramedic coordinator and her attitude toward the job. On November 1, 1979, following an exit interview at which Wagenseller was asked to resign and refused, she was termi-nated.

She appealed her dismissal in letters to her supervisor and to the Hospital administrative and personnel department, answering the Hospital's stated reasons for her termination, claiming violations of the disciplinary procedure contained in the Hospital's personnel policy manual, and requesting reinstatement and other remedies. When this appeal was denied, Wagenseller brought suit against the Hospital, its personnel administrators, and her supervisor, Kay Smith.

Wagenseller, an "at-will" employee, contends that she was fired for reasons which contravene public policy and without legitimate cause related to job perfor-mance. She claims that her termination was wrongful, and that damages are recoverable under both tort and contract theories. The Hospital argues that an "at-will" employee may be fired for cause, without cause, or for "bad" cause. We hold that in the absence of contractual provision such an employee may be fired for good cause or for no cause, but not for "bad" cause.

The Employment-at-Will Doctrine

History

As early as 1562, the English common law presumed that an employment contract containing an annual salary provision or computation was for a one-year term. Murg & Scharman, *Employment at Will: Do the Exceptions Overwhelm the Rule?* 23 B.C. L. REV. 329, 332 (1982). Originally designed for the protection of seasonal farm workers, the English rule expanded over the years to protect factory workers as well. Workers were well protected under this rule, for the one-year presumption was not easy to overcome. . . .

In the early nineteenth century, American courts borrowed the English rule. The legal rationale embodied in the rule was consistent with the nature of the predominant master-servant employment relationship at the time because it reflected the master's duty to make provision for the general well-being of his servants. . . . In addition, the master was under a duty to employ the servant for a term, either a specified or implied time of service, and could not terminate him strictly at will. . . . The late nineteenth century, however, brought the Industrial Revolution; with it came the decline of the master-servant relationship and the rise of the more impersonal employer-employee relationship. In apparent response to the economic changes sweeping the country, American courts abandoned the English rule and adopted the employment-at-will doctrine. Murg & Scharman, *supra* at 334. This new doctrine gave the employer freedom to terminate an at-will employee for any reason, good or bad.

. . . .

Present-Day Status of the At-Will Rule

In recent years there has been apparent dissatisfaction with the absolutist formulation of the common-law at-will rule. . . . Today, courts in three-fifths of the states have recognized some form of a cause of action for wrongful discharge. Lopatka, *The Emerging Law of Wrongful Discharge — A Quadrennial Assessment of the Labor Law Issue of the 80s*, 40 Bus. Law. 1 (1984).

The trend has been to modify the at-will rule by creating exceptions to its operation. Three general exceptions have developed. The most widely accepted approach is the "public policy" exception, which permits recovery upon a finding that the employer's conduct undermined some important public policy. The second exception, based on contract, requires proof of an implied-in-fact promise of employment for a specific duration, as found in the circumstances surrounding the employment relationship, including assurances of job security in company person-nel manuals or memoranda. Under the third approach, courts have found in the employment contract an implied-in-law covenant of "good faith and fair dealing" and have held employers liable in both contract and tort for breach of that covenant. Wagenseller raises all three doctrines.

The Public Policy Exception

The public policy exception to the at-will doctrine began with a narrow rule permitting employees to sue their employers when a statute expressly prohibited their discharge. See *Kouff v. Bethlehem-Alameda Shipyard*, 90 Cal. App. 2d 322, 202 P.2d 1059 (1949) (statute prohibiting discharge for serving as an election officer). This formulation was then expanded to include any discharge in violation of a statutory expression of public policy. See *Petermann v. Teamsters Local 396*, 174 Cal. App. 2d 184, 344 P.2d 25 (1959) (discharge for refusal to commit perjury). Courts later allowed a cause of action for violation of public policy, even in the absence of a specific statutory prohibition. See *Nees v. Hocks*, 272 Or. 210, 536 P.2d 512 (1975) (discharge for being absent from work to serve on jury duty). The New Hampshire Supreme Court announced perhaps the most expansive rule when it held an employer liable for discharging an employee who refused to go out with her foreman. The court concluded that termination "motivated by bad faith or malice or based on retaliation is not [in] the best interest of the economic system or the public good and constitutes a breach of the employment contract." *Monge v. Beebe Rubber Co.*, 114 N.H. 130, 133, 316 A.2d 549, 551 (1974). Although no other court has gone this far, a majority of the states have now either recognized a cause of action based on the public policy exception or have indicated their willingness to consider it, given appropriate facts. The key to an employee's claim in all of these cases is the proper definition of a public policy that has been violated by the employer's actions. . . .

Before deciding whether to adopt the public policy exception, we first consider what kind of discharge would violate the rule. The majority of courts require, as a threshold showing, a "clear mandate" of public policy. . . . The leading case recognizing a public policy exception to the at-will doctrine is *Palmateer v. International Harvester Co.*, 85 Ill. 2d 124, 421 N.E.2d 876 (1981) . . . which holds that an employee stated a cause of action for wrongful discharge when he claimed he was fired for supplying information to police investigating alleged criminal violations by a co-employee. Addressing the issue of what constitutes "clearly mandated public policy," the court stated:

> There is no precise definition of the term. In general, it can be said that public policy concerns what is right and just and what affects the citizens of the State collectively. It is to be found in the State's constitution and statutes and, when they are silent, in its judicial decisions. Although there is no precise line of demarcation dividing matters that are the subject of public policies from matters purely personal, a survey of cases in other States involving retaliatory discharges shows that a matter must strike at the heart of a citizen's social rights, duties, and responsibilities before the tort will be allowed. 85 Ill. 2d at 130, 421 N.E.2d at 878–89.

It is difficult to justify this court's further adherence to a rule which permits an employer to fire someone for "cause morally wrong." So far as we can tell, no court faced with a termination that violated a "clear mandate of public policy" has refused to adopt the public policy exception. Certainly, a court would be hard-pressed to find a rationale to hold that an employer could with impunity fire an employee who refused to commit perjury. Why should the law imply an agreement which would give the employer such power? It may be argued, of course, that our economic system functions best if employers are given wide latitude in dealing with employees. We assume that it is in the public interest that employers continue to have that freedom. We also believe, however, that the interests of the economic system will be fully served if employers may fire for good cause or without cause. The interests of society as a whole will be promoted if employers are forbidden to fire for cause that is "morally wrong."

[The Supreme Court of Arizona decided to adopt a public policy exception to the employment-at-will rule.]

We turn then to the questions of where "public policy" may be found and how it may be recognized and articulated. As the expressions of our founders and those we have elected to our legislature, our state's constitution and statutes embody the public conscience of the people of this state. It is thus in furtherance of their interests to hold that an employer may not with impunity violate the dictates of public policy found in the provisions of our statutory and constitutional law.

We do not believe, however, that expressions of public policy are contained only in the statutory and constitutional law, nor do we believe that all statements made in either a statute or the constitution are expressions of public policy. . . . Other state courts have similarly recognized judicial decisions as a source of public policy. . . .

[The court said that the interest involved must be more than an employee's personal moral or ethical views. It is not enough that an employer asked an employee to do something that she thought was wrong.] Although an employee facing such a quandary may refuse to do the work believed to violate her moral philosophy, she may not also claim a right to continued employment. . . .

However, some legal principles, whether statutory or decisional, have a discernible, comprehensive public purpose. A state's criminal code provides clear examples of such statutes. Thus, courts in other jurisdictions have consistently recognized a cause of action for a discharge in violation of a criminal statute. . . .

In the case before us, Wagenseller refused to participate in activities which arguably would have violated our indecent exposure statute, A.R.S. § 13-1402. She claims that she was fired because of this refusal. The statute provides:

§ 13-1402. Indecent exposure; classifications

A. A person commits indecent exposure if he or she exposes his or her genitals or anus or she exposes the areola or nipple of her breast or breasts and another person is present, and the defendant is reckless about whether such other person, as a reasonable person, would be offended or alarmed by the act.

B. Indecent exposure is a Class 1 misdemeanor. Indecent exposure to a person under the age of fifteen years is a Class 6 felony.

While this statute may not embody a policy which "strikes at the heart of a citizen's social right, duties, and responsibilities" as clearly and forcefully as a statute prohibiting perjury, we believe that it was enacted to preserve and protect the commonly recognized sense of public privacy and decency. . . . The relevant inquiry here is not whether the alleged "mooning" incidents were either felonies or misdemeanors or constituted purely technical violations of the statute, but whether they contravened the important public policy interests embodied in the law. The law enacted by the legislature establishes a clear policy that public exposure of one's anus or genitals is contrary to public standards of morality. We are compelled to conclude that termination of employment for refusal to participate in public exposure of one's buttocks[322] is a termination contrary to the policy of this state, even if, for instance, the employer might have grounds to believe that all of the onlookers were voyeurs and would not be offended. In this situation, there might be no crime, but there would be a violation of public policy to compel the employee to do an act ordinarily proscribed by the law.

From a theoretical standpoint, we emphasize that the "public policy exception" that we adopt does not require the court to make a new contract for the parties. In an at-will situation, the parties have made no express agreement regarding the duration of employment or the grounds for discharge. The common law has presumed that in so doing the parties have intended to allow termination at any time, with or without good cause. It might be more properly argued that the law has recognized an implied covenant to that effect. Whether it be presumption or implied

---

[322] [5] We have little expertise in the techniques of mooning. We cannot say as a matter of law, therefore, whether mooning would always violate the statute by revealing the mooner's anus or genitalia. . . . Compelled exposure of the bare buttocks, on pain of termination of employment, is a sufficient violation of the policy embodied in the statute to support the action.

contractual covenant, we do not disturb it. We simply do not raise a presumption or imply a covenant that would require an employee to do that which public policy forbids or refrain from doing that which it commands.

Thus, in an at-will hiring we continue to recognize the presumption or to imply the covenant of termination at the pleasure of either party, whether with or without cause. Firing for bad cause — one against public policy articulated by constitutional, statutory, or decisional law — is not a right inherent in the at-will contract, or in any other contract, even if expressly provided. See 1 A. CORBIN, CONTRACTS § 7; 6A A. CORBIN, CONTRACTS §§ 1373–75 (1962). Such a termination violates rights guaranteed to the employee by law and is tortious. See PROSSER & KEETON ON TORTS § 92 at 655 (5th ed. 1984).

The "Personnel Policy Manual" Exception

Although an employment contract for an indefinite term is presumed to be terminable at will, that presumption, like any other presumption, is rebuttable by contrary evidence. See Restatement (Second) of Agency § 442; *Leikvold v. Valley View Community Hospital*, 141 Ariz. 544, 547, 688 P.2d 170, 173 (1984). Thus, in addition to relying on the public policy analysis to restrict the operation of the terminable-at-will rule, courts have turned to the employment contract itself, finding in it implied terms that limit the employer's right of discharge. Two types of implied contract terms have been recognized by the courts: implied-in-law terms and implied-in-fact terms. An implied-in-law term arises from a duty imposed by law where the contract itself is silent; it is imposed even though the parties may not have intended it, and it binds the parties to a legally enforceable duty, just as if they had so contracted explicitly. 1 A. CORBIN, CONTRACTS § 17, at 38 (1960). The covenant of good faith and fair dealing, discussed *infra*, is an implied-in-law contract term that has been recognized by a small number of courts in the employment-at-will context.

An implied-in-fact contract term, on the other hand, is one that is inferred from the statements or conduct of the parties. It is not a promise defined by the law, but one made by the parties, though not expressly. Courts have found such terms in an employer's policy statements regarding such things as job security and employee disciplinary procedures, holding that by the conduct of the parties these statements may become part of the contract, supplementing the verbalized at-will agreement, and thus limiting the employer's absolute right to discharge an at-will employee. . . . Arizona is among the jurisdictions that have recognized the implied-in-fact contract term as an exception to the at-will rule. . . .

In October 1978, Scottsdale Memorial Hospital established a four-step disciplinary procedure to achieve the Hospital's stated policy of "provid[ing] fair and consistent discipline as required to assist with the improvement of employees' behavior or performance." Subject to 32 listed exceptions, prior to being terminated a Hospital employee must be given a verbal warning, a written performance warning, a letter of formal reprimand, and a notice of dismissal. The manual further qualifies the mandatory procedure by providing that the 32 exceptions "are not inclusive and are only guidelines." In appealing her dismissal, Wagenseller cited violations of this procedure, but the trial court ruled as a matter of law that the manual had not become part of the employment contract between Wagenseller and the Hospital. The court of appeals held that the Hospital's failure to follow the four-step disciplinary procedure did not violate Wagenseller's contract rights because she failed to prove her reliance on the procedure as a part of her employment contract. We disagree with both of these rulings. . . .

Whether any particular personnel manual modifies any particular employment-at-will relationship and becomes part of the particular employment contract is a question of fact. Evidence relevant to this factual decision includes the language used in the personnel manual as well as the employer's course of conduct and oral representations regarding it. . . . Here, the court of appeals ruled, in effect, that the Hospital had adequately disclaimed any liability for failing to follow the procedure it had established. It found this disclaimer in the final item in the Hospital's list of exceptions to its disciplinary procedure: "These major and minor infractions are not inclusive and are only guidelines." The court concluded that the effect of this "clear" and "conspicuous" provision was "to create, by its terms, no rights at all."

We do not believe this document, read in its entirety, has the clarity that the court of appeals attributed to its individual portions. One reading the document might well infer that the Hospital had established a procedure that would generally apply in disciplinary actions taken against employees. Although such a person would also note the long list of exceptions, he might not conclude from reading the list that an exception would apply in every case so as to swallow the general rule completely. We do not believe that the provision for unarticulated exceptions destroys the entire articulated general policy as a matter of law. Not only does such a result defy common sense, it runs afoul of our reasoning in *Leikvold v. Valley View Community Hospital*, where we addressed this problem directly:

> Employers are certainly free to issue no personnel manual at all or to issue a personnel manual that clearly and conspicuously tells their employees that the manual is not part of the employment contract and that their jobs are terminable at the will of the employer with or without reason. Such actions, either not issuing a personnel manual or issuing one with clear language of limitation, instill no reasonable expectations of job security and do not give employees any reason to rely on representations in the manual. However, if an employer does choose to issue a policy statement, in a manual or otherwise, and, by its language or by the employer's actions, encourages reliance thereon, the employer cannot be free to only selectively abide by it. Having announced a policy, the employer may not treat it as illusory. . . .

The general rule is that the determination whether in a particular case a promise should be implied in fact is a question of fact. 1 A. CORBIN, *supra*, § 17 at 38. . . . Where reasonable minds may draw different conclusions or inferences from undisputed evidentiary facts, a question of fact is presented. . . . We believe that reasonable persons could differ in the inferences and conclusions they would draw from the Hospital's published manual regarding disciplinary policy and procedure. Thus, there are questions of fact as to whether this policy and procedure became a part of Wagenseller's employment contract. . . . The trial court therefore erred in granting summary judgment on this issue.

The court of appeals' resolution of the reliance issue also was incorrect. A party may enforce a contractual provision without showing reliance. . . . The employee's reliance on an announced policy is only one of several factors that are relevant in determining whether a particular policy was intended by the parties to modify an at-will agreement. The employer's course of conduct and oral representations regarding the policy, as well as the words of the policy itself, also may provide evidence of such a modification. . . .

The "Good Faith and Fair Dealing" Exception

We turn next to a consideration of implied-in-law contract terms which may limit an employer's right to discharge an at-will employee. Wagenseller claims that discharge without good cause breaches the implied-in-law covenant of good faith and fair dealing contained in every contract. See Restatement (Second) of Contracts § 205. . . . In the context of this case, she argues that discharge without good cause violates the covenant of good faith and is, therefore, wrongful. The covenant requires that neither party do anything that will injure the right of the other to receive the benefits of their agreement. . . . The duty not to act in bad faith or deal unfairly thus becomes a part of the contract, and, as with any other element of the contract, the remedy for its breach generally is on the contract itself. . . . In certain circumstances, breach of contract, including breach of the covenant of good faith and fair dealing, may provide the basis for a tort claim. . . .

The question whether a duty to terminate only for good cause should be implied into all employment-at-will contracts has received much attention in the case law and other literature. . . . Courts have generally rejected the invitation to imply such a duty in employment contracts, voicing the concern that to do so would place undue restrictions on management and would infringe the employer's "legitimate exercise of management discretion." . . . We think this concern is appropriate. . . .

Tort recovery for breach of the implied covenant of good faith and fair dealing is well established in actions brought on insurance contracts. . . . Courts have been reluctant, however, to extend the tort action beyond the insurance setting. The rationale for permitting tort recovery in insurance contract disputes and not in disputes involving other contracts has been founded largely upon the existence of a "special relationship" between insurer and insured. . . . Were we to adopt such a rule, we fear that we would tread perilously close to abolishing completely the at-will doctrine and establishing by judicial fiat the benefits which employees can and should get only through collective bargaining agreements or tenure provisions. . . . While we do not reject the propriety of such a rule, we are not persuaded that it should be the result of judicial decision.

In reaching this conclusion, however, we do not feel that we should treat employment contracts as a special type of agreement in which the law refuses to imply the covenant of good faith and fair dealing that it implies in all other contracts. As we noted above, the implied-in-law covenant of good faith and fair dealing protects the right of the parties to an agreement to receive the benefits of the agreement that they have entered into. The denial of a party's right to those benefits, whatever they are, will breach the duty of good faith implicit in the contract. Thus, the relevant inquiry always will focus on the contract itself, to determine what the parties did agree to. In the case of an employment-at-will contract, it may be said that the parties have agreed, for example, that the employee will do the work required by the employer and that the employer will provide the necessary working conditions and pay the employee for work done. What cannot be said is that one of the agreed benefits to the at-will employee is a guarantee of continued employment or tenure. The very nature of the at-will agreement precludes any claim for a prospective benefit. Either employer or employee may terminate the contract at any time.

We do, however, recognize an implied covenant of good faith and fair dealing in the employment-at-will contract, although that covenant does not create a duty for the employer to terminate the employee only for good cause. The covenant does not protect the employee from a "no-cause" termination because tenure was never a benefit inherent in the at-will agreement. The covenant does protect an employee from a discharge based on an employer's desire to avoid the payment of benefits already earned by the employee. . . . Thus, plaintiff here has a right to receive the benefits that were a part of her employment agreement with defendant Hospital. To the extent, however, that the benefits represent a claim for prospective employment, her claim must fail. The terminable-at-will contract between her and the Hospital made no promise of continued employment. To the contrary, it was, by its nature, subject to termination by either party at any time, subject only to the legal prohibition that she could not be fired for reasons which contravene public policy.

Thus, because we are concerned not to place undue restrictions on the employer's discretion in managing his workforce and because tenure is contrary to the bargain in an at-will contract, we reject the argument that a no-cause termination breaches the implied covenant of good faith and fair dealing in an employment-at-will relationship. . . .

Summary and Conclusions

The trial court granted summary judgment against Wagenseller on the count alleging the tort of wrongful discharge in violation of public policy. We adopt the "public policy" exception to the at-will termination rule and hold that the trial court erred in granting judgment against plaintiff on this theory. On remand plaintiff will be entitled to a jury trial if she can make a *prima facie* showing that her termination was caused by her refusal to perform some act contrary to public policy, or her performance of some act which, as a matter of public policy, she had a right to do. The obverse, however, is that mere dispute over an issue involving a question of public policy is not equivalent to establishing causation as a matter of law and will not automatically entitle plaintiff to judgment. In the face of conflicting evidence or inferences as to the actual reason for termination, the question of causation will be a question of fact.

The trial court granted summary judgment against Wagenseller on the count alleging breach of implied-in-fact provisions of the contract. We hold that this was error. On this record, there is a jury question as to whether the provisions of the employment manual were part of the contract of employment.

We affirm the grant of summary judgment on the count seeking recovery for breach of the implied covenant of good faith and fair dealing. We recognize that covenant as part of this and other contracts, but do not construe it to give either party to the contract rights — such as tenure — different from those for which they contracted. . . .

For the foregoing reasons, we affirm in part and reverse in part. The decision of the court of appeals is vacated and the case remanded to the trial court for proceedings not inconsistent with this opinion.

HOLOHAN, C.J., dissenting and specially concurring.

The Court of Appeals held in this case that the personnel manual was not, as a matter of law, part of the employment contract. I concur in that position because I find the analysis of the Court of Appeals more convincing than that advanced by the majority of this court. I, therefore, dissent from the opinion of the court on that issue.

On the remaining issues I concur in the result.

NOTES AND QUESTIONS

1.　*Theory of the decision:* Is the majority of the Arizona Supreme Court trying to carry out the likely intention of the parties? (Suppose you conclude that neither party had thought of the situation that prompted the case. Is the court seeking what they would have decided had they thought of the problem?) Is it regulating the employment rules of the hospital for their reasonableness? Is it reviewing the discretion of supervisors?

Is the court carrying out the criminal laws of the State of Arizona? Suppose that instead of "mooning" the audience, the group of nurses were to appear in very revealing bikinis. Assume Ms. Wagenseller always wore very modest swimsuits that revealed little, and assume that the costumes that the nurses were to wear would be embarrassing and personally offensive to her. Indeed, this is what makes the audience respond to the skit. However, someone dressed in this costume would not violate the statute discussed by the court. She is fired because she refused to appear in the bikini that the performers were to wear at the show. Would she have a cause of action under the *Wagenseller* case?

2.　*The public policy exception:* All states except Alabama, Florida, Georgia, Louisiana, New York, and Rhode Island recognize some version of a public policy exception to employment-at-will.[323] State legislation, however, in all of these states but Alabama and Georgia protects most of the activities typically contained within a judicially created public policy exception.[324] Courts in all but one of the jurisdictions that have declined to accept a general public policy exception have

---

[323] Seymour Moskowitz, *Golden Age in the Golden State: Contemporary Legal Developments in Elder Abuse and Neglect*, 36 Loy. L.A. L. Rev. 589, 650 (2003).

[324] Kenneth G. Dau-Schmidt & Timothy A. Haley, *Governance of the Workplace: The Contemporary Regime of Individual Contract*, 28 Comp. Lab. L. & Pol'y J. 313, 338 (2007).

done so on the grounds that adopting a public policy exception should be left to the legislature.[325]

3. *Another approach to public policy?* Wisconsin has adopted a public policy exception, but its interpretation of the doctrine puts it among the states with the most pro-employer approach of those recognizing such a cause of action. In *Brockmeyer v. Dun & Bradstreet,*[326] the Supreme Court of Wisconsin adopted a narrow public policy exception to the employment-at-will rule:

> Courts should proceed cautiously when making public policy determinations. No employer should be subject to suit merely because a discharged employee's conduct was praiseworthy or because the public may have derived some benefit from it.
>
> A plaintiff-employee alleging a wrongful discharge has the burden of proving that the dismissal violates a clear mandate of public policy. Unless the employee can identify a specific declaration of public policy, no cause of action can be stated. The determination of whether the public policy asserted is a well-defined and fundamental one is an issue of law which the trial court [and not the jury] should decide. Once the plaintiff has demonstrated that the conduct that caused the discharge was consistent with a clear and compelling public policy, the burden of proof then shifts to the defendant-employer to prove that the dismissal was for just cause.
>
> We believe that the adoption of a narrowly circumscribed public policy exception properly balances the interests of employees, employers, and the public. Employee job security interests are safeguarded against employer actions that undermine fundamental policy preferences. Employers retain sufficient flexibility to make needed personnel decisions in order to adapt to changing economic conditions. Society also benefits from our holding in a number of ways. A more stable job market is achieved. Well-established public policies are advanced. Finally, the public is protected against frivolous lawsuits since courts will be able to screen cases on motions to dismiss for failure to state a claim or for summary judgment if the discharged employee cannot allege a clear expression of public policy.

The court went on to label the cause of action as one in contract since "[w]e believe that the reinstatement and back pay are the most appropriate remedies for public policy exception wrongful discharges, since the primary concern in these actions is to make the wronged employee 'whole.'" Thus, punitive damages, which could be awarded in a tort action, will not be allowed in Wisconsin. Also, "damages are limited by the concepts of foreseeability and mitigation."

The court then turned to the facts of the case and applied its test. The jury had found that Dun & Bradstreet had wrongfully discharged Brockmeyer and awarded him $250,000 in compensatory damages and $250,000 in punitive damages. The Supreme Court of Wisconsin upheld the Court of Appeals' reversal of the trial court's judgment. It sustained the employer's dismissal of an employee who had

---

[325] *Id.* at 339.

[326] 113 Wis. 2d 561, 335 N.W.2d 834 (1983).

alleged that he had been pressured not to testify honestly in a sex discrimination suit. Brockmeyer contended that he was asked to commit perjury by Dun & Bradstreet's official. The Supreme Court of Wisconsin responded:

> The record is devoid of any evidence demonstrating that Dun & Bradstreet asked Brockmeyer to lie. Admittedly, an inference can be drawn from this record that Dun & Bradstreet was concerned over the fact that Brockmeyer would tell the truth if asked to testify at proceedings concerning his former secretary's sex discrimination claim. This inference is a far cry from the allegation that Dun & Bradstreet wanted Brockmeyer to commit perjury. There is no clearly defined mandate of public policy against discharging an employee because his testimony may be contrary to an employer's interests. Such behavior may be indicative of bad faith, but it is not contrary to established public policies.

Are there likely to be many employees-at-will who will be able to make use of the Wisconsin rule? How, for example, would fired employees-at-will finance a lawsuit? Suppose the fired employee were a factory or clerical worker. Are lawyers in Wisconsin likely to take their case on a contingent fee? Indeed, is the Wisconsin position an exercise in empty symbolism?

An employee did recover under the Wisconsin rule in *Kempfer v. Automated Finishing, Inc.*[327] A supervisor had ordered the employee to drive a truck when the employee did not have a commercial motor vehicle driver's license. The employee had been stopped by a state patrol officer who had noticed that the truck had a cracked windshield. The officer told the employee that because of the weight of the truck, the employee was required to have the commercial license to drive it. Furthermore, further violations could result in personal fines, jail time, or both. The employer's officials later asked the employee to drive the truck on six separate occasions. He refused because he did not have the proper license. He was not told to get one, and he would have had to use AFI's truck to take the test. The plant manager again told the employee to drive the truck, he refused because he lacked the proper license, and the employer suspended the employee for two days. The employee went to the Department of Motor Vehicles, but a DMV official called AFI and explained that the employee needed to appear with a truck of the proper size to take the necessary test for the license. When the employee returned to work, he was told that his position had been eliminated in a cost-cutting effort, and he was fired. The employee sued and the jury found for him. It awarded $22,167 as back pay and benefits and $145,000 for future lost wages and benefits.

The Supreme Court of Wisconsin found that the employee had established that he was fired because he refused to violate a "fundamental and well-defined public policy." Justice Jon Wilcox wrote for the court and noted that it had decided that such a policy could not be found in case law, but the order to drive the truck without the proper license would have violated an important statute. However, Wisconsin does not award tort damages for the public policy cause of action. The *Brockmeyer* case limits recovery for wrongful discharge to reinstatement and back pay unless another remedy is needed to make the employee whole. The court said:

---

[327] 211 Wis. 2d 100, 564 N.W.2d 692 (1997).

We agree that there may be some cases where an award of front pay in lieu of reinstatement is necessary to make the wronged employee whole. However, as *Brockmeyer* limited damages in almost all cases to reinstatement and back pay, front pay can only be available when there is no other avenue to make the employee whole. . . .

Reinstatement is not feasible if the employee cannot be placed in the same or a similar position or if the company refuses to reinstate the employee. However, reinstatement is not infeasible simply because a plaintiff claims that he or she does not get along with the employer or because the plaintiff claims that he or she is not comfortable working for someone who previously terminated him or her.

In those situations where reinstatement is not feasible, an award of front pay is still limited by the concepts of foreseeability and mitigation . . .[328]

The court remanded the case and directed the trial court to determine whether reinstatement was feasible, and if not, to send the case to a jury to determine the amount of future wage loss that the employee suffered as a result of the breach that was foreseeable and not subject to mitigation. Chief Justice Abrahamson and Justice Ann Walsh Bradley concurred in the majority opinion. However, the Chief Justice wrote separately "to suggest several considerations the circuit court might entertain in awarding front pay upon remand . . . " She quoted Judge Posner, who said that courts had traditionally refused to grant specific performance of employment contracts because they did "not want to involve themselves in the industrial equivalent of matrimonial squabbling." She also said that while a major problem in awarding damages for the discharge of an at-will employee was to avoid speculation, the "amount of damages must be decided with all the certainty that the case permits." She quoted a Pennsylvania court as saying: "Substantial justice is better than exact injustice."[329] What would you expect that trial court to do with the Chief Justice's statements about remedy? Upon remand, on October 7, 1997, the trial judge set the case for trial on February 13, 1998. The judge ordered a pretrial conference and ordered alternative dispute resolution, with the judge as mediator. He stated the issues as "back pay? reinstatement? front pay?" On December 30,

---

[328] *Id.* at 120.

[329] The WISCONSIN STATE JOURNAL, Mar. 30, 1997, at 1E, reported while the case was pending before the Supreme Court of Wisconsin after oral argument:

A Waukesha County jury awarded Kempfer $167,167 in damages, including $22,167 in back pay and $145,000 in the money he'll lose until retirement [in taking] lower-paying jobs with other companies. The ruling is opposed by state businesses and Wisconsin Manufacturers and Commerce, the state's largest business organization, which filed a brief in the case. . . . WMC's lawyer, Timothy Costello, told the court the most the employee should get is back pay and reinstatement. He said the case was very important to the group: "The court's decision on the issue of recoverability of future lost earnings in wrongful discharge cases will have an impact on WMC's membership and will represent a significant development in an important area of Wisconsin's employment law."

But Kempfer's lawyer, Joe Welcenbach, and Patricia Meunier, lawyer for the Wisconsin Employment Lawyers Association, which filed a brief in the case, said reinstatement in such cases is often impractical and courts must have the power to give wrongfully fired employees complete damages.

1997, the parties stipulated that "all claims and causes of action set forth in the pleadings, on the merits," were dismissed with prejudice and without costs to any party. On February 3, 1998, the plaintiff's lawyer filed a notice of satisfaction of judgment for $193,107.12. The notice did not specify how this sum was calculated.[330]

4. ***Does implied contract based on an employment handbook trump employment-at-will?*** In the early to mid-1980s, several cases found employers bound by employee handbooks that set out what could be read as promises of job security and multi-stage disciplinary procedures. For example, in *Toussaint v. Blue Cross & Blue Shield of Michigan,* the Supreme Court of Michigan said that the provisions of a personnel manual voluntarily adopted by the employer after it had hired the employee became part of a legally enforceable employment contract.[331] Toussaint had legitimate expectations of job security. He had asked about it when he was hired, and he testified that he was told that he would be with the company "as long as I did my job." Later he asked again, and he was given a copy of the personnel manual which provided for discharge "for just cause only" after warnings, notice, hearings, and procedures. The employer fired Toussaint because its officials suspected him of dishonesty. They did not follow the procedures in the personnel manual. It was unlikely that the employer could have proved dishonesty, but Toussaint's supervisors had lost confidence in him. The Michigan court, by a four-to-three vote, found that Toussaint had shown an implied contract, and it was unnecessary to prove specific reliance on the personnel manual. The dissent saw no contract, but it said that Toussaint might prevail under Restatement (Second) of Contracts § 90 if he could prove reliance on the manual.[332] The Supreme Court of Minnesota, on similar facts in *Pine River State Bank v. Mettile,* found a unilateral contract for the employee.[333] The manual was an offer that the employee accepted by continuing to work at the bank.

Employers adopted such manuals as part of a generalized bureaucratization of the workplace, engendered in part by civil rights laws. Professor Lauren B. Edelman asked why "a growing number of employers have implemented due

---

[330] In *Mackenzie v. Miller Brewing Co.*, 241 Wis. 2d 700, 623 N.W.2d 739 (2001), Justice Jon Wilcox, writing for a majority of the Supreme Court of Wisconsin, also embraced Professor Richard Epstein's argument that employment-at-will benefits employees because it lets them leave at any time for any reason. "The flexibility afforded by the contract at will permits the ceaseless marginal adjustments that are necessary in any ongoing productive activity conducted . . . in conditions of technological and business change." Richard A. Epstein, *In Defense of the Contract at Will*, 51 U. Chi. L. Rev. 947, 969 (1984) ("The employee is not locked into an unfortunate contract if he finds better opportunities elsewhere or if he detects some weakness in the internal structure of the firm."). Justice Wilcox and his colleagues decided that Wisconsin does not recognize a tort of intentional misrepresentation to induce an at-will employee to continue at work. The opinion did recognize that "in another case" an employee handbook might offer a contract remedy or there might be a cause of action based on promissory estoppel.

[331] 408 Mich. 579, 292 N.W.2d 880 (1980). *See also* Ferraro v. Koelsch, 124 Wis. 2d 154, 368 N.W.2d 666 (1985).

[332] Do you think that many employees could prove that they had relied on the procedures for discharge in their employer's personnel manual? Do you think that most employees read or even skim the personnel manual when they are hired? What could an employee show that would count as significant reliance?

[333] 33 N.W.2d 622 (Minn. 1983).

process protections for their nonunion employees in the absence of any direct [legal] mandates to do so?"[334] She said that civil rights laws and questions about the right to hire and fire were generalized into a norm of fair treatment. However, she cautioned that fair treatment became operationalized as meaning *procedure*. She suggested that "due process protections may reinforce employers' control over labor by giving the appearance of fair governance while channeling conflict into a forum that, especially in the nonunion context, is unlikely to produce significant reform."[335] In later work, Edelman and her colleagues suggest that employers adopted procedures as a way to respond to the various civil rights laws that threatened to make them liable for discrimination in hiring and firing and hostility in the workplace.[336] Courts eventually adopted this norm of fair procedure as part of their interpretation of these civil rights laws.[337]

Lawyers specializing in employment law who represented larger organizations sought to cope with the conflict between their clients' desires to appear fair and deal with the civil rights laws by creating procedures and, at the same time, retain the advantages of employment-at-will. The major tool of transaction planners is contract drafting. These lawyers seek the right form of words to produce magic results — that is, results favoring their client, whether or not employees actually know about or agree to the terms in any real sense. Professor Edelman argues that management lawyers frequently seek to contract around legal risk. Employers increasingly include at-will clauses in their employment contracts or even in their application forms, with the result that employees, often unknowingly, waive their right to be terminated only for cause. A similar trend is occurring with respect to mandatory arbitration. Increasingly, employers include pre-dispute mandatory arbitration clauses in their employment contracts, handbooks, or employment applications. In most cases, employees cannot bargain over the terms or opt out of these contracts (other than by exiting the workplace). Thus, pre-dispute mandatory arbitration clauses in essence force employees to waive their statutory rights and allow employers to avoid jury trials and large damage awards.[338] Professor Jonathan Fineman notes: "Although courts are often willing to liberally interpret

---

[334] Lauren B. Edelman, *Legal Environments and Organizational Governance: The Expansion of Due Process in the American Workplace*, 95 Am. J. Soc. 1401, 1402 (1990).

[335] *Id.* at 1436.

[336] *See* Lauren B. Edelman, Steven E. Abraham & Howard S. Erlanger, *Professional Construction of Law: The Inflated Threat of Wrongful Discharge*, 26 Law & Soc'y Rev. 47, 77–78 (1992) ("[P]ersonnel professionals and practicing lawyers have a shared interest in constructing the threat of wrongful discharge in such a way that employers perceive the law as a threat and rely upon those professionals to curb the threat. That threat — and the proffered solution — would help both professions to gain a symbiotic jurisdiction over corporate response to the legal environment."). *See also* Lauren B. Edelman, *Legal Ambiguity and Symbolic Structures: Organizational Mediation of Civil Rights Law*, 97 Am. J. Soc. 1531, 1541 (1992) ("[B]ecause of normative pressure from their legal environments, organizations do not simply ignore or circumvent weak law, but rather construct compliance in a way that, at least in part, fits their interests.").

[337] Lauren B. Edelman, Linda H. Krieger, Scott R. Eliason, Catherine R. Albiston & Virginia Mellema, *When Organizations Rule: Judicial Deference to Institutionalized Employment Structures*, 117 Am. J. Sociology 888 (2011).

[338] Lauren B. Edelman, Working Law: The Managerialization of Civil Rights in the Workplace (forthcoming).

contract theory to combat perceived unfairness in the employment relationship, this approach is limited. To challenge employers' stated intent, courts need ambiguity or conflict. To challenge contract formation, courts need drafting mistakes."[339]

The Arizona court in the *Wagenseller* case finds enough facts alleged so that a jury could find an implied contract that the plaintiff would not be discharged except through a specified procedure that was not followed. Many writers have said that the various state courts are highly inconsistent in how they use the implied contract exception to employment-at-will. Professor Natalie Pedersen analyzed over 100 state and federal cases involving employment handbooks, employment-at-will, and disclaimers seeking to ward off employer liability.[340] She examines six matched pairs of cases with similar facts in which one court has found an implied contract and another has refused to do so. She concludes: "[C]ourts, even when faced with similar fact situations, often decide disclaimer cases differently depending on whether they focus on the objective intent of the employer in including the disclaimer or the reasonable expectations of the employee when faced with the disclaimer in the context of the entire employee handbook." For example, in *Dillon v. Champion Jogbra, Inc.*,[341] the employee manual stated on the first page:

> The policies and procedures contained in this manual constitute guidelines only. They do not constitute part of an employment contract, nor are they intended to make any commitment to any employee concerning how individual employment action can, should, or will be handled. Champion Jogbra offers no employment contracts nor does it guarantee any minimum length of employment. Champion Jogbra reserves the right to terminate any employee at any time "at will, with or without cause."

However, the employer had a "corrective action procedure" that established a progressive discipline system. The Vermont court found that the "boilerplate language" of the disclaimer did not necessarily communicate to employees that there were no job security provisions in light of the inconsistent statements in the manual. Other courts look only to the language of the disclaimer and read it literally, focusing on its "plain meaning." They are concerned primarily with what the employer said rather than what a reasonable employee would take as the meaning in light of everything communicated to her.

Do employees know about employment-at-will, and the right of an employer to fire for good, bad, or no reason? Ian H. Eliasoph reviewed a number of studies of employees' knowledge about the law related to employment.[342] He says that "over the last thirteen years, a number of empirical studies have established that most Americans overestimate the protective power of employment regulations."[343] He

---

[339] Jonathan Fineman, *The Inevitable Demise of the Implied Employment Contract*, 29 BERKELEY J. EMP. & LAB. L. 345, 379 (2008).

[340] Natalie Bucciarelli Pedersen, *A Subjective Approach to Contracts?: How Courts Interpret Employee Handbook Disclaimers*, 26 HOFSTRA LAB. & EMP. L.J. 101, 111 (2008).

[341] 819 A.2d 703 (Vt. 2002).

[342] Ian H. Eliasoph, *Know Your (Lack of) Rights: Reexamining the Causes and Effects of Phantom Employment Rights*, 12 EMP. RTS. & EMP. POL'Y J. 197 (2008).

[343] *Id.* at 198.

also stated, "[E]mployees know that the employment relationship is highly regulated but . . . [they] do not know the specifics of the protections afforded by the law."[344] He continues:

> Some authors argue that recent trends in the labor market have seriously eroded employee expectations of long-term job tenure, calling into doubt whether [assumptions about discharge for cause and how layoffs will be run in case of economic difficulty] . . . remain the dominant paradigm in employment relations. However, even if it is true (as it likely is) that expectations of long-term job tenure have diminished, there is little evidence that norms of fair play and just cause dismissal have been undermined in the process. Indeed, to the contrary, recent years have seen the proliferation of corporate codes and systems of employer self-regulation designed, at least in part, to reassure workers that they will be treated fairly. Thus, . . . [the] thesis that just cause dismissals and concepts of fair play constitute typical employer conduct likely remains well-founded.[345]

Professor Cynthia Estlund looks at employees' misconceptions about their legal rights.[346] For example, "They believe they enjoy something like 'just cause' protection when they are mostly terminable 'at will.' "[347] She says that the gap between employer and employee beliefs and legal reality needs to be dealt with. "That gap is problematic because it allows employers to have it both ways — to enjoy the benefits of employee expectations of legally enforceable job security without legal accountability."

Why are employees often mistaken? Many employees are unlikely to read and understand a personnel manual. They may have unrealistic positive expectations of their new job and their employer. Provisions about discharge may not seem relevant or important when one is happy to have a job. Perhaps all that they gain from the words in manuals is that there is a procedure that the employer says will be fair. Professor Richard Epstein has said: "Nor is there any reason to believe that such contracts are marred by misapprehensions, since employers and employees know the footing on which they have contracted: the phrase 'at will' is two words long and has the convenient virtue of meaning just what it says, no more and no less."[348]

Perhaps this is true, but employees may know that the phrase does not mean what it says literally. No employment today really is completely at will. For example, suppose an employee's supervisor wanted to fire an employee because she was black. The term "at will" would not give the supervisor that right. Perhaps employees translate the term as "at will as long as it is fair," or something along those lines.

---

[344] *Id.* at 221.

[345] *Id.* at 212.

[346] Cynthia L. Estlund, *How Wrong Are Employees About Their Rights, and Why Does It Matter?* 77 N.Y.U. L. Rev. 6 (2002).

[347] *Id.* at 7.

[348] Richard A. Epstein, *In Defense of the Contract at Will*, 51 U. Chi. L. Rev. 947, 955 (1984).

The reported cases suggest that the disclaimers and statements about at-will employment are not always perfectly clear. Perhaps counsel for employers tried to have their cake and eat it too. Perhaps the game is to sneak the disclaimer past the employee but have it available for a judge or arbitrator. Or perhaps lawyers with no ulterior motives have just engaged in sloppy contract drafting.

d. The "covenant of good faith" exception

The Arizona Supreme Court in the *Wagenseller* case recognizes a limited covenant of good faith and fair dealing. It does not prevent termination when there is no proof of just cause. Rather, "[t]he covenant does protect an employee from a discharge based on an employer's desire to avoid the payment of benefits already earned by the employee . . . " For example, in *Fortune v. National Cash Register Co.*,[349] NCR fired a salesman who had worked for the company for 25 years, a day after he placed a large order from a customer that would have entitled him to an extremely large bonus. A verdict for the salesman was affirmed by the Supreme Judicial Court of Massachusetts. The employer's motive for firing the plaintiff was to avoid paying the bonus and was "in bad faith." While these cases do not require just cause to fire an employee and yield only contract damages, when the employer can be shown to have acted to block a commission or the vesting of a bonus or pension plan, large amounts can be involved.

e. Reflecting on the struggle over employment-at-will

As we've seen, courts have spent decades shaping and reshaping the employment-at-will doctrine. Why? What goals do the courts seem to be pursuing in the area of employment for an indefinite term? Are they attempting to carry out the expectations of employees for which employers are responsible? Are they attempting to promote the mobility of labor and competition for jobs to keep job performance up and wages down? Are they following a policy of judicial restraint to leave the area to the power configuration found in American employment relations, promoting "living trees" and avoiding "dismal swamps"? Why hasn't this area been dealt with by legislation? Only two states, Montana[350] and Arizona,[351] have passed

---

[349] 373 Mass. 96, 364 N.E.2d 1251 (1977).

[350] Mont. Code Ann. § 39-2-904(1)(b) (2003). *See* Bradley T. Ewing, Charles M. North & Beck A. Taylor, *The Employment Effects of a "Good Cause" Discharge Standard in Montana*, 59 Indus. & Lab. Rel. Rev. 17 (2005). They argue that Montana employers are better off than employers elsewhere because the statute limits the remedies discharged employees can recover.

[351] Ariz. Rev. Stat. Ann. § 41-1461 to 41-1468 (2004). Professor Jean Braucher calls this statute "very convoluted and unclear." Jean Braucher, *Cowboy Contracts: The Arizona Supreme Court's Grand Tradition of Transactional Fairness*, 50 Ariz. L. Rev. 191, 207 (2008). The Arizona Employment Protection Act (EPA) preserves the tort cause of action for violation of the public policy reflected in a statute, if the statute does not provide its own remedy to employees (e.g., civil rights statutes). The EPA also does not appear to affect the contractual good-faith cause of action recognized in *Wagenseller*, since employment is recognized as contractual by the statute. But when it comes to the theory of a contractual right to job security implied in fact, the EPA requires a writing signed by the employer and the employee or an employment manual that "expresses the intent that it is a contract of employment." This expression of intent could be found in the manual as a whole rather than only from explicit words so stating. Because the statute on this point is in the nature of a Statute of Frauds, it is also possible that the Arizona courts might use § 139 of the Restatement (Second) of Contracts as an exception where an employee can show

statutes dealing with indefinite-term employment, and a proposed uniform act fell flat and was not passed by any state.[352] What does all this teach us about "activist judges" who work either to protect employees or favor the power of employers?[353]

i. *Restatement § 90 to the rescue?*

In *Hunter v. Hayes*,[354] the defendant had offered plaintiff a construction job, which was to begin on June 14, 1971. No ending date of the employment was specified. Defendant's agent told plaintiff to quit her current position at the telephone company so she would be ready to work when called. She did so, but defendant failed to employ her. She was out of work for two months. Relying on *Hoffman v. Red Owl Stores*, the Colorado Court of Appeals found for the plaintiff on the basis of promissory estoppel. It upheld an award of two months' wages.

In *Worley v. Wyoming Bottling Co., Inc.*,[355] Worley worked for more than 15 years as the sales manager for a Coca-Cola distributorship. When he was hired, he completed an employment application that contained an at-will employment disclaimer. About 10 years after he was hired, Worley signed a non-compete agreement that included at-will employment language. Two years after that, in 1993, Wyoming Bottling issued an employee handbook that contained statements that those in Worley's position were at-will employees.

In 1995, the distributorship increased its sales goals and threatened its managers with termination if the goals were not met. Worley's supervisor resigned.

---

reliance on promises made orally or implied in conduct. Arizona has a history of following the RESTATEMENT. The EPA bars the use of the "part performance" doctrine as an exception to its writing requirement, but the Arizona Supreme Court has stated that this doctrine applies only where an equitable remedy is sought and not to actions for damages. Trollope v. Koerner, 106 Ariz. 10, 470 P.2d 91 (1970). *See also* Steven E. Abraham, *The Arizona Employment Protection Act: Another "Wrongful Discharge Statute" That Benefits Employers?* 12 EMP. RTS. & EMP. POL'Y J. 105 (2008).

[352] The Model Employment Termination Act (META) was criticized both as imposing too many burdens on employers and as not protecting employees enough. *See* Stephen F. Befort, *Labor and Employment Law at the Millennium: A Historical Review and Critical Assessment*, 43 B.C. L. REV. 351, 426 (2002).

[353] Judge Richard Posner thinks that conservatives are mistaken when they attack "activist judges" and assert that "[l]egislators make the law; judges find and apply it." He says: "There has never been a time when the courts of the United States, state or federal, behaved consistently in accordance with this idea. Nor could they, for reasons rooted in the nature of law and legal institutions, in the limitations of human knowledge, and in the character of the political system." Richard A. Posner, *The Case Against Strict Constructionism: What Am I? A Potted Plant?* THE NEW REPUBLIC, Sept. 18, 1987, at 23. The term *activist judge* came into modern popular usage in the 1967 nomination of Thurgood Marshall, an African American, to the Supreme Court of the United States. *See* Trevor Parry-Giles, *Character, the Constitution, and the Ideological Embodiment of "Civil Rights" in the 1967 Nomination of Thurgood Marshall to the Supreme Court*, 82 Q. J. SPEECH 364 (1996). Marshall was opposed by a group of senators from the South. They could not assert that no black person was qualified for this position or make the racist attacks that would have been expected only a few years before. They claimed that because of his "judicial activism," he would destroy the rights of Americans. Given all this, is there still some reason that courts should defer to the legislature to make significant policy change? Is it enough that if a state supreme court adopts exceptions to the employment-at-will rule that displease some group heard by the legislature, a statute changing the law could always be passed?

[354] 533 P.2d 952 (Colo. Ct. App. 1975).

[355] 1 P.3d 615 (2000).

Good Example of trying to work through IS THERE AK, after establishing those arguments we move to RS§90

Worley talked with Joe DeCora, the company president, about job security. Worley explained to DeCora that he planned to make some major financial commitments, but he wanted to make sure that his job was secure before he did this. DeCora told Worley to make the financial commitments because his job was secure. He said that the job would remain available as long as Worley wanted it. He repeated these statements at a lunch with another person. A few months later, Worley checked with his new supervisor, asking whether his job performance was satisfactory. The supervisor said that everything was fine. Worley refinanced his home, and he bought a new car and new appliances for his home. Less than a month later, Wyoming Bottling demoted Worley one position level to route manager. The demotion included loss of the use of a company car, loss of the use of a company credit card, and an $11,000 reduction in annual salary. Worley contacted DeCora. DeCora fired him, repeating it three times in the midst of profanity.

Worley sued, asserting a number of theories. The trial court granted summary judgment on all of them. The Supreme Court of Wyoming reversed the trial court's decision on some but not all of his theories. The Supreme Court found that summary judgment was improper because Worley had alleged facts that, if proven, would justify a claim for promissory estoppel. It noted that "a claim for promissory estoppel may fail if a disclaimer, such as one in an employee handbook, makes the employee's reliance on the promise unreasonable." However, in this case, one of the statements in Wyoming Bottling's documents read: "Words or actions which are inconsistent with these rights, by any company employee or representative except the president, are not authorized and may not be relied upon." If the trier of fact found that DeCora, the president of the company, provided the assurances about job security, then Worley's reliance may be considered reasonable, and he arguably acted in justifiable reliance on DeCora's promise.

Promissary estoppel case rule remanded

ii.   *Employment-at-will and the free market*

After studying a great deal about employment-at-will, what do you think of the following scholarly comments?

CASE

In *Kumpf v. Steinhaus*,[356] the Seventh Circuit reviewed a jury verdict in a case in which Kumpf alleged that Steinhaus had wrongfully interfered with his prospects for receiving certain fees. In affirming the trial court decision, Judge Frank Easterbrook, formerly a professor at the University of Chicago Law School, took the opportunity to comment about employment-at-will:

> The privilege to manage corporate affairs is reinforced by the rationale of employment-at-will. Kumpf had no tenure of office. The lack of job security gave him a keen motive to do well. Security of position may diminish that incentive. See Richard A. Epstein, *In Defense of the Contract at Will*, 51 U. CHI. L. REV. 947 (1984). Employment-at-will, like the business judgment doctrine, also keeps debates about business matters out of the hands of courts. People who enter a contract without a fixed term know there is some prospect that their business partners may try to take advantage of them or simply make a blunder in deciding whether to continue the relationship. Yet

---

[356] 779 F.2d 1323 (7th Cir. 1985).

people's concern for their reputation and their ability to make other advantageous contracts in the future leads them to try to avoid both mistakes and opportunistic conduct. Contracting parties may sensibly decide that it is better to tolerate the risk of error — to leave correction to private arrangements — than to create a contractual right to stay in office in the absence of a "good" reason. The reason for a business decision may be hard to prove, and the costs of proof plus the risk of mistaken findings of breach may reduce the productivity of the employment relation.

Many people have concluded otherwise; contracts terminable only for cause are common. But in Wisconsin, courts enforce whichever solution the parties select. A contract at will may be terminated for any reason (including bad faith) or no reason, without judicial review; the only exception is a termination that violates "a fundamental and well-defined public policy as evidenced by existing law." *Brockmeyer v. Dun & Bradstreet.* . . . Greed — the motive Kumpf attributes to Steinhaus — does not violate a "fundamental and well-defined public policy" of Wisconsin. Greed is the foundation of much economic activity, and Adam Smith told us that each person's pursuit of his own interests drives the economic system to produce more and better goods and services for all. . . .

The contention that businesses should be more considerate of their officers should be addressed to the businesses and to legislatures. Some firms will develop reputations for kind treatment of executives, some will be ruthless. Some will seek to treat executives well but find that the exigencies of competition frustrate their plans. The rule of *this* game is that Kumpf was an employee at will and had no right to stay on if his board wanted him gone. . . . Kumpf did not bargain for legal rights against Lincoln Life, and the judge properly declined to allow the jury to convert moral and ethical claims into legal duties.

iii.   *Employment-at-will and the idea of "consent"*

Peter Linzer, writing in the *Georgia Law Review*, commented on Professor Ian Macneil's critique of the idea of "consent" in forming employment relationships.[357] He observed:

> Macneil is not a believer in the state as curer of all ills, and he expressed doubt about my conclusions in no small part because he has a firm belief that no one is truly powerless, and that what we are really dealing with are degrees of relative power. . . . [T]he thrust of the cases, the longevity cases most clearly, but also the retaliatory discharge and personnel handbook cases, is that the employee's relation to a business enterprise is more complex than just a barter of his services for pay. The employee is becoming a part-owner of the business. . . .

> One cannot draw an exact parallel between employees and franchises, since employees are paid for their services, do not make a cash investment, and

---

[357] Peter Linzer, *The Decline of Assent: At-Will Employment as a Case Study of the Breakdown of Private Law Theory*, 20 Ga. L. Rev. 323, 395, 397, 408–09 (1986).

do not normally expect to share directly in the firm's profits. Nonetheless, the employee's investment is in many ways similar to the franchisee's. The longer the employee has worked for a company, the more specific his job skills have become, the less mobile he is, and the more his investment in the firm becomes his only means of livelihood and self-respect. And the more courts are justified in hobbling the at-will doctrine because of the transaction-specific investment and the relationship that has accrued, however unconsciously, between the worker and the firm.

iv. *Farber and Matheson on the employer's need to build "trust"*

Professors Daniel A. Farber and John H. Matheson propose that a "promise is enforceable when made in furtherance of an economic activity."[358] Under this doctrine, they would enforce promises that employers make to employees. They contend:

> [A] mutual interest in a long-term and amicable relationship is part of the explanation that [economists] . . . give for the behavior of the market. For example, classical economics suggests that if someone were to come along and offer to perform an employee's job at a reduced rate, the employer would fire the existing employee and replace him by the lower-cost employee. Yet in reality this never happens. The reason is that the employer cannot afford to take action that will discourage employees from making long-term investments in their jobs. For example, much on-the-job training is actually given by older employees, who will have little incentive to provide such training if they fear their own jobs may be at stake. To maximize the benefits of their relationship, both sides need a certain amount of trust. . . .

> Because trust is essential to our basic economic institutions, it is a public good. One individual breaking trust in a dramatic way, or many individuals breaking trust less dramatically, can lead to short-run benefits for those individuals but create negative externalities. The willingness of others to trust is impaired, requiring them to invest in precautions or insure themselves against the increased risk of betrayal. Such externalities exist because of asymmetrical information: the promisor necessarily has better information about his own trustworthiness than does the promisee. For example, in the short run employers can profit by making commitments to employees, obtaining the resulting benefits, and then reneging. But in the long run, enforcement benefits promisors as a group by fostering the reliance from which they seek to benefit. Conversely, trustworthy individuals confer a social benefit by increasing the general perception of trust, thereby allowing others to decrease such costs.

---

[358] Daniel A. Farber & John H. Matheson, *Beyond Promissory Estoppel: Contract Law and the "Invisible Handshake,"* 52 U. CHI. L. REV. 903, 927, 928–29, 935–36 (1985). Copyright © University of Chicago. Reprinted with permission.

Seen in this light, the cases in which courts have pushed the doctrine of promissory estoppel beyond its stated justification and technical limitations are characterized by a strong need both by the parties and society for a high level of trust. They involve relationships in which one party must depend on the word of the other to engage in socially beneficial reliance. In the employee cases, the socially beneficial reliance takes the form of higher job performance and lower turnover. . . .

[E]conomic actors are free to make any statements they desire without fear of liability, so long as the other party understands that they are not committing themselves, are stating only their current intentions, and may change their mind at any time. In other words, where potential promisors are less than confident of their future conduct, the proposed rule fosters better information transmission by encouraging them to reveal their uncertainties. This information will help to insure that promisors will be trusted only insofar as they are worthy of trust.

Assume that we accept Farber and Matheson's argument about the value of trust for society. Does it follow that all promises by employers to employees must be enforceable to preserve that trust? I face many other-than-legal sanctions if I break my word. Why aren't these sanctions enough to defend the degree of trust needed by society? Moreover, doesn't the employer have an interest in working with people that he or she likes or at least about whom she or he has no strong feelings one way or the other? Some employees' job performance and behavior is not so bad as to present a clear case of just cause for firing but it is mildly disruptive at the workplace. Or worker X's job performance deserves the grade of C or a C+. The employer has a chance to hire worker Y, whose record indicates that she will perform at an A level. Why shouldn't the employer be able to change employees? Would it matter whether the employer and the employee work together in a close relationship and the employer must rely on the employee's skill and discretion, or whether they are more distant and the employee's tasks are more routine and involve relatively little discretion?

During the past two decades many middle managers and professionals have lost their jobs as large corporations have "downsized." Should we conclude that this experience has undercut whatever assumptions employees once had about their employment tenure, or about how much they can or should rely on promises made by their employers?

### v.	*Employment-at-will as protecting the already-protected*

A note in the *Harvard Law Review* offers the following argument:[359]

The public policy exception, as it now exists, represents a very limited attempt to control employer misconduct. It chiefly benefits employees constituting the most privileged third of the United States labor market —

---

[359] Note, *Protecting Employees at Will Against Wrongful Discharge: The Public Policy Exception*, 96 HARV. L. REV. 1931, 1950–51 (1983).

employees who already enjoy protection from the sorts of arbitrary and abusive treatment that the public policy exception is supposed to deter. Moreover, because courts have restricted its reach to only a narrow range of employer misconduct, the public policy exception reaffirms the legitimacy of the employer's otherwise unquestioned authority to fire employees at will.

Yet even when law plainly serves the goal of preserving the existing arrangement of economic and social interests, there may lie within it a kernel of emancipatory power. This potential is present in the public policy exception to the at-will rule. Dual labor market theory has shown that the extension of job security to employees in the secondary market [these jobs are generally not sheltered from competition, are often found in smaller, less stable firms, and involve short promotional ladders] may reduce labor market stratification by improving the working conditions of women, minorities, and other disfavored groups in the secondary labor market. Moreover, the concept of public policy as a limit on employer discretion can raise the expectations of employees who might otherwise believe their rights to be unworthy of vindication. A more expansive application of the public policy exception may thus operate at the levels of both corrective justice and political consciousness to effectuate a change in labor relations that, as commentators have almost unanimously agreed, is long overdue.

Basically as it stands now; these Harvard losers say it only protects people who don't need protection

vi.   *The costs of limiting the at-will rule*

Professors David Autor, John Donohue, and Stewart Schwab studied the impact of adoption of the three exceptions to employment-at-will across all the states involved.[360] Their analysis is careful, detailed, and involves extensive coding of the data. They find little impact on a state adopting the public policy or the good-faith exceptions. However, they "find a modest but robustly negative impact of . . . the implied-contract exception . . . on the employment-to-population ratio in state labor markets. This impact, which averages –0.8 percent to –1.6 percent, exists for all education and gender groups, and is detectable among states adopting at several time intervals during the sample. . . . [W]e find no evidence that these legal doctrines had any significant impact on workers' wages."[361]

Why would a state's courts adopting the implied-contract limitation on employment-at-will cause employers to hire fewer workers? How would employers get the work done?[362] How would they change their practices to blunt the impact of employment-at-will? Wouldn't an implied-contract exception give incumbent workers greater bargaining power because the "alternative to laying off workers

---

[360] David H. Autor, John J. Donohue III, & Stewart J. Schwab, *The Costs of Wrongful-Discharge Laws*, 88 REV. ECON. & STAT. 211 (2006). *See also* Max Schanzenbach, *Exceptions to Employment at Will: Raising Firing Costs or Enforcing Life-Cycle Contracts?* 5 AM. L. & ECON. REV. 470 (2003).

[361] Autor, Donohue, & Schwab, *supra* note 360, at 212.

[362] Thomas J. Miles, *Common Law Exceptions to Employment at Will and U.S. Labor Markets*, 16 J.L. ECON. & ORG. 74 (2000) finds that temporary employment increases by a statistically significant 15 percent following the adoption of the implied-contract exception.

who are pushing for higher wages would trigger the firing cost"?[363]

vii.   *The American rule(s) contrasted with other industrialized nations*

Professor Laura Beth Nielsen studied one multinational corporation's employee termination practices in the United States and in Canada.[364] Canada does not follow the American employment-at-will rule. Canadian employees not fired for cause are entitled to "reasonable notice," which can take the form of notice or monetary compensation. In some situations there is also a right to severance payments. Moreover, Canadian workers' rights to health insurance and disability compensation depend much less on employment. Canadians do not have a clear right to a jury trial, and they are likely to find a civil case diverted to alternative dispute resolution. Damages awarded in civil cases are much lower than in the United States. What is the impact of the two systems on the firm that she studied? She calls the firm PCO. She tells us:

> Although the exact costs remain unknown (and are probably unknowable), they are being directed differently. In PCO Canada, higher expenditures are channeled to employees in the form of more generous granting of probation and more generous severance; they are "paying workers." In PCO U.S., the money is channeled to the work of the legal and quasi-legal professionals employed by PCO U.S. They are "paying lawyers."[365]

Professor Julie Suk looks at the French regulations that make it difficult to fire workers.[366] Employers seldom create new jobs in France because it is so costly to lay off an employee — they tend to replace employees who retire or leave. She argues that "limiting firing discretion increases discriminatory hiring." Young people of North African descent live in segregated housing and receive a poorer education than the average French citizen. Suk explains, "An employer knowing how costly it will be to fire a full-time employee is less likely to hire candidates whom they consider risky hires. This leads to both 'rational' and racially biased failures to hire racial minorities."[367]

The *Financial Times* is published in London. In an article published in 2005, it stated: "America grows while Europe stalls for many reasons, among them disparities in flexibility caused by employment laws. Europe will never recover until

---

[363] Autor, Donohue, & Schwab, *supra* note 360, at 227.

[364] Laura Beth Nielsen, *Paying Workers or Paying Lawyers: Employee Termination Practices in the United States and Canada*, 21 LAW & POL'Y 247 (1999).

[365] The Canadian approach to termination may have another benefit. Allan Lind, Jerald Greenberg, Kimberley S. Scott, & Thomas D. Welchans, *The Winding Road from Employee to Complainant: Situational and Psychological Determinants of Wrongful Termination Claims*, 45 ADMIN. SCI. Q. 557 (2000), find that wrongful termination claims were most strongly correlated with the way workers felt they had been treated at the time of termination and with their expected winnings from such a claim. The approach of the American branch of the firm that Neilsen studied would seem more likely to create plaintiffs than the Canadian branch's way of handing the situation.

[366] Julie C. Suk, *Discrimination at Will: Job Security Protections and Equal Employment Opportunity in Conflict*, 60 STAN. L. REV. 73 (2007).

[367] *Id.* at 97.

employment protection statutes are modernised and politicians restore flexibility to employers and workers."[368]

f. In conclusion . . . a hypothetical

Consider the tale of Ann Vale. The story is based on an actual case.[369] We changed all the names to protect the guilty.

Ms. Ann Vale, until last week, worked for a famous multinational corporation, selling plastics to industrial users. She had worked for this corporation for five years. She quit a high-paying job with another firm to take a position with the multinational. Officials of the multinational recruited her. They said that the multinational rewarded merit and offered a bright future to those who could do the job. Her written contract with the multinational contained no provision defining its duration, and it did not state explicitly that it was an employment-at-will contract. She was given an employee handbook that provided for annual performance reviews, as well as notice of deficiencies in performance and a hearing, before an employee would be fired. Copies of these handbooks were given to all employees.

Until recently, Ms. Vale was on the fast track to success. A group of purchasing agents for companies that bought large amounts of plastics were "her accounts." This meant that she contacted them regularly and sought their orders. Sales people at the multinational were assigned specific geographical regions as "their territories." She was noted for her aggressiveness and skill in closing hard-to-make sales. She was one of the best salespeople in the plastics division of the multinational corporation. Her performance reviews all said that she was an outstanding salesperson. Two months ago, two competing manufacturers of plastics each offered her a job with large raises in base salary, benefits, and commission. She talked to her supervisor at the multinational corporation, and he assured her that her future was assured with the multinational corporation. As a result, she turned down both offers.

[handwritten margin note: Turned down two job offers cuz assured her future was assured]

Last summer, Ms. Vale complained to managers at the multinational corporation about the prostitutes that the multinational furnished to salesmen at the corporation's annual convention in Las Vegas. She also complained many times about what she called "the anti-woman jokes" that managers at her firm frequently told at sales meetings. She objected to the corporation's "casting couch" road to success for less competent women. One of the managers told her that she was not "one of the boys." In addition, she has often told secretaries who work at the multinational's main offices that they should form a union.

A month ago, Ms. Vale sold a very large order of plastics to a customer who wanted to deal with her. Her supervisors decided that the sale was "out of her territory." The customer "belonged" to another salesperson. One of the top officers in the sales department told her that she would get the commission because the

---

[368] Diana Furchtgoot-Roth, *What America's Labour Laws Can Teach Europe*, Financial Times, Aug. 12, 2005, at 11.

[369] The actual case was settled. Ann Vale received a substantial sum in exchange for her signature on a release of liability. However, she did not get returned to the fast track to success in the major corporation for which she formerly worked.

person assigned to the territory could never have closed that sale. However, Ms. Vale's immediate boss gave the commission to Ms. X, in whose territory the sale was made. Those who work with Ms. Vale assume that the boss and Ms. X have a long-term sexual relationship.

Ms. Vale complained to an executive of the multinational who worked at its home office. She mentioned the personal relationship between her boss and Ms. X. Within a week, Ms. Vale was fired. The company did not follow its internal procedure detailed in the employment manual, which called for warning, notice, and a hearing. A vice president of the multinational wrote a letter to Ms. Vale. He said that she was insubordinate and a source of dissension among her fellow employees. He stated that this was an emergency situation, and so usual procedures could not be followed.

Ms. Vale called a good friend who was one of the multinational's executives and told him what had happened. The executive was angry and promised that something would be done. Within a week, a top official of the human resources department offered her another job at her former salary and commission rate. However, the job was in a division of the multinational corporation known as "corporate Siberia." This division has a reputation for making poor products, and newspapers that cover business matters have reported that it is likely to close soon. She rejected the offer of this position.

Ms. Vale comes to your law firm and asks a senior partner what to do. While she has some resources, she cannot invest much in attorney's fees, costs of investigation, and the like. The senior partner and associates who work for him will investigate Ms. Vale's claims under the various federal and state statutes prohibiting discrimination against women. The partner asks you to investigate possible causes of action based on common-law theories. It is unclear which state's law governs the transaction. The corporation's home office is in California. Ms. Vale operated out of the Pacific Coast regional office, which has its headquarters in Arizona. Ms. Vale and the representative of the multinational corporation originally negotiated her employment contract in Wisconsin. Another member of the firm will work on arguments about which state's law applies. You are to consider the common-law theories that courts in each of these states are likely to apply. (Once you discover which state's laws are most helpful to Ms. Vale's case, your colleague will pursue arguments that that state's laws should control this transaction.)

D.   LONG-TERM RELATIONSHIPS IN COMMERCIAL TRANSACTIONS

In this section, we turn from family and employment to buying and selling goods and dealing with ownership and control. These are settings in which we might expect contract law to be central, and the situations brought before the courts to fit neatly into contract rules. Sometimes both of these things will be true. For example, there are contracts designed to allocate the risks of rising or falling markets, and the party who guesses wrong is seldom excused.

Sometimes, contract law stands at the margin of business transactions and exerts some degree of indirect influence. The chance that one might be sued can be one of several factors affecting behavior, even when the businessperson is unsure about the exact risks involved. Contract law can also reinforce other norms and sanctions. However, much behavior in commercial settings is relatively unaffected by the legal enforceability of contracts and rules dealing with performance or damages. In many situations, no one even thinks about law or lawyers until, perhaps, they appear on the scene.

Other-than-legal sanctions channel business behavior in most cases. Many transactions reflect what the economist Arthur Okun called "the invisible hand-shake."[370] For example, a trader can have a long-term relationship with a particular trading partner or be part of a group of traders. These relationships benefit businesspeople. For example, relationships create and draw on other-than-legal norms and sanctions. Those who depart from acceptable practices risk losing a relationship or position within the group of traders.

1. "Braiding": Relational Norms and Sanctions Intertwined with Legal Ones[371]

Jack Ramsey, the retired general manager of S.C. Johnson & Sons (a large company with major international business), told a story about Johnson's practices during the Great Depression of the 1930s. Johnson had long bought containers (what were then called "tin cans") for its products from three companies. All three suffered large losses because of the economic situation in the nation during these times. Johnson could have had the three bid against each other to bring down the cost of containers and increase Johnson's returns on its sales. It did not do this. Rather, it determined which of the three container firms needed Johnson's order the most at that particular time in order to stay in business, and it placed the order with that firm.

Five or six years later, Ramsey noted, things were very different. The United States was at war, and much of the economy was under government control. Steel was rationed, and there were many shortages of products, such as containers for consumer goods. "We never wanted [for] a can," Ramsey said. "They owed us because of how we treated them in the Depression." The companies that made cans were probably also influenced by the potential business that Johnson might place with them once the war was over. Perhaps it was important too that the people who ran Johnson and its three suppliers all knew each other. Notice that the firms did not have legally enforceable contract rights against each other in either the time of the Depression or during World War II. Ramsey stressed the difference between what is beneficial in the short term and long-term interests. Moreover, he saw Johnson's behavior as what was morally called for.

In the past, typically, business relationships were left relatively unstructured — people ordered from their supplier or they made a deal on an exchange. In some situations, however, parties structured their arrangements in great detail. Often

---

[370] ARTHUR OKUN, PRICES & QUANTITIES: A MACROECONOMIC ANALYSIS (The Brookings Institution 1981).

[371] *See* Ronald J. Gilson, Charles F. Sabel & Robert E. Scott, *Braiding: The Interaction of Formal and Informal Contracting in Theory, Practice, and Doctrine*, 110 COLUM. L. REV. 1377 (2010) (collaboration rests on a governance structure that, over time, creates confidence in the capabilities and trust in the character of the counterparty).

this would be the case when powerful third parties were involved, such as those who lend money to finance the deal. However, in these more structured arrangements, the concern was usually for business needs rather than legal enforceability. Even when lawyers prepared elaborate contract documents, the businesspeople and engineers who carried out the transaction often followed conventional practices rather than reading the written contract. Engineers, for example, often read the specifications for making the product and ignored the rest of the documents.

When a dispute arises, taking a legal approach to it can have costs. Our culture seldom approves of making a legal attack against another party who is trying to cooperate in good faith.[372] Some normative vocabularies call on the parties to seek a solution that benefits both or imposes burdens roughly equally on both. Niklas Luhmann argues that going from a cooperative vocabulary to a legal one changes people's reactions. It may make it harder to continue the relationship. One party asserts that she is right and the other person is wrong. Talking the language of rights and legal duties initiates a chain of events that are largely out of the control of the parties and introduces uncertainty. One party is claiming that she need not consider anything other than the law.

Professor Stewart Macaulay interviewed the sales manager for a manufacturer of machine tools:

> [O]ne can get drastic problems in selling machines. For example, when a machine fails to work, a customer is likely to be subject to a great deal of delay. He will refuse to pay for the machine, and he may bill us for downtime. He will be out of production and want the profits he could have made with our machine. But this is not something any lawyer could handle without putting you out of business. This must be handled on a business basis by a salesperson and the person who bought the machine. We don't look for legal loopholes to avoid obligations like this. After all, you are selling reliability and your reputation gets around.

Professor Josh Whitford interviewed a strategic buyer at a major mid-volume OEM (original equipment manufacturer).

> Buyer: We work with that supplier. If there is a manufacturing fault, it is theirs, if engineering is at fault, it is ours.

> JW: Are there disputes about whether or not it is manufacturing or engineering?

> Buyer (laughing): Oh, there's always disputes.

> JW: But you don't call in the lawyers?

> Buyer: No sir. We do not try to cheat our suppliers. We try to be fair and honest.[373]

---

[372] *See* Luhmann, *supra* note 37.

[373] JOSH WHITFORD, THE NEW OLD ECONOMY: NETWORKS, INSTITUTIONS, AND THE ORGANIZATIONAL TRANSFOR-MATION OF AMERICAN MANUFACTURING 87 (Oxford University Press 2006). This is not to say that some

There are other reasons why many businesspeople do not see litigating a contract dispute as a good idea. Even if a party wins, it must usually pay lawyers and expert witness fees. One mid-volume supplier told Professor Josh Whitford: "You get long-term agreements, but I can't outspend them in court.[374] The litigation process is very slow, and a participant will not see any return on her investment in the process for a long time. Many of the firm's managers and engineers will be taken away from their jobs and diverted to playing roles in the litigation. They are not back at the plant making money. Additionally, contract law rules on damages often limit any recovery to far less than what has actually been lost. (Recall *Hadley v. Baxendale* and the requirement for proof of damages with reasonable certainty.) Also, litigation is public, and the firm may be required to disclose things that it would rather keep secret.

Still another reason for the reluctance among businesspeople to litigate a contract dispute is that many legal rules in the field of contracts are very qualitative, and so good arguments can be made for both parties. This means that it is hard to predict whether litigation will be a good gamble. For example, under UCC § 2-615(a), which is covered in more detail in Volume II of this casebook, a seller can be excused from performing "if performance as agreed has been made impracticable by the occurrence of a contingency the non-occurrence of which was a basic assumption on which the contract was made." Was performance "impracticable"? Was non-occurrence of the contingency a "basic assumption"? Both questions require normative judgments about facts, rather than answers that turn on easy-to-establish events in the world.

Finally, all you may accomplish through litigation is to drive the other firm into bankruptcy — where you will recover, at best, a few cents on the dollar of the amount of your judgment. However, businesses do tend to litigate when copyrights or patents are involved.

Interviews by Professor Stewart Macaulay with various businesspeople and their lawyers show, however, that not all of them express disdain for contract and the legal rules governing enforceability.

Interview with a partner in a major law firm with a commercial practice:

Mr. X stated that he was impatient with businessmen who see contract as a scheme by lawyers designed to get fees. He is sick and tired of hearing, "We can deal on the basis of good faith. We can trust old Max."

> Unsophisticated businessmen seem to need to be "burned" to understand the risks they are running. Just because your house has never burned down does not prove that you do not need fire insurance. There is a great need for preventive law, and it could result in long-run savings. Questions do not arise from the lack of good faith. One simply has an honest misunderstanding: people tend not to admit that the other person's position is an honest misunderstanding, they argue, and you have a dispute.

---

lawyers are not masters at mediation, searching for solutions acceptable to both sides and making sure that no one feels cheated.

[374] *Id.*

In about 90 percent of contracts involving the building industry you will have some kind of dispute before the building is up and paid for. One just doesn't know what he is getting. Here contracts are most important. Builders ought to know this because they are in court often enough trying to defend the job they have done. The number of disputes is in direct proportion to the size and complexity of the building. The parties simply cannot define everything called for in a contract to construct a 12-story building. The parties never seem to agree in advance on what kind of guarantee the builder is giving. Builders don't follow plans and specifications; they "interpret them." They get overextended, and then they try to cut corners.

Interview with the general counsel of a nationally known manufacturing firm:

We negotiate overriding agreements to cover all our dealings with the aviation industry or subcontracts relating to it. We are extremely careful. An airframe manufacturer must negotiate with the airlines in great detail as to the warranty it will give them. Obviously, the airframe builders have a fantastic exposure to damage suits if anything goes wrong with the airplane. This exposure backs up to every one of their basic suppliers. The only way to handle this is by a carefully drafted contract defining responsibility and then by insurance to cover the responsibility undertaken. You will get careful contracts, if the businessmen have any sense, whenever there is exposure to serious liability — products liability, the possibility of liability for patent infringement, or the possibility of liability to workmen who come on the premises. Perhaps it is the influence of the insurance company.

Some practices changed about 30 years ago. Prior to that time, most manufacturers were vertically integrated: they bought raw materials and made in their own factories most of the pieces and components that they assembled into their products. Starting in the 1980s, American manufacturers faced great competition from Japan. There came to be great pressure to change the organization of their manufacturing processes. Many U.S. manufacturers outsourced production in order to gain the technical knowledge of their suppliers and to avoid or undermine labor unions. This was the "network" approach.[375] Manufacturers had to decide which

---

[375] *See* Daniel Jutras, *The Legal Dimensions of Everyday Life*, 16 Can. J. of L. & Soc'y 45 (2001). Jutras summarizes in English an article published in French by J.G. Belley, *Le Contrat Entre Droit, Économie et Société* (1998). Jutras reports that Belley studied ALCAN, a large aluminum company. Belley tells the story of a transformation of the economic culture of corporations — from the traditional culture of relationships of trust, confidence, and interdependence to a modern, technocratic culture of quality control, and coordination, driven by fixed objectives of growth. Previous scholarship had emphasized the importance of implicit norms and personal bonds of trust in long-term commercial contracts. Belley underlines the unresolved tension created in those contracts by the introduction of the depersonalized logic of expert systems and explicit demands for quality production while the contract price is reduced over time. Supply contracts at ALCAN are very explicit, but Belley's research shows that the behavior of parties in circumstances of uncertainty is guided by unspoken shared assumptions, which make up the underlying culture of the contract. There is a plurality of such cultures, which together provide structure and depth to the terms of interaction between ALCAN and its suppliers. Next to the juridical culture of the explicit contract, there is, in particular, an economic culture of profitability and pragmatism, at once traditional (resting on interpersonal bonds of trust) and modern (resting on the

suppliers were worth the cost of creating or maintaining a long-term relationship and, conversely, which components could be obtained on the basis of price, by awarding the manufacturing contract to a low bidder.

Suppliers that wanted a long-term relationship generally applied by filling out a form that asked for a great deal of information about what the supplier would bring to the relationship.[376] The buyer would typically ask for the right to inspect the potential supplier's place of business and gain access to the supplier's records, personnel, and facilities. If the potential supplier were successful in its bid to become an official supplier, it would be subject to a Master Supply Agreement (MSA). The MSA is not a contract to buy goods. It is an agreement about how the two firms are going to do business.[377] Much of a typical MSA is made up of provisions designed to break down the barriers between the two firms. The MSA clears a space for extra-legal modes of contract governance.

The structure of an MSA is formal and detailed. Buyers typically invest a great deal in communicating what is required. It is not enough just to specify the product to be delivered on a particular date. The manufacturing processes will be specified. There is intense monitoring; the buyer's engineers spend much time at the supplier's production facilities. John Deere's MSA, for example, requires that a John Deere engineer sign off on several steps involved in the production process, certifying that each step was done properly. The seller's technical personnel are often expected to suggest new techniques for making products, as well as new products that will benefit the buyer. The parties learn about each other through the product design process, as well as sessions devoted to solving problems. Great efforts are made to avoid misunderstandings. Suppliers are rated by the buyer, and there are meetings to explain questions.

The buyer issues an order for those products that are needed immediately; it does not carry a large inventory. The MSA usually gives the buyer a right to cancel any order "for convenience." Some buyers do not specify what they will pay if they cancel orders. They say only that they will pay such charges of the seller "as shall result from an equitable adjustment." Some cancellation clauses require the buyer to agree to pay the contract price for items completed before the cancellation. The buyer will also pay for costs allocable solely to the canceled order, for any work already in process, and any materials purchased for that order that the seller cannot salvage. There are other provisions, but generally when an order is canceled, buyers do not put the seller where it would have been had the contract been performed.

Buyers often have a list of standard charges for various defects in performance. These are authorized as deductions from what the buyer must pay for the goods shipped and accepted. They cover a few defective items in a large order, packaging that does not meet the buyer's requirements, minor delays, and the like. One reason

---

cold technocratic comfort of expert systems). Furthermore, the process of explicitly articulating the terms of cooperation necessarily affects the implicit culture of the relationship.

[376] *See* Lisa Bernstein, *Private Ordering, Social Capital, and Network Governance in Procurement Contracts: A Preliminary Exploration.* (Unpublished manuscript 2015).

[377] Walmart, for example, requires those who become its suppliers to furnish a certificate from an insurance company stating that both the supplier and Walmart are covered for product liability claims.

for making these charges is to gain the attention of those higher up in the seller's organization. The deductions usually signal that these details actually matter and are not something to be left to those who package the goods. More serious failures by the seller ("epidemic breaches") give the buyer much greater rights to take over and minimize the losses. Buyers work with defaulting sellers, doing a "root cause analysis." Buyers hesitate to cancel contracts with suppliers, even those who are seriously deficient. The costs of finding substitute suppliers are great enough that it affects a buyer's judgments about when to cancel.

We can get some understanding of these kinds of collaborative relationships, and what the buyer can do when major problems arise, by considering the story of the Boeing 787 "Dreamliner," which begins in 2003. Boeing designed an elaborate outsourcing process for its radical new airplane design. The 787 was supposed to combine lightweight materials (e.g., carbon fiber as a substitute for aluminum) and fuel-efficient engines to make it 20 percent cheaper to fly and one-third less costly to maintain than older passenger jet planes. The plan was for all of the pieces of the plane to be made outside of Boeing's factories and then shipped to those factories, where Boeing would assemble all of the pieces. The plan was to build a plane out of its components in three days.

The grand outsourcing plan proved to be a disaster. Many of the suppliers had themselves outsourced the engineering to even smaller companies, and these smaller firms proved unable to do all of the necessary work on time. The new carbon-fiber substitute for aluminum proved extremely difficult to deal with for firms that did not have extensive prior experience in working with it. Many suppliers could not conform to Boeing's engineering tolerances. As a result, the parts delivered to Boeing's factory in Washington did not fit together. All of these problems caused production of the 787 to be delayed again and again. The first plane was ultimately delivered to All Nippon Airways, a Japanese airline, on September 25, 2011 — approximately three years late.[378]

Boeing sent large teams of its own people into suppliers' plants to show them how to do the job. Dozens or hundreds of Boeing employees were sent to attack problems at plants in Italy, Japan, and South Carolina. Boeing bought two large suppliers and turned their facilities into Boeing factories.

Spirit AeroSystems Holdings, Inc., was one of Boeing's largest suppliers on the 787 project. The delays caused by other suppliers meant that Boeing was not ready to receive Spirit's performance at its Washington plant. In an April 2008 filing with the Securities and Exchange Commission,[379] Spirit asserted that Boeing had agreed to provide Spirit with cash-advance payments approximating the value of the components that it would have delivered under the original 787 production schedule. The new agreement was initiated with a $124 million cash payment reflected in Spirit's first-quarter 2008 results.

Boeing worked hard to keep its customers for the 787, but some airlines canceled their orders. In October 2011, China Eastern Airlines announced that it was

---

[378] *See* Stephen Brashear, *Finally . . . A First Flight for the 787* [photographs of the ceremonial delivery]. *Available at* stephenbrashear.com/2011/finally-a-first-flight-for-the-787.

[379] Spirit AeroSystems Holdings, Inc., Report (Form 8-K) (Apr. 8, 2008).

canceling orders for 24 of the 787s that it had ordered. However, it replaced this order with a new one for 45 smaller Boeing 737 jets. In a report filed with the Hong Kong Stock Exchange, China Eastern said that it had negotiated "significant price concessions" with Boeing, enabling China Eastern to acquire the smaller planes at a sum that was lower than their 2008 catalog prices (which would normally have been in effect, per the 2008 agreement to buy the 787 Dreamliners).[380]

Obviously, the 787 story reads very differently from what might have happened if Boeing had sued its suppliers for Boeing's lost anticipated profits caused by the suppliers' material breach. Boeing's customers, as far as we know, canceled some orders but did not sue for the profits they would have made flying the 787s had they been delivered on time. Many contracts for the sale of passenger aircraft set a price formula for delays; we do not know the contractual details of Boeing's arrangement with its customers. Boeing finally managed to produce the 787 Dreamliner and deliver finished airplanes to those customers that had not canceled their orders.

So far we have told a relatively positive story about outsourcing and the creation of collaborative relationships between large corporate buyers and their suppliers. However, Professor Josh Whitford tells us:

> In spite of very real efforts by OEMs to reformulate organizational structures and to build collaborative relationships with suppliers, these relationships are nevertheless frequently characterized by "bad waltzing" that differs fundamentally from the simple use of hard bargaining tactics backed up with the threat of exit power. Simple hard bargaining is widely understood by suppliers to be well within the norms of everyday business and predictable enough that it need not undermine collaboration. But interviews with OEMs and suppliers in the American Upper Midwest show that relationships are also systematically plagued by ambiguous signaling and rife with no-holds-barred tactics used by OEMs exploiting vulnerabilities opened up by the new relationships for short-term gain. These deviations, which unequivocally deviate from official firm strategies and which both sides agree should not occur, happen often and unpredictably enough that they virtually force suppliers to hedge their own collaboration, undermining the efforts even of those in OEMs and suppliers who are genuinely working to create systemic change.[381]

Whitford explains some of the practices that undercut collaboration. Some members of the buyer's firm are evaluated by how much they can contribute to the firm's bottom line. They are under great pressure to "make their numbers." Such officials can take information gained from suppliers in networks with a firm's technical personnel and give it to other potential suppliers, so that they can bid less than the supplier who worked with the buyer's officials on how to make the product. They can demand that the accepted suppliers cut their prices by a certain percentage each year, even when this will undercut the production of the new product that the buyer and the supplier have worked out. The new system of

---

[380] *See* David Kesmodel, *China Eastern Cancels Order for 24 Boeing 787 Dreamliner Jets*, WALL STREET JOURNAL, Oct. 17, 2011.

[381] Whitford, *supra* note 373, at 95–96.

industrial production is very much a work in progress.

2.   Contract Law in Action: Vindicating Rights or Provoking Compromise and Settlement?

In Chapter 2, we considered Professor David Campbell's argument that contract remedies are designed, in large part, to provoke one party to help his or her contract partner when the partner is having trouble performing.[382] At best, the aggrieved party will often be pushed to accept a settlement rather than an award of damages. Only in a very limited group of situations will the law order specific performance, and while large awards of damages are possible, few plaintiffs will be able to jump all of the hurdles necessary to gain them. Sometimes, all that such an award would achieve would be to push the defendant into bankruptcy, where the plaintiff might recover little or nothing of its claim.

Indeed, there is a widespread custom whereby buyers can cancel orders if they no longer need the item. Sometimes a buyer who wishes to exercise such a right will offer to pay some of the seller's reliance losses. However, calling off a contract is not always accepted by the seller, and the law of contracts and its remedial system may serve as leverage in unhappy negotiations for a settlement. For example, US Airways made contracts to buy Boeing 737 and 757 aircraft in the early 1980s. From the late 1980s to the mid-1990s, US Airways was in great financial trouble and faced a very real threat of bankruptcy. Several times during this period, Boeing agreed to postpone delivery and payment dates for the aircraft, and the contracts were reworked in other ways. In 1994 and 1995, the contracts were revised so that the planes would not be built until between 1998 and 2005.

However, in November 1996, new management at US Airways selected Airbus, Boeing's major competitor, to supply up to 400 Airbus aircraft to replace a substantial part of US Airways' fleet of planes. Then it told Boeing to "tear up the contracts" for the 737s and 757s. When US Airways failed to make a payment required by the revised contracts in November 1997, Boeing sued for about $450 million.

US Airways, however, asserted that Boeing's refusal to cancel the contract was a departure from a long pattern of practice in the aircraft industry. Boeing, the airline asserted, had more orders than it could fill on time. US Airways' cancellation would allow Boeing to sell the planes it would have built for US Airways to other airlines for a higher price. US Airways asserted that in such a situation, industry custom was to accept a cancellation. US Airways also argued that Boeing's many concessions on delivery dates to US Airways during the life of the contracts waived the basic obligation of US Airways to buy the planes. Boeing denied that contract cancellations were the custom of the industry.[383]

---

[382] *See* Chapter 2, section F.1., *supra.*

[383] Stanley Holmes, *US Airways Says Boeing After Revenge, Not Justice,* SEATTLE TIMES, Nov. 30, 1997, at E1; Frederic M. Biddle, *US Airways Attacks Boeing's Problems with Production in Legal Dispute,* WALL STREET JOURNAL, Nov. 18, 1997, at B10.

[margin notes: One thing to change forems, another to leave for competitor]

Even though Boeing's strategy in the past had been to make concessions to help US Airways cope with its financial difficulties, Boeing still sued US Airways for breach of contract when the endgame was reached. It was one thing to roll over delivery and payment dates in the face of US Airways' grave financial problems. It was something else to tear up the contract entirely so that US Airways could turn to a competitor to supply its need for planes for the foreseeable future.

[margin notes: Settled out of ct. i conceded bound by K]

As usually happens, the parties did not litigate to judgment. They settled the case, but as part of the settlement, US Airways acknowledged that it was bound to the contract with Boeing.[384] Why might this acknowledgment have been important to Boeing? *⇒ for future*

3. Commercial Relationships and Private Governments

[margin note: ADR = Alternative dispute res]

The materials that follow deal with alternative dispute resolution (ADR) in commercial matters. The parties, by contract or by membership in an association, "agree" to submit their disputes to a private legal system rather than to the public courts. The most common types of ADR agreements are agreements either to negotiate, to mediate, or to arbitrate. Some contracts call for a graduated process involving all three of these methods, beginning with informal negotiation and ending with binding arbitration. All types of ADR, however, have become increasingly common in commercial contracts. Businesses often see ADR procedures as saving them time and money, and broad judicial interpretations of statutes regulating ADR, such as the Federal Arbitration Act (the FAA), have reassured parties that their agreements to arbitrate are likely to be enforced. Despite the proliferation of ADR contracts, however, many lawyers remain unfamiliar with the implications and applications of the various types of ADR procedures.

Thomas J. Stipanowich, a former law professor at the University of Kentucky, has identified four questions that law students should consider when studying ADR:[385] *[margin/inline note: 4 Qs when studying ADRs]*

(1) What forms of agreement now exist for out-of-court issue resolution and conflict management?

(2) What roles are played by third-party "interveners" (such as mediators or arbitrators), and what constraints, if any, are placed on their selection?

(3) To what extent are particular kinds of agreements given legal effect, and on what basis?

---

[384] The case was settled in April 1998. US Airways paid Boeing an undisclosed amount, acknowledged that it had breached the contract, and dropped its countersuit against Boeing. Susan Carey, *US Airways Is About to Order Airbus A-330s*, WALL STREET JOURNAL, July 2, 1998, at A3. There was speculation in the press about whether Boeing had so poisoned the relationship by refusing a cancellation that US Airways would not buy aircraft from it in the future. Of course, with only two available suppliers of large passenger aircraft in the world, US Airways would have benefited from at least the tacit threat to buy Boeing planes in any future negotiations with Airbus.

[385] Thomas J. Stipanowich, *Contracts Symposium: Contract and Conflict Management*, 2001 WIS. L. REV. 831, 836. Copyright © 2005 by The Board of Regents of the University of Wisconsin System. Reprinted by permission of the Wisconsin Law Review.

(4) What are the legal results of each particular method of issue resolution? How do courts treat decisions/evaluations by interveners or settlement agreements facilitated by interveners?

Consider these questions while reading the following materials.

a.   Negotiation and mediation

People have often included in their contracts or agreements a duty to negotiate with each other in the event of a future dispute about the contract, or to agree to submit their disputes to a third party for "mediation." In the past, courts often refused to enforce these agreements, characterizing them as indefinite (and unenforceable) "agreements to agree," or as being against public policy. Stipanowich reports that today, however, mediation is the "centerpiece" of court, agency, and private ADR programs.

Mediation, and agreements to engage in less formal negotiation, are not binding dispute-resolution methods. Such agreements usually simply require the parties to attempt to resolve their dispute in some type of structured process prior to resorting to litigation. Agreements to negotiate often require that the parties negotiate "in good faith." Agreements to mediate require parties to use a third-party mediator to facilitate their negotiations. But agreements to negotiate or to participate in mediation do not require parties to reach an agreement at the end of the process, nor do they give a third-party intervener the authority to settle the dispute or to bind the parties to a particular outcome.

This does not mean that negotiation or mediation requirements constitute merely an empty ritual that must be complied with before litigation can commence. Negotiation, far from being an "alternative" form of dispute resolution, is a critical part of a lawyer's day-to-day practice. Most parties to a dispute engage in some type of negotiation, either between lawyers or between the parties themselves, before a lawsuit is filed in court. Advocates of contractually mandated negotiation argue that most contract disputes lend themselves to resolution by this type of direct negotiation, and that a contractual agreement to negotiate in good faith helps to "start the ball rolling." The intervention of a mediator offers parties a chance to settle their differences on a mutually acceptable basis while avoiding much of the cost, delay, and adversarial practices associated with binding arbitration and court trials.[386]

Mediation itself can take many forms. Consider the following excerpt from Stipanowich's work:[387]

> Some years ago, an empirical study of mediated construction cases revealed the extraordinary diversity of the process in a single transactional sector. Reported experiences involved disputes of many different kinds, ranging from $0 to $100,000,000. Although nine-tenths of the proceedings were completed in ten days or less, a few went on for months; process costs varied considerably. Mediators used a variety of different techniques in the

---

[386] *Id.* at 848.

[387] *Id.*

course of facilitating negotiations. The result was usually monetary settlement, although agreements to perform certain work and other solutions were achieved in some cases.

Developing technology has already created new variants of mediation. In eBay's new online dispute resolution program, thousands of cases are being directly negotiated or mediated without the parties ever seeing one another.[388] Mediators facilitate online discussions between parties who are frequently separated by many time zones, over the course of hours or days. Although negotiations usually are conducted in English, multilingual mediators are sometimes employed.

In practice, mediation means different things to different people, and the mediation experience varies greatly depending upon the nature of the problems presented (or the way they are defined), the goals of participants, and the styles and strategies of mediators. Discussions may be narrowly focused on legal or factual questions and the possible outcomes of trial or arbitration, or more broadly aimed to encompass business or personal standards and goals, and perhaps even to empower individuals to deal with one another more effectively in the course of a relationship. Indeed, some view mediation as a vehicle for achieving important human values such as self-awareness and self-transcendence through the process of compromise. Some lawyers find mediation a welcome opportunity to function as a healer of human conflict rather than a "hired gun."

Stipanowich notes that mediators themselves also exhibit a wide variety of behaviors, ranging from avoiding any expression of opinion in the disputes to emphasizing their role as an "agent of reality" and therefore directly stating their opinions of the merits of the parties' positions or the reasonableness of a proposed compromise.[389]

The judicial response to negotiation and mediation agreements has been mixed. Although courts seem to be increasingly willing to direct parties to negotiate or mediate, policing the results of failed processes has proven difficult, particularly with respect to mediated settlement discussions, where strong public policies supporting confidentiality reinforce the natural reluctance of courts to police negotiations.[390] Some courts, citing policies and precedents favoring broad enforceability of *arbitration* agreements, have applied the Federal Arbitration Act (FAA) to agreements to mediate. Other courts have simply (and erroneously) treated mediation and arbitration as synonymous terms.[391] Stipanowich argues that this is inappropriate:[392]

---

[388] [111] *See* Ethan Katsh et al., *E-Commerce, E-Disputes, and E-Dispute Resolution: In the Shadow of "eBay Law,"* 15 Ohio St. J. on Disp. Resol. 708–12 (2000).

[389] Stipanowich, *supra* note 385, at 850.

[390] *Id.* at 869.

[391] *Id.* at 861, *citing* Cecala v. Moore, 982 F. Supp. 609 (N.D. Ill. 1997) (applying the FAA to a mediation agreement without distinguishing the two) and CB Richard Ellis, Inc. v. American Envtl. Waste Mgmt., No. 98-CV-4183 (E.D. N.Y. 1998).

[392] Stipanowich, *supra* note 385, at 862–63.

Modern arbitration statutes are founded on the proposition that private arrangements for final and binding resolution of disputes are a good thing, not only because they relieve courts of a commensurate burden, but because they afford parties considerable latitude in structuring mechanisms for resolving conflict in their own way, according to their own timetable and their own particular needs. These broad principles are applicable not only to binding arbitration, but also to mediation and other ADR processes that hold the promise of an out-of-court resolution in a setting defined by private agreement.

In contrast to arbitration, however, mediation does not effectively operate as an all-purpose substitute for litigation and a guarantee that disputes will be finally resolved in the alternative forum. . . . [P]roblems quickly emerge when one moves beyond a superficial policy analysis and seriously considers the implications of enforcement under the FAA and modern state arbitration statutes — all of which are to varying degrees incompatible with the intent to mediate.

Consider, first of all, the fundamental premise of "enforcing" an agreement to mediate: as reflected in the emerging case law, the judicial order often entails no more than a mandate to sit down together in the presence of a mediator. While the normal incidents of litigation may be temporarily suspended, there is no wholesale substitution of private process for public, only the contingency that a negotiated settlement will end some or all of the litigation.

Mediators very rarely have any authority with respect to motion practice or discovery, and are not empowered to issue subpoenas for the attendance of witnesses or the production of documents; arbitration statutes contemplate the possibility of arbitral subpoenas and enable courts to exert their authority to facilitate such orders. While extended participation in pre-trial activities may be deemed an implied relinquishment of the right to adjudicate disputes through arbitration, the same cannot be said of resort to mediation; in the absence of contrary agreement, resort to mediated negotiation may be had at any point up to and during trial.

As developed in the courts, moreover, the law of arbitration has evolved to protect arbitrators from liability in the course of their arbitral duties . . . although the issue of mediator immunity is much debated, mediators are a far cry from full-fledged judge surrogates . . . the well-recognized concept of quasi-judicial immunity for arbitrators does not necessarily establish a precedent for mediator immunity.

Finally, and most tellingly, arbitration statutes establish a framework for judicial review, vacatur, modification, and enforcement of awards rendered by arbitrators . . . the [FAA] clearly contemplates a judgment rendered through adversary adjudication, not through facilitated negotiation.

What, then, should judges do with contractual agreements to negotiate or mediate disputes? When mediation is part of a multi-step dispute resolution process culminating in arbitration, courts have sometimes compelled mediation as a 'condition precedent' to the right to arbitrate.[393] Other courts have left this decision up to the arbitrator.[394] The more fundamental question, though, is whether courts should force parties into a process intended to achieve cooperation and consensus. Stipanowich cites an Australian tribunal on this issue:

> Conciliation or mediation is essentially consensual, and the opponents of enforceability contend that it is futile to enforce something which requires the co-operation and consent of a party when co-operation and consent cannot be enforced; equally, they say that there can be no loss to the other party if for want of co-operation and consent the consensual process would have led to no result. The proponents of enforceability contend that this misconceives the objectives of alternative dispute resolution, saying that the most fundamental resistance to compromise can wane and turn to co-operation and consent if the dispute is removed from the adversarial procedures of the courts and exposed to procedures designed to promote compromise, in particular where a skilled conciliator or mediator is interposed between the parties. What is enforced is not co-operation and consent but participation in a process from which co-operation and consent might come.

b. Arbitration

Arbitration agreements are quite different than agreements to negotiate or mediate disputes. Although there are some "non-binding" arbitration procedures,[395] arbitration agreements are more often written to be "binding." A binding arbitration agreement means that the parties to the agreement have agreed to forfeit almost all judicial review of their dispute and be bound by the result reached in a private adjudicative process. In other words, an agreement to arbitrate usually operates as a waiver of the right to proceed in court. Thus, while mediators may attempt to cajole or persuade the parties to compromise, arbitrators act more like private judges, hearing each side of a dispute and issuing a decision. They also establish the procedural rules to be followed and determine the schedule or "calendar" under which the process will be conducted.

Soia Mentschikoff's article in the *Columbia Law Review* is the classic study of commercial arbitration.[396] She distinguishes three basic models. The *umpire* type stresses speed and economy. The parties or a trade association select an expert who will be right, or at least will make decisions within a zone of reasonable judgment. In such situations, a quick answer given by someone who knows the trade is more important than "the right answer." For example, in some areas lumber wholesalers and retail lumber yards settle disputes about the quality of lumber by calling in an expert lumber grader to decide whether a shipment complies with the contract. The expert looks at the questioned lumber and announces its quality. The losing party

---

[393] *Id.* at 866.

[394] *Id.*

[395] Stipanowich cites construction contracts and the National Advertising Division of the council of Better Business Bureaus as two areas in which non-binding arbitration procedures are accepted.

[396] Soia Mentschikoff, *Commercial Arbitration*, 61 Colum. L. Rev. 846 (1961).

[handwritten margin notes: "Similar to ct but quicker and less formal", "Arb clauses don't need to be conspicuous", "Group just decides"]

pays the fee, which deters starting the procedure for trivial issues. Under the *adversary* model, the parties offer evidence and argument in hearings, and one or more arbitrators decide. It is roughly analogous to proceedings in court, but procedures can be quicker and less formal. In the *investigatory* model, representatives of an organization, such as a stock exchange, take responsibility for developing evidence and making a decision. We find this model in situations where those who do business value membership in an association. Often the question is whether the association should allow a member to continue to participate in light of its actions.[397]

Many people are enthusiastic about binding arbitration as an answer to some of the problems of the legal system. In the international sphere, binding arbitration seems to some a welcome alternative to litigating in foreign court, permitting parties to select a neutral forum in a mutually convenient location with impartial decision makers and acceptable procedures, and often resulting in an award that is widely enforceable under international conventions.[398] At the national level, a survey of Fortune 1000 companies reveals that binding arbitration is a leading dispute resolution alternative in commercial contracts.[399] According to this survey, representatives of more than two-thirds of responding companies cited savings of money and time as reasons for choosing arbitration. Other reasons included limited discovery, expertise among neutral decision makers, preservation of business relations, avoidance of legal precedents, encouragement of more satisfactory settlements, a "more satisfactory process," and durability of results.

Others are less enthusiastic about commercial arbitration. Consider the following:

Marvin T. Fabyanske & Steven T. Halverson, *Arbitration: Is It an Acceptable Method of Resolving Construction and Contract Disputes?*
16 FORUM — ABA SECTION OF INSURANCE, NEGLIGENCE & COMP. LAW 281 (1980)[400]

Arbitration is intended to provide a forum where decisions are made by experienced professionals, unfettered by technical procedures or rules of law. Accordingly, arbitration is uniquely suited to complex and technical factual disputes. The expertise of the triers of fact, coupled with the informality of the proceeding, allow both parties to delve quickly and deeply into the complex factual situations that frequently surround construction disputes.

---

[397] For studies of trade association arbitration, *see* Lisa Bernstein, *Private Commercial Law in the Cotton Industry: Creating Cooperation Through Rules, Norms, and Institutions*, 99 MICH. L. REV. 1724 (2001); Bernstein, *Opting Out of the Legal System: Extralegal Contractual Relations in the Diamond Industry*, 21 J. LEGAL STUD. 115 (1992).

[398] Stipanowich, *supra* note 385, at 841.

[399] DAVID B. LIPSKY & RONALD L. SEEBER, THE APPROPRIATE RESOLUTION OF CORPORATE DISPUTES: A REPORT ON THE GROWING USE OF ADR BY U.S. CORPORATIONS (Cornell/PERC Institute on Conflict Resolution 1998).

[400] Copyright © 1980 by the American Bar Association. Reprinted by permission of the American Bar Association.

Usually decided on fact, not law

Depends how much dispute

Small = usually faster

Bigger = a lot of times not better

In summary, only works when both want it to

On the other hand, cases that turn on subtle legal theories are not well suited for arbitration. Fine distinctions between competing theories of law are frequently ignored by arbitrators. With few exceptions, arbitrators will decide cases on factual merits and equities rather than legal entitlement. Arbitrators, however, are frequently lawyers, and many arbitrators who are not lawyers have nonetheless accumulated substantial experience in the law either by virtue of their business experience or their participation in arbitration panels. For these reasons, the legal or factual nature of the dispute, standing by itself, provides insufficient grounds for determining whether arbitration is more desirable than litigation in a given case.

Another important factor bearing on the suitability of arbitration for dispute resolution is the amount in controversy. Arbitration, of course, has no jurisdictional amounts, either minimum or maximum, unless the arbitration agreement so provides. Proponents of arbitration frequently tout low costs and speed as primary advantages of arbitration, but experience suggests that the amount in controversy has a great deal to do with the relative speed and economy of the arbitration cases.

In small cases, arbitration can be both faster and more economical than litigation. By dispensing with [the] numerous procedural requirements [of] discovery, and even the need for counsel, arbitration can provide a quick and inexpensive resolution of small disputes.

Where substantial sums of money are involved, however, the relative speed and economy of arbitration becomes doubtful. In such cases most parties retain counsel. Since arbitrators are usually professionals who have other commitments and arbitrators are seldom willing to devote more than a few days a month to a particular case, hearings will frequently stretch out over several months. Hearings are further protracted because, in the absence of provisions for pre-hearing discovery, they usually provide the parties with their first opportunity to conduct discovery. . . . In the last analysis, arbitration is an effective dispute-resolution mechanism only if all the parties involved genuinely want it to work. Both the basis and the strength of arbitration is consent. If it is lacking, arbitration becomes ineffective and resort to the courts is almost inevitable.[401]

———————

The U.S. Supreme Court has read the Federal Arbitration Act as evidencing a strong federal policy favoring arbitration.[402] This has had a tremendous impact on how arbitration agreements are written and interpreted by parties and by state and federal courts. Courts routinely order parties to arbitrate in accordance with ADR agreements, and refuse to hear cases pending arbitration. When arbitration awards are judicially reviewed, courts have imposed strict limits on the scope of that review, discouraging extended appeals and giving arbitrators great flexibility in fashioning awards.[403] Some judges have even allowed arbitrators to impose punitive dam-

———————

[401] [Eds. note: Arbitration using the American Arbitration Association is often as costly and subject to as much delay as litigation. *See* Herbert M. Kritzer & Jill K. Anderson, *The Arbitration Alternative: A Comparative Analysis of Case Processing Time, Disposition Mode, and Cost in the American Arbitration Association and the Courts*, 8 JUST. SYS. J. 6 (1983).]

[402] *See* Stipanowich, *supra* note 385, at 844.

[403] *Id.* at 879.

ages.[404] Also, as we have seen above, courts sometimes extend these policies and principles to agreements to mediate or negotiate.

In addition to interpreting the FAA itself quite broadly, the Supreme Court has also held that the FAA preempts state law in relation to any arbitration agreements within the reach of the Interstate Commerce Clause of the United States Constitution.[405] Thus, states are largely prohibited from placing limits or regulations on arbitration agreements unless the limitations are also applicable to other types of contracts. This has been particularly significant in consumer and employment areas, where boilerplate contract language requiring consumers or employees to submit their claims to arbitration has generated a great deal of controversy. Again, Stipanowich illustrates the problem:[406]

> Private dispute resolution is more than ever a fact of everyday life. Binding arbitration clauses are now a common feature of banking, credit card, financial, health care, insurance and communication service agreements, and agreements for the sale of consumer goods. The traditional image of arbitration as a merchant forum has given way to something akin to a broad-based "surrogate" justice system, supplanting public process in various realms of human endeavor. Recent Supreme Court and appellate court opinions broadening federal arbitration law under the [FAA], coupled with mass-produced standard contracts containing broad arbitration clauses, have extended the umbra of arbitration to encompass nearly the entire spectrum of civil disputes, including tort and statute-based claims.

> Along the way, it has often been observed that "[t]he speed and economy of arbitration . . . could prove helpful to all parties." For this reason, mass claims settlements sometimes provide for resolution of individual claims through customized arbitration processes.

> On the other hand, contract boilerplate requiring consumer or employee claims and controversies to be arbitrated has generated a good deal of controversy in recent years. A private arbitration process may well fall short of parties' reasonable exceptions of fairness and have a dramatic impact on consumers' substantive rights and remedies. The range of concerns raised by arbitration agreements in consumer or employment transactions include awareness of the arbitration agreement and a waiver of the right to trial; access to information about the arbitration program; the independence and impartiality of the decision-makers, and of the administering institution, if any; the quality of the process and the competence of arbitrators; the cost, location, and time frame of arbitration; the right to representation; the fundamental fairness of hearings; access to information (discovery); the nature of arbitral remedies, including the availability of punitive damages in cases where they would be available in court; the availability of class actions; the scope of judicial review of

---

[404] *Id.*

[405] Doctor's Assocs. v. Casarotto, 517 U.S. 681 (1996).

[406] Stipanowich, *supra* note 385, at 888–92.

arbitration awards; and even the availability of binding precedents for the future guidance of actors in various arenas. . . .

In a private justice system . . . the primary determinant of users' experiences is an agreement. The agreement defines the nature of the process, the range of issues to be addressed, the character of the intervener's role, and the method of identifying or appointing individual(s) to play that role. Consensual conflict management is a universe of choices, and its great potential is in the creative exercise of those choices.

There are, however, situations where only one party effectively controls choices about private justice. The paradigm is a dispute resolution provision in a standardized contract prepared and presented by a company or organization to its employees, to franchisees, or to consumers of goods and services. Such provisions often do not involve arm's-length negotiation, but consist of terms presented on a take-it-or-leave-it basis — a classic indicium of the contract of adhesion. . . . Consider, for example, a boilerplate dispute resolution provision in a consumer contract calling for "arbitration under X rules" without explaining the latter or providing information about where to find such rules. . . . Modern dispute resolution procedures often run to dozens of provisions covering many pages, like rules of court. Therefore, such documents are usually incorporated by reference — sometimes a very cryptic reference — in the contract. They are not always easy to locate.

We will return to the subject of arbitration in Chapter 4.

Chapter 4

SOCIAL CONTROL OF FREE CONTRACT

We have already seen a number of limitations on free contract. The material in this chapter explores social control of contract in greater detail. The subject is controversial. Partisans fought political battles from the progressive era through the New Deal in the name of freedom of contract. These arguments, wearing slightly more modern dress, are still with us.

Taking a purely individualistic position, one can argue that because I have various abilities and rights and because society must support those abilities and rights rather than control them, I can make any contract I wish. If I make a good deal, I've won the game. If I make a bad one, that is just the price of freedom. Respect for me as an individual requires honoring my choices however they turn out. Relieving me of bad deals is an attack on my competence and autonomy. There is no reason to assume that legislators, judges, or administrators know more than I do about what is best for me. Furthermore, I can learn from my own mistakes, or those of others. We all benefit if people have reason to plan and deal with risk intelligently. The incentive to do so is reduced if I have no responsibility for my poor choices.

Most think that there is some truth in this position. Few, however, hold it without qualification. While most bargains may be a good thing, some are not. Suppose A and B make a contract to kill C. It could be a rational and cost-effective, although immoral, way for A to deal with problems caused by C. Nonetheless, performance of this contract would invade C's rights. It would injure C's friends and those who depend on C for economic support. Furthermore, everyone in a society has an interest in minimizing murder. There is no reason to allow A to sue B for breach of this contract. Indeed, we want to encourage B to breach it. \ *Late = sick hypo*

Insofar as we justify the institution of contract on the basis of choice, we may want to insist that people make real choices before they are bound to contracts. Suppose A drugs B so that B does not know what B is doing. A guides B's hand to sign a document labeled "Contract." Should the law enforce this bargain? An individualist defense of contract rests on choice. Despite his signature on the document, B's apparent choice was not a real one. Some would want us to examine B's conduct. If B could have avoided the problem, enforcing the transaction might offer an incentive for self-reliance and care. It would be cheaper for B to avoid trouble than to have an official agency bail him out after A took advantage of him. Alternatively, A's fault might offend us enough to warrant denying him any advantage from drugging B.

How far can we push these ideas? Can we say that the legal system should refuse to enforce all contracts that impinge on the interests of those who are not parties to the transaction? Should the legal system refuse to enforce all deals in which the choice of one of the parties was not a real one? These are slippery slopes. Almost all contracts have an impact on people who are not parties to the bargain. What kinds of impact warrant refusing to enforce deals? Also, we can view all choice as both free and constrained at the same time. How many constraints must there be before we see the consent in the transaction as flawed?

Writers and reformers have also advocated social control of contract based on other theories. Some call for making rules or applying them so that we redistribute wealth from the richer to the poorer in our society. Others advocate paternalism or maternalism. They say that legal agencies should take care of some, many, or all people in the society. Rules should ensure that bargains are fair. Some proposals focus on bargaining procedures to help people take care of themselves. Others seek to regulate particular terms or the content of entire contracts so that people do not make mistakes in entering disadvantageous or unfair transactions. Still others would have legal agencies intervene in particular transactions in the name of fairness. Recent developments in behavioral economics may support more social control by documenting identifiable biases in human perception and the influence of framing of situations on how people behave.

People are not equal in wealth, talent, or bargaining skill. A purely individualistic contract law would allow the strong to prey on the weak. It would reward suspicion and penalize trust. It would magnify the advantages that the powerful already have. Distributional and paternal/maternal arguments usually oppose the virtues of individualism. These arguments also present their own slippery slope. How far should we go in trying to redistribute income? How much should we take care of what kinds of people? Must we just intuit that some interventions make sense while others do not?

Partisans in the free contract debate repeatedly make two other kinds of arguments. First, the costs of limiting free contract may be greater than the benefits of regulation. For example, people in trouble may need to borrow money. It is not easy to find creditors willing to deal with people in economic trouble, and regulation will make such loans even less attractive. Regulation in the form of usury laws, which limit the rate of interest lenders can charge, may actually create an illegal loan market. Some high-risk debtors can't borrow money at the legal rate of interest. Loan sharks make loans at illegal rates of interest and, since they cannot use the courts to aid in collecting their debts, they fashion their own private government, relying on threats of physical violence to encourage payment. While state usury restrictions have limited impact because of their preemption by federal banking law, other types of regulation of consumer credit also restrict supply and drive some borrowers to black markets. Consumer demand, in other words, may create supply even over regulatory obstacles.

Second, it is not easy for legal agencies to regulate the process of making contracts or their content. Even assuming we want contracts policed, we must ask whether judges or administrators have the capability to regulate bargains. Suppose that a legislature passes a statute allowing courts to overturn bargains that are unfair. Standards such as "fair," "unreasonable," or "unconscionable" are difficult to define. Even when we fashion working definitions, they can be difficult to apply.

Lawyers face difficulty in proving the circumstances of a transaction, as well as its impact.[1]

In the end, perhaps there are some problems that cannot be solved without basic structural changes in our society that are beyond the power of judges or administrators. Attempting to react on a case-by-case basis might distract us from seeing the need for these changes.

Whatever your initial reaction to these arguments, you must recognize that there is a great deal of social control of contract. Contracts to commit crimes may themselves be crimes. Courts have long refused to enforce most illegal contracts or those against public policy. Antitrust laws forbid contracts that limit competition. The laws of fraud and duress limit bargaining tactics. Contracts with governmental units must contain promises not to discriminate on the grounds of race, sex, or religion. Employers may have to pay a minimum wage. Contracts to buy and sell insurance and corporate securities are subject to elaborate regulation. Obviously, we could offer many other examples.

A.   SOCIAL CONTROL AND THE PUBLIC INTEREST

1.   Illegal Contracts

a.   Introduction

Contracts to commit serious crimes are crimes themselves. Not surprisingly, the courts usually refuse to enforce these contracts. Furthermore, a party to an illegal contract often cannot recover restitution to get back what he has paid to have someone else break the law. Nonetheless, neither the criminal law nor the courts' refusal to enforce illegal contracts deter all of these agreements. People do make deals to murder others. Illegal markets such as the drug trade involve all kinds of bargains. There are private governments offering sanctions that usually deter breaches of these contracts.[2] However, even if we think that few people will be deterred from making such deals by their legal unenforceability, courts' refusals to support them make an important symbolic statement. And yet, the mere fact that the underlying transaction itself is illegal does not automatically lead courts to hold the contracts unenforceable. What factors besides criminality seem to matter to courts asked to enforce an "illegal" contract?

---

[1] Conversely, some laws attempt to prescribe in excruciating detail the exact language that contracts may or must (or must not) contain. The federal "truth in lending" law, for example, contains fine-grained instructions about what certain consumer loan documentation must say. Some worry that this level of detail imposes heavy transaction costs on small lenders and has little real benefit to consumers, who may not read the agreements they sign.

[2] *See* Peter Reuter, *Social Control in Illegal Markets, in* TOWARD A GENERAL THEORY OF SOCIAL CONTROL, vol. II at 29 (Donald Black ed., Academic Press 1984). Two of Reuter's section headings are "The Mafia as a Dispute-Settlement System" and "The Mafia, Arbitration, and Extortion."

b.   Illegality: form and substance

Courts have long extended the illegal-contract doctrine beyond contracts that state openly that their object is to commit crimes. They look through the "form" of the contract (or pleadings about it) to inspect its "substance." *Everet v. Williams* is the celebrated "Highwayman's Case," decided by the Court of Exchequer in 1725. Apparently, the case involved an agreement between two highwaymen to share the expenses and the proceeds of robbery. The pleadings, however, do not say this in so many words.

> "[T]he Bill alleged that 'the plaintiff was skilled in dealing in several commodities, such as plate, rings, watches, etc.; that the defendant applied to him to become a partner; and that they entered into partnership, and it was agreed that they should equally provide all sorts of necessaries, such as horses, saddles, bridles, and equally bear all expenses on the roads and at inns, taverns, alehouses, markets, and fairs; that the plaintiff and the defendant proceeded jointly in the said business with good success on Hounslow Heath, where they dealt with a Gentleman for a gold watch; and afterwards the defendant told the plaintiff that Finchley, in the County of Middlesex, was a good and convenient place to deal in, and that commodities were very plenty at Finchley, and it would be almost clear gain to them; that they went accordingly, and dealt with several Gentlemen for divers watches, rings, swords, canes, hats, cloaks, horses, bridles, saddles, and other things; that about a month afterwards the defendant informed the plaintiff there was a Gentleman at Blackheath who had a good horse, saddle, bridle, watch, sword cane, and other things to dispose of, which he believed might be had for little or no money; that they accordingly went and met with the said Gentleman, and after some small discourse they dealt for the said horse, &c.; that the plaintiff and defendant continued their joint dealings together until Michaelmas, and dealt together at several places . . . to the amount of 2000 pounds and upwards.' . . . The rest of the Bill was in the ordinary form for a partnership account. The Bill is said to have been dismissed, with costs, to be paid by the Counsel who signed it; and the Plaintiff and the Defendant were, it is said, both hanged and one of the Solicitors for the Plaintiff was afterwards transported.
>
> "Another account is that the Solicitor was ordered to be led around Westminster Hall, when the Court was sitting, with the obnoxious Bill cut in strings and hung around his neck."[3]

Moral of the story: If you live by the sword, don't ask a court to help when your partner stabs you in the back. Or is it?

The following case takes an approach different from that taken in *Everet v. Williams*. The plaintiff's lawyer wrote to us that "as far as I was concerned, this was purely a business transaction between two persons who had made a deal for the sale

---

[3] William R. Riddell, *A Legal Scandal Two Hundred Years Ago*, 16 A.B.A. J. 422 (1930). Reprinted from Volume 16 (1930) with permission of the ABA JOURNAL: THE LAWYER'S MAGAZINE, published by the American Bar Association.

of property." The Court agreed, refusing to look through the form of the transaction to its substance.

CARROLL v. BEARDON
Montana Supreme Court
381 P.2d 295 (1963)

HARRISON, J.

This is an appeal from a judgment . . . in favor of plaintiff-respondent [Carroll] and against defendant-appellant [Beardon]. . . .

On March 15, 1960, Edna Carroll . . . and Agnes Beardon . . . executed instruments in writing, one a warranty deed from respondent to appellant, and a note and mortgage back from appellant to respondent for the sale of a building and acreage in the amount of $42,000. A down payment of $8000 was made at the time of the sale, and the note and mortgage provided that the appellant would pay to respondent monthly the sum of $1000 for the months of January through June and $2000 for the months of July through December. The appellant paid one monthly payment. In September 1960, a mortgage foreclosure action was instituted by the respondent setting forth the . . . facts, showing a sum due in the amount of $41,805.53 for the building, personal property, and 50 acres of land located in Toole County.

So far the facts in the case set forth an ordinary real estate transaction with a default by the purchaser, and it is not until the appellant's answer is read that the court finds itself trying to settle a dispute of two madams over a house of prostitution. The appellant alleges by way of her answer that although she secured the deed for the property, gave the note and mortgage, and entered into possession, that the mortgage is absolutely void as contrary to express law, and public policy; that the alleged mortgage was entered into in furtherance of prostitution in violation of the laws of the State of Montana and intended by respondent Carroll and the appellant Beardon so to be, and was entered into by the parties hereto with the knowledge, intent, and purpose on their part that the said property would be used for the purpose of prostitution in violation of the laws of the State of Montana; and that prior to, and on the date of the consummation of this illegal transaction, prostitution was the only activity at the so-called Hillside Ranch.

While neither counsel had the effrontery to parade these indignant madams before the court, their depositions speak for them, and are most enlightening. Both admit that they are madams, in the limited sense of the word, and have operated this valuable piece of property, known as the Hillside Ranch, as a house of prostitution, the respondent some four years prior to the sale, and the appellant since that date. Both admit to the sale of liquor without a state license, but the respondent deposed she had a federal license, leaving the court to wonder whether she is a strong central government supporter, or a more careful businesswoman. The appellant's position concerning these lawful taxes seems to be that her payments going from $1000 per month to $2000 per month during the harvest months and the Christmas season, that she could not afford the luxury of taxation.

Counsel on both sides of the case dig deep in legal lore to convince the court of the righteousness of their client's cause . . . Many courts refuse to aid either party to contracts where the transaction is illegal. . . . A review of the evidence put before the court in this case tempts this court to dismiss the appeal. However, there are many decisions to the effect that where the sale is of property that may or may not be used for an illegal purpose, that it is no defense that the seller knew the purpose of the buyer, without further evidence implicating the seller. . . . In the absence of active participation, the defense of illegality is ordinarily not available to the party who has breached the contract, where the fault and illegality are unilateral on her side of the transaction. . . . The bare knowledge of the purpose for which the property is sold is not enough to raise the valid defense of illegality. . . .

It is also important to consider the fact that the defendant has had the benefit of this contract for several years. Her status naturally does not appeal to the favor of this court, and in order to sustain such a defense a party who has reaped its benefits must show more active participation by the seller than has been shown here. . . .

[T]his same question, raising the illegality of the sale of gambling equipment was before the Supreme Court of Wyoming in the case of *Fuchs v. Goe*, 62 Wyo. 134, 163 P.2d 783. . . . In the *Fuchs* case, as in this case, after the sale of the property, the seller had no connection with the business. The court, quoting from 32 *Am. Jur.* 68–69, 49, in the *Fuchs* case in this connection stated:

> [I]n order to defeat a recovery for rent by the lessor it must be shown that he participated in some degree, however slight, in the wrongful purpose and intended the property be so used, and that mere indifference on his part as to the intended use of the premises is not sufficient to bar his recovery. Mere knowledge on the lessor's part that the lessee will use the premises for an unlawful purpose does not make the lessor a participant in that purpose; for mere knowledge that the lessee may or will use the premises for an unlawful purpose is not of itself sufficient to show that the lessor intended that they must or shall be so used."

. . .

Finding ample evidence in the record to sustain the trial court's findings and conclusions, the judgment appealed from is affirmed. . . .

ADAIR, J. (concurring in part and dissenting in part): I concur in the result, but not in all that is said in the above opinion. This is a case of the pot calling the kettle black. However, the calling of names will not pay the promissory note nor discharge nor invalidate the mortgage upon which this action is brought. Each party to the contract is required to keep her promises and to perform her obligations thereunder. . . .

NOTES AND QUESTIONS

1. ***Explaining the court's decision — what is "active participation"?*** Suppose in *Everet v. Williams*, the Highwayman's Case, Joseph Williams had agreed to supply John Everet with "horses, saddles, bridles" and to "bear all

Question of Harvest season ↑ if is more customers then

expenses on the roads and at inns, taverns, alehouses, markets, and fairs." Everet, in turn, promised to use his skill "in dealing in several commodities" on Hounslow Heath and in Finchley in the County of Middlesex to rob such people as the Gentleman at Blackheath. Would the approach of the Supreme Court of Montana call for the enforcement of their contract?

Suppose, instead, Williams sold Everet "horses, saddles, and bridles" for cash, knowing what Everet planned to do with them. Would this contract be enforceable? What did Ms. Carroll know about what Ms. Beardon was going to do with the property? Shelby, Montana, is in a wheat-growing area; it is a railroad town located 35 miles from the Canadian border, and in 2013, it had a population of 3,294. The Supreme Court of Montana stressed that the vendor was not running the prostitution operation at the Hillside Ranch at the time of the suit. However, the vendor had purchased the property for $6000 and five years later sold it to the buyer for approximately $50,000. In a deposition, the vendor's lawyer questioned Beardon, the buyer. He asked about the $50,000 price for the Hillside Ranch:

Q. Wasn't that a fair price for the property?

A. I wouldn't say that, no. As a house of prostitution, yes, it was.

Seller's lawyer then asked whether his client knew "what your operations might be." Beardon responded: "Oh, yes, she knows." The lawyer asked: "You could do anything you wanted with that property if you so desired, could you not?" Beardon answered: "I couldn't do that and make the payments she expected me to make." The lawyer continued: "And what did you buy at that time? What were you negotiating for?" Beardon said: "I was buying a going business of prostitution." Moreover, the vendor was alleged to have said: "You can make good money here. It is slow in the winter but you can make good money during the harvest season." Remember also that the vendor was to be paid more under the contract during the harvest and holiday seasons when business was likely to be better. Suppose we accept that Agnes Beardon paid Edna Carroll for a going illegal business. Does "the active participation test" allow you to judge whether a court should refuse to enforce a contract in that event?

2. *Explaining the court's decision — the "local option":* To what extent, if at all, does the court's opinion reflect the two judges' attitude about crimes such as gambling or prostitution? Justice Harrison seems to find the transaction amusing, and his opinion is playful. Both opinions seem concerned about "windfalls to the wicked." Madam Beardon is asking to keep a going business, free of the obligation to pay for it. Everet and Williams "were, it was said, both hanged." What was likely to happen to Madam Beardon if the court accepted the defense of illegality? What likely happened when the court refused to accept this defense? Ms. Beardon failed to make the payments required by the contract because she was not making enough at the Hillside Ranch to cover them. She testified that she tried unsuccessfully to negotiate a new payment schedule with Ms. Carroll before the suit was filed.

Usually, we assume laws apply throughout a state. However, when many states repealed laws prohibiting the sale of alcoholic beverages, they expressly allowed counties or cities to exercise local option and continue prohibition. In many (if not all) states, there is a tacit local option of whether to apply state laws governing gambling and prostitution. Most law enforcement is in the hands of local officials. Both police and prosecutors have discretion concerning when to enforce which laws. If a community is at least indifferent to gambling and prostitution, police and prosecutors will often spend little effort trying to prosecute these crimes. When these crimes are prosecuted, sometimes juries refuse to convict.

At the time of the sale, the Hillside Ranch had been in business for about five years. It was located on a road that ran past the local fairground about a mile east of the small city. We can also guess that police and prosecutors knew of its existence and didn't enforce the law. The buyer testified that the place was commonly known as the Hillside Ranch and house of prostitution. "[E]verybody in town knows [what] it is." In effect, the Supreme Court of Montana decided to leave matters to the discretion of law enforcement officials in Shelby, Montana. The citizens who influence affairs there may not find prostitution particularly objectionable when it is out of sight at the Hillside Ranch. They might have felt differently if the Hillside Ranch were too near a school or a church, or if it were a business selling drugs such as crack cocaine and heroin. This explanation is speculative since not a word in the opinion suggests anything of the sort. Although speculative, is it realistic or just cynical? The house at the Hillside Ranch no longer exists; all that remains is some of the foundation and a nice view of the city to the west. The last public house of prostitution operating in downtown Butte, Montana (about 200 miles from Shelby), was not closed until 1982, nearly 20 years after the decision in *Carroll v. Beardon*.[4]

3. *Nevada's local option:* Nevada specifically provides smaller counties a local option for prostitution. Counties with populations under 700,000 may license this type of business.[5]

c. Comparative fault

One of the problems with the defense of illegality is that the punishment may not fit the crime. By the traditional rule of *Everett v. Williams*, the court leaves the parties where it finds them. The maxim *in pari delicto potior est conditio defendentis vel possidentis* translates as "if (when) the parties are in equal guilt, the defendant or the possessor is in a better position." This approach may reward the defendant by leaving him with the fruits of the crime. It may penalize the plaintiff by leaving her out of pocket what she has contributed to the enterprise. Furthermore, courts have long recognized that the traditional rule can be too blunt and unrefined. One party may have planned the criminal transaction while the other just went along. Courts invented ways to make adjustments in the situation in which it finds the parties when they are "not *in pari delicto*." We might call these ways collectively the "not *in pari delicto*" rule.

Professor Leon Trakman[6] notes that New Zealand legislation authorizes a court to grant "relief to any party to an illegal contract . . . as the Court in its discretion

---

[4] John Cloud, *The Oldest Profession Gets a New Museum*, TIME MAGAZINE, August 14, 2000, at 4.

[5] *See* NEV. REV. STAT. ANN. § 244.345 (2011).

[6] Leon Trakman, *The Effect of Illegality in the Law of Contract: Suggestions for Reform*, 55 CAN. B. REV./LA REVUE DU BARREAU CANADIEN 627, 652–54 (1977). Contrast Professor Feinman's criticism of the

thinks just."[7] He says this standard reflects modern common law practice with or without express legislative authorization. Trakman makes a legal realist argument to defend this approach, saying:

> [C]ritics have contended that the exercise of judicial discretion will lead to unwarrantable capriciousness in the decision-making process. In reality, the risk of judicial arbitrariness is significantly reduced in view of the controls inherent within the common law system. Thus, the demand that judges give logical reasons for their decisions achieves both a public scrutiny of the decision-making process and the possibility that unsound judgments will be reversed on appeal. Judicial consistency is maintained by the requirement that courts reflect upon past experiences in the legal system . . . [J]udicial arbitrariness is limited by rules of evidence and procedure [that] require courts to make determinations only after evaluating all relevant evidence, properly elicited and considered.

> Greater difficulty is posed by the suggestion that courts are insufficiently equipped to weigh normative public policy considerations, which often contradict each other and fluctuate with time. Yet, even this criticism is rebutted by the attributes of the living common law. For, the fact that courts are constantly exposed to factual situations forces them to develop the "situation sense" necessary to make essentially "non-legal" decisions. In addition, judicial precedent compels common law judges to reflect upon the significance of previous fact situations. Finally, the rules of evidence require that courts give credence to party witnesses, including experts summoned to give testimony on issues of fact. However, the final fetter upon the judiciary lies in [its] capacity to develop meaningful methods of determining the effects of illegality through the evolutionary process of judicious experimentation and example.

The materials that follow develop what we have called the "not *in pari delicto*" rule. Do you think the materials support Professor Trakman's position? Or do they support the critics who are alarmed by what they see as judicial arbitrariness?

COMA CORP. v. KANSAS DEPARTMENT OF LABOR
Kansas Supreme Court
283 Kan. 625, 154 P.3d 1080 (2007)

Nuss, J.

Cesar Martinez Corral filed a claim for his earned but unpaid wages against his employer, Coma Corporation, d/b/a Burrito Express, and its president, Mario Coria. The Kansas Department of Labor (KDOL) determined that both respondents (Coma) owed Corral wages plus interest and also assessed a civil penalty for a total of $7,657 under the Kansas Wage Payment Act, K.S.A. 44-312 *et seq.*

---

discretionary approach called for by the RESTATEMENT (SECOND) OF CONTRACTS § 90, *supra* Chapter 3, note 203.

[7] *See* THE ILLEGAL CONTRACTS ACT, c. 129, § 7(1), S.N.Z. (1970).

Coma appealed cuz hes undocumented. DC then said cuz hes undoc he only gets the wages.

↳ KDOL appealing that

On Coma's petition for review pursuant to the Kansas Act for Judicial Review and Civil Enforcement of Agency Actions (KJRA), K.S.A. 77-601 *et seq.*, the district court reversed in part. It concluded that because Corral was an undocumented worker not legally permitted to work in the United States he was only entitled to the applicable minimum wage for work performed and was not entitled to a penalty. The KDOL appeals directly to this court under the KJRA. . . . [W]e affirm in part and reverse in part the judgment of the district court. We affirm the judgment of KDOL.

FACTS

Coria = Prez
Crral = Employee

Mario Coria is the president of Coma Corporation, a Wichita enterprise. On May 17, 2004, after Cesar Martinez Corral was fired from his Coma employment, he filed a claim for earned but unpaid wages. Corral alleged that he worked as a cook for Coma from October 2003 to May 12, 2004, at a pay rate of $6 per hour.

Corral testified at a telephone wage hearing conducted by a KDOL hearing officer. Corral stated that the manager, Luis Calderon, agreed to pay him $6 per hour with weekly payment. . . . No one besides Corral testified.

In granting Corral's claim, the hearing officer determined that the evidence presented no issues of fact and awarded wages plus interest. . . . The hearing officer also awarded Corral a penalty of $3,720 for Coma's willful and knowing withholding of his wages. Based upon $3,720 in wages, $217 in interest, and a penalty of $3,720, the hearing officer awarded Corral a total of $7,657 against Coma and Coria as its president. Coma filed a motion to dismiss, or in the alternative, to set aside the initial order, which the Secretary of the KDOL denied. Coma also filed a petition for review that was denied.

Breakdown of wage v. int v. Penalty

Coma then filed a Petition for Judicial Review of Final Order with the district court. There, KDOL stipulated that Corral is an undocumented worker "not legally permitted to work in the United States."

In a 17-page opinion, the district court concluded that the Kansas Wage Payment Act (KWPA), K.S.A. 44-312 *et seq.*, did apply to undocumented workers. It held, however, that Corral was only entitled to the applicable minimum wage for work performed because the employment contract was illegal due to Corral's status as an undocumented worker. The court remanded to KDOL for recalculation at the applicable minimum wage. It also reversed the hearing officer's penalty award, holding that federal immigration policy should prohibit a statutory penalty.

Should be lower to min wage and no stat Penalty Ct. says

ANALYSIS

Issue 1: An undocumented worker's employment contract is enforceable under the Kansas Wage Payment Act.

Coma argues that Corral's employment contract was illegal and unenforceable because he is an illegal alien. Intertwined with this argument is another: Coma claims that federal immigration law preempts the KWPA. The KDOL responds that the district court was correct in concluding that Corral was covered by the KWPA,

Illegals still covered by KWPA KODL says
(immigrants)

used throughout

essentially rejecting the preemption argument. It argues the court erred, however, in concluding that Corral's employment contract was illegal and unenforceable due to his status as an undocumented worker and that Corral therefore was entitled only to minimum wage.

To the extent resolution of the issues necessitates statutory interpretation, this court's review is unlimited. . . . Deference to an agency's interpretation is especially appropriate when "the agency is one of special competence and experience." . . . However, the final construction of a statute always rests with the courts. . . .

Application of the KWPA to undocumented workers
Analysis on this issue below

As mentioned, Coma's "illegal contract" argument is intertwined with its allegation that the KWPA does not apply to Corral because "it contravenes the central policy of federal immigration law," i.e., state law is preempted by federal law. . . . Preemption is a question of law over which we exercise *de novo* review. *Doty v. Frontier Communications, Inc.*, 272 Kan. 880, 888, 36 P.3d 250 (2001).

Because of Coma's reliance upon preemption, it does not dispute that K.S.A. 44-313(b) of the KWPA expansively defines an employee as "*any person* allowed or permitted to work by an employer." (Emphasis added.) Nor does it dispute that pursuant to K.S.A. 44-314(a), an employer is required to pay all wages due to an employee at least once a month. In short, the plain language of the statute does not exclude undocumented workers from the "employee" definition or from the protections of the KWPA. Nor are there any KWPA exceptions to this expansive definition.

Plain language doesn't exclude illegal imm.

Coma's purported trumping argument is instead based upon 8 U.S.C. § 1324a(a) (2000), which makes employment of unauthorized aliens illegal, and *Hoffman Plastic Compounds v. NLRB*, 535 U.S. 137, 122 S. Ct. 1275 (2002). In *Hoffman*, the United States Supreme Court reversed a National Labor Relations Board's (NLRB) award of back pay to an undocumented worker because recovery was "foreclosed by federal immigration policy" as stated in the Immigration Reform and Control Act of 1986 (IRCA). 535 U.S. at 140, 122 S. Ct. 1275. Technically, *Hoffman* itself did not involve preemption, but rather concerned a conflict between competing federal laws: the National Labor Relations Act (NLRA) and IRCA.

There, Hoffman hired Jose Castro based upon documents which purported to verify his authorization to work in the United States. Hoffman subsequently fired Castro for his involvement in a union-organizing campaign. Three years later, the NLRB concluded that Hoffman unlawfully selected four employees, including Castro, for layoff, due to involvement in union activities. As a remedy, the NLRB ordered Hoffman to, among other things, offer reinstatement and back pay to the fired employees. Later, at a compliance meeting before an Administrative Law Judge (ALJ), Castro confirmed he had fraudulently obtained documents to support his employment application. He testified that he was born in Mexico, that he had never been authorized to work in the United States, and that he used a friend's birth certificate to fraudulently obtain a California driver's license and Social Security card. Based upon Castro's acknowledgment, the ALJ determined that the NLRB was precluded from awarding Castro back pay or offering reinstatement, because

In Hoffman Plastics used fraud docs to get the job

such relief was in conflict with the IRCA. Four years later, the NLRB reversed the specific issue of back pay.

In the Supreme Court's analysis, it first discussed *Sure-Tan, Inc. v. NLRB*, 467 U.S. 883, 104 S. Ct. 2803 (1984). In *Sure-Tan*, the Court affirmed the NLRB's determination that the NLRA applied to undocumented workers. 467 U.S. at 892, 104 S.Ct. 2803. . . . After construing *Sure-Tan*, the *Hoffman* court discussed changes that occurred after the case was decided:

> [T]wo years after *Sure-Tan*, Congress enacted IRCA, a comprehensive scheme prohibiting the employment of illegal aliens in the United States. . . . As we have previously noted, IRCA "forcefully" made combating the employment of illegal aliens central to "[t]he policy of immigration law." It did so by establishing an extensive "employment verification system," § 1324a(a)(1), designed to deny employment to aliens who (a) are not lawfully present in the United States, or (b) are not lawfully authorized to work in the United States, § 1324a(h)(3). This verification system is critical to the IRCA regime. To enforce it, IRCA mandates that employers verify the identity and eligibility of all new hires by examining specified documents before they begin work. § 1324a(b). If an alien applicant is unable to present the required documentation, the authorized alien cannot be hired. § 1324a(a)(1). 535 U.S. at 147–48, 122 S.Ct. 1275.

Based on the foregoing analysis, the *Hoffman* court reasoned that as an undocumented worker, Castro did not have the right to a remedy based on the presumption of his continued illegal employment. 535 U.S. at 149, 122 S. Ct. 1275. Thus, wages for work not actually performed were not appropriate.

The court concluded:

> [A]llowing the Board to award back pay to illegal aliens would unduly trench upon explicit statutory prohibitions critical to federal immigration policy, as expressed in IRCA. It would encourage the successful evasion of apprehension by immigration authorities, condone prior violations of the immigration laws, and encourage future violations. However broad the Board's discretion to fashion remedies when dealing only with the NLRA, it is not so unbounded as to authorize this sort of an award." 535 U.S. at 151–52, 122 S. Ct. 1275.

To begin our preemption analysis, we acknowledge that the Supremacy Clause of Article VI of the United States Constitution provides for federal preemption of state law. Preemption may arise through an express provision, by implication, or through conflict between a federal and state law. . . . See also *Doty v. Frontier Communications, Inc.*, 272 Kan. 880, 36 P.3d 250 (2001) ("In the absence of express preemption in a federal law, there is a strong presumption that Congress did not intend to displace state law."). Additionally, "it is well established that the states enjoy 'broad authority under their police powers to regulate . . . employment relationship[s] to protect workers within the state.'" *Madeira v. Affordable Housing Foundation, Inc.*, 469 F.3d 219, 228 (2d Cir. 2006). . . .

. . . . [T]he district court . . . noted that federal courts have consistently upheld the applicability of FLSA protections to undocumented employees. See *Patel v.*

[handwritten margin note: Basically can't award backpay for work not done in an illegal agreement]

Quality Inn South, 846 F.2d 700, 705–06 (11th Cir. 1988) (under the FLSA, undocumented worker was entitled to recover unpaid minimum wages and overtime for work already performed).

The district court also observed that there is little precedent in Kansas upon which to rely. . . . Based upon the weight of what the district court considered "persuasive authority," and the plain language of K.S.A. 44-313(b), the court concluded that like the FLSA, the KWPA applies to undocumented workers. It specifically noted that "the reasoning of many courts that have addressed this question — that the enforcement of employment statutes actually furthers the goals of the IRCA by creating disincentives for employers to hire illegal aliens," and that K.S.A. 44-313(b) "on its face makes no exception for illegal aliens."

We agree. Based upon other jurisdictions' rejection of IRCA preemption of certain state labor laws, coupled with their narrow reading of *Hoffman*, we conclude that under this case's facts, Coma has not overridden the presumption against federal preemption. . . . More specifically, we agree that the KWPA applies to earned, but unpaid, wages of an undocumented worker — the exact question before us. See, e.g., *Zavala v. Wal-Mart Stores, Inc.*, 393 F. Supp. 2d 295 (N.J. 2005); *Flores v. Amigon*, 233 F. Supp. 2d 462; *Zeng Liu v. Donna Karan Intern., Inc.*, 207 F. Supp. 2d 191, 192 (S.D.N.Y. 2002) ("Courts have distinguished between awards of post-termination back pay for work not actually performed and awards of unpaid wages pursuant to the Fair Labor Standards Act.").

Finally, we agree with the rationale set forth in *Flores v. Amigon*, 233 F. Supp. 2d 462, where the court granted FLSA protections to an undocumented worker and determined that payment of unpaid wages for work actually performed furthers the federal immigration policy:

> Indeed, it is arguable that enforcing the FLSA's provisions requiring employers to pay proper wages to undocumented aliens when the work had been performed actually furthers the goal of the IRCA, which requires the employer to discharge any worker upon discovery of the worker's undocumented alien status. 8 U.S.C. § 1324a(a)(2). If employers know that they will not only be subject to civil penalties, 8 U.S.C. § 1324a(e)(4)(A), and criminal prosecution, 8 U.S.C. § 1324a(f)(1), when they hire illegal aliens, but they will also be required to pay them at the same rates as legal workers for work actually performed, there are virtually no incentives left for an employer to hire an undocumented alien in the first instance. Whatever benefit an employer might have gained by paying less than the minimum wage is eliminated and the employer's incentive would be to investigate and obtain proper documentation from each of his workers" *Id.* at 464.

The legality of the employment contract

In an argument heavily intertwined with federal preemption, Coma also asserts that Corral's employment contract is illegal under state law. Specifically, it argues that KDOL regulations require that a contract of employment contain lawful provisions in order to be enforceable. Coma reasons that because Corral does not have a legal right to be or to work in the United States, his contract violates IRCA and is unenforceable under KDOL regulations and state law. In support, it cites *Sweet v. Stormont Vail Regional Medical Center*, 231 Kan. 604, 611, 647 P.2d 1274 (1982) (contracts that are unreasonable or illegal are unenforceable).

The district court appeared to agree with Coma. Despite acknowledging that Corral was an employee under the KWPA, it stated: "[T]he Court's analysis does not end here. The KWPA, unlike many of the employment statutes at issue in the above cited cases, is heavily dependent on the contract between the employer and the employee. Accordingly, a closer examination of Mr. Corral's claim is required."

The district court concluded that Corral's contract was not lawful:

> This court holds as a matter of law that the oral employment contract between Mr. Corral and the Petitioners, for amounts above the minimum wage, *is contrary to the IRCA, and is therefore illegal under Kansas law and unenforceable under the KWPA*. See *Petty v. City of El Dorado*, 270 Kan. 847, 854, 19 P.3d 167, 172 (2001) (court may void those contract provisions which violate the law)." (Emphasis added.)

Even assuming that our rejection of federal preemption on Corral's wage claim does not foreclose Coma's argument that his employment contract violates IRCA, we disagree that IRCA makes the contract illegal and therefore unenforceable. . . .

Prior to IRCA's enactment, the Alaska Supreme Court confronted the issue of whether a contract of employment entered into by a Canadian alien was barred by illegality. *Gates v. Rivers Construction Co., Inc.*, 515 P.2d 1020 (Alaska 1973). The court first discussed the nature of illegal contracts:

> Generally, a party to an illegal contract cannot recover damages for its breach. But as in the case of many such simplifications, the exceptions and qualifications to the general rule are numerous and complex. Thus, when a statute imposes sanctions but does not specifically declare a contract to be invalid, it is necessary to ascertain whether the legislature intended to make unenforceable contracts entered into in violation of the statute. *Id.* at 1021.

The *Gates* court then concluded that enforcement of the employment contract with the Canadian alien was not barred. It looked at the statutory language:

> It is clear that the contract involved here should be enforced. First, it is apparent that *the statute itself does not specifically declare the labor or service contracts of aliens seeking to enter the United States for the purpose of performing such labor or services to be void*. The statute only specifies that aliens who enter this country for such purpose, without having received the necessary certification, "shall be ineligible to receive visas and shall be excluded from admission into the United States." (Emphasis added.) *Id.* at 1021–22.

The court next advanced the concept of equity and fairness to the employee:

> Second, that the appellee [employer], who knowingly participated in an illegal transaction, should be permitted to profit thereby at the expense of the appellant [employee] is a harsh and undesirable consequence of the doctrine that illegal contracts are not to be enforced. *This result, so contrary to general considerations of equity and fairness, should be countenanced only when clearly demonstrated to have been intended by the legislature.* (Emphasis added.) *Id.* at 1022.

Finally, in a general foreshadowing of the benefit described in *Flores*, i.e., of reducing employer incentives to violate the law, the *Gates* court stated:

> Third, since the purpose of this section would appear to be the safeguarding of American labor from unwanted competition, the appellant's contract should be enforced, because such an objective would not be furthered by permitting employers knowingly to employ excludable aliens and then, with impunity, to refuse to pay them for their services. *Indeed, to so hold could well have the opposite effect from the one intended, by encouraging employers to enter into the very type of contracts sought to be prevented.* (Emphasis added.) *Id.* at 1022.

The IRCA and purported illegal employment contracts were specifically at issue in *Majlinger v. Cassino Contracting Corp.*, 25 A.D.3d 14, 802 N.Y.S.2d 56 (2005). There, an injured undocumented worker sued the contractor and site manager for injuries sustained when the worker fell from a scaffold while installing siding. In addressing whether the award of damages for lost wages was preempted by IRCA, the court held that the defendants could not avoid liability merely because of the worker's undocumented status. Within this context, the court also discussed changes to immigration law:

> A federal statute enacted in 1885 . . . which provided that any contract of employment with an undocumented alien was void, was repealed in 1952 with the passage of the INA [Immigration and Nationality Act] . . . The INA, with certain exceptions, makes undocumented aliens who seek to enter this country for the purpose of performing labor ineligible to receive visas or to be admitted into the United States. This alteration of the federal statute indicates that "Congress determined that the exclusion of certain aliens from admission to the United States was a more satisfactory sanction than rendering their contracts void and thus unjustifiably enriching employers of such alien laborers." *Gates v. Rivers Constr. Co.*, 515 P.2d 1020, 1023 (Alaska 1973). While the IRCA subsequently added provisions prohibiting the hiring of undocumented aliens, the IRCA and the regulations that accompany it "do not purport to intrude into the area of what protections a State may afford these aliens." In the absence of an explicit statement of Congress's intent to deprive undocumented aliens of remedies to which they would otherwise be entitled in state courts, such a disability may not be inferred." *Majlinger*, 25 A.D.3d at 21–22.

Majlinger also addressed the specific contract illegality issue: "As between the undocumented worker and the employer . . . there is a contract of employment, under which the worker is entitled to be paid for his or her work." *Id.* at 24. It found unpersuasive the case law barring recovery of damages for lost income gained from

Ask if I go to DH

Also, work itself not illegal matters

illegal activities, observing that "[a]n undocumented alien performing construction work is not an outlaw engaged in illegal activity, such as bookmaking or burglary. Rather, the work itself is lawful and legitimate; it simply happens to be work for which the alien is ineligible or disqualified." *Id.* at 29. The court held the undocumented worker was entitled to proceed with a loss of wages claim. . . .

CASE to show also holds true in this labor sector

Employers' argument that a worker's undocumented status makes his employment contract illegal under IRCA and therefore void and enforceable has been rejected in the related area of workers' compensation as well. In *Design Kitchen v. Lagos*, 388 Md. 718, 882 A.2d 817 (2005), the court concluded that because the IRCA does not specifically prohibit undocumented workers from seeking employment, and the definition of "employee" under state law does not exclude employees who are undocumented workers, the employment contract is not illegal. . . .

Finally, we agree with KDOL's position concerning the strong and longtime Kansas public policy of protecting wages and wage earners. . . . [T]he legislature has created a stiff penalty for employers failing to pay wages already earned: 1 percent of the unpaid wages for every day they are not paid, up to a total of 100 percent. See K.S.A. 44-315(b).

Accordingly, we conclude that to deny or to dilute an action for wages earned but not paid on the ground that such employment contracts are "illegal," would thus directly contravene the public policy of the State of Kansas.

We hold for the above reasons that the district court erred in concluding that Corral's employment contract was illegal under IRCA and therefore not enforceable under the KWPA.

Basically Corral gets everything KDOL originally gave him.

[The court also held that the KDOL did not err in assessing statutory penalties against Coma pursuant to K.S.A. 44-315(b) for willful failure to pay wages earned by an employee; it stated that the statute states no "illegal alien" exception.] . . . The judgment of the district court is affirmed in part and reversed in part. The judgment of the Kansas Department of Labor is affirmed.

NOTES AND QUESTIONS

1. ***Prospective rights:*** Does *Coma Corp.* protect contractual rights to job security? Assume, for example, that a U.S. citizen were employed under an enforceable one-year employment agreement. If she were to be wrongfully terminated prior to the end of the year, expectation would presumptively give her the benefit of her bargain (that is, the balance of one year's wages, less mitigation, etc.). Would we expect the same under the rule of *Coma*? Or does the apparent bargaining disadvantage often associated with the at-will employee implicitly inform the court's analysis? And how should *Coma*'s reasoning extend to workers' compensation and disability benefits? Can undocumented workers recover for race or sex discrimination under federal or state statutes? Is it possible that undocumented aliens might enjoy greater employment protections than U.S. citizens under the employment-at-will doctrine?[8]

---

[8] We discussed the employment-at-will doctrine in Chapter 3, Section C.4., *supra*.

2. ***How valuable are legal rights for undocumented workers?*** Do you think the holding of *Coma Corp.* typically in fact protects workers' rights to recover unpaid wages? Why or why not? Hint: who was the nominal plaintiff?

[handwritten: → CASE #]

3. ***Repentance:*** In *Greenberg v. Evening Post Ass'n,*[9] the court applied another qualification to the illegal contract doctrine based on a balancing of fault and a concern for incentives. The *Hartford Post* employed Fitch to run a contest to increase its circulation. One of the prizes was an automobile worth $2500. Greenberg entered the contest. Fitch told him that only a person willing to put money into the contest could win. If Greenberg were willing to pay Fitch $300, Fitch would see that Greenberg won the automobile. Greenberg paid $300 to Fitch. Two weeks later, Fitch demanded another $100. Greenberg sought legal advice. His lawyer said that he was a party to a fraudulent scheme and should repudiate the whole transaction. Greenberg demanded his money and sued Fitch. Fitch left the state, and so Greenberg sued the publisher of the newspaper. A jury found for Greenberg. The Supreme Court of Connecticut said: "We think the jury might reasonably have found that the defendant actually received the $300 paid by the plaintiff to Fitch, less Fitch's commission of 20 percent — although it seems that the money was not received by the defendant in a lump sum, or with knowledge that it came from the plaintiff." The judgment was affirmed.

The court said that the "question is whether it is not quite as consistent with sound public policy to encourage the prompt repudiation of illegal and immoral contracts by permitting, under such circumstances, the recovery of money paid upon an illegal or immoral consideration, as to declare the money forfeit the moment it is paid, and thus discourage repentance in such cases." The court decided that the trial court had charged the jury correctly. A plaintiff may recover money paid to carry out an illegal or immoral design if the arrangement was repudiated with reasonable promptness. The plaintiff must back out before the other party acts to put into effect any part of the illegal or immoral design.

[handwritten margin note: Basically, if you realize its illegal / decide against BEFORE anything illegal takes place you can recover. Ct. Holds that otherwise you are discouraging penance]

Is this an example supporting Professor Trakman's argument about judicial competence to make the necessary policy judgments in such cases?

KARPINSKI v. COLLINS
California Court of Appeal, First District
252 Cal. App. 2d 711, 60 Cal. Rptr. 846 (1967)

SHOEMAKER, J. *[handwritten: → Dairyman]*

Plaintiff John Karpinski brought this action against defendants Gene and Ruth Collins and the Santa Clara Creamery to recover secret rebates which plaintiff was allegedly compelled to pay defendants in order to secure and retain a Grade A contract for the sale of plaintiff's milk.

Plaintiff, the sole witness at the trial, was a dairyman. Prior to April 1962, he had sold his milk to a cheese factory under a contract entitling him to what in the business is called the Grade B price, which was established by the federal

---

[9] 91 Conn. 371, 99 Atl. 1037 (1917). *[handwritten: Lolz ↓ for right margin case]*

government and was approximately 60 percent of the Grade A price, which was established by the state. (The Grade A price was 44 cents per gallon and the Grade B price 27 cents per gallon.) Plaintiff testified that it was financially impossible for a dairyman in the Santa Clara Valley to remain in business without a Grade A contract.

Agree to A→K w/ Def for 4.5cent kickback per gallon

Around April 1, 1962, defendant Gene Collins, the president of the Santa Clara Creamery, called on plaintiff and offered him a Grade A contract for the sale of his milk if plaintiff would pay him a rebate or "kickback" of 4 1/2 cents a gallon during the life of the contract. Plaintiff accepted the offer because no other Grade A contracts were available and he had no other choice.

On April 1, 1962, a formal contract was prepared whereby plaintiff agreed to sell the Santa Clara Creamery 51,600 pounds of Grade A milk per month, and the creamery agreed to purchase said milk at the Grade A price for the Santa Clara marketing area. The contract was terminable by either party upon 30 days' notice.

Thereafter, plaintiff furnished the milk and was paid the specified price. President Collins would then bill plaintiff for monthly "feeding charges" in an amount equal to the agreed rebate of 4 1/2 cents per gallon of milk delivered. No feeding services were ever performed by Collins or the Santa Clara Creamery.

P gives loan for 1.5cent off per gallon on rebate.

Approximately one year after the contract had gone into effect, Collins informed plaintiff that he needed money to pay off a debt or he would lose the creamery; that if he did not loan him $6,500, Collins would terminate his contract and find another dairyman who could raise the money. Collins promised to repay the loan by reducing the rebate 1 1/2 cents per gallon during the life of plaintiff's contract.

Plaintiff obtained the $6,500 and gave it to Collins in exchange for a promissory note dated April 16, 1963, signed by Collins and his wife. Plaintiff thereafter paid Collins a rebate of only 3 cents per gallon of milk delivered.

Plaintiff subsequently fell behind in the payment of his monthly rebates, making no payments after October 1963. By letter of May 22, 1964, Collins advised plaintiff that his contract had been terminated. Plaintiff was unable to obtain another Grade A milk contract and ultimately disposed of his dairy.

Plaintiff testified that during the life of his contract with the Santa Clara Creamery, his payments to Collins had totaled $10,677.72, which sum consisted of the $6500 loan and $4,177.72 in secret rebates.

Ct awarded rebates and loan value. Def's (creamery/collins) appeal.

Upon the facts, the court concluded that plaintiff was entitled to judgment against defendants Gene and Ruth Collins in the amount of $6,500 and against defendant Gene Collins in the additional amount of $4,177.72.

Judgment was accordingly entered, and defendants Collins appeal therefrom.

Defendants contend that the judgment must be reversed because the trial court erred in its findings that plaintiff was not *in pari delicto* with defendants; that he was a member of the class protected by § 4280, subdivision (a), of the Agricultural Code; and that he was entitled to recover from defendants the sums illegally paid to secure and obtain the Grade A milk contract.

Defendants point out that § 4280, subdivision (a), is applicable to milk producers as well as to milk distributors and prohibits the acceptance as well as the payment of secret rebates, and assert that the evidence in the instant case establishes as a matter of law that plaintiff violated the statute and was therefore *in pari delicto* with defendants. They rely upon . . . (citations omitted) as authority for the general rule that an illegal contract furnishes no basis for an action either in law or in equity. However, in our case, the situation is not one in which the two parties, who were equally at fault, made the joint decision to enter into a transaction violative of § 4280, subdivision (a), of the Agricultural Code. The trial court found that "because of his position," plaintiff was not *in pari delicto* with defendants. It is obvious that by plaintiff's "position," the court had reference to the fact that plaintiff was a small dairyman whose economic survival was dependent upon his ability to obtain a Grade A milk contract in a locality where such contracts were extremely scarce and that he was therefore peculiarly vulnerable to the exertion of economic coercion by a person such as defendant, who was apparently unwilling to do business with any dairyman who would not agree to pay him unlawful rebates. Under these circumstances, we are satisfied that the court correctly determined that the case came within a well-recognized exception to the rule of *in pari delicto* and that since plaintiff was only slightly at fault and defendants were grievously at fault, plaintiff was entitled to recover what he had rendered as performance of the executed illegal transaction. . . .

Defendants also point out that the purpose of the Milk Stabilization Act (Agr. Code, §§ 4200–4420) is to eliminate unfair, unjust, destructive and demoralizing trade practices in the producing, marketing, sale, processing, or distribution of milk, which tend to undermine regulations and standards of the content and purity, and to insure a reasonable amount of stability and prosperity in the marketing of milk. . . . Defendants assert that § 4280, subdivision (a), and certain other provisions of the Milk Stabilization Act that prohibit unfair trade practices, are very similar to the Unfair Practices Act (Bus. & Prof. Code, §§ 17000–17101) and that both acts should be applied in the same manner. Since § 17051 of the Business and Professions Code provides that any contract made in violation of the Unfair Practices Act is illegal and affords no basis for recovery, defendants reason that the same rule should apply to contracts made in violation of § 4280, subdivision (a) of the Agricultural Code.

No provision similar to § 17051 of the Business and Professions Code is contained in the Milk Stabilization Act. Undoubtedly the Legislature in enacting the Milk Stabilization Act saw no necessity for including such a directive and being familiar with the doctrine of *in pari delicto* and the courts' application thereof, left the matters arising under the act to be dealt with by the courts as the facts of each case might warrant.

Judgment affirmed. AGEE and TAYLOR, JJ., concur.

NOTES AND QUESTIONS

1. ***Deterrent effect?*** Would you expect litigation such as the *Karpinski* case to be effective to deter illegal rebate arrangements between producers and distributors of milk?

2. *Public enforcement:* After the illegal kickback arrangement in *Karpinski* came to light, the California Director of Agriculture revoked the distributor's license of the Santa Clara Creamery in 1965. In addition, the California Attorney General brought suits against the creamery's bonding companies for the amount of the rebates, citing *Karpinski*. In one of these cases, the judge directed a verdict against a bonding company; a later poll of the jury revealed that they would have found for the bonding company because the jurors lacked sympathy with producers who entered illegal contracts.

3. *A statutory solution?* In 1967, California enacted a milk pooling statute that gives all producers a share of Grade A prices under pooling plans for each area. The aim is to eliminate incentives for illegal rebate schemes. This statutory scheme is still in effect.[10]

4. *The murky question of who is most at fault:* Richard Danzig investigated the background of the *Karpinski* case[11] and noted that the entire trial took just over one hour. Moreover, Gene Collins, one of the defendants, was a long-haul truck driver, and he could not take the time away from work to attend the trial. Is it likely that the court had enough information upon which to make a judgment about which party was most at fault? While there will be some clear cases, in many situations both parties are likely to have displayed a significant amount of fault. What should a court do then? Are the approaches discussed in Notes 2 and 3, *supra*, more promising ways to have a deterrent effect?

5. *What's in a "grade"?* Danzig's investigation also revealed something that students care about in a slightly different context: what was the difference between "Grade A" and "Grade B"? Answer: nothing, from a qualitative perspective. Danzig learned that in California, in 1960:[12]

> [T]here were two basic kinds of contracts under which a producer might sell his milk: Grade A contracts and Grade B contracts. Since most milk in California has for some time been of the quality required for use as fluid milk, the denomination "Grade A" or "Grade B" refers to the ultimate use of the milk, rather than its quality. Milk purchased under a Grade A contract was distributed as fluid milk; milk purchased under a Grade B contract was used primarily for cheese. The prices paid per gallon under a Grade A contract were always considerably higher than Grade B prices; consequently, such contracts were highly sought after.

---

[10] *See* CAL. FOOD & AGRIC. CODE §§ 62700–62731 (2009), the Gonsalves Milk Pooling Act.

[11] Richard Danzig, THE CAPABILITY PROBLEM IN CONTRACT LAW: FURTHER READINGS ON WELL-KNOWN CASES 134–46 (1st ed., Foundation Press 1978).

[12] *Id.* at 135–36.

2.   Contracts Against Public Policy

a.   Introduction

Courts have long asserted the power to refuse to enforce contracts or provisions in contracts that are against public policy. While the doctrine appears to call for judicial regulation of bargains, courts have used it primarily in limited and well-defined areas. The Restatement (Second) of Contracts, §§ 178–199, deals with the subject. Section 178 sets a general standard, saying that a promise is unenforceable if "the interest in its enforcement is clearly outweighed in the circumstances by a public policy against the enforcement of such terms." It then sets out a complex balancing test. Courts are to weigh such things as the forfeiture that will result if they deny enforcement against the seriousness of any misconduct involved and the extent to which it was deliberate.

Contracts in restraint of trade (§§ 186–188) and contracts that impair family relations (§§ 189–191) are two long-established areas subject to supervision on grounds of public policy. Other promises usually denied enforcement are promises to commit a tort (§ 192); promises to violate a fiduciary duty (§ 193); promises to interfere with the performance of a contract of another (§ 194); terms exempting a party from liability for harm caused intentionally, recklessly, or negligently (§ 195); and terms exempting a party from the legal consequences of misrepresentation (§ 196). Restitution usually is also unavailable "unless denial of restitution would cause disproportionate forfeiture" (§ 197). We deal further with liability exemptions (also known as waivers or releases) and misrepresentation in Sections B.5. and C of this chapter, *infra*.

b.   Covenants by employees not to compete

A classic application of the public policy doctrine involves covenants by employees not to compete after they terminate their employment. What is involved? On one hand, an employer does not have to hire anyone. It can choose to give up this freedom not to hire only if employees agree to particular terms. If it wants to demand such a promise, then, absent fraud or the like, we could view it as an application of free contract. Furthermore, employers seek to protect a real interest by demanding contract provisions against competition by former employees. Employers invest a great deal in training employees, and they expect this investment to pay off in the future. Moreover, employees may learn trade secrets such as manufacturing processes, business strategies, and the characteristics of potential customers. Employees often establish long-term continuing relationships with customers and co-workers, who may follow them when they move to other employers or open their own businesses. Employees get the chance to create and develop these relationships through the investment of employers. An employee who takes advantage of these relationships after leaving the employer may harm the employer. So, employers sometimes seek to protect themselves through contract provisions known as "covenants" (ongoing promises to act or refrain from certain conduct) prohibiting employees from competing with the employer, post-termination.

Nonetheless, courts, in the name of public policy, carefully police employee covenants not to compete. We must ask how and why they do this, and what the likely impact of their effort is.

FULLERTON LUMBER CO. v. TORBORG
Wisconsin Supreme Court
270 Wis. 133, 70 N.W.2d 585 (1955)

Action by plaintiff Fullerton Lumber Company, a foreign corporation, against defendant Albert C. Torborg, for an injunction restraining defendant from breach of contract. Upon findings of fact and conclusions of law filed by the trial court, judgment was entered dismissing plaintiff's complaint. From that judgment plaintiff appeals.

Plaintiff is a Minnesota corporation with its principal office in Minneapolis. It operates a number of retail lumber yards in Wisconsin and other states. Defendant began working for the plaintiff in a managerial capacity in 1938. In December 1942 he entered the military service and when he returned to civilian life in November 1945 he was rehired by the company and placed in charge of a yard at Gaylord, Minnesota. At the time of his rehiring he was advised that the pension plan provided for the company's employees had been made applicable to managers who had been employed five years; that the time spent in military service could be counted in the five-year period required to qualify; and that it was the company's policy to require employment agreements with employees who were eligible to participate in such plans. In March 1946 defendant was transferred to Clintonville, Wisconsin, as manager of the company's yard there. On April 15, 1946, he entered into an employment contract with the company which provided, in part:

> If I cease to be employed by the company for any reason, I will not, for a period of ten years thereafter, work directly or indirectly for any establishment or on my own account handling lumber, building material, or fuel at retail in any city, village, or town, or within a radius of 15 miles thereof, where I have served as manager for the company within a period of five years preceding the date of termination of my employment, unless first obtaining permission, in writing, from the company. . . .

In November 1953 [Torborg] voluntarily quit, advising plaintiff that he intended to open his own lumber yard in that city. He thereafter incorporated the Clintonville Lumber and Supply, Inc. and on December 1, 1953, commenced business in Clintonville, taking with him three other of the plaintiff's Clintonville yard employees.

Plaintiff thereafter brought this action to enjoin defendant from working for the Clintonville Lumber and Supply, Inc., for himself or for any other lumber and fuel business within a radius of 15 miles of Clintonville during a period of 10 years following the termination of his employment by the plaintiff, as provided in that portion of the contract set out above. The trial court found that the restraint as to time was unreasonably long and not reasonably necessary for the fair protection of plaintiff's business, and granted judgment dismissing the complaint. . . .

MARTIN, J. . . .

There is no question that restrictive covenants of the type involved in this contract are lawful and enforceable if they meet the tests of necessity and reasonableness.

As stated in Restatement of Contracts § 516 . . . :

> The following bargains do not impose unreasonable restraint of trade unless effecting, or forming part of a plan to effect, a monopoly: . . . .
>
> > (f) A bargain by an assistant, servant, or agent not to compete with his employer, or principal, during the term of the employment or agency, or thereafter, within such territory and during such time as may be reasonably necessary for the protection of the employer or principal, without imposing undue hardship on the employee or agent.

At § 515 . . . of the same text it is stated:

> A restraint of trade is unreasonable, in the absence of statutory authorization or dominant social or economic justification, if it
>
> > (a) is greater than is required for the protection of the person for whose benefit the restraint is imposed. . . ."

It is established that the burden rests upon the employer to establish both the necessity for, and the reasonableness of, the restrictive covenant he seeks to enforce by enjoining the employee from violating its terms.

Cases such as . . . (citations omitted), where this court has upheld restrictive covenants, are not very helpful in this instance because they grow out of the sale of a business rather than employment. As pointed out in the Restatement of Contracts § 515, Comment (b):

> No identical test of reasonableness applies to bargains for the transfer of land or goods or of a business, on the one hand, and to bargains for employment on the other. The elements that must be considered in order to determine reasonableness differ in the two cases, especially where the employment is of a specialized character, and familiarity and skill in it are assets of the employee. Limitations of his use of these assets are less readily supported than limitations of the use of property or in carrying on a business.

Our court has consistently recognized this difference with respect to applying the test of reasonableness, *Milwaukee Linen Supply Co. v. Ring*, 210 Wis. 467, 246 N.W. 567 (1933), and has allowed a much greater scope of restraint in contracts between vendor and vendee than between employer and employee. As there stated, "There is 'small scope for the restraint of the right to labor and trade and a correspondingly small freedom of contract.' " *Id.* at 469. In all these cases the facts must be carefully scrutinized to determine whether the employee is restrained beyond the point where he could be reasonably anticipated to injure his employer's business. Where the facts warrant such a conclusion this court has held that the entire covenant must fall.

Basically if part is unreasonable can't enforce I think

[I]f full performance of a promise indivisible in terms, would involve unreasonable restraint, the promise is illegal and is not enforceable even for so much of the performance as would be a reasonable restraint." Restatement of Contracts § 518.

We agree with the trial court that the 10-year period of restraint imposed by the instant contract is unreasonably long. There is no case cited where this court has upheld a covenant in an employment contract restricting the employee from engaging in competitive activity for so long a time, and the evidence in this case does not establish that a 10-year restraint is necessary for the protection of plaintiff's business.

It cannot be seriously disputed, however, that defendant was plaintiff's key employee in the Clintonville yard. Being a foreign corporation with all its officers and supervisory employees outside of the state, the plaintiff necessarily depended for the growth and maintenance of goodwill in the Clintonville area upon the efforts and personal assets of the defendant. In the first three years of his employment as manager there he tripled the business of the yard and thereafter (with the exception of 1952 when the entire country experienced a building "boom") he maintained the sales at a level averaging well over $200,000 per year. He terminated his employment at the end of 1953 and immediately commenced operations in Clintonville in competition with the plaintiff. The sales of plaintiff's yard for 1954, based upon its business for the first five months of that year, were estimated at approximately $60,000, a decline of more than two-thirds of the average annual sales of the previous years (excluding the peak year 1952).

Basically Def was 0 for P and clearly shown by diff in results when not there

These facts conclusively show not only that the business of plaintiff's Clintonville yard depended largely on the efforts and customer contacts of the defendant, but that it suffered an irreparable loss when defendant took those efforts and customer contacts, as well as three other employees of plaintiff's yard, into a competitive business immediately after he left its employ.

Defendant states in his brief:

> We concede at this point that plaintiff does have a legitimate interest in its business and goodwill that it is entitled to preserve by exacting a reasonable restrictive covenant from its manager. The testimony in this case clearly shows that defendant has been able to establish a business at Clintonville which has substantially cut into the business of plaintiff. This, of course, was possible because defendant started his business immediately after he quit plaintiff, while all of his connections with the customers of the plaintiff were still strong. It is obvious that if defendant were removed from the scene for any extended period, and his place were taken by another Fullerton manager, the goodwill and trade of the plaintiff would be safe in the hands of the new manager.

Big statement

There has been no case in this court where the facts presented such a clear need for the kind of protection plaintiff thought it was bargaining for when this contract was made. The facts show that it had every reason to anticipate its business would suffer if defendant, after developing and establishing personal relations with its customers in Clintonville, chose to leave its employ and enter into competition with it in that vicinity.

It is, of course, necessary to consider whether the legality of the covenant is open to objection on the ground of coercion or interference with individual liberty. "[I]njunctive relief will not be awarded against breach of a covenant the real purpose of which was to prevent the employee from quitting the employers' service." Annotation 52 A.L.R. 1363.

There is no evidence that such a purpose existed when this contract was drawn and the fact that defendant did in fact terminate the employment to carry on competitive operations shows that the restrictive covenant had no such deterring effect upon him. There is no showing that it had had that effect at any time while he was working for the plaintiff.

The evidence of irreparable damage to the plaintiff is so strong in this case that we have undertaken a thorough reconsideration of the rule that has obtained in Wisconsin — that a covenant imposing an unreasonable restraint is unenforceable in its entirety.

In *General Bronze Corporation v. Schmeling*, 208 Wis. 565, 243 N.W. 469, 470 (1932), where, in the sale of a business, the contract contained a restrictive covenant not to engage in a competitive business within certain states of the United States "or within the Dominion of Canada or the Republic of Mexico," the court found no evidence that the plaintiff had ever had any business in Canada and Mexico. It was held that to the extent that the covenant restricted competition in those countries it was broader than reasonably necessary to protect the goodwill sold. The plaintiff contended that the contract by its terms was divisible and that such portions as were void by reason of being in restraint of trade could be separated and the contract enforced as to the proper territory. This contention was held valid.

The Massachusetts court has applied the rule that if the restrictive agreement as to territory is unreasonable, even though it be indivisible in terms, it is nevertheless enforceable for so much of the performance as would be a reasonable restraint. In *Whiting Milk Companies v. O'Connell*, 277 Mass. 570, 179 N.E. 169, 170 (1931), where the covenant in question restricted an employee from interfering with the business of the employer or selling dairy products to any of its customers, and it was found that the plaintiff's business extended over a large area of the state, the court held that the covenant was too broad. Although the contract was not by its own terms divisible, since it specified the prohibited territory in general terms, the court enjoined its breach to the extent of the customers the defendant had served while in the plaintiff's employ. . . .

In a later case, *Metropolitan Ice Co. v. Ducas*, 291 Mass. 403, 196 N.E. 856, 858 (1935), the rule was extended to the time limitation imposed in a restrictive covenant of an employment contract. Referring to the application of the rule in the Whiting case and others, the court said: "No reason presents itself why the rule of reasonable enforcement as to space should not be applicable to time." Whereas the agreement restriction was for a period of 15 years, the court affirmed the decree of the lower court enjoining the defendant for 18 months from the date of the decree.

In 5 WILLISTON ON CONTRACTS (rev. ed.) §§ 1659 and 1660, the author discusses the divisibility of promises and states that the traditional test of severability is the "blue-penciling" test (which this court applied in the *General Bronze Corporation* case, *supra*.) But he points out that in England, which is the source of this rule . . . , it has been held that:

> . . . where a negative restrictive covenant, indivisible in terms, extended beyond a time that the court in its discretion thought appropriate for an injunction, it granted an injunction for the period during which it deemed that remedy reasonable." § 1659, p. 4683.

. . . Williston, referring to such authority (including most of the cases dealt with above), stated in Vol. 5, § 1660, p. 4683:

> Covenants, in terms unlimited as to time, have sometimes been divided in the way suggested. . . . While the Restatement of Contracts § 518 has accepted the rule laid down by the majority of American courts as stated in the preceding section [i.e., the blue-penciling test], the tendency of the late American cases has been toward the minority view, that the legality of contracts in restraint of trade should not turn upon the mere form of wording but rather upon the reasonableness of giving effect to the indivisible promise to the extent that would be lawful."

. . . It is our considered opinion that this view should be adopted in Wisconsin. While we recognize that the rule of partial enforcement of indivisible promises is a departure from that which this court has adhered to in the past, there is no departure from the general principle that contracts in restraint of trade are void as against public policy if they deprive the public of the restricted party's industry or injure the party himself by precluding him from pursuing his occupation and thus prevent him from supporting himself and his family. Where the terms of a restrictive covenant, not otherwise invalid, restrain an employee beyond either the area or the time within which an employer needs protection from competition by him, it is that excess of territory or time that is contrary to public policy and void.

As set out above, this court has been willing to apply the "blue-pencil" test to area restrictions, *General Bronze Corporation v. Schmeling, supra*, but we do not see why the basic reason for such willingness to enforce a contract after removing terms which are literally divisible should not also exist in the case of indivisible promises where the evidence is ample to support a finding as to the extent the restriction would be necessary and valid. Territory limits are by their nature more susceptible to separate specification than time and are often so expressed, but we see no difficulty in making a finding as to time upon evidence that is available to show the necessity for restraint in that respect.

In considering this rule many authorities point to the danger that its application might tend to encourage employers and purchasers possessing superior bargaining power to insist upon oppressive restrictions. However, these contracts are always subject to the test of whether their purpose is contrary to public policy, and if there is any credible evidence to sustain a finding that they are deliberately unreasonable and oppressive, such covenants must be held invalid whether severable or not.

The judgment is reversed and the cause remanded for a determination by the trial court of the extent of time as to which the restrictive covenant with respect to defendant's operations in Clintonville is reasonable and necessary for plaintiff's protection, and for judgment enjoining defendant from a breach thereof. It appears to us that a minimum period of three years would be supported by the evidence. It was established that after defendant took over the managership of plaintiff's yard in 1945 he built the business to a fairly constant level in that period of time, and it must be assumed that any manager taking his place could accomplish the same thing if the restrictions of the contract were enforced against the defendant during that time. In view of the fact that defendant has engaged in continuous competitive activities since December 1, 1953, employing the advantage gained while he was in the service of the plaintiff, the injunction should run from the date of the judgment rather than the date the employment terminated. . . .

Judgment reversed and cause remanded for further proceedings in accordance with this opinion.

GEHL, J. (dissenting) . . .   [handwritten: DISSENT BEGINS]

It is true, as the majority say, that there has been a tendency on the part of some courts to ascertain whether a contract in restraint of trade is divisible and, if found to be, to hold it unreasonable only to the extent necessary for the protection of the covenantee. Unless that position is limited, however, as it has been by this court, it gives effect to the court's notion as to what should be included in the contract, rather than to the intent of the parties as expressed in the contract, the parties who, had they desired a narrower or a broader provision, should and could have expressed it in the writing. If the provision is to be treated as being divisible, such purpose must be found in the contract itself; that quality should not be supplied by the court simply because it might be considered that the parties should have made broader or narrower provision against possible competition than they did. That is the rule of this state.

General Bronze Corporation v. Schmeling . . . was an action brought by a corporation to restrain former stockholders from competition. The defendants had been the principal stockholders of a manufacturing corporation which had sold its assets to the plaintiff. By the terms of the agreement it was provided that the defendants would not within 15 years from the date of the transfer engage in competition with the plaintiff in the United States, the District of Columbia, the Dominion of Canada, and the Republic of Mexico. . . . The action was brought to restrain the defendants from violating the provisions of the covenant. The court said:

> There is no evidence that the business of this company extended into Canada or Mexico, and to the extent that the covenant restricts competition in these countries, it is broader than is reasonably necessary to protect the goodwill sold. However, it is contended by the plaintiff that the contract by its own terms is divisible, and that the portions of the contract which are void by reason of being in restraint of trade may readily be separated and dropped, and the contract enforced as to the proper territory. . . . We have concluded that this contention is valid. The parties have adopted as one unit of the restrictive agreement the states and territories of the United States and the District of Columbia, descriptive in a territorial sense of the entire

[handwritten margin note: Basically establishs severability as valid in Wisco, unlike by]

United States; as a second unit the Dominion of Canada, and as a third unit the Republic of Mexico. These areas are disjunctively described and furnish a proper basis, under the doctrine of the foregoing cases, for dividing the covenant and enforcing it in the territory that is coextensive with the business of the old company.

It will be observed that the court said and pointed out very clearly that the contract "by its own terms is divisible." It could not be questioned that if the divisibility as to area should appear in the contract itself, the same requirement should apply as to time. This case is cited in the opinion of the majority, but the majority omits to refer to the fact that the court based its conclusion upon the fact that the contract was by its own terms divisible. . . .

I have found no Wisconsin case which suggests that the court, rather than the parties who made the contract, should be permitted to substitute arbitrarily for the parties a provision making an indivisible covenant divisible. The citation of text authorities and of cases from other jurisdictions "is but misplaced industry." They are of no help to this court, which has so clearly stated the rule that if a covenant is to be treated as being divisible and therefore enforceable to the extent that it is a reasonable restriction, the fact of divisibility must appear from the contract itself. If it can be said that a single provision as to time, 10 years as is this case, is divisible and it is possible to read that quality out of the terms of the contract, then it is only reasonable to ask, how could a provision indivisible as to time be effectively expressed?

It is apparent that the majority have construed the contract and applied a rule in the light of what has taken place since its execution. It occurs to me to inquire: as of what time are we to determine that the terms of a contract are or are not unreasonable? Is it to be determined as of the time of its execution, or as of a later time? May we say that a contract is void and then, not because of its terms, but because of the manner in which one of the parties to it has subsequently construed its terms, or because he has violated its provisions to the loss of the other party, still hold it enforceable in whole or in part? I doubt it. . . .

It would seem that if a provision of a contract valid when made cannot be rendered invalid even by legislative action, one invalid when made cannot be validated, in whole or in part, by action of the parties.

The mere fact that developments subsequent to the execution of the contract show that the parties, or one of them, should have made a better bargain for himself does not affect the situation.

I would affirm.

NOTES AND QUESTIONS

1. *The legislature responds:* In response to *Fullerton Lumber*, the Wisconsin legislature in 1957 passed Wis. Stat. § 103.465, which provides that a covenant not to compete by an assistant, servant, or agent is enforceable only "if the restrictions imposed are reasonably necessary for the protection of the employer" and that "[a]ny covenant . . . imposing an unreasonable restraint is illegal, void and

unenforceable even as to any part of the covenant or performance that would be a reasonable restraint." The Wisconsin Supreme Court interpreted this statute in *Star Direct, Inc. v. Dal Pra*,[13] holding that an unenforceable "business clause" (prohibiting a former employee from engaging in a "substantially similar" business activity in the employee's former sales territory even though not in competition with the employer) was divisible from a "customer clause" (prohibiting the employee from soliciting customers of the employer) and from a "confidentiality clause" (prohibiting use of information such as marketing techniques, customer lists, and trade secrets), and thus the latter two clauses were enforceable notwithstanding substantial overlap among the three clauses. Two justices dissented. Chief Justice Shirley Abrahamson, in her dissenting opinion, noted that the purpose of the statute was to place "the onus on employers to draft reasonable restrictive employment covenants." She also quoted from another opinion of the court: "A principal argument against giving effect to reasonable aspects of a restraint is that the employer can fashion ominous covenants which affect the mobility of employees because of their *in terrorem* effect on employees who respect contractual obligations and their effect on competitors who do not wish to risk legal difficulties." How would you expect the Wisconsin statute, as interpreted in *Star Direct*, to affect the drafting strategies of employers?

2. *Aftermath in* **Fullerton:** On remand, Albert Torborg was ordered not to compete with Fullerton Lumber for three years. Torborg then sent a letter to the Secretary of State of Wisconsin withdrawing as Secretary-Treasurer of Clintonville Lumber and Supply. In the next year's annual report for the company, Betty Torborg, with the same address as Albert, was listed as vice president, and she continued to hold various officer positions for the company for some years. Why didn't the lawyers for Fullerton Lumber also ask to enjoin Betty Torborg from running Clintonville Lumber and Supply? After the court order against Albert expired, he again appeared in the company's annual reports as Secretary-Treasurer and later as President and the company continued in business for decades. Meanwhile, Fullerton Lumber's presence in Clintonville gradually faded away.

3. *Balancing the equities:* The Nebraska Supreme Court, in *Philip G. Johnson & Co. v. Salmen*, listed factors to balance in judging whether or not to enforce a covenant not to compete.[14] A court should consider: (1) the degree of inequality of bargaining power; (2) the risk of the employer actually losing customers as a result of the competition; (3) the extent of respective participation by the parties in securing and retaining customers; (4) the good faith of the employer; (5) the existence of general knowledge about the identity of customers; (6) the nature and extent of the business position held by the employee promising not to compete; (7) the employee's training, health, and education, and the needs of his or her family; (8) the current conditions of employment; (9) the necessity of the employee changing his calling or residence if the covenant is enforced; and (10) the correspondence of the restraint found in the contract with the need for protecting legitimate interests of the employer.

---

[13] 319 Wis. 2d 274, 767 N.W.2d 898 (2009); *see also* Metso Minerals Indus., Inc. v. FLSmidth-Excel LLC, 733 F. Supp. 2d 980 (E.D. Wis. 2010).

[14] 211 Neb. 123, 317 N.W.2d 900 (1982).

What are the consequences of standards that call for balancing so many factors?[15] Professor Rachel Arnow-Richman says that if courts are going to evaluate the fairness of noncompete agreements, they must "closely investigat[e] at least three broad aspects of the formation process: the ability of the employee to bargain regarding the agreement's terms, the appropriateness of the scope of the restraint as of the time of formation, and the consideration provided by the employer in exchange for the noncompete."[16]

4. *A flat rule:* Under California Business and Professions Code § 16600 (2015), "every contract by which anyone is restrained from engaging in a lawful profession, trade, or business of any kind is to that extent void." What are the advantages of prohibiting the enforcement of employee restrictive covenants? Do you see any disadvantages? Would this California statute deter firms from doing business there when they had employees who might be free to leave and take their talents to a competitor? Even if such firms were not deterred from doing business in, say, Silicon Valley, might the statute impose a cost that could injure such firms, causing them to pay their employees less? How might you determine whether this was true? It has been reported that California employers are more likely than employers in other states to have employees sign contracts agreeing not to disclose trade secrets and to be more aggressive than other employers in trying to enforce such agreements.[17] Do you think trade secret agreements can be an adequate substitute, from an employer's perspective, for an employee restrictive covenant?

An economic efficiency argument is sometimes made to support the enforceability of covenants not to compete. If we do not enforce such covenants (assuming they are "reasonable"), those who might start businesses (e.g., technology whizzes) may decline to do so, fearing that they will end up like Fullerton Lumber, losing valued customers (or expertise) when an employee leaves.[18]

California effectively forbids such covenants, and so economic theory might predict that California should see depressed job growth. As is well known, however, it has been the most innovative state in the nation for many years, with far greater growth in sectors (such as technology) that would seem especially vulnerable to employee defection. Does California embarrass economic theory on this score, or does it simply suggest that other legal (or extra-legal) mechanisms are at work? Can you think of economic arguments for a flat rule such as California's?

5. *Sandwiched in between:* Recently, it appears that employers are starting to demand non-compete agreements even from lower-wage workers. Jimmy John's, a popular sandwich chain, has its employees sign a covenant not to compete that has a fairly large scope. Employees who sign the covenant agree not to work for a

[handwritten margin note: basically doesn't enforce any noncompete as a flat rule (Cali)]

---

[15] *See generally* Jeffrey G. Grody, *Partial Enforcement of Post-Employment Restrictive Covenants,* 15 COLUM. J.L. & SOC. PROBS. 181 (1979).

[16] Rachel S. Arnow-Richman, *Bargaining for Loyalty in the Information Age: A Reconsideration of the Role of Substantive Fairness in Enforcing Employee Noncompetes,* 80 OR. L. REV. 1163, 1234 (2001).

[17] Ronald J. Gilson, *The Legal Infrastructure of High Technology Industrial Districts: Silicon Valley, Route 128 and Covenants Not to Compete,* 74 N.Y.U. L. REV. 575 (1999).

[18] *See* Christina L. Wu, Comment, *Noncompete Agreements in California: Should California Courts Uphold Choice of Law Provisions Specifying Another State's Law?,* 51 UCLA L. REV. 593, 611 (2003); *see also* John Dwight Ingram, *Covenants Not to Compete,* 36 AKRON L. REV. 49, 78 (2002).

competitor (defined as any business that derives at least 10 percent of its sales from sandwiches), that is located within three miles of any Jimmy John's location, for a period of two years following the employee's departure from the sandwich chain.[19] Although it appears the chain does not regularly enforce the agreement, at the present time it would effectively prevent former Jimmy John's employees from making sandwiches for pay within the city limits of Chicago, Minneapolis, and Denver.

6. *Liquidated damages to the rescue?* Yet another possible strategy for employers is to provide for liquidated damages for enforcement of a covenant not to compete. In one case, *Willard Packing Co. v. Javier*,[20] an employer sought $50,000 in liquidated damages from a former employee, a packaging salesperson who went to work for a competitor. The Maryland court held that the employer had not met its burden of proving that the liquidated damages clause was a reasonable estimate of its loss, particularly in light of the inequality of bargaining power between the parties. It noted these arguments by the appellant-employer:

> Appellant put forth three bases in arguing for the reasonableness of the liquidated damages provision at issue. First, appellant alleged that, in an earlier case, the cost of litigating a breached non-compete provision against a former employee was approximately $50,000. Second, appellant alleged that $50,000 was a reasonable estimate of the expense incurred in hiring and training a salesman like Javier. Lastly, and we think particularly telling, appellant conceded that the covenant had been taken from employment contracts utilized by a competitor . . . because it was a persuasive valuation of appellant's damages.

The court found that the clause was not reasonable in light of anticipated or actual damages of the employer and was meant to "penalize and punish" the employee for going to work for a competitor.[21]

In another case, *Pollack v. Calimag*,[22] a court upheld a liquidated damages clause for $25,000 plus attorney's fees against an osteopathic physician named Dr. Pollack, who operated a pain clinic for another physician, a neurologist who had bought the clinic. After Dr. Pollack's contract was not renewed, he joined another pain clinic and advertised in Racine, the city where he had previously practiced, in violation of a covenant not to compete for one year within a 20-mile radius of his prior location. The Wisconsin court held that the covenant was reasonable to protect the neurologist's patient list and goodwill in the clinic, and that the $25,000 in liquidated

---

[19] *See* Dave Jamieson, Huffington Post, *Jimmy John's "Oppressive" Noncompete Agreement Survives Court Challenge*, Apr. 10, 2015, huffingtonpost.com/2015/04/10/jimmy-johns-noncompete-agreement_n_7042112.html; Dave Jamieson, Huffington Post, *Jimmy John's Noncompete Agreement, All Mapped Out*, Oct. 17, 2014, huffingtonpost.com/2014/10/17/jimmy-johns-noncompete-map_n_6005598.html.

[20] 169 Md. App. 109, 899 A.2d 940 (Md. App. 2004).

[21] More recently, the Maryland courts have *upheld* liquidated damages clauses in this context, finding that the employee seeking to escape the clause "failed to present evidence that the liquidated damages clause was unreasonable in any respect." *See* CAS Severn, Inc. v. Awalt, 213 Md. App. 683, 702–03, 75 A.3d 382, 393 (2013).

[22] 157 Wis. 2d 222, 458 N.W.2d 591 (Wis. App. 1990).

damages, about 18 percent of Dr. Pollack's annual salary, was also reasonable in light of the difficulty of estimating how many patients might follow him and also in light of evidence of actual harm of perhaps $21,000 in drawing away patients. The court also noted that the liquidated damages had been negotiated down by Dr. Pollack from a proposed $200,000.[23]

B.   SOCIAL CONTROL, CONTRACT, AND CHOICE

1.   Introduction

Individual freedom turns on having a large degree of choice. Choice is always limited. We cannot choose to live forever or to repeal the law of gravity. We bargain in the context of our experiences and existing social and economic situations. Nonetheless, those who value personal freedom celebrate maximizing choice. Ideally, contract coordinates choices so that both parties are better off. We are both free to choose whether or not to make a contract and what its terms should be. You seek the salary I will pay and find the tasks I wish performed enjoyable. I see you as a diligent and skillful employee well worth what I pay you. When we add a market with other employers and other employees, then I cannot pay you too little nor can you demand too much. Other potential contracts create a frame of reference affecting our satisfaction with our arrangement.

Perhaps paradoxically, the values of free choice and free contract demand some social control of the process. Suppose, for example, you did not want to make a contract with me. However, your words and actions caused me to think you had agreed to my proposals. We could honor free choice to the maximum and say that since there had been no meeting of the minds, there was no deal. However, this position would protect you at my expense if I had reasonably relied on what I had thought was our bargain. Moreover, since choice is a subjective matter, you could back out if you were willing to lie about whether you had intended to contract. There are many possible solutions to these problems. A legal system could require people to make choices in a certain form so they are less likely to make mistakes. It could limit your freedom by requiring you to use reasonable care in communication to see that you do not cause harm to me. It could hold you responsible for my reasonable interpretations of your words and conduct. We have already touched on this problem in *Hawkins v. McGee*, and we will develop it further in the second volume of these materials. We mention it here only to remind you that even the objective theory of contracts is a form of social control of the process. Under it, a person may commit a contract that she did not intend to make.

A system designed to promote and protect free choice must go further. Some people cannot exercise choice and protect themselves. We may worry whether a contract between an adult and a five-year-old child is likely to produce the benefits

---

[23] Some courts view interference with the doctor-patient relationship as a strong public policy concern of its own, likely to outweigh the interest in enforcing a contract, particularly using injunctive relief. *See* Valley Medical Specialists v. Farber, 197 Ariz. 363, 982 P.2d 1277 (1999). Enforcement of damages, however, would not necessarily raise the same degree of concern.

of free contract. We may worry whether those who are mentally ill can choose in their own best interests.

Once we start down this road, however, we encounter a problem. Children and those who are mentally ill are not the only people who may not be able to act in their own best interests. People have different capacities to choose what is prudent or best for themselves. Some are smarter than others. Some are honest and trusting, and others may take advantage of these admirable qualities. Some like the thrill of taking unreasonable risks.

Moreover, contracts affect third parties who have no say in the negotiations. Professor Frank H. Knight was a founder of the Chicago school of economics, which celebrates free enterprise and challenges governmental regulation. Nonetheless, Knight often pointed out that people frequently do not act for themselves alone. Rather, their choices benefit or injure members of their families as well. In his words:[24]

> [A] rather small fraction of the population of any modern nation enter into contracts on their own responsibility. Our "individualism" is really "familism"; all minors, the aged, and numerous persons in other classes, including for practical purposes the majority of adult women,[25] have their status-determining bargains made for them by other persons. The family is still the unit in production and consumption. It is hardly necessary to point out that all arguments for free contract are nullified or actually reversed whenever one person contracts on behalf of another.

For example, a father's money-losing business contract (or his gambling debts) may limit his daughter's chances for education. While she is in no way responsible for her father's choices, the consequences of those choices may affect her life. In holding a father to the consequences of his choices, courts may deny the daughter's freedom to choose.

We might ask in every case whether the contracting parties had the capability of choosing wisely. There are two concerns with this approach. We may worry about allowing judges or jurors to decide whether your choices are reasonable. Some insist that you are the only one who can decide what you value. We may also worry about the burden on commerce and on the courts if we must examine the bargaining skill of all those who make contracts that turn out poorly. Some insist that as long as I do nothing illegal and commit no torts, the fruits of my bargaining skill belong to me. You got a bad deal, but I got a good one. There is debate about my obligation to consider your interests when we make a contract and when we perform it. Our responses may differ as context changes. For example, we may accept self-interest as the only guide when two horse-traders wheel and deal. We may hesitate to allow self-interest to govern in transactions between, say, an attorney and her client.

---

[24] Frank H. Knight, *The Ethics of Competition*, in The Ethics of Competition and Other Essays 41, 49 (Allen & Unwin 1951). Knight also said: "The family is the minimum effective social unit, and a vital part of the social problem is allocating responsibility for all those who cannot — or even will not — take adequate responsibility for themselves." Frank H. Knight, Intelligence and Democratic Action 160 (Harvard University Press 1960).

[25] [Eds. note: This essay was published originally in 1923.]

Freedom also implies that I cannot interfere with your choice. I may put a gun to your head and insist that you make a contract with me. I may trick you into making a choice. I may be able to influence your understanding of the transaction so you think it advantageous when in fact it is not. I may lie or I may deceive by half-truths. Some find the situation harder to resolve when I do not coerce or trick you myself. Instead, I take advantage of a situation where your choices are constrained or where I know that you misunderstand the contract and its likely consequences. We can relieve the burden on courts and support the security of transactions by imposing a heavy burden of self-reliance. However, the more the legal system moves in this direction, the harder it is to justify its actions in terms of freedom and choice. Most of us do not "choose" to make decisions with guns to our heads.

As always, real problems involve conflicting values. Free choice may not be the only value involved. Some want to make it easier to run large organizations. Others may want to take care of the disadvantaged, either by fashioning rules in their favor or on a case-by-case basis.[26]

We will look at the idea of free choice and free contract, and at the degree of social control of contract implicit within it. The rules are sufficiently flexible to allow very different views to affect the results without changing the legal formula. Furthermore, views have changed over time. Professor Duncan Kennedy comments on the indeterminacy we find in modern law:[27]

> One way of conceiving of the transition from Classical to modern legal thought is through the imagery of core and periphery. Classical individualism dealt with the issues of community versus autonomy, regulation versus facilitation and paternalism versus self-determination by affirming the existence of a core of legal freedom which was equated with firm adherence to autonomy, facilitation, and self-determination. The existence of countertendencies was acknowledged, but in a backhanded way. By its "very nature," freedom must have limits; these could be derived as implications from that nature; and they would then constitute a periphery of exceptions to the core doctrines.
>
> What distinguishes the modern situation is the breakdown of the conceptual boundary between the core and the periphery, so that all the conflicting positions are at least potentially relevant to all issues. The Classical concepts oriented us to one ethos or the other — to core or periphery — and then permitted consistent argument within that point of view, with a few hard cases occurring at the borderline. Now, each of the conflicting visions claims universal relevance, but is unable to establish hegemony anywhere.

---

[26] *See* Duncan Kennedy, *Distributive and Paternalist Motives in Contract and Tort Law, with Special Reference to Compulsory Terms and Unequal Bargaining Power*, 41 Md. L. Rev. 563 (1982); Roberto Unger, *The Critical Legal Studies Movement*, 96 Harv. L. Rev. 561 (1983).

[27] Duncan Kennedy, *Form and Substance in Private Law Adjudication*, 89 Harv. L. Rev. 1685, 1737 (1976).

2.   Capacity to Contract — *[New]*

A system championing free choice must face those people who cannot choose in their own best interests. Few would want to uphold contracts between a capable adult and someone who was severely mentally ill or a very young child. Granting this, the legal system then faces a typical line-drawing problem with the typical difficulties. How do we define incapacity in an adult? When does one cease being a child subject to protection? Do we want to pay the price of case-by-case determination, or can we have rules that make matters clear?

Furthermore, to what extent do, or should, courts consider policies other than choice when they deal with capacity? United States Circuit Judge, and former law professor, Richard Posner rejected a claim that demanding self-reliance always serves to make the market function better. *Sutliff, Inc. v. Donovan Companies, Inc.*[28] involved the adequacy of a criminal complaint alleging mail fraud.

[reject the claim that self-reliance always makes mkt function better]

> [T]he complaint alleges that the defendants, knowing that Mrs. Sutliff was psychologically incapacitated (perhaps having driven her to this state) and desiring to injure their competitors by getting them to extend credit to Sutliff [Inc.] that it could not repay, inveigled Mrs. Sutliff into selling oil to defendants below its [Sutliff, Inc.'s] cost. The defendants tell us that *this was no more than driving a hard bargain; that they did society a favor in driving from the market a businesswoman too weak-minded to know that you cannot flourish if you buy dear and sell cheap*; and that if they are guilty of a federal crime so is the consumer who buys a product below what he thinks are the seller's costs. This argument ignores, however, the allegations respecting Mrs. Sutliff's mental state. If you contract with someone who lacks the mental capacity to enter into a legally enforceable contract, not only is the contract voidable on grounds of incapacity; it is voidable on grounds of fraud, provided that the other party took advantage of the mental incapacity when he made the contract. (Emphasis added.)

Do you read Judge Posner's opinion as requiring a case-by-case appraisal of the weakness and strength of all bargainers? When you read the material in later sections dealing with duress, misrepresentation, and failing to read documents, remember the defendant's argument. Do the courts accept the idea that it is a good thing to drive from the market businesspeople who are too weak-minded? Is there anything to the argument? Why do teachers in professional schools give low grades to students who do poorly?

a.   Mental incapacity to contract

The law of mental capacity to contract reflects changing views about mental illness. Courts based earlier decisions on ideas about mental capacity and personal responsibility that Freudians later attacked. If a person could understand what he was doing, his choices were binding. For example, in *American Granite Co. v. Kringel,*[29] a creditor sued on two promissory notes. The trial court found Kringel

[CASE]

---

[28] 727 F.2d 648 (7th Cir. 1984).

[29] 156 Wis. 94, 144 N.W. 204 (1914).

competent to do business when he signed the notes. The evidence showed Kringel was severely afflicted by "a disorder commonly affecting the mind." A short time after the notes were signed, he was placed under guardianship. He was declared insane and sent to a mental hospital, where he died a few months after the notes had been executed.

Nonetheless, the Supreme Court of Wisconsin affirmed the trial court. It said "a person who, in general, is insane, may bind himself by contract made during a lucid interval rendering him capable of appreciating the nature of his acts and exercising judgment thereto." Notice that the Supreme Court of Wisconsin said nothing about what the one receiving the notes knew about Kringel's condition nor the fairness of the transaction. Some today would question the reality of an apparent lucid interval during which he seemed capable of appreciating situations and exercising judgment. However, if I appear lucid and you know nothing about my mental problems, you have an interest in the benefit of your bargain with me.

The Restatement (Second) of Contracts § 15 attempts to fashion a modern statement of the impact of mental illness on capacity to contract. Members of the advisory group considering § 15 suggested that the Reporter update the statement of the law on mental capacity. There had been significant changes in psychiatric thought, which had been reflected in the criminal law defense of insanity. Appellate courts see relatively few cases involving mental capacity in civil actions. Trial courts or lawyers in their offices handle most of them. The Restatement could make a contribution by suggesting a modern approach. Courts could consider whether they should revise traditional statements of the rules in light of changes in views about mental illness and changes in the criminal law standards. Professor Robert Braucher, the Reporter who drafted § 15, accepted this suggestion. His draft, as polished by the various committees and members of the American Law Institute, is as follows:

§ 15. Mental Illness or Defect

(1) A person incurs only voidable contractual duties by entering into a transaction if by reason of mental illness or defect

(a) he is unable to understand in a reasonable manner the nature and consequences of the transaction, or

(b) he is unable to act in a reasonable manner in relation to the transaction and the other party has reason to know of his condition.

(2) Where the contract is made on fair terms and the other party is without knowledge of the mental illness or defect, the power of avoidance under Subsection (1) terminates to the extent that the contract has been so performed in whole or in part or circumstances have so changed that avoidance would be inequitable. In such a case a court may grant relief as justice requires.

Comment:

a. Rationale. A contract made by a person who is mentally incompetent requires the reconciliation of two conflicting policies: the protection of justified expectations and of the security of transactions, and the protection of persons unable to protect themselves against imposition. Each policy has sometimes prevailed to a greater extent than is stated in this Section. . . .

b. The standard of competency. . . . Where no guardian has been appointed, there is full contractual capacity in any case unless the mental illness or defect has affected the particular transaction: a person may be able to understand almost nothing, or only simple or routine transactions, or he may be incompetent only with respect to a particular type of transaction. Even though understanding is complete, he may lack capacity to control his acts in the way that the normal individual can and does control them; in such cases the incapacity makes the contract voidable only if the other party has reason to know of his condition. Where a person has some understanding of a particular transaction [that] is affected by mental illness or defect, the controlling consideration is whether the transaction in its result is one [that] a reasonably competent person might have made. . . .

c. Proof of incompetency. . . . [W]hen there is mental illness or defect but some understanding . . . the critical fact often is departure from the normal pattern of similar transactions, and particularly inadequacy of consideration.

d. Operative effect of incompetency. . . . Regardless of the other party's knowledge or good faith and regardless of the fairness of the terms, the incompetent person on regaining full capacity may affirm or disaffirm the contract, or the power to affirm or disaffirm may be exercised on his behalf by his guardian or after his death by his personal representative. . . .

e. Effect of performance. Where the contract has been performed in whole or in part, avoidance is permitted only on equitable terms. . . . Any benefits still retained by the incompetent must be restored or paid for, and restitution must be made for any necessaries furnished under the contract. . . .

NOTES AND QUESTIONS

1. *New York applies the Restatement's second test, involving lack of control:* In *Ortelere v. Teachers' Retirement Board*,[30] the New York Court of Appeals applied the Restatement's test concerning lack of control, despite an ability to understand, to a teacher who was on leave for mental illness when she elected maximum retirement benefits, payable to her during her life, and then died two months later, leaving nothing for her husband of 38 years. He had left his job to take care of her. Mrs. Ortelere suffered from involutional psychosis, melancholia type. She suffered a nervous breakdown at age 60 and took a leave of absence, toward the end of which she made the retirement election and then began receiving retirement benefits. She was extremely depressed and unable to care for herself, so her husband had given up his job as an electrician to stay home with her. The court explained its reasoning for ordering a new trial under the "lack of control" test as follows:

---

[30] 25 N.Y.2d 196, 303 N.Y.S.2d 362, 250 N.E.2d 460 (N.Y. 1969).

The avoidance of duties under an agreement entered into by those who have done so by reason of mental illness, but who have understanding, depends on balancing competing policy considerations. There must be stability in contractual relations and protection of the expectations of parties who bargain in good faith. On the other hand, it is also desirable to protect persons who may understand the nature of the transaction but who, due to mental illness, cannot control their conduct. Hence, there should be relief only if the other party knew or was put on notice as to the contractor's mental illness. Thus, the Restatement provision for avoidance contemplates that "the other party has reason to know" of the mental illness. . . .

When, however, the other party is without knowledge of the contractor's mental illness and the agreement is made on fair terms, the proposed Restatement rule is: "The power of avoidance under subsection (1) terminates to the extent that the contract has been so performed in whole or in part or the circumstances have so changed that avoidance would be inequitable. In such a case a court may grant relief on such equitable terms as the situation requires." . . .

The system was, or should have been, fully aware of Mrs. Ortelere's condition. They, or the Board of Education, knew of her leave of absence for medical reasons and the resort to staff psychiatrists by the Board of Education. Hence, the other of the conditions for avoidance is satisfied.

Chief Judge Charles D. Breitel, who wrote the majority decision for the New York Court of Appeals, was an adviser to the Restatement (Second) of Contracts and participated in the discussions of § 15, which he cited in its tentative draft form (unchanged in the final version). In the second-to-last paragraph in his opinion in the *Ortelere* case, Judge Breitel said, "Of course, nothing less serious than medically classified psychosis should suffice or else few contracts would be invulnerable to some kind of psychological attack." Is this an amendment or an application of the text of § 15?

The dissenting opinion stressed that not only did Mrs. Ortelere show a good understanding of her election but that it was, in the dissenter's view, necessary to provide enough to support two retired persons.

2. ***The career of the* Ortelere *doctrine:*** Lower New York courts have struggled with a number of cases involving the *Ortelere* doctrine. *Tomasino v. New York State Employees' Retirement System*[31] involved a claim by the estranged wife of a 22-year employee of the state. He made no election of benefits prior to his death, which meant that he received maximum lifetime benefits and a modest death benefit. The wife sought to have the election changed to increase the death benefit on the ground that he had been mentally ill at the time of his failure to elect. Although there was evidence that the system knew of the employee's psychosis, which impaired his decision-making capacity, the Court of Appeals affirmed denial of the widow's claim. They distinguished *Ortelere* on the ground that "Mr. and Mrs. Ortelere were interdependent and deeply devoted each to the other and real partners in an ideal marriage of many years." In view of the marital separation in the *Tomasino* case,

---

[31] 87 App. Div. 2d 675, 448 N.Y.S. 819, *aff'd*, 57 N.Y.2d 753 (1982).

the court presumed that the employee would have chosen the option yielding the largest returns in his lifetime.

In another case, *Pentinen v. New York State Employees' Retirement System*,[32] a petitioner sought to change an election under a state pension plan, claiming, through counsel, that petitioner's mental condition was essentially like that of Mrs. Ortelere, making the election voidable. The Appellate Division affirmed a refusal to permit the change. It found that though the petitioner's mental condition was in fact comparable to Mrs. Ortelere's, the system had no notice of this condition. In addition, the system had purchased an annuity for her, and "thus circumstances have so changed that avoidance of petitioner's election would be inequitable."

Finally, in a third case, *Keith v. New York State Teachers' Retirement System*,[33] the court found that a trial should be held to determine whether an employee's election of benefits could be overturned. Though there was no allegation that the system had reason to know of the retiree's mental condition at the time it accepted the application, the court noted that the *Ortelere* decision adopted the rule of the Restatement (Second) of Contracts, which provides that where the other party does not know of the mental illness, the power to avoid terminates only to the extent that the contract has been so performed in whole or in part or circumstances have changed such that avoidance would be inequitable. "[P]laintiff must still be permitted to put in proof of his wife's mental condition and to show that nullification would not be inequitable."

3. *The success of the Restatement approach:* The approach of Restatement § 15 has been remarkably successful in the courts. Professor Gregory Maggs researched its reception and found 22 citations of § 15, only one of them negative.[34] The Pennsylvania Supreme Court, in *Estate of McGovern v. Commonwealth State Employees' Retirement Board*, said, "This Court has never adopted Section 15 of the Restatement, which requires a post-hoc determination of reasonableness, and we decline to do so now."[35]

b. Contracts made under the influence of drugs

Alcohol and other drugs can affect our capacity to make the choices involved in free contract. We might wish to distinguish several situations. Suppose a person is under the influence of alcohol or other drugs that affect mental capacity. However, the other party either does not know this or does not realize the extent of the person's incapacity to make choices. Or suppose the other party is the one who has supplied the drug. For example, seller takes buyer to a restaurant. Seller suggests pre-dinner drinks, several bottles of wine with dinner, and an after-dinner drink. Then seller asks buyer to sign a contract.

---

[32] 60 App. Div. 2d 366, 401 N.Y.S. 587 (1978).

[33] 46 App. Div. 2d 938 (1974).

[34] *See* Gregory E. Maggs, *Ipse Dixit: The Restatement (Second) of Contracts and the Modern Development of Contract Law*, 66 Geo. Wash. L. Rev. 508, 519 (1998).

[35] 517 A.2d 523, 526 (Pa. 1986).

Harlow v. Kingston[36] suggests that courts have long overturned transactions in extreme cases. The court found that plaintiff had deeded his interest in real estate to defendant for $200. The fair value of the interest was $1388. For 10 days before the transaction, plaintiff had been on a prolonged spree and had been grossly intoxicated. When he signed the deed, he was not appreciably under the influence of liquor. However, he had been out of money for several days and had exhausted his credit. Plaintiff suggested the transaction. Immediately after he obtained the $200, he started on another drunken debauch that lasted two weeks. The trial court determined that by reason of his debauch, plaintiff had such a consuming thirst for liquor that his mind did not act normally, and he did not appreciate what he was doing. It ordered the property reconveyed after plaintiff had repaid $200 plus interest. The judgment was affirmed. The Wisconsin Supreme Court said "it is manifest that such disparity between value and consideration paid shows a grossly inadequate consideration, and the facts support the inference that defendant at the time of purchase fully realized that he was obtaining such a bargain. He acquainted himself with the nature of the property, and no doubt understood what was its actual value before the deal was consummated."

The Restatement (Second) of Contracts § 16 deals with intoxicated persons. Essentially, the text is the same as § 15(1) governing mental incapacity, but there is no provision analogous to § 15(2). Thus, in most instances the other party must have "reason to know that by reason of intoxication" he is unable to understand the nature and consequences of the transaction or act in a reasonable manner in relation to it. However, the comment notes: "If the intoxication is so extreme as to prevent any manifestation of assent, there is no contract. Otherwise the other party is affected only by intoxication of which he has reason to know." It explains that "voluntary intoxication not accompanied by any other disability has been thought less excusable than mental illness." The Reporter's Note suggests that the critical factor is the conduct of the sober party rather than the inability of the party in the grip of alcohol. It continues: "the problem seems closer to that of persons of mild mental retardation or dull normal intelligence where extra protection should be given rather than capacity denied." The Comment states: "Use of drugs may raise similar problems."

c.   Contracts made with minors — infancy

Voidable contracts: A contract made with a minor is voidable at the minor's election. (The defense is often called *infancy,* but it applies to anyone who has not reached the age of majority.) This is a flat rule. Intelligent and experienced people who are 17 years and 364 days old can disaffirm. Immature people who are 18 years and one day old cannot. This is true even when the adult in the transaction has no reason to suspect the minor's age. Furthermore, the transaction is voidable, not void. If the minor wants to back out of the deal, he or she can do so. If the minor does not want to back out, the adult must go forward with the contract. The minor can bring an action to avoid the transaction and recover any money paid to the adult. The minor also can assert infancy as a defense when the adult sues on the contract.

---

[36] 169 Wis. 521, 173 N.W. 308 (1919).

In many instances minority is a surrogate for defenses such as fraud, duress, breach of warranty, or unconscionability, which we will study later. Unlike those defenses, the person seeking to get out of a contract need prove only his or her age. Usually, the matter is so clear that litigation can be avoided or any trial will be simple for the minor's lawyer to handle.

Professor Anthony Kronman explains the rule as working "to protect children from their own shortsightedness and lack of judgment." He notes: "However great their eventual powers of autonomous self-control, persons have a natural history in which they undergo moral and psychological development along predictable lines and normally acquire the various capacities — including judgment or moral imagination — without which freedom in any meaningful sense is impossible."[37] He continues:

> A child's ability to harm himself through imprudent purchases is limited by the resources he happens to have at any given moment, resources that usually take time to accumulate. The time required to save for a substantial purchase itself functions as a kind of cooling-off period by providing an opportunity for reflection and by increasing the likelihood of parental intervention. If a child were allowed to make binding contracts, his spending power — and hence his capacity to harm himself by spending foolishly — would no longer be constrained by the limits of his present wealth. And since a contract can be made in an instant (unlike accumulation, which requires time), parents would have less control over the purchases their children make.[38]

How does this rule differ from those applicable to the mentally infirm?[39] What might account for these differences? *Don't have to prove anything but age*

Restitution: Suppose a minor makes a contract with an adult. The child defaults, the adult sues for breach, and the minor defends successfully on the ground of infancy. Is the adult entitled to restitution of any benefits conferred on the minor? *Halbman v. Lemke* suggests the sometimes harsh results of contracting with a minor.[40] *→ CASE #9 Harshness of minors + deals*

Michael Lemke owned a service station where James Halbman, a minor, worked. Lemke sold a car to Halbman for $1250. Halbman paid Lemke $1000 and promised to pay $25 a week until he paid the balance. Halbman took possession of the car. About five weeks later, a connecting rod in the engine broke, and Halbman took the car to a garage where it was repaired at a cost of $637.40. Halbman did not pay the repair bill, and the car remained at the garage. Halbman wrote Lemke disaffirming the contract, and he demanded that Lemke return all the money that Halbman had paid. About six months later, the garage removed the engine and transmission to satisfy its garageman's lien. It then towed what remained of the vehicle to the

---

[37] Anthony Kronman, *Paternalism and the Law of Contracts*, 92 Yale L.J. 763, 795–96 (1983).

[38] *Id.* at 788 n.79.

[39] *Compare* Walter D. Navin Jr., *The Contracts of Minors Viewed from the Perspective of Fair Exchange*, 50 N.C. L. Rev. 517 (1972), criticizing the rule.

[40] 99 Wis. 2d 241, 298 N.W.2d 562 (1980).

residence of Halbman's father. Halbman asked Lemke several times to take the vehicle, but Lemke refused. During the time the car was at the garage or later when it was at Halbman's father's home, it was vandalized, making it a total loss.

The Supreme Court of Wisconsin held that Halbman was entitled to the return of the money he had paid Lemke. In addition, a disaffirming minor need only return so much of the goods as is possible; Halbman did not have to make restitution for use of the car or depreciation in its value. Many other states would also reach this result. However, others have statutes that require restoration of any consideration received as a condition to disaffirming a contract.

In some states, minors are liable for misrepresenting their age to an adult. While they may disaffirm their contracts, they are still responsible for their torts. In these states, minors' claims for restitution are set off against adults' claims for tort damages. Automobile dealers often state on standard form contracts that the buyer represents that he or she is above 18 (or 21 if this is the age of majority). When we discuss misrepresentation later in this course, consider whether such a clause on a standard form should trigger tort liability in light of the requirements for establishing such a cause of action.

Necessaries: Minors cannot avoid liability on contracts they make for necessaries. This exception to avoidability is intended to give them the ability to provide for their basic needs. This liability can be viewed as grounded in the substantive law of restitution, based on the benefit received, and thus should be for the fair market value of the necessaries rather than the contract price. Courts usually restrict the category of necessaries to clothing, food, and shelter. They usually do not expand it to include expensive and discretionary items such as automobiles and stereo systems, though there are some cases to the contrary.

3. Duress

a. The search for a standard

Another way to exercise social control of contract is through the doctrine of "duress": society may not wish to enforce promises made under conditions of excessive threat. This, however, leads to the difficult question: what makes a threat "excessive"?

Professor Patrick Atiyah sketches some of the history of the doctrine of duress in his history of the ideas found in British and American contract law. He notes:[41]

> [Duress] came to be explained as being [an illustration] of defective assent, or an unfree will. In the eighteenth century . . . [this doctrine] had appeared generally to be based on simple ideas of fairness. A man who was coerced . . . was not likely to obtain a fair return for his payment. But now that the fairness of an exchange was itself coming to be treated as not a matter for the Courts anyhow, . . . [d]uress . . . [was] whittled away in the nineteenth century as [a defense] . . . to actions on executory contracts till virtually nothing was left. . . .

---

[41] PATRICK ATIYAH, THE RISE AND FALL OF FREEDOM OF CONTRACT 434–36 (Oxford University Press 1979).

[T]he result . . . of the tendency to treat coercion as something affecting the free will, was unfortunate. The idea that a man's will is "overborne" by certain types of pressure and not others is both in logic indefensible, and in practice impossible of application. The reality is that some forms of pressure are in conformity with the social and economic system and the moral ideas of the community, and others are not. The line can be only drawn by distinguishing between different kinds of pressure, not by attempting to analyze the effect of the pressures on a man's mind. The result was to make it virtually impossible for a sensible law of duress to develop at all during this period. In practice, however, it mattered little, for duress almost disappeared from the law of contract altogether during the nineteenth century.

The doctrine of duress is still sometimes approached as if it embodied a judicial definition of free choice or free will. We believe the readings that follow demonstrate that it is more helpful to see the duress doctrine as an effort to establish the boundary between proper and improper advantage-taking.[42] To the extent this is true, however, ask yourself: What distinguishes the doctrine of "duress" from doctrines invalidating contracts on grounds of fraud or misrepresentation or "undue influence"? As you will see, these are different legal doctrines, analyzed and argued by lawyers (and rationalized by judges) in different ways.

Professor Robert Hale pointed out in 1923 that we can view "property" as legally supported duress.[43] You want my automobile. You may be willing to pay what everyone would agree is a reasonable price for it. Nonetheless, the law gives me the privilege to keep the car from you. Or I can keep it unless you pay my unreasonable price. This protection — my property right — is a major part of my bargaining power. This is true even though your situation, and my knowledge of it, allows me to "take advantage" of you. The classic doctrine — what Professor Kennedy would call the "core" — says that a threat to do what you are legally entitled to do cannot be duress.

At the other extreme, if I threaten to kill or injure you unless you make a contract, the resulting agreement will not be enforceable. Though the result might be rationalized on the ground that you lacked free will, or did not have free choice to enter into the contract, it is easy also to justify non-enforcement on the ground that the contract resulted from improper advantage-taking. Threatening to kill or injure someone is both a crime and a tort.

These examples seem to draw a sharp line. However, to use Professor Duncan Kennedy's term again, there is a "periphery" of uncertainty. Courts have branded

---

[42] Common law judges in the late 19th and early 20th centuries solved a particular kind of duress problem through the doctrine of consideration. A and B make a contract. B refuses to perform unless he is paid more than the contract price. A promises to pay the added amount, and B performs. A then refuses to carry out his promise. A's promise would not be supported by consideration under the pre-existing obligation rule. In this way, Professor Grant Gilmore tells us, courts could apply an apparently objective rule and avoid having to deal with issues of fairness. GRANT GILMORE, THE DEATH OF CONTRACT 42, 48, 76 (Ohio State University Press 1974).

[43] Robert L. Hale, *Coercion and Distribution in a Supposedly Non-Coercive State*, 38 POL. SCI. Q. 470 (1923). *See also* Hale, *Bargaining, Duress and Economic Liberty*, 43 COLUM. L. REV. 603 (1943).

Not all threats that constitute duress also constitute crime or tort

as duress some threats of actions that would not be crimes or torts. Indeed, threats of inflicting some crimes and torts are less coercive than other threats.

MITCHELL v. C.C. SANITATION CO.
Texas Court of Civil Appeals
430 S.W.2d 933 (1968)

CASE 6

JOHNSON, J.

This is a summary judgment case in which the appellant, R.L. Mitchell, brought action for personal injury damages against William W. Crane and C.C. Sanitation Co., Inc. Mitchell's damages were allegedly caused by the negligence of William W. Crane, while he, Crane, was driving a truck in the course and scope of his employment for C.C. Sanitation Company. At the time of the accident in question, Mitchell was driving a truck in the course and scope of his employment for Herrin Transportation Company.

Signed releases for $ following collision

Subsequent to the collision in question, Mitchell signed two releases. The first was in favor of William W. Crane and C.C. Sanitation Company. It was signed by both Mitchell and Herrin Transportation Company and was for $388.65. The second release was also in favor of William W. Crane and C.C. Sanitation Company but it was signed only by Mitchell, and was for $62.12. Therefore the instant case was not only an action for damages but also an action to set aside the releases which the appellant had executed in favor of the appellees.

By Sum J. TC said no damages, appealed

Appellees, defendants below, filed a motion for summary judgment asserting that the releases signed by Mitchell and the acceptance of the checks paid pursuant to the releases barred any recovery by him. The trial court, taking into consideration the depositions on file, the affidavits, the pleadings, and other stipulations made by the parties, granted the motion for summary judgment denying all relief to the plaintiff. The essential question before this court is whether or not the record reveals a genuine issue of fact to have been raised which would enable the appellant to avoid the enforceability of such releases.

Being a case determined by summary judgment, we must resolve all doubts as to the existence of a genuine issue as to a material fact against the movant, appellees here. . . . Accepting as true that evidence which tends to support appellant's position and viewing the evidence in the light most favorable to him, the following situation is presented.

Appellant alleged that at the time of the occurrence in question, he was driving a truck in the course and scope of his employment for Herrin Transportation Company. As he was in the process of passing another truck driven by the defendant, Crane, who was in the course and scope of his employment for the defendant C.C. Sanitation Company, the defendant's truck suddenly and without warning was negligently steered to the left by defendant Crane, thus proximately causing the accident that resulted in serious and permanent injuries to him, the appellant. Numerous specific acts of negligence were alleged against the driver, Crane. The appellant alleged his damages to be in the sum of $40,000.00, which included damages for pain and suffering, lost wages, loss of earning capacity, and past and future medical expenses.

As to the releases, Mitchell alleged that they were signed by him because of duress and fraud imposed upon him by his employer, Herrin Transportation Company. Herrin handled its own claim service through one Ross C. Hall, under the name of Southwestern Claims Adjustment Company. After the accident, Hall advised C.C. Sanitation of the damages to Herrin's truck and to Mitchell, and placed C.C. Sanitation on notice of "Herrin's subrogation interest for all property damage inflicted upon its equipment and all workmen's compensation payments to or on behalf of its driver, Mr. Mitchell." By letter, Hall advised C.C. Sanitation and its insurance company, Maryland Casualty Company, of Herrin's truck damage of $281.65, that Herrin had paid Mitchell's physician, Dr. Cobb, $107.00, and that Herrin was therefore due $388.65. Thereafter Hall advised one Patrick Gorski, an adjuster for Maryland Casualty Company, that Mitchell was expecting to be paid $62.12 which he, Mitchell, had paid for his doctor out of his own pocket.

Maryland Casualty, acting by and through Gorski, prepared the proposed releases. The first was in the sum of $388.65 to be executed by Herrin and Mitchell, and the second was in the sum of $62.12 to be executed only by Mitchell. These were then transmitted from Gorski to Hall so that they might be signed by Herrin and by Mitchell. Hall apparently undertook the responsibility of obtaining Mitchell's signature on both releases. After the two releases were signed they were returned to Maryland Casualty Company, who then issued the two checks. The first was mailed directly to Herrin and the second directly to Mitchell. At no time during the negotiations outlined did Maryland Casualty Company or its adjuster Gorski have any personal conversation with, or see Mitchell.

The allegations of duress and fraud find their primary support in the deposition and affidavit of the appellant, Mitchell. According to Mitchell, he was called to Hall's office and when he went there Hall had the two previously prepared releases in hand. Hall threatened that if Mitchell did not settle for the amounts stated in the releases and sign them that he, Mitchell, would be "through," that is, he would lose his job. Further, that "Ross Hall just told me that it was a release so they could get their money for the truck and I could keep my job." When asked if anyone for Herrin Transportation Company talked to him about the execution of the releases, Mitchell responded, "Well, before I signed them Ross Hall blew his stack because I refused to sign them. He had Eldon Brown call me and put pressure on me." He then testified that Eldon Brown was "second in command" for Herrin Transportation Company. He further testified, "Well, I was informed that I would either sign these releases or I wouldn't have a job." He was asked, "Now, were you told anything else that may have caused you to sign the releases?" He responded, "Nothing except if *they* didn't get *their* money I didn't have no job." (Emphasis added.)

Mitchell stated that during this conversation and prior to signing the releases, Hall telephoned someone representing C.C. Sanitation and Crane and: "What Mr. Hall said over the telephone was that he had finally convinced me that it would be better to sign it. In other words, it was either sign the release or not have a job." He continued, "Whoever he talked to on the phone, he said I prefer to sign the releases than lose my job." By affidavit, Mitchell identified Patrick Gorski, the adjuster for Maryland Casualty Company, as the person with whom Hall was speaking on the telephone. Mitchell also testified to Hall's statements that he, Hall, was handling the matter for C.C. Sanitation and William Crane, was working on behalf of them, was "taking care" of it for them, and was getting the releases signed for them.

Mitchell testified that he would not have signed the releases had Hall not told him that he was going to lose his job if he didn't sign, that he did not feel that he was being adequately compensated for the injuries he sustained in the accident and that the only reason he would sign releases like those that he did sign would be to keep his job. By affidavit Mitchell stated, "I told Mr. Hall nothing was being paid me for the pain and suffering I had experienced or for my future doctor's bills," but, "he was insistent that I sign the releases so that Herrin Transportation could get the money for their truck." Mitchell stated, "Had he not threatened me with my job I would not have signed the releases. His threat caused me to do something (sign the releases) which was against my own free will and accord."

Mitchell further alleged that at the time Hall made the threats against his job, he did so with the knowledge, consent, and acquiescence of the insurance company for the appellees, Maryland Casualty Company, who was acting by and through Gorski, their insurance adjuster. Mitchell alleged that not only did Gorski know of the threats but after such threats were made, Maryland Casualty Company accepted the benefits arising therefrom by accepting the releases and attempting to enforce them. Mitchell alleged that Hall, at the time he procured the execution of releases, was acting as the agent of Maryland Casualty Company. Appellant alleged further, as the basis of the fraud and/or inadequate consideration, that the amount of the releases went solely to compensate Herrin Transportation Company for its expenses, and the appellant and Herrin Transportation Company, for the amount of the doctor's bills to date; that no cash was paid to the appellant in addition to the above-mentioned amounts. Lastly, appellant alleged that the appellees and his employer, Herrin Transportation Company, acted in a conspiracy coercing him into signing the releases.

It is a general rule that contracts obtained through duress or coercion are voidable and this rule is applicable to releases. . . .

"Any coercion of another, either mental, physical, or otherwise, causing him to act contrary to his own free will or to submit to a situation or conditions against his own volition or interests, constitutes 'duress.' " *Hailey v. Fenner & Beane*, 246 S.W. 412 (Tex. Civ. App. 1922). However, there is authority stating: "There can be no duress unless there is a threat to do some act which the party threatening has no legal right to do." *Dale v. Simon*, 267 S.W. 467 (Tex. Com. App. 1924). Appellee contends that duress cannot exist because Herrin Transportation Company was at liberty to discharge the appellant at any time and for any reason they so desired, for he was not shown to be more than an employee at will. Stated another way, that the employer Herrin had the right to discharge the appellant at any time and the threat to do what they had the legal right to do cannot constitute duress or fraud.

As the disposition of the instant case was made on appellee's motion for summary judgment, applying the well-known principles previously set forth, the following conclusions find support in the record and may be validly and helpfully made: (1) the employer Herrin had the right to discharge appellant at any time it desired; (2) there was a very real compulsion, economic and otherwise, here brought to bear on the appellant by his employer; (3) it was the force of this constraint alone, that caused appellant to do what he otherwise would not have considered doing; (4) this compulsion was brought to bear by the employer Herrin, working in concert with the defendant, C.C. Sanitation; (5) the employer Herrin did what it here did for its own economic benefit and advantage, and (6) the effect of such action was to effectively terminate and destroy a valid claim and otherwise good cause of action possessed by the appellant.

"Although an employer, acting singly, has the undoubted right to discharge an employee or one of his family, the coercion arising from a threat to do so, when employed as a means to force the employee to sign a release of an action which he has instituted against him or another employer is unlawful, and, under circumstances showing that such means in fact overcame the employee's resistance and will, may constitute duress." 20 A.L.R.2d 743, 751. We believe this reasoning is applicable to the instant case, and though no Texas cases directly in point are found, believe that substantial authority is otherwise available. . . .

In *Perkins Oil Co. of Delaware v. Fitzgerald*, 197 Ark. 14, 121 S.W.2d 877, an employee who was an oiler at a cottonseed oil mill lost both arms in a machine accident at the mill. To induce the employee to release the company, the mill superintendent told him that if he consulted an attorney, or tried to sue the company, his stepfather, the sole support of plaintiff's invalid mother, would be discharged, and the company would prevent his re-employment in any other like business. Such evidence was held sufficient to warrant submission to the jury on the question of whether the employee signed the release under duress or coercion.

In the case at bar there was obvious opportunity for employer oppression to be brought against the employee. The parties stood on no equal footing, there was great economic disparity between them, and there was no equality of bargaining positions. The appellant undoubtedly was the weaker party, the threat to discharge him was very real, and he was fully justified in expecting that he would be immediately discharged.

In addition, the employer, Herrin Transportation Company, had a direct economic interest in their employee signing the releases, and this was the reason for doing what the company did. Absent the releases being signed by Mitchell, Herrin would not be paid the damages to its truck ($281.65) or the doctor's bills it had previously paid ($107.00). The major portion of the money received for signing the releases went to Herrin Transportation Company, with only $62.12 being paid to appellant. Even this sum was for doctor's bills that appellant had previously paid out of his own pocket as a result of the accident in question. There was no consideration of, nor compensation for, the most important elements of damages allegedly suffered by appellant, these being mental and physical pain and suffering and reduced capacity to work.

In addition, there is evidence in the record from which it might properly be concluded that the defendant C.C. Sanitation not only knew of the constraint and compulsion that was applied to Mitchell by his employer, but participated in it, and later accepted its economic benefits.

[handwritten margin note: Threat to fire can be coercion or duress even if its legal(?) in similar cases at least]

[handwritten star symbol in circle]

It is the opinion of the majority of this court that even where the right of an employer to discharge an employee is unquestioned, duress and coercion may be exercised by the employer by threats to discharge the employee, where circumstances such as are here presented appear. We cannot conclude that an employer with the opportunity for oppression on an employee that here appears, may use such power for his own economic interest, and yet conclude that no question of duress or coercion arises. Where there is such an inequality in the terms, sacrifice of benefits, and rights on the part of the employee, inadequacy of consideration, and advantage taken of the weaker party, we cannot conclude that no fact situation of duress or coercion exists.

It is the opinion of the majority of this court that under the circumstances here presented the existence of duress and coercion sufficient for the avoidance of the releases was a genuine issue of fact, which was raised by the record. There being such issue of fact, under the law applicable to summary judgment, this cause must be reversed and remanded.

Reversed and remanded. *[handwritten: → Overturn / remand ↳ Its issue of fact whether coercion. Shouldn't be SJ case]*

TUNKS, C.J., dissenting.

I respectfully dissent.

The facts of this case are accurately stated in the majority opinion. Those facts show that the Maryland Casualty Company, insurer for the appellees, was confronted with two claims asserted by two different claimants growing out of one accident. The carrier declined to pay one claimant until the other claim was settled. Its conduct in that respect was not at all unreasonable. It is obvious that an important factor in the settlement of claims is the avoidance of possible expense to be incurred in defending suits. The carrier could not fully avail itself of the benefits in that respect by settling one claim and defending the other. Not only did the conduct of the carrier constitute a reasonable exercise of business judgment but it was conduct clearly within its legal rights.

[handwritten margin note: Basically that it was in Herrin War into shouldn't be used against them]

The majority seems to place emphasis on the fact that it was to the financial interest of Herrin Transportation Company to get the plaintiff to release his claim. I would emphasize that fact as sustaining the validity and propriety of Herrin's conduct, rather than tainting it. It is uncontroverted that Herrin had the lawful right to terminate Mitchell's employment without any cause. It should follow, *a fortiori*, that they had a right to terminate his employment unless he would take such action as would permit them to recover on their claim. In my opinion their conduct would be more subject to attack if they, having no financial interest in the matter, had threatened to fire Mitchell because of personal spite or ill will or simply because they were permitting Maryland Casualty Company to avail itself of a lawful right to discharge which they, as employers at will, had.

As the two actors in this situation, the carrier and the employer, each acting individually, were acting within their legal rights, so were they, acting in concert, within the bounds of lawfulness. The majority opinion cites authorities for the proposition that an employer's threat to discharge an employee at will is not duress. Neither is any other threat to do any other lawful act duress. It may be assumed that the record supports a finding of fact to the effect that Maryland Casualty Company refused to pay Herrin until Mitchell had settled his claim for the purpose of inducing Herrin to exercise its influence in getting Mitchell to settle for the amount offered. At least Maryland Casualty Company got the benefit of Herrin's exercise of its influence. Maryland Casualty Company, however, did not induce Herrin to do or threaten to do something unlawful to influence Mitchell to settle.

Nor is the appellant's contention that his settlement was involuntary because it was made under economic compulsion sound. In *McKee, General Contractor v. Patterson*, 153 Tex. 517, 271 S.W.2d 391, it was held that a workman's acceptance or retaining employment in the face of known and appreciated dangers was voluntary though done under the economic necessity's of earning a livelihood. Thus, Mitchell's settlement of his claim to avoid losing his job was, nevertheless, voluntary.

I would affirm the judgment of the trial court.

NOTES AND QUESTIONS

1. ***What is a wrongful threat?*** *Mitchell* expands the concept of duress past threats to commit crimes or torts. This poses the problem, in Professor Dalton's words, of "isolating just those kinds of impairment [of bargaining power] that the law is prepared to redress without feeling that the whole structure of bargaining between unequals is put in jeopardy."[44] Suppose the truck driver in the *Mitchell* case had been represented by a lawyer and had received some compensation for his injuries. Should the case then have come out the other way?

2. ***Wrongful, but not illegal, threats:*** Bargaining involves offering rewards and punishments — the proverbial "carrots" and "sticks." Lawyers are people who can cause trouble. Thus, when they offer to settle a dispute, there is at least the tacit threat of litigation if the other side refuses the offer. Are threats of litigation in and of themselves a form of duress? How is a court — with a distinct interest in the presence and process of litigation — to decide?

In *Wolf v. Marlton Corp.*,[45] a husband and wife sued to recover a down payment of $2450. They had made this payment pursuant to a contract to buy a house to be built by Marlton Corporation. The plaintiffs sought to cancel their contract because they were having marital difficulties. Marlton sought to hold them to their bargain until the couple's lawyer threatened that, if the couple were forced to conclude the purchase they would arrange a subsequent resale to "a purchaser who would be undesirable in [that] tract, and that [Marlton] would not be happy with the results." The lawyer also told Marlton, "It will be the last tract that you will ever build in New Jersey, and it will be the last house that you will sell in this tract." Marlton then sold the house to a third party. Marlton sought to keep the down payment, arguing that its failure to sue the couple for breach of contract was caused by their lawyer's threats, which constituted duress. The trial court ruled in favor of the plaintiffs, finding Marlton's promise to cancel to be enforceable. The appellate court reversed,

---

[44] Clare Dalton, *An Essay in the Deconstruction of Contract Doctrine*, 94 Yale L.J. 997, 1031 (1985).

[45] 57 N.J. Super. 278, 154 A.2d 625 (1959).

finding that the threat by the buyers might constitute duress. The appellate court observed:

> Plaintiffs assert that, once they bought the house, they had a legal right to sell it to whomever they wished. They rely on the familiar general rule to the effect that a threat to do what one has a legal right to do does not constitute duress. . . . That proposition, however, is not an entirely correct statement of the law of duress as it has developed in this jurisdiction. Under the modern view, acts or threats cannot constitute duress unless they are wrongful; but a threat may be wrongful even though the act threatened is lawful. We have come to deal, in terms of the business compulsion doctrine, with acts and threats that are wrongful, not necessarily in a legal, but in a moral or equitable sense. . . .
>
> The sale of a development home to an "undesirable purchaser" is, of course, a perfectly legal act regardless of any adverse effect it may have on the fortunes of the developer's enterprise. But where a party for purely malicious and unconscionable motives threatens to resell such a home to a purchaser, specially selected because he would be undesirable, for the sole purpose of injuring the builder's business, fundamental fairness requires the conclusion that his conduct in making this threat be deemed "wrongful," as the term is used in the law of duress.

[handwritten margin note: Basically the P's/couple saying that reselling to shitty owners isn't illegal is insufficient to prove its not wrong/duress]

Many people reading this case assume that the plaintiff's lawyer was threatening to sell the house to a member of a minority group. The court said that a threat may be wrongful, even though the act threatened is lawful. If this is true, by what standard do we measure wrongfulness? Suppose a borrower has fallen behind on payments on a loan to provide working capital for a business. The bank "threatens" to refuse to renew the loan unless the borrower gives a mortgage on her home. The bank subsequently seeks to foreclose the mortgage on the residence. Can the borrower argue that it gave the mortgage only under duress? Suppose a homeowner signs a promissory note to pay an extremely high price for a pump to try to save property from a flood? Can the homeowner argue that it signed the note under duress? How can this be distinguished from *Wolf v. Marlton*?

3.   *Threats of prosecution as the lever:* In Ibsen's play *A Doll's House*, originally produced in 1879, Nora borrows money from Nils Krogstad, a lawyer. Under their agreement, Nora's father was to cosign the note, thereby adding his promise to Nora's. The father was very ill. Nora forged his signature because she was sure that he would sign. Nora used the money to take her husband, Torvald, to Italy when he was ill. Nils works for Torvald. Nora persuades Torvald to find a job for her old friend, Kristine. Torvald decides to fire Nils and give Kristine Nils's job. Nils then threatens Nora. If she cannot persuade Torvald not to fire Nils, Nils will tell Torvald about the loan and the forgery. It is clear that he is implicitly threatening to involve the criminal law. Looking at Ibsen's play in light of the common law of duress, has Nils used duress to prompt Nora to persuade Torvald not to fire Nils? In more modern times, the story usually involves an employee who has embezzled money. The employer, and sometimes his or her lawyer, discovers this. The employee is told that she or he must repay the money or the employer will call the police. Duress, or just efficient debt collection?

[handwritten note: Good Q ➝ be even better if we had some semblance of an answer]

4. ***The Restatement's approach:*** The Restatement (Second) of Contracts § 175 says that a contract is voidable if "a party's manifestation of assent is induced by an improper threat by the other party that leaves the victim no reasonable alternative." Obviously, this standard turns on the definition of *improper.* Section 176 provides:

(1) A threat is improper if

(a) what is threatened is a crime or a tort, or the threat itself would be a crime or a tort if it resulted in obtaining property,

(b) what is threatened is a criminal prosecution,

(c) what is threatened is the use of civil process and the threat is made in bad faith, or

(d) the threat is a breach of the duty of good faith and fair dealing under a contract with the recipient.

(2) A threat is improper if the resulting exchange is not on fair terms, and

(a) the threatened act would harm the recipient and would not significantly benefit the party making the threat,

(b) the effectiveness of the threat in inducing the manifestation of assent is significantly increased by prior unfair dealing by the party making the threat, or

(c) what is threatened is otherwise a use of power for illegitimate ends.

Professor Clare Dalton criticizes the Restatement's approach.[46] She looks at the kinds of threats covered by the Restatement. She finds that the tests turn on "unfair exchange," and highly uncertain measures of appropriate conduct such as "unfair dealing" or "the use of power for illegitimate ends. . . . These raise the very questions they were supposed to answer: What uses of power are illegitimate, what kinds of pressure are unfair, in the contractual context."[47]

Compare Professor Dalton's criticism with Professor Kronman's statement: "One who believes, as Mill did and I do, that some paternalistic restrictions on contractual freedom are not only permissible but morally required, must supply a standard or principle for evaluating paternalistic arguments in particular cases; only in this way can the legitimacy of paternalism be established and its limits defined."[48] Contrast both Dalton's and Kronman's positions with Professor Trakman's praise of an open-ended approach in the areas of illegality and public policy. (Professor Trakman's praise is quoted immediately preceding *Coma Corporation v. Department of Labor, supra.*)[49] Can we do better than telling judges to make *ad hoc* judgments about fairness with a presumption that contracts should be upheld? Is the *Mitchell* case an example of an *ad hoc* approach? If so, and you find that

---

[46] *See* Dalton, *supra* note 44, at 1032–36.

[47] *Id.* at 1035.

[48] Anthony Kronman, *Paternalism and the Law of Contracts*, 92 Yale L.J. 763, 765 (1983).

[49] *See* Trakman, *supra* note 6.

problematic, what should the court have done instead?

b.   The Wisconsin rule?

Sometimes, as we have seen, cases raising issues of state law are brought in federal courts under diversity jurisdiction (involving parties from two different states), requiring the federal courts to determine what state law is on the issue in question. The Seventh Circuit, in the case that follows, acknowledges that Wisconsin contract law governs. We shall have occasion to examine how faithfully it applies that law.

THE SELMER CO. v. BLAKESLEE-MIDWEST CO.
United States Court of Appeals, Seventh Circuit
704 F.2d 924 (1983)

Posner, J.

This appeal by the plaintiff from summary judgment for the defendants in a diversity case requires us to consider the meaning, under Wisconsin contract law, of "economic duress" as a defense to a settlement of a contract dispute.

On this appeal, we must take as true the following facts. The plaintiff, Selmer, agreed to act as a subcontractor on a construction project for which the defendant Blakeslee-Midwest Prestressed Concrete Company was the general contractor. Under the contract between Blakeslee-Midwest and Selmer, Selmer was to receive $210,000 for erecting prestressed concrete materials supplied to it by Blakeslee-Midwest. Blakeslee-Midwest failed to fulfill its contractual obligations; among other things, it was tardy in supplying Selmer with the prestressed concrete materials. Selmer could have terminated the contract without penalty but instead agreed orally with Blakeslee-Midwest to complete its work, provided Blakeslee-Midwest would pay Selmer for the extra costs of completion due to Blakeslee-Midwest's defaults. When the job was completed, Selmer demanded payment of $120,000. Blakeslee-Midwest offered $67,000 and refused to budge from this offer. Selmer, because it was in desperate financial straits, accepted the offer.

Two and a half years later Selmer brought this suit against Blakeslee-Midwest (the other defendants' liability, being derivative from Blakeslee-Midwest's, does not require separate consideration), claiming that its extra costs had amounted to $150,000 ($120,000 being merely a settlement offer), and asking for that amount minus the $67,000 it had received, plus consequential and punitive damages. Although Selmer, presumably in order to be able to claim such damages, describes this as a tort rather than a contract action, it seems really to be a suit on Blakeslee-Midwest's alleged oral promise to reimburse Selmer in full for the extra costs of completing the original contract after Blakeslee-Midwest defaulted. But the characterization is unimportant. Selmer concedes that, whatever its suit is, it is barred by the settlement agreement if, as the district court held, that agreement is valid. The only question is whether there is a triable issue as to whether the settlement agreement is invalid because procured by "economic duress."

If you extract a promise by means of a threat, the promise is unenforceable. This is not, as so often stated, *see, e.g., Totem Marine Tug & Barge, Inc. v. Alyeska Pipeline Serv. Co.,* 584 P.2d 15, 22 (Alaska 1978), because such a promise is involuntary, unless "involuntary" is a conclusion rather than the description of a mental state. If the threat is ferocious ("your money or your life") and believed, the victim may be desperately eager to fend it off with a promise. Such promises are made unenforceable in order to discourage threats by making them less profitable. The fundamental issue in a duress case is therefore not the victim's state of mind but whether the statement that induced the promise is the kind of offer to deal that we want to discourage, and hence that we call a "threat." Selmer argues that Blakeslee-Midwest said to it in effect, "give up $53,000 of your claim for extras [$120,000 minus $67,000], or you will get nothing." This has the verbal form of a threat but is easily recast as a promise innocuous on its face — "I promise to pay you $67,000 for a release of your claim." There is a practical argument against treating such a statement as a threat: it will make an inference of duress inescapable in any negotiation where one party makes an offer from which it refuses to budge, for the other party will always be able to argue that he settled only because there was a (figurative) gun at his head. It would not matter whether the party refusing to budge was the payor like Blakeslee-Midwest or the promisor like Selmer. If Selmer had refused to complete the job without being paid exorbitantly for the extras and Blakeslee-Midwest had complied with this demand because financial catastrophe would have loomed if Selmer had walked off the job, we would have the same case. A vast number of contract settlements would be subject to being ripped open upon an allegation of duress if Selmer's argument were accepted.

Sensitive — maybe oversensitive — to this danger, the older cases held that a threat not to honor a contract could not be considered duress. . . . But the principle was not absolute, as is shown by *Alaska Packers' Ass'n v. Domenico,* 117 Fed. 99 (9th Cir. 1902). Sailors and fishermen (the libelants) "agreed in writing, for a certain stated compensation, to render their services to the appellant in remote waters where the season for conducting fishing operations is extremely short, and in which enterprise the appellant had a large amount of money invested; and, after having entered upon the discharge of their contract, and at a time when it was impossible for the appellant to secure other men in their places, the libelants, without any valid cause, absolutely refused to continue the services they were under contract to perform unless the appellant would consent to pay them more money." *Id.* at 102. The appellant agreed, but later reneged, and the libelants sued. They lost; the court refused to enforce the new agreement. Although the technical ground of decision was the absence of fresh consideration for the modified agreement, it seems apparent both from the quoted language and from a reference on the same page to coercion that the court's underlying concern was that the modified agreement had been procured by duress in the form of the threat to break the original contract. *Cf.* Farnsworth, CONTRACTS 271 (1982).

Alaska Packers' Ass'n shows that because the legal remedies for breach of contract are not always adequate, a refusal to honor a contract may force the other party to the contract to surrender his rights — in *Alaska Packers' Ass'n,* the appellant's right to the libelants' labor at the agreed wage. It undermines the institution of contract to allow a contract party to use the threat of breach to get the contract modified in his favor not because anything has happened to require modification in the mutual interest of the parties but simply because the other party, unless he knuckles under to the threat, will incur costs for which he will have no adequate legal remedy. If contractual protections are illusory, people will be reluctant to make contracts. Allowing contract modifications to be voided in circumstances such as those in *Alaska Packers' Ass'n* assures prospective contract parties that signing a contract is not stepping into a trap, and by thus encouraging people to make contracts promotes the efficient allocation of resources.

Capps v. Georgia Pac. Corp., 253 Or. 248, 453 P.2d 935 (1969), illustrates the principle of *Alaska Packers' Ass'n* in the context of settling contract disputes. The defendant promised to give the plaintiff, as a commission for finding a suitable lessee for a piece of real estate, 5 percent of the total rental plus one-half of the first month's rent. The plaintiff found a suitable lessee and the lease was signed. Under the terms of the commission arrangement the defendant owed the plaintiff $157,000, but he paid only $5,000 and got a release from the plaintiff of the rest. The plaintiff later sued for the balance of the $157,000, alleging that when requesting payment of the agreed-upon commission he had "informed Defendant that due to Plaintiff's adverse financial condition, he was in danger of immediately losing other personal property through repossession and foreclosure unless funds from Defendant were immediately made available for the purpose of paying these creditors." 253 Or. at 252, 453 P.2d at 937. But "Defendant, through its agent . . . advised Plaintiff that though he was entitled to the sums demanded in Plaintiff's Complaint, unless he signed the purported release set forth in Defendant's Answer, Plaintiff would receive no part thereof, inasmuch as Defendant had extensive resources and powerful and brilliant attorneys who would and could prevent Plaintiff in any subsequent legal proceedings from obtaining payment of all or any portion of said sums." *Id.* We can disregard the reference to the defendant's "powerful and brilliant attorneys" yet agree with the Oregon Supreme Court that the confluence of the plaintiff's necessitous financial condition, the defendant's acknowledged indebtedness for the full $157,000, and the settlement of the indebtedness for less than three cents on the dollar — with no suggestion that the defendant did not have the money to pay the debt in full — showed duress. The case did not involve the settlement of a genuine dispute, but, as in *Alaska Packers' Ass'n*, an attempt to exploit the contract promisee's lack of an adequate legal remedy.

Although *Capps* is not a Wisconsin case, we have no reason to think that Wisconsin courts would reach a different result. *Cf. Mendelson v. Blatz Brewing Co.*, 9 Wis. 2d 487, 494, 101 N.W.2d 805, 809 (1960); *Wurtz v. Fleischman*, 97 Wis. 2d 100, 109–11, 293 N.W.2d 155, 160 (1980). But the only feature that the present case shares with *Capps* is that the plaintiff was in financial difficulties. Since Blakeslee-Midwest did not acknowledge that it owed Selmer $120,000, and since the settlement exceeded 50 percent of Selmer's demand, the terms of the settlement are not unreasonable on their face, as in *Capps*. Thus the question is starkly posed whether financial difficulty can by itself justify setting aside a settlement on grounds of duress. It cannot. "The mere stress of business conditions will not constitute duress where the defendant was not responsible for the conditions." *Johnson, Drake & Piper, Inc. v. United States*, 531 F.2d 1037, 1042 (Ct. Cl. 1976) (per curiam). The adverse effect on the finality of settlements and hence on the willingness of parties to settle their contract disputes without litigation would be great if the cash needs of one party were alone enough to entitle him to a trial on the validity of the settlement. In particular, people who desperately wanted to settle for cash — who simply could not afford to litigate — would be unable to settle, because they could not enter into a binding settlement; being desperate, they could always get it set aside later on grounds of duress. It is a detriment, not a benefit, to one's long-run interests not to be able to make a binding commitment.

Matters stand differently when the complaining party's financial distress is due to the other party's conduct. Although Selmer claims that it was the extra expense caused by Blakeslee-Midwest's breaches of the original contract that put it in a financial vise, it could have walked away from the contract without loss or penalty when Blakeslee-Midwest broke the contract. Selmer was not forced by its contract to remain on the job, and was not prevented by circumstances from walking away from the contract, as the appellant in *Alaska Packers' Ass'n* had been; it stayed on the job for extra pay. We do not know why Selmer was unable to weather the crisis that arose when Blakeslee-Midwest refused to pay $120,000 for Selmer's extra expenses — whether Selmer was undercapitalized or overborrowed or what — but Blakeslee-Midwest cannot be held responsible for whatever it was that made Selmer so necessitous, when, as we have said, Selmer need not have embarked on the extended contract.

[We have deleted two paragraphs from the opinion in which the court rejects Selmer's argument that Blakeslee-Midwest's withholding of "retainage" constituted "duress of goods." The argument, though an interesting one, was discussed in a passage more confusing than illuminating.]

Affirmed.

NOTES AND QUESTIONS

1. ***Judge Posner and Law and Economics:*** Judge Richard Posner is a former professor of law at the University of Chicago. He was appointed to the United States Court of Appeals for the Seventh Circuit by President Reagan in 1981. Judge Posner is routinely characterized as the most widely cited legal authority in recent history; his influence is hard to overstate.[50] Professors Stephen Choi and Mitu Gulati tell us something of Judge Posner:[51]

> If obscurity defines the careers of most judges, notoriety defines that of Judge Richard A. Posner of the Seventh Circuit Court of Appeals. When his opinions are discussed, whether in an academic context or in the media, his name is likely to be invoked. This notoriety is such that he has been profiled in the pages of the *New Yorker*, debated Ronald Dworkin in the *New York*

---

[50] Fred R. Shapiro, *The Most-Cited Legal Books Published Since 1978*, 29 J. LEGAL STUD. 397, 397–98 (2000).

[51] Stephen J. Choi & G. Mitu Gulati, *Mr. Justice Posner? Unpacking the Statistics*, 61 N.Y.U. ANN. SURV. AM. L. 19, 19–20 (2005). *See also* Stephen J. Choi & G. Mitu Gulati, *Ranking Judges According to Citation Bias (As a Means to Reduce Bias)*, 82 NOTRE DAME L. REV. 1279, 1299 (2007) (stating that "Richard Posner, who shows [up] at the top of almost every citation ranking of either judges or legal academics, shows up" as the most frequently cited judicial opinion writer by the United States Court of Appeals judges of the opposite political party).

Review of Books, excoriated the 9/11 Commission Report in the pages of the *New York Times Book Review*, criticized the field of critical race theory in the pages of the *New Republic*, and used the opportunity of delivering the Holmes lectures at Harvard Law School to condemn the entire field of moral philosophy as producing work of little or no value to legal analysis. He has written best-selling books ranging from his classic treatise on the economic analysis of law to books covering sex, literature, aging, the federal courts, public intellectuals, and moral philosophy, all the way to the Monica Lewinsky affair.

An earlier Wall Street Journal article provides some context:[52]

CHICAGO — Judge Richard A. Posner has little use for words like fairness and justice. "Terms which have no content," he calls them. What America's lawyers and judges need, he says, is a healthy dose of free-market thinking.

From the bench of the U.S. Court of Appeals for the Seventh Circuit here, Judge Posner applies a standard of economic efficiency in cases where many others fail to see markets at play. He calibrates social costs and benefits on questions of religious expression and privacy. . . .

In a highly controversial 1983 dissent, he argued against the widespread practice of appointing free counsel to represent prisoners who bring civil-rights suits. If the prisoner can't retain a lawyer on a contingency-fee basis, he wrote, "the natural inference to draw is that he doesn't have a good case."

Such opinions are part of what the 47-year-old judge calls his self-assumed mission to "raise the level of economic literacy" in the federal judiciary. They have also drawn attention to "Law and Economics," an intellectual movement of which Judge Posner is a leading theorist and tireless booster. . . .

Law and Economics "is the most important thing that has happened in legal thought since the New Deal," says Prof. Bruce A. Ackerman of [Yale Law School]. "It's the most important thing in legal education since the birth of Harvard Law School."

Prof. Ackerman, however, is a leading critic of Judge Posner. Although the professor has nothing against economic thinking in the courtroom, he says, he refers to Judge Posner's approach as "pseudo-empirical" reasoning.[53]

---

[52] Paul M. Barrett, *Influential Ideas: A Movement Called "Law and Economics" Sways Legal Circles*, WALL STREET JOURNAL, Aug. 4, 1986, at 1, col. 1. Reprinted by permission of WALL STREET JOURNAL, Copyright © 1986 Dow Jones & Company, Inc. All Rights Reserved Worldwide.

[53] [Eds. note: Ackerman is suggesting that Posner's empirical assumptions are questionable. For example, Professor Robert Ellickson undertook an empirical examination of one of the classic economics and law axioms, the "Coase Theorem." *See* Robert C. Ellickson, *Of Coase and Cattle: Dispute Resolution Among Neighbors in Shasta County*, 38 STAN. L. REV. 623 (1986). Coase's proposition asserts that when transaction costs are zero, a change in the rule of liability will have no effect on the allocation of resources. Coase used as an example a conflict between two neighbors — a rancher running cattle and a farmer raising crops. The parable suggests that when transaction costs are low, parties will respond to a new rule by agreeing to an exchange of property rights that perpetuates the prior efficient allocation

Many Law and Economics practitioners praise the work of Judge Posner as a source of inspiration. In more than 100 scholarly articles and 10 books, the judge has applied economics to almost every branch of the law.[54] A friend at the University of Chicago calls him an "academic entrepreneur" who "was very self-conscious about creating a school of thought" with Law and Economics.

For a response to some early law and economics writing, including Posner's, see Duncan Kennedy and Frank Michelman, *Are Property and Contract Efficient?*[55] Professor Arthur Leff reviewed Posner's *Economic Analysis of Law.*[56] He said that the closest analogue to Posner's approach was the picaresque novel, such as Henry Fielding's Tom Jones. In such novels the "hero sets out into a world of complexity and brings to bear on successive segments of it the power of his own particular personal vision. The world presents itself as a series of problems; to each problem that vision acts as a form of solution; and the problem having been dispatched, our hero passes on to the next adventure." Posner's hero, of course, is economic analysis. It solves any and all problems. Leff asks "what pressures in contemporary legal scholarship might be responsible for the appearance, now, of four hundred pages of tunnel vision . . . " He concludes: "Since its basic intellectual technique is the substitution of definitions for both normative and empirical propositions, I would call it American Legal Nominalism." For further discussion of Judge Posner, see Larissa MacFarquhar, *The Bench Burner: How Did a Judge With Such Subversive Ideas Become a Leading Influence on American Legal Opinion?*[57] MacFarquhar quotes John Donohue, a Stanford law professor, as saying "A little bit of empirical support goes a long way for him." On the other hand, Judge Posner appears to be rethinking his fundamental commitments in view of the economic crisis of 2008, writing, "We are learning that we need a more active and intelligent government to keep our model of a capitalist economy from running off the rails."[58]

The financial crisis of 2008 created an intellectual problem for law and economics. Professor Jonathan Lipson explained in 2010:[59]

---

of resources. Ellickson studied these transactions in Shasta County. He found that a change in animal trespass law fails to affect resource allocation, not because transaction costs are low, but because they are very high. Parties had long-term continuing relationships that enabled them to enforce informal norms and so potential disputants ignored the formal law. Ellickson stresses that Ronald Coase is well aware of the limitations of his proposition. However, Ellickson cites work by Professor Posner that seems to assume that the Coase Theorem describes the likely empirical situation. Ackerman, of course, does not suggest that all of Professor/Judge Posner's work is flawed empirically.]

[54] [Eds. note: Posner was a law professor from 1969 to 1982, about 13 years. If he wrote 100 articles in that period, this would average a little more than seven a year, a remarkable output.]

[55] 8 HOFSTRA L. REV. 711 (1980).

[56] Arthur Leff, *Economic Analysis of Law: Some Realism About Nominalism*, 60 VA. L. REV. 451, 452, 459 (1974).

[57] THE NEW YORKER, Dec. 10, 2001, at 10.

[58] RICHARD A. POSNER, A FAILURE OF CAPITALISM: THE CRISIS OF '08 AND THE DESCENT INTO DEPRESSION (2009).

[59] *See* Jonathan C. Lipson, *The Great Repression: The Crisis of Richard Posner*, HUFFINGTON POST, huffingtonpost.com/peter-j-liacouras/the-great-repression-the_b_644925.html (accessed September 20, 2015).

Since the crash of 2008, Judge Posner, who sits on the Seventh Circuit Court of Appeals in Chicago and teaches at the University of Chicago Law School, has written scores of articles and blogs — and two books — on the financial crisis, including [in 2010] *The Crisis of Capitalist Democracy*. Throughout, Judge Posner surprised many by insisting that we are in a depression caused by bad government policies that were, in turn, based on bad economics. Only heavy government spending can get us out.   *Wild one was conservative*

Because Posner is a prominent public intellectual, what he says about the financial crisis gets attention. Views have been mixed. Some did not like that he broke with his conservative past, embracing large stimulus packages. Others viewed this as a refreshing change of heart.

Either way, critics tend to ignore a basic flaw in Posner's work here, which is that he fails to mention his role — and that of legal academics generally — in creating and popularizing the policies he now criticizes. Posner has, in short, produced a "culpa" without a "mea."

*   *   *

Law and Economics was [] an important link in the intellectual chain that led to the deregulatory fervor of the past 30 years. Yet, Posner omits this vital piece of the story — and his starring role in it — from his major accounts of the financial crisis. Except for a footnote which acknowledges that "some of" his work "succumbed to [the] fallacy" that markets are axiomatically superior to regulation, it is as though neither he nor the Law and Economics movement ever existed. The financial crisis is, according to Posner, the fault of virtually everyone except Law and Economics.

With re-regulation on the horizon, Posner may recognize that the next real fight is about intellectual liability for the crisis. Because Law and Economics played a role in building a system he now views as flawed, he needs to tell a story that insulates (and thus exonerates) his movement. His version — which we can call the Great Repression — would set the rhetorical parameters of the discussion going forward. That discussion blames the government and the economists, but not the lawyers and legal academics — who were often both ardent advocates for, and implementers of, deregulation.

We shall touch briefly in Section E of this chapter (on unconscionability) on what this re-regulation looks like in consumer financial services contracts. For now, it is enough to ask: Would the post-crisis Judge Posner decide *Selmer* as he did originally? Or do crises beget broader and deeper changes in thought and behavior?

2.   ***The doctrinal nature of Judge Posner's approach:***   Does Judge Posner apply a "will theory" test in *Selmer*? Is his approach consistent with the Restatement (Second) of Contracts § 175?

3.   ***Judicial restraint?***   Judge Posner in *Selmer* is considering a case brought to federal court under diversity of citizenship jurisdiction. He says he is applying

Wisconsin law and cites *Wurtz v. Fleischman*,[60] decided just three years earlier, for the proposition that "we have no reason to think that Wisconsin courts would reach a different result." His citation begins with the signal "*Cf.*," which literally means "compare" and is appropriate where the authority is supportive by analogy, with a parenthetical explanation highly recommended (Judge Posner gives none). The *Wurtz* decision focused on the Wisconsin Court of Appeals' error in finding facts and remanded the case to the trial court to make factual determinations, with these substantive directions on the law of duress:

> Among the basic elements of economic duress which the trial court should expressly consider on remand are those listed by Williston . . . § 1617 at 704:
>
> > 1. The party alleging economic duress must show that he has been the victim of a wrongful or unlawful act or threat, and
>
> > 2. Such act or threat must be one which deprives the victim of his unfettered will.
>
> As a direct result of these elements, the party threatened must be compelled to make a disproportionate exchange of values or to give up something for nothing. If the payment or exchange is made with the hope of obtaining a gain, there is not duress; it must be made solely for the purpose of protecting the victim's business or property interests. Finally, the party threatened must have no adequate legal remedy. . . .

Williston emphasizes that merely driving a hard bargain or taking advantage of another's financial difficulty is not duress, as Judge Robert W. Warren noted recently in a decision from the Eastern District of Wisconsin, holding there was no economic duress because there was no wrongful act:

> Duress involves "wrongful acts . . . that compel a person to manifest apparent assent to a transaction without his volition or cause such fear as to preclude him from exercising free will and judgment in entering into a transaction." Restatement of Contracts § 493 (1932). . . . *Federal Deposit Ins. Corp. v. Balistreri*, 470 F. Supp. 752, 758 (E.D. Wis. 1979).

Recent decisions by the Wisconsin Court of Appeals treat *Wurtz* as stating a four-part test for economic duress: "The first element of such a cause of action is a wrongful or unlawful act. . . . The second element is that the victim was deprived, by the unlawful act, of his or her 'unfettered will.' . . . Third, that there resulted an unfair exchange, and fourth, that the threatened party has no adequate legal remedy."[61]

Why did Judge Posner cite *Wurtz* with a "*Cf.*" signal? Did he apply the substantive analysis of the *Wurtz* case? If not, would it make a difference if he applied the four-part test *Wurtz* took from Williston? Compare Judge Posner's

---

[60] 97 Wis. 2d 100, 293 N.W.2d 155 (1980).

[61] Mancini v. Mathews, 306 Wis. 2d 850, 743 N.W.2d 167 (Ct. App. 2007); *see also* Vaughn v. Electronic Technologies Intern., L.L.C., 269 Wis. 2d 890, 675 N.W.2d 810 (2004).

methodology in *Selmer* to that in *Lake River v. Carborundum* in Chapter 2, applying the Illinois rule on liquidated damages.

4.   *Something fishy:* Judge Posner uses the *Alaska Packers* case as an illustration of his position. The original compensation promised the fishermen in that case was either $50 or $60 for the season plus two cents per red salmon caught; while in Alaska the fishermen demanded and received promises of $100 for the season. The U.S. Court of Appeals for the Ninth Circuit explained:

> On the trial in the court below, the libelants [the fishermen] undertook to show that the fishing nets provided by the respondent were defective, and that it was on that account that they demanded increased wages. On that point, the evidence was substantially conflicting, and the finding of the court was against the libelants, the court saying:
>
> > "The contention of libelants that the nets provided them were rotten and unserviceable is not sustained by the evidence. The defendants' interest required that libelants should be provided with every facility necessary to their success as fishermen, for on such success depended the profits defendant would be able to realize that season from its packing plant, and the large capital invested therein. In view of this self-evident fact, it is highly improbable that the defendant gave libelants rotten and unserviceable nets with which to fish. It follows from this finding that libelants were not justified in refusing performance of their original contract."

The Ninth Circuit declined to disturb the fact-finding of the trial court. Did the trial court engage in fact-finding, or theoretical economic analysis?

For an empirical analysis of the case that suggests that it may be much more complex than Judge Posner's parable, see Debora L. Threedy, *A Fish Story: Alaska Packers' Association v. Domenico.*[62] Professor Threedy argues that the conventional story of the case rests on the assumption that the ship's owner was dependent on the fishermen and had they refused to work, it would have suffered significant losses. This is unlikely to have been the case. The Pyramid Harbor plant, which was to receive the fish caught, had a limited capacity to can fish and there was no way to store excess catch that could not be canned. Moreover, the Pyramid Harbor plant could and did buy salmon from the local Chilkat and Chilkoot tribes. Professor Threedy suggests that it is likely that the fishermen were Italian immigrants and Italian-Americans recruited by a labor contractor in San Francisco. They probably had very poor information about wages and conditions of employment in Alaska when they agreed to leave San Francisco, and that probably contributed to their strike.

5.   *Professor Ian Macneil and relational concerns:* Professor Ian Macneil discussed contractual solidarity in his lectures at Northwestern University.[63]

---

[62]   2000 Utah L. Rev. 185.

[63]   Ian R. Macneil, The New Social Contract, 45, 46–47, 91, 92, 94, 102–03 (1980). Copyright © 1980 by the Yale University Press. Reprinted with the permission of the Yale University Press.

Consider the functions of the duress doctrine in light of his position. Macneil tells us:

> One of the sources of this norm [of mutuality] lies in contractual solidarity; contractual solidarity cannot survive in the face of perceptions that one side constantly gets too good a deal. What constitutes too good a deal varies greatly; the medieval peasants from whom most of us descend accepted more unevenness than we would in modern America, although we seem to put up with a lot. But if anything is plain from history it is that the more an exchange system is perceived as wrongly uneven the more its beneficiaries must depend on external force to maintain it. . . .
>
> Organic solidarity consists of a common belief in effective future interdependence. . . .
>
> It may be noted that organic solidarity is pinned on psychology — not on sociology, economics, law, politics, or force, but on psychology. Such solidary[64] beliefs exist as long as each person in a relation can give an affirmative answer to the following question: Do I think conditions will continue to exist whereby each of us will desire to and be able to depend on the other? . . . Closely related to the notion of law as a back-up system seldom used actively, but always used passively, is law's function as a relatively precise expression — an index if you will — of the great underlying and diffuse sea of custom and social practices in which human affairs are conducted. . . . Contract law, for example, says to all in our society: it is important that you pay your bills. The message is perhaps more vital to those who normally do than to those who do not. It preserves their sense of organic solidarity, whereas those not paying bills have, in a measure, already lost that sense. . . .
>
> The solidary belief cannot survive long in the face of recognition that other participants in the relation are both willing and able to do unlimited or immense harm to the putative believer in order to achieve very limited gains for themselves. No longer is it possible to answer affirmatively the key question: Do I think conditions will continue to exist whereby each of us will desire to and be able to depend on the other?
>
> It should be noted that disproportionate harm does not mean any harm. Some harm to others is inherent in human relations and is built into the process of exchange itself. For example, any negotiations respecting a deal can be stated in terms of harm: "Unless you pay my asking price for the 10,000 square feet of vinyl flooring you wish to purchase, I shall withhold it and impose on you whatever harm follows from your not securing it from me." In the ordinary case, this proposal will not, however, be viewed as imposing harm. . . .
>
> Affirmative views of exchange can easily change and parties be seen as trading in harm rather than in good. This happens, for instance, whenever

---

[64] [Eds. note: *Solidary*, adj. Characterized by or involving community of responsibilities and interests. WEBSTER'S NEW UNIVERSAL UNABRIDGED DICTIONARY.]

one side is seen as hogging the exchange-surplus or otherwise misusing power. Medieval outrage against forestalling and regrating, modern complaints of oil company profiteering, or beliefs that one social class "gets too much," rapidly convert the psychology of exchange from that of goods to that of harms. When this happens the solidary belief is in danger since people may begin to question the benefits of continued interdependence and hence its very existence, at least on present terms.

In what ways, if at all, are the positions of Judge Posner and Professor Macneil opposed?

6. *Professor Gordon, contract theory, and ideology:* Professor Robert Gordon offers a challenge to traditional contract theory and doctrine, urging that they have not yet responded to the insights of Professors Macaulay and Macneil.[65]

> [T]he relational perspective's revelation of a social world of semi-autonomous contracting cultures, governed by relations of cooperative organic solidarity and of pervasive hierarchical domination, is deeply upsetting to the core premises of our liberal social order. Contract law has traditionally been one of the theatres — a small, elite theatre, to be sure, compared to television or Chamber of Commerce lunches — in which those premises are given public expression. . . .
>
> If you accept this account, if you stop thinking of contract law as a pathetically inadequate attempt by legal academics to structure the dealings of the commercial world and think of it instead as a (relatively modest) platform for the expression of ideology, then its doctrines become interesting again for what they can reveal about the society's official values. (Of course, at least as interesting if not more so for the same purpose, would be less elevated, "field level" manifestations of legal ideology, such as advice given in lawyers' offices; but these are obviously a lot harder to study.) . . .
>
> In short, the law embodies a set of fantasies about the world that become real when people act upon them as if they are real: when, for example, people accept the terms of a deal imposed upon them by powerful others as the product of circumstances and their own volition rather than simply of the power of others, or when they abandon a lifelong trading or business partner because the relation is no longer profitable. Freedom of contract means, among other things, never having to say you are sorry.
>
> Some theorists have even advanced a bold hypothesis of a specific historical causal relationship between the fantasy world of political-legal ideological discourse about contracts and the social world of contracting: they contend that encouraging people to deal with one another as strangers progressively erodes the underlying relations of solidarity, reciprocity, and trust upon which capitalist economies essentially depend.

---

[65] Robert W. Gordon, *Macaulay, Macneil, and the Discovery of Solidarity and Power in Contract Law*, 1985 Wis. L. Rev. 565, 575–76, 578–79. Copyright © 1985 by The Board of Regents of the University of Wisconsin System. Reprinted by permission of the Wisconsin Law Review.

4. Undue Influence

The doctrine of "undue influence" is another instance of social control of contract. Undue influence can play a role in relational contracts when judges see the situation as falling outside an impersonal market setting. The rule is hardly precise; there must be something other than an impersonal market relationship. People can use bargaining power but not too much. The court must see the weakness of the party wanting out of a deal as excusable. While we might see it as a special case of duress, courts often treat it as a distinct way to attack some types of contracts. How, exactly, do we draw doctrinal lines between the seemingly similar problems created by "duress" and by "undue influence"?

[handwritten: similar, but not same as duress]

The doctrine plays its major role in gifts and wills. For example, an elderly person becomes attached to his doctor and alienated from his children and grandchildren. The person changes his will, leaving a large bequest to the doctor, and then dies. The children and grandchildren contest the will, claiming that the doctor exercised undue influence to gain a bequest. Since an older person often has a special relationship with his or her doctor, courts struggle with many of these cases every year.[66] The chance of a contested will, of course, prompts many settlements under which doctors, lawyers, nurses, and friendly neighbors share the bequest with family members.

[handwritten: elderly leaving will is ex on how diff than duress]

Undue influence can also be raised as grounds to avoid a contract. In *Frowen v. Blank,*[67] the vendor sought to rescind the sale of a farm because of a breach of the duties involved in a confidential relationship. The trial court denied rescission, but the Supreme Court of Pennsylvania reversed. The vendor was an 86-year-old woman suffering from loss of hearing and sight. She had only two or three years of formal education and little business education. The purchaser and his wife bought the adjoining farm in the early 1960s. A close social relationship developed between the older woman and the young couple. The vendor taught the young couple farm-related crafts. The couple helped her with farm chores and often drove her to local social events.

[handwritten: Ct CASE → UI can be used to avoid K]

The couple drafted a one-page document stating that the vendor agreed to sell the farm to them for $15,000. The vendor signed. About a year later, the purchasers drove the vendor to their lawyer's office, where she signed a formal document without reading it. The fair market value of the farm was $35,000. There was "dependence or trust, justifiably reposed." The case was remanded to give the purchasers an opportunity to establish that the transaction was "fair, conscientious, and beyond the reach of suspicion."

The couple who bought the farm seemed to have taken advantage of a close relationship with a weak woman who had no independent advice, and the court protected her trust in them by requiring them to establish why the price was so low and that the transaction was fair. By setting the standard at a level of fairness,

---

[66] *See* Thomas L. Shaffer, *Undue Influence, Confidential Relationship, and the Psychology of Transference*, 45 Notre Dame L. Rev. 197 (1970). *Compare* McClamroch v. McClamroch, 476 N.E.2d 514 (Ct. App. Ind. 1985), where the person unsuccessfully charged with undue influence was a second wife.

[67] 493 Pa. 137, 145, 149, 425 A.2d 412 (1981).

it effectively made them fiduciaries. A fiduciary is a person with an obligation to look out for the interests of another, such as the relationship of a lawyer with a client and a parent with a child. Fiduciaries are typically held to high standards of fairness in dealings with those for whom they have responsibility. The law also recognizes another type of relationship, called a relationship of confidence, with slightly lower responsibilities, such as to make full disclosure and state only opinions truly held. Siblings and close friends are often, but not always, held to have confidential relationships.

Professor Ethan Leib proposes that the law should reinforce friendship in a number of ways, including, in many instances, treating friends as fiduciaries who hold legally enforceable duties to each other.[68] Leib confronts the "crowding out" argument, namely, that formal legal intervention could crowd out development of trust. He states the argument against his position as follows: "If law *replaces* trust, a regime of trust enforcement actually undermines the very important brand of trust it was seeking to protect!"[69] Leib is skeptical that law would *replace* trust. He argues: "Friendship . . . provides so many of its own incentives for entry (and it is relatively easy to exit when the costs grow too great) that it is hard to imagine legal regulations actually deterring people from establishing and developing friendships."[70] He points out that rather than crowding out, legal rights may complement trust, particularly when legal rights are costly to assert and, when asserted, yield uncertain results.[71] Do you agree that legal regulation in the context of friendship is unlikely to interfere with development of these relationships? Is legal reinforcement of relationships of trust a good idea, or is it too fraught with peril? If it is a good idea, is contract law the right category?

As suggested above, undue influence is sometimes very close to duress. In *Odorizzi v. Bloomfield School District*,[72] the court found that an elementary school teacher had stated a claim for undue influence by the school district in obtaining his agreement to resign. The teacher had been arrested on charges of homosexual activity in 1964. The superintendent of the district and principal of the school came to the teacher's apartment after he had been awake for 40 hours going through arrest, questioning, and booking. They claimed they were there to help. They said he must resign immediately, without consulting an attorney first, to avoid publicity as part of discharge proceedings and the resulting embarrassment and humiliation. The court said that these alleged facts, if true, made out a case of overpersuasion.

[handwritten margin note: Ask him to resign for crime of homo, very similar to durress]

Professor E. Allan Farnsworth of Columbia Law School, who was the Reporter for the second half of the Restatement (Second) of Contracts, discussed the relationship between undue influence and duress.[73] He noted that a court could have reached much the same result in the *Odorizzi* case using an expanded

---

[68] *See* Ethan J. Leib, *Friendship & The Law*, 54 UCLA L. Rev. 631 (2007); Leib, *Friends as Fiduciaries*, 86 Wash. U. L.R. 665 (2009).

[69] Leib, *Friends as Fiduciaries*, *supra* note 68, at 726.

[70] *Id.* at 728.

[71] *Id.* at 730–31.

[72] 246 Cal. App. 2d 123, 54 Cal. Rptr. 533 (Cal. App., 2nd Dist. 1966).

[73] E. Allan Farnsworth, *Coercion in Contract Law*, 5 U. Ark. Little Rock L. Rev. 329 (1982).

doctrine of duress rather than undue influence.

> The liberalization of the requirement that the threat be one that the law condemns would permit the court to find that the school board's threat to publicize any proceedings against Odorizzi and hurt his chances of obtaining another job was an improper one on the ground that doing so would harm Odorizzi and would not significantly benefit the school board. And the liberalization of the requirement that the threat be sufficiently grave to justify the victim's assent would permit the court to conclude that Odorizzi had no reasonable alternative but to resign in the face of the improper threat.

> It is therefore a likely consequence of the liberalization of the requirements of duress that courts and litigants will place more emphasis on the coercive nature of transactions that were previously subject to attack only on the grounds of undue influence. The doctrine of duress may, in the long run, swallow up much of what has previously been considered to be undue influence.

b/c durress has been liberalized, makes undue influence more rare

Professor Farnsworth may be correct that the doctrine of duress will ultimately "swallow up" undue influence. Yet, the fact remains that lawyers and judges — and bar examiners — continue to recognize a distinction between the two. Based on what you've read thus far, can you articulate that distinction? If so, do you think it is meaningful? If not — that is, you can't describe what differentiates the two doctrines — why not? Do you feel unduly influenced one way or the other? If so, by what?

5. Misrepresentation   *↙ New Topic*

Most people agree that there should be social control of contract (e.g., regulation) to prevent and remedy fraud. Even those who want a wide area in which bargainers are free to exercise choices and power accept some limitations on dishonesty. We can provoke controversy, however, when we consider how far to carry this idea.

Those who believe in choice and individualism could view the law of misrepresentation in a number of ways. The virtues of free contract flow from situations where both parties understand the facts and risks. Then they fashion a deal responding to them. If I trick you into signing a contract, I have robbed you of free choice. The formal deal will be but an empty shell. It will not reflect your assumptions and expectations. Moreover, I know that it does not. I am trying to impose my will on you by trickery and cheating. My conduct has little, if any, social value. There is no reason to encourage it.

Nonetheless, the legal system may insist that you take care of yourself. It may deny remedies for fraud that you could have detected or avoided. This may serve several functions. Courts lighten their workload by turning you away. Courts can give you incentives to use care and be suspicious. If you respond to these incentives, your behavior will help the market work better at less cost.[74]

Arg. against asserting misrep is it encourages care if deny claim on this ground

---

[74] In the words of Judge Posner: "Even in the case of deliberate misrepresentations, a requirement

People could also lie abt. it beng misrep

Furthermore, courts seek to protect transactions from invalid claims of fraud made by dishonest people seeking to get out of a bad deal. When I discover I've made a bad deal, I may want to get out. I may lie about what you said, charging you with misrepresentations you did not make. Courts can impose hard-to-prove requirements and demand clear proof. Moreover, one faced with a bad deal may go through a very human process of self-deception. I may convince myself that you must have said certain things that, in fact, you did not say. Courts may wish to avoid having to search for truth by imposing heavy self-reliance rules.

Moreover, American attitudes toward fraud are contradictory. Fraud is bad and often criminal. Yet the amusing con man is a character found in fiction and film. Statements such as "you cannot cheat an honest man" also reflect attitudes towards bargainers and those claiming the protection of courts. We suspect larceny in the hearts of both seller and buyer. It is easy to worry about the honest buyer cheated by the used car dealer. It is also easy to forget that the buyer is often trying to trade in a car with a defective transmission, hoping that the used car dealer does not discover it before they make a deal. Anyone who has been a buyer or seller (or both) on Craigslist knows the duality of this worry.

Nonetheless, we should recognize the practical consequences of the choices being made. If courts impose a high burden of proof to establish difficult-to-prove requirements, few lawsuits will succeed. If they accept the ordinary civil burden of proof and demand only easy-to-prove requirements, those asserting misrepresentation will win more cases. Who benefits from making misrepresentation hard to establish? Who benefits from making it easier to establish? The impact of these choices will benefit some and hurt others. This impact may not be random.

Fraud is often an orphan in the law school curriculum. Contracts teachers see it as part of torts. Torts teachers see their mission as exploring negligence and auto accidents. They either omit the subject or teach it quickly. Nonetheless, dealing with misrepresentation is an important part of social control of contract. Even what critics see as the flaws of the law of misrepresentation are significant. The flaws have prompted a great deal of legislation, ranging from federal and state securities regulation to false advertising statutes.

Tort | Fraud doctrine

Professor Kennedy's "core" and "periphery" ideas discussed above have special importance in this area.[75] The classic tort of fraud — the core doctrine — grants relief where the defendant (a) has wrongfully made (b) a material misrepresentation of (c) fact on which (d) the plaintiff had a right to rely. Then plaintiff must prove (e) reliance on the misrepresentation, which (f) caused (g) injury.

Until the middle of the 20th century, plaintiffs faced serious difficulties dealing with all of these ideas. The rule was *caveat emptor* — let the buyer beware. For

---

that the plaintiff prove reasonable reliance . . . serves a healthy purpose. Legal proceedings are costly, and it is cheaper for a potential victim of misrepresentation to take very inexpensive precautions than to allow him to shut his eyes to the obvious and then sue." Amoco Oil Co. v. Ashcraft, 791 F.2d 519, 522 (7th Cir. 1986).

[75] *See* Kennedy, *supra* note 27.

example, the statement had to be intentionally false; an honest mistake would not be fraudulent. It is not easy to prove that defendant *intended* to make a false statement. If (like most law students) you are taking criminal law, there is a good chance you know how difficult it is to show "intent." Moreover, the false statement had to be "material." Materiality is a complex idea which suggests that the legal system judges a statement's significance in the transaction. It must be a statement of fact. Opinions and predictions are usually not enough. Of course, often it is not easy to distinguish between assertions of fact and opinions (see the *Vokes* case in section B.7. of this chapter, *infra*). Perhaps most importantly, plaintiff had to take reasonable steps toward self-protection. She had to inspect the subject of the contract and find flaws for herself. She could not trust a seller's statements. She had to read and understand all documents. She had to discover clauses that were inconsistent with oral representations. Finally, a plaintiff had to prove that her reliance caused injury of a tangible kind. The common law added to all this difficulty by requiring that a plaintiff prove fraud by "clear and convincing" evidence. This is a heavier burden than the one courts impose on plaintiffs in most civil cases (a "preponderance" of the evidence).[76]

By the end of the 20th century, courts had questioned, softened, or even abandoned almost all the elements of the classic tort. The periphery of exceptions makes it hard to state a modern law of misrepresentation. Sellers are responsible in some states for innocent misrepresentations. For example, the Supreme Court of Rhode Island recognized a right to rescind and recover what was paid when a vendor of real estate and her agent told the buyers there was no termite problem, even though there was no evidence that the vendor or agent were aware of the termite problem that did exist.[77] The Court stated that simple justice demands that when both vendor and vendee are innocent, the one making the false statement should bear the loss of the benefits of the transaction. "The speaker who uses the unqualified statement does so at his peril. The risk of falsity is his." He is strictly accountable for his words. It is an absolute liability to achieve certain goals.[78]

---

[76] Lawyers sometimes think of the difference quantitatively. "Preponderance" means, roughly, a bit more than 50 percent. The evidence need not be very strong. "Clear and convincing" means that the evidence must be stronger than 51 percent, say two-thirds. The most stringent evidentiary test comes from criminal law: "beyond a reasonable doubt," a phrase that suggests a very high evidentiary burden for the government when seeking to convict someone of a crime. Why do you think the legal system uses different evidentiary burdens for different types of problems (e.g., contract versus criminal)? Does that say something about what is at stake?

[77] *See* Halpert v. Rosenthal, 107 R.I. 406, 417, 267 A.2d 730 (1970).

[78] Remedies for innocent misrepresentation are often limited to rescission, but not always. For example, in Maser v. Lind, 181 Neb. 365, 148 N.W.2d 831 (1967), the vendors represented that buildings were in sound condition although termites had damaged the buildings seriously. The court allowed the purchasers to recover damages although they could not prove the vendors knew there were termites. It did not limit the purchasers to rescinding the transaction.

In many situations, rescission for innocent misrepresentation is a welcome remedy. However, it often has a major defect. Rescission may not create a fund large enough so that a successful vendee can pay an attorney. The purchaser may recover what she paid. However, after she pays her lawyer, she will not be where she was before she bought a house infested with termites.

The distinction between a statement of fact and one of opinion is another traditional element of the tort of fraud that has sometimes been relaxed in modern times. Today, in some circumstances, the seller will be liable for the failure to honestly state her opinion. *Vokes v. Arthur Murray, infra*, may be an example of such a holding.

Victims of intentional misrepresentation often have many remedies. They can sue for the tort of fraud. Most jurisdictions will protect the victim's expectation interest in fashioning remedies.[79] The victim is entitled to the benefit of the bargain, measured by the difference in the value of the thing misrepresented and the value it would have had if the representation had been true. A few jurisdictions limit recovery in tort actions to "out-of-pocket" damages, roughly a measure of the plaintiff's reliance losses (perhaps the cost of repairing the thing represented). For a discussion of this point, see *Beardmore v. T.D. Burgess Co.*[80] In more modern times it has become not uncommon for courts to award punitive damages for intentional misrepresentation.[81]

---

[79] Section 2-721 of the UCC codifies this rule, providing that the remedies of Article 2 for non-fraudulent breach can be used for material misrepresentation or fraud and that a claim for rescission can be combined with a claim for damages. Some courts, however, have adopted an "economic loss" rule that cuts off intentional fraud recovery in the absence of personal injury, relegating the victim to her contract remedies, if any. *See, e.g.*, Below v. Norton, 310 Wis. 2d 713, 751 N.W.2d 351 (2008) (discussed further in Note 3 following *Boud v. SDNCO, Inc., infra*).

[80] 245 Md. 387, 226 A.2d 329 (1967).

[81] Many states have statutes that provide greater remedies for misrepresentations than the common law. Some of these statutes are limited to cases involving consumers, while others can be used by businesses complaining about the practices of other businesses. Some states model their statutes on the Federal Trade Commission Act, prohibiting "unfair methods of competition . . . and unfair or deceptive practices." Others broadly prohibit consumer fraud or unconscionable consumer practices. Still others, based on the Uniform Deceptive Trade Practices Act, specifically prohibit 11 deceptive practices and contain, in addition, a catch-all prohibition against "any other conduct which similarly creates a likelihood of confusion or of misunderstanding." Most of these statutes are enforced by the state attorney general or by administrative agencies. However, individual plaintiffs can often bring private lawsuits based on these statutes. The elements of a statutory cause of action are often easier to establish than the classic tort of fraud. Furthermore, a plaintiff who wins her case can often recover reasonable attorney's fees. Many members of the bar, however, are unaware of the possibilities under these statutes.

Section 100.18 of the Wisconsin Statutes is an example of a statute prohibiting deceptive practices. It provides, in part:

> No person . . . with intent to sell . . . any real estate, merchandise, securities, employment, [or] service . . . shall make, [or] publish . . . in a newspaper, magazine or other publication, or in the form of a book, notice, handbill, poster, bill, circular, pamphlet, letter, sign, placard, card, label, or over any radio or television station, or in any other way similar or dissimilar to the foregoing, [a] . . . representation of any kind to the public relating to such purchase, [or] sale . . . which . . . representation contains any assertion, representation or statement of fact which is untrue, deceptive or misleading.

The section does not apply to insurance, or to real estate brokers who can bring themselves within an exemption spelled out at § 100.18(12)(b). The statute provides for enforcement by the attorney general. However, individuals can also bring private actions. If they win, they can recover reasonable attorney's fees. Obviously, the text and interpretations of these statutes and administrative regulations will differ from state to state. All we can do in these materials is alert you to the existence of these alternatives to difficult actions based on misrepresentation. You should never consider a misrepresentation action without first reading the applicable statutes and administrative regulations to see whether they provide better tools than the common law.

The following cases raise another difficult question in the law of misrepresentation: when must a party to a contract reveal information that it has reason to believe is not known or appreciated by the other party? Can it be misrepresentation simply to remain silent?

OBDE v. SCHLEMEYER
Washington Supreme Court
56 Wash. 2d 449, 353 P.2d 672 (1960)

FINLEY, J.

Plaintiffs, Mr. and Mrs. Fred Obde, brought this action to recover damages for the alleged fraudulent concealment of termite infestation in an apartment house purchased by them from the defendants, Mr. and Mrs. Robert Schlemeyer. Plaintiffs assert that the building was infested at the time of the purchase; that defendants were well apprised of the termite condition, but fraudulently concealed it from the plaintiffs.

After a trial on the merits, the trial court entered findings of fact and conclusions of law sustaining the plaintiffs' claim, and awarded them a judgment for damages in the amount of $3,950. The defendants appealed. Their assignments of error may be compartmentalized, roughly, into two categories: (1) those going to the question of liability, and (2) those relating to the amount of damages to be awarded if liability is established.

First, as to the question of liability: The Schlemeyers concede that, shortly after they purchased the property from a Mr. Ayars on an installment contract in April 1954, they discovered substantial termite infestation in the premises. The Schlemeyers contend, however, that they immediately took steps to eradicate the termites, and that, at the time of the sale to the Obdes in November 1954, they had no reason to believe that these steps had not completely remedied the situation. We are not convinced of the merit of this contention.

The record reveals that when the Schlemeyers discovered the termite condition they engaged the services of a Mr. Senske, a specialist in pest control. He effected some measures to eradicate the termites, and made some repairs in the apartment house. Thereafter, there was no easily apparent or surface evidence of termite damage. However, portions of the findings of fact entered by the trial court read as follows:

> Senske had advised Schlemeyer that in order to obtain a complete job it would be necessary to drill the holes and pump the fluid into all parts of the basement floors as well as the basement walls. Part of the basement was used as a basement apartment. Senske informed Schlemeyer that the floors should be taken up in the apartment and the cement flooring under the wood floors should be treated in the same manner as the remainder of the basement. Schlemeyer did not care to go to the expense of tearing up the floors to do this and therefore this portion of the basement was not treated.

Senske also told Schlemeyer even though the job were done completely, including treating the portion of the basement which was occupied by the apartment, to be sure of success, it would be necessary to make inspections regularly for a period of a year. Until these inspections were made for this period of time the success of the process could not be determined. Considering the job was not completed as mentioned, Senske would give Schlemeyer no assurance of success and advised him that he would make no guarantee under the circumstances.

No error has been assigned to the above findings of fact. Consequently, they will be considered as the established facts of the case. . . . The pattern thus established is hardly compatible with the Schlemeyers' claim that they had no reason to believe that their efforts to remedy the termite condition were not completely successful.

The Schlemeyers urge that, in any event, as sellers, they had no duty to inform the Obdes of the termite condition. They emphasize that it is undisputed that the purchasers asked no questions respecting the possibility of termites. They rely on a Massachusetts case involving a substantially similar factual situation, *Swinton v. Whitinsville Sav. Bank*, 311 Mass. 677, 42 N.E.2d 808 (1942). Applying the traditional doctrine of caveat emptor — namely, that, as between parties dealing at arms' length (as vendor and purchaser), there is no duty to speak, in the absence of a request for information — the Massachusetts court held that a vendor of real property has no duty to disclose to a prospective purchaser the fact of a latent termite condition in the premises.

Without doubt, the parties in the instant case were dealing at arms' length. Nevertheless, and notwithstanding the reasoning of the Massachusetts court above noted, we are convinced that the defendants had a duty to inform the plaintiffs of the termite condition. In *Perkins v. Marsh*, 179 Wash. 362, 37 P.2d 689 (1934), a case involving parties dealing at arms' length as landlord and tenant, we held that:

> Where there are concealed defects in demised premises, dangerous to the property, health, or life of the tenant, which defects are known to the landlord when the lease is made, but unknown to the tenant, and which a careful examination on his part would not disclose, it is the landlord's duty to disclose them to the tenant before leasing, and his failure to do so amounts to a fraud."

We deem this rule to be equally applicable to the vendor-purchaser relationship. See Keeton, *Fraud — Concealment and Non-Disclosure*, 15 TEX. L. REV. 1, 14–16 (Dec. 1936). In this article Professor Keeton also aptly summarized the modern judicial trend away from a strict application of caveat emptor by saying:

> It is of course apparent that the content of the maxim "caveat emptor," used in its broader meaning of imposing risks on both parties to a transaction, has been greatly limited since its origin. When Lord Cairns stated in *Peek v. Gurney* that there was no duty to disclose facts, however morally censurable their non-disclosure may be, he was stating the law as shaped by an individualistic philosophy based upon freedom of contract. It was not concerned with morals. In the present stage of the law, the decisions show a drawing away from this idea, and there can be seen an attempt by many

courts to reach a just result in so far as possible, but yet maintaining the degree of certainty which the law must have. The statement may often be found that if either party to a contract or sale conceals or suppresses a material fact that he is in good faith bound to disclose then his silence is fraudulent.

The attitude of the courts toward non-disclosure is undergoing a change, and contrary to Lord Cairns's famous remark it would seem that the object of the law in these cases should be to impose on parties to the transaction a duty to speak whenever justice, equity, and fair dealing demand it. *Id.* at 31.

A termite infestation of a frame building, such as that involved in the instant case, is manifestly a serious and dangerous condition. One of the Schlemeyers' own witnesses, Mr. Hoefer, who at the time was a building inspector for the city of Spokane, testified that ". . . if termites are not checked in their damage, they can cause a complete collapse of a building . . . they would simply eat up the wood." Further, at the time of the sale of the premises, the condition was clearly latent — not readily observable upon reasonable inspection. As we have noted, all superficial or surface evidence of the condition had been removed by reason of the efforts of Senske, the pest control specialist. Under the circumstances, we are satisfied that "justice, equity, and fair dealing," to use Professor Keeton's language, demanded that the Schlemeyers speak — that they inform prospective purchasers, such as the Obdes, of the condition, regardless of the latter's failure to ask any questions relative to the possibility of termites. . . .

The Schlemeyers' final contentions, relating to the issue of liability, emphasize the Obdes' conduct after they discovered the termite condition. Under the purchase agreement with the Schlemeyers, the Obdes paid $5,000 in cash, and gave their promissory note for $2,250 to the Schlemeyers. In addition, they assumed the balance due on the installment contract, under which the Schlemeyers had previously acquired the property from Ayars. This amounted to $34,750. After they discovered the termites (some six weeks subsequent to taking possession of the premises in November 1954), the Obdes continued for a time to make payments on the Ayars contract. They then called in Senske to examine the condition — not knowing that he had previously worked on the premises at the instance of the Schlemeyers. From Senske the Obdes learned for the first time that the Schlemeyers had known of the termite infestation prior to the sale. Obdes then ceased performance of the Ayars contract, and allowed the property to revert to Ayars under a forfeiture provision in the installment contract.

The Schlemeyers contend that by continuing to make payments on the Ayars contract after they discovered the termites the Obdes waived any right to recovery for fraud. This argument might have some merit if the Obdes were seeking to rescind the purchase contract. . . . However, this is not an action for rescission; it is a suit for damages, and thus is not barred by conduct constituting an affirmance of the contract. . . .

For the reasons hereinbefore set forth, we hold that the trial court committed no error in determining that the respondents (Obdes) were entitled to recover damages against the appellants (Schlemeyers) upon the theory of fraudulent concealment. However, there remains the question of the proper amount of damages to be awarded. The trial court found that:

> [B]ecause of the termite condition the value [of the premises] has been reduced to the extent of $3950.00 and the plaintiffs have been damaged to that extent, and in that amount.

As hereinbefore noted, judgment was thereupon entered for the respondents in that amount.

The appellants concede that the measure of damages in a case of this type is the difference between the actual value of the property and what the property would have been worth had the misrepresentations been true. . . .

The judgment awarding damages of $3,950 is well within the limits of the testimony in the record relating to damages. The Obdes have not cross-appealed. The judgment of the trial court should be affirmed in all respects. It is so ordered.

WEAVER, C. J., ROSELLINI, and FOSTER, JJ., concur. HILL, J., concurs in the result.

NOTES AND QUESTIONS

1. ***The law of termites:*** Judge Finley of the Supreme Court of Washington begins his opinion in *Hughes v. Stusser* as follows:[82]

> Of the forms of animal life known to modern science, few, if any, classifications other than Homo sapiens have been the subject of as much legal controversy as the members of the order Isoptera. The species involved in this particular lawsuit does not appear in the record, but it is likely it was from the genus Reticulitermes of the family of Rhinotermitidae, known to the nonbiologically oriented as "termites." The wooden edifices of man represent nothing more to these despicable insects than an abundant source of cellulose, which is their principal food.

There is an annotation in 22 A.L.R. 3d 972 on "Duty of Vendor of Real Estate to Give Purchaser Information as to Termite Infestation." The annotation lists 120 cases decided between 1952 and 2009. This annotation, of course, does not cover all reported cases involving termites but only those where a duty to give accurate information about them was in issue. The courts in the deep South seem less likely to give relief to a buyer than those elsewhere. Why might this be the case? The case law shows that American courts are divided about whether a home owner has any duty to disclose what she knows about termites when selling the house. Once again, we must note that the United States is a federal system, and often there is no one clear rule followed by all of the states. The rules of contract law often differ from state to state, and of course they also change over time.

2. ***Silent misrepresentation in Washington:*** The Supreme Court of Washington clarified its *Obde* decision in *Hughes v. Stusser*.[83] Purchasers of a house sued vendors for damages, alleging fraudulent failure to disclose a concealed dry rot and

---

[82] 68 Wash. 2d 707, 415 P.2d 89 (1966).

[83] *Id.*

termite condition. There was enough evidence to support the trial judge's finding that the Stussers had no knowledge of the condition at the time of sale. Thus, "there could be no affirmative duty to disclose to Mr. and Mrs. Hughes the conditions of which the Stussers had no knowledge! Correlatively, the Stussers could not conceal a condition unknown to them."

In *Mitchell v. Straith*,[84] the court interpreted the *Obde* case also to require proof that "the undisclosed fact was a material fact to the extent that it substantially affected adversely the value of the property or operated to materially impair or defeat the purpose of the transaction." It also pointed out that the *Obde* case "relied on a finding that the purchaser had no knowledge of the alleged defect and that it was a defect a reasonable inspection would not disclose."

3.   *Warranty, another theory:* Article 2 of the Uniform Commercial Code contains an elaborate scheme of express and implied warranties, as well as provisions for reconciling warranties and disclaiming them.[85] It provides that descriptions, affirmations of fact, and promises about goods can constitute express warranties,[86] and that the law supplies implied warranties, such as a warranty of fitness for the ordinary purposes for which the particular goods are used.[87] There are also common law warranties, express and implied. The law of warranty, unlike that of fraudulent misrepresentation, does not inquire into the state of mind of the one making a warranty, looking for dishonesty or at least negligence. Warranty is thus a "strict liability" theory; one can make an honest mistake in giving a warranty and still be liable. The Restatement takes a broad approach to misrepresentation, making contracts voidable by recipients of either fraudulent or material misrepresentations, thus treating misrepresentation as much like warranty.[88]

In *House v. Thornton*, the court found that a builder impliedly warrants that a new house's foundations are firm and secure so the house is structurally safe for occupation.[89] Thus, the buyer of the house could recover damages without proof that the builder knew of the defective condition or made any affirmative statements about it. In a sense, when a builder offers to sell a new house it impliedly represents that the building is placed on adequate foundations to keep it from sinking or sliding down a hill. A structure on inadequate foundations isn't a new house.

Warranties in sales of houses depend on state law, most of it case law with a lot of nuance. The Washington court limited its rule in *Klos v. Gockel*.[90] The court explained that the essence of the *House* doctrine was that "the vendor-builder be a person regularly engaged in building, so that the sale is commercial rather than

---

[84] 40 Wash. App. 405, 411–12, 698 P.2d 609, 613 (1985).

[85] *See* UCC §§ 2-313 to 2-318.

[86] UCC § 2-313.

[87] UCC § 2-314(2)(c). An implied warranty is a promise read into a contract; this is a nice but misleading way of saying it is imposed by law.

[88] RESTATEMENT (SECOND) OF CONTRACTS § 162, 164 (1981).

[89] 76 Wash. 2d 428, 457 P.2d 199 (1969). *See* Joseph C. Brown Jr., *The Implied Warranty of Habitability Doctrine in Residential Property Conveyances: Policy-Backed Change Proposals*, 62 WASH. L. REV. 743 (1987).

[90] 87 Wash. 2d 567, 570, 554 P.2d 1349, 1352 (1976).

casual or personal in nature." It noted that the sale must be of a new house. The sale must be nearly contemporaneous with completion. An intervening tenancy must not interrupt the transaction unless the builder-vendor created such an intervening tenancy for the primary purpose of promoting the sale of the property.

Thus, in Washington, an individual selling a house must disclose known defective conditions such as termites. However, the buyer must prove that the vendor knew or should have known of them. An owner selling an older house does not impliedly promise it to be free from defects. A builder selling a new house, however, is liable for structural defects, even without proof of knowledge. Why did the court draw these lines? Are they based on choice, paternalism, or something else?

4. **Seller's disclosure forms:** The precise problem raised by *Obde v. Schlemeyer* is less likely to come up in many states today. Sellers of used residential property often deal through real estate agents. The National Association of Realtors estimated that two-thirds of all suits filed after a real estate transaction allege misrepresentation or a failure to disclose defects in the property. Buyers who think they have been misled about a house often are not satisfied to sue the seller. Indeed, often the seller has moved to another state and is hard to sue, or the seller may no longer have sufficient assets to satisfy a judgment. Buyers, as a result, almost always sue the real estate agent for alleged misrepresentations or failures to disclose what they knew or ought to have known. As a result, a number of large real estate brokerages began requiring sellers who engaged their services to fill out elaborate disclosure forms. Sellers would check boxes on the forms indicating that they knew of a defect in the house. Copies were given to potential buyers. Real estate agents then could ward off suits or defend those that were brought. They could prove that buyers had been told about defects, and sellers could no longer remain silent. If a seller did not indicate that there was a defect, the seller was making a positive representation about the quality of the house. Real estate agents could defend against claims of misrepresentation or failure to disclose by asserting that they had only passed along the seller's claims about his or her house.

In 1985, California passed legislation requiring sellers to make such disclosures.[91] Since 1991, the National Association of Realtors has lobbied the state legislatures seeking laws requiring sellers to complete mandated forms, and many have done so.

Suppose a seller makes a false statement in a required disclosure statement. What are the consequences? Some statutes may require no more than that real estate brokers must use forms approved by a state commission. What happens when a seller fails to use the form? Or makes untrue statements on the form? Are buyers left to their remedies for fraud or innocent misrepresentation based on a seller's answers on the disclosure form?[92]

---

[91] Cal. Civ. Code §§ 1102–1102.17.

[92] Vance A. Fisher, in *A Closer Look at Michigan's Seller Disclosure Act,* found that the Michigan statute in effect when he wrote was unclear. Michigan Lawyers Weekly, March 21, 1994, p. 2. The Act calls for disclosures, but fails to provide the consequences of a seller's failure to disclose or of an erroneous statement. "Presumably, the Legislature meant to relegate the result to the case law of Michigan concerning misrepresentation and nondisclosure." The statute provides that no transfer shall be invalidated because of noncompliance with the Act. Apparently, a buyer must assert rights based on

5. *Disclosures in used car sales:* Many states also require disclosures of defects in used car sales by dealers. Arizona combines disclosure with an implied warranty of merchantability (see UCC § 2-314, which states, among other things, that this warranty requires that the goods be "fit for the ordinary purposes for which such goods are used") for 15 days or 500 miles, whichever comes earlier. Parts of a used car can only be excluded from this warranty by disclosure of a specific defect.[93] Thus, an Arizona used car dealer can only disclaim the implied warranty of merchantability by disclosing particular defects; a blanket disclaimer (see UCC § 2-316) does not work.

6. *Remedies in* **Obde:** Avoidance of the contract is one remedy for misrepresentation. The Obdes did not seek to avoid the contract; the court refers to this in terms of not seeking "rescission," but rescission is a misleading term because it can also refer to a mutual agreement to undo a contract. The Restatement therefore refers to the contract being ⟨voidable⟩ by the recipient of a fraudulent or material misrepresentation and provides for restitution for any benefit conferred.[94]

[handwritten margin note: In this case not seeking to make K void, but rather seeking damages]

The Obdes sought damages and not avoidance. Were damages in the case based on the expectation interest or something else? Would the Obdes have received more if they had avoided the contract and sought restitution? Should they have been able to both avoid the contract (and get restitution) *and* get damages for not getting a termite-free house?

7. *Professor Kronman on the duty to disclose:* Professor Anthony Kronman notes that the common law features inconsistent rules.[95] On one hand, I cannot snap up your offer, knowing you have made a mistake. For example, you write me, offering to sell goods for $1.25 a unit. Suppose any reasonable person in my position would know that you meant the price to be $2.15 a unit. Your typist just transposed the 1 and 2 in writing the price. My attempted acceptance would not create a contract at $1.25 a unit. However, if all I said in my letter responding to your offer was "I accept," my acceptance might create a contract at $2.15 a unit. I might be responsible for leading you to believe we had a deal at that price.

On the other hand, there is great inconsistency about my duty to disclose material facts likely to affect your decision to enter a contract. For example, I know my house is infested with termites or roaches. I should be aware that you would not buy it if you were aware of the condition. Can I conclude a binding contract with you if I fail to tell you about the termites or roaches? In many states, like Washington, the answer is no.

Suppose a buyer thinks there is oil on seller's land. It buys the property at a price that does not reflect its value as a source of oil. Is there a duty to disclose? Does it matter if the seller is a farmer with little wealth and the buyer is a multinational oil company with great assets?

---

misrepresentation before the closing when a deed is signed.

[93] Ariz. Rev. Stat. Ann. § 44-1261.

[94] Restatement (Second) of Contracts §§ 164, 376 (1981).

[95] Anthony Kronman, *Mistake, Disclosure, Information, and the Law of Contracts*, 7 J. Legal Stud. 1 (1978).

Kronman suggests that "where the knowledgeable party's contract rights are enforced despite his failure to disclose a known mistake, the knowledge involved is typically the product of a costly search. A rule permitting nondisclosure is the only effective way of providing an incentive to invest in the production of such knowledge."[96] Buyers often spend a good deal of money, for example, searching for land that might contain valuable minerals. Kronman offers an example of this. Texas Gulf Sulphur conducted expensive aerial surveys revealing a geological anomaly associated with valuable ore deposits. Texas Gulf Sulphur paid the estate of Murray Hendrie $500 for a two-year option to buy the mineral rights for $18,000 plus 10 percent of the profits made on exploitation. When the optioned property proved to be extremely valuable, the estate sued, alleging that Texas Gulf Sulphur had intentionally misled the seller by failing to disclose the promising geological information. (The case was settled.) Kronman notes that buyers in such cases would be less likely to invest in costly searches for information if they were required to disclose that information to the seller. Buyers expect to recover the search costs, in part at least, from the increase in value of the land attributable to the discovery of minerals on it. (It is important to remember that the searchers must also recover the costs of unsuccessful searches from the proceeds of those that prove successful.)

When extractive industries seek to buy land because it has or may have valuable minerals under the surface, they typically use an agent who does not disclose who the principal is. Why do you suppose this is? The law generally finds no misrepresentation due to there being an undisclosed principal in such cases. Is this legal approach consistent with Kronman's theory?

Kronman discusses *Obde v. Schlemeyer.*[97] He argues that requiring disclosure of latent defects such as those involved there makes sense from an economic perspective. Where a seller knows of a defect that the buyer does not, the seller is the party best able to avoid the buyer's mistake at least cost. "A disclosure requirement is unlikely to have a substantial effect on the level of investment by homeowners in the detection of termites. . . . In most cases, a homeowner will have an adequate incentive to check for termites even if the law requires him to disclose what he discovers." He will want to protect his own investment in the house. Kronman notes: "Even where neither party has knowledge of the defect, it may be efficient to allocate to the seller the risk of a mistaken belief that no defect exists, on the grounds that of the two parties he is the likely to be the cheapest mistake-preventer [because of his superior access to information]."

8. *Professor Scheppelle's study of Kronman's theory:* Professor Kim Scheppelle studied cases involving the conscious withholding of information.[98] She calls this the problem of "strategic secrets." She subjected Kronman's theory of "cheapest mistake-preventer" to the test of a sample of about 100 reported cases drawn from the legal encyclopedias *American Jurisprudence 2d* and *Corpus Juris Secundum,* supplemented by those cases frequently cited in the secondary literature. She concluded that the case law allows information to be kept secret if it could

---

[96] *Id.* at 9.

[97] *Id.* at 24–25.

[98] Kim Lane Scheppele, Legal Secrets: Equality and Efficiency in the Common Law (University of Chicago Press 1988).

be obtained with roughly equal efforts by both parties. Sellers have to disclose latent but not obvious defects, but buyers rarely have to disclose. This principle, however, is more theoretical than actual. Courts do not recognize inequality of resources at the parties' command. Large oil companies can buy land from small landowners without disclosing the results of research. The courts reason that the information about subsurface oil is available to anyone who chooses to look. They refuse to consider that some can afford the costs of looking far better than others. Does this approach on the part of the courts at least partially overlap with Kronman's recommended approach?

6. Good Faith   *New Topic*

MARKET STREET ASSOCIATES v. FREY
United States Court of Appeals, Seventh Circuit
941 F.2d 588 (1991)

Case AB good faith

POSNER, J.

Market Street Associates Limited Partnership and its general partner appeal from a judgment for the defendants, General Electric Pension Trust and its trustees, entered upon cross-motions for summary judgment in a diversity suit that pivots on the doctrine of "good faith" performance of a contract. *Cf.* Robert Summers, *"'Good Faith' in General Contract Law and the Sales Provisions of the Uniform Commercial Code,"* 54 VA. L. REV. 195, 232–43 (1968). Wisconsin law applies — common law rather than Uniform Commercial Code, because the contract is for land rather than for goods. . . .

Using UI common law cuz sale of land → not goods

In 1968, J.C. Penney Company, the retail chain, entered into a sale and leaseback arrangement with General Electric Pension Trust in order to finance Penney's growth. Under the arrangement Penney sold properties to the pension trust, which the trust then leased back to Penney for a term of 25 years. Paragraph 34 of the lease entitles the lessee to "request Lessor [the pension trust] to finance the costs and expenses of construction of additional Improvements upon the Premises," provided the amount of the costs and expenses is at least $250,000. Upon receiving the request, the pension trust "agrees to give reasonable consideration to providing the financing of such additional Improvements and Lessor and Lessee shall negotiate in good faith concerning the construction of such Improvements and the financing by Lessor of such costs and expenses." Paragraph 34 goes on to provide that, should the negotiations fail, the lessee shall be entitled to repurchase the property at a price roughly equal to the price at which Penney sold it to the pension trust in the first place, plus 6 percent a year for each year since the original purchase. So if the average annual appreciation in the property exceeded 6 percent, a breakdown in negotiations over the financing of improvements would entitle Penney to buy back the property for less than its market value (assuming it had sold the property to the pension trust in the first place at its then market value).

One of these leases was for a shopping center in Milwaukee. In 1987 Penney assigned this lease to Market Street Associates, which the following year received an inquiry from a drugstore chain that wanted to open a store in the shopping center, provided (as is customary) that Market Street Associates built the store for it. Whether Market Street Associates was pessimistic about obtaining financing from the pension trust, still the lessor of the shopping center, or for other reasons, it initially sought financing for the project from other sources. But they were unwilling to lend the necessary funds without a mortgage on the shopping center, which Market Street Associates could not give because it was not the owner but only the lessee. It decided therefore to try to buy the property back from the pension trust. Market Street Associates' general partner, Orenstein, tried to call David Erb of the pension trust, who was responsible for the property in question. Erb did not return his calls, so Orenstein wrote him, expressing an interest in buying the property and asking him to "review your file on this matter and call me so that we can discuss it further." At first, Erb did not reply. Eventually Orenstein did reach Erb, who promised to review the file and get back to him. A few days later an associate of Erb called Orenstein and indicated an interest in selling the property for $3 million, which Orenstein considered much too high.

That was in June of 1988. On July 28, Market Street Associates wrote a letter to the pension trust formally requesting funding for $2 million in improvements to the shopping center. The letter made no reference to paragraph 34 of the lease; indeed, it did not mention the lease. The letter asked Erb to call Orenstein to discuss the matter. Erb, in what was becoming a habit of unresponsiveness, did not call. On August 16, Orenstein sent a second letter — certified mail, return receipt requested — again requesting financing and this time referring to the lease, though not expressly to paragraph 34. The heart of the letter is the following two sentences: "The purpose of this letter is to ask again that you advise us immediately if you are willing to provide the financing pursuant to the lease. If you are willing, we propose to enter into negotiation to amend the ground lease appropriately." The very next day, Market Street Associates received from Erb a letter, dated August 10, turning down the original request for financing on the ground that it did not "meet our current investment criteria": the pension trust was not interested in making loans for less than $7 million. On August 22, Orenstein replied to Erb by letter, noting that his letter of August 10 and Erb's letter of August 16 had evidently crossed in the mails, expressing disappointment at the turn-down, and stating that Market Street Associates would seek financing elsewhere. That was the last contact between the parties until September 27, when Orenstein sent Erb a letter stating that Market Street Associates was exercising the option granted it by paragraph 34 to purchase the property upon the terms specified in that paragraph in the event that negotiations over financing broke down.

The pension trust refused to sell, and this suit to compel specific performance followed. Apparently the price computed by the formula in paragraph 34 is only $1 million. The market value must be higher, or Market Street Associates wouldn't be trying to coerce conveyance at the paragraph 34 price; whether it is as high as $3 million, however, the record does not reveal.

The district judge granted summary judgment for the pension trust on two grounds that he believed to be separate although closely related. The first was that, by failing in its correspondence with the pension trust to mention paragraph 34 of the lease, Market Street Associates had prevented the negotiations over financing that are a condition precedent to the lessee's exercise of the purchase option from taking place. Second, this same failure violated the duty of good faith, which the common law of Wisconsin, as of other states, reads into every contract. . . . Restatement (Second) of Contracts § 205 (1981); 2 E. Allan Farnsworth, FARNSWORTH ON CONTRACTS § 7.17a (1990). In support of both grounds the judge emphasized a statement by Orenstein in his deposition that it had occurred to him that Erb mightn't know about paragraph 34, though this was unlikely (Orenstein testified) because Erb or someone else at the pension trust would probably check the file and discover the paragraph and realize that if the trust refused to negotiate over the request for financing, Market Street Associates, as Penney's assignee, would be entitled to walk off with the property for (perhaps) a song. The judge inferred that Market Street Associates didn't want financing from the pension trust — that it just wanted an opportunity to buy the property at a bargain price and hoped that the pension trust wouldn't realize the implications of turning down the request for financing. Market Street Associates should, the judge opined, have advised the pension trust that it was requesting financing pursuant to paragraph 34, so that the trust would understand the penalty for refusing to negotiate.

We begin our analysis by setting to one side two extreme contentions by the parties. The pension trust argues that the option to purchase created by paragraph 34 cannot be exercised until negotiations over financing break down; there were no negotiations; therefore they did not break down; therefore Market Street Associates had no right to exercise the option. This argument misreads the contract. Although the option to purchase is indeed contingent, paragraph 34 requires the pension trust, upon demand by the lessee for the financing of improvements worth at least $250,000, "to give reasonable consideration to providing the financing." The lessor who fails to give reasonable consideration and thereby prevents the negotiations from taking place is breaking the contract; and a contracting party cannot be allowed to use his own breach to gain an advantage by impairing the rights that the contract confers on the other party. . . . Often, it is true, if one party breaks the contract, the other can walk away from it without liability, can in other words exercise self-help. *First National Bank v. Continental Illinois National Bank*, 933 F.2d 466, 469 (7th Cir. 1991). But he is not required to follow that course. He can stand on his contract rights.

But what exactly are those rights in this case? . . . Market Street Associates argues, with equal unreason as it seems to us, that it could not have broken the contract because paragraph 34 contains no express requirement that in requesting financing the lessee mention the lease or paragraph 34 or otherwise alert the lessor to the consequences of his failing to give reasonable consideration to granting the request. There is indeed no such requirement (all that the contract requires is a demand). But no one says there is. The pension trust's argument, which the district judge bought, is that either as a matter of simple contract interpretation or under the compulsion of the doctrine of good faith, a provision requiring Market Street Associates to remind the pension trust of paragraph 34 should be read into the lease.

It seems to us that these are one ground rather than two. A court has to have a reason to interpolate a clause into a contract. The only reason that has been suggested here is that it is necessary to prevent Market Street Associates from reaping a reward for what the pension trust believes to have been Market Street's bad faith. So we must consider the meaning of the contract duty of "good faith." The Wisconsin cases are cryptic as to its meaning though emphatic about its existence, so we must cast our net wider. We do so mindful of Learned Hand's warning, that "such words as 'fraud,' 'good faith,' 'whim,' 'caprice,' 'arbitrary action,' and 'legal fraud' . . . obscure the issue." *Thompson-Starrett Co. v. La Belle Iron Works*, 17 F.2d 536, 541 (2d Cir. 1927). Indeed they do. Summers, *supra*, at 207–20; 2 FARNSWORTH ON CONTRACTS, *supra*, § 7.17a. The particular confusion to which the vaguely moralistic overtones of "good faith" give rise is the belief that every contract establishes a fiduciary relationship. A fiduciary is required to treat his principal as if the principal were he, and therefore he may not take advantage of the principal's incapacity, ignorance, inexperience, or even naivete. . . . If Market Street Associates were the fiduciary of General Electric Pension Trust, then (we may assume) it could not take advantage of Mr. Erb's apparent ignorance of paragraph 34, however exasperating Erb's failure to return Orenstein's phone calls was and however negligent Erb or his associates were in failing to read the lease before turning down Orenstein's request for financing.

But it is unlikely that Wisconsin wishes, in the name of good faith, to make every contract signatory his brother's keeper, especially when the brother is the immense and sophisticated General Electric Pension Trust, whose lofty indifference to small (less than $7 million) transactions is the signifier of its grandeur. In fact the law contemplates that people frequently will take advantage of the ignorance of those with whom they contract, without thereby incurring liability. Restatement, *supra*, § 161, Comment D. The duty of honesty, of good faith even expansively conceived, is not a duty of candor. You can make a binding contract to purchase something you know your seller undervalues. . . . Anthony T. Kronman, *Mistake, Disclosure, Information, and the Law of Contracts,*" 7 J. LEGAL STUD. 1 (1978). That of course is a question about formation, not performance, and the particular duty of good faith under examination here relates to the latter rather than to the former. But even after you have signed a contract, you are not obliged to become an altruist toward the other party and relax the terms if he gets into trouble in performing his side of the bargain. . . .

But it is one thing to say that you can exploit your superior knowledge of the market — for if you cannot, you will not be able to recoup the investment you made in obtaining that knowledge — or that you are not required to spend money bailing out a contract partner who has gotten into trouble. It is another thing to say that you can take deliberate advantage of an oversight by your contract partner concerning his rights under the contract. Such taking advantage is not the exploitation of superior knowledge or the avoidance of unbargained-for expense; it is sharp dealing. Like theft, it has no social product, and also like theft it induces costly defensive expenditures, in the form of overelaborate disclaimers or investigations into the trustworthiness of a prospective contract partner, just as the prospect of theft induces expenditures on locks. See generally Steven J. Burton, *Breach of Contract and the Common Law Duty to Perform in Good Faith*, 94 HARV. L. REV. 369, 393 (1980).

The form of sharp dealing that we are discussing might or might not be actionable as fraud or deceit. That is a question of tort law and there the rule is that if the information is readily available to both parties the failure of one to disclose it to the other, even if done in the knowledge that the other party is acting on mistaken premises, is not actionable. . . . All of these cases, however . . . involve failure to disclose something in the negotiations leading up to the signing of the contract, rather than failure to disclose after the contract has been signed. . . . The distinction is important, as we explained in *Maksym v. Loesch*, 937 F.2d 1237, 1242 (7th Cir. 1991). Before the contract is signed, the parties confront each other with a natural wariness. Neither expects the other to be particularly forthcoming, and therefore there is no deception when one is not. Afterwards the situation is different. The parties are now in a cooperative relationship, the costs of which will be considerably reduced by a measure of trust. So each lowers his guard a bit, and now silence is more apt to be deceptive. . . .

Moreover, this is a contract case rather than a tort case, and conduct that might not rise to the level of fraud may nonetheless violate the duty of good faith in dealing with one's contractual partners and thereby give rise to a remedy under contract law. Burton, *supra*, at 372 n.17. This duty is, as it were, halfway between a fiduciary duty (the duty of utmost good faith) and the duty merely to refrain from active fraud. Despite its moralistic overtones it is no more the injection of moral principles into contract law than the fiduciary concept itself is. . . . It would be quixotic as well as presumptuous for judges to undertake through contract law to raise the ethical standards of the nation's businesspeople. The concept of the duty of good faith, like the concept of fiduciary duty, is a stab at approximating the terms the parties would have negotiated had they foreseen the circumstances that have given rise to their dispute. The parties want to minimize the costs of performance. To the extent that a doctrine of good faith designed to do this by reducing defensive expenditures is a reasonable measure to this end, interpolating it into the contract advances the parties' joint goal.

It is true that an essential function of contracts is to allocate risk, and would be defeated if courts treated the materializing of a bargained-over, allocated risk as a misfortune the burden of which is required to be shared between the parties (as it might be within a family, for example) rather than borne entirely by the party to whom the risk had been allocated by mutual agreement. But contracts do not just allocate risk. They also (or some of them) set in motion a cooperative enterprise, which may to some extent place one party at the other's mercy. "The parties to a contract are embarked on a cooperative venture, and a minimum of cooperativeness in the event unforeseen problems arise at the performance stage is required, even if not an explicit duty of the contract." *AMPAT/Midwest, Inc. v. Illinois Tool Works, Inc.*, 896 F.2d 1035, 1041 (7th Cir. 1990). The office of the doctrine of good faith is to forbid the kinds of opportunistic behavior that a mutually dependent, cooperative relationship might enable in the absence of rule. " 'Good faith' is a compact reference to an implied undertaking not to take opportunistic advantage in a way that could not have been contemplated at the time of drafting, and which therefore was not resolved explicitly by the parties." *Kham & Nate's Shoes No. 2, Inc. v. First Bank of Whiting*, 908 F.2d 1351, 1357 (7th Cir. 1990). The contractual duty of good faith is thus not some newfangled bit of welfare-state paternalism or (*pace* Duncan Kennedy, *Form and Substance in Private Law Adjudication*, 89 HARV. L. REV. 1685, 1721 [1976]) the sediment of an altruistic strain in contract law, and we are therefore not surprised to find the essentials of the modern doctrine well established in 19th-century cases. . . .

The emphasis we are placing on postcontractual versus precontractual conduct helps explain the pattern that is observed when the duty of contractual good faith is considered in all its variety, encompassing not only good faith in the performance of a contract but also good faith in its formation. Summers, *supra*, at 220–32. . . . The formation or negotiation stage is precontractual, and here the duty is minimized. . . . At the formation of the contract the parties are dealing in present realities; performance still lies in the future. As performance unfolds, circumstances change, often unforeseeably; the explicit terms of the contract become progressively less apt to the governance of the parties' relationship; and the role of implied conditions — and with it the scope and bite of the good-faith doctrine — grows. . . .

The dispositive question in the present case is simply whether Market Street Associates tried to trick the pension trust and succeeded in doing so. If it did, this would be the type of opportunistic behavior in an ongoing contractual relationship that would violate the duty of good faith performance, however the duty is formulated. There is much common sense in Judge Reynolds' conclusion that Market Street Associates did just that.[99] The situation as he saw it was as follows. Market Street Associates didn't want financing from the pension trust (initially it had looked elsewhere, remember), and when it learned it couldn't get the financing without owning the property, it decided to try to buy the property. But the pension trust set a stiff price, so Orenstein decided to trick the pension trust into selling at the bargain price fixed in paragraph 34 by requesting financing and hoping that the pension trust would turn the request down without noticing the paragraph. . . .

The only problem with this recital is that it construes the facts as favorably to the pension trust as the record will permit, and that of course is not the right standard for summary judgment. The facts must be construed as favorably to the nonmoving party, to Market Street Associates, as the record permits. . . . When that is done, a different picture emerges. On Market Street Associates' construal of the record, $3 million was a grossly excessive price for the property, and while $1 million might be a bargain it would not confer so great a windfall as to warrant an inference that if the pension trust had known about paragraph 34 it never would have turned down Market Street Associates' request for financing cold. And in fact the pension trust may have known about paragraph 34, and either it didn't care or it believed that unless the request mentioned that paragraph the pension trust would incur no liability by turning it down. Market Street Associates may have assumed and have been entitled to assume that in reviewing a request for financing from one of its lessees the pension trust would take the time to read the lease to see whether it bore on the request. Market Street Associates did not desire financing from the pension trust initially — that is undeniable — yet when it discovered that it could not get financing elsewhere unless it had the title to the property it may have realized that it would have to negotiate with the pension trust over financing before it could hope to buy the property at the price specified in the lease.

On this interpretation of the facts there was no bad faith on the part of Market

---

[99] [Eds. note: Judge Reynolds was the trial judge.]

Street Associates. It acted honestly, reasonably, without ulterior motive, in the face of circumstances as they actually and reasonably appeared to it. The fault was the pension trust's incredible inattention, which misled Market Street Associates into believing that the pension trust had no interest in financing the improvements regardless of the purchase option. We do not usually excuse contracting parties from failing to read and understand the contents of their contract; and in the end what this case comes down to — or so at least it can be strongly argued — is that an immensely sophisticated enterprise simply failed to read the contract. On the other hand, such enterprises make mistakes just like the rest of us, and deliberately to take advantage of your contracting partner's mistake during the performance stage (for we are not talking about taking advantage of superior knowledge at the formation stage) is a breach of good faith. To be able to correct your contract partner's mistake at zero cost to yourself, and decide not to do so, is a species of opportunistic behavior that the parties would have expressly forbidden in the contract had they foreseen it. The immensely long term of the lease amplified the possibility of errors but did not license either party to take advantage of them.

The district judge jumped the gun in choosing between these alternative characterizations. The essential issue bearing on Market Street Associates' good faith was Orenstein's state of mind, a type of inquiry that ordinarily cannot be concluded on summary judgment, and could not be here. If Orenstein believed that Erb knew or would surely find out about paragraph 34, it was not dishonest or opportunistic to fail to flag that paragraph, or even to fail to mention the lease, in his correspondence and (rare) conversations with Erb, especially given the uninterest in dealing with Market Street Associates that Erb fairly radiated. To decide what Orenstein believed, a trial is necessary. As for the pension trust's intimation that a bench trial (for remember that this is an equity case, since the only relief sought by the plaintiff is specific performance) will add no illumination beyond what the summary judgment proceeding has done, this overlooks the fact that at trial the judge will for the first time have a chance to see the witnesses whose depositions he has read, to hear their testimony elaborated, and to assess their believability.

SJ is inappropriate

The judgment is reversed and the case is remanded for further proceedings consistent with this opinion.

NOTES AND QUESTIONS

1. ***Remand:*** On remand, the trial judge found that Mr. Orenstein, Market Street's general partner, had been trying to trick the defendant by failing to mention section 34 of the lease. On appeal this finding was affirmed.[100]

Found against MSA again on remand

2. ***Distinguishing performance from formation:*** Interpreting the duty of good faith, Judge Posner emphasizes a distinction between formation and performance cases. Does this distinction make sense to you? What justification is there for permitting knowing exploitation of ignorance when entering into a contract? Review, in this connection, the views of Professor Kronman summarized in Note 7 following *Obde v. Schlemeyer*, and also review the decision in *Hoffman v. Red Owl*

---

[100] Market Street Associates v. Frey, 21 F.3d 782 (7th Cir. 1994).

Stores, in Chapter 3, section C.1.a., *supra*.

Professor Kate O'Neill has written an article in which she discusses Judge Posner's rhetorical skills in general and how in particular he uses them in the *Market Street* case.[101] Posner talks about a duty to read, but for all we know, the pension trust's officials may have read the contract when they negotiated it, so that the trust's management mistakes were more in not training its employees or in not having better risk management procedures. O'Neill adds:

> The appeal "pivoted" on the trial court's evaluation of Market Street's good faith, but Judge Posner prefers not to discuss the case on those terms. By focusing initially on the paradox that the [t]rust might win despite its carelessness, he diverts the reader's attention from Market Street's "gotcha" tactics, and he contrives a doctrine that allows him to shift the analysis from the moralistic vocabulary of good faith to the new, economic vocabulary of efficiency. The effect of this rather elaborate framing is to remind and persuade the reader that there is no generalized duty to be one's "brother's keeper," and the duty of good faith during performance is merely a default rule about efficiency.

O'Neill also focuses on how Judge Posner sets up the issue to make it seem interesting and important (and therefore a good candidate for inclusion in a casebook or citation by other courts). What techniques do you notice along these lines? This is a question you could ask about many of Judge Posner's opinions, and, for that matter, many opinions that end up in casebooks.

3. Subsequent Wisconsin cases: The Wisconsin intermediate appellate courts have decided two similar cases after the *Market Street Associates* case. In *Nauga v. Westel Milwaukee Co., Inc.*,[102] a dealer had sued a distributor for breach of contract and for violation of the Wisconsin Fair Dealership Act. The distributor then offered a new dealership agreement to all its dealers. The lengthy form contract stated, as paragraph 30.10, that any dealer renewing its dealership released the distributor from any existing claims. This would have had the effect of ending the dealer's lawsuits against the distributor. No attempt was made to call the plaintiff dealer's attention to this provision, but it was discovered nonetheless by his lawyer. The lawyer then typed a clause at the bottom of one of the pages of the form contract stating that the plaintiff dealer would release all of its existing rights in exchange for a payment of $250,000. The plaintiff dealer signed the revised form and returned it to the distributor. The distributor's lawyer did not see the amendment of the form, and the distributor executed a renewal of the dealership. The plaintiff dealer sued for $250,000. The trial court refused to enforce the provision requiring the payment because the parties had not come to a meeting of the minds. The appellate court reversed in a two-to-one decision. "Westel's negligence does not relieve it of contractual obligations, and . . . Westel's true intentions do not render the new agency agreement unenforceable." The court may have reacted to its view of the good faith of the parties in a footnote: "While claiming

---

[101] Kate O'Neill, *Rhetoric Counts: What We Should Teach When We Teach Posner*, 39 SETON HALL L. REV. 507, 545 (2009).

[102] 216 Wis. 2d 306, 576 N.W.2d 573 (1998).

that Nauga never could have realistically expected the settlement, Westel at the same time suggests that Nauga somehow was willing to relinquish all claims, pursuant to paragraph 30.10, in exchange for nothing."

In *Hennig v. Ahearn*,[103] a firm was negotiating to hire a new chief executive officer. Both sides were represented by lawyers, and they exchanged numerous drafts. Changes in the drafts were always highlighted and explained. The CEO thought that the parties had agreed on all issues and had a deal. The president of the firm altered nine words in the middle of a paragraph in a way that greatly reduced the compensation that the CEO would receive. The president delivered the final version of the written contract to the CEO without calling any attention to the alteration. The CEO signed the contract without noticing the change. When he discovered the change, he sued for misrepresentation and sought reformation. The trial court granted the firm's motion for summary judgment because the terms of the contract were fully disclosed on the face of the written document and there was no duty to call the CEO's attention to the change. The appellate court reversed and remanded for a jury trial. It cited an earlier Wisconsin Supreme Court decision as setting a standard for the duty to disclose adverse facts: "[T]he advantage taken of the plaintiff's ignorance . . . [must be] so shocking to the ethical sense of the community, and . . . so extreme and unfair, as to amount to a form of swindling, in which the plaintiff is led by appearances into a bargain that is a trap, of whose essence and substance he is unaware . . ." The appellate court found that a jury  could find a duty to point out the last-minute changes to the CEO's employment contract. It continued: "Courts should refuse to act for the relief of one who blindly acts and a plaintiff may not close his eyes to what is obviously discoverable by him, but there is not a rule of law that a party must read each and every word of successive drafts of a complex document. This would greatly add to the time and expense of consummating commercial transactions."

Is the *Nauga* case consistent with the *Hennig* decision? Neither case cites Judge Posner's decision in *Market Street Associates*. The *Hennig* case relies on misrepresentation law rather than the duty of good faith. See *Obde v. Schlemeyer*, in Section B.5. of this chapter, *supra*. Is the distinction Judge Posner draws between application of the duty of good faith in performance and formation cases good law in Wisconsin?

7. Most of the Theories at Once: A Review

So far, we have presented various approaches to social control of contract as distinct legal categories. A lawyer can ask whether her client lacked capacity, agreed under duress or undue influence, made a decision on the basis of misrepresentation, or perhaps claim breach of an obligation of good faith. As so often is true, common law categories are not bounded by bright, distinct lines. A particular case may almost fit in a number of them. The following case should prompt reflection and review of the material presented in the preceding sections of this chapter.

---

[103] 230 Wis. 2d 149, 601 N.W.2d 14 (1999).

VOKES v. ARTHUR MURRAY, INC.
Florida Court of Appeals
212 So. 2d 906 (1968)

PIERCE, J.

This is an appeal by Audrey E. Vokes, plaintiff below, from a final order dismissing with prejudice, for failure to state a cause of action, her fourth amended complaint, hereinafter referred to as plaintiff's complaint.

Defendant Arthur Murray, Inc., a corporation, authorizes the operation through-out the nation of dancing schools under the name of "Arthur Murray School of Dancing" through local franchised operators, one of whom was defendant J.P. Davenport, whose dancing establishment was in Clearwater.

Plaintiff Mrs. Audrey E. Vokes, a widow of 51 years and without family, had a yen to be "an accomplished dancer" with the hopes of finding "new interest in life." So, on February 10, 1961, a dubious fate, with the assist of a motivated acquaintance, procured her to attend a "dance party" at Davenport's "School of Dancing" where she whiled away the pleasant hours, sometimes in a private room, absorbing his accomplished sales technique, during which her grace and poise were elaborated upon and her rosy future as "an excellent dancer" was painted for her in vivid and glowing colors. As an incident to this interlude, he sold her eight half-hour dance lessons to be utilized within one calendar month therefrom, for the sum of $14.50 cash in hand paid, obviously a baited "come-on."

Thus she embarked upon an almost endless pursuit of the terpsichorean art during which, over a period of less than sixteen months, she was sold fourteen "dance courses," totalling in the aggregate 2302 hours of dancing lessons for a total cash outlay of $31,090.45, all at Davenport's dance emporium. All of these fourteen courses were evidenced by execution of a written "Enrollment Agreement — Arthur Murray's School of Dancing" with the addendum in heavy black print, "No one will be informed that you are taking dancing lessons. Your relations with us are held in strict confidence," setting forth the number of "dancing lessons" and the "lessons in rhythm sessions" currently sold to her from time to time, and always of course accompanied by payment of cash of the realm.

These dance lesson contracts and the monetary consideration therefor of over $31,000 were procured from her by means and methods of Davenport and his associates that went beyond the unsavory, yet legally permissible, perimeter of "sales puffing" and intruded well into the forbidden area of undue influence, the suggestion of falsehood, the suppression of truth, and the free exercise of rational judgment, if what plaintiff alleged in her complaint was true. From the time of her first contact with the dancing school in February 1961, she was influenced unwittingly by a constant and continuous barrage of flattery, false praise, excessive compliments, and panegyric encomiums, to such extent that it would be not only inequitable, but unconscionable, for a Court exercising inherent chancery power to allow such contracts to stand.

She was incessantly subjected to overreaching blandishment and cajolery. She was assured she had "grace and poise"; that she was "rapidly improving and developing in her dancing skill"; that the additional lessons would "make her a beautiful dancer, capable of dancing with the most accomplished dancers"; that she was "rapidly progressing in the development of her dancing skill and gracefulness," etc., etc. She was given "dance aptitude tests" for the ostensible purpose of "determining" the number of remaining hours of instruction needed by her from time to time.

At one point she was sold 545 additional hours of dancing lessons to be entitled to award of the "Bronze Medal" signifying that she had reached "the Bronze Standard," a supposed designation of dance achievement by students of Arthur Murray, Inc.

Later she was sold an additional 926 hours in order to gain the "Silver Medal," indicating she had reached "the Silver Standard," at a cost of $12,501.35.

At one point, while she still had to her credit about 900 unused hours of instructions, she was induced to purchase an additional 24 hours of lessons to participate in a trip to Miami at her own expense, where she would be "given the opportunity to dance with members of the Miami Studio."

She was induced at another point to purchase an additional 126 hours of Lessons in order to be not only eligible for the Miami trip but also to become "a life member of the Arthur Murray Studio," carrying with it certain dubious emoluments, at a further cost of $1,752.30.

At another point, while she still had over 1,000 unused hours of instruction, she was induced to buy 151 additional hours at a cost of $2,049.00 to be eligible for a "Student Trip to Trinidad" — at her own expense, as she later learned.

Also, when she still had 1100 unused hours to her credit, she was prevailed upon to purchase an additional 347 hours at a cost of $4,235.74, to qualify her to receive a "Gold Medal" for achievement, indicating she had advanced to "the Gold Standard."

On another occasion, while she still had over 1200 unused hours, she was induced to buy an additional 175 hours of instruction at a cost of $2,472.75 to be eligible "to take a trip to Mexico."

Finally, sandwiched in between other lesser sales promotions, she was influenced to buy an additional 481 hours of instruction at a cost of $6,523.81 in order to "be classified as a Gold Bar Member, the ultimate achievement of the dancing studio."

All the foregoing sales promotions, illustrative of the entire 14 separate contracts, were procured by defendant Davenport and Arthur Murray, Inc., by false representations to her that she was improving in her dancing ability, that she had excellent potential, that she was responding to instructions in dancing grace, and that they were developing her into a beautiful dancer, whereas in truth and in fact she did not develop in her dancing ability, she had no "dance aptitude," and in fact had difficulty in "hearing the musical beat." The complaint alleged that such representations to her "were in fact false and contrary to the plaintiff's true ability, the truth of plaintiff's ability being fully known to the defendants, but withheld from the plaintiff for the sole and specific intent to deceive and defraud the plaintiff and to induce her in the purchasing of additional hours of dance lessons." It was averred that the lessons were sold to her "in total disregard to the true physical, rhythm, and mental ability of the plaintiff." In other words, while she first exulted that she was entering the "spring of her life," she finally was awakened to the fact there was "spring" neither in her life nor in her feet.

The complaint prayed that the Court decree the dance contracts to be null and void and to be cancelled, that an accounting be had, and judgment entered against the defendants "for that portion of the $31,090.45 not charged against specific hours of instruction given to the plaintiff." The Court held the complaint not to state a cause of action and dismissed it with prejudice. We disagree and reverse.

The material allegations of the complaint must, of course, be accepted as true for the purpose of testing its legal sufficiency. Defendants contend that contracts can only be rescinded for fraud or misrepresentation when the alleged misrepresentation is as to a material fact, rather than an opinion, prediction, or expectation, and that the statements and representations set forth at length in the complaint were in the category of "trade puffing," within its legal orbit.

It is true that "generally a misrepresentation, to be actionable, must be one of fact rather than of opinion." *Tonkovich v. South Florida Citrus Industries, Inc.*, Fla. App. 1966, 185 So. 2d 710; *Kutner v. Kalish*, Fla. App. 1965, 173 So. 2d 763. But this rule has significant qualifications, applicable here. It does not apply where there is a fiduciary relationship between the parties, or where there has been some artifice or trick employed by the representor, or where the parties do not in general deal at "arms' length" as we understand the phrase, or where the representee does not have equal opportunity to become apprised of the truth or falsity of the fact represented. 14 FLA. JUR. FRAUD AND DECEIT, § 28; *Kitchen v. Long*, 1914, 67 Fla. 72, 64 So. 429. As stated by Judge Allen of this Court in *Ramel v. Chasebrook Construction Company*, Fla. App. 1961, 135 So. 2d 876: "A statement of a party having . . . superior knowledge may be regarded as a statement of fact although it would be considered as opinion if the parties were dealing on equal terms."

It could be reasonably supposed here that defendants had "superior knowledge" as to whether plaintiff had "dance potential" and as to whether she was noticeably improving in the art of terpsichore. And it would be a reasonable inference from the undenied averments of the complaint that the flowery eulogiums heaped upon her by defendants as a prelude to her contracting for 1944 additional hours of instruction in order to attain the rank of the Bronze Standard, thence to the bracket of the Silver Standard, thence to the class of the Gold Bar Standard, and finally to the crowning plateau of a Life Member of the Studio, proceeded as much or more from the urge to "ring the cash register" as from any honest or realistic appraisal of her dancing prowess or a factual representation of her progress.

Even in contractual situations where a party to a transaction owes no duty to disclose facts within his knowledge or to answer inquiries respecting such facts, the law is if he undertakes to do so he must disclose the whole truth. *Ramel v. Chasebrook Construction Company, supra; Beagle v. Bagwell*, Fla. App. 1964, 169 So. 2d 43. From the face of the complaint, it should have been reasonably apparent to defendants that her vast outlay of cash for the many hundreds of additional hours of instruction was not justified by her slow and awkward progress, which she would have been made well aware of if they had spoken the "whole truth."

In *Hirschman v. Hodges, etc.*, 59 Fla. 517, 51 So. 550 (1910), it was said that "what is plainly injurious to good faith ought to be considered as a fraud sufficient to impeach a contract," and that an improvident agreement may be avoided "because of surprise, or mistake, want of freedom, undue influence, the suggestion of falsehood, or the suppression of truth."

We repeat that where parties are dealing on a contractual basis at arm's length with no inequities or inherently unfair practices employed, the Courts will in general "leave the parties where they find themselves." But in the case *sub judice*, from the allegations of the unanswered complaint, we cannot say that enough of the accompanying ingredients, as mentioned in the foregoing authorities, were not present which otherwise would have barred the equitable arm of the Court to her. In our view, from the showing made in her complaint, plaintiff is entitled to her day in court.

It accordingly follows that the order dismissing plaintiff's last amended complaint with prejudice should be and is reversed.

Reversed. LILES, C. J., and MANN, J., concur.

NOTES AND QUESTIONS

1. *Review:* Counsel for Arthur Murray argued that Mrs. Vokes was "not justified in relying upon statements of a dancing instructor to the effect that she has good dancing aptitude and is progressing well in the development of her dancing skills where she continually has difficulty in hearing the musical beat, is therefore unable to acquire any ability to learn different dance steps, and does not in fact develop in her dancing ability." What, if anything, is wrong with this argument? Could Mrs. Vokes's lawyer argue plausibly that she lacked capacity to make this contract? That she was the victim of duress? Did Arthur Murray violate a duty of good faith owed to Mrs. Vokes?

Compare *Parker v. Arthur Murray, Inc.*[104] Plaintiff was a 37-year-old college-educated bachelor who lived alone in a one-room attic apartment. His instructors regularly praised and encouraged him, despite his lack of progress. He executed contract extensions and new contracts with Arthur Murray. An automobile accident severely injured plaintiff. At that time he had contracted for a total of 2734 hours of lessons, for which he had paid $24,812.80.

The trial judge dismissed plaintiff's cause of action for fraud and his demand for punitive damages. The appellate court affirmed. It said that statements that plaintiff had "exceptional potential to be a fine and accomplished dancer" and was a "natural-born dancer" were not fraud. These were only opinions, and plaintiff did not have a right to rely. The court took into account the business relationship of the parties as well as the educational background of plaintiff. However, the court affirmed the trial court's finding excusing plaintiff from performance because of his

---

[104] 10 Ill. App. 3d 1000, 295 N.E.2d 487 (1973).

injury.[105] This prompted rescission of the contracts and restitution of all amounts paid.

How does the *Parker* case differ from the *Vokes* decision? What are the courts assuming about Mr. Parker and Mrs. Vokes? Why did the court consider Parker's educational background?

2. ***Dance studios versus gullible, lonely people:*** While it may seem hard to believe, the legal problem in the *Vokes* case is not uncommon. In 1960, the Federal Trade Commission brought a deceptive practices complaint against Arthur Murray, Inc., and its officers.[106] It noted that Murray was the licensor of some 450 studios throughout the world. The complaint charged that the respondents had employed the following techniques to sell courses, which were sometimes used to mislead and coerce purchasers:

> 1. The use of "relay salesmanship," involving a number of Arthur Murray representatives who sign up a lone prospect by force of numbers and unrelenting sales talks, sometimes aided by hidden listening devices monitoring the conversation with the pupil;

> 2. The use of so-called "analyses," "studio competitions," and similar purported objective methods of judging dancing ability, which actually exist to get the "winner" or "successful candidate" to buy future lessons;

> 3. The use of blank or partially filled-out contract forms, and by refusing to answer or evading questions as to amount due or payable so that pupils are misled as to the amount of their financial obligations;

> 4. By falsely assuring prospects that a given course will enable him to achieve a certain "standard" of dancing proficiency when it is planned that the prospects will be subjected to further coercive sales efforts before both the given course is completed and the "standard" reached.

The FTC and Arthur Murray, Inc. settled the proceeding by a consent order.[107]

On October 27, 1999, the ABC News program "20/20" ran a 15-minute segment on a Florida dance studio chain in the Tampa area (not Arthur Murray) that was using techniques very similar to those used in the Vokes case. Several women were interviewed who had signed a series of contracts totalling between $80,000 and $100,000. The local sheriff investigated. He charged one of the owners with the misdemeanor "exploitation of the elderly" for entering into such contracts with one customer, who was suffering from Alzheimer's disease. The sheriff believed no crime had been committed in the other cases, though the women who consented to be

_____

[105] A party to a contract may be, in some circumstances, excused from performance when circumstances have so changed that the purpose of the performance can no longer be achieved, and achievement of that purpose was clearly central to the agreement. This is sometimes referred to as the "frustration of purpose" doctrine. It means, for example, that I might not be liable to pay rental for a racing car which I had rented for purposes of driving it in the Indianapolis 500 if the Indianapolis 500 was canceled because of a natural disaster. This excuse for non-performance is the subject of investigation as part of Volume II of these materials.

[106] Federal Trade Commission, Ann. Rep. 60 (1960).

[107] *See* CCH Trade Reg. Rept. Par. 28,965 (1961); NEW YORK TIMES, Aug. 3, 1960, at 14, col. 3.

interviewed on the television show all regretted their contracts and wanted their money back. At the time of the television broadcast, the studio was refusing to return the money.

3.   *Statutory solutions:* In the early 1960s, the California Assembly Interim Committee on the Judiciary studied dance and health studios. It found:

> The opportunity to make a quick dollar at the expense of the lonely, credulous, or impressionable customer has led to practices that form a pattern of overreaching and misrepresentation seriously close to fraud and extortion . . .

> They [long-term contracts] offer an irresistible temptation to the fraudulent operator to use high-pressure salesmanship, sign up all the customers he can for the largest amounts and longest terms that can be extracted, then close the studio or curtail services enough to discourage his newly acquired clientele.

The Committee then recommended the passage of legislation regulating dance studio contracts.[108] Some key provisions today are:[109]

§ 1812.53. Payments

(a) No contract for dance studio lessons and other services shall require payments or financing by the buyer over a period in excess of one year from the date the contract is entered into, nor shall the term of any contract be measured by the life of the buyer. However, the lessons and other services to be rendered to the buyer under the contract may extend over a period not to exceed seven years from the date the contract is entered into.

(b) All contracts for dance studio lessons and other services that may be in effect between the same seller and the same buyer, the terms of which overlap for any period, shall be considered as one contract for the purposes of this title.

§ 1812.54. Contents

(a) Every contract for dance studio lessons and other services shall provide that performance of the agreed-upon lessons will begin within six months from the date the contract is entered into.

(b) A contract for dance studio lessons and other services may be canceled by the student at any time provided he or she gives written notice to the dance studio at the address specified in the contract. When a contract for dance studio lessons and other services is canceled the dance studio shall calculate the refund on the contract, if any, on a *pro rata* basis. The dance studio shall refund any moneys owed to the student within 10 days of

---

[108]   A draft of the Act was prepared for the Committee by students at Stanford Law School, and a law regulating both health and dance studios was enacted in 1961. The 1969 enactment of the Dance Studio Act divided the regulation of the two industries. The entire text of the current Act can be found at CAL. CIV. CODE §§ 1812.50 to 1812.69 (2009).

[109]   CAL. CIV. CODE (2009).

Statutes regarding dance studios

receiving the cancellation notice, unless the student owes the dance studio money for studio lessons or other services received prior to the cancellation, in which case any moneys owed the dance studio shall be deducted by the dance studio from the refund owed to the student and the balance, if any, shall be refunded as specified above. A dance studio shall not charge a cancellation fee, or other fee, for cancellation of the contract by the student.

(c) Every contract for dance studio lessons and other services shall contain a written statement of the hourly rate charged for each type of lesson for which the student has contracted. If the contract includes dance studio lessons that are sold at different per-hour rates, the contract shall contain separate hourly rates for each different type of lesson sold. All other services for which the student has contracted that are not capable of a per-hour charge shall be set forth in writing in specific terms. The statement shall be contained in the dance studio contract before the contract is signed by the buyer.

(d) Every dance studio subject to Sections 1812.64 and 1812.65 shall include in every contract for dance studio lessons or other services a statement that the studio is bonded and that information concerning the bond may be obtained by writing to the office of the Secretary of State.

The statute also requires that a written contract be used and that a copy be given to the customer.[110] In addition to the general right to cancel as to future lessons provided by the statute, § 1812.57 also requires that there be a clause in the contract providing for relief from payment obligations for lessons not yet received in the event of disability or death. In §§ 1812.62–1812.64, the statute provides for private civil actions with treble damages and reasonable attorney's fees for buyers of lessons injured in violation of the act and also for enforcement proceedings by the state attorney general.

The statute survived challenges by Arthur Murray, Inc.[111] Would you expect the statute to be more effective in altering dance studio practices than precedents like *Vokes v. Arthur Murray*?

4. ***Regulation by the market:*** Most national corporations guard their reputa-

---

[110] CAL. CIV. CODE § 1812.52.

[111] In People v. Arthur Murray, Inc., 238 Cal. App. 2d 333, 340, 47 Cal. Rptr. 700, 705 (1965), the court upheld an injunction against selling lifetime contracts and doing other acts prohibited by the Act. The court found that Murray's method of doing business "is calculated to aid and abet the violations which are committed by the dance studios." It also found that the statute was constitutional. In Beck v. Arthur Murray, Inc., 245 Cal. App. 2d 976, 977, 54 Cal. Rptr. 328, 329 (1966), Murray had its licensees post a sign saying they were responsible for "all obligations of any kind respecting the business of this studio." The court found that this did not avoid Arthur Murray, Inc.'s liability for violating the Dance Studio Act. *See also* Nichols v. Arthur Murray, Inc., 56 Cal. Rptr. 728 (1967); Staples v. Arthur Murray, Inc., 253 Cal. App. 2d 507, 61 Cal. Rptr. 103 (1967). In Porter v. Arthur Murray, Inc., 249 Cal. App. 2d 410, 57 Cal. Rptr. 554 (1967), Arthur Murray, Inc., changed its contract with those who were running local studios. Nonetheless, the court found that Arthur Murray, Inc., was still responsible for the violations of the Dance Studio Act by those licensed to run a studio with the Arthur Murray name. Finally, in Holland v. Nelson, 5 Cal. App. 3d 308, 85 Cal. Rptr. 117 (1970), Arthur Murray's lawyers argued unsuccessfully that a one-year statute of limitations applied to claims under the Dance Studio Act. The court added attorney's fees of $1500 for the appeal to those awarded for the trial.

tion. In theory, at least, those who fail to satisfy their customers will suffer the penalties of the impersonal market. Whatever the merits of the allegations, there are a great many cases similar to the *Vokes* decision involving Arthur Murray dance studios. Why did the old and the lonely continue to go to the dance studios and buy expensive long-term courses of dancing instruction? Professor Gordon says: "[O]ur sense of experience is always pushing up against the legal categories, and potentially forcing alternative understandings of what is going on."[112] He continues:[113]

> Through the briefly sketched images of the court, our rational consumer has been transformed into a lonely, vulnerable woman in search of excitement and companionship — the dance studio, from a seller of dancing skills, into a sort of surrogate lover. A 51-year-old widow who would not dream of going, for example, to a singles bar wants safe and respectable ways to find male companionship. Learning how to dance is such a way. The dance studio becomes not just a way of getting there, but the destination itself: a place where attractive and charming instructors discover in her unsuspected graces and talents, and encourage her to feel desirable and at home among friends. They put her in a hierarchy of achievement and reward her efforts with medals and promotions. Was she really misled by being told how graceful and talented she was? Would things have been better, and she happier, if she had been given a coldly critical appraisal of her dancing ability? Perhaps the flattery and attention, even the lies if one must label a seducer's compliments as such, were not a distortion of the service the studio should have been rendering her, but an essential part of the service itself. The commodity the studio men are supplying is much more than dancing skills; it is the sensation of being alive and exciting.

Younger people often enter similar long-term contracts with health or exercise studios. Both California and New York (and probably many other states) specifically regulate these contracts by statute.[114]

One prominent fitness company was investigated by the Attorney General of New York in 2004, after that office had received more than 600 complaints over a five-year period. The company agreed to reform a number of sales and advertising practices and pay $200,000 for the cost of the investigation. The *New York Times* reported problems that a reader faced when she wanted to cancel her month-to-month gym contract after she moved from New York to California. She had to contact a central office, and she sat on hold for more than 30 minutes on three occasions, including one hour-long wait. She finally had her credit card company cancel the monthly electronic payments, and this prompted the fitness company to deal with her. The documents that it sent were misleading. The *New York Times*

---

[112] Robert Gordon, *Unfreezing Legal Reality: Critical Approaches to Law*, 15 Fla. St. U. L. Rev. 195, 204 (1987).

[113] *Id.* at 205.

[114] *See, e.g.,* Faer v. Vertical Fitness & Racquet Club, Ltd., 119 Misc.2d 295, 462 N.Y.S.2d 784 (Civ. Ct. City of N.Y. 1983).

contacted the company, and its representative said that it would change its practices.[115]

C. SOCIAL CONTROL IN THE GUISE OF SEEKING CHOICE: FORM CONTRACTS AND CHOICE

Stewart Macaulay, *Private Legislation and the Duty to Read — Business Run by IBM Machine, the Law of Contracts, and Credit Cards*
19 Vand. L. Rev. 1051 (1966)[116]

"It will not do for a man to enter into a contract, and, when called upon to abide by its conditions, say that he did not read it when he signed it, or did not know what it contained."[117] This rallying cry often is sounded in contracts and restitution opinions. Sometimes it makes such good sense that it is axiomatic. Yet in common with all grand slogans, there are situations where it just doesn't fit. For example, where the one who signs cannot read and has reason to trust another who tricks him by misreading the document, most courts have thought that the limits of the duty to read and understand have been reached. Undoubtedly courts would find other boundaries to the principle, if asked to do so. Imagine, for example, a purchase order form printed on gray paper. On the back are a number of terms and conditions printed in such light gray ink that they can be seen only by holding the paper at an angle to the light. Clearly, if a court ever were to enforce any of these terms and conditions, it would be marching to some ideology other than "choice." More difficult are the cases where the words are more easily read and understood but where it is probable that only the most suspicious will discover and understand them. This describes many form contracts. Organizations often attempt to use such forms and contract ideology to legislate privately. Sometimes this is successful. How then should we decide what effect to give the seldom-read form contract?

The following case is a decision of the House of Lords, which was the highest court in the United Kingdom until the Supreme Court of the United Kingdom was created in 2009. Usually five Law Lords heard the case and each issued an opinion. Only three opinions (or "speeches," as they are called) are reproduced here: those of Lord Reid and Lord Devlin in full, followed by an excerpt from Lord Hodson's opinion.

---

[115] David Segal, *The Haggler: When Canceling a Contract is a Workout*, N.Y. Times, Jan. 10, 2009, at B6.

[116] Excerpt from the Introduction.

[117] [1] Sanger v. Dun, 47 Wis. 615, 620, 3 N.W. 388, 389 (1879).

McCUTCHEON v. DAVID MacBRAYNE LTD.

Hluh?   House of Lords
[1964] 1 W.L.R. 125

[Eds. note: McCutcheon (the appellant) was a Scottish farmer who attempted to ship his car on the ferry *Lochiel*. When the boat went down, he sued its owner and operator, MacBrayne. MacBrayne lost in the trial court, but won an appeal at the intermediate level. This appeal, to the House of Lords, followed.]

The facts are set out in their Lordships' opinions.

Their Lordships took time for consideration.

oral K

LORD REID.

My Lords, the appellant is a farm grieve in Islay. While on the mainland in October 1960, he asked his brother-in-law, Mr. McSporran, a farmer in Islay, to have his car sent by the respondents to West Loch Tarbert. Mr. McSporran took the car to Port Askaig. He found in the respondent's office there the purser of their vessel *Lochiel*, who quoted the freight for a return journey for the car. He paid the money, obtained a receipt, and delivered the car to the respondents. It was shipped on the *Lochiel* but the vessel never reached West Loch Tarbert. She sank, owing to negligent navigation by the respondents' servants, and the car was a total loss. The appellant sues for its value, agreed at 480 pounds.

The question is, what was the contract between the parties? The contract was an oral one. No document was signed or changed hands until the contract was completed. I agree with the unanimous view of the learned judges of the Court of Session that 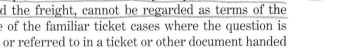 the terms of the receipt, which was made out by the purser and handed to Mr. McSporran after he paid the freight, cannot be regarded as terms of the contract. So the case is not one of the familiar ticket cases where the question is whether conditions endorsed on or referred to in a ticket or other document handed to the consignor in making the contract are binding on the consignor. If conditions not mentioned when this contract was made are to be added to or regarded as part of this contract it must be for some reason different from those principles that are now well settled in ticket cases. If this oral contract stands unqualified there can be no doubt that the respondents are liable for the damage caused by the negligence of their servants.

The respondents' case is that their elaborate printed conditions form part of this contract. If they do, then, admittedly, they exclude liability in this case. I think I can fairly summarise the evidence on this matter. The respondents exhibit copies of these conditions in their office, but neither the appellant nor his agent, Mr. McSporran, had read these notices, and I agree that they can play no part in the decision of this case. Their practice was to require consignors to sign risk notes which included these conditions before accepting any goods for carriage, but on this occasion no risk note was signed. The respondents' clerkess, knowing that Mr. McSporran was bringing the car for shipment, made out a risk note for his signature, but when he arrived she was not there and he dealt with the purser of the *Lochiel*, who was in the office. He asked for a return passage for the car. The purser quoted a charge of some six pounds. He paid that sum and then the purser made out and gave him a receipt which he put in his pocket without looking at it. He then delivered the car. The purser forgot to ask him to sign the risk note.

The Lord Ordinary believed the evidence of Mr. McSporran and the appellant. Mr. McSporran had consigned goods of various kinds on a number of previous occasions. He said that sometimes he had signed a note, sometimes he had not. On one occasion he had sent his own car. A risk note for that consignment was produced, signed by him. He had never read the risk notes signed by him. He said: "I sort of just signed it at the time as a matter of form." He admitted that he knew he was signing in connection with some conditions but he did not know what they were. In particular, he did not know that he was agreeing to send the goods at owner's risk. The appellant had consigned goods on four previous occasions. On three of them he was acting on behalf of his employer. On the other occasion he had sent his own car. Each time he had signed a risk note. He also admitted that he knew there were conditions but said that he did not know what they were.

The respondents contend that, by reason of the knowledge thus gained by the appellant and his agent in these previous transactions, the appellant is bound by their conditions. But this case differs essentially from the ticket cases. There, the carrier in making the contract hands over a document containing or referring to conditions that he intends to be part of the contract. So if the consignor or passenger, when accepting the document, knows or ought as a reasonable man to know that that is the carrier's intention, he can hardly deny that the conditions are part of the contract, or claim, in the absence of special circumstances, to be in a better position than he would be if he had read the document. But here, in making the contract neither party referred to, or indeed had in mind, any additional terms, and the contract was complete and fully effective without any additional terms. If it could be said that when making the contract Mr. McSporran knew that the respondents always required a risk note to be signed and knew that the purser was simply forgetting to put it before him for signature, then it might be said that neither he nor his principal could take advantage of the error of the other party of which he was aware. But counsel frankly admitted that he could not put his case as high as that.

The only other ground on which it would seem possible to import these conditions is that based on a course of dealing. If two parties have made a series of similar contracts each containing certain conditions, and then they make another without expressly referring to those conditions it may be that those conditions ought to be implied. If the officious bystander had asked them whether they had intended to leave out the conditions this time, both must, as honest men, have said "of course not." But again the facts here will not support that ground. According to Mr. McSporran, there had been no constant course of dealing; sometimes he was asked to sign and sometimes not. And, moreover, he did not know what the conditions were. This time he was offered an oral contract without any reference to conditions, and he accepted the offer in good faith.

The respondents also rely on the appellant's previous knowledge. I doubt whether it is possible to spell out a course of dealing in his case. In all but one of the previous cases he had been acting on behalf of his employer in sending a different kind of goods and he did not know that the respondents always sought to insist on excluding liability for their own negligence. So it cannot be said that when he asked his agent to make a contract for him he knew that this or, indeed, any other special term would be included in it. He left his agent a free hand to contract, and I see nothing to prevent him from taking advantage of the contract that his agent in fact made. "The judicial task is not to discover the actual intentions of each party; it is to decide what each was reasonably entitled to conclude from the attitude of the other" (*Gloag on Contract*, 2nd ed., p. 7). In this case I do not think that either party was reasonably bound or entitled to conclude from the attitude of the other, as known to him, that these conditions were intended by the other party to be part of this contract.

Lord Devlin.

My Lords, when a person in the Isle of Islay wishes to send goods to the mainland he goes into the office of MacBrayne (the respondents) in Port Askaig which is conveniently combined with the local post office. There he is presented with a document headed "conditions" containing three or four thousand words of small print divided into 27 paragraphs. Beneath them there is a space for the sender's signature which he puts below his statement in quite legible print that he thereby agrees to ship on the conditions stated above. The appellant, Mr. McCutcheon, described the negotiations which preceded the making of this formidable contract in the following terms: "Q. Tell us about that document; how did you come to sign it? A. You just walk in the office and the document is filled up ready and all you have to do is to sign your name and go out. Q. Did you ever read the conditions? A. No. Q. Did you know what was in them? A. No."

There are many other passages in which Mr. McCutcheon and his brother-in-law, Mr. McSporran, endeavour more or less successfully to appease the forensic astonishment aroused by this statement. People shipping calves, Mr. McCutcheon said (he was dealing with an occasion when he had shipped 36 calves), had not much time to give to the reading. Asked to deal with another occasion when he was unhampered by livestock, he said that people generally just tried to be in time for the boat's sailing; it would, he thought, take half a day to read and understand the conditions and then he would miss the boat. In another part of his evidence he went so far as to say that if everybody took time to read the document, "MacBrayne's office would be packed out the door." Mr. McSporran evidently thought the whole matter rather academic because, as he pointed out, there was no other way to send a car.

There came a day, October 8, 1960, when one of the respondents' vessels was negligently sailed into a rock and sank. She had on board a car belonging to Mr. McCutcheon which he had got Mr. McSporran to ship for him, and the car was a total loss. It would be a strangely generous set of conditions in which the persistent reader, after wading through the verbiage, could not find something to protect the carrier against "any loss . . . wheresoever or whensoever occurring"; and condition 19 by itself is enough to absolve the respondents several times over for all their negligence. It is conceded that if the form had been signed as usual, the appellant would have had no case. But, by a stroke of ill luck for the respondents, it was upon this day of all days that they omitted to get Mr. McSporran to sign the conditions. What difference does that make?

If it were possible for your Lordships to escape from the world of make-believe which the law has created into the real world in which transactions of this sort are actually done, the answer would be short and simple. It should make no difference whatever. This sort of document is not meant to be read, still less to be understood. Its signature is in truth about as significant as a handshake that marks the formal conclusion of a bargain.

Your Lordships were referred to the dictum of BLACKBURN J. in *Harris v. Great Western Railway Co.*[118] The passage is as follows: "And it is clear law that where there is a writing, into which the terms of any agreement are reduced, the terms are to be regulated by that writing. And though one of the parties may not have read the writing, yet, in general, he is bound to the other by those terms; and that, I apprehend, is on the ground that, by assenting to the contract thus reduced to writing, he represents to the other side that he has made himself acquainted with the contents of that writing and assents to them, and so induces the other side to act upon that representation by entering into the contract with him, and is consequently precluded from denying that he did make himself acquainted with those terms. But then the preclusion only exists when the case is brought within the rule so carefully and accurately laid down by PARKE B., in delivering the judgment of the Exchequer in *Freeman v. Cooke*,[119] that is, if he 'means his representation to be acted upon, and it is acted upon accordingly: or if, whatever a man's real intentions may be, he so conduct himself that a reasonable man would take the representation to be true, and believe that it was meant that he should act upon it, and did act upon it as true.' "

If the ordinary law of estoppel was applicable to this case, it might well be argued that the circumstances leave no room for any representation by the sender on which the carrier acted. I believe that any other member of the public in Mr. McCutcheon's place — and this goes for lawyers as well as for laymen — would have found himself compelled to give the same sort of answers as Mr. McCutcheon gave; and I doubt if any carrier who serves out documents of this type could honestly say that he acted in the belief that the recipient had "made himself acquainted with the contents." But BLACKBURN J. was dealing with an unsigned document, a cloakroom ticket. Unless your Lordships are to disapprove the decision of the Court of Appeal in *L'Estrange v. F. Graucob Ltd.*[120] — and there has been no suggestion in this case that you should — the law is clear, without any recourse to the doctrine of estoppel, that a signature to a contract is conclusive.

This is a matter that is relevant to the way in which the respondents put their case. They say that the previous dealings between themselves and the appellant, being always on the terms of their "risk note," as they call their written conditions, the contract between themselves and the appellant must be deemed to import the same conditions. In my opinion, the bare fact that there have been previous dealings

----

[118] [16] [1876] 1 Q.B.D. 515, 530.

[119] [17] [1848] 2 Ex. 654.

[120] [19] [1834] 2 K.B. 394, C.A.

between the parties does not assist the respondents at all. The fact that a man has made a contract in the same form 99 times (let alone the three or four times which are here alleged) will not of itself affect the hundredth contract in which the form is not used. Previous dealings are relevant only if they prove knowledge of the terms, actual and not constructive, and assent to them. If a term is not expressed in a contract, there is only one other way in which it can come into it and that is by implication. No implication can be made against a party of a term that was unknown to him. If previous dealings show that a man knew of and agreed to a term on 99 occasions there is a basis for saying that it can be imported into the hundredth contract without an express statement. It may or may not be sufficient to justify the importation, — that depends on the circumstances; but at least by proving knowledge the essential beginning is made. Without knowledge there is nothing.

It is for the purpose of proving knowledge that the respondents rely on the dictum of Blackburn, J. which I have cited. My Lords, in spite of the great authority of Blackburn, J., I think that this is a dictum which some day your Lordships may have to examine more closely. It seems to me that when a party assents to a document forming the whole or a part of his contract, he is bound by the terms of the document, read or unread, signed or unsigned, simply because they are in the contract; and it is unnecessary and possibly misleading to say that he is bound by them because he represents to the other party that he has made himself acquainted with them. But if there be an estoppel of this sort, its effect is, in my opinion, limited to the contract in relation to which the representation is made; and it cannot (unless of course there be something else on which the estoppel is founded besides the mere receipt of the document) assist the other party in relation to other transactions. The respondents in the present case have quite failed to prove that the appellant made himself acquainted with the conditions they had introduced into previous dealings. He is not estopped from saying that, for good reasons or bad, he signed the previous contracts without the slightest idea of what was in them. If that is so, previous dealings are no evidence of knowledge and so are of little or no use to the respondents in this case.

I say "of little or no use" because the appellant did admit that he knew that there were some conditions, though he did not know what they were. He certainly did not know that they were conditions that exempted the respondents from liability for their own negligence, though I suppose, if he had thought about them at all, he would have known that they probably exempted the respondents from the strict liability of a carrier. Most people know that carriers exact some conditions and it does not matter in this case whether Mr. McCutcheon's knowledge was general knowledge of this sort or was derived from previous dealings. Your Lordships can therefore leave previous dealings out of it and ask yourself simply what is the position of a man who, with that amount of general knowledge, apparently makes a contract into which no conditions are expressly inserted?

The answer must surely be that either he does not make a contract at all because the parties are not *ad idem*, or he makes the contract without the conditions. You cannot have a contract subject to uncommunicated conditions, the terms of which are known only to one side.

It is at this point, I think, that their Lordships in the Second Division fell into error. The Lord Justice-Clerk said:[121] "It is, I think, well settled that, if A contracts with B for the carriage by B of A's goods in the knowledge, gained through previous experience of similar transactions, that B carries goods subject to conditions, A is bound by these conditions under this later contract, if it is of a similar nature to those which have gone before, in the absence of agreement or information to the contrary. This applies even if A, knowing that there are conditions, does not take the trouble to ascertain precisely what these conditions are." Similarly Lord MacIntosh said:[122] "In these circumstances, I am of opinion, following what I understand to be the law as laid down in *Parker v. South Eastern Railway Co.*,[123] and particularly by BAGGALLAY L.J., that the pursuer being aware, by reason of his own previous experience and of that of the agent who happened to be acting for him in the present transaction, that goods were carried on the defenders' vessels subject to certain conditions, and having been given no reason to think that these conditions were not still operative on October 8, 1960, was bound by the conditions, although, as was proved to have been the case, he had never at any time acquainted himself with their purport."

My Lords, I think, with great respect, that this is to introduce a new and fundamentally erroneous principle into the law of contract. There can be no conditions in any contract unless they are brought into it by expression, incorporation, or implication. They are not brought into it simply because one party has inserted them into similar transactions in the past and has not given the other party any reason to think that he will not want to insert them again. The error is based, I think, on a misunderstanding of what are commonly called the ticket cases; I say this because the single authority cited for the proposition is one of the leading ticket cases, *Parker v. South Eastern Railway Co.* The question in these cases is whether or not the passenger has accepted the ticket as a contractual document. If he knows that it contains conditions of some sort, he must know that it is meant to be contractual. If he accepts it as a contractual document, then prima facie (I am not dealing with questions of reasonable notice) he is bound by the conditions that are printed on it or incorporated in it by sufficient reference to some other document, whether he has inquired about them or not. That is all that BAGGALLAY, L.J., is saying in *Parker v. South Eastern Railway Co.*[124]

In the present case there is no contractual document at all. There is not so much as a peg on which to hang any terms that are not expressed in the contract nor a phrase that is capable of expansion. It is as if the appellant had been accepted as a passenger without being given a ticket at all. There is, then, no special contract and the contract is the ordinary one which the law imposes on carriers. As BAGGALLAY, L.J., said: "This clearly would be the nature of the contract if no ticket were delivered, as occasionally happens."[125]

If a man is given a blank ticket without conditions or any reference to them, even

[121] [21] [1962] S.C. 506, 512.

[122] [22] *Id.* at 516.

[123] [23] 2 C.P.D. 416, 425.

[124] [24] *Id.* at 425.

[125] [25] *Id.* at 424.

if he knows in detail what the conditions usually exacted are, he is not, in the absence of any allegation of fraud or of that sort of mistake for which the law gives relief, bound by such conditions. It may seem a narrow and artificial line that divides a ticket that is blank on the back from one that says "For conditions see time-tables," or something of that sort, that has been held to be enough notice. I agree that it is an artificial line and one that has little relevance to everyday conditions. It may be beyond your Lordships' power to make the artificial line more natural: but at least you can see that it is drawn fairly for both sides and that there is not one law for individuals and another for organisations that can issue printed documents. If the respondents had remembered to issue a risk note in this case, they would have invited your Lordships to give a curt answer to any complaint by the appellant. He might say that the terms were unfair and unreasonable, that he had never voluntarily agreed to them, that it was impossible to read or understand them and that anyway if he had tried to negotiate any change the respondents would not have listened to him. The respondents would expect him to be told that he had made his contract and must abide by it. Now the boot is on the other foot. It is just as legitimate, but also just as vain, for the respondents to say that it was only a slip on their part, that it is unfair and unreasonable of the appellant to take advantage of it and that he knew perfectly well that they never carried goods except on conditions. The law must give the same answer: they must abide by the contract they made. What is sauce for the goose is sauce for the gander. It will remain unpalatable sauce for both animals until the legislature, if the courts cannot do it, intervenes to secure that when contracts are made in circumstances in which there is no scope for free negotiation of the terms, they are made upon terms that are clear, fair and reasonable and settled independently as such. That is what Parliament has done in the case of carriage of goods by rail and on the high seas.

I have now given my opinion on the main point in the case and the one on which the respondents succeeded below. On the other points on which the respondents failed below and which they put forward again as grounds for dismissing the claim, I have nothing to add to what your Lordships have already said. In my opinion, the appeal should be allowed.

LORD HODSON.

My Lords, the decision of the Second Division of the Inner House in favour of the defenders seems to me to involve an extension of the application of the doctrine of "course of dealing" which is not warranted by the facts of this case. . . .

The law as it stands appears hard on the holders of tickets who, unless they are exceptional persons, will not take pains to make an examination of a ticket offered to them to see if any conditions are imposed. It would be scarcely tolerable to take the further step of treating a contracting party as if he had signed and so bound himself by the terms of a document with conditions embodied in it, when, as here, he has done no such thing but may be supposed, having regard to his previous experience, to have been willing to sign what was put before him if he had been asked.

Can't rely on prior dealings only to know condition

NOTES AND QUESTIONS

1. *The background of the case:* A map of the Inner Hebrides shows the isolation of Islay. It is about a two-hour-and-10-minute boat trip from Port Askaig to West Tarbert. West Tarbert is about 150 miles from Glasgow on a road around a loch. Indeed, although Port Askaig, West Tarbert, and Glasgow are about on the same latitude, one must drive about 85 miles north of West Tarbert before one can turn southeast for Glasgow. Islay is almost directly north of Ballycastle in Northern Ireland.

Others who had signed the risk note doubtless lost valuable property when MacBrayne's boat sank.[126] Isn't it capricious to allow Mr. McCutcheon to recover for his lost car but deny recovery to all the others who suffered such severe losses when the boat sank? Would it make more sense to hold a lottery and allow the winner to recover his or her loss? Or is the case itself an odd form of lottery?

2. *Deep background:* If you really want a sense of the impact of the sinking of the *Lochiel* on this modest community, go to this blog all about the vessel and the people associated with it: lochiel1960.blogspot.com.

You can see a film from the late 1940s and early 1950s about the people of the Isle of Islay, and at about five minutes into it, the *Lochiel* sails into the harbor at Port Askaig to the tune of Auld Lang Syne, played on bagpipes. You will see period cars, trucks, and people and even a picture of the sunken *Lochiel* with only its bridge out of water.

YAUGER v. SKIING ENTERPRISES, INC.
Wisconsin Supreme Court
206 Wis. 2d 76, 557 N.W.2d 60 (1996)

WILLIAM A. BABLITCH, JUSTICE.

Michael and Brenda Yauger (the Yaugers), seek review of a Court of Appeals decision holding that a liability waiver signed by Michael Yauger effectively relieved Skiing Enterprises, Inc., d/b/a Hidden Valley (Hidden Valley) of liability for its alleged negligence in the death of the Yaugers' then eleven-year-old daughter, Tara. Hidden Valley argues that the exculpatory clause unambiguously relieves them from liability for the type of accident that gave rise to this litigation. The Yaugers argue that the ambiguity in the language of the exculpatory contract renders it unenforceable, and therefore it does not protect Hidden Valley from a negligence claim. We conclude that the exculpatory contract signed by Michael Yauger is void as against public policy for two reasons: (1) it failed to clearly, unambiguously, and unmistakably explain to him that he was accepting the risk of Hidden Valley's negligence; (2) the form looked at in its entirety failed to alert the signer to the nature and significance of the document being signed. Accordingly, we reverse and remand.

---

[126] We know, for example, that one farmer lost four years' savings when his 40 sheep drowned. *See* JOHN MCPHEE, THE CROFTER AND THE LAIRD 32–33 (Farrar, Straus & Giroux 1970).

The relevant facts are not in dispute. On October 8, 1992, Michael Yauger purchased a 1992–93 season family ski pass at Hidden Valley's ski shop. The application form asked for the name, age, and relationship of his family members. He filled in the names of his daughters, eight-year-old Felicia and ten-year-old Tara, and his wife, Brenda Yauger. Immediately following the space provided for this information was the clause in question.[127] It provided:

"In support of this application for membership, I agree that:

"1. There are certain inherent risks in skiing and that we agree to hold Hidden Valley Ski Area/Skiing Enterprises Inc. harmless on account of any injury incurred by me or my Family member on the Hidden Valley Ski Area premises."

There was nothing conspicuous about the paragraph containing the waiver. It was one paragraph in a form containing five separate paragraphs. Although the waiver paragraph was the first paragraph of text, it did not stand out from the rest of the form in any manner. It did not require a separate signature.

On March 7, 1993, Tara was skiing at Hidden Valley Ski Area when she allegedly collided with the concrete base of a chair lift tower at the end of a ski run. She died from injuries sustained in the collision.

The Yaugers filed a wrongful death suit in circuit court alleging that Hidden Valley negligently failed to pad the side of the lift tower. Hidden Valley filed a motion for summary judgment based upon the exculpatory clause contained in the application for the season family ski pass signed by Michael Yauger. The circuit court . . . granted the motion for summary judgment, finding the exculpatory clause valid and binding on both Michael and Brenda Yauger. The Court of Appeals held that the exculpatory contract barred the Yaugers from suing Hidden Valley for negligence, and upheld the summary judgment finding that the term "inherent risks in skiing" plainly and simply described the risk of colliding with a fixed object while skiing. *Yauger v. Skiing Enterprises, Inc.*, 196 Wis. 2d 485, 499, 538 N.W.2d 834 (1995). We disagree.

This case presents one issue: whether, as a matter of public policy, the form Michael Yauger signed bars the Yaugers' claim against Hidden Valley.

[I]f the exculpatory contract is void as a matter of law, then it would be inappropriate to grant the defendants' summary judgment motion insofar as there remains a material issue of fact. We conclude that, as a matter of law, the form Michael Yauger signed was void as against public policy and, therefore, the clause does not bar the Yaugers' claim against Hidden Valley.

Exculpatory contracts are not favored by the law because they tend to allow conduct below the acceptable standard of care. *Richards v. Richards*, 181 Wis. 2d 1007, 1015, 513 N.W.2d 118 (1994). However, exculpatory contracts are not automatically void and unenforceable. *Id.* Rather, a court closely examines whether such agreements violate public policy and construes them strictly against the party seeking to rely on them. *Id.*

---

[127] [Eds. note: *See* Note 1 following the case for the reproduced application form.]

Wisconsin law on exculpatory contracts has recently been thoroughly reviewed. There is no need to reiterate the basic principles here. An examination of [the] three most recent cases involving exculpatory contracts as a defense to a negligence action leads us to the conclusion that the form signed by Michael Yauger is void as against public policy.

These cases, in different ways, involved an exculpatory clause that failed to disclose to the signers exactly what rights they were waiving. In the first case, *Arnold v. Shawano County Agr. Soc'y*, 111 Wis. 2d 203, 330 N.W.2d 773 (1983), the court held an exculpatory contract unenforceable because the accident that occurred was not "within the contemplation of the parties" when they signed the exculpatory agreement. In contrast, in *Dobratz v. Thomson*, 161 Wis. 2d 502, 468 N.W.2d 654 (1991), the court struck down on summary judgment a broad release on the ground that it was ambiguous and unclear, and that, as a matter of law, no contract was formed. Finally, in *Richards*, *supra*, the court concluded that the exculpatory contract was void as against public policy because its overbroad, general terms created ambiguity and uncertainty as to what the signer was releasing. . . .

Among the principles that emerge from these cases, two are relevant to our determination in this case. First, the waiver must clearly, unambiguously, and unmistakably inform the signer of what is being waived. Second, the form, looked at in its entirety, must alert the signer to the nature and significance of what is being signed. The waiver in question fails in both respects. Thus, the court finds this waiver void as against public policy under either of these principles.

Addressing the first principle, we conclude that the waiver fails to clearly, unambiguously, and unmistakably inform the signer that he is waiving all claims against Hidden Valley due to their negligence. Although Hidden Valley argues that the form unambiguously relieves them from all liability for whatever cause, including their own negligence, nowhere in the form does the word "negligence" appear. Indeed, the form fails to exhibit any language expressly indicating Michael Yauger's intent to release Hidden Valley from its own negligence.

Although the contract uses the term "inherent risks in skiing," nowhere in the contract is that term defined. Hidden Valley argues that the type of accident which led to Tara's injuries, collision with a fixed object, is inherent in the sport of skiing and therefore within the contemplation of the parties. That certainly is a plausible interpretation, but it is not the only plausible interpretation. Equally plausible is that the effect of the "inherent risks" language was sufficient only to negate the possibility of a strict liability claim based on an inherently dangerous activity, or, again equally plausible, that such term referred only to the hidden dangers of skiing not attributable to the owner's negligence.

The ambiguity of the phrase "inherent risks of skiing" is seen in a review of other cases interpreting this term. The highest court of New Jersey defined "inherent risks of skiing" as those risks that "cannot be removed through the exercise of due care if the sport is to be enjoyed." *Brett v. Great American Recreation, Inc.*, 144 N.J. 479, 677 A.2d 705, 715 (1996) (interpreting the New Jersey Ski Statute). The essence of the Yaugers' tort claim is that the danger from the lift tower could have been removed by placing padding around the entire lift tower. Similarly, the

Supreme Court of Vermont expressly found that a ski owner's negligence is not an inherent risk of skiing. *Dalury v. S-K-I, Ltd.*, 670 A.2d 795, 800 (1995).

In contrast, the Michigan Court of Appeals held that the "dangers that inhere in the [sport of skiing]" include natural conditions and "types of equipment that are inherent parts of a ski area, such as lift towers." *Schmitz v. Cannonsburg Skiing Corp.*, 170 Mich. App. 692, 428 N.W.2d 742 (1988). If judges disagree on the meaning of the term "inherent risks," how can this court infer that a reasonable person would understand what rights he or she was signing away?

Given the well-established principle that exculpatory contracts are construed strictly against the party seeking to rely on them, and given the ambiguous nature of the term "inherent risks of skiing," we must conclude that this waiver was void as against public policy because it failed to clearly, unambiguously, and unmistakably inform Michael Yauger of the rights he was waiving. . . . A valid exculpatory contract must be clear, unambiguous, and unmistakable to the layperson. This form failed to unambiguously inform Michael Yauger that he was prospectively absolving Hidden Valley from responsibility for its negligence. The form absolved Hidden Valley from the inherent risks of skiing, but failed to state whether Hidden Valley's negligence was one of the inherent risks of skiing to which the clause referred.

The second principle that emerges from our prior cases that is relevant here is that the form, looked at in its entirety, must clearly and unequivocally communicate to the signer the nature and significance of the document being signed. This form violates that principle in a number of respects.

First, the form was a one-page form entitled "APPLICATION." Thus, just as in *Richards*, this form was meant to serve two purposes: (1) an application for a season pass; and (2) a release of liability. Just as in *Richards*, this dual function is not made clear in the title of the contract, which merely states, "APPLICATION." The written terms indicate very clearly that this contract is more than a mere application for a season pass. As we stated in *Richards*, "the release should have been conspicuously labeled as such to put the person signing the form on notice . . . Identifying and distinguishing clearly between those two contractual arrangements could have provided important protection against a signatory's inadvertent agreement to the release." *Richards*, 181 Wis. 2d at 1017, 513 N.W.2d 118.

Additionally, there was nothing conspicuous about the paragraph containing the waiver. It was one paragraph in a form containing five separate paragraphs. It did not stand out from the rest of the form in any manner. It did not require a separate signature.

The form, looked at in its entirety, must be such that a reviewing court can say with certainty that the signer was fully aware of the nature and the significance of the document being signed. The combination of the above factors leads us to conclude that we cannot say with any degree of certainty that a reasonable person would be aware of the nature and significance of the waiver at the time of its execution.

While the law grudgingly accepts the proposition that people may contract away their right to recovery for negligently caused injuries, the document must clearly, unambiguously, and unmistakably express this intention. Furthermore, the document when looked at in its entirety must clearly and unequivocally communicate the nature and significance of the waiver. This form before us fails in both respects. Accordingly, it is void as against public policy.[128] We remand to the circuit court for a trial on the issues of negligence and contributory negligence.

The decision of the court of appeals is reversed and the cause remanded to the circuit court for proceedings consistent with this opinion.

NOTES AND QUESTIONS

1. *The Yaugers' application:* The following is a copy of the document that was at the heart of the case.

---

[128] [3] Petitioner raises two other issues: (1) enforceability of the exculpatory clause against Michael Yauger's non-signing wife, Brenda Yauger, and (2) enforceability of the exculpatory clause with respect to claims arising under Wisconsin's Safe Place Statute. Because we find for the Petitioners on other grounds, we need not reach these issues.

2. ***Race to the bottom?*** States with a big skiing industry tend to have statutes addressing the responsibilities of ski operators to at least clarify and in some instances reduce their liability.[129]

3. ***Inconsistency in the laws of different jurisdictions:*** Suppose that McSporran had both read and signed the contract before consigning McCutcheon's automobile on that fateful day. No doubt the House of Lords would have held McCutcheon bound to the terms of the contract and denied recovery. But how would the *McCutcheon* case have been decided in Wisconsin, after the decision in *Yauger v. Skiing Enterprises*? Would the Wisconsin courts limit the holding in *Yauger* to cases in which the plaintiff incurred personal injury, or would they apply it to property loss cases as well? All the Wisconsin precedents cited in *Yauger* were personal injury cases. In a personal injury context, the Wisconsin Supreme Court reaffirmed its *Yauger* holding in *Atkins v. Swimwest Family Fitness Center.*[130]

In some states, principles like that established in *Yauger* apply in property damage cases as well. Some state court decisions have prohibited exculpation of negligence liability clauses entirely. In *Dalury v. S-K-I Ltd.*,[131] a case involving personal injury, the Vermont Supreme Court stated its rationale so as to cover property damage exclusions as well.

Statutes or administrative regulations change many of the traditional rules in various industries, not just in skiing. For example, the Indiana Code, § 32-8-28-1, addresses the limited liability of hotel keepers for guests' property. The hotel may offer a safe in which guests may place valuable property. If it conspicuously posts a notice in each room of the availability of the safe and that the hotel is not liable unless articles are tendered for safekeeping, then it is not liable.

4. ***"Plain English" laws:*** New York and several other states have responded to the problems of incomprehensible forms by adopting a "plain English" law.[132] The statute requires that a consumer contract must be drafted in a "clear and coherent manner using words with common and everyday meanings," and "appropriately divided and captioned by its various sections." One law review note, written a year after the statute's passage, suggests relatively widespread compliance.[133] Most firms surveyed revised their forms because of the law. Most also were pleased with the results. The note concludes:

> The benefits of contracts written in plain English are undeniable. For the consumer, the obvious benefits are the avoidance of frustration and unfair surprise. The benefits to business, while not so obvious, are equally worthwhile. Most importantly, the use of plain English is fundamental good business. The movement should generate goodwill and foster confidence

---

[129] *See* Lori J. Henkel, *Ski resort's liability for skier's injuries resulting from condition of ski run or slope*, 55 A.L.R. 4th 632 (originally published in 1987 and updated through 2015).

[130] 277 Wis. 2d 303, 691 N.W.2d 334 (2005).

[131] 670 A.2d 795 (Vt. 1995).

[132] *See* N.Y. Gen. Obligation Law § 5-702 (McKinney Supp. 1984–85).

[133] Rosemary Moukad, *New York's Plain English Law*, 8 Fordham Urb. L.J. 451, 462–63 (1979). *See also* Jeffrey Davis, *Protecting Consumers from Overdisclosure and Gobbledygook: An Empirical Look at the Simplification of Consumer-Credit Contracts*, 63 Va. L. Rev. 841 (1977).

and trust in business. Consumers are much more likely to abide by terms which they understood from the beginning. Businessmen and employees will spend less time explaining clauses, answering complaints, and defending themselves in lawsuits. Businesses will be in a much stronger position to enforce contracts when the consumer's obligations have been clearly spelled out.

A leading printer of legal forms revised them to follow the New York and New Jersey plain-language laws. He said that New York's law "has not been an instrument of social change. It works for the middle-class consumers who realize the system works for them." A lawyer who drafted plain-language form contracts argues, however, that the law "has helped people without their realizing it."

We can get a flavor of the differences by comparing an older form with a new one drafted after the plain-language laws. Both clauses are designed to sell a house "as is." The seller is not responsible for defects. The older, traditional provision reads:

> This contract is entered into with the purchaser's full knowledge as to the value of the land, and the buildings and improvements thereon, and not upon any representations as to the value, character, quality or condition thereof, other than as may be expressly provided herein.

The plain-language version of the same clause states:

> The Buyer has inspected the Property or has had the Property inspected by others. Except for any rights of inspection reserved elsewhere in this Contract, the Buyer accepts the property "as is." The Seller makes no claim or promise about the condition or value of the Property.[134]

5. *Do disclosure and plain language make a difference?* Can we expect plain language and bold type to make much of a difference? Will these be an effective type of regulation? Professor William Whitford argues:[135]

> [P]recontract disclosure is most often required only in the written document called the contract. Sellers have long known that it is precisely in the contract, and only in the contract, that information consumers are not supposed to notice is to be put. Admittedly, sellers have often buried unfavorable information in small type. But the use of large, bold type, commonly required by disclosure regulations, will rarely communicate information prior to the signing of the contract unless the consumer is searching for the information and has reason to expect it to be in the

---

[134] NEW YORK TIMES, Nov.17, 1981, sec. 8, p. 1, col. 1, and p. 31, cols. 1–4. *See also* Burt A. Leete, *Plain Language Legislation: A Comparison of Approaches*, 18 AM. BUS. L.J. 511 (1981). For a criticism of plain-language approaches, *see* David M. LaPrairie, *Taking the "Plain Language" Movement Too Far: The Michigan Legislature's Unnecessary Application of the Plain Language Doctrine to Consumer Contracts*, 45 WAYNE L. REV. 1927, 1952 (2000) (arguing that the concept of plain language is too imprecise and that "the function of this bill will prove detrimental to consumers because the contract drafters will directly pass on the litigation costs associated with this misapplied doctrine. Finally, more pragmatic solutions such as forces of the free market economy, consumer responsibility, and continuing education sufficiently promote productive contractual relationships between consumers and contract drafters.").

[135] William C. Whitford, *The Functions of Disclosure Regulation in Consumer Transactions*, 1973 WIS. L. REV. 400, 425–26.

contract. In nearly all consumer transactions — and to a very great extent in all contractual transactions — the effective agreement, an oral one, is made before the buyer ever sees the written contract. To the parties, the signing of the written contract is usually only a ritual, roughly equivalent to a handshake. The written contract is likely to be read carefully enough to be understood at some time subsequent to its signing, if at all. Even in the rare case in which a consumer actually reads the contract before signing, it must be remembered that he usually views himself as already morally committed. If he comes across information in the written contract which ordinarily would persuade him not to sign, it puts him in a conflict situation and one which, in accordance with the theory of cognitive dissonance, he may resolve by discounting the disclosed information. Certainly in this situation, unless the information pertains to a buying desire valued very highly by the consumer, he is likely to be receptive to a conflict-resolving suggestion by a salesman that the disclosed information is not really significant and is only included because the law so requires.

Whitford distinguishes a predictive from a normative model of buyer behavior. If those seeking to aid consumers accept people as they are, they must seek information about how people make decisions and whether items that might be put in bold type would be significant to most people. If those drafting regulations are operating on the basis of a normative model, they base their decisions about what items to be put in bold type on how they think buyers ought to behave. He notes that a great deal of disclosure regulation seems to be based on a normative model of behavior and seems to have little impact on actual behavior.

Would Whitford expect the disclosures required by *Yauger* to be effective? In an interview with the lawyer for the defendant in that case, who represents many ski hill operators in Wisconsin, we learned that the ski hill industry did not seek legislative relief from the decision in *Yauger*. But neither did the industry abandon exculpatory clauses. Rather, the ski hills redrafted their exculpatory clauses to mention "negligence" specifically, in a bold manner in a separate paragraph that must be separately initialed. Do you think Wisconsin consumers now have a better understanding of the terms to which they are agreeing when they purchase a ski hill ticket?

6. *The role of insurance:* In *Yauger*, the plaintiffs' daughter was tragically killed in the accident that led to the litigation. In many similar cases the consumer is injured and incurs medical expenses. If the consumer is covered by medical insurance, who benefits when an exculpatory clause is declared invalid? Is this question at all relevant in considering what should be the rules governing the formation of consumer contracts?

PROCD, INC. v. ZEIDENBERG
United States Court of Appeals, Seventh Circuit
86 F.3d 1447 (1996)

EASTERBROOK, CIRCUIT JUDGE.

Must buyers of computer software obey the terms of shrinkwrap licenses? The district court held not, for two reasons: first, they are not contracts because the licenses are inside the box rather than printed on the outside; second, federal law forbids enforcement even if the licenses are contracts. 908 F. Supp. 640 (W.D. Wis. 1996). The parties and numerous amici curiae have briefed many other issues, but these are the only two that matter — and we disagree with the district judge's conclusion on each. Shrinkwrap licenses are enforceable unless their terms are objectionable on grounds applicable to contracts in general (for example, if they violate a rule of positive law, or if they are unconscionable). Because no one argues that the terms of the license at issue here are troublesome, we remand with instructions to enter judgment for the plaintiff.

I

ProCD, the plaintiff, has compiled information from more than 3,000 telephone directories into a computer database. We may assume that this database cannot be copyrighted, although it is more complex, contains more information (nine-digit zip codes and census industrial codes), is organized differently, and therefore is more original than the single alphabetical directory at issue in *Feist Publications, Inc. v. Rural Telephone Service Co.*, 499 U.S. 340. . . .[136] ProCD sells a version of the database, called SelectPhone™, on CD-ROM discs. (CD-ROM means "compact disc — read only memory.") The "shrinkwrap license" gets its name from the fact that retail software packages are covered in plastic or cellophane "shrinkwrap," and some vendors, though not ProCD, have written licenses that become effective as soon as the customer tears the wrapping from the package. Vendors prefer "end user license," but we use the more common term.) A proprietary method of compressing the data serves as effective encryption too. Customers decrypt and use the data with the aid of an application program that ProCD has written. This program, which is copyrighted, searches the database in response to users' criteria (such as "find all people named Tatum in Tennessee, plus all firms with 'Door Systems' in the corporate name"). The resulting lists (or, as ProCD prefers, "listings") can be read and manipulated by other software, such as word processing programs.

The database in SelectPhone™ cost more than $10 million to compile and is expensive to keep current. It is much more valuable to some users than to others.

---

[136] [Eds. note: In *Feist Publications*, the U.S. Supreme Court held that the telephone listings in an ordinary telephone book could not be copyrighted — this information is in the public domain. It was the *Feist* decision that allowed the plaintiff to include on its computer database information that it obtained from other telephone directories without paying for the information.]

The combination of names, addresses, and SIC codes[137] enables manufacturers to compile lists of potential customers. Manufacturers and retailers pay high prices to specialized information intermediaries for such mailing lists; ProCD offers a potentially cheaper alternative. People with nothing to sell could use the database as a substitute for calling long distance information, or as a way to look up old friends who have moved to unknown towns, or just as an electronic substitute for the local phone book. ProCD decided to engage in price discrimination, selling its database to the general public for personal use at a low price (approximately $150 for the set of five discs) while selling information to the trade for a higher price. It has adopted some intermediate strategies too: access to the SelectPhone™ database is available via the America Online service for the price America Online charges to its clients (approximately $3 per hour), but this service has been tailored to be useful only to the general public.

If ProCD had to recover all of its costs and make a profit by charging a single price — that is, if it could not charge more to commercial users than to the general public — it would have to raise the price substantially over $150. The ensuing reduction in sales would harm consumers who value the information at, say, $200. They get consumer surplus of $50 under the current arrangement but would cease to buy if the price rose substantially. If because of high elasticity of demand in the consumer segment of the market the only way to make a profit turned out to be a price attractive to commercial users alone, then all consumers would lose out — and so would the commercial clients, who would have to pay more for the listings because ProCD could not obtain any contribution toward costs from the consumer market.

To make price discrimination work, however, the seller must be able to control arbitrage. An air carrier sells tickets for less to vacationers than to business travelers, using advance purchase and Saturday-night-stay requirements to distinguish the categories. A producer of movies segments the market by time, releasing first to theaters, then to pay-per-view services, next to the videotape and laserdisc market, and finally to cable and commercial TV. Vendors of computer software have a harder task. Anyone can walk into a retail store and buy a box. Customers do not wear tags saying "commercial user" or "consumer user." Anyway, even a commercial-user-detector at the door would not work, because a consumer could buy the software and resell to a commercial user. That arbitrage would break down the price discrimination and drive up the minimum price at which ProCD would sell to anyone.

Instead of tinkering with the product and letting users sort themselves — for example, furnishing current data at a high price that would be attractive only to commercial customers, and two-year-old data at a low price — ProCD turned to the institution of contract. Every box containing its consumer product declares that the software comes with restrictions stated in an enclosed license. This license, which is encoded on the CD-ROM disks as well as printed in the manual, and which appears on a user's screen every time the software runs, limits use of the application program and listings to non-commercial purposes.

---

[137] [Eds. note: An SIC code is a standardized industrial code used in the census. It identifies what businesses an entity participates in.]

Matthew Zeidenberg bought a consumer package of SelectPhone™ in 1994 from a retail outlet in Madison, Wisconsin, but decided to ignore the license. He formed Silken Mountain Web Services, Inc., to resell the information in the SelectPhone™ database. The corporation makes the database available on the Internet to anyone willing to pay its price — which, needless to say, is less than ProCD charges its commercial customers.[138] Zeidenberg has purchased two additional SelectPhone™ packages, each with an updated version of the database, and made the latest information available over the World Wide Web, for a price, through his corporation. ProCD filed this suit seeking an injunction against further dissemination that exceeds the rights specified in the licenses (identical in each of the three packages Zeidenberg purchased). The district court held the licenses ineffectual because their terms do not appear on the outside of the packages. The court added that the second and third licenses stand no different from the first, even though they are identical, because they might have been different, and a purchaser does not agree to — and cannot be bound by — terms that were secret at the time of purchase. 908 F. Supp. at 654.

II

Following the district court, we treat the licenses as ordinary contracts accompanying the sale of products, and therefore as governed by the common law of contracts and the Uniform Commercial Code. Whether there are legal differences between "contracts" and "licenses" (which may matter under the copyright doctrine of first sale) is a subject for another day. *See Microsoft Corp. v. Harmony Computers & Electronics, Inc.*, 846 F. Supp. 208 (E.D.N.Y.1994). . . . Zeidenberg . . . argue[s], and the district court held, that placing the package of software on the shelf is an "offer," which the customer "accepts" by paying the asking price and leaving the store with the goods. *Peeters v. State*, 154 Wis. 111, 142 N.W. 181 (1913). In Wisconsin, as elsewhere, a contract includes only the terms on which the parties have agreed. One cannot agree to hidden terms, the judge concluded. So far, so good — but one of the terms to which Zeidenberg agreed by purchasing the software is that the transaction was subject to a license. Zeidenberg's position therefore must be that the printed terms on the outside of a box are the parties' contract — except for printed terms that refer to or incorporate other terms. But why would Wisconsin fetter the parties' choice in this way? Vendors can put the entire terms of a contract on the outside of a box only by using microscopic type, removing other information that buyers might find more useful (such as what the software does, and on which computers it works), or both. The "Read Me" file included with most software, describing system requirements and potential incompatibilities, may be equivalent to 10 pages of type; warranties and license restrictions take still more space. Notice on the outside, terms on the inside, and a right to return the software for a refund if the terms are unacceptable (a right that the license expressly extends), may be a means of doing business valuable to buyers and sellers alike. *See* E. Allan

---

[138] [Eds. note: Judge Easterbrook makes a mistake here in his statement of the facts. Zeidenberg's corporation never did charge a fee for use of its database. Zeidenberg had planned to sell advertising to be posted on the website, but ProCD obtained an injunction against further maintenance of the website before Zeidenberg sold any advertising. There is no reason to believe that Judge Easterbrook would have decided this case differently if he had correctly understood these facts.]

Farnsworth, 1 *Farnsworth on Contracts* § 4.26 (1990); Restatement (Second) of Contracts § 211, Comment A (1981) ("Standardization of agreements serves many of the same functions as standardization of goods and services; both are essential to a system of mass production and distribution. Scarce and costly time and skill can be devoted to a class of transactions rather than the details of individual transactions."). Doubtless a state could forbid the use of standard contracts in the software business, but we do not think that Wisconsin has done so.

Transactions in which the exchange of money precedes the communication of detailed terms are common. Consider the purchase of insurance. The buyer goes to an agent, who explains the essentials (amount of coverage, number of years) and remits the premium to the home office, which sends back a policy. On the district judge's understanding, the terms of the policy are irrelevant because the insured paid before receiving them. Yet the device of payment, often with a "binder" (so that the insurance takes effect immediately even though the home office reserves the right to withdraw coverage later), in advance of the policy, serves buyers' interests by accelerating effectiveness and reducing transactions costs. Or consider the purchase of an airline ticket. The traveler calls the carrier or an agent, is quoted a price, reserves a seat, pays, and gets a ticket, in that order. The ticket contains elaborate terms, which the traveler can reject by canceling the reservation. To use the ticket is to accept the terms, even terms that in retrospect are disadvantageous. See *Carnival Cruise Lines, Inc. v. Shute*, 499 U.S. 585 (1991). . . . Just so with a ticket to a concert. The back of the ticket states that the patron promises not to record the concert; to attend is to agree. A theater that detects a violation will confiscate the tape and escort the violator to the exit. One could arrange things so that every concertgoer signs this promise before forking over the money, but that cumbersome way of doing things not only would lengthen queues and raise prices but also would scotch the sale of tickets by phone or electronic data service.

Consumer goods work the same way. Someone who wants to buy a radio set visits a store, pays, and walks out with a box. Inside the box is a leaflet containing some terms, the most important of which usually is the warranty, read for the first time in the comfort of home. By Zeidenberg's lights, the warranty in the box is irrelevant; every consumer gets the standard warranty implied by the UCC in the event the contract is silent; yet so far as we are aware no state disregards warranties furnished with consumer products. Drugs come with a list of ingredients on the outside and an elaborate package insert on the inside. The package insert describes drug interactions, contraindications, and other vital information — but, if Zeidenberg is right, the purchaser need not read the package insert, because it is not part of the contract.

Next consider the software industry itself. Only a minority of sales take place over the counter, where there are boxes to peruse. A customer may place an order by phone in response to a line item in a catalog or a review in a magazine. Much software is ordered over the Internet by purchasers who have never seen a box. Increasingly software arrives by wire. There is no box; there is only a stream of electrons, a collection of information that includes data, an application program, instructions, many limitations ("MegaPixel 3.14159 cannot be used with BytePusher 2.718"), and the terms of sale. The user purchases a serial number, which activates the software's features. On Zeidenberg's arguments, these unboxed sales are unfettered by terms — so the seller has made a broad warranty and must pay consequential damages for any shortfalls in performance, two "promises" that if taken seriously would drive prices through the ceiling or return transactions to the horse-and-buggy age.

According to the district court, the UCC does not countenance the sequence of money now, terms later. (Wisconsin's version of the UCC does not differ from the Official Version in any material respect, so we use the regular numbering system. Wis. Stat. § 402.201 corresponds to UCC § 2-201, and other citations are easy to derive.) One of the court's reasons — that by proposing as part of the draft Article 2B a new UCC § 2-203 that would explicitly validate standard-form user licenses, the American Law Institute and the National Conference of Commissioners on Uniform [State] Laws have conceded the invalidity of shrinkwrap licenses under current law . . . depends on a faulty inference. To propose a change in a law's *text* is not necessarily to propose a change in the law's *effect*. New words may be designed to fortify the current rule with a more precise text that curtails uncertainty. . . . [T]he place to start is § 2-204(1): "A contract for sale of goods may be made in any manner sufficient to show agreement, including conduct by both parties which recognizes the existence of such a contract." A vendor, as master of the offer, may invite acceptance by conduct, and may propose limitations on the kind of conduct that constitutes acceptance. A buyer may accept by performing the acts the vendor proposes to treat as acceptance. And that is what happened. ProCD proposed a contract that a buyer would accept by using the software after having an opportunity to read the license at leisure. This Zeidenberg did. He had no choice, because the software splashed the license on the screen and would not let him proceed without indicating acceptance. So although the district judge was right to say that a contract can be, and often is, formed simply by paying the price and walking out of the store, the UCC permits contracts to be formed in other ways. ProCD proposed such a different way, and without protest Zeidenberg agreed. Ours is not a case in which a consumer opens a package to find an insert saying "you owe us an extra $10,000" and the seller files suit to collect. Any buyer finding such a demand can prevent formation of the contract by returning the package, as can any consumer who concludes that the terms of the license make the software worth less than the purchase price. Nothing in the UCC requires a seller to maximize the buyer's net gains. . . .

Some portions of the UCC impose additional requirements on the way parties agree on terms. A disclaimer of the implied warranty of merchantability must be "conspicuous." UCC § 2-316(2), incorporating UCC § 1-201(10). Promises to make firm offers, or to negate oral modifications, must be "separately signed." UCC §§ 2-205, 2-209(2). These special provisos reinforce the impression that, so far as the UCC is concerned, other terms may be as inconspicuous as the forum-selection clause on the back of the cruise ship ticket in *Carnival Lines*. Zeidenberg has not located any Wisconsin case — for that matter, any case in any state — holding that under the UCC the ordinary terms found in shrinkwrap licenses require any special prominence, or otherwise are to be undercut rather than enforced. In the end, the terms of the license are conceptually identical to the contents of the package. Just as no court would dream of saying that SelectPhone™ must contain 3,100 phone books rather than 3,000, or must have data no more than 30 days old, or must sell for $100 rather than $150 — although any of these changes would be welcomed by the customer, if all other things were held constant — so, we believe, Wisconsin would not let the buyer pick and choose among terms. Terms of use are no less a part of "the product" than are the size of the database and the speed with which the software compiles listings. Competition among vendors, not judicial revision of a package's contents, is how consumers are protected in a market economy. *Digital Equipment Corp. v. Uniq Digital Technologies, Inc.*, 73 F.3d 756 (7th Cir. 1996). ProCD has rivals, which may elect to compete by offering superior software, monthly updates, improved terms of use, lower price, or a better compromise among these elements. As we stressed above, adjusting terms in buyers' favor might help Matthew Zeidenberg today (he already has the software) but would lead to a response, such as a higher price, that might make consumers as a whole worse off.

III

The district court held that, even if Wisconsin treats shrinkwrap licenses as contracts, § 301(a) of the Copyright Act, 17 U.S.C. § 301(a), prevents their enforcement. 908 F. Supp. at 656–59. The relevant part of § 301(a) preempts any "legal or equitable rights [under state law] that are equivalent to any of the exclusive rights within the general scope of copyright." [Discussion of this issue is omitted. The court concluded that "a simple two-party contract is not 'equivalent to any of the exclusive rights within the general scope of copyright' and therefore may be enforced."]

Reversed and Remanded.

NOTES AND QUESTIONS

1.   *The decision below:* In the District Court opinion, District Judge Barbara Crabb concluded that the contract was formed when Zeidenberg purchased the box containing the CD-ROM. Since he had not had an opportunity to inspect the terms of the license at the time, these terms were not deemed part of the contract at the time of formation. Because Zeidenberg later had an opportunity to inspect the terms of the license (after he opened the box containing the CD-ROM), Judge Crabb treated the license terms as proposals to modify or alter the existing contract. She considered whether these proposals could be considered part of the contract in this way, deeming Zeidenberg's failure to object to the terms of the license as an acceptance of the proposed modification or alteration. Applying both UCC §§ 2-207 and 2-209, Judge Crabb concluded that Zeidenberg's failure to object could not be deemed an acceptance. As an interpretation of those UCC sections, Judge Crabb's decision is in accord with leading interpretations (involving software purchases) from other jurisdictions. See *Arizona Retail Systems v. Software Link*[139] and *Step-Saver Data Systems v. Wyse Technology*.[140] On appeal, Judge Easterbrook avoided interpretation of these sections altogether by holding that there was no contract formed until after Zeidenberg failed to object to the license

---

[139] 831 F. Supp. 759 (D. Ariz. 1993).

[140] 939 F.2d 91 (3d Cir. 1991).

terms. Hence there was no need to look to the UCC sections concerning proposals to modify or alter a contract.

Imagine a purchase of a CD-ROM where the seller failed to enclose a license agreement in the box, due to some slipup, though the box still stated in small print that a license agreement was enclosed. Would a contract then be formed when the buyer purchased the CD-ROM at the checkout register? What would Judge Easterbrook say? If a contract would be formed at purchase in this hypothetical case, why is a contract not formed at the point in time in *ProCD v. Zeidenberg*?

2.   *Some additional facts:* Professor William Whitford, one of the authors of this casebook, conducted interviews with Matt Zeidenberg and his lawyer and learned a great deal of interesting background.[141] Matt Zeidenberg was a graduate student in computer science at the time of this case. He got the idea of setting up his website when he read an account of the decision in *Feist Publications v. Rural Telephone Service*, described in the first footnote in the *ProCD* decision, in a user's manual written by ProCD. The *Feist* decision held that telephone directories could not be copyrighted, and Zeidenberg realized that this meant that ProCD did not have a property interest in the telephone numbers contained in ProCD's database. He then purchased another separate telephone number database, combined the telephone number data for California from that database with the California numbers recorded in ProCD's product, and created his website. Zeidenberg never did charge for access to his website. He had intended to sell advertising, but his website was enjoined before he had accomplished that.

Soon after learning of Zeidenberg's website, ProCD hired a large Boston law firm and sued Zeidenberg in Wisconsin. Zeidenberg had little money and was represented for only a token payment by a friend who had just passed the bar exam and had not previously litigated a case. ProCD's lawyers took Zeidenberg's deposition in a day-long proceeding that Zeidenberg remembers as "like a trial." The lawyers accused Zeidenberg of criminal offenses in the press and threatened lawsuits for a million dollars (or more). Zeidenberg later offered to accept a permanent injunction against the website if ProCD dropped their lawsuit, but the lawyers for ProCD insisted on payment of ProCD's legal expenses, then over $100,000. So Zeidenberg moved for summary judgment, won at trial, but lost on appeal. His lawyer, David Austin (Dave), described the appeal as follows to Professor Whitford (Bill):[142]

[Bill:] Did you undertake to do the appeal?

[Dave:] I did not want to do the appeal. I thought I had done well enough in the district court. I didn't want to press my luck in the circuit court. I had no experience in law school with a circuit court argument. So I prevailed upon Matt to get another attorney to handle the appeal. And for some foolish reason I kept my name on the case in the Seventh Circuit. Then it came about that a week before the oral argument, this guy totally bailed out on the case and. . . .

---

[141] *See* William Whitford, ProCD v. Zeidenberg *in Context*, 2004 Wis. L. Rev. 821. You can hear the interviews at https://mediaspace.wisc.edu/media/cd.v.zeidenberg/0_tyoqxki6.

[142] *Id.* at 833–34.

[Bill:] He did the briefing, this other attorney. . . .

[Dave:] He did all the briefing, and then a week before the argument he called me up and said, "I'm leaving the country. Here's the file. You've got to do the oral argument."

[Bill:] So you actually did the oral argument in the Seventh Circuit without having written the briefs.

[Dave:] That's right.

[Bill:] How much time was allotted for oral argument?

[Dave:] Looking back, we can see this had become a very important case and apparently the court felt it was at the time. They allowed half an hour on each side, which was double the normal amount of time for argument.

[Bill:] Do you have any idea why?

[Dave:] I don't know why. There was never any indication from the court why.

[Bill:] Were there any amici in the case?

[Dave:] There were four amici; there were three on ProCD's side and one on our side.

[Bill:] And who were the amici?

[Dave:] There were some that I would call the heavy hitters on the other side: the Business Software Alliance, which is the dozen or 15 biggest software producers in the country, and another trade association that was about 1200 software distributors.

[Bill:] And on your side?

[Dave:] And on our side, the Committee for Interoperable Systems. Mark Lemley [a law professor who is now on the faculty of Stanford Law School], who had helped us in the trial court, was the attorney for that group and wrote that brief.

[Bill:] Do you think it's reasonable to speculate that the fact that these amicus briefs were filed might have had something to do with the extended argument?

[Dave:] It seems likely.

[Bill:] Did those amici attorneys argue?

[Dave:] No. ProCD and we argued; but that was all.

[Bill:] Can you describe what the argument was like, as an existential experience?

[Dave:] As an existential experience, on a scale of one to ten — it was the worst day of my life. You know, I admit that I was in over my head and didn't really know what was going to happen. The phrase I used at the time and continued to use is that Judge Easterbrook hazed me. It was a pretty awful experience.

[Bill:] There were a lot of questions?

[Dave:] There were a lot of questions. He made it plain that he thought we were in the wrong and he was very aggressive with us. And the other odd thing, I thought, was that it was a three-judge panel, and Judge Easterbrook was the only one that talked all day. The other two were completely silent.

After Zeidenberg lost the appeal, the parties did enter into a settlement, but Zeidenberg is not at liberty, because of the terms of the settlement, to reveal its terms. Zeidenberg never made a penny from the website, but he also avoided bankruptcy. He returned to his graduate studies. Why do you think ProCD refused to settle before summary judgment and before the appeal, even though Zeidenberg agreed to a permanent injunction against his website? Did ProCD expect to recover over $100,000 in attorney fees (incurred before the summary judgment motion) from a grad student? Do you think it recovered from Matt the additional attorney's fees for itself at the summary judgment phase and for the appeal? What did ProCD and the trade groups on its side get by pursuing the appeal, probably at significant expense? Is it likely ProCD and the trade groups planned an appeal to the Seventh Circuit from the outset?

3. *How important is the notice on the box?* Would it matter if ProCD did not include a notice on the box? In the actual case, ProCD did have a notice on the box, albeit in small print, indicating that there was a license enclosed in the box. Would the case have been decided in Zeidenberg's favor if there had been no notice on the box? Before answering this question, read the next case.

4. *Relevance of Wisconsin law: ProCD* was decided six months before the Wisconsin Supreme Court decision in *Yauger v. Ski Enterprises.* The opinion in *ProCD* cites none of the Wisconsin precedents discussed in *Yauger.* Of course, *ProCD* is treated as a UCC case at least in part, and the Wisconsin cases discussed in *Yauger* are not. Does that make the non-UCC Wisconsin cases irrelevant to the result in *ProCD*? And do you think *ProCD* is still good law in Wisconsin, given the later Wisconsin Supreme Court decisions in *Yauger* and in *Atkins v. Swimwest*?[143]

Judge Easterbrook relied almost exclusively on the text of Article 2 of the UCC. He noted that some terms must be conspicuous or separately signed. He took this to mean that other terms need not be conspicuous. However, is this good technical lawyering? The judge quotes § 2-204(1). He failed to deal with § 1-201(3) [§ 1-201(b)(3) in Revised Article 1]. Why is it relevant? Turn back to the excerpt from Professor Macaulay's article with which we began this section. Would Judge Easterbrook say that terms and conditions in such light gray ink that they could be read only by holding the paper at an angle to the light would be part of a contract? Would § 2-204(1) call for this result? Suppose the terms and conditions were printed in invisible ink and could only be read if the paper were treated with a chemical that

---

[143] 277 Wis. 2d 303, 691 N.W.2d 334 (2005) (affirming the *Yauger* holding). *See* Note 3 following *Yauger v. Skiing Enterprises, Inc., supra.*

made them visible. What would Judge Easterbrook and § 2-204(1) say then? To what extent, if at all, does Judge Easterbrook's decision turn on the law of Wisconsin?

5. *How adequate is the market to deal with standard forms?* Judge Easterbrook states that "competition among vendors, not judicial revision of a package's contents, is how consumers are protected in a market economy." Do you agree? How well do you think the marketplace protects consumers from unfair terms in software license agreements?

6. *Proposed Article 2B morphs into UCITA:* Judge Easterbrook referred to a proposed amendment to the Uniform Commercial Code that would have ratified standard form licenses. This proposed amendment was part of a proposed Article 2B to the UCC. Article 2B was never promulgated by the sponsors of the UCC, because the American Law Institute (ALI) refused to endorse it after objections were raised that it was too favorable to the software industry. The other sponsor of the UCC — the Uniform Law Commission (ULC), which was then known as the National Conference of Commissioners on Uniform State Laws, or NCCUSL — then promulgated the same draft legislation, without significant substantive change, as the Uniform Computer Information Transactions Act (UCITA).[144] This uniform act was endorsed by the ULC at its annual meeting in July 1999 and recommended for adoption by the various states. As of 2010, UCITA had been adopted by only two states — Virginia and Maryland. As we shall see after considering the next case, the ALI has since weighed in with its own project in the area, called Principles of the Law of Software Contracts, approved by the ALI membership in 2009 and published by the ALI in 2010. UCITA is now viewed as a dead letter.

HILL v. GATEWAY 2000, INC.
United States Court of Appeals, Seventh Circuit
105 F.3d 1147 (1997)

EASTERBROOK, CIRCUIT JUDGE.

A customer picks up the phone, orders a computer, and gives a credit card number. Presently a box arrives, containing the computer and a list of terms, said to govern unless the customer returns the computer within 30 days. Are these terms effective as the parties' contract, or is the contract term-free because the order-taker did not read any terms over the phone and elicit the customer's assent?

One of the terms in the box containing a Gateway 2000 system was an arbitration clause. Rich and Enza Hill, the customers, kept the computer more than 30 days before complaining about its components and performance. They filed suit in federal court arguing, among other things, that the product's shortcomings make Gateway a racketeer (mail and wire fraud are said to be the predicate offenses), leading to treble damages under RICO for the Hills and a class of all other purchasers. Gateway asked the district court to enforce the arbitration clause; the judge refused, writing that "[t]he present record is insufficient to support a finding of a

---

[144] The ULC is described in Chapter 2, Section A.1., *supra.*

valid arbitration agreement between the parties or that the plaintiffs were given adequate notice of the arbitration clause." Gateway took an immediate appeal, as is its right. 9 U.S.C. § 16(a)(1)(A).

The Hills say that the arbitration clause did not stand out: they concede noticing the statement of terms but deny reading it closely enough to discover the agreement to arbitrate, and they ask us to conclude that they therefore may go to court. Yet an agreement to arbitrate must be enforced "save upon such grounds as exist at law or in equity for the revocation of any contract." 9 U.S.C. § 2. *Doctor's Associates, Inc. v. Casarotto*, 517 U.S. 681 (1996), holds that this provision of the Federal Arbitration Act is inconsistent with any requirement that an arbitration clause be prominent. A contract need not be read to be effective; people who accept take the risk that the unread terms may in retrospect prove unwelcome. . . . Terms inside Gateway's box stand or fall together. If they constitute the parties' contract because the Hills had an opportunity to return the computer after reading them, then all must be enforced.

ProCD, Inc. v. Zeidenberg, 86 F.3d 1447 (7th Cir. 1996), holds that terms inside a box of software bind consumers who use the software after an opportunity to read the terms and to reject them by returning the product. Likewise, *Carnival Cruise Lines, Inc. v. Shute*, 499 U.S. 585 (1991), enforces a forum-selection clause that was included among three pages of terms attached to a cruise ship ticket. *ProCD* and *Carnival Cruise Lines* exemplify the many commercial transactions in which people pay for products with terms to follow; *ProCD* discusses others. 86 F.3d at 1451–52. The district court concluded in *ProCD* that the contract is formed when the consumer pays for the software; as a result, the court held, only terms known to the consumer at that moment are part of the contract, and provisos inside the box do not count. Although this is one way a contract could be formed, it is not the only way: "A vendor, as master of the offer, may invite acceptance by conduct, and may propose limitations on the kind of conduct that constitutes acceptance. A buyer may accept by performing the acts the vendor proposes to treat as acceptance." *Id.* at 1452. Gateway shipped computers with the same sort of accept-or-return offer ProCD made to users of its software. *ProCD* relied on the Uniform Commercial Code rather than any peculiarities of Wisconsin law; both Illinois and South Dakota, the two states whose law might govern relations between Gateway and the Hills, have adopted the UCC; neither side has pointed us to any atypical doctrines in those states that might be pertinent; *ProCD* therefore applies to this dispute.

Plaintiffs ask us to limit *ProCD* to software, but where's the sense in that? *ProCD* is about the law of contract, not the law of software. Payment preceding the revelation of full terms is common for air transportation, insurance, and many other endeavors. Practical considerations support allowing vendors to enclose the full legal terms with their products. Cashiers cannot be expected to read legal documents to customers before ringing up sales. If the staff at the other end of the phone for direct-sales operations such as Gateway's had to read the four-page statement of terms before taking the buyer's credit card number, the droning voice would anesthetize rather than enlighten many potential buyers. Others would hang up in a rage over the waste of their time. And oral recitation would not avoid customers' assertions (whether true or feigned) that the clerk did not read term X to them, or that they did not remember or understand it. Writing provides benefits for both sides of commercial transactions. Customers as a group are better off when vendors skip costly and ineffectual steps such as telephonic recitation, and use instead a simple approve-or-return device. Competent adults are bound by such documents, read or unread. For what little it is worth, we add that the box from Gateway was crammed with software. The computer came with an operating system, without which it was useful only as a boat anchor. . . . Gateway also included many application programs. So the Hills' effort to limit *ProCD* to software would not avail them factually, even if it were sound legally — which it is not.

For their second sally, the Hills contend that *ProCD* should be limited to executory contracts (to licenses in particular), and therefore does not apply because both parties' performance of this contract was complete when the box arrived at their home. This is legally and factually wrong: legally because the question at hand concerns the formation of the contract rather than its performance, and factually because both contracts were incompletely performed. *ProCD* did not depend on the fact that the seller characterized the transaction as a license rather than as a contract; we treated it as a contract for the sale of goods and reserved the question whether for other purposes a "license" characterization might be preferable. . . . All debates about characterization to one side, the transaction in *ProCD* was no more executory than the one here: Zeidenberg paid for the software and walked out of the store with a box under his arm, so if arrival of the box with the product ends the time for revelation of contractual terms, then the time ended in *ProCD* before Zeidenberg opened the box. But of course ProCD had not completed performance with delivery of the box, and neither had Gateway. One element of the transaction was the warranty, which obliges sellers to fix defects in their products. The Hills have invoked Gateway's warranty and are not satisfied with its response, so they are not well positioned to say that Gateway's obligations were fulfilled when the motor carrier unloaded the box. What is more, both ProCD and Gateway promised to help customers to use their products. Long-term service and information obligations are common in the computer business, on both hardware and software sides. Gateway offers "lifetime service" and has a round-the-clock telephone hotline to fulfil this promise. Some vendors spend more money helping customers use their products than on developing and manufacturing them. The document in Gateway's box includes promises of future performance that some consumers value highly; these promises bind Gateway just as the arbitration clause binds the Hills. . . .

At oral argument the Hills propounded still another distinction: the box containing ProCD's software displayed a notice that additional terms were within, while the box containing Gateway's computer did not. The difference is functional, not legal. Consumers browsing the aisles of a store can look at the box, and if they are unwilling to deal with the prospect of additional terms can leave the box alone, avoiding the transaction[] costs of returning the package after reviewing its contents. Gateway's box, by contrast, is just a shipping carton; it is not on display anywhere. Its function is to protect the product during transit, and the information on its sides is for the use of handlers . . . rather than would-be purchasers.

Perhaps the Hills would have had a better argument if they were first alerted to the bundling of hardware and legal-ware after opening the box and wanted to return the computer in order to avoid disagreeable terms, but were dissuaded by the expense of shipping. What the remedy would be in such a case — could it exceed the shipping charges? — is an interesting question, but one that need not detain us because the Hills knew before they ordered the computer that the carton would include some important terms, and they did not seek to discover these in advance. Gateway's ads state that their products come with limited warranties and lifetime support. How limited was the warranty — 30 days, with service contingent on shipping the computer back, or five years, with free onsite service? What sort of support was offered? Shoppers have three principal ways to discover these things. First, they can ask the vendor to send a copy before deciding whether to buy. . . . [T]he Hills do not contend that Gateway would have refused to enclose the remaining terms too. Concealment would be bad for business, scaring some customers away and leading to excess returns from others. Second, shoppers can consult public sources (computer magazines, the websites of vendors) that may contain this information. Third, they may inspect the documents after the product's delivery. Like Zeidenberg, the Hills took the third option. By keeping the computer beyond 30 days, the Hills accepted Gateway's offer, including the arbitration clause.

[T]he decision of the district court is vacated, and this case is remanded with instructions to compel the Hills to submit their dispute to arbitration.

NOTES AND QUESTIONS

1. *Are English and American law different?* Recall the decision of the House of Lords in *McCutcheon v. MacBrayne, supra.* Assuming that case is still good law, what result in England under the facts of *ProCD*, and under *Hill v. Gateway*? If you think English law in this area is different than the law as stated by these cases, which is preferable from a policy perspective? Why?

2. *Are* **ProCD** *and* **Hill** *dated?* At their time in the early years of the Internet, *ProCD* and *Hill* were controversial. For a case detailing their technical errors under Article 2, see *Klocek v. Gateway.*[145] *Klocek* focused in part on UCC § 2-206(1)(b), which was ignored in the Seventh Circuit decisions.

Since then, the worlds of law and technology have continued to develop rapidly. In 2009, the American Law Institute completed a project called Principles of the Law of Software Contracts (the *Principles*), which provides, in § 2.02(c):[146]

> A transferee will be deemed to have adopted a standard form as a contract if
>
> (1) the standard form is reasonably accessible electronically prior to initiation of the transfer at issue;
>
> (2) upon initiating the transfer, the transferee has reasonable notice of and access to the standard form before payment or, if there is no payment, before completion of the transfer;
>
> (3) in the case of an electronic transfer of software, the transferee signifies agreement at the end of or adjacent to the electronic standard

---

[145] 104 F. Supp. 2d 1332 (D. Kan. 2000).

[146] AM. LAW INST., PRINCIPLES OF THE LAW OF SOFTWARE CONTRACTS (2010).

form, or in the case of a standard form printed on or attached to packaged software or separately wrapped from the software, the transferee does not exercise the opportunity to return the software unopened for a full refund within a reasonable time after the transfer; and

    (4) the transferee can store and reproduce the standard form if presented electronically.

These elements are joined by an "and," meaning that the first is operative in all cases; the standard form should be reasonably accessible (typically on the vendor's Internet site) prior to the time a customer initiates a transfer. Does this answer Judge Easterbrook's concern in *Hill* with the impracticality of reading terms over the telephone? Presumably, even in a telephone order, the operator could direct a customer to the company's website to see terms if the customer desired to do so before completing the order. With in-store purchases, boxes could specify websites at which the terms could be found, so that customers who cared could wait to make a purchase until after going home and reading them. Is Internet availability of terms likely to introduce some policing of them?

Meanwhile, consumers have largely moved away from "shrinkwrap" contracts — such as those in *ProCD* and *Hill* — in which terms would follow payment, to "clickwrap" contracts, in which one must click "I agree" prior to payment. In *Specht v. Netscape Communications Corp.*,[147] the court described a clickwrap license as follows:

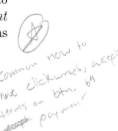

    A clickwrap license presents the user with a message on his or her computer screen, requiring that the user manifest his or her assent to the terms of the license agreement by clicking on an icon. The product cannot be obtained or used unless and until the icon is clicked. For example, when a user attempts to obtain Netscape's Communicator or Navigator, a web page appears containing the full text of the Communicator/Navigator license agreement. Plainly visible on the screen is the query, "Do you accept all the terms of the preceding license agreement? If so, click on the Yes button. If you select No, Setup will close." Below this text are three buttons or icons: one labeled "Back" and used to return to an earlier step of the download preparation; one labeled "No," which if clicked, terminates the download; and one labeled "Yes," which if clicked, allows the download to proceed. Unless the user clicks "Yes," indicating his or her assent to the license agreement, the user cannot obtain the software.

Professor Mark Lemley (mentioned in the interview with David Austin in Note 2 following *ProCD v. Zeidenberg, supra*), surveying the situation 10 years ago, observed: "Every court to consider the issue has found 'clickwrap' licenses . . . enforceable."[148] Do you think that courts simply do not care about consumers who fail to read terms when offered? Or are there other policing mechanisms at work? Have the ALI *Principles* become the de facto law of consumer Internet contract-

---

[147] 150 F. Supp. 2d 585, 593–94 (S.D.N.Y. 2001), *aff'd*, 306 F.3d 17 (2d Cir. 2002).

[148] Mark A. Lemley, *Terms of Use*, 91 Minn. L. Rev. 459, 459 (2006).

ing? How often do you read the terms of an Internet contract before clicking "I agree"?

3. *Gateway's arbitration clause and the Federal Arbitration Act:* The arbitration clause included in Gateway's contract with Mr. Hill was found to be unconscionable in *Brower v. Gateway 2000*.[149] The unconscionability issue was not raised by the lawyers for the Hills in the case you just read, *Hill v. Gateway 2000*, and was not considered by the court. Is it an issue the court should have considered *sua sponte*?

Judge Easterbrook refers to the Federal Arbitration Act (FAA). Basically, the FAA is a federal statute that prevents states from subjecting arbitration agreements to any regulation that is not targeted at contracts generally, including regulation that would require arbitration clauses to be more prominently disclosed than other contract terms. We will examine the effects of arbitration clauses in section E of this chapter, which deals with unconscionability.

4. Carnival Cruise Lines v. Shute: The opinion mentions a 1991 U.S. Supreme Court decision in *Carnival Cruise Lines v. Shute*.[150] Plaintiffs, residents of the state of Washington, purchased tickets for a cruise off the western coast of Mexico. The ticket, which they received in the mail, contained a forum selection clause requiring any suits between the parties to be litigated in Florida. When plaintiffs sought to sue in Washington for injuries incurred while aboard, the suit was enjoined and the forum selection clause upheld. Because the cruise was on open seas, the case was governed by admiralty law, which is federal law. Admiralty law requires that the terms of contracts be "fundamentally fair," and the U.S. Supreme Court held there was no fundamental unfairness in requiring plaintiffs to litigate their case in Florida. Plaintiffs stipulated in the case that they had a reasonable opportunity to read the contract at a time when they could return the ticket and get a full refund. For a case that distinguishes *Carnival Cruise Lines* in a situation where the plaintiffs could only get a 50 percent refund when a ticket containing a forum selection clause arrived, see *Johnson v. Holland American Line*.[151]

5. *The market again:* Recall that in *ProCD* Judge Easterbrook argued that the market was the appropriate protector of the consumer interest in standard transactions. Many years ago, Professors Alan Schwartz and Louis Wilde[152] argued that a market of substantial size will contain a significant number of buyers who will read and understand the implications of the terms and conditions offered by the seller. If these buyers shop for deals with favorable contract terms, the market is sufficiently competitive, and sellers will not be able to customize their forms to provide better terms only for the sophisticated buyers. Instead, sellers will have to write their forms to benefit all buyers; if they do not, they will lose sales to those who read and understand. Thus, all buyers gain the terms that informed buyers

---

[149] 246 A.D.2d 246, 676 N.Y.S.2d 569 (1998).

[150] 499 U.S. 585 (1991). For a critique of the reasoning in this case, see Jean Braucher, *The Afterlife of Contract*, 90 Nw. U. L. Rev. 49, 61–68 (1995).

[151] 206 Wis. 2d 562, 577 N.W.2d 475 (1996).

[152] Alan Schwartz & Louis L. Wilde, *Intervening in Markets on the Basis of Imperfect Information: A Legal and Economic Analysis*, 127 U. Pa. L. Rev. 630 (1979).

want. This result is likely better than one produced by courts or other legal agencies, the authors argued.

Professor W. David Slawson responded:[153]

> The firm of which I was a member when I was a practicing lawyer represented three corporate clients that used standard forms which, it happened, I drafted. One of the clients was a bank which used a wide variety of forms for different aspects of its business. To the best of my recollection, no one in any of the corporations or in the law firm ever suggested that the forms should be drafted other than as one-sidedly in the interests of the corporate client as possible. Nor did anyone ever report a customer or other business firm with which any of the corporations had dealt as objecting to anything in any of their forms or wanting to change them. In no case in which special arrangements were made with a very large buyer or borrower were the favorable terms extended to other dealings of the same kind. Moreover, I cannot even conceive of a situation in which it would have been profitable for the corporations we represented to make their forms more favorable to the interests of all customers merely because special arrangements occasionally had to be made for some.

Does Slawson convince you that Schwartz and Wilde are wrong by this argument? Whether or not you are willing to concede that this kind of market pressure produces the best results possible, would you accept that it could have some influence? Do you know of examples of competition on the terms of standard form contracts? An additional point is that sellers in some markets may be able to segment readers and non-readers of standard forms, something that has become easier on the Internet with the ability to track what customers are reading, with the result that readers may not benefit non-readers.

For the Schwartz/Wilde theory to work, at least a reasonable number of consumers would have to know something about the terms of the contracts to which they are parties, and do something about those terms (e.g., shop elsewhere if unhappy with them). Recent scholarship has revealed that this is highly unlikely to happen. Instead, if "end user license agreements" are any indication, Professors Yannis Bakos, Florencia Marotta-Wurgler, and David R. Trossen have found that almost no one reads them.[154] Nor is it reasonable to expect that consumers would do so. Scholars find that standard form contracts are long and difficult to read, averaging around 2,000 words, and require a graduate degree to understand them (as measured by Flesch-Kinkaid readability scores).[155] Professors Omri Ben-Shahar and Carl E. Schneider have argued that consumers would be better off relying on "expert opinion" websites, such as Yelp and Amazon.[156] These websites,

---

[153] W. David Slawson, *The New Meaning of Contract: The Transformation of Contract Law by Standard Forms*, 46 U. PITT. L. REV. 44 (1984).

[154] Yannis Bakos, Florencia Marotta-Wurgler, & David R. Trossen, *Does Anyone Read the Fine Print?, Consumer Attention to Standard-Form Contracts*, 43 J. LEGAL STUD. 1 (2014).

[155] Florencia Marotta-Wurgler & Robert Taylor, *Set in Stone? Change and Innovation in Consumer Standard-Form Contracts*, 88 N.Y.U. L. REV. 240 (2013).

[156] OMRI BEN-SHAHAR & CARL E. SCHNEIDER, MORE THAN YOU WANTED TO KNOW: THE FAILURE OF

rather than contracts or contract doctrine, may tell consumers what they really need to know.

6. *Ian Macneil on contracts of adhesion:* Professor Ian Macneil offers an approach to the problems of consumer "contracts of adhesion" based on concepts of relationship and status.[157] He says that consumers of goods and services in a modern economy are bureaucrats operating within a private government. Bureaucracy, as he uses the term, "is a particular form of governance of human affairs dominated by reasoned and detailed planning. A bureaucrat is anyone participating in the affairs so governed."[158] If Macneil's image of a "bureaucrat" troubles you, you can substitute the idea of a citizen of a private government governed by its rules and sanctions, which he or she may not know when the relationship begins. Perhaps this describes your relationship to your university.

Consumer goods and services are often accompanied by documents, sometimes called contracts, explaining the relationship's plan. These documents give instructions about using the product, and they tell consumers what they can and cannot do if anything goes wrong. Macneil argues that when consumers buy products, they accept both the known and unknown natures of those products and both the known and unknown documentary terms that come with them.

In a liberal state, this view of the consequences of citizenship in a private government as a consumer is troubling. If courts hold consumers bound to "contracts" defined by the standard form documents that accompany consumer products, any element of choice or responsibility for misleading others is fictional in all but a few limiting cases. Consumers do not choose the details of the relationship. Nor are consumers responsible for misleading suppliers of goods and services. Those who draft and use form contracts know that their customers are unlikely to read and understand these documents.

However, if courts do not hold consumers bound to these documents, then some other form of planning must be substituted. Under liberal theory, if we do not rely on the parties, only the state can supply the terms governing these transactions. This solution has costs, which we may not want to pay.

Macneil insists that there are competing policies involved in consumer transactions. Firms such as General Motors and Honda must be able to supply large quantities of goods at low prices. This is the consumer mission. It limits what society can do in overseeing the status of consumers as they deal with large corporations. Society cannot regulate in ways that might destroy the large automobile companies or so transform them that they cannot perform their consumer mission.

These corporations serve the consumer mission, but their motive is also a desire

---

MANDATED DISCLOSURE (Princeton University Press 2014).

[157] Ian Macneil, *Bureaucracy and Contracts of Adhesion*, 22 OSGOODE HALL L.J. 5 (1984). Macneil there discusses the *McCutcheon* case: "As Mr. McCutcheon said of the 27 paragraphs of conditions in MacBrayne's shipping documents, 'Och well, the reading and understanding would be taking half a day, and then we would be missing the boat altogether.' " *Id.* at 6. Macneil concludes: "[A]ny court saying that consumers 'ought' to read the terms of long contracts of adhesion can only be making a very poor joke." *Id.*

[158] *Id.* at 8.

to reap profit, power, growth, and internal employment. Macneil continues: "The consumer vote in the marketplace is a powerful force towards harmony of motivation and mission, but far from all-powerful. And to the extent there is disharmony, public intervention must be considered. Considered, mind you, not automatically chosen."[159]

We might want to abandon contractual ideas but hold consumers to the terms of the form documents that accompany the goods they buy. A buyer of a car consents to entering a relationship and accepts the manufacturer's plan for it, whether or not the buyer understands that plan. We might want to regulate so that the manufacturer's plan could not run too far counter to the consumer's reasonable expectations about what is involved in such a purchase.[160]

Macneil points out that his relational approach should not surprise us:[161]

> Liberal society has always recognized numerous legitimate relations into which entry is by consent, but the content of which is largely unknown at the time the consent was given. This is the idea of joining a relation. We can join a law firm or a university faculty or any other employment relation; we can join the army; we can join a corporation by buying its shares; we can join in holy matrimony. In each instance we can do so in spite of large-scale ignorance about the restraints we are accepting.

He argues that we might add the consumer relationship to this list and thus avoid the legitimating fictions of contract, choice, or responsibility for misleading others. In their place, he would substitute the legitimation of a valuable social relationship with some market and, perhaps, some governmental discipline.

Should we accept Macneil's approach and abandon contract concepts when we deal with risk notes, insurance policies, and the documents accompanying consumer products, with their warranty disclaimers and remedy limitations? Is Macneil's approach fundamentally different from Judge Easterbrook's, or from Schwartz and Wilde's (*see* Note 5, *supra*)? Is Macneil's theory more sophisticated, more grounded in reality?

Are you willing to abandon notions of consent and choice to the particular terms of a transaction as necessary for the formation of contracts? Some have argued that, insofar as form contracts are concerned, the law should place the burden of justifying any departures from "background law" — the law that would apply in the absence of agreement — on the drafter of the agreement.[162] The following case arguably takes at least a small step in that direction. Do you find this approach promising?

---

[159] *Id.* at 26.

[160] A similar approach is taken by Arthur Leff, *Contract As A Thing*, 19 Am. U. L. Rev. 131 (1970). Professor Leff suggested that the law should look at standard form contracts much as it looks at goods. There should be "implied warranties" respecting the quality of a contract, much as there are respecting the quality of goods. Compare UCC § 2-314, discussed in section D.2.a. of this chapter, *infra*.

[161] Macneil, *supra* note 157, at 20–21.

[162] *See* Todd Rakoff, *Contracts of Adhesion: An Essay in Reconstruction*, 96 Harv. L. Rev. 1173, 1229, 1235, 1243 (1983).

C & J FERTILIZER, INC. v. ALLIED MUT. INS. CO.
Iowa Supreme Court
227 N.W.2d 169 (1975)

REYNOLDSON, J.

[handwritten margin note: Reversing dec for def.]

This action to recover for burglary loss under two separate insurance policies was tried to the court, resulting in a finding [that] plaintiff had failed to establish a burglary within the policy definitions. Plaintiff appeals from judgment entered for defendant. We reverse and remand.

Trial court made certain findings of fact in support of its conclusion reached. Plaintiff operated a fertilizer plant in Olds, Iowa. At time of loss, plaintiff was insured under policies issued by defendant and titled "BROAD FORM STORE-KEEPERS POLICY" and "MERCANTILE BURGLARY AND ROBBERY POLICY." Each policy defined "burglary" as meaning:

> . . . the felonious abstraction of insured property (1) from within the premises by a person making felonious entry therein by actual force and violence, of which force and violence there are visible marks made by tools, explosives, electricity, or chemicals upon, or physical damage to, the exterior of the premises at the place of such entry. . . .

On Saturday, April 18, 1970, all exterior doors to the building were locked when plaintiff's employees left the premises at the end of the business day. The following day, Sunday, April 19, 1970, one of plaintiff's employees was at the plant and found all doors locked and secure. On Monday, April 20, 1970, when the employees reported for work, the exterior doors were locked, but the front office door was unlocked.

There were truck tire tread marks visible in the mud in the driveway leading to and from the plexiglas door entrance to the warehouse. It was demonstrated this door could be forced open without leaving visible marks or physical damage.

[handwritten margin note: Basically the felon got in w/out visible damage to the exterior of building]

There were no visible marks on the exterior of the building made by tools, explosives, electricity, or chemicals, and there was no physical damage to the exterior of the building to evidence felonious entry into the building by force and violence.

Chemicals had been stored in an interior room of the warehouse. The door to this room, which had been locked, was physically damaged and carried visible marks made by tools. Chemicals had been taken at a net loss to plaintiff in the sum of $9,582. Office and shop equipment valued at $400.30 was also taken from the building.

Trial court held the policy definition of "burglary" was unambiguous, there was nothing in the record "upon which to base a finding that the door to plaintiff's place of business was entered feloniously, by actual force and violence," and, applying the policy language, found for defendant.

Certain other facts in the record were apparently deemed irrelevant by trial court because of its view [that] the applicable law required it to enforce the policy provision. Because we conclude different rules of law apply, we also consider those facts.

The "BROAD FORM STOREKEEPERS POLICY" was issued April 14, 1969; the "MERCANTILE BURGLARY AND ROBBERY POLICY" on April 14, 1970. Those policies are in evidence. Prior policies apparently were first purchased in 1968. The agent, who had power to bind insurance coverage for defendant, was told plaintiff would be handling farm chemicals. After inspecting the building then used by plaintiff for storage he made certain suggestions regarding security. There ensued a conversation in which he pointed out there had to be visible evidence of burglary. There was no testimony by anyone that plaintiff was then or thereafter informed [that] the policy to be delivered would define burglary to require "visible marks made by tools, explosives, electricity, or chemicals upon, or physical damage to, the exterior of the premises at the place of . . . entry."

The import of this conversation with defendant's agent when the coverage was sold is best confirmed by the agent's complete and vocally-expressed surprise when defendant denied coverage. From what the agent saw (tire tracks and marks on the interior of the building) and his contacts with the investigating officers ". . . the thought didn't enter my mind that it wasn't covered . . ." From the trial testimony it was obvious the only understanding was that there should be some hard evidence of a third-party burglary vis-a-vis an "inside job." The latter was in this instance effectively ruled out when the thief was required to break an interior door lock to gain access to the chemicals.

The agent testified the insurance was purchased and "the policy was sent out afterwards." The president of plaintiff corporation, a 37-year-old farmer with a high school education, looked at that portion of the policy setting out coverages, including coverage for burglary loss, the amounts of insurance, and the "location and description." He could not recall reading the fine print defining "burglary" on page three of the policy. . . .

Extrinsic evidence that throws light on the situation of the parties, the antecedent negotiations, the attendant circumstances and the objects they were thereby striving to attain is necessarily to be regarded as relevant to ascertain the actual significance and proper legal meaning of the agreement. . . .

The trial court never made a finding [that] there was or was not a burglary. We have noted its examination of the evidence was tailored to fit the policy "definition" of burglary: " 'Burglary' means the felonious abstraction of insured property (1) from within the premises by a person making felonious entry therein by actual force and violence, of which force and violence there are visible marks. . . ." (Emphasis supplied.)

Nor did trial court consider the evidence in light of the layman's concept of burglary (who might well consider a stealing intruder in his home or business premises as a burglar, whether or not the door was entered by force and violence) or the legal definition of burglary, hereinafter referred to. Trial court made no determination regarding burglary in those contexts.

Insofar as trial court was construing the policy — that being a matter of law for the court — we are not bound by its conclusions. . . . Neither are we bound by trial court's rule [that] this case is controlled by the fine print "definition" of burglary, if that rule was erroneously applied below. . . .

And if the definition of "burglary" in defendant's policy is not enforceable here, then trial court's finding [that] there was no evidence of forcible entry through an outside door is not controlling in the disposition of this case.

Plaintiff's theories of recovery based on "reasonable expectations," implied warranty, and unconscionability must be viewed in light of accelerating change in the field of contracts.

I. *Revolution in formation of contractual relationships.*

Many of our principles for resolving conflicts relating to written contracts were formulated at an early time when parties of equal strength negotiated in the historical sequence of offer, acceptance, and reduction to writing. The concept that both parties assented to the resulting document had solid footing in fact.

Only recently has the sweeping change in the inception of the document received widespread recognition:

> Standard form contracts probably account for more than 99 percent of all contracts now made. Most persons have difficulty remembering the last time they contracted other than by standard form; except for casual oral agreements, they probably never have. But if they are active, they contract by standard form several times a day. Parking lot and theater tickets, package receipts, department store charge slips, and gas station credit card purchase slips are all standard form contracts.

> . . . .

> The contracting still imagined by courts and law teachers as typical, in which both parties participate in choosing the language of their entire agreement, is no longer of much more than historical importance." W. David Slawson, *Standard Form Contracts and Democratic Control of Lawmaking Power*, 84 Harv. L. Rev. 529 (1971). . . .

It is generally recognized the insured will not read the detailed, cross-referenced, standardized, mass-produced insurance form, nor understand it if he does. 7 Williston on Contracts § 906B, p. 300 ("But where the document thus delivered to him is a contract of insurance the majority rule is that the insured is not bound to know its contents"); 3 Corbin on Contracts § 559, pp. 265–66 ("One who applies for an insurance policy . . . may not even read the policy, the number of its terms and the fineness of its print being such as to discourage him"); Note, *Unconscionable Contracts: The Uniform Commercial Code*, 45 Iowa L. Rev. 843, 844 (1960) ("It is probably a safe assertion that most involved standardized form contracts are never read by the party who 'adheres' to them. In such situations, the proponent of the form is free to dictate terms most advantageous to himself.") . . .

The concept that persons must obey public laws enacted by their own representatives does not offend a fundamental sense of justice: an inherent element of assent pervades the process.

But the inevitable result of enforcing all provisions of the adhesion contract, frequently, as here, delivered subsequent to the transaction and containing provisions never assented to, would be an abdication of judicial responsibility in face of basic unfairness and a recognition that persons' rights shall be controlled by private lawmakers without the consent, express or implied, of those affected. . . . A question is also raised whether a court may constitutionally allow that power to exist in private hands except where appropriate safeguards are present, including a right to meaningful judicial review. See W. David Slawson, *supra* at 553.

The statutory requirement that the form of policies be approved by the commissioner of insurance . . . neither resolves the issue whether the fine print provisions nullify the insurance bargained for in a given case nor ousts the court from necessary jurisdiction. . . . In this connection it has been pertinently stated:

> Insurance contracts continue to be contracts of adhesion, under which the insured is left little choice beyond electing among standardized provisions offered to him, even when the standard forms are prescribed by public officials rather than insurers. Moreover, although statutory and administrative regulations have made increasing inroads on the insurer's autonomy by prescribing some kinds of provisions and proscribing others, most insurance policy provisions are still drafted by insurers. Regulation is relatively weak in most instances, and even the provisions prescribed or approved by legislative or administrative action ordinarily are in essence adoptions, outright or slightly modified, of proposals made by insurers' draftsmen.

> Under such circumstances as these, judicial regulation of contracts of adhesion, whether concerning insurance or some other kind of transaction, remains appropriate. Keeton, *Insurance Law Rights At Variance With Policy Provisions*, 83 Harv. L. Rev. 961, 966–67 (1970). . . .

The mass-produced boilerplate "contracts," necessitated and spawned by the explosive growth of complex business transactions in a burgeoning population left courts frequently frustrated in attempting to arrive at just results by applying many of the traditional contract-construing stratagems. As long as 15 years ago Professor Llewellyn, reflecting on this situation in his book *The Common Law Tradition — Deciding Appeals*, wrote:

> What the story shows thus far is first, scholars persistently off-base while judges grope over well-nigh a century in irregular but dogged fashion for escape from a recurring discomfort of imbalance that rests on what is in fact substantial nonagreement despite perfect semblance of agreement. Karl Llewellyn, The Common Law Tradition — Deciding Appeals 367–68 (Little Brown & Co. 1960).

> . . . .

The answer, I suggest, is this: Instead of thinking about "assent" to boilerplate clauses, we can recognize that so far as concerns the specific, there is no assent at all. What has in fact been assented to, specifically, are the few dickered terms, and the broad type of transaction, and but one thing more. That one thing more is a blanket assent (not a specific assent) to any not unreasonable or indecent terms the seller may have on his form, which do not alter or eviscerate the reasonable meaning of the dickered terms. The fine print which has not been read has no business to cut under the reasonable meaning of those dickered terms which constitute the dominant and only real expression of agreement, but much of it commonly belongs in. *Id.* at 370.

In fairness to the often-discerned ability of the common law to develop solutions for changing demands, it should be noted appellate courts take cases as they come, constrained by issues the litigants formulated in trial court — a point not infrequently overlooked by academicians. Nor can a lawyer in the ordinary case be faulted for not risking a client's cause on an uncharted course when there is a reasonable prospect of reaching a fair result through familiar channels of long-accepted legal principles, for example, those grounded on ambiguity in language, the duty to define limitations or exclusions in clear and explicit terms, and interpretation of language from the viewpoint of an ordinary person, not a specialist or expert. . . .

Plaintiff's claim [that] it should be granted relief under the legal doctrines of reasonable expectations, implied warranty, and unconscionability should be viewed against the above backdrop.

II. Reasonable expectations.

This court adopted the doctrine of reasonable expectations in *Rodman v. State Farm Mutual Ins. Co.*, 208 N.W.2d 903, 905–08 (Iowa 1973). The *Rodman* court approved the following articulation of that concept: "The objectively reasonable expectations of applicants and intended beneficiaries regarding the terms of insurance contracts will be honored even though painstaking study of the policy provisions would have negated those expectations." *Id.* at 906.

At Comment F to § 237[163] of the Restatement (Second) of Contracts . . . we find the following analysis of the reasonable expectations doctrine:

> Although customers typically adhere to standardized agreements and are bound by them without even appearing to know the standard terms in detail, they are not bound to unknown terms which are beyond the range of reasonable expectation. A debtor who delivers a check to his creditor with the amount blank does not authorize the insertion of an infinite figure. Similarly, a party who adheres to the other party's standard terms does not assent to a term if the other party has reason to believe that the adhering party would not have accepted the agreement if he had known that the agreement contained the particular term. Such a belief or assumption may be shown by the prior negotiations or inferred from the circumstances. Reason to believe may be inferred from the fact that the term is bizarre or oppressive, from the fact that it eviscerates the non-standard terms explicitly agreed to, or from the fact that it eliminates the dominant

---

[163] [Eds. note: This citation is to the Tentative Draft of the RESTATEMENT (SECOND) OF CONTRACTS § 237, which became § 211 in the final version; this comment was rewritten, though to the same effect.]

purpose of the transaction. The inference is reinforced if the adhering party never had an opportunity to read the term, or if it is illegible or otherwise hidden from view. This rule is closely related to the policy against unconscionable terms and the rule of interpretation against the draftsman.

Nor can it be asserted the above doctrine does not apply here because plaintiff knew the policy contained the provision now complained of and cannot be heard to say it reasonably expected what it knew was not there. A search of the record discloses no such knowledge.

The evidence does show, as above noted, a "dicker" for burglary insurance coverage on chemicals and equipment. The negotiation was for what was actually expressed in the policies' "Insuring Agreements": the insurer's promise "To pay for loss by burglary or by robbery of a watchman, while the premises are not open for business, of merchandise, furniture, fixtures, and equipment within the premises. . . ."

In addition, the conversation included statements from which the plaintiff should have understood defendant's obligation to pay would not arise where the burglary was an "inside job." Thus the following exclusion should have been reasonably anticipated:

> Exclusions
>
> This policy does not apply: . . . (b) to loss due to any fraudulent, dishonest or criminal act by any Insured, a partner therein, or an officer, employee, director, trustee, or authorized representative thereof. . . .

But there was nothing relating to the negotiations with defendant's agent which would have led plaintiff to reasonably anticipate defendant would bury within the definition of "burglary" another exclusion denying coverage when, no matter how extensive the proof of a third-party burglary, no marks were left on the exterior of the premises. This escape clause, here triggered by the burglar's talent (an investigating law officer, apparently acquainted with the current *modus operandi*, gained access to the steel building without leaving any marks by leaning on the overhead plexiglas door while simultaneously turning the locked handle), was never read to or by plaintiff's personnel, nor was the substance explained by defendant's agent.

Moreover, the burglary "definition" which crept into this policy comports neither with the concept a layman might have of that crime, nor with a legal interpretation. *See State v. Murray*, 222 Iowa 925, 931, 270 N.W. 355, 358 (1936) ("We have held that even though the door was partially open, by opening it farther, in order to enter the building, this is a sufficient breaking to comply with the demands of the statute"); *State v. Ferguson*, 149 Iowa 476, 478–79, 128 N.W. 840, 841–42 (1910) ("It need not appear that this office was an independent building, for it is well known that it is burglary for one to break and enter an inner door or window, although the culprit entered through an open outer door. . . ."); *see State v. Hougland*, 197 N.W.2d 364, 365 (Iowa 1972).

The most plaintiff might have reasonably anticipated was a policy requirement of visual evidence (abundant here) indicating the burglary was an "outside" not an "inside" job. The exclusion in issue, masking as a definition, makes insurer's obligation to pay turn on the skill of the burglar, not on the event the parties bargained for: a bona fide third-party burglary resulting in loss of plaintiff's chemicals and equipment.

The "reasonable expectations" attention to the basic agreement, to the concept of substance over form, was appropriately applied by this court for the insurer's benefit in *Central Bearings Co. v. Wolverine Insurance Company*, 179 N.W.2d 443 (Iowa 1970), a case antedating *Rodman*. We there reversed a judgment for the insured which trial court apparently grounded on a claimed ambiguity in the policy. In denying coverage on what was essentially a products liability claim where the insured purchased only a "Premises-Operations" policy (without any misrepresentation, misunderstanding or overreaching) we said at page 449 of 179 N.W.2d:

> In summation we think the insured as a reasonable person would understand the policy coverage purchased meant the insured was not covered for loss if the "accident" with concomitant damage to a victim occurred away from the premises and after the operation or sale was complete.

The same rationale of reasonable expectations should be applied when it would operate to the advantage of the insured. Appropriately applied to this case, the doctrine demands reversal and judgment for plaintiff.

[The court went on to consider, and apply, doctrines of implied warranty and unconscionability. Both of these doctrines will be discussed later in these materials. After you have read the materials on implied warranty and unconscionability you should return to this case and consider how you believe they might be applicable.]

We reverse and remand for judgment in conformance herewith. . . .

LeGrand, Justice (dissenting). I dissent from the result reached by the majority because it ignores virtually every rule by which we have heretofore adjudicated such cases and affords plaintiff *ex post facto* insurance coverage which it not only did not buy but which it knew it did not buy. . . .

While it may be very well to talk in grand terms about "mass advertising" by insurance companies and "incessant" assurances as to coverage which mislead the "unwary," particularly about "fine-print" provisions, such discussion should somehow be related to the case under review. Our primary duty, after all, is to resolve this dispute for these litigants under this record.

There is total silence in this case concerning any of the practices the majority finds offensive; nor is there any claim plaintiff was beguiled by such conduct into believing it had more protection than it actually did.

The record is even stronger against the majority's fine-print argument, the stereotype accusation which serves as a coup de grace in all insurance cases. Except for larger type on the face sheet and black (but not larger) print to designate divisions and sub-headings, the entire policies are of one size and style of print. . . .

Nor can the doctrine of reasonable expectations be applied here. We adopted that rule in *Rodman v. State Farm Mutual Automobile Insurance Company*, 208 N.W.2d 903, 906, 907 (Iowa 1973). We refused, however to apply it in that case, where we said:

> The real question here is whether the principle of reasonable expectations should be extended to cases where an ordinary layman would not misunderstand his coverage from a reading of the policy and where there are no circumstances attributable to the insurer which foster coverage expectations. Plaintiff does not contend he misunderstood the policy. He did not read it. He now asserts in retrospect that if he had read it he would not have understood it. He does not say he was misled by conduct or representations of the insurer. He simply asked the trial court to rewrite the policy to cover his loss because if he had purchased his automobile insurance from another company the loss would have been covered, he did not know it was not covered, and if he had known it was not covered he would have purchased a different policy. The trial court declined to do so. We believe the trial court correctly refused in these circumstances to extend the principle of reasonable expectations to impose liability.

Yet here the majority would extend the doctrine far beyond the point of refusal in *Rodman*. Here we have affirmative and unequivocal testimony from an officer and director of the plaintiff corporation that he knew the disputed provision was in the policies because "it was just like the insurance policy I have on my farm."

I cannot agree plaintiff may now assert it reasonably expected from these policies something it knew was not there.

[The dissent went on to reject the majority's application of both the implied warranty and unconscionability theories.]

NOTES AND QUESTIONS

1. ***Applications to areas other than insurance:*** Can we apply the approach of the *C & J Fertilizer* case to form contracts in areas other than insurance? In *Elliott Leases Cars, Inc. v. Quigley*, the Supreme Court of Rhode Island extended it to a lease of an automobile.[164] John Quigley, in his capacity as president of Rhode Island Buckle, Inc., leased an automobile from Elliott. The wife of an officer of the corporation drove the car with her husband's permission. She had an accident caused by her negligence. Elliott Leases Cars sued her for the total cost of repairing the car. She denied liability, asserting that the lease required Elliott to provide collision insurance for her benefit. The trial court, relying on an explicit provision in the contract, ruled there was no obligation to provide collision insurance for her benefit. Defendant was found liable. The Supreme Court of Rhode Island reversed. Two justices dissented.

Elliott Leases Cars used two forms for its leasing. One was an "Automobile Leasing Order." It was a single-page summary of the transaction. It contained a list of 18 items that were followed by a check mark in one of two columns. The first was headed "HERE IS WHAT ELLIOTT PROVIDES," and the second, "HERE IS WHAT CUSTOMER PAYS FOR." Included in items to be paid for by Elliott was

---

[164] 373 A.2d 810 (R.I. 1977).

"ACCIDENT REPAIRS — 100/deduct — Due to Collision (or Upset) per Accident." The second document was the formal lease. It consisted of 28 provisions in small print covering two full pages. Clause 2 required the lessee to pay for any loss or damage to the automobile caused by negligence.

The majority said that courts construe ambiguous or conflicting provisions against the author of those provisions. Its opinion said:

> It is common knowledge, and so should have been known to plaintiff, that the detailed provisions of insurance contracts are seldom read by consumers. *C & J Fertilizer, Inc. v. Allied Mut. Ins. Co.* . . . The plaintiff should have known that the leasing order, which was a simple, highly readable summary of the transaction, would be relied upon by its customers. The plaintiff could easily have avoided any ambiguity in the contract, and hence avoided creating a reasonable expectation of coverage, by noting the exclusion of negligence on the face of the leasing order.[165]

The dissent argued that the rule of construction against the drafter was a rule of last resort. There was no reason to extend the rules governing insurance to routine form contracts in common everyday use. The opinion continued:[166]

> [T]he majority's expressed solicitude for consumers is irrelevant to the resolution of this case. In particular, their statement that "the detailed provisions of insurance contracts are seldom read by consumers" is strikingly inapposite to the present context. I repeat that this is not an insurance contract. It is a commercial automobile lease, signed by a businessman — who presumably had his eyes open when he signed it — in his capacity as a corporate president. I would hold him to his bargain. . . .

The *Elliot Leases Cars* case is an exception. For the most part, courts have not extended the doctrine of reasonable expectations beyond insurance cases. A well-known exception is Arizona, where a line of cases have extended the doctrine to all form contracts. When an attempt was made in the drafting of a proposed revised Article 2 to interject the Arizona approach into the UCC, there were strong objections from many seller groups. The drafting effort has been abandoned.

2. ***Reasonable expectations in Arizona:*** Arizona has more state court decisions using the reasonable expectations doctrine than any other state. The leading case is *Darner Motor Sales, Inc. v. Universal Underwriters Ins. Co.*,[167] an insurance case in which the insurance agent allegedly assured the insured business that its automotive leasing customers had coverage up to a certain level that the insurer later denied, based on policy terms. The court held that the insured had a valid cause of action based on the reasonable expectations doctrine. The insured's principal admitted never reading the policy, saying "it's like reading a book" and stating that, following his conversations with the insurance agent assuring him of coverage, "I didn't think I needed to." Darner's office manager testified that she never really read the policy either and saw little need to do so in view of the fact that

---

[165] *Id.* at 813.

[166] *Id.* at 816.

[167] 140 Ariz. 383, 682 P.2d 388 (1984).

the insurance agent "would occasionally appear, remove pages from the loose-leaf binder and insert new pages." *Darner* is a classic case of conflict between boilerplate and oral assurances, albeit assurances to a business, not a consumer.

Another important Arizona case is *Broemmer v. Abortion Services of Phoenix, Ltd.*,[168] which did not involve insurance. Rather, a 21-year-old patient signed an agreement to arbitrate before an ob-gyn and then suffered a punctured uterus during her abortion procedure. The Court held that the plaintiff, who was under competing pressures from her parents and boyfriend at the time of the procedure, had no reasonable expectation that a medical malpractice claim would be subject to arbitration. She was not orally advised to the contrary as in *Darner*, but the court found that the abortion clinic did not adequately inform her that she was giving up her right to trial by jury in the event of medical malpractice. Which of these two cases, *Darner* or *Broemmer*, involves a broader application of the reasonable expectations doctrine? *Darner* involved insurance of a business and an agent's representation contrary to the policy, while *Broemmer* involved a consumer who was not given advice contrary to the form contract, although she was in a high-stress situation when she signed an "arbitration agreement." She later said that she was still not sure what arbitration is.

3. ***The insurance context and mass disaster:*** Insurance cases remain the most promising for use of the reasonable expectations doctrine, on the theory that a customer buys coverage of losses, not a lawsuit over technical and counterintuitive policy exclusions. Of course, insurance companies base their prices on risk assessment, and having to cover a risk they did not accurately anticipate can be devastating. A recent example occurred in the aftermath of Hurricane Katrina, which caused widespread property damage, in addition to loss of life, in New Orleans and nearby parts of the Gulf Coast. In his book *The Ascent of Money*,[169] Niall Ferguson tells the story of several insurance companies who had insured wind damage to property but not flood damage. They denied nearly all Katrina-related claims, despite indications that most of the damage was caused by wind hours before the flooding began. The insurers cited a nearly inscrutable fine-print policy exclusion for flooding "whether other causes acted concurrently or in a sequence with the excluded event to produce the loss . . . " In other words, they took the position that because the loss from wind was in a sequence with loss from flooding, the wind damage was not covered. Richard F. Scruggs, a lawyer once known as the "King of Torts" because of his successful litigation against tobacco companies, set up his "Scruggs Katrina Group" to sue on behalf of those denied coverage, but his efforts collapsed when he and several associates were indicted on charges of trying to bribe a judge.

4. ***Reaching the desired result by construction of the meaning of contracts:*** Even if we assume that particular provisions in a contract are valid, courts then must determine what those provisions mean. The proper interpretation frequently is not obvious. Where contract terms are deemed ambiguous, there may be room for a court to favor the interpretation that produces what it sees as the fair result.

---

[168]   173 Ariz. 148, 840 P.2d 1013 (1992).

[169]   NIALL FERGUSON, THE ASCENT OF MONEY: A FINANCIAL HISTORY OF THE WORLD 177–83 (Penguin 2008).

Sometimes, when courts want to avoid a particular result, they strive mightily to find ambiguity where none would seem evident. Then they construe the "ambiguous" provision in the contract so as to avoid the result they deem unfair.

The classic illustration of creative interpretation to avoid an undesired result is in Shakespeare's *Merchant of Venice*. We left the story hanging in Chapter 2 of these materials. As you will recall, Shylock sued to enforce his bond. It called for Antonio to forfeit one pound of flesh upon non-payment of his debt. Shylock rejected the Court's plea to be merciful. Then Portia appeared on the scene, disguised as a doctor of laws. She was the newly won wife of Bassanio, Antonio's good friend. She was, however, so effectively disguised that nobody recognized her. The Court permitted her to conduct the proceedings, assuming her to be an expert in such matters.[170]

> Shylock. *My deeds upon my head! I crave the law.*
> *The penalty and forfeit of my bond.*
>
> Portia. *Is he not able to discharge the money?*
>
> Bassanio. *Yes, here I tender it for him in the court;*
>
>   . . . .
>
> *Wrest once the law to your authority:*
> *To do a great right, do a little wrong,*
> *And curb this cruel devil of his will.*
>
> Portia. *It must not be. There is no power in Venice*
> *Can alter a decree established:*
> *'Twill be recorded for a precedent,*
> *And many an error by the same example*
> *Will rush into the state. It cannot be.*
>
> Shylock. *A Daniel come to judgment! yea, a Daniel!*
> *O wise young judge, how I do honor thee!*
>
> Portia. *I pray you, let me look upon the bond.*
>
> Shylock. *Here 'tis, most reverend doctor; here it is.*
>
>   . . . .
>
> Portia. *Why, this bond is forfeit;*
> *And lawfully by this the Jew may claim*
> *A pound of flesh, to be by him cut off*
> *Nearest the merchant's heart. Be merciful:*
> *Take thrice thy money; bid me tear the bond.*
>
> Shylock. *When it is paid according to the tenor,*
> *It doth appear you are a worthy judge;*
> *You know the law, your exposition*
> *Hath been most sound: I charge you by the law,*
> *Whereof you are a well-deserving pillar,*

---

[170] William Shakespeare, The Merchant of Venice, act 4, sc. 1, ll. 2147–2263.

Proceed to judgment: by my soul I swear
There is no power in the tongue of man
To alter me. I stay here on my bond.

. . . .

Portia. *For, the intent and purpose of the law*
Hath full relation to the penalty,
Which here appeareth due upon the bond.

Shylock. *'Tis very true! O wise and upright judge!*
How much more elder art thou than thy looks!

Portia. *Therefore lay bare your bosom.*
Shylock. *Ay, 'his breast:'*
So says the bond: — doth it not, noble judge? —
'Nearest his heart': those are the very words.

Portia. *It is so. Are there balance here to weigh*
The flesh?

. . . .

Portia. *A pound of that same merchant's flesh is thine:*
The court awards it, and the law doth give it.

Shylock. *Most rightful judge!*

Portia. *And you must cut this flesh from off his breast:*
The law allows it, and the court awards it.

Shylock. *Most learned judge! A sentence! Come, prepare!*

Portia. *Tarry a little: there is something else.*
This bond doth give thee here no jot of blood;
The words expressly are 'a pound of flesh':
Take then thy bond, take thou thy pound of flesh:
But in the cutting it, if thou dost shed
One drop of Christian blood, thy lands and goods
Are, by the laws of Venice, confiscate
Unto the state of Venice.

Gratiano. [a friend of Antonio] *O upright judge!*

Mark, Jew: *O learned judge!*

Shylock. *Is that the law?*

Portia. *Thyself shalt see the act:*
For, as thou urgest justice, be assur'd
Thou shalt have justice, more than thou desir'st.

At this point Shylock abandoned his suit for enforcement of the bond, but the judicial proceeding transformed from a civil suit into a criminal prosecution of Shylock, and led to his impoverishment and forced conversion. For these further developments of the story you will have to see or read the play. We confine ourselves here to the "contractual" aspect of the proceeding.

Portia purports to interpret the contract provision, and her reading of the bond is literal. However, if the purpose of contract interpretation is to discern the intention of the parties at the time the contract was made, she misinterpreted it. Bassanio beseeched Portia "To do a great right, do a little wrong." Portia responded: "It must not be." But did it be? Was the result consistent with the expectations of Antonio and Shylock when they arranged the loan? Would Shylock have given Antonio credit on the security of a pound of flesh without the right to draw blood? Did Antonio have any reason to think Shylock would?[171]

If Portia misinterpreted the contract, then courts have followed her example many times since. This is particularly true when the contract is a printed standard form and a court sees the parties as unequal in bargaining power. Professor Karl Llewellyn wrote vividly about such contract reading, grouping it with a number of other techniques for reaching the right result. He wrote that:[172]

> First, since they [such techniques] all rest on the admission that the clauses in question are permissible in purpose and content, they invite the draftsman to recur to the attack. Give him time, and he will make the grade. Second, since they do not face the issue, they fail to accumulate either experience or authority in the needed direction: that of marking out for any given type of transaction what the minimum decencies are [that] a court will insist upon as essential to an enforceable bargain of a given type, or as being inherent in a bargain of that type. Third, since they purport to construe, and do not really construe, nor are intended to, . . . they seriously embarrass later efforts . . . to get at the true meaning of those wholly legitimate contracts and clauses which call for their meaning to be got at instead of avoided. . . .
>
> Covert tools are never reliable tools.

When Llewellyn drafted Article 2 of the Uniform Commercial Code, he sought to provide reliable tools to deal with problems such as those posed by standard form contracts. In the next sections we will have occasion to judge his skill as a tool maker.

D. WARRANTY, DISCLAIMERS, AND REMEDY LIMITATIONS: THE UCC PATTERN

1. Warranties as a Tool to Guard Expectations

Legislatures and courts regulate the quality of goods or services supplied by sellers through the legal device called *warranty*. Sometimes sellers make detailed promises about the quality of the goods they will deliver under a contract. For

---

[171] *See* RUDOLF VON JHERING, THE STRUGGLE FOR LAW 76–78, 86–88, 1–1ii (Lalor trans. 1915) ("[T]he Jew is cheated out of his legal right . . . True, it is done in the interest of humanity, but does chicanery cease to be chicanery because it is practiced in the name of humanity?").

[172] Karl Llewellyn, Book Review, 52 HARV. L. REV. 700, 701–03 (1939).

example, a seller may explicitly promise that a machine will produce a given number of units per hour or is free from defects in workmanship and materials. Often, however, contracts for the sale of goods have few, if any, express provisions about quality. Furthermore, they say nothing about the buyer's rights and the seller's duties if there are problems with the goods. What happens then? The law could say that it is up to the buyer to bargain for express guarantees. It could rule that in the absence of express provisions concerning quality, the buyer takes the product "as is" and "with all faults." However, whatever the virtues of this hard-line position, it would fly in the face of the ways sellers promote their products. The seller works hard to create buyers' expectations that seller produces high-quality goods. Advertisements and salespersons' statements attempt to affect buyers' views of quality. Expectations arise, though they differ depending on the circumstances and are not the same with respect to new, as opposed to used, goods.

While we find warranties elsewhere, their usual territory is sales of goods. Courts have long held sellers of goods to some duty to provide products of at least minimal quality. Often judges talked of implied promises flowing from the buyer's reasonable expectations in a particular transaction. More skeptical writers argue that warranties are imposed promises, enforced for reasons of policy. Social control of contract is still the topic before us. Traditionally, courts did not hold sellers of real estate to warrant the quality of the buildings involved. As we've noted in the materials on misrepresentation, courts in some states hold commercial sellers of real estate to warrant at least a minimum quality. Judges may be imposing regulation on transactions between professionals and amateurs. Contracts for services may not involve warranties as such, although many service providers disclaim implied warranties, just in case. At any rate, courts must often interpret the obligations assumed when the parties dispute whether the one providing services has defectively performed. In this section, we will focus on warranties in sales of goods.

As you now know, sales of goods are governed by Article 2 of the Uniform Commercial Code. You can best understand the UCC warranty scheme, explained below, by trying to solve a problem. What do the materials in this section say about the solution of the XYZ v. ABC case, below? (This is a difficult problem. You should read UCC §§ 2-313, 2-314, 2-315, 2-316, 2-317, 2-714(2), and 2-719.)

ABC Manufacturing Company (ABC) makes and sells production machinery ordered by its customers. XYZ Widget Co., Inc. (XYZ) negotiated with ABC, seeking a contract to buy a production machine capable of converting "R-grade" steel into widget frames. Representatives of the firms reached agreement. An ABC engineer wrote the order on a form document written by ABC's lawyers. On the form he described the machine sold as a "widget frame stamping machine capable of using 'R-grade' steel, produced according to the plans and specifications attached to this document." ABC's engineers prepared these plans and specifications for this contract after lengthy negotiations with XYZ's engineers. At the bottom of the form document, just above the line for XYZ's signature, the following printed language appeared: "ABC agrees to replace all defective parts for 30 days, without charge for parts or labor, which shall be the exclusive remedy if any part is defective. There are NO OTHER REPRESENTATIONS OR

WARRANTIES, express or implied, accompanying this sale. This contract is the final and complete expression of the parties' agreement." Authorized representatives of both ABC and XYZ signed the form.

ABC manufactured the machine and delivered it to XYZ within the time specified in the contract. XYZ paid the full purchase price upon delivery. XYZ installed the machine properly and attempted to stamp widget frames using R-grade steel. It soon discovered that the machine was not capable of stamping acceptable widget frames from R-grade steel. XYZ cannot use a different grade of steel in its product. XYZ immediately notified ABC that the machine was defective, and it explained the problem in detail. XYZ asked ABC to honor its warranty. ABC sent a representative to XYZ's factory, and she inspected the machine. Based on her report, ABC refused to accept return of the machine or to repair it. ABC explained that it had built the machine according to plans and specifications (which nowhere contained a requirement that the machine be capable of using R-grade steel), and there were no defective parts. Both parties now agree that no machine manufactured according to the plans and specifications attached to their contract could stamp acceptable widget frames from R-grade steel. To use R-grade steel, the machine would need higher-quality parts. These parts have slightly different measurements from the parts they would replace, so repair of the existing widget frame stamping machine is not possible. Only a completely new machine could use R-grade steel.

XYZ sued ABC for the price of the machine. XYZ also claimed as damages its lost profits for the time it had taken a third company to manufacture a widget frame stamping machine that would meet its needs. How likely is it that XYZ will win the remedies it seeks? What will it argue? How will ABC defend?[173]

2. Warranties, Express and Implied

The Uniform Commercial Code attempts to balance the expectations of buyers with the freedom of sellers to limit the risks they assume in putting products on the market. Several sections deal with creating express and implied warranties. These focus on the buyer's expectations. Nonetheless, you may detect some social control of contract as well. Then the Code attempts to regulate how a seller can disclaim warranties or limit the remedies a buyer may have for any defect in the goods. Lawyers must work with many interrelated Code sections in order to make a technically adequate argument.

a. The buyer's expectations and fair dealing: creating warranties

Sellers may make express or implied warranties when they sell goods. First, § 2-313(1) says sellers create express warranties in a number of ways:

---

[173] One of the authors of these materials sketched some notes on this problem. His answer ran seven single-spaced typed pages. Much is concealed in these three innocent paragraphs.

(a) Any affirmation of fact or promise made by the seller to the buyer which relates to the goods and becomes part of the basis of the bargain creates an express warranty that the goods shall conform to the affirmation or promise.

(b) Any description of the goods which is made part of the basis of the bargain creates an express warranty that the goods shall conform to the description.

(c) Any sample or model which is made part of the basis of the bargain creates an express warranty that the whole of the goods shall conform to the sample or model.

On the other hand, subsection (2) says "an affirmation merely of the value of the goods or a statement purporting to be merely the seller's opinion or commendation of the goods does not create a warranty."

What does this mean? If seller states that a car gets better than 35 miles per gallon on the highway, it has breached a warranty if the car gets only 25 miles per gallon. (On the other hand, EPA fuel-efficiency measures of miles per gallon are based on ideal conditions and are required under federal law, so that a customer who gets mileage per gallon that is less than an EPA rating does not have a strong case for breach of warranty.) If seller promises to deliver a brand-new Chevrolet four-door sedan, it cannot perform by delivering a used Chevrolet station wagon. The UCC makes it clear that this liability does not turn on the use of the word "warranty" or the intention of the seller to back its goods. However, statements such as "I could sell this car for more than I'm asking," "I think the car ought to get around 35 miles per gallon," or "This is a fine automobile" do not create express warranties. Absent effective disclaimers, sellers are bound by affirmations of fact, promises, and descriptions of the goods. They are not bound by opinions and statements commending the goods.

The Code goes further and says sellers can make implied warranties, too. Under § 2-314, merchant sellers impliedly warrant that goods are "merchantable." The definition of merchantability has six factors. Probably the two most important are that the goods "pass without objection in the trade under the contract description" and also "are fit for the ordinary purposes for which such goods are used."

The other important implied warranty is "fitness for particular purpose." Section 2-315 tells us that sellers who know "any particular purpose for which the goods are required and that the buyer is relying on the seller's skill or judgment to select or furnish suitable goods" make such a warranty.

Again, all this seems designed to protect the likely expectations of a reasonable buyer. However, we might also justify imposing warranties to police the fairness of transactions. Courts may preserve the integrity of the market by allowing buyers to trust sellers rather than demanding to have everything spelled out in detail. For example, suppose a used car dealer contracts to sell a one-year-old Jeep. The implied warranty of merchantability allows the buyer to rely on getting whatever "passes without objection in the trade" under that description. Suppose the Jeep that is tendered lacks effective brakes. A court might hold that the Jeep does not comply with the implied warranty of merchantability because the court believes it is undesirable for cars in an unsafe condition to be sold without explicit warning to the buyer. A court might so hold even though a typical buyer might have no opinion about whether a used car with unsafe brakes "passes without objection in the trade." In other words, it may be that more than the buyer's expectation is being protected. Furthermore, a car without effective brakes is not fit for driving in ordinary ways, so it is not fit for the ordinary purposes for which cars are used.

b. The seller's free contract and fair dealing — warranty disclaimers and remedy limitations

So far, so good. Sellers must honor their buyers' reasonable expectations, and perhaps social concerns about fair dealing in the marketplace. But the Code's drafters also wanted to honor free contract. Sellers ought to be able to limit their obligations so they can control costs and buyers should be able to accept risks in exchange for lower prices. And what of those sellers who create expectations that the goods are of high quality and then hide clauses in form contracts contradicting those understandings? Again, we face the problem of the conflict between the real deal and the paper deal. The drafters tried to balance the competing interests by saying that sellers could tailor their liability, but they had to do so "conspicuously," so buyers would have a fighting chance to understand just what they were buying. Whether the drafters succeeded in the latter objective is the subject of debate. In addition, the drafters may have introduced some direct regulation, restricting some remedy limitations no matter how conspicuously disclosed by the seller.

How did the drafters of the UCC attempt to regulate limitations of liability? By creating a distinction between a clause that *disclaims* warranties and one that grants warranties but *limits remedies*. Many find this distinction confusing. But the difference is critical to understanding the Code's regulation of the risks of selling goods. Section 2-316 governs exclusion or modification of warranties. Section 2-719 deals with modification or limitation of remedies. The tests differ. As a result, a lawyer must first classify a contract clause as either a disclaimer or a remedy limitation to consider whether it is valid.

For example, suppose a farmer sells a 1938 Packard, which has been in the barn for years, to a buyer who restores old cars. The farmer has been to law school. He tells the buyer that the Packard is being sold "as is," and "with all flaws and faults." Furthermore, he makes clear that he does not know anything about its mechanical condition. In the Code's terms, the seller has disclaimed all warranties. He is refusing expressly to guarantee anything about the quality of the remains of the Packard. The farmer has disclaimed any warranties under UCC § 2-316(3)(a).

Alternatively, suppose a buyer purchases a new Chevrolet from a dealer. General Motors makes a number of promises about the quality of the automobile. These are warranties, and GM does not try to disclaim them. However, suppose it provides in the contract that within 50,000 miles or five years it will replace or repair defective parts or workmanship on the drive train of the car. After the car has been driven for that distance or time, General Motors' obligations cease. The contract also provides that buyer may not recover consequential damages for loss of the use of the car. GM has made a warranty, but it has limited the remedy for its breach. Whether courts would enforce this limitation would turn on all three subsections of UCC § 2-719.

Just to make things more confusing, lawyers often draft remedy limitations in the form of warranty disclaimers. For example, a fairly common clause provides that "seller will replace or repair defective items for one year from the date of delivery. There are no other warranties, either express or implied." Literally, the first clause says nothing about warranty.[174] Promising to replace and repair defective goods for a year is a statement about remedy. This language attempts to say that the buyer gets one remedy for a limited time and no other. Yet the seller called the clause a warranty and said there were no other ones. Could a court interpret such a clause as not disclaiming any warranties? Go back and reread the ABC/XYZ problem (and your answer), above. Do you see the problem(s)?

c.   The necessary steps

We can summarize this discussion by stressing the logical structure of these provisions of the UCC. There is a series of steps, and lawyers must take them in order. Sections or subsections of the UCC do not exist in isolation. We repeat to emphasize the point — there is a series of steps, and you must take them in order:

First, lawyers must decide whether, absent disclaimers, the seller gave any warranties. If there is a warranty, you must classify it. Is it an express or an implied warranty? If it is an implied warranty, is it one of merchantability or fitness for particular purpose? (Express and implied warranties also may overlap or conflict. We sort this out by applying § 2-317.) Of course there can be more than one type of warranty; a contract might contain four express warranties and an implied warranty of merchantability, for example.

Second, lawyers must consider whether the type of warranty given has been disclaimed successfully. We test disclaimers of express warranties against § 2-316(1). Sections 2-316(2) and (3) control disclaimers of implied warranties.

Finally, lawyers must ask whether a seller has effectively limited remedies for the breach of any warranties not successfully disclaimed, under § 2-719.

As you might expect after some experience with the Code, this outline of simple steps conceals many difficult issues. To resolve them, lawyers must refer to many other Code sections that we have not discussed here. Whatever its virtues, the Code's analysis of warranty is complex and calls for first-class lawyering skills.[175] If matters were not difficult enough, warranties in consumer transactions add other layers of complexity. There are federal and state statutes and regulations that add to and subtract from the UCC's approach, some of which we will elaborate on below.

You may find much of this discussion abstract and difficult to follow. It should make more sense after you consider some cases that present actual transactions and try your hand at the ABC/XYZ problem, if you have not done so already.

---

[174] We could read the language as promising impliedly that the goods are not defective. If a court accepts this interpretation, there is an express warranty that the goods are not defective, under UCC § 2-313.

[175] For an indication of the complexity and challenges, *see* Charles J. Goetz *et al.*, *Article Two Warranties in Commercial Transactions: An Update*, 72 Cornell L. Rev. 1159 (1987) (a 167-page analysis of UCC warranty problems).

3. Conspicuous Disclaimers and Conscionable Remedy Limitations

HUNT v. PERKINS MACHINERY CO., INC.
Massachusetts Supreme Judicial Court
352 Mass. 535, 226 N.E.2d 228 (1967)

CUTTER, J.

Hunt, an experienced commercial fisherman, got in touch with the defendant (Perkins), a distributor of Caterpillar Tractor Company's products. He was considering the purchase of a diesel engine for his fishing boat. In the fall of 1960, Perkins's sales manager, one Rideout, went to Hunt's house in Orleans to acquaint him with the various Caterpillar diesel engines available. At Rideout's suggestion, Hunt went to Maine to look at a boat equipped with such an engine. In January 1961, Hunt signed a purchase order for one Caterpillar Model D330 engine with a 1.2 to 1 reduction gear (instead of one reduction gear ordinarily supplied by the manufacturer) and certain specified accessories. The written portion of the purchase order was prepared (except for the signatures) by Rideout. It was on a "pad of paper containing several copies separated by carbon paper."

Hunt did not read anything on the back of the order when he signed it. "The original and all . . . copies of the . . . [o]rder were taken by Rideout . . . for signature by an official" of Perkins. Hunt received a fully executed copy of the order by mail a few days later.

The face of the purchase order contains a statement of the property sold, acknowledgment of a $500 deposit, a statement of the balance ($4,095) due, and certain miscellaneous information. In the center of the face of the order in bold face type capitals appears the statement "BOTH THIS ORDER AND ITS ACCEPTANCE ARE SUBJECT TO 'TERMS AND CONDITIONS' STATED IN THIS ORDER." On the reverse side of the order at the top in the same bold face type capitals appear the words "TERMS AND CONDITIONS." Underneath those words there are 11 numbered paragraphs. Included among the numbered paragraphs are those set out in the margin.[176]

After Hunt had received his executed copy of the order, he took his boat to

---

[176] [1] The relevant terms and conditions are the following: "1. *Acceptance.* This order is subject to acceptance by Seller only at Seller's place of business in Massachusetts and shall become a binding contract only when a copy has been accepted in writing and . . . returned to Buyer. 2. *All Agreements.* This written order when accepted by Seller shall be the . . . exclusive statement of all terms of the agreement between the parties other than such additional agreements as may be contained in any contracts, notes, or other documents specified herein. No representations of any kind have been made except as set forth in this order or in the other documents specified herein. 3. WARRANTIES. SELLER MAKES NO WARRANTIES (INCLUDING . . . ANY WARRANTIES AS TO MERCHANTABILITY OR FITNESS) EITHER EXPRESS OR IMPLIED WITH RESPECT TO THE PROPERTY UNLESS ENDORSED HEREON IN WRITING. BUYER SHALL BE LIMITED TO THE WARRANTIES OF THE RESPECTIVE MANUFACTURERS OF THE PRODUCTS SOLD. . . . 6. *Limitation of Liability.* Seller shall not be liable for any property damage or for any . . . injuries . . . suffered in connection with the operation or installation of the [p]roperty. . . ."

Plymouth Marine Railway (Marine) to have it prepared for the new engine. Seven or eight days later Hunt by telephone learned from Rideout that there would be a delay in delivery. Rideout then told Hunt that he could tear up the contract and forget the engine if he wanted to do so. Hunt decided to go through with the purchase because his boat was already at Marine and the old engine had been removed.

The engine was delivered to Marine on March 6, 1961, and was thereafter installed in the boat by Marine. This installation work included everything that was necessary to connect the engine, with the exception of the initial starting. That was done by employees of Perkins. Marine was not connected with, nor acting for, Perkins at any time. Its work was not controlled by Perkins. It was engaged by and paid by Hunt.

After the engine was installed a series of mechanical problems arose, each of which was corrected by Perkins at no expense to Hunt other than the time involved while the repairs were being made. The engine, when running, gave off excessive quantities of heavy black smoke, which caused the boat to become dirty, inside and out, and rendered Hunt's work on the boat unpleasant. This condition persisted until the removal of the engine. At Hunt's request Perkins, on several occasions and by a variety of means, attempted without success to curtail the smoking.

About July 20, 1961, the engine was removed by Hunt and put on the dock at Marine's plant. Hunt called Perkins and reported that he had removed the engine and advised Perkins to get it. The engine is still on Marine's premises.

In July 1961, Hunt purchased a new engine from another manufacturer. This new engine has performed satisfactorily.

Hunt's evidence of damages consisted of a showing of cash payments to Marine of $761.49 for installation work and testimony that he lost $250 each day when he was prevented from fishing as a result of Perkins' work on the boat. Perkins worked on the boat on about 10 different occasions between the installation of the engine and June 1961.

The trial judge denied motions for directed verdicts in this action in two counts, count 1 for breach of an implied warranty of merchantability and count 2 for breach of an implied warranty of fitness for a particular purpose. The jury returned verdicts for $5,357. Perkins brings before us exceptions to the denial of directed verdicts and to the judge's refusal to order verdicts entered for Perkins under leave reserved. There was evidence from which the facts stated above could have been found.

1. This case presents issues under the Uniform Commercial Code . . . concerning excluding or modifying (a) the implied warranty of merchantability under . . . § 2-314, and (b) the implied warranty under . . . § 2-315, that goods shall be fit for a particular purpose. Section 2-316(2) reads, in part: "(2) . . . [T]o exclude or modify the implied warranty of merchantability or any part of it the language must mention merchantability and in case of a writing must be conspicuous, and to exclude or modify any implied warranty of fitness the exclusion must be by a writing and conspicuous. Language to exclude all implied warranties of fitness is sufficient if it states, for example, that 'There are no warranties which extend beyond the

description on the face hereof' " (emphasis supplied). Section 2-316(2) must be read with § 1-201(10), which provides, in part: " 'Conspicuous': A term . . . is conspicuous when it is so written that a reasonable person against whom it is to operate ought to have noticed it. A printed heading in capitals (as: NON-NEGOTIABLE BILL OF LADING) is conspicuous. Language in the body of a form is 'conspicuous' if it is in larger or other contrasting type of color. . . . Whether a term or clause is 'conspicuous' . . . is for decision by the court" (emphasis supplied). . . . The first question for decision is whether the disclaimer of the warranties on the back of this purchase order was "conspicuous."

Some light is shed upon the meaning of "conspicuous" in § 1-201(10) by the official comment on the subsection, which says in part, "This is intended to indicate some of the methods of making a term attention-calling. But the test is whether attention can reasonably be expected to be called to it." . . .

Under § 2-316(2) read with the last sentence of § 1-201(10), it is a question of law for the court whether a provision is conspicuous. We are in as good a position to decide that issue as the trial judge, for a photographic copy of both sides of the purchase order is before us. We decide the issue by applying the statutory test under § 1-201(10) of what is conspicuous, *viz.* whether "a reasonable person against whom . . . [the disclaimer] is to operate ought to have noticed it."

In the language of the official comment . . . the boldface printing on the front of the purchase order (although adequate in size and contrast with the rest of the printing on the form) was not in words sufficient to call attention to the language on the back of the form. That language would naturally be concealed because the forms were part of a pad of paper when Hunt signed the paper. There was no reference whatsoever on the front of the order to the "Terms and Conditions" as being on the back of the order, and the quoted words "Terms and Conditions" might have been thought to apply to other small-type provisions on the front of the order unless Hunt had happened to turn over the form and look at the back of the order. His first reasonable opportunity to do this was when the executed form was returned to him.

In the opinion of a majority of the court, the provisions on the front of the purchase order did not make adequate reference to the provisions on the back of the order to draw attention to the latter. Hence the provisions on the back of the order cannot be said to be conspicuous although printed in an adequate size and style of type. The disclaimer was not effective.

2. Upon the evidence, the jury could reasonably conclude that the continued smoking of the engine was caused by a condition that constituted a breach both of the warranty of merchantability and of the warranty of fitness for a particular purpose. A smoking marine engine can hardly be regarded as of merchantable quality when sold by a distributor of such engines who is unable to cure the defect after persistent efforts. It could be found that Perkins, through Rideout, was fully aware of Hunt's requirements and his purpose in buying the engine and that Hunt relied on Perkins to guide him in its selection. . . . No evidence summarized in the bill of exceptions suggests that any injury to the engine may have been caused by Marine's work in installing it in Hunt's boat. Verdicts could not have been directed for Perkins.

Exceptions overruled.

NOTES AND QUESTIONS

1. **Conspicuousness:** Suppose the front of the form used in *Hunt v. Perkins Machinery Co.* had prominently referred to terms and conditions "on the reverse side of this order." Would the case have come out differently?

Should it matter if a survey shows that most buyers will not read any contractual terms, even if printed in larger and contrasting type? The court in *Armco, Inc. v. New Horizon Development Co. of Va., Inc.,*[177] said: "Because the excluding language in the contract is in larger type, we hold as a matter of law that it is conspicuous."

Section 2-316(2) requires a valid disclaimer to mention "merchantability." Would most businesspeople understand the meaning of that word? Would most consumers? Could a court, relying on the comment to § 1-201(10) [now § 1-201(b)(10) in Revised Article 1] that is emphasized in *Hunt*, hold that a disclaimer using the word "merchantability" was not conspicuous?

2. **"As is" disclaimers:** A seller can disclaim the implied warranty of merchantability or fitness for particular purpose without meeting all the tests of § 2-316(2). Under subsection (3)(a), a seller can exclude all implied warranties "by expressions like 'as is', 'with all faults' or other language which in common understanding calls the buyer's attention to the exclusion of warranties and makes plain that there is no implied warranty." Official Comment 7 says: "Such terms in ordinary commercial usage are understood to mean that the buyer takes the entire risk as to the quality of the goods involved." Notice, too, that subsection (3)(c) allows exclusion or modification of warranties by course of dealing (§ 1-303(b)), course of performance (§ 2-303(a)) or usage of trade (§ 1-303(c)). That is, the risk could be placed on a buyer by the way the parties have dealt in the past, by the way they have performed the particular contract, or by methods of dealing "having such regularity of observance" as to justify an expectation that it will be observed with respect to this transaction. Nonetheless, most sellers draft their implied warranty disclaimers to comply with § 2-316(2) rather than rely on § 2-316(3). Few sellers of new products want to offer them "as is." Many see their warranty as a selling tool.

3. **"As is" disclaimers and conspicuousness:** *Gindy Mfg. Corp. v. Cardinale Trucking Corp.*[178] involved the sale of new trailers to a commercial buyer. Seller's printed form contract used in the sale contained an invalid disclaimer of implied warranties under § 2-316(2); the clause intended as a disclaimer did not mention merchantability and was not conspicuous. The issue considered by the court was whether § 2-316(3) requires an "as is" disclaimer to be conspicuous. UCC § 2-316(3) does not expressly say so. Nonetheless, a requirement that a disclaimer be conspicuous is consistent with the purpose of the Code, as well as its legislative history. There is reason to believe that the omission of a clear conspicuousness

---

[177] 331 S.E.2d 456, 459 (Va. 1985).

[178] 11 N.J. Super. 383, 396–99, 268 A.2d 345, 352–54 (1970).

requirement arose inadvertently when a single section was broken into sections 2 and 3. As the court said:

> It does not make sense to require conspicuous language when a warranty is disclaimed by use of the words "merchantability" or "fitness" and not when a term like "as is" is used to accomplish the same result. It serves no intelligible design to protect buyers by conspicuous language when the term "merchantability" is used, but to allow an effective disclaimer when the term "as is" is buried in fine print. Nor does it make sense to require conspicuous language to disclaim the implied warranties of merchantability and fitness and not impose a similar requirement to disclaim other implied warranties that arise by course of dealing or usage of trade. The expectations of the buyer need as much protection in one case as in another. My preference, therefore, is to find that there is a requirement of conspicuousness when terms like "as is" are used to exclude an implied warranty of merchantability or fitness. It seems reasonable to say that to avoid these implied warranties the requirements of subsection (2) must be met, except that expressions like "as is" will be given effect in addition to the expressions specified in subsection (2). This interpretation, nevertheless, would still leave intact the exclusion of implied warranties arising from a course of dealing or usage of trade by expressions like "as is," whether conspicuous or not. It would appear desirable, to eliminate all doubt in this area, for the legislature to amend N.J.S.A. 12A:2-316 so as to include an express requirement of conspicuous language when a writing is used to exclude or modify any and all implied warranties. In any case, an interpretation requiring conspicuousness to avoid the warranties of merchantability and fitness still leaves open the effect of the disclaimer clause here on the implied warranties arising under § 2-314(3). . . .

4. *Limited remedies that fail of their essential purpose:* Sellers frequently warrant their goods but limit the remedy for any defects to replacement or repair at their option. If they take this step, almost certainly they will continue and state they are not liable for consequential or incidental damages. UCC §§ 2-719(2) and (3) regulate these clauses. First, if a limited remedy fails of its essential purpose, "remedy may be had as provided in this Act." Second: "Consequential damages may be limited or excluded unless the limitation or exclusion is unconscionable." The section continues: "Limitation of consequential damages for injury to the person in the case of consumer goods is *prima facie* unconscionable, but limitation of damages where the loss is commercial is not."

Many of the first cases to interpret these provisions involved consumers who had purchased defective automobiles or other expensive goods. They took their vehicles to dealers for repair again and again. The dealers kept the vehicles for a long time and could not successfully repair them. For example, in *Murray v. Holiday Rambler, Inc.*,[179] plaintiffs purchased a 22-foot 1973 Avenger motorhome for $11,007.15. They took possession in January 1974, and by July the vehicle had been returned to the dealer nine or ten times. In July, they took a trip to Colorado and experienced more difficulty, including a brake failure on a mountain road. When

---

[179] 83 Wis. 2d 406, 265 N.W.2d 513 (1978).

they returned home, they complained. Arrangements were made to take the vehicle to the factory in Indiana for repairs. The manufacturer, however, told the plaintiffs they would have to pick up the vehicle in Indiana themselves. Plaintiffs consulted a lawyer and brought a lawsuit to recover the cost of the vehicle and damages for loss of use.

The trial court found that when a buyer gives a seller reasonable opportunity to repair, but the vehicle fails to operate as a new vehicle free of defects should, the limited remedy of replacement or repair fails of its essential purpose under § 2-719. This meant that the buyers could revoke their acceptance under § 2-608 and recover what they had paid. They also recovered $2500 for loss of use of the vehicle.

The Supreme Court of Wisconsin found that the recovery for loss of use was an award of consequential damages. It then said that "although an express warranty excludes consequential damages, when the exclusive contractual remedy fails, the buyer may recover consequential damages under [§ 2-715], as though the limitation had never existed."[180] In essence, § 2-719(2) says a limited remedy fails of its essential purpose when there is not "a fair quantum of remedy for breach of the obligations or duties outlined in the contract" or when "an apparently fair and reasonable clause because of circumstances fails in its purpose or operates to deprive either party of the substantial value of the bargain."[181] When there is such a failure, the statute says "remedy may be had as provided in this Act." Section 2-715, allowing consequential damages, is a remedy provided in the Uniform Commercial Code. Thus, plaintiffs may make use of it.[182]

Consumers seldom have significant consequential damages.[183] Business purchasers, however, often have claims for the profits they would have made had a machine not been defective. Sellers of commercial products usually disclaim liability for consequential damages. When courts encountered commercial cases where a seller could not repair defective goods within a reasonable time, many declined to follow the reasoning in cases such as *Murray v. Holiday Rambler*. For example, in *Chatlos Systems, Inc. v. National Cash Register Corp.*,[184] NCR sold a computer system to a manufacturer. It was to be "up and running" by March 1975. About a year and a half later, only one of the six promised functions had been implemented and there were difficulties even with it. Chatlos demanded that NCR remove the computer, and NCR refused. Chatlos sued, seeking lost profits as consequential damages. The trial court awarded this. The court of appeals reversed.

It agreed that the limited remedy had failed of its essential purpose. However, it said:[185]

---

[180] *Id.* at 432, 265 N.W.2d at 526.

[181] Official Comment 1 to § 2-719.

[182] However, the court reversed the judgment for $2500 because the amount was speculative in light of the evidence submitted.

[183] An exception is when a consumer suffers personal injury as a result of a defect in, or the failure of, some potentially dangerous product.

[184] 635 F.2d 1081 (3d Cir. 1980).

[185] *Id.* at 1086.

THESE pages are discussion of whe limiting remedies / avoiding consequence under
warranties is appropriate.

632   SOCIAL CONTROL OF FREE CONTRACT   CH. 4

The limited remedy of repair and a consequential damages exclusion are two discrete ways of attempting to limit recovery for breach of warranty. . . . The Code, moreover, tests each by a different standard. The former survives unless it fails of its essential purpose, while the latter is valid unless it is unconscionable. We therefore see no reason to hold, as a general proposition, that the failure of the limited remedy provided in the contract, without more, invalidates a wholly distinct term in the agreement excluding consequential damages.

The court then looked at the situation in the case. It stressed that this was a commercial case between substantial business concerns. There was no great disparity in the parties' bargaining power or sophistication. Chatlos engineers had some appreciation of the problems in installing a computer system. "Some disruption of normal business routines, expenditure of employee time, and impairment of efficiency cannot be considered highly unusual or unforeseeable in a faulty computer installation."[186] There was no element of surprise since the contract expressed the limitation in a short and easily understood document. The seller did not act unreasonably or in bad faith. Thus, there was no reason not to enforce the parties' allocation of risk.[187]

Chatlos could recover a buyer's remedy under § 2-714(2). However, this remedy would not include consequential damages. Disclaimers of consequential damages are not affected by § 2-719(2) since they are governed by subsection (3). Thus, Chatlos could recover the difference "between the value of the goods accepted and the value they would have had if they had been as warranted . . ." The court remanded the case for a finding on the difference in values.[188]

In *Fiorito Bros., Inc. v. Fruehauf Corp.*,[189] the court took an approach that can be understood as a compromise between the holdings in *Holiday Rambler* and *Chatlos Systems*. Fruehauf sold Fiorito Bros. dump truck bodies for carrying wet concrete to highway construction sites. The bodies were covered under a five-year warranty, but seller disclaimed liability for incidental or consequential damages. When the bodies were put in use on dump trucks, they bulged and bowed when filled with cement and the hydraulic hoists failed. Cracks and tears also appeared in the corners and welds of the bodies. Fiorito notified Fruehauf of the problems but received no response. It wrote letters. Finally, a Fruehauf service manager came to the shop, examined the bodies, and said that the defects were not covered under warranty. Letters were exchanged but Fruehauf denied responsibility.

The trial court found that the limited remedy of replacement or repair had failed of its essential purpose. "[T]he facts show nothing but a callous disregard by

---

[186] *Id.* at 1087.

[187] For a very similar approach, see Xerox Corp. v. Hawkes, 475 A.2d 7 (N.H. 1984).

[188] The trial court found that the system delivered was worth $6000, but if it had been as warranted, it would have been worth $207,826.50. Another appeal followed and in a second opinion (670 F.2d 1304 (3d Cir. 1982)), the court affirmed the trial court's verdict. The principal issue in the second appeal arose from the fact that the price for the system was less than $50,000. Apparently the NCR salesforce had been extravagant in representing its virtues!

[189] 747 F.2d 1309 (9th Cir. 1984).

[Fruehauf] for the purposes for which the exclusive repair-or-replacement remedy was designed — to ensure that [Fiorito] would acquire defect-free trucks."[190] The court of appeals affirmed this finding.

The court of appeals then found that the trial court had correctly concluded that the failure of the limited remedy invalidated Fruehauf's disclaimer of consequential damages. Fruehauf claimed that a disclaimer of consequential damages was always valid unless it was unconscionable. Moreover, the clause was not oppressive at the beginning because of the relatively equal bargaining power of the parties. The court of appeals said, however, that each case and each contract must be judged on its own merits. It quoted the trial judge's opinion with approval:[191]

> Under the circumstances of each contract, are the exclusive-remedy and damage-exclusion terms separable elements of risk allocation . . . [or] are they inseparable parts of a unitary package of risk allocation? In the current case, it does not make sense to view the exclusive-remedy and consequential-damage provisions independently. The purpose of the parties in agreeing to this exclusive-remedy provision was to ensure that the Plaintiff would not suffer from downtime and other such consequential harms that follow from defective conditions in the trucks. . . . *It cannot be maintained that it was the parties' intention that Defendant be enabled to avoid all consequential liability for breach by first agreeing to an alternative remedy provision designed to avoid consequential harms, and then scuttling that alternative remedy through its recalcitrance in honoring the agreement.* (Emphasis added.)

Are these decisions based on enforcing the choice of the parties, social control of bargaining, facilitating big business, or something else?

4. Parol Evidence, Warranties, and Standard Forms

What happens if the seller promises something to the buyer in the course of negotiations that differs materially from what ends up in the written contract? This is, in simple terms, the problem the "parol evidence rule" seeks to solve.

The "parol evidence rule" is a vast body of doctrine concerning how much emphasis to put on writings in interpretation of contracts. The Restatement (Second) of Contracts takes 10 sections, §§ 209–218, to set the doctrine forth and generally takes a liberal approach to admission of parol evidence, both to add to writings and to explain them. The UCC's version is condensed into one section, § 2-202, but depends on concepts that receive further elaboration in the Restatement. The parol evidence doctrine is complex even from any one perspective, but to make things even more difficult, there are competing schools of thought about how much to use parol evidence.

A core concept in this body of law is that sometimes parties "integrate" their terms into a final writing, which might be either complete or partial. The paradigm

---

[190] *Id.* at 1312.

[191] *Id.* at 1315. The court followed the same approach in *Milgard Tempering, Inc. v. Selas Corp. of America*, 761 F.2d 553 (9th Cir. 1985).

PAROLE EV.= Diff between how its framed vs. whats actually in physical doc.

envisioned is of a fully negotiated agreement, where at the end of the process the parties carefully decide what the final terms are and put them in a final writing; a long way from this ideal case is the non-negotiated deal in which a business uses a pre-drafted standard form. The concept of integration has two parts: a "complete integration" is a full and final statement of terms; a "partial integration" is final on the terms it includes, but it is not complete, meaning that side terms can be proved. The line between these two types of integration is fuzzy. A "merger clause" is a contract term that attempts to create a bright line by stating that the agreement is a complete integration, but the courts are divided on how much weight to give such a term, particularly in cases involving standard forms with merger clauses. The Restatement, for example, says in Comment B to § 210 that a writing cannot prove its own completeness, but some courts treat a merger clause as conclusive or nearly so.

When there is an integration, parol evidence (anything outside the final writing, including oral statements and preliminary writings) cannot contradict it. On the other hand, parol evidence can be used to explain the meaning of a writing, even if integrated. Among the difficulties in this body of law is the question of when to view a writing as an integration. Absent a merger clause, courts that take a more "four corners" approach may look at the writing to see if it appears complete; if it appears to be detailed and comprehensive, such courts will not look outside it for alleged side terms. Other courts look at all parol evidence to see if the story about a side term is plausible; if they find the story credible, they will let the jury hear it and decide.

Another troubling issue is whether an integrated writing must appear ambiguous before parol evidence can be used to explain its meaning; most courts recognize that sometimes parol evidence will reveal ambiguity. Some go further and look at any proffered parol evidence to see whether it shows a credible meaning, and if so, as with evidence of credible side terms, allow the jury to decide. Finally, the difference between a contradiction and an explanation may be in the eye of the beholder, so allowing explanations but not contradictions just makes lawyers who are trying to get in parol evidence characterize the purpose of the evidence as explanation.

Competing views about the reliability of juries may explain the different approaches to parol evidence to a significant extent. Furthermore, commercial predictability as a value drives some courts to cut off inquiry into alleged oral side terms and alleged oral discussions about the meaning of terms when there is a complete-looking writing that appears to have a "plain meaning."

The parol evidence rule is covered in more detail in Volume II. For present purposes, it is an important part of the law relevant to both warranties and standard form contracts. The concept of the "real deal" and the "paper deal" may once more help you to understand what is at stake. Drafters want their forms, and just their forms, to spell out rights; if the law takes this approach, however, it risks providing a roadmap for legally sanctioned deceptive practices in which salespeople and advertising promise the world, while the fine print taketh away. The following case, dealing with a luxury yacht rather than the working man's boat involved in *Hunt*, shows the potential for a vast gap between the buyer's expectations based on how the seller frames the deal and what a standard form actually delivers — and when a court will refuse to consider "extrinsic" evidence (e.g., a brochure separate from the written contract).

BOUD v. SDNCO, INC.
Utah Supreme Court
54 P.3d 1131 (2002)

DURRANT, ASSOCIATE CHIEF JUSTICE.

INTRODUCTION

Appellant Joseph Boud seeks rescission of his contractual agreement to purchase a luxury yacht from appellee KCS International, Inc., d/b/a Cruisers Yachts ("Cruisers"), because of mechanical and electrical problems with the yacht. Boud appeals the district court's grant of summary judgment in favor of Cruisers. This case presents three main questions. First, did a sales brochure containing a photograph of the model Boud purchased and an accompanying caption describing the yacht create an express warranty, and if so, was that express warranty disclaimed? Second, did Cruisers engage in deceptive sales practices by including the photograph and caption in its sales brochure? Third, did the photograph and accompanying caption constitute negligent misrepresentations?

We conclude that an express warranty was not created by the brochure and that even were this the case, the parties' written contract effectively disclaimed any warranty other than the limited warranty provided for in the contract itself. Because no express warranty was created, we further conclude that Boud's allegations that Cruisers engaged in deceptive sales practices or made negligent misrepresentations also fail. We therefore affirm the district court's decision granting summary judgment in favor of Cruisers.

BACKGROUND

In December 1998, Boud visited Wasatch Marine, a Salt Lake City retailer run by SDNCO, Inc., that sells yachts manufactured by Cruisers. Wasatch Marine gave Boud a copy of Cruisers' 1999 sales brochure. Boud read and reviewed this brochure, paying particular attention to a page that contained a photograph of Cruisers' 3375 Esprit model apparently moving at a high rate of speed. Accompanying the photograph was a caption that read as follows:

> Offering the best performance and cruising accommodations in its class, the 3375 Esprit offers a choice of either stern drive or inboard power, superb handling and sleeping accommodations for six.

Due in part to the depictions in the brochure, Boud agreed to buy a 3375 Esprit model yacht for over $150,000. In late December 1998, he put down a $15,000 deposit and agreed to take delivery of the yacht in the spring of 1999. On May 10, 1999, Boud paid the balance of the sales price; he then took the yacht for a test drive and signed a sales contract on May 20. This contract indicated that Boud would receive a $476 refund, as he had overpaid. During the test drive on May 20, 1999, and a subsequent test drive approximately a week later, the yacht manifested several electrical and mechanical problems. Pursuant to a limited warranty that accompanied the written contract, Wasatch Marine serviced the yacht and attempted to fix the problems.

A subsequent test drive of the yacht in early June revealed that problems still existed with the yacht. Boud claims that these problems included (1) difficulty shifting gears, (2) the system alarm going off at idling speed, (3) partial failure of the air conditioning system, (4) unexplained sounding of the carbon monoxide detector, (5) a malfunctioning generator, and (6) misalignment of the rear door. Due to these mechanical problems, Boud sought to rescind the sales agreement. Cruisers responded by offering to repair or replace any defective parts as per the limited warranty. Boud then commenced this action.

In his amended complaint, Boud relied on three independent theories. First, he argued that the photograph and caption were themselves an express warranty, and that Cruisers and Wasatch Marine failed to provide him with a yacht that satisfied that warranty. Second, he asserted that, by putting forth the photograph and caption, Cruisers had engaged in deceptive sales practices in violation of section 13-11-4 of the Utah Code. Finally, Boud alleged that the photograph and accompanying language amounted to negligent misrepresentations made by Cruisers.

The district court heard arguments on Cruisers' motion for summary judgment and granted the motion on the ground that the materials in the brochure amounted to mere sales talk, or puffery, which could not give rise to an express warranty. The court further concluded that because the referenced portion of the brochure was not specific enough to create an express warranty, Boud's alternative arguments also failed. Boud appeals these rulings.

ANALYSIS

I. ISSUES PRESENTED/STANDARD OF REVIEW

On appeal, Boud claims that the district court erred in three respects. First, he argues that the district court erred in ruling that the photograph and caption in Cruisers' sales brochure did not amount to an express warranty. Second, he maintains that the district court should have found that Cruisers engaged in deceptive sales practices in violation of section 13-11-4 of the Utah Commercial Code. Finally, Boud contends that the district court incorrectly concluded that the photograph and caption did not constitute negligent misrepresentations. . . .

II. BOUD MAY NOT RELY ON THE PHOTOGRAPH AND CAPTION AS AN EXPRESS WARRANTY

The district court concluded that the photograph and caption contained in Cruisers' brochure did not provide an express warranty on which Boud could rely. We agree for two reasons.

A. The Photograph and Accompanying Caption Did Not Create an Express Warranty.

The creation of express warranties by affirmation or promise is governed by section 70A-2-313 of the Utah Code, which adopts the Uniform Commercial Code's provisions governing express warranties. Subsection 70A-2-313(1)(a), which governs promotional materials, states that an "affirmation of fact or promise made by [a] seller . . . [that] becomes part of the basis of [a] bargain creates an express warranty." Utah Code Ann. § 70A-2-313(1)(a) (1999). The next subsection places a limitation on this rule, however; it states that an "affirmation merely of the value of the goods or a statement purporting to be merely the *seller's opinion* or commendation of the goods does not create [an express] warranty." *Id.* § 70A-2-313(2). (Emphasis added.) Thus, the determination of whether an express warranty has been created ultimately hinges upon an examination of whether representations made by the seller were mere statements of opinion or were, rather, promises or affirmations of fact. In order to make this determination, we must examine the actual language and images set forth in Cruisers' brochure.

To qualify as an affirmation of fact, a statement must be objective in nature, i.e., verifiable or capable of being proven true or false. Similarly, to be relied upon as a promise, a statement must be highly specific or definite. The photograph and caption contained in Cruisers' brochure are not objective or specific enough to qualify as either facts or promises; the statements made in the caption are merely opinions, and the photograph makes no additional assertions with regard to the problems of which Boud has complained.

Cruisers' brochure contains language characteristic of an opinion. Specifically, its assertions that the 3375 Esprit offers the "best performance" and "superb handling" rely on inherently subjective words. *See Royal Bus. Machs., Inc. v. Lorraine Corp.*, 633 F.2d 34, 42 (7th Cir. 1980) ("General statements to the effect that goods are 'the best' . . . are generally regarded as expressions of the seller's opinion or 'the puffing of his wares' and do not create an express warranty."). While representations that a boat is the "fastest in its class" or "most powerful in its class" could be objectively tested for their truth and could therefore qualify as affirmations of fact, an assertion that a boat is "best in its class" cannot. The word "best" is a description that must ultimately be measured against some opinion or other imprecise standard, and "superb" is a near synonym subject to the same qualification. *Cf. Martin Rispens & Son v. Hall Farms, Inc.*, 621 N.E.2d 1078, 1083 (Ind. 1993) ("[T]he statement 'top quality seeds' is a 'classic example of puffery.' "). Similarly, "performance" is not a single quality, but rather embodies numerous qualities a boat may possess, and different people may place different weight on each individual quality. Reasonable people could therefore disagree and legitimately argue that several different boats in a given class perform "best" based on personal preferences that would be impossible to discount or disprove. As such, it would be unreasonable as a matter of law for anyone to rely on such a statement as one of fact. Accordingly, the language contained in the caption at issue is a mere statement of opinion.

Moreover, because the photograph does not make any factual representations with respect to the problems Boud has alleged, it does not create an express warranty on which Boud could sustain his claims. While the photograph depicts a boat moving across a body of water, it makes no representations regarding mechanical or electrical systems; nor does it provide any representations as to quality or reliability.

Consequently, we agree with the district court that the brochure lacks the specificity necessary to have created an express warranty. The proper source of redress for the yacht's mechanical and electrical problems is the limited warranty.

B. By Signing the Contract, Boud Disclaimed Any Express Warranty That Might Have Been Created and Agreed That the Contract Was an Integration of the Final Terms of the Parties' Agreement.

Even if we were to conclude that the photograph and caption created an express warranty, Boud disclaimed any express warranty that might have been created during the negotiation process by signing the written sales agreement. This court has held that "terms that might otherwise be considered a basis of the bargain are not express warranties if the final written contract effectively disclaims and/or excludes any such warranties." *Rawson v. Conover*, 2001 UT 24, ¶ 56, 20 P.3d 876 (Utah 2001).

The contract entered into between the parties included the following language directly above the signature line on which Boud signed:

> Purchaser agrees that his contract includes all of the terms, conditions, and warranties on both the face and reverse side hereof, that this agreement cancels and supersedes any prior agreement and as of the date hereof comprises the complete and exclusive statement of the terms of the agreement relating to the subject matter covered hereby. PURCHASER BY HIS/HER EXECUTION OF THIS AGREEMENT ACKNOWL-EDGES THAT HE/SHE HAS READ ITS TERMS, CONDITIONS, AND WARRANTIES BOTH ON THE FACE AND THE REVERSE SIDE HEREOF AND A [sic] HAS RECEIVED A TRUE COPY OF THIS AGREEMENT, AND FURTHER AGREES TO PAY THE 'BALANCE DUE' SET FORTH ABOVE ON OR BEFORE THE DATE SPECIFIED.

Further, the contract clearly stated the following in bold capital letters:

> **NO WARRANTIES, EXPRESS OR IMPLIED, ARE MADE OR WILL BE DEEMED TO HAVE BEEN MADE BY EITHER SELLER OR THE MANUFACTURER OF THE NEW MOTOR VEHICLE . . . EXCEPTING ONLY THE CURRENT PRINTED WARRANTY . . . WHICH WARRANTY IS INCORPORATED HEREIN AND . . . A COPY OF WHICH WILL BE DELIVERED TO PURCHASER AT THE TIME OF DELIVERY . . . AND THE REMEDIES SET FORTH IN SUCH WARRANTY WILL BE THE ONLY REMEDIES AVAIL-ABLE.**

Boud argues that he is not bound by this disclaimer because (1) evidence of prior terms should replace the limited warranty, (2) he signed the contract under duress, and (3) the contract was not accompanied by adequate consideration. We reject each of these arguments. We conclude that, by signing the sales contract, Boud certified that he accepted the limited warranty provision and disclaimed any prior express warranty that might have been created.

1. The Parol Evidence Rule Precludes the Introduction of Contradictory Terms

To begin with, Boud's attacks on the validity of the sales contract fail because the parol evidence rule precludes a search for additional or contradictory terms outside of the four corners of a written contract absent some proof of fraud or mistake. See *Semenov v. Hill*, 1999 UT 58, ¶ 12, 982 P.2d 578 ("[T]he general rule pertaining to acceptance of an offer by signing is that 'where a person signs a document, he is not permitted to show that he did not know its terms, and in the absence of fraud or mistake he will be bound by all its provisions, even though he has not read the agreement and does not know its contents.' ") . . .

No evidence of fraud or mistake has been presented in this case; Boud therefore cannot avoid the effect of the parol evidence rule nor claim that the parties agreed to any terms other than those included in the written contract.

2. Boud Did Not Sign the Contract Under Duress

Boud next alleges that he signed the sales contract under duress and was forced to pay for the yacht in advance of signing on the threat of being denied delivery. However, he conceded to the district court that he was not obligated to pay the full sales price up front, but chose to do so to ensure that he would be able to "lock in" the best price possible. This concession forecloses Boud's argument because the mere fact that he was motivated to sign the sales agreement in order to obtain a favorable price does not implicate duress under Utah law. . . .

III. BECAUSE THE PHOTOGRAPH AND CAPTION FAIL TO CREATE AN EXPRESS WARRANTY, THEY DO NOT CONSTITUTE MATERIAL REPRESENTATIONS THAT WOULD IMPLICATE DECEPTIVE SALES PRACTICES OR NEGLIGENT MISREPRESENTATIONS.

With respect to his assertions that Cruisers engaged in deceptive sales practices and made negligent misrepresentations, Boud has conceded in this appeal as well as to the district court that the validity of all three of his arguments hinges on his claim that the language and photograph in the brochure were specific enough to create an express warranty. Because we have determined that the photograph and caption did not create an express warranty, Boud's alternative arguments fail as a result of his concession. We therefore affirm the district court's decision to grant summary judgment in favor of Cruisers.

CONCLUSION

We conclude that the photograph and caption contained in Cruisers' sales brochure were mere statements of opinion and did not create an express warranty. Moreover, even if they did, because Boud signed the written sales contract and thereby accepted the limited warranty associated with it, he expressly disclaimed any prior express warranty. Finally, because Boud has conceded that his alternative arguments depend upon his claim that the brochure created an express warranty, we hold that his causes of action for deceptive sales practices under the Utah Consumer Sales Practices Act and negligent misrepresentation also fail. For all these reasons, the decision of the district court is affirmed.

NOTES AND QUESTIONS

1. *The two issues in* Boud: The court in *Boud* treated as "puffing" the picture of the boat going at a high rate of speed and the accompanying caption language about "best performance" and "superb handling." Would the case have been decided differently if the brochure had promised "flawless electrical and mechanical systems"? Would the parol evidence rule have operated in the same way? Can a seller make an oral express warranty and then exclude it using a standard form contract with a merger clause and stating that there are no express warranties other than those in the form? If so, is the expectation that the customer will get the seller to change the writing or otherwise be bound by the standard form? Would many consumers know that they should do that? Would many hesitate to show such distrust of the salesperson? Would most salespeople have the authority to make such a change? One function of the parol evidence rule may be to help lawyers drafting documents to ward off liability that might be created by a salesperson's statements attempting to close a deal and earn a commission. If this is the reason for disclaimers and remedy limitations in form contracts, should the law enable lawyers to do this?[192] Can we justify cases such as *Boud* on the ground that disappointed consumers can lie about what the salesperson said to them?

2. *Fraud as an exception:* In addition to exceptions to the parol evidence rule for proof of side terms when a writing is only partially integrated and for explanation of terms even in a complete integration, there are many other exceptions to the parol evidence rule, such as to show fraud, mistake, duress, or "other invalidating cause," as the Restatement puts it in § 214(d). Why didn't misrepresentation or deception work as exceptions in *Boud?*

In the variation on *Boud* discussed in Note 1, involving a seller making an express warranty orally but then excluding it in a standard form with a merger clause, could the plaintiff still recover for misrepresentation? The court in *Halpert v. Rosenthal*[193] (in which a seller innocently, but erroneously, advised a buyer that the house was free from termites) discussed the effect of a merger clause on misrepresentation:[194]

> The plaintiff's second contention is to the effect that even if an innocent misrepresentation without knowledge of its falsity may under certain circumstances entitle the misrepresentee to relief by way of rescission,

---

[192] *See* Lawrence M. Solan, *The Written Contract as Safe Harbor for Dishonest Conduct*, 77 CHI.-KENT L. REV. 87 (2001).

[193] 107 R.I. 406, 267 A.2d 730 (1970).

[194] *Id.* at 415–16, 267 A.2d at 735.

defendant cannot maintain his action because the sales agreement contains a merger clause. This provision immediately precedes the testimonium clause and provides that the contract "contains the entire agreement between the parties, and that it is subject to no understandings, conditions, or representations other than those expressly stated herein." The plaintiff argues that in order to enable a purchaser to rescind a contract containing a merger clause because of a misrepresentation, proof of a fraudulent misrepresentation must be shown. We find no merit in this argument. . . .

As we observed before, the availability of the remedy of rescission is motivated by the obvious inequity of allowing a person who has made the innocent misrepresentation to retain the fruits of the bargain induced thereby. If we are to permit a party to rescind a contract which is the result of an innocent misrepresentation, the "boilerplate" found in the merger clause shall not bar the use of this remedy.

Not all states recognize a cause of action for innocent misrepresentation. Furthermore, some states that do recognize this cause of action nonetheless prohibit introduction of evidence of oral representations when a contract containing a merger clause has been signed. In other words, some courts, unlike the court in *Halpert v. Rosenthal*, invoke the parol evidence rule to bar a remedy in innocent misrepresentation as well as warranty. However, a very solid exception to the parol evidence rule is that fraud, meaning intentionally making misrepresentations, can be proved notwithstanding the use of an apparently complete integration, even one using a merger clause. And, speaking of termites, recall the *Obde* case, in section B.5. of this chapter, *supra*. Would it have mattered if the Schlemeyers (the defendant-sellers) had made a parol evidence objection? If not, why not?

3. *An impediment to the fraud theory:* Even if parol evidence of fraud can come in, some courts bar tort recovery based on the "economic loss doctrine," which limits parties to their contract remedies. In *Below v. Norton*,[195] a four-to-three majority of the Wisconsin Supreme Court held that a residential home buyer could not recover in tort for intentional fraud because the loss was economic and did not involve personal injury.[196] Although some courts, most of them federal, have enthusiastically adopted this approach to liability containment, Judge Richard Posner has explained[197] that the origin of the recent idea of applying an economic loss rule to common law intentional fraud misuses dicta in a U.S. Supreme Court admiralty products liability case, *East River S.S. Corp. v. Transamerica Delaval, Inc.*[198] Some lower federal courts treated broad language in that opinion as if it were a statute not limited by the facts of the case. In products liability law under either strict liability or negligence, many courts restrict plaintiffs who suffer only

---

[195] 310 Wis. 2d 713, 751 N.W.2d 351 (2008).

[196] The state of Wisconsin has superseded *Below* in the context of residential real property contracts, permitting tort damages in such cases. *See* Wis. Stat. § 895.10 (2009). Section 895.10 (2) provides: "In addition to any other remedies available under law, a transferee in a residential real estate transaction may maintain an action in tort against the real estate transferor for fraud committed, or an intentional misrepresentation made, by the transferor in the residential real estate transaction."

[197] *See* All-Tech Telecom, Inc. v. Amway Corp., 174 F.3d 862, 866–67 (7th Cir. 1999).

[198] 476 U.S. 858 (1986).

pecuniary harm to their warranty rights, if any, but this idea makes little sense in the law of intentional fraud, which is quintessentially about pecuniary loss in the form of being intentionally misled into a transaction and about deterrence of wrongdoing.[199] The UCC makes it clear that in the realm of sales of goods, there is no rule against fraud recovery in tort as an alternative; the UCC takes pains to say that defrauded buyers can choose to use remedies available under Article 2 for nonfraudulent breach.[200] If a fraud cause of action would not lie where there is a contract, there would be no need to extend expectation-based remedies to fraud actions. The UCC treats contract and tort as alternative remedies from which a defrauded party to a contract can choose. Practical reasons for customers to turn to tort include disclaimer of warranties, limitation of remedies, and having a shot at punitive damages.

4.   ***Implied warranties to the rescue?*** Why couldn't implied warranties be used in the *Boud* case? Consider that question now under the UCC and then return to it after reading the next section. Isn't a yacht a consumer product under the Magnuson-Moss Warranty Improvement Act? Did the seller comply with the act? Could the buyer have used the implied warranty of merchantability? If so, with what remedy?

5.   Regulating Warranties in Consumer Transactions

Many reformers and scholars think that the Uniform Commercial Code's provisions on warranties, disclaimers, and remedy limitations are inadequate to protect consumers. The United States Congress has taken steps to further regulate some or all warranties in consumer transactions.[201] We can ask whether these steps are effective or wise.

The Magnuson-Moss Act: The United States Congress held hearings on automobile warranties several times in the late 1960s and early 1970s. Consumer protection advocates proposed regulation of automobile industry practices, but they were unsuccessful. Then the focus of the legislative battle widened, and advocates proposed regulation of all warranties given by manufacturers of consumer products.[202] Congress passed the Magnuson-Moss Warranty

---

[199] *See* Jean Braucher, *Deception, Economic Loss and Mass-Market Customers: Consumer Protection Statutes as Persuasive Authority in the Common Law of Fraud*, 48 Ariz. L. Rev. 829, 836 (2006) (also arguing that it is even easier to find that state consumer protection statutes' remedies were not meant to be restricted to cases of personal injury and therefore apply where the loss is only pecuniary).

[200] UCC § 2-721.

[201] Some states, like California, have also enacted statutes that regulate consumer warranties.

[202] *See* Donald P. Rothschild, *The Magnuson-Moss Warranty Act: Does It Balance Warrantor and Consumer Interests?*, 44 Geo. Wash. L. Rev. 335, 350–53 (1976), which says that four studies influenced Congress. They showed that consumers could not understand rights, duties, and remedies under the warranties being used, and that existing consumer remedies were impractical. The four studies were William C. Whitford, *Law and the Consumer Transaction: A Case Study of the Automobile Warranty*, 1968 Wis. L. Rev. 1006; FTC, Report of The Task Force on Appliance Warranties and Service (1969); FTC, Report on Automobile Warranties (1970); Staff of Subcomm. on Commerce & Finance, House Comm. on Interstate & Foreign Commerce, 93d Cong., 2d Sess., Report on Consumer Product Warranties (1974).

Improvement Act.[203]

As we should expect, the Act was a compromise. To get any statute passed, consumer advocates accepted disclosure regulation. Manufacturers' representatives could not oppose a statute designed to block deception. Disclosure regulation fits free market ideology. Informed consumers will pay for that measure of protection against defective products that they find valuable.

Under the Magnuson-Moss Act, a "supplier" of a "consumer product" need not give any "written warranty."[204] However, if a business is a supplier offering a new consumer product, and if it does offer a written warranty, then it must "clearly and conspicuously designate" that warranty as either a "full" or a "limited" one.[205] The drafters of the statute hoped to create simple terms that consumers would understand. If a supplier wanted to offer an attractive full warranty to gain market share, it would have to meet federal requirements.[206] For example, a supplier giving a full warranty must remedy any defect within a reasonable time without charge to the customer. If the supplier cannot do this after a reasonable number of attempts, then the customer can elect a refund of what she paid or a replacement of the product. This is a "lemon law" type of remedy allowing the customer to exit or get a replacement, also provided by state laws discussed later in this section. Any exclusion of consequential damages must appear conspicuously on the face of the written full warranty.

If a supplier is unwilling to grant all of these rights to consumers, it must call its warranty a "limited" one. Those who drafted the statute hoped that competition would push manufacturers to offer full warranties rather than those stigmatized as limited ones. Originally, the proposed statute required sellers to identify less-than-full warranties by words showing that they were second-rate. However, the suppliers' lobbyists battled and changed the term to the neutral phrase "limited warranty."

There is one part of the limited warranty under Magnuson-Moss, however, that has some substantive teeth. If a supplier gives any written warranty, full or limited, it cannot disclaim or modify any implied warranties nor limit their duration to less than "the duration of a written warranty of reasonable duration."[207] This means that the implied warranty of merchantability supplied by the UCC is mandatory if the supplier gives a written warranty. Most suppliers have offered only limited warranties.

The Magnuson-Moss Act says nothing about limiting the remedies offered for implied warranties.[208] On first impression, we might think that remedy limitations

---

[203] 15 U.S.C. §§ 2301 to 2312 (first enacted in 1975).

[204] The statute defines all of these terms. In addition, there are regulations that amplify and explain. For example, the provisions that regulate a warranty's content apply only to consumer goods costing more than $10 (excluding tax).

[205] 15 U.S.C. § 2303.

[206] 15 U.S.C. § 2304 lists the requirements for a full warranty.

[207] See 15 U.S.C. § 2308(a).

[208] Remember that under the UCC, sellers can offer attractive warranties but limit remedies to

are still governed only by the Uniform Commercial Code. The Federal Trade Commission (which has rule-making powers) has indicated it interprets Magnuson-Moss to require exclusions or limitations of consequential damages to be conspicuous. In 1975 the FTC published rules[209] requiring "[a]ny warrantor warranting to a consumer by means of a written warranty a consumer product actually costing the consumer more than $15.00 shall clearly and conspicuously disclose [a number of things] in a single document in simple and readily understood language."[210] A warrantor must state what it will do in the event of a failure to conform with the written warranty and what the consumer must do. In addition, under both full and limited written warranties a supplier must disclose "[a]ny exclusions of or limitations on relief such as incidental or consequential damages, accompanied by the following statement . . . 'Some states do not allow the exclusion or limitation of incidental or consequential damages, so the above limitation or exclusion may not apply to you.' "[211]

Thus, the Magnuson-Moss Act, and the FTC's administrative regulations, grant consumers a number of rights beyond those found in the Uniform Commercial Code.[212] But how are consumers to enforce them? The Magnuson-Moss Act creates a federal cause of action for "a consumer who is damaged by the failure of a supplier . . . to comply with any obligation under this title, or under a written warranty, implied warranty, or service contract." However, the statute grants the federal courts jurisdiction to hear claims under its provisions only if the amount in controversy is more than $50,000. Congress did not intend to burden the federal courts with claims based on defective automobiles, recreational vehicles, and appliances.

Because of the jurisdictional limit in federal court, most consumers must sue for breach of warranty in state courts.[213] In the state courts, consumers proceed under the Uniform Commercial Code's provisions on warranties, disclaimers, and remedy limitations, as well as under the Magnuson-Moss Warranty Act. To use the latter, lawyers for consumers often have to educate state trial judges in the requirements of the federal statute.

Furthermore, the Magnuson-Moss Act provides that a court may award attorney's fees to a consumer who prevails. Several courts have found that this part of the federal statute applies in an action brought in a state court where part of the case was based on the federal act.[214] Often these decisions involve a basic UCC

---

replacement or repair at their option. UCC § 2-719(1)(a).

[209] *See* 16 CFR §§ 700.1 to 703.8.

[210] 16 CFR § 701.3.

[211] 16 CFR § 701.03(8).

[212] For example, the court in Checker Taxi Co., Inc. v. Checker Motors Sales Corp., 376 F. Supp. 997 (D. Mass. 1974), says that a remedy limitation need not be conspicuous under UCC § 2-719(2). Remedy limitations must be conspicuous under the FTC regulations.

[213] 15 U.S.C. § 2310(d)(1) says that a consumer who is damaged by the failure of a supplier to honor any obligation under the statute — or under a written warranty, implied warranty, or service contract — may bring suit for damages and other legal and equitable relief in any court of competent jurisdiction in any state.

[214] *See, e.g.*, Volkswagen of America, Inc. v. Harrell, 431 So. 2d 156 (Ala. 1983); Sherer v. De Salvo,

warranty, disclaimer, and remedy limitation analysis, with the Magnuson-Moss Act occupying only a minor role. Nonetheless, the federal statute serves as a springboard for attorney's fees.[215]

The statute has had some impact. Though there are few reported cases of individuals having brought claims under the Magnuson-Moss Act, there have been class actions brought representing all the buyers of particular products. Litigation may be a poor measure of the success or failure of the statute. Almost all consumer products come with written warranties drafted by lawyers who have read the statute. Many, if not most, warranties are easier to read and understand today than before Congress passed the statute. Many firms have tried to communicate to consumers what is and is not covered by the warranty. Consumer advocates believe the statute is useful.[216]

Nonetheless, the statute primarily calls for disclosure regulation. Its underlying theory assumes the behavior of informed, rational consumers in a competitive market. Again we face what Professor William Whitford calls the distinction between predictive and normative theories. Should we evaluate the statute by what real consumers are likely to do or what reasonable consumers ought to do?[217] Is it enough if manufacturers fear that a small group of consumers will read, understand, and refuse to buy if warranties are unsatisfactory? Perhaps in a mass market it will be difficult for manufacturers to make special deals for these few fully informed rational consumers, and their diligence will prompt suppliers to offer better warranties to everyone.

We could make a very different argument in view of the hopes of the consumer advocates who struggled to regulate consumer product warranties. Magnuson-Moss stands as a strong example of symbolic legislation. Congress wanted to cool out the consumer advocates pressing for action when consumer protection was a popular issue. At the same time, many representatives and senators did not want to offend big business. Congress solved its problem by passing a statute that required suppliers of consumer products to redraft their warranties. This benefited business lawyers by making more work for them. Nonetheless, it offered most consumers little benefit. Suppliers advertise and market products proclaiming their virtues. They create expectations of quality. At the same time, they undercut these expectations by warranty disclaimers and remedy limitations. All the redrafting demanded by Magnuson-Moss will not offset the expectations created by advertising and marketing strategies.

---

634 S.W.2d 149 (Ark. App. 1982); Black v. Don Schmid Motor, Inc., 232 Kan. 458, 657 P.2d 517 (1983).

[215]   *See* Sherer v. De Salvo, 634 S.W.2d 149 (Ark. App. 1982).

[216]   *See* National Consumer Law Center, *12 Reasons to Love the Magnuson-Moss Warranty Act*, 11 J. CONSUMER & COM. L. 127 (2008) (listing as the two top reasons that it provides for attorney's fees and prevents disclaimer of implied warranties if a written warranty is given).

[217]   Geraint Howells, *The Potential and Limits of Consumer Empowerment by Information*, 32 J. L. & SOC'Y 349 (2005) ("[M]any consumers . . . have a limited ability to understand the information. Information strategies are clearly problematic for those who find it difficult to read. Moreover, all of us have limits on our ability to process information. . . . Much information is provided in a manner that simply washes over the heads of consumers.").

Furthermore, the statute seems to grant individuals private rights, but few situations will involve enough money to make it worth trying to use the rights created by the statute. Indeed, Magnuson-Moss could be argued to be an example of mystification to aid big business in riding out the tide of reform. To what extent, if at all, is this argument unfair? What factual and normative assumptions are involved? Which, if any, seem questionable?

A major issue under Magnuson-Moss in recent years has been whether actions under the federal statute can be forced into binding arbitration under arbitration clauses. We will discuss reservations about consumer arbitration later in this chapter. Even though the Federal Trade Commission has issued a regulation under Magnuson-Moss stating that informal dispute resolution under the act cannot be binding on any party,[218] two U.S. Courts of Appeals have held that the Federal Arbitration Act still makes Magnuson-Moss claims subject to arbitration.[219] However, other courts have refused to follow this authority and do not require arbitration of Magnuson-Moss claims.[220]

Lemon laws and automobile warranties: So-called "lemon laws" are another example of attempts to regulate warranties to benefit consumers. Typically, automobile manufacturers offer warranties of a specified duration but limit remedies to the replacement or repair of defective parts. Representatives of the manufacturers talk of the interchangeability of parts and insist all cars can be repaired. Consumer advocates view this as a comforting fantasy. All 50 states have passed lemon laws.[221] Most of these laws provide the consumer with remedies, including the right to return the car if the dealer's repeated efforts to solve recurring problems prove to be ineffective. Rights under "lemon laws" are typically in addition to rights granted under the UCC or the contract of sale. Professor Joan Vogel surveyed their provisions and expressed doubt as to their value.[222] A consumer must exhaust any remedies possible under a manufacturer's private consumer-dispute mechanism. Private government often prevents litigation by

---

[218] 16 C.F.R. § 703.5(j) (first enacted in 1981).

[219] Walton v. Rose Mobile Homes, L.L.C., 298 F.3d 470 (5th Cir. 2002); Davis v. Southern Energy Homes, Inc., 305 F.3d 1268 (11th Cir. 2002). *See also* Jonathan D. Grossberg, *The Magnuson-Moss Warranty Act, The Federal Arbitration Act, and the Future of Consumer Protection*, 93 CORNELL L. REV. 659 (2008). *See also* Hemphill v. Ford Motor Co., 41 Kan. App. 2d 726, 206 P.3d 1 (2009); Jones v. GMC, 640 F. Supp. 2d 1124 (D. Ariz. 2009); Seney v. Rent-A-Center, Inc., 909 F. Supp. 2d 444 (D. Md. 2012).

[220] *See* Higgs v. The Warranty Group, 2007 U.S. Dist. LEXIS 50064 (S.D. Ohio, July 11, 2007); Rickard v. Teynor's Homes, Inc., 279 F. Supp. 2d 910 (N.D. Ohio 2003); Browne v. Kine Tysons Imports, Inc., 190 F. Supp. 2d 827 (E.D. Va. 2002); Koons Ford of Baltimore, Inc. v. Lobach, 919 A.2d 722 (Md. 2007); Simpson v. MSA of Myrtle Beach, Inc., 644 S.E.2d 663 (S.C. 2007); Tucker v. Ford Motor Co., 72 Va. Cir. 420 (2007). In Kolev v. Euromotors West/The Auto Gallery, 658 F.3d 1024 (9th Cir. 2011), the Ninth Circuit initially reached the conclusion that Magnuson-Moss claims were not subject to mandatory arbitration, choosing not to adopt the reasoning in *Walton* and *Davis* (*see supra* note 219), but the court's opinion was withdrawn *sua sponte* in Kolev v. Euromotors West/The Auto Gallery, 676 F.3d 867 (9th Cir. 2012) to await the decision of the California Supreme Court in Sanchez v. Valencia Holding Co., L.L.C., 2014 Cal. LEXIS 1964 (Cal. Mar. 19, 2014) (pending).

[221] *See* Louis J. Sirico Jr., *Automobile Lemon Laws: An Annotated Bibliography*, 8 LOY. CONSUMER L. REV. 39 (1996).

[222] Joan Vogel, *Squeezing Consumers: Lemon Laws, Consumer Warranties, and a Proposal for Reform*, 1985 ARIZ. ST. L.J. 589.

providing meaningless steps for consumers. As a result, they are cooled out and walk away. She says: "In many respects, they [lemon laws] simply restate the present law. In other respects, they are more restrictive than alternative legal remedies."[223] She continues:[224]

> If lawmakers wish to provide increased protection to purchasers of automobiles, there are certain modifications which would make the lemon laws more effective: (1) clear rules or standards; (2) presumptions that ease the burden of proof, (3) a minimum of technicalities; and (4) a choice between a refund and other damages or a replacement vehicle. They could also publicize consumers' rights under the improved laws.

Professor Jean Braucher criticizes consumer product warranty law based on a legal rights model, which produces warranties that are not well designed for consumers to use themselves when making demands for relief from sellers. She argues that the law should be framed to encourage and assist consumers who complain to the seller.[225] The UCC's implied warranty of merchantability is vague as to what is covered and for how long, and remedy limitations referring to "incidental and consequential damages" are incomprehensible to consumers. Magnuson-Moss then incorporates these UCC concepts into its disclosure scheme, leading to warranties that are not in plain language. Braucher argues that warranties should be required to contain instructions to consumers about how to complain, a description of what consumers can expect from the product, and clear and specific remedies for product quality defects — clarity that also makes a legal claim easier to establish if a lawsuit is ultimately brought.

Have lemon laws had an impact? One indication that lemon laws have had a big impact is that state attorneys general, lemon law administrators, and consumer advocates have become concerned about recycling of lemons (bought back by automakers) into the used-car market. They have urged creation of a system of tracking these cars so that used car buyers will be informed if they are buying a lemon.[226] In 2001, George A. Akerlof won the Nobel Prize in Economic Sciences for a paper called "The Market for Lemons," dealing with just this problem and discussing lemon laws as regulation designed to address market failure due to information asymmetries.

There has long been skepticism, however, about how much benefit consumers derive from lemon laws. In January 1993, the magazine *Consumer Reports* said: "Weak laws, including many that allow auto manufacturers to run the arbitration process; poor oversight by the states; and miles of red tape have stymied consumers at every turn."[227] Its study showed that consumers win much more often in states where there are government-run lemon law arbitration programs than in states

Often lemon law fails b/c automaker runs arb bote

---

[223] *Id.* at 644.

[224] *Id.* at 645.

[225] Jean Braucher, *An Informal Resolution Model of Consumer Product Warranty Law*, 1985 Wis. L. Rev. 1405.

[226] Christopher Jensen, *Government Urged to Update Buyers' Guide*, New York Times, Automobiles Section, p. 1 (Dec. 13, 2009).

[227] 58 Consumer Reports, January 1993, at 40.

where the auto makers run the arbitration programs.

Professor Stewart Macaulay notes in an article that all states and the District of Columbia have lemon laws covering automobiles, some of which also cover motorcycles, and adds:[228]

Not all lemons equal man

Lolz

> The Center for Auto Safety rates these laws. . . . It found the California law to be the best. . . . "New vehicles in California can be classified as lemons in the first 18 months or 18,000 miles, and consumers can sue after two failed attempts at fixing a safety defect." . . . The center ranked the Illinois law 49 out of 51. . . . Under Illinois law, the dealer gets four chances to fix the car, and there is no exception for safety defects.

Macaulay also says, "Lemon laws favor consumers willing to deal with paper-work, walk into a situation that is totally foreign to them, and face a manufacturer's representative who has the advantage of experience."[229]

States that run lemon law programs certainly claim great benefits for consumers. For example, New York's Attorney General issued a report in 2003 stating that consumers in that state's new car arbitration program won 65.4 percent of cases and recovered over $10 million in that one year, and that over the previous 17 years, they had won 67 percent of cases and recovered a total of nearly $185 million.[230] In litigation, the Wisconsin Supreme Court upheld a judgment of $74,371 when Chrysler failed to replace a defective minivan within 30 days after a consumer's demand. The van cost about $15,000; the judgment included lawyer's fees and twice the consumer's pecuniary loss. See *Hughes v. Chrysler Motors Corp.*[231] In another case, the Wisconsin Court of Appeals also strictly applied the 30-day period for refund or replacement, saying, "There are no excuses."[232] In addition to reported recoveries in arbitration programs and litigation, lemon laws may also be an important influence on how manufacturers treat customers, settling complaints without resort to dispute resolution.

Consumers who must go through a lemon law process are unlikely to buy another car from the manufacturer whose dealers could not repair their car. Moreover, in many states an agency publishes rankings on lemon law claims adjusted for the number of a particular make and model sold in the state. A Texas official commented: "It's quite possible one reason that manufacturers such as General Motors, Chrysler, and Ford are settling a lot of cases is that they want to have a low lemon index. They have a tendency to be more proactive. . . . Some of them [other

---

[228] Stewart Macaulay, *Freedom From Contract: Solutions in Search of a Problem?* 2004 Wis. L. Rev. 777, 815 & n.141 (citing and quoting Rick Popely, *Lawyers Sour on State Lemon Law; Illinois' Protections are Too Weak to Provide Any Benefit*, Chicago Tribune, June 1, 2003, at 1).

[229] *Id.* at 816 & n.146 (citing and quoting Peter Lewis, *Lemon Law Leaves Sour Taste for Owner: Driver of Brake-Troubled Car Fails to Prove Her Case*, Seattle Times, Oct. 14, 2002, at B1).

[230] *Annual Report — 2003, New York's New Car Lemon Law Arbitration Program*, http://www.lemonlawclaims.com/2003-New-York-state-report-on-the-lemon-law.htm

[231] 197 Wis. 2d 973, 542 N.W.2d 148 (1996).

[232] Chariton v. Saturn Corp., 238 Wis. 2d 27, 32, 615 N.W.2d 209, 2000 WI App 148 (Wis. Ct. App. 2000).

manufacturers] are slower to catch on."[233] Lemon laws, of course, are not the only reason that manufacturers have worked harder in recent years than in the past to improve the service offered by their dealers. Repeated unsuccessful trips to a dealer's service department produce only unhappy buyers who are unlikely to buy the same brand of car again.

Regulation of warranties — costs and benefits: Are all these attempts to regulate warranties wise? Disclosure regulation rests on the idea that consumers will be able to make better choices. Undoubtedly, redrafting forms and making material available to consumers costs money. However, we can wonder whether the law forces manufacturers to waste most of this effort. As noted *supra* in Section C of this chapter, there is growing evidence that consumers do not read standard form contracts. Perhaps manufacturers are influenced by the chance that a few prospective purchasers might read the warranty coverage. Perhaps they fear that consumer activists might publicize what they view as substandard warranty coverage.

Substantive regulation of warranties raises a number of other issues. All states have adopted lemon laws to regulate the performance of automobile warranties. The goal is to force dealers to repair automobiles successfully and promptly. Consumers may expect this, and manufacturers may be responsible for creating these expectations. Nonetheless, the obligation adds to the cost of distributing automobiles. Manufacturers face the threat of having to repair cars successfully and promptly or suffering penalties. As a result they may invest in better quality control at their factories and better service management and technology. Manufacturers may keep stocks of parts available and offer consulting services to dealers on difficult-to-solve repair problems. This may raise the price of automobiles for everyone. Those consumers willing to gamble that their car would not be a lemon cannot choose lower prices for bigger risks.

Consumers face many bureaucratic or administrative problems in enforcing warranty rights. Manufacturers reward officials for keeping down warranty costs. It is difficult for the manufacturers to reward them for retaining consumer goodwill. Delays often result from difficulties in running a parts system. Manufacturers strive to reduce the costs of maintaining large inventories of parts that they may never sell. Shipping a small part of little value to a dealer may be very expensive, and manufacturers try to combine shipments of various orders to dealers to cut these costs. Some problems are extremely difficult to diagnose. For example, some malfunctions come and go. Unless the dealer can see the product while it is experiencing the problem, it is almost impossible to uncover the cause of these intermittent difficulties.[234]

Finally, manufacturers seek to police the way dealers administer warranties. Dealers must fill out forms justifying certain repairs before the manufacturers will reimburse them. Dealers must obtain approval from a manufacturer's agent before

---

[233] THE HOUSTON POST, Nov. 24, 1994, at A52.

[234] Kenneth McNeil & Richard E. *Miller, The Profitability of Consumer Protection: Warranty Policy in the Auto Industry,* 25 ADMIN. SCI. Q. 407 (1980) ("Manufacturers often signal dealers that they don't care about service by placing undue emphasis on short-term cost control.").

they do certain costly warranty work. While these steps hold down costs, they do create incentives to deny warranty claims or to minimize efforts to solve consumers' problems.[235]

Any successful reform would have to deal with these bureaucratic incentives to minimize warranty expenses. However, if a reform did succeed, it might increase warranty expenses. Manufacturers would deal with these increased costs in some way. Suppose the public learned more about consumer complaints dealing with particular products and their defects. For example, statistics on problems with products could be gathered and published. Would this be a better way to deal with the problem, as compared to considering individual cases one by one?

E. UNCONSCIONABILITY

More people are comfortable with a liberal theory of free contract when the parties have some rough economic equality. This is sometimes referred to as "equality of bargaining power," but of course contracts often involve little or no bargaining, especially when there is inequality of power. At any rate, the theory of free contract works better if both parties have some measure of resources beyond those needed to purchase a minimum of food, clothing, and shelter. Suppose seller and buyer are both wealthy people. Seller offers what she thinks is her rare violin to buyer. Buyer examines the violin carefully. Then buyer agrees to purchase it for about the current market value of a rare instrument. The violin is an old copy of a rare violin, worth much less. A court could decide that both parties made mistakes and rescind the sale. It could, on the other hand, decide that buyer assumed the risk and hold him to the bargain. While the losing party will be unhappy, the court's decision is unlikely to make a significant change in the way the parties live. The loser's material situation will be much the same as before.

Things are different when one of the parties is poor. Seller may be trying to convert her one asset into cash so she can command food and shelter. If the transaction is rescinded, she may face a desperate situation. Or a wealthy seller may offer a poor buyer food, shelter, clothing, or some of the things that make life more enjoyable. Poor buyers may have few choices about whom to buy from or sell to. They may lack skill and experience in appraising the quality and value of goods. Their continuing goodwill may be worth little, and so others can exploit them in a particular transaction without concern about future business.

During the late 1950s and early 1960s, wealthy and middle-class Americans "discovered" the poor. President Lyndon Johnson even waged a "war on poverty." Public interest lawyers were some of the important warriors against poverty during the 1960s and 1970s. They used many bodies of law as tools to attack what they saw as wrong in American society. One important tool was the doctrine of unconscionability, found in § 2-302 of the Uniform Commercial Code. We will look at the cases and the reactions of scholars. We will ask what one can say for and against attacking important social problems by attacking particular contracts. Whatever our politics make us see as ends, as lawyers we must be concerned with means as well. There

---

[235] *See* William C. Whitford, *Law and the Consumer Transaction: A Case Study of the Automobile Warranty*, 1968 Wis. L. Rev. 1006.

are no cost-free magic solutions. If we really want greater economic equality, are contract rules sufficient to get us there? How do businesses deal with the costs of contract rules? Taxes and transfer payments through social welfare programs are more direct routes to equality of distribution, although obviously perhaps even more controversial.

The doctrine of unconscionability was in its early days most famously used in efforts to provide increased judicial oversight of retailing to the poor. The case you will read below, *Williams v. Walker-Thomas Furniture Co.*, involved an "installment sale" contract with certain features the court found to be unconscionable. Retail installment sale contracts are less common today than they were in the past (e.g., the 1960s, the time of the *Williams* case). They first became popular because they enabled consumers to purchase beyond their current earning power. The deal was usually in the form of a sale coupled with a secured transaction.[236] The retailer would sell an item (e.g., a television) for a purchase price that the consumer would pay in installments over time. The seller usually had a lien on the goods sold (and perhaps other goods owned by the customer), which secured payment. If the consumer made all payments required by the contract (e.g., principal plus interest, and perhaps other charges), the consumer would then own the item outright. If the customer missed a payment, the seller would then have the right to "foreclose" its lien, which meant seizing the property in question.[237] Often, as in *Williams*, this involved a suit to "replevy" the goods, which is the technical form of the action required to enable a secured creditor (such as a seller under an installment sale contract) to take possession of property securing the unpaid purchase price (which is effectively a loan).

Although installment sales contracts were used with middle-class consumers, they were then — and now — most important among low-income purchasers, who often had low, fixed incomes that constrained their purchasing power. Today, these sorts of contracts are largely obsolete among the middle class, except in the case of cars and other big-ticket items (such as recreational boats). Consumers who are able to get credit cards — those in the middle class — will tend to use their credit cards to make retail purchases when they cannot (or do not want to) pay cash.

Low-income consumers, by contrast, may not have access to credit cards. The modern version of the installment sale is the so-called "rent-to-own" (RTO) contract. In 2011, Charles Harwood, deputy director of the Federal Trade Commission's Bureau of Consumer Protection, testified about the rent-to-own industry, which is the subject of the early cases on unconscionability.[238] The Commission's written statement included the following background, which helps to

---

[236] "Secured transactions" in personal property are transactions in which personal property secures payment or performance of an obligation. They are largely governed by Article 9 of the Uniform Commercial Code, a subject worthy of its own course in most law schools.

[237] You saw liens discussed in, among others, the *Lake River* case in Chapter 2, section D, *supra*. Note that under Article 9 of the Uniform Commercial Code, a secured creditor has the right to use so-called "self-help" repossession — in other words, to seize the collateral without ever going to court — if it can do so without a "breach of peace." UCC § 9-609(b)(2).

[238] *See* Fed. Trade Comm'n, *Prepared Statement on Rent-to-Own Transactions Before the Financial Institutions and Consumer Credit Subcommittee of the House Financial Services Committee*, July 26, 2011, at 3–4, https://www.ftc.gov/sites/default/files/documents/public_statements/prepared-statement-

explain the industry, as well as some of the issues early unconscionability cases wrestled with.

Rent to own

Backup

The RTO industry consists of dealers that rent consumer products with an option to buy. These products have traditionally included furniture, appliances, home electronics, jewelry, and computers. Some dealers may specialize in offering other particular types of products, such as musical instruments, tires and wheels, or automobiles.

In recent years, the RTO industry has gradually expanded its offerings to encompass a broader range of products. The Association of Progressive Rental Organizations (APRO), an RTO industry trade association representing many RTO stores, reports that the RTO model is being adapted to other product lines outside the traditional ones, including homes, fine art, bicycles, storage sheds, and riding lawnmowers.

RTO agreements typically do not require any down payment or credit check, thus providing consumers with immediate access to household goods for a weekly or monthly payment. Generally, RTO agreements are self-renewing on a weekly or monthly basis, and consumers are under no obligation to continue making payments beyond the current weekly or monthly period. RTO transactions may be attractive to consumers who cannot afford a cash purchase, may be unable to qualify for traditional credit, or are unable or unwilling to wait until they can save enough money for a purchase.

RTO agreements provide consumers with the option to purchase the goods, in most cases either by continuing to make payments for a specified period of time, usually 12 to 24 months, or by making an early payment of some specified proportion of the remaining payments. APRO reports that some RTO stores have begun to offer more payment options to consumers for purchasing merchandise, including the option to purchase goods within three to six months instead of the typical period of 12 to 24 months. APRO estimates that in 2009 there were approximately 8,600 RTO stores in the United States and Canada, serving more than four million customers and producing $7 billion in annual revenues.

Important questions about RTO contracts involve whether the poor pay more (too much more?) than middle-class consumers for the items they purchase through these contracts, and the quality of their experience with the retailer if they happen to default. The same FTC report explains that although most RTO customers (75 percent) were satisfied with their experience with RTO transactions, 19 percent of all RTO customers interviewed were dissatisfied with their experience, and most cited high prices as the reason. Complaints about high prices were made by 27 percent of all RTO customers, including nearly 70 percent of dissatisfied customers. Fewer customers complained about problems with the merchandise or repair service, the treatment received from store employees, the imposition of hidden or added costs, or other issues. Nearly half of all RTO customers had made at least one late payment. Sixty-four percent of customers who made late payments reported

federal-trade-commission-rent-own-transactions/110726renttoowntestimony.pdf.

that the treatment they received from the store when they were late was either "very good" or "good," and another 20 percent reported that the treatment was "fair." Fifteen percent of late-paying customers reported being treated poorly when they were late, including 11 percent who indicated possibly abusive collection practices.

The RTO industry typically justifies charging higher prices to its consumer market on grounds that they present a greater credit risk than the average consumer. Given the purchaser/borrower's limited income, the risks of default — and a loss to the retailer — are greater than they would be in installment sales to purchasers with higher incomes. Greater risk justifies a greater purchase price, the argument goes. At the same time, it appears that when the consumer is in default, parties to retail installment contracts often avoid formal legal proceedings. In many (perhaps most) cases, the consumer agrees to "throw the keys on the table," and the seller takes back the property in question, without resorting to the legal process. Once the consumer relinquishes the property, the important question becomes liability for the so-called "deficiency" — the difference between the value of the property reacquired by the seller and the total amount due. As you read *Williams v. Walker-Thomas*, consider whether Judge Wright's concerns about terms in the parties' installment sale contract might apply to RTO agreements today.

1. The Origins

WILLIAMS v. WALKER-THOMAS FURNITURE CO.

United States Court of Appeals, District of Columbia Circuit
350 F.2d 445 (D.C. Cir. 1965)

J. Skelly Wright, C.J.

Appellee, Walker-Thomas Furniture Company, operates a retail furniture store in the District of Columbia. During the period from 1957 to 1962 each appellant in these cases purchased a number of household items from Walker-Thomas, for which payment was to be made in installments. The terms of each purchase were contained in a printed form contract that set forth the value of the purchased item and purported to lease the item to appellant for a stipulated monthly rent payment. The contract then provided, in substance, that title would remain in Walker-Thomas until the total of all the monthly payments made equaled the stated value of the item, at which time appellants could take title. In the event of a default in the payment of any monthly installment, Walker-Thomas could repossess the item.

Pay monthly rent until total = value then get title → Repo if default

The contract further provided that "the amount of each periodical installment payment to be made by [purchaser] to the Company under this present lease shall be inclusive of and not in addition to the amount of each installment payment to be made by [purchaser] under such prior leases, bills, or accounts; *and all payments now and hereafter made by [purchaser] shall be credited pro rata on all outstanding leases, bills, and accounts* due the Company by [purchaser] at the time each such payment is made." (Emphasis added.) The effect of this rather obscure provision was to keep a balance due on every item purchased until the balance due on all items, whenever purchased, was liquidated. As a result, the debt incurred at the time of purchase of each item was secured by the right to repossess all the items previously purchased by the same purchaser, and each new item purchased automatically became subject to a security interest arising out of the previous dealings.

On May 12, 1962, appellant Thorne purchased an item described as a Daveno, three tables, and two lamps, having total stated value of $391.10. Shortly thereafter, he defaulted on his monthly payments and appellee sought to replevy all the items purchased since the first transaction in 1958. Similarly, on April 17, 1962, appellant Williams bought a stereo set of stated value of $514.95.[239] She too defaulted shortly thereafter, and appellee sought to replevy all the items purchased since December 1957. The Court of General Sessions granted judgment for appellee. The District of Columbia Court of Appeals affirmed, and we granted appellants' motion for leave to appeal to this court.

Appellants' principal contention, rejected by both the trial and the appellate courts below, is that these contracts, or at least some of them, are unconscionable and, hence, not enforceable. In its opinion in *Williams v. Walker-Thomas Furniture Company*, 198 A.2d 914, 916 (1964), the District of Columbia Court of Appeals explained its rejection of this contention as follows:

> Appellant's second argument presents a more serious question. The record reveals that prior to the last purchase appellant had reduced the balance in her account to $164. The last purchase, a stereo set, raised the balance due to $678. Significantly, at the time of this and the preceding purchases, appellee was aware of appellant's financial position. The reverse side of the stereo contract listed the name of appellant's social worker and her $218 monthly stipend from the government. Nevertheless, with full knowledge that appellant had to feed, clothe, and support both herself and seven children on this amount, appellee sold her a $514 stereo set.

> We cannot condemn too strongly appellee's conduct. It raises serious questions of sharp practice and irresponsible business dealings. A review of the legislation in the District of Columbia affecting retail sales and the pertinent decisions of the highest court in this jurisdiction disclose, however, no ground upon which this court can declare the contracts in question contrary to public policy. We note that were the Maryland Retail Installment Sales Act, Art. 83 §§ 128–153, or its equivalent, in force in the District of Columbia, we could grant appellant appropriate relief. We think Congress should consider corrective legislation to protect the public from such exploitive contracts as were utilized in the case at bar.

We do not agree that the court lacked the power to refuse enforcement to contracts found to be unconscionable. In other jurisdictions, it has been held as a matter of common law that unconscionable contracts are not enforceable. While no decision of this court so holding has been found, the notion that an unconscionable bargain should not be given full enforcement is by no means novel. In *Scott v.*

---

[239] [1] At the time of this purchase her account showed a balance of $164 still owing from her prior purchases. The total of all the purchases made over the years in question came to $1,800. The total payments amounted to $1,400.

United States, 79 U.S. (12 Wall.) 443, 445 (1870), the Supreme Court stated: "If a contract be unreasonable and unconscionable, but not void for fraud, a court of law will give to the party who sues for its breach damages, not according to its letter, but only such as he is equitably entitled to. . . . "

Since we have never adopted or rejected such a rule, the question here presented is actually one of first impression.

Congress has recently enacted the Uniform Commercial Code, which specifically provides that the court may refuse to enforce a contract which it finds to be unconscionable at the time it was made. 28 D.C. Code § 2-302 (Supp. IV 1965). The enactment of this section, which occurred subsequent to the contracts here in suit, does not mean that the common law of the District of Columbia was otherwise at the time of enactment, nor does it preclude the court from adopting a similar rule in the exercise of its powers to develop the common law for the District of Columbia. In fact, in view of the absence of prior authority on the point, we consider the congressional adoption of § 2-302 persuasive authority for following the rationale of the cases from which the section is explicitly derived. Accordingly, we hold that where the element of unconscionability is present at the time a contract is made, the contract should not be enforced.

Unconscionability has generally been recognized to include an absence of meaningful choice on the part of one of the parties together with contract terms which are unreasonably favorable to the other party.[240] Whether a meaningful choice is present in a particular case can only be determined by consideration of all the circumstances surrounding the transaction. In many cases the meaningfulness of the choice is negated by a gross inequality of bargaining power.[241] The manner in which the contract was entered is also relevant to this consideration. Did each party to the contract, considering his obvious education or lack of it, have a reasonable opportunity to understand the terms of the contract, or were the important terms hidden in a maze of fine print and minimized by deceptive sales practices? Ordinarily, one who signs an agreement without full knowledge of its terms might be held to assume the risk that he has entered a one-sided bargain. But when a party of little bargaining power, and hence little real choice, signs a commercially unreasonable contract with little or no knowledge of its terms, it is hardly likely that his consent, or even an objective manifestation of his consent, was ever given to all the terms. In such a case the usual rule that the terms of the agreement are not to be questioned should be abandoned and the court should consider whether the terms of the contract are so unfair that enforcement should be withheld.

---

[240] [6] *See* Henningsen v. Bloomfield Motors, Inc.; Campbell Soup Co. v. Wentz.

[241] [7] *See* Henningsen v. Bloomfield Motors, Inc., 161 A.2d at 86, and authorities there cited. Inquiry into the relative bargaining power of the two parties is not an inquiry wholly divorced from the general question of unconscionability, since a one-sided bargain is itself evidence of the inequality of the bargaining parties. This fact was vaguely recognized in the common law doctrine of intrinsic fraud, that is, fraud which can be presumed from the grossly unfair nature of the terms of the contract. See the oft-quoted statement of Lord Hardwicke in Earl of Chesterfield v. Janssen, 28 Eng. Rep. 82, 100 (1751): "[Fraud] may be apparent from the intrinsic nature and subject of the bargain itself; such as no man in his senses and not under delusion would make. . . . "

In determining reasonableness or fairness, the primary concern must be with the terms of the contract considered in light of the circumstances existing when the contract was made. The test is not simple, nor can it be mechanically applied. The terms are to be considered "in the light of the general commercial background and the commercial needs of the particular trade or case."[242] Corbin suggests the test as being whether the terms are "so extreme as to appear unconscionable according to the mores and business practices of the time and place." 1 CORBIN ON CONTRACTS, § 128 (1963). We think this formulation correctly states the test to be applied in those cases where no meaningful choice was exercised upon entering the contract.

Remand to fig out more detail of circs that might be made in uncon

Because the trial court and the appellate court did not feel that enforcement could be refused, no findings were made on the possible unconscionability of the contracts in these cases. Since the record is not sufficient for our deciding the issue as a matter of law, the cases must be remanded to the trial court for further proceedings.

So ordered.

DANAHER, C.J. (dissenting):

The District of Columbia Court of Appeals obviously was as unhappy about the situation here presented as any of us can possibly be. Its opinion in the Williams case, quoted in the majority text, concludes: "We think Congress should consider corrective legislation to protect the public from such exploitive contracts as were utilized in the case at bar."

Dissent = DC'cA opinion

My view is thus summed up by an able court which made no finding that there had actually been sharp practice. Rather the appellant seems to have known precisely where she stood.

There are many aspects of public policy here involved. What is a luxury to some may seem an outright necessity to others. Is public oversight to be required of the expenditures of relief funds? A washing machine, e.g., in the hands of a relief client might become a fruitful source of income. Many relief clients may well need credit, and certain business establishments will take long chances on the sale of items, expecting their pricing policies will afford a degree of protection commensurate with the risk. . . .

I mention such matters only to emphasize the desirability of a cautious approach to any such problem, particularly since the law for so long has allowed parties such great latitude in making their own contracts. I dare say there must annually be thousands upon thousands of installment credit transactions in this jurisdiction, and one can only speculate as to the effect the decision in these cases will have.

I join the District of Columbia Court of Appeals in its disposition of the issues.

---

[242] [11] Comment, UCC § 2-307 [sic]. [Eds. note: The language quoted in the text of the opinion is from Comment 1, UCC § 2-302.]

Quimbee: If an element of uncon exists at formation is it enforceable? NOPE

NOTES AND QUESTIONS

1. ***The poor go shopping:*** Professor D.I. Greenberg studied Walker-Thomas Furniture Company's operations.[243] The store, which sold appliances and furniture, was located on Seventh Street in the "easy credit" corridor of downtown Washington, D.C.

Walker-Thomas marketed through about 30 door-to-door people who were both sales representatives and collection agents. They had from 15,000 to 20,000 working accounts. The store had an average yearly sales volume of $4 million. Its business derived almost completely from welfare, Social Security, and Supplemental Security Income recipients, as well as segments of the working poor. Few of these people could obtain credit for major purchases in normal retail stores.

Walker-Thomas found it profitable to deal with its customers. It offered credit to them, and it had a means of collecting a high percentage of what was due. Since its customers' prime source of income was the monthly benefit check, its salespeople scheduled collection for days when checks were likely to arrive. These salespeople carried money and cashed the check while deducting the required payment. This benefited the poor, who had difficulty cashing checks.

The salespersons provided intangible psychological rewards for customers by personalizing interaction. Low-income customers may be misunderstood at retail stores because of language difficulties. Security guards watch them suspiciously. Clerks ignore them or indicate that they are worthless customers. The Walker-Thomas person who came to the apartment, however, was friendly, helpful, and willing to simplify procedures. However, Greenberg argues that the salesperson controlled the interaction. The salesperson would not tell these customers the total price, emphasizing the amount of the monthly payment. The salesperson knew the income of the customer and saw the apartment. The salesperson could suggest that the customer needed a new television set or a new couch. Often the customer signed a contract and the salesperson selected the particular appliance or item of furniture for them.

When the time for collection came, the salesperson could allow extra time when there was good reason for the delay. However, if Walker-Thomas thought a customer should pay, it was expert in many debt collection techniques. It used a series of letters with increasing threats. They telephoned debtors, calling very early in the morning or late in the evening. They called customers' friends and relatives and asked why payments were not being made.

Walker-Thomas seldom gave warranty service on the goods. The salesperson would attempt to fix various items, adding the cost of repairs to the monthly payments where it would not be seen. Often the salesperson kept the payment booklet and revised it to add charges. Those who paid on time got things fixed as a reward. The salesperson blamed the customer: the children were rough on the item, or the customer failed to operate the item properly. However, they told good customers that the salesperson could do them a favor and get the item fixed.

---

[243] D.I. Greenberg, *Easy Terms, Hard Times: Complaint Handling in the Ghetto*, in No Access to Law: Alternatives to the American Judicial System 379 (Laura Nader ed., Academic Press 1980).

If a customer complained to a legal services or social agency, Walker-Thomas responded using its power. It threatened to end the customer's access to credit. It threatened to be inflexible about prompt payments in the future. Walker-Thomas employed six people, called "the pimps," to assemble information about customers who might present problems. For example, a customer complained to the Federal Trade Commission about Walker-Thomas's practices. The management called the customer and threatened to tell her social worker that her husband was working on a construction site in Virginia. The customer's status could change from "husband's whereabouts unknown" to that of an ex-welfare recipient. While the husband was not contributing anything to her, she would have to establish this by going through procedures at the welfare office. Welfare kept down its case load by being arbitrary, so those facing any new hearing ran the risk of a wrong decision. The customer withdrew the complaint.

Greenberg's conclusion warns about focusing on Walker-Thomas. It is worth remembering as we work through the following material:[244]

> Consider that labor and insurance costs, shoplifting, inability to secure lines of credit, and bad debts combine to push business out of the ghetto and make profit a virtually impossible goal except for . . . [a] firm like Walker-Thomas. . . . The complaints of poor people . . . represent a "trickle-down" from the choices made by the politically and economically powerful. The complaints of the poor therefore derive from the same sources as their poverty. To castigate Walker-Thomas . . . is ultimately to criticize the political and economic choices we make as a society.

2. *Walker-Thomas's goals in drafting the contract clause:* Here are some excerpts from Professor Richard A. Epstein's article *Unconscionability: A Critical Appraisal*:[245]

> One sort of clause that has come under . . . scrutiny is the so-called "add-on" clause used in consumer credit sales. These clauses govern the security interest taken back by the seller, and, in one common form, provide that all previous goods purchased by the buyer from the seller will secure the debts incurred with the current purchase. The security agreement also provides that each payment made with respect to any of the items purchased would be applied against all outstanding balances, allowing the seller in effect to retain his security interest in all the goods sold until the debts with respect to all items are discharged. A single default on a single payment could trigger the [seller's] right to possess all the goods subject to the comprehensive security arrangement.
>
> Although agreements of this kind can, and have, been attacked on unconscionability grounds, they make good sense in the cases to which they apply. One of the major risks to the seller of personal property is that the good sold will lose value . . . more rapidly than the purchase price is paid off. . . . The seller, therefore, who takes back a security interest only in the

---

[244] *Id.* at 14.

[245] 18 J.L. & Econ. 293, 306–08 (1975) (footnotes omitted). Published by The University of Chicago. Copyright © 1975 by The University of Chicago. All rights reserved.

goods sold, runs the real risk that repossession of the single item sold will still leave him with a loss on the transaction as a whole. . . . One way to handle this problem is to require the purchaser of the goods to make a larger cash down payment, but that, of course, is something which many buyers, particularly those of limited means, do not want to do. Another alternative is for the buyer to provide the seller with additional collateral; yet here the best collateral is doubtless in goods sold by the seller to the buyer. Other goods already in the possession of the buyer may be of uncertain value, and they may well be subject to prior liens. Again, they may be of a sort that the seller cannot conveniently resell in the ordinary course of his business. . . . The "add-on" clause allows both parties to benefit from the reduction in costs in the setting up of a security arrangement.

why they do the "add on" apply to everything structure

The case for the add-on clause is strengthened, moreover, when we note its legal effects. As between the buyer and seller the clause allows the seller to collect upon his unpaid debt without having to avail himself of the awkward procedures established for unsecured creditors. The clause assures the seller that the value he has furnished the buyer will, if need be, first be used to satisfy his own claims. . . . The sense of these clauses . . . is demonstrated anew, moreover, once we realize that they operate within one very strong constraint . . . which restricts the creditor in a secured transaction to the recovery of principal, interest, and costs in cases of default by the buyer.

Professor Epstein seems to assume the main purpose of an add-on clause is to enable the creditor to collect more of its debt if it is necessary for the creditor to collect through judicial action. Do you agree that that is the main purpose or function of these clauses? Consider your answer in the light of the next question, focusing on what Walker-Thomas actually would have seized.

3. *Procedural posture and Walker-Thomas's goals in the lawsuit:* In *Williams*, Walker-Thomas was the plaintiff, seeking to "replevy" items purchased by Thorne and Williams. As noted above, replevin is a legal procedure whereby the plaintiff, asserting a possessory interest (e.g., title), seeks to recover possession of goods from someone who is not entitled to possess them. The "writ of replevin" is the order sought by the plaintiff to entitle it to take the defendants' property.

Walker Thom is P

The writ issued by the lower court in the *Williams* case would have enabled Walker-Thomas to seize the following: one wallet, two pairs of draperies, one apron set, one pot holder set, one set of rugs, one pair of draperies, one 2 x 6 folding bed, one chest, one 9 x 12 linoleum rug, two pairs of curtains, four sheets, one WS20 portable fan, two pairs of curtains, one Royal portable typewriter, two gun and holster sets (presumably toys), one metal bed, one inner-spring mattress, four chrome kitchen chairs, one bath mat set, shower curtains, one Speed Queen washing machine, and one Admiral stereo.[246]

Many of these items seem to have little resale value. Why was Walker-Thomas

---

[246] *See* Pierre Dostert, *Appellate Restatement of Unconscionability: Civil Legal Aid at Work*, 54 A.B.A. J. 1183 (1968).

interested in repossessing such things as used shower curtains and children's toys? Does the excerpt from Professor Epstein in Note 2, *supra*, provide an answer to this question? Do you think Walker-Thomas might have reasons for including an add-on clause in its contract in addition (or alternatively) to the reason suggested by Professor Epstein? Is the answer to these questions relevant to an unconscionability analysis?

4. *The fate of add-on clauses:* The "add-on" clause challenged in the *Williams* case is sometimes called a "cross-collateral" clause.[247] Such clauses are now regulated by statute in many states. For example, the Arizona Retail Installment Sales Transactions Act (A.R.S. § 44-6002c(6)) provides that "goods purchased under the previous contract or contracts may be security for the goods purchased under the subsequent contract, but only until such time as the total of payments under the previous contract or contracts is fully paid." The Uniform Commercial Code, also, restricts to some extent the use of add-on clauses in the consumer setting. *See* U.C.C. § 9-204(b)(1). Why do you think legislatures thought it appropriate to regulate these clauses?

5. *Law and Economics and unconscionability:* Professor Epstein's views in Note 2, *supra*, may be associated with the law and economics school of thought, of which he is a part. One might think that law and economics would be hostile to the doctrine of unconscionability on grounds such as those asserted by Professor Epstein (e.g., that it impairs freedom of contract). Consider, however, this observation from Professor Russell Korobkin:[248]

> Some students will contend that the law-and-economics emphasis on whether a term is efficient from an ex ante perspective is inconsistent with the term "unconscionability," which itself seems to have a moral connotation absent from any analysis of ex ante efficiency. But in the context of unconscionability, a distinction between moral and economic considerations is not so obvious. Consider the following propositions:
>
> (1) It *is not* unconscionable for Walker-Thomas to include a cross-collateralization clause in its standard form contract if the resulting market-driven price/term combination makes buyers as a class better off than they otherwise would be, even if the term imposes a hardship ex post on some particular buyers, like Williams, who default.
>
> (2) It *is* unconscionable, on the other hand, for Walker-Thomas to include a cross-collateralization clause in its standard form contract if the resulting market-driven price/term combination makes buyers as a class worse off than they otherwise would be.

6. *The intersection of race, class, and gender:* Many readers who know the demographics of Washington, D.C., assume Ora Lee Williams is African American.

---

[247] Commercial lawyers sometimes refer to these as "cross-collateral" clauses, because they mean that one item of property can secure obligations under more than one contract — that is, the item in question can serve as collateral that "crosses" multiple obligations or contracts.

[248] Russell Korobkin, *A "Traditional" and "Behavioral" Law-and-Economics Analysis of* Williams v. Walker-Thomas Furniture Company, 26 U. Haw. L. Rev. 441, 468 (2004).

Professor Blake Morant confirms this fact on the basis of a conversation with a law professor colleague who worked in the legal services office at the time and met Ms. Williams.[249] Does the fact of her race matter? Professor Deborah Waire Post has argued that it is important because it is part of the "inequality of bargaining power" in the transaction and in the deals of other African Americans, particularly when they are also poor. She says, "[W]e continue to teach students about 'meaningful choice' with reference to class, certainly, and to education, because [they are] explicitly referenced in the case, but without reference to the targeting of African American communities by commercial predators."[250] In the home mortgage market, for example, the practice of "reverse redlining" involves targeting racial minorities for subprime loans even when they would normally qualify for prime mortgages or when they cannot afford the mortgages being offered.[251] Post also argues that it is best to acknowledge that race, gender, and class all play a role in reactions to *Williams v. Walker-Thomas*; then we can forthrightly assess whether negative stereotypes are in play: "[T]he welfare mother has assumed mythic proportions in American culture. When we teach this case, the myth looms in the background, overpowering whatever facts contradict the myth."

One of the ways the myth may enter into the reasoning of the court is in the quote from the District of Columbia Court of Appeals to the effect that it was outrageous (a "sharp practice" and "irresponsible") to sell Ms. Williams a $514 stereo when she was a welfare mother with a stipend of $218 a month to support herself and seven children. However, in a footnote in the case, we learn that Ms. Williams had paid $1400 on prior purchases and had reduced her balance to $164. In other words, Ms. Williams repaid a great deal of debt on a low income. Thus, she may have been a good credit risk. In addition, perhaps the stereo was affordable for her at the time of the transaction, for example if the payments were spread out over five years to make them sufficiently low per payment period. She may have suffered some sort of financial shock after the stereo purchase that made her no longer able to pay. If she was a good credit risk and could afford the payments at the time of the purchase, does that make the transaction conscionable? Or is the problem the way the add-on term was phrased? If so, could the problem be fixed with better disclosure?

Professor Post writes that reading the case transports her back to her own childhood "as a poor black person living among other working-class white and black families on an integrated street in a small city." She says:[252]

> My parents were poor — not stupid — and like Ora Lee Williams they dealt regularly with a person from a company like Walker-Thomas. I am pretty sure the extension of credit to my parents had nothing to do with income,

[249] Blake Morant, *The Relevance of Race and Disparity in Discussions of Contract Law*, 31 New Eng. L. Rev. 889, n.208 (1997).

[250] Deborah Waire Post, *Freeing Ora Lee Williams*, in Contracting Law (Amy Hilsman Kastely, Deborah Waire Post, and Sharon Kang Hom, eds., Carolina Academic Press 2000).

[251] Nicole Lutes Fuentes, *Defrauding the American Dream: Predatory Lending in Latino Communities and Reform of California's Lending Law*, 97 Cal. L. Rev. 1279, 1287–89 (2009).

[252] Deborah Waire Post, *The Square Deal Furniture Company*, in Contracting Law 638–39 (Amy Hilsman Kastely, Deborah Waire Post, & Sharon Kang Hom, eds., Carolina Academic Press 2000).

assets, debt, or prior credit history. It had a lot more to do with the personal relationship between them and the salesman from the Square Deal Furniture Company . . . When he came, the salesman sat at the kitchen table and drank coffee with my Dad. He talked about lots of things besides the purchases and payments my parents made. . . . [H]e seemed like a family friend. He listened to my parents when they explained they couldn't make a payment that week but would double up the next week.

Post remembers variation in the quality of the goods sold: "The furniture was shoddy, the clothes were fine . . . " In addition, her impression is that the implicit expectations were that customers made payments unless there was a catastrophe, and that the store would not only give extensions but also take back a purchase if a person just couldn't afford it. So it was not within expectations that the store would send a truck and try to take everything away. Overall, based on her childhood experience with a low-income retailer that did not act so harshly, Professor Post believes that Walker-Thomas "did violence by charging too much; it did violence by pressuring people to buy more than they could afford; it did violence by threatening harm; it did harm by disregarding friendships." Rather than an absence of meaningful choice, she says, "[T]he key to the decision in *Williams* is surprise. I might even go so far as to call it betrayal." How is this analysis similar to and different from the relational contract approach of Professor Ian Macneil, discussed several times elsewhere in this chapter?

7. ***Unconscionability as a common-law doctrine:*** *Williams* applies the UCC's unconscionability section as persuasive authority concerning the common law. As a technical matter, why doesn't it apply the UCC directly? The Restatement (Second) of Contracts § 208 now treats unconscionability as part of the common law of contracts; it is not a doctrine restricted to the sale of goods.

8. ***Unconscionability and warranty disclaimers:*** Is the doctrine of unconscionability available to check possible abuses of disclaimers of warranty? Before reading further, you might see if you can construct for yourself, out of the provisions of the UCC and its comments, the arguments on both sides of this question.

Many argue that warranty disclaimers are not vulnerable to application of the unconscionability doctrine because § 2-316(2) indicates what is necessary for a warranty disclaimer to be valid, and the requirement that it be "not unconscionable" — which was inserted in § 2-719(3), dealing with limitations on consequential damages — is conspicuously absent. Some courts have accepted this view.[253] Other courts have rejected the same arguments, finding unconscionability to be a limitation on warranty disclaimers. Even if the warranty disclaimer might survive the challenge of § 2-302, plaintiffs might still prevail either on a theory of strict product liability (if the claim is for other than economic loss), or under the terms of consumer legislation, either state or federal.

---

[253] *See, e.g.*, Avery v. Aladdin Prod. Div., 128 Ga. App. 266, 196 S.E.2d 357 (1973); Tacoma Boatbldg. Co. v. Delta Fishing Col, 1980 U.S. Dist. LEXIS 17830 (W.D. Wash. Jan. 4, 1980).

2. Challenges to Unconscionability: Ambiguity and Arbitration

The effectiveness of the unconscionability doctrine in providing adequate relief has been the topic of much debate. While many academics and social liberals embraced the doctrine as a means of improving the economic plight of the poor, others worried that the doctrine was vague, untethered to concrete principles of common law or legislative mandate. Many believed that the death knell for unconscionability was sounded by a series of recent Supreme Court cases upholding arbitration clauses over unconscionability challenges.[254] These decisions would, in effect, take the unconscionability determination away from judges. Let us consider both perspectives.

a. Ambiguity

"Unconscionability analysis," Anne Fleming writes, "and the balancing it entailed, smacked of freewheeling judicial policymaking, rather than neutral or efficiency-guided judging."[255] Professor Fleming was echoing the sentiments of commercial law professor Arthur Leff.[256] She states:[257]

> Leff delivered the most devastating critique of the Code provision on unconscionability. Cataloging in painstaking detail the U.C.C. drafters' many missteps in preparing the text and commentary of section 2-302, Leff concluded that the provision suffered from "amorphous unintelligibility." In Leff's view, the final draft invited judges to rely on their own "emotional state" to determine which terms were permissible. By permitting judges to "police contracts on a clause-by-clause basis," the provision demanded they decide whether particular terms should be allowed as a matter of policy. The term "unconscionable" — a "highly abstract word" — provided no concrete guidelines to help resolve questions that were essentially "problems of social policy." It invited a court to be "nondisclosive about the basis of its decision even to itself." Finding little guidance in section 2-302 as drafted, Leff offered his own framework to help courts in analyzing unconscionability claims. Leff's distinction — between procedural and substantive unconscionability — has dominated thinking about the issue ever since. In the case of *Williams*, Leff approved the outcome, but not the

[Handwritten margin note: Claim uncon analysis not well founded / is random]

---

[254] Rent-A-Center, West, Inc. v. Jackson, 561 U.S. 63, 130 S. Ct. 2772, 177 L. Ed. 2d 403 (2010); AT&T Mobility LLC v. Concepcion, 563 U.S. 333, 131 S. Ct. 1740, 179 L. Ed. 2d 742 (2011); Am. Express Co. v. Italian Colors Rest., 133 S. Ct. 2304, 186 L. Ed. 2d 417 (2013).

[255] Anne Fleming, *The Rise and Fall of Unconscionability as the "Law of the Poor,"* 102 Geo. L.J. 1383, 1430–31 (2014).

[256] Arthur Allen Leff, *Unconscionability and the Code — The Emperor's New Clause*, 115 U. Pa. L. Rev. 485 (1967). *See also* Arthur Leff, *Unconscionability and the Crowd — Consumers and the Common Law Tradition*, 31 U. Pitt. L. Rev. 349, 349–58 (1970) ("One cannot think of a more expensive and frustrating course than to seek to regulate goods or 'contract' quality through repeated lawsuits against inventive 'wrongdoers.' Wouldn't it be easier and far more effective, if one finds these cross-collateral clauses, or some others, offensive in consumer transactions, just to face one's conclusion and regulate them out of existence, in a manner no lawyer could conscientiously avoid?").

[257] Fleming, *supra* note 255, at 1422–24.

method of reaching it. He agreed that there was sufficient evidence of procedural unconscionability to merit remand. The nature of the substantive unconscionability was less apparent, however. Most likely, the court viewed the whole transaction as substantively unfair, because Walker-Thomas Furniture knew at the time of the sale that Williams was on relief and could not afford the stereo. Leff did not object to the court treating welfare recipients as a special "class" for purposes of contract law. He argued that such distinctions were "exceedingly common in the law (not to mention life)." Rather, he opposed the method of imposing these controls — regulation "via the judicial bureaucracy, on an ad hoc case-by-case basis essentially unrestrained by legislative or administrative guidance." Furthermore, few such cases would make it to a judge because only consumers with free legal representation could afford to test the legality of their contract terms in court.

It would be better to let legislatures, rather than judges, make such political decisions and ban certain contract terms outright. Indeed, these contracts were not really contracts at all, Leff argued. They were more like "products," things. These were not bargained-for exchanges in the traditional contract law model. Nor would it be desirable to make consumers bargain for contract terms, which would increase the cost of these transactions. Rather, Leff argued, legislatures should face the policy questions raised by such "products" and decide what terms were off-limits, much like they would regulate the minimum quality of goods for sale.

In a 1981 article, Professor William Whitford argued that Article 2's unconscionability standard was a vague provision, made even less workable by the statutory directive to consider the entire context of the transaction.[258] This enabled courts to distinguish any precedent, based on a variation in circumstance. Moreover, the ambiguity of the standard made it unlikely that merchants would alter their practices voluntarily. Rather, they would "give themselves the benefit of the doubt" that they were not doing anything unconscionable. While unconscionability defenses might induce settlements that benefited individual consumers who were fortunate enough to be represented by counsel, the very nature of settlement meant that there would be no precedent binding on the population of those who sold to the poor. To have a broader impact on unconscionable practices, one would need instruments different from the traditional lawsuit.

More recently, in a tribute to Professor Jean Braucher, Whitford observed that Braucher, like many scholars, worried that the ambiguity and vagueness inherent in a standard like "unconscionability" would fail to protect many who might need it:[259]

> [Braucher] made this point most often by discussing the limited impact of the unconscionability standard of the UCC, Article 2. What could change practices on the ground, [she] believed, were rules — specific, inflexible

---

[258] William C. Whitford, *Structuring Consumer Protection Legislation to Maximize Effectiveness*, 1981 WIS. L. REV. 1018.

[259] William C. Whitford, *Jean Braucher's Contracts World View*, 58 ARIZ. L. REV. 13, 26 (2016).

directions to commercial parties about how to behave (e.g., what terms to include or not to include in a [standard form contract]). The greatest advantage of specific rules is that they are partially self-enforcing because, if told specifically and unambiguously what to do, many merchants will obey even if there is little fear of sanction for disobedience — perhaps from a sense of law-abidingness, perhaps from a fear of bad publicity, or for some other reason. The specific rules [Braucher] favored could, and sometimes do, come from direct legislation, but [her] preference was to implement a flexible statutory standard through administrative regulations.

As we shall see in Section E.3. of this chapter, *infra*, this is where the law seems to be heading.

b. Arbitration

Despite its vagueness, and thus its unpredictability in litigation, the unconscionability doctrine continued to be raised quite frequently by attorneys representing poor consumers sued by creditors. An unconscionability defense often raised an issue that could be settled on summary judgment, and it often yielded a compromise settlement. In more recent years, consumer lawyers had some success in using the unconscionability defense to challenge arbitration clauses in consumer and employment contracts. Consumers and employees tried to use unconscionability as a means to attack mandatory, pre-dispute arbitration provisions, on the basis of both lack of understanding of what arbitration means (not getting a day in court and instead having to use a private forum) and unfair arbitration rules — such as remote locations and high fees that make it impractical to use the forum at all — to try to show both procedural and substantive unconscionability. And they particularly focused on increasingly common clauses in arbitration agreements that foreclosed class actions, in court or in arbitration proceedings, by a group of consumers or employees similarly disadvantaged by a particular contract term or practice. Reread section D.3. of Chapter 3, *supra*, concerning the Federal Arbitration Act and the increasing use of arbitration clauses in financial, medical, insurance, and communication services as well as employment contracts.

Since 2010, the Supreme Court has made it quite difficult for consumer plaintiffs to claim successfully that arbitration clauses should be struck on grounds of unconscionability. A recent article by David Horton and Andrea Cann Chandrasekher concisely explains why, and what this means:[260]

> Consider three recent cases filed by consumers against large companies. John Feeney accused a computer manufacturer of charging tens of thousands of its customers an illegal $13 sales tax.[261] Elizabeth Dean brought a class action against a private, for-profit vocational school for misleading its students about the costs and marketability of their de-

---

[260] David Horton & Andrea Cann Chandrasekher, *After the Revolution: An Empirical Study of Consumer Arbitration*, 104 Geo. L.J. 57, 58–62 (2015).

[261] [1] *See* Plaintiffs' Memorandum in Support of Motion for Reconsideration of Orders Granting Defendants' Motions to Compel Arbitration, Feeney v. Dell Inc., No. 03-01158, 2007 WL 6048106, at *3 (Mass. Super. Ct. Nov. 30, 2007).

grees.[262] Ernestine Hawkins sued a bank after she was injured by an accident in its lobby.[263] Anyone who has tracked the evolution of the U.S. civil justice system can predict what happened next. The businesses did not deny the plaintiffs' allegations or debunk their legal theories. Instead, they moved to compel arbitration.

The use of private dispute resolution as the first line of defense against consumer lawsuits has long been controversial. In 1925, Congress passed the Federal Arbitration Act (FAA) to abolish common law rules that made it impossible to obtain specific performance of an agreement to arbitrate. The statute lay largely dormant until the 1980s, when the U.S. Supreme Court held that it preempts state law, governs statutory claims, and embodies a "liberal federal policy favoring arbitration." Countless firms added arbitration clauses to their contracts, making arbitration "a phenomenon that pervade[s] virtually every corner of the daily economy." Some Justices, business groups, and the defense bar applauded this development, arguing that arbitration's speed, flexibility, and affordability pave the way for customers to pursue claims. But other courts, plaintiffs' lawyers, and consumer advocates objected that abridged procedures thwart substantive rights, and that arbitrators — who, unlike judges, are paid by the case — are reluctant to rule against the repeat playing firms that may select or veto them again in the future.

Since 2010, these issues have been thrust back into the spotlight. For decades, judges maintained the legitimacy of alternative dispute resolution by policing arbitration clauses for fairness. If a consumer proved that arbitral expenses or one-sided procedures thwarted her rights, a court would strike down all or part of the arbitration clause under the unconscionability doctrine. But in 2010, the [U.S. Supreme] Court held in *Rent-A-Center, West, Inc. v. Jackson* that drafters could bypass this layer of judicial review by delegating questions about the scope or validity of the arbitration clause to the arbitrator.[264] By allowing private judges to define their own powers, the Court rejected concerns that they are biased against consumers. Similarly, until 2011, most jurisdictions refused to enforce class arbitration waivers when plaintiffs asserted numerous low-value claims. These judges reasoned that because small-dollar grievances will either be aggregated or abandoned, class arbitration waivers liberated firms from liability. However, in *AT&T Mobility LLC v. Concepcion*[265] and *American Express v. Italian Colors Restaurant (Italian Colors)*[266] the Court made class arbitration waivers bulletproof, placing the onus on customers to initiate their own arbitrations rather than ride the wake of class proceedings.

---

[262] [2] *See* Dean v. Draughons Junior Coll., Inc., 917 F. Supp. 2d 751, 753 (M.D. Tenn. 2013).

[263] [3] Hawkins v. Region's, 944 F. Supp. 2d 528, 529 (N.D. Miss. 2013).

[264] [14] *See* 561 U.S. 63, 72, 130 S. Ct. 2772, 177 L. Ed. 2d 403 (2010).

[265] [17] 563 U.S. 333, 131 S. Ct. 1740, 179 L. Ed. 2d 742 (2011).

[266] [18] 133 S. Ct. 2304, 186 L. Ed. 2d 417 (2013).

The cases from the first paragraph of this [excerpt] illustrate the profound impact of the Court's recent FAA jurisprudence. In *Feeney*, the Massachusetts Supreme Judicial Court held that *Concepcion* and *Italian Colors* required each plaintiff to pursue their small-dollar lawsuits in individual arbitration. The state high court speculated that few customers would do so, and called this result "untenable," but felt bound to obey "a controlling statement of Federal law."

Similarly, in *Dean*, the plaintiff urged a district judge in Tennessee to exempt her and the other former students from arbitration because they were "buried in debt" and could not afford to pay the arbitrator's fees. Yet the defendant's arbitration clause stated that its "scope or enforceability . . . shall be determined by the arbitrator, and not by a court." The judge reasoned that, as paradoxical as it sounds, under *Rent-A-Center*, the issue of whether the plaintiffs should be arbitrating was for the arbitrator to decide.[267] The court sent the matter to the private tribunal, but not before flying a red flag of protest:[268]

> [T]his holding present[s] a serious fairness issue. . . . [T]he court is concerned that one or more of the named plaintiffs in this action will not be able to afford the out-of-pocket costs to arbitrate, even under conservative cost assumptions. Indeed, several of the plaintiffs have represented that they have no income and no unencumbered assets whatsoever. . . . While required by the FAA, this result strikes the court as manifestly unjust and, perhaps, deserving of legislative attention.

However, the Mississippi district court in *Hawkins* had no such misgivings. The plaintiff asserted that she could not be forced to arbitrate her tort claim because she had closed her account at the bank where she fell three years before the incident.[269] She contended that there was no contract — and therefore no agreement to arbitrate — between her and the institution. The court held that this argument was irrelevant because the plaintiff's original deposit agreement provided that "[a]ny dispute regarding whether a particular controversy is subject to arbitration . . . shall be decided by the arbitrator(s)."[270] The court sent the dispute to arbitration and defended this result:[271]

> The Supreme Court's decision[s] . . . might be regarded by some as creating a legal "black hole" which inevitably sucks in disputes and sends them to arbitration. . . . [However,] while many plaintiffs seem to regard arbitration as the place where "lawsuits go to die," at least one empirical study of consumer arbitrations conducted by the

---

[267] [24] *See* Dean v. Draughons Junior Coll., Inc., 917 F. Supp. 2d 751, 765 (M.D. Tenn. 2013).

[268] [25] *Id.* at 765.

[269] [26] Hawkins v. Region's, 944 F. Supp. 2d 528, 530 (N.D. Miss. 2013).

[270] [28] *See id.*

[271] [29] *Id.* at 531–32 (internal quotation marks omitted).

American Arbitration Association found, among other things, that consumers won some relief in 53.3 percent of the cases they filed and recovered an average of $19,255.

These opinions reveal that the Court's reading of the FAA inspires strong, divergent reactions. But they also highlight a flaw in the fabric of this debate. Both critics and proponents of the Court have only the dimmest sense of what actually happens in the extrajudicial forum. Are the many commentators who have condemned *Concepcion* and *Italian Colors* correct that class arbitration waivers "deny a willing plaintiff any and all practical means of pursuing a claim"?[272] Or is individual arbitration superior to the class action because it is faster, cheaper, and allows consumers to act pro se? Is the expansion of arbitral sovereignty in *Rent-A-Center* unwise because arbitrators favor repeat players? Or do private judges resolve cases in a "completely fair and impartial manner"?[273] These are empirical questions about a system that does not lend itself to empirical inquiry.

NOTES AND QUESTIONS

1. ***Shedding some light — repeat players:*** Horton and Chandrasekher were able to gain some empirical insight. They studied about 5,000 consumer arbitrations conducted by the American Arbitration Association (AAA) between 2009 and 2013. Among other things, they found that "repeat players" win more often and pay less in damages than other defendants. But why does being a repeat player matter?

Are you more or less likely to win a game if you play it more often than your opponent? As we've noted elsewhere, Marc Galanter has explained that one reason the "haves" come out ahead in litigation is because they develop expertise in, and familiarity with, that process.[274] Is there any reason to think that arbitration would be different?

2. ***Arbitration and the common-law tradition:*** Much of what you have read in this course has come from common law courts. These institutions often (though not always, of course) publish reasoned opinions that then perform what some scholars call an educative or expressive function.[275] They tell future readers (including potential judges, litigants, lawyers, and law students) how a particular dispute was resolved, thereby performing a predictive service. For all of its weaknesses — as discussed in section B.1. of this chapter, *supra*, some scholars criticize the indeterminacy of common law precedent — the common law has at least provided a "public" mechanism for developing and learning the law.[276]

---

[272] [30] Feeney v. Dell Inc., 465 Mass. 470, 989 N.E.2d 439, 454 (2013).

[273] [33] Hawkins v. Region's, 944 F. Supp. 2d 528, 532 (N.D. Miss. 2013).

[274] *Supra* Chapter 3, note 198.

[275] *See, e.g.*, Christopher L. Eisgruber, *Is the Supreme Court an Educative Institution?*, 67 N.Y.U. L. Rev. 961 (1992); Jonathan C. Lipson, *The Expressive Function of Directors' Duties to Creditors*, 12 Stan. J. L. Fin. & B. 224 (2007).

[276] *See, e.g.*, David Luban, *Settlements and the Erosion of the Public Realm*, 83 Geo. L.J. 2619, 2623 (1995) ("precedents and legal rules are public goods. Although the original litigants of the cases 'purchase' the rules, future litigants use these rules without paying.").

A key criticism of arbitration is therefore not merely that repeat players may win excessively, but also that it is, as Professor Stipanowich has argued, a "hermetically sealed black box."[277] Arbitrators do not usually publish opinions, and so we know neither the force of precedent nor the precedential force of arbitral awards. William Landes and Richard Posner have argued that leaving adjudication solely to arbitration would under-produce precedent:[278]

> [P]rivate judges [arbitrators] may have little incentive to produce precedents. They will strive for a fair result between the parties in order to preserve a reputation for impartiality, but why should they make any effort to explain the result in a way that would provide guidance for future parties? To do so would confer an external, an uncompensated, benefit not only on future parties but also on competing judges.

How might arbitration affect the development of the common law? What becomes of common law in a world with a diminishing "stock" of precedent?

3.   *Arbitration and unconscionability:* If Professor Leff was correct, and the principal problem with unconscionability doctrine was that it was ambiguous, why would arbitration be any better? After all, if it is in fact a "black box," there is no particular reason to believe that arbitrators feel themselves bound to follow precedent, much less produce it. If that is the case, why would arbitration offer any greater certainty of outcome for litigants? Why might repeat players care less about predictability than "one-off" litigants in arbitration? What, besides precedent, might predict outcomes here? Whom does precedent — as created by common law courts — serve besides the litigants?

4.   *Class (-action) consciousness:* The Horton and Chandrasekher study discusses recent Supreme Court cases on both arbitration and class action lawsuit waivers. A class action is a lawsuit commenced on behalf of a large number of plaintiffs. It is subject to special rules of civil procedure (Federal Rule of Civil Procedure 23, in the case of lawsuits commenced in United States district courts). The elements required to "certify" (create) a class are complex, and beyond the scope of this class. Why might the class action lawsuit be especially important in cases of unconscionability? Consider the following: If, as in *Williams*, plaintiffs seek merely to escape onerous contract terms, and they are impoverished to begin with, how are the lawyers to be paid?

Historically, class action lawsuits often sought affirmative recoveries, of which a portion went to the plaintiff's lawyers. The class action lawsuit was for a time viewed as an important mechanism to vindicate private rights and redress widespread violations of consumer protections.[279] This form of litigation has, however, been

---

[277] Thomas J. Stipanowich, *The Third Arbitration Trilogy: Stolt-Nielsen, Rent-A-Center, Concepcion and the Future of American Arbitration*, 22 Am. Rev. Int'l Arb. 323, 328–30, 367–70, 380–86 (2012).

[278] William M. Landes & Richard A. Posner, *Adjudication as a Private Good*, 8 J. Legal Stud. 235, 238 (1979).

[279] *See* Stephen B. Burbank & Sean Farhang, *Class Actions and the Counterrevolution Against Federal Litigation*, University of Pennsylvania Law School, Public Law Research Paper No. 15-12 (June 18, 2015), http://ssrn.com/abstract=2622201 or http://dx.doi.org/10.2139/ssrn.2622201 (accessed October 13, 2015).

criticized on a variety of grounds, including that such suits appear to some to be more effective at enriching the lawyers who commence them than in protecting the subject classes. If individuals can waive the right to pursue a class action lawsuit, leaving no class actions in contract, what incentives do lawyers have to take these cases?

3. Public Enforcement and the Resurrection(?) of Unconscionability: The Field of Consumer Financial Protection

a. State intervention in consumer financial services contracts

There is no denying the potential power of arbitration clauses (especially when coupled with class-action waivers) in private litigation. They may effectively define the outer boundary of the private use of the unconscionability doctrine to exercise social control of contract. But public actors — state attorneys general and the federal Consumer Financial Protection Bureau — are not bound by arbitration clauses. It appears that they are now increasingly inclined to police consumer finance contracts that they consider to be unconscionable, notwithstanding the presence of such clauses.

Consumer financial services have long been regulated by a complex web of state and federal laws. Your law school probably has more than one course devoted to these subjects, in particular classes on consumer protection, banking, and bankruptcy. We obviously do not think your contracts professor expects you to have mastered these subjects. Yet, few contracting contexts bring together as many of the questions that have concerned us — e.g., what promises legal institutions should recognize, and what they should do if they find the promises socially unacceptable — as consumer financial services. These contracts will include credit card agreements, student loan agreements, and — if you are "unbanked" or "underbanked" (terms explained in the next case) — payday or "signature" loans.

STATE OF NEW MEXICO EX REL. KING v. B&B INVESTMENT GROUP, INC.
New Mexico Supreme Court
329 P.3d 658 (2014)

CHÁVEZ, J.

In January 2006, two former payday lenders, B&B Investment Group, Inc., and American Cash Loans, LLC (Defendants), began to market and originate high-cost signature loans of $50 to $300, primarily to less-educated and financially unsophisticated individuals, obscuring from them the details of the cost of such loans. The loans were for twelve months, payable biweekly, and carried annual percentage rates (APRs) ranging from 1,147.14 [percent] to 1,500 percent. The Attorney General's Office (the State) sued Defendants, alleging that the signature loan products were procedurally and substantively unconscionable under the common

Common law at play

law and that they violated the Unfair Practices Act (UPA), NMSA 1978, Sections 57-12-1 to -26 (1967, as amended through 2009).

The district court found that Defendants' marketing and loan origination procedures were unconscionable and enjoined certain of its practices in the future, but declined to find the high-cost loans substantively unconscionable, concluding that it is the Legislature's responsibility to determine limits on interest rates. Both parties appealed. We affirm the district court's finding of procedural unconscionability. However, we reverse the district court's refusal to find that the loans were substantively unconscionable because under the UPA, courts have the responsibility to determine whether a contract results in a gross disparity between the value received by a person and the price paid. We conclude that the interest rates in this case are substantively unconscionable and violate the UPA.

I. BACKGROUND

Defendants market, offer, and originate high-interest, small-principal loans that they call "signature loans," from retail storefronts in Albuquerque, Farmington, and Hobbs, New Mexico. Signature loans are unsecured loans which require only the signature of the borrower, along with verification of employment, home address, identity, and references. Borrowers take out loans of $50 to $300 in principal, which are scheduled for repayment in biweekly installments over a year. Signature loans carry APRs between 1,147.14 and 1,500 percent.

Defendants are subprime lenders from Illinois who opened several payday lending operations in New Mexico in the early 2000s because, according to company president James Bartlett, "there was no usury cap" here. Before 2006, Defendants' loan portfolios were predominantly "payday loans," which, like signature loans, are small-principal, high-interest loans. See Nathalie Martin, *1000% Interest — Good While Supplies Last: A Study of Payday Loan Practices and Solutions*, 52 ARIZ. L. REV. 563, 564 (2010). Payday loans differ from signature loans primarily in the length of time they take to mature: payday loan terms are between fourteen and thirty-five days, whereas Defendants' signature loans are yearlong. Prior to 2007, when legislation was passed to limit payday lending, payday loans could be rolled over indefinitely, which essentially turned them into medium- to long-term loans that had the effect of keeping the borrower in debt for extended periods of time, similar to the signature loans at issue here.

Defendants converted their loan products from payday to signature loans in Illinois in 2005, after the Illinois legislature enacted its Payday Loan Reform Act. Defendants also converted their loan products from payday to signature loans in New Mexico just before the New Mexico Legislature implemented extensive payday loan reforms in 2007. Signature loan products are not subject to the restrictions placed on payday loans by the 2007 amendments to the Small Loan Act because they do not meet the definition of payday loans. By 2008, Defendants no longer marketed payday loans at their stores. Defendants admitted their signature loans "definitely could be a substitute product" for payday loans.

Defendants extend signature loans to the working poor; they lend exclusively to people who provide proof of steady employment but who, by definition, are either unbanked or underbanked. The Federal Deposit Insurance Corporation (FDIC) defines unbanked households as those without a checking or savings account, and underbanked households as those that have a checking or savings account but rely on alternative financial services. Federal Deposit Insurance Corporation, 2011 FDIC National Survey of Unbanked and Underbanked Households, Executive Summary at 3 n.2 (Sept. 2012), http://www.fdic.gov/householdsurvey/. The State's expert testified, and Defendants admit, that signature loans are "alternative financial services." All signature loan borrowers are at least underbanked, and those borrowers without a checking or savings account are unbanked. These borrowers are highly likely to live in poverty: in New Mexico, one-third of all unbanked households and almost one-quarter of all underbanked households earn less than $15,000 per year. Borrowers' testimony bears out the fact that Defendants target the working poor.

One borrower, Oscar Wellito, testified that he took out a signature loan from Defendants after he went bankrupt. He was supporting school-aged children while trying to service debt obligations with two other small loan companies. He earned about $9 an hour at a Safeway grocery store, which was not enough money to make ends meet, yet too much money to qualify for public assistance. "That's why," he testified, "I had no choice of getting these loans, to feed my kids, to live from one paycheck to another paycheck." He needed money for groceries, gas, laundry soap, and "whatever we need to survive from one payday to another payday." Mr. Wellito borrowed $100 from Defendants. His loan carried a 1,147.14 APR and required repayment in twenty-six biweekly installments of $40.16 with a final payment of $55.34. Thus, the $100 loan carried a total finance charge of $999.71.

Another borrower, Henrietta Charley, took out a loan from Defendants for $200 that carried the same 1,147.14 APR as Mr. Wellito's loan. Ms. Charley, a medical assistant and mother of three, earned $10.71 per hour working thirty-two hours per week in the emergency department of the San Juan Regional Medical Center. She earned around $615 in take-home pay every two weeks, while her monthly expenses, excluding food and gas, exceeded $1,000. Ms. Charley's ex-husband would only pay child support "every now and then," and when she did not receive that supplemental income, she would fall behind on her bills. She needed a loan to buy groceries and gas. Defendants gave her a $200 signature loan with a total finance charge of $2,160.04.

After borrowers brought complaints to the Attorney General, the State sued Defendants under the UPA, which prohibits "[u]nfair or deceptive trade practices and unconscionable trade practices in the conduct of any trade or commerce." Section 57-12-3. Unconscionable trade practices are defined in relevant part as an "extension of credit . . . that to a person's detriment: (1) takes advantage of the lack of knowledge, ability, experience or capacity of a person to a grossly unfair degree; or (2) results in a gross disparity between the value received by a person and the price paid." Section 57-12-2(E). The State identified numerous business practices that it argued were procedurally unconscionable, and alleged that the loan terms were substantively unconscionable. The State sought restitution, civil penalties, and injunctive relief. The State also sued Defendants for violating New Mexico's common law of substantive and procedural unconscionability.

(handwritten margin note: DC found Procedural Uncon not Subs Uncon)

The district court adjudicated liability in a four-day bench trial, and found that . . . the loans were not substantively unconscionable, but they were procedurally unconscionable under common law. The evidence adduced at trial is discussed below.

[Eds. note: We omit the discussion of the standard of review. The court reasoned that "by both statute and case law, we review whether a contract is unconscionable as a matter of law."]

III. DISCUSSION

A. There was substantial evidence to support the district court's judgment that Defendants' loans were procedurally unconscionable. . . .

An unconscionable trade practice is any extension of credit that "takes advantage of the lack of knowledge, ability, experience or capacity of a person to a grossly unfair degree" and is detrimental to the borrower. Defendants challenge the sufficiency of the evidence for the district court's finding that they violated [New Mexico's prohibition on procedurally unconscionable contract terms]. To support the district court's ruling, there must be substantial evidence that the borrowers lacked knowledge, ability, experience, or capacity in credit consumption; that Defendants took advantage of borrowers' deficits in those areas; and that these practices took advantage of borrowers to a grossly unfair degree to the borrowers' detriment. We conclude that substantial evidence supports the district court's findings as to each of these elements.

(handwritten margin note: Elements of Proc. Uncon.)

1. Evidence of borrowers' lack of financial sophistication

(handwritten margin note: Element #1)

There was substantial evidence that the borrowers lacked knowledge, ability, experience, or capacity in credit consumption. The district court heard from Defendants that a "signature loan primarily is for someone that is an unbanked person [or] underbanked." As discussed above, all signature loan borrowers are by definition underbanked because they are utilizing alternative financial services. Ms. Charley is an example of an underbanked borrower because although she had access to a bank account, she only used it to receive child support payments. A subset of Defendants' borrowers are unbanked, like Mr. Wellito, who testified he never had a bank account because he could not afford to open one. The district court heard evidence about the demographic characteristics of unbanked and under-banked New Mexicans, as well as their behavioral and cognitive biases, which were borne out by borrower testimony. We will discuss each piece of demographic and cognitive evidence in turn.

(handwritten margin note: Admitted its for un/under banked)

Demographically, unbanked and underbanked New Mexicans have significantly less education than the general population, are disproportionately living in poverty, and are more likely to be people of color. Their education levels are lower: the State presented evidence that in over 25 percent of unbanked and underbanked households, no one holds a high school degree, and in only a handful of unbanked households — just over 9 percent — does anyone have any college education at all. They are more likely to be poor: 27.9 percent of unbanked households and 24.2

(handwritten margin note: Demo of these people = poor, POC, less edu)

percent of underbanked households in New Mexico lived on less than $15,000 per year in 2009. Over 50 percent of underbanked households live on less than $30,000 per year. They are also more likely to belong to an ethnic minority: 41.6 percent of Hispanic households are unbanked or underbanked, and 58.3 percent of "other" households (defined as non-Hispanic, non-black, and non-white, which is a category that includes Native Americans) are unbanked or underbanked.

Behaviorally and cognitively, unbanked and underbanked New Mexicans exhibit heuristic biases that work to their detriment. The State's expert, Professor Christopher Peterson, testified that these borrowers exhibit certain cognitive biases that lead them to make decisions that are contrary to their interests. They exhibit unrealistic optimism, or fundamental attribution error, meaning that they overestimate their ability to control future circumstances and underestimate their exposure to risk. Thus, these borrowers have unrealistic expectations about their ability to repay these loans. They also exhibit temporal biases, meaning they tend to focus on short-term gains, while discounting future losses they might suffer. Thus, borrowers focus on the promise of quick cash, and fail to make more considered judgments about the long-term costs of the loan. They also are subject to "framing" and "anchoring" effects, meaning that the way the price of a loan is framed at the outset may distort the prospective borrower's perception of the cost, and the borrower will retain that initial perception. If the cost initially is framed as being very low, such as $1.50 per day, a borrower will "anchor" his or her expectations on that claim and have difficulty reassessing the true costs once more information becomes available. Finally, borrowers are subject to information overload, meaning that when they are presented with a technically complex loan agreement, they cease trying to understand the terms at all because they realize they will not be able to understand all of the pricing features.

These cognitive biases were confirmed in a New Mexico–specific study of borrower perceptions at the point of sale in the high-cost lending environment, which Professor Peterson relied on to formulate his opinion. *See* Martin, *supra*, at 596–613. In that study of 109 borrowers, Professor Martin found that 75 percent of borrowers could not identify the APR of their small-principal, high-interest loan at the point of sale, or mistakenly believed that the interest rate was between one and 100 percent. *Id.* at 600–01. Additionally, borrowers could not reliably distinguish whether their loans were payday or installment loans, suggesting that the labels — as far as borrowers were concerned — are a distinction without a difference. *Id.* at 586 n.123.

Moreover, these cognitive biases were consistent with borrower testimony. Mr. Wellito and Ms. Charley testified that they thought they would be able to pay off their loans early, which is consistent with the unrealistic optimism bias described by Professor Peterson. Evidence of temporal bias was shown by Mr. Wellito's testimony that he took out the loan because Defendants' advertisements made it "look so easy," like "the money's there and . . . you just walk in and you just get it . . . [and] you pay it all off." Ms. Charley also testified that she took out the signature loan because it looked like an "easy" way out of her financial distress. The theory of framing and anchoring effects and information overload was consistent with statements from borrowers who testified that they focused on the biweekly payment amount and did not consider the long-term costs of the loan. Borrowers also testified that loan origination at Defendants' stores took about 10 minutes and was a hurried "sign here, sign there" process, which is further evidence that the borrowers may have been subject to information overload at the time of loan origination.

Info overload at play as well [handwritten margin note]

Beyond cognitive biases, borrowers' simple lack of knowledge, experience, ability, or capacity in credit transactions was evident from their testimony. Mr. Wellito, who had never had a bank account in his life, could not accurately describe how interest is calculated, stating that interest is "when you borrow money . . . you pay a little bit more to have them lend you the money." He did not know that interest is quoted in terms of a percentage, and did not understand that it is better for the buyer if the number is lower. Ms. Charley had not taken out a small loan before and did not understand that her loan would require sixteen interest-only payments. Another borrower, Rose Atcitty, understood only the amount she would have to pay and the date she would have to start repayment when she took out her signature loan; she was not told about the interest rate or the finance charge, and did not understand that it was a year-long loan. This testimony shows that these were not sophisticated borrowers, but borrowers who lacked knowledge of basic consumer finance concepts and had little experience in banking and credit markets.

Lack general knowledge exp. in this area. [handwritten margin note]

2. Evidence of Defendants' exploitation of borrowers' disadvantage

There was substantial evidence that Defendants took advantage of borrowers' deficits. Defendants directed their employees to describe the loan cost in terms of a misleading daily rate. Employees were instructed to tell customers that interest rates are typically "between $1.00 and $1.50 per day, per one hundred you borrow." Defendants admitted that this was a factually inaccurate rate. At $1 per day, the finance charge for one year would be $365, and at $1.50 per day, the finance charge would be $547.50, but Defendants knew that the actual finance charge for one year would be at least $1,000. Defendants would also advertise that they were selling loans at 50 percent off, when in fact the only thing that was 50 percent off was the interest on the first installment payment on the loan.

Lied a/b how much per day as well as discount [handwritten margin note]

Defendants aggressively pursued borrowers to get them to increase the principal of their loans. "Maximize Every Customer's Principle [sic] Balance" and "maximize every opportunity that presents itself" was the mandate. Defendants directed employees to take time every day to give every customer a "courtesy call" to "make them aware of the possibility of rewriting their loan if there is availability on their account." Employees were also directed to "CALL ACTIVE FILES TO IN-CREASE PRINCIPAL" with the objective of "increasing the principal amount borrowed to build store." The script for the courtesy calls was as follows:

> Your account balance as of today is $____, and your credit available is $____. Renewing your loan with us today, Mr./Mrs. ____, would put an extra $____ in your pocket, which I'm sure would come in handy with back to school, last-minute vacations or anything else that comes up towards the end of Summer. Would you like me to get things ready for you to come in today and take care of this?

At least one store employee described a practice of calling customers who were one payment away from paying off their loans to encourage them to take out another loan.

Defendants also instructed their employees to withhold amortization schedules from customers. The store manual instructed, "PRINT OUT THE AMORTIZA-TION SCHEDULE FOR THE FILE, BUT NEVER GIVE ONE TO A CUS-TOMER!" Mr. Bartlett claimed that this entire instruction was a "misprint" in the 2007 store manual, and explained that the reason he had included it again in the 2010 version is that it was an instruction he had "overlooked when revising" the manual. He stated that although "that is exactly what [the store manual] says," Defendants actually train their employees to give out amortization schedules "to everybody." Borrowers, however, testified that they had not received amortization schedules. The district court did not credit Mr. Bartlett's testimony, finding instead that Defendants have a practice of withholding the schedules.

Amortization schedules revealed the signature loans were interest-only loans for extended periods of time. For example, the amortization schedule in Ms. Charley's file showed that she would have to make sixteen biweekly payments of $90.68 each before any of her payments would be allocated toward her principal. According to her amortization schedule, on the seventeenth biweekly payment, she would finally pay off the first $1.56 toward her principal. Thus, Ms. Charley would have to make timely payments totaling $1,541.56 over thirty-four weeks (seventeen biweekly payments) before her loan balance would fall below the principal she borrowed. Defendants did not explain this to Ms. Charley, nor did they give her a copy of the amortization schedule.

All of these practices were mandated by Defendants' own confidential employee manuals, demonstrating that they were systematic company policies, as opposed to isolated incidents. These practices were confirmed by the testimony of both store employees and borrowers.

3. Evidence of gross unfairness and detriment

There was substantial evidence that Defendants' practices took advantage of borrowers to a grossly unfair degree. We consider whether borrowers were taken advantage of to a grossly unfair degree by looking at practices in the aggregate, as well as the borrowers' characteristics. . . . The pattern of conduct by Defendants in this case shows they were leveraging the borrowers' cognitive and behavioral weaknesses to Defendants' advantage, and that the borrowers were clearly among the most financially distressed people in New Mexico. This evidence supported a reasonable inference that Defendants were taking advantage of borrowers to a "grossly unfair degree."

Defendants argue that the State failed to prove detriment because it "offered no evidence as to whether the individual borrower thought the loan transaction worked to his or her detriment." The UPA does not require a subjective, individualized showing of detriment. . . . We may presume detriment from the evidence that Defendants' corporate practices took unfair advantage of borrowers' disadvantages to a gross degree. . . .

For the same reasons, there was also substantial evidence supporting the finding of procedural unconscionability as understood in common law. Procedural unconscionability may be found where there was inequality in the contract formation. Analyzing procedural unconscionability requires the court to look beyond the four corners of the contract and examine factors "including the relative bargaining strength, sophistication of the parties, and the extent to which either party felt free to accept or decline terms demanded by the other." As discussed at length above, the relative bargaining strength and sophistication of the parties is unequal. Moreover, borrowers are presented with Hobson's choice: either accept the quadruple-digit interest rates, or walk away from the loan. The substantive terms are preprinted on a standard form, which is entirely nonnegotiable. The interest rates are set by drop-down menus in a computer program that precludes any modification of the offered rate. Employees are forbidden from manually overriding the computer to make fee adjustments without written permission from the companies' owners: manual overrides "will be considered in violation of company policy and could result with . . . criminal charges brought against the employee and or termination." Because these contracts are prepared entirely by Defendants, who have superior bargaining power, and are offered to the weaker party on a take-it-or-leave-it basis, Defendants' loans are contracts of adhesion. "Adhesion contracts generally warrant heightened judicial scrutiny because the drafting party is in a superior bargaining position," *Rivera v. Am. Gen. Fin. Servs., Inc.,* 2011-NMSC-033, ¶ 44, 150 N.M. 398, 259 P.3d 803, and although they will not be found unconscionable in every case, "an adhesion contract is procedurally unconscionable and unenforceable when the terms are patently unfair to the weaker party." *Id.* Under these circumstances, there is substantial evidence that Defendants' loans are procedurally unconscionable under common law.

B. The district court's permanent injunction is an appropriate remedy.

The UPA grants the State the right to seek restitution, civil penalties, and injunctive relief for unfair trade practices. The district court granted the State a permanent injunction.

. . . .

The district court permanently prohibited Defendants from (1) targeting borrowers to try to increase the amount of their principal debt obligation until the borrower's file had become inactive for at least sixty days; (2) quoting the cost of signature loans "in terms of a daily or other nominal amount . . . or in any other amount than that which is mandated by the federal Truth in Lending Act," in advertising materials or during loan origination; (3) engaging in any practice that focuses the borrower's attention on the loan's installment payment obligation "without also clearly, conspicuously, and fully disclosing and explaining the cost of the loan if repaid over the course of the full repayment term"; and (4) representing that the loans will be in any way "easy" to repay. The district court also ordered Defendants to (1) provide all borrowers with a copy of the amortization schedule; (2) provide information regarding a substantive legal defense and contact information for the Attorney General's Office when communicating with a borrower in connection with debt collection; and (3) revise employee manuals to reflect these changes.

Because there was substantial evidence supporting the district court's findings that Defendants' lending practices were procedurally unconscionable, the district court had the authority to grant this injunctive relief pursuant to Section 57-12-8(B). The injunction attempts to remedy Defendants' procedurally unconscionable practices and is narrowly tailored to address each practice. We see nothing improper about the injunction.

C. The loans were substantively unconscionable under common law and the UPA.

The district court concluded that it was precluded from ruling on substantive unconscionability absent an express statutory prohibition of the interest rates at issue, and without considering the evidence on each individual loan issued by Defendants. We disagree with both conclusions.

"Unconscionability is an equitable doctrine, rooted in public policy, which allows courts to render unenforceable an agreement that is unreasonably favorable to one party while precluding a meaningful choice of the other party." *Cordova v. World Finance Corporation of New Mexico*, 2009-NMSC-021, ¶ 21, 146 N.M. 256, 208 P.3d 901. Substantive unconscionability is found where the contract terms themselves are "illegal, contrary to public policy, or grossly unfair." *Id.* ¶ 22. In determining whether a contract term is substantively unconscionable, courts examine "whether the contract terms are commercially reasonable and fair, the purpose and effect of the terms, the one-sidedness of the terms, and other similar public policy concerns." *Id.* "Contract provisions that unreasonably benefit one party over another are substantively unconscionable." *Id.* ¶ 25. Thus, substantive unconscionability can be found by examining the contract terms on their face — a simple task when, as here, all substantive contract terms were nonnegotiable, and embedded in identical boilerplate language. *See id.* ¶ 22. The test for substantive unconscionability as outlined in *Cordova* simply asks whether the contract term "is grossly unreasonable and against our public policy under the circumstances." *Id.* ¶ 31. We hold it is grossly unreasonable and against public policy to offer installment loans at 1,147.14 to 1,500 percent interest for the following reasons.

Courts are not prohibited from deciding whether a contract is grossly unreasonable or against public policy simply because there is not a statute that specifically limits contract terms. In a landmark case on substantive unconscionability, *Williams v. Walker-Thomas Furniture Co.*, the District of Columbia Circuit Court reversed the District of Columbia Court of Appeals on precisely this issue. In that case, the court of appeals had determined that, although it "could not condemn too strongly appellee's conduct" in selling a woman a $514 stereo set "with full knowledge that appellant had to feed, clothe and support both herself and seven children" on a $218 monthly income, it would not find the contract unconscionable because it found no caselaw or legislation that would support a declaration that the contract at issue was contrary to public policy. The circuit court reversed, stating "We do not agree that the court lacked the power to refuse enforcement of contracts found to be unconscionable." Even in the absence of binding precedent or statutory power, the circuit court held that "the notion that an unconscionable bargain should not be given full enforcement is by no means novel." We agree with the reasoning of *Williams*. Ruling on substantive unconscionability is an inherent equitable power of the court, and does not require prior legislative action. "Equity supplements the common law; its rules do not contradict the common law; rather, they aim at securing substantial justice when the strict rule of common law might work hardship." Larry A. DiMatteo, *The History of Natural Law Theory: Transforming Embedded Influences into a Fuller Understanding of Modern Contract Law*, 60 U. PITT. L. REV. 839, 890 (1999) (internal quotation marks and citation omitted). Although there is not a specific statute specifying a limit on acceptable interest rates for the types of signature loans in this case, in addition to our caselaw addressing unconscionability, the Legislature has empowered courts to adjudicate cases involving claims of unconscionable trade practices under the UPA.

In determining the public policy behind the UPA, we must first examine the statute's plain language. The statute expressly prohibits extensions of credit that take advantage of borrowers' weaknesses "to a grossly unfair degree" or that result in "a gross disparity" between the value and the price. The UPA is a law that prohibits the economic exploitation of others. The language of the UPA evinces a legislative recognition that, under certain conditions, the market is truly not free, leaving it for courts to determine when the market is not free, and empowering courts to stop and preclude those who prey on the desperation of others from being rewarded with windfall profits.

The district court determined that the signature loans do not result in a gross disparity between the value and the price because borrowers could pay off the loans early, and they "obtained a value beyond the face value, or even the time value, of the money borrowed — the ability to buy groceries for their children now, the ability to buy gas to get to a new job, and the ability to pay off a cell phone." In adopting this view, the district court was following a subjective theory of value, under which the more desperate a person is for money, the more "value" that person receives from a loan. Thus, hypothetically a high-cost loan could violate the statute if a person borrows money for betting on blackjack, because the "value" that person receives would be low compared to the price of the loan, whereas the same high-cost loan sold to a single mother who needs to feed her children could not violate the statute, because the "value" that mother receives would be high compared to the price of the loan. Under that erroneous reading of the statute, consumer exploitation would be legal in direct proportion to the extent of the consumer's desperation: the poorer the person, the more acceptable the exploitation. Such a result cannot be consonant with the consumer-protective legislative intent behind the UPA. It is not the use to which the loan is put that makes its value low or high, but the terms of the loan itself.

Under an objective, not a subjective, reading of the UPA, Defendants' signature loans are low-value products. First, these loans are extremely expensive. The least expensive signature loan carries a 1,147.14 APR, meaning a loan of $100 carries a finance charge of $999.71. Second, Defendants do not report positive repayments to credit reporting agencies. Thus, borrowers who succeed in bearing the exorbitant costs associated with these loans and who make good-faith efforts to repay them can never improve their credit scores. Borrowers who fail to pay, however, can have their credit scores negatively impacted. They can be sued and have their wages garnished. They will also be liable for Defendants' costs of collecting on the debt, including attorney fees. Third, there is a $25 bounced check or automatic clearing-

Discussion of all of the subs. uncon terms w/in loan itself

house fee that can be added to the cost of the loan each time a check is returned for insufficient funds, and there is a 5 percent penalty fee for each late payment, each of which potentially increase the cost of these loans. Fourth, there is an acceleration-upon-default clause which provides that if a borrower falls behind on his or her payments over the year, then the full amount of the debt — principal and interest — comes due immediately. All of these loan features, in combination with the quadruple-digit interest rates, make it a low-value product regardless of how the borrower uses the principal. Defendants point out that people who take out mortgages will, like borrowers here, pay several times the principal in interest payments over the life of their loan. However, unlike a mortgage loan, borrowers are not gaining an asset when taking out a signature loan; rather, they are taking on liability. The value the borrower receives from a signature loan consists of a small amount of principal — never more than $300 — and an enormous amount of risk. Therefore, these loans are objectively low-value products and are grossly disproportionate to their price.

No hard cap on int rates doesn't mean can charge whatever

Defendants further contend it is not the public policy of this state to prohibit usurious interest rates because the Legislature removed the interest rate cap in 1981. In this argument lies the implicit assertion that by removing the interest rate cap, the Legislature was stating that there is *no* interest rate that would violate public policy. Indeed, Defendants' expert testified that interest rates of 11,000 percent or even 11,000,000 percent would be acceptable under our statutory scheme.[280] If we were to accept Defendants' argument, we would have to hold that the doctrine of unconscionability as it exists at common law and in the UPA does not apply to the extension of credit. We decline to do so because to do so would thwart New Mexico public policy as expressed in the UPA and other legislation.

. . . .

The UCC . . . addresses substantive unconscionability. The New Mexico Legislature adopted the UCC's unconscionability doctrine in 1961; it codifies the courts' broad remedial power to refuse to enforce an unconscionable contract, strike the offending clause, or limit the application of the offending clause to avoid an unconscionable result. Section 55-2-302. . . . Although Section 55-2-302 pertains to the sale of goods, it was enacted prior to the UPA sections dealing with unconscionability. Therefore, we can infer that when it enacted the unconscionability clause of the UPA, the Legislature intended to allow the courts the same flexibility in determining whether a contract extending credit is unconscionable.

. . . .

In 2007, the Legislature amended the Small Loan Act [the 1955 act regulating the New Mexico small loan industry] to try to address the payday loan crisis in New Mexico. The amendments cap the effective interest rate on payday loans at about 400 percent by limiting fees and interest on payday loans to $15.50 per $100

---

[280] [4] In an example of the unlimited nature of this argument, Defendants' expert, Professor Thomas Lehman, also posited that it would be acceptable for a borrower to agree to harvest a kidney in exchange for $100. However, he stopped short of endorsing freedom to contract for one's own involuntary servitude, stating that although one could enter such a contract, one could "break that bond at any time they want."

borrowed, plus an additional $0.50 per loan for fees charged by the consumer-information database provider. Payday lenders are required to take into account the borrower's financial position, and they cannot extend loans exceeding 25 percent of the borrower's gross monthly income. However, the effective fee cap and other consumer protections built into the Small Loan Act only apply to payday loans, defined as loans with a duration of fourteen to thirty-five days, for which the consumer receives the loan principal and in exchange gives the lender a personal check or debit authorization for the amount of the loan plus interest and fees.

. . . .

The Legislature did not repeal all statutes protecting consumers from usurious practices: far from it, the Legislature empowered the Attorney General and private citizens to fight unconscionable practices through the UPA; it ratified the court's inherent equitable power to invalidate a contract on unconscionability grounds under the UCC; it maintained a prohibition on excessive charges and set a reasonable default interest rate of 15 percent under the Money Act; and it set a de facto interest rate cap on [payday loans] with the 2007 amendments to the Small Loan Act. Contrary to Defendants' contention that the repeal of the interest rate cap demonstrates a public policy in favor of unlimited interest rates, the statutes when viewed as a whole demonstrate a public policy that is consumer-protective and anti-usurious as it always has been. A contrary public policy that permitted excessive charges, usurious interest rates, or exploitation of naive borrowers would be inequitable, particularly in New Mexico where a greater percentage of people are struggling in poverty, and where more households are unbanked and under-banked than almost anywhere in the nation. Professor Peterson testified that "Defendants' signature loan product is among the most expensive loan products offered in the recorded history of human civilization." For comparison, interest rates that were considered high in the mid-twentieth century — rates used for high-risk borrowers on unsecured loans — were between 18 and 42 percent. Mafia loan sharks in New York City at the height of mafia power charged 250 percent interest. It is contrary to our public policy, and therefore unconscionable as a matter of law, for these historically anomalous interest rates to be charged in our state. We next address the appropriate remedy or remedies for the substantively unconscionable loans.

D. Restitution is the appropriate remedy for the procedural and substantive unconscionability of the signature loans in this case.

During the remedies phase of trial, the State requested that the district court invalidate all of the loans as the fruit of unconscionable lending practices and return the parties to their precontract status. Thus, the State sought restitution in the form of a full refund for borrowers of all money paid in excess of the principal on their loans. The district court denied restitution by any measure, reasoning that: (1) complete avoidance of the loans was improper because it would result in borrowers paying no interest; (2) the State's proposed remedy ignored the subjective value borrowers received, and would be a windfall to borrowers; (3) any refunds to borrowers would have to be offset by the subjective value they received; and (4) full refund restitution would be inequitable because it would put Defendants out of business. The final question is whether the district court abused its discretion in failing to grant restitution.

An abuse of discretion occurs "when the trial court's decision is clearly untenable or contrary to logic and reason." In this case, the district court was correct in determining that . . . the loans were procedurally unconscionable. On that basis alone, the district court could have voided the contracts entirely. Loans need not be both procedurally and substantively unconscionable to be invalidated by a court. *Cordova* ("[T]here is no absolute requirement in our law that both [substantive and procedural unconscionability] must be present to the same degree or that they both be present at all" in order to invalidate a contract.). Thus, where, as in this case, there is overwhelming evidence that the loans were procedurally unconscionable, no evidence of substantive unconscionability is needed in order to invalidate the contract. However, in this case, we hold that the interest rate terms were substantively unconscionable. Given the fact that these loans were both substantively and procedurally unconscionable, it would not have been an abuse of discretion to invalidate the entirety of the contracts.

. . . In order to facilitate the consumer-protective legislative purpose of the UPA, there was ample reason to grant restitution to borrowers for Defendants' unconscionable trade practices. It would not further the purpose of the UPA under these circumstances to allow Defendants to retain the full profits of their unconscionable trade practices. Thus, the district court abused its discretion in failing to grant any form of restitution. Nevertheless, we agree with the district court that it would be inequitable to allow borrowers to pay no interest at all.

When a contract term is unconscionable, like the 1,147.14 to 1,500 percent interest rates in this case, the court "may refuse to enforce the contract, or may enforce the remainder of the contract without the unconscionable term, or may so limit the application of any unconscionable term as to avoid any unconscionable result." *Padilla v. State Farm Mut. Auto. Ins. Co.*, 2003-NMSC-011, ¶ 15, 133 N.M. 661, 68 P.3d 901 (internal quotation marks and citations omitted). We decline to grant a windfall to all borrowers by allowing them to completely avoid the contracts. We hold instead that the quadruple-digit interest rate, a substantively unconscionable term, shall be stricken from the contracts of all borrowers. We then enforce the remainder of the contract without the unconscionable term.

The district court avoided calculating restitution, calling the task "arbitrary and unjustified" without precise figures to draw upon. However, the New Mexico statutes provide a default interest rate that allows "private lenders to charge interest on money debts at the legal rate where the contract is silent on the issue." *Martinez v. Albuquerque Collection Servs., Inc.*, 867 F. Supp. 1495, 1508 (D.N.M. 1994). Fifteen percent is the maximum allowable default interest rate. Section 56-8-3(A) ("The rate of interest, in the absence of a written contract fixing a different rate, shall be not more than fifteen percent annually . . . on money due by contract."). . . . Because the unconscionable interest rates in Defendants' loans are invalid terms, these contracts are silent with respect to rates. We apply the statutory default interest rate of 15 percent simple annual interest to these loans.

Defendants must refund all money collected by Defendants on their signature loans in excess of 15 percent of the loan principal as restitution for their unconscionable trade practices. We recognize that the district court could have fashioned a remedy whereby the borrowers would pay less for these loans by either setting a default interest rate lower than the statutory maximum of 15 percent, or by imposing an amortization schedule on the loans under which the total finance charge on the 15 percent simple interest loans would amount to less than 15 percent of the whole principal. We decline to do so here for the sake of equity and to prevent delay. Instead, Defendants will keep the maximum allowable interest of 15 percent under Section 56-8-3 and refund the remainder of the monies that the borrowers paid on their loans that is over 15 percent of the principal. For example, Oscar Wellito's $100 loan with 1,147.14 APR is now rewritten as a $100 loan with 15 APR. With simple interest, he therefore owes $115 on the contract. He paid Defendants a total of $160.64. Defendants must refund $45.64 to Mr. Wellito, which is the difference between the monies he paid on their unconscionable contract, $160.64, and the monies he owes under the reformed contract, $115. Because these contracts are unconscionable, Defendants must also refund any penalties or fees they collected from borrowers that were associated with missed, late, or partial payments.

IV. CONCLUSION

We hold that loans bearing interest rates of 1,147.14 to 1,500 percent contravene the public policy of the State of New Mexico, and the interest rate term in Defendants' signature loans is substantively unconscionable and invalid. We therefore reverse the district court's ruling on substantive unconscionability. We affirm the district court's ruling that Defendants engaged in procedurally unconscionable trade practices, and uphold the permanent injunction granted against Defendants. Accordingly, we affirm in part, reverse in part, and remand to the district court for a determination of damages in accordance with this opinion.

NOTES AND QUESTIONS

1. ***Who is the plaintiff?*** This case was styled *State of New Mexico ex rel. King v. B&B Investment Group.* "Ex rel" is law-Latin for *ex relatione*, meaning "upon being related" or, more loosely, "on behalf of." The phrase signifies that the suit was commenced by the state on behalf of a private party that sought the relief in the first place. We will return to this question below, but why at this point do you think that the borrowers (i.e., Wellito and Charley) did not sue in their own capacity?

2. ***The source of law:*** Is this a contract case? In *B&B Investment,* the State of New Mexico sued B&B under New Mexico's Unfair Practices Act (UPA), NMSA 1978, Sections 57-12-1 to -26 (1967, as amended through 2009). The opinion has an ample discussion of unconscionability. But do you think that unconscionability, as a cause of action in isolation, would have produced the same outcome? If not, does unconscionability have any independent significance as a doctrine? If so, what work does a statute such as New Mexico's UPA do in this sort of lawsuit?

3. ***Why was this in court at all (of arbitration, again)?*** If, as is likely, B&B Investment's loan agreements contained arbitration (and delegation) clauses, why was this in court at all? Doesn't the *Rent-A-Center* case, mentioned above, mean

that only an arbitrator can decide whether arbitration is, itself, unconscionable? Perhaps the answer is that the New Mexico attorney general was not bound by the arbitration clause. Does this, then, help to explain who the plaintiff was, and why? Can you think of an argument that would force the state, even in its *ex rel.* capacity, to arbitrate, assuming the contract contained arbitration and delegation clauses?

4. ***The remedy — restitution:*** In *Williams v. Walker-Thomas*, the defendants (Williams and Thorne) did not seek affirmative recoveries. Instead, it appears they put up unconscionability as a defense to Walker-Thomas's replevin action. In *B&B Investment*, by contrast, the State of New Mexico sought not only to enjoin future lending above a certain interest rate, but also to require defendants to refund amounts to consumers in excess of the state's 15 percent default interest rate. This is an example of restitution without rescission, or an explicit finding of "unjust enrichment." On what theory do we justify this sort of remedy? Consider, in this regard, the result in *Fullerton Lumber v. Torborg*, in section A.2.b. of this chapter, *supra.* Do you see a similarity? If so, what, if anything, justifies it?

5. ***The remedy — the default rate of interest:*** The court in *B&B Investment* awarded the consumers the difference between the contract rate and the "default rate" of 15 percent when the contract contained no specific provision awarding a rate of default interest. "Default interest" is usually a rate of interest prescribed by contract that applies going forward after a debtor has defaulted under a loan agreement. It is usually higher than the rate that applies absent a default. Why did the *B&B Investment* court choose the statutory default rate? Why not, for example, rewrite the contract to impose a more market-based interest rate, such as an average of actual default rates charged to actual consumer borrowers in New Mexico?

6. ***Who else matters?*** The court in *B&B Investment* does not indicate whether the loan agreements contained class-action waivers, of the sort held enforceable in *Concepcion*, discussed *supra.* If there had been one, how and why would the remedy in *B&B Investment* have gotten around it? Or does (or should) the result in *B&B Investment* benefit only Mr. Wellito and Ms. Charley? We do not know who else B&B or American Cash, the nominal defendants, had agreements with, or how many other "signature lenders" like B&B and American Cash there were in New Mexico. If, however, we assume that there were many borrowers and a fair number of other lenders, what effect would this decision have on them and their relationships? Is this the functional equivalent of a class-action lawsuit? Perhaps something even more powerful? How would these borrowers and lenders know that they were implicitly affected by this decision?

7. ***Financial condition versus cognition:*** As noted above, the early unconscionability cases, such as *Williams*, seemed to turn in part on the financial condition and educational levels of the consumer-parties to the challenged contracts. They were poor and with limited education, whereas the retailer (or other party) was not. *B&B Investment* seems to focus more explicitly on behavioral and cognitive elements in its analysis. Here, the borrowers were not merely poor and uneducated, but may also have suffered from "unrealistic optimism," "unrealistic expectations about their ability to repay" and a distorted "framing" of the price of the loan, among other things. But isn't that often true in contracting? How far do we want to

take the idea that systematic psychological biases may be the basis for relief from promissory liability?

As Professor Stewart Macaulay has observed:[281]

> We have to ask how, and whether, social scientists can help legal scholars find out what they want to know without running risks of making mistakes that are far too great. Sometimes all the social scientist need do is to hand the legal scholar an article or a chapter in a book. Often, however, what appears in such places must be translated for those who have not mastered the language. You seldom can just grab a "fact" from social science and "plug it in" to a law review article without running a real risk of error.

b. Dodd-Frank and the consumer financial protection bureau

State actors (e.g., the New Mexico attorney general) are not the only public agents seeking to redress what they perceive to be serious problems in consumer financial services contracts. In the wake of the financial crisis of 2008, Congress enacted the Dodd-Frank Wall Street Reform and Consumer Protection Act of 2010 (Dodd-Frank). Dodd-Frank seeks to regulate many aspects of financial services. Among other things, it took seriously the suggestion of law professor (now Senator) Elizabeth Warren (with Oren Bar-Gill) that Congress create a Consumer Financial Protection Bureau (CFPB).[282] According to its website, the CFPB "is focused on one goal: watching out for American consumers in the market for consumer financial products and services."[283] Among other things, the CFPB:

- Writes rules, supervises companies, and enforces federal consumer financial protection laws[284]
- Restricts unfair, deceptive, or abusive acts or practices
- Takes consumer complaints
- Promotes financial education
- Researches consumer behavior
- Monitors financial markets for new risks to consumers
- Enforces laws that outlaw discrimination and other unfair treatment in consumer finance

A recent paper by Professors Jean Braucher and Angela Littwin explains the substantive limits to the CFPB's regulatory authority:[285]

---

[281] Stewart Macaulay, *A New Legal Realism: Elegant Models and the Messy Law in Action*, UC-Irvine New Legal Realism 10th Anniversary Conference (2014).

[282] Oren Bar-Gill & Elizabeth Warren, *Making Credit Safer*, 157 U. Pa. L. Rev. 1 (2008).

[283] *See* consumerfinance.gov/the-bureau/creatingthebureau.

[284] There are certain "federal consumer financial protection laws" for which the CFPB does not have enforcement or supervision authority: for example, the Fair Housing Act and the Servicemembers Civil Relief Act.

[285] Jean Braucher & Angela Littwin, *Examination as a Method of Consumer Protection*, 87 Temp. L. Rev. 807, 829–32 (2015) (footnotes omitted).

[Dodd-Frank] grants the CFPB . . . the power to regulate unfair, deceptive, and abusive practices (UDAAP) by the entities it regulates. These concepts are themselves broad standards that nevertheless contain enough substantive content to be useful. Because they are standards, the CFPB can use them to regulate new practices for which there is no specific authority or statutory command. But while they may sound vague to the untrained ear, the UDAAP standards are not nearly as imprecise as the unconscionability standard. Two of them (unfair and deceptive) have had well-settled definitions since the 1980s, and two of them (unfair and abusive) are defined in the Dodd-Frank Act. The deception and unfairness concepts are from the Federal Trade Commission Act (FTC Act) and have been the subject of policy statements and case law. There is some overlap among the three terms, but they do have distinct meanings.

Deception liberalizes the common law of misrepresentation, for example to cover acts or practices likely to mislead average consumers in the target audience even if there has not been any actual misleading and no deceptive intent. It also enables preventive regulation. The CFPB is making use of this history by following an FTC policy statement on the meaning of deception.

Unfairness focuses on likely substantial consumer injury that is not reasonably avoidable or outweighed by countervailing benefits; the FTC Act and the Dodd-Frank Act use essentially the same definition. And while this statutory definition is itself vague, both agencies have supplied concrete interpretations. The FTC has been refining its approach in dialogue with the courts and Congress for more than eight decades, while the CFPB appears to be making up for lost time. In a 1980 policy letter to Congress, the FTC offered a consolidated interpretation that later became the basis for the statutory definition of unfairness. The CFPB has built on the FTC's approach and added a few features of its own. The FTC defined substantial harm generally as monetary (or health and safety), rather than emotional, injury. The CFPB adopts a similar course, although it states that emotional harm could be enough in the right circumstances and emphasizes that the risk of substantial harm satisfies the test; actual injury is not required. The FTC restricted unavoidable injuries to those that undermined "the free exercise of consumer decision making." Similarly, the CFPB considers injury not reasonably avoidable when a practice "interferes with or hinders a consumer's ability to make informed decisions or take action to avoid that injury." The Bureau also adds that injuries are not reasonably avoidable when consumers can only avoid them by spending significant monetary or other resources. When balancing potential benefits, the FTC considered a practice's potential cost savings to consumers as well as the potential costs of regulation to companies and society as a whole. The CFPB also includes potential consumer cost savings and the cost of regulation in its cost-benefit analysis. The Bureau additionally mentions "a wider availability of products and services resulting from competition" as a possible offsetting benefit.

In contrast with unfairness and deception, the abusiveness concept is new. But not only does the Dodd-Frank Act define abusiveness, the Act defines it to prohibit a specific type of consumer lending practice that has become increasingly prevalent in recent years. Abusiveness addresses harms stemming from the consumer's cognitive biases identified by behavioral economics. The statutory definition has multiple alternatives, the most important of which is that an act or practice must not take unreasonable advantage of "a lack of understanding on the part of the consumer of the material risks, costs, or conditions of the product or service." Deception appears to already cover this behavior, but abuse's emphasis on consumer understanding clarifies that even accurate disclosure is not enough if consumers misunderstand how a product will work. In other words, abusive practices are those that depend on companies understanding consumers better than consumers understand themselves and using that knowledge to profit from consumers' blind spots about their own cognition and behavior.

The CFPB has provided additional clarity by identifying examples of evidence that a practice may be abusive: (1) if profitability depends on back-end penalty fees, or more generally, if a pricing structure makes it difficult for consumers to understand total costs; and (2) when credit is extended without the expectation that consumers will be able to pay. Obscuring the total price has featured prominently in the revolving credit card business model, while lending without regard to ability to pay characterizes subprime mortgage loans during the pre-crisis bubble, much revolving credit card debt, and subprime automobile loans today.

Recall the discussion of arbitration and unconscionability, *supra*. In section 1028(a) of Dodd-Frank, Congress instructed the CFPB to study "the use of agreements providing for arbitration of any future dispute . . . in connection with the offering or providing of consumer financial products or services," and to report to Congress on this, which it did in March 2015.[286] In doing so, the CFPB looked at thousands of arbitrations involving consumer financial services, such as credit cards, checking accounts/debit cards, payday loans, prepaid cards, private student loans, and auto loans between 2010 and 2012. Although the findings are too extensive to detail here, consider several:

- Consumers report that dispute resolution plays little to no role in choosing the credit card they use most frequently.

- Consumers are generally unaware of whether their credit card contracts include arbitration clauses. Consumers with such clauses in their agreements generally either do not know whether they can sue in court or wrongly believe that they can do so.

*   *   *

- Of the 341 [sampled arbitration] cases filed in 2010 and 2011 that were resolved by an arbitrator and where [CFPB was] able to ascertain the outcome, consumers obtained relief regarding their affirmative claims in 32

---

[286] Consumer Financial Protection Bureau Arbitration Study (Mar. 2015) [CFPB Arbitration Report], www.consumerfinance.gov/reports/arbitration-study-report-to-congress-2015.

disputes.[287] Consumers obtained debt forbearance in 46 cases (in five of which the consumers also obtained affirmative relief). The total amount of affirmative relief awarded was $172,433 and the total debt forbearance was $189,107.[288]

- Of the 52 disputes filed in 2010 and 2011 that involved consumer affirmative claims of $1000 or less, arbitrators resolved 19, granting affirmative relief to consumers in four such disputes.[289]

- Of the 244 cases in which companies made claims or counterclaims that were resolved by arbitrators in a manner that [CFPB was] able to determine, companies obtained relief in 227 disputes. The total amount of such relief was $2,806,662.[290]

In other words, companies that used arbitration to seek affirmative relief against consumers succeeded about 93 percent of the time. Consumers who sought affirmative relief against companies, by contrast, succeeded less than 10 percent of the time. However, this report also finds that consumers may not fare much better in court. In 82 of the 1,205 individual federal cases for which the CFPB analyzed outcomes (6.8 percent) . . . a consumer obtained a judgment against a company party through a summary judgment motion, a default judgment, or a trial. (Most were default judgments, and there were only two trials.)[291] The CFPB noted that it had limited information about the quality of the claims or various other factors that might have affected outcomes. This may, however, help to explain why consumer financial services companies prefer to use arbitration over litigation.

At least one response from the CFPB has been to consider proposing rules that would prohibit class-action waivers in consumer financial services contracts.[292] Concerned that "arbitration agreements effectively prohibit class proceedings, including litigation, and that they prevent many consumers from obtaining remedies when they are harmed by the providers of consumer financial products or services . . . [t]he [CFPB] has prelimin[arily] determined that a regulation that would prohibit the application of pre-dispute arbitration agreements to class litigation in court would protect consumers [and] serve the public interest."[293] The CFPB proposal would not prevent consumers and financial service providers from agreeing to arbitration, either on an individual basis or as a class, "as long as class litigation remains an option."

---

[287] *Id.* at 12.

[288] *Id.*

[289] *Id.*

[290] *Id.*

[291] *Id.* at 8.

[292] *See* Consumer Financial Protection Bureau, Small Business Advisory Review Panel for Potential Rulemaking on Arbitration Agreements (Oct. 7, 2015), http://files.consumerfinance.gov/f/201510_cfpb_small-business-review-panel-packet-explaining-the-proposal-under-consideration.pdf.

[293] *Id.* at 4.

NOTES AND QUESTIONS

1. *How does the CFPB relate to unconscionability?* Braucher and Littwin describe the CFPB's standards as "not nearly as imprecise as unconscionability." Are they broad enough to accommodate any situation to which the unconscionability doctrine could apply? Could the CFPB regulate the activity described in *B&B Investment*? While the CFPB has authority to regulate "unfair," "deceptive," and "abusive" practices, there are limits to what it can do. It has limited authority, for example, to directly regulate interest rates.[294]

2. *Examination:* Professors Braucher and Littwin implicitly argue that an important advantage of modern public intervention is that it need not be traditional civil litigation. Instead:[295]

> One of the CFPB's most powerful tools is supervision, which enables the Bureau to examine financial institutions' compliance with consumer protection law on an ongoing basis. Dedicated consumer protection examination is a new development in the law, one with potential to have a major impact on compliance. Although examination is time-consuming and commands devotion of resources both by the agency and [by] regulated entities, it is still less resource-consuming than litigation. It thus provides a relatively cost-effective way for an agency to obtain both changes in company practices and compensation for victims. In other words, for the first time in U.S. history, a federal regulator with a commitment to consumer protection has access to real-time company compliance information as well as the tools to remedy any deficits it finds.

> *   *   *

> Examiners gather information from an impressive variety of sources: (1) CFPB work products such as the most recent Risk Assessment, prior examination reports, and information on enforcement; (2) complaint information from the CFPB, the FTC Consumer Sentinel, and the Better Business Bureau, as well as other federal and state agencies; and (3) public information, including that from securities filings, newspaper articles, websites, blog postings, as well as industry publications with information on credit ratings, product performance, and areas of profitability. Only after conducting this exhaustive external review do examiners ask the supervised entity for information. . . .

> [E]xaminers are instructed to assess legal risks, by reviewing for potential UDAAPs, regulatory noncompliance, and discrimination. Full-scope examinations culminate with a determination of a "compliance rating," a numerical evaluation of a company's current compliance with federal financial consumer law and systems for ensuring compliance in the future. These

---

[294] The Dodd-Frank Act, section 1027(o), provides that "No provision of this title shall be construed as conferring authority on the [CFPB] to establish a usury limit applicable to an extension of credit offered or made by a covered person to a consumer, unless explicitly authorized by law." 12 U.S.C. § 5517(o) (2010).

[295] Braucher & Littwin, *supra* note 285, at 808, 836–37, 837–38.

ratings provide another way the Bureau maximizes the compliance effect of its supervision resources. Examiners apply uniform criteria, regardless of industry, in order to effectuate the purpose of the rating system: "[T]o help identify those institutions whose compliance with Federal consumer financial law displays weaknesses requiring special supervisory attention."

The examination reports in which the CFPB communicates its findings to supervised companies likely further increases company compliance in two ways. First, a company's compliance rating provides the organizing principle for the examination report the Bureau uses to communicate its findings. Companies presenting little risk of noncompliance receive brief reports, while companies presenting increasing degrees of risk receive increasingly longer reports. The tone of a report's conclusion about a company should also match the compliance rating. Second, . . . examiners [are instructed to] "clearly cite statutory or regulatory violations," and to state "specific expectations," including a timeframe, when company attention or corrective action is required. . . . The more precise the feedback on regulatory violations, the less able companies are to give themselves the benefit of the doubt and the more pressure it places on company actors' self-image as law-abiding citizens.

* * *

Finally, even once an examination is complete, supervised entities are still subject to ongoing monitoring, which closes the risk-prioritization feedback loop. For non-banks, the Bureau conducts product and market analyses to inform its ongoing risk assessment, which in turn informs the next round of examination scheduling. For large banks, the goal is to "maintain reasonably current information" about their risk profiles through periodic checks that may include meetings and telephone calls. The CFPB monitors banks at least once per quarter and places some of them under continuous supervision, with CFPB examiners present on a full-time basis.

What are some of the likely effects of examination on financial services firms and their customers? Notice that, like arbitration, examination is a largely private matter: the results are not likely to be made public. Does this alter your view of "public good" concerns about arbitration? Or, does it suggest that the important questions lie elsewhere?

3. *Commitment:* Braucher and Littwin's analysis of the CFPB's examination function argued that "public enforcement is crucial." They point out that "only one factor . . . might predict successful public enforcement: commitment of the regulatory agency. . . . Without commitment, consumer protection would not occur."[296] What factors ultimately determine the character of a public agency's commitment to its regulatory agenda? Is commitment purely political? If so, to what extent can or should we trust the vindication of private rights to majoritarian rule? If not, what other factors affect commitment in this context? If litigants are not litigating for themselves — as the plaintiff in a breach of contract suit might — for

---

[296] *Id.* at 809.

whom are they acting? What are their incentives and how do we monitor them?[297] And what is supposed to happen if, for political reasons, regulators change their commitments?

4. *The takeaway — unconscionability and social control:* We have now traveled quite a distance from where we began. The Washington, D.C., of *Williams v. Walker-Thomas* is not the Washington, D.C., of the CFPB. (Or is it?) Students understandably want a "takeaway." This is not easy when considering social control of contract generally, or in the guise of unconscionability doctrine and its modern developments, in particular. How we exercise "social control" of contract is one of the most difficult questions we face in contract law because it challenges the traditional structure of contractual relations as involving two parties — buyer and seller, for example. Whenever we agree that some social control of contract is appropriate, we are in effect saying that third parties — whether they are judges, regulators, or the "community" — get a say in what two persons can and cannot agree to.

Moreover, modern social control aimed at deterring or redressing unconscionable contracting appears to challenge common law techniques for resolving ostensibly private, two-party contract disputes. Historically, as you have seen, this was the work of courts. Today, it appears that we place more of this work in the hands of arbitrators and regulators than in the past. Few among us would advocate abandoning the common law system of *stare decisis* (unless, of course, that is what you think arbitration does). But as we ask legislatures such as Congress to create regulatory entities such as the CFPB to set *ex ante* limits on what consumer contracts may do, and state attorneys general (such as that in New Mexico) to enforce consumer protection statutes *ex post*, we must ask: Are we merely supplementing the common law tradition of judge-made, incremental law — or displacing it? Is the phrase "consumer contract" destined to become a contradiction in terms?

Your contracts course cannot answer these questions; you will spend much of your career thinking about these and related matters. Nevertheless, two observations may help. First, it appears that contract is never a purely private affair. While courts and commentators may understandably characterize contract as a form of "private ordering" and adjudication of contract disputes as a form of "private law," contracts and contract law always have social implications. There are some promises society does not want enforced. That is social control of contract. Thus, the important question in the first instance is to consider what classes of promises, and what promissory conditions, might lead "society" to worry? It may be that contract is an awkward weapon in the "war on poverty." Yet, it seems equally true that we all recognize (public?) limits to private arrangements. As law students and lawyers, your job will in part be to recognize those limits, and the doctrines and principles that inform them.

Second, and perhaps more prosaically, unconscionability and its modern expres-

---

[297] *Id.* Braucher and Littwin's analysis draws on an earlier paper by Professor Whitford. William C. Whitford, *Structuring Consumer Protection Legislation to Maximize Effectiveness*, 1981 Wis. L. Rev. 1018, which set forth a framework for conceptualizing and implementing consumer protection legislation.

sion — through activities undertaken by agencies such as the CFPB — may evidence a shift in actors, but not necessarily a fundamental transformation of the role of social norms in policing contracts. Unconscionability doctrine seems to be telling us that some promises are so one-sided, so harmful to one of the parties, that even if no other doctrine — such as fraud, misrepresentation, or duress — is available, there is an outer boundary: our conscience. This, of course, leads inevitably to more difficult questions, beyond the scope of this class, but with which you will wrestle throughout your careers: Whose conscience, exactly, counts for this purpose? Ours alone, or that of other actors involved in these problems? Is it merely the "conscience of the king" that we care about, and if so, who is "king" for this purpose?[298] How do we know our conscience and how do we know when — and when not — to act on it?

---

[298] Lest you think you can complete these materials without a bit more Shakespeare, consider Hamlet's famous words:

> I'll have grounds
> More relative than this — the play's the thing
> Wherein I'll catch the conscience of the King.

William Shakespeare, HAMLET, act 2, sc. ii, ll. 1678–80.

TABLE OF CASES

[References are to pages.]

[References are to pages.]

[References are to pages.]

[References are to pages.]

[References are to pages.]

[References are to pages.]

TABLE OF STATUTES

[References are to pages.]

[References are to pages.]

[References are to pages.]

[References are to pages.]

INDEX

[References are to sections.]

[References are to sections.]

[References are to sections.]

[References are to sections.]